LITIGATION LIBRARY

FOSKETT ON COMPROMISE

FOSKETT ON COMPROMISE

LITIGATION LIBRARY

NINTH EDITION

THE HON. SIR DAVID FOSKETT, LL.B., F.C.I.Arb., F.K.C.
Formerly a Justice of the High Court, Queen's Bench Division
A Bencher and former Treasurer of Gray's Inn

and contributors

SWEET & MAXWELL

THOMSON REUTERS

First Edition 1980 by David Foskett
Second Edition 1985 by David Foskett
Third Edition 1991 by David Foskett
Fourth Edition 1996 by David Foskett
Fifth Edition 2002 by David Foskett
Sixth Edition 2005 by David Foskett
Seventh Edition 2010 by David Foskett
Eighth Edition 2015 by David Foskett
Ninth Edition 2020 by David Foskett

Published and typeset in 2020 by Thomson Reuters (Professional) Limited
Sweet & Maxwell, 6th Floor, 5 Canada Square, London, E14 5AQ,
Thomson Reuters (Professional) UK Limited (Registered in England & Wales,
Company No 1679046.
Registered Office and address for service: 2nd Floor, 1 Mark Square,
Leonard Street, London EC2A 4EG

Printed and bound by CPI Group (UK) Ltd, Croydon, CR0 4YY.

For further information on our products and services, visit
www.sweetandmaxwell.co.uk

No natural forests were destroyed to make this product; only farmed timber
was used and replanted.

A CIP catalogue record for this book is available from the British Library.

ISBN: 9780414072657

CONSULTANT EDITOR

THE HON. SIR DAVID FOSKETT, LL.B., F.C.I.Arb., F.K.C.
Formerly a Justice of the High Court, Queen's Bench Division
A Bencher and former Treasurer of Gray's Inn

GENERAL EDITOR

DR JOHN SORABJI, M.A. (Oxon), MPhil, LL.M
Principal Legal Adviser to the Lord Chief Justice
and the Master of the Rolls
of Inner Temple, Barrister

CONTRIBUTORS

DAVID HODGE QC, B.A. (Oxon), B.C.L.
A Specialist Chancery Circuit Judge on the Northern Circuit
Chancellor for the Diocese of Oxford, Deputy Chancellor for the Diocese of Blackburn
Bencher of Lincoln's Inn

ADRIAN LYNCH QC, LL.B.
of Gray's Inn, Barrister
A Recorder

WILLIAM EDIS QC, M.A. (Oxon), Dip. Law (City University)
of Lincoln's Inn, Barrister,
A Recorder

BRIE STEVENS-HOARE QC, LL.B., LL.M.
Barrister, a Fee Paid Tribunal Judge
Bencher of Lincoln's Inn

NICHOLAS ALLEN QC, M.A. (Cantab), LL.M. (Cantab), M.C.I.Arb.
of Middle Temple, Barrister,
A Recorder

JAMES STRACHAN QC, M.A. (Oxon)
of Middle Temple, Barrister
A Deputy High Court Judge

TOM MONTAGU-SMITH QC, M.A. (Oxon)
of Lincoln's Inn, Barrister

ROSANNA FOSKETT M.A. (Cantab), MPhil (Cantab), Dip.Law (City University)
of Lincoln's Inn, Barrister

CONSULTANT EDITOR

THE HON. SIR DAVID [illegible]

[illegible]

"Let us never negotiate out of fear. But let us never fear to negotiate."
President John F. Kennedy

"A good compromise ... is like a good sentence; or a good piece of music. Everybody can recognize it. They say, 'Huh. It Works. It makes sense'."
President Barack Obama

Foreword to the First Edition

"I'm happy to be able to tell your Lordship that you will not be troubled by this case; the parties have settled their differences." Those words, so welcome to the judicial ear mean much more, however, than an unexpected round of golf for the judge. If it were not that a high proportion of cases are compromised long before they reach court the administration of justice would soon grind to a halt; the courts would be overwhelmed by the volume of work. Moreover, the skilful practitioner, be he barrister or solicitor, who can accurately gauge the strength of his own case and that of his opponent will often be able to save his client great trouble and expense by judicious and timely compromise.

When one realises the importance of these skills, and how much of some practitioners' time is taken up in attempts to settle litigation, it is surprising that there is so little written guidance on the subject. It may look easy, but there is much to learn and many pitfalls.

Mr Foskett has in his comprehensive and scholarly review covered every aspect of the subject, not overlooking the vital area of professional ethics. The reputation of being a straightforward honest negotiator is worth any number of dubiously achieved settlements.

This is a book which anyone handling litigation would do well to read.

The Right Hon. Lord Lane, A.F.C.,
Lord Chief Justice of England

Foreword to the Fourth Edition

The law loves compromise.

It has good reason to do so, since a settlement agreement freely made between both parties to a dispute ordinarily commands a degree of willing acceptance denied to an order imposed on one party by court decision. A party who settles forgoes the chance of total victory, but avoids the anxiety, risk, uncertainty and expenditure of time which is inherent in almost any contested action, and escapes the danger of total defeat.

The law reflects this philosophy, by making it hard for a party to withdraw from a settlement agreement, as from any other agreement, and by giving special standing to an agreement embodied, by consent, in an order of the court. Rules of practice are framed so as to encourage settlement, by exposing the substantial loser of an action to a heavy burden of costs and enabling the maker of a reasonable offer, even if the offer is refused, to obtain some protection against that burden.

But there is, as always, a catch. To negotiate a final and binding settlement agreement; to make sure that all necessary matters are covered; to express the terms clearly and unambiguously; to make sure that the agreement is simply and inexpensively enforceable; to advise where one party claims that he has been misled or pressured into making an agreement by the other side; all this may call for as much skill, including legal skill, as fighting the action.

In this, as in other legal fields, there is no substitute for a sound grasp of legal principle, an understanding of the special rules governing the subject matter and a knowledge of the up-to-date case law. That is what this valuable book provides, and that is why a Fourth Edition is so welcome.

If, as is greatly to be hoped, the movement towards settlement of disputes out of court, by mediation or conciliation, gathers pace, the learning which this book contains will become even more relevant and necessary. It is the right book, in the right place, at the right time.

The Right Honourable Lord Bingham of Cornhill
Lord Chief Justice of England
The Law Courts
The Strand
London
June 4, 1996

Foreword to the Eighth Edition

35 years after the first edition it is a privilege to welcome this new edition under the title *Foskett on Compromise*, published in the 800th anniversary year of Magna Carta. That is indeed an appropriate anniversary for the new edition because Magna Carta was an early example of a compromise agreement, even if it was an agreement between a King and rebellious barons and a Welsh Prince. It has emerged into one of the fundamental documents underpinning the rule of law. However it is easy to forget that initial attempts were made to set it aside as obtained by duress (a subject in its modern context covered in chapter 4 of this work) and that its various clauses can be seen as providing examples of possibly the longest surviving compromise agreement ever achieved.

In modern times Lord Bingham, in writing a Foreword to an earlier edition of this book, spoke of the importance of parties trying to settle their disputes. Some years on, it is not enough to stress the importance of settling disputes. In the light of the great increase in legal costs over the intervening years, parties will often be driven to compromise their disputes as they cannot afford to do otherwise.

Many lawyers acting for parties who are intent on compromise assume that they know enough to be able to draft the agreement settling the dispute; well known phrases such as "without prejudice to the rights of the parties" and "in full and final settlement" are terms most lawyers will have learnt in their early days of training as forming the bedrock of a compromise agreement. Few, however, appreciate that the law relating to compromise was never that simple. These days it is certainly not simple. No lawyer can do his client a greater disservice than to arrive at a compromise of a dispute that does not settle that dispute, as the client is then faced with yet further litigation on top of the possibility that the original dispute will be re-opened.

Any lawyer attempting to reach a compromise of a dispute or of litigation should therefore become familiar with the ever increasing complexity of the law relating to compromise. There can be no better place to do this than by use of this text. In its comprehensive coverage, there are invaluable chapters which provide considerable assistance. CPR Part 36 is but one example of a detailed and up to date review – it covers all the recent revisions, including those which came into force on April 6, 2015. There is also a very useful chapter on resolution by agreement of Administrative Court proceedings; one of the many topical subjects in this chapter is the section on costs which clearly explains the approach the courts now take.

Apart from matters of strict law, there is very sound guidance on professional ethics and responsibilities. The achievement of a successful outcome of a dispute through a settlement is most easily reached where the lawyers trust each other; the greatest litigation solicitors are those who are universally respected for their integrity and adherence to professional standards. They are the lawyers who served their clients best. I cannot commend the reading of this chapter too highly as providing a clear pathway through the difficulties that can arise where integrity is not the touchstone for all involved.

The Rt. Hon. Lord Thomas of Cwmgiedd
Lord Chief Justice of England and Wales
May 3, 2015

Preface to the Ninth Edition

2020 represents the 40th anniversary of the publication of the First edition of this work. Whilst we seem to live in an increasingly confrontational period in some areas of life, both nationally and internationally, the impetus for parties to litigation or arbitral proceedings to resolve their differences before the final hearing is no less strong now than it was then. Whilst the process of settlement, whether achieved through direct negotiation or facilitated by mediation or some other form of ADR, so often bears fruit even when, as now, disputes seem to have become even more complex, there remain pitfalls and unanticipated nuances that need to be identified and addressed in that process. We hope this new edition will help in that regard.

There have been one or two changes in the team of contributors since the last edition. His Honour Judge David Hodge QC (formerly of Maitland Chambers) has been joined by Rosanna Foskett, also of Maitland Chambers, in the authorship of Chapter 23. James Strachan QC, of 39 Essex Chambers, has taken over Chapter 33 from Nigel Giffin QC. Nicholas Allen QC, of 29 Bedford Row, has taken over Chapters 24 and 26 from Charles Hyde QC. I am very grateful to all of them for coming on board and I should like to extend my thanks to Nigel and Charles for their past contributions and, of course, to David for his continued support. Brie Stevens-Hoare QC, who has considerable experience in the field, kindly agreed to review Chapter 25 in addition to her work on Chapters 29 and 30. I have re-joined the writing team on Chapter 32 with Tom Montagu-Smith QC, of 24 Old Buildings, and he and I have produced a new Chapter 36 entitled 'The settlement of international commercial disputes'. It contains an extensive analysis of the UN Convention on International Settlement Agreements resulting from Mediation ('the Singapore Convention') and of the role of the New York Convention in the enforcement of agreed arbitral awards. I am, of course, extremely grateful to Adrian Lynch QC, of 11 King's Bench Walk, and William Edis QC, of 1 Crown Office Row, for their continuing contributions.

Dr John Sorabji has assumed the role of General Editor for this edition and has brought to bear his unrivalled knowledge of the law and practice of civil litigation, both in the UK and elsewhere, in respect of many of the chapters. I am very grateful to him.

I am as ever grateful to the publishers for their continuing interest and support and to those responsible for preparing the Tables and the Index.

As I said in the Preface to the last edition, and I fear I must do the same in relation to this edition, with the constant publication of judgments at all levels, it is very difficult to specify with precision a date upon which a book of this nature is up-to-date. It has been possible to make some references to cases reported up to 1 November 2019 and I believe the text is broadly up-to-date as at that date.

Finally, my travels to Singapore, Hong Kong and Malaysia, in particular, over the last year or so have demonstrated how much reliance is placed upon this book in those jurisdictions and how the same or similar issues over dispute resolution arise worldwide.

Our researches for this edition have shown continuing reliance upon it in other jurisdictions too, particularly those influenced by the English common law. We have tried where possible to incorporate references to relevant cases from those jurisdictions. We all have much to learn from each other.

David Foskett
39 Essex Chambers
81 Chancery Lane
London WC2A 1DD
22 November 2019

TABLE OF CONTENTS

PART 4:

THE SETTLEMENT PROCESS IN CIVIL JUSTICE

PART 5:

ROLE OF LEGAL ADVISERS IN COMPROMISE

PART 6:

INSURANCE INTERESTS AND COMPROMISE

PART 7:

CHANCERY LITIGATION

PART 8:

MATRIMONIAL, FAMILY AND INHERITANCE DISPUTES

PART 10:

EMPLOYMENT CONTRACTS AND COMPROMISE

PART 11:

LANDLORD AND TENANT AND DISPUTES OVER LAND

PART 12:

CONSTRUCTION LITIGATION

PART 13:

ARBITRATIONS

PART 14:

ADMINISTRATIVE COURT PROCEEDINGS

PART 15:

THE SETTLEMENT OF APPEALS, THE ROLE OF ADR AND THE SETTLEMENT OF CROSS-BORDER DISPUTES

APPENDICES

TABLE OF CASES

TABLE OF CASES

TABLE OF STATUTES

TABLE OF STATUTORY INSTRUMENTS

PART 1: LEGAL FOUNDATION AND CONSEQUENCES OF COMPROMISES

CHAPTER 1

Introduction

Compromise can be defined as the settlement of a dispute by mutual concession[1] or a "coming to terms, or arrangement of a dispute, by concessions on both sides".[2] The essential foundation for a legally binding compromise is the law of contract. The combined effect of this definition and the assertion of the principle that the true foundation of compromise is the law of contract[3] is good for most purposes although it does not comprehend all matters discussed in this work. A more practical and, perhaps, more apt definition for present purposes would be that a compromise involves the complete or partial resolution by agreement of differences[4] before final adjudication by a court or tribunal of competent jurisdiction. However, the search for a suitable definition may be a somewhat barren exercise: identifying the contexts in which "compromise" operates may be more useful. **1-01**

Broadly speaking, compromise occurs most frequently in the private law context[5] where disputes arise between individuals or other legal *personae*. The law is the framework of rules by reference to which disputes are resolved. Courts and other tribunals exist for the purpose of administering the law and thereby resolving disputes. Since 1999 and the introduction of the Civil Procedure Rules (CPR) governing practice and procedure in civil proceedings, a case-managed system of civil justice has been in place in England and Wales. It is a system that is based essentially upon an adversarial process.[6] In that system it is for the parties to bring their disputes before the appropriate forum. Procedural rules in the CPR govern the **1-02**

---

1 See *Shorter Oxford Dictionary*.

2 *Oxford English Dictionary*. In *Gurney v Grimmer* (1932) 38 Com. Cas. 12 at 18, Lawrence LJ said that when a matter has been compromised it "assumes that a mutual concession has been made by both parties and that each party has got something less than he claimed". In *NFU Development Trust, Re* [1972] 1 W.L.R. 1548 at 1555, Brightman J, as he then was, said that "the word 'compromise' implies some element of accommodation on each side". See also *Alabama, New Orleans, Texas and Pacific Junction Ry Co, Re* [1891] 1 Ch. 213 at 243. And see Ch.2.

3 Evans LJ quoted with approval a similar passage in earlier editions in *Korea Foreign Insurance Co v Omne Re SA* [1999] Lloyd's Rep. I.R. 509, noted at para.8-08. See also *Gay Choon Ing v Loh Sze Ti Terence Peter* [2009] 2 SLR(R) 332 and *Real Estate Consortium Pte Ltd v East Coast Properties Pte Ltd and another* [2010] SGHC 373.

4 "Differences" for this purpose are taken to include differences during the interim stages of litigation. In the Arbitration Act 1996 the expression "dispute" is defined as including "any difference": see Ch.32. In *Garlick v Royal Trust Bank* unreported 10 February 1999 CA, Peter Gibson LJ said that it had been undisputed that, "a compromise is merely a contract which emerges from the course of negotiations, that there must be some underlying dispute before a true compromise could be said to have emerged [and] that a compromise is designed to bring an end to the dispute".

5 For the distinction between private and public law remedies, see *O'Reilly v Mackman* [1983] 2 A.C. 237 and *Cocks v Thanet DC* [1983] 2 A.C. 286. cf. *Roy v Kensington and Chelsea and Westminster Family Practitioner Committee* [1992] 1 A.C. 624, *British Steel Plc v Customs and Excise Commissioners (No.1)* [1997] 2 All E.R. 366, *Trustees of the Dennis Rye Pension Fund v Sheffield City Council* [1998] 1 W.L.R. 840.

6 The system is based on recommendations made by Lord Woolf in Access to Justice-Final Report 1996 (the Final Report to the Lord Chancellor on the civil justice system in England and Wales).

form and manner in which disputes are litigated. These are designed to identify and clarify the issues between the parties, to encourage a state of readiness for the trial of those issues and to assist thereby the ultimate resolution of the particular dispute or disputes from which the litigation arose. Subject to the existence of any right of appeal and the pursuit of such an appeal to its conclusion, the decision or judgment of the appropriate tribunal represents the final word on the matter as between the parties. The matter is said to be res judicata.[7] It cannot be ventilated again. The only matter which might occasion further recourse to the tribunal is the enforcement of the decision or judgment or some incidental question such as costs. Very similar consequences follow if the parties choose arbitration to resolve their dispute.[8]

1-03 However, the civil justice system does not provide merely a managed framework aimed at enabling parties to litigate their disputes to judgment, but a structure that is also designed to facilitate settlement.[9] At any stage of the whole process the parties may draw back from asking the court or other tribunal to adjudicate upon their dispute.[10] They may, by agreement, resolve it themselves. Indeed, they may have resolved it before embarking on any litigious process. Except in certain cases[11] parties have complete freedom to resolve their disputes consensually and without interference from the court. Having resolved their dispute in this way it is no less binding upon them and final than if a court had resolved it for them through a binding judgment.[12]

1-04 Whilst in many cases the agreement represents the final resolution of the original dispute, questions can arise on issues such as whether some aspect of the prior negotiations invalidates the compromise, precisely what the compromise means, the manner of its enforcement and so on. In consequence a body of law, founded essentially on the law of contract, has grown up with special reference to the situation of parties engaged in, or who have engaged in, the resolution or attempted resolution of their disputes. This constitutes the subject matter of the law of compromise. The manner in which parties conclude their agreement and the use to which they put the court process to give effect to it, or to set it aside, constitute features of the practice of compromise.

1-05 Compromise is not confined solely to the private law context. The volume of litigation in the public law sector inevitably leads to situations in which the parties achieve a complete or partial resolution of the differences leading to that litigation. Whether this is compromise *stricto sensu* is debatable, but it is an area that merits attention.[13]

---

7 The full Latin expression is *res judicata pro veritae accipitur*: a thing adjudicated is received as the truth. See Ch.6.

8 See Ch.32.

9 See Ch.13.

10 However, the fact that parties compromise litigation between the conclusion of the trial and before a reserved judgment is given may not necessarily result in the court not handing down the judgment: *Prudential Assurance Co Ltd v McBains Cooper* [2000] 1 W.L.R. 2000 CA. See also *Gurney Consulting Engineers (A Firm) v Gleeds Health & Safety Ltd* [2006] EWHC 536 (TCC); 108 Con. L.R. 58. See also *R (S) v General Teaching Council for England* [2013] EWHC 2779 (Admin).

11 See, e.g. Ch.27.

12 See Ch.6.

13 See Ch.33.

CHAPTER 2

Nature of a Dispute

MUST BE A DISPUTE BEFORE A COMPROMISE

A compromise in the true sense of the term does not arise until some dispute or difference of view exists between the parties which, by agreement, they then resolve.[1] It is not necessary for there to be pending litigation,[2] but there must be some "actual" or "potential" dispute.[3] The meaning to be given to the word "potential" in this context is of some importance.[4] **2-01**

ACTUAL DISPUTE

An "actual" dispute will not exist until a claim is asserted by one party which is "disputed" by the other. Where no such dispute about an issue can be discerned, no subsequent agreement between the parties will be found to have compromised that issue.[5] This can be illustrated by a number of examples from varying contexts: **2-02**

In *Smith v Smith*,[6] following a divorce, W made two applications to the court in respect of the former matrimonial home: one was under s.17 of the Married Women's Property Act 1882, by virtue of which she claimed a beneficial interest in it; the other was under the divorce jurisdiction by virtue of which she claimed a property adjustment order in relation to it. At that time she made no application for lump sum provision. When the applications came to be heard in April 1971, it transpired that because of certain charges on the house its net value at that time was nil. W abandoned the two applications and acknowledged, as part of a consent order, that she had no beneficial interest in the house. Some two years later, after the house had increased substantially in value, she applied for leave to claim a lump sum, the only source of such a lump sum being the net proceeds of sale of the house. H sought to allege that she was precluded from doing so by virtue of the consent order made in 1971 and said, in effect, that she had agreed as part of the compromise not to seek a lump sum. This argument was rejected on the basis that merely **2-03**

---

1 See para.1-01. There is a close relationship between this proposition and the principle that consideration is required to sustain the validity of a compromise: see para.3-07 onwards.

2 *Cook v Wright* (1861) 1 B. & S. 559, *Mercantile Investment and General Trust Co v International Co of Mexico* [1893] 1 Ch. 484 at 494.

3 In two cases concerning alleged compromises of shareholders' rights, the Court of Appeal emphasised that any rearrangement of those rights could not be said to be a true compromise unless a dispute as to those rights or their enforcement existed: *Sneath v Valley Gold Ltd* [1893] 1 Ch. 477, *Mercantile Investment and General Trust Co* [1893] 1 Ch. 484. See also *Chapman v Chapman* [1995] A.C. 429, referred to at para.23-21.

4 See para.2-08 onwards.

5 This issue may also arise in connection with whether a purported "without prejudice" offer is admissible in evidence. If there is no dispute, or no extant dispute, at the time it is made it will not be subject to the "without prejudice" privilege: see paras 19-12—19-22.

6 *Smith v Smith* (1974) 5 Fam. Law 125 CA. See also *Cloutte v Storey* [1911] 1 Ch. 18 CA.

abandoning claims for specific relief in relation to the property could not be construed as agreeing not to claim a lump sum from its proceeds of sale.

In other words, at the time of the agreement in 1971, W had not asserted a claim for relief by way of lump sum provision and there was thus no "dispute" about it. It follows, therefore, that this claim could not have been compromised.[7]

2-04 In other cases a fair analysis of the parties' discussions may reveal that, whatever other specific differences lie between them, certain matters are not in dispute and may even be admitted. These undisputed and admitted matters cannot thereafter be invested with a contentious character in order to found an argument that they have been the subject of a compromise. This situation arises not infrequently where a sum of money is in truth paid "on account" of some (yet to be determined) final figure and an attempt is then made to suggest that it was tendered or paid "in full and final settlement" of an alleged dispute.[8] The following cases illustrate the way in which the court will react to such a suggestion:

2-05 In *Newton Moor Construction v Charlton*,[9] C did building works for D and submitted a bill for £18,612 comprised of the price for the works originally ordered plus sums for extra items with deductions for items omitted. On 25 October, D's solicitors wrote saying that he was prepared to pay £8,847 and set out how this sum was arrived at. The letter indicated that he took the tender amount for the original work (£11,020) and made certain deductions for items omitted. He made a further deduction for some delay which he claimed to be entitled to set off and added a series of sums for extras, two of which he said were agreed figures and the remainder at figures he said were reasonable. The letter concluded as follows:

> "In these circumstances [D] has handed to me for despatch to you a cheque for £8,847 in full and final settlement of your account concerning the work ... If you are not prepared to accept this payment we have instructions to accept service of any proceedings concerning same. Will you please acknowledge receipt of this letter and cheque."

The cheque was received by C, paid into C's account and met. On 30 October, C's solicitors wrote acknowledging the letter and saying this: "With regard to the cheque for £8,847 our clients are accepting this cheque in part payment." In due course C sued for the balance of the bill and was met by the defence that there had been an accord and satisfaction by acceptance of the cheque sent in full and final settlement. The Court of Appeal held that there had been no accord and satisfaction. Sir David Cairns said that the letter of 25 October, when properly analysed, was no more than an admission that the sum of £8,847 was due for the reasons set out in the letter. There was, therefore, no consideration "for any agreement that could be said to be implied from the letter of 25 October, the cheque and the acceptance of that cheque". Eveleigh LJ said that the cheque was not accepted on the basis upon which it was offered and the parties were not, therefore, *ad idem*. Lawton LJ said that there was no evidence of accord and satisfaction.

2-06 In *Neuchatel Asphalte Co Ltd v Barnett*,[10] C, a company with its head office in London, contracted through its Birmingham office to do certain work for D at an agreed price of £250. The total amount charged was £259 to take account of an extra item. After the works

---

7 A party who should have disputed a matter at the time of a compromise reflected in a consent order or judgment may be prevented from disputing it later: see para.6-07 onwards.

8 This part of this paragraph was cited with approval in *Ferguson v Davies* [1997] 1 All E.R. 315 CA, noted at para.2-07. An analysis of this kind needs to be contrasted with the approach that may be required to determine whether the "without prejudice" privilege applies to certain communications between the parties. There is a significant body of authority (largely based on strong policy objectives) that it is not appropriate to "dissect" out admissions from other material in otherwise "without prejudice" discussions: see, e.g. para.19-51.

9 *Newton Moor Construction v Charlton* (1981) CAT 555. And see fn.11. Also see para.3-12 onwards.

10 *Neuchatel Asphalte Co Ltd v Barnett* [1957] 1 W.L.R. 356.

were completed D objected to the additional £9 and had some queries in relation to the main works carried out. Initially D sent a cheque for £125 expressly "on account" pending a reply to the queries he had raised. D discussed the queries with C's representative in Birmingham, but they had not been resolved by the time the London office had sent out a statement for the outstanding amount of £134. D returned the statement to the London office asking it to liaise with the representative in Birmingham. About a week later, but before the Birmingham representative had dealt with the matter, D sent a letter and a cheque for £75 to C's London office. The letter was as follows:

> "With further reference to account, in spite of repeated requests for allowance to which I am entitled, you have failed to advise me in this matter. I am therefore enclosing my further cheque for £75 in respect of this work."

On the back of the cheque D had typed the words "in full and final settlement of account" and made provision for a signature and date. Upon receipt of the cheque, a secretary indorsed it by rubber stamp over a 2d stamp and signed it. In proceedings brought by C for the balance, D sought to argue that, having presented the cheque for payment,[11] C must be taken to have settled the dispute. One of the facts found by the trial judge was that a reduction of £59 was far greater than any allowance C was likely to grant D in relation to the disputed items. The Court of Appeal held that, having regard to the terms of the letter sent by D with his cheque, it was plain that the £75 was sent on account and not by way of a settlement proposal.

In *Ferguson v Davies*,[12] C and D entered into a contract whereby C sold his stock of specialist records, tapes and discs to D in return for D's promise to provide C with similar goods up to the value of £600 by a certain date in default of which D was to pay to C the value of the goods supplied by C in cash. That value was in the region of £1,700. In fact D only delivered goods to the value of £143.50 and made a single payment of £5. C had originally limited his claim to £486.50 (possibly to keep within the small claims jurisdiction) and issued a default summons in Form N1. When Form N1 was sent to D it was accompanied by Form 9B which, inter alia, asked the question: "How much of the claim do you dispute?" D originally ticked the box, "I dispute the full amount claimed", but then crossed the tick out and initialed the erasure. He then ticked the second box opposite, "I admit the amount of £ ..." and inserted £150. D did not complete certain parts of the form that followed, but then answered a later question, "Do you dispute the claim because you have already paid it?", with the answer, "Yes, I paid £450 to the plaintiff over this period", giving details of when the sums were paid. The trial judge, who found the facts as indicated above, rejected this assertion. D did send a cheque for £150 to C as he was encouraged to do by Form 9B which indicated that, "If [he disputed] part only of the claim [he] must either pay the amount admitted to [C] ... [and] send this defence to the court" or, "complete the ... admission form and send it to the court with this defence". D wrote two letters on the day he sent the cheque (17 February), one to C enclosing the cheque which he described, "as a full payment on the County Court Summons" and expressing the hope that, "this will now resolve the matter". The other letter was to the court in which he indicated that he did not dispute the fact that he owed C money, but that he did dispute the amount being claimed. C, who discussed the position with a member of the county court staff, took the view that he was entitled to accept the cheque in part payment of the larger sum and to pursue that larger sum. He presented the cheque and following its clearance he wrote to D informing him that he was proposing to enlarge his claim to a sum in excess of £1,500. In due course he was given leave to amend his claim to increase it to £1,745.79. A defence of accord and satisfaction met this claim. This was not dealt with as a preliminary point. The judge found that a further £1,400 was due to C from D, but held that the presentation for payment of the cheque for £150 compromised the claim and the action failed. The Court of Appeal held that this conclusion was wrong. The sending by D of the cheque for £150 was simply an unequivocal and formal admission of indebted- **2-07**

---

11 For other cases concerning cheques sent "in full and final settlement", see para.3-30 onwards.

12 See fn.8.

ness and he was not giving C any additional benefit on top. Accordingly (per Henry LJ), there was no consideration for the accord suggested. Evans LJ expressed no view on the question of lack of consideration, but was unable to interpret D's letter to C as containing an unequivocal offer to pay £150 only upon the basis that, if C accepted it, he would withdraw the balance of the claim. C was entitled to understand D's offer as simply being to the effect that £150 was admittedly due, and was being paid, leaving the balance in dispute.

POTENTIAL DISPUTE

2-08 Parties frequently seek to compromise "potential" issues between them even if those issues have not yet been elevated to the status of an actual dispute. A familiar and well-established formula for settling disputes is in the following (or similar) terms:

> "A agrees to accept from B the sum of [figure] in full and final settlement of all claims which he has or may have arising from [the specified incident or other state of affairs]."[13]

The intention of such wording is plain. It is intended that the payment should discharge finally all claims that have not merely already been advanced, but also those which might subsequently be advanced in connection with whatever incident or state of affairs had brought the parties into dispute. It follows that the intention of the agreement underlying the use of this formula is that an issue not yet identified or formulated is also to be regarded as comprehended in the settlement. The phraseology has been subjected to judicial scrutiny.

2-09 In *Kitchen Design and Advice Ltd v Lea Valley Water Co*,[14] C sustained damage to its stock, fixtures and fittings at its premises as a result of flooding caused by a burst water main owned by D. C made a claim against its own insurers initially only for the physical damage arising from the flooding and this claim was settled by the insurers for about £18,000. C's insurers, who were subrogated to C's rights against D, sought to recover that sum from D's insurers. After negotiations D's insurers paid C's insurers the sum of £15,000 and the latter signed a form of discharge which expressly stated that the sum of £15,000 was accepted,

> "in full satisfaction, liquidation and discharge of all claims we have or may have against [D] in connection with a burst water main in [place identified] on [date recorded]".

Some four months after this agreement was concluded, C advanced to its insurers for the first time a claim for loss of profit in consequence of business interruption. This was settled as between C and its insurers for about £17,000 and C's insurers then sought to claim this from D's insurers. The latter took the point that the entirety of C's claim had been set-

---

13 Another form sometimes seen in personal injuries cases is, "in settlement [or full and final settlement or full satisfaction and discharge] of all claims, whether now or hereafter to become manifest, arising directly or indirectly from [the defined accident]": see, e.g. *Saunders v Ford Motor Co* [1970] 1 Lloyd's Rep. 379, *Arrale v Costain Civil Engineering Ltd* [1976] 1 Lloyd's Rep. 98 CA. In *Line Trust Corp Ltd v Fielding* unreported 26 July 1999 CA, the provision in the Tomlin order the subject of the argument was in the following terms: "All parties ... release all claims which they or any of them have or may have against each other in respect of the subject matter of this action or arising out of these proceedings." As Peter Gibson LJ said, the use of the expression "may have" showed that the settlement comprehended "any future claim".

14 *Kitchen Design and Advice Ltd v Lea Valley Water Co* [1989] 2 Lloyd's Rep. 221. In *Ter Yin Wei v Lim Leet Fang* [2012] SGHC 82, C accepted a certain sum from insurers "in full and final settlement of all claims we/I have or may have against D" arising from an accident. This was held to embrace C's personal injuries claim.

tled by the payment of the sum of £15,000 having regard to the terms of the form of discharge. Phillips J, as he then was, held that D's insurers were correct in this contention. One of the arguments advanced on behalf of C's insurers was that the phrase "all claims we have or may have" meant that the settlement was restricted to claims which C's insurers "either had advanced or were in a position to advance at the time the form of discharge was signed" and that the subject matter of the agreement "was limited to the claims that were actually discussed" between the insurers' representatives. In relation to these arguments Phillips J said that the phrase,

> "was clearly designed to cover, not merely claims actually advanced in relation to the burst main, but other claims not advanced which might be advanced".

He went on to say that the fact that the insurers' representatives had only been negotiating in respect of specific items of physical damage "cannot detract from the natural meaning of the phrase".

This conclusion was in line with long-established practice: the "buying off" of a potential claim has long been recognised as a matter of importance and the courts have never stood in the way of this being achieved in appropriate circumstances.[15] **2-10**

The House of Lords has confirmed this approach as potentially applicable to claims of which the parties could not at the time of the compromise have been aware. It has been said that, in principle and provided the appropriate language is used, a party may be bound by a compromise agreement supported by valuable consideration in which he agrees,

> "to release claims or rights of which he is unaware and of which he could not be aware [and] even claims which could not on the facts known to the parties have been imagined".[16]

The phraseology of an agreement giving rise to such a consequence will, of course, depend upon the subject matter of the dispute giving rise to the agreement and to the general nature of the agreement into which the parties have entered. A clause along the following lines[17] may have efficacy in this regard:

> "This agreement is in full and final settlement of all claims and potential claims of whatsoever nature and kind (including interest, costs and any claims that at the date hereof have not or may not have been foreseen or may not have been capable of being foreseen, either factually or legally, by the parties hereto) which the parties have or may have against each other under or in respect of or arising out of or in connection with, whether directly or indirectly, [the specified and identified matters giving rise to the dispute] and without prejudice the generality of the foregoing, the parties hereto agree not to commence or prosecute any proceedings against one another arising out of or in connection with such matters."

The release of an unforeseen claim may be achieved even in circumstances where a formula of the kind referred to above has not been used expressly by the parties: **2-11**

---

15 cf. para.5-22 onwards. An argument that a provision such as that referred to in para.2-08 must satisfy the "reasonableness test" within the Unfair Contract Terms Act 1977 in order to be binding was rejected in *Tudor Grange Holdings Ltd v Citibank NA* [1992] Ch. 53.

16 *Bank of Credit and Commercial International SA v Ali* [2002] 1 A.C. 251, per Lord Bingham of Cornhill, with whom Lord Browne-Wilkinson agreed, at 259. See also Lord Nicholls of Birkenhead at 265 and Lord Clyde at 282. Lord Hoffmann, who dissented in the result, was also of the view that a release could operate effectively to exclude a claim that could not have been foreseen at the time of the release. For further consideration of this case, including the form of the release, see para.5-22 onwards.

17 Adapted from the clause considered in *Heaton v AXA Equity and Law Life* [2002] 2 A.C. 329. See para.6-39 onwards.

In *Bristow v Grout*,[18] C was injured in an accident in January 1982 in respect of which there was no issue concerning D's liability. C's solicitors wrote to D's insurers indicating that C claimed "damages for the personal injury, losses, expenses and inconvenience arising from the accident". At that stage C's injuries appeared to be confined to his face. After further correspondence, C's solicitors wrote to the insurers saying that C "is prepared to accept your offer in the sum of £1,500" in relation to general damages. In that letter there was further reference to certain expenses and disbursements and also to special damages. After further correspondence C's solicitors wrote again confirming that C was prepared to accept general damages,

> "already agreed at £1,500 together with special damages in the sum of £147 comprising examination fees £12, telephone calls £15 and the travelling expenses. The overall settlement figure is therefore £1,647 ... subject to payment of costs".

The letter indicated that the costs were £565.01. The next day D's insurers sent two cheques to C's solicitors for £1,647 and £565.01 respectively, both of which were presented and met. At that time, unbeknown to C, he was beginning to suffer from a condition of the hip possibly attributable to the accident. In 1985 a consultant orthopaedic surgeon concluded that his symptoms, which by then had substantially increased, were as a result of the accident. The Court of Appeal held that C was not entitled to seek damages either for the "original" injuries or the further symptoms since it was plain that the agreement was intended to be in full and final settlement of his claim in negligence for personal injuries arising out of the accident in January 1982 which was the claim made in the letter before action. May LJ said that it was,

> "quite clear ... that [C] cannot in subsequent proceedings be heard to say that, as a result of the accident and claim so compromised, he in fact sustained further damage of which he was earlier unaware".

THE UNARTICULATED DISPUTE?

2-12 It has been suggested above[19] that the absence of a dispute, actual or potential, precludes the emergence of a compromise in its true sense. An actual dispute[20] will invariably be articulated expressly by the parties. Even a potential dispute[21] will be articulated expressly in the sense that the parties will have identified the essential legal and factual matrix or substratum from which the potential dispute might arise.[22] An argument has been advanced[23] for what is, on one view, a third situation, namely, one where parties reach an agreement "without [having spelt] out a dispute, [but sensing] that an underlying problem might grow into a fully articulated disagreement".[24]

2-13 The distinction between this situation and that of a compromise of a potential dispute as defined above[25] may be that no "underlying problem" has been contemplated by the parties in respect of the latter: each has effectively said to the

---

18 *Bristow v Grout* (1987) CAT 1134; 1987 WL 748563; *The Times*, 9 November 1987 CA. See also *O'Boyle v Leiper*, *The Times*, 26 January 1990 CA.

19 See para.2-01 onwards.

20 See paras 2-02—2-07.

21 See paras 2-08—2-11.

22 In a straightforward personal injury case, for example, the parties will identify the material accident and the overall claim for damages (as was done in *Bristow v Grout*: see para.2-11). By settling all claims that the claimant has or may have the parties have expressly articulated the potential existence of claims going beyond those actually formulated at the time of the settlement: see *Kitchen Design and Advice Ltd* [1989] 2 Lloyd's Rep. 221 at para.2-09.

23 N.H. Andrews, "Mistaken settlement of disputable claims" (1989) 4 L.M.C.L.Q. 431.

24 Andrews, "Mistaken settlement of disputable claims" (1989) 4 L.M.C.L.Q. 431.

25 See fn.22.

other:

> "If there is something arising from the state of affairs that brought us into dispute which we have not yet identified, we expressly forego any further claims or counterclaims arising therefrom."

In the former situation each party is effectively recognising internally that some dispute might emerge from the shadows, but neither has raised it expressly with the other or in a way that identifies the area in shadow. Andrews argues[26] that an agreement reached in such a situation should be characterised as an "implied settlement", the word "settlement" being preferred to "compromise" because of the latter's association with the need for disputation to exist before a compromise can be said to have arisen. An "implied settlement" is defined as one where an agreement is made "in circumstances of doubt", a classic example being afforded by the payment made by an insurer to an insured who has made a claim under the contract of insurance between them. The payment made by the insurer is generally to be regarded as closing the matter[27] even if possible disputes as to the liability to make payment exist, albeit in unarticulated form.

For many practical purposes the distinction between the compromise of a potential dispute and an implied settlement as defined[28] would be of no great importance: the law will strive to uphold an agreement plainly designed to bring to an end any latent disputation between the parties. The difficulty with the foregoing formulation of an implied settlement is that it does not sit happily with a number of well-established authorities.[29] It may be thought that the existence of an actual or potential dispute remains the foundation of a true compromise and that a settlement of a claim under an insurance policy should be seen as in a category of its own,[30] whilst recognising that in many such cases a true compromise of a disputed liability will take place and in others something closely analogous thereto will result. Since it is now clear that even "unimagined" claims (which, by definition, could not have been articulated so as to give rise to a dispute at the time of the compromise[31]) can be the subject of a compromise, there can be no doubt that unarticulated disputes may be the subject of a true compromise. **2-14**

Law or Fact

A dispute may involve questions of law, of fact, or a combination of both. The dispute may be conducted orally or by written communications and within or outwith the context of litigation. **2-15**

The assertions, denials and counter-assertions comprising the dispute need have no foundation in fact or in law provided they are made in good faith.[32] If a party to a compromise attempts to escape its consequences by alleging that the claim had no legal or factual foundation, the court will decline to investigate such an **2-16**

---

26 Andrews, "Mistaken settlement of disputable claims" (1989) 4 L.M.C.L.Q. 431.

27 cf. *Woolwich Building Society v IRC* [1993] A.C. 70 at 165, per Lord Goff of Chieveley. See also para. 22-19

28 See para.2-13.

29 eg., *Huddersfield Banking Co v Lister* [1895] 2 Ch. 273, referred to at para.4-17. And see Andrews, "Mistaken settlement of disputable claims" (1989) 4 L.M.C.L.Q. 431, 445–449.

30 See para.22-19.

31 See para.2-10.

32 The proposition in the text should not be confused with the principle that a fundamental mistake, going to the root of the compromise itself, may vitiate the compromise: see Ch.4. For proviso as to good faith, see para.2-19.

allegation.[33] In many cases, for example, a claimant will allege the fact of the defendant's negligence which the defendant denies. The law does not permit a defendant who has compromised a claimant's claim for damages based on the alleged negligence subsequently to pursue the suggestion that he was not in fact negligent for the purpose of avoiding the compromise. Not infrequently, in cases between landlord and tenant, the tenant will seek to claim damages for the failure of the landlord to effect certain external repairs in breach of an alleged implied covenant to that effect. In many situations the law implies no such covenant and yet the landlord might, for example, reduce his own claim for arrears of rent against the tenant because of the tenant's claim. He would not be permitted subsequently to allege that the compromise of the rent claim should be set aside because the tenant's claim was unfounded in law.

2-17 In *Binder v Alachouzos*,[34] D borrowed a total of £65,000 from C, relatives of C and companies with which C was closely associated. D gave cheques by way of repayment of the loans and agreed interest, but the cheques were not met. The various lenders commenced actions against D on the dishonoured cheques. In his defence, D alleged that the loans were made in the course of carrying on the business of moneylending and were void and unenforceable. Shortly before the trial of those actions an agreement was reached which provided, inter alia, that the actions should be discontinued and that D should pay C the sum of £86,565, with interest at 18 per cent, by instalments of £10,000 per month payable on a particular day each month. It was further expressly agreed by D that: (a) none of the transactions the subject of the actions was a transaction to which the Moneylenders Acts applied; and (b) no defence should be raised in any action on the agreement other than as to the quantum of the moneys that had been paid. D paid two or three instalments and then defaulted. In C's action to recover the balance of the sums owing under the agreement, D sought to raise again the issue of the Moneylenders Acts and suggested that the compromise was not binding. The Court of Appeal held that he was not entitled to put forward these arguments since there had been a bona fide compromise of an issue of fact in the previous action, namely whether the original loans were unlawful money-lending transactions.

2-18 In *Colchester BC v Smith*,[35] C and D had been in dispute about D's occupation of certain land. D had asserted through his solicitors that he had acquired possessory title to the land, an assertion rejected by C. In due course, after further correspondence and a threat by C to bring possession proceedings, D entered into a tenancy agreement in relation to the land and, as part of that agreement, he acknowledged that he had "not gained any right title or interest to or in it by adverse possession". That agreement was made in November 1983. In November 1984 C instituted proceedings seeking possession of the land relying upon the terms of the tenancy agreement. In those proceedings D sought to argue, inter alia, that he had acquired possessory title to the land. At first instance it was held on the evidence that D had, prior to the tenancy agreement, acquired possessory title to certain parts of the land, but that he was estopped by contract or convention from disputing C's title to it having regard to the agreement. The Court of Appeal held, following *Binder v Alachouzos*, that there had been a bona fide compromise of a disputed issue in the agreement of November 1983 and that D was prevented from going behind it.

Must be bona fide

2-19 Lack of good faith in the assertion of a claim or the maintenance of a denial, in

---

33 For example *Huddersfield Banking Co v Lister* [1895] 2 Ch. 273 at 278 (fact), *Holsworthy UDC v Holsworthy RDC* [1907] 2 Ch. 62 at 73 (law). See also *Norfolk Finance Ltd v Newton* Unreported 15 October 1998 CA.

34 *Binder v Alachouzos* [1972] 2 Q.B. 151. See also *Panyiatou v Sony Music Entertainment (UK) Ltd, The Times,* 30 June 1994 and *FPH Law (a Firm) v Brown (t/a Integrum Law)* [2016] EWHC 1681 (QB); [2016] 5 Costs L.O. 733 at [29] per Slade J.

35 *Colchester BC v Smith* [1992] Ch. 421.

circumstances where there is no foundation in fact or law to support them, may operate to invalidate a compromise founded thereon.[36] It would seem that, provided a claimant believes that he has a right to make the claim he asserts, even if he has little confidence in its ultimate success, a compromise of it is valid.[37] If, on the other hand, he makes a claim which he knows to be unfounded and derives an advantage from the compromise of the claim, his conduct will be considered fraudulent and the compromise liable to be set aside.[38] In the former case the compromise will be upheld even if the party against whom the claim is made believes that it has no foundation. By compromising it, he puts an end to troublesome litigation.[39] In the latter case, however, if the claim's lack of foundation is known by the other party, any agreement purporting to be based upon it cannot truly be said to be a compromise since no real dispute as such exists.

The legal effect of such an agreement will often arise in connection with third-party rights.[40] As between the parties it may be operative.[41]

---

36 *Wade v Simeon* (1846) 2 C. B. 548, *Cook v Wright* (1861) 30 L. J. (Q.B.) 321; (1861) 1 B. & S. 559, *Callisher v Bischoffsheim* (1869) L.R. 5 Q.B. 449, *Blythe Ex p. Banner, Re* (1881) 17 Ch. D. 480, *Holsworthy UDC* [1907] 2 Ch. 62, *Binder v Alachouzos* [1972] 2 Q.B. 151. See para.3-11.

37 *Callisher* (1869) L.R. 5 Q.B. 449, *Blyth Ex p. Banner, Re* (1881) 17 Ch. D. 480. In *Freedman v Union Group Plc* [1997] E.G.C.S. 28, Peter Gibson LJ said that it is "common for a person genuinely to believe in the rightness of a claim, but still to harbour doubts whether it would in fact succeed".

38 *Callisher* (1869) L.R. 5 Q.B. 449, per Cockburn C.J. at 452, *Wade v Simeon* (1846) 2 C.B. 548. See Ch.4.

39 See Ch.3.

40 See Ch.6.

41 See Ch.6. On the one hand, it could be argued that, since no consideration is furnished by either party, the apparent agreement is a *nudum pactum*; on the other hand, the agreement may be seen simply as the equivalent of a release of an "unimagined" claim: see para.2-14.

CHAPTER 3

Essential Requirements of a Valid Compromise

INTRODUCTION

3-01 Since a compromise is a contract, the ordinary principles of contract law apply with as much force as in other contractual contexts. Under the ordinary law a contract will not be found to have arisen unless:

(i) consideration exists[1];
(ii) an agreement can be identified which is complete and certain;
(iii) the parties intend to create legal relations; and
(iv) in some cases, certain formalities have been observed.[2]

The significance of each of these requirements in the context of compromise will be examined briefly.

CONSIDERATION

3-02 The usual approach to consideration under the general law is to define it as the accrual of some benefit to one party or the suffering of some detriment by the other.[3] Consideration may consist of the exchange of mutual promises or the performance by one party of an act in return for a promise by the other to do some act.[4] In standard terminology, consideration must "move from the promisee".[5]

Promised or actual forbearance to sue

3-03 In compromise, consideration is often provided by the promised or actual forbearance of one party to pursue a claim against another in return for some promised or actual act by the other.[6] Such act may constitute a benefit to the claimant or a detri-

---

1 Except, of course, in cases of contracts under seal.
2 *Chitty*, Vol.1, Chs 2, 4 and 5.
3 *Currie v Misa* (1875) L.R. 10 Ex. 153 at 162, per Lush J.
4 *Chitty*, Vol.1, paras 4-008 to 4-009.
5 *Chitty*, Vol.1, para.4-037 onwards. It need not, but usually does, "move to the promisor".
6 Any doubt concerning the efficacy of a promise as constituting good consideration was resolved by the decision in *British Russian Gazette and Trade Outlook Ltd v Associated Newspapers Ltd* [1933] 2 K.B. 616. A promised or actual forbearance from pursuing a claim against a third party in return for a promised or actual act by another party will furnish good consideration (cf. *Oliver v Davis* [1949] 2 K.B. 727 at 743) although the doctrine of privity of contract may preclude the third party from enforcing the agreement thus reached: see Ch.6.

ment to the performer or indeed both. The promised or actual forbearance may be for a specified time or, where no time is specified, for a reasonable time.[7]

3-04 An example of a promised forbearance is afforded by a situation in which in return for a promise by a creditor to forbear from taking immediate proceedings on a debt, the debtor promises to create, or actually creates, a charge on property in favour of the creditor for the amount of the debt.[8] The respective benefits and detriments are obvious.

3-05 An example of an actual forbearance arises where a creditor forbears in fact from taking immediate proceedings on a debt, though not in pursuance of an express promise to that effect, on the basis of which the debtor promises to create a charge on his house for the amount of the debt. The actual forbearance is said to constitute the consideration for the debtor's promise.[9] It must, however, be referable to the debtor's promise[10] and arise (probably)[11] from an express or implied request therefor by him.

3-06 In *Combe v Combe*,[12] H, following a divorce, promised W permanent alimony at the rate of £100 per annum. When he failed to keep his promise, W sought to enforce it as an agreement arguing, amongst other things, that she had given consideration for it by her forbearance to take proceedings for maintenance. The Court of Appeal held, on this argument, that the alleged consideration did not exist because H had not requested W, expressly or impliedly, to forbear from taking proceedings and the actual forbearance could not be said to be referable to H's promise.[13]

Compromise proper

3-07 The foregoing discussion has focused on situations where the promised or actual forbearance to sue has been met by an act which was not itself a promised or actual forbearance to raise some defence to the intended claim or to pursue some counterclaim. However, matters such as these manifestly represent good consideration for the original claimant's promised or actual forbearance to sue. In this situation, where consideration of this nature "moves each way", it can legitimately be said that a contract of compromise has been concluded by the parties. Such consideration has been described judicially thus:

3-08 "Every day a compromise is effected on the grounds that the party making it has a chance of succeeding in it, and if he bona fide believes he has a fair chance of success, he has a reasonable ground for suing, and his forbearance to sue will constitute a good consideration. When such a person forbears to sue he gives up what he believes to be a right of action, and the other party gets an advantage, and, instead of being annoyed with an action, he escapes from the vexations incident to it."[14]

3-09 "[I]f an intending litigant bona fide forbears a right to litigate a question of law or fact

---

7 *Fullerton v Provincial Bank of Ireland* [1903] A.C. 309 at 313.

8 cf. *Wigan v England & Scottish Law Life Assurance Association* [1909] 1 Ch. 291 at 297–298.

9 See *Alliance Bank v Broom* (1864) 2 Drew & Sm. 289; *Wyvern Developments, Re* [1974] 1 W.L.R. 1097 at 1103–1104; cf. the majority of the Court of Appeal in *Miles v New Zealand Alford Estate Co* (1886) 32 Ch. D. 26 and the suggested distinction between it and the *Alliance Bank* case in *Chitty*, Vol.1, para.4-058.

10 *Combe v Combe* [1951] 2 K.B. 215, *Wigan* [1909] 1 Ch. 291.

11 *Combe* [1951] 2 K.B. 215, *Fullerton* [1903] A.C. 309, cf. *Broom* (1864) 2 Drew & Sm. 289.

12 See fn.10.

13 Even if W had agreed not to proceed for maintenance as a direct result of a request by H, public policy would have prevented enforcement of the agreement: see *Combe* [1951] 2 K.B. 215, per Asquith LJ at 226 and see Ch.24.

14 *Callisher* (1870) L.R. 5 Q.B. 449 at 452, per Cockburn CJ.

which it is not vexatious or frivolous to litigate, he does give up something of value. It is a mistake to suppose it is not an advantage, which a suitor is capable of appreciating, to be able to litigate his claim, even if he turns out to be wrong. It seems to me it is equally a mistake to suppose that it is not sometimes a disadvantage to a man to have to defend an action even if in the end he succeeds in his defence; and I think therefore that the reality of the claim which is given up must be measured, not by the state of the law as it is ultimately discovered to be, but by the state of the knowledge of the person who at the time has to judge and make the concession. Otherwise you would have to try the whole cause to know if the man had a right to compromise it."[15]

No consideration

The adequacy of the consideration given or received is not ordinarily open to question.[16] Consideration must, however, be real. As such there are circumstances in which the court will decline to uphold the existence of a consideration that apparently exists. **3-10**

Baseless, frivolous, vexatious or illegal claim

It would seem that a forbearance from pursuing a claim (a) known by the claimant to be baseless[17] or (b) which is vexatious or frivolous[18] would constitute no consideration for a compromise based upon it. Equally, a forbearance to pursue an illegal claim, for example, one made illegal by statute, would represent no consideration.[19] So too a forbearance which itself is prohibited by law or is contrary to public policy is no consideration.[20] **3-11**

Existing debts and part payment thereof

Under the general law of contract past consideration is no consideration unless given at the request of the promisor.[21] As noted earlier, an actual forbearance to sue will constitute consideration only if afforded at the request of the debtor.[22] Thus, an actual abstention from pursuing an existing debt will be good consideration for a debtor's promise, for example, to give security for it, only if it results from some express or implied request therefor. **3-12**

It should be recalled in this context that, in general terms, an agreement to accept part payment of a debt or liquidated demand is not binding because no consideration is furnished by the debtor.[23] This would seem to be so even if, as a matter of fact, the creditor is content to avoid the process of litigation with a view **3-13**

---

15 *Miles v New Zealand Alford Estate Co* (1885) 32 Ch. D. 266 at 291, per Bowen LJ. See the analysis of the facts in *Technocrats International Inc v Fredic Ltd* [2004] EWHC 692 (QB) at [30]–[33].

16 *Chitty*, Vol.1, paras 4-014–4-021. See also *Stephens v Bateman* (1778) 1 Bro. C.C. 22 and *Naylor v Winch* (1824) 1 Sim. & St. 555.

17 See para.2-19. However, forbearing to pursue a defence subsequently held to be without merit is good consideration: *Simantob v Shavleyan* [2019] EWCA Civ 1105; [2019] 6 WLUK 458 at [43]–[53].

18 See fn.15.

19 *Hyams v Coombes* (1912) 28 T.L.R. 413, *Burrell & Son v Leven* (1926) 42 T.L.R. 407, *Poteliakhoff v Teakle* [1938] 2 K.B. 816. See *Chitty*, Vol.1, para.4-051 and see Ch.4.

20 For example, Matrimonial Causes Act 1973 s.34, discussed in Ch.24. See *Chitty*, Vol.1, para.4-056.

21 *Chitty*, Vol.1, para.4-026 onwards.

22 See para.3-03 onwards.

23 *Foakes v Beer* (1884) 9 App. Cas. 605, *D & C Builders Ltd v Rees* [1966] 2 Q.B. 617.

to securing the money indisputably due to him.[24] If, however, the debtor gives something other than mere part payment of the debt, for example, he pays at a different time or place or in a different currency, sufficient consideration is furnished.[25] There are, furthermore, a number of exceptions to the general rule expressed above and the doctrine of equitable estoppel may intervene to protect the debtor.[26] An agreement of the nature under discussion may not, perhaps, in any event be regarded as a compromise in the true sense of the term. There is no dispute settled by mutual concession.[27]

3-14 In *Tiney Engineering Ltd v Amods Knitting Machines Ltd*,[28] C and D engaged in a transaction involving the sale of a knitting machine. C's case was that it had been agreed that upon sale of the machine a commission of 10 per cent of the price should be paid. D's case was that 5 per cent was the agreed percentage. The sale went through and C submitted an invoice to D on the basis of 10 per cent. A meeting took place at which C's representative initialled the invoice, which had been amended to 5 per cent commission, underneath the words "accepted in full and final settlement". £3,000 was then paid immediately, but C thereafter claimed the balance of a commission based on 10 per cent. It was found as a fact at the trial that the original agreement had been that a 10 per cent commission would be paid. The Court of Appeal held that, on the facts found, a sum based upon a 10 per cent commission was admittedly due and all that was given when the sum of £3,000 was paid was part payment of that sum. There was, accordingly, no consideration for the agreement to accept the lesser sum and C was entitled to the balance.

3-15 In *Arrale v Costain Civil Engineering Ltd*,[29] C was injured in an accident when employed by D in the building of a harbour wall at Dubai in the Persian Gulf as a result of which his left arm had to be amputated. According to the Workmen's Compensation Ordnance of the Trucial States 1965, which was operative in Dubai, C was entitled to a fixed sum of money (calculated by reference to a schedule) by way of compensation for his injuries. A provision of the Ordnance entitled D, if they elected to do so, to seek to prove

> "to the Court that [C] deliberately contravened instructions issued to safeguard his health and person or displayed serious negligence in executing those instructions",

whereupon C would not have been entitled to compensation under the Ordnance. As a matter of policy D had decided not to rely on this provision. The sterling equivalent of the sum to which C thus became entitled was £490. This sum was paid to C upon C signing a receipt acknowledging that the sum was accepted

> "in full satisfaction and discharge of all claims in respect of personal injury whether now or hereafter to become manifest arising directly or indirectly from"

the accident. C thereafter sought to pursue a claim for compensation at common law. D argued that C could not do so having regard to the terms of the receipt. The Court of Appeal held that C was entitled to proceed. The majority[30] held that the receipt, on its true construction, did not operate to exclude the common law claim.[31] All members of the court held that if the receipt did so operate, D had given no consideration for any such agreement. Lord Denning MR[32] appeared to equate the position with accepting a lesser sum in discharge of a greater sum, drawing attention to the fact that D had paid C the exact

---

24 cf. paras 3-07–3-09.

25 *Chitty*, Vol.1, para.4-117 onwards.

26 *Chitty*, Vol.1, paras 4-130–4-138.

27 See para.1-01.

28 *Tiney Engineering Ltd v Amods Knitting Machines Ltd* (1986) CAT 440, [1987] C.L.Y. 412. In *Ferguson v Davies* [1997] 1 All E.R. 315, Henry LJ (with whom Aldous LJ agreed) based his decision upon the ground that no consideration was furnished by D.

29 *Arrale v Costain Civil Engineering Ltd* [1976] 1 Lloyd's Rep. 98 CA.

30 Lord Denning MR and Stephenson LJ.

31 This aspect of the decision is noted further in paras 5-32 and 5-34.

32 *Arrale* [1976] Lloyd's Rep. 98 at 102.

sum to which he was entitled under the Ordnance. However, he did go on to suggest that this was a conclusion that could only be reached if the two claims were "to be regarded as severed into two or combined into one" which, he continued, "would be a poor way of deciding whether an agreement is binding". He preferred to regard the position as one of inequality of bargaining power, where no one had explained to C that he might have a claim at common law, and thus one in which there could have been no agreement to bargain away the common law claim. Geoffrey Lane LJ (as he then was), having taken the view that C had promised not to sue at common law, said that D gave no consideration because: (a) by paying the sum under the Ordnance, they were doing no more than performing an obligation already cast upon them by law; and (b) having decided in this case never to invoke the provision referred to above, they gave nothing up in this regard in return for C's promise.[33]

On the issue of consideration Stephenson LJ agreed with the reasons given by Lord Denning MR and Geoffrey Lane LJ, but was not prepared to regard it as a case of inequality of bargaining power having regard to certain findings of fact made by the trial judge.[34]

Arrale's case is a difficult one in some respects, particularly having regard to the differing judicial views and emphases on the various issues canvassed.[35] On the question of consideration, the first reason given by Geoffrey Lane LJ (with which Stephenson LJ agreed) is arguably the most persuasive and most consistent with ordinary contractual principles.[36] The second reason is also consistent with the principle that illusory consideration is no consideration,[37] but there are features of this principle that require further examination in the context of compromise.[38] **3-16**

There are other examples in the reported cases of situations where this issue has arisen for consideration: **3-17**

In *Broderick, Re*,[39] the Inland Revenue obtained judgment for nearly £14,000 and costs against B on the basis of an assessment to tax. Shortly after issuing enforcement proceedings, B's solicitors asked the Revenue for, and were granted, eight weeks to arrange settlement. Some two weeks later B's solicitors sent a "without prejudice" letter to the Revenue stating that B was in a position to make an offer of £7,500, in settlement of the amount due. The Revenue replied saying that the amount offered would be accepted without prejudice, but that B's proposals for clearing the balance would be expected within about two months. Shortly before the expiration of the deadline for these further proposals, B's solicitors sent a cheque for £7,500, "in full and final settlement of all monies due" in the enforcement proceedings. The cheque was presented and paid into an Inland Revenue account. A few days later the Revenue wrote to B's solicitors asking for proposals as to the balance. In subsequent bankruptcy proceedings B contended that there had been an accord and satisfaction. Carswell J. held that: (i) there had been no accord and satisfaction[40] and (ii) if there had been an agreement to accept £7,500 in settlement, there was no consideration for that agreement.

---

33 *Arrale* [1976] Lloyd's Rep. 98 at 106.

34 *Arrale* [1976] Lloyd's Rep. 98 at 104–105. Any reference in the judgments to the principle of "inequality of bargaining power" must be read in the light of *National Westminster Bank Plc v Morgan* [1985] A.C. 686 at 708.

35 It was referred to without disapproval in the narrative of relevant cases by Lord Bingham of Cornhill in *Ali* [2002] 1 A.C. 251 at [16]. See further at para.5-23 onwards.

36 *Chitty*, Vol.1, para.4-123 onwards. cf. *Williams v Roffey Bros and Nicholls (Contractors) Ltd* [1991] 1 Q.B. 1 CA.

37 *Chitty*, Vol.1, para.4-023.

38 See para.3-20.

39 *Broderick, Re* [1986] 6 N.I.JB. 36.

40 See para.3-32 onwards.

3-18 In *Selectmove, Re*[41] S Co was in debt to the Inland Revenue for unpaid PAYE and NIC. Discussions took place in about July 1991 as to how the debt might be discharged. S Co contended that it had been agreed in those discussions that the Revenue would take no action on the debt in return for a promise that payment of the debt would be made by instalments of £1,000 per month from February 1992 together with future PAYE and NIC contributions as they fell due. Payments were made pursuant to the alleged agreement, although some were late, until the Revenue demanded payment of the debt in full and presented a winding-up petition. It was contended on S Co's behalf that, since the Revenue would have received a practical benefit from receiving the instalment payments, there was good consideration for the Revenue's alleged promise not to enforce the debt. The Court of Appeal held that, although the facts did not support the existence of the alleged promise, even if they had done so this argument had to be rejected because it had been raised and rejected by the House of Lords in *Foakes v Beer*.[42]

Intention to pursue claim?

3-19 One final matter arises in the context of the question whether consideration exists to support a compromise. Does a person who bona fide sets up a claim against another, but who does not in fact intend to pursue it to court, furnish consideration by "forbearing" from pursuing it? An example would be afforded where, say, an elderly lady is injured as the result of another person's alleged negligence and is advised by her legal advisers that she has a reasonable case for claiming damages. Although she is prepared for her solicitors to intimate a claim, and even commence proceedings on her behalf, in the hope that some offer of compromise is made, because of her age and fear of giving evidence in court she is firm in her intention of not pursuing the claim to court. Assuming such facts to be susceptible of proof, would any compromise of the apparent claim be considered a nullity on the basis that she had furnished no consideration?

3-20 There is some authority[43] to suggest that no consideration is furnished in such a situation. In *Arrale's* case[44] one basis for the Court of Appeal's decision was that since the defendants had no intention of raising a form of defence to one part of the plaintiff's overall claim, they were not entitled to say that by not raising it they had furnished consideration for his promise not to pursue the rest of his claim.[45] It is submitted that this was a plainly correct analysis of the situation in that case and reflects the principle that illusory consideration is no consideration.[46] However, it is not thought that this establishes (any more than do the other authorities) that an intention to pursue a claim (or, of course, a defence) to court must be maintained throughout the period until a compromise is concluded. Indeed, other authority[47] suggests that the "reality of the claim made and the bona fides of the compromise" represent the real consideration.

---

41 *Selectmove, Re* [1995] 1 W.L.R. 474; and see *Rock Advertising Ltd v MWB Business Exchange Centres Ltd* [2018] UKSC 24; [2018] 2 W.L.R. 1603; *Chitty*, Vol.1, para.4-117 onwards, and *Simantob v Shavleyan* [2019] EWCA Civ 1105. See Peel, "Part Payment of a debt is no consideration" (1994) 110 L.Q.R. 353.

42 See fn.23.

43 *Miles* (1886) L.R. 32 Ch. D. 266 at 291, per Bowen LJ who refers to an "intending litigant". In *Cook v Wright* (1861) 1 B. & S. 559 at 569 reference is made to a claim which is "bona fide intended to pursue". See also *Syros Shipping Co SA v Elaghill Trading Co; The Proodos C* [1980] 2 Lloyd's Rep. 390 at 392.

44 See fn.29.

45 "It is no consideration to refrain from a course of action which it was never intended to pursue": *Arrale* [1976] 1 Lloyd's Rep. 98, per Geoffrey Lane LJ at 106.

46 See fn.37.

47 *Cook v Wright* (1861) 1 B. & S. 559 at 570, per Blackburn J, adopted by Fry LJ in *Miles* (1886) L.R. 32 Ch. D. 266.

Arguably consideration is furnished in a situation such as that described. It might fairly be regarded as furnished by the giving up of the right on the part of the claimant to a change of heart about not proceeding, such right existing, of course, until the expiration of the relevant limitation period or until the claim is dismissed for want of prosecution. Needless to say, the potential defendant "buys off" the risk of such a change of heart although he will probably regard it as "buying off" an intended claim.[48] Arguably the correct view is that a person is entitled to pursue a bona fide claim to the point of compromise and that thereafter his intention to pursue the claim to court cannot be called into question. 3-21

AN IDENTIFIABLE AGREEMENT

General

In many instances the existence of a compromise will not be in doubt. Usually it will be found in, or evidenced by, an exchange of written communications, a written memorandum of agreement or a consent order or judgment. In some circumstances, however, it may be difficult to ascertain whether the parties have in fact concluded an agreement. The essential task is to determine whether the parties' negotiations have crystallised into a contractually binding agreement.[49] In order to achieve this the traditional approach, applying an objective test, is to seek to identify a definite offer by one party and a definite acceptance of that offer by the other party.[50] The refinements of this approach are not considered in this work.[51] Some examples taken from cases involving compromise will be considered below. Each involves the exercise of construing the parties' negotiations objectively.[52] 3-22

The court will look at the whole course of the negotiations to see whether agreement is reached at any point.[53] If such a point is identified, the mere fact that negotiations are continued thereafter will not of itself affect the existence of the agreement already concluded.[54] If the continued negotiations disclose an agreed rescission of that agreement then the position is different.[55]

---

48 In *Garlick v Royal Trust Bank* (unreported 10 February 1999) the Court of Appeal quoted the view expressed in the text without express approval, but equally without express disapproval. In the circumstances of that case it was said that there was "no evidence that [D] had decided not to proceed, or never intended to proceed" in relation to the particular matter in dispute.

49 See para.3-70.

50 *RTS Flexible Systems Ltd v Molkerei Alois Muller GmbH & Co KG* [2010] UKSC 14; [2010] 1 W.L.R. 753, especially per Lord Clarke at [45] onwards. This traditional approach may not always be that helpful: see *New Zealand Shipping Co Ltd v A.M. Satterthwaite & Co Ltd* [1975] A.C. 154 at 167, per Lord Wilberforce, *Butler Machine Tool v Ex-Cell-O Corp (England)* [1979] 1 W.L.R. 401 at 404, per Lord Denning MR. But see *Gibson v Manchester City Council* [1979] 1 W.L.R. 294 HL.

51 See *Chitty*, Vol.1, Ch.2, especially, para.2-002 onwards.

52 The objective nature of the exercise is exemplified in *O.T. Africa Line Ltd v Vickers Plc* [1996] 1 Lloyd's Rep. 700, where Mance J, as he then was, held that D was bound by an agreement arising from acceptance by C of a mistaken offer of £150,000 in settlement made by D's solicitor when D's intention was that $155,000 should be offered. See para.4-27. See also *Huyton SA v Peter Cremer GmbH & Co* [1999] 1 Lloyd's Rep. 620 referred to at para.4-61 fn.152.

53 *Hussey v Horne-Payne* (1879) 4 App. Cas. 311, *Shears v Shears* (1973) CAT 288, *Bushwall Properties Ltd v Vortex Properties Ltd* [1976] 1 W.L.R. 591 CA.

54 *James Miller & Partners Ltd v Whitworth Street Estates (Manchester) Ltd* [1970] A.C. 583, *RS Flexible Systems Ltd v Molkerei Alois Muller GmbH* [2010] UKSC 13, [2010] 1 W.L.R. 735 at [45]. In *Newbury v Sun Microsystems* [2013] EWHC 2180 (QB) Lewis J held that in construing correspond-

SOME EXAMPLES

Binding agreements

3-23 In the following cases[56] the court concluded that a binding compromise had been achieved:

In *Shears v Shears*,[57] during the pendency of proceedings brought by W under s.17 of the Married Women's Property Act 1882, solicitors' letters to the following effect were exchanged:

(a) from W indicating that she would be prepared to accept £500 as one lump sum in settlement of her claim, expressing the hope that H would do everything possible to raise the sum so that the matter could be disposed of once and for all;
(b) a reply from H indicating that he would be able to raise £500 "within the next two months", but indicating that he needed time to make arrangements, and inviting W's solicitors to take instructions;
(c) from W saying that she would accept £500 cash and "appreciates it may take a few weeks to raise that amount";
(d) a number of letters from H thereafter asking if (but not insisting that) W would accept a £50 reduction on account of some liability of the parties to a third party.

The Court of Appeal held, construing the correspondence as a whole, that a concluded agreement that W would accept £500 in full settlement of her claim to be paid "within a reasonable time" of (c) could be discerned.

3-24 In *Capon v Evans*,[58] C was involved in a road traffic accident for which D was responsible. C's car was damaged and she also sustained personal injuries. The damage to her car was covered by her own insurance policy, but the claims she wished to advance for loss of use of the car and for her personal injuries represented uninsured losses. D was not covered by a policy of insurance in relation to this accident. C instructed solicitors to pursue her uninsured losses, her insurers having met the cost of repairing the damage to her car. C's insurers sought to recover their outlay (some £1,646) from D separately. D instructed solicitors to deal with the claims being made against him and correspondence ensued between those solicitors, on the one hand, and C's solicitors and C's insurers, on the other. The following material letters passed:

2 March—D's solicitors wrote to C's insurers saying that they would like to discuss "the question of your outlay and [C's] claim for uninsured losses". They asked whether they should communicate with the insurers or C's solicitors in this regard.

4 March—C's insurers replied saying that D's solicitors should communicate with C's solicitors concerning the uninsured losses and with them (the insurers) regarding their outlay.

9 March—D's solicitors wrote: (a) to C's solicitors expressing their understanding that they (C's solicitors) were communicating with other insurers as agents for the Motor Insurers Bureau in connection with the personal injury claims and asked for details of the other uninsured losses; and (b) C's insurers asking for details of their outlay.

---

ence between C and D to decide whether a binding agreement to settle a dispute had been concluded, it was not permissible or of any assistance to look at the parties' subsequent conduct. See also *Chitty*, Vol.1, paras 2-027 to 2-028.

55 *Davies v Sweet* [1962] 2 Q.B. 300, *Shears* (1973) CAT 288. A useful summary of the principles applicable in this context can be found in *Reass Sarl v Markel International Insurance Co Ltd* [2007] 8 WLUK 80 (7 August 2007), per Cooke J.

56 See also *Reass Sarl* [2007] 8 WLUK 80 and *Littlefair, Williamson & Beardall v Vinamul* [2006] EWCA Civ 31.

57 *Shears v Shears* (1973) CAT 288.

58 *Capon v Evans* [1986] 4 WLUK 41; [1987] C.L.Y. 413.

12 March—C's insurers wrote to D's solicitors giving the figure of £1,646 as their outlay.

31 March—C's solicitors replied to (a) above indicating that hiring charges for an alternative vehicle represented the only uninsured losses being pursued against D which were not covered by the Motor Insurers Bureau.

3 June—D's solicitors wrote to C's solicitors offering a sum in respect of vehicle hire. (The letter did not purport to deal with anything else.)

6 July—D's solicitors wrote to C's insurers disputing the quantum of their outlay, but indicating that D would be prepared to discharge whatever liability he may have to them by instalment payments.

12 August—C's solicitors replied to D's solicitors' letter of June 3, saying that C would be prepared to "concede a proportion of the hire charges and would accept £100 plus VAT towards those charges". The letter concluded with these words:

> "If the above is acceptable to your client, we can say that there will be no other claim by our client on yours arising out of this accident."

17 September—D's solicitors wrote back to C's solicitors indicating acceptance of the proposal in the letter of 12 August, "on the basis that there will be no other claim by your client on ours arising out of this accident". In this letter they sent a cheque for £115 (i.e. £100 plus VAT) which they asked C's solicitors to hold to their order until C had signed a form of "receipt and indemnity" which acknowledged that the sum of £115 was "in full and final settlement of all ... claims against [D] arising from the motor accident". The form of receipt was duly signed and the cheque presented and met.

In due course C's insurers sought to pursue their outlay against D and were met by the defence that there had been an accord and satisfaction in respect of all C's losses, including the insured losses. On the trial of the preliminary point, the trial judge held that there had been no compromise of the insured losses and in arriving at that conclusion he had received evidence concerning C's state of mind when effecting the settlement with D. The Court of Appeal also held that there had been no settlement of the insured losses, but said that C's **3-25**

> "subjective understanding as to the effect of the words used [in the settlement agreement] ... cannot have been relevant and admissible evidence, in the absence of any plea of mistake or rectification".

It was further held that the agreement was not to be found solely in the receipt but it comprised of: (a) the offer in the letter of 12 August; (b) the counter-offer in the letter of 17 September; and (c) the acceptance of that counter-offer by the signing of the receipt and the acceptance of the cheque. The letter of 12 August dealt solely with C's uninsured losses relating to hiring charges and prior thereto D's solicitors had been "manifestly content to treat the [claim for damage to the car] as being the claim of the insurers themselves", something evidenced by the previous correspondence. It was said that,

> "a reasonable person, standing in the shoes of the offeree, would reasonably have construed the offer in the letter of September 17 ... in the same sense as [C's] solicitors' letter of August 12, ... namely that it related to the uninsured losses only".[59]

It was permissible to look at the letter enclosing the receipt to determine its true effect.[60]

In *Tomlin v Standard Telephones and Cables Ltd*,[61] C sustained injuries on board D's ship in an accident in June 1964. Negotiations ensued between C's solicitor and D's insurers **3-26**

---

[59] Relying upon *Reardon Smith Line Ltd v Yngvar Hansen-Tangen* [1976] 1 W.L.R. 989 at 996–997.

[60] Relying on *Neuchatel Asphalte Co Ltd v Barnett* [1957] 1 W.L.R. 356, noted at para.2-06.

[61] *Tomlin v Standard Telephones and Cables Ltd* [1969] 1 W.L.R. 1378. This case is further referred to in para.19-28 in relation to the circumstances in which the "without prejudice" veil can be lifted. An interesting contrast to this decision, in which part of a dispute was held to have been compromised, is afforded by *Bunge SA v Kruse* [1980] 2 Lloyd's Rep. 142 CA, affirming [1977] 1

before proceedings were issued. In a letter from the insurers to C's solicitor they said that they were "only prepared to deal with the case on a 50/50 basis" and then went on to make an offer of a specific sum of money. C's solicitor replied in these terms:

> "Whilst, as you appreciate, I take the opposite view ... on the question of liability, my client has instructed me to say that he will agree to settle his case on a 50/50 basis as you propose and accordingly this leaves only the question of quantum to be disposed of."

There was no letter subsequent to that letter in which the proposition of liability being agreed on a 50/50 basis was accepted specifically. However, there were letters from D's insurers thereafter referring to the "50/50 agreement come to between us for settlement of this claim" and to the effect that it had been agreed that it was a "50/50 case". The suggestion that all that was left was quantum was never rejected or controverted in the subsequent correspondence. The Court of Appeal[62] held that a concluded agreement on the issue of liability had been reached, the counter-offer contained in the letter from C's solicitor having been accepted by the course of correspondence thereafter. Sir Gordon Willmer said[63] that:

> "[O]n the whole ... those repeated recitals of the existence of an agreement can be, and should be, construed as an acceptance of [C's] counter-offer.[64]"

No binding agreement

3-27 In the following cases no binding agreement was found:

In *Azzarito v Pinkett & Eastern British Road Services Ltd*,[65] there were written negotiations between C's solicitors and D's insurers concerning C's personal injuries claim. D's solicitors offered "£800 inclusive in full and final settlement of your client's claim", after stating that they considered special damages to be approximately £384 and general damages to be £400. C's solicitors replied saying that their client "is prepared to accept £800 plus our costs herein in settlement of this claim". They then indicated a precise figure for costs and the constituent elements of that sum. D's solicitors replied sending a cheque for £800 "in full and final settlement of his claim" and raised a query as to one of the constituent elements of the costs figure. After further correspondence, D's solicitors said that they would be prepared to agree a lesser sum for costs than the figure suggested by C's solicitors. By then, C had decided not to accept the sum offered, and the cheque for £800, which had not been cashed, was returned. The Court of Appeal held that the correspondence, on its true construction, did not give rise to an agreement by C to be bound by the figure of £800 for his damages. His solicitors' first letter amounted to a counter-offer to the effect that he was prepared to accept £800 plus the specified figure for costs in full and final settlement of his claim. That counter-offer was never accepted by D's insurers.

Lloyd's Rep. 492. In that case an issue arose as to whether the whole or merely part of a commercial dispute had been compromised. The Court of Appeal held that the commercial background to the negotiations showed that the whole dispute was intended to be compromised even though the literal interpretation of the telexes constituting the agreement did not suggest this.

62 Danckwerts LJ and Sir Gordon Willmer. Ormrod J dissented on the construction of the correspondence.

63 *Tomlin* [1969] 1 W.L.R. 1378 at 1387.

64 The correspondence carried the suggestion that there had been some telephone contact between C's solicitor and the insurers although there was no evidence of this. In the absence of such evidence, the acceptance of the offer can best be seen as one manifested by conduct: see *Chitty*, Vol.1, para.2-030.

65 *Azzarito v Pinkett & Eastern British Road Services Ltd* (1979) CAT 628. See also para.3-50.

In *Ferguson v Davies*,[66] Evans LJ held that C was entitled to treat the sending by D of the cheque for £150 as merely being in respect of an undisputed amount and not as an unequivocal offer of a sum in final settlement of the whole of C's claim. **3-28**

In *Cherkas v F & P Barretta*,[67] D, floor contractors, did flooring work at C's property. C raised complaints about the work, which D disputed. Arrangements were made for D to return to the property to carry out remedial works. D alleged that they had agreed to do this in order to resolve all outstanding issues. C, however, asserted that they had agreed to D's return, but not so as to preclude them from seeking to recover from D their outlay in terms of costs arising from the investigation and the pursuit of their complaints. The correspondence between the parties' solicitors that preceded D's return to the property indicated that D did not wish to contribute to C's outlay, but that whilst C were happy for D to return, they wanted reimbursement of their outlay. The Court of Appeal held that there was no binding agreement of compromise. **3-29**

Presentation of cheque sent in settlement

The issue

A question that frequently arises in this context is whether the presentation of a cheque sent "in full and final settlement" of a dispute amounts to an unqualified acceptance of the offer reflected in the sending of that cheque on those terms. The question is often posed on the basis of whether the presentation of the cheque for payment constitutes an "accord and satisfaction" of the disputed claim.[68] Having regard to the classic definition of "accord and satisfaction",[69] and indeed to the ordinary contractual principles reflected in that definition, the issue is more accurately stated as being confined initially to whether an accord has been reached in the circumstances, satisfaction depending on whether acceptance of the cheque per se is sufficient or whether payment on presentation of the cheque is required.[70] **3-30**

Whether an "accord" has been reached depends on whether, construed objectively, the actions of the recipient of the cheque constitute acceptance of the offer reflected in the sending of the cheque. Before this issue arises for determination two preliminary matters may need to be considered[71]:

---

66 See para.2-07 and fnn.70 and 81. See also *Clarke v Nationwide Building Society* (1998) 76 P. & C.R. D5, where sending a cheque purportedly "in full and final settlement" was held to be merely a gesture of goodwill.

67 *Cherkas v F & P Barretta* [2000] 5 WLUK 308 (12 May 2000) (Buxton LJ and Hooper J).

68 See, e.g. *Auriema Ltd v Haigh and Ringrose Ltd* (1988) 4 Const. L.J. 200 at para.3-42.

69 "Accord and satisfaction is the purchase of a release from an obligation whether arising under a contract or tort or by means of any valuable consideration, not being the actual performance of the obligation itself. The accord is the agreement by which the obligation is discharged. The satisfaction is the consideration which makes the agreement operative": *British Russian Gazette and Trade Outlook Ltd v Associated Newspapers Ltd* [1933] 2 K.B. 616 at 643.

70 There is a presumption that a payment made by cheque is conditional on the cheque being honoured, but the presumption can be rebutted by showing an express or implied intention that the cheque is taken in total satisfaction of the relevant liability: *Charge Card Services Ltd, Re* [1989] Ch. 497; *Chitty*, Vol.1, para.21-075. An interesting question that might arise in this context is whether an offeree of a cheque sent "in full and final settlement", and who decides to present the cheque, thereby binds himself to the amount proffered on the cheque as the settlement sum in the event of it being dishonoured. Provided there is nothing in the circumstances to displace the foregoing presumption, it is thought that he would not be so bound.

71 These two issues may merge in some circumstances: see, e.g. *Ferguson v Davies* [1997] 1 All E.R. 315, per Evans LJ, referred to in para.2-07 and fn.28.

(i) Cheque must be offered in "full and final settlement"

3-31 The evidence must show that a definite offer has been made to settle on a "full and final" basis. Without this no question of an equivalent acceptance on that basis can arise.

In *Rustenburg Platinum Mines Ltd v South African Airways and Pan American World Airways Inc*,[72] C were the owners of two boxes of platinum which were flown into Heathrow Airport from South Africa by D1 and were due to be flown to the United States by D2. Whilst the boxes were in the effective custody of D2, one was stolen. C sought the value of the lost platinum (about £60,000) from their insurers who, in due course, made claims against D1 and D2. By a letter, D2 authorised D1 to settle the claim and advised them that they (D2) regarded their maximum liability to be about £200 having regard to the terms of the Warsaw Convention. A few weeks later D1 sent a cheque in that sum to C's insurers' agents, informing them of the terms of D2's letter. On the reverse side of the cheque was a short printed form of receipt including the words, "In payment of claim TC 1546/70". The agents forwarded the cheque to C's insurers who signed the receipt and banked the cheque. In the insurers' subsequent subrogated action to recover the full amount of the claim, D2 contended, inter alia, that the claim had been settled by the signing of the receipt and the acceptance of the cheque. Ackner J (as he then was) held[73] that D1's letter to C's insurers' agent did not constitute an unequivocal offer for the full and final settlement of C's claim. The Court of Appeal confirmed this view. Sir David Cairns said[74] that:

> "Very clear words would be needed to show that an offer of [£200] was to be understood as an offer to settle a claim amounting to [£60,000] ... The only possible offer was [D1's letter to C's insurers' agents], and this did not make it at all plain that the [£200] was offered in full and final settlement."

(ii) Cheque offered "in full and final settlement" must seek to settle a dispute

3-32 The need for there to have been an actual or potential dispute before a compromise can be said to have arisen has been noted previously.[75] If a cheque is sent purporting to be "in full and final settlement" of a dispute, but on closer analysis the background shows that the sending of the cheque merely evidences an admission that the amount on the cheque is owing and that there is no true dispute, then no overall settlement will have been concluded by acceptance of the cheque. This was the situation in *Newton Moor Construction Ltd v Charlton*[76] and *Neuchatel Asphalte Co Ltd v Barnett*.[77]

How is the issue determined?

3-33 On the assumption that an offer "in full and final settlement" of some real dispute is clearly made at the time the cheque is sent, will its acceptance and/or presentation amount to an acceptance of the offer?

---

72 *Rustenburg Platinum Mines Ltd v South African Airways and Pan American World Airways Inc* [1979] 1 Lloyd's Rep. 19 CA.

73 *Rustenburg Platinum Mines* [1977] 1 Lloyd's Rep. 564 Commercial Ct.

74 *Rustenburg Platinum Mines* [1979] 1 Lloyd's Rep. 19 at 25 CA.

75 See para.2-01 onwards.

76 Certainly so far as Sir David Cairns was concerned: see para.2-05.

77 See para.2-06.

(a) Fact or law?

Despite an observation made by Lord Denning MR in one case to the contrary,[78] the balance of authority supports the proposition that neither of these acts of itself, as a matter of law, constitutes an acceptance. Whether there has been an "accord" by virtue of the acceptance and/or presentation of the cheque is a question of fact determined on the evidence in each case where the issue arises. Many years ago the matter was put authoritatively in this way[79]: 3-34

> "If a person sends a sum of money on the terms that it is to be taken, if at all, in satisfaction of a larger claim; and if the money is kept, it is a question of fact as to the terms upon which it is so kept. Accord and satisfaction imply an agreement to take the money in satisfaction of the claim in respect of which it is sent. If accord is a question of agreement, there must be either two minds agreeing or one of the two persons acting in such a way as to induce the other to think that the money is taken in satisfaction of the claim, and to cause him to act upon that view. In either case it is a question of fact."

In *Bunge SA v Kruse*[80] Lord Denning MR said of the foregoing passage:

> "I do not agree [that the question of accord and satisfaction is one of fact]. At any rate, when everything is on paper, in the telexes and correspondence between the parties, it is a question of law."

This comment has been the subject of further analysis by the Court of Appeal in two subsequent cases. In *Pereira v Inspirations East Ltd*[81] Rose LJ (with whom Glidewell and Nolan LJJ agreed) said this:

> "For my part, save in relation to analysis of the matter as being a question of law or fact, I do not see anything in Lord Denning's judgment which is inconsistent with the approach of Bowen LJ in *Day v McLea*. In any event, it seems to me that although ultimately whether there is accord and satisfaction must be a matter of law, equally clearly, the resolution of that legal question must depend upon the facts of the particular case."

Further, in *Stour Valley Builders v Stuart*[82] Lloyd LJ, as he then was, having referred to the final sentence of the quotation from Lord Denning's judgment referred to above, said this:

> "The qualification is important. The construction of correspondence is always a question of law. But there is nothing in *Bunge v Kruse* to support the view that accord and satisfaction is a question of law in every case… . *Day v McLea* has not, in my opinion, been qualified by *Bunge v Kruse* except in the sense which I have already mentioned in relation to negotiations conducted in writing."[83]

---

78 See *Bunge SA* [1977] 1 Lloyd's Rep. 492 at 495.

79 *Day v McLea* (1889) 22 Q.B.D. 610 at 613, per Bowen LJ. Lord Esher MR gave a judgment to the same effect (at 612–613) and Fry LJ (at 613) agreed that the earlier unreported case of *Miller v Davies* was conclusive on the issue.

80 *Bunge SA* [1977] 1 Lloyd's Rep. 492 at 495.

81 *Pereira v Inspirations East Ltd* (1992) CAT 1048. See para.3-44.

82 *Stour Valley Builders v Stuart* [1992] 12 WLUK 396; [2003] T.C.L.R. 8; *Independent*, 9 February 1993, noted at para.3-40. See also *Ferguson v Davies* [1997] 1 All E.R. 315, referred to in para.2-07, per Evans LJ at 325.

83 There does not appear to be any significant conflict between the views of the Court of Appeal in *Pereira* (1992) CAT 1048 and those expressed in *Stour Valley Builders v Stuart* [1992] 12 WLUK 396; [2003] T.C.L.R. 8. If there is, some interesting questions of precedent would arise. The judgment in *Pereira* was given on 9 November 1992, some six weeks before the judgment in *Stour Valley Builders*. The former case was not cited in the latter, but equally the earlier Court of Appeal deci-

(b) The resolution of the issue of fact

3-35 Since the issue is one of fact then, unless there is some irrebuttable presumption that the acceptance and/or presentation of such a cheque is to be taken as acceptance of the terms upon which it is offered, each case will depend upon its own facts. It is clear from the authorities already referred to and from those further cases to which reference will be made below, that no such irrebuttable presumption operates: if such a presumption were to operate it would effectively negate the rejection by the courts of the proposition that acceptance and/or presentation of the cheque itself constitutes acceptance as a matter of law.[84]

3-36 The starting point for addressing the analysis of the facts in any case where the issue falls for consideration is that an *objective* construction must be placed on the material events:

> In *Bell v Galynski and Kings (A.) Loft Extensions*,[85] C lived in a semi-detached house. D1 either lived in or controlled the other half of the building. C became aware that damage had occurred to the party wall in his loft and that certain rubble had been deposited on the insulating material covering the floor of the loft, as a result of loft conversion works carried out in D1's part of the building by D2. C informed D1's solicitors that he held D1 responsible and said that he would forward the account for the remedial works in due course. He also notified them that he would additionally claim compensation for "any further deterioration of my property due ... to the development work already carried out". The account for the remedial works was subsequently sent and C sought reimbursement. In his letter C expressly made his claim "without prejudice to any further claim which might result from the building work affixed to my property". D2 sent a cheque to C for the amount of the account under cover of a letter which stated that it was sent "in full and final settlement of your claim against [D1] with regard to damage caused to party wall". Some three weeks later, and before the cheque had been cleared through C's bank, D2 wrote advising C that they would not be held responsible,
>
> > "for any further claims for any damage allegedly arising due to construction of the loft conversion unless we are allowed to inspect such 'alleged damage' prior to repair".
>
> Thereafter the cheque was cleared. In due course C sought to claim from D1 and D2 further damages arising from the original loft conversion works and the issue arose as to whether any such claim had been compromised by the acceptance of the cheque. The Court of Appeal held that such claim had indeed been compromised. Since the cheque was tendered "in full and final settlement" and C did not make clear his intention at that stage of claiming further compensation, his action,
>
> > "in clearing the cheque without any demur or further qualification must be regarded as excluding him from prosecuting a further claim for alleged additional damage caused [by D1 and D2] (per Edmund Davies LJ)."
>
> Megaw LJ emphasised that the words and actions of C must be judged objectively and without regard to what C may have intended and understood.

---

sion in *Neuchatel Asphalte Co Ltd* [1957] 1 W.L.R. 356 (to which decision Denning LJ was a party) in which *Day v McLea* (1889) 22 QBD 611 was cited and relied upon by Morris LJ, was not cited in *Pereira*. The *Neuchatel Asphalte* decision was cited and relied upon in *Stour Valley Builders*.

84 In *Pereira* (1992) CAT 1048, Rose LJ said that: "Any presumption that might otherwise have arisen that payment of the cheque into the Plaintiff's bank account ... gave rise to an inference that he was accepting the Defendant's offer was plainly rebutted by him simultaneously sending his letter to the Defendants."

85 *Bell v Galynski and Kings (A.) Loft Extensions* [1974] 2 Lloyd's Rep. 13 CA. See also per Lloyd LJ in *Stour Valley Builders* [1992] 12 WLUK 396; [2003] T.C.L.R. 8: "As with any other bilateral contract, what matters is not what the creditor himself intends but what, by his words and conduct, he has led the other party as a reasonable person ... to believe."

The approach thus adopted to the question of the effect of the acceptance of a cheque would seem to be that the presentation for payment of a cheque tendered "in full and final settlement" of a dispute, without demur or qualification, will be taken as an *objective* manifestation of an intention to accept the offer of settlement thus made. This approach is further illustrated by the following cases: **3-37**

In *Upfield v Marshall*,[86] the parties were in dispute about the balance due under an outstanding account. D wrote to C enclosing a cheque for £167 "in full and final settlement of the work done so far and the items supplied to date". C paid in the cheque and issued no response to the letter for seven weeks when solicitors he had instructed in the meantime wrote saying that the sum was not accepted "in full and final settlement". The Court of Appeal held that the payment in of the cheque amounted to an acceptance of the offer and there was a binding agreement. (The agreement, of course, related only to the matters which were then in dispute, i.e. "the work done so far and the items supplied to date".)

In *Merkuria Foreign Trade Corp v Dateline Electric Co Ltd*,[87] D1 sent to C a cheque for £6,696 under cover of a letter of 4 July 1975 expressed to be "in full and final settlement" of any claims against D2 and, in effect, said that if the cheque was presented to D2's bank in Jersey it would be cleared pursuant to the terms of the letter enclosing the cheque. That letter had been preceded by a telex making the same offer and a further letter to the same effect was sent on 17 July 1975. C did present the cheque for payment and it was cleared on 23 July. Subsequently, C sought to argue that it had received the money merely as part payment of its claim. The Court of Appeal rejected this argument: **3-38**

per Stephenson LJ:

> "[T]hey did not qualify or seek to qualify in any way, as they could have done, the terms under which they were accepting it. They did not say 'We are accepting it without prejudice to other claims'; they did not say 'We are accepting it on account."

Per Robert Goff LJ:

> "[B]y paying the cheque into their bank account without in any way objecting that they were not receiving it on those terms [i.e. in the letter] the plaintiffs clearly bound themselves by those terms."

In each of the foregoing cases there was a clearly definable and not insignificant delay between the receipt of and/or the payment in of the cheque and the subsequent manifestation of an intention not to accept the proceeds of the cheque other than as part payment. In *Bell v Galynski*[88] the plaintiff had retained the cheque for over three weeks and thereafter paid it into his bank. The question arises whether there is any clear dividing line between those cases where the delay is not sufficient to give rise to the inference of acceptance and those where it is. The answer was provided by Lloyd LJ in *Stour Valley Builders v Stuart*[89]: **3-39**

> "Cashing the cheque is always strong evidence of acceptance, especially if it is not accompanied by immediate rejection of the offer. Retention of the cheque without rejection is also strong evidence of acceptance depending on the length of the delay. But neither of these factors are conclusive; and it would ... be artificial to draw a hard and fast line between cases where the payment is accompanied by immediate rejection of the offer and cases where objection comes within a day or a few days."

---

86 *Upfield v Marshall* (1976) CAT 142.

87 *Merkuria Foreign Trade Corp v Dateline Electric Co Ltd* (1979) CAT 413.

88 See para.3-36.

89 See fn.82.

3-40 In that case, C, a small firm of builders, carried out some work for D at his home. On 5 July 1991 C sent D an itemised bill which showed an amount of £10,204 after certain payments on account had been taken into account. D queried a number of items which had been charged as extras and complained about other items for which he claimed compensation. On 18 July, C sent a detailed reply in which it was accepted that there had been some very minor errors in the original account. The revised account came to £10,163. On 23 July, D sent a detailed reply, the amount in dispute being about £3,000. D made an offer to settle in the sum of £8,471 in the following terms:

> "I am prepared to settle this matter now. I am enclosing a cheque in full and final settlement of all charges for £8,471. This figure includes all charges, compensation, savings and does not leave any retention outstanding."

The cheque arrived on 25 July, and one of C's proprietors (C1) gave it to his secretary to pay in. He spoke to his fellow proprietor the same day and contacted his solicitor the following day, sending him the papers. On 29 July, the cheque had been cleared. On 31 July, the solicitor advised C1 by telephone and C1 then spoke to D on the telephone saying that the cheque could not be accepted in full and final settlement. D asked why the cheque had been paid in and C1 said he needed the money. On 1 August, C wrote a letter before action claiming the difference between £8,471 and £10,163. The judge found as a fact that there had been no agreement between the parties that the cheque was to be accepted in full and final satisfaction of C's claim. The Court of Appeal held that this finding was open to the judge on the facts and would not be disturbed. It was held that the judge had asked himself the correct question, namely whether what C had done had caused D to think that the money had been taken in satisfaction of the claim and that he was entitled, on the evidence, to conclude that it did not.

3-41 The following cases also illustrate circumstances in which the court has concluded that no settlement has arisen from the presentation of a cheque purportedly sent "in full and final settlement":

In *Day v McLea*,[90] C was claiming a considerable sum from D. Before proceedings were commenced D sent a cheque for £102 18s 6d, being less than the amount claimed, stating that it was in full satisfaction of all demands and enclosing a form of receipt to be signed by C in those terms. C replied saying that the cheque was taken "on account" and had been placed to D's credit, a receipt on account being sent together with a request for the balance of the claim. The Court of Appeal held that, the matter being one of fact, the judge had been entitled to conclude that there had been no accord and satisfaction.

3-42 In *Auriema Ltd v Haigh and Ringrose Ltd*,[91] D contracted with T to install high-level alarms for spheres at T's oil refinery. D subcontracted the supply of the detectors to C for a total sum of just over £9,900. Following the supply and installation of the alarms a dispute arose between C and D. D alleged that they had incurred expenses of £5,205 because of defects in the detectors. C denied liability for these expenses, the basis for this denial of liability being set out in a detailed letter. This detailed letter did not come to the attention of the person within D who wrote to C in the following terms:

> "In order that this matter may be concluded we enclose a cheque to cover the differences between [the contract sum which C claimed and the sum of £5,205]. Your banking of the cheque will be taken as acceptance of our proposal as full and final settlement and we would waive the right to pursue further costs."

C replied in the following terms:

---

[90] (1889) 22 Q.B.D. 610. See para.3-34 and fn.79.

[91] (1988) 4 Const. L.J. 200.

"We have accepted this payment as part-payment towards our invoice [for the full amount of the claim] ... and do not accept the suggestion that this was in full and final settlement of our invoice."

That letter appears to have been written on the day the cheque was banked. HH Judge James Fox-Andrews QC, official referee, held that there was evidence, in the form of C's letter in reply, that C did not intend to accept the offer and that there had not been the necessary accord:

"If the cheque had been banked without demur or qualification by [C], that would have been compelling evidence that [C] intended to accept [D's] offer."

In *Broderick, Re*[92] the principal ground for the decision was that the essential element for an accord and satisfaction was missing as there was no agreement between the minds of the parties, and the Inland Revenue had done nothing to induce B's solicitors to think that the money was taken in satisfaction of the claim. **3-43**

In *Pereira v Inspirations East Ltd*,[93] C booked a touring holiday through D, travel agents. The holiday took place in December 1989. C did not regard the holiday as successful and upon his return made various complaints to D. He asked D to refund his money "plus costs and losses". By a letter of 6 January 1990 D sent a cheque for £225 to C "in full and final settlement of this matter". On 24 March 1990, C paid the cheque into his bank account and sent a letter to D dated 11 January 1990, saying that the cheque was "accepted on account", claiming the balance of the monies he had paid to D and indicating that he was awaiting D's "revised offer in short course". The letter did not say that C was paying the cheque into his account. C's letter was received by D on 26 March 1990 and the cheque was cleared by debit of D's bank account on 27 March 1990, after 15.00. The Court of Appeal held that, assessing C's conduct objectively, the simultaneous sending of the letter with the payment of the cheque into his bank showed clearly that he was not accepting D's offer. **3-44**

The American rule

The balance of authority in the United States is that: **3-45**

"[As] a matter of law, the use or retention of [a cheque sent on condition that it is accepted in full and final settlement of a dispute] by the creditor, with knowledge of the condition, is regarded as an assent to it."[94]

The contention that this rule applies (or should apply) in the English courts has been rejected twice by the Court of Appeal.[95] The advantage of certainty that the operation of the rule would bring has been acknowledged. Lloyd LJ said this in *Stour Valley Builders v Stuart*[96]:

"I can see the advantages of having such a rule. But there are analytical and conceptual difficulties. Accord and satisfaction depends on the debtor establishing an agreement between the parties whereby the creditor undertakes for valuable consideration to accept a sum less than the amount of his claim ... If the creditor at the very moment of paying in the cheque makes clear that he is not assenting to the condition imposed by the debtor, how can it be said that, objectively, he has accepted the debtor's offer?"

---

92 *Broderick, Re* [1986] 6 N.I.J.B. 36; [1987] C.L.Y. 2644; discussed at para.3-17.

93 See fn.81.

94 *Williston on Contracts*, 4th edn, para.1854, *Hudson v Yonkers Fruit Co* (1932) 179 North Eastern Reps. 373.

95 It was rejected explicitly in *Stour Valley Builders* [1992] 12 WLUK 396; [2003] T.C.L.R. 8 and implicitly in *Pereira v Inspirations East Ltd* (1992) CAT 1048.

96 *Stour Valley* [1992] 12 WLUK 396; [2003] T.C.L.R. 8.

3-46 The debate about which approach is the better one and which is more consistent with established contractual principles[97] highlights two classic confrontations: first, that between the objective and subjective analyses of a set of facts; secondly, that between the need for certainty in the law (particularly in commercial dealings) and the desire for flexibility to meet the perceived justice of a particular situation. As things stand, the English courts have elected for the flexibility that is denied by the American rule. That flexibility enables the court in appropriate circumstances to prevent advantage being taken by a debtor of the precarious financial situation of the creditor. Cash flow is the lifeblood of many small businesses and the sending of a cheque for a lesser sum than the claim purporting to be "in full and final settlement", may in reality be no more than an attempt to put pressure on the creditor in need of an immediate injection of revenue to sustain the business.

Conversion of the cheque or its proceeds

3-47 A consequence of the American rule[98] is that the recipient of a cheque sent in full and final settlement who banks that cheque in violation of the condition imposed by the sender is guilty of converting the cheque or its proceeds.[99] That the same legal consequence may flow from the same factual situation under the English law appears to have been acknowledged by the English courts.[100] Whilst in *Pereira v Inspirations East Ltd*[101] the Court of Appeal appeared to accept that where the facts of a particular case supported the conclusion that a conversion had taken place,[102] that conclusion may have a bearing on the overall legal consequences, in *Stour Valley Builders v Stuart*[103] the contrary view was taken. Lloyd LJ said this:

> "[D] argues that by paying in the cheque ... with knowledge of the conditions attached to the payment, the creditor acts unlawfully. But suppose he does; suppose the payment in is a conversion of the cheque or its proceeds. How does that help the debtor to establish that the creditor has accepted the condition which the debtor imposed?"

3-48 The only answer that can be given to the question posed by Lloyd LJ in the passage referred to is that, by acting unlawfully, the creditor disentitles himself from contending that he accepted the cheque on a different basis from that on which it was offered.[104] However, there is a circularity about the argument which, it is submitted, is broken by concentrating, as the English courts do, on whether an accord (a meeting of minds) has been established. Whilst that factual issue remains at the forefront of the court's consideration, it is respectfully submitted that Lloyd LJ's approach in the *Stour Valley* case is correct and logical and that whether

---

97 See, e.g. David Andrews, "Cheques sent in settlement" (1991) 13 C.J.Q. 7.

98 See para.3-45.

99 *Hudson* (1932) 179 North Eastern Reps. 373 at 375, per Cardozo CJ.

100 *Pereira v Inspirations East Ltd* (1992) CAT 1048, where, on the facts, the Court of Appeal suggested that, "the highest that ... it can be put against [C] ... is that the paying in of the cheque by him may have been attempted conversion". Whilst the chose in action that is evidenced by the existence of a cheque cannot be converted, the cheque itself can and the true owner can recover the full extent of any loss thus occasioned: *Clerk & Lindsell on Torts*, 21st edn (2014), para.17-38.

101 See fn.100.

102 For example, where the recipient of the cheque pays it in before communicating to the sender his intention merely to accept it on account, thus depriving the sender of the opportunity of stopping the cheque. In this situation Nolan LJ said that "other considerations might well have arisen".

103 See fn.82.

104 cf. *Homeguard Products (NZ) Ltd v Kiwi Packaging Ltd* [1981] 2 N.Z.L.R. 322, per Mahon J.

conversion has occurred in the circumstances plays no part in determining the outcome of that issue.[105]

A COMPLETE AND CERTAIN AGREEMENT

General principle

Although it may be possible to distil from the parties' negotiations an apparent agreement, the agreement may not be sufficiently complete or certain to enable it to be upheld by the court. The position under the general law of contract has been stated thus: **3-49**

> "[U]nless all the material terms of the contract are agreed there is no binding obligation. An agreement to agree in future is not a contract; nor is there a contract if a material term is neither settled nor implied by law and the document contains no machinery for ascertaining it."[106]

Failure to agree all material terms

Where it is plain that a material element in the negotiations remains unresolved, the court is likely to hold that no concluded agreement has been achieved because a material term has not been agreed. **3-50**

> In *Yorwerth v Sonnyplaster*,[107] D wrote to C's solicitors enclosing a cheque for £112 as an ex gratia payment saying that they did not consider that they were in any way liable for C's costs. C's solicitors replied acknowledging receipt of the cheque saying that they were "taking instructions regarding costs". They paid in the cheque within a few days but did not communicate with D's solicitors again for four-and-a-half months, when they wrote saying that £112 was not an acceptable settlement figure. The Court of Appeal held that there was no concluded agreement because the question of costs was outstanding and, in the circumstances, the payment in of the cheque and the silence for four-and-a-half months could not be construed as an acceptance.[108]

In the normal course of events, the court will not imply a term as to the payment of costs.[109]

Terms too vague

Where the parties' agreement is expressed in terms that are too vague to be enforced, the court will decline to hold that a sufficiently certain agreement has been **3-51**

---

105 A similar approach was adopted in *Stour Valley Builders* [1992] 12 WLUK 396; [2003] T.C.L.R. 8 to the argument that the payment-in of the cheque in the situation that forms the basis for the present discussion constitutes a breach of s.21(2)(b) of the Bills of Exchange Act 1908. Lloyd LJ said that the section "does not help [D] establish substantively an agreement on the part of the creditor to accept a lesser sum in satisfaction of his claim".

106 *Foley v Classique Coaches Ltd* [1934] 2 K.B. 1 at 3, per Maugham LJ. For an example of where a purported agreement of compromise fell foul of this requirement, see *Jackson v Thakrar* [2007] EWHC 271 (TCC); [2007] B.P.I.R. 167.

107 *Yorweth v Sonnyplaster* (1973) CAT 255. See also *Gannon v Chubb Fire Ltd* [1996] P.I.Q.R. P108 CA.

108 cf. para.3-27 onwards.

109 See paras 5-60–5-61.

reached.[110]

In *Wilson & Whitworth Ltd v Express & Independent Newspapers Ltd*,[111] C and D were newspaper publishers who became involved in a passing-off action in 1936. C's claim was dismissed at first instance, but its appeal was settled by a consent order in "Tomlin" form in which one of the scheduled terms was to the effect that C would not do certain things in connection with the presentation of their newspapers and associated advertising "to any further extent than at the commencement of this action". When the matter had first been mentioned to the Court of Appeal it appeared to have been the parties' intention that this obligation should be recorded as an undertaking to the court. The Court of Appeal was unwilling to accept an undertaking in such vague terms and suggested that the parties agree more specific terms or, perhaps, deal with the settlement in a way that did not require an undertaking to the court. The parties were unable to agree more precise terms but asked the court to make a Tomlin order with the term indicated above as part of the schedule. The Court of Appeal made the order. In 1968 D alleged that C was acting in breach of the term and sought an injunction restraining C from breaking the agreement. Plowman J held that, having regard to the observations of the Court of Appeal in 1936, an injunction could not be granted to enforce an obligation so vaguely expressed.

3-52 In *Tadmor v Tadmor*,[112] an order was made on W's application for an ouster order against H in the following terms:

> "Upon hearing counsel for the parties
>
> And upon [cross undertakings by H and W not to assault molest or otherwise interfere with one another]
>
> It is directed that [W] do occupy the first floor flat at the matrimonial home ... (without [H] or the tenant) and that [H] do occupy such parts of the ground floor as he can arrange with the said tenant, subject to the tenant's approval."

The order was never implemented in that W never returned to the matrimonial home, the tenant never moved out of his part of the first floor flat (possibly because he had some form of statutory protection) and no arrangement was made between H and the tenant concerning the occupation of the ground floor. W wanted the matter looked at on the merits, but H took the point that this was precluded because the order was a consent order. The Court of Appeal held that it was not a consent order because: (a) it did not contain a recital to that effect[113]; and (b) because a true consent order was equal to a contract between the parties and this order was too uncertain and subject to many conditions "such as the tenant moving from the first floor to the ground floor and arrangements being made with the tenant".

3-53 In *Assi v Leeds Metropolitan University*,[114] C became a full-time research student with D in 1991. Following various disputes C was told by D in 1992 that it was being recommended that the government funding for his work should cease and that he should not continue as a research student. C invoked D's grievance procedure and an apparent compromise was reached under which, on C's case, D would enrol him and grant him a three-year bursary subject to the selection of a suitable research topic and the appointment of a suitable supervisor. C complained that, in breach of that agreement, D had failed

---

[110] *Chitty*, Vol.1, para.2-148 onwards. An argument to this effect was advanced and rejected in relation to the compromise considered in *Snelling v John Snelling Ltd* [1973] 1 Q.B. 87, the facts of which are recorded at para.3-69. See also *Hutchinson v Tamosius* [1999] 5 WLUK 349 (24 May 1999), where HH Judge Hegarty QC, sitting as a judge of the High Court, rejected an argument to this effect in the context of the result of settlement discussions in relation to a partnership dispute.

[111] *Wilson & Whitworth Ltd v Express & Independent Newspapers Ltd* [1969] 1 W.L.R. 197.

[112] *Tadmor v Tadmor* (1976) CAT 432. The point that this was an interlocutory and an executory order does not appear to have been taken on W's behalf: see, e.g. para.24-13.

[113] This is generally thought not necessarily to be fatal: see para.10-04.

[114] *Assi v Leeds Metropolitan University* [2001] EWCA Civ 641.

to provide him with a suitable supervisor and claimed damages for breach of contract. The Court of Appeal held that the judge had been correct in holding that the agreement reached was invalid for uncertainty in that it was not legally enforceable until a suitable research topic and supervisor had been identified.

However, where a provision in an agreement is merely incapable of any precise meaning, but can be severed from the rest of the agreement without doing violence to it, the court will do so.[115] **3-54**

Agreement to agree and the "future document"

As indicated above,[116] an agreement to agree in the future is not a contract. For example, an agreement by the parties to stay[117] the proceedings between them "on terms that the issues arising therein be resolved by agreement" would be unlikely to be upheld. This would constitute nothing more than an agreement to agree or negotiate.[118] **3-55**

Problems occasionally arise when the parties have compromised their dispute but speak or write in terms which contemplate the drawing-up of some further document setting the seal, as it were, on their agreement. The question arises whether the compromise is immediately binding or not binding until such document is executed. The question has been formulated thus: **3-56**

> "[I]t is a question of construction whether the execution of the further contract is a condition or term of the bargain or whether it is a mere expression of the desire of the parties as to the manner in which the transaction already agreed to will in fact go through. In the former case there is no enforceable contract either because the condition is unfulfilled or because the law does not recognise a contract to enter into a contract. In the latter case there is a binding contract and the reference to the more formal document may be ignored."[119]

Since the question is one of construction with a view to ascertaining the intention of the parties, it is impossible to describe any particular situation which arises in the context of compromise as being in one category or the other.[120] The crucial factor is the significance attached by the parties to the future act. That is determined by construing the agreement as a whole.[121]

---

115 *Nicolene v Simmonds* [1953] 1 Q.B. 543. See *Chitty*, Vol.1, paras 2-153 and 2-155.

116 See para.3-49.

117 See Ch.9.

118 *Walford v Miles* [1992] 2 A.C. 128, where the House of Lords upheld the well-established principle that a bare agreement to negotiate was unenforceable. See *Chitty*, Vol.1, paras 2-144–2-146. cf. *Cable & Wireless Plc v IBM United Kingdom Ltd* [2002] EWHC 2059 (Comm); [2002] CLC 1319, where Colman J upheld an agreement that the parties would "attempt in good faith to resolve the dispute or claim through an Alternative Dispute Resolution (ADR) procedure as recommended to the Parties by [CEDR]". See also *Beta Investments SA v Transmedia Europe Inc* [2003] EWHC 3066 (Ch) distinguished in *Bezant v Rausing* [2007] EWHC 1118 (QB).

119 *Von Hatzfeldt-Wildenburg v Alexander* [1912] 1 Ch. 284 at 288. See *Chitty*, Vol.1, para.2-124 owards.

120 See, e.g. *Behar, Ellis & Parnell v Territorial Investments Ltd* (1973) CAT 237 noted in para.29-20. In *Bishop v Berkshire Health Authority* [1999] P.I.Q.R. P92, Douglas Brown J held that the then standard form of consent order entered into when a claimant is considering a structured settlement following agreement on the award of damages on a conventional basis is nothing more than an agreement to agree and thus does not constitute a binding obligation on the part of the claimant to accept that sum. Cf. *Gardiner v South Essex Health Authority* unreported 10 December 1998 and *Heselwood v Collett* [1999] P.I.Q.R. Q136, where the form of agreed order contained an undertaking on behalf of the claimant to limit the claim to the agreed conventional figure. See further Ch.27.

121 *Chitty*, Vol.1, para.13-041 onwards. See, e.g., *Newbury v Sun Microsystems* [2013] EWHC 2180

3-57 An agreement between husband and wife to enter into a separation agreement on specified terms has been held to be binding.

In *Morton v Morton*,[122] W had brought proceedings against H in a magistrates' court in 1930 for maintenance for herself and their son. The proceedings were compromised outside court and the terms were reflected in a document entitled, "Heads of agreement" which was drawn up and signed by the respective solicitors. After reciting W's agreement to withdraw her summons, the document recorded that H and W "hereby mutually agree to enter a separation deed containing the following clauses", and the various terms were set out. Although the terms were carried out, no formal agreement was ever prepared or executed. In subsequent proceedings it was argued that the document was nothing more than a contract to contract. A Divisional Court of the Probate, Divorce and Admiralty Division held that there was a binding agreement (subject to the ultimate jurisdiction of the court). Lord Merriman P[123]:

> "[T]he commonest thing in the world, in these matrimonial causes, whether in the courts below or in this court, is to draw up heads of agreement, which are afterwards to be put into more solemn form, if the parties so require; but to say ... that this is nothing more than a contract to make a contract seems to me to be impossible ... Every requisite of the agreement between the parties was here and I think it is the clearest possible case of a concluded agreement, which no doubt either party could have insisted on being put into more formal shape."[124]

Problem of the "conditional" compromise

3-58 Could it be argued on the foregoing basis that a compromise agreement that, on its proper construction, contains a condition that a consent order or judgment reflecting it be made in due course, is not binding? The question is considered elsewhere,[125] but the answer is "no". Arguably this is analogous to the position of a contract made subject to the fulfilment of some future condition which may or may not be satisfied. Such an agreement is not regarded as too vague or uncertain. It may have a number of different effects depending on how the agreement is interpreted.

Not binding until future event

3-59 If the parties expressly or impliedly stipulate that their compromise should not be binding upon them until the happening of some event, for example, the approval of, or concurrence with its terms by, a third party, or until it has been reduced to writing,[126] effect will be given to that stipulation and either party may withdraw from the agreement up to the moment of fulfilment of the condition.

(QB); [2013] C.I.L.L. 3425.

122 *Morton v Morton* [1942] 1 All E.R. 273. And see *Xydhias v Xydhias* [1999] 2 All E.R. 386 CA, discussed in Ch.32. Where parties negotiate on the basis that a binding agreement will come into existence only when the wording of a contemplated consent order is agreed, then in the absence of agreement to such wording no binding contract of compromise will have arisen: *Dalgety Foods Holland BV v Deb-its Ltd* [1994] F.S.R. 125.

123 *Morton* [1942] 1 All E.R. 273 at 273.

124 For settlements in matrimonial cases generally, see Ch.32. For a case where some heads of terms recorded at the end of a mediation were held to be sufficiently clear and certain, and complying with s.2 of the Law of Property (Miscellaneous Provisions) Act 1989 to be binding, see *Abberley v Abberley* [2019] EWHC 1564 (Ch). See also Ch.30.

125 See Ch.5, para.5-48 onwards.

126 Most mediation agreements contain a term to this effect. See Ch. 35

In *Plumley v Horrell*,[127] T, by his will, left the bulk of his property to the six children of his two sisters. By a subsequent will, made about three months later, he left the bulk of his property to his half-sister, H. H's husband sought to prove the second will. This was opposed by two children of T's two sisters of the full blood, and proceedings were commenced. During the trial a compromise was effected, the terms of which were indorsed on the brief of counsel for one of the parties and signed and assented to by the others. The effect of the compromise was that H's husband would be entitled to prove the will upon his undertaking to charge the property passing under the will in favour of each of the six children of his full sisters for equal sums of £500, only two of those children being party to the proceedings. Although the other four children assented to the arrangement, none signed the agreement. After the agreement two of the children who were not parties to the previous proceedings entered caveats against the probate to which, under the compromise, H's husband would otherwise have been entitled. One of the children who had been a party to the compromise sought specific performance against H's husband of the obligation under the compromise to pay the sum of £500. Lord Romilly held: (i) that the compromise was conditional upon the second will being admitted to probate; (ii) that since not all the children of the full sisters were parties to the agreement, it could only become binding on all parties if they all accepted it; and (iii) since certain of the children had repudiated the arrangement, it bound no one. **3-60**

Binding obligation to await future event

Alternatively, the parties may enter into a compromise, the operation of which is suspended until the fulfilment of the condition. There is a binding obligation on the parties to await the fulfilment of the condition. **3-61**

In *Smallman v Smallman*,[128] the parties to a matrimonial dispute agreed all the essential terms of a compromise and expressed it to be dependent "on the approval of the court". The Court of Appeal rejected the argument that the agreement was not binding unless and until it was approved by the court. Lord Denning MR[129] expressed the position this way:

> "There is an agreement but the operation of it is suspended until the Court approves it. It is the duty of one party or the other to bring the agreement before the Court for approval. If the Court approves it, it is binding on the parties. If the court does not approve it, it is not binding. But, pending the application to the court, it remains a binding agreement which neither party can disavow."

Compromise unilaterally binding until future event

The agreement may provide for the acceptance by one party of an obligation immediately binding upon him but the final compromise of the dispute being dependent on the fulfilment of a condition by the other. For example, A may agree with B that he will accept £1,000 in full settlement of his claim for unliquidated damages if B pays that sum into court within 28 days. A would not be permitted to resile from **3-62**

---

[127] *Plumley v Horrell* (1869) 20 L.T. 473. See also *Benstall v Swain* (1829) Tamlyn 288 at 295, cf. *Pym v Campbell* (1856) 6 E. & B. 370.

[128] *Smallman v Smallman* [1972] Fam. 25, cf. *Amey v Amey* [1992] 2 F.L.R. 89.

[129] *Smallman* [1972] Fam. 25 at 31. Where the intention of the parties is that a settlement already achieved should be formalised in a deed, the delivery by one party to the other of a signed deed as an escrow on condition that the other party signs it results in the party delivering the deed being bound irrevocably not to withdraw from the agreement: see *Silver Queen Maritime Ltd v Persia Petroleum Services Plc* [2010] EWHC 2867 (QB). cf. *Dietz v Lennig Chemicals* [1969] 1 A.C. 170 where the House of Lords held that an agreement of an infant's claim requiring the approval of the court under what was then RSC Ord.80 was not binding until the court gave its approval. Lord Pearson said (at 190) that "either party could lawfully have repudiated [the agreement] at any time before the court approved it". See further at Ch.27.

his agreement until B had the opportunity of fulfilling the condition.[130] If B paid the money into court within the prescribed period the compromise would be final.

Compromise immediately binding defeasible on condition subsequent

3-63 Finally, the parties may enter into an immediately binding compromise which remains so until the fulfilment (more usually the failure) of some condition which causes it to cease to be binding. For example, one party to a dispute concerning the title to property (real or personal) may compromise the claim of the other by agreeing to pay him a specified sum within a specified period following the sale of the property, each party agreeing that neither shall be bound by the sum if the property realises less than a certain price. Parties to a claim for a liquidated sum may similarly agree that the creditor shall have in his favour a consent judgment for the full amount of the debt subject to a provision that the debtor may, within a specified period, pay a lesser sum in satisfaction of the claim, in default of which payment the creditor may enforce the judgment for the whole sum.[131]

In each of the situations referred to above, though the fulfilment (or failure) of the relevant condition may be uncertain, the terms of the compromise are sufficiently clear and complete for the appropriate effect to be given to it.[132]

3-64 In *Bartlett v Conley*,[133] C and her late husband lent D1 and D2 £180,000 in November 1989 following their financial difficulties in the light of the problems at Lloyd's. C instituted proceedings for the recovery of £117,000, being the balance of the foregoing sum outstanding, and the trial was due to commence on 11 August 1997. An agreement was reached on the morning of the trial which was recorded in a document entitled "Draft Heads of Agreement". The document was in these terms:

> "The parties are agreed to compromise [C's] claims in these actions on the following terms, subject to
>
> (1) [D1's and D2's] bank ... (a) agreeing to the imposition of a second charge in favour of [C] as set out below; (b) agreeing to a ceiling upon the level of borrowings secured by way of its first charge being fixed at a maximum of £150,000 during the lifetime of the second charge referred to above;
> (2) the parties agreeing upon the precise form of the charge to be entered into;
> (3) [D1 and D2] retaining their Legal Aid status."
>
> "1. The Defendants and each of them do agree to pay to the Plaintiff the sum of £117,000 ('the principal sum') on a date no later than 11th day of August 2003.
> 2. In default of the payment as above of the principal sum on or before 11/8/03, the Defendants and each of them will become liable to pay on 12/8/03 the sum of £150,000 ('the default sum').
> 3. The Defendants and each of them agree to execute a legal charge upon the property known as Southlands Farm, Moretonhampstead, Devon to secure the payment of the principal and default sum.
> 4. No order for costs.

---

[130] See the analysis of this type of situation under the general law of contract by Diplock LJ in *United Dominions Trust (Commercial) Ltd v Eagle Aircraft Services Ltd* [1968] 1 W.L.R. 74 at 83–84. The use of the word "agree" in the text will be noted. If A merely offered B the opportunity of compromising on the terms suggested and B did not signify acceptance of the proposal, the question of revocability of the offer might arise prior to B actually paying the money into court: see, e.g. *Chitty*, Vol.1, para.2-083 onwards.

[131] *South American and Mexican Co Ex p. Bank of England, Re* [1895] 1 Ch. 37.

[132] For the rights and obligations of the parties in the event of the fulfilment or, as appropriate, non-fulfilment of the relevant condition, see Ch.8.

[133] *Bartlett v Conley* unreported 2 July 1999, QBENI 1999/0193/1.

5. Legal Aid Taxation of the Defendants' costs.
6. Liberty to apply as to the interpretation and timing of this order."

No consent order giving effect to this draft was drawn up. Subsequent correspondence between the parties' solicitors showed that the intention underlying the provision concerning D1's and D2's "Legal Aid status" was that that status should remain until the making of the consent order whereupon their certificates would be discharged.

In June 1998 the Legal Aid Board decided that D1 and D2 were no longer entitled to Legal Aid and their certificates were discharged. C reinstated her proceedings against D1 and D2 on the basis that the condition for the compromise, namely the retention of their Legal Aid status, no longer obtained and, accordingly, there was no longer any effective agreement.

The Court of Appeal held that C was entitled to take that position since once D1's and D2's Legal Aid certificates ceased to operate for whatever reason prior to the making of the consent order, the condition in the agreement ceased to be satisfied. The court proceeded on the assumption, without deciding, that the original agreement was binding subject to the fulfilment of the various conditions.

Compromise of part of dispute

It is quite possible for the parties expressly to compromise a particular element or elements in their dispute without arriving at an overall settlement.[134] This in no way results in the particular compromise being regarded as incomplete. In accident cases involving personal injury, for example, the parties not infrequently agree an apportionment of liability, the assessment of damages being left to the court.[135] Where the question arises as to what was compromised the question is one of construction of the parties' agreement.[136] **3-65**

The foregoing situation must, of course, be contrasted with that in which a material part of the dispute remains unresolved at a time when, as one of the parties subsequently seeks to argue, a complete agreement has been concluded.[137] **3-66**

Agreement reached in "without prejudice" negotiations

A not unknown misapprehension is that a "without prejudice" agreement is neither complete nor binding until confirmed by an "open" agreement. This is not so. Once a "without prejudice" offer[138] is accepted, a complete contract is established which is binding on both parties.[139] **3-67**

INTENTION TO CREATE LEGAL RELATIONS

Under the ordinary law of contract an agreement will not be enforced unless the parties intended to create a legally binding contract. The test for determining the existence of the intention is an objective one.[140] The problem of whether such an intention exists will rarely arise in the context of compromise. The dispute will usu- **3-68**

---

[134] Positive encouragement to settle issues within a case is given in the CPR: see Ch.13.
[135] *Tomlin v Standard Telephones* [1969] 1 W.L.R. 1378.
[136] See Ch.5.
[137] See para.3-50.
[138] See Ch.19.
[139] See, e.g. *Tomlin* [1969] 1 W.L.R. 1378.
[140] *Chitty*, Vol.1, para.2-161 onwards.

ally be sufficiently constituted, either by way of correspondence involving solicitors or actual litigation, for it to be abundantly clear that any compromise is intended to affect the legal relations of the parties.[141] The issue has, however, arisen in a number of cases concerning spouses, civil partners or others whose lives are connected in a domestic or "family" sense in relation to, as it were, amicable domestic arrangements.[142] Since the essence of compromise is the resolution of differences, it is not thought that this aspect of the law has much significance in this context. It is quite possible, of course, for members of a family to compromise a dispute, and intend thereby to be bound contractually, without the intervention of legal advisers.[143]

3-69 In *Snelling v John Snelling Ltd*,[144] C, D2 and D3, who were brothers, were directors of a family company, D1. Over a period of years, having regard to the policy of the brothers not to draw all of their earnings from the business, substantial loan accounts built up in favour of each. Serious differences arose between the brothers about the running of the company, culminating in C writing a letter to his father (who was chairman of the company) and to D2 and D3 in very uncomplimentary terms so far as the latter were concerned, but at the same time putting forward suggestions for reorganising the business. C threatened that if the principle of his proposals was not agreed to by a certain date, he would resign and withdraw his assets. This letter was written at a time when D1 was in the final stage of negotiations for the raising of additional finance for its operations by way of mortgage from a finance company. Efforts were made to overcome the differences between the brothers and on the same day as the mortgage was completed an agreement, prepared by D3 without legal assistance, was signed by all three. The agreement provided, inter alia, that in the event of any director resigning voluntarily he would immediately forfeit all monies due to him from D1 and its associated companies. It was further provided that the agreement would remain in force until the loan from the finance company had been repaid. About three months later C resigned his directorship and, in due course, sought to recover the balance outstanding on his loan account. It was contended on C's behalf that the agreement was not binding as it was not intended to give rise to legal relations. Ormrod J (as he then was) held that the agreement was intended to have legal effect and drew attention to the following factors that led to this conclusion: (i) the relationship between C and D2 and D3 had been destroyed by dissensions before the agreement was signed; (ii) although drafted by a layman, the agreement contained words and phrases (including reference to "the court") which suggested that legal consequences were intended to flow from it.

3-70 There is as yet no reported English case in which a party to negotiations towards a compromise has sought to elevate a "comfort letter"[145] or a "letter of intent"[146] into a contractually binding commitment. The precise legal status of such a document is not finally settled and the effect of any such letter may be very much affected by the specific facts of the case. Generally it might be thought that the use of expres-

---

141 See, e.g. *Bushwall Properties Ltd v Vortex Ltd* [1976] 1 W.L.R. 591. But see *Orion Insurance Co Plc v Sphere Drake Insurance Plc* [1992] 1 Lloyd's Rep. 239, where the Court of Appeal upheld a finding that an agreement made at a meeting of representatives of various insurance companies—the meeting having been designed to resolve differences over liabilities arising from the participation of the companies in two earlier insurance pool agreements—was a "goodwill agreement" only and was not intended to affect the legal relations of the parties. Also see *Jackson v Thakrar* [2007] EWHC 271 (TCC); 113 Con. L.R. 58.

142 *Chitty*, Vol.1, para.2-179 onwards.

143 *Snelling* [1973] 1 Q.B. 87.

144 *Snelling* [1973] 1 Q.B. 87.

145 *Kleinwort Benson Ltd v Malaysia Mining Corp Berhad* [1989] 1 W.L.R. 379 CA.

146 *Wilson Smithett & Cape (Sugar) Ltd v Bangladesh Sugar and Food Industries Corp* [1976] 1 Lloyd's Rep. 378.

sions such as "comfort" and, perhaps to a lesser extent, "intent" in relation to a letter or other similar communication would be regarded as negativing any intent to create legal relations in regard to its contents.[147]

FORMALITIES

Little or no formality is required for a contract to be upheld under English law.[148] Thus few situations arise where parties desirous of compromising their disputes need to have regard to the observance of any formalities. Three areas merit some attention: 3-71

Land

Any compromise involving a "sale or other disposition of an interest in land"[149] must be made in writing and "only by incorporating all the terms which the parties have expressly agreed in one document or, where contracts are exchanged, in each".[150] It is permissible for the terms to be incorporated into the relevant document by reference "to some other document",[151] but the document incorporating the terms "must be signed by or on behalf of each party to the contract".[152] Should any of these formalities not be observed there will be no contract. 3-72

In any case where a compromise involves a transfer of an acknowledged title or the creation of a lease,[153] these provisions must be observed. The most likely areas in which these matters will be of concern are the settlement of boundary disputes[154] and the compromise of landlord and tenant actions.[155] 3-73

Guarantee

A contract of guarantee must be in writing or evidenced by writing. Such a contract involves, on the part of the guarantor, a "promise to answer for the debt, 3-74

---

147 In *Associated British Ports v Ferryways NV, MSC Belgium NV* [2009] EWCA Civ 189, [2009] 1 Lloyd's Rep. 595 Maurice Kay LJ, with whom Lord Clarke MR and Jacob LJ agreed, said as follows: "I regard a letter of comfort, properly so called, as one that does not give rise to contractual liability. The label used by the parties is not necessarily determinative. It is a matter of construction of the document as a whole." *Chitty*, Vol.1, para.2-133.

148 *Chitty*, Vol.1, Ch.5.

149 The grant of an option to acquire an interest in land comes within the meaning of the section, but the notice by which such an option is exercised does not: *Spiro v Glencrown Properties Ltd* [1991] Ch.537, *Farrage v North Wiltshire DC* (1992) 64 P. & C.R. 527.

150 Law of Property (Miscellaneous Provisions) Act 1989 s.2(1). The Act affects all such transactions entered into after 26 September 1989. See *Orton v Collins* [2007] 1 W.L.R. 2953 for the relationship between these provisions and CPR Pt 36.

151 Law of Property (Miscellaneous Provisions) Act 1989 s.2(2).

152 Law of Property (Miscellaneous Provisions) Act 1989 s.2(3).

153 Other than an agreement to create a short lease (i.e. less than three years) within s.54(2) of the Law of Property Act 1925: s.2(5)(a). This includes a periodic tenancy. However, a "boundary agreement" is probably excluded from this requirement. In *Joyce v Rigolli* [2004] EWCA Civ 79, the Court of Appeal confirmed that the agreement concerned was "an agreement that merely demarcated the boundary. It did not purport to be a contract to convey any land from the appellant to the respondent. The parties' purpose was to fix the boundary at about the place where they thought it ought to have been". See further at Ch.30 and also *Nweze v Nwoko* [2004] EWCA Civ 379.

154 See Ch.30.

155 See Ch.29.

default or miscarriage of another person".[156] Thus any compromise involving the introduction of a third party to act as guarantor of the obligations of one of the parties must comply with the statute to be enforceable as against him.

DEEDS

3-75 Where parties decide for whatever reason to embody their agreement in a formal deed, the provisions of s.1 of the Law of Property (Miscellaneous Provisions) Act 1989[157] must be observed. In summary, these provisions require the deed to:

(a) make it clear on its face that it is intended to be a deed[158]; and
(b) be executed validly in accordance with the Act.[159]

The Act does not apply to deeds effected before s.1 became operative.[160]

---

156 Statute of Frauds 1677 s.4. See *Chitty*, Vol.2, Ch.44.
157 The Act applies to all deeds, not just those relating to land or property.
158 Law of Property (Miscellaneous Provisions) Act 1989 s.1(2)(a).
159 Law of Property (Miscellaneous Provisions) Act 1989 s.1(2)(b) and (3).
160 Law of Property (Miscellaneous Provisions) Act 1989 s.1(11).

CHAPTER 4

Impeachment of a Compromise

While parties may appear to have reached a complete and valid compromise, circumstances may arise, as they do under the ordinary law of contract, which render that apparent agreement ineffectual. Those circumstances are now examined. **4-01**

INCAPACITY[1]

CHILDREN[2]

A child is not as a matter of law bound by a compromise.[3] Any such agreement is voidable at his option.[4] It would, however, be capable of ratification on attaining majority.[5] Nonetheless, a minor may become bound by a compromise of a dispute affecting him if the court approves the agreement.[6] **4-02**

PERSONS WITH IMPAIRED MENTAL FUNCTIONING

At common law, a mentally disordered person will be held to a contract unless he did not know what he was doing and the other party was aware of the incapacity which resulted in him not knowing what he was doing at the time he entered into the contract. If the mentally disordered person can establish this, the contract would be regarded as voidable at his option.[7] An otherwise voidable contract for this reason may be ratified by the mentally disordered person after he has recovered or during a rational period.[8] **4-03**

A person who "lacks capacity in relation to a matter" is someone who "at the material time ... is unable to make a decision for himself in relation to the matter **4-04**

---

1 For a general analysis, see *Chitty*, Vol.1, Ch.8.

2 The word "child" is used in the text in place of either "minor" or "infant" to accord with the more modern approach of the CPR: see r.21.1(2)(b). A "child" is a person under the age of 18 years, see Family Law Reform Act 1969.

3 *Overton v Bannister* (1844) 3 Ha. 504, *Mattei v Vautro* (1898) 78 L.T. 682.

4 *Chitty*, Vol.1, paras 9–005 and 9–036 onwards. See also *Rhodes v Swithenbank* (1889) 22 Q.B.D. 577.

5 Minors' Contracts Act 1987 s.1(1)(a).

6 See Ch.27. See CPR r.21.10.

7 *Imperial Loan Co Ltd v Stone* [1892] 1 Q.B. 599, where the language used to describe someone suffering from a mental disorder is considerably out-dated and old-fashioned. Nonetheless, the common law principles are set out in that case. See also *Hart v O'Connor* [1985] A.C. 1000 PC. The need for reference to common law principles in the context of compromise is likely to be rare. The Mental Capacity Act 2005 is likely to be relevant to most situations that arise. For a case where a party to a compromise agreement claimed subsequently to have lacked capacity to enter into the agreement, see *Wadhwani v Ingenious Media Holdings Ltd* [2018] EWHC 350 (QB).

8 *Matthews v Baxter* (1873) L.R. 8 Ex. 132. Cf. the analogous situation concerning children above.

because of an impairment of, or a disturbance in the functioning of, the mind or brain."[9] Following the entry into force of the Mental Capacity Act 2005 the term "patient" is no longer used. Someone whose mental functioning brings him within the provisions of the Act is a "protected party" in any litigation and will have to act through a "litigation friend".[10] In *Dunhill v Burgin (Rev 1)* the UK Supreme Court affirmed that where an individual is a "protected party" (or a child) and fails to act through a "litigation friend" any settlement entered into must be approved by the court under CPR. 21.11 for it to be binding.[11] This is the case whether (or not) the individual or the other party were aware of the fact of the mental incapacity. For the purposes of CPR r.21.10 the fact that the settlement was contained within a consent order did not amount to court approval. Where it is unclear whether an individual is a "protected party" the court under its inherent jurisdiction may approve a settlement. Such a settlement will be valid, for the purposes of CPR r.21.10, if it subsequently becomes apparent that the individual was, at the relevant time, a "protected party".[12]

4-05 A judge cannot enter a consent to an order on behalf of a litigant before him because the litigant's counsel cannot obtain instructions and the judge feels that entering the consent is in that person's best interests.[13]

LEGAL ADVISERS[14]

4-06 Neither a solicitor nor a barrister has any implied or ostensible authority to compromise some matter "collateral to the action" in question.[15]

NON-LEGAL ADVISERS AND REPRESENTATIVES

4-07 Pursuant to s.54 of the Taxes Management Act 1970 an accountant may have actual authority to compromise a dispute between his taxpayer client and the Revenue. Equally, in certain circumstances, the taxpayer may have held out an accountant apparently acting for him as having authority to enter into such an agreement, even though in fact the accountant had no express authority to do so.[16]

---

9 Mental Capacity Act 2005 s.2(1). Section 3 sets out a detailed framework for determining whether someone "is unable to make a decision for himself".

10 See Ch.27.

11 *Dunhill v Burgin (Rev 1)* [2014] 1 W.L.R. 933 (UKSC), para.20. See CPR r.21.10. For details concerning the relevant procedure where a party is mentally incapacitated, see para 10-22 onwards. See also para.27-16 onwards.

12 *Coles v Perfect & Ors* [2013] EWHC 1955 (QB). In that case neither party alleged that the claimant lacked capacity, but both parties were anxious to secure the approval of the court to the settlement so that they could be assured that the settlement was valid, final and binding. The course adopted in that case is often followed also where there is some element of doubt about the relevant party's capacity, but a trial of the issue is considered to be unnecessary or disproportionately expensive."

13 *Woodhead v Woodhead* (1978) CAT 147.

14 For the role of legal advisers and others in securing a "compromise agreement" in the employment setting, see Ch.28. See *Nesbitt v Holt* [2007] EWCA Civ 249; [2007] P.N.L.R. 24 in relation to a possible claim by a litigant represented by a Citizens Advice Bureau caseworker who, it was alleged, settled a claim under the Disability Discrimination Act 1995 against the litigant's former employers without the litigant's authority.

15 See para.21-16.

16 *Inland Revenue Commissioners v West* [1991] STC 357 CA; cf. *Sheppard v Inland Revenue Commissioners* [1992] 3 All E.R. 58. For "ostensible authority" to operate to bind a principal it is necessary for the principal to hold the agent out as having authority. No representation by the agent as to the extent of his authority can amount to a holding-out by his principal: *Selectmove Ltd, Re* [1995]

Expert witnesses

An expert witness engaged by a party, who takes part in a discussion with an expert witness instructed by another party to the litigation pursuant to a direction of the court, has no power to bind the party by whom he is instructed on any aspect of the case, unless the parties agree to be bound.[17] The practical effect of an agreement between experts may be effectively to bind a party, and indeed where a single expert is jointly instructed (whether by agreement or by direction of the court)[18] this practical consequence may be felt more acutely. However, the strict legal position in terms of an expert's authority is that he cannot bind the party or parties by whom he is instructed in relation either to the whole case or in respect of the issue or issues he is asked to address. **4-08**

Companies

A trading company has an implied power to compromise claims brought by or against it.[19] Whilst there was at one time the possibility of the doctrine of ultra vires vitiating a compromise entered into by a company,[20] this possibility has effectively been removed by s.39 of the Companies Act 2006. It provides that the "validity of an act done by a company shall not be called into question by reason of anything in the company's constitution". The extent to which an individual director or employee has capacity to bind a company to a compromise will depend on the particular circumstances of the case.[21] **4-09**

Local authorities

A local authority's action may fall foul of the ultra vires doctrine. A local authority may act only within the powers conferred upon it by statute. Where it acts beyond those powers the doctrine of ultra vires, the object of which is "the protection of the public",[22] will invalidate the act in question. Whilst it is perfectly permissible for a local authority to compromise disputes in which it becomes involved, entering into a compromise that lies beyond its powers is ultra vires and the agreement apparently reached will be struck down as void ab initio.[23] **4-10**

---

1 W.L.R. 474 at 478. See also *HMRC v Southern Cross Employment Agency Ltd* [2015] UKUT 0122 (TCC).

17 CPR r.35.12(5).

18 CPR rr.35.7 and 35.8. See *D (A Child) v Walker* [2000] 1 W.L.R. 1382 CA, but cf. *W v Oldham MBC* [2005] EWCA Civ 1247; [2006] 1 F.L.R. 543 in the family law setting.

19 *Dixon v Evans* (1872) L.R. 5 H.L. 606, *Bath's Case* (1878) 8 Ch. D. 334.

20 *GNW Central Rail Co v Charlebois* [1899] A.C. 114, *Jon Beauforte (London) Ltd, Re* [1953] Ch. 131.

21 In *Hurst Stores and Interiors Ltd v M.L. Europe Ltd* [2004] EWCA Civ 490; [2004] B.L.R. 249 the issue arose as to whether the "project manager" of a company engaged to refit the toilet facilities in a large building had the authority to bind the company to a compromise.

22 *Hazell v Hammersmith and Fulham LBC* [1992] 2 A.C. 1 at 36, per Lord Templeman. See also para.33-07 onwards.

23 *Eastbourne BC v Foster* unreported 20 December 2000, Colin Mackay QC, as he then was, sitting as a deputy High Court judge. In this case the local authority entered into a "Compromise Agreement" with one of its senior employees under which he received a financial package on his ceasing employment which went beyond what the local authority could properly and legitimately have agreed with him. It was common ground at the trial that the agreement was void ab initio. For the decision on appeal to the Court of Appeal, see *Eastbourne BC v Foster* [2001] EWCA Civ 1091. See also *Rose Gibb v Maidstone and Tunbridge Wells NHS Trust* [2009] EWHC 862 (QB).

Partners

4-11 A view traditionally expressed,[24] namely, that one partner may not compromise proceedings brought by or against the firm may be over-simplistic.[25] Since the settlement of a dispute with a partnership may arguably be seen as part of the ordinary business of most types of firm,[26] it may be thought that a third party may ordinarily compromise a claim by or against a firm in the confidence that it would bind all partners even though he may not know whether all the partners either knew of or expressly approved it. However, an arrangement going beyond the usual nature of a compromise,[27] or one which was, to the knowledge of the other party to the settlement, in fraud of the other partners,[28] would be liable to be set aside.

Representative parties

4-12 Where a party represents others who have "the same interest in a claim",[29] a consent order or judgment reflecting a compromise of that claim will "unless the court otherwise directs"[30] be binding,

> "on all persons represented in the claim … but may only be enforced by or against a person who is not a party to the claim with the permission of the court".[31]

Although the express approval of the court to a settlement of such a claim is not required, the court retains a degree of control over the effect of such a settlement both on parties represented in the claim and those who were not parties in the action. In proceedings to which CPR r.19.7 applies[32] the court's approval of a proposed settlement by a representative party is required.[33] Such approval will be given "where [the court] is satisfied that the settlement is for the benefit of all the represented persons".[34] Similar further protection to the represented parties is given under this rule as is afforded under CPR r.19.6 in relation to the binding nature of any judgment and its enforceability.[35]

Represented parties acting personally

4-13 Individual parties who have solicitors acting for them may, if they are sui juris,

---

24 See para.4-08 of the 3rd edition and 79 *Halsbury's Laws*, 5th edn (2008), para.55.

25 This view is based on *Crane v Lewis* (1887) 36 W.R. 480.

26 cf. Partnership Act 1980 s.5 and *Lindley and Banks on Partnership*, 20th edn (London: Sweet & Maxwell, 2017), para. 12–11 onwards. Since a partner in general terms has an implied authority to commence legal proceedings in the name of the firm (Lindley, para.14–71), it would seem illogical if a similar power to compromise those proceedings did not exist: see Lindley, para.14–72. However, the position may be different where proceedings are brought *against* a partnership. It appears that one party may not bind a partnership to a consent judgment against it: Lindley, para.14–77.

27 See *Niemann v Niemann* (1890) 43 Ch. D. 198. The headnote of this case reads as follows: "There is no power in one partner, in the absence of special authority from his co-partners or evidence of a special course of dealing, to accept shares in a company even though fully paid up in satisfaction of a debt due to the firm."

28 Lindley, 2017, para.14–72.

29 CPR r.19.6(1).

30 CPR r.19.6(4).

31 CPR r.19.6(4)(a) and (b).

32 Those relating to the estate of a deceased person, property subject to a trust or the meaning of a document (including a statute): CPR r.19.7(1).

33 CPR r.19.7(5).

34 CPR r.19.7(6). See *Archer & Others v Travis Perkins PLC & Others* [2014] EWHC 1362 (Ch); [2014] Pens. L.R. 311 at [16].

35 CPR r.19.7(7).

compromise an action without the intervention of their solicitors.[36] If their motives are dishonest with a view to depriving the solicitors of their costs or defeating their lien, the court will intervene for the solicitors' protection.[37]

MISTAKE

General

Mistakes occur in the contractual context in a number of ways. A clear and comprehensive classification of the various types of mistake that can operate to invalidate a contract is elusive.[38] In general terms the law recognises (i) mistakes where the parties have come to an agreement, but on the basis of some shared false assumption of fact, law[39] or the existence of a state of affairs which renders performance of the agreement the parties contemplated impossible[40] and (ii) mistakes where there has been some misunderstanding about the terms of the agreement. So far as the latter are concerned, the mistake may either be mutual in the sense that both parties have confused what the other intended or unilateral in the sense that only one of them has confused what was intended. Where there has been a mutual mistake or mutual misunderstanding the contract will be regarded as void ab initio.[41] The position in the case of a unilateral mistake is less clear, but relief may be afforded in certain circumstances.[42] **4-14**

Relief sought or given

Prior to *Great Peace Shipping Ltd v Tsavliris Salvage (International) Ltd*[43] ("*The Great Peace*") there had been a debate for many years about whether there was a separate equitable jurisdiction to set aside an agreement on the basis of a mutual (or common) mistake.[44] Since that case it is now clear that such a jurisdiction does not exist.[45] Where an operative mutual mistake (or misunderstanding) is found to have occurred, the contract will be void ab initio. Where there is disagreement about **4-15**

---

36 *Brunsdon v Allard* (1859) 2 Ell. & Ell. 19, *Sullivan v Pearson* (1868) L.R. 4 Q.B. 153, *The Hope* (1883) 8 P.D. 144.

37 *Margetson and Jones, Re* [1897] 2 Ch. 314 per Kekewich J: "[T]he Courts have uniformly held ... that if the solicitor for the one party meets the principal on the other side and a bargain is made, that bargain is good. It cannot be said that the principal's authority is gone, because such a thing as that is impossible; and therefore, whether there is a litigation pending or not, if the solicitor for the defendant meets the plaintiff and effects a compromise with him, that compromise is binding upon the plaintiff or the defendant, as the case may be, notwithstanding that up to that time he had been represented by a solicitor. That is as consonant with common sense as the rule itself; but what the Court has also said is that it must be done honestly and in a straightforward way to get rid of the litigation for the sake of peace, and not with a view to depriving the solicitor of his costs. If the one solicitor meeting the party on the other side, or the two parties compromise knowing of the lien of the solicitor and intending to defeat it, that shall not be allowed; and the only question, therefore, is whether that was the intention."

38 *Chitty*, Vol.1, para. 6–001 onwards.

39 See para.4-20.

40 *Great Peace Shipping Ltd v Tsavliris Salvage (International) Ltd* [2003] Q.B. 679 ("*The Great Peace*").

41 *Chitty*, Vol.1, paras.6-008-6–009.

42 See para.4-22.

43 *The Great Peace* [2003] Q.B. 679.

44 *Chitty*, Vol.1, Ch.6, esp. para.6-055 onwards.

45 "If coherence is to be restored to this area of our law, it can only be by declaring that there is no jurisdiction to grant rescission of a contract on the ground of common mistake where that contract

whether a mistake or misunderstanding of this nature occurred, the relief that the party asserting it will seek would seem to be a declaration to that effect, the setting aside of any such agreement (and any order or judgment made pursuant thereto) and an order directing repayment of any money paid thereunder.[46] Where a party asserts an operative unilateral mistake, his remedy is likely to be rectification of (as he would say) the erroneously expressed written agreement of compromise.[47] For a party resisting the attempts of the other to enforce the compromise, an operative unilateral mistake might afford a defence either to a claim for damages or to one for specific performance.[48]

Mistake in compromise

Mutual mistake about fundamental matter

Fact

4-16 A shared misapprehension of fact which goes to the root of the compromise renders the agreement void:

In *Allcard v Walker*,[49] a consent order was made in matrimonial proceedings following a divorce varying a post-nuptial settlement of certain property. The consent order was made on the mistaken assumption by all concerned that certain other property was bound by the settlement. In fact it was not so bound and Stirling J held that the consent order made on this false premise should be set aside on terms. The contention that the mistake was one of law was rejected (private right of ownership being held to be a matter of fact), but Stirling J said, in any event, that a mistake of law would not to be fatal to the application to set aside the order.

4-17 In *Huddersfield Banking Co Ltd v Henry Lister & Son Ltd*,[50] a consent order for the sale of a number of looms in a factory was made in the liquidation of the company to which the factory belonged. It was made upon the erroneous assumption that the looms were not fixtures. In fact, as subsequently appeared, they had been wrongfully loosened by a third party. The Court of Appeal held that the order had been made on the basis of a mutual mistake of fact and that the order should be set aside.

---

is valid and enforceable on ordinary principles of contract law": *The Great Peace* [2003] Q.B. 679 at [157], per Lord Phillips MR. He went on to say that an "equitable jurisdiction to grant rescission on terms where a common fundamental mistake has induced a contract gives greater flexibility than a doctrine of common law which holds the contract void in such circumstances ... there is scope for legislation to give greater flexibility to our law of mistake than the common law allows".

46 For a review of the remedies available when a compromise is treated as void ab initio, see *Eastbourne BC v Foster (No.1)* [2001] EWCA Civ 1091; [2002] I.C.R. 234. See case comment by Dharmananda, 'Contradictions in considering conduct void under compromise' (2002) L.Q.R. 118.

47 *Chitty*, Vol.1, para. 3-089 onwards. See paras 4-31—4-35.

48 *Chitty*, Vol.1, para.6-061. Such a defendant could counterclaim for rectification: cf. *Roberts, Re* [1905] 1 Ch. 704.

49 *Allcard v Walker* [1896] 2 Ch. 369.

50 *Huddersfield Banking Co Ltd v Henry Lister & Son Ltd* [1895] 2 Ch. 273. In earlier editions of this work the case of *Magee v Pennine Insurance Co Ltd* [1969] 2 Q.B. 507 was given as an example of an operative false and fundamental assumption of fact that invalidated a compromise. Since the basis of the decision in this case can no longer be regarded as good law following *The Great Peace* [2003] Q.B. 679, it is not now put forward as an example in this context. It would be interesting to see how similar facts would be decided on the basis of the law as it now is to be regarded. But the case of *Galloway v Galloway* (1914) 30 T.L.R. 531 (separation deed void because both parties assumed that they were validly married) is probably to be considered as correct whatever approach to the law applicable to mistake is adopted.

It was said by Kay LJ[51]:

> "It seems to me that, both on principle and on authority, when once the Court finds that an agreement has been come to between parties who were under a common mistake of material fact, the Court may set it aside, and the Court has ample jurisdiction to set aside the order founded upon that agreement."

4-18 In *Grains & Fourrages SA v Huyton*,[52] C were buyers and D were sellers, pursuant to two separate contracts, of Chinese cotton expellers. The first contract was for 10,000 tonnes and the second for 1,983 tonnes respectively. The standard terms of the Grain and Feed Trade Association contract, upon which the parties traded, provided that the quality was to be, "final on representative samples drawn at discharge and analysed in London". Samples were taken at the port of discharge by jointly instructed superintendents and sent to London for analysis. On 5 August 1993 the analysts issued two certificates of analysis in respect of the expellers and extractions. On receiving the certificates and on re-checking, D advised C that there appeared to have been a typing error with the result that the results of the analyses had been interchanged, pointing out that the tonnages did not correspond with the commodity certified on each certificate. D asked that the analysts issue new and amended certificates. C took this up with the analysts who stated that the results corresponded with the samples provided and that the superintendents may have interchanged the labels on the samples. Proceeding on the assumption that this is what had happened, C and D agreed to treat each analysis as corresponding to the other contract. Payment was made on that basis. However, it emerged later that, contrary to the common assumption made by C and D, there was no transposition of results in relation to the cargoes named in the two certificates, but merely an incorrect transposition of the tonnages for each cargo. Mance J, as he then was, held that the agreement reached, which did not in the circumstances involve any element of compromise, should be set aside on the ground of a "common and fundamental mistake".

Opinion

4-19 Arguably, a mutual mistake of opinion will not vitiate a compromise, though what differentiates an opinion from fact or, in some circumstances, law may not always be that easy to determine:

In *Cooper v Cooper (Preece)*,[53] H agreed to buy off any claim which W might have in the former matrimonial home for £400. The agreement was made in January 1972 and the agreed sum plus interest was to be paid by June 1972. Whilst the negotiations continued during 1971 both parties thought that the value of the house was about £4,000 (the sum outstanding on mortgage being about £3,800). In June 1972 H sold the property for £8,650. W sought to resile from the agreement on the basis that there had been a mutual mistake of fact, namely the value of the house. The Court of Appeal held that there had been no mistake of fact, merely one of opinion as to the value of the property. It was said that they both knew the house and all the material facts (for example, that it was very damp).[54]

---

51 *Huddersfield Banking* [1895] 2 Ch. 273 at 284. In one of the nicer metaphors to be found in the literature of the law reports, Vaughan Williams J said this at first instance: "To say that the Court can set aside the agreement ... but that it cannot set aside an order which was the creature of that agreement, seems to me to be giving the branch an existence which is independent of the tree."

52 *Grains & Fourrages SA v Huyton* [1997] 1 Lloyd's Rep. 628, cf. *The Ypatia Halcoussi* [1985] 2 Lloyd's Rep. 364 where no mutual mistake could be shown.

53 *Cooper v Cooper (Preece)* (1973) CAT 425B; [1973] 12 WLUK 66; [1974] C.L.Y. 90u.

54 cf. *Warren v Warren* (1983) 13 Fam. Law 49 (where the Court of Appeal granted W leave to appeal out of time against the making of a lump sum order based upon an agreed valuation of the former matrimonial home, when that valuation was exceeded on sale some eight months later by approaching 100 per cent. Griffiths LJ, as he then was, described the case as "atypical because of the

Law

4-20 Characterising a mistake as one of law in contradistinction to one of fact or of opinion can be a difficult exercise.[55] For the purposes of the law of restitution the distinction between a mistake of law and a mistake of fact has been held by the House of Lords to be no longer maintainable.[56] Against that background the Court of Appeal held in *Brennan v Bolt Burdon*[57] that a mutual mistake of law could in principle invalidate a compromise although there was no operative mistake of law in that case.[58] It is plainly an uncomfortable consequence that this principle, if applied too readily, could undermine the finality normally associated with a compromise.[59] Indeed, there are indications in the judgments that had an exception to the general principle based upon "public policy" been proposed in argument, it would have afforded an answer to the issues raised in the case.[60] However, the case is authority for the principle articulated, albeit one the application of which is likely to be scrutinised with particular care when raised. It is part of the everyday process of the compromise of actual or threatened litigation that views are taken on each side about the state of the law or its applicability to the facts of the particular case. Indeed, these views are frequently ventured in negotiation. It remains important to appreciate that the mere fact that parties compromise a dispute involving competing assertions of law which have debatable validity will not undermine the compromise. Provided the assertions are made in good faith[61] there would be no obvious grounds for calling the compromise into question. Since it is necessary for a mutual mistake of law to render performance of the agreement impossible in the way the parties contemplated before the court will intervene to set it aside,[62] it is difficult to envisage how this would ordinarily arise in the case of a compromise.[63]

---

extraordinary discrepancy"). Whatever the correctness of *Cooper v Cooper* (1973) CAT 425B; [1973] 12 WLUK 66; [1974] C.L.Y. 90u may have been on the facts, and indeed on the principle of whether a mistake as to opinion can vitiate an agreement, it is thought that in the matrimonial finance context a significant discrepancy between a sale price of property and the value attributed to it by the parties in their negotiations leading to a consent order may afford a ground for setting aside the consent order, provided the order was substantially different from the order that would have been made if the true value had been known: see *Livesey v Jenkins* [1985] A.C. 424 and para.24-117 onwards. cf. *L v L* (1981) 11 Fam. Law 57 (Balcombe J). See also *Edmonds v Edmonds* (1990) Fam. Law 473, where *Warren v Warren* was distinguished and attention drawn to *Barder v Caluori* [1988] A.C. 20. In many cases the precise boundary between a mistake of opinion and a mistake of fact will be difficult to identify: see, e.g. the discussion in *Chitty*, Vol.1, para.6–002 onwards.

55 *Chitty*, Vol.1, paras 6–052 and 29–041.

56 *Kleinwort Benson Ltd v Lincoln City Council* [1999] 1 A.C. 153 HL.

57 *Brennan v Bolt Burdon* [2005] Q.B. 303.

58 It is easier to assert the principle than to identify the circumstances in which a mistake of law could invalidate a compromise. Suppose that A and B settle a dispute before proceedings are issued against the background of the shared erroneous belief that the limitation period applicable to the dispute in question had not expired. Would that be a mistake of law? If so, would it be right for the compromise to be set aside?

59 *Brennan* [2005] Q.B. 303, per Maurice Kay LJ at [22], per Bodey J at [39] and per Sedley LJ at [61]–[63].

60 *Brennan* [2005] Q.B. 303, per Maurice Kay LJ at [23] and per Bodey J at [52].

61 See para.2-19.

62 See para.4-14.

63 *Brennan* [2005] Q.B. 303 per Maurice Kay LJ at [22] and per Sedley LJ at [59]–[60]. Sedley LJ said this at [60]: "I think that in cases of mutual mistake of law a different test may be necessary. The equivalent question needs to be whether, had the parties appreciated that the law was what it is now known to be, there would still have been an intelligible basis for their agreement. This seems to me to come as close as one can come to what was identified as being at issue in the *Great Peace* case, at p.691, para.32: a common mistaken assumption (in that case one of fact) which renders the service

Mutual misunderstanding of terms

One situation that falls to be considered under the general heading of "mutual mistake" arises where each party interprets and accepts the offer of the other in a completely different sense from that which was intended. In such a situation, no contract comes into existence. An example would be afforded where A and B have two separate and distinct disputes running concurrently. A makes an offer of compromise intended to deal with both disputes; B believes that A is attempting to compromise one dispute only and accepts on that basis, and the actual agreement is inconclusive. Clearly there would be no contract, the parties being treated as not *ad idem*.[64] **4-21**

Unilateral mistake

This sub-heading embraces the situation where the mistake about the terms of the agreement is unilateral in the sense that only one party has confused what was intended. Following *The Great Peace*[65] it is plain that, whatever other jurisdiction for giving relief to the mistaken party may exist, an equitable jurisdiction to set aside the agreement cannot now be invoked.[66] There is, however, some uncertainty about the way the courts will deal with this situation. Where one party to a compromise is labouring under some misapprehension about its terms that is known to, or has in some way been encouraged by, the other party, it is arguable that there is no genuine agreement between them even though, viewed objectively, it would appear that an agreement has been concluded.[67] That could render the whole agreement void ab initio or, alternatively, result in an agreement upon the basis of the **4-22**

---

that will be provided if the contract is performed something different from the performance that the parties contemplated." In *Kyle Bay Ltd (t/a Astons Nightclub) v Underwriters* [2007] EWCA Civ 57, Neuberger LJ at [23], drew attention to the differing views of Maurice Kay and Sedley LJJ on this issue. He put the matter thus: "In paragraph [22] of his judgment, Maurice Kay LJ gave three reasons why the *Great Peace* decision gave rise to difficulties for the claimant, the first of which was that it was 'quite simply not a case of impossibility of performance. The compromise has at all times remained performable ...'. Sedley LJ, however, was more concerned about the application of the 'impossibility of performance' test in cases of common mistake of law—see at paragraphs [60] to [61]. At the end of paragraph [59], he had identified the 'difficulty ... in seeing how the effect of [a common mistake of law ... on an agreement by which litigation is compromised] can be equiparated with the impossibility of a contractual venture'." Neuberger LJ (with whom Ward and Wilson LJJ agreed) said that it was unnecessary "on this appeal to decide which view is preferable" but expressed the view that "ultimately, the two approaches may essentially amount to the same thing."

64 In previous editions the case of *Hickman v Berens* [1895] 2 Ch. 638 had been advanced as an example of the application of this principle. However, *Chitty* suggested (32nd edn, Vol.1, para.5-072 fn.322) that this case would not be followed today because of the objective nature of the test required by *The Great Peace* [2003] Q.B. 679 and since the compromise agreement did express "exactly what one of the parties meant". This approach might still afford a solution to the problems associated with a compromise of claims arising from a dispute which apparently settles both insured and uninsured losses, when one party intended that it should be so and the other did not so intend: cf. para.3-24. However, the actual terms of the agreement, properly construed, will probably determine the outcome of any such issue.

65 See fn.40.

66 See fn.45. See also on unilateral mistake in a compromise situation, *Statoil ASA v Louis Dreyfus Energy Services LP (The Hariette N)* [2008] 2 Lloyd's Rep. 685.

67 This would seem to apply to a unilateral mistake of law affecting the appreciation by one party of the terms of a compromise, which is known to the other party: *Stone v Godfrey* (1854) 5 De G.M. & G. 76 at 90. A mistake as to the effect of the compromise will not of itself do so: *Taylor v Taylor* (1976) CAT 228A; *Powell v Smith* (1872) L.R. 14 Eq. 85; *Hart v Hart* (1881) 18 Ch. D. 670.

understanding of the mistaken party for whom the remedy of rectification may be available in relation to any written agreement made pursuant to the negotiations.[68]

4-23 The cases to which reference is made below must now be viewed in the light of the restatement of the law of mistake in *The Great Peace* and the proposition that a mistake of law may now afford grounds for treating a compromise as void.

4-24 In *Wilding v Sanderson*,[69] a consent order was made directing the taking of accounts between the parties. One party thought that a particular form of account had been agreed not involving the payment of interest. The other party intended the converse. The terms of the consent order, on their true construction, showed that interest was to be charged. The Court of Appeal held, however, that the mistake of one party as to the meaning of the words of the consent order had been contributed to by the other because of certain letters written on their behalf prior to the compromise, the minutes of judgment prepared by them and some remarks of their counsel. There was no real agreement between the parties.[70]

4-25 Where, however, the unilateral mistake is not known to, or contributed to by, the other party and can, therefore, be seen as a one-sided mistake simpliciter, the compromise will ordinarily[71] be upheld.

In *Taylor v Taylor*,[72] negotiations took place between the solicitors acting for H and W with a view to compromising financial issues. A concluded agreement was arrived at in correspondence whereby W would give up her right to periodical payments for herself (but not for the children) if H would transfer the matrimonial home into her sole name subject to a charge in his favour for a specified sum. H in fact entered into the agreement thinking that W had relinquished her rights to periodical payments for the children as well, his solicitors not having made this clear in the negotiations. The Court of Appeal held that H could not go behind the correspondence and say that he was mistaken about its effect. It was not a case of mutual or common mistake. It was a mistake of H himself "not known to the other party, nor contributed to by her".[73]

4-26 In *Olympia Sauna Shipping Co SA v Shinwa Kaiun Kaisha Ltd (The Ypatia Halcoussi)*,[74] C chartered its vessel to D under a time charter on the New York Produce Exchange form for one round trip carrying a cargo of coal. The vessel arrived in Vancouver to load coal in March 1981, but there was a delay in berthing with the result that D claimed that the vessel had been off-hire for something over 13 days. On 8 July D submitted a hire statement to C which showed a deduction of $226,088 in respect of time lost at Vancouver and $28,636 in respect of bunkers. After an allowance for commission (which appears from the report to have been $5,652, representing 2.5 per cent of $226,088), the total deduction was shown as $249,072. The net result, if D was entitled to make these deductions, was a balance in D's favour of about $74,000. If the deductions were not permissible, the amount recoverable by C from D would be diminished by the $74,000 balance owed to D. This balance was not the subject of discussion or correspondence at that time. C and D were unable to agree on the deductions D was entitled to make for off-hire and bunkers and in July 1981 the dispute was referred to arbitration in London. C's points of claim claimed the amount deducted in respect of off-hire (less the commission), but at that stage made no reference to the deduction in respect of bunkers. In the points of defence and counterclaim D contended that the deductions were permissible and advanced a substantial (but unparticularised) counterclaim, but did not counterclaim for the $74,000 balance. The

---

68 *Chitty*, paras 6-060 and 3-069 onwards. It may also afford a defence to a claim for specific performance: para.6-061.

69 *Wilding v Sanderson* [1897] 2 Ch. 534.

70 See *Wilding* [1897] 2 Ch. 534, per Lindley LJ at 550.

71 *Chitty*, paras 3-001—3-003 and 3-069 onwards.

72 *Taylor v Taylor* (1976) CAT 228A.

73 per Lord Denning MR.

74 *The Ypatia Halcoussi* [1985] 2 Lloyd's Rep. 364.

arbitration was due to take place on 17 and 18 June 1982. Negotiations with a view to resolving the dispute started in March 1982 and at about that time C gave notice of its intention to increase its claim in order to pursue the deduction of $28,636 in respect of bunkers, thus making its total claim in the sum of $249,072. At no time during the negotiations between March and June 1982, when the compromise agreement hereafter referred to was concluded, did either party make reference to the $74,000 balance. On 8 June, C indicated to D's solicitors by telex that C would be

> "prepared to accept [$]195,000 in total and final settlement of all outstanding claims and amounts whatsoever arising out of the ... time charter, both parties to forgo all claims and demands against the other".

On June 9, D's solicitors replied by telex saying that D "accepts the terms of settlement" and indicating that the money would be paid on or before June 18. The cheque that D proffered to discharge the debt under the compromise was for $195,000 less the $74,000 balance which D said was not comprehended by the settlement, but which in fact D had overlooked and forgotten about at the time of the settlement. C refused to accept this and sued for the whole sum of $195,000. D counterclaimed for rectification of the agreement alleging common mistake or unilateral mistake. Bingham J (as he then was) held: (a) that there could have been no common mistake because D, having forgotten about it, had no intention with regard to the $74,000 balance at any relevant time before the compromise agreement, and C either had no intention with regard to it or did have intention, being that it should not be deducted from the sum to be paid; (b) if there was a unilateral mistake (which there could not have been because D had forgotten about the $74,000 balance), P had no actual knowledge of such mistake.

In *OT Africa Line Ltd v Vickers Plc*,[75] C and D had been negotiating the settlement of a dispute about the delayed shipment of four battle tanks from England to Nigeria. The claim was for about US $700,000 plus interest and costs, and the trial was fixed for January 15, 1996. In November 1995 D paid into court the sum of US $103,000 in settlement of the claim. This was not accepted and on 8 December, C offered to settle for approximately US $185,000 for total detention costs plus a contribution to fixed costs of US $280,000, interest and costs. This offer was expressed to be open for 14 days. Various other discussions took place thereafter in which the figures mentioned by, or on behalf of, each side were expressed in US dollars. On December 22, D's solicitors faxed an offer to C's solicitors for "the total sum of £150,000 (including the sum in court)", the offer being expressed to be open until 4 January unless withdrawn sooner. An offer of £150,000 was not what D intended. It was intended that an offer of US $155,000, which had previously been made in oral discussions, be repeated. D's solicitors' fax was a mistake. D sought to argue, inter alia, that the agreement reached ought to be set aside on the grounds of unilateral mistake. Mance J, as he then was, held that since C "were ... not aware of, or in a position where they shut their eyes to, or responsible for or at fault in respect of any mistake made on [D's] side", there were no grounds for setting the agreement aside. **4-27**

Traditionally, an interlocutory[76] consent order made on the basis of a purely unilateral mistake not known to, or contributed to, by the other party can be set aside or varied.[77] Where, however, the consent order reflects a true compromise, a purely unilateral mistake will be unlikely to afford grounds for the intervention of the court.[78] **4-28**

Another instance of a unilateral mistake operating to defeat a compromise would arise where a successful plea of *non est factum* could be raised in relation, say, to **4-29**

---

[75] *OT Africa Line Ltd v Vickers Plc* [1996] 1 Lloyd's Rep. 700. See also *EasyFind (NSW) Pty Ltd v Paterson* (1987) 11 N.S.W.L.R. 98.
[76] In other words, interim.
[77] See paras 6-21—6-24 and the implications of this in matrimonial finance cases at para.24-25 onwards.
[78] See para.4-22.

proceedings to enforce the terms of a deed of compromise. In general terms,[79] a party who has signed a document essentially or fundamentally different from what was intended by him to be signed will not be bound by its terms. The plea does not, of course, avail a person who seeks merely to allege that he did not read the agreement or did not understand the scope or effect of its terms.[80]

Mistaken record of compromise

4-30 Having reached agreement on all issues, the parties may proceed to incorporate the terms of the agreement in a formal written agreement. Where proceedings are extant they may wish to embody in a consent order or judgment such terms as are capable of embodiment in a court order or judgment. The situation may arise where the written agreement or court order does not properly and accurately reflect the agreement reached.

4-31 So far as a written agreement is concerned, if its inaccuracy has arisen as the result of a mutual mistake of the parties the court may well order its rectification.[81] Equally, if the document is inaccurate because of the mistake of one party which is known to the other who does not draw attention to the mistake, the court will order rectification because it would be inequitable not to do so.[82]

4-32 If a court order or judgment does not properly reflect the parties' agreement the court may have jurisdiction to amend it under the "slip rule"[83] or under its inherent jurisdiction.[84]

4-33 The principles and practice reflected in the foregoing two paragraphs have been applied in the context of an incorrectly drafted Tomlin order:

> In *Islam v Askar*,[85] C and D were partners in a restaurant business. In October 1991 C gave notice of dissolution of the partnership and in November 1991 instituted proceedings for its winding-up. Various negotiations took place resulting in an exchange of faxes between solicitors by virtue of which D agreed to "buy out" C's interest in the partnership for £67,000. That sum was to be payable as to £20,000 immediately and the balance at the rate of £350 per week. It was also agreed that C would accept responsibility for a loan from his bank which had been used in connection with the partnership. D's solicitors suggested that a Tomlin order should be made and sent a draft to C's solicitors. That draft incorrectly provided for a starting figure for payment of the balance of £40,000 rather than

79 *Chitty*, Vol.1, paras 3-004 and 3-049 onwards.

80 *Chitty*, Vol.1, para.13-002. A misrepresentation as to the effect of a compromise may operate to invalidate it, however: see *Hirschfeld v The London, Brighton and South Coast Ry Co* (1876) 2 Q.B.D. 1 discussed at para.4-46.

81 *Chitty*, Vol.1, para.3-057 onwards. See also *Craddock Bros v Hunt* [1923] 2 Ch. 136, *US v Motor Trucks Ltd* [1924] A.C. 196. In *FSHC Group Holdings Ltd v Glas Trust Corporation Ltd* [2019] EWCA Civ 1361, the Court of Appeal clarified the test to be applied in determining whether rectification will be ordered on the grounds of common or mutual mistake. It was not, as Lord Hoffmann had said in *Chartbrook Ltd v Persimmon Homes Ltd* [2009] UKHL 38 a purely objective test, but one involving the issue of whether, when they executed the relevant document, the parties had a common intention in respect of a particular matter which, by mistake, the document did not accurately record. It is necessary to show not only that each party to the contract had the same actual intention, but also that there was an "outward expression of accord". The background is dealt with fully in Ch.24 at paras 24-97 – 24-99.

82 *Thomas Bates Ltd v Wyndham's Ltd* [1981] 1 W.L.R. 505 CA. See also *Riverlate Properties v Paul* [1975] Ch. 133 CA; *Islam v Askar* [1994] 10 WLUK 130; *The Times*, 20 October 1994.

83 CPR r.40.12.

84 *The Bellcairn* (1885) 10 P.D. 161, *Ainsworth v Wilding* [1896] 1 Ch. 673, *South American and Mexican Bank Ex p. Bank of England, Re* [1895] 1 Ch. 37 at 45, *Saunders v Saunders* (1978) 8 Fam. Law 206. See also *Islam v Askar* [1994] 10 WLUK 130; *The Times*, 20 October 1994.

85 *Islam v Askar* [1994] 10 WLUK 130; *The Times*, 20 October 1994. For Tomlin orders, see Chs 9 and 11.

£47,000, monthly payments of the balance and an indemnity by C in relation to creditors other than the bank. The Tomlin order was made incorporating those mistakes in the schedule to the order, C's solicitors having failed to notice them. Shortly afterwards C's solicitors noticed the mistake as to the starting figure for the balance and drew the attention of D's solicitors to the mistake. A fresh Tomlin order was made rectifying this mistake, but the other two went unnoticed at that stage. When C's solicitors were eventually alerted to these other two mistakes, D's solicitors declined to agree to the rectification of the schedule to the Tomlin order, contending that the failure of C's solicitors to note and correct the mistakes earlier resulted in a binding agreement. It was further contended that, if this argument were wrong, but the agreement originally made had been incorrectly reflected in the Tomlin order, a fresh action was necessary to achieve rectification of the order. Finally, it was contended that there was no inherent jurisdiction to correct the schedule to the order as the schedule was not part of the order. The Court of Appeal rejected each of these arguments and held that: (1) where the Tomlin order "mistakenly did not reflect the agreement correctly and the counter-party is aware of that fact, his conscience being affected in equity, and he seeks to take advantage of that mistake", there is an inherent jurisdiction to correct the Tomlin order; (2) whilst the schedule to the order may not be part of the order, it is part of the record of the court and is consequently amenable to the inherent jurisdiction.

In the normal course of events, the court will play no part in the drafting of the terms reflected in a Tomlin order schedule. This will be a matter for the parties. Even if the parties include a provision which, for example, is too vaguely expressed to be capable of enforcement,[86] the court will not ordinarily decline to make the order requested despite the difficulties which may subsequently arise.[87] However, it is not unusual for the court to propose alterations to draft consent orders prepared by the parties. The fact that such alterations are proposed and accepted does not render the order a nullity. The same principle applies when the court makes alterations to the schedule to a Tomlin order in order to give effect to the intention of the parties and to which no objection is subsequently taken. 4-34

In *Allied Irish Bank v Hughes and Fountain*,[88] D1's hotel was charged to C as mortgagees. After the terms of the mortgage had not been complied with C instituted proceedings for possession of the property. Discussions took place between C, D1 and D2's solicitors, D2 being D1's husband. In due course an agreement of compromise was reached which was to be incorporated into a Tomlin order. In order to give effect to the agreement D2 was to become a party to the proceedings brought by C. The agreement contained provisions for the payment of various sums by D1 and D2 upon or by certain dates. One of the provisions was in terms that "[the] Defendants will pay" to C a certain sum by a certain date and a subsequent term was that "[the] Defendants will further pay" to C interest upon that sum between the date of the agreement and the date for payment. When the proposed Tomlin order, in the schedule to which these two terms appeared, was placed before the district judge he added the words "jointly and severally" in relation to the obligations undertaken by D1 and D2 in respect of each of these two terms. He also added the provision into the order that there should be no order as to costs save that D1's costs should be taxed in accordance with the Legal Aid Regulations. TheTomlin order was thus made and entered into the court records. It was sent to the parties, including solicitors acting for D1 and D2. Those solicitors, who had not been in attendance before the district judge, raised no objection to the alterations and proceeded to tax their costs in accordance with the additional part of the order added by the district judge. The Court of Appeal held that what had occurred had not rendered the Tomlin order a nullity and, in any event, the order, 4-35

---

86 *Wilson and Whitworth Ltd v Express and Independent Newspapers Ltd* [1969] 1 W.L.R. 197 noted at para.3-51.

87 *Wilson and Whitworth* [1969] 1 W.L.R. 197.

88 *Allied Irish Bank v Hughes and Fountain* (1994) CAT 1055.

having been referred back to D1 and D2's solicitors who acted upon it and took no point upon it, must in the circumstances be taken to have been accepted by the parties.

4-36 Where, of course, the provisions of a Tomlin order schedule are clear and unambiguous and truly reflect the parties' prior agreement, there are no grounds for altering the terms thus recorded.[89]

MISREPRESENTATION

General

4-37 A false representation of a material fact, made prior to a compromise and which induces it, may, at the instance of the party misled, operate to vitiate the compromise. The misrepresentation may be set up as a defence to a claim for specific performance of the agreement or as the basis of a claim to have it set aside. If any loss has been occasioned by the misrepresentation it may give rise to a claim for damages (for fraudulent or negligent misrepresentation) or an indemnity (in the case of innocent misrepresentation).[90] This latter aspect is unlikely to have much practical significance in the context of compromise. If the agreement has been embodied or reflected in a court order or judgment, the order or judgment may be set aside.[91]

Are compromises contracts uberrimae fidei?

4-38 Before looking at some instances of misrepresentation in this context, the question of whether contracts of compromise are uberrimae fidei must be considered. Ordinarily, the non-disclosure of a material fact will not constitute a misrepresentation[92] unless it makes that which is represented false.[93] But in certain classes of contract—called contracts uberrimae fidei—there must be full disclosure of all material facts. Without such disclosure a contract of this type is voidable. It has been suggested[94] that compromises belong to this class. However, modern textbooks[95] do not put ordinary compromises of disputes into this category. All the cases relied upon as supporting the view that compromises are contracts uberrimae fidei[96] involved compromises of disputed rights under a will or settlement, often where infant beneficiaries were concerned. The Court of Chancery, as a court of equity, insisted on full disclosure in such cases before being prepared to uphold any agreements reached.[97] There is a strong argument that to extend these authorities to sug-

---

89 *Nolan Davis Ltd v Catton* unreported 2001 WL 676767 6 March 2001 TCC.

90 *Chitty*, Vol.1, para.7-046 onwards.

91 See Ch.12.

92 See, e.g. per Lord Atkin in *Bell v Lever Bros Ltd* [1932] A.C. 161 at 227.

93 *Dimmock v Hallett* (1866) L.R. 2 Ch. App. 21.

94 Edwards, *The Law of Compromise and Family Settlements* (1925), pp.141–147, and Kerr, *Fraud and Mistake*, 7th edn (1952), p.96.

95 See, e.g. *Chitty*, Vol.1, para.7-158 onwards.

96 For example *Gibbons v Caunt* (1799) 4 Ves. 849, *Brooke v Mostyn* (1864) 2 De G.J. & S. 373, *Gordon v Gordon* (1816–19) 3 Swans. 400, *Goymour v Pigge* (1844) 13 L.J. Ch. 322.

97 In *Marshall v Marshall* unreported 8 October 1998 CA, Thorpe LJ said this: "When the misfortune of a contested probate action falls on a family, the pressures and stresses are, in many respects, similar to those that afflict a family torn by contested proceedings following the dissolution of a marriage. In my judgment, the negotiation of compromise of such proceedings, whether in the Family Divi-

gest that all compromises belong to this class is inappropriate.[98] However, it is to be noted that in *Bank of Credit and Commercial International SA v Ali*[99] there were suggestions[100] that a general release[101] should only be held to be operative if the party giving the release is unaware of any claim that the party to whom the release is granted may have. As things stand, it cannot be said that these suggestions would translate into a universally applicable proposition of law and the issue may require sustained argument in a case where it arises before a definitive position can be stated.[102]

The view that compromises generally are not contracts uberrimae fidei is supported by *Turner v Green*,[103] where a compromise of an action for an account was held to be specifically enforceable notwithstanding the suppression of a material fact prior to the conclusion of the compromise by the party seeking specific performance. Chitty J, having cited the general proposition that mere silence in relation to a material fact is not a ground for rescission or a defence to specific performance unless there is "an obligation to disclose", said[104] that "[i]t cannot be contended that [there was] ... any obligation to disclose" the material fact in that case. There is a further passage in the judgment[105] from which it is plain that the learned judge did not regard the contract of compromise in that case as requiring uberrima fides. Furthermore, in *Wales v Wadham*,[106] Tudor Evans J had to consider the question of whether at common law a compromise of financial differences between estranged spouses was one requiring uberrima fides. He concluded that it was not. His decision was reinforced by the fact that, in the particular case, the parties had not insisted on full disclosure. Given that whether a contract was to be **4-39**

---

sion or the Chancery Division, must be characterised by candour and not jeopardised by side deals, concealed from one or more of the negotiating parties. In other words, I would hold that there was a duty of full and frank disclosure of facts and circumstances relevant to the weighing of a proposal for the formation of the compromise."

98 See, e.g. the comments of Rimer J in *Clarion Ltd v National Provident Institution* [2000] 1 W.L.R. 1888.

99 *Ali* [2002] 1 A.C. 251.

100 *Ali* [2002] 1 A.C. 251, per Lord Nicholls of Birkenhead at [31]–[32] and Lord Hoffmann at [69]–[70].

101 See para.5-22 onwards.

102 *Ali* [2002] 1 A.C. 251, Lord Bingham of Cornhill (with whom Lord Browne-Wilkinson agreed) at [20] and Lord Clyde at [87] declined to express concluded views on the issue. And see *Chitty*, Vol.1, para.7-183.

103 *Turner v Green* [1895] 2 Ch. 205. See N. Andrews, *Principles of Civil Procedure* (1994), para.13-047. The rationale for this principle was, it is respectfully submitted, put well by Rimer J, as he then was, in *Clarion Ltd v National Provident Institution* [2000] 1 W.L.R. 1888 at 1905: "The compromise of litigation is a contractual exercise in which it is the commonest thing for each side to be aware of facts and matters of which it either knows or at least suspects the other side is ignorant. If each side knew all that the other side knew then either no or only a very different compromise would be reached. In the negotiation of such compromises the parties must be careful not to make any misrepresentations. But there is in my view no general duty imposed upon them in the nature of a duty of disclosure. The negotiations are in the nature of an arm's length commercial bargain. Each party has to look after his own interests and neither owes a duty of care to the other." He also made the following observation: "It would in my view be astonishing if, in the ordinary case, a defendant could later set aside a compromise merely because he had learnt from some 'loose talk at a Bar function' that he had materially overpaid a claimant who, unbeknown to him but well known to the claimant's advisers, probably could not have proved his case at all." See also *Radhakrishnan v University of Calgary Faculty Association*, 2002 ABCA 182 (Court of Appeal of Alberta).

104 *Turner* [1895] 2 Ch. 205 at 208. And see also *Silver Queen Maritime Ltd v Persia Petroleum Services Plc* [2010] EWHC 2867 (QB) at [130]–[140], per Lindblom J.

105 *Turner* [1895] 2 Ch. 205 at 209.

106 *Wales v Wadham* [1977] 1 W.L.R. 199, not criticised on this point by the House of Lords in *Livesey* [1985] A.C. 424, but distinguished in a somewhat different context in *Inclusive Technology v Williamson* [2009] EWCA Civ 718; [2010] 1 P. & C.R. 2.

regarded as requiring uberrima fides "must depend upon its substantial character and how it came to be effected",[107] the learned judge concluded that this one was not.[108]

4-40 A suppression of a fact or document which, if its existence were revealed, would destroy totally (rather than, perhaps, merely undermine to some extent) a claim being advanced by a claimant would involve the claimant in pursuing a claim which he knew to be unfounded. A compromise of such a claim could be invalidated.[109]

4-41 It would appear, therefore, that generally each case would have to be looked at on its own facts to see whether full disclosure was being insisted upon by the parties. In the general run of litigation this is unlikely to be so and indeed negotiations might be hindered by such insistence. Two areas where full disclosure would seem to be required as a matter of law are:

(a) the compromise of a partnership dispute[110]; and
(b) a compromise involving the actual or potential transfer of title to land.[111]

Some examples

4-42 It has already been noted[112] that the assertion of a claim known by the claimant to be baseless, which induces a compromise, will be regarded in law as a fraudulent misrepresentation. Opinions may, of course, differ as to the validity of assertions made. Generally, a statement of unfounded opinion which induces a contract will not be an operative misrepresentation.[113] If, however, a person represents that he holds an opinion when in fact he does not, that will constitute a false representation.[114] The dividing line between statements of opinion and fact may be difficult to determine, particularly where the representor is in a better position than the representee to assess the accuracy and validity of the statement.[115]

---

107 *Seaton v Heath* [1899] 1 Q.B. 782 at 792, per Romer LJ. See *Palmer v University of Surrey* unreported CC; 2014 WL 1097173, where the issue turned on whether a compromise agreement reached in respect of a personal injury claim could be characterised as a contract of insurance. Recorder James Watson QC, sitting as a judge of the County Court, held that it did not. It did not because it did not, applying the dicta of Sir Robert Megarry VC in *The Medical Defence Union Ltd v Department of Trade* [1980] 1 Ch. 80 at 90, have the "hallmarks"' of an insurance contract.

108 In *Livesey* [1985] A.C. 424, a statutory duty of disclosure was said to arise from the provisions of the Matrimonial Causes Act 1973 s.25. To the extent to which *Wales v Wadham* [1977] 1 W.L.R. 199 was contrary to this view it was disapproved by the House of Lords, but no doubt was cast upon the general proposition referred to in the text.

109 See para.2-19. There is continuing obligation on parties during litigation to disclose documents that come to their notice: CPR r.31.11. A failure to disclose a material document discovered after the original list of documents is served, or which comes into existence thereafter, could afford grounds for alleging a misrepresentation: see Andrews, *Principles of Civil Procedure*, 1994, para.13–049. Andrews' account arises from a discussion of the position under the RSC. Its rationale is however equally applicable under the CPR.

110 *Chitty*, Vol.1, para.7-181.

111 *Chitty*, Vol.1, para.7-175. See Ch.30.

112 See para.2-19.

113 *Anderson v Pacific Fire and Marine Insurance Co* (1872) L.R. 7 C.P. 65. "When an opinion is expressed the person who expresses it either does or does not know facts which justify that opinion. The existence of those facts, and his state of knowledge in relation to them, are themselves facts capable of being misrepresented by implication by the expression of opinion ... Sometimes an expression of opinion may carry with it no implication other than that the opinion is genuinely held. But on other occasions, as in this case, the circumstances may be such as to give rise to the implied representation that the person knew of facts which justified his opinion": *BG Plc v Nelson Group Services (Maintenance) Ltd* [2002] EWCA Civ 547, per Kennedy LJ.

114 *Chitty*, Vol.1, paras 6-008—6-009.

115 cf. *Brown v Raphael* [1958] Ch. 636, *Esso Petroleum Co Ltd v Mardon* [1976] Q.B. 801, *Chitty*,

Where, during the course of negotiations, a representation is made which at the time is true but which subsequently becomes false, a failure to disclose the changed position would be, in effect, a misrepresentation.[116] 4-43

In *Gilbert v Endean*,[117] a claimant had, in effect, obtained a judgment against a debtor in a certain sum. Thereafter he agreed to accept a lesser sum on the basis of the debtor's represented poor financial position. It was known by all parties that the debtor's father was a wealthy man but that he had refused to help his son. Before the compromise agreement was signed the father died. The debtor's solicitor knew this at the time of the signing but failed to disclose it to the claimant's solicitor. The Court of Appeal held that the failure to disclose what was clearly a material fact given the earlier position was, in effect, a misrepresentation.

A statement of intention as to future conduct is not a representation of fact unless the intention of the person making the statement is, at the time of making it, the opposite of what is stated. Thus a party to negotiations with a view to compromise who states his existing intention accurately and honestly but who thereafter, but before the agreement is concluded, changes his mind is not under a duty to disclose it to the other party.[118] A representation by a party that he possesses a settled intention to pursue (or not to pursue) a particular course of conduct when no such settled intention exists can amount to a misrepresentation.[119] 4-44

The legal effect of a misrepresentation of law has hitherto been somewhat uncertain. As in the case of a mistake of law,[120] the dividing line between a misrepresentation of law and one of fact or opinion is often difficult to identify.[121] However, if a statement can fairly be characterised as one of law, such a statement, if incorrect or misleading, has usually been regarded as incapable of amounting to an actionable misrepresentation.[122] However, developments in the law of restitution[123] suggest that the distinction between a mistake of fact and one of law is not sustainable. It would seem to follow that such a distinction could not now also be made in the context of misrepresentation.[124] If that is a correct analysis of the recent authorities, a misrepresentation of law must now be regarded as capable of being relied upon to set aside an agreement concluded in reliance upon it. Since representations of law are frequently made in precontractual negotiations with a view to compromise, it is likely that the court will approach with considerable caution any proposition that an incorrect assertion of law constitutes an actionable misrepresentation in this context.[125] 4-45

Where, however, a misrepresentation is made as to the legal effect of a compromise, particularly where the representee is not independently legally advised, there are circumstances in which the court will intervene: 4-46

Vol.1, paras 7-007 to 7-010.

116 It might also be considered to give rise to a unilateral mistake of fact on the part of the party misled known to, or contributed to, by the other party: para.4-25 onwards.

117 *Gilbert v Endean* (1878) 9 Ch. D. 259. See also *With v O'Flanagan* [1936] Ch. 575 CA; *Davies v London and Provincial Marine Insurance Co* (1878) 9 Ch. D. 469, *Dietz v Lennig Chemicals Ltd* [1969] 1 A.C. 170, considered at para.4-48.

118 *Wadham* [1977] 1 W.L.R. 199 at 211.

119 cf. *Livesey* [1985] A.C. 424.

120 See para.4-20.

121 *Chitty*, Vol.1, para.7-017.

122 *Beesly v Hallwood Estates Ltd* [1960] 1 W.L.R. 549.

123 *Kleinwort Benson Ltd v Lincoln City Council* [1999] 1 A.C. 153 HL, *Pankhania v Hackney London Borough Council* [2002] EWHC 2441 (Ch).

124 *Chitty*, Vol.1, para.7-017.

125 cf. para.19-50.

In *Hirschfeld v The London, Brighton and South Coast Ry Co*,[126] C was injured when travelling as a passenger in one of D's trains. Not long after the accident a representative of D called on C to see if C intended to make a claim. C said that he did and after discussion he agreed to accept a certain sum from D in full satisfaction of his claims. He signed a deed of release. Thereafter C sought to pursue a claim for a greater sum, alleging that D's representative had told him that if his injuries proved to be more serious than anticipated he could, notwithstanding the terms of the release, seek and obtain greater compensation. It was held[127] that C was entitled to rely upon the misrepresentation to avoid the terms of the release.

4-47 In *Saunders v Ford Motor Co Ltd*[128] C suffered an injury in the course of his employment by D. D's insurers had an office at D's works. A representative of those insurers had a conversation with C during which C agreed to accept £200 in full settlement of all his claims. The insurers' representative told C that the sum was "only for pain and suffering and for [his] absence from work" and, in effect, that if C's condition got worse the position could be reviewed. Paull J held that C was not bound by the agreement because either there was attached to the agreement an understanding that he could come back if his condition deteriorated or because the parties were not *ad idem*.[129]

A misrepresentation may arise in a variety of ways:

4-48 In *Dietz v Lennig Chemicals Ltd*[130] a claim by a widow, on behalf of herself and her child, under the Fatal Accidents Act, arising from the death of her husband, was compromised and, in due course, put before the court for approval. At the time the agreement was concluded she had not remarried, but by the time it was put before the court she had. She had not told her solicitors, who at all times up to and including the court hearing believed that she was unmarried. Indeed, the title of the court papers remained in her old surname. The House of Lords held that the failure to disclose the changed situation (albeit completely innocent) and the use of the old surname in the court proceedings constituted a misrepresentation.

4-49 In *Roberts, Re*,[131] a solicitor misread or misunderstood counsel's opinion on a particular matter and thereby misrepresented its effect to one of a number of legatees he was advising. On the faith of what was represented a particular legatee entered into a compromise of her claims against the estate with other legatees. The Court of Appeal held that it should be set aside.

4-50 Needless to say, once a representation had been made it will be operative only if:

(a) it has been addressed to the party misled; and
(b) it induced the compromise.

These will be matters of fact to be determined.[132]

---

126 *Hirschfield v The London, Brighton and South Coast Ry Co* (1876) 2 Q.B.D. 1. See also *West London Commercial Bank v Kitson* (1884) 13 Q.B.D. 360 at 362–363.

127 Mellor and Lush JJ.

128 *Saunders v Ford Motor Co Ltd* [1970] 1 Lloyd's Rep. 379.

129 In *Arrale v Costain Civil Engineering Ltd* [1976] 1 Lloyd's Rep. 98 at 104–105, Stephenson LJ said that he regarded the decision in *Saunders* [1970] 1 Lloyd's Rep. 379 "as based on a misrepresentation inducing the signing of the receipt ... and I would respectfully agree with it". This is indeed arguably the better view of what fell for determination in the *Saunders* case.

130 *Dietz* [1969] 1 A.C. 170. See also para.27-15.

131 *Roberts, Re* [1905] 1 Ch. 704.

132 See, e.g. the analysis of the evidence covering these two matters in *Wales v Wadham* [1977] 1 W.L.R. 199 at 212-214.

Relief available

The principal equitable relief available in respect of any form of misrepresentation (whether fraudulent, negligent or innocent) is that of rescission. Provided the party misled has not affirmed the compromise or been guilty of undue delay, or third-party rights have not intervened, or a substantial restoration of the status quo has not become impossible, the court will be prepared to set it aside together with any consent order or judgment based upon it.[133] Since for most practical purposes in the context of compromise that remedy (with appropriate consequential directions) is the one which will be sought, it is not proposed to examine the circumstances in which damages may fall to be awarded for a misrepresentation.[134] **4-51**

DURESS AND UNDUE INFLUENCE

General

Certain forms of duress upon a contracting party have always operated to vitiate the agreement at common law.[135] Other forms of undue influence and pressure may operate to do so in equity. The precise extent of the circumstances in which undue influence and pressure operate are difficult to define.[136] Indeed, any attempt to do so has been firmly rejected by the House of Lords.[137] Each case depends upon its own particular facts. Whether the matter be approached on the basis of evidence of a particular factual situation or a presumption of undue influence in certain circumstances, the court will intervene only if an unfair advantage has been taken of one party by the other (in the sense of domination or victimisation) leading to a manifestly disadvantageous transaction. The concept of "inequality of bargaining power"[138] was also firmly rejected. **4-52**

All earlier cases raising the issue of undue influence must be considered to be subject to this restatement of the law. As with the concept of "economic duress",[139] with which undue influence to some extent overlaps, it may have a significance in the context of compromise.[140] **4-53**

Examples in the context of compromise

Threat of proceedings

Where a debt has arisen in circumstances which might render the debtor liable to criminal proceedings (for example, where a company employee or director has misappropriated company funds for his own use), a threat of prosecution will not **4-54**

---

[133] *Chitty*, Vol.1, para.7-103 onwards. Also *Huddersfield Banking Co v Henry Lister* [1895] 2 Ch. 273, referred to at para.4-17.

[134] *Chitty*, Vol.1, para.7-046 onwards.

[135] For example actual or threatened violence to the person or a near relative.

[136] *Chitty*, Vol.1, Ch.8.

[137] *National Westminster Bank Plc v Morgan* [1985] 1 A.C. 686.

[138] *Lloyds Bank Ltd v Bundy* [1975] Q.B. 326 at 339, per Lord Denning MR.

[139] See para.4-62 onwards.

[140] cf. *Backhouse v Backhouse* [1978] 1 W.L.R. 243 at 252 (Balcombe J). See also *Horry v Tate & Lyle Refineries Ltd* [1982] 2 Lloyd's Rep. 416.

necessarily invalidate a compromise of the claim.[141] It will depend on the circumstances in which the threat is made.[142]

4-55 A threat of civil proceedings will not, of course, ordinarily operate to invalidate a compromise of the claim[143] although in rare circumstances the threat may be uttered in a way that constitutes duress.[144] A compromise of an unfounded claim known to be so by the claimant will be ineffective[145] and consequently a threat to pursue such a claim which results in a compromise will invalidate the agreement.

4-56 In *Brent v Brent*,[146] C was the son of TB who died without making provision for his widow and family. On TB's death C became absolutely entitled to premises comprised in a settlement made by one of TB's forbears. He remained in possession of those premises for some 21 years until he entered into a contract to sell them. For some 14 years following his father's death C provided his mother, HB, with an annual allowance and, after this was discontinued, with certain other things and small sums of money. Some years after the allowance as such was discontinued, a conveyancer called Snell, acting on behalf of HB, caused a distress to be put upon the premises alleging arrears of the allowance. C, who was alarmed at this and at Snell's threats to sell his stock, signed an agreement prepared by Snell to pay the sum claimed together with the costs of the distress. Shortly thereafter Snell represented to C that HB and others had a claim to part of the property and that they were about to take proceedings. The claims advanced were unfounded and Snell knew this. As a result of Snell's representation C entered into a further agreement whereby the property was to be sold and the various "claimants", together with Snell, were to receive shares in the proceeds of sale. The Lord Chancellor held that the agreement could not be supported and should be set aside as a result of Snell's "threats and intimidation" on HB's behalf.

Threat of unlawful act

4-57 A compromise induced by a threat to do or abstain from doing something which it is unlawful to do or abstain from doing, when the party agreeing has no option but to agree, will be set aside:

4-58 In *Ormes v Beadel*,[147] a building contractor in the course of erection of a building asked the architect for money, to which he was lawfully entitled, to pay his workmen. The money was urgently required. The architect threatened not to pay him unless he gave up the contract on distinctly disadvantageous terms. The agreement was set aside.

4-59 In *D&C Builders Ltd v Rees*,[148] C was a small firm of builders which had done some work for D. It was lawfully entitled to £482 for the work it had done. After several months of

---

141 *Flower v Sadler* (1882) 10 Q.B.D. 572, distinguishing *Williams v Bayley* (1866) L.R. 1 H.L. 200 and following *Ward v Lloyd* (1843) 7 Scott. N R. 499. An agreement not to prosecute may be illegal: see para.4-77.

142 *Chitty*, Vol.1, para.8-049 onwards.

143 cf. *Chitty*, Vol.1, para.8-051. See *Lau Siu Keung Vincent v John Ming Shun Vincent* [2015] HKDC 1002.

144 *Daniel v Drew* [2005] EWCA Civ 507; [2005] 2 F.C.R. 365.

145 See para.2-19. "It is one thing for a person to threaten a claim or defence in which that person has no confidence at all. It is a quite different thing for a person to intimate a claim or defence which, whilst the person recognises that it raises a doubtful or undecided point, he or she also believes in and intends to pursue it in court if necessary": *Simantob v Shavleyan* [2019] EWCA Civ 1105 at [49].

146 *Brent v Brent* (1841) 10 L.J. Ch. 84.

147 *Ormes v Beadel* (1860) 2 Giff. 166, reversed on appeal on the basis, in effect, that the contractor had affirmed the agreement: 2 De G.F. & J. 333.

148 *D&C Builders Ltd v Rees* [1966] 2 Q.B. 617. This case could be seen as one involving "economic duress": see para.4–66. See also *Occidental Worldwide Investment Corp v Skibs A/S Avanti (The Siboen and The Sibotre)* [1976] 1 Lloyd's Rep. 293 at 335.See also *Carillion Construction Ltd v Felix (UK) Ltd*, noted at para. 31-80.

delay, and at a time when C was in a parlous financial state, D told C that it could have £300 or it would get nothing. It accepted the sum in full settlement. The Court of Appeal held that C was not estopped from suing for the balance. D had unfairly taken advantage of C's position.

A threat that goods unlawfully detained will not be released unless some payment is made will invalidate the contract.[149] If, however, there is a genuine dispute between the parties as to whether the detention is unlawful, a valid compromise involving the release of the goods and payment may be made.[150] **4-60**

Threat of otherwise lawful act

This is a difficult concept but nonetheless one that cannot be ignored in this context. Prima facie it is difficult to see why a person may not threaten to do something which is lawful in order to induce another person to come to an agreement with him. A threat of civil proceedings is plainly lawful and a compromise of those threatened proceedings will not be set aside save in the rare circumstances where the manner of the threat constitutes duress.[151] Equally there may be rare situations in which the threat of an otherwise lawful act goes far beyond what is either normal or reasonable behaviour or, in the particular context in question, what is reasonable in relation to the dispute the parties are endeavouring to settle.[152] It appears[153] that the US courts are more willing to employ this concept than their English counterparts. Chitty records a case in which a settlement of an injured employee's claim for damages at a manifestly low figure, procured by an otherwise lawful threat to dismiss him, was set aside on this ground.[154] **4-61**

Economic duress

The pressure applied in each of the cases referred to in paras 4-58 and 4-59 was of an economic nature. It is now clearly established that, **4-62**

---

149 *Somes v British Empire Shipping Co* (1860) 8 H.L.C. 338, *Green v Duckett* (1883) 11 QBD 275.

150 *Atlee v Backhouse* (1838) 3 M. & W. 633.

151 See para.4-55; *Chitty*, Vol.1, para.8-051; *Drew v Daniel* [2005] EWCA Civ 507; [2005] 2 F.C.R. 365 at [40] and *Lau Siu Keung Vincent v John Ming Shun Vincent* [2015] HKDC 1002.

152 In *CTN Cash and Carry Ltd v Gallagher Ltd* [1994] 4 All E.R. 713, Steyn LJ, as he then was, said that: "Outside the field of protected relationships, and in a purely commercial context, it might be a relatively rare case in which 'lawful act duress' can be established. And it might be particularly difficult to establish duress if the defendant bona fide considered that this demand was valid. In this complex and changing branch of the law I deliberately refrain from saying 'never'." In *Huyton SA v Peter Cremer GmbH & Co* [1999] 1 Lloyd's Rep. 620, a case involving the suggestion that a compromise was voidable on the grounds of economic duress, Mance J, as he then was, said at 637, having quoted Steyn LJ's words, that the proposition that: "[G]ood or bad faith may be particularly relevant when considering whether a case might represent a rare example of 'lawful act duress' is not difficult to accept. Even in cases where the pressure relied on is an actual or threatened breach of duty, it seems to me better not to exclude the possibility that the state of mind of the person applying such pressure may in some circumstances be significant, whether or not the other innocent party correctly appreciated such state of mind. 'Never' in this context also seems too strong a word." A little earlier in his judgment the learned judge had said this: "The law will of course be cautious about re-opening an apparent compromise made in good faith on both sides. But it seems, on the one hand, questionable whether a 'compromise' achieved by one party who does not believe that he had at least an arguable case is a compromise at all—though it may be upheld if there is other consideration ... and, on the other hand, difficult to accept that illegitimate pressure applied by a party who believes bona fide in his case could never give grounds for relief against an apparent compromise."

153 See *Chitty*, Vol.1, para.8-046.

154 *Mitchell v CC Sanitation Co* (1968) 430 S.W. (2d) 933.

"economic pressure may be sufficient to amount to duress for this purpose, provided at least that the economic pressure may be characterised as illegitimate and has constituted a significant cause inducing the [claimant] to enter into the relevant contract".[155]

The suggestion that the coercion must have been such as to vitiate his consent[156] has been criticised and its utility in this context questioned.[157] However, whatever the precise parameters of the concept of economic duress may be, it could clearly have considerable significance in the context of compromise.

4-63 The dividing line between the type of economic pressure that is illegitimate and that which is legitimate may not always be easy to identify. Many pressures will be brought to bear in negotiations within a commercial context (including, of course, negotiations with a view to compromising a dispute, actual or potential) which will be regarded as both commonplace and acceptable.[158] Each case will depend upon its own facts, but the essential question will be whether the actual economic pressure exerted in the particular circumstances left the party upon whom it was imposed with no real choice (or no reasonable alternative) but to enter into the compromise.[159] Examples can be found on each side of the dividing line:

4-64 In *Dorimix Srl v Visage Imports Ltd*,[160] C was an Italian company trading as a supplier of ladies' and men's clothing. D, a UK-based company, was an importer and wholesaler of such clothing. D placed orders with C for the delivery of goods over the period July to September 1989 so that the clothing could be in the retail market for the autumn/winter season. Delays in delivery occurred and the parties were in dispute about responsibility for these delays. On 1 November, a compromise was reached and recorded in the following terms:

"1. *Re Ladies Shipments* It was agreed today that all goods received into [D's] warehouse by Tuesday 7th November 1989 will be accepted at ordered price. Any goods received between Tuesday 7th November and Tuesday 21st November 1989 are subject to 25% discount. Any goods shipped after Friday 17th November 1989 are to be shipped free of charge.

2. *Re Mens Shipments*
   a. [not relevant].
   b. Re all other mens outstanding purchase orders. If these goods are shipped before Friday 3rd November 1989 they are subject to 25% discount. If these goods are shipped after Friday 3rd November 1989 they are subject to 30% discount up until Friday 17th November 1989, after Friday 17th November any outstanding menswear orders will be shipped free of charge."

Because C had been concerned that D would not accept late delivery of the goods ordered earlier in the year, it had been looking for other outlets in the United Kingdom. C learned that garments such as those it was expecting to be delivered were on sale elsewhere at prices considerably lower than those at which C was proposing to sell them. D told C that it had been placed in an impossible situation as a result, but exaggerated the effect which this situation would have upon it to place pressure on C to agree, under threat of refusal by D to accept further deliveries or to pay the full price for those goods already shipped, to allow D a further discount. C agreed to a further significant discount on 8

---

[155] *Dimskal Shipping Co SA v ITWF ("The Evia Luck")* [1992] A.C. 152 at 165, per Lord Goff of Chieveley.

[156] Beatson, *The Use and Abuse of Unjust Enrichment* (1991), pp.113–117; Birks (1990) 3 L.M.C.L.Q. 342.

[157] See fn.155.

[158] *Chitty*, Vol.1, paras 8-008 and 8-024.

[159] *Chitty*, Vol.1, para.8-032 onwards.

[160] *Dorimix Srl v Visage Imports Ltd* unreported 18 May 1999 CA.

November. HH Judge Diamond QC found that D's threat constituted "substantial and heavy economic pressure" on C which amounted to "illegitimate economic pressure". It constituted a threat not to perform the agreement of 1 November and amounted to a repudiation of that contract. It left C with only two practical alternatives: either to submit to D's demand or to accept the repudiation and sue for damages, the latter course being "financially unattractive and potentially disastrous". Although C lost the case on another issue and took that issue to the Court of Appeal, D did not appeal against the foregoing conclusion.

In *Hennessey v Craigmyle & Co Ltd*,[161] A was told by R that he would be summarily dismissed as from a week later, that his pay would stop, he would lose the use of his car and he would get no reference. The option was to be treated as having been made redundant with certain associated financial benefits. That option would only be available if he signed an agreement prepared by a conciliation officer of ACAS under s.134 of the Employment Protection (Consolidation) Act 1978, giving up his right to take proceedings before an industrial tribunal. He took legal advice, signed the agreement and was subsequently dismissed on the grounds of redundancy. Subsequently, A sought to argue, inter alia, that the agreement was voidable at common law on the grounds of "economic duress". The Court of Appeal held that the industrial tribunal had been entitled to reject this argument because A's will was not overborne: he had an alternative, albeit an unattractive one, of complaining to the industrial tribunal and drawing social security in the meantime. **4-65**

A compromise entered into as a result of the undue influence of one party over the other may be set aside at the instance of the party subjected to the undue influence.[162] The utility of making the classification frequently made[163] between situations in which actual undue influence operates and where (subject to disproof) it is presumed to have operated because of the relationship of the parties, has been questioned and labelled as "confusing" by the House of Lords.[164] The issue is essentially one of fact depending on, **4-66**

> "the nature of the alleged undue influence, the personality of the parties, their relationship, the extent to which the transaction cannot readily be accounted for by the ordinary motives of ordinary persons, and all the circumstances of the case",

presumptions in certain circumstances merely constituting tools in resolving the issue.[165] Recourse to the question whether a transaction is to the "manifest disadvantage" of the person influenced[166] has also been said not to be helpful.[167] Where undue influence is established the transaction may be set aside unless the person influenced loses the right to rescind.[168]

When the issue of undue influence arises the availability of independent legal advice to the party subjected to the influence has always been regarded as a material, though not always conclusive, factor in determining whether the influence oper- **4-67**

---

[161] *Hennessey v Craigmyle & Co Ltd* [1986] I.C.R. 461. It is questionable whether the decision in this case would be the same now following *Dimskal* see fn.155. A case in which alleged "economic duress" in the context of a compromise was not upheld is *Hutchinson v Tamosious* unreported 24 May 1999: see para.3-51 fn.110.

[162] *Chitty*, Vol.1, para.8-058 onwards.

[163] *Barclays Bank Plc v O'Brien* [1994] 1 A.C. 180 at 189-190, per Lord Browne-Wilkinson.

[164] *Royal Bank of Scotland v Etridge* [2001] UKHL 44; [2002] 2 A.C. 773.

[165] *Royal Bank of Scotland* per Lord Nicholls of Birkenhead at [13], per Lord Clyde at [92], per Lord Hobhouse of Woodborough at [98] and per Lord Scott of Foscote at [107].

[166] *National Westminster Bank Plc* [1985] 1 A.C. 686 at 704, per Lord Scarman.

[167] *Royal Bank of Scotland* [2001], per Lord Nicholls of Birkenhead at [26] UKHL 44; [2002] 2 A.C. 773.

[168] *CIBC Mortgages Plc v Pitt* [1994] 1 A.C. 200. See para.4-70.

ated as a matter of fact.[169] Detailed guidance on the duties of solicitors in the context of husband and wife cases has now been given.[170] It will be a question of fact in every case whether, when advice has been taken, it has had an "emancipating effect" in relation to the undue influence exercised.[171]

4-68 Undue influence is perhaps, most likely to arise where members of a family are in dispute; but it could as easily arise where a bank and its customer compromise certain differences.[172] It has been held to operate in a case where an unrepresented employee compromised his personal injuries claim with his employers' insurance company.[173]

Husband and wife

4-69 Not infrequently allegations are made that arrangements apparently made between parties to a matrimonial dispute were made as the result of the undue influence or pressure exerted by one party over the other. It is well-established that, as a matter of law, there is no presumption of undue influence between husband and wife.[174] However, in many cases a wife may well be able to demonstrate that she reposed trust and confidence in her husband in relation to their financial affairs such that undue influence is to be presumed.[175] Nonetheless, married (or other close personal) relationships may differ in respect of the responsibilities in these matters and each case will be looked at on its own facts.[176]

Effect

4-70 Where a compromise has been entered into as the result of duress or undue influence it becomes voidable at the option of the party so subjected. Early steps to disavow the apparent agreement must be taken otherwise it may be held to have been ratified or affirmed.[177]

---

169 *Powell v Powell* [1900] 1 Ch. 243, but now to read subject to *Royal Bank of Scotland* [2001] UKHL 44; [2002] 2 A.C. 773.

170 *Royal Bank of Scotland* [2001] UKHL 44; [2002] 2 A.C. 773.

171 *Royal Bank of Scotland* [2001] UKHL 44; [2002] 2 A.C. 773, per Lord Nicholls of Birkenhead at [20]. See also *Boustany v Piggott* (1995) 69 P. & C.R. 298 PC. Merely having the opportunity to take advice may not suffice: *Claughton v Price* (1998) 30 H.L.R. 396. In that case Nourse LJ said: "[T]aking independent legal advice is neither always necessary nor always sufficient to rebut the presumption of undue influence. In many cases, I would say in most cases, it will be sufficient. But here it is clear that it was not, for the simple reason that [the influencer] could not reasonably have believed that a solicitor acting for [the influenced] would have advised him to go ahead without a crucial form of protection which had been offered originally and which there was every reason to believe would be given if requested." See also *Credit Lyonnais Bank Nederland NV v Burch* [1997] 1 All E.R. 144.

172 cf. *National Westminster Bank Plc* [1985] 1 A.C. 686.

173 *Horry* [1982] 2 Lloyd's Rep. 416 (Peter Pain J): a settlement was set aside where an employee accepted a low offer of compensation (a) without independent legal advice and (b) in ignorance of the contents of the insurers' medical report on him which was not shown to him.

174 *Royal Bank of Scotland* [2001] UKHL 44; [2002] 2 A.C. 773, per Lord Nicholls of Birkenhead at [19].

175 *Barclays Bank Plc* [1994] 1 A.C. 180.

176 *Royal Bank of Scotland* [2001] UKHL 44; [2002] 2 A.C. 773. And see Ch.24.

177 *Ormes v Beadel* (on appeal) (1860) 2 De G.F. & J. 333, *Occidental Worldwide Investment Corp v Skibs A/S Avanti* [1976] 1 Lloyd's Rep. 293, *North Ocean Shipping Co Ltd v Hyundai Construction Co Ltd* [1979] Q.B. 705. See *Chitty*, Vol.1, para.7-054.

ILLEGALITY

General

A court will not enforce a contract which, or the purpose of which, is illegal either under statute or under the general law.[178] Parties who are genuinely agreed on a compromise of their differences need to have an eye for any possible illegality if they wish it to be capable of enforcement.[179] The jurisdiction of the court to sever an illegal part of an agreement leaving the rest intact and capable of enforcement is somewhat limited.[180] **4-71**

Compromise of disputes involving issues of illegality

There is a distinction between a compromise which is itself illegal and a compromise of a dispute which gives rise to questions of illegality. The former, of course, falls within the general principle stated above. The latter will ordinarily be upheld. **4-72**

In *Binder v Alachouzos*,[181] the facts of which have previously been given,[182] the Court of Appeal rejected D's argument that the compromise itself was illegal, tainted, he suggested, by the illegality that he alleged had affected the original financial transactions involving C.

Furthermore, at least for practical purposes, a distinction should be drawn between a compromise which is itself illegal and the compromise of a dispute on a contract which is indisputably illegal. The distinction may be more readily understood by reference to examples: **4-73**

(a) A and B have a dispute about the position of their boundary. A agrees not to commence proceedings for trespass against B in return for the latter's promise to destroy by fire a shed belonging to C, another neighbour. This is an illegal compromise of a legitimate dispute.
(b) A and B agree that A shall transport B's goods for reward in a vehicle that both parties know is not permitted by law to carry the weight of the goods in question. During the journey the vehicle topples over and the load is damaged.[183] A agrees to pay B £100,000 in return for agreeing not to sue for damage to B's goods. The original contract (or its performance)[184] was illegal, but the compromise is of itself prima facie legitimate.

Having made the distinction from the practical point of view, it should be noted that the legal effect is the same in each case: the compromise is illegal and would be unenforceable.[185] In the first, the purpose of the contract of compromise is illegal. **4-74**

---

[178] *Chitty*, Vol.1, Ch.16.
[179] *Tinsley v Milligan* [1994] 1 A.C. 340 at 362 HL.
[180] *Chitty*, Vol.1, para.16-236 onwards. See *Carney v Herbert* [1985] A.C. 301 PC.
[181] *Binder v Alachouzos* [1972] 2 Q.B. 151. See also *FPH Law v Brown (t/a Integrum Law)* [2016] EWHC 1681 (QB); [2016] 5 Costs L.O. 733, a case involving a bona fide compromise of an issue concerning the enforceability of a conditional fee agreement.
[182] See para.2-17.
[183] See *Ashmore, Benson, Pease & Co Ltd v AV Dawson Ltd* [1973] 1 W.L.R. 828 CA.
[184] *Ashmore* [1973] 1 W.L.R. 828 CA.
[185] *Chitty*, Vol.1, para.16-015.

In the second, the consideration for the compromise (the forbearance to sue on an illegal contract) is illegal.[186]

Illegal compromises

Ousting jurisdiction

4-75 An agreement which purports to remove any recourse to the courts in the event of a dispute is void.[187] However, appropriately drafted arbitration clauses[188] or dispute-resolution clauses[189] may result in the determination of disputes by persons other than judicial *personae*. Not infrequently, terms of compromise provide for the settlement of disputes arising therefrom by an arbitrator, for example in cases where one party is obliged to carry out work under the terms of the agreement.

Matrimonial financial provision

4-76 Parties to a matrimonial dispute may not "contract out" of the right to apply to the court for financial relief.[190]

Stifling a prosecution

4-77 A dispute may give rise to both civil and criminal law consequences. A purported compromise of the civil aspects of a dispute will be void if it contains an express or implied term to the effect that no prosecution will be launched or that the ap-

---

186 *Poteliakhoff v Teakle* [1938] 2 K.B. 816, *Hill v William Hill (Park Lane) Ltd* [1949] A.C. 530. See Ch.3.

187 *Lee v Showmen's Guild of Great Britain* [1952] 2 Q.B. 249; *Chitty*, Vol.1, paras 16-073 onwards. Any attempt by a "public authority" to impose on an individual party to a compromise of a dispute an obligation not to pursue the authority to court for a remedy for breach would almost certainly constitute a violation of art.6(1) of the European Convention on Human Rights and Fundamental Freedoms. Following the introduction of the CPR, the jurisdictions of the High Court and county court became a great deal closer in many areas. It is thought that it would not be contrary to public policy, and thus not a void provision, for parties to a dispute effectively to prevent the court from awarding the proper measure of damages, or the full extent of any relief, by agreeing to transfer the dispute from the High Court to the county court on the express condition that the claimant limits his claim for relief to that available in the county court: cf. *Basaran v Nevar Investments Ltd* (1979) CAT 181. Indeed, parties not infrequently agree that a dispute should be dealt with on the small claims track (or indeed the fast track) even though the damages might otherwise exceed the relevant limit in order to avoid the costs consequences of the track appropriate to the true value of the claim.

188 Now governed by the Arbitration Act 1996. See *Chitty*, Vol.1, Ch.17, esp. para.17-074. And see Ch.32.

189 *Channel Tunnel Group Ltd v Balfour Beatty Construction Ltd* [1993] A.C. 334, where it was held that the court has an inherent jurisdiction to inhibit proceedings brought in breach of an agreed method of resolving disputes. Parties to commercial agreements frequently provide for the determination by experts of issues that may arise during the currency of the contract: e.g. *Jones v Sherwood Computer Services Plc* [1992] 1 W.L.R. 277, *Nikko Hotels UK v MEPC Plc* (1991) 28 E.G. 86, *Amoco (UK) Exploration Co v Amerada Hess Ltd* [1994] 1 Lloyd's Rep. 330. The terms of the agreement may result in an expert having to answer mixed questions of fact and law: *Norwich Union Life Insurance Society v P&O Property Holdings* (1993) 13 E.G. 108 CA, *Amoco (UK) Exploration Co v Amerada Hess Ltd* above, cf. *Neste Production Ltd v Shell UK Ltd* [1994] 1 Lloyd's Rep. 447. A clause which seems to exclude completely the jurisdiction of the court from, e.g. reviewing the decision of the expert where there had been fraud or bias would be invalid: *Chitty*, Vol.1, para.16–075. See generally Kendall (1993) 109 L.Q.R. 385. See also *Cott UK Ltd v F.E. Barber Ltd* [1997] 3 All E.R. 540 and *Halifax Financial Services Ltd v Intuitive Systems Ltd* [1999] 1 All E.R. (Comm) 303.

190 See Ch.24.

propriate authorities will not be notified.[191] Indeed, it would appear that both parties to such an agreement could be guilty of conspiring to pervert the course of justice.[192] In a compromise of a dispute giving rise potentially to criminal proceedings in addition to the civil claims, great care should be taken to ensure that any agreement reached is clearly understood and expressed to be in respect solely of the civil claims.

Bankruptcy

A compromise tending to obstruct the course of bankruptcy proceedings is illegal and unenforceable: **4-78**

In *Kearley v Thomson*,[193] an agreement between a friend of the bankrupt and the petitioning creditor's solicitors that he should pay them their costs in return for their not opposing the bankrupt's discharge was held by the Court of Appeal to be unenforceable.

Assignment of right of action

A compromise involving the assignment by one party to the other of a right of action against another may be illegal. It may offend the rule which generally prohibits champertous agreements.[194] Broadly speaking, the principle applied is that an assignment of this nature will not be struck down if the assignee has a "genuine commercial interest in taking the assignment and in enforcing it for his own benefit".[195] **4-79**

In *Brownton Ltd v Edward Moore Inbucon Ltd*,[196] C, who were commodity brokers, sought and obtained advice from D1, who were computer systems consultants, concerning the installation of a computer system for their business. D1 recommended various manufacturers including D2. As a result, C entered into a contract with D2 for the supply, installation and maintenance of a computer system manufactured by them. The system never worked, was inadequate for C's needs and was scrapped. C sued D1 for damages for breach of contract, and negligence in connection with the advice given. D1 denied liability and alleged that any damages suffered by C were caused by D2's breach of their contract with C. C thereupon introduced D2 into the proceedings alleging breach of contract. D2 denied liability, alleging that what had been supplied was in accordance with **4-80**

---

[191] *Keir v Leeman* (1846) 9 Q.B. 371, *Windhill Local Board of Health v Vint* (1890) 45 Ch. D. 351 CA, *Rawlings v Coal Consumers Association* (1874) 30 L.T. 469, *Williams v Bayley* (1866) L.R. 1 H.L. 200, *Jones v Merionethshire Permanent Benefit BS* [1892] 1 Ch. 173. See *Chitty*, Vol.1, paras 16-039 onwards. In *Australia and New Zealand Banking Group Ltd v Compagnie Noga d'Importation et d'Exportation S.A., Nessim D Gaon* [2007] EWHC 293 (Comm); [2007] 1 Lloyd's Rep. 487 the court rejected an argument that a provision in a settlement agreement had the effect of stifling a prosecution.

[192] *R. v Panayitou and Antoniades* [1973] 1 W.L.R. 1032. See criticism of this decision by Professor Glanville Williams QC (1975) C.L.R. 609. And also see Hudson, "Contractual Compromises of Criminal Liability" (1980) 43 M.L.R. 532.

[193] *Kearley v Thomson* (1890) 24 Q.B.D. 742. See *Chitty*, Vol.1, para.16-070.

[194] *Chitty*, Vol.1, para.16-076 onwards. Given the introduction of conditional fee and damage-based agreements (the latter under the Legal Aid and Sentencing of Offenders Act 2012) in many areas of litigation, the approach of the courts to maintenance and champerty has changed and will continue to change: see *Giles v Thompson* [1994] 1 A.C. 142 at 164. However, cf. *Awwad v Geraghty & Co* [2001] Q.B. 570 CA, in relation to a "contingency fee". And see in relation to "conditional fees", *Kellar v Williams* [2004] UKPC 30 at [21], per Lord Carswell.

[195] *Trendtex Trading Corp v Credit Suisse* [1982] A.C. 679 at 703, per Lord Roskill. See also *Chitty*, Vol.1, para.16–057 onwards and *Massai Aviation Services v Attorney General* [2007] UKPC 12; [2007] 5 LRC 179.

[196] *Brownton Ltd v Edward Moore Inbucon Ltd* [1985] 3 All E.R. 499. See also *South East Thames Regional Health Authority v Y.J. Lovell (London) Ltd* (1985) 32 B.L.R. 127.

the contract, and denying that they had been made aware of C's requirements. They denied that they had been obliged contractually to provide a system fit for any particular purpose, but alleged that the goods supplied were of merchantable quality. D1 issued third-party proceedings against D2 and D2 issued a contribution notice against D1. Shortly before the trial (which was likely to be prolonged) D1 paid into court £302,002 in satisfaction of all the causes of action in respect of which C claimed against D1. C were prepared to accept this in settlement of their claims against both D1 and D2 provided they could secure a satisfactory arrangement with regard to their costs against D2 and D2's costs against them. D2 were unwilling to forgo their costs against C. Before C gave notice of acceptance of the payment into court an agreement was entered into between P and D1 whereby C would accept the sum in court on the usual terms as to costs, but would at the same time grant to D1 an assignment of their cause of action against D2. Notice of the assignment was given to D2, and D1 made it clear that all that they would be seeking was "an appropriate contribution in respect of the sum paid out in settlement" which they asserted would be to the extent of one half of the sum paid. At the trial, when D1 sought leave to amend the statement of claim to plead the agreement, the judge refused the application, accepting D2's contention that the agreement was champertous. The Court of Appeal, allowing D1's appeal, held that, looking at the totality of the transaction, D1 had a genuine commercial interest in taking the assignment. Although the contracts between C and D1 and C and D2 were separate, they arose out of the same commercial transaction and both D1 and D2 were sued in respect of the same damage. Consequently, any sum recovered by C from D2 would reduce the sum recoverable from D1 and, therefore, immediately before the assignment D1 had a genuine commercial interest in reducing the amount of their own loss. It was also said[197] that it was not fatal to such an agreement that the assignee might be better off or make a profit as a result.

4-81 Where a liquidator of a company or the trustee in bankruptcy of a bankrupt enters into such an arrangement, such an assignment will be valid.[198]

Restrictive trade practices

4-82 There is a substantial body of legislation, both European and within the United Kingdom, dealing with anti-competitive practices.[199] The common law continues to strike down agreements in unreasonable restraint of trade.[200] Plainly, any compromise, or any term within a compromise, which offends this framework of law will be susceptible to the argument that it is unenforceable.[201]

Employment law

4-83 The common law approach to covenants in unreasonable restraint of trade apply to the employer–employee relationship and, in particular, to the position of the employee after the termination of the contract of employment.[202] Any compromise of a dispute between an employer and an employee that offends the principles

---

[197] *Brownton* [1985] 3 All E.R. 499 at 506, per Sir John Megaw and at 508–509, per Lloyd LJ Sir John Donaldson MR agreed with both judgments.

[198] *Norglen Ltd v Reeds Rains Prudential* [1999] 2 A.C. 1. In that case *Advanced Technology Structures Ltd v Cray Valley Products Ltd* [1993] B.C.L.C. 723 was overruled.

[199] *Chitty*, Vol.2, Ch.43; Whish & Bailey, *Competition Law*, 9th edn (OUP, 2018); Bellamy & Child, European Union Law of Competition, 8th edn (OUP, 2018). See Competition Act 1998.

[200] *Chitty*, Vol.1, para.16-196 onwards.

[201] cf. *Topliss Showers Ltd v Gessey & Son* [1982] I.C.R. 501, noted in para.3-44 of the 4th edition of this work, where a compromise involving restrictions on the ability of certain parties to sell goods other than at certain specified prices would have been unenforceable because of a failure to register the agreement pursuant to the Restrictive Trade Practices Act 1976 (now repealed by the Competition Act 1998).

[202] *Chitty*, Vol.1, para.16-135 onwards.

encompassed within this approach will be unenforceable. Equally, certain agreements seeking to preclude the right of a dismissed employee to apply to an employment tribunal are unenforceable.[203]

[203] See Ch.28.

CHAPTER 5

Terms of a Compromise

PRELIMINARY

5-01 It is often necessary for a court to construe the terms of a contract of compromise in order to determine its true effect and not infrequently the question arises of whether a term should be implied in order to give effect to what is perceived to be the agreement reached between the parties.

CONSTRUCTION[1]

General problems and approach

5-02 Subsequent to the conclusion of a compromise, questions may arise as to its meaning and effect. This can occur even when those with the highest calibre of legal expertise have been responsible for the drafting of the agreement.[2] The task is to ascertain the common intention of the parties by construing the agreement.

5-03 The means by which this objective is attained in the general contractual setting were the subject of restatement in *Investor's Compensation Scheme Ltd v West Bromwich Building Society*.[3] Lord Hoffmann spelt out the principles in the following way[4]:

> "I do not think that the fundamental change which has overtaken this branch of the law, particularly as a result of the speeches of Lord Wilberforce in *Prenn v Simmonds* [1971] 1 W.L.R 1381, 1384–1386 and *Reardon Smith Line Ltd v Yngvar Hansen-Tangen* [1976] 1 W.L.R 989, is always sufficiently appreciated. The result has been, subject to one important exception, to assimilate the way in which such documents are interpreted by judges to the common sense principles by which any serious utterance would be interpreted in ordinary life. Almost all the old intellectual baggage of 'legal' interpretation has been discarded. The principles may be summarised as follows.
>
> 5-04 (1) Interpretation is the ascertainment of the meaning which the document would convey to a reasonable person having all the background knowledge which would reasonably have been available to the parties in the situation in which they were at the time of the contract.
>
> 5-05 (2) The background was famously referred to by Lord Wilberforce as the 'matrix of fact', but this phrase is, if anything, an understated description of what the

---

1 See also Ch.6. See Lewison, *The Interpretation of Contracts* (6th edition).

2 See, e.g. *Wilson and Whitworth* [1969] 1 W.L.R. 197, noted at para.3-51, where the later to become Lord Denning MR had played a part in the drafting.

3 *Investor's Compensation Scheme Ltd v West Bromwich Building Society* [1998] 1 W.L.R. 896 HL.

4 *Investor's Compensation Scheme* at 912–913. Lord Goff of Chievely, Lord Hope of Craighead and Lord Clyde expressly agreed with Lord Hoffmann's speech.

background may include. Subject to the requirement that it should have been reasonably available to the parties and to the exception to be mentioned next, it includes absolutely anything which would have affected the way in which the language of the document would have been understood by a reasonable man.[5]

5-06 (3) The law excludes from the admissible background the previous negotiations of the parties and their declarations of subjective intent. They are admissible only in an action for rectification. The law makes this distinction for reasons of practical policy and, in this respect only, legal interpretation differs from the way we would interpret utterances in ordinary life. The boundaries of this exception are in some respects unclear. But this is not the occasion on which to explore them.[6]

5-07 (4) The meaning which a document (or any other utterance) would convey to a reasonable man is not the same thing as the meaning of its words. The meaning of words is a matter of dictionaries and grammars; the meaning of the document is what the parties using those words against the relevant background would reasonably have been understood to mean. The background may not merely enable the reasonable man to choose between the possible meanings of words which are ambiguous but even (as occasionally happens in ordinary life) to conclude that the parties must, for whatever reason, have used the wrong words or syntax: see *Mannai Investments Co Ltd v Eagle Star Life Assurance Co Ltd* [1997] A.C. 749.

5-08 (5) The 'rule' that words should be given their 'natural and ordinary meaning' reflects the common sense proposition that we do not easily accept that people have made linguistic mistakes, particularly in formal documents. On the other hand, if one would nevertheless conclude from the background that something must have gone wrong with the language, the law does not require judges to attribute to the parties an intention which they plainly could not have had. Lord Diplock made this point more vigorously when he said in *Antaios Compania Naviera S.A. v Salen Rederierna A.B.* [1985] A.C. 191, 201:

> 'if detailed semantic and syntactical analysis of words in a commercial contract is going to lead to a conclusion that flouts business commonsense, it must be made to yield to business commonsense.[7]'"

5-09 This summary of the general principles of construction[8] continues to be treated as an authoritative framework within which issues concerning the interpretation of a compromise should be judged.[9] Whilst it is essentially a restatement of established principles in contemporary language, the "old intellectual baggage" associated with certain older canons of construction has been jettisoned in favour of a more down-to-earth, common-sense approach to determining what the parties meant by what

---

5 In *Ali* [2002] 1 A.C. 251 at [39] Lord Hoffmann emphasised that he "meant anything which a reasonable man would have regarded as *relevant*" (Lord Hoffmann's emphasis).

6 See now para.5-10 onwards.

7 For a case where "commercial sense" was regarded as important to the construction of the settlement agreement see *Independiente Ltd v Music Trading On-Line (HK) Ltd* [2008] 1 W.L.R. 608. See also *Chartbrook Ltd v Persimmon Homes Ltd* [2009] 1 A.C. 1101.

8 per Lord Bingham of Cornhill at [8].

9 These principles were reaffirmed in *Chartbrook Ltd v Persimmon Homes Ltd* [2009] 1 A.C. 1101: see fn.11 and para.5-13. And see *Rainy Sky SA v Kookmin Bank* [2011] UKSC 50; [2011] W.L.R. 2900 at [20]–[22] per Lord Clarke JSC, as applied in *Hellenic Hull Mutual Association Plc v Starlight Shipping Co* [2014] EWHC 3068 (Comm) at [49] onwards. per Flaux J. Also see *Arnold v Britton* [2015] UKSC 36; [2015] A.C. 1619 at [15] and *Wood v Capita Insurance Services Ltd* [2017] UKSC 24; [2017] A.C. 1173 at [8]–[15], affirming that *Arnold v Brittan* had not departed from the approach set out in *Rainy Sky*. The court had to determine the question whether which of two possible constructions of a compromise agreement was appropriate. The interpretation consistent with 'business common sense' was to be preferred. There is a helpful summary of the relevant principles in *Lukoil Asia Pacific PTE Ltd v Ocean Tankers (PTE) Ltd* [2018] EWHC 163 (Comm); [2018] 2 All E.R. (Comm) 108. See also fn.73.

they said. It does mean that some of the older authorities have to be viewed in a somewhat less rigid way than might have been the case hitherto.[10]

Subjective intentions or understandings, negotiations and extrinsic evidence

It remains established law that in order to determine the common intention of the parties to an agreement reduced to writing, evidence of the pre-contractual negotiations as an aid to construction is inadmissible.[11] This principle will apply to negotiations leading to a compromise whether concluded purely as a written contract or as an agreement embodied in a consent order or judgment. It follows that the intention of the parties must be determined by reference to the document or order itself: extrinsic evidence of what may or may not have been in the minds of the parties at the time of their agreement is not admissible for this purpose.[12] In the context of compromise this can be illustrated in a number of cases: **5-10**

In *Arrale v Costain Civil Engineering Ltd*,[13] the facts of which have been given previously,[14] the Court of Appeal held that in so far as the trial judge had taken into account evidence concerning the negotiations in order to construe the terms of the form of discharge, he was wrong to have done so. The evidence may have been relevant to the issues of misrepresentation and non est factum also raised, but should have been ignored for the purposes of construction.[15] It was also said[16] that it was doubtful whether the fact that the parties had permitted the giving of such evidence without objection rendered the same admissible for such purposes. **5-11**

In *Capon v Evans*,[17] the facts of which have also been given previously,[18] the Court of Appeal held that the judge should not have received evidence of C's "subjective understand- **5-12**

---

10 *Chitty*, Vol.1, para.13-041 onwards.

11 This principle was reaffirmed by the House of Lords in *Chartbrook Ltd* [2009] 1 A.C. 1101. Lord Hoffmann, with whom all their Lordships agreed, said at [41] that, "there is no clearly established case for departing from the exclusionary rule". He recognised that the rule can have the effect "[T]hat parties are sometimes held bound by a contract in terms which, upon a full investigation of the course of negotiations, a reasonable observer would not have taken them to have intended." However, he said that "[A] system which sometimes allows this to happen may be justified in the more general interest of economy and predictability in obtaining advice and adjudicating disputes." He concluded by saying: "It is, after all, usually possible to avoid surprises by carefully reading the documents before signing them and there are the safety nets of rectification and estoppel by convention." In that case the House of Lords concluded that the contractual term in issue contained "a grammatical ambiguity which must be resolved by considering the business purpose" of the contract (at [12]). The decision and the affirmation of the principle is not without its detractors: see, e.g. McLauchlan (2010) L.Q.R. 8–14.

12 A passage to like effect in the 3rd edition was quoted with approval in *Dattani v Trio Supermarkets Ltd* [1998] I.R.L.R. 23 CA, referred to at para.5-15. See also *British Movietonews Ltd v London and District Cinemas Ltd* [1952] A.C. 166, *General Accident Fire and Life Assurance Corp v IRC* [1963] 1 W.L.R. 1207 CA, cf. *Reardon Smith Line Ltd v Yngvar Hansen-Tangen* [1976] 1 W.L.R. 989 at 995–997. See also *Cadmus Shipping Co Ltd v Lakeview Trading Co SA* (1979) CAT 317: it was held not legitimate to look at a contemporaneous note of party's representative to aid construction of an undertaking that formed part of an agreed order.

13 *Arrale* [1976] 1 Lloyd's Rep. 98 CA.

14 See para.3-15.

15 *Arrale* [1976] 1 Lloyd's Rep. 98 per Lord Denning MR at 101, per Stephenson LJ at 103–104 and per Geoffrey Lane LJ at 105.

16 *Arrale* [1976] 1 Lloyd's Rep. 98 per Stephenson LJ at 104.

17 *Capon v Evans* (1986) CAT 413; [1987] C.L.Y. 413.

18 See para.3-24.

ing as to the effect of the words used" in the agreement. This evidence was neither relevant nor admissible "in the absence any plea of mistake or rectification".

5-13 In *Rees v West Glamorgan CC*,[19] a personal injuries claim brought by C against D was settled in correspondence in April/May 1991 between C's solicitors and D's insurers on the basis that C would accept "£33,000 in full and final settlement of his claim together with [costs, details of which were supplied in the letter]". The letter from C's solicitor concluded with the words, "I await cheques to conclude this matter". On 31 May 1991 the Compensation Recovery Unit issued a certificate to D's insurers showing that, in respect of a compensation payment made in the week ending 7 June 1991, the sum to be deducted and paid to the Compensation Recovery Unit pursuant to s.22 of the Social Security Act 1989 (effective from 3 September 1990) was just over £10,000. C refused to accept any other sum than £33,000 and disputed D's right to deduct the amount provided for on the certificate. At first instance it was held that the contract of compromise, on its true construction, meant that C would receive £33,000 "in his hand" and that D would pay an additional sum to the Compensation Recovery Unit. In construing the agreement the recorder asked himself what P's solicitor had in mind when referring to the "cheques to conclude this matter" other than one for £33,000 and further said that the offer did not specify any deduction to be made. The Court of Appeal held the recorder was wrong to conclude as he did:

(1) There was nothing in the correspondence to support the conclusion that C was to receive £33,000 "in his hand": the letters recorded an agreement to settle C's claim for £33,000 and s.22 of the 1989 Act simply directed what was to be done in performance of that agreement.
(2) The subjective state of mind of C's solicitor was not the correct test to apply and was irrelevant.

These cases represent illustrations of the way the general exclusionary rule operates.[20] In *Chartbrook Ltd v Persimmon Homes Ltd*[21] Lord Hoffmann said this:

> "The rule excludes evidence of what was said or done during the course of negotiating the agreement for the purpose of drawing inferences about what the contract meant. It does not exclude the use of such evidence for other purposes: for example, to establish that a fact which may be relevant as background was known to the parties, or to support a claim for rectification or estoppel. These are not exceptions to the rule. They operate outside it."

5-14 It has always been the case that extrinsic evidence may be admitted to assist in identifying the commercial purpose of the contract[22] and in the context of compromise such evidence has been admitted (a) to explain the meaning to be attached to an ambiguous word or expression and (b) to identify the disputes which the parties, by their agreement, were endeavouring to resolve.[23]

---

19 *Rees v West Glamorgan CC* [1994] P.I.Q.R. 37.

20 See per Lord Hoffmann at fn.10.

21 See fn.8.

22 In *Prenn v Simmonds* [1971] 1 W.L.R. 1381, Lord Wilberforce said that whilst "evidence of negotiations, or of the parties' intentions ... ought not to be received" it could be received if "[R]estricted to evidence of the factual background known to the parties at or before the date of the contract, including evidence of the 'genesis' and objectively the 'aim' of the transaction."

23 *Chitty*, Vol.1, para.13-108 onwards. In *National Bank of Sharjah v Dellborg* (1997) CAT 1320, Saville LJ, as he then was, said that "where the words the parties have used are ambiguous or, read literally, are meaningless or nonsensical, the surrounding circumstances must be considered in order to select the appropriate meaning or to try to give the words meaning or sense". For the admissibility or otherwise of "without prejudice" negotiations in this context, see *Oceanbulk Shipping and Trading SA v TMT Asia Ltd* [2011] 1 A.C. 662. And see para.19-29.

In *Dattani v Trio Supermarkets Ltd*,[24] C had instituted proceedings for unfair dismissal against D. These came before an industrial tribunal on 9 November 1992. Before final adjudication a settlement was reached by which C was to be paid £5,000 by D. The formal record of the tribunal was in the following terms: **5-15**

> "This case has been settled on the basis that the Respondent pay the Applicant the sum of £5,000 at the rate of £1,000 per month, the first payment to be made on 16 November 1992. The Applicant remains free to return to the Tribunal should the sum agreed not be paid within the agreed time limits."

A further handwritten document addressed to C by a director of D and dated the same day as the settlement was reached recorded as follows:

> "In consideration of your accepting the sum of £5,000 from Trio Supermarkets Ltd in settlement of your claim for unfair dismissal by Trio Supermarket Limited in five installments [sic] of £1,000 per month I as director of Trio Supermarkets Limited hereby personally guarantee payment of each of the said sums of £1,000."

The terms of C's complaint to the industrial tribunal contained the allegation that certain wages were outstanding, but he did not pursue a claim for unpaid wages in the unfair dismissal proceedings although it would have been open to him to do so. About one year later C launched county court proceedings seeking unpaid wages of £11,800. D argued, inter alia, that this claim was embraced within the compromise made on 9 November 1992. D's counsel at the tribunal hearing had made two statements about the negotiations. In the first he indicated that negotiations during the luncheon adjournment broke down when C's solicitor made it clear that C would accept the sum of £3,500 offered, but only on the basis that it would be without prejudice to any other claim that C might bring in the county court. Counsel went on to say that the "less favourable settlement" in the sum of £5,000 was agreed when further evidence had been given and the tribunal had indicated informally that it was minded to find for C. His second statement was made after being reminded of the other document dated 9 November 1992 referred to above. Of that C said this:

> "Since writing my earlier statement I have now been shown [the document dated] 9th November 1992 which records the agreement made between [C's solicitor] and myself on behalf of Trio Supermarkets Limited. I can accordingly state that no basis for a settlement was discussed between us at the second adjournment other than that it was in respect of the Applicant's claim then being heard at the Industrial Tribunal."

The Court of Appeal held that the statements of D's counsel were relevant and admissible on the issue of the identification of the claim compromised and, accordingly, that only the unfair dismissal claim was the subject of the agreement.[25]

Where the basis upon which an offer of settlement was made becomes an issue, it would seem that the course of the negotiations[26] and other extrinsic evidence[27] will be admissible to resolve that issue. **5-16**

---

24 *Dattani* [1998] I.R.L.R. 23.

25 *Dattani* [1998] I.R.L.R. per Mummery LJ at [52] of the judgment: "Taking account of its object, language, context and background this agreement should be construed as limited to a compromise of the unfair dismissal claim. Counsel's agreed statement is highly material on the issue of identification of the claim compromised. There was an initial offer to settle for £3,500. That was not accepted. An express reservation was made by [C's] solicitor of the right to bring proceedings in the county court. The sum, which was finally agreed at £5,000 was described by counsel for the company at that time as being 'less favourable' to the company. That was after [D's director] had given evidence and the tribunal had given an indication that they would find against the company."

26 See paras 3-24 onwards.

27 See, e.g. *Neuchatel Asphalte Co Ltd* [1957] 1 W.L.R. 356 noted at para.2-06.

Post-compromise words and deeds

5-17 It is a well-established principle[28] that the words and deeds of parties *after* the conclusion of a contract cannot be used as an aid to the construction of the contract.[29]

"Rules" of construction

5-18 In the light of the restatement of the principles underlying the approach to the construction of contracts generally,[30] it is no longer appropriate to describe as "rules" the propositions that have hitherto been treated as regulating the interpretation of contracts.[31] Nonetheless, many of the propositions traditionally called "rules of construction" will continue, as guidelines,[32] to inform the task of the court when seeking to put the correct interpretation on the parties' agreement. The propositions of particular relevance when considering a compromise have usually been the following:

(a) words are to be given their natural and ordinary meaning unless the result is absurd or the agreement is inconsistent within itself;
(b) words are to be interpreted in such a way as to effectuate the agreement rather than to invalidate it;
(c) the agreement should be considered as a whole, the meaning of words to be taken from their context with a view, if possible, to giving effect to the whole of it.

5-19 An example of the way in which the traditional approach led to an obviously common-sense result is afforded by the following case:

> In *Morss v Morss*,[33] parties to a matrimonial case had compromised on terms which provided, inter alia, that H would in due course make available for W's "use" a house then in the course of construction "rent free for her life or until ... debarred by the court from access to the children of the family". As part of the agreement H undertook to furnish the house, to pay its outgoings and to maintain the insurance on the property and its contents. The Court of Appeal held, construing the agreement as a whole, that the word "use" meant "use as a residence and not otherwise". H was released from his undertaking to the court after W had ceased using the property herself as a residence, having gone to live with another man.

5-20 It needs to be emphasised that the process of construction and reference to the applicable principles only become necessary when there is uncertainty or ambiguity about the terms recorded by the parties. It has been said[34] that,

> "where words used have an unambiguous and sensible meaning as a matter of ordinary language [there would be] serious objections in an approach which would permit the surrounding circumstances to alter that meaning".

The strained interpretation of ordinary language should not be the end product of the process of construction.

---

28 Not controverted by anything said in *Investors Compensation Scheme Ltd v West Bromwich Building Society* [1998] 1 W.L.R. 896.
29 *Chitty*, Vol.1, at para.13-136. See also *Arrale* [1976] 1 Lloyd's Rep. 98 at 103–104.
30 See para.5-03 onwards.
31 *Chitty*, Vol.1, para.13-042.
32 *Chitty*, Vol.1, para.13-042.
33 *Morss v Morss* [1972] Fam. 264, in particular the judgment of Megaw LJ at 277–279.
34 *National Bank of Sharjah v Dellborg* (1997) CAT 1320.

It is important to emphasise also that reference to cases in which the court has reached a particular conclusion in relation to a particular word or phrase will be of limited assistance in other cases. In this area, in particular, authorities "must be read in the context of their peculiar facts".[35] That having been said, certain phrases, hallowed by long and frequent usage, are likely to receive substantially the same response by way of construction in most compromises in which they appear. An obvious example would be the well-established formula "in full and final settlement of all claims that [C] has or may have arising from the accident".[36] Another example might be where parties agree a settlement "in respect of the subject-matter" of the action between them. Here a court is likely to interpret the words "in respect of" as connoting the widest possible connection between the settlement and the subject-matter of the action.[37] 5-21

Releases

A compromise agreement will often contain a release of future demands and liabilities arising out of the dispute that has led to the compromise. Not infrequently such a release is expressed in very general terms.[38] In construing the meaning of a "release" in *Bank of Credit and Commercial International SA v Ali*[39] Lord Bingham of Cornhill said this[40]: 5-22

> "In construing this provision, as any other contractual provision, the object of the court is to give effect to what the contracting parties intended. To ascertain the intention of the parties the court reads the terms of the contract as a whole, giving the words used their natural and ordinary meaning in the context of the agreement, the parties' relationship and all the relevant facts surrounding the transaction so far as known to the parties. To ascertain the parties' intentions the court does not of course inquire into the parties' subjective states of mind but makes an objective judgment based on the materials already identified."

The release by one party of another from liability arising from whatever state of affairs brought them into dispute is, of course, the very essence of compromise.[41] Usually, parties will wish to see a resolution that wipes the slate clean and indeed that prevents further matters of disputation being added to the slate.[42] Many formulae have been devised to secure this objective, some fairly short, some more 5-23

---

35 *Ali* [2002] 1 A.C. 251, per Lord Bingham of Cornhill at [17].

36 See para.2-08 onwards. Though cf. *Multiplex Constructions (UK) Ltd v Cleveland Bridge UK Ltd* [2006] EWHC 1341 (TCC); 107 Con. L.R. 1.

37 *Line Trust Corp v Fielding* unreported 26 July 1999 CA. cf. *Multiplex Constructions (UK) Ltd* [2006] EWHC 1341 (TCC) at [568]–[572].

38 See para.5-23.

39 *Ali* [2002] 1 A.C. 251. See also *Satyam Computer Services Ltd v Upaid Systems Ltd* [2008] EWCA Civ 487 at [79].

40 *Ali* [2002] 1 A.C. 251 at [8].

41 See para.1-01 and para.6-01.

42 cf. *Ali* [2002] 1 A.C. 251, per Lord Nicholls of Birkenhead at [23]: "General releases are often entered into when parties are settling a dispute which has arisen between them, or when a relationship between them, such as employment or partnership, has come to an end. They want to wipe the slate clean. Likewise, the problem which has arisen in this case is typical. The problem concerns a claim which subsequently came to light but whose existence was not known or suspected by either party at the time the release was given. The emergence of this unsuspected claim gives rise to a question which has confronted the courts on many occasions. The question is whether the context in which the general release was given is apt to cut down the apparently all-embracing scope of the words of the release."

extensive.[43] Any such formula may be characterised as a "general release".[44] Releases of this nature have been utilised for very many years in a variety of contexts.[45] In some of the older authorities[46] there emerged the suggestion that there was a particular "rule of construction" applicable to deeds of release confining the ambit of the release to matters within the contemplation of the party making the release and in respect of which he had knowledge. Whatever the historical context in which these statements of principle found expression, the contemporary view is that no special rule of construction applies to a release. In *Bank of Credit and Commercial International SA v Ali*,[47] Lord Nicholls of Birkenhead said this[48]:

> "[T]here is no room today for the application of any special 'rules' of interpretation in the case of general releases. There is no room for any special rules because there is now no occasion for them. A general release is a term in a contract. The meaning to be given to the words used in a contract is the meaning which ought reasonably to be ascribed to those words having due regard to the purpose of the contract and the circumstances in which the contract was made. This general principle is as much applicable to a general release as to any other contractual term. Why ever should it not be?"

5-24 The case in which the foregoing words appeared is an important contemporary illustration of the circumstances in which a general form of release is agreed[49] but which can then give rise to difficult problems of interpretation:

> C was an employee of the bank from June 1985 to June 1990. Following an extensive reorganisation of its worldwide business during the spring and early summer of 1990, and following consultation with ACAS and C's trade union, C was sent a redundancy notice terminating his employment with effect from 30 June 1990. The notice set out the terms of the redundancy package offered totalling £9,910. An additional option was offered, namely a further month's gross salary if he was willing to sign an ACAS form (COT-3)44 acknowledging that the payment from the bank was in full and final settlement. Having discussed the matter briefly with an ACAS official, C agreed to accept this additional sum (£2,772) and signed the COT-3 form in the following terms:
>
> "[C] agrees to accept the terms set out in the documents attached in full and final set-

---

43 *Ali* [2002] 1 A.C. 251, per Lord Hoffmann at [38]. In *Heaton v AXA Equity & Law Life Assurance Society Plc* [2002] 2 A.C. 329, the release in the settlement agreement was in these terms: "Each of the parties hereto hereby unconditionally and irrevocably releases and discharges each other, and their respective directors, officers and employees from all or any liabilities, actions, causes of action, suits, demands of whatever nature or kind and howsoever and whenever arising which any of them may be entitled to make, assert or pursue in any jurisdiction whatsoever in relation to or in any way connected with the matter specified in clause 2.1 above." Clause 2.1 provided that the "agreement is in full and final settlement of all claims and potential claims of whatsoever nature and kind (including interest and costs) which the parties have or may have against each other under or in respect of or arising out of or in connection with, whether directly or indirectly" in relation to certain identified and enumerated matters. In *Marsden v Barclays Bank Plc* [2016] EWHC 1601 (QB); [2016] 2 Lloyd's Rep. 420, a release in a compromise agreement concerning a claim for alleged Swaps mis-selling was worded as follows: "in full and final settlement of all complaints, claims and causes of action which arise directly or indirectly, or may arise, out of or are in any way connected with the Swaps". It was held to apply to claims said to arise from alleged fraud.

44 See fn.37.

45 See, in particular, the historical review of the authorities in the speech of Lord Bingham of Cornhill in *Ali* [2002] 1 A.C. 251 at [10]–[16].

46 See the cases referred to in *Chitty*, Vol.1, at para.22-005.

47 See fn.37.

48 *Ali* [2002] 1 A.C. 251 at [26]. See also Lord Bingham of Cornhill (with whom Lord Browne-Wilkinson agreed) at [17], Lord Hoffmann (who dissented in the result) at [54]–[57] and Lord Clyde at [79].

49 See Ch.28. See also *Priory Caring Services Ltd v Capita Property Services Ltd* [2010] EWCA Civ 226; 129 Con. L.R. 81.

tlement of all or any claims whether under statute, common law or in equity of whatsoever nature that exist or may exist and, in particular, all or any claims rights or applications of whatsoever nature that the applicant has or may have or has made or could make in or to the industrial tribunal, except [his] rights under [the bank's] pension scheme."

Unknown to C (and to the general body of D's employees) D's business had been carried on for a number of years in a dishonest and corrupt manner and had been seriously insolvent. In July 1991 the bank was put into compulsory liquidation. A number of former employees (including C) sought to claim in the liquidation for damages for handicap in the labour market caused by the stigma that association with D was likely to cause (known colloquially as "the stigma claims"). The liquidators of the bank rejected the claims, but in speeches delivered on 12 June 1997[50] the House of Lords held that such claims could proceed in principle. The liquidators then sought to argue, in relation to those former employees who had signed the form of release referred to above, that any such claim had thus been compromised. C's case was selected as a test case. The assumed facts included that D knew at the time of the agreement with C that its business was being carried out dishonestly and corruptly, that C did not know this and that he could not have been expected to appreciate that it might have been so carried out. The House of Lords held (Lord Hoffmann dissenting) that C's claim was not covered by the release.

Lord Bingham of Cornhill, having reviewed the old authorities (including *Turner v Turner and Arrale v Costain Civil Engineering Ltd*,[51] both of which are noted below[52]), and having expressed himself as noted above,[53] said that he shared the reluctance of the judges in those earlier cases "to infer that a party intended to give up something which neither he, nor the other party, knew or could know that he had".[54] He expressed himself thus[55]: **5-25**

"What, then, of the claim for stigma damages which lies at the heart of this appeal? The bank, through its senior employees, is fixed with knowledge of the bank's insolvency and nefarious practices, although it seems unlikely that those negotiating with the employees were alert to these facts, very carefully concealed from the world. [C] had no such knowledge. Neither the bank, even when fixed with such knowledge, nor [C] could realistically have supposed that such a claim lay within the realm of practical possibility. On a fair construction of this document I cannot conclude that the parties intended to provide for the release of rights and the surrender of claims which they could never have had in contemplation at all. If the parties had sought to achieve so extravagant a result they should in my opinion have used language which left no room for doubt and which might at least have alerted [C] to the true effect of what (on that hypothesis) he was agreeing."

Lord Nicholls of Birkenhead expressed himself as follows[56]: **5-26**

"I consider these parties are to be taken to have contracted on the basis of the law as it then stood. To my mind there is something inherently unattractive in treating these parties as having intended to include within the release a claim which, as a matter of law, did not then exist and whose existence could not then have been foreseen. This employee signed an informal release when he lost his job, in return for an additional month's pay. The ambit of the release should be kept within reasonable bounds. [C] cannot reason-

---

50 *Mahmud v Bank of Credit and Commercial International SA* [1998] A.C. 20. In that case, according to Lord Nicholls of Birkenhead in *Ali* [2002] 1 A.C. 251 at [33], the House of Lords "developed or, put more bluntly, changed the law".

51 *Turner* (1880) 14 Ch. D. 829 and *Arrale* [1976] 1 Lloyd's Rep. 98, respectively.

52 See paras 5-30 and 5-32.

53 See para.5-22.

54 *Ali* [2002] 1 A.C. 251 at [17].

55 *Ali* [2002] 1 A.C. 251 at [19].

56 *Ali* [2002] 1 A.C. 251 at [35].

ably be regarded as having taken upon himself the risk of a subsequent retrospective change in the law. A claim arising out of such a change cannot be regarded as having been within the contemplation of the parties."

5-27 Lord Clyde was of the same view[57]:

"The stigma claim is one which neither party could have contemplated even as a possibility as the law stood at the time when the agreement was made. At that time it would not be known whether or not the employee would have any difficulty at all in finding alternative employment. The bank's conduct had not yet achieved the notoriety which could create the stigma. But even if those facts had been even suspected as a possibility the prospect of any liability falling on the bank to a former employee is something which must have been far beyond the reasonable contemplation of the parties. Even without formulating any definition of the precise scope of the agreement, it seems to me that if the parties had intended to cut out a claim of whose existence they could have no knowledge they would have expressed that intention in words more precise than the generalities which they in fact used."

5-28 Whilst the facts of the case may have been unusual—indeed unique in the sense that they are unlikely to be replicated precisely in another case—the expressions of principle concerning the way in which releases of this nature are to be interpreted are of considerable importance. A contemporary approach to the process of construction yielded what many may regard as a just result on a preliminary issue in a highly unusual situation. The principles thus enunciated will, of course, fall to be applied henceforth in other more mundane and less obviously meritorious cases.

5-29 All previous authorities must now be read in the light of the speeches in *Bank of Credit and Commercial International SA v Ali*. It is to be noted, however, that the majority was of the opinion articulated specifically by Lord Bingham of Cornhill (referred to in para.5-25) that the decisions in many of those previous authorities reflected a disinclination on the part of the court "to infer that a party intended to give up something which neither he, nor the other party, knew or could know that he had".

5-30 In *Turner v Turner*,[58] disputes arose concerning the provisions made in T's will. In July 1868 a compromise of those disputes was achieved whereby the persons interested under the will, in consideration of certain payments by T's executrix, released by deed all claims on the estate "which they ... then had, or could, should, or might at any time or times have". T had been one of the next of kin of J.M.W. Turner, RA, and was entitled to one-fifth of the latter's estate. Part of that estate consisted of certain plates, pictures and engravings, which had been sold to J in 1858 for £2,500, of which T had received £500. In 1873, J put these items up for auction and received about £40,000. A suit was thereafter maintained against J by J.M.W. Turner's next of kin (including T's executrix) to have the sale to him set aside. In 1877, a decree to that effect was made with the result that T's executrix became entitled to a one-fifth share in the proceeds of the auction. It was common ground that when the deed of release was executed in July 1868 none of the parties was aware of the value of the items or of any right to set aside the original sale. Malins VC held that the one-fifth share of the proceeds of the auction was not subject to the general release because,

"it has always been the rule of this Court to construe releases and documents of that kind with regard to the intention of the parties, and to the state of the property which was known at the time".[59]

---

57 *Ali* [2002] 1 A.C. 251 at [86]. cf. paras 31–30 onwards.

58 *Turner v Turner* (1880) 14 Ch. D. 829.

59 *Turner* (1880) 14 Ch. D. 829 at 834.

All T's executrix had achieved under the deed of release was a "release of all claims and demands in respect of property which was then known to exist".[60]

In *Directors of the London and South Western Ry Co v Blackmore*,[61] in 1861, acting under compulsory purchase powers, D purchased some of C's land for railway purposes. In 1862, D sold to C some other areas of land. Various disputes arose between the parties culminating in an agreement in 1864. It contained various provisions concerning the erection and maintenance of boundary walls between C's land and D's land and also a release by C "of all claims and demands therein mentioned, or for or on any other account or ground whatsoever". In 1866 the land originally purchased by D from C became surplus to requirements and D proposed to sell it. C wanted to exercise a statutory right of pre-emption pursuant to the Act under which it had originally been purchased. D argued, inter alia, that any such right had been surrendered under the general release. In his opinion Lord Westbury said this:[62] **5-31**

> "The general words in a release are limited always to that thing or those things which were specially in the contemplation of the parties at the time when the release was given. But a dispute that had not emerged, or a question which had not at all arisen, cannot be considered as bound and concluded by the anticipatory words of a general release.[63]"

In *Arrale v Costain Civil Engineering Ltd*,[64] the facts of which have been given elsewhere,[65] Lord Denning MR was of the view that there could not have been an agreement to release the common law claim because no one gave any thought to it.[66] **5-32**

Plainly, whatever may have been in the minds of the parties at the time the terms of a release are agreed, the release should not be interpreted so as to defeat the very object it set out to achieve: **5-33**

In *Perkins, Re*,[67] L assigned the residue of a lease to A1 who, in due course, assigned the then residue of the term to A2. Each assignment contained a covenant by the assignee to pay the rent and to keep his assignor indemnified in respect of any breaches of the covenants in the lease. A2 died in December 1895 and A1 was adjudicated bankrupt in June 1897. After A1's bankruptcy, A2's executors assigned the then residue of the term to a man of straw who did not pay the rent or perform the covenants. L was required to pay, and did pay, the outstanding amounts for rent and insurance premiums under the lease. He pursued A1, through his trustee in bankruptcy, for these sums. A compromise was achieved whereby L took an assignment of A1's right to indemnity from A2 in return for which L released A1's estate in bankruptcy "from all claims and demands under or in respect of" A1's obligations to him under the (first) assignment. In L's action seeking a declaration that A2's estate was liable to him for payments made and to be made under the lease, it was argued by A2's executors that the release was to be construed as releasing all liability of A1 or his estate in bankruptcy to L under the covenants with L, with the effect that A2's executors were discharged from all liability under the covenant to indemnify A1. The Court of Appeal held that the release in the deed "although couched in very general terms, must, if possible, be so construed as not to defeat the object or

---

60 *Turner* (1880) 14 Ch. D. 829 at 836; cf. para.2-08 onwards.

61 *Directors of the London and South Western Ry Co v Blackmore* (1870) L.R. 4 H.L. 610.

62 *Blackmore* (1870) L.R. 4 H.L. 610 at 623–624.

63 In *Ali* [2002] 1 A.C. 251, Lord Hoffmann (at [42]) said of the first sentence of this quotation from Lord Westbury's speech: "This is rather a sweeping statement. It is almost always dangerous to say 'always'. But, in cases of a release given in connection with the settlement of a dispute, it is a fair generalisation."

64 *Arrale* [1976] 1 Lloyd's Rep. 98.

65 See para.3-15.

66 *Arrale* [1976] 1 Lloyd's Rep. 98 at 102.

67 *Perkins, Re* [1898] 2 Ch. 182.

purpose of the deed of which it forms part". Since the preservation of the right to sue A2's executors was essential to L's "recovery ... of the asset assigned to him, and which asset he is to take in satisfaction of all demands", the "estate released must exclude that asset".[68]

The "contra proferentem" rule[69]

5-34 Despite the move away from the continued use of Latin expressions in everyday legal language, the phrase "*contra proferentem*" continues to trip off the tongue of lawyers engaged in commercial matters, although it is now often referred to simply as "construction against (the) grantor".[70] The more important issue is whether the principle it enshrines still has a role to play in the construction of agreements. Expressed shortly and simply, the principle applied to the resolution of an ambiguity in an agreement which cannot be resolved by other principles of construction is that the ambiguity is resolved against the party responsible for putting it forward.

In *Arrale v Costain Civil Engineering Ltd*,[71] the majority held that any ambiguity in the receipt put forward by D should be resolved against D.

5-35 The principle enshrines a pragmatic and workable means of resolving justly an ambiguity in a written document in a way that would appeal to the hypothetical reasonable man faced with having to choose between two alternative meanings.[72] On that basis the principle has a future.

Relevance of jurisdiction of court when construing consent order or judgment

5-36 The general approach to the construction of a consent order or judgment is broadly the same as that of the construction of a contract of compromise.[73] Since a consent order or judgment is itself evidence of the agreement it embodies or reflects, there would be no objection in principle to evidence of the terms of that agreement being received to assist in resolving any ambiguity in the terms of the order or judgment.[74] Where, however, there is a patent conflict between the terms of the order and the antecedent agreement, and the conflict is not susceptible of resolu-

---

68 *Perkins, Re* [1898] 2 Ch. 182, per Sir Nathaniel Lindley MR, giving the reserved judgment of the court, at 190.

69 *Chitty*, Vol.1, para.13-095 onwards.

70 See, e.g. *McHale v Cadogan* [2010] EWCA Civ 14 at [11]. In *Lexi Holdings Plc v Stainforth* [2006] EWCA Civ 988 at [17] Carnwath LJ described the "so-called 'contra proferentem' rule" as one of the "tools" made available by the law to decide on "the intended purpose of the [agreement] as understood by both parties".

71 *Arrale* [1976] 1 Lloyd's Rep. 98.

72 cf. proposition 4 in Lord Hoffmann's summary in *Investors Compensation Scheme Ltd* set out in para.5-07.

73 In *Sirius International Insurance Co (Publ) v FAI General Insurance Ltd* [2004] UKHL 54; [2004] 1 W.L.R. 3251, in the context of construing a Tomlin order, Lord Steyn (with whom Lords Nicholls of Birkenhead and Walker of Gestingthorpe agreed specifically and with whom, on the approach to construction Lords Bingham of Cornhill and Brown of Eaton-under-Heywood also agreed) said this at [18]: "The settlement contained in the Tomlin order must be construed as a commercial instrument. The aim of the inquiry is not to probe the real intentions of the parties but to ascertain the contextual meaning of the relevant contractual language. The inquiry is objective: the question is what a reasonable person, circumstanced as the actual parties were, would have understood the parties to have meant by the use of specific language. The answer to that question is to be gathered from the text under consideration and its relevant contextual scene." See also *Weston v Dayman* [2006] EWCA Civ 1165 at [5]; *Viagogo AG v Competition and Markets Authority* [2019] EWHC 1706 (Ch) and *Pourghazi v Kamyab* [2019] EWHC 1300 (Ch) (interpretation of a Tomlin order).

74 For example *Cloutte v Storey* [1911] 1 Ch. 18 at 25–26.

tion by rectification of one or other,[75] the question arises as to which would prevail. It is difficult to give an answer which would necessarily apply in every situation of such an unusual nature, but overall the order or judgment would probably prevail. As the final stage of the process by which the parties have sought to put to rest their previous disputation, they must be taken to have submitted themselves consensually to the court's jurisdiction.[76] The consent order or judgment then falls to be interpreted in the way in which an order or judgment of a like nature, but not expressed to be by consent, would be interpreted.[77] If there is any doubt about whether the order or judgment is within the powers of the court, it should be construed as being limited to the jurisdiction of the court and be enforced only to that extent.[78]

Consistent with the principle that, when parties agree that a consent order or a judgment should be made, they are to be taken as submitting themselves to the ordinary jurisdiction of the court, the court will approach the interpretation of the consent order or judgment by reference to the court's ordinary jurisdiction. **5-37**

In *Allsuch v Kaye*,[79] at a time when different scales of costs were awarded in respect of different levels of award, an order by consent in the county court provided for payment of costs "to be taxed on scale 2". The Court of Appeal held that, properly construed, such an order did not preclude the exercise on taxation of the discretion on discretionary items provided for in relation to scale 2 costs by the then Ord.38 r.9 of the County Court Rules. **5-38**

In *Tucker v Woodroof*,[80] a building dispute between C, the builder, and D, the employer, was compromised by the acceptance by C of £1,600 and of D's undertaking to pay C's costs of the action "on an indemnity basis to be taxed if not agreed". The Court of Appeal held that the effect of this agreement was not that taxation was to be at large, but it should be on the appropriate scale (scale 2), but on an indemnity basis. The discretion conferred by the then Ord.38 r.9,[81] was not precluded. **5-39**

In *Caudery v Finnerty*,[82] a consent judgment, reflecting the settlement of an action for breach of promise of marriage and an action for monies lent, was entered in the following terms: **5-40**

"By consent, it is ordered that judgment should be entered for [C] for £1,250, with costs of both actions to be taxed, to be paid by [D] by 8 equal payments half-yearly, the first of such payments to be made within a month of July 19, 1888."

A further provision under the order related to the maintenance of premiums under a policy of security and the order continued as follows:

"Execution not to issue provided that the payments of the instalments and of the

---

75 See para.4-30 onwards.

76 See *Chanel Ltd v F. W. Woolworth* [1981] 1 W.L.R. 485 and 491 CA. In *Cornhill Insurance Plc v Barclay* (1992) CAT 948 (noted more fully at para.6-05), Beldam LJ said that "[when] the court is asked to make an order enforceable by the parties to give effect to their agreement, the parties should in the absence of express reservation be taken to have intended that the order has the same effect as it would have had if made after the court had resolved the underlying issues between them". See also per Staughton LJ in *Balkanbank v Taher (No.2)* [1995] 1 W.L.R. 1056 at 1063. Though cf. *Morris v Wentworth-Stanley* [1999] Q.B. 1004 CA, considered in more detail at para.6-29 onwards.

77 A proposition noted with approval by HH Judge Humphrey LLoyd QC, OR, in *Wallace v Brian Gale & Associates* [1997] 2 Costs L.R. 15 at [25] (decision upheld on appeal, *Wallace v Brian Gale & Associates* [1998] 2 Costs L.R. 53), in the context of the question whether reference to "costs in the action" in a Tomlin Order encompassed the later costs of enforcement.

78 *Hinde v Hinde* [1953] 1 All E.R. 171 at 178.

79 *Allsuch v Kaye* (1978) CAT 840.

80 *Tucker v Woodroof* [1993] 2 WLUK 341; *The Times*, 18 March 1993.

81 Now see CPR r.44.3.

82 *Caudery v Finnerty* (1892) L.J.Q.B. 496; (1892) 66 L.J. 684.

premiums were regularly kept up; but that in case default were made in the payment of any instalment [C] be at liberty to issue execution for the whole amount remaining unpaid."

D commenced paying the required instalments. After payment of the first instalment C intimated a claim for interest upon the whole sum under ss.17 and 18 of the Judgments Act 1838. D denied liability to make such further payment and the issue was agreed to be left until all payments had been made. It was held that the order could not be construed so as to include interest since the instalments were to be of equal amounts. Per Collins J: "The equality of the instalments prima facie excludes payment of interest, which would vary according to the amount remaining unpaid.

5-41 In *Balkanbank v Taher (No.2)*,[83] C, a bank, issued proceedings in Ireland against various defendants, D, claiming the return of certain monies that were alleged to belong to it and damages for fraud arising out of a joint venture agreement. C sought and obtained from the Irish court a *Mareva* injunction restraining D from dealing with their assets within the jurisdiction of the Irish court. Shortly after obtaining this injunction, C obtained a worldwide Mareva injunction from the English court in aid of its substantive proceedings in Ireland pursuant to s.25 of the Civil Jursidiction and Judgment Act 1982. The *Mareva* injunction was granted on the basis of various undertakings by C, including an undertaking in damages in the usual form, namely,

> "to abide by any order which this court may make as to damages, in case this court may hereafter be of the opinion that the Defendants or any of them have suffered any by reason of this order which the [claimant] ought to pay".

Following the substantive trial, at which C's principal allegations of fraud failed, the Irish *Mareva* injunction was discharged and the Irish court directed an inquiry as to damages suffered by D arising from the injunction. Some three months later a consent order was made in the English court discharging the worldwide *Mareva* injunction and ordering that,

> "there be an inquiry as to what damages [D] have ... suffered as a result of the making of the [*Mareva* order] which [C] ought to pay".

An issue arose thereafter as to whether the terms of this consent order precluded the court from considering, as a matter of discretion, whether the undertaking as to damages should be enforced. The Court of Appeal held that the order did not preclude such consideration. It was well established that when it came to enforcing an undertaking as to damages there were two separate points to consider: (i) as a matter of discretion, should the court order that the undertaking be enforced? (ii) if so, what loss had the defendants suffered in terms of money, was it caused by the order and was it too remote? Per Beldam LJ:

> "[T]he question is whether on the construction of the agreed order ... the parties must be taken to have agreed that the court on the enquiry as to damages should only be concerned with the second question ... namely, the amount of the damages, or whether the court can enquire into the first question, namely, whether the undertaking should be enforced."

Beldam LJ said that the following factors had to be taken into account:

> "[F]irstly, that the parties had agreed that there would be an enquiry before a judge in the terms of the undertaking and the conventional order which was made. Secondly, the proceedings were unusual because the injunction was originally obtained pursuant to s.25 of the Civil Jurisdiction and Judgments Act 1982, when it was not expected by the parties that there would be proceedings in this jurisdiction ... There was, therefore, no action or proceeding in this country in which a judge trying the case would

[83] *Balkanbank v Taher (No.2)* [1995] 1 W.L.R. 1056. The first instance decision is reported at [1994] 4 All E.R. 239. See also *Cornhill Insurance Plc v Barclay* [1992] 10 WLUK 64, CA, noted at para.6-05.

> be in a position to consider the matters bearing on the exercise of the discretion whether to enforce the undertaking. Thirdly ... the words of the undertaking and the order 'which the [claimant] ought to pay' are capable of including the exercise by the court of its discretion."

Beldam LJ said further that, in the absence of any specific reference to the question of discretion in the correspondence leading up to the agreed order or on the occasion when the judge was asked to make that agreed order, "the terms of the order are wide enough to and do in fact include both questions".

IMPLIED TERMS

General

In addition to problems caused by imprecise or ambiguous drafting, parties may omit to include in their agreement a term which is necessary to render it effectual or complete. In these circumstances the court will be prepared to imply such term or terms as may be necessary to render the agreement effective[84] or complete[85] in the manner in which the parties are presumed to have intended.[86] The court cannot, however, rewrite the parties' agreement, a principle sometimes overlooked by those contending for the existence of an implied term. **5-42**

Implications as to time

Unless an agreement expressly provides that an obligation is to be fulfilled within a specified time or can be construed as such,[87] a term will be implied that the obligation must be fulfilled within a reasonable time.[88] What is a reasonable time depends on the circumstances.[89] **5-43**

Consistent with the approach referred to above,[90] where parties agree to an order or judgment they will be taken to have submitted themselves to the usual rules and jurisdiction associated with such an order or judgment unless they have agreed otherwise. If they have agreed otherwise, that will ordinarily be apparent from the terms of the order or judgment agreed. Where there is no agreement to the contrary reflected in the judgment or order itself (or no rule within the CPR makes provision to the contrary), a consent order or judgment for the payment of a sum of money (including costs) must be complied with within 14 days of its date.[91] A consent order requiring an act (other than the payment of money) to be performed must specify the time within which the act is to be performed.[92] Under the previous rules[93] a judgment entered in default of compliance with an order of this nature which did not specify a time for compliance would be set aside, the original order **5-44**

---

84 *The Moorcock* (1889) 14 P.D. 64.

85 *Liverpool City Council v Irwin* [1977] A.C. 239.

86 *Chitty*, Vol.1, para.14-06 onwards. And see *Marks & Spencer Plc v BNP Paribas Securities Services Trust Co (Jersey) Ltd* [2015] UKSC 72; [2016] A.C. 742; *Ali v Petroleum Company of Trinidad and Tobago* [2017] UKPC 2; [2017] I.C.R. 531 at [5].

87 As in *Board v Hoey* [1948] W.N. 448; (1949) 65 T.L.R. 43.

88 *Chitty*, Vol.1, para.21-021. See, e.g. *Shears* (1973) CAT 288, noted at para.3-23.

89 *Chitty*, Vol.1, para.21-021.

90 See para.5-36 onwards.

91 CPR r.40.11.

92 CPR PD 40B para.8.1.

93 RSC Ord.42 r.2; CCR Ord.22 r.3.

being treated as a nullity since it was incapable of enforcement.[94] Under the CPR a failure to comply with a rule or practice direction "does not invalidate any step taken in the proceedings unless the court so orders".[95] The practice in relation to the enforcement of mandatory orders under the CPR has not changed from that prevailing under the former rules.[96] If the antecedent agreement failed to contain an express term as to the time for performance of the obligation to be set out in the consent order, the court would imply an obligation to perform the obligation within a reasonable time[97] and alter the order accordingly upon application. If the antecedent agreement did contain an express provision concerning the time for compliance, but the subsequent consent order failed to reflect this, the order could be amended under CPR r.40.12.[98] However, until the order was thus modified it would be incapable of enforcement.

"Permission to apply"[99] omitted

5-45 Parties may, when drawing up the order designed to embody and give effect to their agreement, omit inadvertently the words "permission to apply". The incorporation of these words into the order enables the court to make further orders for the purpose of working out the order.[100] If the parties omit the expression, would the court imply it and entertain an application as if it had been expressly reserved? In cases of orders not made by consent which are not of a final character and which may require further orders for their working out, it is clear that the words will be implied[101] and permission given, if appropriate, to amend the order under the "slip rule".[102] There would seem no reason in principle why the same should not apply to consent orders of a similar character.

5-46 The implication of such a provision, in the circumstances indicated, should not be confused with the question of whether the expression might be implied where the parties agree to stay proceedings between them upon agreed terms, but omit to provide for it in relation to the enforcement of those terms.[103] It is clear that if the stay imposed consensually is absolute and unqualified (i.e. without the addition of words "save for the purposes of enforcing the agreed terms") and no "permission to apply" is reserved, the court will not imply such provision into the order.[104] If, however, the stay is qualified in the sense indicated, but the words "permission to apply for the purpose of enforcing the terms" are omitted, would the court imply them? On the basis of the approach discussed in the preceding paragraph, there is no reason in principle why it should not. It would merely involve the addition of a

---

94 *Hitachi Sales (UK) Ltd v Mitsui Osk Lines Ltd* [1986] 2 Lloyd's Rep. 574 CA.

95 CPR r.3.10.

96 *The White Book* 2019 Vol.1 (Thomson Reuters) at para.40.11.1 maintains the applicability of *Hitachi Sales (UK) Ltd* [1986] 2 Lloyd's Rep. 574 where CPR PDB para.8.1 applies as authority for the proposition that an order made without a date requires rectification by way of a further order.

97 See para.5-43.

98 See *Bristol-Myers Squibb Co v Baker Norton Pharmaceuticals Inc* [2001] EWCA Civ 414, *Markos v Goodfellow (No.2)*[2002] EWCA Civ 1542; (2002) 146 S.J.L.B. 231.

99 In pre-CPR terminology the expression was "liberty to apply".

100 *Cristel v Cristel* [1951] 2 K.B. 725; *Potts v Potts* (1976) 6 Fam. Law 217 CA. It does not enable the court to vary or alter the original order.

101 *Penrice v Williams* (1883) 23 Ch. D. 353 at 356–357, explaining *Fritz v Hobson* (1880) 14 Ch. D. 542.

102 CPR r.40.12; *Websdell v Jenkins* (1902) 46 S.J. 484.

103 See para.9-18 onwards.

104 *Hearn, Re* (1913) 108 L.T. 452 and 737 CA; *E.F. Phillips Ltd v Clarke* [1970] Ch. 322. But see *Atkinson v Castan, The Times,* 17 April 1991, considered at para.11-30 onwards.

term to the agreement reflected in the consent order which is necessary to render it effectual or complete.[105]

No implication of consent order or judgment

The mere fact that a compromise has been reached whilst proceedings are pending will not, without more, result in a consent order or judgment being made to give effect to the agreement. A term to the effect that an order should be made will not be implied[106]; express provision to this effect will be required.[107] It follows that merely because a judge is told that terms have been agreed, those terms will not necessarily be incorporated in an order or judgment.[108] **5-47**

Implied term pending agreed order?

Assuming that a compromise contains an express term to the effect that an appropriate consent order or judgment will be made in due course, will the court use an implied term to bridge the gap between the time when the compromise is concluded and the making of the order? The problem, which has already been highlighted to some extent[109] may be illustrated by a simple example: **5-48**

> A and B agree in correspondence that B will compromise A's claim for damages for personal injuries by payment to A of the sum of £25,000 inclusive of costs. It is stipulated by A and agreed by B (and thus a condition of the compromise) that a consent judgment in A's favour for £25,000, with no order as to costs, should be entered. What happens if A or B repents of this bargain before the judgment is entered?

If the agreement were construed merely as an agreement to agree, i.e. to agree to the judgment being entered in the proposed form on the day when the application for judgment is to be made, then it would not be binding and either party could change his mind before judgment is entered.[110] However, this would be an unmeritorious position to take. **5-49**

The situation is readily met by regarding the agreement as immediately binding upon both A and B, one of the terms being that A will in due course accept in his favour a judgment for £25,000 and that B will consent to it being entered against him. By supporting this express term with an implied term to the effect that both parties will co-operate in securing the agreed judgment (or, conversely, that neither will prevent its realisation), each would be protected from the consequences of an attempted withdrawal from the agreement by the other. If A evinced an intention not to accept the judgment in due course, or refused to do so, and attempted to **5-50**

---

105 See para.5-42.

106 *McCallum v Country Residences Ltd* [1965] 1 W.L.R. 657 CA. The making of a consent order or judgment is not necessary to render an agreement of compromise effectual since means of enforcement (pursuant to a fresh action) exist to enable such an agreement to be effective. For the same reason it could not be said that such an agreement was incomplete. There may, however, be situations in which the express terms of the agreement so clearly contemplated the making of an order or judgment (even though not expressly saying so) that "it goes without saying" that this was intended: cf. *Chitty*, Vol.1, para.13-008. In this sense and in this kind of situation it is submitted that the court might "imply" a term to the relevant effect.

107 *Graves v Graves* (1893) 69 L.T. 420. And see Ch.11.

108 *Green v Rozen* [1955] 1 W.L.R. 741.

109 See para.3-58 onwards.

110 See para.3-58 onwards.

proceed with his claim, B could set up the agreement as a defence if he so chose or he could apply to stay the proceedings.[111]

5-51 If B failed to consent to the judgment, or evinced an intention not to do so in due course, the question of A's remedy arises. There would be little doubt that he could sue upon the agreement in a fresh action and obtain judgment[112] or, in the circumstances, treat himself as discharged from his obligations under the agreement and pursue his original claim.[113] If he wished to hold B to the bargain struck, the commencement of a fresh action, with the associated additional costs and delay, would not be an attractive course. Would it be possible for him to invite the court to enter judgment in his favour, either by consent or otherwise, without taking this unappealing course of action?

5-52 Although there is little direct authority on the issue of whether an implied term of the nature referred to above would be held to exist in the type of situation described, the general law would support it[114] as would the analogous situation disclosed by a case such as *Smallman v Smallman*.[115] Furthermore, in *Hargrave v Hargrave*,[116] Lord Langdale MR, dealing with an argument to the effect that a compromise which provided that its terms should, if necessary, be made a rule of court,[117] was not binding if it were not made a rule of court, said this: "It is unnecessary that such an agreement should ripen into an order of court before it can be made available."

5-53 If, therefore, such a term is to be implied, does the court have jurisdiction to enter judgment in A's favour on the basis of the prior agreement even though B is no longer a consenting party to it? On one view of the decision of the Court of Appeal in *McCallum v Country Residences Ltd*[118] the answer would appear to be "no". However, closer analysis[119] and subsequent dicta in another case[120] suggest that this is not a correct reading of that decision.

5-54 In *McCallum v Country Residences Ltd*, C, a student architect, claimed damages and other relief against D, a property development company. D denied C's claim and counterclaimed for damages for defective work. Attempts were made to resolve the dispute in correspondence. The first offer made on D's behalf was for £400 plus C's costs to date. The offers were gradually increased over the ensuing months to £900, with no specific reference to costs save on one occasion when D's solicitors said that if the particular offer (£800) was not accepted, they had instructions to pay that sum into court forthwith. C's solicitors, when replying to the final offer of £900 made by D's solicitors, indicated that it was "of course, accepted on the understanding that [D] will pay the costs incurred to date". They also drew attention to the fact that, as C was legally aided, an order for legal aid taxation would be needed. They said that they would,

> "issue a formal summons before the Official Referee that terms of settlement have been arrived at so that we can obtain the necessary order".

---

111 See Ch.11. Where the parties agreed to a compromise which was "to be recorded in a suitably worded agreement", that was not a condition of the agreement, but an expression of the wishes of the parties that there be a formal record of what had been agreed: *Newbury v Sun Microsystems* [2013] EWHC 2180 (QB); [2013] C.I.L.L. 3425. See para.3-56.

112 See Ch.11.

113 See Ch.8. Since the obtaining of a judgment was a condition imposed by A, the failure to satisfy this condition would give A this right if he accepted B's repudiation.

114 *Chitty*, Vol.1, paras 14-012 and 14-013.

115 *Smallman* [1972] Fam. 25, discussed at para.3-61.

116 *Hargrave* (1850) 12 Beav. 408 at 413.

117 See para.9-08.

118 *McCallum* [1965] 1 W.L.R. 657.

119 See para.5-57 onwards.

120 *Howard & Wyndham v Healthworks UK* [1989] 8 WLUK 78; [1990] 4 CL 376 per O'Connor and Stocker LJJ. See para.5-56.

They asked for D's cheque in settlement. The cheque was not forthcoming and D's solicitors made further complaints about C's work. C's solicitors took the line that the matter had been settled and, in due course, issued a summons seeking an order in Tomlin form staying the proceeding upon terms that D was to pay C £900 plus his taxed costs, with a legal aid taxation of C's costs. Apart from acknowledging service of the summons, D's solicitors said nothing further on the matter. When the matter came before the court, D's representative did not feel able to consent to the making of the Tomlin order (saying that he was not happy about the position on costs and that the compromise was not fully agreed or concluded). The official referee nevertheless made the order, considering that there had been an agreement to settle at £900 plus costs. The Court of Appeal (Danckwerts LJ dissenting) held that the official referee had no jurisdiction to make the order. The majority (Lord Denning MR and Winn LJ) took the view, on the correspondence, that whilst a concluded compromise had been achieved in the sum of £900 plus costs, there had been no agreement, express or implied, that a Tomlin order should be made.[121] There had been a simple compromise which gave rise to a new cause of action and which required a new action for the purposes of enforcement:

> "In the absence of a consent to the order, as distinct from a consent to the agreement, I do not think the Court has jurisdiction to make an order ... Of course, if there could have been found a consent to the order being made, it would have been a different matter.[122]"

5-55 On the facts of *McCallum* no consent to the making of the Tomlin order was forthcoming on the day the court was invited to make such an order. Equally, the view of the majority was that there was no agreement at the time the compromise was concluded that such an order represented the means by which the compromise was to be implemented. To that extent the case does not address directly the issue presently under consideration. However, the case has been said to support the proposition that no order can be made in favour of an applicant in the category to which A in the example above[123] belongs where B reneges upon the agreement. This proposition has been rejected.

5-56 In *Howard of Wyndham v Healthworks UK*,[124] solicitors for C and D entered into written and oral negotiations with a view to resolving certain proceedings and did indeed reach agreement. The primary issue for the court was whether agreement had been reached on a certain date or on a subsequent date. If the conclusion had been that the agreement had been achieved on the subsequent date, then the agreement would have included a provision that a Tomlin order would be made in the form prepared by one of the solicitors. By the time the Tomlin order was sought from the court, D was unwilling to give his consent. It was argued on his behalf that, following *McCallum*, there was no jurisdiction to make the order. The Court of Appeal held that the agreement had in fact been concluded at the earlier of the two possible times and that, accordingly, the question did not arise. However, it was said that, had the agreement been reached at that later stage, with the provision for the Tomlin order included, there would have been "a term of that agreement that a Tomlin order should be made, and that the necessary consent was present". The court would have had jurisdiction to make such an order. It was said that where parties agree that terms of settlement are to be embodied in a Tomlin order,

> "it is not open, when one party seeks to get the order registered[125] by the Court for the purposes of enforcement, to a party who has previously consented to go back on his consent".

---

121 Danckwerts LJ construed the correspondence as a final agreement to pay £900 plus costs, together with an implied agreement that the action should be brought to an end in the cheapest and quickest way, namely by a summons in the Tomlin form.

122 *McCallum* [1965] 1 W.L.R. 657 at 660.

123 See para.5-48.

124 *Howard & Wyndham v Healthworks UK* [1989] 8 WLUK 78; [1990] 4 CL 376.

125 Although the word "registered" was used in O'Connor LJ's judgment, it appears that this carries no

5-57 In the foregoing case, *McCallum* was explained on the basis that,

> "the Court cannot have been satisfied that there was a true consent as to the cost part of the order and this lack of consent was manifested by the hesitancy of [D's representative] to consent to the costs order".

It is indeed clear that in *McCallum* no consent was forthcoming on D's behalf to the order sought on C's behalf and, furthermore, that the costs aspect was what lay at the root of D's unwillingness to agree to the order or even to accept that an agreement had been reached. However, all members of the court in *McCallum*[126] proceeded on the basis that a concluded agreement including the costs aspect had been reached. Some other explanation, therefore, is required for the conclusion that there was no jurisdiction to make the Tomlin order in that case. The explanation would appear to be that the majority was unable to find that there was, as part of the compromise itself, any term that a Tomlin order should be made. Danckwerts LJ had been prepared to find an implied agreement to this effect[127] and it seems clear that Winn LJ would have been prepared to regard the court as having jurisdiction to make such an order if he had felt that the compromise could have been construed as Danckwerts LJ had construed it.[128] Lord Denning MR said that the position would have been different "if there could have been found a consent to the order being made".[129]

5-58 On this basis it would seem that a court would have jurisdiction to make an appropriate consent order giving effect to a previously concluded compromise notwithstanding the lack of formal consent to the making of the order by one of the parties, provided there was an express or implied term in that agreement that the order should be made. The court would find the consent to the order or judgment *in the original agreement*, a consent which, having regard to the implied term as to co-operation referred to previously,[130] is to be regarded as irrevocable. Any residual doubt there may be about the juridical basis for this approach can be dispelled by consideration of the following: using the example that gave rise to this discussion,[131] B was agreeing at the time of the compromise to consent to a judgment for £25,000 in the extant action. It would make a nonsense of that agreement

---

further significance than the word "made".

126 *McCallum* [1965] 1 W.L.R. 657, per Lord Denning MR at 660, per Danckwerts LJ at 662 and per Winn LJ at 662.

127 See fn.121.

128 *McCallum* [1965] 1 W.L.R. 657 at 663.

129 See fn.122. In *Atkinson v Castan, The Times,* 17 April 1991, considered in detail at para.11-30, Staughton LJ said that in *McCallum* [1965] 1 W.L.R. 657 the court "by a majority held that the correspondence did not reveal an agreement to an order in Tomlin form".

130 See para.5-50. In *Cook v Cook* (1984) 14 Fam. Law 121, W had agreed in a deed of separation made prior to the institution of divorce proceedings that she would transfer her interest in the matrimonial home to H in return for £5,000 whereupon all her claims for financial provision would be dismissed. She received the £5,000 pursuant to the agreement and then instituted divorce proceedings as agreed. After dissolution of the marriage she gave notice of her claims for financial provision, submitting that the deed was void and that the court should not approve the agreement it reflected. At first instance her claims were rejected and an order dismissing them, including periodical payments, was made. (Note: this case was before s.25A of the Matrimonial Causes Act 1973 came into effect and was heard when the law was that a periodical payments claim could only be dismissed by consent.) On appeal W argued that the court should not have dismissed her periodical payments claim because she had resiled from the previous agreement. The Court of Appeal held that W's consent to the dismissal of the claim could be found *in the deed* and that there was, therefore, jurisdiction to make the order.

131 See para.5-48.

if B could resile from that position and argue that A should commence a fresh action to secure his (A's) rights under the agreement.[132]

Although each of the two cases considered above concerned the proposed making of a Tomlin order, no practical or logical distinction could be drawn between agreements contemplating that form of consent order and any other form of order: the legal analysis of a compromise that includes provision for the making of any form of consent order or judgment must be the same. **5-59**

If, of course, the agreement was construed as conditional in the sense that, until judgment is entered, there is no binding agreement, the position would be different.[133]

Costs

Whilst a court will always deal with the question of costs in contested proceedings, it is, of course, something for the parties to resolve by agreement if they settle those proceedings. If they do not mention it at all in their negotiations or their agreement, the only conclusion would seem to be that each side must bear its own costs. It is not necessary, in order to give efficacy to the agreement, for the court to imply a term relating to costs.[134] **5-60**

In *Somerset v Ley*,[135] disputed proceedings concerning a will were compromised and the court approved the settlement on behalf of an infant respondent. The proceedings were conducted in chambers, leading counsel having been briefed on behalf of several of the parties. The consent order embodying the compromise, although making provision for C's costs to be taxed and paid out of T's residuary estate, did not make express provision for the payment of leading counsel's fees, something required by the relevant Costs Rules in relation to proceedings in chambers. Cross J (as he then was) held that a provision that the fees of leading counsel were to be met could not be implied into the terms of settlement. **5-61**

If the matter of costs has been raised in negotiations and remains outstanding there may well be no concluded agreement.[136] An offer (which was accepted) to pay "reasonable costs" in a personal injuries claim was held to mean "costs to be taxed if not agreed".[137] **5-62**

---

[132] In *Atkinson v Castan*, the Court of Appeal held that where parties agree that their agreement should be (and is) set out in full in the recitals to a consent order, that of itself gives the court power to make orders in aid of the enforcement of the agreement in the existing action rather than requiring the institution of a fresh action. This case is considered fully at para.11-30 onwards.

[133] See para.3-58.

[134] On the court's approach where parties to a compromise cannot agree costs, see para.9-03 onwards.

[135] *Somerset v Levy* [1964] 1 W.L.R. 640.

[136] *Yorweth v Sonnyplaster* (1973) CAT 255 noted at para.3-50.

[137] *Zaniewski v Scales* (1969) 113 S.J. 525. See also *Gannon v Chubb Fire Ltd* [1996] P.I.Q.R. P108 CA.

CHAPTER 6

Effects of a Compromise

EFFECTS AS BETWEEN THE PARTIES

End of dispute

An unimpeached compromise represents the end of the dispute or disputes from which it arose.[1] Any issues of fact or law that may have formed the subject matter of the original dispute are buried beneath the surface of the compromise.[2] The court will not permit them to be raised afresh in the context of a new action.[3] If the parties have agreed that their original dispute may be resurrected in certain circumstances then, of course, the position may be different.[4] The principle has been neatly stated judicially on a number of occasions: **6-01**

In *Plumley v Horrell*,[5] Lord Romilly MR said this:

> "Prima facie everybody would suppose that a compromise means that the question is not to be tried over again. That is the first meaning of compromise. When I compromise a law suit with my adversary, I mean that the question is not to be tried over again."

In *Knowles v Roberts*,[6] Bowen LJ expressed the position thus:

> "As soon as you have ended a dispute by a compromise you have disposed of it."

This principle applies whether or not litigation was commenced in relation to the dispute[7] and, if it was, whether or not the compromise has been embodied in a consent order or judgment of the court.[8] The foundation of the principle lies in two aspects of public policy: the need for there to be an end to disputation[9] and the desirability of parties being held to their bargains. Where parties compromise without embodying their agreement in a court order or judgment, the latter aspect dominates the picture. Where the compromise is embodied in a judgment or order, both aspects **6-02**

---

1 This sentence was cited with approval in *Prudential Assurance Co Ltd v McBains Cooper* [2000] 1 W.L.R. 2000 at 2005 CA per Brooke LJ with whom Peter Gibson and Robert Walker LJJ agreed. See also *Gay Choon Ing v Loh Sze Ti Terence Peter* [2009] 2 SLR(R) 332 (CA), *Schindler Lifts (Hong Kong) Ltd v Nikko Services Ltd* [2013] HKCA 678 (Lam V-P) and *Chun Yue Benjamin v Fok Chun Wan Ian and others* [2014] HKCFI 2 (Poon J).

2 See *Ovlas SA v Strand (London) Ltd* [2009] EWHC 1564 (Ch).

3 See paras 1-02 and 2-16.

4 See para.8-02 onwards.

5 *Plumley v Horrell* (1869) 20 L.T. 473 noted at para.3-60.

6 *Knowles v Roberts* (1888) 38 Ch. D. 263 at 272.

7 *Cook v Wright* (1861) 1 B. & S. 559, *Knowles* (1888) 38 Ch. D. 263.

8 *Dixon v Evans* (1872) L.R. 5 H.L. 606, *Holsworthy UDC v Holsworthy RDC* [1907] 2 Ch. 62.

9 *Interest reipublicae ut sit finis litium.* See per Lord Diplock in *Thrasyvoulou v Secretary of State for the Environment* [1990] 2 A.C. 273 at 289.

are present, the former finding particular expression in the doctrine of res judicata.[10] This doctrine applies to a judgment or order notwithstanding that it is made pursuant to an agreement between the parties.[11] However, the nature and content of the agreement of compromise will be of particular relevance to the application of the doctrine in this context, both in its narrow and its wider sense.[12]

The consequences of an attempt by one party to ignore the existence of a compromise (whether or not embodied in an order or judgment) will be considered in due course.[13]

Identifying the disputes resolved[14]

6-03 An important aspect of the whole subject of compromise is the need, which may arise subsequent to the making of a compromise, for a court to identify precisely the disputes that have been settled.[15] The end result contemplated by this process of identification is the same whether the court is considering a compromise embodied in a consent order or judgment or one which is not. There may, of course, be differences in the materials which the court will have available and be prepared to examine for this purpose in each case. There may also be a possible distinction between the two situations regarding the effect of the parties apparently neglecting to compromise a matter which could and should have been raised in their dispute.[16]

Where there is no consent order or judgment

6-04 Where a compromise is effected other than by a consent order or judgment, the court will have a variety of materials to examine: first and foremost, of course, will be the agreement itself, whether comprised in some formal document or merely the one or two communications which crystallised (or evidenced) the agreement.[17] Indeed, if the agreement was oral, the precise words used on the material occasion must be examined. However, an agreement's phraseology may not always yield the answer to the question in hand. As observed previously,[18] in the normal course of events the parties' negotiations are inadmissible as an aid to construction of an agreement. However, they are relevant and admissible to assist in resolving any ambiguity of phraseology in the agreement or to identify the disputes the parties intended to resolve.[19] It is axiomatic that the analysis of these materials is an objective one, the subjective intentions of each party being irrelevant. An objective analysis of the "factual matrix" that formed the background to the compromise is required to enable the disputes settled to be identified.[20]

---

10 For the full expression, see Ch.1, fn.7.

11 *South American and Mexican Co Ex p. Bank of England, Re* [1895] 1 Ch. 37 CA (and see Ch. 36 fn. 41).*Kinch v Walcott* [1929] A.C. 482 PC.

12 See para.6-07 onwards.

13 See Ch.8.

14 Paragraphs 6-03, 6-04 and 6-06 were cited with approval in *Dattani* [1998] I.R.L.R. 240 at 243–244 CA.

15 See Ch.5.

16 See para.6-07 onwards.

17 See Ch.3.

18 See Ch.5, para.5-06 onwards.

19 An example of this approach is afforded by the case of *Capon v Evans* [1986] 4 WLUK 41; [1987] C.L.Y. 413 noted at paras 3-24 and 3-25, where the issue was whether both insured and uninsured losses arising from an accident had been compromised.

20 See para.5-03 onwards. See also *Reardon Smith Line v Hansen-Tangen* [1976] 1 W.L.R. 989 HL,

Where there is an agreed order or judgment

The same issue can arise where a consent order or judgment is agreed designed to reflect the compromise of the disputes between the parties. In the normal course of events, a consent order or judgment must be construed, as with the agreement it embodies, without direct evidence of the parties' intentions, although evidence of "surrounding circumstances" may be admissible.[21] The consent order itself may furnish evidence of the dispute or disputes it resolves.[22] Sometimes the parties will have drawn up a formal agreement which, it was proposed, should be effectuated by the order. Reference to that agreement may be made to determine the extent of the disputes compromised.[23] If not, then the materials referred to in the preceding paragraph will be analysed. **6-05**

In *Cornhill Insurance Plc v Barclay*,[24] C obtained an ex parte *Mareva* injunction against D1, D2 and D3 and gave the usual undertaking in damages. All defendants sought an order discharging the injunction on the basis that there was no evidence to support the suggestion that there was a risk that they would dissipate their assets. After the application had progressed for a while agreement was reached upon the basis that a sum of money (£1.3 million) be placed in an account in the joint names of the parties' solicitors, whereupon the *Mareva* injunction against D1 and D2 would be discharged. The injunction against D3 (a limited company) was agreed to continue with the proviso that it could continue to discharge its legitimate business expenses. A consent order was drawn up reflecting this, but making no express reference to the undertakings as to damages in the original *Mareva* order. Subsequently D1 sought to enforce the undertaking as to damages against C, contending that the consent order had not resulted in a discharge of that undertaking. The Court of Appeal held that the consent order, when construed in the light of the surround-

---

Prenn v Simmonds [1971] 1 W.L.R. 1381 HL. And see *Knowles* (1888) 38 Ch. D. 263. In *Cornhill Insurance Plc v Barclay* [1992] 10 WLUK 64, CA, noted at para.6-05, Beldam LJ said that "[the] scope of an agreement of compromise by parties to proceedings before the Court is to be sought from its construction according to the principles used to determine the meaning of any other agreement. The intention of the parties is to be gathered from the terms of the agreement and such of the surrounding circumstances as may properly be called in aid". Stuart-Smith LJ stated: "It is common ground that in construing the consent order which embodied the agreement reached between the parties the Court must have regard to the surrounding circumstances in which the agreement was reached which includes 'evidence as to the nature of the disputes compromised by the order': Plowman J in *General Accident Fire and Life Assurance Corporation v I.R.C.* [1963] 1 W.L.R. 421, 431."

21 *General Accident Fire and Life Assurance Corp v IRC* [1963] 1 W.L.R. 421 and 1207.

22 *River Ribble Joint Committee v Croston UDC* [1897] 1 Q.B. 251; *Smith v Smith* (1974) 5 Fam. Law 125 CA.

23 *Cloutte v Storey* [1911] 1 Ch. 18 (the deed of agreement referred to questions "now in dispute" between the parties and the eventual court order confirming the compromise was construed as so referring), referred to without disapproval by Lord Bingham of Cornhill in *Ali* [2002] 1 A.C. 251 at [14]. In *Cloutte v Storey* Farwell LJ (with whom Cozens-Hardy MR and Fletcher Moulton LJ agreed) said at 34 that, "[it] is not in accordance with principle or authority to construe deeds of compromise of ascertained specific questions so as to deprive any party thereto of any right not then in dispute and not in contemplation by any of the parties to such deed".

24 *Cornhill Insurance Plc v Barclay* [1992] 10 WLUK 64, CA. cf. *Balkanbank v Taher (No.2)* [1995] 1 W.L.R. 1056. In *Line Trust Corp Ltd v Fielding* [1999] 7 WLUK 549, CA, an issue arose as to whether a release in the schedule to a Tomlin order by which all parties released "all claims which they or any of them have or may have against each other in respect of the subject matter of this action or arising out of these proceedings" embraced claims for secret profit against certain defendants. The Tomlin order had been made on 6 October 1992 embodying a settlement reached in a substantial action in which those defendants had also been defendants. On 5 October 1992 a contribution notice was served upon one of those defendants in which a claim for secret profit had been intimated. The Court of Appeal treated the contribution notice as part of the factual background against which the Tomlin order was made and held that, objectively construed, the release was intended to embrace a compromise of the claim in respect of the secret profit given that it was a claim which arose "in respect of" the subject matter of the earlier action.

ing circumstances, was intended to compromise all matters arising from the grant of the injunction and the application to set it aside. Stuart-Smith LJ stated:

> "The effect of the compromise was that in consideration of [C] abandoning such right as it had to an injunction until trial, the defendants agreed to abandon such rights as they had to apply for a discharge and to pay £1.3m into a joint account. The abandonment of such rights necessarily involved the abandonment of the contentions of fact upon which they were based."

6-06 Whilst it is extremely unlikely to arise in practice now, there have been occasions in the past when a consent order or judgment has appeared almost, as it were, out of the blue with the most insubstantial evidence of its background. Should this situation arise then, unless by inference from such evidence as there may be, the court can determine the disputes compromised, it would appear that all matters between the parties, except the terms of the actual judgment or order itself, are at large.[25]

MATTERS LEFT OUT[26]

6-07 Not infrequently the analysis of the appropriate materials will disclose that the parties expressly or by necessary implication compromised certain matters of dispute but not others. In some cases it will be clear that certain matters were expressly or by implication not made part of the compromise.[27] However, there may be cases where, on any objective view, the parties could and should have dealt with a particular matter but neglected to do so. To what extent will they be permitted by the court to litigate that matter on some future occasion?

6-08 There is, at least in principle, a distinction between a compromise of a dispute achieved before the commencement of proceedings and one achieved thereafter. In the former situation (which will be governed solely by the law of contract), unless the court can imply a term that a particular matter was compromised, the agreement as construed must stand: the court will not rewrite the parties' bargain. It may

---

25 cf. *Goucher v Clayton* (1865) 13 W.R. 336, where in an action for the infringement of a patent D submitted to judgment against him and it appeared from the record that the validity of the patent had been not put in issue. It was held in a subsequent proceedings by C against D for a fresh infringement that D was not estopped from contesting the validity of the patent.

26 The analysis contained in this paragraph in the 4th edition (and which is substantially repeated here) was adopted with approval in *Dattani* [1998] I.R.L.R. 240 at 243 CA. However, that analysis must now be read in the light of *Johnson v Gore Wood & Co (A Firm)* [2002] 2 A.C. 1 HL, referred to in para.6-12 onwards, in which the House of Lords made it clear that the *Henderson v Henderson* principle could apply even though the first action resulted "in a compromise and not a judgment" (per Lord Bingham of Cornhill at 32). See also per Lord Millett at 59. In that case the proceedings in the first action were compromised by means of a written settlement agreement during the sixth week of the trial. It is not clear what order of the court, if any, was made. Usually, in this kind of situation, an order staying all further proceedings is made. However, it is not thought that the formal manner in which the proceedings are terminated is relevant. What is important is that there should have been proceedings which ultimately ended in a settlement. It follows that the alternative ground for the decision in *Dattani*, discussed at para.5-15, namely that the "decision" of the industrial tribunal was not a true decision, nor was it an order or judgment, to which the doctrine of res judicata applied, cannot now be regarded as the correct basis for rejecting the argument that C was precluded from pursuing his claim.

27 For example *Worman v Worman* (1889) 43 Ch. D. 296 (where an issue as to the impropriety of an investment was left out of account at the time of an earlier compromise). And see *Smith v Smith* (1974) 5 Fam. Law 125 CA, noted at para.2-03.

be possible for the agreement to be effective without the matter in question having been embraced within it.[28]

Where, however, proceedings have been commenced and a settlement is achieved thereafter, what has traditionally been regarded as an extension of the doctrine of res judicata may operate to prevent the matter being litigated in a second action.[29] The principle applied is often referred to as the rule in *Henderson v Henderson*. In that case Sir James Wigram VC said this[30]: **6-09**

> "[W]here a given matter becomes the subject of litigation in, and adjudication by, a court of competent jurisdiction, the court requires the parties to that litigation to bring forward their whole case, and will not (except under special circumstances) permit the same parties to open the same subject of litigation in respect of matter which might have been brought forward as part of the subject in contest, but which was not brought forward, only because they have, from negligence, inadvertence, or even accident, omitted part of their case. The plea of res judicata applies, except in special cases, not only to points upon which the court was actually required by the parties to form an opinion and pronounce a judgment, but to every point which properly belonged to the subject of litigation, and which the parties exercising reasonable diligence, might have brought forward at the time." **6-10**

In *Greenhalgh v Mallard*,[31] it was said: **6-11**

> "[R]es judicata for this purpose is not confined to the issues which the court is actually asked to decide, but ... it covers issues or facts which are so clearly part of the subject matter of the litigation and so clearly could have been raised that it would be an abuse of the process of the court to allow a new proceeding to be started in respect of them."

These statements and subsequent expositions of the rule in *Henderson v Henderson* were reviewed by the House of Lords in *Johnson v Gore Wood & Co (A Firm)*,[32] a case in which the previous proceedings had resulted in a compromise. Before considering the facts of the case[33] the contemporary approach to the rule should be noted. Lord Bingham of Cornhill[34] said this: **6-12**

> "It may very well be ... that what is now taken to be the rule in *Henderson v Henderson* has diverged from the ruling which Wigram V-C made, which was addressed to res judicata. But *Henderson v Henderson* abuse of process, as now understood, although separate and distinct from cause of action estoppel and issue estoppel, has much in common with them. The underlying public interest is the same: that there should be finality in litigation and that a party should not be twice vexed in the same matter. This public interest is reinforced by the current emphasis on efficiency and economy in the conduct of litigation, in the interests of the parties and the public as a whole. The bringing of a claim or the raising of a defence in later proceedings may, without more, amount to abuse if the court is satisfied (the onus being on the party alleging abuse) that the claim or defence should have been raised in the earlier proceedings if it was to be raised at all. I would not accept that it is necessary, before abuse may be found, to identify any additional element such as a collateral attack on a previous decision or some dishonesty, but where those elements are present the later proceedings will be much more obviously

---

28 See para.5-42 onwards.

29 See para.9-43 for an example where res judicata was held not to apply.

30 *Henderson v Henderson* (1843) 3 Hare 100 at 115.

31 *Greenhalgh v Mallard* [1947] 2 All E.R. 255 at 257. See also *Yat Tung Investment Co v Dao Heng Bank* [1975] A.C. 581 PC. cf. *Lawlor v Gray* [1984] 3 All E.R. 345. And see *Arnold v National Westminster Bank Plc* [1991] 2 A.C. 93 HL.

32 *Johnson v Gore Wood & Co (A Firm)* [2002] 2 A.C. 1 HL.

33 See para.6-17.

34 *Johnson* [2002] 2 A.C. 1 at 30–31.

abusive, and there will rarely be a finding of abuse unless the later proceeding involves what the court regards as unjust harassment of a party. It is, however, wrong to hold that because a matter could have been raised in earlier proceedings it should have been, so as to render the raising of it in later proceedings necessarily abusive. That is to adopt too dogmatic an approach to what should in my opinion be a broad, merits-based judgment which takes account of the public and private interests involved and also takes account of all the facts of the case, focusing attention on the crucial question whether, in all the circumstances, a party is misusing or abusing the process of the court by seeking to raise before it the issue which could have been raised before. As one cannot comprehensively list all possible forms of abuse, so one cannot formulate any hard and fast rule to determine whether, on given facts, abuse is to be found or not. Thus while I would accept that lack of funds would not ordinarily excuse a failure to raise in earlier proceedings an issue which could and should have been raised then, I would not regard it as necessarily irrelevant, particularly if it appears that the lack of funds has been caused by the party against whom it is sought to claim. While the result may often be the same, it is in my view preferable to ask whether in all the circumstances a party's conduct is an abuse than to ask whether the conduct is an abuse and then, if it is, to ask whether the abuse is excused or justified by special circumstances. Properly applied, and whatever the legitimacy of its descent, the rule has in my view a valuable part to play in protecting the interests of justice."

6-13 Lord Millett put the matter thus[35]:

"It is one thing to refuse to allow a party to relitigate a question which has already been decided; it is quite another to deny him the opportunity of litigating for the first time a question which has not previously been adjudicated upon. This latter (though not the former) is prima facie a denial of the citizen's right of access to the court conferred by the common law and guaranteed by article 6 of the Convention for the Protection of Human Rights and Fundamental Freedoms (1953). While, therefore, the doctrine of res judicata in all its branches may properly be regarded as a rule of substantive law, applicable in all save exceptional circumstances, the doctrine now under consideration can be no more than a procedural rule based on the need to protect the process of the court from abuse and the defendant from oppression."

6-14 As already indicated,[36] the House of Lords made it clear that the principle embodied in the rule in *Henderson v Henderson* could be applied where the first action concluded in a settlement. Lord Bingham of Cornhill put the considerations in this context as follows[37]:

"An important purpose of the rule is to protect a defendant against the harassment necessarily involved in repeated actions concerning the same subject matter. A second action is not the less harassing because the defendant has been driven or thought it prudent to settle the first; often, indeed, that outcome would make a second action the more harassing."

6-15 Lord Millett, having said that the principle was capable of applying where the first action was settled, said this[38]:

"Here it is necessary to protect the integrity of the settlement and to prevent the defendant from being misled into believing that he was achieving a complete settlement of the matter in dispute when an unsuspected part remained outstanding."

6-16 The rule in *Henderson v Henderson* was traditionally identified as having ap-

---

35 *Johnson* [2002] 2 A.C. 1 at 59.
36 See fn.25.
37 *Johnson* [2002] 2 A.C. 1 at 32–33.
38 *Johnson* [2002] 2 A.C. 1 at 59.

plication where a matter or issue "could and should" have been raised in the earlier litigation.[39] Where the settlement of such an action did not expressly deal with the matter that ought to have been raised, the argument in the second action was to the effect that the party then seeking to raise it was precluded from doing so.[40] Following *Johnson v Gore Wood & Co (A Firm)* it is clear that that argument may, in some circumstances, still be maintained and may indeed succeed, although "too mechanical an approach" to the argument with little regard to the overall balance of justice is an approach which has been disavowed.[41] However, it is equally clear that where parties expressly agree to exclude from the settlement of the previous action the very matter about which complaint is made when it is raised in subsequent proceedings, the court will be very unlikely to treat those subsequent proceedings as an abuse of the process of the court.

In *Johnson v Gore Wood & Co (A Firm)*,[42] C had conducted a property development business through a company, W Ltd. W Ltd was C's corporate embodiment. D was a firm of solicitors retained by C to act on W Ltd's behalf in connection with the proposed purchase of a piece of land for development purposes. D was also retained to act for and advise C in his personal capacity.[43] The property deal broke down and W Ltd commenced proceedings for professional negligence against D in January 1991. Those proceedings came to trial in 1992. In addition to the claim of W Ltd, C maintained that he had a personal claim against D arising from its alleged professional negligence. That claim was not brought at the same time or in the same proceedings as that brought by W Ltd, but it had been intimated on C's behalf at a very early stage in those proceedings when it was said that it would be pursued "in due course". In December 1991 C obtained a legal aid certificate to bring the personal claim. This was notified to D whose insurers, without admission, invited C's solicitors to give full details of the quantum of the claim. This was done. On the eve of the trial of W Ltd's claim, C's solicitors wrote to D's solicitors indicating that his personal claim would be pursued whether W Ltd's claim culminated in a judgment or settlement. The trial of W Ltd's claim began in October 1992 and was still proceeding in November 1992 when discussions took place about the possibility of an overall settlement embracing W Ltd's claim and C's claim. At a meeting on 1 December 1992, agreement was reached that C's claim would be capped at £250,000 exclusive of interest and costs, but that it was to be regarded as a separate claim. On December 2 W Ltd's claim was compromised by means of a settlement agreement which contained terms: (a) which capped C's personal claim as previously agreed; and (b) maintained confidentiality in relation to the agreement except "[in] connection with any action which [C] may bring against [D]". C issued a writ against D in April 1993 in respect of his personal claim. When those proceedings were well-advanced D indicated that it was proposing to apply to strike out the claim as an abuse of the process of the court. In relation to the argument that the rule in *Henderson v Henderson* should lead to C's claim being struck out, the House of Lords held unanimously that this should not be so. The parties to the settlement of W Ltd's action (in reality C and D) had proceeded on the basis of an underlying assumption that a further proceeding by C would not be an abuse of process. The settlement agreement itself contained terms which only made sense on the assumption that C was likely to make a personal claim. It would be unjust to permit D to resile from that assumption. **6-17**

---

39 See, e.g. the approach of the Court of Appeal in *Johnson* [2002] 2 A.C. 1 referred to at [81] in the opinions of the House of Lords.

40 An argument to this effect was advanced in *Worman v Worman* (1889) 43 Ch. D. 296, but on the facts was held not to apply. See also *Talbot v Berkshire CC* [1994] Q.B. 290.

41 *Johnson* [2002] 2 A.C. 1 at 34. See *Henley v Bloom* [2010] EWCA Civ 202; [2010] 1 W.L.R. 1770 where a claim for damages for disrepair brought by a former tenant against his former landlord was deliberately held back at the time of negotiating a possession order, but was held to be an abuse in new proceedings.

42 See fn.41. See also *Perry v Day* [2004] EWHC 1398 (Ch); [2005] B.C.C. 375.

43 Since the proceedings, which led to the arguments in the House of Lords, were in the nature of a strike out application this fact was assumed for the purposes of the argument.

Other effects of a compromise

6-18 The principal effect in law of an unimpeached compromise has been stated.[44] Not only does it represent, in general terms, finality so far as the original dispute is concerned, it represents a new situation giving rise to new causes of action.[45] The practical and procedural aspects of particular methods of compromise will be considered in due course.[46] A number of ancillary effects of compromise must not be overlooked and can conveniently be summarised here. Some arise directly because of the existence of a consent order or judgment; others arise in the context of the compromise remaining entirely contractual, no consent order or judgment having been made.

Deriving from consent order or judgment

6-19 Those matters which arise from the existence of a consent order or judgment can be summarised as follows:

Fresh proceedings to set aside[47]

6-20 A judgment or order by consent is binding until set aside.[48] Fresh proceedings must be commenced in order to set aside a final judgment or order by consent.[49] If it appears, before a proposed consent judgment or order has been drawn up or sealed, that a consent has been given against the background of any matter which would vitiate a contract of compromise, that consent may be withdrawn with the permission of the court and the order or judgment set aside.[50] Such an application will be entertained if instituted prior to, or contemporaneously with, the drawing-up or sealing of the order.[51] In matrimonial finance proceedings, if it becomes apparent before a consent order is perfected that the order has been obtained by fraud, it

---

44 See paras 6-01 and 6-02.

45 *McCallum* [1965] 1 W.L.R. 657 at 660.

46 See Chs 9 and 10.

47 For the practice, see Ch.12.

48 *Kinch v Walcott* [1929] A.C. 482 PC, *IRC v Hoogstraten* [1985] Q.B. 1077 CA.

49 *Huddersfield Banking Co v Henry Lister* [1895] 2 Ch. 273, *Wilding v Sanderson* [1897] 2 Ch. 534, *Ainsworth v Wilding* [1896] 1 Ch. 673, *Page v Page* (1972) CAT 383, *Kennedy v Claude Williams Motors Ltd* (1975) CAT 135, *Kuwait Airways Corp v Iraqi Airways Co (No.2)* [2001] 1 W.L.R. 429 HL. It cannot be set aside on appeal: *Elstein's Affairs, Re* [1945] 1 All E.R. 272. cf. *De Lasala v De Lasala* [1980] A.C. 546. In *Skinner v The Thames Valley and Aldershot Co Ltd* [1995] 7 WLUK 96, CA, C's personal injuries claim against D1 was compromised on the basis that D1 would pay £525,000 and costs. A consent order was entered to that effect. During subsequent discussions as to the costs to be charged by C's solicitors, D1's solicitors considered that they had made a mistake in agreeing to pay costs because it seemed that C's solicitors may have agreed to act for the particular claimant for no charge. D1 sought leave to appeal against the consent order on that basis. In refusing the application for leave to appeal the Court of Appeal held that the only way in which D1 could challenge the agreed order as to costs was by bringing a fresh action.

50 *Holt v Jesse* (1876) 3 Ch. D. 177, *Lewis v Lewis* (1890) 45 Ch. D. 281, *Hickman v Berens* [1895] 2 Ch. 638; *Stewart v Kennedy* (1890) 15 App. Cas. 75, *Neale v Gordon Lennox* [1902] A.C. 465, *Moore v Peachey* (1892) 66 L.T. 198, *Shepherd v Robinson* [1919] 1 K.B. 474, *Dietz* [1969] A.C. 170. See also para.29-18 onwards: "there is long-standing jurisprudence in the United Kingdom establishing that a court may, before entry of a judgment or the drawing of an order has been completed, reconsider the matter and amend its order if thought fit to do so": per Lord Scott of Foscote in *Bundhoo v Mauritius* [2007] 4 WLUK 420, PC (Mauritius).

51 *Shepherd* [1919] 1 K.B. 474, *Marsden v Marsden* [1972] Fam. 280. The cases confirming the jurisdiction of the court to intervene in these circumstances were decided when "perfection" of the order or judgment represented the time when this jurisdiction ceased to be available. The word "perfect" or "perfection" does not now appear in the CPR. Subject to the power of the court to

is established that the court should not go on to perfect the order but should proceed to re-hear the proceedings. This approach should be followed unless the court concludes that the innocent party was aware of the actual position before the consent order was entered into or that a reasonable person would not have been influenced by the fraud.[52]

An interim order[53] may be made by consent. Can such an order be set aside? The CPR have not changed the substantive law. It follows that pre-CPR authorities are relevant to the question of the legal status of a consensual interim order. **6-21**

An interim order made by consent may have a true contractual foundation; but equally it may simply reflect an acceptance by the parties that the order made is the correct order to make in the circumstances without the trappings of an underlying contract.[54] It may be necessary for the court to examine the basis of an interim order made by consent to see whether there is a true contractual foundation. It is rare for the parties to utilise the machinery of such an order to conclude a final compromise of their dispute, but there is no reason in principle why they should not do so. If it is plain that the parties did intend to conclude the whole case or, more usually, some issue (for example, liability) by means of an interim order made by consent, then full effect will be given to that contractual foundation underlying the order.[55] When, however, there is no such contractual foundation,[56] or the contractual foundation shows that the parties are expressly submitting themselves to the jurisdiction of the **6-22**

---

dispense with the need to do so, every judgment or order must be "drawn up": CPR r.40.3(1). Every order that is drawn up, including a consent order made pursuant to r.40.6, must be "sealed": CPR rr.40.2, 40.3 and 40.6(2). It is submitted that the jurisdiction of the court to intervene in the circumstances mentioned will certainly exist until the order in question is "drawn up" and probably until it is "sealed": cf. *Stewart v Engel* [2000] 1 W.L.R. 2268. See also *Kirin Amgen Inc v Transkaryotic Therapies Inc* [2002] R.P.C. 2.

52 *Sharland v Sharland* [2015] UKSC 60; [2016] A.C 871 at [37] onwards. See para.24-88.

53 An interim order for this purpose is one that would have been called an "interlocutory order" before the CPR.

54 *Siebe Gorman Ltd v Pneupac Ltd* [1982] 1 W.L.R. 185 CA. Lord Denning MR, with whom Eveleigh and Templeman LJJ agreed, said this at 189: "We have had a discussion about 'consent orders.' It should be clearly understood by the profession that, when an order is expressed to be made 'by consent', it is ambiguous. There are two meanings to the words 'by consent.' That was observed by Lord Greene MR in *Chandless-Chandless v Nicholson* [1942] 2 K.B. 321, 324. One meaning is this: the words 'by consent' may evidence a real contract between the parties. In such a case the court will only interfere with such an order on the same grounds as it would with any other contract. The other meaning is this: the words 'by consent' may mean 'the parties hereto not objecting.' In such a case there is no real contract between the parties. The order can be altered or varied by the court in the same circumstances as any other order that is made by the court without the consent of the parties. In every case it is necessary to discover which meaning is used. Does the order evidence a real contract between the parties? Or does it only evidence an order made without objection?" The continued potential relevance of this distinction was acknowledged in *Pannone LLP v Aardvark Digital Ltd* [2011] EWCA Civ 803; [2011] 1 W.L.R. 2275, where at [27]–[29] the Court of Appeal confirmed that the court has power under CPR rr 3.1(2)(a) and 3.8(1) to extend time for compliance, or grant relief from sanctions where there has been failure to comply, with a procedural obligation contained in a consent order. The order required C to and serve its reply and defence to counterclaim by a certain time on a certain date in default of which the claim would be struck out and D would have permission to enter judgment in full on its counterclaim. See further at fnn.62–66. See also *Sentosa Building Construction Pte Ltd v DJ Builders & Contractors Pte Ltd* [2015] SGHCR 18.

55 *Purcell v FC Trigell* [1971] 1 Q.B. 358. In that case, it was plain from the correspondence prior to the making of the consent order that the defendants were agreeing to their defence on liability being struck out if they failed to answer some interrogatories within a certain period. It was an agreement going to a substantive issue in the case for which consideration was given on each side: see per Winn and Buckley LJJ in particular. And see *Tigner-Roche & Co v Spiro* (1982) 126 S.J. 526 CA; cf. *Greater London Council v Rush and Tompkins* (1984) 128 S.J. 722.

56 For example where the words "by consent" merely evidence an order made without objection: *Siebe Gorman Ltd* [1982] 1 W.L.R. 185, *Chandless-Chandless* [1942] 2 K.B. 321 at 324.

court to intervene further in the proceedings,[57] or that there is no contractual foundation depriving the court of the right to intervene further in the proceedings,[58] the dispute and any relevant issue remains at large.

6-23 Prior to the CPR the courts had always retained somewhat wider powers of interference with what were termed interlocutory consent orders than in the case of final consent orders. This reflected an exercise of the inherent jurisdiction by which the court retained a general control over interlocutory orders notwithstanding that they had been made by consent.[59] The approach manifested itself in various ways. For example, it was held that a mistake "on one side only" may afford grounds for setting aside the order.[60] Alternatively, rather than set aside the order, the court might decline to enforce it on the grounds that it would be inequitable to do so.[61]

6-24 The decision in *Pannone LLP v Aardvark Digital Ltd*[62] has confirmed that the court's powers in this regard have not diminished under the CPR. The question of whether the court has the power under this jurisdiction to vary "a genuine settlement of a substantive dispute as to the parties rights"[63] and, if so, to what extent it may do so remains an issue for resolution at the appellate level.[64] At the very least it is likely that the jurisdiction would be exercised very sparingly[65] given the intention that the CPR were not intended to interfere with the parties' freedom to contract on whatever terms they choose.[66]

---

57 cf. *Chanel Ltd v FW Woolworth & Co* [1981] 1 W.L.R. 485 CA: an agreed order was made incorporating an undertaking by D2 not to do certain things "until judgment ... or until further order in the meantime". On the assumption that the order had a contractual foundation, it was held that the order evidenced the underlying agreement which was itself to the effect that the undertaking should bind D2 until judgment or further order. See also para.5-36 onwards.

58 *Siebe Gorman Ltd* [1982] 1 W.L.R. 185, per Eveleigh and Templeman LJJ.

59 *Purcell* [1971] 1 Q.B. 358, *Burnholme and Forder Ltd v Warley* (1977) CAT 236A, *Greater London Council v Rush and Tomkins* (1984) 128 S.J. 722 CA.

60 *Purcell* [1971] 1 Q.B. 358, per Lord Denning MR, *Mullins v Howell* (1879) 11 Ch. D. 763 at 766, *Brister v Brister* [1970] 1 W.L.R. 664.

61 The view Buckley LJ took in *Purcell* [1971] 1 Q.B. 358, of what was done in *Mullins* (1879) 11 Ch. D. 763. There must be evidence to show that it would be inequitable for the order to stand before the court will interfere: *Basaran v Nevar Investments Ltd* (1979) CAT 181.

62 See fn.54. As followed by the Court of Appeal in *Safin (Fursecroft) Ltd v Badrig's Estate* [2015] EWCA Civ 739; [2016] L. & T.R. 11 at [42] onwards, which explained that the power to vary consent orders under the CPR applied to both types of such order identified under the RSC by the Court of Appeal in *Siebe Gorman & Co Ltd v Pneupac Ltd* [1982] 1 W.L.R. 185, i.e. both case management consent orders and consent orders that deal with the substantive issues in a dispute.

63 *Pannone LLP* at para.27.

64 In *Weston v Dayman* [2006] EWCA Civ 1165; [2008] 1 BCLC 250, the Court of Appeal assumed without deciding that the court had such a power, but declined to exercise it, noting that "a bargain freely made should be upheld: see para.25.

65 *Pannone LLP* at para.27 where the following was said: "Assuming that there is a power so to do, where the settlement is embodied in an order of the court, it can rarely be appropriate for the court to intervene further than to the extent to which the contract can, by its own terms or pursuant to general contractual principles, be modified or discharged in the light of changed circumstances." See also *Beacon v Service Insurance Co Ltd* [2014] EWHC 2435 (QB).

66 See, e.g. para.14-03. See also para.4-21. In *Ropac Ltd v Inntrepreneur Pub Co (CPC) Ltd* [2001] C.P. Rep. 51, Neuberger J, appears to have concluded that an agreed "unless order" providing that T should be ordered to deliver up possession of premises to L unless a sum of money was paid to L by a specified date (time being expressly made of the essence), which he concluded was a "consent order of a binding nature", was, in principle, capable of being modified by the court in the sense of extending the time for compliance by T of the obligation to pay the sum of money. Having so decided (it appears), he decided not to extend the time for compliance. The transcript of the judgment is not entirely satisfactory and the case was complicated by the intervention of the jurisdiction to grant T relief from forfeiture notwithstanding the order for possession. The decision was not disapproved

Appeals

Virtually every appeal from a court order now requires permission to appeal.[67] It follows that a proposed appeal against the making of any consent order or judgment also requires permission to appeal.[68] The grounds of any appeal from a final consent order or judgment would doubtless be subjected to particularly close scrutiny. **6-25**

A consent order or judgment with implications for other parties

A consent order or judgment may have legal and practical implications for parties other than those to whom strictly it applies. Those parties may or may not have been introduced into the proceedings by the time the consent order or judgment is made. **6-26**

Since, in general terms, the rules (statutory or otherwise) governing orders or judgments made by the court following contested proceedings apply to those made by consent, parties who agree to an order or judgment are generally taken to have accepted that the normal rules applicable to such an order or judgment will apply.[69] If those rules have implications for other parties, generally those implications will also apply in relation to a consent order or judgment. **6-27**

That approach may not, however, be of universal application. For example, the Civil Liability (Contribution) Act 1978 provides that in relation to a claim for debt or damage a judgment against one person liable in respect of the debt or damage, **6-28**

> "shall not be a bar to an action, or to the continuance of an action, against any other person who is (apart from any such bar) jointly liable with him in respect of the same debt or damage".[70]

It might be thought that if A and B settle a claim by A for debt or damage in respect of which B and C are jointly liable expressly on the basis that a judgment against B is entered, they are to be taken to be recognising and agreeing that A's right to claim against C may proceed (subject to any sanction in costs that might be imposed upon A if more than one action is brought to establish C's liability if this could have been achieved in one action).[71] However, it has been held that this is not necessarily so.

In *Morris v Wentworth-Stanley*,[72] C contracted to carry out work on land farmed in partnership by D1, his brother and his brother's wife, D2. D2 took no active part in the partnership. In 1991 the brother died and D1 continued the farming business. By September 1992 substantial sums were outstanding in respect of invoices submitted by C for his work. D1 gave notice terminating C's contract which he (C) treated as a repudiation. In July 1992 he, through his company, had commenced an action against the partnership for about £12,000 and interest in respect of work done up to that time. In **6-29**

---

as such by the Court of Appeal in *Pannone LLP* (see paras 29-30), but it was observed that "the consent order there under consideration represented the compromise of a substantive dispute, not an agreed modus vivendi in relation to a case management decision in preparation for trial." The approach taken in *Ropac* was applied by the Court of Appeal in *Safin (Fursecroft) Ltd* [2015] EWCA Civ 739; [2016] L. & T.R. 11. See also *Shah v Chafer* [2018] EWCA Civ 1334 at [13] and *Riordan v Moon Beevor* [2018] EWHC 1452 (QB).

67 CPR r.52.3(1). See *Tanfern Ltd v Cameron-MacDonald* [2000] 1 W.L.R. 1311 at [20]–[22].

68 This was a specific requirement under the RSC Ord.59 r.1B(1)(b).

69 See para.5-36.

70 Civil Liability (Contribution) Act 1978 s.3.

71 Civil Liability (Contribution) Act 1978 s.4.

72 *Morris v Wentworth-Stanley* [1999] Q.B. 1004 CA.

February 1993 he commenced an action against D1, D1's brother and D2 "trading as the Stonards Farm Partnership" for about £48,000 plus interest. D1's solicitors informed C's solicitors that the brother had died and that the partnership with D2 had been dissolved in December 1991. They suggested that to avoid the cost of seeking instructions from the brother's personal representatives and from D2, C might wish to delete the brother's name and D2's name from the writ. C did so and the proceedings continued against D1 "trading as the Stonards Farm Partnership". D1 made a counterclaim on behalf of the partnership alleging breach of contract and negligent advice. During a period when the trial of the consolidated claims was adjourned part heard, a settlement was negotiated against the background of D1 being in financial difficulties. D1 agreed to pay £60,000 (about 75 per cent of the claim inclusive of interest), to abandon his counterclaim and to pay C's costs. The sum of £60,000 was to be paid in two instalments of £30,000 each. A judgment giving effect to this agreement was entered on 13 November 1995. On 28 November 1995 it was indicated on D1's behalf that he could not pay the agreed sums and was contemplating an individual voluntary arrangement under the Insolvency Act 1986. In January 1996 it was agreed that D1's son would pay £45,000 "in full and final settlement of the judgment". It was not suggested on C's behalf to D1 at the time of the original settlement, or to D1 or his son at this stage, that he intended to pursue D2 in respect of the balance of his claim. He did subsequently make such a claim giving credit for the sums received. The Court of Appeal held that, having failed to make any express reservation of the right to proceed against D2 at the time of the original settlement,[73] C's right to pursue a claim against her for the joint liability of the partnership was lost in the accord and satisfaction thus achieved and that s.3 of the Civil Liability (Contribution) Act 1978 did not permit the claim to be brought.[74]

6-30 As will be apparent from the discussion below,[75] the legal principles applicable in the general area of the settlement of cases arising from joint, concurrent and several obligations have been considered by the House of Lords. The principle in *EWA (A Debtor), Re*,[76] which underlay the primary basis for the decision in *Morris v Wentworth-Stanley*, did not fall for review by the House of Lords and, accordingly, the principle remains good law despite being much criticised.[77] If the need in the settlement agreement for an express reservation of the right to pursue the

---

[73] See fn.75.

[74] Although not necessary for the purposes of its decision, the Court of Appeal also held that C's second action amounted to an abuse of the process of the court within the rule in *Henderson v Henderson* (1843) 3 Hare 100 (see para.6-08 onwards). It is at least questionable whether this view of the circumstances in *Morris v Wentworth-Stanley* could survive the restatement of the rule in *Henderson v Henderson* in *Johnson v Gore Wood & Co (A Firm)*. Lord Millett said at 119: "The rule in *Henderson v Henderson* ... cannot sensibly be extended to the case where the defendants are different. There is then no question of double vexation. It may be reasonable and sensible for a plaintiff to proceed against A first, if that is a relatively simple claim, in order to use the proceeds to finance a more complex claim against B. On the other hand, it would I think normally be regarded as oppressive or an abuse of process for a plaintiff to pursue his claims against a single defendant separately in order to use the proceeds of the first action to finance the second, at least where the issues largely overlap so as to form, in Sir James Wigram VC's words ... 'the same subject of litigation'."

[75] See para.6-36 onwards. Until then this area of the law was characterised as "developing": *Cape & Dalgleish v Fitzgerald* [2002] 2 Lloyd's Rep. PN 110, per Simon Brown LJ In *Minton v Kenburgh Investments (Northern) Ltd* [2001] B.C.C. 648 CA, Robert Walker LJ said that it was a "difficult and developing area".

[76] *EWA (A Debtor), Re* [1901] 2 K.B. 642.

[77] The decision was described by Professor Glanville Williams QC as "extraordinary" in *Joint Obligations* (1949). The Law Commission, in its report, *The Law of Contract: Report on Contribution*, Law Com.79 (1977), described the rule as "somewhat technical" and said that "a plaintiff may find that settling with one tortfeasor prevents him from proceeding against the others although this was not what he really intended". The report recorded that the suggestion had been made that "it was time the common law rule on which this doctrine is founded should be abolished". In the event the Law Commission decided not to accede to this proposal (which, it said, "clearly has some force") because

other joint debtor had been disavowed, the whole basis for the decision concerning the effect of the settlement agreement reached would have been undermined. However, the question remains of how objectively to construe an agreement[78] containing a term which appears to sanction proceeding against D2 notwithstanding the settlement with D1 (namely, that a consent judgment should be made in due course to which s.3 of the Civil Liability (Contribution) Act 1978 applies), but which does not contain the express or implied term required by law to permit that course to be taken. The argument that an agreement containing a term that a consent judgment would be made must mean that the consequences provided for by s.3 have been accepted by the parties or, conversely, that unless they have expressly agreed to restrict the effect of the judgment it must have the same effect as one obtained adversely, was described as having "considerable force".[79] It was, however, rejected in the circumstances of the case.

Where a claimant is permitted to,[80] and does, maintain concurrent claims against a number of parties, he must give credit for sums received pursuant to any settlement or settlements reached with some, but not all, of those parties if he pursues to judgment another party (or parties) in respect of those concurrent claims.[81] **6-31**

As already indicated,[82] a judgment in a representative action is binding on all the parties represented, but it cannot be enforced without the court's permission against anyone not a party to the proceedings. **6-32**

It should be noted that an agreed order for possession may be enforceable against all those found on the relevant premises irrespective of whether they were parties to the agreement giving rise to the order.[83] **6-33**

Deriving from compromise with no consequent consent order or judgment

Those ancillary matters that may derive from the existence of a compromise concluded other than by means of a court order or judgment can be summarised thus: **6-34**

---

it had no immediate bearing on rights of contribution with which its report was primarily concerned. The Commission's view, expressed in para.43 of its report, was that the problem was "not so serious as in the case of release by judgment because whereas release by accord and satisfaction involves the satisfaction of the claim, release by judgment operates even where the judgment is unsatisfied". That proposition is, of course, correct where there is satisfaction of the claim following the accord. In *Morris* there was no satisfaction.

78 The decision was given before *Ali* [2002] 1 A.C. 251, discussed at para.5-24. Applying also the test of what the reasonable man, armed with all the relevant facts and considerations, would have said of the settlement, it is at least arguable that he would have said that C was not intending to release any party other than D1 from liability to pay him what was due. See also *Crooks v Newdigate Properties Ltd* [2009] EWCA Civ 283; [2009] C.P. Rep. 34.

79 The identity of leading counsel for the unsuccessful appellant will be noted.

80 See para.6-36 onwards.

81 *Townsend v Stone Toms & Partners* (1984) 27 B.L.R. 26 CA, *Banque Keyser Ullman SA v Skandia (UK) Insurance Co Ltd* [1988] 1 F.T.L.R. 360. See further on the manner in which credit is to be given in such cases, para.6-55 onwards.

82 See para.4-12.

83 *R. v Wandsworth County Court Ex p. Wandsworth LBC* [1975] 1 W.L.R. 1314. See also *Thompson v Elmbridge BC* [1987] 1 W.L.R. 1425 CA, and *Wiltshire CC v Frazer (No.2)* [1986] 1 W.L.R. 109. See Ch.29.

Fresh action to set aside

6-35 Where parties are unable to agree that, for whatever reason,[84] their agreement should be set aside and treated as rescinded, a fresh action instituted for the purpose will be required.[85]

Effects in connection with other parties

6-36 An agreement between a claimant and some, but not all, of the parties to a dispute may have an impact upon: (i) the claimant's right to proceed against the other parties; and (ii) the rights of those other parties to contributions in respect of the sum paid to the claimant in settlement. The general problem can be expressed as determining the extent to which a settlement between A and B in a dispute that also involves (or potentially involves) C precludes (or does not preclude, as the case may be):

(a) a claim by B against C for a contribution to his outlay in the settlement with A;
(b) a further claim directly by A against C in respect of loss or damage said by A to have been sustained as the result of some joint wrongdoing, or some concurrent wrongdoings, by B and C;
(c) if a claim by A against C is not precluded, a claim by C against B for contribution to his (C's) outlay towards A.

6-37 The paying party under a compromise will usually want to know that his liability for any further payment is at an end, though he may wish to preserve a right to claim a contribution to his liability from some other party. The party who has sustained loss or damage may be content to regard his settlement with one party as satisfying his claim fully, or he may wish to regard it as merely partial satisfaction with the opportunity to pursue the balance of his loss from another party. The law has been clarified significantly by the decision of the House of Lords in *Heaton v AXA Equity and Law Life*.[86] It still remains, however, more complex than it should be.[87]

6-38 The rules governing a settlement not embodied in a consent order or judgment are unaffected by the Civil Liability (Contribution) Act 1978. The relevant part of that Act (dealing with claims in respect of debt or damage against a number of parties) applies only to a judgment.[88] It is, nonetheless, the subsequent claim for a contribution (made pursuant to the Act)[89] brought against one or other of the parties to the original settlement by a party pursued for the first time subsequently that frequently brings into focus the scope and effect of the previous settlement.[90]

---

84 See Ch.4.

85 See Ch.12.

86 *Heaton* [2002] 2 A.C. 329. See *Crooks v Newdigate Properties Ltd* [2009] EWCA Civ 283; [2009] C.P. Rep. 34.

87 See, e.g. the comments of Steyn LJ in *Watts v Aldington* [1993] 12 WLUK 197; [1999] L. & T.R. 578, quoted by Auld LJ in *Jameson v Central Electricity Generating Board* [1998] Q.B. 323 at 336–337. See paras 6-42–6-43.

88 Civil Liability (Contribution) Act 1978 s.3. See para.6-28.

89 Civil Liability (Contribution) Act 1978 s.1.

90 See, e.g. *Cape & Dalgleish (A Firm) v Fitzgerald* [2001] Lloyd's Rep. PN 110: D was, until his summary dismissal for gross misconduct (the perpetration of large scale systematic fraud), the managing director of a group of companies, I. I issued proceedings against D, but within days a settlement was agreed whereby D surrendered his 10% holding in the group and each party mutually released each other from any claims. I, on behalf of the members of the group, released D from "any

(i) Concurrent (or successive) contract-breakers and concurrent tortfeasors When a court has to determine whether a further claim, including a contribution claim, has or has not been precluded by a settlement between A and B, its "primary focus of attention" will be upon the "terms of the settlement agreement between A and B ... construed in its appropriate factual context".[91] In *Heaton v Axa Equity and Law Life* Lord Bingham of Cornhill drew together a number of propositions that inform the process by which the postulated agreement between A and B may be interpreted. The case itself was one involving successive contract-breakers in the sense that each was in breach, or allegedly in breach, consecutively of separate contracts, but the statements of principle went beyond purely that situation and dealt also with the position of concurrent tortfeasors.[92] Lord Bingham said this[93]: 6-39

> "In considering whether a sum accepted under a compromise agreement should be taken to fix the full measure of A's loss, so as to preclude action against C in tort in respect of the same damage, and so as to restrict any action against C in contract in respect of the same damage to a claim for nominal damages, the terms of the settlement agreement between A and B must be the primary focus of attention, and the agreement must be construed in its appropriate factual context. In construing it various significant points must in my opinion be borne clearly in mind:
>
> (1) The release of one concurrent tortfeasor does not have the effect in law of releasing another concurrent tortfeasor and the release of one contract-breaker does not have the effect in law of releasing a successive contract-breaker.
> (2) An agreement made between A and B will not affect A's rights against C unless either (a) A agrees to forgo or waive rights which he would otherwise enjoy against C, in which case his agreement is enforceable by B, or (b) the agreement falls within that limited class of contracts which either at common law or by virtue of the Contracts (Rights of Third Parties) Act 1999 is enforceable by C as a third party.
> (3) The use of clear and comprehensive language to preclude the pursuit of claims and cross-claims as between A and B has little bearing on the question whether

and all claims, rights and remedies which it has now or may have in the future, known or unknown ... arising from his employment or office as director with, or as a shareholder of, any of them, or from the matters referred to in the [proceedings], or under the Shareholders' Agreement, or in any other way whatever, and any and all claims for expenses, legal costs or damages, arising from any of the same". Some while later I brought proceedings against its former auditors, C, alleging breach of duty in failing to detect D's frauds. C then issued contribution proceedings against D under the 1978 Act. The Court of Appeal held that I was not precluded by the agreement from pursuing the claim against C.

91 *Heaton* [2002] 2 A.C. 329 at [9], per Lord Bingham of Cornhill. Presumably this means adopting the approach to the construction of a contract as set out in *Investors Compensation Scheme Ltd* [1998] 1 W.L.R. 896 at 912–913, as modified in *BCCI v Ali* [2001] A.C. 251: see para.5-03 onwards.

92 Concurrent (or several) tortfeasors (in contradistinction to joint tortfeasors) commit separate tortious acts which cause or contribute to the same damage: *Clerk & Lindsell on Torts*, 22nd edn (2018), para.4–07 onwards. *Heaton* dealt with the issue of concurrent tortfeasors because the case of *Jameson v Central Electricity Generating Board* [2000] 1 A.C. 455 HL, which had been raised in argument, had been understood by some to indicate that the rule which applies to joint tortfeasors applied also to concurrent tortfeasors: see, e.g. the 5th edn of this work at paras 6-42–6-57.

93 *Heaton* [2002] 2 A.C. 329 at [9]. Where contract breakers can be regarded as successive in the sense that each is (or is allegedly) in breach consecutively of separate contracts, it is possible that the claims made are linked and the losses occasioned by the breaches overlap. Adjustments may have to be made to ensure against double recovery, but subject to that there is nothing to prevent a claimant who has settled with one such contract breaker from proceeding against the others. Indeed, where the damages obtainable against the succeeding contract breakers may only be nominal, there would be nothing wrong in principle for the claimant to proceed in order to obtain a declaration of the court that a breach of contract had been committed provided the pursuit of the action could not be characterised as an abuse of the process of the court.

the agreement represents the full measure of A's loss. The more inadequate the compensation agreed to be paid by B, the greater the need for B to protect himself against any possibility of further action by A to obtain a full measure of redress.

(4) While an express reservation by A of his right to sue C will fortify the inference that A is not treating the sum recovered from B as representing the full measure of his loss, the absence of such a reservation is of lesser and perhaps of no significance, since there is no need for A to reserve a right to do that which A is in the ordinary way fully entitled to do without any such reservation.

(5) If B, on compromising A's claim, wishes to protect himself against any claim against him by C claiming contribution, he may achieve that end either (a) by obtaining an enforceable undertaking by A not to pursue any claim against C relating to the subject matter of the compromise, or (b) by obtaining an indemnity from A against any liability to which B may become subject relating to the subject matter of the compromise."

6-40 The case of *Jameson v Central Electricity Generating Board*[94] must now be seen in the light of the decision and analysis in *Heaton*.

J worked for five years for E. During that time, he was required by E to work at various locations including two power stations owned and occupied by D. During his employment, and during the period he worked at D's power stations, he was subject to exposure to asbestos. In 1987 J developed symptoms of malignant mesothelioma from which he died in April 1988. Before his death he had brought proceedings for damages for personal injuries against E alleging exposure to asbestos at various premises including those of D negligently and in breach of statutory duty. Shortly before his death he accepted £80,000 plus costs from E, the sum being expressed in a Tomlin order to be "in full and final settlement and satisfaction of all causes of action in respect of which [J] claims in the statement of claim". J's claim on the basis of full liability would have been worth approximately £130,000 and the sum of £80,000 was accepted to reflect the risks associated with the possibility of failing to establish liability against E. In April 1989, a year after J's death, the executors of his estate sought to bring proceedings against D seeking damages on behalf of J's widow under the Fatal Accidents Act, the claim being valued at about £142,000. The exposure to asbestos dust relied upon in this action was the same as part of the exposure relied upon in the previous action. The allegations of negligence and breach of statutory duty against D were similar, but not identical, to those previously made against E. D sought to argue that the settlement achieved in the action against E precluded pursuit of the claim against D.

D's argument prevailed in the House of Lords. In *Heaton* Lord Bingham said that, properly understood, the reasoning in *Jameson* was as follows[95]:

"(1) Proof of damage is an essential step in establishing a claim in tortious negligence ...

(2) Such a claim is a claim for unliquidated damages ...

(3) Such a claim is liquidated when either judgment is given for a specific sum or a specific sum is accepted in a compromise ...

(4) A judgment on such a claim will ordinarily be taken to fix the full measure of a claimant's loss ...

(5) A sum accepted in settlement of such a claim may also fix the full measure of a

---

[94] *Jameson* [2000] 1 A.C. 455 HL. There can be no doubt that the tortfeasors in this case were rightly treated as concurrent, nor that the damage which ensued (the terminal illness and subsequent death of Mr Jameson) was the same whichever tort caused it; but it should be noted that the nature of the damages claim in each situation was different. Mr Jameson's personal claim was for damages for personal injuries. The claim brought by his estate on behalf of his wife was for the lost dependency.

[95] *Heaton* [2002] 2 A.C. 329 at [8].

claimant's loss ... whether it does so or not depends on the proper construction of the compromise agreement in its context ...

(6) On the facts of [J's] case, the sum accepted from [E] in settlement was to be taken as representing the full measure of [J's] loss: it followed that [J's] claim in tortious negligence was extinguished and he had no claim which could be pursued against [D]."[96]

(ii) Joint tortfeasors On the law as it stands, it is clear that a release of one joint tortfeasor[97] by way of accord and satisfaction will operate to release all the others.[98] The rationale for the rule is that the cause of action against the joint tortfeasors is "one and indivisible"[99] and that it is extinguished by settlement with one of the tortfeasors. Where a claimant wishes to preserve the possibility of pursuing any of the other joint tortfeasors he must expressly (or impliedly[100]) reserve his right to do so at the time of the settlement. The rule has been subjected to trenchant criticism[101]: **6-41**

"These appeals illustrate the absurdity of the rule that the release of one of two joint and several tortfeasors operates as a release of the other. In Victorian times judges of great distinction reasoned that in a case involving joint and several liability of joint tortfeasors there is only a single cause of action, and accordingly a release of one of two joint tortfeasors extinguishes that single cause of action, or as it was usually put, releases the other joint tortfeasors. The rule has been relaxed by statute. The fact that joint tortfeasors can be sued successively heavily compromised the perceived rule of logic. But the old rule apparently still survives. In truth there is no inexorable march of logic. In a less formalistic age it is now clear that the question whether the release of a joint tortfeasor should operate to release the other tortfeasor is a policy issue. Either solution is logically defensible. But good sense, fairness and respect for the reasonable expectations of contracting parties suggests that the best solution is that the release of a joint tortfeasor should not release the other tortfeasor. On this basis the consequence that the unreleased tortfeasor may bring an action for contribution against the released tortfeasor must be faced. As far as the unreleased tortfeasor is concerned the settlement between the plaintiff and the released tortfeasor is res inter alios acta. If this solution is not perfect, it at least has the merit of promoting more sensible results than any other solution: see Glanville Williams, *Joint* **6-42**

---

[96] See *Vanden Recycling Ltd v Bevin Tumulty* [2017] EWCA Civ 354; [2017] C.P. Rep. 33 at [37]–[51], applying both *Jameson* [2000] 1 A.C. 455 and *Heaton* [2002] 2 A.C. 329. In that case a consent order was in reality a judgment by consent. Payment of the amount of damages fixed in the judgment by one tortfeasor barred further proceedings against other tortfeasors for the same damage. See also *Wright v Barts Health NHS Trust* [2016] EWHC 1834 (QB), Edis J.

[97] The expression being used in the sense that the tortfeasors have committed the same wrongful act for which they are jointly and severally liable for the whole of the damage thus occasioned. See *Crooks v Newdigate Properties Ltd* [2009] EWCA Civ 283; [2009] C.P. Rep. 34.

[98] *Clerk & Lindsell on Torts*, 22nd edn (2018), para.4–10 onwards.

[99] *Duck v Mayeu* [1892] 2 Q.B. 511 at 513, *Apley Estates Co Ltd v De Bernales* [1947] Ch. 217 at 220–221, *Gardiner v Moore* [1969] 1 Q.B. 55. See also *Jameson v Central Electricity Generating Board* [1998] Q.B. 323 at 335.

[100] *Gardiner v Moore* [1969] 1 Q.B. 55.

[101] *Watts* [1993] 12 WLUK 197; [1999] L. & T.R. 578, per Steyn LJ quoted (and agreed with) by Auld LJ in *Jameson v Central Electricity Generating Board* [1998] Q.B. 323 at 336–337. Auld LJ said that the rule as to joint tortfeasors is "in retreat". However, in *Gladman Commercial Properties v Fisher Hargreaves Proctor & Ors* [2013] EWCA Civ 1466; [2014] C.P. Rep. 13, the Court of Appeal was not invited to review the correctness of *Watts*. However, at [39]–[41] the court indicated (per Briggs LJ) why it was not appropriate to imply a reservation in that case given that all the parties to the agreement were legally advised and represented during the settlement negotiations so that they "must reasonably be supposed to have understood the legal consequences of a settlement with some, but not all, joint tortfeasors." Longmore LJ observed at [84] that the established rule is more likely to be a "trap for the unwary" for an unrepresented litigant whereas in a case such as the instant case "in which commercial firms or companies are represented by sophisticated legal teams, that consideration is much less powerful." The case highlights the need for an express reservation of a right to pursue a joint tortfeasor if that is what is sought.

Obligations (1949), pp. 137-138. The absurd consequences of applying the rule of logic invariably led judges, in the best common law tradition, to devise ways of escaping the rigours of its application. The first was the invention of the distinction between an agreement operating as a release of one joint tortfeasor from liability (which resulted in the discharge of the other joint tortfeasor from liability) and an agreement not to sue one joint tortfeasor (which did not involve a discharge of the other). The second technique was the creation of the rule that, even if the agreement operates as a release of one joint tortfeasor, nevertheless the other tortfeasor was not released if the agreement contained a reservation of the plaintiff's rights against the other tortfeasor. In combination these two subsidiary rules, generously interpreted, have ensured that in the majority of cases satisfactory solutions are achieved. But plainly the law is not in a satisfactory state. It is true that a claimant, who engages sophisticated lawyers, can by suitably drafted contractual stipulations avoid the application of the primary rule. But the rule is undoubtedly a trap for the unwary. And for those who are aware of the problem it is a potential disincentive to entering into bona fide and reasonable compromises. The rule requires re-examination, notably in the light of the suspect logic on which it was founded and, in any event, on the basis that the rationale of the rule disappeared once the 'one cause of action' theory was undermined by the statute which authorised successive actions against joint tortfeasors. The point is of considerable importance since it potentially affects a large number of transactions. But it seems to me that binding authority compels me to approach the problem in the traditional way."

6-43 In *Watts v Aldington*,[102] R had been plaintiff in defamation proceedings against A1 and A2. He had succeeded and in November 1989 was awarded £1.5 million against A1 and A2, together with his costs to be taxed if not agreed. R obtained an injunction against both A1 and A2 preventing repetition of the defamatory material. As at the entry of the judgment: (i) R became entitled to enforce the judgment; and (ii) A1 and A2 each became entitled to bring contribution proceedings against the other pursuant to the Civil Liability (Contribution) Act 1978, provided they did so within two years of the judgment. In September 1990, A2 was adjudicated bankrupt upon his own petition. In December 1990, A1 was adjudicated bankrupt on R's petition, relying upon the damages element of the judgment of November 1989. A1 instituted an appeal against this adjudication. Following a finding that A1 had breached the injunction against him, he was ordered to pay R indemnity costs. A1 intimated an intention to appeal against that order for costs and also indicated an intention to apply for leave to appeal out of time against the November 1989 judgment. A1 also, having failed to secure a variation of the terms of the injunction, intimated an intention to appeal against that refusal. Negotiations took place in early 1991 which led to a settlement of all outstanding issues between R and A1. The agreement recited all the orders referred to above, including the judgment of November 1989, and it provided, inter alia, that R would accept a certain sum of money from A1 which he undertook to accept

> "in full and final settlement of the judgment and orders referred to above and any liability howsoever arising before today's date which could involve any payment by [A1] directly or indirectly to [R]".

One of the other terms was that the bankruptcy order against A1 would be annulled. This agreement was implemented. An issue arose subsequently as to whether the agreement had the effect of releasing A2 from his liability under the November 1989 judgment. The Court of Appeal held that it did not. The objective construction of the agreement, having regard to the surrounding circumstances and the express words of the agreement, was that the parties to the agreement were not intending that A2 should be forthwith discharged from all further liability. Neill LJ stated: "The agreement was plainly subject to an implied term that [R's] rights against [A2] would be reserved." Steyn LJ stated: "The implied term is established. It is the equivalent of an express reservation." The court eschewed any attempt to categorise the agreement as a release or discharge, on the one hand, or merely

---

[102] *Watts* [1993] 12 WLUK 197; [1999] L. & T.R. 578.

an agreement not to sue A1 or to enforce the judgment against him, on the other. It was said that the true inquiry was to determine the meaning and effect of the agreement.

This case involved the question of the effect upon the liability of a judgment debtor (who, with his fellow judgment debtor, was jointly and severally liable to the judgment creditor) of a release by the judgment creditor of the other judgment debtor.[103] Its relevance in the present context is to note the antipathy of the Court of Appeal towards the traditional rule relating to joint tortfeasors, the need for its re-examination and the undesirability of extending its ambit. **6-44**

(iii) Joint contractors A compromise by way of an accord and satisfaction between a claimant and one or more of a number of joint, or joint and several, contractors discharges his claim against all. **6-45**

In *Deanplan Ltd v Mahmoud*,[104] L demised factory premises to T for 20 years. The lease contained the normal covenant for the payment of rent and the usual qualified covenant against assignment, with a proviso that every assignment should contain a covenant by the assignee directly with L to observe and perform the covenants and conditions of the lease. Some two years after the original lease was granted T (with L's consent) assigned the lease to D2, a company, which duly entered into the required covenant with L. Some 12 years later, and with L's agreement, D2 assigned the residue of the term to D1. D1 entered into direct covenants with L as was required. D1 fell into arrears with the rent and L obtained judgment in the county court for part of the rent owed. In due course the bailiffs took walking possession of the premises. Negotiations between L and D1 resulted in an agreement whereby L accepted certain goods (which in due course it sold) "in full and final settlement of all claims and demands against [D1] under the terms of the lease" and D1's surrender of the lease. L then sought to recover the balance of the rent from D2. HH Judge Paul Baker QC, sitting as a High Court judge, held that L was not entitled to recover the balance from D2. The agreement with D1 operated as a release, by way of accord and satisfaction, of all covenantors undertaking the same obligation. Since there were no words reserving rights against any other parties in the agreement between L and D1, and no surrounding circumstances rebutting the prima facie effect of the agreement, the agreement must take effect accordingly. **6-46**

Judge Baker QC summarised the law in this way[105]: **6-47**

"[A] release of one joint contractor releases the others. There is only one obligation. A release may be under seal or by accord and satisfaction. A covenant not to sue is not a release. It is merely a contract between the creditor and the joint debtor which does not affect the liabilities of the other joint contractors or their rights of contribution or indemnity against their co-contractor. It is a question of the construction of the contract between the creditor and joint debtor in the light of the surrounding circumstances whether the contract amounts to a release or merely a contract not to sue."[106]

This statement must now be read subject to the judgments of the Court of Appeal in *Watts v Aldington* in which the categorisation of the agreement as a release or a contract not to sue was said no longer to be called for.[107] **6-48**

---

[103] See also *Johnson v Davies* [1999] Ch. 117 at 127.

[104] *Deanplan Ltd v Mahmoud* [1993] Ch. 151. See also *Johnson v Davies* [1999] Ch. 117.

[105] *Deanplan* [1993] Ch. 151 at 170.

[106] *Watters v Smith* (1831) 2 B. & Ad. 889, *Nicholson v Revill* (1836) 4 Ad. & E. 675, *EWA (A Debtor), Re* [1901] 2 K.B. 642.

[107] See fn.101.

6-49 **(iv) Contribution claims between defendants and other parties**[108] As has been indicated,[109] it is frequently the case that the subsequent claim for a contribution against the original settling party by a party not a party to the original settlement brings into focus the terms of the original settlement. It is important to note that when one of two or more potential defendants to a claim for damage (whether the allegation is of joint or several liability) makes or agrees to make a payment in bona fide compromise of the claim, he may claim contribution from the others provided "that he would have been liable assuming that the factual basis of the claim against him could be established".[110] That proviso was apparently[111] added during the progress through its Parliamentary stages of the Bill which led to the Civil Liability (Contribution) Act 1978 as a means by which compromises based solely on the possibility of liability under foreign law were to be excluded from the potentiality of a contribution claim. The phraseology is, however, sufficiently wide to exclude compromises based on doubts as to the legal liability of the relevant defendant under English law.

6-50 It is also of significance to note that where the potential defendant to a claim for damage settles with the claimant and the claimant then (as he is entitled to do) commences proceedings against another defendant, that other defendant may seek contribution from the first defendant who has settled.

6-51 In *Logan v Uttlesford DC*,[112] C was employed by D Council and whilst working for it, was struck by a car driven by the third party. The third party settled C's claim for £2,000 before litigation commenced. C subsequently commenced proceedings against D alleging that the accident was caused by its negligence. D denied liability but brought in the third party claiming contribution. The third party applied to strike out the claim for contribution on the basis that, having settled C's claim as against him, D could not claim contribution. The Court of Appeal held that s.1(3) of the Civil Liability (Contribution) Act 1978 gave D a claim against the third party if C could show that D was liable. The section was not to be read as if the following words were added after "since the time when the damage occurred"—otherwise than by a judgment on the merits or by reason of a bona fide settlement.

6-52 The statutory requirement, pursuant to s.1(1) of the 1978 Act, is that any claim for a contribution must relate to "the same damage" as that in respect of which the claimant for the contribution was himself liable. The correct approach to this requirement was considered by the House of Lords in *Royal Brompton NHS Trust v Hammond*.[113] Lord Bingham of Cornhill referred[114] to the proposition,

> "that one important object of the 1978 Act was to widen the classes of person between whom claims for contribution would lie and to enlarge the hitherto restricted category of causes of action capable of giving rise to such a claim".

However, he emphasised that it is

> "a constant theme of the law of contribution from the beginning that B's claim to share with others his liability to A rests upon the fact that they (whether equally with B or not) are subject to a common liability to A".

---

108 See para.6-28 onwards.
109 See para.6-38.
110 Civil Liability (Contribution) Act 1978 s.1(4).
111 See A.M. Dugdale, "The Civil Liability (Contribution) Act 1978" (1979) 42 M.L.R. 182. See also *BRB (Residuary) Ltd v Connex South Eastern Ltd* [2008] 1 W.L.R. 2867 at [11]–[12].
112 *Logan v Uttlesford DC* [1984] 1 WLUK 929; (1984) 134 N.L.J. 500; *The Times*, 21 February 1984.
113 *Royal Brompton NHS Trust v Hammond* [2002] 1 W.L.R. 1397 HL.
114 *Royal Brompton NHS Trust* [2002] 1 W.L.R. 1397 at [5].

He said[115] that the three questions to ask are:

> "(1) What damage has A suffered? (2) Is B liable to A in respect of that damage? (3) Is C also liable to A in respect of that damage or some of it?"

He added the following observation:

> "I do not think it matters greatly whether, in phrasing these questions, one speaks (as the 1978 Act does) of 'damage' or of 'loss' or 'harm', provided it is borne in mind that 'damage' does not mean 'damages' (as pointed out by Roch LJ in *Birse Construction Ltd v Haiste Ltd* [1996] 1 W.L.R 675, 682) and that B's right to contribution by C depends on the damage, loss or harm for which B is liable to A corresponding (even if in part only) with the damage, loss or harm for which C is liable to A. This seems to me to accord with the underlying equity of the situation: it is obviously fair that C contributes to B a fair share of what both B and C owe in law to A, but obviously unfair that C should contribute to B any share of what B may owe in law to A but C does not."

(v) Joint contractor claimants If a claimant is one of a number of joint contractors, a settlement with him by someone liable under the contract would not operate as a discharge of the obligations. However, any subsequent claim[116] for the whole amount of the debt would, in effect, require credit to be given for the amount paid under the settlement[117] assuming that the interests of the claimants are truly joint. **6-53**

(vi) Torts (Interference with Goods) Act 1977 In a claim under the Torts (Interference With Goods) Act 1977 for a wrongful interference with goods, the claimant's title to the goods is extinguished by payment of a sum in compromise of the claim.[118] A settlement between the bailor of a chattel and a party who damaged the chattel in respect of damage thus caused, will bind the bailee of the chattel in respect of any claims arising from the bailment even though the settlement is expressed to be "without prejudice" to the bailee's claim.[119] **6-54**

Financial accounting involving other parties following a settlement

Where a claimant settles a claim against one or other of a number of parties against whom he is maintaining claims, he must generally bring into account the sums achieved from such a settlement if he is entitled to (and does) pursue to judgment any of the remaining parties to the action. In a case where a claimant has concurrent claims against more than one defendant, the whole amount recovered under a settlement with one must be brought into account in any claim against another.[120] However, the question of how sums such as these are to be treated is not always straightforward. **6-55**

---

115 *Royal Brompton NHS Trust* [2002] 1 W.L.R. 1397 at [6].

116 CPR r.19.3, provides that "[where] a claimant claims a remedy to which some other person is jointly entitled with him, all persons jointly entitled to the remedy must be parties unless the court orders otherwise".

117 cf. *Steeds v Steeds* (1899) 22 Q.B.D. 537; *Powell v Brodhurst* [1901] 2 Ch. 160. See further at para.6-70 onwards.

118 Torts (Interference with Goods) Act 1977 s.5.

119 *O'Sullivan v Williams* [1992] 3 All E.R. 385 CA.

120 *Townsend v Stone Toms & Partners* (1984) 27 B.L.R. 26 CA, *Banque Keyser Ullman SA v Skandia (UK) Insurance Co Ltd* [1988] 1 F.T.L.R. 360, Steyn J, *Crooks v Newdigate Properties Ltd* [2009] EWCA Civ 283; [2009] C.P. Rep. 34.

6-56 In *Townsend v Stone Toms & Partners*,[121] C appointed D1 as architects and D2 as building contractors in connection with certain building works, C and D2 in due course becoming parties to a JCT prime cost contract. C was dissatisfied with the quality of the works done and the ultimate cost and commenced proceedings against D1 and D2. The claim against D1 was for damages for defective design, defective supervision (both of D2 and a plumbing contractor) and for over-certification of monies paid to D2. The claims against D2 in contract were for defective work, its failure to rectify that work and a claim for sums allegedly overpaid. There was a substantial degree of overlapping between the claims against D1 and D2 where allegations of defective supervision and defective work were made respectively, on the one hand, and also in respect of overcertification and overpayment, on the other. D2 counterclaimed for a sum that it contended was the balance outstanding under the contract. In due course D2 paid the total sum of £30,000 into court in satisfaction of all the causes of action in respect of which C claimed and after taking into account its counterclaim. C accepted this sum and a consent order was made for the payment out of that sum, together with costs up to a specified date and the dismissal of the counterclaim. At the trial against D1 the judge found that had C pursued his claim against D2 to trial, he would have established a concurrent and co-extensive liability between D2 and D1 of about £25,000. (In C's pleaded case against D2 the amount claimed totalled about £229,000.) Given this finding, taken with the fact that C had already received £30,000 plus costs from D2, the judge decided that C had no further claim against D1 in respect of matters where its liability was concurrent and co-extensive with D2. Judgment was given against D1 for some £8,700 in relation to matters in respect of which there was no concurrent and co-extensive liability with D2. The Court of Appeal held that the judge's approach was correct and rejected suggestions:

(i) that if the £30,000 fell to be taken into account at all, it should only be taken into account at the time of executing the judgment against D1;
(i) that it should be ignored altogether because it was impossible to say how much (if any) of the sum was attributable to claims for which D2 was responsible; and
(i) that if it was to be taken into account at all, it should be attributed to each claim against D1 in the proportion which £30,000 bore to the total amount of the claims brought against D2.

6-57 The judgments are not entirely easy to distil into a series of succinct propositions.[122] It was emphasised that if it should be thought appropriate in any case to seek to apportion an amount received in settlement between the various claims advanced by a claimant, the onus is on the claimant to put forward material in support of the apportionment for which he contends.[123] Where the amount received in settlement resulted from the acceptance of a payment into court, attention was drawn to the opportunity for a claimant to obtain an order of the court under what was then RSC Ord.22 r.1(5), directing the party who made the payment into court to amend the notice to specify "the sum paid in respect of each cause of action".[124] Oliver LJ also made it plain that, even though the task of carrying out such an apportionment "may not be altogether straightforward", it was one

---

[121] See fn.120.

[122] This may arise from the fact that the judge below approached the task in hand largely in the way he had apparently been invited to do on C's behalf, yet that approach was the subject of criticism on C's behalf in the Court of Appeal: see *Townsend* (1984) 27 B.L.R. 26 CA per Oliver LJ at 42. Purchas LJ, at 52, made it clear that the determination of this sort of issue "must depend very much upon the context and the conduct of each individual case" and it would be "unwise for this court to lay down general rules".

[123] See *Townsend* (1984) 27 B.L.R. 26 CA, per Oliver LJ at 41, per Purchas LJ at 51 and 53 and per Waller LJ at 56.

[124] Payments into court under CPR Pt 36 were abolished in 2007. Since then both claimants and defendants may only make Pt 36 offers. See Ch.14.

which had to be attempted on the material available.[125] In carrying out that task, should it arise, Purchas LJ said that the court "must restrict its attention to the effective benefits received by" the claimant.[126] In *Otkritie International Investment Management Ltd v Urumov*,[127] Eder J expressed reservations about an alternative approach suggested by Oliver LJ to that which had been taken by the judge, and which the Court of Appeal had endorsed. Oliver LJ suggested in the light of Lord Denning's judgment in *Bryanston Finance Ltd v de Vries*[128] that a viable alternative would be to have entered judgment for the whole amount of damages, but to then make provision for execution to be for no more than was appropriate having taken account of any amount received by way of settlement.[129] As Eder J put it, while such an alternative was at the least "not unobjectionable" and may in some circumstances be justified,[130]

> "in the ordinary course, ... if relevant recoveries are made prior to judgment they operate to reduce the damage suffered by the claimant and thereby reduce the amount of any judgment that the claimant is entitled to. I accept that this is not necessarily a hard-and-fast rule; ..."

In *Banque Keyser Ullman SA v Skandia (UK) Insurance Co Ltd*,[131] syndicates of banks of which C was a member, succeeded in actions against two insurers of which D was one on the issues of liability and causation, quantum being left for subsequent adjudication save that damages would be in a sum equivalent to the amounts that would have been recoverable under certain insurance policies. At the conclusion of the trial it was ordered, inter alia, that D pay 40 per cent of C's costs. The purpose of the insurance policies had been to provide C with protection in the event of the failure of certain corporate borrowers to repay substantial loans. The insurances had been arranged by brokers, B, who were originally defendants in the proceedings. C's claims against B were settled on the first day of the trial on the basis that B accepted liability in the sum of £10.5 million and this sum was paid on the express basis that it was in full and final settlement of C's claims "including the claims for costs". Under this settlement C received just over £3 million. C and D disagreed about the credit to be given by C for the sum received from B. Of that sum a little over £480,000 represented C's agreed costs of the action against B. C contended that that sum should be deducted from the credit that would otherwise have to be given to D since it had represented an additional separate claim against B. C also contended that the unrecovered costs of its action against D (i.e. the remaining 60 per cent)—some £416,000—should also represent a deduction from the necessary credit on the basis that, had it pursued B to trial, C would have recovered such unrecovered costs from B. Steyn J, as he then was, held that a deduction of the amount of C's agreed costs of the action against B should be made from the credit to be given since it represented a separate and additional claim against B; but that the unrecovered costs of the action against D were not to be deducted since C had not shown that a claim for such costs against B would have been sustainable. Referring to *Townsend*, Steyn J said that the **6-58**

> "principle appeared to be that if a plaintiff who received payment from one of two tortfeasors established an additional separate claim against him, the payment was al-

---

125 *Townsend* (1984) 27 B.L.R. 26 at 41.

126 *Townsend* (1984) 27 B.L.R. 26 at 53.

127 [2014] EWHC 755 (Comm) at [9]-[10].

128 (1975) Q.B. at 703

129 *Townsend* (1984) 27 B.L.R. 26 at 39.

130 *Otkritie International Investment Management Ltd v Urumov* [2014] EWHC 755 (Comm) at [9]-[10].

131 See fn.120. See first instance decision on the merits at *Banque Keyser Ullman* [1990] 1 Q.B. 665. D eventually abandoned its appeal. The other defendant succeeded in the Court of Appeal and House of Lords: [1991] 2 A.C. 249.

located first to that claim, and credit must be given in favour of the second tortfeasor only for the excess necessarily referable to the overlapping claim."

Preservation of Rights Against Other Parties in Partial Settlements of Multi-Party Litigation—Some Illustrations

6-59 Litigation, particularly commercial and construction litigation, has become increasingly complex. The complexity frequently arises from the number of parties that become involved. An all-embracing settlement is often not easy to achieve. Some of the problems that can arise have already been highlighted[132] and others remain to be discussed.[133] The path to the preservation of rights against parties other than those to whom the settlement applies can occasionally be somewhat perilous. Equally, the fact that rights are preserved in certain situations can lead to the appearance, at least, of injustice. Two cases in the field of construction litigation illustrate how problems such as these may arise.

6-60 In *Hydrocarbons Great Britain Ltd v Cammel Laird Shipbuilders and Automotive Products Ltd (t/a AP Precision Hydraulics)*,[134] C took delivery in March 1985 of an accommodation vessel for use in a sea-based gas field. The vessel was a platform with four legs which were lowered to stand on the sea bed, the platform itself being capable of being jacked up above the sea by means of hydraulic jacking units. The vessel was manufactured by D who had subcontracted the design and supply of the jacking units to 3P1. 3P1 employed 4P1 to design, manufacture and supply 24 heavy-duty, double-action hydraulic cylinders for the jacking units and 4P1, in its turn, subcontracted the manufacture and supply of 48 cast steel clevises (which formed part of the hydraulic cylinders) to 4P2. By an agreement between 4P1 and 4P4, 4P4 witnessed the testing of the clevises and issued certificates in respect of them. In April 1986 cracks were discovered in a number of clevises and the accommodation vessel was taken out of service for repair. It did not return to service until March 1987. C sued D, who served a third-party notice on 3P1 claiming an indemnity. 3P1 served fourth-party proceedings on 4P1, who served contribution claims against 4P2 and 4P4. In May 1989 C's claim against D was settled for £5.17 million. In November 1990, 3P1 and 4P1 entered into an agreement which provided, inter alia, as follows:

> "[4P1] admit their liability to [3P1] in the event that [3P1] are held liable to [D] ... to indemnify [3P1] against [D's] claim against [3P1] ... The amount of [4P1's] liability to [3P1] shall be limited to the amount of that sum of money to which [4P1] are or may become entitled under or by virtue of any order or judgment made or entered or any term of any settlement agreement made in the action in [4P1's] name against any other fourth party."

In January 1991 D's claim against 3P1 was settled for £5 million.

At the trial between the remaining parties preliminary issues arose as to whether, by virtue of the above agreement: (a) 4P1 could recover anything but nominal damages from 4P2 and/or 4P4 in respect of its liability to 3P1; or (b) 4P1 could be entitled to recover any indemnity or contribution from 4P2 and/or 4P4 in respect of such liability.

The Court of Appeal held:

(1) On the true construction of the agreement 4P1 admitted its liability to indemnify 3P1 if the latter was held liable to D.
(2) 3P1 was held liable to D for £5 million.

---

132 See para.4-79 onwards (assignment); para.6-26 onwards (contribution proceedings); para.6-55 onwards (financial accounting).

133 See Ch.31.

134 *Hydrocarbons Great Britain Ltd v Cammel Laird Shipbuilders and Automotive Products Ltd* (1991) 53 B.L.R. 84.

(3) The amount of 4P1's loss was, therefore, £5 million, subject to any challenge to the reasonableness of the settlement between D and 3P1.
(4) 4P1's claim against 4P2 and/or 4P4 was for an indemnity in respect of the above loss of £5 million.
(5) By the above agreement 3P1 limited its claim against 4P1 to the sum for which 4P1 might obtain judgment against 4P2 and 4P4.
(6) The answer to each of the questions raised in the preliminary issues was "yes".

In *Wessex Regional Health Authority v HLM Design Ltd*,[135] C engaged D and 3P1 as architects and main contractor respectively in connection with the construction of a hospital. 3P1 engaged S as subcontractor. The contracts between C and 3P1 and 3P1 and S were JCT contracts containing arbitration clauses. The contract overran by 84 weeks at which stage practical completion was certified. D granted 3P1 an extension of time for 74 weeks and agreed to 3P1 giving S an equivalent extension. In July 1989 3P1 began arbitration proceedings against C claiming a further 10 weeks' extension. C counterclaimed, contending that 3P1 was entitled only to a 30-week extension of time and that 44 weeks had been incorrectly granted by D. C also counterclaimed for just under £1 million in respect of defective work. In February 1992, shortly before the arbitration, C and 3P1 settled their disputes upon terms that C paid to 3P1 a further £1.65 million, each side bearing its own costs. The extension of time granted by D was left unchanged. The agreement was incorporated into a consent award.[136] In May 1992 C issued proceedings against D alleging that, as a result of D's breaches of contract and negligence, C had overpaid 3P1 and sought recovery of those sums from D. P contended that those sums included the sums C had agreed to pay 3P1 in the arbitration proceedings which had been settled. D raised the following defences: **6-61**

(i) C's losses arose from the compromise in the arbitration proceedings and that if it was incorrectly made it was C's fault;
(ii) alternatively, C had failed to mitigate its loss;
(iii) C, as employer under a JCT contract, had no independent cause of action against his architect for over-certification save in limited circumstances (for example the contractor's insolvency);
(iv) the arbitration would establish the true contractual entitlement as between employer and contractor.

D brought third-party proceedings against 3P1 seeking, inter alia, a contribution under the Civil Liability (Contribution) Act 1978. In interlocutory proceedings a number of preliminary issues fell for determination, including the question of whether the consent award in the arbitration proceedings precluded D from proceeding. HH Judge Fox-Andrews QC, official referee, held that since C, as employer, had independent, concurrent and unlimited causes of action arising out of certification against both D (as architect) and 3P1 (as main contractor), C's claims were not precluded by the existence of the consent award. Had C and D wished to provide for this it should have been included within their contract. For the same reason, C's proceedings were not an abuse of the process of the court.

135 *Wessex Regional Health Authority v HLM Design Ltd* (1995) 71 B.L.R. 84.
136 See Ch.32.

EFFECTS UPON AND IN CONNECTION WITH THIRD PARTIES

6-62 Some effects of a compromise, upon persons not directly parties to it, have already been considered.[137] Those instances concerned situations where the third party was to some extent a party to the dispute out of which the compromise arose. The discussion hereafter concerns third parties correctly so called: persons or parties concerned neither with the original dispute nor with the process of compromise. The issues may conveniently be discussed in relation to four questions:

(1) How, if at all, may a compromise impose liabilities upon a third party?
(2) How, if at all, may a third party acquire rights under compromise?
(3) What rights, if any, does a third party have to impeach a compromise?
(4) What effects, if any, are felt by a third party who has become interested in the subject of a compromise following its impeachment by one of the parties to it?

Each will be considered separately.

Imposition of liability

6-63 The doctrine of privity of contract[138] generally precludes the imposition of contractual liabilities upon a third party by parties to the contract. This principle is unaffected by the Contracts (Rights of Third Parties) Act 1999 to which reference is made below. There may, of course, be a number of situations where the practical effect of an agreement of compromise between two parties may have an adverse effect upon a third party.[139]

Acquisition of rights

6-64 The same doctrine (privity of contract) has, in general terms, precluded a third party from suing to obtain the benefits which, by their contract, the parties have sought to confer upon him. Notwithstanding the efforts of Lord Denning MR[140] to displace it, the doctrine and its consequences has largely remained intact at common law.[141] However, the Contracts (Rights of Third Parties) Act 1999, in the circumstances in which it applies,[142] makes a substantial inroad into the effects of the doctrine.

6-65 In the normal course of events, the only objects of benefit under a compromise will be the parties themselves. However, there may be circumstances in which a third party may be the person whom they agree to benefit.

A not wholly unlikely example would be afforded where, say, two estranged brothers, A and B, become embroiled in proceedings over the ownership of a motor car. A alleges joint ownership by reason of a contribution to the purchase price; B, in whose name the car is

---

137 See para.6-26 onwards.
138 *Chitty*, Vol.1, paras 18–021–18-022 and 18–139 onwards.
139 See, e.g. para.6-33.
140 *Drive Yourself Hire Co (London) Ltd v Strutt* [1954] 1 Q.B. 250, *Beswick v Beswick* [1966] Ch. 538 CA.
141 *Dunlop Pneumatic Tyre Co Ltd v Selfridge and Co Ltd* [1915] A.C. 847, *Beswick v Beswick* [1968] A.C. 58 HL, *Scruttons Ltd v Midland Silicones Ltd* [1962] A.C. 446. See *Chitty*, Vol.1, para.18–046 onwards. Though see *Linden Gardens Trust v Lenasta Sludge Disposals Ltd* [1994] A.C. 85.
142 See para.6-82 onwards.

registered, alleges sole ownership, saying that any contribution made by A was really a contribution by their mother, she being the source of the funds. They eventually come to an agreement whereby A agrees not to pursue his claim in return for a promise by B to pay the mother £1,000. Could this promise be enforced if B failed to keep it?

The common law doctrine of privity of contract would suggest that the mother, certainly, would have no right to enforce it. Unless the court was prepared to find that A was a trustee of the contractual right in favour of his mother, in which case proceedings could be taken with A and B as defendants,[143] there would appear to be nothing that the mother could do. The concept of the trust of a contractual right, as a device for circumventing the rigours of the doctrine of privity of contract, has met with less and less favour in the courts.[144] **6-66**

The position now[145] would appear to be that if the contract between A and B expressly provided that the mother may enforce the agreement,[146] and that she is expressly identified by name within it,[147] then she may indeed do so "in her own right".[148] **6-67**

Indeed, even if there is no express agreement to the above effect within a contract, but a term "purports to confer a benefit" on a third party, then that party may enforce the contract in his own right unless **6-68**

> "on a proper construction of the contract it appears that the parties did not intend the term to be enforceable by the third party".[149]

The parties to the original contract cannot rescind or vary it without the consent of the third party subject to certain powers of the court to dispense with such consent.[150] Equally, the existence of a term that complies with s.1 of the Act does not affect the right of the promisee to enforce any term in the contract.[151] **6-69**

Although a somewhat homely example was given in para.6-65, there is plainly considerable scope for the effect of the Act to be felt in compromises of all kinds, particularly in the commercial setting. For example, it is possible to envisage circumstances in which it may be utilised to circumvent the problems associated with lifting the veil of incorporation. Parties will need to give careful consideration to the drafting of compromises that mention third parties to ensure either that the Act does apply, if that is what is desired, or that it does not, if it is not the intention. **6-70**

It seems that if two parties compromise their differences, one of the terms being that a third party should not be sued in respect of some matter by one of the parties, the third party can effectively claim the benefit of that term provided the correct procedural steps are taken and all parties are before the court: **6-71**

In *Snelling v John Snelling Ltd*,[152] the facts of which have been given elsewhere,[153] C had sued the company, D1, for the monies outstanding on his loan account. D2 and D3, his **6-72**

---

[143] *Vandepitte v Preferred Accident Insurance Corp of New York* [1933] A.C. 70 at 79.
[144] *Vandepitte* [1933] A.C. 70, *Schebsman, Re* [1944] Ch. 83.
[145] Generally the Act applies to all contracts entered into from 11 May 2000 onwards: Contracts (Rights of Third Parties) Act 1999 s.10(2).
[146] Contracts (Rights of Third Parties) Act 1999 s.1(1)(a).
[147] Contracts (Rights of Third Parties) Act 1999 s.1(3).
[148] Contracts (Rights of Third Parties) Act 1999 s.1(1).
[149] Contracts (Rights of Third Parties) Act 1999 s.1(1)(b) and (2).
[150] Contracts (Rights of Third Parties) Act 1999 s.2.
[151] Contracts (Rights of Third Parties) Act 1999 s.4.
[152] *Snelling* [1973] 1 Q.B. 87.
[153] See para.3-69.

brothers, applied to be joined as defendants to the action, adopted the defence that D1 had put in (pleading the agreement) and counterclaimed for a declaration that the sums which C claimed had been "forfeited" pursuant to the terms of that agreement. Ormrod J (as he then was) held that, although D1 could not rely upon the agreement, not being a party to it, D2 and D3 could and, since all parties were before the court, there was jurisdiction to grant a stay of C's claim. Since, however, the reality was that C's claim failed, an order dismissing it was made.

6-73 Where a third party compromises a claim made by A against B and pays A the agreed sum, the court will intervene to prevent A pursuing B for the full amount.

In *Hirachand Punamchand v Temple*,[154] C were money-lenders carrying on business in India. D borrowed money from them and gave them a promissory note in return. He also borrowed money from them on the security of a bond. When D failed to repay the loans with interest C approached D's father for payment at a time when the statement of account showed the total indebtedness to be Rs 3,600. After certain correspondence D's father sent a banker's draft in C's favour for a sum less than the amount claimed under the promissory note in full settlement of the claim. C took the draft and cashed it, keeping the money. C then pursued D for the balance under the loan. The Court of Appeal held that C could not pursue D for the balance on the basis that the debt was extinguished by the payment by D's father[155]; or that to permit the action would be a fraud on the father or an abuse of the process of the court[156]; or that from the moment of the cashing of the draft C would hold any monies received on the promissory note on trust for D's father and, since it was plain that he did not wish his son to pay anything further under the promissory note, C had no right to pursue the matter.[157]

Impeachment by or on behalf of third parties

6-74 Since, generally, parties cannot by virtue of a compromise impose liabilities upon a third party, a third party can rarely, if ever, have any legitimate interest in its impeachment (or, for that matter, its enforcement). However, since compromises almost invariably involve the payment of money or the disposition of property by one party to the other, the practical effect may be to diminish a fund upon which others may have legitimate claims. In some circumstances the court may intervene at the instance of a third party or on his behalf, usually in the context of bankruptcy or family disputes.

Bankruptcy

6-75 The most important area in which third parties may be interested in a diminishing fund is where a party to a compromise has become bankrupt since effecting the compromise. Such a person may, under the guise of compromising a dispute, deliberately seek to prefer one creditor over the others or simply put out of their reach a fund upon which they have claims. The trustee in bankruptcy is responsible for discovering, realising and distributing the bankrupt's property amongst his credi-

---

154 *Hirachand Punamchand v Temple* [1911] 2 K.B. 330. See also *Barclays Bank Plc v Willowbrook International Ltd, Financial Times,* 9 July 1985 (Walton J). In *Stour Valley Builders v Stuart* [2003] T.C.L.R. 8, Lloyd LJ said that the ratio decidendi in the *Hirachand* case "is not easy to discern". Though see *Morris v Wentworth-Stanley* [1999] Q.B. 1004 at 1018.

155 *Hirachand* [1911] 2 K.B. 330 at 339–340 and 340–341, per Fletcher Moulton and Farwell LJJ, respectively, relying upon *Cook v Lister* (1863) 13 C.B.(N.S.) 543. Vaughan Williams LJ founded his decision upon other grounds, but expressly said that a defence to the claim on this basis "might be set up": at 337–338.

156 *Hirachand* [1911] 2 K.B. 330.

157 See *Hirachand* [1911] 2 K.B. 330, per Vaughan Williams LJ at 337.

tors in accordance with accepted principles. He may seek the court's aid in impeaching such a transaction[158] even though, it seems, it would not otherwise be open to attack.[159] The court's jurisdiction to "look behind" a compromise at the behest of the bankrupt himself or on his behalf will be used sparingly and only in "special circumstances" where the bankrupt was advised on it by his counsel.[160]

The intervention of the court will frequently be invited by the trustee in bankruptcy when a husband, who thereafter becomes bankrupt, has compromised certain disputes with his wife in such a way that all or a substantial part of the matrimonial assets become vested in her or the children. A transfer or settlement of such property made pursuant to a consent order to that effect may still be open to impeachment under s.339 of the Insolvency Act 1986.[161] Such a consent order may be made only in proceedings for divorce or judicial separation. It is, of course, possible for a husband and wife living together amicably, but in the knowledge that the husband may become bankrupt before long, to "compromise" proceedings brought by the wife[162] to determine the extent of her interest in the matrimonial home which is in the husband's sole name. She may have made sufficient contributions to its acquisition, pursuant to an express or implied agreement that she should have a share in its beneficial ownership, to entitle her to an interest.[163] What would be the effect of a consent order declaring her interest to be 99 per cent when a court would not have assessed it at more than, say, 25 per cent? It is submitted, on the basis of the approach set out above,[164] that the court would look behind the agreement to the realities.[165] **6-76**

The same approach would doubtless be adopted in respect of a "compromise" of claims by parties other than spouses to shared ownership of property made in similar circumstances. **6-77**

Family disputes

The estrangement of a family offers a fertile environment for the growth of arrangements whereby assets "disappear", legitimate claims thereby being frustrated. **6-78**

---

158 Insolvency Act 1986 ss.339–342.

159 *Blythe Ex p. Banner, Re* (1881) 17 Ch. D. 480, *Hawkins Ex p. Troup, Re* [1895] 1 Q.B. 404, *Lennox Ex p. Lennox, Re* (1885) 16 Q.B.D. 315 (see particularly, per Cotton LJ). Whether as between parties the compromise would be binding was left open in *Banner*, though in *Hawkins* Lord Esher MR, at 408, indicated that it would be: cf. para.2-19.

160 *A Debtor, Re* [1929] 1 Ch. 123 (some evidence of impropriety or lack of knowledge of facts on the part of counsel necessary), *Gregory Ex p. Norton v Trustee, Re* [1935] Ch. 65. But where a consent order is made by virtue of which W's claim for periodical payments is dismissed and in return she obtains substantially more than that to which she otherwise would have been entitled by way of capital and property provision, she will have given valuable consideration and the transactions may be immune from attack: *Abbott, Re* [1983] Ch. 45. See also *Windle, Re* [1975] 1 W.L.R. 1628 and cf. *Kumar, Re* [1993] 1 W.L.R. 224.

161 Matrimonial Causes Act 1973 s.39. In *Kumar (A Bankrupt), Re* [1993] 1 W.L.R. 224, Ferris J pursuant to s.339 of the Insolvency Act 1986, set aside a disposition by H by deed to W of his interest in the matrimonial home, the transfer being held to have been at an undervalue. A transfer of property order made by consent (or indeed other than by consent) between the date of the presentation of the bankruptcy petition against a husband and the date when the bankruptcy order is made constitutes a "disposition of property" within s.284 of the Insolvency Act 1986 and is, accordingly, void unless made with the consent, or subsequent ratification, of the Bankruptcy Court: *Flint (A Bankrupt), Re* [1993] Ch. 319.

162 Under the Married Women's Property Act 1882 s.17.

163 The interest would be held on resulting or constructive trust by the husband for the wife and so would not form a part of his estate: Insolvency Act 1986 s.283(1) and (3).

164 The authorities referred to in fn.155.

165 cf. *Densham, Re* [1975] 1 W.L.R. 1519.

Claims under the Matrimonial Causes Act 1973 ("the 1973 Act") and the Inheritance (Provision for Family and Dependants) Act 1975 ("the 1975 Act") depend on the existence of assets from which they can be met. Provisions exist under each Act to enable the impeachment or reversal of transactions intended to prevent or frustrate such claims.[166]

6-79 Voluntary transfers of assets are usually caught by these provisions,[167] but transfers for valuable consideration to persons acting in good faith and without notice of the dishonest intention remain inviolate, certainly in proceedings under the 1973 Act[168] and probably[169] under the 1975 Act. A genuine compromise of a dispute, whereby assets upon which such claims might be made are completely or substantially dissipated, would seem to be incapable of challenge by the claimant. But what of a compromise based on a concocted dispute? Or of a compromise of a genuine dispute whereunder the whole of the assets are transferred subject to an "undertaking" about the return of a proportion in due course? Or of a compromise of a genuine dispute in which the party against whom such claims are made is more than necessarily generous to the other party to the dispute?

6-80 In the first and second postulated situations there would be little difficulty in holding that there was no consideration for the compromise or that there was a lack of good faith. But the third situation could present difficulties. It is perhaps best illustrated by an example:

> H, who is old, uninsured and estranged from W, injures a young boy when he negligently drops something from his first-floor window to the street below. Knowing that he (H) has not long to live, he compromises the boy's claim for £100,000, his savings and only capital, when the claim was worth only £1,000. He does this intending to frustrate W's claim although the boy's advisers and representatives do not know this and accept in good faith.

Arguably such a compromise could not be impeached under the 1973 Act[170] but that an order under s.10(2) of the 1975 Act might well be made.

Other situations

6-81 Equity has always retained for itself the jurisdiction to grant relief against the consequences of fraud however it is sought to be covered.[171] A fraudulent dissipation of assets under cover of a compromise could, presumably, be set aside at the instance of a third party injuriously affected.[172]

Effects of impeachment by parties on third parties

6-82 By virtue of a compromise, A receives an item of property from B. A then sells

---

166 1973 Act s.37; 1975 Act s.10.

167 1973 Act s.37(4); 1975 Act s.10(2)(b).

168 1973 Act s.37(4); 1975 Act s.10(2)(b).

169 Under the 1975 Act a disposition made other than for "full valuable consideration" to a donee "may" result in an order that the donee, in effect, repays any money received or restores any property transferred: s.10(2). The court's discretion whether to exercise its powers will take into account "the circumstances in which the disposition was made, ... the relationship ... of the donee to the deceased, the conduct ... of the donee and all the other circumstances of the case": s.10(6).

170 Although, for what it is worth in the circumstances, his conduct in dissipating the assets in this way could be taken into account in W's application for financial relief: *Martin v Martin* [1976] Fam. 335.

171 See Kerr, *Fraud and Mistake*, 7th edn (1952), p.6, quoted in *Cadogan v Cadogan* [1977] 1 W.L.R. 1051 at 1061 CA.

172 cf. *Blenkinsopp v Blenkinsopp* (1852) 1 De G.M. & G. 495.

it to C. If B then discovers the existence of a ground for impeaching the compromise and wishes to do so, what is the legal position?

The answer depends on the effect in law of the ground for impeachment. If its effect is to render the compromise merely voidable (for example, in the case of misrepresentation), the intervention of C's rights will operate to prevent its rescission,[173] provided C acted in good faith.[174] In this case C's position is secure. If, however, the compromise is void (for example, for mistake) A will have acquired no title to pass on to C.[175] **6-83**

It would appear that even if grounds exist for the setting aside of a consent order or judgment, it will not be so set aside, certainly at the joint instance of the parties, if a third party is likely to be prejudiced.[176] Where the original consent judgment sought to be set aside involved a third party, it is incumbent on the applicant to ensure that the third party is joined as a respondent to the application or that their interests are in some way protected.[177] **6-84**

EFFECTS IN CONNECTION WITH ASSIGNMENT

As has already been observed,[178] the parties to a compromise will normally anticipate receiving the benefits from it and indeed performing the obligations under it. Occasionally, however, one party or the other may wish to place another in his shoes for the purpose of carrying it out or receiving the benefits. To what extent can this be done? **6-85**

In general terms a party cannot shift the burdens of a contract onto the shoulders of another without the consent of the other contracting party.[179] If, however, an analysis of the terms of the contract, its subject matter and other material circumstances suggests that the identity of the performer of the obligations is of no particular importance, performance by a substitute will suffice.[180] This is known as vicarious performance: it is not really an example of assignment.[181] Thus, for example, a building dispute might be compromised on terms which provide, inter alia, for the completion by the builder of certain items of work. Depending on the circumstances, vicarious performance by another builder may suffice. **6-86**

At common law the benefit of a contract could not be assigned without the agreement of both contracting parties; in equity, subject to certain exceptions, it could. These exceptions still obtain notwithstanding the existence of the statutory form of assignment under the Law of Property Act 1925[182] and some may be of relevance in the context of compromise. **6-87**

It would appear that parties to a contract may provide expressly that the benefits

---

173 *Babcock v Lawson* (1880) 5 Q.B.D. 284, *L.G. Clarke, Re* [1967] Ch. 1121. And see *Stone v Godfrey* (1854) 5 De G.M. & G. 76.

174 *Scholefield v Templer* (1859) 4 De G.J.E. 429.

175 For example *Cundy v Lindsay* (1878) 3 App. Cas. 459.

176 *The Bellcairn* (1885) 10 P.D. 161, *Hammond v Schofield* [1891] 1 Q.B. 453.

177 *Ranasingham v Cooray* (1978) CAT 302.

178 See para.6-80.

179 *Robson v Drummond* (1831) 2 B. & Ad. 303, *Tolhurst v Associated Portland Cement Manufacturers Ltd* [1902] 2 K.B. 660 CA and [1903] A.C. 414 HL.

180 *Davies v Collins* [1945] 1 All E.R. 247.

181 *Davies* [1945] 1 All E.R. 247 at 249; *Chitty*, Vol.1, para.19–082 onwards.

182 Law of Property Act 1925 s.136. The machinery of assignment is outside the scope of this work: see, e.g. *Chitty*, Vol.1, Ch.19.

arising are not to be assignable.[183] This principle could, if the parties so wished, be extended to a compromise.

6-88 If the identity of a person entitled to the benefit of a contract is material to the person upon whom rests the burden, the benefit will not be assignable. The subjective wishes of the parties are, however, ignored. For example, if A compromises his dispute with B by virtue of which B owes him a sum of money, A will be entitled to assign the right to the money to C even though C intends to use the right to make B bankrupt.[184]

6-89 It is usually said that a "bare right to litigate" is not assignable since such an assignment would savour of maintenance or champerty.[185] That broad statement of principle still appears to be the law although the approach of the House of Lords in *Trendtex Trading Corp v Credit Suisse*[186] has resulted in a less rigid approach to the question.[187] In any event, the broad statement of principle had, prior to that decision, been subject to a number of significant exceptions. For example, a simple debt, which represents in effect merely a right to litigate, is assignable.[188] Thus a debt under a compromise can be assigned. A right to litigate ancillary to a transfer of property can be assigned.[189] Thus rights arising from the compromise of a boundary dispute between owners of adjacent properties would seem to be assignable provided some transfer of property is or may be involved.[190]

6-90 The right of a wife to maintenance is not assignable on the grounds of public policy.[191]

6-91 Superimposed upon the general principles of the law of contract must be the rules governing the assignability or otherwise of consent judgments. It is clear that a judgment debt is assignable,[192] as indeed is a judgment for costs to be assessed if assessed.[193] A mere right to apply for costs is not assignable.[194] Where a part only of a judgment debt is assigned, the assignee will not be able to take enforcement proceedings without joining the assignor: the law permits only of execution in respect of the whole of a judgment debt.[195]

6-92 Assignment of rights and liabilities under a compromise may take place by operation of law on the death of one or other or both of the parties. Whilst not all rights and liabilities can be enforced by the estate,[196] a simple debt can be pursued and a judgment debt can be enforced.

6-93 Equally, by operation of law the trustee in bankruptcy of a bankrupt is the statu-

---

183 cf. *United Dominions Trust Ltd v Parkway Motors* [1955] 1 W.L.R. 719.

184 cf. *Fitzroy v Cave* [1905] 2 K.B. 364. The leading authority on the subject is *Tolhurst v Associated Portland Cement Manufacturers Ltd* [1902] 2 K.B. 660.

185 *Chitty*, para.19–050 onwards.

186 *Trendtex Trading Corp v Credit Suisse* [1982] A.C. 679. See Ch.4, para.4-83, and the case of *Brownton Ltd v Edward Moore Inbucon Ltd* [1985] 3 All E.R. 499.

187 See *Camdex International Ltd v Bank of Zambia (No.1)* [1998] Q.B. 22 CA, and *Zabihi v Janzemini* [2009] EWHC 3471 (Ch).

188 For example *Fitzroy* [1905] 2 K.B. 364.

189 *Dawson v Great Northern and City Railway* [1905] 1 K.B. 260, *Glegg v Bromley* [1912] 3 K.B. 474, *Defries v Milne* [1913] 1 Ch. 98, *Ellis v Torrington* [1920] 1 K.B. 399.

190 See Ch.30 below.

191 *Watkins v Watkins* [1896] P. 222, *Clark v Clark* [1906] P. 331. The principle doubtless applies to all parties capable of pursuing financial relief in family proceedings: see Ch.24.

192 *Goodman v Robinson* (1868) 18 QBD 332, *Harley v Samson* (1914) 30 T.L.R. 450. Whether an assignee of a judgment debt is in an identical position to the original judgment creditor is open to question: *Forster v Baker* [1910] 2 K.B. 636 at 642.

193 *Hambleton v Brown* [1917] 2 K.B. 93.

194 *Marley, Re* [1952] 1 All E.R. 1057, cf. *Brownton Ltd v Edward Moore Inbucon Ltd* [1985] 3 All E.R. 499, discussed at para.4-80.

195 *Forster v Baker*. *Chitty*, Vol.1, para.19–015.

196 *Chitty*, Vol.1, para.20–001 onwards.

tory assignee of his choses in action.[197] The trustee in bankruptcy may reassign the chose in action to the bankrupt.[198]

6-94 The resolution of a dispute by means of a consent judgment of a court outside the United Kingdom is a bar to proceedings on the cause of action thus compromised provided the judgment is enforceable and entitled to recognition in England and Wales (or, where appropriate, Northern Ireland).[199]

---

[197] *Chitty*, Vol.1 para.20–016 onwards.

[198] *Stein v Blake* [1996] 1 A.C. 243 HL.

[199] Civil Jurisdiction and Judgments Act 1982 s.34. For foreign arbitral awards, see Arbitration Act 1950 s.36. See also Ch. 32 and Ch.36.

CHAPTER 7

Satisfaction and Discharge of Obligations Under a Compromise

This chapter is concerned with situations in respect of which it can properly be said that: **7-01**

(a) a party to a compromise has discharged or satisfied his obligations under it; or
(b) circumstances have arisen by virtue of which the law no longer demands performance of those obligations.[1]

PERFORMANCE

The construction of a compromise to determine the extent of the obligations imposed thereunder have already been examined.[2] Once the extent of an obligation has been ascertained, the general principle, subject to the maxim de minimis non curat lex, is that complete and precise performance is essential. The other party will be bound to accept that performance as discharging the performer's obligations under the contract. In the absence of that performance, the other party will be entitled to say that there has been a breach of contract and the consequences of that will need to be addressed.[3] Normally, the nature and extent of the act or acts required to constitute performance of an obligation under a contract of compromise will be clear from the agreement. However, there will be situations in which the nature and extent of the obligations have not been spelt out with clarity and the court will have to decide what was intended. **7-02**

Payment by cheque or credit card

The provision of a cheque in satisfaction of an obligation to pay money under a compromise may raise the question of whether the provision of the cheque itself is a sufficient discharge of the obligation or whether the receipt of cleared funds after presentation for payment of the cheque by the recipient is necessary.[4] Should money be paid by credit or debit card the question will also arise whether acceptance of payment by such a method discharges the obligation.[5] **7-03**

---

1 *Chitty*, Vol.1, Pt 7.
2 See Ch.5.
3 See Ch.8.
4 *Chitty*, Vol.1, para.21–075 onwards.
5 *Chitty*, Vol.1, para.21-084. See *Re Charge Card Services Ltd* [1989] Ch. 497.

Payment by instalments

7-04 A compromise may provide for the satisfaction of an obligation to pay a sum of money by means of instalment payments.[6] In the normal course of events, the parties will have specified what is to happen in the event of less than complete payment of the sequence of instalments.[7] In this situation it will be plain, if it be what was agreed, that full and precise performance of the obligation is required. Where, however, the contract does not provide for what is to happen in the event of less than full payment, the question could arise whether virtually full performance is sufficient. The situation is best illustrated by an example:

> A and B resolve a boundary dispute over a strip of land in respect of which B asserts possessory title by an agreement whereby, upon payment to A by B of the sum of £10,000 by equal monthly instalments, A will execute a deed of conveyance of a specified part of the disputed strip of land to B. Apart from this, the agreement is silent about what should happen if B defaults in the payments. B makes nine of the 10 payments and then defaults.

Despite the apparent injustice to B in having discharged his obligation to the extent of 90%, it is not thought that A would be under any obligation to execute the deed of conveyance. Unless the court was prepared to import into the situation the concept of "substantial performance" of an entire contract[8] or some approach analogous to that provided for in s.31(2) of the Sale of Goods Act 1979 (concerning contracts for the sale of goods by instalments),[9] nothing less than full and precise performance of B's obligation would suffice to trigger the performance of A's obligation.[10]

"Entire" compromise

7-05 If a contract of compromise is construed as "entire", i.e. that performance by one party is conditional upon full performance by the other, the failure by the latter fully to perform will entitle the former to treat himself as discharged from any performance on his part. For example, A and B compromise their differences over certain building work being done by B for A on the terms that A will pay B a sum of money if B completes a hot water system in his (A's) house which C had started but failed to complete.[11] Unless B performs substantially his obligation, i.e. does the work such that any defects and the costs of rectifying them are relatively small, A will not be obliged to pay him the agreed sum and will be regarded as discharged

---

6 See, e.g. *Horizon Technologies International Ltd v Lucky Wealth Consultants Ltd* [1992] 1 W.L.R. 24, PC, noted at para.11–26. See also *Korea Foreign Insurance Co v Omne Re SA* [1999] EWCA Civ 1166; [1999] Lloyd's Rep IR 509, noted at para.8–08.

7 For example that the whole sum becomes due upon default in one payment (as in *Horizon Technologies International Ltd v Lucky Wealth Consultants Ltd* [1992] 1 W.L.R. 24) or that the party to whom the payments are to be made shall be entitled to resort to his original claim (credits to be given for payments received).

8 *Chitty*, Vol.1, para.21–033 onwards. It is thought that this is unlikely in this situation, though cf. para.7–05.

9 Also see, s.26 of the Consumer Rights Act 2015. Benjamin, *Sale of Goods*, 10th edn, para.8–065 onwards, and 14-105. Also see *Chitty*, Vol.1, para.24–046. Again, it is thought that this is unlikely.

10 It is difficult to see how B could secure repayment of the £9,000 paid unless some restitutionary remedy could be relied upon. The question of the title to the disputed strip of land might, at first blush, seem difficult. However, it is submitted that the court would hold that the effect of the compromise was that in consideration of D's promise to convey part of the land to B upon completion of the payments, B gave up his right to assert ownership of the whole of the disputed strip by possessory title: cf. *Cornhill Insurance Plc v Barclay* (1888) 38 Ch. D., noted at para.6–05.

11 cf. *Bolton v Mahadeva* [1972] 1 W.L.R. 1009. See *Chitty*, para.21–034.

from so doing. If B does perform the work substantially he will be entitled to the agreed sum less the cost of rectifying the defects.

Agreement collateral to compromise

It should be noted that a party who complies with an obligation under a contract of compromise, but who fails to honour an agreement collateral to that contract, will still be regarded as having discharged the obligation under the compromise. **7-06**

In *Guy v Walker*,[12] C was a stock and share dealer who was in possession of a certificate of railway stock which D alleged belonged to her. She obtained an interlocutory injunction preventing C from parting with the certificate. C then advanced a claim against D for £1,955 which he alleged to be due in respect of certain dealings in stocks and shares. She disputed the claim, but a compromise was reached and she paid C £1,000 "in full discharge of all claims ... and costs". C thereafter sought to pursue D for the balance of his claim, asserting that he had agreed to accept the reduced sum on the terms of D signing a written retraction of certain charges of fraud which she had made publicly against him, and that she had not carried out that part of the agreement. The Court of Appeal held that C's action should be stayed. If there had been the agreement on the part of D as C alleged, it did not form part of the agreement embodied in the receipt. Any such agreement was a collateral agreement and C could bring an action for damages for breach of it.

Mutually dependent obligations

Just as a failure to fulfil an obligation under a collateral contract will not afford a basis for alleging a breach of the main contract of compromise, the failure to honour an obligation under a compromise which is independent of the performance by the other party of his obligations will not afford grounds for disregarding the agreement. This is a situation which is not likely to arise frequently since, in most cases, obligations under agreements are construed as mutually dependent.[13] **7-07**

DISCHARGE OTHER THAN BY PERFORMANCE

The circumstances in which complete or substantial performance of the obligations under a compromise are no longer expected by law and where the compromise is discharged can be summarised as follows: **7-08**

(a) where the parties enter into a deed of release[14];
(b) where the parties enter into a fresh accord and satisfaction (in effect, a new compromise);
(c) where the parties agree to release each other from performance or further performance under the compromise (i.e. rescission) whether or not a new agreement is made thereafter;
(d) where the parties agree to vary the terms of the compromise;
(e) where waiver or estoppel operate to relieve a party from being obliged to perform an obligation;
(f) where there is an operative frustration of the compromise.

A detailed analysis of each of these situations is unnecessary for the purposes of

---

[12] *Guy v Walker* (1892) 8 T.L.R. 314.
[13] *Chitty*, paras 24-035–24-037.
[14] For the interpretation of releases, see para.5–22 onwards.

this work.[15] The most likely areas for dispute in the context of compromise would be where (e) and (f) arguably arise. The essential features of each should be noted although the following resumé is not intended to be exhaustive.

7-09 Waiver occurs where a party to an agreement leads the other party to believe that he will not insist on his strict entitlement to treat the agreement as repudiated.[16] It disentitles the party forbearing from going back on his promise and insisting on his strict rights under the agreement.

7-10 Estoppel is not dissimilar to waiver but usually arises without an express request for forbearance when one party, by his words or conduct, induces the other to believe that strict compliance with the terms of the compromise will not be required. Putting the matter very broadly, if in all the circumstances it would be inequitable to allow the forbearing party to resile from the position he has taken, he will be precluded from insisting on strict performance.[17]

7-11 Frustration occurs when circumstances arise after the making of an agreement which render performance impossible or so totally different from that which was contemplated as to make performance inappropriate. If the changed circumstances render performance merely more difficult, onerous or expensive, the agreement will not be frustrated. Equally, the impossibility of giving effect to a subsidiary term of a compromise does not frustrate the whole agreement.[18] Examples of circumstances giving rise to frustration are afforded by the destruction of the subject matter of the agreement, the death of a party to an agreement requiring personal performance and supervening illegality. But frustration will not be found where it has been induced by one or other of the parties to the agreement.[19]

7-12 In the matrimonial context it should be noted that a subsequent decree of divorce or nullity will not frustrate a prior compromise in the form of a separation agreement under which provision is made for maintenance payments.[20]

---

15 *Chitty*, Vol.1, Chs 22 and 23.

16 *Chitty*, Vol.1, para.24-007 onwards.

17 For a detailed appraisal, see *Chitty*, Vol.1, para.3-130 onwards.

18 *Willis v Willis* [1928] P.10, CA.

19 See, generally, *Chitty*, Vol.1, Ch.23.

20 *May v May* [1929] 2 K.B. 386, *Adams v Adams* [1941] 1 K.B. 386. It may afford grounds for a variation of the agreement under Matrimonial Causes Act 1973 s.35. See Ch.24.

CHAPTER 8

Effects of a Breach of a Compromise

GENERAL

The purpose of a compromise is to put an end to the parties' dispute.[1] Such cause or causes of action as each had, or may have had, prior to the conclusion of the agreement are discharged and, if the compromise is embodied in a consent judgment, those causes of action become merged in the judgment.[2] New causes of action arise from the existence of the compromise.[3] Do these principles mean that one party's original claim or claims can never be reasserted in the event of the compromise being disregarded by the other? **8-01**

Given the normal meaning, purpose and effect of a compromise, the natural inference is that the parties' common intention is that the compromise will henceforth govern their legal relationship in connection with the disputes in which they had been engaged. Accordingly, those disputes would still be regarded as "dead" even in the event of breach of the compromise.[4] In these circumstances, recourse to the original claims will not be permitted unless, upon a true construction of the compromise, it is clear that this is what the parties intended. In this context, whilst the matter is primarily one of construction, the nature of the consideration furnished by the parties may operate as a pointer. **8-02**

PROMISED OR ACTUAL ACTS

In the discussion on consideration,[5] attention was drawn to the fact that consideration usually furnished in the context of a compromise is the promised or actual forbearance of one party to pursue a claim against another in return for some promised or actual act by the other.[6] If the promised or actual forbearance to pursue the claim is construed as being in return for the promised performance of some act by the other party, such agreement will be regarded as one involving the immediate discharge of the claim.[7] Where, however, the promised or actual forbearance is construed as being in return for the actual performance of some act by the other **8-03**

---

1 See paras 6-01 and 6-02.

2 *Thoday v Thoday* [1964] P. 181 at 197–198, per Diplock LJ; *Virgin Atlantic Airways Ltd v Zodiac Seats UK Ltd (formerly Contour Aerospace Ltd)* [2013] UKSC 46; [2014] A.C. 160 at [17], per Lord Sumption: "... there is the doctrine of merger, which treats a cause of action as extinguished once judgment has been given on it, and the claimant's sole right as being a right on the judgment." See also *Turf Club Auto Emporium Pte Ltd v Yeo Boong Hua* [2017] SGCA 21 at [153] and *Chitty*, Vol.1, para.25-007.

3 *McCallum v Country Residences* [1965] 1 W.L.R. 657 at 660. See para.5-54 onwards.

4 See, e.g. *Supamarl Ltd v Federated Homes Ltd* (1981) 9 Con. L.R. 25.

5 See para.3-02 onwards.

6 See para.3-03.

7 *Sibtree v Tripp* (1846) 15 M. & W. 23, *Crowther v Farrer* (1850) 15 Q.B. 677, *Henderson v Stobart*

party, the claim forborne will not be discharged until such performance takes place.[8] The propositions may be illustrated by reference to two simple examples:

(a) A agrees not to pursue his claim[9] against B in return for B's promise to pay A the sum of £10,000 within 28 days;
(b) A agrees not to pursue his claim against B if B pays to A the sum of £10,000 within 28 days.

If B fails to make the payment within the period specified, A's remedy under (a) would merely be to sue B for damages upon the compromise. Under (b) he would have the option of accepting B's repudiation of the agreement, treating himself as discharged from further performance of his obligations and reasserting his original claim, or of affirming the compromise and suing upon it.[10]

8-04 Although the illustrations given above involve merely the actual or promised payment of a sum of money, the analysis will be to the same effect where more complex terms are involved. Where there is a clear and unconditional discharge, abandonment or release of a claim by one party in return for the promised performance by the other of a series of acts, that original claim can never be revived. Where the agreement involves merely the suspension of the claim pending the carrying-out of the acts by the other party then the claim may not be lost forever.

8-05 In *Fraser v Elgen Tavern Property Ltd*,[11] C's claim for unliquidated damages against several defendants was settled upon terms of settlement which provided for a certain sum to be paid to C's solicitors within 21 days, time to be of the essence. The terms of settlement stated:

> "The defendants to pay and the plaintiffs to accept the sum of $315,000 in full settlement of the plaintiff's claim" and "subject to an order for the taxation and payment of the plaintiffs costs, action to be struck out."

The sum was not paid on the due date. C's solicitors gave notice that this non-payment constituted a repudiation of the terms of settlement and that C contended that he was no longer bound by the settlement. Late tender of the sum was refused. The defendants contended that there was accord and satisfaction in that C had agreed to accept their promise to pay the sum in satisfaction of the claim. Murphy J held that: (1) since time had expressly been made of the essence, it was a condition of the settlement that payment should be within 21 days; (2) on a true construction of the agreement C was not agreeing to accept the promise of the defendants to pay the sum: he was agreeing to accept payment within 21 days, time being of the essence.

8-06 In *Hopmeyer v Silverman*,[12] a claim for possession under the Landlord and Tenant Act 1954 (to which, it appears, there was no defence) was the subject of a "compromise": the claim was adjourned upon certain terms with liberty to restore. The terms were that T undertook: (1) to enter into a new tenancy agreement upon the terms of the draft tenancy agreement attached to the order within one month (the reference in the draft agreement to the inventory being understood to relate to an inventory drawn up by T and agreed between the parties within that period of one month); and (2) to pay L's costs. T simply

---

(1850) 5 Ex. 99. And see *Morris v Baron and Co* [1918] A.C. 1 at 35, per Lord Atkinson, and *British Russian Gazette Ltd v Associated Newspapers Ltd* [1933] 2 K.B. 616. See *Chitty*, Vol.1, para.22-015.

8 *Morris v Baron and Co* [1918] A.C. 1, *British Russian Gazette Ltd* [1933] 2 K.B. 616.

9 A claim which, if liquidated, is disputed or alternatively unliquidated: see para.3-12 onwards.

10 He is not bound to accept the repudiation and revert to the original claim: *Smith v Shirley and Baylis* (1875) 32 L.T. 234, noted at para.8-10. See also *Turf Club Auto Emporium Pte Ltd v Yeo Boong Hua* [2017] SGCA 21 at [154].

11 *Fraser v Elgen Tavern Property Ltd* [1982] V.R. 398 (Supreme Court of Victoria).

12 *Hopmeyer v Silverman* (1980) CAT 147; [1980] 2 WLUK 289.

failed, despite encouragement from L's solicitors, to produce the inventory. L restored his claim for possession and an order was granted. The Court of Appeal held that there had been an accord but no satisfaction since T had failed to produce the inventory.

Generally speaking, therefore, a compromise agreement will discharge all original claims and counterclaims unless it expressly provides for their revival in the event of breach.[13] Where a party wishes to be able to revive his original claim in the event of the other party's failure to comply with his obligations under the compromise, he would be well-advised to insist that a term to that effect should be incorporated.[14] Any judgment or order made reflecting an agreement of this nature would need to be drafted so as to give effect to this intention. **8-07**

In *Korea Foreign Insurance Co v Omne Re SA*,[15] D were reinsurers and C was the reinsured. They compromised certain disputes that arose between them under a number of reinsurance contracts in an agreement entitled "Commutation and Release Agreement". Under this agreement D agreed to pay C the sum of $1.35 million in full and final settlement of the outstanding claims. That sum was to be paid as to $100,000 on the execution of the agreement and the balance of $1,250,000 was to be paid in 12 instalments, 11 of $100,000 each and a final one of $150,000. The initial sum of $100,000 was paid but none of the further instalments was paid. The following clauses appeared in the agreement: **8-08**

(i) "It is a condition precedent to this [agreement] that in the event [that D] makes default in [the payment] of USD 100,000.00 ... upon execution of this Agreement and/or any of the instalments within 5 to 10 bank working days from the ... dates [specified in the agreement] from [any] reason whatsoever, this [agreement] shall be wholly null and void, and [C] shall be entitled to reserve its full rights without prejudice to its rights under the Reinsurance Agreements and the claims recoveries."
(ii) "[C] and [D] in consideration of the execution of this Agreement by both parties hereto and upon the payment [specified], shall release and discharge each other ... from all past, present and future adjustments, obligations, offsets, actions, causes of action ... which either party ever had, now have, or hereafter may have ... it being the intention of the parties that this release operate as a full and final settlement of both parties' current and future liabilities and which arise out of the Reinsurance Agreements as defined."

Following D's failure to pay any of the instalments after the initial payment C instituted proceedings for the balance of $1.25 million. An issue arose as to whether C was entitled to sue D under the agreement (which provided that it became "null and void" in the event of a default by D) or whether C was obliged to revert to the original claims and pursue D in respect of those claims. D contended for the latter interpretation basing their argument on the proposition that, once they had been in default, the agreement was "null and void". The Court of Appeal held that since the general law of contract gave C the right upon D's repudiatory breach to elect whether to affirm the compromise agreement and to sue upon it, or to treat it as wholly discharged and to revert to the original claims, the clause referred to under (i) above gave D no basis for arguing that C was obliged to rely upon the original claims. It made no commercial sense to interpret that clause in the manner contended for by D since D could, by their own default, discharge their own liabilities under it and C would never have had any right to bring proceedings under it.

Where an agreement, on its proper construction, does provide for recourse to the **8-09**

---

[13] This sentence was cited with approval in *Korea Foreign Insurance Co v Omne Re Sa* [1999] EWCA Civ 1166; [1999] Lloyd's Rep. I.R. 509 per Evans LJ.

[14] In *Korea Foreign Insurance Co* CA, no express provision to this effect was incorporated in the agreement. However, the agreement was construed in such a way as to have this effect.

[15] *Korea Foreign Insurance Co v Omne Re Sa* [1999] EWCA Civ 1166; [1999] Lloyd's Rep. I.R. 509.

original claim in the event of a breach by the other party, the question arises as to whether the innocent party is thereby obliged to revert to that claim or whether he can proceed to enforce the compromise. Whilst it would not be impossible to conceive of an agreement which expressly provided that the innocent party in such a situation *must* revert to the original claim, the most likely formulation of such an agreement is that he *may* do so. If this is not spelt out expressly, it is likely to be implied in the sense that it is the obvious inference to be drawn from the agreement.[16] In this situation it would appear that the innocent party may elect between reverting to the original claim and pursuing his rights under the compromise.

8-10 In *Smith v Shirley and Baylis*,[17] C had resisted the grant of probate of the will and codicils of which D were executors. At the trial of the matter a compromise was concluded in the following terms:

> "In consideration of [C] withdrawing from opposition to proof of the will and codicils, [D] undertake to pay [C], within fourteen days, the sum of [£5,850], and a further sum of [£750] for costs; and thereupon [C] and the other residuary legatees will, if so required, release by deed all claim to the residue. Probate not to issue until after payment of the above sums, and the case to be adjourned for that purpose. In default of payment of the above sums within the time specified [C] to be entitled to have the case called on for hearing, and to take a verdict by consent upon all the issues."

D made default in payment and C sued upon the agreement and obtained judgment for £6,600. D appealed, arguing that the compromise merely entitled C either to the agreed sums, if paid, or to a verdict by consent in default of payment, but not to a right to the sums if not so paid. C argued that the true construction of the agreement was to the effect that D were absolutely bound to pay the agreed sums for a particular consideration, but that, if they should make default, C was to have another remedy, beyond and in addition to the ordinary remedy, by way of action for breach of promise to pay. The Court of Exchequer[18] held that the true construction of the compromise was as C had contended and that, accordingly, C was entitled to judgment.

ANTICIPATORY BREACH OF COMPROMISE

8-11 When an agreement permits recourse to the original claim in the event of a breach then, provided the specified breach is committed, the innocent party may elect to pursue his original claim or proceed on the compromise.[19] Is it necessary in every case to await the non-fulfilment of the particular obligation before the election is made? In accordance with the ordinary principles of the law of contract in relation to anticipatory breach, it would seem that, in certain circumstances, the end of the agreed period for performance need not be awaited. Where a party upon whom the obligation rests: (a) renounces the compromise; or (b) does or omits to do something which renders performance of the obligation impossible the other party may treat the particular circumstances as a repudiation and act accordingly.[20]

---

16 *Chitty*, Vol.1, para.14-008.

17 *Smith v Shirley and Baylis* (1875) 32 L.T. 234. See also *Korea Foreign Insurance Co* [1999] Lloyd's Rep. I.R. 509.

18 Cleasby, Pollock and Amphlett BB.

19 *Shirley and Baylis* (1875) 32 L.T. 234.

20 *Chitty*, Vol.1, para.24-031.

Renunciation

> "A renunciation of a contract occurs when one party by words or conduct evinces an intention not to perform, or expressly declares that he is or will be unable to perform, his obligations under the contract in some essential respect."[21] **8-12**

Thus, where A agrees to accept £10,000 from B in settlement of his claim and costs if B pays this sum within 28 days, B will be held to have renounced the compromise if, within the 28-day period, he shows that he does not in fact intend to make the payment.[22]

Self-created impossibility

Where a party to a contract, whether deliberately or otherwise, but, in any event, by his own act or default, creates circumstances which render performance by him impossible, he will be regarded as having repudiated the contract.[23] Such impossibility may arise at any time before performance is complete. An example of a non-deliberate impossibility is afforded by a compromise whereunder one party agrees to transfer to the other certain items of property, but before transfer a judgment creditor seizes the property in execution,[24] or the party upon whom the obligation to transfer rests is made bankrupt.[25] Either event will be regarded as a repudiation. **8-13**

Implied term as to co-operation

A further aspect of this part of the law has already been highlighted.[26] The court will normally imply into any agreement a term to the effect that neither party will prevent performance or, looking at the matter the other way, that each party will do all that is reasonably necessary to see that it is carried out.[27] Thus, where a compromise provides that a court order shall be obtained or the agreement is "subject to the approval of the court", a term will be implied to the effect that both parties will co-operate in bringing the matter before the court and, where appropriate, in seeking its approval.[28] Any failure to do so will constitute a repudiation.[29] **8-14**

INNOCENT PARTY'S CHOICE IF AVAILABLE

Where an innocent party finds himself in the position of being able to elect whether to pursue his original claim or to proceed under or by virtue of the **8-15**

---

21 *Chitty*, Vol.1, para.24-018.

22 The problem of failure to make instalment payments is considered at para.7-04.

23 *Universal Cargo Carriers Corp v Citati* [1957] 2 Q.B. 401.

24 cf. *Keys v Harwood* (1846) 2 C.B. 905; 135 E.R. 1201.

25 *Powell v Marshall Parkes & Co* [1899] 1 Q.B. 710.

26 See para.5-48 onwards.

27 *Stirling v Maitland* (1864) 5 B. & S. 840; 122 E.R. 1043, CtQB; *Barque Quilpué, Ltd v Brown* [1904] 2 K.B. 264, CA; *Chitty*, Vol.1, paras 14-012–14-013. For the general approach to implication, see *Marks & Spencer Plc v BNP Paribas Securities Services Trust Co (Jersey) Ltd* [2015] UKSC 72; [2016] A.C. 742.

28 *Smallman v Smallman* [1972] Fam. 25. See also Ch.24.

29 It will be a question of construction in cases of this nature whether the agreement consists of mutual promises to agree to the order sought, or whether it consists of an agreement by one party not to pursue fully his claims in return for the act of consent of the other party to the agreed order when the court is invited to make it. See para.3-58 onwards.

compromise, careful consideration will have to be given to the practical and financial advantages of each course.[30] Indeed, those implications will probably have been considered before entering into the compromise in the first instance. Further, where the option to reassert the original claim is contemplated, care must be taken by the legal advisers of the innocent party in the drafting of letters to the guilty party or his advisers after becoming aware of his breach. Any statement or act which recognises unequivocally the continued existence of the compromise (such as continuing to request performance) after a repudiation in the sense referred to will result in an implied affirmation of the agreement precluding recourse to the original claim.[31]

30 The remedies available to an innocent party under or by virtue of the compromise are considered in Ch.11.

31 *Chitty*, Vol.1, paras 24-003-24-004. For an analysis of a situation in which the issue of affirmation arose in the context of the discussion of a possible compromise of a dispute arising from a breach of contract, see *Bell Electric Ltd v Aweco Appliance Systems* [2002] EWHC 872 (QB); [2002] EU. L.R. 443.

PART 2: MACHINERY, PRACTICE AND ENFORCEMENT OF A COMPROMISE

This part is concerned with the various means by which compromises are effectuated, the manner of achieving the course chosen and the steps which may be taken thereafter to enforce it.

CHAPTER 9

Means by which Compromises are Effectuated

GENERAL AND PRELIMINARY

This chapter is concerned with the means by which parties to a compromise give effect to their agreement. Before turning to the methods most commonly used, some preliminary matters should be noted. **9-01**

THE AIM

Once a settlement has been achieved, the parties will need to ensure that: **9-02**

(a) the terms are properly and accurately recorded; and
(b) insofar as the mere recording of the terms is not sufficient for the purpose of achieving the agreed means of enforcement, the terms are embodied in some suitable document, court or arbitral order to enable expeditious enforcement.

When a settlement of court proceedings is reached, the parties will usually agree to a machinery by virtue of which enforcement of the terms can be achieved within those proceedings rather than leaving the matter to be dealt with in fresh proceedings.[1]

COSTS

In the normal course of events, the agreement will make specific provision in relation to the legal costs incurred. Absent of any such provision, the court will not imply a term in relation to costs, the natural inference being that each party will bear its own costs.[2] **9-03**

With the advent of the "issues-based" nature of the court's jurisdiction on costs following the introduction of the CPR[3] parties do from time to time agree all substantive matters except costs and then invite the court to determine that issue, often on the basis of written submissions[4]. There are divided views about the desirability of the practice. The difficulties faced by a court in this situation were set out by Mummery LJ in a case decided before the introduction of the CPR.[5] He said this: **9-04**

---

1 See para.6-20.
2 See para.5-60.
3 CPR r.44.3(3) and (4).
4 See, e.g. *Carlisle & Cumbria United Independent Supporters' Society Ltd v CUFC Holdings Ltd* [2010] EWCA Civ 463; [2011] B.C.C. 855.
5 *Butcher v Wolfe* [1999] C.P.L.R. 112, CA.

"All lawyers learn from experience that costs are often a stumbling block in negotiating a settlement of proceedings. A judge who is informed by the parties that they have agreed everything except costs may be placed in a difficult position. On the one hand, he may take the view that, if the parties have not agreed everything, including costs, then they have not settled their case: they must either reach an agreement on costs or, failing that, go on with the case. This is a matter for the discretion of the judge. He may be entitled in some circumstances to adopt that position in the hope that the case will not go on and that a settlement on costs will be achieved. On the other hand, a judge may not wish to risk jeopardising the settlement, and may agree to ... decide the costs issue for the parties. There can be problems; as the case has not run its full course, the judge has not heard all the evidence and all the argument. He may face difficulty in knowing what materials he should take into account in the exercise of his judicial discretion."

The issue was revisited in a case after the introduction of the CPR.[6] Mummery LJ again uttered words of caution[7]:

"The arguments advanced on this appeal have demonstrated the real difficulties inherent in asking a judge to exercise his discretion in respect of the costs of an action, which he has not tried. There are, no doubt, straightforward cases in which it is reasonably clear from the terms of the settlement that there is a winner and a loser in the litigation. In most cases of that description the parties themselves will realistically recognise the result and the costs will be agreed. There will be no need to involve the judge in any decision on costs. If he becomes involved, because the parties cannot agree and ask him to resolve the costs dispute, the decision is not usually a difficult one for him to make.

There are, however, more complex cases (and this is such a case) in which it will be difficult for the judge to decide who is the winner and who is the loser without embarking on a course, which comes close to conducting a trial of the action that the parties intended to avoid by their compromise. The truth often is that neither side has won or lost. It is also true that a considerable number of cases are settled by the parties in the belief that the terms of settlement represent a victory, or at least a vindication of their position, in the litigation, or in the belief that they have not lost; or, at the very least, in the belief that the other side has not won.

In my judgment, in all but straightforward compromises, which are, in general, unlikely to involve him, a judge is entitled to say to the parties 'If you have not reached an agreement on costs, you have not settled your dispute. The action must go on, unless your compromise covers costs as well.'

The disposition of a judge to help parties in negotiations for a settlement is understood and applauded. Good intentions are not, however, risk free. If acted upon too readily, commendable judicial intentions can make things far worse than they would have been if the judge had adopted the unpopular stance of requiring the parties to confront the realities of their litigation situation. The judge has a discretion to decline to do what the parties ask him to do. If, on the one hand, the action is for damages, it will be relatively easy for the judge to tell from the size of the settlement sum and from the litigation history (offers, payments in and so on) how the costs should be borne. As I have already said, it would be relatively unusual for the parties themselves not to agree on the costs of such cases. In more complex cases, however, involving a number of issues and claims for discretionary equitable relief, the costs position is much more difficult for the judge to resolve without actually trying the case."[8]

---

6 *BCT Software Solutions Ltd v C Brewer and Sons Ltd* [2003] EWCA Civ 939; [2004] C.P. Rep. 2. See also *Promar International Ltd v Clarke* [2006] EWCA Civ 332, *Venture Finance Plc v Mead* [2005] EWCA Civ 325; [2006] 3 Costs L.R. 389, *Bray (t/a Building Co) v Bishop* [2009] EWCA Civ 768; [2009] T.C.L.R. 9, *Powles v Reeves* [2016] EWCA Civ 1375; [2017] 1 Costs L.R. 19.

7 *BCT Software Solutions* [2003] EWCA Civ 939; [2004] C.P. Rep. 2 at [4]–[7].

8 Chadwick LJ made similar observations at [24]–[26].

More recently, in *Gossage v Bishton*[9] Lewison LJ endorsed these reservations[10]: 9-05

"Unfortunately, however, the parties could not agree how the legal costs could be dealt with. They agreed that the question of costs should be dealt with by the district judge. This is, in my judgment, bad practice which puts the court in a very difficult position. Except in obvious cases it is very difficult for the court to make a just order for costs without going into the merits of litigation. The whole purpose of a settlement is to avoid the court having to undertake that task. If the case is obvious then the parties ought to be able to agree how the costs should be borne. The court does, of course, have power to make an order for costs even after the substantive dispute has been settled, but it is a discretionary power which the court may choose not to exercise."

However, a countervailing view was expressed by Lord Neuberger, Master of the Rolls, as follows[11]: 9-06

"I am not at all sure that I would subscribe to Lord Justice Lewison's disapproval or characterisation of bad practice of parties settling all their issues save as to costs and leaving the question of costs to be determined by the court. Parties to litigation should be encouraged to settle as many issues as they can and if they can settle all issues except costs it would be wrong to discourage them from doing so. I would prefer to say that where parties reach an agreement which involves all issues save as to costs being agreed then, as the cases which Lewison LJ has cited demonstrate, first they should be encouraged to try and settle the issue of costs but, secondly, if they cannot do so then they should appreciate that there is a real risk that the court will make no order for costs."

Notwithstanding the reservations that the courts have expressed concerning this approach, guidance has been given concerning the proper approach to be taken when it is necessary for the court to determine costs where a claim has settled before trial. Initially, this guidance was given in the context of public law proceedings in the administrative court.[12] The Court of Appeal in *Powles v Reeves*[13] has now confirmed that that public law approach, which was set out in principles articulated by Scott Baker J in *R. (Boxall) v Waltham Forest LBC*,[14] as adapted to private law proceedings by the Court of Appeal in *Brawley v Marczynski*[15] and in *R (M) v Croydon LBC* should be adopted.[16] Where parties have proceeded on this basis, the judge has acceded to the invitation and made an award of costs, the question arises whether the parties should be able to appeal against that decision. There was a suggestion in a matrimonial finance case[17] that an appeal was prohibited in such circumstances because leaving the question of costs to the judge was part of the compromise. However, the Court of Appeal in *BCT Software Solutions Ltd v C Brewer and Sons Ltd* has said that "there is no such hard and fast limit to [its] jurisdiction ...".[18] Accordingly, there is no formal prohibition to an appeal. However, Mummery LJ in that case went on to state that the Court of Appeal, 9-07

9 [2012] EWCA Civ 717.

10 [2012] EWCA Civ 717, Lewison LJ, at [8].

11 [2012] EWCA Civ 717 at [31]–[32].

12 cf. paras 33-20–33-23, for the test and discussion.

13 [2016] EWCA Civ 1375; [2017] 1 Costs L.R. 19 at [18]–[20].

14 [2001] 4 C.C.L. Rep. 258.

15 [2002] EWCA Civ 756; 2003] 1 W.L.R. 813 at [21].

16 [2012] EWCA Civ 595; [2012] 1 W.L.R. 2607 at [60]–[63] per Lord Neuberger MR and at [77] per Stanley Burnton LJ.

17 *Denne v Denne* (1977) CAT 474B.

18 [2003] EWCA Civ 939; [2004] C.P. Rep. 2.

> "is entitled to approach an appeal against a costs order, which has been made as part of a compromise, with an even greater degree of reluctance than is usually the case when it is asked to interfere with the discretion of the trial judge".[19]

The consequence of this was that as the parties had agreed to the judge determining the costs, it was "reasonable to expect them to accept his decision, unless it can be shown that the result is, in all the circumstances, manifestly unjust."[20] Absent "manifest injustice" an appellate court should not interfere with the exercise of the judge's costs discretion.[21] As Chadwick LJ observed in *Venture Finance Plc v Mead*, recognised the "hurdle",[22] which a party who has invited the court to decide costs upon settlement before trial must overcome if an appellate court is to interfere with a trial judge's discretion.

9-08 An agreement to an order for costs entails a somewhat open-ended commitment.[23] Not infrequently the party agreeable to paying his opponent's costs would, in principle, prefer a more clearly defined obligation. This can be achieved either by agreeing an overall settlement sum inclusive of costs with no order as to costs, or by agreeing a specific sum as to costs.

Where either or both parties are in receipt of Legal Aid Agency funding, an order for an appropriate public funding assessment will be required.[24]

THE METHODS OF COMPROMISE

EXCHANGE OF WRITTEN COMMUNICATIONS

9-09 Not infrequently, particularly when no proceedings are in existence, solicitors will engage in a formal exchange of correspondence (in hard or electronic form) confirming an agreement. Strictly speaking, this adds nothing to the agreement already reached and is unnecessary. However, it is often felt to be a convenient way of evidencing finality and is useful in that respect. An example would be afforded by a letter or email from a claimant's solicitor stating that his client agrees to accept £10,000 "in full and final settlement of all claims which he has or may have against [the defendant] arising from the accident on [date] and costs", such com-

---

19 [2003] EWCA Civ 939; [2004] C.P. Rep. 2 at [8]. A successful appeal was pursued against an order made in these circumstances in *Carlisle & Cumbria United Independent Supporters' Society Ltd v CUFC Holdings Ltd*: see fn.4.

20 [2003] EWCA Civ 939; [2004] C.P. Rep. 2 at [8].

21 [2003] EWCA Civ 939; [2004] C.P. Rep. 2 at [15]. Mummery LJ's approach was followed in *Venture Finance Plc v Mead* [2005] EWCA Civ 325; [2006] 3 Costs L.R. 389 and *Bray (t/a Building Co) v Bishop* [2009] EWCA Civ 768; [2009] T.C.L.R. 9, and *Powles v Reeves* [2016] EWCA Civ 1375; [2017] 1 Costs L.R. 19. In the last of the three judgments, the Court of Appeal noted that Gross LJ in *Patience v Tanner* [2016] EWCA Civ 158; [2016] 2 Costs L.R. 311 at [33] had queried whether Mummery LJ had intended "manifest injustice" to be a threshold test. As David Richards LJ noted at in *Powles v Reeves* at [25], the Court of Appeal in *Patience v Tanner* was not referred to its previous decisions in either *Venture Finance* or *Bray*.

22 [2005] EWCA Civ 325; [2006] 3 Costs L.R. 389 at [25].

23 The commitment includes one to pay interest at the judgment rate from the date the order for costs is made, even though the amount to be paid under that order will not be ascertained until the completion of detailed assessment: *Hunt v R.M. Douglas (Roofing) Ltd* [1990] A.C. 398. (In the *Hunt* case the proceedings had been settled in Tomlin form, one of the terms being that D was to pay C the costs of the action to be taxed if not agreed.)

24 See, e.g. Precedent No.1 at para.A1-01 in Appendix 1.

munication being in reply to one from the defendant's solicitor seeking confirmation of the agreement in those terms.[25]

A DEED OR MEMORANDUM OF AGREEMENT

In some circumstances, particularly where the terms of compromise are not entirely straightforward, the parties may enter into a formal deed.[26] **9-10**

This is often a convenient method of finalising the compromise of a partnership or boundary dispute which has not reached the stage of proceedings. It is not, of course, necessary in every case that the formalities of a deed should be observed. A memorandum of agreement drafted in terms normally associated with the content of a deed would, provided it is signed by or on behalf of both parties, be quite sufficient.

MAKING AN AGREEMENT AN ORDER OR RULE OF COURT

Where proceedings are in existence, the incorporation, so far as possible, of the terms of a compromise in the court record is often regarded as important, particularly from the point of view of enforcement. It has been suggested[27] that the parties may consent to an order directing themselves to perform the various obligations provided for under the settlement. Where the obligations sought to be imposed by the order are such as could have been imposed by the court under its normal jurisdiction, such a course is unobjectionable. However, it is clear that parties cannot by consent confer upon the court a jurisdiction which it does not otherwise possess.[28] Where terms go beyond the court's normal jurisdiction, yet the parties desire the agreement to be readily enforceable without the need to bring a fresh action, some other approach needs to be adopted. One such approach has been for a consent order to be made directing that the agreement "be filed and made a rule of court".[29] Specific agreement to this effect is necessary.[30] The agreement is still a contract but is enforceable in the proceedings without the necessity of a fresh action.[31] The procedure is very similar to that of scheduling the terms of the agreement to a Tomlin order.[32] It is, however, an old and rarely used procedure and its disadvantage is that there is a division of judicial opinion about the precise manner in which enforcement may be achieved.[33] **9-11**

SIMPLE CONSENT JUDGMENT FOR THE PAYMENT OF MONEY

This method will frequently be adopted where the basis of the agreement is the straightforward payment of a sum of money by one party to the other. It has the advantage from the judgment creditor's point of view of an immediate right to enforcement in default of payment. **9-12**

---

[25] See para.2-08 onwards.

[26] Certain formalities must be observed: see para.3-75. See also *Silver Queen Maritime Ltd v Persia Petroleum Services Plc* [2010] EWHC 2867 (QB) and Ch.30.

[27] *Green v Rozen* [1955] 1 W.L.R. 741 at 744. See also *Atkinson, The Times*, 17 April 1991, considered in detail at para.11-30.

[28] See para.9-19 onwards and para.10-06 onwards.

[29] See Precedent No.17 in the 4th edn of this work.

[30] *Graves v Graves* (1893) 69 L.T. 420.

[31] *Shaw, Re* [1918] P. 47: "The effect of making the terms a rule of Court enables the terms to be summarily enforced without the necessity of bringing an action".

[32] See para.9-18 onwards.

[33] See para.11-06 onwards. Indeed it is, perhaps, for this reason that this particular mechanism is hardly ever adopted.

9-13 Where there is any doubt about the other party's willingness to pay the agreed sum, it is prudent to insist upon a straightforward consent judgment with no provision as to time for payment.[34] The consequences of registration of the judgment[35] will be avoided by the judgment debtor if he pays immediately.

9-14 This is a convenient point to note again the difference between a consent order or judgment and one to which the party against whom it is entered merely submits. The latter is not a judgment or order by consent.[36] Where there is a true agreement between the parties reflected in a consent order or judgment, the order or judgment does not itself constitute a contract. It affords evidence of the contract upon which it is based and it has been said that the contract is "not less a contract and subject to the incidents of a contract because there is superadded the command of a judge".[37] A submission to judgment may involve one party accepting that the other party is entitled to the judgment, or a conscious decision by that party not to pursue a defence to the claim, but it does not necessarily have the contractual foundation which lies at the root of a consent judgment.

Consent judgment providing time for payment

9-15 A party may be prepared to allow the other party time to pay the agreed sum whilst still wishing to have the security of an enforceable judgment without further application to the court. This can be achieved in a number of ways:

(a) by entering a consent judgment specifying the time within which the judgment debtor shall pay the agreed sum[38];
(b) by entering a consent judgment with no provision as to time subject to a direction in one or other of the following terms:
  (i) that the judgment not be drawn up for the agreed period;
  (ii) that the judgment lies in the court office for the agreed period;
  (iii) that execution is stayed for the agreed period.

A more usual alternative to one or other of these directions would be afforded by the recording of an undertaking by the judgment creditor not to enforce the judgment for the agreed period.[39]

9-16 In each instance, a failure on the judgment debtor's part to pay the sum within the agreed period would entitle the judgment creditor to take immediate enforcement proceedings.[40]

9-17 In some cases time will be afforded to a judgment debtor by an agreement whereby payments are made by instalments.[41] The usual method of securing the position of the judgment creditor is for there to be a forthwith judgment for the

---

34 The standard form of judgment provides for payment to be made within 14 days: CPR r.40.11. If no such period is contemplated under the consent judgment, care will have to be taken to ensure that the terms of the judgment drawn up by the court accurately reflect the terms of the draft agreed judgment and provide for payment forthwith.

35 See Register of Judgments, Orders and Fines Regulations 2005 (SI 2005/3595).

36 *Chandless-Chandless* [1942] 2 K.B. 321 at 324; *Levi v Taylor* (1904) 116 L.T.Jo. 64. See para.6-22 fns.54 and 55. See also *Siebe-Gorman Ltd* [1982] 1 W.L.R. 185, CA.

37 *Wentworth v Bullen* (1829) 9 B. & C. 840 at 850, *Lievesley v Gilmore* (1866) L.R. 1 C.P. 570, *Conolan v Leyland* (1884) 27 Ch. D. 632, *Worthington & Co v Abbot* [1910] 1 Ch. 588, *Brister v Brister* [1970] 1 W.L.R. 664. See also *Horizon Technologies International Ltd v Lucky Wealth Consultants Ltd* [1992] 1 W.L.R. 24, PC and *Islam v Askar* (1994) CAT 1240; *The Times,* 20 October 1994, *Qayoumi v Qayoumi* (20 December 2002, ChD, unreported.)

38 CPR r.40.11.

39 See Precedent No.2 at para.A1-02 in Appendix 1, modified to include the undertaking.

40 See Ch.11.

41 cf. *South American & Mexican Co, Re* [1895] 1 Ch. 37 and *Horizon Technologies International Ltd*

whole of the agreed sum, execution of which is directed to be stayed on condition that the judgment debtor pays an agreed figure at periodic intervals with a provision that the stay on execution be removed in the event of a default in one of the periodic payments.[42]

Payment of money without judgment

The payee may not insist that judgment is entered immediately against the payer. A convenient method of securing the creditor's position in such a case is for a consent order to be made staying the proceedings[43] as follows: **9-18**

(a) upon terms that the agreed sum is paid within a specified period with permission to remove the stay and enter judgment in that sum if not so paid;
(b) upon terms that the agreed sum is paid within a specified period in default of which the stay is removed and the proceedings restored; or
(c) upon terms scheduled to the order of the court save for the purpose of enforcement, with permission to apply for such purpose, the terms scheduled (or indorsed) being that the one party agrees to pay the other the agreed sum within the specified period.

The third method is more usually adopted where the terms of the agreement are somewhat complex and it is felt that full reference to them in the order is unnecessary or impossible.[44] However, it is also appropriate in cases involving the payment of a sum of money (possibly by instalments) where the parties do not want public reference to be made to it either on the face of the order or by their representatives.[45] It is not a judgment and cannot, without more, be enforced as such.[46] **9-19**

Consent judgment or order involving terms other than mere payment of money, including Tomlin order

A compromise will often comprise a series of terms not all of which involve the direct payment of money. Equally, terms of compromise often provide for arrangements which could not have been made the subject of a direct court order or judgment. For example, an action brought by the hirer (on hire-purchase) of a car against the finance company and the garage which originally supplied it in respect of alleged defects might be compromised on terms which include acceptance by the hirer of another car in exchange for the one of which complaint was made, with certain financial adjustments between the parties. Clearly, such an agreement is possible and enforceable as a pure contractual agreement, but a court order directing the exchange of cars could not have been made. This problem does not arise where the parties are agreed on the manner in which a specific jurisdiction of the court is to be exercised in order to give effect to their compromise. In such a case an ap- **9-20**

[1992] 1 W.L.R. 24 PC. See CPR r.40.11(a).

42 It is not always advisable for a judgment creditor to insist that in default of any one payment the whole balance becomes due because the judgment debtor may be able to use this to secure his own bankruptcy.

43 For the significance and meaning of a "stay", see para.9-26 onwards.

44 The order is a Tomlin order: see para.9-20 onwards.

45 But note para.10-28 onwards and, in particular, para.10-30.

46 See para.11-22 onwards.

propriate provision to the relevant effect may appear in the consent order or judgment.[47]

9-21 In cases where some or all of the terms of the compromise go beyond that which could be provided for by means of a straightforward consent order or judgment, care must be taken in selecting the most appropriate machinery for giving effect to the agreement. Where an agreement is reached which contains provisions of this nature, it is not good practice (nor indeed lawful) merely to recite the terms of the agreement in a document purporting to be a consent order or judgment and placing the words "by consent it is ordered" or by "by consent it is adjudged" at the beginning of the document.[48] A consent order or judgment drawn up in a way that has not focused clearly upon whether any or all of its constituent provisions are within the normal jurisdiction of the court can present great problems when the question of enforcement arises.[49]

9-22 A variety of means exist by which terms of an agreement that cannot be effected as an order or judgment within the normal jurisdiction of the court can be made amenable to the jurisdiction of the court for the purposes of enforcement. For example, provided it is sufficiently clearly expressed for the purposes of subsequent enforcement,[50] a court will be prepared to accept an undertaking given by a party to the court which assumes an obligation going beyond what the court might have imposed upon that party by order.[51] Reference has already been made[52] to the procedure by which an agreement may be filed and made a rule of court, although it should be noted that this approach is now rarely, if ever, adopted.[53]

9-23 The method most commonly adopted to effectuate a compromise involving terms going beyond the court's normal jurisdiction is to incorporate the agreement into a "Tomlin order".[54] This provides for a consensual stay of the proceedings on the agreed terms save for the purpose of carrying the agreed terms into effect, permission to apply to the court for this purpose being reserved.[55] The terms are usually incorporated into a schedule to the order or are recorded in a separate document[56] which is identified clearly on the face of the order. The great advantage of this procedure is that it enables the enforcement of the terms of the settlement *within the existing action* by a summary procedure. The terms may, of course, be complex and, as already indicated above, can be of a nature which go beyond the normal jurisdiction of the court. Indeed, the terms of settlement can go outside the ambit of the original dispute between the parties.[57]

---

47 Although this arises most frequently in compromises of financial proceedings in the family jurisdiction, it can also arise in connection with, for example, disputes to which the Torts (Interference with Goods) Act 1977 or the Consumer Credit Act 1974 apply.

48 This is what was done by the district judge in relation to the draft consent order presented to the court in *Atkinson v Castan, The Times,* 17 April 1991, noted at para.11-30.

49 See, e.g. para.10-11.

50 *Wilson and Whitworth* [1969] 1 W.L.R. 197 noted at para.3-51.

51 Cf. para.24-57.

52 See para.9-09.

53 See para.9-09.

54 Named after Tomlin J.

55 Precedent No.3 at para.A1-03 in Appendix 1. In *Marchant v Marchant* (1967) CAT 26, Danckwerts LJ expressed the view that the words "liberty to apply" without more are ineffective to keep alive the proceedings for the purposes of enforcement. The full expression "liberty to apply for the purpose of enforcing the said terms" must be used. cf. para.11-29. The expression "permission to apply" reflects post-CPR terminology.

56 See Precedent No.3 at para.A1-03 in Appendix 1.

57 *EF Phillips & Sons v Clarke* [1970] Ch. 322.

Regular use has been made of the Tomlin form of order for many years.[58] The structure of the Tomlin order itself represents something of a compromise between competing legal and practical considerations. It is well established that once a compromise has been concluded a new legal relationship between the parties comes into existence replacing the previous relationship of disputation.[59] In the event of a failure by one of the parties to honour the agreement, the position in law is that the innocent party will have a cause of action represented by an action for damages, for specific performance or for an injunction or other relief depending upon the circumstances.[60] In the ordinary way, a cause of action is pursued procedurally by means of a new action. However, it would be something of a perversion of the whole idea of compromise if the full procedural panoply arising from the institution of new proceedings[61] was necessary in this situation. New proceedings in the form of a fresh action would be cumbersome and would, in most cases, result in unjustified delay in the implementation of the agreement.[62] But for the machinery afforded by a Tomlin order, parties to an agreement containing provisions which could not be made the subject of direct provision within a consent order would be forced to institute fresh proceedings for the purposes of enforcement. **9-24**

The nature and effect of a Tomlin order was considered by the Court of Appeal in *Hollingsworth v Humphrey*[63]: **9-25**

> Proceedings between C and D concerning the ownership of a property they had once shared, and which was subject to a joint mortgage, were compromised in Tomlin form on 27 October 1978. The material terms appearing in the schedule to the order were as follows:
>
> (a) The property should be sold within three months from the date of the order, D to have conduct of the sale.
> (b) Out of the proceeds of sale (as defined) C should receive £5,500, the balance to go to D, whereupon C was to be indemnified by D against liability under the joint mortgage.
>
> The order was not entered until 15 June 1979. D did nothing about the sale except to indicate in June 1979 that he was getting vacant possession from certain tenants to enable a sale to take place. Correspondence ensued between solicitors until about January 1982 during the course of which C's solicitors threatened proceedings for contempt. Nothing further happened until June 1983 when C's solicitors wrote a further letter. Finally, in June 1985, C served a notice of motion seeking:
>
> (a) an order lifting the stay so that she could proceed to trial; alternatively
> (b) an order that the terms be carried into effect with consequential directions;
> (c) an inquiry as to damages occasioned to C by D's delay in effecting the sale.
>
> Mervyn Davies J refused to order (a) but ordered specific performance of the provisions in the schedule, substituting a new date for compliance. He also awarded C damages in an amount equal to 13.5 per cent per annum on the £5,500 from January 27, 1979.

---

58 At least since 1927 (*Practice Note* [1927] W.N. 290) and probably very much longer: See David Foskett QC, "*The Tomlin Order: Three Score Years and Ten*", London Common Law and Commercial Bar Association Lecture, 19 November 1997, given to mark the 70th anniversary of the Tomlin order, reproduced in Appendix 6 to the 6th edn of this work.

59 See paras 6-01 and 6-02.

60 See Ch.11.

61 Including the payment of court fees on the institution of proceedings, the need for exchange of pleadings, disclosure and so on.

62 Arguably, any such action would be subject to the relevant Pre-Action Protocol.

63 *Hollingsworth v Humphrey* (1987) CAT 1244, *Independent*, 21 December 1987 CA. See also *Wagstaff v Colls* [2003] EWCA Civ 469.

The Court of Appeal held that he was correct save to the extent of having awarded damages: that aspect had to be pursued by way of separate action.

9-26 On the issue of whether the stay should have been removed Fox LJ expressed himself in this way, having recorded that there was no question in the instant case of the vitiation of the compromise by "for example, fraud or mistake":

> "The first question ... is the meaning of the agreement reached between the parties. That agreement ... consists not only in the scheduled terms of the compromise, but includes the provision for the stay itself which is an integral part of the compromise."

Having referred to the wording of the consent order, he continued as follows:

> "As between the parties, ... while the action is not discontinued or dismissed, the bargain was that the action would not be resorted to thereafter save for the purpose of enforcing the terms. That is the plain meaning of the language used ... The liberty to apply for the purpose of enforcing the terms gave [C] a summary method of securing compliance."

9-27 The argument that the compromise was merely a contract for the sale of C's beneficial interest in the property was rejected. That had been a matter in dispute and, as Fox LJ observed, C had "asserted a cause of action and gave that up in consideration of the provisions of the Tomlin order". The reason why it was necessary for there to be a fresh action to claim damages for breach of the agreement reflected in the schedule to the Tomlin order was that a claim for damages did not represent enforcement of the agreement: the original action was only kept alive for that purpose and for no other. As he put it:

> "[U]nder the terms of the Tomlin order the only jurisdiction which [the judge] had in this action was to make an order for the purpose of carrying into effect the terms of compromise. An award of damages is not carrying the terms into effect. It is granting a remedy for breach of contract. In my view any claim by [the plaintiff] for breach of contract must be pursued in a separate action."

9-28 The decision of the Court of Appeal concerning the need for a fresh action to pursue a claim for damages for breach of a provision in a Tomlin order schedule is arguably a somewhat restrictive interpretation of the words of a Tomlin order. Indeed, when the CPR were first drafted, the restrictive effect of this ruling was recognised and an effort made to circumvent it in the situation where a Pt 36 offer is accepted.[64] There is some authority to the effect that the overriding objective[65] enables the court to take a different view from that expressed in *Hollingsworth v Humphrey*.[66]

9-29 In *The Bargain Pages Ltd v Midland Independent Newspapers Ltd*[67] a passing-off action between C and D was settled by means of a Tomlin order in 1996. The terms of settle-

---

64 See para.15-29. The precedent for a Tomlin order put forward in the 5th edn (and which continues to appear in this edition (see Precedent No.3 at para.A1-03 in Appendix 1), contains a provision in these terms: "AND IT IS RECORDED that the parties have agreed that any claim for breach of contract arising from an alleged breach of the terms set out in [the Schedule to this order] [the above mentioned document] may, unless the court orders otherwise, be dealt with by way of an application to the court without the need to start a new claim." This is designed to circumvent the effect of *Hollingsworth* (1987) CAT 1244; *Independent*, 21 December 1987.

65 CPR r.1.1.

66 *Bargain Pages Ltd v Midland Independent Newspapers Ltd* [2003] EWHC 1887 (Ch); [2004] F.S.R. 6.

67 *Bargain Pages* [2003] EWHC 1887 (Ch); [2004] F.S.R. 6. Although see *Community Care North East*

ment scheduled to the order imposed restrictions on D as to the name and get-up under which it might publish and distribute its papers. In addition it was required to procure that its parent, subsidiary and associated companies controlled by it should be bound by the terms of the agreement as if they themselves were party to it. The order provided in conventional terms that all further proceedings in the action were stayed "except for the purpose of carrying the said terms into effect" and for that purpose the parties were to be at liberty to apply. During the next six years corporate reorganisations took place on both sides. Issues arose between successors to C and D as to whether there were breaches by D's successors of the terms of the Tomlin order and, if so, how they might be pursued. On the issue of how C might pursue claims for damages against D, Sir Andrew Morritt VC held that a fresh action would not be necessary. He put matters thus[68]:

> "The first passing off action gave rise to a settlement to which effect was given by the Tomlin order. The Tomlin order is as much a part of the case as the original issues as to passing off. In my view it follows that the overriding objective applies as much to issues arising from the Tomlin order as it did to the original dispute about passing off. It appears to me to be contrary to the overriding objective to require that the remedy of damages for the breach of a term of the compromise be pursued in a second action if a remedy by way of mandatory injunction to enforce the terms of the compromise can be pursued in the first. Each arises from the terms of settlement scheduled to the Tomlin order. It is not suggested that those terms are liable to be set aside. Accordingly I do not consider that the decision of the Court of Appeal in *Hollingsworth v Humphrey* ... would preclude an order for an enquiry as to damages sustained by [C] in consequence of a breach of the terms of the Agreement."

Irrespective of the issues concerning a potential claim for damages arising from breach of a Tomlin order, parties wishing to utilise the convenient machinery for enforcement afforded by such an order would be well-advised to use the standard form of words associated with it.[69] Since the effect of those words is so clearly established, it would be less than sensible to utilise some variant lest the court should be inclined to interpret the agreement underlying the consent order in a different manner from that which was intended. The importance of the words used in the usual form of Tomlin order is that a *conditional* stay of the proceedings is provided for, the action remaining alive for the purposes of enforcement.[70] The effect of a "stay" of proceedings in a context other than that of a Tomlin order has been much debated,[71] but the position now appears to be settled: an *absolute* or an *unconditional* stay is not to be equated with a dismissal or discontinuance of proceedings.[72] An operative stay prevents the action from moving forward any further,[73] or resuming "its active life",[74] without an order of the court, such an order not being granted lightly[75] and only in a "proper case".[76] The Court of Appeal has 9-30

v Durham County Council [2010] EWHC 959 (QB); [2012] 1 W.L.R. 338 at [27], where doubt was expressed as to whether CPR r.1.1, or CPR r.1.4, could be relied on to vary "the terms of the agreement in the schedule to a Tomlin Order which have been freely entered into by the parties as a binding contract"

68 *Bargain Pages* [2003] EWHC 1887 (Ch); [2004] F.S.R. 6 at [44].

69 See Precedent No.3 at para.A1-03 in Appendix 1.

70 See para.9-19.

71 See, e.g. *Lambert v Mainland Market Deliveries Ltd* [1977] 1 W.L.R. 825 CA. See also *Wagstaff* [2003] EWCA Civ 469.

72 *Rofa Sport Management AG v DHL International (UK) Ltd* [1989] 1 W.L.R. 902 CA.

73 *Lambert* [1977] 1 W.L.R. 825, per Lawton LJ at 834.

74 *Rofa Sport Management AG* [1989] 1 W.L.R. 902, per Neill LJ at 911.

75 See *Lambert* [1977] 1 W.L.R. 825, per Megaw and Lawton LJJ.

76 *Derrick v Williams* [1939] 2 All E.R. 559, *Cooper v Williams* [1963] 2 Q.B. 567, *Lambert* [1977] 1 W.L.R. 825. A former bankrupt, who takes an assignment of a right of action against certain persons

drawn attention to the "great difficulties" that would be faced by a party seeking the removal of a stay to an action "stayed by consent following a compromise".[77] Consistent with the analysis of the effect of a Tomlin order in *Hollingsworth v Humphrey*,[78] it is submitted that the "great difficulties" would lie in suggesting that the compromise itself was in some way conditional and not conclusive of the action and/or that the stay could be removed for the purpose of proceeding with the original claim.[79] Any form of words that gives rise to an absolute or unconditional stay of the proceedings will result in the need for a fresh action to enforce the terms of any agreement scheduled to the order.[80]

9-31 In *Hearn, Re*,[81] W had instituted proceedings by way of originating summons dated 21 October 1908 to determine, inter alia, whether H, from whom she was separated, had forfeited his life interest in an annuity of £500 provided for under his father's will, that annuity having been secured by the appropriation of certain properties. H was also entitled to a one-sixth share in the residue of the estate, his entitlement to that share being secured upon other properties. Those proceedings were compromised and a consent order was made on 15 June 1909 under which all further proceedings were stayed upon the terms mentioned in a schedule to the order. The terms provided, inter alia, that W should receive £315 per annum during the joint lives of H and W, such sum to be paid out of the income from the properties upon which H's annuity and his share of the residue were secured. It was also agreed that the trustees of the will of H's father (P) should take over the collection of the rents from, and the general management of, the properties securing H's annuity. H was left in possession of the properties securing his share of the residue. By early 1910 the income from the properties securing the annuity was insufficient to pay the annuity in full after provision for prior charges had been made. The full amount of W's entitlement to £315 per annum under the agreement was not paid and, through her solicitors, she asked H to make good the deficiency out of the rents and profits of the property upon which his share of the residue was secured. This request was in accordance with the terms of the agreement reflected in the schedule to the order. H did not comply with this request and W issued a summons within the action stayed by the consent order seeking an order that H should give up possession of the properties securing or representing his one-sixth share of the residue, or that a receiver should be appointed in respect of those properties, so that the sums outstanding could be made good and the future payments rendered secure. There was no defence to W's application on the merits, but H took the point that the original action had been brought to an end by the consent order of 15 June 1909 and that an action for specific performance would be required to secure enforcement of those terms. Sargant J held that W was not entitled to obtain the relief she sought by motion or summons in the original proceedings and that independent proceedings were required. The Court of Appeal held that Sargant J. was "perfectly right" in this decision.[82]

9-32 It should be noted that the consent order made in *Hearn, Re* did not provide for the qualified stay of proceedings required for a Tomlin order.[83] Equally, although the parties incorporated their agreement in the court record (namely, the schedule

---

from his trustee in bankruptcy, is in no better position to apply to lift the stay imposed by a Tomlin order and to proceed against those persons than is his trustee in bankruptcy: *Ross (A Bankrupt), Re* [1998] B.C.C. 29 CA, relying upon *Selig v Lion* [1891] 1 Q.B. 513.

77 *Rofa Sport Management AG* [1998] 1 W.L.R. 902 at 911.

78 See para.9-26.

79 See *Alan Williams Entertainment Ltd v Hurd* [2006] EWHC 81 (Ch); [2006] E.M.L.R. 15, per David Richards J at [75].

80 *Morton v Quick* (1878) 26 W.R. 441, *Green v Rozen* [1955] 1 W.L.R. 741 at 745–746. But see para.11-29.

81 *Hearn, Re* (1913) 108 L.T. 452 and 737.

82 *Hearn, Re* (1913) 108 L.T. 737 at 738.

83 See para.9-21 onwards.

to the order),[84] no suggestion was made that this gave the court a jurisdiction to grant relief by way of enforcement of the agreement without the need for a fresh action.[85]

A compromise embodied in a Tomlin order is just as susceptible to being set aside on any of the usual invalidating grounds[86] as any other compromise. The question arises of whether, as in most other cases,[87] a fresh action is required to set aside the order in such circumstances, or whether an application to remove the stay is the correct procedural course to adopt. It may be thought logical that, just as a judgment or other order by consent demands the institution of a fresh action for this purpose, so too would a settlement incorporated in a Tomlin order. Nonetheless, it appears to be possible for the matter to be dealt with purely by way of application. A stay imposed by virtue of the acceptance by one party of a Pt 36 payment may be set aside by application in the action.[88] Although not referring specifically to the procedural steps necessary for the purpose, in *Hollingsworth v Humphrey*[89] Fox LJ said that it was, 9-33

> "clear that a stay imposed as part of a compromise of an action may be lifted if the compromise is vitiated by, for example, mistake or fraud".

Whilst there is much to be said for this convenient approach from the practical point of view, it must be borne in mind that any process by which an agreement, or an order embodying that agreement, is sought to be set aside involves the assertion of a new cause of action based on whatever invalidating ground is relied upon. This would, in the normal course of events, require the institution of fresh proceedings. One answer to those proceedings might be the expiration of the appropriate limitation period. Presumably, such a point could also be taken in the context of an application to remove a stay in the circumstances under discussion.[90] 9-34

As emphasised below,[91] the schedule to a Tomlin order forms part of the court record and is amenable to the inherent jurisdiction of the court for the purposes of amendment in appropriate circumstances.[92] However, it is thought that those circumstances are confined principally to correcting an obvious error in the phraseology of the schedule such that it does not reflect the antecedent agreement of the parties.[93] Otherwise the power to alter the contractual terms set out in the schedule is ordinarily limited to the circumstances in which there is "a remedy in relation to that contract".[94] 9-35

---

84 *Islam* (1994) CAT 1240.
85 cf. *Atkinson*, *The Times*, 17 April 1991, discussed at para. 11-29 onwards.
86 See Ch.4.
87 See Ch.12.
88 cf. *Derrick v Williams* [1939] 2 All E.R. 559, *Lambert* [1977] 1 W.L.R. 825.
89 See para.9-23.
90 Since a limitation point must, in the ordinary course of events, be pleaded, there must, it is submitted, be a clear written intimation of the facts alleged to support the defence to the application.
91 See para.10-31.
92 See para.4-37 onwards.
93 As occurred in *Islam v Askar*, noted at para.4-33.
94 See *Community Care North East v Durham County Council* [2010] EWHC 959 (QB); [2012] 1 W.L.R. 338, an approach endorsed in *Watson v Sadiq* [2013] EWCA Civ 822. In *Community Care North East*, Ramsey J suggested that "if the terms of the consent order part of the Tomlin order included an express liberty to apply to vary the terms of the schedule either generally or in particular circumstances, the court would have the power to do so." That would, it is thought, undoubtedly be so although any such provision in the order would be extremely unusual given that the whole purpose of a compromise reflected in Tomlin order is for the parties to have spelt out the terms upon which they are agreed with no discretion being left to the court other, perhaps, than in relation to enforce-

9-36 The question of whether and, if so, what is the appropriate limitation period for enforcement of terms contained in the settlement that is embodied in a Tomlin order has been unresolved until recently. In The *Bargain Pages Ltd v Midland Independent Newspapers Ltd*,[95] it was suggested that enforcement of such terms were subject to the Limitation Act 1980. Notwithstanding that, until *Bostani v Pieper*,[96] there was no authoritative decision on the question. In *Bostani*, the dispute was settled on the basis that payments totalling US$33 million were to be paid to the claimant. The sum was to be paid in six instalments, only two of which were made. The settlement terms provided that in the event of non-payment judgment could be entered against the defendant. Just short of six years from the date of the last instalment payment that was made the claimant applied for judgment. The application was resisted on, amongst other grounds, the ground that it was statute-barred. Jacob J noted that there was no decisive authority on the limitation question. He concluded that a settlement contained in a schedule to a Tomlin order was a simple contract. As such it was subject to the six-year time limit set out in s.5 of the Limitation Act 1980.[97] He went on to affirm that since no new claim was being advanced and that all that was being sought was for a judgment in the sum scheduled to the Tomlin Order, neither s.35(3) of the 1980 Act nor CPR r.17(4) applied to the application.[98] This decision is consistent with the well-established proposition that the terms of a Tomlin order schedule retain a contractual status until converted by an application to the court into an enforceable court order.[99] The decision does not address directly the question of what would have occurred if the provision in the Tomlin order schedule had been converted into an enforceable judgment, but execution of the judgment had been delayed significantly.

OTHER CASES

9-37 Other orders to which parties may consent in complete or partial resolution of the compromise involve adjournment, withdrawal, discontinuance or dismissal of the proceedings.

Adjournment

9-38 A party may be prepared for the trial of his claim (or the hearing of any interim application) to be adjourned generally (with liberty to restore) or for a specified period to enable the other party to carry out the terms of the agreement. A provision would normally be made whereby the claimant would undertake to apply for the discontinuance or dismissal of the claim on fulfilment of the terms by the other party. Should the terms not be carried out, the original claim could proceed.[100]

Many applications for an interim injunction are compromised on the basis of an adjournment of the application upon certain undertakings.[101]

---

ment of the terms of the agreement.

95 [2003] EWHC 1887 (Ch); [2004] F.S.R. 6.

96 [2019] EWHC 547 (Comm); [2019] 4 W.L.R. 44.

97 [2019] EWHC 547 (Comm); [2019] 4 W.L.R. 44 at [54]–[56].

98 [2019] EWHC 547 (Comm); [2019] 4 W.L.R. 44 at [59]–[60]. Also see *Starlight Shipping Co v Allianz Marine & Aviation* [2011] EWHC 3381 (Comm); [2012] 2 All E.R. (Comm) 608.

99 See paras 11-22–11-28. See also *Jeffrey Cartwright v Venduct Engineering Ltd* [2018] EWCA Civ 1654 and *Shah v Chafer* [2018] EWCA Civ 1334.

100 For example, *Hopmeyer v Silverman* (1980) CAT 147, noted at para.8-06.

101 See para.11-34 onwards.

Withdrawal or discontinuance

Subject to the appropriate rule,[102] an action may be withdrawn or discontinued by consent either unconditionally or upon terms. Both have the effect of putting an end to the proceedings even for the purposes of enforcement of any agreed terms unless they are "kept alive" specifically for such purpose.[103] Neither course precludes the commencement of fresh proceedings based on the same cause of action unless, on a true construction of the terms of the agreement underlying the consent, it is clear that a discharge of all claims was intended.[104] **9-39**

In *Apple Computer Inc v Popiolek*,[105] C issued a writ against D seeking orders restraining him from selling computers, computer equipment and computer programmes not of C's manufacture under the name "Apple" and from passing off as manufactured by C similar items. C also claimed damages. At the hearing of C's summons for interlocutory relief in the terms of the indorsement on the writ, D consented to a perpetual injunction in the terms of the relief sought in the writ in consideration of which C agreed to, and did, file a notice of discontinuance of the action. In subsequent proceedings against D for alleged breaches of the injunction occurring after the notice of discontinuance, D sought to argue that the injunction did not survive the discontinuance and that, accordingly, no enforcement proceedings could be taken. In the Supreme Court of Victoria, Nicholson J held that the injunction, which was a final order intended to dispose of part of C's claim, was not affected by the discontinuance: at the time of the agreement only the claim for damages remained alive and it was only that part of the subject-matter of the action which was affected by the notice of discontinuance. **9-40**

In *The Ardandhu*,[106] a collision occurred between two vessels, K and A. The owners of K brought an action for damages against the owners of A. An agreement was drawn up between the respective solicitors in which the solicitors for A's owners said that they consented "to this action being discontinued without costs on the ground of inevitable accident". An order was subsequently made in the following terms: "Upon consent of both solicitors, it is ordered that this action be discontinued, without costs, on the ground of inevitable accident". The question arose subsequently of whether the agreement and the order giving effect to it represented a mutual release of all claims or whether, as the owners of K argued, there was merely a discontinuance with all matters remaining potentially open. The House of Lords held that parties must be taken to have intended the words of the agreement and the order to have their natural and ordinary meaning, namely that of a discontinuance, leaving the possibility for each party to reassert its rights. Had the parties' solicitors used the words "this action should be dismissed", then no further proceedings would have been possible. **9-41**

In *Macedonia Maritime Co v Austin & Pickersgill Ltd (The Fayrouz I–IV)*,[107] C were foreign shipowners for whom D constructed four vessels under separate contracts. C contended that at the time each of the vessels was delivered each was defective in a **9-42**

---

[102] CPR Pt 38. In *Ernst & Young v Butte Mining Plc* [1997] 1 W.L.R. 1485, Robert Walker J set aside as an abuse of the process of the court a notice of discontinuance of C's claim against D designed to frustrate the service by D of a substantial counterclaim which, but for the existence of C's claim, would have been statute-barred. The counterclaim could have been pursued provided C's claim was continued by virtue of s.35 of the Limitation Act 1980. The notice of discontinuance was served after a consent order had been agreed between C and D setting aside a judgment on C's claim obtained in default of defence.

[103] A "stay" is preferable in the circumstances and more certain in its effect: see para.9-26 onwards.

[104] *The Ardandhu* (1887) 12 App. Cas. 256.

[105] *Apple Computer Inc v Popiolek* [1984] V.R. 156 Supreme Court of Victoria.

[106] *Owners of Cargo of Kronprinz v Owners of the Kronprinz (The Ardandhu)* (1887) 12 App. Cas. 256. See also *Ako v Rothschild Asset Management Ltd* [2002] EWCA Civ 236; [2002] I.C.R. 899 at [29].

[107] *Macedonia Maritime Co v Austin & Pickersgill (Fayrouz I–IV)* [1989] 2 Lloyd's Rep. 73.

number of respects, including the welding. They claimed damages against D for about £3 million. D sought security for costs in the sum of £480,000 up to summons for directions stage (excluding discovery), but not beyond, approximately £350,000 of which was attributable to weld investigations on each of the vessels. C, who were in financial difficulties, indicated to D their willingness to withdraw some of their claims and provided D with a list set out under two headings entitled "claims to be withdrawn" and "claims which will be pursued". The welding claims were to be dropped on all vessels bar one and the one to be pursued involved a less costly weld investigation than the others. C offered D its reasonable costs to date in relation to the claims to be withdrawn and invited D to confirm its agreement in principle. C threatened to issue a summons returnable at the same time as D's summons for security, the costs of which would be sought if D failed to agree. D responded by accepting the offer and, following further discussions, C confirmed that their total claim after the withdrawals was $528,000 plus interest and costs. As a result D reduced its claim for security for costs to £75,000, including discovery, and agreement was reached that £45,000 of security should be provided. An order by consent in relation to the security was made subsequently and C were given leave to withdraw certain of the claims. C then sought to revive some of the withdrawn claims, including all those relating to welding. Hirst J, as he then was, held that they were not entitled to do so. They had carefully chosen which of the claims they were going to pursue, bearing in mind all the financial implications and those relating to the prospects of success, as a result of which they reduced substantially their potential liability to provide security for costs. The commercial background indicated "a permanent abandonment [of the claims withdrawn] and not a mere pause pending possible revival of the plaintiffs' fortunes".

Dismissal

9-43 The effect of a dismissal of proceedings by consent[108] operates in the same way as a dismissal by adjudication, namely that the cause of action dies with the dismissal. The doctrine of res judicata applies and precludes the commencement of fresh proceedings upon the same or substantially the same grounds.[109] A straightforward consent order dismissing a claim for want of prosecution will not preclude fresh proceedings unless a true compromise underlies the consent.[110]

"No order"

9-44 The expression "no order" is frequently used in the context of interim applications and parties do, from time to time, agree that "no order" should be made "by consent". Where this occurs in relation to an ordinary interim application the expression will usually be taken to imply that the parties have agreed that there is no (or no longer) reason for making an order at that time on the particular application hitherto being pursued. When it is used in the context of the final resolution of the differences between parties, it can give rise to problems because of its somewhat ambiguous meaning.[111] It is best avoided in that latter context.

---

108 CPR r.40.6.

109 *The Ardandhu* (1887) 12 App. Cas. 256, *The Bellcairn* (1885) 10 P.D. 161. See also *Kinch v Walcott* [1929] A.C. 482 PC and *Cohen v Jonesco* [1926] 1 K.B. 119 at 125. In *Zurich Insurance Co Plc v Hayward* [2011] EWCA Civ 641; [2011] C.P. Rep. 39, the doctrine of res judicata did not prevent the second action which was designed to impeach the settlement of the original action in which fraud had been alleged against the claimant on the ground that the settlement had itself been obtained by fraud of the same nature alleged in the original action

110 *Magnus v National Bank of Scotland* (1888) 57 L.J. Ch. 902.

111 See para.24-54 and also *Atkinson, The Times,* 17 April 1991, noted at para.11-30.

CHAPTER 10

Practice of Compromise

GENERAL

Once parties have agreed the essential terms of their compromise and have chosen the machinery by which it is to be implemented, the question arises of how, in practice, the machinery is set in place. Different practical steps will have to be taken depending on the stage at which the agreement is finalised and on the practice of the particular court or tribunal, if any, in which proceedings are extant. If no proceedings are involved and some written agreement is contemplated, this will, in the normal course of events, be arranged between the parties' advisers or, in some cases, by the mediator if a mediator has facilitated the agreement. The focus of this chapter will be to deal with the position when court proceedings are involved.[1] A number of preliminary, but significant, matters should be considered first. **10-01**

Attitude of the courts to compromise

The courts welcome and encourage compromise. It is in the interests of parties to disputes and to the civil justice system as a whole. It is thus in the private interest of parties and a public good, a theme articulated on many occasions, most recently by Sharp LJ in *Mionis v Democratic Press SA*.[2] The reasons are manifest. In some instances[3] the approval of the court is necessary for a compromise to be effective. Generally speaking, however, this is not necessary and the court is not concerned with the terms of the compromise. This is a matter for the parties. Since they created the dispute, they can dispose of it as they please.[4] Indeed, it appears **10-02**

---

1 For the practice in relation to mediated settlements and settlements of arbitral proceedings, see Chs 32,35 and 36.

2 [2017] EWCA Civ 1194; [2018] Q.B. 662 at [88], citing Lord Bingham's preface to the 4th edn of this work, and at [89], in which Sharp LJ emphasised the public interest in settlement, "I would add that settlement does not only serve the private interests of the litigants, but the administration of justice and the public interest more generally, by freeing court resources for other cases. The law therefore encourages and facilitates the mutual resolution of disputes by various means, for very sound reasons of public policy; and there is obviously an important public interest in the finality of settlement". The promotion of both private and public interests in the promotion of settlement is a feature of the CPR, e.g., it is a feature of the overriding objective (CPR r.1.1(2)(e)) and of active case management, which requires the court to help "the parties to settle the whole or part of the case" (CPR r.1.4(2)(f)).

3 See, e.g. Chs 24 and 27.

4 However, the court retains a discretion to hand down judgment publicly notwithstanding that the parties settle the case after receiving a draft judgment for suggested correction but before it is handed down formally: *Prudential Assurance Co Ltd v McBains Cooper* [2000] 1 W.L.R. 2000, CA, *Gurney Consulting Engineers v Gleeds Health & Safety Ltd* [2006] EWHC 536 (TCC); 108 Con. L.R. 58, *Greenwich Inc Ltd v Dowling* [2014] EWHC 2451 (Ch). It is not however appropriate to view the

that the court cannot decline to enter a consent order or judgment merely because it is suspicious of the terms or disapproves of them.[5] If the court is asked to make an order outside its jurisdiction,[6] or which is illegal, then it can properly decline to do so.

As a matter of practice, the court has ordinarily not been prepared to make a binding declaration of right by consent,[7] although this practice is now less strictly followed.[8] Where any proposed consent order or judgment affects the status of any of the parties the court would wish to be informed of the facts and law applicable before making the order.[9] Thus, although a court may make suggestions about the proposed terms of a compromise,[10] it cannot refuse to give effect to them by means of an order or judgment desired by the parties.[11] In *Arthur J.S. Hall v Simons* in the

---

circulation of a draft judgment as a "staging post" on the way to settlement: *R (S) v General Teaching Council for England* [2013] EWHC 2779 (Admin) at [26]–[27]. Also see *Prudential Assurance Co Ltd* at [28]. In certain circumstances a court may continue to hand down a judgment where the parties have settled the dispute on condition that judgment is not given, see *F&C Alternative Investments (Holdings) Ltd v Barthelemy* [2011] EWHC 1851 (Ch); [2012] Bus. L.R. 884.

5 *Noel v Becker* [1971] 1 W.L.R. 355 CA. See also *South American & Mexican Co, Re* [1895] 1 Ch. 37, where it was acknowledged that agreed terms do not have to be mentioned by counsel to the court. See, e.g. *Correa v BP Plc* [2019] EWHC 232 (QB). *Bruce v Worthing BC* (1994) 26 H.L.R. 223 at 228, per Staughton LJ: "In our adversarial system a judge who is asked to make a consent order should do so, provided that the parties are of full age and understanding and that the order is not illegal, immoral or so equivocal as likely to give rise to further dispute."

6 *Noel v Becker* [1971] 1 W.L.R. 355, per Davies LJ at 357, *Hinde v Hinde* [1953] 1 All E.R. 175. See further at para. 10-06 onwards.

7 *Wallersteiner v Moir* [1974] 1 W.L.R. 991. cf. *Patten v Burke Publishing* [1991] 1 W.L.R. 541. See also para.23-40.

8 See, e.g. *Animatrix Ltd v O'Kelly* [2008] EWCA Civ 1415, where it was said to be no more than a rule of practice not to make declarations by consent, and that the court could so grant a declaration where it was necessary to do justice. Also see *Hayim v Couch* [2009] EWHC 1040 (Ch) at [17], where the principles to be derived from the authorities governing the grant of declarations by consent were said to be:

> "...
> (1) That the rule that a court should not grant a declaration except after a trial was only ever a rule of practice.
> (2) That the rule should not be followed if following it would deny the claimant the fullest justice to which he is entitled.
> (3) That the rule is less strong since the coming into force of the CPR than it was when the RSC held sway.
> (4) That where the parties' consent to (or agree not to oppose) the grant of declaratory relief and that consent forms part of a bona fide commercial bargain entered into between them to avoid the need for a trial, the Court is likely to consider it necessary to grant the declarations sought in order to do justice between them."

And see *Vince v Revenue and Customs Commissioners* [2016] EWHC 3144 (Ch), para.23-43 and para.30-13.

9 *R. v Bloomsbury and Marylebone County Court Ex p. Blackburne* (1984) 14 H.L.R. 56.

10 cf. *Practice Direction (Ch.D.) (Minutes of Order)* [1960] 1 W.L.R. 1168, "1. Where minutes of order have been settled by counsel the registrar should not interfere in any way with the minutes unless it appears to him that they do not carry out the intention of the judge or are defective in form. If the registrar is not satisfied he should refer the minutes back to counsel through the solicitors with his proposed amendments. Should the registrar and counsel be unable to agree the minutes, the matter should be mentioned to the judge. 2. In the case of terms scheduled to a consent order these terms represent an arrangement between the parties, and the registrar is not concerned to approve them, although he may properly offer suggestions upon them if it appears to him that they may cause some difficulty."

11 A refusal by a court to make such an order could, presumably, be enforced by a mandatory order, and an order in terms different in substance from those desired by the parties could be the subject of an appeal: cf. *Noel v Becker* [1971] 1 W.L.R. 355. Indeed, a refusal to make an order at all could itself be regarded as an order dismissing a joint application of the parties for a consent order or judg-

Court of Appeal,[12] Lord Bingham of Cornhill CJ, having referred to the equivalent passage in the 4th edition of this work and to *Noel v Becker*,[13] said this[14]:

> "Adult parties of sound mind may ordinarily settle proceedings by an agreement made wholly out of court ... They may for a variety of reasons choose to embody their agreement in a consent judgment of the court; this will not in the ordinary way call for any exercise of judgment by the court."

REALITY OF THE CONSENT

Before the court will enter a consent order or judgment it must be satisfied that the appropriate consents have been given.[15] Without such consents no order can be made and the court cannot consent on behalf of a party.[16] Where parties are physically before the court, either in person or by representation, it is usual for the court to ask directly for confirmation of the consents. The consent of an unrepresented party is no less real than that of a represented party, but the court may enquire a little further to ensure that such consent is given voluntarily.[17] **10-03**

If the parties are not physically before the court, but have invited the making of an order by consent, the draft order submitted to the court must be signed by the solicitors or counsel acting for each of the parties to the order.[18] If the consenting party is a litigant in person, they must sign the proposed order.[19] Unless the court has any reason to doubt the authenticity of the signature or that the consent was given voluntarily, the order will be made.[20]

RECORDING OF THE CONSENT

Where a judgment or order truly represents the result of mutual consents, the fact of its consensual nature should be recorded on the face of the order or judgment.[21] The failure to do so will not affect the fact that it is of such a nature[22] and the court will be prepared to investigate the background if necessary to determine the true position.[23] **10-04**

---

ment such that an appeal would lie.

12 *Arthur J.S. Hall v Simons* [2002] 1 A.C. 615.

13 *Noel* [1971] 1 W.L.R. 355.

14 *Noel* [1971] 1 W.L.R. 355 at [20]. The implications of the judgments in the House of Lords in *Hall v Simons* in the context of compromise are dealt with in Ch.21.

15 cf. CPR Pt 40 PD 40B para.3.2.

16 *Woodhead v Woodhead* (1978) CAT 147.

17 The consent of a litigant in person to the making by a district judge of the county court of an injunction must be "real, genuine and informed"; non-dissent is not sufficient: *Simons and Simons v Winder and Winder* (27 July 1982) CAT 369; [1982] 7 WLUK 277 at [8], per Stephenson LJ.

18 See CPR Pt 40 PD 40B para.3.4(3)(a). See further at para.10-17 onwards for the practice.

19 See CPR Pt 40 PD 40B para.3.4(3)(b).

20 It has long ceased to be the practice that the personal attendance of a litigant in person before a judge is required, or that his signature is attested by a solicitor, before a consent order will be made. cf. para.24-50.

21 See CPR Pt 40 PD 40B para.3.4(2); *Michel v Mutch* (1886) 54 L.T. 45, *Darley (Trustee of Baines) v Tulley* (1923) 155 L.T. Jo. 128; *Chandless-Chandless v Nicholson* [1942] 2 K.B. 321 at 324, CA, per Lord Greene MR, "If an order is made by consent the practice should invariably be that it should on the face of it be expressed so to have been made. When the court finds an order which is not expressed to be made by consent it certainly is not going to treat it as a consent order unless it is satisfied that it was in fact a consent order". See further at para.10-17 onwards.

22 *Darley v Tulley* (1923) 155 L.T. Jo. 128.

23 *Magnus v National Bank of Scotland* (1888) 57 L.J. Ch.902 at 904; and see *Chandless-Chandless v Nicholson* [1942] 2 K.B. 321 at 324, CA.

The distinction between a consent order or judgment and one to which a party "submits" has already been noted.[24] The mere fact that a party submits to an order or judgment does not accord it the status of one "by consent". This is so even if the submission is made pursuant to an agreement. The fact that an order or judgment is made "by consent" may have a number of practical and procedural implications.[25]

Indorsement of counsels' briefs

10-05 In those distant days before laptop computers or tablet devices were taken to court habitually by counsel, the practice of indorsing counsels' briefs with the terms of an agreed order was often employed.[26] It is thought that this will rarely, if ever, be a technique adopted in contemporary times. However, if it is ever utilised the usual practice would be for each counsel to sign each other's indorsement. This precaution obviates the difficulties that might otherwise arise where the indorsement on one brief differs substantially from that on the other. In such an event, the court would historically not hear evidence of what was really intended and any order made in purported pursuance of the indorsements was regarded as a nullity.[27]

Jurisdiction

10-06 It has already been observed[28] that a court must enter a judgment or make an order by consent in the terms desired by the parties unless problems of jurisdiction (or illegality) arise. It is important, therefore, in practice for parties to ensure that no such problems remain before placing a draft agreed order or judgment before a court. Indeed, where problems of this nature have not been resolved, the court will often invite parties to reconsider the position and put matters in order.[29]

Problems of this nature can arise in a number of ways.

(i) The forum itself

10-07 Parties may find themselves inviting a court to make an order or judgment outside the normal jurisdiction of that particular court or about which there is some doubt as to its jurisdiction. This will usually arise, if at all, in the county court. The problem is readily resolved by the filing of a memorandum pursuant to the appropriate section of the County Courts Act 1984.[30] Properly speaking, the agreement should be made before the judgment or order is made,[31] although it would appear that a failure to do so, and no point being taken by any party, would not render the order a nullity.[32]

---

24 See para.9-14.

25 See Ch.6 and Ch.12.

26 *Green v Rozen* [1955] 1 W.L.R. 741.

27 *Practice Note* [1884] W.N. 91.

28 At para.10-02.

29 However, it is not unknown for the parties and the court to overlook a jurisdictional problem: see, e.g. *IRC v Hoogstraten* [1985] Q.B. 1077 noted at para.10-10. This can give rise to further difficulties at a later stage, particularly with regard to enforcement: e.g. *Hinde v Hinde* [1953] 1 W.L.R. 175; [1953] 1 All E.R. 175 noted at para.10-11.

30 County Courts Act 1984 s.18 or 24.

31 cf. *R. v Willes (Judge) Ex p. Abbey National Building Society* [1954] 1 W.L.R. 136.

32 cf. *Williams v Settle* [1960] 1 W.L.R. 1072. In *Gurmit Singh v Satnam Singh* [2004] EWCA Civ 544, on an application for permission to appeal, Auld LJ held that CPR Pts 10 and 11, taken together, mean that a failure to dispute the county court's jurisdiction is to be taken to have accepted it.

(ii) Tribunal within the appropriate forum

A judge of the High Court or the county court possesses all the powers within the relevant jurisdiction. A master and district judge, or equivalent judge, each possess a limited jurisdiction and, in some cases, an extended jurisdiction by the consent of the parties.[33] Parties should ensure that the correct tribunal is invited to make the order. In cases of doubt the directions of the court may be sought. 10-08

(iii) Terms of the order or judgment are outside the ordinary jurisdiction[34]

It has already been noted[35] that the parties cannot by consent confer on the court a jurisdiction which it does not otherwise possess. If the point is noted, the court could properly decline to make an order outside its jurisdiction.[36] The rationale for this position is presumably that the court would not wish to, nor would wish to be seen to, act in a way that was arguably unlawful. 10-09

In *IRC v Hoogstraten*,[37] C sued D for over £2.5 million, being the sum allegedly due in respect of unpaid taxes and interest, and obtained a *Mareva* order restraining any disposition of D's assets up to the amount claimed. Subsequently, D made certain dispositions of property in breach of this order. C sought his committal to prison for contempt, alternatively for the sequestration of his property. At a resumed hearing of this notice of motion negotiations took place and an agreement was reached. D accepted that he had been in breach of the order, but he contended (and this was common ground) that he had purged his contempt by, in effect, arranging for the recovery of the property the subject of the previous dispositions. In the circumstances C agreed not to seek D's committal to prison whilst he agreed to the sequestration of all his property. An agreed order to this effect was made by the judge. The Court of Appeal held that whilst the agreement was made in good faith and represented a sensible and constructive outcome of a contested committal application, the order "ought never to have been made" because an order for sequestration, under the then RSC Ord.45 rr.1 and 5 could only be made against a person who was in contempt of court. At the time the agreed order was made, D was no longer in contempt of court. The order was, however, a valid order of the court until set aside.[38] 10-10

From the point of view of a client whose legal advisers have led him into the making of such an order, there may be unwanted consequences, particularly in connection with difficulties concerning enforcement. 10-11

In *Hinde v Hinde*,[39] a consent order was made in 1936, upon W's application for maintenance from H, in a specified sum and was expressed to be payable to her "until remarriage". After H's death in 1952 no further payments were made and W, not having remarried, sought to enforce the order against H's estate. The Court of Appeal held that insofar as the consent order purported to confer upon W the right to receive payments from H beyond their "joint lives"—the period for which the court ordinarily had jurisdiction

---

33 CPR r.2.4 and CPR Pt 2 PD 2B para.1.3 and *The White Book* 2019, Vol.1, para.2.4.1 onwards.

34 "Jurisdiction" in this context is used in the narrow sense of the term: per Diplock LJ in *Garthwaite v Garthwaite* [1964] P. 356 at 387.

35 See para.9-20 onwards.

36 *Noel* [1971] 1 W.L.R. 355 at 357.

37 *IRC v Hoogstraten* [1985] Q.B. 1077.

38 See also *Isaacs v Robertson* [1985] A.C. 97 PC, cf. *Nicholls v Kinsey* [1994] Q.B. 600 CA.

39 *Hinde* [1953] 1 W.L.R. 175; [1953] All E.R. 171. See also *Sugden v Sugden* [1957] P. 129 at 137, per Hodson LJ See more generally in the family law context in Ch.24.

to provide[40] —the order was of no effect notwithstanding that it was made by consent.[41] Enforcement could not, therefore take place.

(iv) Terms of the order or judgment are outside the jurisdiction in the particular case

10-12 The consent order the parties invite a court to make may contain an order that the court would ordinarily have jurisdiction to make but not in the context of the specific claims and counterclaims advanced in the particular proceedings. An example is where a claim by a landlord against a tenant for damages for breach of a repairing covenant (and nothing more) is compromised on the basis that the tenant vacates the property. If the landlord wishes to obtain an order for possession (to which the tenant is prepared to consent or submit) to secure his position under the agreement, an appropriate amendment to the proceedings, or the institution of fresh proceedings (doubtless waiving all formalities), would usually be considered necessary to enable the court to make an order for possession.

10-13 Nothing very formal or expensive would be required for the court to accept the existence of the appropriate jurisdiction to make the order. A sentence in the preamble to a consent order to the effect that the parties have agreed to treat the existing proceedings as proceedings for the particular relief claimed, "abridging all time and waiving all formalities" would doubtless suffice. In some circumstances the court may require that a formal pleading be filed or an appropriate amendment be made to the existing proceedings, a suitable undertaking that this will be done being given.

10-14 In certain situations the permission of the court may be required before a new or amended pleading is filed. This will be dealt with by consent.

10-15 If attention is paid by the legal advisers of parties to a compromise to the jurisdictional aspects of any proposed consent order or judgment, no difficulty is likely to be found in the making and subsequent enforcement of the order. Much expense and frustration (particularly on the part of the lay client) will be saved by having everything in order.

10-16 The foregoing discussion has been directed at matters which, logically, are preliminary and incidental to the making of a consent order or judgment. Attention is now turned briefly to the practical aspects of securing the order or judgment once its terms have been agreed and all jurisdictional problems resolved.

PRACTICE OF OBTAINING A CONSENT ORDER

10-17 Where the proposed consent order or judgment is one of a number of fairly straightforward forms provided for in the rules,[42] and provided none of the parties is a litigant in person, nor is the approval of the court as such to the order required,

---

40 Supreme Court of Judicature (Consolidation) Act 1925 s.190(2). See now Matrimonial Causes Act 1973 s.28(1)(a).

41 Such a provision could have been made in an agreement (*Kirk v Eustace* [1937] A.C. 491) and still could be (cf. Matrimonial Causes Act 1973 s.36), but *not* as part of an order.

42 CPR r.40.6(3). It will be noted that (b)(ii) refers to an order for "the stay of proceedings on agreed terms, disposing of the proceedings, whether those terms are recorded in a schedule to the order or elsewhere". This is intended to refer to a Tomlin order. The words "or elsewhere" were inserted to cater for the situation in which the parties (as they do with increasing frequency) wish to record the substance of their agreement other than in the schedule to the order (which is part of the court record and open for inspection) and thus keep it confidential: see para.10-28 onwards.

a court officer may enter and seal the order.[43] If this procedure is followed, the order or judgment will not bear the name and judicial title of the person who made it,[44] because, of course, it will not have received any judicial scrutiny and will not have received any judicial authority as such. The order will, however, have the full authority of the court.

Where the foregoing procedure is adopted, the court officer will be concerned to ensure that the proposed order falls fairly and squarely within the terms of CPR r.40.6(3). If there is any doubt, he will refer the order to the master, district judge or judge. It will also be of concern to the court officer to ensure that none of the parties is a litigant in person. The purported making of an order pursuant to this procedure when one of the parties is a litigant in person would probably invalidate the order.[45] **10-18**

Where a represented party agrees a proposed consent order with a litigant in person, it would be prudent for the solicitor drawing up the order for submission to the court to write a covering letter to the court stating expressly that r.40.6(2) does not apply. This should ensure that judicial scrutiny is given to the order. The fact that it has been presented to a master, district judge or judge should be checked when the order is returned by the court.[46]

When the provisions of r.40.6(2) and (3) do not apply, an application to the court should be made.[47] The application, which will usually be dealt with by a master or district judge, can be dealt with without a hearing.[48] All applications are governed by CPR Pt 23. Since all parties are agreed that the particular consent order should be made, it is likely that the application will be made without serving an application notice.[49] The agreed order must be drawn up in the agreed terms, be expressed to be "by consent" and be signed by the legal representative acting for each party to whom the order relates or by the party if he is a litigant in person.[50] Where all parties affected by the order have written to the court consenting to the making of the order, a draft of which has been filed with the court, the draft will be treated as having been signed by all parties.[51] As indicated above, so far as litigants in person are concerned, the practice prior to the CPR had been for the court to accept a consent order signed by a litigant in person when satisfied that the signature was genuine and that the consent was also genuine and voluntarily given.[52] That practice continues. The master or district judge would be entitled to ask the litigant in person to attend before him, or to ask for some second written confirmation of agreement, if he had any reservations about the matter. **10-19**

Information required by court

The CPR Pt 23A Practice Direction places upon the parties who wish to follow the procedures available in CPR r.40.6 the onus of ensuring that the court is provided "with any material it needs to be satisfied that it is appropriate to make **10-20**

---

43 CPR r.40.6(2).

44 CPR r.40.2(1)(c).

45 *National Westminster Bank Plc v Smillie* (unreported 4 February 1999), and see *National Westminster Bank Plc v Smillie* [2001] EWCA Civ 1300.

46 *National Westminster Bank Plc v Smillie* (unreported 4 February 1999).

47 CPR r.40.6(5).

48 CPR r.40.6(6); CPR r.23.8(a).

49 CPR Pt 23 PD 23A para.3(3).

50 CPR r.40.6(7).

51 CPR Pt 23 PD 23A para.10.2.

52 See para.10-03.

the order".[53] This might include, for example, reference to some particular authority or statutory provision so as to demonstrate that the court does have jurisdiction to make a particular order which, at first sight, might seem unusual.

Settlements reached just before or during trial

10-21 Where a settlement is not achieved until just before or during the trial, the practice will vary slightly depending upon whether the court's approval to the settlement is required. If approval is not required, the judge will have been told by the advocates that a settlement has been reached and they will usually prepare a draft agreed order or judgment. That will be presented to the judge in open court who, provided he is satisfied that it displays all the proper features of a valid consent order or judgment,[54] will proceed to make the order. It is not strictly necessary for any terms of the settlement to be mentioned in open court, whether or not they appear on the face of the draft order.[55] Once an order is made it is a public document and is available for scrutiny, a factor which sometimes impels the parties to adopt a procedure designed to ensure confidentiality.[56] Where approval is required, the trial judge will be invited to give that approval.[57]

Settlements requiring approval of the court

10-22 A settlement involving a child or protected party may be concluded prior to the commencement of proceedings. If so, the approval of the court will still be required for the agreement to be binding. The CPR Pt 21 Practice Direction sets out the procedure to be adopted[58] and the information required. The Practice Direction deals with the information required when the settlement is of a claim arising from an accident. The information may need to be amplified where the claim arose out of alleged clinical negligence. For example, an issue which frequently arises in this context is causation. The defence may accept the alleged negligence (either in whole or in part), but denies that it caused or materially contributed to the condition of which complaint is made. Where the claimant is prepared to make a discount to reflect the risks of an adverse finding, the court will need to be informed about this and about how the claimant's advisers see the issue.[59]

10-23 Where counsel has advised on the settlement, it is normal for counsel's opinion to be placed before the court. It is not usually shown to the opposing side.

10-24 Where the settlement is concluded after the institution of proceedings, an application for approval will have to be made. If the settlement is concluded well before the trial, the application can be dealt with by the master or district judge under CPR r.40.6. In cases of difficulty, the application might be referred to a judge. If the settlement is achieved at or shortly before trial, the approval will be sought from the trial judge.

---

53 CPR Pt 23 PD 23A para.10.4. A letter is usually acceptable for this purpose.
54 See para.10-06 onwards.
55 See para.10-02.
56 See paras 10-28 onwards.
57 See para.10-22 and Ch.27.
58 CPR Pt 21 PD 21 paras 6.1–6.3: see Appendix 3.
59 See Ch.27.

NOTIFICATION OF SETTLEMENT TO COURT

Where a settlement is reached which disposes of the whole claim for which a date or "window" has been fixed for trial, the parties must notify the listing officer for the trial court immediately.[60] Where a sealed order giving effect to the settlement has been obtained, a copy of the sealed order should be filed with the listing officer.[61] **10-25**

A settlement of an appeal to the Court of Appeal should also be notified to the court as soon as possible.[62] **10-26**

SETTLEMENT OF APPEALS

The practice applicable when an appeal is made from a Master or district judge to a judge, or of any appeal to the Court of Appeal, is dealt with in Ch.34. **10-27**

CONFIDENTIALITY

Parties may wish to keep the terms of their compromise confidential. There are two aspects that require to be considered: first, the agreement as to confidentiality itself; secondly, the means by which that agreement is given effect in any consent order reflecting it. **10-28**

As between the parties, an express term as to confidentiality will usually be agreed if required. This will take the form appropriate to the nature of the case, but will normally provide that the terms of the compromise remain confidential to the parties save as may be necessary for the purposes of its implementation and as may be required by a court or other competent authority.[63] In *Horizon Technologies International Ltd v Lucky Wealth Consultants Ltd*,[64] the following provision appeared in the deed of settlement underlying the Tomlin order made in that case: **10-29**

> "All parties hereto acknowledge that the provisions in this Deed of Settlement are confidential to all the parties hereto to include all officers, directors and servants thereof and each party undertakes in favour of all the others not to disclose any of these provisions to any person not a party to this deed, save as may be necessary for the purpose of implementing this Deed of Settlement. It is hereby agreed that neither party shall be in breach of this clause by disclosing any matters contained herein if compelled to do so by any Court or authority of competent jurisdiction."

If the compromise remains entirely contractual, the means of enforcing any threatened breach of the confidentiality clause would be by means of an application for an interim injunction in the context of a fresh action to enforce the **10-30**

---

60 CPR r.39.10(1).

61 CPR r.39.10(2).

62 This consideration applies where the parties settle the appeal whilst the court has reserved its judgment following the arguments: *HFC Bank Plc v HSBC Bank Plc,* [2000] C.P.L.R. 197, CA.

63 For example, HMRC.

64 *Horizon Technologies International Ltd* [1992] 1 W.L.R. 24, 28, PC. Another variant on this theme is as follows: "The parties are agreed that the terms of this settlement are to remain confidential between them and their legal advisers and are not to be disclosed in any circumstances to any other person without the prior written consent of all parties hereto or the permission of the court, such permission to be sought upon notice to all other parties." Also see, *Thakrar v Ciro Citterio Menswear Plc (In Administration)* [2002] EWHC 1975 (Ch) at [32] on *Horizon* generally.

agreement. If the agreement is embodied in some form of agreed order, the means of enforcement will depend upon the form of that order. If the confidentiality clause appears as a provision within the schedule to a Tomlin order, then an injunction may be sought since the terms of the schedule are contractual in status. Technically it would be possible to convert such a provision into an enforceable order by means of obtaining a mandatory order,[65] but this would offer no practical advantage over the obtaining of an injunction. Once an injunction has been obtained following a breach or threatened breach, notice of the existence of the injunction can be given to others (for example, the Press, other media outlets or internet providers) who might otherwise be a conduit for the publication of the terms. Where, despite the apparent agreement between the parties as to confidentiality, there is doubt about the good faith of one or other of the parties, the existence of undertakings to the court may offer the most effective medium for the prevention of disclosure of the terms of the agreement.

10-31 There are a number of types of case where the parties wish to ensure that no publicity is given to the terms of their settlement. Anything said in open court about a settlement can, of course, be reported. As already indicated,[66] in most cases it is not necessary for the terms of settlement to be mentioned in open court. However, any consent order or judgment will form part of the court record which is available for subsequent scrutiny. For example, the schedule to a Tomlin order, whilst not strictly part of the immediately enforceable court order, is part of the court record.[67] If the normal form of Tomlin order is utilised, a direction from the court could be obtained to the effect that the schedule to the order "be not released" to any party other than the parties or their advisers.[68] If concern is felt about the efficacy of this direction, the best approach would be to ensure that the terms which would otherwise be scheduled to the order are incorporated on a separate document, suitably identified on the face of the Tomlin order.[69]

---

65 See para.11-22 onwards.

66 See fn.5.

67 *Islam v Askar* (1994) CAT 1240; *The Times*, 20 October 1994; see para.4.33.

68 Sir David Foskett was once involved in a case as Counsel in which Sir Michael Davies suggested that such a direction be made where the parties wished the terms of the schedule to the Tomlin order to be kept confidential.

69 See Precedent No.3 at para.A1-03 in Appendix 1.

CHAPTER 11

Enforcement of a Compromise

GENERAL

Where the terms of a compromise permit recourse to the original claim in the event of non-compliance with the agreement,[1] the innocent party will have the option of deciding whether to follow that course or to pursue such remedies as may be available under the compromise.[2] The discussion that follows presupposes a decision by the innocent party to rely upon his rights under the compromise. 11-01

The manner in which those rights may be enforced or otherwise relied upon[3] will to some extent depend upon the machinery chosen for giving effect to the compromise.[4] The essential primary consideration is whether or not what is to be enforced or relied upon is a contract, an order or a judgment.

WHERE THE COMPROMISE IS ENTIRELY CONTRACTUAL

In the event that the compromise is entirely contractual, the usual remedies for breach of contract will be available depending on the circumstances.[5] Damages will often be the appropriate remedy, although there may be situations in which specific performance or an injunction will be granted. 11-02

Where a party to a compromise attempts to ignore its existence, either by continuing or commencing proceedings, the other party may either set up the agreement as a defence to the claim or apply to the court to stay the proceedings.[6] In the latter event the party seeking to establish the existence of the compromise will usually apply for an order staying the proceedings. The question of whether a binding agreement exists is normally directed to be tried as a preliminary issue. Where no application to such effect is made, but the pleadings disclose that the issue exists, a 11-03

---

1 See Ch.8.

2 See para.8-09.

3 cf. para.36-37, fn.96.

4 See Ch.9.

5 *Chitty*, Vol.1, Pt 8.

6 *Eden v Naish* (1878) L.R. 7 Ch. D. 781, *Baker v Baker* (1886) 55 L.T. 723, *Mathews, Re* [1905] 2 Ch.460, *Guy v Walker* (1892) 8 T.L.R. 314. See also *Snelling* [1973] 1 Q.B. 87, noted at para.6-72. Where proceedings are extant and the claimant wishes to allege that an agreement has been reached compromising those proceedings, he may seek a determination of the point as a preliminary issue in those proceedings without the need for a fresh action. If the point is determined in his favour, an order staying the proceedings will be made and a declaration given as to the terms of the compromise. This was the course followed in the unreported case of *Metrostore Ltd v British Railways Board* Unreported January 20, 1989. See also *Eden v Naish* (1878) L.R. 7 Ch. D. 781 and *Walsh v Hall* [2016] EWHC 1759 (Ch). Enforcement of the compromise as such would require a fresh action. cf. para.11-29.

direction to this effect may be made.[7] When the question arises whether an appeal to the Court of Appeal has been compromised, it can be dealt with by way of a preliminary application to stay all further proceedings.[8]

WHERE THERE IS A CONSENT ORDER OR JUDGMENT

11-04 The courses open in respect of the enforcement of a consent order or judgment depend upon the form the order or judgment takes. It is likely that these courses will have been taken into account when the form of order was formulated. As previously indicated,[9] unless the parties expressly agree and provide otherwise ordinarily they will be taken to have agreed that any consent order or judgment drawn up to embody their compromise will take effect as if the court itself had made it following a contested hearing. In other words, the normal jurisdiction and practice of the court applies to any such order or judgment.

11-05 The enforcement processes available to a party wishing to take proceedings arising from a failure by the other party to comply with an order or judgment will be governed by the relevant provisions of the CPR.[10]

WHERE AN AGREEMENT IS FILED AND MADE A RULE OF COURT

11-06 As has been observed previously,[11] the procedure of filing and making an agreement a rule of court is rarely, if ever, utilised in contemporary times, certainly in mainstream civil litigation. The analysis that follows indicates why that is so, but also may assist where an issue does arise of the effect of such an agreement if it should arise.

11-07 Where the agreement as a whole has been filed and made a rule of court the enforcement process will depend on the provision within the agreement sought to be enforced. Where a particular provision has been made the subject of an order, then the enforcement process applicable to an order of that nature will be appropriate. Where a particular provision has not been made an order, but nonetheless remains part of the agreement, the approach will be similar to that which is appropriate to the enforcement of provisions in the schedule to a Tomlin order[12]: subject to one possible exception,[13] a further order of the court, converting the contractual obligation into an enforceable order, will be needed before enforcement steps can be taken.

Status of an agreement made a rule of court

11-08 The foregoing view is, it is thought, the better one. There is, however, a divergence of view on the authorities as to the precise status of an agreement made a rule of court: is it equivalent to an order and enforceable as such or is it still merely an agreement which requires further steps to be taken in relation to it before it

---

7 *Tomlin* [1969] 1 W.L.R. 1378.
8 cf. *Harte v Harte* (1976) CAT 423A.
9 See para.5-36 onwards.
10 CPR Pt 70 onwards.
11 See para.9-11 fn. 33.
12 See para.11-22 onwards.
13 See para.11-21.

becomes an order or equivalent to an order?[14] That it is the latter rather than the former is, however, supported by strong authority and accords with established principles and practice:

> In *Shaw, Re*,[15] the precise question of the status of the provisions of such an agreement fell to be considered. The question, essentially, was whether or not payments made under provisions of an agreement made a rule of court were, for the purposes of taxation provisions, made under an order of the court. The Court of Appeal held that the payments were *not* made under an order and that the agreement was still a contract and nothing more. It was said[16] that the effect of making an agreement a rule of court was to enable enforcement of its provisions in a summary way without the need for a fresh action. **11-09**

It follows that the provisions of an agreement made a rule of court are accorded a status identical to the status of the provisions in a Tomlin order schedule,[17] the whole purpose of a Tomlin order being to enable enforcement of those provisions *within the existing action* and without the need for a new action. **11-10**

Some support for the view that making an agreement a rule of court does not accord it the status of an order of the court may be found, albeit obiter, in *Jessel v Jessel*.[18] **11-11**

> In *Jessel v Jessel*, minutes of an order recording a matrimonial settlement were ordered to be made a rule of court. One provision, which H sought to uphold,[19] was an undertaking by W not to apply to increase a consent order for periodical payments made previously and an acknowledgment that the provision made in that order was to be in settlement of all her claims for periodical payments. One of H's arguments was that the making of the agreement a rule of court validated what was otherwise a void provision. The Court of Appeal held that the original order was a continuing order and dismissed H's contentions on that basis. However, all members of the court[20] doubted whether making a provision such as this a rule of court would validate it.[21] **11-12**

The contrary view seems to have been taken in *Royal Society of Literature v Lowenthal*[22] and *Herbert v Herbert*.[23] **11-13**

> In *Royal Society of Literature v Lowenthal*, a summons to enforce a provision of an agreement made a rule of court was taken out under the former RSC Ord.45 r.8.[24] It was argued at first instance that making a compromise a rule of court had the effect of making it an order and thus enforceable under that particular provision of the RSC. At first instance Jupp J held that, the terms of the compromise had to be treated as though they were themselves orders of the court and the point was conceded by counsel in the Court of Appeal. Since the decision of Jupp J is not reported, and the matter was not argued in the

---

14 The practice derives from the old probate practice about which there is little evidence in contemporary books.

15 *Shaw, Re* [1918] P. 47 CA. See also *Croft v Croft* (1922) 38 T.L.R. 648 and *Aspden (Inspector of Taxes) v Hildesley* [1982] 1 W.L.R. 264.

16 *Shaw, Re* [1918] P 47, per Warrington LJ at 53–54, and at 53, per Swinfen-Eady LJ.

17 See para.9-21 onwards.

18 *Jessel v Jessel* [1979] 1 W.L.R. 1148 CA.

19 On the basis of *Minton v Minton* [1979] A.C. 593 HL, as to which see Ch.24.

20 See *Jessel* [1979] 1 W.L.R. 1148: Lord Denning MR, Browne and Geoffrey Lane LJJ at 1154, 1155 and 1156 respectively.

21 i.e. the provision would *not* have assumed the status of an order.

22 *Royal Society of Literature v Lowenthal* (1978) CAT 182.

23 *Herbert v Herbert* (1978) 122 S.J. 826.

24 This rule related to the enforcement, amongst other things, of a "mandatory order" or a "judgment or order".

Court of Appeal, it is thought that little weight can be attached to it. It is not clear whether *Shaw, Re* was cited at first instance: if it was not, the decision was clearly per incuriam.

11-14 In *Herbert v Herbert Herbert v Herbert* (1978) 122 S.J. 826, it was held that an agreement which had been made a rule of court had the same effect as an order or judgment and was enforceable as such. A summons to commit for an alleged breach of one of its terms was allowed to proceed. Although the argument to the contrary effect was advanced, it is clear that neither *Shaw, Re* nor *Dashwood v Dashwood*[25] was cited in support. Had they been cited, the decision might well have been different.[26]

Order or rule of court

11-15 It is possible that some confusion has arisen in this context by the use on some occasions in the older cases of the expressions "order of court" and "rule of court" as more or less synonymous.[27] They are occasionally run together. In *Smythe v Smythe*,[28] an action for judicial separation was compromised before trial upon certain terms, one of which was that the respondent was to pay the petitioner's taxed costs. It was provided that the agreement "may be made a rule of the High Court". The report shows[29] that an order was made subsequently "making the agreement of compromise an order of the Queen's Bench Division" and that thereafter it was "duly made an order". Counsel for the respondent argued there was no power to make the terms of compromise "a rule of court". Sir James Hannen, giving the leading judgment, referred to the long-established practice of making such agreements "a rule of court" and went on to say that he did not doubt that he "could have made this agreement an order of court".

11-16 Despite the apparent interchangeability of the two expressions, the case of *Smythe v Smythe* supports the view that a further order is required before a provision in an agreement made a rule of court becomes an order. The case concerned a provision which without doubt was within the jurisdiction of the court to make, and this may, of course, afford an explanation for the use of expressions suggesting that the agreement itself could be made an order of court. It is noteworthy that Sir James Hannen, when referring to the practice, said[30] that agreements of compromise "frequently contain clauses providing that the agreement may be made a rule of court or that a judge's order may be obtained, if necessary",[31] reflecting the very real distinction between the two.

11-17 If the converse view were taken it would mean that, by something of a "backdoor" method, parties could make an obligation under an agreement immediately enforceable as a court order when such an obligation could not have been made the subject of an order under the normal jurisdiction of the court. As has been observed,[32] this cannot be done. Furthermore, an agreement which is a contract for one purpose[33] must surely be a contract for all purposes.[34]

---

25 *Dashwood v Dashwood* [1927] W.N. 276.

26 The term of the agreement alleged to have been breached was one by which H agreed not to remove certain items from the matrimonial home. It could have been an undertaking to W, not an undertaking to the court: cf. *Marchant v Marchant* (1967) CAT 26, at para.11-36.

27 For example, *Green v Rozen* [1955] 1 W.L.R. 741 at 743, per Slade J (which, incidentally, was cited in *Herbert v Herbert* (1978) 122 S.J. 826). See also fn.37.

28 *Smythe v Smythe* (1887) 18 Q.B.D. 544 CA.

29 *Smythe* (1887) 18 Q.B.D. 544 at 545.

30 *Smythe* (1887) 18 Q.B.D. 544 at 546.

31 Words echoed by Barnes J in *Graves v Graves* (1893) 69 L.T. 420.

32 See para.9-20 onwards.

33 *Shaw, Re* [1918] P. 47 CA.

Enforcement

If the foregoing analysis is correct then, it is thought, the enforcement of a provision (other, perhaps, than one for the payment of money)[35] in an agreement made a rule of court has two stages: (1) the obtaining of an appropriate court order directing compliance with the provision and (2) in the event of non-compliance, the institution of the appropriate enforcement process. **11-18**

The first order will doubtless be in the form of a mandatory order, an injunction or an order for specific performance if the provision is one requiring an act to be performed, the order fixing a time for performance. The party seeking such order may, of course, invite the court to provide for what is to happen in the case of default.[36] Subject to the one matter referred to below, if the provision of the agreement was that a sum of money be paid over within a particular period and it was not so paid, the court could simply grant judgment for the sum. If the provision was that the other party perform a particular act within a specified period and that act is not carried out, the court could grant an appropriate sum by way of compensation for the breach.

The precise approach will depend on the provision sought to be enforced. The important point is that some further court order is necessary to secure redress, but that that order may be obtained in the existing action (by application) rather than the institution of a completely fresh action. **11-19**

It has to be acknowledged that if the view expressed above is correct, a somewhat cumbrous process to enforce is necessary involving, possibly, two applications to the court. However, matters of convenience cannot override the juridical basis of the process. At all events, of course, it is no more inconvenient than seeking to enforce the provisions of a Tomlin order schedule.[37] There is, as observed above, no reason why a default provision should not be incorporated in the order made by the court when an application to enforce the agreement is made. **11-20**

Although the burden of the foregoing discussion has been to the effect that provisions in an agreement made a rule of court are still contractual in effect, it is possible that provisions by virtue of which "any sum of money, or any costs, charges or expenses" are payable to "any person" are directly enforceable as judgments. The provisions of the Judgments Act 1838 s.18 apply to "all rules of courts of common law" whereby sums such as those specified above are payable. The persons to whom such sums are payable are "deemed judgment creditors within the meaning of" the Act.[38] The precise significance of these provisions in the present context is **11-21**

---

34 Once the terms of an agreement have been embodied in a consent order their legal effect is derived from the order not the agreement: *De Lasala v De Lasala* [1980] A.C. 546. This expression of principle has led to the view being expressed in two Family Division cases that the agreement made a rule of court thereby becomes an order: see Ch.24. Nonetheless, it is generally thought that the underlying agreement still has contractual force in contexts other than the matrimonial context: see para.11-26.

35 See para.11-21.

36 Once an order has been made it is important to bear in mind the words of Megaw LJ in *Royal Society of Literature v Lowenthal* (1978) CAT 182: "The Court has jurisdiction ... to take whatever measures are appropriate, having regard to the circumstances of the case and bearing in mind the necessity of looking fairly to the interests of both parties, to see that a party in whose favour an order of the Court has been made shall not be left to suffer by reason of a breach of that order by another party. The Court is not to be hampered by technicalities of procedure." See also para.11-30.

37 See para.11-22 onwards.

38 Quoted in full in *Hunt v Douglas (Roofing) Ltd* [1990] A.C. 398. In *Legal Aid Board v Russell* [1990] 2 Q.B. 607, Lord Donaldson of Lymington MR said that at the time the 1838 Act was enacted "rules" was a term "denoting decisions or rulings by the judiciary on a case by case basis, as is clear from

a little doubtful and in practice, it is thought, recourse should be had to an order for payment before enforcement steps are contemplated.

Where the terms are incorporated in a Tomlin order

11-22 Where parties agree that a Tomlin order should be made, traditionally the terms of the agreement have been scheduled to the order staying the proceedings.[39] Those terms do not thereby become orders of the court and cannot, for example, be enforced directly by proceedings for contempt. In the event of default, the party wishing to enforce any of the scheduled terms as an order must apply to the court under the "permission to apply" provision in the order for such order or direction as may be appropriate to convert the contractual obligation into one enforceable by judicial process.[40]

11-23 Where the term sought to be enforced is one requiring the payment of money, the court will make an order that the sum be paid.[41] Unless the court specifies a different date for compliance, such an order will be enforceable after 14 days have elapsed from the date of the order.[42] Where the term relates to the performance of some other act, an order directing performance[43] must be obtained before proceedings for committal or for relief under any other provision[44] are instituted. Equally, where the term provides that a certain act shall not be performed, an injunction restraining commission must be obtained before the issue of any further enforcement process. Where the term relates to the execution of any conveyance, contract or other document, the court may direct its execution by the relevant party in the first instance, and, thereafter, in default of compliance, nominate another person to do so.[45]

11-24 The court will decline to enforce terms that are too vague.[46] It is possible that the court would entertain a claim for damages arising from an alleged breach of a Tomlin order without requiring the institution of a fresh action.[47]

11-25 Circumstances may arise in which a party prima facie obliged to comply with a provision in a Tomlin order schedule will seek to resist the making by the court of an order to enforce that provision. Non-compliance with some other provision in the schedule by the party seeking the order for enforcement may, in some circumstances, constitute a basis for the court refusing to make the order. This will depend upon an analysis of the contract reflected in the schedule. The question has arisen of whether terms forming part of the agreement between the parties, but not incorporated in the schedule to the Tomlin order, may be relied upon to resist the making of such an order.

---

contemporary law reports which constantly conclude with such expressions as 'rule nisi', 'rule absolute' or 'rule discharged' and it is clearly in this sense that section 18 refers to 'rules of courts of common law'". This view was endorsed by the House of Lords: [1991] 2 A.C. 317 at 326.

39 See para.9-23.

40 *Dashwood v Dashwood* [1927] W.N. 276. See also *Pubmaster Ltd v Gibb* [2002] EWHC 2236 (Ch) and *Bostani v Pieper* [2019] EWHC 547 (Comm), considered at para.9-36.

41 The order made in *EF Phillips & Sons Ltd v Clarke* [1970] Ch. 322 and the order sought in *Bostani v Pieper* [2019] EWHC 547 (Comm).

42 CPR r.40.11.

43 CPR PD 40B para.8.1.

44 CPR PD 40B para.9.1.

45 Senior Courts Act 1981 s.39.

46 See para.3-51; *Wilson & Whitworth Ltd v Express and Independent Newspapers Ltd* [1969] 1 W.L.R. 197.

47 See paras 9-27—9-29.

In *Horizon Technologies International Ltd v Lucky Wealth Consultants Ltd*,[48] C and D settled certain proceedings between them by means of a deed of settlement which itself included a provision that upon execution of the deed both parties would apply jointly to the court for an order in the Tomlin form. The terms of the Tomlin order and its schedule were set out in one of the eight substantive clauses of the deed of settlement. The terms to be incorporated in the schedule provided, inter alia, for a series of payments to be made by D on or before specified dates, the first two such payments being direct to C and the remaining seven payments to a Chinese company. It was provided that default in payment of any of the sums would result in all the specified sums becoming due and payable forthwith. The other substantive clauses of the deed of settlement were to come into operation upon the making of the Tomlin order. One of those clauses provided that the terms set out in the deed were "interdependent on each other" and that "breach or failure to observe any of the provisions ... shall forthwith discharge the parties of the other part from further performance". The Tomlin order was duly made and D made the first of the payments provided for in the schedule. Before the second payment fell due, a director of D (who was a party to the deed) alleged that C had failed to comply with one of the provisions of the deed (which was not incorporated in the schedule to the Tomlin order) and D, relying upon the clause referred to above, claimed to be released from any further performance of its obligations. On the issue of whether D was prima facie entitled to rely upon the clause referred to in order to resist C's claim for an order to enforce the provisions of the Tomlin order, the Judicial Committee of the Privy Council held that D was so entitled. It was said that the schedule to the Tomlin order was, **11-26**

> "clearly an integral part of the deed, but put, as it were, in parenthesis to take advantage of the Tomlin order procedure for summary judgment, so that the payments could be quickly and cheaply enforced".

As part of the deed the provisions in the schedule remained "subject to all its provisions", including that referred to above.

Parties who agree to a Tomlin order will usually seek to secure enforcement of its provisions in the manner described above.[49] However, it should be recalled that the agreement which led to the making of the Tomlin order still retains its own independent existence.[50] It follows that, in appropriate circumstances, a party may choose to seek a remedy under that agreement rather than pursuant to the Tomlin order. **11-27**

In *Islam v Askar*, the facts of which have been given previously,[51] C sought to overcome the procedural difficulties he was experiencing by commencing a fresh action based upon the agreement reached in the exchange of faxes. The Court of Appeal held that, whilst the normal remedy would be to enforce the Tomlin order, there was no reason in principle why C should not be granted a remedy in this separate action. **11-28**

Where the terms are part of an order that does not reflect finality

Whilst it might normally be anticipated that a party who had agreed to an **11-29**

---

48 *Horizon Technologies* [1992] 1 W.L.R. 24 PC, cf. *Hammond v Travers* unreported 7 May 1999 (Latham J), where C sought unsuccessfully to argue that there were terms outside the Tomlin order made that constituted collateral warranties.

49 See para.11-22.

50 "Thus, as is common ground, the contract of settlement is capable of being distinct from the Tomlin order or any agreement to procure it. An example of such distinct contracts is afforded by *Horizon Technologies Ltd v Lucky Wealth Consultants Ltd* ...": per Sir Andrew Morritt VC in *Thakrar v Ciro Citterio Menswear* [2002] EWHC 1975 (Ch).

51 See para.4-33.

adjournment of his claim to enable agreed terms to be carried out would restore his claim in default of those terms being fulfilled, there is no reason in principle why he should not take steps to enforce the agreed terms.[52] The same would apply to a withdrawal or discontinuance upon agreed terms. Enforcement could not take place in the context of the adjourned, withdrawn or discontinued proceedings: a fresh action would be necessary.

Agreed order that recites the terms of agreement

11-30 In certain circumstances it appears that the mere recitation of the terms of an agreement in an order will be sufficient to enable enforcement of these in the existing action.

In *Atkinson v Castan*,[53] C and D had been in dispute about a sycamore tree that grew on D's property close to its boundary with C's property. The tree grew close to a garage on C's land and at some stage the roots penetrated the garage, causing damage. On the advice of a tree surgeon, C, through their solicitors, requested D to have the tree removed. C commenced proceedings for nuisance in the county court after D had not taken steps to have the tree removed. In due course D received advice from a chartered surveyor, which, amongst other things, accepted that in the long term, removal of the tree was the only action to be adopted. In April 1988, D's solicitors wrote to C's solicitors confirming that D would remove the tree and meet the cost of the remedial work. Shortly after that letter was written, D filed an admission in the county court in the form of a defence, which admitted the allegations in the particulars of claim save as to the question of damages. C's solicitors prepared a draft consent order which was headed "Draft Consent Order" and was in the following terms:

> "UPON the defendants having within the defence filed herein admitted paragraphs 1 to 6 (inclusive) of the plaintiffs' particulars of claim in this action
>
> AND UPON the defendants having agreed to have removed at their expense the sycamore tree referred to in the aforesaid particulars of claim and each and every part thereof (including the roots)
>
> AND UPON the defendants having agreed to pay for the remedial work required to the garage of the plaintiffs as a result of the damage caused by the said tree and the removal of that tree and further to make good at their own expense any damage caused to the property of the plaintiffs as a result of and during the removal of the said tree and the aforesaid remedial work
>
> IT IS ORDERED that there be no order save that the defendants to pay the plaintiffs' costs of and incidental to the claim and to the action herein such costs to be taxed on Scale 3 if not agreed.
>
> WE, the undersigned hereby CONSENT to an order in the aforementioned terms."

This draft order was in due course signed by the parties' respective solicitors and submitted to the court. The order drawn up by the court and signed by the registrar in June 1988 differed from the draft consent order in that: (a) the words "By Consent It Is Ordered That" were inserted before the preamble or recitals; and (b) the word "further" was inserted in the expression "It Is Ordered" where the question of costs was provided for. Neither party at that stage complained about the form of the order drawn up by the court. Subsequently D obtained further expert advice indicating that no remedial work was necessary and neither was the removal of the tree. Consequently D took no steps to implement the agreement previously made. In July 1989, C took out an application in the existing action seeking orders that D should forthwith remove the sycamore tree and that there should be judgment for C for damages to be assessed. In March 1990, the county court

---

[52] *Shirley and Baylis* (1875) 32 L.T. 234 considered in para.8-10.
[53] *Atkinson* [1991] 4 WLUK 62; *The Times*, 17 April 1991.

judge made orders in the terms sought by C. D, who wished to take any point open to them in law to avoid the removal of the tree, had argued that, in the circumstances, C should have brought a fresh action to enforce the agreement and that they could not do so in the existing action. This argument was repeated on appeal, attention being drawn on behalf of D to the facts that:

(i) C had not adopted one of the well-established methods of settling an action which obviated the need for a fresh action for the purposes of enforcement[54];
(ii) the draft consent order provided for "no order" save in respect of costs; and;
(iii) no "liberty to apply" was provided for.

Whilst doubting whether it was open to D to argue that the matter should be dealt with on the basis of the draft consent order rather than the order actually made by the county court, the Court of Appeal dealt with the appeal on the basis of the terms of the draft order. The Court of Appeal held that a fresh action was not necessary in the circumstances. Since the parties agreed that the order made by the court should recite the agreed terms, that was sufficient to enable those terms to be enforced by obtaining an appropriate order in the existing action.

The result in this case represented a robust despatch by the court of an unmeritorious point taken by parties trying to delay compliance with freely undertaken obligations. However, it is questionable whether the reasons given for the decision are entirely consistent with established authority and practice.[55] The recitals to the order were effectively treated by the Court of Appeal as the equivalent of terms scheduled to a Tomlin order[56] or contained in an agreement filed and made a rule of court,[57] even though it is plain that the agreed order was not (and, apparently, not intended to be) a Tomlin order nor one directing that the agreement "be filed and made a rule of court". In his judgment, Woolf LJ (with whom Staughton LJ agreed), having referred to the practice of filing and making an agreement a rule of court, said that it was clear beyond doubt that, **11-31**

"there is a long-established practice of compromising actions by making the agreement part of the decision of the court or, as it is often said, making it a rule of court".

This is, of course, entirely correct; but hitherto the mere recitation of the terms of the agreement in the preamble to a consent order would, unless those terms had been framed as undertakings to the court,[58] normally have been looked upon simply as a means of recording what the parties' agreement had been, rather than as affording the means by which summary orders for enforcement of those terms could be achieved. The means by which parties had hitherto ensured that summary orders could be secured in aid of enforcement of the contractual obligations of a compromise was to agree that a Tomlin order should be made or that the agreement should be filed and made a rule of court. In either situation the court has normally looked for an express term to this effect within the compromise.[59] In *Atkinson* it seems that the Court of Appeal construed the agreement reflected in the draft consent order as involving either an express or an implied term to the effect that the terms set out in the recitals would be enforceable within the action. The mat-

---

[54] See paras 9-02 and 11-22.
[55] For example, *Hearn, Re* (1913) 108 L.T. 452 and 737, noted at para.9-31, does not appear to have been cited in *Atkinson*. And see the comments made in para.9-28.
[56] See para.9-21 onwards.
[57] See para.9-11.
[58] See para.11-34 onwards.
[59] See paras 5-47 and 9-11.

ter was put thus by Woolf LJ:

11-32 "It is clear from [the draft order] first of all that the compromise was set out in full in the recitals; secondly, that it was intended that the compromise so set out should be included as part of the record of the decision of the court; thirdly, that the purpose of this being done was to ensure that the compromise would have the added status which results from a compromise being part of or incorporated into a decision of the court; fourthly, that the obvious purpose of this added status was to put the plaintiffs in a position where they would have the advantage, which would not otherwise be available, of going back to the court in the existing action to have the compromise enforced if the court was prepared to make the necessary orders to achieve this result; and fifthly and finally, that there should be liberty to apply for the purposes of enforcing the action."

11-33 That was, of course, the construction placed upon the agreement reached in that particular case. Since it appears that there was no defence to the claim brought by C in the first place (save, perhaps, as to the precise relief sought), it would seem to be, with respect, an entirely sensible and suitably purposive construction. Indeed, although the point does not appear to have been taken, the use of the expression "no order" might well have been held to connote the possibility of recourse to the court for an order in the event of the terms reflected in the recital not being complied with.[60] However, it is thought that the decision ought to be confined largely to its own facts: parties ought to be capable of choosing and securing a mechanism for the enforcement of their compromise about the nature of which there should be no need for prolonged debate.

Injunction by consent or undertaking

11-34 An injunction by consent may be enforced in the same manner as one obtained adversely, namely by sequestration or committal. Because of the serious nature of these remedies the rules governing them must ordinarily be strictly observed.[61] However, technical breaches of the rules which do not prejudice the person in breach may not prevent appropriate enforcement.[62]

11-35 An undertaking to the court is enforceable in the same manner,[63] the only difference being that the undertaking does not have to be served on the person giving it before steps to commit for breach can be taken.[64] Furthermore, since an undertaking to the court is to be treated as an order of the court, enforcement processes other than committal may be taken where appropriate.[65]

11-36 It should clearly be understood that an order for committal can be made only where there has been an undertaking to the court:

In *Marchant v Marchant*,[66] H and W compromised proceedings brought by W against H on the basis of alleged wilful neglect to provide her with reasonable maintenance. The compromise consisted of a withdrawal of the summons on terms which included an

---

60 See para.9-43.

61 *Amberley Construction Ltd v Beamish* [2003] EWCA Civ 1267, *McIlraith v Grady* [1968] 1 Q.B. 468, *Wellington v Wellington* (1978) 122 S.J. 296 CA, *Cinderby v Cinderby* (1978) 122 S.J. 436 CA.

62 *Nicholls v Nicholls* [1997] 1 W.L.R. 314 CA, *C v E* [2009] EWHC 2718 (QB).

63 *Neath Canal Co v Ynisarwed Resolven Colliery Co* (1875) 10 Ch. App. 450, *Milburn v Newton Colliery Ltd* (1908) 52 S.J. 317.

64 *D v A&Co* [1900] 1 Ch. 484, *Launder, Re* (1908) 98 L.T. 554. See also *Hussain v Hussain* [1986] Fam. 134.

65 *Gandolfo v Gandolfo* [1981] Q.B. 359. See *M v M (Enforcement: Judgment Summons)* [1993] Fam. Law 469.

66 *Marchant v Marchant* (1967) CAT 26.

undertaking by H "not to resort to the matrimonial home as from July 31, 1964 or to molest W", the words "liberty to apply" also being incorporated. The Court of Appeal held that W could not apply to commit H to prison for an alleged breach of the undertaking because it was not an undertaking to the court.

PART 3: PRACTICE ON IMPEACHMENT OF A COMPROMISE

CHAPTER 12

Practice on Setting Aside a Compromise

12-01 Assuming that grounds exist for setting aside a compromise,[1] the question of the practice to be followed to achieve this arises.

The practice varies according to whether or not the compromise remains purely contractual in status or whether it has been embodied in a consent order or judgment.

SETTING ASIDE A COMPROMISE AGREEMENT

12-02 The procedure for seeking a judicial rescission of a compromise agreement is identical to that required in relation to any other contract. A fresh action is needed seeking an order setting aside the agreement with consequential directions.[2] Where appropriate, a counterclaim for the same purpose may be raised.[3]

SETTING ASIDE A COMPROMISE EMBODIED IN A CONSENT ORDER OR JUDGMENT

12-03 Prior to the drawing-up or sealing of a consent order or judgment there is a limited jurisdiction to set aside such an order or judgment.[4] An application seeking such relief must be issued prior to, or contemporaneously with, the drawing-up or sealing of the order.[5]

12-04 After the drawing-up or sealing of the order, a final order or judgment by consent may be set aside only in a fresh action commenced for that purpose.[6] The relief sought will depend on the circumstances but will, in all probability, be the appropriate relief[7] in relation to the agreement underlying the order or judgment and an order setting it aside.[8]

---

1 See Ch.4.

2 The principal remedy sought would be either a declaration of invalidity or an order setting aside the agreement (i.e. rescission) with consequential directions. The remedy granted may, of course, be different: e.g. damages in lieu of rescission in circumstances to which the Misrepresentation Act 1967 s.2(2) applies. See Ch.4.

3 *Roberts, Re* [1905] 1 Ch. 704. cf. *Kleinwort Benson Ltd v Lincoln City Council* [1999] 2 A.C. 349, on the principle established in *Roberts*.

4 See, e.g. *Sharland v Sharland* [2016] A.C. 871, noted at para.24-92. See also para.6-20 and para.21-17 onwards.

5 See para.6-20 and para.21-17 onwards.

6 See para.6-20.

7 See fn.2.

8 The interests of third parties must be protected: see para.6-84.

Interim order

12-05 An interim order may be set aside by an application in the action in appropriate circumstances.[9] However, if the order has been made without mistake on either side, the court will not set it aside (thus giving it its full contractual effect) but may decline to enforce it if it would be inequitable to do so.[10] The application would seek the appropriate relief and should be supported by evidence.

Tomlin order

12-06 Since the effect of a Tomlin order is generally determinative of the rights of the parties to an action following its resolution by agreement, such an order is, it is submitted, in effect a final order and thus, strictly speaking, the institution of a fresh action is necessary to set aside the order if an invalidating ground is said to exist.[11] However, it is possible that an application to remove the stay on any of the usual invalidating grounds may be made by a simple application in the action.[12] There is little practical difference between the two procedures.

Costs when agreement or order set aside

12-07 Where proceedings to set aside a compromise are successful, the court will examine carefully the question of the incidence of costs. The victor may not always be easy to identify.[13]

---

[9] See para.6-21 onwards.

[10] See para.6-21 onwards.

[11] See para.6-20. An order may occasionally appear to be a Tomlin order whereas, on proper analysis, it is not: *Vanden Recycling Ltd v Kras Recycling BV* [2017] EWCA Civ 354; [2017] C.P. Rep. 33.

[12] See paras 9-33–9-35.

[13] cf. *Hickman v Berens* [1895] 2 Ch. 638.

PART 4: THE SETTLEMENT PROCESS IN CIVIL JUSTICE

CHAPTER 13

Present Landscape in Civil Litigation

For as long as litigation has taken place there has always been an impetus on the part of the parties to reach an accommodation if possible.[1] Leaving aside all other factors, the high level of costs involved in pursuing a case to a full trial or arbitral hearing has always operated as an incentive to settle, particularly where the outcome of the case is difficult to predict. Making a settlement offer, particularly on the part of a defendant to an action, effective in relation to the costs of the action if not accepted, has long been an important feature in the litigation landscape. The system of payments into court[2] in relation to claims for damages that had been in place since at least 1933[3] and the development of Calderbank offers[4] represented the most prominent features in that landscape before the reforms embodied in the CPR were implemented in April 1999. The most significant part of the CPR relating to the process of settlement was Pt 36, the aim of which was to help "encourage reasonable and early settlement of proceedings"[5]. In 2007 fundamental changes were made to Pt 36, not least the abolition of payments into court,[6] aimed at further encouraging and facilitating settlement.[7] **13-01**

The pre-CPR practice worked well, albeit settlement often took place at a late stage in the chronology of an action.[8] Many of the positive features of that system were incorporated into the CPR in 1999, in some cases with modifications appropriate to a case-managed system of civil justice subject to the CPR's overriding objective. Some additional features were also set in place. **13-02**

As a result of the reforms effected in 1999 the civil litigation landscape changed significantly, not least because the promotion of settlement, and particularly early settlement, became a central feature of that landscape.[9] The increased emphasis **13-03**

---

1 For comment on the public interest in settlement see, *D v NSPCC* [1987] A.C. 171, 232 See also para.10-02. Prior to the CPR's introduction the vast majority of cases commenced were resolved other than by trial. In 1996, for instance, only about 2–3% of the cases commenced in the Queen's Bench Division were set down for trial and of those nearly 90% were resolved by settlement. While the Annual Judicial Statistics are not wholly clear it appears that of the approximately 1,000 cases listed for trial, about 50% were resolved following trial, whereas about the same proportion settled "at the doors of the court" or during the trial.

2 See the 4th edn of this work, Ch.10.

3 See *Cumper v Pothecary* [1941] 2 K.B. 58.

4 See the 4th edn of this work, Ch.9.

5 H. Woolf, *Access to Justice: Interim Report to the Lord Chancellor on the Civil Justice System in England and Wales* (HMSO) (1995), Ch.24, para.1.

6 The movement away from payments into court formalised by the amendments to CPR Pt 36 made in April 2007 followed on from the decisions in *Crouch v King's Healthcare NHS Trust* [2005] 1 W.L.R. 2015, *Trustees of Stokes Pensions Fund v Western Power Distribution (South West) Plc* [2005] 1 W.L.R. 3595.

7 See Ch.14.

8 fn.1.

9 CPR PD— Pre-action Conduct para.8.1.

given to it from the Heilbron & Hodge and Woolf Reports to the Jackson and, most recently, Briggs Reports[10] has, as the first of the four reports suggested, worked to implement a "philosophy of litigation [that] should be primarily to encourage settlement of disputes whether through the court process or by alternative means of dispute resolution".[11] One consequence of this cultural shift has been that it appears that fewer cases are being dealt with in court,[12] which if correct means that more cases are being settled or, at least, are being settled earlier. If that is so, one of the main objectives of the civil justice reforms has largely been achieved.[13]

Whilst changed funding arrangements over the last decade or so for certain types of litigation will have made a substantial impact on the number of claims instituted, the structures and approach put in place by the civil justice reforms have had an impact on the process of settlement itself. As indicated above, the principal structure put in place to aid settlement was Pt 36.[14] Another significant influence was the general costs regime of the CPR. Another increasing influence on the settlement process has been the encouragement by the courts of the use of alternative dispute resolution (ADR), principally mediation[15], an emphasis that is only ever likely to increase.[16]

Before considering these features in the present landscape in the context of settlement, a number of preliminary matters need to be noted.

NEGOTIATION

13-04 Every settlement emerges from a negotiating process. It has been a hallmark of the justice system that the parties may conduct their negotiations ordinarily without revealing to the court their content, including any offers made within them, in the event that a full trial is necessary. This traditional approach continues to find expression in the present system. Every Pt 36 offer[17] is treated automatically as "without prejudice save as to costs"[18] (although, of course, not every offer of settlement is made pursuant to Pt 36[19]) and it cannot be revealed to the court until the trial is concluded.[20] It follows that a thorough understanding of the "without prejudice" rule

10 M. Briggs, *Civil Courts Structure Review: Final Report* (July 2016) Ch.6 at p.58 onwards.

11 H. Heilbron & H. Hodge, *Civil Justice on Trial—A Case for Change* (1993) Joint report of The Bar Council and Law Society at 6.

12 See the quarterly court statistics, previously the Annual Judicial Statistics at *https://www.gov.uk/government/collections/civil-justice-statistics-quarterly* [Accessed 18 November 2019]. Caution should be adopted, however, in relying upon them as evidence of settlement rates: see, R. Jackson, *Review of Civil Litigation Costs—Preliminary Report* (May 2009), Vol.1, Ch.5, "Establishing how many civil claims are brought and how many are contested is not easy." It follows that establishing how many cases that are commenced are settled is itself not an easy task save to say that it is almost certain that the vast majority are resolved without trial.

13 See fn.1.

14 See para.14-02.

15 See Ch.35.

16 See *Faidi v Elliot Corporation* [2012] EWCA Civ 287; [2012] H.L.R. 27 at [39] per Ward LJ. Further promotion of the use of ADR is being effected by, for instance, the publication of S. Blake et al, *The Jackson ADR Handbook* (2016, OUP) and the further increase in emphasis on settlement in M. Briggs, *Chancery Modernisation Review—Final Report* (2013, Judicial Office), Ch.5 and M. Briggs, *Civil Courts Structure Review: Final Report* (July 2016) Ch.6. See further at Ch.35.

17 See Ch.15.

18 CPR r.36.16(1); see para.14-06 onwards.

19 See paras 14-02—14-05 and Ch.26.

20 See CPR r.36.16(2), CPR r.52.22(1) and para.14-08.

is necessary both in relation to Pt 36 and to settlements concluded outside Pt 36, including those facilitated by mediation.[21]

EXCHANGE OF INFORMATION

Generally speaking, a settlement that is satisfactory to both parties will occur only when each party to a dispute has had a fair opportunity to appraise the strengths and weaknesses of his own case and that of his opponent. Whilst opposing sides will still frequently arrive at differing perceptions of those strengths and weaknesses, the process often reveals an acceptable middle ground resulting in a compromise. A "fair opportunity" to appraise a case depends at least partly upon the availability of relevant information and documentation to each party. A system designed to encourage the early settlement of disputes will, as a basic minimum, require the earliest possible exchange of relevant information and documentation.[22] Inadequate disclosure of information and documentation before negotiations take place will often result in dissatisfaction on the part of one or other of the parties with the settlement achieved and can foment "post-settlement remorse".[23] **13-05**

Pre-action Protocols operate in a number of areas of litigation,[24] some of which[25] account for the largest number of civil cases instituted.[26] They were introduced in order "to enable [parties] to obtain the information they reasonably need in order to enter into an appropriate settlement".[27] Their existence, supported by effective judicial sanctions in the event of non-compliance,[28] has been a significant influence on the earlier settlement of the particular type of litigation to which it relates. **13-06**

The absence of a relevant pre-action protocol (not least due to the existence and general applicability of the Practice Direction— Pre-Action Conduct) does not preclude the court from penalising in costs a party whose conduct in not providing relevant information prior to the commencement of proceedings has disabled the making of an informed pre-action offer or an informed evaluation of a claimant's offer.[29] **13-07**

---

21 See Ch.18.

22 CPR PD—Pre-action Conduct, para.3(d).

23 An expression coined by Sir Thomas Bingham MR, as he then was, in *Arthur J.S. Hall & Co v Simons* [2002] 1 A.C. 615 at 643.

24 Protocols now exist in relation to Resolution of Package Travel Claims, Construction and Engineering Disputes, Debt Claims, Media and Communications Claims, Personal Injury Claims, Clinical Disputes, Professional Negligence, Judicial Review, Disease and Illness Claims, Housing Disrepair Cases, , Possession Claims based on Mortgage or Home Purchase Plan Arrears in Respect of Residential Property, Dilapidations, Possession Claims by Social Landlords, Low Value Personal Injury Claims in Road Traffic Accidents, and Low Value Personal Injury Claims in Employers Liability and Public Liability Claims. The CPR PD—Pre-Action Conduct complements the Protocols.

25 For example, personal injury litigation and litigation arising from alleged clinical negligence.

26 Defined in the Glossary to the CPR as "[s]tatements of understanding between legal practitioners and others about pre-action practice and which are approved by a relevant practice direction".

27 H. Woolf, *Access to Justice: Final Report to the Lord Chancellor on the Civil Justice System in England and Wales* (HMSO) (1996), Ch.10, para.1.

28 The extent to which a pre-action protocol has been complied with is a factor the court must take into account in deciding what, if any, order for costs to make (CPR r.44.2(5)(a)) and which it will consider when deciding an application for relief from a sanction imposed for a failure to comply with any rule, practice direction or court order: CPR r.3.9(1)(a) and (b). CPR r.3.1(3)–(7) contains provisions enabling the court, in appropriate circumstances, to order a party to pay a sum of money into court if that party has, without good reason, failed to comply, inter alia, with "a relevant pre-action protocol".

29 CPR r.44.2(5) is wide enough to cover this.

PRE-ACTION COSTS

13-08 Since the present discussion is focused primarily on the pre-action stage, it is important to note that the costs ordered to be paid by one party to another may include "costs incurred *before* proceedings have begun".[30] Since considerably more pre-action activity than occurred formerly is encouraged under the post-CPR system, it is only right that the costs arising in connection with a dispute should embrace appropriately incurred costs in that early stage. They will, of course, be subject to summary or detailed assessment by the court if they are not agreed. However, the significant point is that whilst a "cost shifting" principle continues to apply to civil litigation[31] no party to a dispute can consider that they are immune from paying their opponent's costs merely because they are being incurred during a period when no proceedings are on foot. Interest on those costs can be awarded.[32]

INDEMNITY COSTS

13-09 The opportunity to obtain, or the potential to be condemned in, indemnity costs[33] is a factor that may induce a party to make a realistic appraisal of the strength of his case. Built into the rules concerning claimants' offers[34] is a structure requiring the court, subject to its ultimate discretion, to award indemnity costs (plus enhanced interest on any damages and upon those costs) if the claimant achieves more than their offer.[35] Does a similar opportunity exist for a defendant to obtain indemnity costs?

13-10 The mere rejection by a claimant of what in the event proves to have been a reasonable offer is not, without more, sufficient to entitle the court to award indemnity costs in the defendant's favour. In *Excelsior Commercial and Industrial Holdings v Salisbury Hammer Aspden & Johnson*[36] Waller LJ said this:

> "The question will always be: is there something in the conduct of the action or the circumstances of the case which takes the case out of the norm in a way which justifies an order for indemnity costs?"

In that case an award of indemnity costs was held to have been appropriate because the claimant had proceeded with what was a very speculative claim, but had recovered merely nominal damages of £2 against the fifth defendant, and failed entirely against the other defendant who was then involved in the proceedings, against the background of various attempts by the defendants to settle it, culminat-

---

30 CPR r.44.2(6)(d).

31 The expression used in the Jackson report to characterise the proposition that the loser pays the successful party's costs.

32 CPR r.44.2(6)(g).

33 CPR r.44.3(2) and 44.3(3) provide for costs to be awarded on either a standard or indemnity basis. The former is, following the introduction of the Jackson reforms in April 2013, subject to the proportionality test, which is set out in CPR r.44.3(5). This applies to cases that commenced after that date.

34 CPR r.36.13 and r.36.14.

35 See, generally, Ch.17.

36 *Excelsior Commercial and Industrial Holdings* [2002] EWCA Civ 879; [2002] C.P. Rep. 67 at [39], and see Lord Woolf MR at [32].

ing in a joint payment into court of £100,000.[37] The test formulated by Waller LJ has been applied consistently.[38]

Some of the principles applicable to the issue of whether to award indemnity costs were summarised in *Elvanite Full Circle Ltd v Amec Earth & Environmental (UK) Ltd* by Coulson J: 13-11

"The principles relating to indemnity costs ... can be summarised as follows:

(a) Indemnity costs are appropriate only where the conduct of a paying party is unreasonable "to a high degree. 'Unreasonable' in this context does not mean merely wrong or misguided in hindsight": see Simon Brown LJ (as he then was) in *Kiam v MGN Ltd* [2002] 1 W.L.R. 2810.

(b) The court must therefore decide whether there is something in the conduct of the action, or the circumstances of the case in general, which takes it out of the norm in a way which justifies an order for indemnity costs: see Waller LJ in *Excelsior Commercial and Industrial Holdings Ltd v Salisbury Hammer Aspden and Johnson* [2002] EWCA (Civ) 879.

(c) The pursuit of a weak claim will not usually, on its own, justify an order for indemnity costs, provided that the claim was at least arguable. But the pursuit of a hopeless claim (or a claim which the party pursuing it should have realised was hopeless) may well lead to such an order: see, for example, *Wates Construction Ltd v HGP Greentree Alchurch Evans Ltd* [2006] BLR 45.

(d) If a claimant casts its claim disproportionately wide, and requires the defendant to meet such a claim, there was no injustice in denying the claimant the benefit of an assessment on a proportionate basis given that, in such circumstances, the claimant had forfeited its rights to the benefit of the doubt on reasonableness: see *Digicel (St Lucia) Ltd v Cable and Wireless PLC* [2010] EWHC 888 (Ch)." [39]

This summary was described as a "helpful if not absolutely exhaustive summary" by Akenhead J in *Courtwell Properties Ltd v Greencore PF (UK) Ltd*.[40] He said that to this list "can be added a number of other specific and general points"[41]: 13-12

"(i) The discretion to award indemnity costs is a wide one and must be exercised taking into account all the circumstances and considering the matters complained of in the context of the overall litigation (see *Three Rivers DC v the Governor of the Bank of England* [2006] EWHC 816 (Comm) and *Digicel* ...

(ii) Dishonesty or moral blame does not have to be established to justify indemnity costs (*Reid Minty v Taylor* [2002] 1 W.L.R. 2800).

(iii) The conduct of experts can justify an order for indemnity costs in respect of costs generated by them (see *Williams v Jervis* [2009] EWHC 1837 (QB)).

(iv) A failure to comply with Pre-Action Protocol requirements could result in indemnity costs being awarded.

(v) A refusal to mediate or engage in mediation or some other alternative dispute resolution process could justify an award of indemnity costs."

---

37 *Reid Minty v Taylor* [2002] 1 W.L.R. 2800 and *Kiam v MGN (No.2)* [2002] 1 W.L.R. 2810.

38 See, e.g. *Corby Group Litigation DC v Corby* [2009] EWHC 2109 (TCC), Akenhead J, *Janis Williams v Calvin Jervis (Lex Komatsu)* [2009] EWHC 1837 (QB), Roderick Evans J, *Colour Quest Ltd v Total Downstream UK Plc* [2009] EWHC 823 (Comm), David Steel J; *Jerrard v Blyth* [2014] EWHC 647 (QB), Sir David Eady.

39 *Elvanite Full Circle Ltd v Amec Earth & Environmental (UK) Ltd* [2013] EWHC 1643 (TCC); [2013] 4 All E.R. 765 at [16]. cf, *Euroption Strategic Fund Ltd v Skandinaviska Enskilda Banken AB* [2012] EWHC 749 (Comm) at [11]-[15] and *Bank of Ireland v Watts Group Plc* [2017] EWHC 2472 (TCC) at [6].

40 *Courtwell Properties Ltd v Greencore PF (UK) Ltd* [2014] EWHC 184 (TCC); [2014] 2 Costs L.O. 289 at [22].

41 *Courtwell Properties Ltd v Greencore PF (UK) Ltd* [2014] EWHC 184 (TCC); [2014] 2 Costs L.O. 289 at [23].

CHAPTER 14

Structure of CPR Part 36

INTRODUCTION

Part 36 of the CPR contains a structure by virtue of which an offer of settlement, whether made by a claimant or a defendant, may be effective on the issue of the costs of securing an appropriate judgment if not accepted. **14-01**

Since its introduction in 1999 it has been subject to a number of substantive revisions. In its original form it replaced Ord.22 of the Rules of the Supreme Court and Ord.11 of the County Court Rules in relation to payments into court in respect of money claims and introduced provisions concerning offers to settle in respect of non-money claims.

The first significant revision occurred in 2007, when the need to make any payment of money into court in respect of a money claim was abolished. Those revisions took effect on 6 April 2007.[1] Further significant revisions took effect in 2010 and 2013. In 2010 section II of Pt 36 was added. That revision took effect on 30 April 2010.[2] In 2013, revisions consequent to the Jackson cost reforms were introduced. They took effect on 1 April 2013.[3] Most recently, on 6 April 2015, a further substantive revision was introduced.[4] Subject to a small number of transitional provisions, it replaced the then extant Pt 36 in its entirety.[5]

Unless indicated otherwise references to Pt 36 in this and the following chapters are to the version in force from April 2015.

---

1 See the Civil Procedure (Amendment No.3) Rules 2006 (SI 2006/3435). The amendment, in effect, codified the consequences of the decisions in *Crouch v King's Healthcare NHS Trust* [2004] EWCA Civ 1332; [2004] 1 W.L.R. 2015 and *Trustees of Stoke Pension Fund v Western Power Distribution (South West) Plc* [2005] EWCA Civ 854; [2005] 1 W.L.R. 3595.

2 See the Civil Procedure (Amendment) Rules 2010 (SI 2010/621).

3 See the Civil Procedure (Amendment) Rules 2013 (SI 2013/262).

4 See the Civil Procedure (Amendment No.8) Rules 2014 (SI 2014/3299). A new Practice Direction, CPR PD 36, supplementing the 2015 Pt 36, came into force on 6 April 2015: see 78th Update, Practice Direction Making Document. Prior to the amendments in 2015, the Practice Direction was numbered as CPR PD 36A. This reflected the fact that a CPR PD 36B, contained transitional provisions, was operative from 2007 until 2015 (see 79th Update, Practice Direction Making Document).

5 See para.18(1) and (2) of the Civil Procedure (Amendment No.8) Rules 2014 (SI 2014/3299) for details concerning the transitional provisions.

NOT A COMPLETE CODE FOR EFFECTIVE OFFERS OF SETTLEMENT

14-02 While Part 36 is a self-contained code[6] it does not, however, represent a complete code for determining the effect that an offer to settle may have upon the costs of or associated with the litigation to which it relates.

First, Pt 36, strictly speaking, concerns the effect of an offer to settle on the costs of *the substantive dispute*, not upon any discrete interim applications that might be made before the trial or any summary judgment application takes place.[7] An offer in relation to an interim application would ordinarily fall to be assessed within the court's general discretion as to costs under CPR r.44.2.[8] It is, however, clear now that an offer made under Pt 36 can be made in respect of the costs of a dispute, where there is a substantive dispute between the parties as to those costs or elements of the Bill of Costs.[9]

Second, whilst any party who wishes that his offer to settle the substantive dispute is judged by reference to the provisions of Pt 36 would be well advised to ensure that it is made precisely in accordance with those provisions, that will not necessarily mean that an offer that does not comply with it becomes irrelevant in relation to costs or that the costs consequences that would have arisen had the offer been in accordance with Pt 36 offer may not, in practice, arise.[10] Neither the 2007 nor the 2015 revisions replicated the former provision that entitled the court to give effect to the normal consequences of Pt 36 if an offer was not strictly in ac-

---

6 See CPR r.36.1(1); *Flynn v Scougall* [2004] EWCA Civ 873; [2004] 1 W.L.R. 3069 CA, *Gibbon v Manchester City Council* [2010] EWCA Civ 726; [2010] 1 W.L.R. 2081 CA, McQuater, "The future of Part 36: Part 2" (2007) J.P.I.L. 193; and Ch.16. In *Wilson v Ministry of Defence* [2013] C.P. Rep. 33, HH Judge Iain Hughes QC, sitting on appeal in the County Court at Winchester held, at [32], that while Pt 36 was a self-contained code, that did not mean that it was separate from the remainder of the CPR. Its terms were to be interpreted consistently with the manner in which such terms and phrases were used and interpreted throughout the CPR. See to similar effect *Global Assets Advisory Services Ltd and Another v Grandlane Developments Limited and Others* [2019] EWCA Civ 1764 where Asplin LJ (with whom Patten LJ and Sir Rupert Jackson agreed) said at [32]: "... there is nothing in the terms of CPR Part 36 which suggests that it is entirely freestanding and that all costs consequences of the acceptance of a Part 36 offer are to be found within the four corners of CPR Part 36 itself".

7 A Pt 36 offer must be in respect of the *claim* made, part of it or an issue within it (CPR r.36.2) and the provision that deals with the costs consequences of a failure to accept such an offer (CPR r.36.14) operates in relation to how the *judgment* compares with the offer. A judgment may, of course, be made following an application for summary judgment: CPR Pt 24.

8 See fn.13.

9 In *White v Wincott Galliford Ltd* [2019] EWHC B6 (Costs), Deputy Costs Master Friston considered a Pt 36 offer made in respect of solicitors' hourly rates within detailed costs proceedings.

10 The court will, however, take a purposive approach to interpretation of the terms of a Pt 36 offer, such that, as Stanley Burnton LJ explained in *C v D* [2011] EWCA Civ 646; [2012] 1 W.L.R. 1962 at [84] and approved by Lord Neuberger MR in *Howell & Ors v Lees-Millais & Ors* [2011] EWCA Civ 786; [2011] 4 Costs LO 456 at [25], "Any ambiguity in an offer purporting to be a Part 36 offer should be construed so far as reasonably possible as complying with Part 36. Once it is accepted that a time-limited offer does not comply with Part 36, one must approach the interpretation of the offer in this case on the basis that the party making the offer, and the party receiving it, appreciated that fact." See, however, *Thewlis v Groupama Insurance Co Ltd* [2012] EWHC 3 (TCC); [2012] B.L.R. 259, where there was a failure to comply with a mandatory requirement of what was then CPR r.36.2(2). In such a circumstance, HHJ Behrens held that the approach taken in *C v D* was inapplicable. Where there are serious procedural errors in terms of compliance with the formal requirements of CPR Pt 36, see also *Carillion JM Ltd v PHI Group Ltd* (also *known as PHI Group Ltd v Robert West Consulting Ltd*) [2012] EWCA Civ 588; [2012] C.P. Rep. 37 (fn.27). See also *Shaw v Merthyr Tydfil County Borough* [2014] EWCA Civ 1678; [2015] P.I.Q.R. P8; *Dutton v Minards* [2015] EWCA Civ 984; [2015] 6 Costs L.R. 1047.

cordance with its provisions.[11] As a consequence, to the extent that an offer does not comply with the requirements of Pt 36 it cannot have the costs consequences provided for within Pt 36.[12] However, the court is entitled (and indeed obliged) to take into account "any admissible offer to settle" drawn to its attention within the overall discretion as to costs under Pt 44.[13]

Third, Pt 36 says nothing directly about the costs consequences where a claimant (who may or may not have made his own Pt 36 offer,[14] but who cannot at all events point to an offer of his own which is "at least as advantageous" to him as the judgment obtained)[15] achieves more than the defendant's Pt 36 offer. Whilst the claimant in this situation is ordinarily to be regarded as the successful party and the defendant the "unsuccessful party", with the result that the latter will be ordered to pay the former's costs,[16] Pt 44 requires the court to consider the various matters set out in that Part before exercising its discretion as to costs. There may be circumstances[17] which would dictate a departure from the general rule.

Fourth, Pt 36 does not apply where a claim is allocated to the small claims track under CPR r.27(2)(1)(g).

Finally, the Court of Appeal confirmed in *Commissioners for HM Revenue and Customs v Blue Sphere Global Ltd* that Pt 36 offers can be made in appellate proceedings irrespective of the type of proceedings from which the appeal originated. It had been argued that since the appeal arose from a decision reached in the VAT and Duties Tribunal (rather than from civil proceedings to which the CPR applied) it was not permissible to apply Pt 36 on an appeal from that tribunal to the Court of Appeal. The court concluded that if it had been intended to exclude the application of Pt 36 to appeals, in either the High Court or Court of Appeal, from

---

[11] The pre-2007 CPR r.36.1(2). The present formulation, now contained in CPR r.36.2(2), is as follows: "Nothing in this Section prevents a party making an offer to settle in whatever way that party chooses, but if the offer is not made in accordance with rule 36.5, it will not have the consequences specified in this Section."

[12] There is a "signpost" at the foot of CPR r.36.2(2) in the following terms: "(Rule 44.2 requires the court to consider an offer to settle that does not have the costs consequences set out in this Section in deciding what order to make about costs.)"

[13] CPR r.44.2(4)(c) provides that: "In deciding what order (if any) to make about costs, the court will have regard to all the circumstances, including ... any admissible offer to settle made by a party which is drawn to the court's attention, and which is not an offer to which costs consequences under Part 36 apply." This approach was adopted to a technically non-compliant Pt 36 offer in *Huntley v Simmonds* [2009] EWHC 406 (QB), Underhill J. It was, however, noted that while the effect of this provision can be relied on to apply the same cost consequences as would have been applicable if a valid Pt 36 offer was in place, this arises as a matter of the court's discretion under CPR r.44. Also see *AF v BG* [2009] EWCA Civ 757; [2010] 2 Costs L.R. 164. The approach in *Huntley* was disavowed, however, by the Court of Appeal in *F&C (Holdings) Ltd v Barthelemy (Costs)* [2012] EWCA Civ 843; [2013] 1 W.L.R. 548 at [63], where Davis LJ reiterated that as a general rule only a valid Pt 36 offer, which complied fully with the formal requirements of the Part, would attract the cost consequences provided for in Pt 36. Except in cases where there were "de minimis errors" it would not generally be permissible to rely on the discretion under CPR r.44.(2) for this purpose.

[14] For claimants' offers, see, in particular, para.17-18 onwards.

[15] See Ch.17.

[16] CPR r.44.2(2)(a).

[17] The court may, for example, make adverse orders for costs against a successful claimant in relation to certain issues that may have been lost despite the overall victory (r.44.2(4) and (5)) and/or award merely a proportion of the claimant's costs, one potential reason for the latter course being an unreasonable refusal to consider an offer of settlement or to negotiate when an offer worthy of consideration is made: see *Codent Ltd v Lyson Ltd* [2005] EWCA Civ 1835; [2006] C.P. Rep. 33. The situation where a claimant does "beat" a defendant's Pt 36 offer, but by a narrow margin at a disproportionate cost, is considered later: see para.17-12 onwards.

tribunals to which the CPR did not apply, the rules would have so stated. They did not so provide and hence Pt 36 applied.[18]

FREEDOM OF CONTRACT

14-03 Given that Pt 36 does not provide a complete code for determining the effect on costs of an offer to settle, it follows that a party may make an offer in a way that deliberately avoids some or all of its provisions. Rule 36.2(2) makes it plain that the existence of Pt 36 does not prevent a party making an offer to settle in whatever way he chooses. A pure "without prejudice" offer[19] would be outside Pt 36 and would not, of course, be capable of being referred to on the question of the costs between the parties.[20] An *open* offer would, strictly speaking, be outside Pt 36,[21] although an offeror who wished to secure the advantages of Pt 36 would doubtless spell out that the intention behind the offer is that it should have all the other consequences of Pt 36. Any offer made *orally* would not be within Pt 36.[22] A claimant's offer which expressly disavowed reliance on the provisions permitting the court to award higher interest if the court's award was better than the offer[23] would not, strictly speaking, be within Pt 36. An offer that does not provide the time required by the rule for consideration of the offer[24] or which altered the deemed inclusion of interest until the end of the period specified in either r.36.5(1)(c) or r.36.5(2)[25] where the offer is a sum of money[26] would not be a Pt 36 offer.

14-04 It follows, therefore, that a party generally needs expressly to opt into Pt 36 in order to guarantee that the court will treat the offer as one to which Pt 36 applies.[27] There is a mandatory requirement in Rule 36.5(1)(b) to "make clear" that an offer is "made pursuant to" Pt 36. This requirement is ostensibly not as onerous as its predecessor, which required that an offer intended to be made "in accordance with" Pt 36 had to "state on its face that it [was] intended to have the consequences of Part 36".[28] An offer that complied with all the other aspects of r.36.5 could be interpreted as making clear that it was made pursuant to Pt 36. However, the absence of specific reference to that fact leaves scope for the argument that the offer should not be treated as a Pt 36 offer. Despite the relaxation in the wording in r.36.5(1)(b), which may legitimately be seen as endeavouring to ensure that technical challenges to the validity of offers that do not follow the exact wording of its

---

18 CPR r.36.4; *Commissioners for HM Revenue and Customs v Blue Sphere Global Ltd* [2010] EWCA Civ 1448; [2011] 2 Costs L.O. 182 at [7]-[9].

19 The intention of the Rules is to preserve the "without prejudice" privilege. For the "without prejudice" rule, see Ch.19.

20 *Cutts v Head* [1984] Ch. 290 CA. It may still be possible to refer to a pure "without prejudice" offer on the issues that arise under s.11(1) of the Access to Justice Act 1999 (which replaced s.17(1) of the Legal Aid Act 1988): see *McCallum* [1971] C.L.Y. 9360.

21 *HTC Corp v Yozmot 33 Ltd (Costs)* [2010] EWHC 1057 (Pat).

22 CPR r.36.5(1)(a).

23 CPR r.36.5(1)(b). See Ch.17.

24 CPR r.36.5(1)(c). See para.15-11 onwards.

25 CPR r36.5(4); see para.15-08.

26 CPR r.36.5(4).

27 Compliance with the provisions of what was, prior to 2015, CPR r.36(2) and is now CPR r.36.5 is mandatory in order to bring an offer to settle within Pt 36: *Carillion JM Ltd v PHI Group Ltd* (also known as *PHI Group Ltd v Robert West Consulting Ltd*) [2012] EWCA Civ 588; [2012] C.P. Rep. 37 at [25]. See also fns 10 and 13.

28 CPR r.36.2(2)(b).

predecessor are less likely to succeed post-April 2015,[29] the better approach remains for the offeror to ensure that any offer intended to be a Pt 36 offer includes an express reference to it being an offer made pursuant to Pt 36. This is particularly important as any offer held to fall outside Pt 36 for non-compliance with the requirements of r.36.5 will require the offeror to invite the exercise of the court's wider discretion under Pt 44 where an offer is not expressed in these terms.[30]

14-05 Whilst generally Pt 36 maintains and upholds the principle of freedom of contract, the normal right of an offeror to withdraw an offer made at any time prior to acceptance[31] is restricted during the "relevant period"[32] of a Pt 36 offer by the need to seek the permission of the court to do so.[33] This restriction applies, at least in theory, to a Pt 36 offer made "before the commencement of proceedings"[34] although it is unclear how, from a practical point of view, the offeree could apply to the court for permission to withdraw the offer within a period as short as 21 days from the time the offer is made.[35] Unless expressly withdrawn, a Pt 36 offer remains open even where the offeree has rejected the offer.[36] Implied withdrawal has no application to Pt 36,[37] nor does a counter-offer made under Pt 36 bring to an end the validity of a previously made offer.[38] although a Pt 36 offer may amount to an implied withdrawal of a prior offer that was not made under Pt 36 (e.g. a previous "without prejudice" offer, Calderbank offer, or open offer).[39] As a consequence a number of valid Pt 36 offers may be in place at any one time.[40] A Pt 36 offer may, however, be "automatically withdrawn" according to terms specified in the offer, subject to the offeree not having already "served notice of acceptance."[41]

---

29 See *Thewlis v Groupama* [2012] EWHC 3 (TCC), [2012] BLR 259. And see fns 10 and 13.

30 See fn.14.

31 *Chitty*, Vol.1, para.2-094.

32 See paras 15-11-15-14.

33 See Ch.16. This provision marks a change in the practice embodied in the original version of Pt 36: see *Scammell v Dicker* [2001] 1 W.L.R. 631, where the Court of Appeal (Aldous and Mance LJJ) held that the CPR "do not prevent a Part 36 offer being withdrawn at any time prior to acceptance". The issue of the relevance of a withdrawn offer on the issue of costs is dealt with at paras 17-02-17-06.

34 CPR r.36.7(1). See also *Solomon v Cromwell Group Plc* [2011] EWCA Civ 1585; [2012] 1 W.L.R. 1048 at [15] where it was held that the effect of accepting a Pt 36 offer made before a claim has been issued is that the claimant is entitled to recover the costs he has incurred in contemplation of the proceedings up to the date of acceptance in so far as they would have formed part of his recoverable costs if proceedings had already been issued. And see Sorabji, Solomon and Oliver on the interaction between CPR 36 and CPR 44 and 45 (2012) CJQ (2) 135.

35 CPR PD 36 (see para.14-16) does not deal with this situation. As an application to withdraw the offer it would need to be made by way of an application under CPR r.23: see CPR PD 36A para.2.2(1) and CPR PD 23A para.5.

36 *Gibbon v Manchester City Council* [2010] EWCA Civ 726; [2010] W.L.R. 2081 at [16].

37 *Gibbon* [2010] EWCA Civ 726; [2010] W.L.R. 2081 at [17]–[18].

38 *Gibbon* [2010] EWCA Civ 726; [2010] W.L.R. 2081 at [16].

39 *Db UK Bank Ltd (t/a Db Mortgages) v Jacobs Solicitors* [2016] EWHC 1614 (Ch); [2016] 4 W.L.R. 184 at [25]–[27], Andrew Hochauser QC, sitting as a deputy judge of the High Court held, "... In my judgment, because one is dealing with an initial common law offer, the impact on it of any counter-offer has to be addressed by reference to common law principles. A Pt 36 counter offer is still a counter-offer". The "initial common law offer" in that case was a Calderbank offer and not one made pursuant to Pt 36: [10].

40 See *Epsom College* [2011] EWCA Civ 1449; and see CPR r.36.9(5)(a).

41 In *C v D* [2011] EWCA Civ 646; [2012] 1 W.L.R. 1962, Rix LJ explained that it was not possible within the terms of the pre-2015 Pt 36 to make a time-limited offer. It was, however, permissible to specify within a Pt 36 Offer that it would remain open for a specified period, but only if by this was meant that the offeror would not seek to withdraw it during that period. If, on the proper construction of the offer, what was meant was that the offer would lapse upon expiry of the specified period, that would take the offer outside Pt 36. And see *Epsom College v Pierse Contracting Southern Ltd*

PRIVILEGED NATURE OF OFFERS WITHIN PART 36

14-06 A Pt 36 offer will be treated as being "without prejudice except as to costs".[42] This means that whilst it can be referred to the court on the issue of costs,[43] it cannot be referred to on any other issue except in the very restricted circumstances that the law permits.[44] The purpose of retaining the "without prejudice" privilege is to enable negotiations to take place on a "cards on the table" basis without fear that anything said or done will be translated into some kind of admission upon which the recipient of the offer seeks to rely at trial.[45] The advantage to the offeror of being able to refer to the offer on the question of costs is that the offeree's conduct in rejecting it can be fully reflected in any order as to costs at the trial if the offer is not bettered.[46] Under the former practice, which doubtless continues, offers of this nature may be referred to in appropriate circumstances during the pre-trial period.[47]

14-07 With the exception of certain specific situations,[48] the general rule is that the fact that a Pt 36 offer has been made, and the terms of such an offer, must not be communicated "to the trial judge until the case has been decided".[49] The purpose of the rule is, of course, to try to ensure that the trial judge is not influenced by knowledge of the offer made. Since the rule refers specifically to the trial judge, which includes any "judge (if any) allocated in advance to conduct the trial"[50] there is within the rules no prohibition, in appropriate circumstances, against drawing the attention of a judge, master or district judge exercising pre-trial case management functions to the existence (and indeed the terms) of a Pt 36 offer. Under the former practice a payment into court could be referred to in an application for an interim payment (once liability has been admitted or established)[51] and "without prejudice" correspondence could be used in response to an application to strike out for want of prosecution.[52] There would seem no reason why the principles underlying that practice should not continue to be followed.

NON-DISCLOSURE TO TRIAL JUDGE OR COURT OF APPEAL

14-08 The rule as to non-disclosure is expressed in apparently mandatory terms[53] as was its predecessor in the Rules of the Supreme Court,[54] but the practice, certainly in relation to inadvertent or apparently tactical disclosure during a trial, has been to

---

[2011] EWCA Civ 1449 at [66]. CPR r.36.9(4)(b) now permits offers to specify the express terms of withdrawal.

42 CPR r.36.16(1).

43 Cf. *Calderbank v Calderbank* [1976] Fam. 93, *Cutts v Head* [1984] Ch. 290, CA.

44 See Ch.19.

45 See Ch.19.

46 See Ch.17.

47 See para.19-64 onwards.

48 See para.14-11.

49 CPR r.36.16(2).

50 CPR r.36.3(f).

51 See para.19-68.

52 See paras 19-64-19-65.

53 "The fact that a Part 36 offer has been made ... *must not* be communicated to the trial judge...": CPR r.36.16(2) (emphasis added). See CPR r.52.22 for the comparable provision concerning non-disclosure in appeal proceedings. But see fn.56.

54 RSC Ord.22 r.7(1).

treat the rule as directory rather than mandatory.[55] Thus where, by inadvertence or otherwise, the rule had been breached, the practice has been for the trial judge to exercise a discretion as to whether to hear the case further. Where satisfied that no injustice would be done, particularly if the knowledge could be put to one side for the purpose of making his decision, the trial judge could proceed.[56] It is thought that this practice continues, certainly in relation to an inadvertent or an apparently tactical disclosure of an offer (whether under Pt 36 or otherwise) during the trial. In *Garratt v Saxby*,[57] the Court of Appeal emphasised that a judge who learns inadvertently of a Pt 36 offer needs to have regard to the overriding objective "in deciding how to exercise [his] discretion to continue with the hearing or to recuse himself". The following additional guidance was given[58]:

> "It is for the judge to decide in each case whether the disclosure of a Pt 36 offer ... makes a fair trial impossible and whether justice demands that he recuse himself. But judges should not be too ready to reach such a conclusion; the delay and extra cost occasioned by a recusal may be very considerable. Moreover, when exercising their discretion, judges should remind themselves that they ought to have little difficulty in analysing and deciding the issues in the case on their merits without being influenced by their knowledge of the amount of the Pt 36 offer."

The question of the practice adopted since the 2007 revision of Pt 36 was implemented, where a "set-piece" application to accept or withdraw a previously unaccepted Pt 36 offer is made shortly before or at the trial, is dealt with below.[59] **14-09**

In order to ensure that disclosure of a Pt 36 offer during the course of a trial does not come to the attention of a judge in any further hearing in the course of proceedings, such as a quantum hearing before a judge other than the judge before whom the liability hearing was heard or an appeal hearing, a number of protective steps can be taken i.e through "suitable redactions to judgments, transcripts and documents"[60] of and disclosed in the hearing. The possibility also exists for any such hearing to be held in private in order to eliminate such a risk. It would, however, require "a strong case ... to be made out in order to override the basic and important principle that justice should be done in public"[61] to order that such a hearing be heard in private. **14-10**

EXCEPTIONS TO THE RULE AS TO NON-DISCLOSURE PROVIDED FOR IN RULES

The existence of a suitably expressed Pt 36 offer would be a relevant factor for the trial judge if the defence of tender before claim[62] was raised. Accordingly, in **14-11**

---

55 *AB v CD* [2011] EWHC 602 (Ch) at [16].

56 *Millensted v Grosvenor Place (Park Lane) Ltd* [1937] 1 K.B. 717 CA; *An Action for Negligence, Re, The Times*, 5 March 1993, Knox J.

57 *Garratt v Saxby* [2004] 1 W.L.R. 2152.

58 *Garratt* [2004] 1 W.L.R. 2152.

59 See para.14-15 onwards.

60 *32 Red Plc (A Gibraltar Company) v WHG (International) Ltd & Ors* [2011] EWHC 665 (Ch) at [8].

61 [2011] EWHC 665 (Ch) at [7], Henderson J.

62 This is described in the Glossary to the Rules as being: "A defence that, before the claimant started proceedings, the defendant unconditionally offered to the claimant the amount due or, if no specified amount is claimed, an amount sufficient to satisfy the claim."

this situation the rule against disclosure of a Pt 36 offer is expressly stated to be inapplicable.[63]

14-12 The second situation for which the rules provide an exception to the general rule is where the proceedings have been stayed "under r.36.14 following acceptance of a Part 36 offer".[64] By the time proceedings have been stayed under r.36.14,[65] it would be extremely rare for a "trial judge" to become involved subsequently. It is possible, however, that a judge allocated in advance to conduct the trial might be drawn into issues concerning the validity of the stay following the apparent acceptance of an offer.[66]

14-13 The third situation provided for in the rules in which the normal rule is relaxed is "where the offeror and the offeree agree in writing that it should not apply".[67]

14-14 Finally, the normal rules are relaxed in a number of situations where "the case has not been decided".[68] This provision was introduced in the 2015 revisions. Where "any part of, or issue in, a case has been decided" the fact and terms of a Pt 36 offer that relates only to the decided parts or issues may be disclosed to the trial judge.[69] As such it allows, for instance, Pt 36 offers relating to preliminary issues, or to matters determined at a split trial, to be disclosed and for the costs of the proceedings relating to that specific issue or those issues to be determined at that time rather than at the overall conclusion of the claim.[70] The fact that there are other Pt 36 offers in the proceedings may also be disclosed in such circumstances, although their terms "must not" be disclosed.[71]

APPLICATION TO ACCEPT OR WITHDRAW A PART 36 OFFER BEFORE OR DURING TRIAL

14-15 Under the practice prior to the introduction of the CPR (and indeed under that obtaining following their implementation in their original form) where a party wished to accept a previously unaccepted Pt 36 payment at the commencement of or during the trial, the existence of the rule against disclosure of the Pt 36 payment to the trial judge did not prevent the application for permission being made to the trial judge. The RSC that governed the position prior to the CPR had been interpreted by the Court of Appeal in a way that required a plaintiff who wanted to accept a payment into court during a trial to obtain the consent of the defendant

---

63 CPR r.36.16(3)(a).

64 CPR r.36.16(3)(b).

65 See para.15-27 onwards.

66 For the practice in relation to an application to withdraw an offer during "the relevant period" or for permission to accept a CPR Pt 36 offer where permission to accept is required, see Ch.16.

67 CPR r.36.16(3)(c). And see *Virgin Atlantic Airways Ltd v Jet Airways (India) Ltd & Ors* [2012] EWHC 3318 (Pat); [2013] 1 W.L.R. 1005, where due to disclosure of one of the terms of a Pt 36 offer in related procedures the claimant was held to have waived the privilege concerning disclosure of the entire terms of the offer, see paras 22 onwards.

68 CPR r.36.16(3)(d).

69 CPR r.36.16(3)(d)(i) and (ii).

70 The new provision thus resolves the question of the proper approach to take to disclosure where there is a split trial that arose under the pre-2015 Pt 36. For the detail of which see: *AB v CD* [2011] EWHC 602 (Ch) at [17]–[18], *Reed Baker Plc & Ors v AXA Insurance UK Plc & Ors* [2012] EWHC 2715 (Comm); [2012] 6 Costs L.R. 1023 at [19], and *Beasley v Alexander* [2012] EWHC 2715 (QB), [2013] 1 WLR 762 at [12]–[14]. An illustration of the approach to split trial situations under the post-2015 Pt 36 can be found in *Interactive Technology Corp Ltd v Ferster* [2017] EWHC 1510 (Ch).

71 CPR r.36.16(4)(a) and (b).

before making the application.[72] The view of the majority of the Court of Appeal was clearly influenced by a desire not to permit a plaintiff to try to gain a tactical advantage when a case was going badly by applying to take the payment into court, thus bringing it to the attention of the trial judge, and then seeking a re-trial before a different judge. However, the dissenting view drew attention to the lack of anything in the RSC that required the defendant's consent to such an application and to the existence of the discretion of the court to continue with the trial notwithstanding the judicial knowledge thus gained.[73] Under the original version of the CPR there was nothing that required the consent of the defendant before a claimant could make such an application during a trial and the practice that had obtained hitherto continued to be adopted: the trial judge would consider the application and, if it was refused, would then consider whether it was necessary to recuse himself.[74]

The Pt 36 Practice Direction provides that any application for permission to withdraw a Pt 36 offer[75] or any application to accept a Pt 36 offer where permission is required[76] specifies that any such application "must" be made: **14-16**

(1) by making an application under Pt 23, which must be dealt with by a judge other than the trial judge, unless the parties agree that such judge may hear the application;
(2) at a trial or other hearing, provided that it is not to the trial judge, unless the parties agree that such judge may hear the application.[77]

Whilst the assignment of either kind of application to a judge other than the trial judge is relatively easy if the application is made some while before the trial date, there could be logistical difficulties if, during a trial, the parties could not agree that such an application should be decided by the trial judge. Previous practice would have enabled the trial judge to consider applications of this nature and indeed, whilst judicial knowledge of the Pt 36 offer would thus have been gained, there would be much to be said for the trial judge deciding such an application: since it would be likely to involve considering to what extent the circumstances of the litigation have changed since the offer in question was made or rejected,[78] no one is normally better placed to assess this than the judge hearing the trial. Whether the Practice Direction was intended to alter this practice is an issue that awaits authoritative determination.[79] **14-17**

---

[72] *Gaskins v British Aluminium Co* [1976] Q.B. 524, per Lord Denning MR and Orr LJ Browne LJ dissented on the point, taking the view that a claimant could apply during the trial to take out a payment into court "whether or not the defendant consents".

[73] See para.14-08.

[74] See para.14-08. See the course taken by HH Judge Kershaw QC in *Capital Bank Plc v Stickland* [2005] 1 W.L.R. 3914 referred to at [2].

[75] See para.16-03.

[76] See Ch.16.

[77] CPR PD 36 paras 2.2 and 3.2. The definition of "trial judge" is that given in Pt 36 itself, see CPR r.36.3(f).

[78] See paras 16-03-16-04.

[79] See *The White Book* 2019, Vol.2. para.12-43.

CHAPTER 15

The Making, Acceptance and Consequences of an Effective CPR Part 36 Offer

INTRODUCTION

This chapter deals with the essential requirements of a valid Pt 36 offer, how it is made, how it is accepted and its effect once accepted. It deals essentially with those circumstances where the court has little, if any, supervisory role in the Pt 36 process. Those circumstances are dealt with in Ch.17. **15-01**

Care is needed to ensure that the mandatory requirements of Pt 36 are fully complied with as the Court of Appeal has emphasised that the rules in Pt 36 are not to be given a liberal interpretation simply to achieve what may be perceived to be the right answer in a given case. As Coulson LJ put it in *Hertel v Saunders*,[1] **15-02**

> "[Part 36] is a prescriptive regime which can have draconian consequences for those who fail to comply with it. That tends to suggest that the court should be wary of liberally construing the rules within Part 36 simply to achieve what might appear, at first glance, to be a pragmatic answer on the facts of a particular case."

An offer that does not comply with certain essential requirements will not be a Pt 36 offer and will not attract the normal costs consequences of Pt 36[2] although, as previously indicated,[3] an offer that is non-compliant may still be of relevance to the issue of costs. Where, however, a Pt 36 offer contains proposed terms going beyond the the formal requirements of Pt 36, as long as any such additional terms are consistent with the mandatory, formal, requirements, they will not invalidate the offer as a Pt 36 offer.[4]

---

1 [2018] EWCA Civ 1831; [2018] 1 W.L.R. 5852 at [37]. Also see *Hislop v Purde* [2018] EWCA Civ 1726; [2019] 1 W.L.R. 201 and *Cartwright v Venduct Engineering Ltd* [2018] EWCA Civ 1654; [2018] 1 W.L.R. 6137.

2 See paras 14–03—14–05. See, for instance, *James v James* [2018] EWHC 242 (Ch); [2018] 1 Costs L.R. 175 at [12]–[16], where HHJ Matthews, sitting as a judge of the High Court, held that an offer was not a valid Pt 36 offer as one of its terms concerning the consequences of acceptance of the offer differed from those prescribed in Pt 36 itself.

3 See para.14–02.

4 See *Horne v Prescot (No.1) Ltd* [2019] EWHC 1322 (QB); [2019] 1 W.L.R. 4808 per Nicol J at [64]: "...while Part 36 is prescriptive, no case cited [to me] suggested that the inclusion of additional words which did not conflict with the mandatory requirements or the operation of the scheme (to the extent that that is different) would mean that an offer was not a valid Part 36 offer."

FORM

15-03 A Pt 36 offer must be in writing.[5]

MATTERS TO WHICH A PART 36 OFFER CAN RELATE

15-04 A Pt 36 offer may "relate to the whole of the claim or to part of it or to an issue that arises in it" and, if it relates to a part or issue, it must state to which part or issue it relates.[6] If it takes account of any counterclaim, it must so state.[7] It can relate solely to liability.[8] It can be made in respect of distinct claims brought by individual claimants against a common defendant, where the intention is to settle both claims by paying a sum of money to the claimants' jointly.[9] Except where the claim is a personal injury claim in which the defendant wishes to offer periodical payments and/or provisional damages as part of the proposed settlement[10], a Pt 36 offer by a defendant to pay a sum of money in settlement of a claim "must be an offer to pay a single sum of money".[11]

15-05 Separate Pt 36 offers need to be made for first instance and appellate

---

5 CPR r.36.5(1)(a).

6 CPR r.36.5(1)(d); and see CPR r.36.2(3). A Pt 36 offer should relate only to the substantive claim, and as such it should not contain terms relating to costs: *Mitchell v James* [2002] EWCA Civ 997; [2004] W.L.R. 158; *Bellamy v Sheffield Teaching Hospitals NHS Trust* [2003] EWCA Civ 1124; *French v Groupama Insurance Co Ltd* [2011] EWCA Civ 1119; [2012] C.P. Rep. 2, and *Knight v Knight* [2019] EWHC 1545 (Ch). A Pt 36 offer can be made where there is a substantive dispute concerning the costs of a claim, and indeed in respect of a specific issue concerning costs, such as the solicitors' hourly rates: see *White v Wincott Galliford Ltd* [2019] EWHC B6 (Costs), and para.14-02.

7 CPR r.36.5(1)(e). CPR r.36.2(3)(a) makes it clear that a Pt 36 offer can be made in respect of a counterclaim and an additional claim. In *Calonne Construction Ltd v Dawnus Southern Ltd* [2019] EWCA Civ 754; [2019] 1 W.L.R. 4793, Asplin LJ confirmed at [33]–[37] that an effective Pt 36 offer can be made in respect of a counterclaim and an additional claim that had not yet been commenced or pleaded. To hold otherwise, it was said, would have been to contradict the express words of CPR r.36.7 (which permits Pt 36 offers to be made in respect of claims before they are commenced), CPR r.36.2(3)(a), and CPR r.20.3. In reaching her decision, with which Flaux and Hamblen LJJ agreed, Asplin LJ distinguished the case from *Hertel v Saunders* [2018] EWCA Civ 1831; [2018] 1 W.L.R. 5852 where at [33] a differently constituted Court of Appeal held that "the words 'claim', 'part of a claim'; and 'issue' [referred] to pleaded claims, parts of claims or issues, and not other claims or issues which may have been intimated in some way but never pleaded". It was observed in *Calonne* at [37] that the case of *AF v BG* [2009] EWCA Civ 757, [2010] 2 Costs L.R. 164 was not referred to the court in *Hertel*. Although Asplin LJ at [42] said that "the decision in *Hertel* is not directly relevant to the circumstances under consideration in this appeal and did not address them", it is, with respect, questionable whether *Hertel* can stand in the light of the judgments in *AF* and *Calonne*.

8 Prior to 2015 this was provided for expressly in the then CPR r.36.2(5). This rule was not incorporated into the 2015 revision. It is apparent that the wording of both CPR r.36.2(3) and r.36.5(1)(d) assume that offers may relate to discrete issues such as liability.

9 *Ali v Channel 5 Broadcast Ltd* [2018] EWHC 840 (Ch); [2018] 2 Costs L.R. 373. In that case the two claims were parallel claims arising out of the same events against the common defendant brought by a married couple (see [41]). Where, however, there is no connection between the claimants and the nature and extent of any damages claimed differ to a material extent, it is likely that a court would not follow this approach. It is arguable, however, that this decision could form the basis upon which the courts could develop a collective settlement regime under CPR Pt 36 applicable to representative claims brought under CPR r.19.6.

10 See CPR r.36.18(3) and r.36.19(1). And see para.15–10.

11 CPR r.36.6(1). An offer to pay a single sum of money "that includes an offer to pay all or part of the sum at a date later than 14 days following the date of acceptance will not be treated as a Part 36 offer unless the offeree accepts the offer": CPR r.36.6(2). See also Ch.27.

proceedings.[12] Prior to the introduction of the 2015 version of Pt 36 it was held that where a Pt 36 offer is made to settle the claim in appellate proceedings it may be relevant to a future re-trial. As Foskett J said in *Uren v Corporate Leisure (UK) Ltd*,[13]

> "I do not see why, in appropriate circumstances, a Part 36 offer in the context of a pending appeal cannot have an impact on the cost of a subsequent re-trial directed by the Court of Appeal following that appeal. There does not appear to be anything in Part 36 that prevents this."[14]

"THE WHOLE OF THE CLAIM"

The natural meaning of this expression connotes all issues that arise directly in the proceedings.[15] It should be recalled that even issues which could have been raised, but were not raised specifically in the proceedings, could be treated as "settled" once a Pt 36 offer has been accepted.[16] **15-06**

In most cases, the "whole of the claim" will embrace primary liability, contributory negligence (where applicable), causation of loss and all issues relating to the remoteness and quantification of damages. Where relief in the form of an injunction or other equitable remedy is sought, it will include that relief as well. **15-07**

INTEREST

Pt 36 does not require the offer to state anything specific in relation to the issue of interest. CPR r.36.5(4)[17] provides that a Pt 36 offer "which offers to pay or offers to accept a sum of money will be treated as inclusive of all interest" until (a) the date on which the period stated under r.36.5(1)(c) expires[18] or (b) if r.36.5(2) applies,[19] a date 21 days after the date the offer was made. In *Calonne Construc-* **15-08**

---

12 CPR r.36.4. And see CPR r.52.22. See also para.14-08.

13 [2013] All E.R. (D) 66 (Apr) at [20]. It was noted that if this were wrong then the offer made in appeal proceedings would be a valid Calderbank offer and capable of being taken account under CPR r.44.2(4)(c).

14 The wording of CPR r.36.4(1), which makes explicit provision for the pre-2015 practice that Pt 36 offers may be made in appeal proceedings but is otherwise in the same terms as the pre-2015 CPR r.36.3(4) does not appear to have altered the basis on which that decision was reached.

15 CPR r.36.5(1)(d). In *Bentley Design Consultants Ltd v Sansom* [2018] EWHC 2238 (TCC); [2018] 6 Costs L.O. 743, an offer to settle a claim that had been made to compromise one aspect of C's claim against D was subsequently purported to be accepted by D in respect of that claim and another claim. The court rejected the argument that the words "the whole of this claim" in the offer meant both aspects of the claim.

16 i.e. the kind of issues that might be treated as res judicata in the wider sense of the principle in *Henderson v Henderson* (1843) 3 Hare 100. See para.6–08 onwards.

17 This provision was described by Nicol J in *Horne v Prescot (No.1) Ltd* [2019] EWHC 1322 (QB); [2019] 1 W.L.R. 4808, as one that does not involve a mandatory requirement, unlike the requirements of r.36.5(1), and merely provides that the absence of any reference to interest in an offer simply means that the offer will be "treated" as inclusive of interest until the relevant date. In order to achieve a different result it would be prudent to specify that an offer is exclusive of interest ([66]–[67]).

18 See para.15–11. The original version of Pt 36 did, however, require this.

19 Which provides that CPR r.36.5(1)(c) "does not apply if the offer is made less than 21 days before the start of the trial".

tion Ltd v Dawnus Southern Ltd,[20] the Court of Appeal held that CPR r.36.5(4) did not preclude an offeror from including express provision for interest following the expiry of the relevant period. The converse (namely, the exclusion of interest from a Pt 36 Offer) is also valid.[21]

PERSONAL INJURY CLAIMS

15-09 In relation to a personal injury claim which includes a claim for future pecuniary loss or where an offer to settle a claim for provisional damages is made, Pt 36 requires that certain information is set out in the offer.[22] Equally, r.36.22 requires that the status of any "recoverable amounts" or "deductible amounts" in a Pt 36 offer should be specified.[23]

INTERIM PAYMENTS

15-10 Under the original version of Pt 36, the Pt 36 payment notice was required to state whether any interim payment already made had been taken into account where a Pt 36 payment had been made in respect of a money claim.[24] No equivalent requirement now appears in Pt 36 in relation to a Pt 36 offer in respect of a money claim. It had been suggested[25] that this omission arose because a payment of money into court is no longer required. It is not thought that that would necessarily represent a sound reason for omitting a comparable provision in the rule as presently formulated but since an "interim payment" is, by definition, a payment "on account of any damages, debt or other sum (except costs) which the court may hold the defendant liable to pay",[26] the natural meaning of this expression would suggest that any interim payment is to be regarded as part of the final sum awarded. However, notwithstanding the lack of specific reference in the rules to the status of an interim payment in any Pt 36 offer, it would doubtless be open to an offeror to indicate the position expressly if it was felt that any uncertainty should be avoided.

TIME FOR ACCEPTANCE

15-11 The 2007 revision of Pt 36 introduced the concept of the "relevant period". This is now defined[27] in the case of an offer made not less than 21 days before trial as "the period stated under rule 36.5(1)(c) or such longer period as the parties agree" or where the offer is made "otherwise" (in other words, within 21 days of the trial) as "the period up to end of such trial". Rule 36.5(1)(c) requires a valid Pt 36 offer to

---

20 [2019] EWCA Civ 754; [2019] 1 W.L.R. 4793 at [43]–[47].
21 See fn.17.
22 CPR r.36.5(3), r.36.18 and r.36.19. See Ch.27.
23 CPR r.36.5(3).
24 CPR r.36.6(2)(d), see, for instance, *The White Book* 2006, Vol.1, para.36.6.
25 *The White Book* 2009, Vol.1, para.25.8.4. This proposition does not appear in later editions.
26 CPR r.25.1(1)(k).
27 CPR r.36.3(1)(g).

"specify a period of not less than 21 days within which the defendant will be liable for the claimant's costs in accordance with rule 36.13 or 36.20 if the offer is accepted".[28]

Except where an offeree has already "served notice of acceptance", a Pt 36 offer may be withdrawn or its terms changed "to be less advantageous to the offeree".[29] This can be done either before[30] or after[31] the relevant period expires by way of written notice of withdrawal or the change of terms.[32] Service is to be effected pursuant to CPR Pt 6.[33]

Where the notice of withdrawal or change in terms is served prior to the relevant period's expiry, it takes effect on the expiry of that period.[34] If, however, the offeree serves notice of acceptance of the offer that is subject to the notice of withdrawal or change of terms prior to expiry of the relevant period, the court's permission is required to give effect to the withdrawal or change in terms, and thereby frustrate the attempt to accept the offer.[35] Such permission may only be granted where there "has been a change of circumstances since the making of the original offer and that it is in the interest of justice" to do so.[36] **15-12**

Where the notice of withdrawal or change of terms is served after the relevant period has expired, the court's permission to withdraw is not required.[37] This can be effected in two ways: first, through specifically providing for withdrawal or change of terms after the relevant period expires within the Pt 36 offer itself[38]; and secondly, by separate notice. The withdrawal or change in terms takes effect either upon service of the notice or according to the terms specified in the offer itself.[39] **15-13**

Since the "relevant period" was introduced it has had the effect of retaining the long-standing principle that for an offer to have effect on the issue of costs it should give the offeree an adequate time to consider its merits. The period of 21 days has long been regarded as the minimum period that ought ideally to be provided to the offeree. It follows that an offer made in excess of 21 days before the trial must "specify a period of not less than 21 days within which the defendant will be liable for the claimant's costs"[40] until acceptance for such an offer to be a valid Pt 36 offer. Any shorter period specified in the offer would, subject to the power of the court to abridge any time provided for in the rules or under the court's inherent **15-14**

---

[28] Particular care needs to be taken in expressing the fact that an offer is open for not less than 21 days: see, *C v D* [2011] EWCA Civ 646; [2012] 1 W.L.R. 1962.

[29] CPR r.36.9(5) provides that a change in terms of an offer that "make it more advantageous to the offeree" is deemed to be a fresh offer and one that does not effect the withdrawal of the original offer.

[30] CPR r.36.10(1). See Ch.16.

[31] CPR r.36.9(1).

[32] CPR r.36.9(2) and r.36.10(1).

[33] See *Sutton Jigsaw Transport Ltd v Croydon London Borough Council* [2013] EWHC 874 (QB), where service of notice of acceptance was not effected in accordance with Pt 6 and, as a consequence, the Pt 36 offer that the claimant wished to accept was validly withdrawn before the purported service of a written notice of acceptance. HH Judge McKenna, sitting as a judge of the High Court, refused to dispense with service or to permit the purported service to stand as retrospective substituted service.

[34] CPR r.36.10(1) and (2)(a).

[35] CPR r.36.10(2)(b). An application to withdraw must be on notice to the offeree, see *Evans v Royal Wolverhampton Hospitals NHS Foundation Trust* [2014] EWHC 3185 (QB); [2015] 1 W.L.R. 4659 per Leggatt J at [42].

[36] CPR r.36.10(3). See para.16–05 onwards.

[37] CPR r.36.9(4)(a).

[38] CPR r.36.9(4)(b).

[39] CPR r.36.9(3) and (4).

[40] CPR r.36.5(1)(c).

jurisdiction,[41] render the offer outside Pt 36 though not necessarily irrelevant on the issue of costs pursuant to the general discretion conferred by Pt 44.[42] As indicated above,[43] an offer made within the 21-day period before trial will be subject to a "relevant period" until the end of the trial. This would have the effect of depriving the offeror of the right to withdraw the offer at any stage during the trial without the permission of the court.[44] Whilst that position may be acceptable to the offeror, if the ability to make an informed offer as late as within the 21-day period before trial is caused by, for example, the delayed supply of information, expert reports or documents on the part of the intended offeree,[45] the court will often be invited by the offeror to abridge the period that would otherwise constitute the "relevant period".

THE MAKING OF THE OFFER

15-15 A Pt 36 offer can be made in CPR Form N242A.[46] More often than not, such an offer is made in a letter. In order to minimise the possibility that an offer may be held not to be compliant with the mandatory, technical provisions of Pt 36, through any inadvertent failure to comply with its formal requirements, use of the Form is obviously less risky than relying upon the composition of another form of communication.[47]

15-16 A Pt 36 offer is made when it is served, pursuant to the provisions of CPR Pt 6, on the offeree.[48]

CLARIFICATION OF THE OFFER

15-17 It is open to the offeree to "request the offeror to clarify the offer"[49] which the offeror is obliged to do within seven days of receiving the request failing which the offeree may apply for an order that the request is answered unless the trial has started.[50] Where clarification is sought and provided, it should be fully considered

---

41 CPR r.3.1(2)(a), (e) and/or (m) would probably confer this power upon the court. CPR r.36.17(7)(c) assumes the existence of a power to abridge the relevant period. In any event, the inherent jurisdiction would probably operate as a backstop if it were felt necessary: cf. *Proetta v Times Newspapers Ltd* [1991] 1 W.L.R. 337, CA, and *R (Kumar) v Secretary of State for Constitutional Affairs* [2006] EWCA Civ 990; [2007] 1 W.L.R. 536 at [62], where the Court of Appeal noted that in exceptional circumstances the inherent jurisdiction, in that case to protect the court from abuse of process, could be relied on as a backstop where rules provided an otherwise complete code.

42 See para.14-02 fn.12. Cf. *Codent Ltd v Lyson Ltd* [2005] EWCA Civ 1835; [2006] C.P. Rep. 33, decided under the original version of CPR Pt 36.

43 See para.15–11.

44 fn.31.

45 cf. *King v Weston-Howell* [1989] 1 W.L.R. 579.

46 CPR PD 36 para.1.1.

47 On the consequences of non-compliance with the mandatory requirements of Pt 36 see, for instance, *Huntley v Simmonds* [2009] EWHC 406 (QB), *Carillion JM Ltd v PHI Group Ltd (also known as PHI Group Ltd v Robert West Consulting Ltd)* [2012] EWCA Civ 588; [2012] C.P. Rep. 37, *Thewlis v Groupama* [2012] EWHC 3 (TCC); [2012] B.L.R. 259; see para.14–04.

48 CPR r.36.7(2). See the signpost following CPR r.36.7(2), which provides that "(Part 6 provides detailed rules about service of documents.)".

49 CPR r.36.8(1).

50 CPR r.36.8(2).

in construing the Pt 36 offer.[51] Construction of a Pt 36 offer, as construction of a contract, requires the court to adopt an objective approach as explained by Tugendhat J in *Rosario v Nadell Patisserie Ltd*[52]:

> "While the provisions of Part 36 are not part of the law of contract, they are made against the background of that law. The need to apply an objective test is one of the rules which apply in both contexts. Under the objective test, a party may be bound if his words or conduct are such as to induce a reasonable person to believe that he intends to be bound, even though he in fact has no such intention."

Whilst CPR r.36.8(1) is framed to permit clarification of "the offer", the court will not wish to encourage detailed and wide-ranging questions about an offer made under the guise of seeking "clarification". Whilst it is impossible to be definitive, it is likely that the court will, in the first instance, ask itself the broad question of whether making the order will help the parties to settle the whole or part of the case.[53] This may narrow down to the issue of whether the terms of the offer are in any material respect unclear or ambiguous such that the offeree would be at a disadvantage in considering it.[54] If that is indeed the conclusion at which the court arrives, a clarification order would be likely. Where a party has provided information sufficient to clarify any ambiguity or unclear issue, it is unlikely that a subsequent refusal to provide further clarification would be viewed by the court as unreasonable.[55] **15-18**

The question will arise of what an offeree should do when an offer is arguably ambiguous, but the offeree is of the view that the argument as to ambiguity should be answered in his favour. From a purely contractual point of view, the offeree would be entitled to accept the offer as it stands and, subject to any issues as to mistake or misrepresentation, the contract thus formed would be binding.[56] The offeree would then have to take his chances in the argument as to the true meaning of the agreement in the event of a dispute about it. However, if the offeree elected not to accept the offer, it is unlikely that the court would be receptive to the argument, when the issue of costs is determined at the end of the trial, that the offer was not accepted because it was unclear or ambiguous. The remedy for that problem would be the seeking of clarification and the failure to do so, where it was plainly the appropriate course, would undoubtedly be one of the "circumstances"[57] that could be taken into account on costs. The culture embodied in the CPR demands a sensible and meaningful dialogue, particularly where settlement is concerned.[58] **15-19**

In making a Pt 36 offer particular care needs to be taken where the offeree is a **15-20**

---

[51] *Bailes v Bloom* [2015] 11 WLUK 560 (QB) per Simler J.

[52] [2010] EWHC 1886 (QB) at [34].

[53] CPR r.1.4(2)(f).

[54] See, e.g. *Kinetics Technology v Cross Seas Shipping* [2001] 2 Lloyd's Rep. 313, (Comm).

[55] *Bailes v Bloom* [2015] 11 WLUK 560, (QB).

[56] It is thought that in most cases where no further involvement of the court is contemplated other than enforcement of the terms of the agreement it is right to say that ordinarily a contract of compromise has been concluded. The suggestions that this may not necessarily be so made in *Orton v Collins* [2007] 1 W.L.R. 2953 and *Warren v The Random House Group Ltd* [2009] Q.B. 600 were made in particular contexts that may not apply to the generality of cases. At all events, the normal consequence of the acceptance of an offer intended to create a bargain is that a contract is thus formed.

[57] CPR r.44.2(4).

[58] See *Hertsmere Primary Care Trust v Administrators of Balasumbramanium's Estate* [2005] EWHC 320 (Ch); [2005] 3 All E.R. 274 at [11], for discussion on the parties' duty to co-operate in respect of Pt 36, albeit in the context a failure by one party to properly inform the other of a procedural error in good time for it to be rectified. It is suggested that the duty applies to the same extent in respect of situations where clarification of an arguably ambiguous offer arises for consideration.

litigant-in-person. In *Kunaka v Barclays Bank*[59] the Court of Appeal held that in such circumstances Barclays Bank ought to have pointed out to the claimant the cost consequences that would ordinarily flow from his acceptance of the offer. As Longmore LJ went on to hold, given a failure to do so, it was appropriate to make an 'otherwise' order under what was then r.36.10(5).[60] Given the increasing volume of litigation conducted by litigants-in-person, care of this nature by parties who are legally represented is increasingly likely to be needed in explaining the general effect and consequences of Pt 36 offers.

EFFECT OF ESTOPPEL ON CHALLENGING COMPLIANCE WITH FORMAL REQUIREMENTS OF PART 36

15-21 Where an offeror draws an offeree's attention to the need to raise any points of non-compliance with the formal requirements of CPR r.36.5, they may be estopped from challenging the validity of the offer at a later stage.[61]

ACCEPTANCE OF A PART 36 OFFER

15-22 In certain circumstances[62] the court's permission is required before a Pt 36 offer may be accepted. In all other circumstances a Pt 36 offer "is accepted by serving written notice of the acceptance on the offeror".[63] There is a requirement that the notice is "filed with the court where the case is proceeding".[64] In the situation where the permission of the court to accept an offer is not required a Pt 36 offer, "may be accepted at any time (whether or not the offeree has subsequently made a different offer), unless it has already been withdrawn".[65]

15-23 Where there has been a trial that has not decided all the issues in the proceedings (for example, where there has been a split trial or a trial of a preliminary issue) any Pt 36 offer relating to the issues determined at that trial is not capable of being accepted.[66] If there are any other extant Pt 36 offers, which relate to other issues in the proceedings, "unless the parties agree" any other such offer "cannot be accepted earlier than 7 clear days after judgment is given or handed down" in the trial of the preliminary issue or split trial.[67]

15-24 Unless the parties agree otherwise, a Pt 36 offer may not be accepted after the end of the trial but before judgment is handed down.[68]

15-25 Proceedings must, however, be extant for a Pt 36 offer to be capable of being

---

59 [2010] EWCA Civ 1035; [2011] 2 Costs L.R. 179 at [7]–[10].

60 Now see CPR r.36.13(5).

61 *Seeff v Ho* [2011] EWCA Civ 401; [2011] 4 Costs L.O. 443 at [12] per Thomas LJ as applied by Arnold J in *Ali* [2018] EWHC 840 (Ch); [2018] 2 Costs L.R. 373 at [42]–[44].

62 See Ch.16. A previously rejected CPR Pt 36 offer that has not been withdrawn may be accepted subsequently: *Sampla v Rushmoor BC* [2008] EWHC 2616 (TCC), *Gibbon v Manchester City Council* [2010] EWCA Civ 726; [2010] W.L.R. 2081 at [16]. In most cases this will require the permission of the court, the giving of which will depend on whether the circumstances have changed sufficiently to make it unjust to do so: para.16–03 onwards.

63 CPR r.36.11(1).

64 CPR PD 36 para.3.1.

65 CPR r.36.11(2). See para.15–12 on withdrawal of a Pt 36 offer.

66 CPR r.36.12.

67 CPR r.36.12(3).

68 CPR r.36.9(5).

accepted. Where a claim or a statement of case has been discontinued[69] or struck out or where a party has failed to comply with an "unless order" that brings the claim to an end,[70] a Pt 36 offer can no longer be accepted. This has been held to be the case even where a successful application for relief from sanctions under r.3.9 could revive the claim.[71] Where it appears likely that a party may not be in a position to comply with an "unless order" it has been said that it may be in their "best interests to accept the offer forthwith". Such acceptance would, it is said, "tend to promote ... the overriding objective."[72]

THE EFFECT OF ACCEPTANCE OF A PART 36 OFFER

Except in those circumstances where the court has a role in deciding whether a Pt 36 offer may be accepted by the offeree,[73] and except in those circumstances where there is a degree of discretion left with the court in relation to costs,[74] there are certain automatic consequences flowing from acceptance of an effective Pt 36 offer. **15-26**

Subject to limited exceptions,[75] where the Pt 36 offer (whether made by a claimant or defendant) relates to the whole of the claim[76] and is accepted within the relevant period,[77] **15-27**

---

69 *SuperGroup Plc v Just Enough Software Corp* [2014] EWHC 3260 (Comm): Flaux J explained in an obiter observation that C was not able to accept a Pt 36 offer made by D in respect of the claim and taking into account D's counterclaim following service of C's notice of discontinuance of the claim because at that stage only the counterclaim remained in existence.

70 *Joyce v West Bus Coach Services Ltd* [2012] EWHC 404 (QB); [2012] 3 Costs L.R. 540 at [33]–[41].

71 *Joyce* [2012] EWHC 404 (QB); [2012] 3 Costs L.R. 540 per Kenneth Parker J at [34]–[35], "... The reason why the dismissal of the claim or the entry of judgment precludes the acceptance of a Part 36 offer is that on dismissal or entry of judgment the claim is to all intents and purposes at an end. But that is also the position where a statement of case or claim has been struck out under an 'unless' order ... Nor am I impressed by any argument that CPR 3.9 (relief from sanctions) was intended to hold a claim that has been struck out on life support, so to speak, awaiting the ministering dispensation of relief by the Court so as to obviate final extinction. That is how practitioners may, without proper justification, have come to view it. A claim that has been struck out is in law at an end. CPR 3.9 provides for an exceptional judicial discretion to reinstate a claim, on terms, if there is a sufficiently compelling case." As he went on to explain at [37], if a claim struck out consequent upon an "unless order" was revived following a successful application for relief from sanctions under CPR r.3.9, the Pt 36 offer would also be reactivated assuming that it had not otherwise been formally withdrawn.

72 *Joyce* [2012] EWHC 404 (QB); [2012] 3 Costs L.R. 540 at [40]. See *Newland Shipping & Forwarding Ltd v Toba Trading FZC* [2014] EWHC 864 (Comm), where two consolidated claims were subject to default judgment and relief from sanctions revived only one of them. In such a case a global Pt 36 offer to settle made prior to the default judgment was held to be inoperative following judgment on the merits in the revived claim. Leggatt J at [12]–[16] explained that in such circumstances a fresh Pt 36 offer, in respect of the revived claim, ought to have been made following the successful relief from sanction claim. As he put it, "It does not seem to me, however, that CPR 36.14(1) is apt to cover a situation where two different judgments are given at different times in two separate actions so as to enable the judgments to be aggregated and treated as if they were one."

73 See Ch.16.

74 See para.14–02.

75 The exceptions arise where CPR r.36.20 applies i.e. Section III of Part 45 applies, or CPR r.36(13)(2) or (4) applies.

76 See paras 15–06 and 15–07.

77 See paras 15–11 and 15–14.

"the claimant will be entitled to the costs of the proceedings (including their recoverable pre-action costs) up to the date on which notice of acceptance was served on the offeror".[78]

Save where a fixed costs regime governs recoverability, the costs will "be assessed on the standard basis if the amount of costs is not agreed".[79]

15-28 Acceptance of a Pt 36 offer "that is or that includes an offer to pay or accept a single sum of money" involves an obligation on the defendant to pay the claimant that sum "within 14 days of the date of ... acceptance".[80] Where a Pt 36 offer "which relates to the whole claim is accepted" the claim will be "stayed upon the terms of the offer".[81] If the accepted sum is not paid within 14 days or such other period as has been agreed "the claimant may enter judgment for the unpaid sum".[82]

15-29 Where an accepted Pt 36 offer contains provisions other than for the payment of

---

78 CPR r.36.13(1). See also *Solomon v Cromwell Group Plc* [2011] EWCA Civ 1585; [2012] 1W.L.R. 1048 noted para.14–05. In *Global Assets Advisory Services Ltd and Another v Grandlane Developments Limited and Others* [2019] EWCA Civ 1764, CA, it was held that there is jurisdiction to order an interim payment on account of costs pursuant to CPR r 44.2(8) where a Part 36 offer has been accepted within the relevant period, thus overruling *J P Finnegan v Spiers (t/a Frank Spiers Licensed Conveyancers)* [2018] EWHC 3064; [2018] 6 Costs L.O. 729.

79 CPR r.36.13(3). There is no provision in this situation for obtaining indemnity costs: see *Dyson Ltd v Hoover Ltd* [2002] EWHC 2229 (Ch); [2003] F.S.R. 21 Jacob J, as he then was, in relation to the identical provision under the original version of CPR Pt 36. This has been seen by some as potentially causing an injustice where a claimant has made his own Pt 36 offer which is not accepted by the defendant, but then the defendant makes a Pt 36 offer which exceeds that which the claimant in his offer said he would accept. If the claimant accepts the defendant's offer he can achieve only standard costs, whereas by accepting it is he is achieving more than his own offer—something which, in the ordinary course of events, would result in an entitlement to indemnity costs and enhanced interest: see para.17–18 onwards. In *Dyson*, where, as required under the original version of Pt 36, the defendant paid money into court, Jacob J suggested that the route out of the difficulty would be for the claimant not to take the money paid in as such, but to write to the defendant indicating the basis upon which the money was to be taken out. If the defendant did not agree to that basis then an application could be made to the court for directions.

80 CPR r.36.14(6) and 36.14(6)(a). Where the court makes an order under r.41.2 (an order for an award of provisional damages) or r.41.8 (order for an award of periodical payments), then the obligation is to pay any single lump sum part of the order within 14 days of the order "unless the court orders otherwise": r.36.11(6)(b). In *Titmus v General Motors UK Ltd* [2016] EWHC 2021 (QB) at [25–[26] it was confirmed the 14-day period could not be extended under CPR Pt 3. The only basis on which the 14-day period could be extended was that set out in CPR r.36.14(6). Laing J went on to hold at [28] that the court had no power under CPR Pt 36 or under CPR r.3.1(2)(a) to order the sum due under CPR r.36.14 to be paid into court.

81 CPR r.36.14(2). A similar approach arises where a Pt 36 offer "which relates to part only of the claim" is accepted: r.36.11(3). This is the equivalent of a rule-imposed Tomlin order.

82 CPR r.36.14(7). The effect of this rule is expressed in permissive terms. However, where the claimant has accepted the offer and is content to receive the sum offered, it is convenient to have the facility to enter judgment readily if the payment is not forthcoming within the stipulated period: see *The White Book* 2019, Vol.1, para.36.14 onwards. The effect of the rules appears to be that once a valid and effective CPR Pt 36 offer is accepted a contract of compromise is concluded and it is that contract that henceforth governs the relationship of the parties. This is, of course, the normal effect of reaching a compromise: see paras 6–01, 6–02 and 6–18. It does not appear that a failure on the part of a defendant to pay the sum offered gives the claimant the opportunity to regard the compromise as no longer binding since the claim is stayed "upon the terms of the offer" once the offer is accepted: see fn.69. The question remains of the situation where the claimant is minded to accept the sum offered *if it is paid within the 14-day period* and would wish to preserve the right to revert to claiming the full value of the claim if it is not. The offeree may be unsure whether the offeror is good for the money. This was one of the broad issues raised in the cases of *Crouch v King's Healthcare NHS Trust* [2005] 1 W.L.R. 2015 CA, and *The Trustees of Stokes Pension Fund v Western Power Distribution (South West) Plc* [2005] 1 W.L.R. 3595 CA, each of which pre-dated the 2007 revision to CPR Pt 36. In the latter case Dyson LJ said: "The best way for a claimant to test the genuineness of an offer and the defendant's ability to pay is to accept the offer (or at least to do so conditionally on payment being forthcoming) and see what happens." Given the way both the 2007 revision and the present, 2015, versions are drafted, the route of conditional acceptance would, it is thought, be the

a sum of money,

> "a party [who] alleges that the other party has not honoured the terms of the offer ... may apply to enforce the terms of the offer without the need for a new claim".[83]

This rule is expressed slightly differently from its predecessor[84] which provided that where a Pt 36 offer had been accepted and one party alleged that the other had not "honoured the terms of the offer" and that he (the innocent party) was "entitled to a remedy for breach of contract", he "may claim the remedy by applying to the court without the need to start a new claim" unless the court ordered otherwise. This formulation had been designed to overcome the potential consequences of the arguably restrictive interpretation placed on the meaning of the words "enforcing the terms" of a Tomlin order in *Hollingsworth v Humphrey*.[85] The impression gained from a first reading of the present formulation is that it is intended as merely a shortened version of the original rule and that no fundamental change was intended. However, it is arguable that the omission in the present formulation of the reference to an entitlement "to a remedy for breach of contract" in consequence of not honouring the terms of the offer was intended to confine the right to apply to the court to pure enforcement and not to claiming a remedy for breach of contract.[86] Whilst the issue awaits authoritative determination, it would be unfortunate if a fresh claim was now to be regarded as the necessary step to seeking damages for an alleged breach of an accepted Pt 36 offer. It may be that the present formulation was intended to embody the approach taken by Sir Andrew Morritt VC in *Bargain Pages Ltd v Midland Independent Newspapers Ltd*[87] where it was held that the overriding objective enabled the making of an order for an inquiry as to damages sustained as the result of an alleged breach of a provision in the schedule to a Tomlin order without the need for a fresh claim.

---

safer route for a claimant faced with uncertainty about the defendant's financial status.

83 CPR r.36.14(8), which is in the same terms as its immediate predecessor, introduced in 2007, CPR r.36.11(8).

84 The original CPR r.36.15(6).

85 See para.9–26.

86 See "Enforcing Settlement Agreements" in *Civil Procedure News 2007*, 5–6 May 2007.

87 See para.9–29. In *Orton* [2007] 1 W.L.R. 2953, a partnership dispute was resolved by the acceptance by the defendant partners of a Pt 36 offer made by C that he would withdraw dissolution notices that he had served in return: (i) for being paid the value of his interests in certain office premises at a valuation; (ii) an indemnity "from and against all monies misappropriated by his wife and any consequential losses and expenses"; and (iii) the payment to him of an additional capital sum. A dispute then arose about the terms of the indemnity and C took the point that there was no effective settlement agreement at all because the Pt 36 offer and notice of acceptance, which involved a disposition of an interest in land, did not comply with s.2 of the Law of Property (Miscellaneous Provisions) Act 1989: see Ch.30. Peter Prescott QC, sitting as a deputy judge of the High Court, held that, whilst "in the vast majority of cases" acceptance of a Pt 36 offer probably does create an enforceable contract, where it does not (as in the instant case), the parties must be taken to have submitted to the consequences of choosing the Pt 36 machinery, namely, that if the offer is accepted the court may enforce it. It creates a binding settlement under the court's rules that the court can enforce. Reliance was placed on the overriding objective and the inherent jurisdiction of the court.

CHAPTER 16

The Court's Supervisory Role in CPR Part 36

INTRODUCTION

The purpose of CPR Pt 36 is to provide a clear and certain structure for making an offer which, if accepted, has well-defined consequences. Indeed this was the purpose of the rules relating to payments into court prior to the implementation of the CPR. A well-known procedure assists and facilitates settlement. To that extent the role of the court as an adjudicatory or supervisory body should be minimal. In the pre-CPR era the payment into court of a sum of money was always required in relation to a claim for damages. The money could not be removed from court without the permission of the court, nor could it be accepted without the court's permission after the usual 21-day period.[1] Whether the payment into court amounted simply to an offer to settle on terms[2] or whether there was no true contractual analogy,[3] the role of the court when a payment into court was accepted within the stipulated period was extremely limited. Its principal role was supervising what happened to the money in court if the defendant wished effectively to withdraw or alter the offer constituted by the payment into court or if, on further reflection, the claimant wished to accept it. The same considerations did not apply to offers in cases not involving a claim for damages where a payment of money into court was not required. **16-01**

---

1 Both under the RSC and the CPR, the usual period given for consideration of the offer reflected either in a payment into court (under the RSC), a Pt 36 payment (under the original version of Pt 36) or now in a Pt 36 offer is 21 days. See para.15–11.

2 In *A Martin French v Kingswood Hill* [1961] 1 Q.B. 96, Devlin LJ said this at 103: "A payment into court is simply an offer to dispose of the claim on terms. If the defendant were free to formulate the terms himself, he could make his offer in whatever form he liked ... But if he seeks to effect his compromise under the rules which permit a payment into court, he must make his offer according to the rules."

3 In *Cumper v Pothecary* [1941] 2 K.B. 58, Goddard LJ said at 67: "[T]here is nothing contractual about payment into court. It is wholly a procedural matter and has no true analogy to a settlement arranged between the parties out of court, which, of course, does constitute a contract." And see, *Gibbon v Manchester City Council* [2010] EWCA Civ 726; [2010] 1 W.L.R. 2081 CA, Moore-Bick LJ said at [5]–[6]: "Part 36 is drafted as a self-contained code ... Basic concepts of offer and acceptance clearly underpin Part 36, but that is inevitable given that it contains a voluntary procedure under which either party may take the initiative to bring about a consensual resolution of the dispute. Such concepts are part of the landscape in which everyone conducts their daily life. It does not follow, however, that Part 36 should be understood as incorporating all the rules of law governing the formation of contracts, some of which are quite technical in nature. Indeed, it is not desirable that it should do so. Certainty is as much to be commended in procedural as in substantive law, especially, perhaps, in a procedural code which must be understood and followed by ordinary citizens who wish to conduct their own litigation. In my view, Part 36 was drafted with these considerations in mind and is to be read and understood according to its terms without importing other rules derived from the general law, save where that was clearly intended."

16-02 A similar regime applied under the original version of Pt 36 which required the payment of money into court by way of an effective offer to settle a money claim. A Pt 36 payment could be withdrawn only with the permission of the court[4] and, unless the parties agreed the liability for costs, a Pt 36 payment could only be accepted by a claimant after the usual 21-day period if the court gave permission.[5] Similar provisions were put in place for claimants' Pt 36 offers and Pt 36 offers generally, neither form of offer requiring the payment of money into court.[6] The difference between the court's supervisory role in relation to a Pt 36 payment compared with that in relation to a Pt 36 offer was that the latter could be withdrawn at any time without the permission of the court.[7]

THE TEST APPLIED TO THE WITHDRAWAL OR LATE ACCEPTANCE OF A PART 36 OFFER

16-03 In relation to the issue of whether to permit the withdrawal of or reduction in a Pt 36 payment or to permit the late acceptance of a previously non-accepted Pt 36 payment, the test for the success of the application was effectively the same. The guiding factor was the change, if any, in the claimant's prospects in the action between the date of the Pt 36 payment and the date of the application to permit withdrawal by the defendant or acceptance by the claimant. In *Flynn v Scougall*,[8] the Court of Appeal considered the circumstances in which it is appropriate to give permission for a Pt 36 payment to be withdrawn. It held that, "the same considerations apply to giving permission to withdraw money in court as to refusing permission to take it out" and that:

> "Goddard LJ's phrase [in *Cumper v Pothecary*[9]] 'a sufficient change of circumstance since the money was paid to make it just that the defendant should have an opportunity of withdrawing or reducing his payment' was to be adopted as consistent with the overriding objective."

16-04 This approach was followed in *Capital Bank Plc v Stickland*.[10]

> In that case C, as mortgagee, brought proceedings against D for interfering with the bank's immediate right to possession of a British registered vessel over which it held a charge. The claim form was issued in early 2003 for delivery-up of the vessel or payment of its value, limited to £88,818.12, plus interest. In June 2003 C's solicitors made a Pt 36 offer

---

4 The then CPR r.36.6(5).

5 The then CPR r.36.11(2)(b).

6 The then CPR rr.36.11 and 12.

7 *Scammell v Dicker* [2001] 1 W.L.R. 631. In the context of a boundary dispute, D made a CPR Pt 36 offer by a letter dated March 9, 2000 in relation to a trial listed for 20 March 2000. The letter drew attention to the fact that, because the offer was made less than 21 days before the trial, it could only be accepted if the parties could agree the liability as to costs or if the court gave permission. By a letter dated 13 March 2000 D withdrew the offer. C argued that it could not be withdrawn unilaterally until a reasonable period had elapsed. The Court of Appeal (Aldous and Mance LJJ) held that D was entitled to withdraw the offer at any time prior to acceptance.

8 *Flynn v Scougall* [2004] 1 W.L.R. 3069.

9 *Cumper* [1941] 2 K.B. 58. Goddard LJ said, at 70, that "the defendant must show that there are good reasons for his application, such as the discovery of further evidence which puts a wholly different complexion on the case or a change in legal outlook brought about by a new judicial decision". He said that, "apart from matters such as fraud or mistake affecting the original payment, the court should consider whether there is a sufficient change of circumstance since the money was paid to make it just that the defendant should have an opportunity of withdrawing or reducing his payment".

10 *Capital Bank Plc v Stickland* [2005] 1 W.L.R. 3914.

offering to accept £85,000 including interest. D did not respond, but put in a defence in which the only point of substance taken was that the vessel in respect of which the proceedings were brought was not the same vessel as had been mortgaged to the bank. D did not respond when the offer was repeated in December 2003. He did not co-operate with C in relation to its desire to inspect the vessel or with orders of the court designed to facilitate this. However, in January 2004 C managed to inspect the vessel when it emerged that the vessel was clearly the mortgaged vessel. Two days before the trial fixed in February 2004 D purported to accept the offers made in June and December 2003 even though each had expired. D made an application at the trial, which was opposed by C, for permission to accept those offers. HH Judge Kershaw QC refused the application on the grounds that the strength of the claim had altered for the better from the bank's point of view, the defendant's persistent flouting of the court's orders, the absence of any security for payment of the £85,000 if he were to decide that it could be accepted and the lateness of the application made on the day of the trial. The Court of Appeal upheld the exercise of the judge's discretion.

Longmore LJ said,[11] rejecting the submission that permission to accept out of time should only be refused if a claimant withdraws or reduces his Pt 36 offer (or a defendant applies to withdraw or reduces his payment-in and is allowed to do so), that

> "the court's discretion should not be narrowed by saying that it can only be exercised if a claimant is to be treated as withdrawing his offer (or if a defendant is to be regarded as entitled to withdraw or reduce his payment-in) but the discretion should rather be as wide as possible so as to advance the overriding objective of dealing with cases justly".[12]

He added that the

> "fact that there has been a change of circumstance is certainly relevant and may well be the most important factor to be taken into account"

and here new evidence (which D had been endeavouring to delay) emerged confirming the identity of the vessel.

THE COURT'S CURRENT SUPERVISORY ROLE

16-05 The court's supervisory role in relation to the withdrawal of a Pt 36 offer is now restricted to an application to that effect made during the "relevant period".[13] Since the "relevant period" will generally be 21 days, it will probably be a rare situation where the circumstances of the litigation will have changed so significantly in such a short period of time for the court to be faced with many applications of this

---

[11] *Capital Bank Plc* at [14].

[12] Referring with approval to para.18–11 in the 5th edn of this work which contained the following proposition: "The guiding factor was the change, if any, in the plaintiff's prospects in the action between the date of the payment in and the date of the application for withdrawal. It is likely, it is thought, that this will still remain a central factor in the court's approach to any such application under the new rules. However, given the nature of case management and the obligation on the parties to help further the overriding objective it is possible that the court would entertain such an application on wider grounds. If, for example, a claimant failed to give proper disclosure of documents in support of his claim, that may afford grounds for concluding that it would be unfair to hold a defendant to a particular Part 36 payment."

[13] See paras 15–11—15–14.

nature.[14] However, the test identified in *Flynn v Scougall*[15] and *Capital Bank Plc v Stickland*[16] and now codified in Rule 36.10(3) will continue to be applied when such an application falls to be determined.[17]

16-06 The approach to an application to accept a Pt 36 offer during trial is subject to a similar approach. Unless the offeror has limited the offer as one that may be accepted only within a stipulated period (which could itself be the "relevant period"), the offer will continue to be available for acceptance thereafter until it is withdrawn.[18] Given the proposition, if valid, that a withdrawn Pt 36 offer will have no, or no significant, impact on the issue of costs at a subsequent trial,[19] most offerors will wish to maintain their offer as an offer that might be accepted (albeit on revised terms as to costs if accepted)[20] notwithstanding its non-acceptance during the "relevant period". It will be open to an offeror to argue that the circumstances of the litigation have changed sufficiently adversely to the offeree that permission to accept it should not be given. In *Houghton v Donoghue (t/a Haulage & Plant Hire Ltd)*[21] consideration was given to the approach the court should take to such an application made during the course of a trial. Having considered the authorities on the approach applicable under the two previous versions of CPR Pt 36,[22] Morgan J concluded that ordinarily the court would be reluctant to permit an offeree to accept a Pt 36 offer not having accepted it prior to trial. Whilst he accepted that there were arguments in favour of permitting a mid-trial acceptance of a Pt 36 offer, such as the saving of court time (albeit a limited amount in such circumstances), where it was apparent that the offeree saw "the way the wind is blowing in the trial" and as a consequence changed their approach to the offer, that amounted to "change of circumstances which [meant] that it may no longer be appropriate to allow the offeree to accept the offer which is still on the table subject to the court's permission".[23] As he explained it[24]:

> "I think that the philosophy exists that where a claimant decides to take his chances with the trial and then repents of his earlier decision to turn down the offer of settlement because the trial, he thinks, is going less well or more badly than predicted, that the court will often take the view that it is not right to give permission to impose a settlement on the reluctant defendant."

The court's approach to such applications, particularly those where the offeror objects to the grant of permission to accept, is thus one that will require strong

---

14 CPR r.36.10(1).

15 See para.16–03.

16 See para.16–04.

17 See *Evans v Royal Wolverhampton Hospitals NHS Foundation Trust* [2014] EWHC 3185 (QB); [2015] 1 W.L.R. 4659 per Leggatt J at [52]: "The test to be applied when the court is considering whether to give a party permission to withdraw a Part 36 offer is whether there has been a sufficient change of circumstances to make it just to permit the party to withdraw its offer. That test was set out by the Court of Appeal in relation to payments into court in *Cumper v Pothecary* [1941] 2 K.B. 58 at 70 ... This test was adopted in relation to Part 36 payments by the Court of Appeal in *Flynn v Scougall* [2004] 1 W.L.R. 3069, 3079 at para 39. I see no reason why the test should be different in relation to a Part 36 offer ..." And see para.16–07.

18 CPR r.36.11(2). See fn.26.

19 See paras 17–02—17–06.

20 See para.16–08.

21 [2017] EWHC 1738 (Ch); [2017] 5 Costs L.R. 857 at [5]–[11].

22 Those authorities were: *Capital Bank Plc v Stickland* [2004] EWCA Civ 1677; [2005] 1 W.L.R. 3914 at [44]–[55]; *Sampla v Rushmoor Borough Council* [2008] EWHC 2616 (TCC) at [16]–[17], and *Nulty v v Milton Keynes BC* [2012] EWHC 730 (QB) at [18].

23 *Houghton* [2017] EWHC 1738 (Ch); [2017] 5 Costs L.R. 857 at [7].

24 *Houghton* [2017] EWHC 1738 (Ch); [2017] 5 Costs L.R. 857 at [10].

justification on the part of the offeree to persuade it to exercise its discretion to permit an offer to be accepted mid-trial.

Since a Pt 36 offer can be withdrawn after the "relevant period" has expired,[25] would it be open to an offeror to frustrate an intimated application by the offeree during a trial[26] to accept the offer by withdrawing it before the application is heard? Whilst the issue, if it ever arises, remains to be determined authoritatively, the likelihood is that the court would regard the issue or intimation of the application as the moment at which the offer is "frozen" pending consideration in due course of the application on its merits.[27] Where such an offer was made within 21 days before the beginning of the trial the "relevant period" extends to the end of the trial.[28] **16-07**

THE COSTS WHEN SUCH AN APPLICATION IS SUCCESSFUL OR WHEN PERMISSION TO ACCEPT IS REQUIRED

The costs of a contested application either for permission to withdraw or change a Pt 36 offer or to accept such an offer when permission to accept it is required will, generally speaking and subject to any particular factors associated with the case, follow the event. However, so far as the costs of the case as a whole are concerned, there is a significant "steer" in the CPR towards the standard position adopted in practice for many years (and which will often be agreed),[29] namely, that the claimant will be entitled to the costs of the proceedings[30] up to the date on which the relevant period expired and will be liable for the defendant's (assumed to be the offeror) costs for the period from the date of expiry of the relevant period to the date of acceptance "unless the court orders otherwise"[31], in respect of which it will be **16-08**

---

25 CPR r.36.9(4).

26 CPR r.36.11(3).

27 This proposition is consistent with the decision of Robert Englehart QC, sitting as a deputy judge of the High Court in *Erghani SA v Sauflon Pharmaceuticals* [2010] 7 WLUK 547, ChD at [10]. The question that arose was whether the court had jurisdiction to allow a Pt 36 offer to be withdrawn after written notice had been given by the offeree that the offer had been accepted. Applying the approach taken by the Court of Appeal in *Flynn v Scougall* (see para.16-03) the deputy judge held that there was such a jurisdiction. It should however "be exercised only in the most exceptional circumstances" and only "on the justice of the case …". Given a radical change in the nature of the case from the time it had been pleaded to the point in time when the Pt 36 offer was said to have been accepted, it was appropriate in the circumstances of that case to grant the application to withdraw.

28 See para.15–11.

29 CPR r.36.13(4).

30 "Costs of the proceedings" in the context of the predecessor to the current CPR r.36.13 was held in *Jean Mary Doris Haynes (Personal Representative of the Estate of Brian Haynes Deceased) v Department for Business Innovation and Skills* [2014] EWHC 643 (QB); [2014] 3 Costs L.R. 475 at [21] per Jay J, to mean "the costs of proceeding against the defendant against whom the deemed order has been made". In that case there were multiple defendants and the claimant accepted an offer made by one defendant. In such circumstances the costs order could not encompass the claimant's costs against all the defendants.

31 CPR r.36.13(4)(b) and (5). See *Matthews v Metal Improvements Co Inc* [2007] EWCA Civ 215 where the Court of Appeal held that C, who wished to accept a Pt 36 payment some while after the normal 21-day period because of new evidence concerning his life expectancy, should have been ordered to pay D's costs after the end of that 21-day period. Neither party had acted unreasonably in the circumstances, but it was wrong simply to decide the issue of costs on the basis of whether C had acted reasonably. There had to be material upon which it could be said that it was "unjust" to depart from the normal rule. In *Kunaka v Barclays Bank Plc* [2010] EWCA Civ 1035; [2011] 2 Costs

for the offeror to persuade the court to do so.[32] The same approach is likely to be adopted, at least as the starting position, where the parties cannot agree the order as to costs either where a Pt 36 offer made less than 21 days before the start of trial is accepted[33] or where a Pt 36 offer, whenever made, is accepted during the trial with the court's permission.[34]

OTHER INSTANCES WHERE THE COURT'S PERMISSION TO ACCEPT IS NEEDED

16-09 The court's permission to accept an offer (irrespective of whether the parties have agreed the liability for costs) made to a child or protected party is required before the settlement is valid.[35]

16-10 Where a defendant makes a Pt 36 offer and states that the offer is intended to include any deductible amounts[36] (as defined in r.36.22(1)(d)), but the relevant period has expired and further deductible amounts have been paid to the claimant since the date of the offer, the permission of the court to accept the offer is

---

L.R .179 the Court of Appeal held that it would only be an exceptional case, where "the fairness of the situation" demanded it, that the court depart from the normal rule. In *Lumb v Hampsey* [2011] EWHC 2808 (QB) Lang J at [6]–[7], as endorsed by the Court of Appeal in *SG v Hewitt* [2012] EWCA Civ 1053; [2013] 1 All E.R. at [20]–[22], explained that the test to be adopted in determining this question under r.36.10(5) was a similar one to that which arose under r.36.14 [now r.36.17]; it is "whether the usual costs order set out in Rule 36.10 (5) [now r.36.13.5] should be departed from because it would be unjust for the Claimant to pay the Defendant's costs after the expiry of the relevant period, in the particular circumstances of this case. Such a departure would be the exception rather than the rule." In the light of this, the factors set out in what is now CPR r.36.17(5)(a)–(d), and given its introduction in 2015 CPR r.36.17(5)(e) are germane to what is now the CPR r.36.13(5) test: see CPR r.36.17(6). In applying those five factors the court should apply the principles articulated in *Smith v Trafford Housing Trust* [2012] EWHC 3320 (Ch); (2012) S.J.L.B 31 at [13] as endorsed by the Court of Appeal in *Webb v Liverpool Women's NHS Foundation Trust* [2016] EWCA Civ 365; [2016] 1 W.L.R. 3899 at [38]. See *Optical Express Ltd v Associated Newspapers Ltd* [2017] EWHC 2707 (QB) Warby J at [12]–[13]. The case of *SG* raised the question of whether an infant claimant, who suffered a brain injury at the age of 6, but whose prognosis for the future did not become reasonably clear until he was 14, ought to pay the defendant's costs after a pre-action Pt 36 offer made when he was 12. The Court of Appeal held (per Pill LJ at [94]) that "[justice] between the parties required ... that the claimant should have his costs until a clear prognosis could be offered to the court and a settlement recommended." See also *Dutton v Minards* [2015] EWCA Civ 984; [2015] 6 Costs L.R. 1047 at [15] onwards.

32 *Tiuta Plc v Rawlinson & Hunter (A Firm)* [2016] EWHC 3480 (QB) per Andrew Baker J at [14]; *Optical Express Ltd v Associated Newspapers Ltd* [2017] EWHC 2707 (QB) at [11]. In *Tuson v Murphy* [2018] EWCA Civ 1461; [2018] 4 Costs L.R. 733 the Court of Appeal considered whether it would be unjust to depart from the usual award where there was dishonesty on the part of a claimant offeree. It held, in the circumstances where the defendant offeror was aware of the dishonesty before making the Pt 36 offer, that it would not be unjust to make the usual order. In reaching its decision, Bean LJ at [32]–[35], with whom Sales and Underhill LJJ agreed, endorsed the approach taken in *Tiuta* at [29]–[30] by Andrew Baker J. As Bean LJ summarised the position at [35], "I agree entirely with what Andrew Baker J said in *Tiuta*. In particular, he was right to emphasise the difference between: a) a case where the facts known to the defendant's advisers at the time of the Part 36 offer do not change significantly during the period before the delayed acceptance; and b) a case where the defendant's advisers' assessment at the time of making the Part 36 offer of the true value of the case, based on the facts then known to them, is upset or undermined by subsequent events or subsequently discovered facts. In the first type of case it is highly unlikely to be unjust to apply the default costs rule."

33 CPR r.36.13(4)(a).

34 See fn.41.

35 CPR r.21.10. See Ch.27.

36 CPR r.36.22(3)(b).

required.[37] The same applies when an apportionment of sums offered in respect of claims under the Fatal Accidents Act 1976 and the Law Reform (Miscellaneous Provisions) Act 1934 is required under CPR r.41.3A.[38]

Where the claimant wishes to accept a Pt 36 offer made by one or more, but not all, of a number of defendants,[39] if the circumstances set out in r.36.15(2)[40] or (3)[41] obtain, the offer may be accepted without obtaining the court's permission. In any other situation, the court's permission is required.[42] **16-11**

In the first of the two situations where the permission of the court is *not* required all the defendants are content with the acceptance by the claimant of the sum offered and that he should have his costs. Equally, the claimant is content not to continue his claims against those who were not directly party to the offer. As between the defendants there may, of course, be outstanding disputes—for example, as to contribution or indemnity. Where a claimant has pursued a number of defendants jointly or alternatively (or indeed jointly and alternatively), it would be unusual for there to remain anything in issue between him and those defendants once a settlement has been achieved. In the second situation where the permission of the court is *not* required (where several liability[43] is alleged against some or all of those defendants) the position is different. Several liability connotes a separate claim and where a claimant accepts a Pt 36 offer in respect of such a claim within the "relevant period" he may do so without the court's permission and will be entitled to his costs as well as being able to continue with a separate claim against the others provided the law permits this in the particular context.[44] The costs to which the claimant will be entitled are, as already indicated,[45] the "costs of the proceedings up to the date on which notice of acceptance was served on the offeror". This is likely to be interpreted as the costs attributable to the claim against the particular defendant whose several liability is discharged by acceptance of his offer. In other words, the expression "costs of the proceedings" would be limited to the costs of proceedings against *that* defendant in respect of *that* liability.[46] **16-12**

The circumstances in which a claimant may accept a Pt 36 offer made by one or **16-13**

---

37 CPR r.36.11(3)(b).

38 CPR r.36.11(3)(c).

39 CPR r.36.15(1).

40 If the defendants are *sued jointly or in the alternative* and the claimant: (a) discontinues his claim against those defendants who have not made the offer; and (b) those defendants give written consent to the acceptance of the offer. "Joint liability" is described in the Glossary to the CPR as being a situation in which "parties ... share a single liability" for which each can be held wholly liable. The expression "sued jointly" was interpreted under the RSC as being sued "in respect of a joint liability", not merely being joined together in the same proceedings: *Townsend v Stone Toms & Partners* [1981] 1 W.L.R. 1153 CA.

41 If the claimant's case is that the defendants have a *several* liability to him and he is entitled to and does continue with his claims against the other defendants.

42 CPR r.36.15(4).

43 "A person who is severally liable with others may remain liable for the whole claim even where judgment has been obtained against the others": Glossary to CPR.

44 As to the legal entitlement, see generally Ch.6 and para.6–38 onwards, in particular.

45 See para.15-27.

46 The forerunner of the rule within the CPR used the expression "costs of the action" which was derived from RSC Ord.62 r.5(4). That provision was interpreted as referring to the costs of the action "against that defendant": *QBE Ltd v Mediterranean Insurance* [1992] 1 W.L.R. 573; *Carrs Bury St Edmunds Ltd v Whitworth Partnership* (1997) 13 Const. L.J. 199. This was to prevent possible injustice to a paying in defendant. It is submitted that the expression "costs of the proceedings" is even more susceptible to this interpretation than was the expression "costs of the action". A defendant who wishes to make the position absolutely clear might wish to phrase his Pt 36 offer in a way which demonstrates that the payment is made in respect of that "part of the claim" which relates to him. See fn.30.

more, but not all, of several defendants without needing the permission of the court have been identified.[47] In any case the claimant must apply to the court for an order permitting acceptance of the offer.[48] The purpose of this requirement, which largely mirrors the former requirements of the RSC,[49] is to enable the court to resolve any outstanding issue as to costs. An example of a situation in which the court might be required to adjudicate is where the claimant wants to accept a Pt 36 offer made by one of two defendants sued in the alternative, but there is an issue between the defendant making the offer and the claimant as to who should be responsible for the costs of the other defendant. Under the former practice, the question as to primary liability for those costs was resolved on the basis of whether it was reasonable for the claimant to have joined the defendant whose costs are in issue. Once that had been resolved in the claimant's favour the remaining matter for consideration was whether the non-offering defendant recovered his costs directly against the defendant who made the offer or against the claimant, who then recovered them against the defendant who made the offer.[50] Similar and other issues will continue to arise and will need to be resolved by the court at the permission stage.[51]

16-14 The court's permission is required to accept a Pt 36 offer in any case where the trial has started.[52]

16-15 The CPR provide[53] that where,

> "the court gives permission [to accept a Pt 36 offer where permission is required], unless all the parties have agreed costs, the court will make an order dealing with costs, and may order that the costs consequences set out in rule 36.10[54] will apply".

The court's full discretion under Pt 44 plainly exists in this situation, but consideration of the consequences set out in r.36.10 will probably operate as a starting-point for considering the exercise of that discretion.

16-16 Where a Pt 36 offer is accepted with the court's permission, there is no power to enter judgment under Pt 36: the claim is subject to a stay under r.36.14.[55]

---

47 See paras 16-11 and 16–12.
48 See fn.40.
49 RSC Ord.22 r.4.
50 See, e.g. *Goldsworthy v Brickell* [1987] Ch. 378 at 418.
51 CPR r.36.11(4).
52 CPR r.36.11(3)(d).
53 CPR r.36.11(4).
54 See para.15–27.
55 *Jolly v Harsco* [2012] EWHC 3086 (QB); [2013] 1 Costs L.R. 115 per Cranston J at [14] in respect of what was then CPR r.36.11.

CHAPTER 17

The Effect of a CPR Part 36 Offer after a Trial

INTRODUCTION

Chapters 14–16 have dealt essentially with how a CPR Pt 36 offer is made, accepted and otherwise supervised by the court prior to a trial or prior to the end of the trial. It is now necessary to consider the position in relation to, or the consequences of, an unaccepted Pt 36 offer after the end of the substantive trial. This will involve considering what effect, if any, a withdrawn Pt 36 offer may have in relation to the costs of the proceedings and the consequences of failing to match or beat a Pt 36 offer at the trial. **17-01**

THE WITHDRAWN OR ALTERED OFFER

When the RSC governed the consequences of making a payment into court,[1] such a payment could not be withdrawn without the court's permission. Where the court gave permission for this to occur, the question arose of what effect, if any, the withdrawn payment into court could have on the issue of costs after the trial at which the claimant failed to match (or better) the payment into court. In *Garner v Cleggs*[2] the Court of Appeal held that the payment into court was relevant to the issue of costs only in regard to those costs incurred between the date of payment in and the date after which the defendants would have been likely to oppose successfully an application by the plaintiff to take the money out of court. Otherwise the costs of the trial fell to be assessed without reference to the existence of the payment into court. This general approach continued to be followed under the original version of Pt 36 when a payment into court (a Pt 36 payment) was required in relation to a money claim.[3] So far as a Pt 36 offer (in contradistinction to a Pt 36 payment) under the original version of Pt 36 was concerned, the rules provided that if a Pt 36 offer was withdrawn "it [would] not have the consequences set out in this part".[4] That formulation would have been apt to embrace a claimant's Pt 36 offer in a money claim. **17-02**

It was suggested[5] that there were anomalies in the position as between the effect of withdrawn Pt 36 payments and withdrawn Pt 36 offers in respect of the possible costs consequences following a trial. It is correct to say that there were. They **17-03**

---

1 See para.16-01.
2 *Garner v Cleggs* [1983] 1 W.L.R. 862.
3 *Capital Bank Plc* [2005] 1 W.L.R. 3914.
4 The then CPR r.36.5(8).
5 See Zuckerman, CPR 36 offers, (2005) C.J.Q. 167.

arose, however, from the policy decision made at the time of the drafting of the original version of Pt 36 which required a payment of money into court in respect of an offer in a money claim, the need for the paying party to obtain permission to withdraw that sum of money if it wished to do so and the corresponding lack of need to seek the permission of the court to withdraw a Pt 36 offer (in other words, an offer in a claim other than one for money). Once that policy was changed, as it was in April 2007,[6] the playing field became the same.

17-04 The current Pt 36 provides (in similar, but not identical, terms to those in the original version) for the normal costs consequences where a claimant fails to obtain a judgment more advantageous than a defendant's Pt 36 offer or where judgment against the defendant is at least as advantageous to the claimant as the proposals contained in a claimant's Pt 36 offer (unless in either event those consequences are considered "unjust").[7] The 2015 revision of the rule introduced an additional factor for the court to consider in carrying out this assessment, namely, r.36.17(5)(e), which requires consideration to be given to the question of whether the offer was a "genuine attempt to settle proceedings". It would appear that the clear intention is to focus on the question whether the Pt 36 offer under consideration was no more than a tactical manoeuvre and whether, as a consequence, the normal cost consequences ought to be disapplied.[8]

17-05 Replicating the former provision in relation to Pt 36 offers,[9] r.36.17(7) provides that those normal costs consequences

> "do not apply to a Part 36 offer ... (a) which has been withdrawn; (b) which has been changed so that its terms are less advantageous to the offeree where the offeree has beaten the less advantageous offer; [or] (c) made less than 21 days before trial, unless the court has abridged the relevant period."

That clear provision should, however, be read subject to the "signpost" appearing in parentheses at the conclusion of r.36.17 to the effect that:

> "Rule 44.2 requires the court to consider an offer to settle that does not have the costs consequences set out in this Section in deciding what order to make about costs."

As already observed,[10] the court is entitled (and indeed obliged) to take into account "any admissible offer to settle" drawn to its attention within the overall discretion as to costs under Pt 44.2. Where a Pt 36 offer is withdrawn it ceases "to attract the consequences set out in CPR r.36.14 ... [and it] then constitutes such an "admissible offer to settle" within CPR r.44.3(4)(c)"[11], now r.44.2(4)(c).[12]

17-06 In considering the potential relevance on costs of a withdrawn Pt 36 offer under r.44.2(4)(c) the court will need to be alive to the playing of tactical games by, in particular, the withdrawal of such offers for no good reason.

---

6 See para.14-01.
7 See CPR r.36.17(4).
8 See para.17-38 onwards.
9 See para.17-02.
10 See para.14-02.
11 *Fox v Foundation Piling Ltd* [2011] EWCA Civ 790 at [53], per Jackson LJ.
12 For a summary of the relevant principles applicable to a consideration of the question of costs under CPR r.44(2) "in a case like this", namely, one involving a subrogated claim for insured losses and a separate uninsured claim, see *Brit Inns Ltd v BDW Trading Ltd (No.2)* [2012] EWHC 2489 (TCC); [2013] 1 Costs L.R. 72 at [44]. Also see *Sugar Hut Group Ltd v AJ Insurance* [2014] EWHC 3775 (Comm).

THE EFFECT OF FAILING TO MATCH OR BEAT AN EXTANT PART 36 OFFER

An extant Part 36 offer

An extant Pt 36 offer for this purpose is one that complies with the requirements of Pt 36[13] and has not been withdrawn.[14] Where a Pt 36 offer is altered, it constitutes a new offer. The rules provide that, except where the "relevant period" has expired, "change of terms [of a Part 36 offer] takes effect when it is served on the offeree."[15] Given the need to serve notice of the change in terms, pursuant to Pt 6, and the requirement for Pt 36 offers to be in writing,[16] any such change will necessarily have to be reduced to writing. **17-07**

The general position

The CPR provide incentives to offerors to make and offerees to accept reasonable Pt 36 offers. Proceeding to court and achieving the same as, or no more than, that which had previously been offered represents no victory and no sensible use of the parties' resources or those of the court. Accordingly, built into the rules is a strong presumption that in that event the offeree will be obliged to meet the costs of the proceedings after he ought reasonably to have accepted the offeror's offer. **17-08**

Where the judgment ultimately obtained by a claimant (either following a trial or on an application for summary judgment) is no more advantageous than a defendant's Pt 36 offer or is at least as advantageous to the claimant as the proposals contained in his own Pt 36 offer,[17] certain consequences are provided for in the rules. In the former situation, the defendant is essentially seen as the victor; in the latter, the claimant is seen as the victor. **17-09**

In assessing who is the victor the court must not treat a claimant who fails to achieve what he or she has offered to accept as the losing party. In *Rolf v De Guerin*,[18] the Court of Appeal explained that were a judge to take an offeror's failure to beat their own offer into account in determining who should pay the costs he or **17-10**

---

13 See Ch.15.

14 A rejected or unaccepted offer is not to be regarded as "withdrawn" within the rule such that it loses its costs potency: *Pankhurst v White* [2010] EWHC 311 (QB), Macduff J. However, Jackson LJ in *Fox v Foundation Piling Ltd* [2011] EWCA Civ 790; [2011] C.P. Rep. 41 at [42] said this: "In my view, *Pankhurst* is not authority for the proposition that a party which withdraws its CPR Pt 36 offer under what is now CPR r.36.3(6) can reap the benefits of CPR r.36.14". Since April 2015 the relevant provisions are CPR r.36.9(4) and r.36.17 respectively.

15 CPR r.36.9(3). And see CPR r.36.10(2) where the "relevant period" has expired.

16 See para.15-03.

17 CPR r.36.17(1).

18 [2011] EWCA Civ 78; [2011] C.P. Rep. 24 at [34]–[34] per Rix LJ, "[34] The judge did err fundamentally in his appreciation of the significance of Mrs Rolf's Pt 36 offer. The Pt 36 mechanism provides a formal, regulated, procedure for a party, including a claimant, to express a willingness to accept something less than total success in his open position in the litigation. If the offer is not accepted and the offeror does better in the final result than his offer, he is entitled, unless the court considers it would he unjust, to costs on an indemnity basis from the expiry of the 'relevant period' (i.e. a basic three weeks, unless the offer extends it) plus interest at an enhanced rate up to 10 per cent above base rate. Therefore there are advantages to a party in pitching his offer realistically, and there are potential disadvantages to an offeree in declining the offer. However, there is nothing about the procedure which states that an offeror is to be prejudiced as to costs because he has expressed his willingness to accept less than his open position. That would make the procedure a most dangerous one to use. The judge's ruling that the incidence of costs should change at the expiry of the relevant period of three weeks confirms the illogicality of his decision ... [35]. Moreover, the

she would "err fundamentally". Offerors cannot, consequently, be penalised in costs under the court's general discretion contained in r.44.2(4)(c) in such circumstances.

Claimant achieves no advantage over defendant's offer

17-11 Subject to r.36.21,[19] where a claimant "fails to obtain a judgment more advantageous than a defendant's Part 36 offer"[20] then, subject to certain exceptions within r.36.17,[21] the court will order that the defendant is entitled to his costs, including "any recoverable pre-action costs" from the date on which the relevant period expired and interest on those costs "unless it considers it unjust to do so".[22] In assessing the rate of interest applicable under CPR r.17(3)(b), the court cannot award interest at an enhanced rate, such as would be available to an award of interest to which CPR r.17)4(c) applied.[23]

17-12 What constitutes a failure "to obtain a judgment more advantageous than" a defendant's Pt 36 offer?[24] It is instructive, in the first instance, to see how the present formulation of the rule compares with the original version. In the original version, when it was generally[25] necessary to make a payment of money into court to constitute an effective offer in a claim for money, the rule[26] provided that where at trial a claimant (a) failed to "better a Part 36 payment" or (b) failed to "obtain a judgment ... more advantageous than a defendant's Part 36 offer" the court would order the claimant to pay any costs incurred by the defendant after the latest date on which the payment or offer could have been accepted without needing the permission of the court (in other words, within what is now effectively the "relevant

---

consequences of a Pt 36 offer are regulated by Pt 36 itself. Thus, CPR r.44.3(4)(c), which states that in deciding what order to make about costs, the court must have regard to all the circumstances including 'any admissible offer to settle ... which is *not* an offer to which costs consequences under Pt 36 apply' (emphasis added), would make no sense if the offer to settle were to be held against the offeror." See also fn.22. It is not entirely clear from the report whether Mrs Rolf's counsel drew the judge's attention to her offer or whether the defendant did. Strictly speaking, given that it was a Pt 36 offer and thus "without prejudice save as to costs", the privilege attaching to it could only be waived by her and, accordingly, it would not have been "admissible" if the defendant had put it forward.

19 i.e. where a claim no longer continues under the RTA or EL/PL Protocols.

20 CPR r.36.17(1)(a).

21 CPR r.36.17(7) and (8).

22 CPR r.36.17(3). See further at paras 17-12 – 17-16 for the interpretation of this requirement. Generally, the only offer considered by the court in this situation is the defendant's offer. A claimant who beats the defendant's offer by a significant amount is not penalised by the fact that he achieved significantly less than his own offer: see *Quorum AS v Schramm (No.2)* [2002] 2 Lloyd's Rep. 72, where C offered to accept $3.6 million, excluding matters of interest, by way of a Pt 36 offer and D made a Pt 36 payment of $600,000. Judgment was given in C's favour for $1.4 million. Thomas J, as he then was, declined to make a comparison between the award and the various offers. He concluded that C had to come to court to obtain the award that bettered D's offer by a substantial amount and awarded C its costs. For a situation where, in a personal injuries claim, C obtained a judgment "more advantageous" than his own offer, but less advantageous than D's subsequent offer, see *Pankhurst* [2010] EWHC 311 (QB) and *Pankhurst v White* [2010] EWCA Civ 1445; [2011] P.I.Q.R. Q2.

23 *Marathon Asset Management LLP v Seddon* [2017] EWHC 479 (Comm); [2017] 2 Costs L.R. 255 at [16]–[20] per Leggatt J.

24 For the situation in relation to offers in personal injury cases where there is a mixed lump sum and periodical payments element, see Ch.27.

25 Though see *Crouch v King's Healthcare NHS Trust* [2004] EWCA Civ 1332; [2005] 1 W.L.R. 2015, CA.

26 The then CPR r.36.20(1).

period")[27] unless it considered it unjust to do so.[28] The starting-point in relation to a claim for money or damages would be whether the claimant had achieved more than the amount of the Pt 36 payment.[29] If so, he would have "bettered" the offer. There were, however, cases where a marginal improvement on a Pt 36 payment at disproportionate expense would result in the court exercising its discretion adversely to the claimant[30] and cases where other factors militated against making an order in the claimant's favour notwithstanding that the Pt 36 payment was "bettered".[31] In *Straker v Tudor Rose*,[32] a case decided before the revised version

---

[27] See para.15-11.

[28] The then CPR r.36.20(2).

[29] In *Blackham v Entrepose UK* [2004] EWCA Civ 1109; [2005] C.P. Rep. 7, the Court of Appeal affirmed the approach that had obtained prior to the CPR, namely that when comparing the value of a judgment obtained following a trial with the value of a Pt 36 payment plus interest made previously, it is important to "compare like with like" (per Brooke LJ) and not to allow the interest that has accumulated since the date of the Pt 36 payment to count in deciding whether the Pt 36 payment has been bettered. As it was put at [10]: "If the defendants paid in, say, £39,000 plus £1,000 interest calculated up to the last day when the claimant could have accepted the payment without having to obtain permission, then if the claimant only received at trial £38,800 plus £950 interest up to that date, he will not have bettered the Pt 36 payment. It would be a misuse of language to say that he bettered it because he received at trial £38,800 plus £950 plus a further £500 of interest between the date he should have accepted the payment in and the date of trial." At [13], Brooke LJ continued thus: "when a judge applies this rule he should first ask himself what the payment into court represented ... and then consider whether the amount for which he has directed judgment to be entered, as compared with that payment, is less than that amount".

[30] This occurred before the introduction of the CPR in 1999: see *Charm Maritime Inc v Elborne Mitchell* [1997] 7 WLUK 447; [1997] C.L.Y. 555. C sued D, its former solicitors, for damages of approximately $20 million representing its alleged losses arising from D's negligence in permitting C's claim in another action to be dismissed for want of prosecution. The trial lasted 30 days. One of the main issues was whether an allegation of fraud in the earlier action would have been sustained. Detailed expert accountancy reports were prepared, and lengthy expert evidence was given, in relation to this issue. The net result was that C achieved a judgment for $841,070. D had made payments into court totalling $822,368, the final increase being made in August 1995 before the trial commenced in the autumn: C, therefore, "beat" the payment into court by about $19,000. Per Swinton Thomas LJ: "[T]he basic rule [is] that costs follow the event and ... a Plaintiff who recovers more than the payment in will recover his costs unless there are special circumstances or it appears to the court that some different order should be made. There remains a discretion which must be exercised judicially but the courts are not tied in a mathematical straight jacket. In this case the Plaintiff has ... beaten the payment in by a few thousand dollars. On the facts of this case ... any reasonable bystander or onlooker, if told that the Plaintiff had recovered a few thousand dollars more than [it] had been offered well before the trial began, would ... take the view that the Plaintiff should pay the costs incurred since the date the offer was made." However, in the circumstances of the case, bearing in mind that "the [plaintiff was] clearly at fault in that [it] should have accepted the sum ... offered" and that: "[T]he defendants were at fault in not paying into court the amount that was eventually recovered by the [plaintiff], broad justice can be achieved between the parties ... by ordering that the Defendants pay the Plaintiff's costs to the date of the payment into court, and that each party should bear its own costs thereafter."

[31] See, e.g. *Painting v University of Oxford* [2005] EWCA Civ 161; [2005] 3 Costs L.R. 394 where C had sustained injuries in an accident and had sought damages in excess of £400,000. A CPR Pt 36 payment of just over £184,000 was made by D shortly before the trial, but on the basis of surveillance evidence D was granted permission to withdraw a very substantial part of the Pt 36 payment leaving £10,000 in court. At trial C maintained her claim for £400,000. The court found that C had intentionally exaggerated her injuries and awarded just over £23,000. C was awarded her full costs because she "bettered" the Pt 36 payment. The Court of Appeal held that the correct order in the case should have been that C should have her costs to the date of the Pt 36 payment, but that she should pay D's costs thereafter. Maurice Kay LJ said: "[A]t no stage did [C] manifest any willingness to negotiate or to put forward a counter-proposal to the Part 36 payment. No one can compel a claimant to take such steps. However to contest and lose an issue of exaggeration without having made ever a counter-proposal is a matter of some significance in this kind of litigation. It must not be assumed that beating a Part 36 payment is conclusive. It is a factor and will often be conclusive, but

of Pt 36 came into effect, C achieved an award of about £13,500 inclusive of interest against the background of a Pt 36 payment of £9,000 made soon after the commencement of proceedings. The trial judge had awarded C only his costs up until a date some months prior to commencement of the proceedings and no costs thereafter. Waller LJ said this:

> "3. ... in the pre-CPR world one would have had no hesitation is saying the judge must have gone wrong. A payment into court was the touchstone in relation to costs—if it was beaten by a plaintiff, the plaintiff got their costs; if the plaintiff failed to beat it the defendant got their costs. There was hardly an exception to that rule.
>
> 4. The position under the CPR is not the same. Part 36 deals with payments in. That rule however does not give any guidance as to what should flow from a situation in which a claimant obtains a money judgment in excess of the sum in court. For that guidance one must go to CPR 44.3."

In that case, C had been unwilling to engage constructively in negotiations and had not complied with the relevant pre-action protocol. The Court of Appeal substituted an order that that C should have 60 per cent of his costs from the date of the Pt 36 offer, the trial judge's order for the period up until that date not being disturbed.

17-13 With the need to make a payment into court abrogated as from 6 April 2007, the question of what was the correct approach in assessing whether a judgment obtained is "more advantageous than" a Pt 36 offer when the offer is a sum of money. The issue arose directly in *Carver v BAA Plc*.[33]

> C pursued damages for personal injuries in an action in which liability had been admitted. She had been claiming in the region of £15,000–£20,000 but was awarded a little short of £4,700 inclusive of interest. This exceeded a Pt 36 payment[34] by £51. There was no suggestion that C was deliberately exaggerating her claim (since she was relying on expert medical advice in support of her approach), but she gained no significant advantage by pursuing the claim to court. C's solicitors had indicated shortly before the trial that their base costs were £35,000 plus disbursements of £10,000, but since the success fee under their conditional fee arrangement was 100 per cent, the net effect was that they were seeking costs in the region of £80,000 plus VAT. The trial judge ordered C to pay D's costs of the claim after the time for accepting the Pt 36 payment had expired and made no order for costs for the prior period covered by an earlier Calderbank offer.[35] The Court of Appeal upheld this exercise of his discretion.

Ward LJ concluded, in summary, that money was not "the sole criterion"[36] in assessing success. A broader approach could be taken, one which permitted the court to engage in a "more wide-ranging review of all the facts and circumstances of the case in deciding whether the judgment, which is the fruit of the litigation, was worth the fight."[37]

17-14 The decision in *Carver v BAA Plc*, despite being held to be of general applica-

---

one has to have regard to all the circumstances of the case."

[32] *Straker v Tudor Rose* [2007] EWCA Civ 368; [2007] C.P. Rep. 32. See also *Jackson v Ministry of Defence* [2006] EWCA Civ 46.

[33] *Carver v BAA Plc* [2008] EWCA Civ 412; [2009] 1 W.L.R. 113. cf. *Morgan v UPS* [2008] EWCA Civ 1476; [2009] 3 Costs L.R. 384 where *Carver* was distinguished on the facts.

[34] The effective offer was made during 2006 when the original version of CPR Pt 36 applied—hence the need for a Pt 36 payment. However, by the time the matter came to trial in 2007 the new version applied: *Carver* [2008] EWCA Civ 412; [2009] 1 W.L.R. 113 at [21].

[35] See para.18-05 onwards.

[36] *Carver* [2008] EWCA Civ 412; [2009] 1 W.L.R. 113 at [31].

[37] *Carver* [2008] EWCA Civ 412; [2009] 1 W.L.R. 113 at [30].

tion in *Multiplex Constructions (UK) Ltd v Cleveland Bridge UK Ltd*,[38] was subject to a significant degree of criticism, it being said to have introduced an unacceptable degree of uncertainty into the operation of the rule.[39] In the light of that criticism the Court of Appeal first gave a narrow interpretation of the approach set out in *Carver v BAA Plc* in *Gibbon v Manchester City Council*.[40] The status quo ante was restored by the introduction of what is now r.36.17(2),[41] which provides that

> "in relation to any money claim or money element of a claim, 'more advantageous' means better in money terms by any amount, however small, and 'at least as advantageous' shall be construed accordingly."[42]

It follows, therefore, that the court is required simply to ask itself whether the amount awarded by way of the judgment is greater, in financial terms, than the offer made. In doing so, as the Court of Appeal in *Gibbon v Manchester City Council* made clear, when the court assesses whether the judgment is greater than the offer, where the offer was inclusive of interest it must determine the interest due on the claim in order to ensure that parity of comparison.[43] In *JLE (A Child) v Warrington and Halton Hospitals NHS Foundation Trust*,[44] Stewart J, allowing an appeal from a deputy Costs Master, rejected an attempt to reintroduce a degree of discretion in determining whether an offer was at "least as advantageous" as a claimant's Pt 36 offer. The deputy Costs Master had considered the question by reference to the margin by which the offer had been beaten in relation to the amount of the costs incurred. Stewart J rejected this approach, emphasising that to adopt it

---

38 [2008] EWHC 2280 (TCC); 122 Con. L.R. 88.

39 See Jackson LJ's review which revealed disquiet in the profession about the effect of the decision in *Carver* [2008] EWCA Civ 412; [2009] 1 W.L.R. 113 (see *Preliminary Report*, Vol.1, para.17.16). In his *Final Report* he referred to the "unwelcome degree of uncertainty [introduced] into the Part 36 regime" by the decision and recommended that its effect "should be reversed either judicially ... or by rule change". It should be made clear, he said, "that in any purely monetary case 'more advantageous' ... means better in financial terms by any amount, however small".

40 [2010] EWCA Civ 726; [2010] 1 W.L.R. 2081. See Sorabji, *W(h)ither Carver?:CPR 36, the law of contract and certainty in Gibbon v Manchester City Council* [2010] EWCA Civ 726; (2011) CJQ (2) 124.

41 Originally introduced as CPR r.36.14(1A). See *Hammersmatch Properties (Welwyn) Ltd v Saint-Gobain Ceramics and Plastics Ltd* [2013] EWHC 2227 (TCC); [2013] 5 Costs L.R. 758 per Ramsey J at [5]–[8]. At [36] Ramsey J went on expressly to disapprove of the seventh of Jackson J's eight principles set out at [72] of *Multiplex Construction (UK) v Cleveland Bridge UK* [2008] EWHC 2280 (TCC) as being derived from *Carver* [2009] 1 W.L.R. 113. Although also see *Sugar Hut Group Ltd v AJ Insurance* [2014] EWHC 3775 (Comm) per Eder J at [18]–[21].

42 CPR r.36.14(1A) was however only applicable to offers made on or after 1 October 2011: the Civil Procedure (Amendment No.2) Rules 2011 (SI 1979/2011). Offers made prior to that remain subject to the more broad-textured approach set out in *Carver* [2009] 1 W.L.R. 113 as explained by *Gibbon v Manchester City Council* [2010] EWCA Civ 726; [2010] W.L.R. 2081.

43 [2010] EWCA Civ 726; [2010] W.L.R. 2081 at [36] per Moore-Bick L.J., "The claimant eventually obtained judgment in the principal sum of £8,375.94 after deducting the various items of the counterclaim, including the sum of £1,000 awarded to Mr. and Mrs. Reeves by way of damages for the interference with the use and enjoyment of their home. (The latter claim was added by amendment shortly before the trial began.) At the time it was made the May offer (which included interest) represented a principal sum of £7,789.46, allowing for interest at 4% for 9 months. (Although the District Judge awarded interest at a rate of 8% that was in my view considerably higher than could have been expected. However, if one were to deduct interest at that rate, the principal sum would be reduced even farther.) Viewed in that light, at the time it was made the May offer fell £1,586.48 short of the amount which the claimant was entitled to recover on its final account and £586.48 short of the amount for which it eventually obtained judgment, even after deducting the sum awarded to Mr. and Mrs. Reeves for interference with the use and enjoyment of their home." And see *Acre 1127 Ltd (in liquidation) (formerly Castle Galleries Ltd) v De Montford Fine Art Limited* [2011] EWCA Civ 130 per Tomlinson LJ at [6].

44 [2019] EWHC 1582 (QB); [2019] Costs L.R. 829 [40]–[44].

would be to reintroduce the approach taken in *Carver*, which had been expressly rejected by the revisions to CPR r.36.17(2) following the Jackson Costs Reforms. It is now clear that the CPR takes a bright line approach to determining the question whether the amount awarded in a judgment is better than that made in the offer.

17-15 The approach taken in money claims is not, however, that which is adopted in non-money claims or claims that do not embrace solely an offer of money. In such claims a broad view has always been required when assessing whether an offer has been beaten.[45]

17-16 Where a claimant has failed to obtain a judgment more advantageous than a defendant's Pt 36 offer the question, if it arises, is whether the court "considers it unjust" to make the normal costs order in favour of the defendant.[46] In *Smith v Trafford Housing Trust*[47] Briggs J noted that there was no authority on the application of the "injustice test" in what was at the time r.36.14(4) and is now r.36.17(5). He went on, however, to summarise the applicable principles,[48] as:

> "a) The question is not whether it was reasonable for the claimant to refuse the offer. Rather, the question is whether, having regard to all the circumstances and looking at the matter as it affects both parties, an order that the claimant should pay the costs would be unjust: see *Matthews v Metal Improvements Co. Inc* [2007] EWCA Civ 215, per Stanley Burnton J (sitting as an additional judge of the Court of Appeal) at paragraph 32.
>
> b) Each case will turn on its own circumstances, but the court should be trying to assess 'who in reality is the unsuccessful party and who has been responsible for the fact that costs have been incurred which should not have been': see *Factortame v Secretary of State* [2002] EWCA Civ 22, per Walker LJ at paragraph 27.
>
> c) The court is not constrained by the list of potentially relevant factors in Part 36.14(4) to have regard only to the circumstances of the making of the offer or the provision or otherwise of relevant information in relation to it. There is no limit to the types of circumstances which may, in a particular case, make it unjust that the ordinary consequences set out in Part 36.14 should follow: see *Lilleyman v Lilleyman (judgment on costs)* [2012] EWHC 1056 (Ch) at paragraph 16.
>
> d) Nonetheless, the court does not have an unfettered discretion to depart from the ordinary cost consequences set out in Part 36.14. The burden on a claimant who has failed to beat the defendant's Part 36 offer to show injustice is a formidable obstacle to the obtaining of a different costs order. If that were not so, then the salutary purpose of Part 36, in promoting compromise and the avoidance of unnecessary expenditure of costs and court time, would be undermined."[49]

In *Lilleyman v Lilleyman* Briggs J had explained, in respect of the third principle above, that when considering the question of whether it is unjust to make such a costs order the court is required to take account of the matters now set out in

---

[45] See, e.g. *Neave v Neave* [2003] EWCA Civ 325; (2003) 100(14) L.S.G. 27, *Diageo North America Inc v Intercontinental Brands (ICB) Ltd (Costs)* [2010] EWHC 172 (Pat), where the main issue between the parties concerned the grant of injunctive relief. Arnold J at [9] considered the nature of the injunction granted "broadly" in assessing whether the Pt 36 offer had been beaten.

[46] *The Procter & Gamble Co v Svenska Cellulosa AB SCA* [2012] EWHC 2839 (Ch); [2013] 1 W.L.R. 1464 per Hildyard J at [55] onwards: the court cannot go behind the formal status of the parties as claimant and defendant to ascertain the appropriate compliance with Pt 36. In assessing whether it would be "unjust" to make a costs order in favour of the defendant the court can, however, assess which party was in reality the defendant in the claim.

[47] [2012] EWHC 3320 (Ch); (2012) 156(46) S.J.L.B. 31, as accepted by Akenhead J in *Bellway Homes Ltd v Seymour (Civil Engineering Contractors) Ltd* [2013] EWHC 1890 (TCC); [2013] T.C.L.R. 8 at [30]–[31].

[48] [2012] EWHC 3320 (Ch); (2012) 156(46) S.J.L.B. 31 at [13].

[49] Briggs J's four principles were endorsed by the Court of Appeal in *Webb v Liverpool Women's NHS Foundation Trust* [2016] EWCA Civ 365; [2016] 1 W.L.R. 3899 at [38].

r.36.17(5)(a)–(e).[50] The court is, however, by virtue of the requirement to take account of all the circumstances specified in r.36.17(5),[51] able to "take a broader view in an appropriate case" than specified in the subparagraphs to the rule. As he said, the court is "not entirely disabled from having regard to questions of justice or injustice arising from the manner in which the offering party has made use of its costs expenditure prima facie now recoverable from the unsuccessful offeree, in the pursuit of its defence to the claim."[52]

In *White v Wincott Galliford Ltd*[53] Deputy Master Friston provided the following detailed summary of the case law that has developed following *Smith v Trafford Housing Trust* dealing with in the injustice test in the context of detailed assessment proceedings[54]:

> "'I summarise my understanding of the law relating to the injustice test in detailed assessment proceedings in the following way (and in doing so, I refer to authorities concerning Part 36 offers made in other types of proceedings):
>
> i) The burden is on the party seeking to rely on injustice: I note that both Andrew Baker J and Warby J have explained that the burden is on the party who seeks to persuade the court that an award would be unjust (see *Tiuta Plc v Rawlinson & Hunter (a firm)* [2016] EWHC 3480 (QB), at [14] and *Optical Express v Associated Newspapers (Costs)* [2017] EWHC 2707 (QB), at [11] respectively). For the reasons set out immediately below, that burden is a heavy one.
>
> ii) 'Formidable obstacle': Briggs J has said that 'the burden ... to show injustice is a formidable obstacle' (see *Smith v Trafford Housing Trust* [2012] EWHC 3320, at [13(d)]. This was cited with approval by Gross LJ in *Briggs v CEF Holdings Ltd* [2017] EWCA Civ 2363, at [20]) and was also adopted by Eder J (see *Ted Baker plc v AXA Insurance UK plc* [2014] EWHC 4178 (Comm), at [16], [17] and [23]).
>
> iii) Specific factors to be taken into account: CPR, r 36.17(5) gives specific guidance as to the factors that the court ought to take into account. Those factors are:
>
> a) the terms of any Part 36 offer;
>
> b) the stage in the proceedings at which any Part 36 offer was made, including, in particular, how long before the assessment started the offer was made;
>
> c) the information available to the parties at the time when the Part 36 offer was made;
>
> d) the conduct of the parties with regard to the giving of or refusal to give information for the purposes of enabling the offer to be made or evaluated; and
>
> e) whether the offer was a genuine attempt to settle the proceedings.
>
> I pause here to note that that these factors relate either to the terms and content of the offer in question, or to the circumstances in which it was made and considered. They make no mention of the factors extraneous to the offer.
>
> iv) The requirement to look at the terms of the offer: In a similar vein, I note that in *Cashman v Mid Essex Hospital Services NHS Trust* [2015] EWHC 1312 (QB) at [24] Slade J has explained that when applying the injustice test, it is the terms of the offer that are relevant, not the level of the costs claimed or the amount disallowed on assessment.
>
> v) Harshness of results: Eady J has explained that while a judge may consider the effect of CPR Part 36 to be harsh, that fact would not be a reason for denying the offeror the benefits of having made the offer (*Downing v Peterborough &*

---

50 At the time they were the matters referred to in CPR r.36.14(4)(a)–(d).

51 Then CPR r.36.14(4).

52 *Lilleyman v Lilleyman (No.2)* [2012] EWHC 1056 (Ch); [2012] 1 W.L.R. 2801 per Briggs J at [16].

53 [2019] EWHC B6 (Costs),

54 [2019] EWHC B6 (Costs) at [20]–[21].

Stamford Hospitals NHS Foundation Trust [2014] EWHC Civ 4216 (QB), at [61] onwards, per Eady J).

vi) The need to take into account all the relevant factors: Black LJ has said that the 'factors specifically identified [in CPR, r 36.17(5)] as relevant cast quite a wide net on their own but they are not the only matters that fall for consideration and [that] anything else which is relevant must be considered as well' (see *SG v Hewitt* [2012] EWCA Civ 1053, at [29]). Indeed, Vos C has explained that the court is required to take into account all of the relevant circumstances: see *OMV Petrom SA v Glencore International AG* [2017] EWCA Civ 195, at [25].

vii) Disaggregation: I note that both Vos C and Slade J have explained that the factors that the court may take into account will not necessarily be the same for each of the benefits under CPR 36.17(4): see *OMV Petrom SA v Glencore International AG* [2017] EWCA Civ 195, at [25] and *Cashman* at [19]. Indeed, Sir Colin Mackay has explained that the injustice test is to be (or at least may be) applied individually to each of those benefits rather than globally; this means that it is open to the court to allow the offeror the advantage of as many or as few of those benefits as would be appropriate on the facts of the case in hand: see *RXDX v Northampton Borough Council* [2015] EWHC 2938 (QB) at [8] and [9].

[21] In summary, when applying the injustice test in a detailed assessment in which a party has 'beaten' a Part 36 offer, the following principles will apply: the court must recognise that the offeree must shift a 'formidable obstacle' in order to satisfy the injustice test; the court should take into account all the relevant circumstances, but its principal focus should be on the terms and content of the offer (and the circumstances in it was made and considered) rather than the outcome of the assessment; and, where appropriate, when applying the injustice test to each of the benefits in CPR, r 36.17(4), the court may take into account factors specific to each of those benefits."

Defendant fails to achieve advantage over claimant's offer

17-17 The financial incentive for a defendant to make a Pt 36 offer is to avoid paying more of the costs of the litigation than is necessary or fair. The financial incentive for a claimant to accept a reasonable Pt 36 offer from a defendant is to avoid the risk of paying the defendant's costs after rejecting it. Whether those costs are payable on the indemnity basis ordinarily depends on whether "there something in the conduct of the action or the circumstances of the case which takes the case out of the norm" and the mere rejection of what proves to have been a reasonable offer is not sufficient to justify such an order.[55]

17-18 Prior to the CPR, the court was, in some limited circumstances, prepared to award a claimant who made an offer indemnity costs after the date of expiry of the offer if the offer was ultimately bettered at trial.[56] However, this was an unusual order for the court to make. The consequence was that if the result of a trial, despite any offer made by the claimant, was that he merely obtained his costs on the usual basis, there would be no incentive to him to make any concession by way of an offer and little incentive to the defendant to accept it. The opportunity to make such an order in favour of a claimant who made an offer of settlement was provided for expressly in the original version of the CPR in the event of the defendant being held liable for more, or upon terms more advantageous to the claimant, than the proposals contained in the claimant's offer.[57] Indeed somewhat more controversially the CPR

---

55 See para.13-10.

56 *McDonnell v Woodhouse and Jones* [1995] 4 WLUK 147; *The Times*, 25 May 1995, (QB) per Waterhouse J.

57 The original CPR r.36.21(1). The word "more" was used in sub-paras (a) and (b) of this rule. It fol-

gave the court the power in this situation to award a higher than normal rate of interest on any sum of money awarded and upon any indemnity costs awarded.[58] That general approach survived the 2007 and 2015 revisions to the CPR.

Where a claimant obtains a judgment against the defendant which is "at least as advantageous" to the claimant as the proposals contained in his own Pt 36 offer, r.36.17(4)[59] provides that "the court must, unless it considers it unjust to do so", order that the claimant is entitled to: (a) interest on the whole or part of any sum of money (excluding interest) awarded at a rate not exceeding 10% above base rate for some or all of the period starting with the date on which the relevant period expired; (b) costs, including any recoverable pre-action costs, on the indemnity basis from the date on which the relevant period expired[60]; (c) interest on those costs **17-19**

---

lowed that, strictly speaking, r.36.21 would not become engaged if the claimant merely matched his offer at trial. However, such an offer would clearly have been seen to have been a reasonable one in the light of the result of the trial and one that the defendant ought to have accepted. Given that the court had the power to award indemnity costs where a party has behaved unreasonably and had the power to award interest at such rate as it considered just (see *Petrotrade Inc v Texaco Ltd* [2002] 1 W.L.R. 947) there was no reason why orders similar to those contemplated in paras (2) and (3) of the then CPR r.36.21 should not have been made in this situation. Indeed, that was the conclusion reached in *Read v Edmed* [2004] EWHC 3274 (QB); [2006] 2 Costs L.R. 201, Bell J. C had offered to accept an apportionment of liability between herself and D on the basis of 50:50. That was rejected but represented the effect of the judgment of the court at trial. Per Bell J: "In my judgment, as a matter of general principle, where in a relatively uncomplicated claim for damages for personal injury and consequential losses such as this, the claimant makes a valid Part 36 offer or other admissible offer to settle an issue of liability at a given proportion of his or her claim, and the defendant refuses that offer and the court gives judgment for precisely that proportion of the claim, the claimant should be entitled to the benefit of an award of indemnity costs from the time of expiry of the offer and some interest on those costs just as he or she would if Part 36.21 had applied to the matter, in order to ensure, so far as possible, that she is not out of pocket, unless there is some particular circumstance, for instance a significant change in the complexion of the case or some unreasonable conduct by or on behalf of the claimant, which would make that conclusion unfair."

58 The controversy arose from a perception that a claimant who was awarded higher interest on his damages if he "beat" his own offer was the recipient of a windfall arising, in effect, from a previously placed wager. The loser was a defendant who was merely exercising his right to contest the claim. These concerns became less when it emerged that the additional interest potentially payable (10% above base rate) was considerably less than was once proposed in relation to certain levels of award. In *Access to Justice, Interim Report* (July 1995) Lord Woolf had suggested that the uplift should be 10% above the rate that would otherwise be awarded on awards up to £50,000, 5% from £50,000 to £100,000 and then 2.5% thereafter. In *Access to Justice, Final Report* (July 1996) he recommended 25% above the rate otherwise payable on awards up to £10,000, 15% from £10,000 to £50,000 and 5% thereafter. The rate would thus have tapered on an award exceeding £10,000, a 5% uplift on the normal rate being the maximum uplift once £50,000 was exceeded. The other area of controversy arose from the suggestion that the rule reflected a breach of art.6 of the European Convention for the Protection of Human Rights and Fundamental Freedoms on the basis that it caused an inequality of treatment as between a claimant and a defendant. The fact that the argument has not been advanced since the CPR's introduction suggests that it may not be considered maintainable although it remains the case that there are those who believe that Pt 36 is more favourable to claimants than to defendants. Jackson LJ's *Final Report* at 425–427 recommended a 10% uplift on damages below £500,000 where a claimant made an adequate offer which the defendant rejects. Above £500,000 "there may be a case for scaling down the uplift". In the event the recommendation was implemented by s.55 of the Legal Aid, Sentencing and Punishment of Offenders Act 2012, the Offer to Settle in Civil Proceedings Order 2013 (SI 93/2013) and, specifically, the "additional amount" payable under what was at the time it was introduced CPR r.36.14(3)(d) and is currently CPR r.36.17(4)(d). Given this reform an argument based on inequality of treatment is likely to be difficult to sustain.

59 Previously CPR r.36.14(3).

60 Under the pre-2015 version of CPR Pt 36 the effect of the ultimate predecessor of what is now CPR r.36.17(4)(b), the then CPR r.36.21(3)(a), the reference to costs was explained as referring to such costs as were are ordered to be paid through an application of what is now CPR 44.2. To determine

at a rate not exceeding 10% above base rate; and (d) an additional amount where the claim has been decided and no prior order has been made under it.[61] The additional amount is limited to a maximum of £75,000 and is calculated "by applying a prescribed percentage" either to the "sum awarded to the claimant by the court" or to the "sum awarded to the claimant by the court in respect of costs" where there has been no monetary award in the claim. The prescribed percentage differs depending on the sum awarded. Where the sum awarded is an amount up to £500,000 it is 10% of the amount awarded. Where the sum awarded is above £500,000 it is 5 per cent of that amount, and 10% of the amount up to £500,000.[62]

17-20 The foregoing provision does not apply to a withdrawn Pt 36 offer or one

> "which has been changed so that its terms are less advantageous to the offeree where the offeree has beaten the less advantageous offer"

or one "made less than 21 days before trial, unless the court has abridged the relevant period".[63]

17-21 Where, however, the terms of r.36.17(4) fall to be implemented, the word "must"[64] reflects a presumption that the consequences set out in the rule will follow unless it is considered unjust. Subject to that latter proviso, there are two areas where the court has a discretion in operating this provision: the first relates to the

---

that question at that time thus required, as Tomlinson J explained in *Kastor Navigation Co Ltd & Anor v AGF M.A.T. & Ors* [2003] EWHC 472 (Comm) at [26]–[27, the court to first determine what costs were recoverable under the version of CPR Pt 44 then in force and then to determine the discretion that arose under CPR Pt 36. That approach was affirmed by the Court of Appeal in *Kastor Navigation Co Ltd & Anor v AXA Global Risks Ltd & Ors* [2004] EWCA Civ 277; [2004] Lloyd's Rep. I.R. 481 per Rix LJ at [135]–[138]. In *Webb v Liverpool Women's NHS Foundation Trust* [2016] EWCA Civ 365; [2016] 1 W.L.R. 3899, the Court of Appeal held that that approach was no longer valid due to the nature of the amendments effected to CPR Pt 36 in 2015 and amendments to CPR Pt 44 following the Jackson Costs reforms. The correct approach to determining costs under CPR r.36.17(4)(b) was simply to start with CPR Pt 36; there was to be no attempt to determine the level of costs under CPR r.44.2 before then going on to determine the question of costs under CPR Pt 36. As Lewison LJ explained at [37]-[38], "[37] In deciding what costs order to make under 36.14 , the Court does not first exercise its discretion under Part 44 . Its only discretion is that conferred by Part 36 itself. The alternative construction requires the Court first to exercise its discretion under Part 44, on the basis of all the circumstances of the case, and then to exercise its discretion under Part 36, again having regard to all the circumstances of the case. This makes no sense. [38] It follows from the above, and in particular that Part 36 is a self-contained code, that the discretion under 36.14 relates not only to the basis of assessment of costs, but also to the determination of what costs are to be assessed. I agree with the Judge that Part 36 does not preclude the making of an issue-based or proportionate costs order. However, a successful claimant is to be deprived of all or part of her costs only if the court considers that would be unjust for her to be awarded all or that part of her costs. That decision falls to be made having regard to "all the circumstances of the case". In exercising its discretion, the Court must take into account that the unsuccessful defendant could have avoided the costs of the trial if it had accepted the claimant's Part 36 offer, as it could and should have done. The principles were aptly summarised by Briggs J (as he then was) in *Smith v Trafford Housing Trust* [2012] EWHC 3320 (Ch) ..."

[61] See fn.46. In *JLE (A Child) v Warrington and Halton Hospitals NHS Foundation Trust* [2019] EWHC 1582 (QB); [2019] Costs L.R. 829, Stewart J in obiter took the view that the additional payment was an all-or-nothing payment, and that contrary to the approach taken by Deputy Costs Master Friston in *White v Wincott Galliford Ltd* [2019] EWHC B6 (Costs), there was no power to make a partial award under CPR r.17(4)(d).

[62] Also see the Offer to Settle in Civil Proceedings Order 2013 (SI 93/2013) art.3. The total amount payable is subject to an upper limit of £75,000: see CPR r.36.17(4)(d) and art.3(5) of the 2013 Order.

[63] CPR r.36.17(7). See, however, paras 17-04 and 17-05.

[64] Previously the rule referred to "will" rather than "must". The change in language was introduced in 2015. It does not however reflect a change in meaning or emphasis, but rather a change in drafting style used in the CPR as a whole: see CPR PD 2D.

amount of the sum of money to which, and the period over which, the higher rate of interest is applicable; the second being in relation to the actual rate of interest itself.

The amount on which, and the period for which, increased interest is payable

The enhanced rate of interest may be ordered to be paid, **17-22**

> "on the whole or part of any sum of money (excluding interest) awarded ... for some or all of the period starting with the date on which the relevant period expired".[65]

This gives the court a wide discretion in relation to the sum of money on which the increased interest can be paid. It can, however, be paid only "in respect of items in the judgment which already merit some award of interest."[66] At the top end of the scale, the court could award increased interest on the whole amount of the award, not merely on the difference between the amount referred to in the offer and the amount of the award. Equally, it can relate to any part of the sum awarded. The period over which it can be ordered is, however, confined to the period after the end of the "relevant period". The court can choose the whole or part of that period.

The rate of interest

The rule provides that the interest capable of being awarded may be "at a rate not exceeding 10% above base rate". This means that the court may add up to 10% to the applicable base rate. It does not mean that the court is restricted to adding merely 10% of the applicable base rate.[67] The rule does not specify the date on which the base rate is to be determined. If it has varied during the period between the end of the relevant period and the date of the award, doubtless an average could be taken. **17-23**

How are these choices made?

As with all powers conferred by the CPR, the court must seek to give effect to the overriding objective when it makes its choice.[68] This remains the case notwithstanding the statement in r.36.1 that Pt 36 forms a self-contained code: it is a self-contained code in terms of its relationship with the law of contract not the CPR. The requirement in CPR r.1.2, with the emphasis in the overriding objective of the need to save expense and on the need for court to allot an appropriate amount of its resources to each case, connotes in the context of this rule a concern that the parties should have focused on the resolution of their dispute.[69] **17-24**

---

65 CPR r.36(17)(4)(a).

66 *Pankhurst v White* [2010] EWCA Civ 1445, per Jackson LJ at [37] affirming *McPhilemy v Times Newspapers Ltd* [2001] EWCA Civ 933; [2002] 1 W.L.R. 934 at [17]–[21] and [28].

67 If the applicable base rate is, say, 6%, the court could award interest up to the rate of 16%. It would not be restricted to 6.6%. The court is not bound to make an award by reference to the base rate: see *Pankhurst* [2010] EWHC 311 (QB); [2010] 3 Costs L.R. 402. See *Assetco Plc v Grant Thornton UK LLP* [2019] EWHC 592 (Comm); [2019] 1 Costs L.R. 197.

68 CPR r.1.2.

69 In *Richard Little v George Little Sebire & Co* [1999] 10 WLUK 581; *The Times*, 17 November 1999, the following view was expressed: "Many of the features of the overriding objective are more directly applicable to the pre-trial and trial periods of a case than to a decision made after a case has effectively been concluded. On the other hand, since one of the factors mentioned in the overriding

17-25 The approach to the way in which the then r.36.21 was to be applied was set out by the Court of Appeal in *Petrotrade Inc v Texaco Ltd*,[70] in which the leading judgment was given by Lord Woolf MR. It was a commercial case in which C had made a Pt 36 offer (to accept just short of $143,000 inclusive of interest) that was not accepted by D but which C bettered (by about $7,000) on a summary judgment application. Since r.36.21 applied only to a judgment obtained "at trial", the rule did not strictly apply to the situation that obtained at the conclusion of the summary judgment application. The Court of Appeal concluded that the judge had been wrong not to award indemnity costs and a higher rate of interest. The following general observations of Lord Woolf MR are of relevance in this context, although it must be recalled that when he referred to Pt 36.21 he was referring to what is now r.36.17[71]:

17-26 "[I]t would be wrong to regard the rule as producing penal consequences. An order for indemnity costs does not enable a claimant to receive more costs than he has incurred. Its practical effect is to avoid his costs being assessed at a lesser figure. When assessing costs on the standard basis the court will only allow costs 'which are proportionate to the matters in issue' and 'resolve any doubt which it may have as to whether costs were reasonably incurred or reasonably proportionate in amount in favour of the paying party'. On the other hand, where the costs are assessed on an indemnity basis, the issue of proportionality does not have to be considered. The court only considers whether the costs were unreasonably incurred or for an unreasonable amount. The court will then resolve any doubt in favour of the receiving party. Even on an indemnity basis, however, the receiving party is restricted to recovering only the amount of costs which have been incurred (see Part 44.4 and Part 44.5).

The ability of the court to award costs on an indemnity basis and interest at an enhanced rate should not be regarded as penal because orders for costs, even when made on an indemnity basis, never actually compensate a claimant for having to come to court to bring proceedings. The very process of being involved in court proceedings inevitably has an impact on a claimant, whether he is a private individual or a multi-national corporation A claimant would be better off had he not become involved in court proceedings. Part of the culture of the CPR is to encourage parties to avoid proceedings unless it is unreasonable for them to do otherwise. In the case of an individual proceedings necessarily involve inconvenience and frequently involve anxiety and distress. These are not taken into account when assessing costs on the normal basis. In the case of a corporation, corporation senior officials and other staff inevitably will be diverted from their normal duties as a consequence of the proceedings. The disruption this causes to a corporation is not recoverable under an order for costs.

The power to order indemnity costs or higher rate interest is a means of achieving a fairer result for a claimant. If a defendant involves a claimant in proceedings after an offer has been made, and in the event, the result is no more favourable to the defendant than

---

objective is the saving of expense, the powers conferred by the rules are likely to be interpreted by the Courts in a way that encourages settlement. Settlement is achieved only if parties focus properly on the strengths and weaknesses of their respective cases. The powers conferred by r.36.21 are plainly designed to sharpen that focus. Unless the discretions conferred by the rule are exercised in a way that makes a material, albeit proportionate, difference to the eventual award in the case, the rule itself would become redundant." This view must be read in the light of the subsequent authoritative decision of the Court of Appeal in *Petrotrade Inc v Texaco Ltd* [2002] 1 W.L.R. 947, but, with diffidence, it is not thought that the essence of the view has been affected by that decision.

70 *Petrotrade Inc v Texaco Ltd* [2002] 1 W.L.R. 947. cf. Moore-Bick J in *Earl v Cantor Fitzgerald International* [2000] 5 WLUK 423 (QB), where he said that "whereas an award of standard interest is intended to be purely compensatory, an award of enhanced interest is more in the nature of a penalty for failing to compromise the proceedings". See also *Hussain v Heywood* [2001] 2 WLUK 518; [2001] 7 C.L. 73 (County Court).

71 *Petrotrade* [2002] 1 W.L.R. 947 at [62]–[65]. See also para.13-09 onwards.

that which would have been achieved if the claimant's offer had been accepted without the need for those proceedings, the message of Part 36.21 is that, prima facie, it is just to make an indemnity order for costs and for interest at an enhanced rate to be awarded. However, the indemnity order need not be for the entire proceedings nor, as I have already indicated, need the award of interest be for a particular period or at a particular rate. It must not however exceed the figure of 10 per cent referred to in Part 36.

There are circumstances where a just result is no order for costs or no interest even where the award exceeds an offer made by a claimant. Part 36.21 does no more than indicate the order which is to be made by the court unless it considers it is unjust to make that order. The general message of Part 36.21, when it applies, is that the court will usually order a higher rate of interest than the going rate. As to what the additional rate of interest should be, it is not possible to give specific guidance. Reference for general guidance has to be made to the terms of Part 36.21 and, in particular, to the provisions of paragraph (5)."

Later in his judgment Lord Woolf gave some further indications of the factors that might be relevant to determining the rate of additional interest if r.36.21 applies. He said this[72]: **17-27**

"If it is accepted that a court has power to depart from the going rate because of a claimant's offer, the question then arises as to what additional interest it would be appropriate to offer? Quite clearly it should not exceed the 10 per cent referred to in Part 36.21. The court would have to take into account all the circumstances in considering whether it would be just to make an order of enhanced interest. Those include the matters which are set out in Part 36.21(5) ...

The amount of the claim is ... a relevant factor. If a claim is small, enhanced interest has to be at a higher rate than if the claim is large, otherwise the additional advantage for the claimant will not be achieved."[73]

The underlying rationale for what was then r.36.21 was also the subject of consideration by the Court of Appeal in *McPhilemy v Times Newspapers Ltd*[74] where Chadwick LJ said this: **17-28**

"It is plain ... that paragraphs (2) and (3) of CPR 36.21 —in conjunction with paragraph (4)—are intended to provide an incentive to a claimant to make a Part 36 offer. The incentive is that a claimant who has made a Part 36 offer (which is not accepted) and who succeeds at trial in beating his own offer stands to receive more than he would have received if he had not made the offer. Conversely, a defendant who refuses a Part 36 offer made by a claimant and who fails to beat that offer at trial is at risk of being ordered to pay more than he would have been ordered to pay if the offer had not been made. But those incentives have to be set in the context that ... CPR 36.21 is not to be regarded as producing penal consequences. The powers conferred by the rule ... are intended to provide 'a means of achieving a fairer result for a claimant' [quoting Lord Woolf's judgment above]. Exercise of the powers cannot achieve 'a fairer result' if it leads to the claimant receiving more than can properly be regarded as a full and complete recompense for having to resort to, to pursue and to endure the strain and anxiety of, legal proceedings. An exercise of the powers which led to the claimant receiving more than could properly be regarded as compensation, in that enlarged sense, would, necessarily in my view, be penal in nature. It could only be supported on the basis that there was a need to punish the defendant by requiring him to pay an amount which went beyond any amount needed to compensate the claimant. But, subject to the limitation that the powers are intended to be used in order to achieve a fairer result for the claimant and not to punish the defendant, it is plain that

---

72 *Petrotrade* [2002] 1 W.L.R. 947 at [75] and [77].

73 See also fn.58 and the quotations from Lord Woolf's interim and final reports.

74 *McPhilemy* [2001] EWCA Civ 933; [2002] 1 W.L.R. 934 at [19] and [21].

they are to be used in order to redress elements, otherwise inherent in the legal process, which can properly be regarded as unfair."

17-29 His conclusion was that:

"[T]he power to award interest under paragraph (2) of CPR 36.21 at an enhanced rate ... is conferred in order to enable the court, in a case to which CPR 36.21 applies, to redress the element of perceived unfairness, otherwise inherent in the legal process, which arises from the fact that damages, costs (even costs on an indemnity basis) and statutory interest will not compensate the successful claimant for the inconvenience, anxiety and distress of having to resort to and pursue proceedings which he had sought to avoid by an offer to settle on terms which (as events turned out) were less advantageous to him than the judgment which he achieved."

17-30 In the same case Simon Brown LJ, as he then was,[75] said that regarding the rule as "penal" and that exercising it implied "condemnation of the defendant's conduct" reflected a misunderstanding of the rationale of the rule.[76] He said:

"It is not designed to punish unreasonable conduct but rather as an incentive to encourage claimants to make, and defendants to accept, appropriate offers of settlement. That incentive plainly cannot work unless the non-acceptance of what ultimately proves to have been a sufficient offer ordinarily advantages the claimant in the respects set out in the rule."

17-31 Notwithstanding those views, it would appear also that the nature of the defence put forward may be relevant,[77] as is the manner in which the claimant has advanced his case.[78]

17-32 Although in *Petrotrade* the Court of Appeal was unwilling to give specific guidance on what the additional rate of interest should be in any case,[79] it indicated that it would be wrong to take 10% above base rate as the starting point.[80]

---

75 *McPhilemy* [2001] EWCA Civ 933; [2002] 1 W.L.R. 934 at [28].

76 Also see *Downing v Peterborough & Stamford Hospitals NHS Foundation Trust* [2014] EWHC 4216 (QB); [2015] 2 Costs L.O. 203 per Sir David Eady at [60] "Mr Porter referred to the indemnity costs provision as 'punitive' in character. In one sense he is right, but one must be careful in the use of language in this context. It is quite clear that this rule, which obviously has legislative sanction, was not intended to 'punish' only conduct which is deemed in some way morally reprehensible or which was in breach of a rule or statutory requirement. A decision was taken, as a matter of public policy, to impose sanctions in order to encourage and facilitate the settlement of litigation and, correspondingly, to avoid parties incurring the costs involved in going to trial and also to save court time. Indemnity costs are, therefore, bound sometimes to be payable under CPR 36.14(3)(b) because an assessment of the merits proves not to have been justified or simply because an informed guess as to the outcome turns out to be wrong."

77 *Petrotrade Inc* [2002] 1 W.L.R. 947 at [76]. See also the comments of Moore-Bick J in *Earl v Cantor Fitzgerald International* [2000] 5 WLUK 423 (QB), where he said that "it is appropriate when exercising the discretion under paragraph (2) to take into account, among other things, the conduct of the defendant in pursuing the matter to trial". In the context of that case he said that he "did not think that [the defendant's] conduct in continuing the litigation" warranted "a maximum award of enhanced interest" against the background of a submission that the case "raised serious issues of fact and law". In that case, where the award exclusive of interest was taken to be £500,000, an award of the maximum enhanced interest (16%) for the relevant period would have yielded an award of over £53,000. The enhanced interest was awarded at the rate of 5% above base rate (11% in total), yielding a rounded-down figure of £35,000.

78 *Petrotrade Inc* [2002] 1 W.L.R. 947 at [76].

79 The award made was 4% above base rate for a period of 12 months, that period running from the time that a judgment had been given in the Court of Appeal on a previous occasion in relation to the particular litigation. Awards at 4–5% above base rate are fairly frequent, though see fn.61. For examples of where the full 10% uplift was awarded see *Taylor v Rive Droite Music Ltd* [2006]

In relation to enhanced interest on any indemnity costs awarded, it is no answer to the claim for enhanced interest that, at all material times, the claimant had been in receipt of legal aid (and thus not personally out of pocket) and that an award of enhanced interest could only provide a windfall to the Legal Services Commission.[81] 17-33

UNJUST TO MAKE THE ORDER?

The logical sequence of questions for the court to ask and answer would seem to be as follows: 17-34

(i) Has the claimant obtained a judgment at least as advantageous to him as the proposals contained in his own Pt 36 offer?
(ii) If so, is it unjust for an order for enhanced interest to be made?
(iii) If not, what should the amount of that interest be, on what sum and for what period?

It is likely that (ii) and (iii) will merge to some degree. The court is obliged to "take into account all the circumstances of the case",[82] including certain specific matters, in deciding whether it would be unjust to make the orders for enhanced interest, indemnity costs and the additional amount.[83] 17-35

The specific matters to which the court will have regard are the terms of the offer and the stage in the proceedings in which it was made, the information available to the parties at the time of the offer and the conduct of the parties with regard to the giving or refusing of information for the purpose of enabling the offer to be evaluated.[84] The rule is doubtless designed to benefit the claimant who makes a bona 17-36

EWHC 2089 (Ch) and *Socimer International Bank Ltd (In Liquidation) v Standard Bank London Ltd* [2006] EWHC 2896 (Comm). In the *Socimer* case Gloster J said: "The purpose of CPR 36.21 is clearly to require parties to give very serious consideration to compromising claims or parts thereof, with penal consequences if they unreasonably fail to do so." cf. para.17-25 onwards.

80 In *Richard Little* [1999] 10 WLUK 581, *The Times,* 17 November 1999, the following view was advanced in relation to the approach to be adopted to choosing the appropriate rate of enhanced interest: "Whilst there are a number of ways in which the issue might be approached, one that strikes me as appropriate is to start with the proposition that enhanced interest of 10% above base rate will be awarded on the whole of the judgment sum (excluding interest) from the earliest date when it can be awarded and then to evaluate whether the effect of doing so will itself work an injustice or result in a disproportionate advantage to the claimant or a disproportionate disadvantage to the defendant." In that case the offer had been to accept £30,000 inclusive of interest and the award was for £50,000 inclusive of interest. In *Cantor Fitzgerald International* [2000] 5 WLUK 423 (QB),, Moore-Bick J said that he was not "persuaded that the court should award the maximum amount by way of enhanced interest unless there is some reason not to do so", but agreed that "it is ... necessary to stand back and consider whether, viewed in the round, any given award would provide a disproportionate benefit to the claimant or impose a disproportionate burden on the defendant". In *Petrotrade Inc* [2002] 1 W.L.R. 947, Lord Woolf referred to *Richard Little* and to the suggestion that "the court should take as the starting point 10% above base rate" and said that it was not an approach he would endorse.

81 *Cantor Fitzgerald International* [2000] 5 WLUK 423 (QB), per Moore-Bick J.

82 See fn.51.

83 CPR r.36.17(5).

84 When judging whether to award indemnity costs and/or enhanced interest and/or an additional amount when a claimant obtains a judgment at least as advantageous as his CPR Pt 36 offer the court is enjoined to consider the "information available to the parties at the time when the Part 36 offer was made": r.36.17(5)(c). The importance of disclosure of information and documentation to enable an offeree to assess an offer has been emphasised: see, e.g. *Ford v GKR Construction* [2000] 1 W.L.R. 1397; *Amber v Stacey* [2001] 1 W.L.R. 1225. It can potentially have an impact on costs: see

fide attempt to settle his claim at a reasonable figure. A failure to supply proper information so that the offer can be evaluated can hardly be said to be acting bona fide[85]. Equally, the court is likely to be slow to assist a claimant who formulates an enormous claim, but who offers to accept something very small by comparison and then achieves slightly more than that figure. Again, this would hardly seem to be bona fide negotiation. A claimant who puts forward a whole series of offers (perhaps all on the same date), hoping that one will be exceeded so as to attract the benefits of the rule, is unlikely to receive an enthusiastic response from the court either.

17-37 In assessing the question whether it is unjust to order an additional amount under r.36.17(4)(d), the court will not take account of the amount of costs claimed. As Warby J said in *Elsevier Ltd v Munro (Supplementary Judgment)*,[86]

> "I do not believe ... that the mere scale of the costs claimed can have a bearing on the decision I have to make. Those costs will be assessed if not agreed, and no more than a reasonable sum will be payable."

It appears, furthermore, following the decision in *Feltham v Bouskall*,[87] that the manner in which an offer was beaten will not be taken into account in assessing whether to make an additional award: the fact that the offer in issue had only just been beaten was of no relevance to the question whether it was unjust to make the additional award. It was, however, held to be relevant in answering that question, and ultimately determining in that case that it was unjust to make the award, that the Pt 36 offer had been made late in the proceedings, that a central issue in the claim was only raised at trial and that disclosure of certain highly relevant documents was not made until the "eve of the commencement of the trial".[88]

Factortame Ltd v Secretary of State for the Environment [2002] 1 W.L.R. 2438. However, if the court concludes that the absence of the information or documentation at the time of the offer made no difference to the offeree's decision not to accept it, then the costs implications are unlikely to be significant. It could have an impact on the question of whether to award indemnity costs other than in the circumstances of an offer to which r.36.17 applies. In *The Maersk Co Ltd v Wilson* [2004] EWCA Civ 313, the discretion was exercised against the claimant because the claimant succeeded in beating his own offer only by a late change of approach to the case.

85 This would appear to have been a significant factor in the decision in *Thinc Group Ltd v Jeremy Kingdom* [2013] EWCA Civ 1306. Both C and D appealed against various costs orders made by the trial judge, the material order for present purposes being an order that D should pay 20% of C's costs on the indemnity basis from a date a few weeks after C's offer to accept a sum from D inclusive of interest that was exceeded (largely because of the interest element) at trial some 5–6 months later. It followed that C obtained an award "at least as advantageous" as his offer. However, C failed to respond to a request from D's solicitors on the day of the offer in these terms: "please confirm what your costs are in order that we may properly consider the offer made." The Court of Appeal upheld the decision of the trial judge to reflect the failure of C to respond to this reasonable request as one of the reasons for not awarding C his full costs after the offer was made. It is respectfully submitted that this decision on this issue was plainly correct. However, in the course of an ex tempore judgment given on 29 October 2013, with which Arden and Ryder LJJ agreed, Macur LJ said that "[the] phrase "unless it considers it unjust to do so" in CPR 36.14 (2) and (3) bear the obvious interpretation of "unless and to the extent of."" The equivalent terminology in the CPR updated on 1 April 2013 is now contained in CPR 36.17(4). Whether it was appropriate to seek to place that gloss on the long-established words in Part 36 as it existed prior to 1 April 2013 is, with respect, debateable, but it is submitted that the gloss cannot be taken forward into the interpretation of CPR 36.17(4) for the reasons given by Stewart J in *JLE (A Child) v Warrington and Halton Hospitals NHS Foundation Trust* [2019] EWHC 1582 (QB); [2019] Costs L.R. 829, [74]-[76].

86 [2014] EWHC 2728 (QB); [2014] 5 Costs L.O. 797 at [8].

87 [2013] EWHC 3086 (Ch); [2014] 1 Costs L.O. 29 per Charles Hollander QC sitting as a deputy judge of the High Court.

88 [2013] EWHC 3086 (Ch); [2014] 1 Costs L.O. 29 at [13]–[16].

THE "TACTICAL OFFER"

The opportunity to secure enhanced interest on any damages awarded, indemnity costs and enhanced interest on the costs is one that a claimant and his advisers may strive to seize. Efforts to secure those advantages may go beyond merely seeking in good faith to put forward an offer based upon a genuine evaluation of the risks involved in the dispute. It is in this context that the "tactical offer" has emerged. It has to be recalled that an offer is an "offer to settle"—in other words, an offer to accept something *less* than the full value of the claim or the full award sought.[89] The offer must, as Henderson J said in *AB v CD*, "contain some genuine element of concession on the part of the claimant, to which a significant value can be attached in the context of the litigation ... which it is in the [offeror's] power to give up at the time when the offer is made."[90] Offers to settle for the full amount claimed, plainly, do not satisfy that requirement and cannot amount to genuine offers. Rule 36.17(5)(e) appears to have been introduced specifically to deter the making of such tactical offers in focusing on the need, as part of determining whether it is unjust to make the normal order for costs, to consider whether a Pt 36 offer was a genuine settlement attempt. Prior to its introduction in 2015 such a factor would have been a matter for the court to assess as one of "all the circumstances of the case". **17-38**

The more difficult question for the court is where the offer is very close in value to the full amount claimed. It might be thought that in determining such a question the court would be assisted by evidence as to what was said between the parties in any discussions surrounding the offer or any relevant negotiations. However, the provision of such information is ordinarily within the scope of the "without prejudice" privilege (which is a valuable privilege as an aid to encouraging settlement and not to be set aside lightly[91]) and, as Foskett J, noted in *JMX v Norfolk and Norwich Hospitals NHS Foundation Trust*, unlikely in any event to assist the determination of the question whether the Pt 36 offer was a genuine offer to settle or a mere tactical device.[92] In such circumstances, the issue arises as to whether such an offer is to be regarded as merely "tactical", in the sense of being made simply to try to secure the advantages conferred by r.36.17, or whether it is an offer that ought to be recognised as a genuine attempt to settle the proceedings.[93] In *Huck v* **17-39**

---

89 An offer by a claimant to accept 100% of his claim would not constitute an "offer to settle" since settlement implies making some concession: see *East West Corp v Dampskibselskabet (No.2)* [2002] 2 Lloyd's Rep. 222, where Thomas J said that to engage these provisions there must be some "offer to settle in the ordinary sense of the word". Even if such an offer is seen as an offer to settle, it will not have been "beaten" when 100% liability is established at trial: see *Gaynor v Blackpool FC Ltd* unreported 10 April 2002 Oldham County Court, HH Judge Armitage QC (report via Lawtel)—although the test now, of course, is whether the judgment obtained is "at least as advantageous" as the offer. See also the *East West Corp* case. An offer to accept 99.9% of a claim might founder upon a similar basis: see *Huck v Robson* [2002] EWCA Civ 398; [2002] 3 All E.R. 263. Cf. fn.88. In *MR v Commissioner of Police of the Metropolis* [2019] EWHC 1970 (QB) a Pt 36 offer to settle by C for nil damages on the basis D should admit that C had been subject to false imprisonment was held to be a genuine offer.

90 *AB v CD* [2011] EWHC 602 (Ch) at [22]–[23].

91 See Ch.19.

92 [2018] EWHC 185 (QB); [2018] 1 Costs L.R. 81, at [18].

93 It is, perhaps, legitimate to ask the question whether it matters. In *Huck v Robson* [2002] EWCA Civ 398; [2002] 3 All E.R. 263, Jonathan Parker LJ said that: "[I]n order to qualify for the incentives provided by paragraphs (2) and (3) of [CPR r.36.21] a claimant's Part 36 offer must represent at the very least a genuine and realistic attempt by the claimant to resolve the dispute by agreement. Such an offer is to be contrasted with one which creates no real opportunity for settlement but is merely a tactical step designed to secure the benefit of the incentives."

Robson[94] the claimant in a road traffic accident case offered to accept a judgment for 95 per cent of the full value of the claim, the only issue on liability being that of contributory negligence. Although a finding of 5 per cent contributory negligence is unknown, the majority of the Court of Appeal concluded that this should be viewed as a genuine offer. Tuckey LJ said:

> "[In] this type of litigation a Claimant with a strong case will often be prepared to accept a discount from the full value of the claim to reflect the uncertainties of litigation. Such offers are not usually based on the likely apportionment of liability but merely reflect the reality that most claimants prefer certainty to the ordeal of a trial and uncertainty about its outcome. If such a discount is offered and rejected there is nothing unjust in allowing the claimant to receive the incentives to which he or she is entitled under the Rules."

17-40 The dividing line between a genuine and a "tactical" offer is not always easy to determine and the introduction of a specific rule requiring consideration of the question whether an offer was "tactical" does nothing to assist in that determination.[95] It needs to be acknowledged that even a 1 per cent discount on a very large sum is itself a large sum.[96] A very small concession on the line of a boundary in a boundary dispute could be regarded as a significant matter. Each case will depend on its own facts.[97] While the court is likely to consider the question whether an offer was "tactical" more systematically than before the introduction of r.36.17(5)(e), it is likely that the court will remain cautious in characterising an offer as merely "tactical" and thus not effective in relation to the exercise of the powers under r.36.17.[98]

---

94 *Huck* [2002] EWCA Civ 398; [2002] 3 All E.R. 263.

95 See *Wharton v Bancroft* [2012] EWHC 91 (Ch); [2012] W.T.L.R. 727 per Norris J at [2] "The concept [of a "tactical offer"] is not an easy one to apply. All Part 36 offers are tactical in the sense that they are designed to take advantage of the incentives provided by Part 36. A low offer in a case where the offeror considers that the offeree's position has no merit cannot be written off as self-evidently 'merely a tactical step'".

96 cf. per Bell J in *Read v Edmed* [2004] EWHC 3274 (QB); [2006] 2 Costs L.R. 201 at [27]: "A 1% or even a 0.1% concession from a realistic apportionment can mean a four or five figure sum in the seven figure claims which are not uncommon today." In the period since that observation was made, figures reaching eight figures are not unfamiliar and there is always the question, in personal injuries' claims, of significant annual periodical payments for care. In *Jockey Club Racecourse Ltd v Willmott Dixon Construction Ltd* [2016] EWHC 167 (TCC); [2016] 4 W.L.R. 43 a 5% discount was held to be a genuine offer to settle the question of liability in a design and build dispute that was valued at approximately £5 million.

97 In *JMX* [2018] EWHC 185 (QB); [2018] 1 Costs L.R. 81 at [14]–[17], Foskett J held that in the circumstances of a medical negligence claim that he characterised as being "likely to run into several million pounds on a traditional lump-sum basis", a Pt 36 offer which provided for a 10% discount on the issue of liability was a genuine offer to settle the issue of liability.

98 *Read* [2004] EWHC 3274 (QB); [2006] 2 Costs L.R. 201 at [23], where there was anecdotal evidence that: "[I]t was the settled practice for litigators acting for claimants to make offers such as 49%, 65%, 74% and so on, to guard against findings of one half, one third and one quarter and so on of contributory negligence because of the clear wording of Part 36.21." As Bell J observed, at [26], "it does seem to me to be absurd if the wording of 36.21(1) has led to a practice of claimants offering to take marginally less than 75, 50, 33.3 or 25%, or some other familiar fraction, simply to gain the benefit of Part 36.21". The wording of r.36.17 is, of course, now different.

CHAPTER 18

Offers Outside CPR Part 36

Attention has already been drawn to the possibility that a party may, for whatever reason, deliberately choose not to make his offer of settlement within CPR Pt 36.[1] For example, a party may wish to commence negotiations without making the threat that, if his offer is not accepted, it may be referred to the court on the issue of costs or, if it is a claimant's offer, that it should carry with it the prospect of enhanced interest and indemnity costs.[2] A straightforward "without prejudice" offer[3] may be advanced in the early stages of trying to resolve a dispute and it is, of course, possible that a party might choose to make a traditional Calderbank offer[4] in an ordinary piece of civil litigation.[5] Settlement meetings, whether with or without the intervention of a mediator, have become common events in all forms of litigation and they are invariably conducted on a "without prejudice" basis. For these reasons, and for the reason that Pt 36 offers[6] are treated automatically as "without prejudice except as to costs",[7] it is necessary to have an appreciation of the limits and effect of the "without prejudice" privilege. This will be dealt with in Ch.19. **18-01**

For present purposes, it is proposed to put forward a brief review of the law and practice applicable to the relevance and, where appropriate, assessment of three types of offer which, strictly speaking, fall outside Pt 36: **18-02**

(i) a "without prejudice" offer;
(ii) a Calderbank offer;
(iii) an open offer.

As observed in the review of Pt 36,[8] the CPR provide that: **18-03**

> "[In] deciding what order (if any) to make about costs, the court will have regard to all the circumstances, including ... any admissible offer to settle made by a party which is drawn to the court's attention, and which is not an offer to which costs consequences under Part 36 apply."[9]

A party is, therefore, entitled to draw to the court's attention any admissible of-

---

1 See para.14-03.
2 See para.23-09 onwards.
3 See para.18-04.
4 See para.18-05.
5 The Calderbank offer can still be an effective form of offer in family finance proceedings albeit in much more limited circumstances than once was the case: see Ch.26.
6 See Ch.17.
7 See para.14-06.
8 See para.14-02.
9 CPR r.44.2(4)(c); See *Reed Executive Plc v Reed Business Information Ltd* [2004] EWCA Civ 887; [2004] W.L.R. 3026 per Jacob LJ para.35.

fer to settle which falls outside Pt 36 when inviting it to consider how to exercise its general discretion as to costs and the court must take it into account.[10]

A "WITHOUT PREJUDICE" OFFER

18-04 It has been a long-established principle that an offer made "without prejudice" cannot be referred to on the question of costs without the consent of both parties.[11] It follows that a pure "without prejudice" offer is not admissible on any issue as to costs[12] without the consent of both parties. The privilege afforded to "without prejudice" negotiations may be set aside in certain situations,[13] but the underlying philosophy of the rule is to enable "cards on the table" negotiations to take place without the fear that concessions made for the purposes of trying to reach an accommodation can then be used at trial to the disadvantage of the party making them.[14]

A CALDERBANK OFFER

18-05 This is an offer expressed to be "without prejudice except [or save] as to costs". In other words, it is intended to have all the features of a pure "without prejudice" offer,[15] but enables reference to it to be made on the issue of costs if it is not accepted. An offer of settlement of this nature first gained more widespread recognition following a Family Division case,[16] although it had been used fairly widely in other divisions and its use had been commended and encouraged.[17] A challenge to the validity of such an offer in relation to costs failed in *Cutts v Head*[18] and, following that case, the Rules of the Supreme Court and the County Court Rules were

---

10 *French v Groupama Insurance Company Ltd* [2011] EWCA Civ 1119; [2012] C.P. Rep 2, *Coward v Phaestos Ltd* [2014] EWCA Civ 1256; [2015] C.P. Rep. 2. A close analysis of what was achieved at trial in comparison with what was offered in the Calderbank offer is necessary. See paras 18-05—18-07.

11 *Cory v Bretton* (1830) 4 C. & P. 462, *Paddock v Forrester* (1842) 3 Man. & G. 903, *Hoghton v Hoghton* (1852) 15 Beav. 278 at 321, *Jones v Foxall* (1852) 15 Beav. 388 at 396, *Walker v Wilsher* (1889) L.R. 23 Q.B.D. 335, *Stotesbury v Turner* [1943] K.B. 370, *Computer Machinery Co Ltd v Drescher* [1983] 1 W.L.R. 1379 at 1382–1383, *Cutts v Head* [1984] Ch.290, *Rush v Tompkins* [1989] A.C. 1280, *Muller v Linsley and Mortimer* [1996] 1 P.N.L.R. 74, *Ofulue v Bossert* [2009] 1 A.C. 990.

12 But see fn.20 in Ch.14.

13 See para.19-23 onwards.

14 See para.19-03.

15 See para.18-04 and Ch.19.

16 *Calderbank v Calderbank* [1976] Fam. 93. It is extraordinary that Mrs Calderbank should have lent her former husband's family name (probably in perpetuity if the Chancery Division permits it) to something which she never in fact did! Her effective offer for the purposes of costs was an open one. It is, perhaps, even more ironic that Calderbank offers no longer have the effectiveness in the Family Division that they once had, see: FPR r.28.3(8); *J v J (Divorce: Ancillary Relief: Costs Management)* [2014] EWHC 3654 (Fam); [2015] Fam. Law 372 at [55]; and Ch.26. See also *McDonnell v McDonnell* [1977] 1 W.L.R. 34.

17 *Computer Machinery Co Ltd v Drescher* [1983] 1 W.L.R. 1379 at 1382–1383, per Sir Robert Megarry VC. Under the RSC the court would not, however, declare at an interlocutory stage that such an offer will be considered on the question of costs in due course: *Corby DC v Holst & Co Ltd* [1985] 1 W.L.R. 427 CA.

18 *Cutts* [1984] Ch. 290.

each extended to make express provision for an offer of this nature.[19] The Calderbank offer became the blueprint for the Pt 36 offer.[20] A Calderbank offer is, of course, admissible on the question of costs and must, accordingly, be taken into account by the court if it is relevant to do so.[21]

Shortly before the CPR came into force[22] the Court of Appeal had the opportunity to review the practice applicable to the assessment of a Calderbank offer in relation to the question of costs.[23] For an offer to have been effective in relation to the costs of the litigation the essential test in this context is that propounded by Sir Thomas Bingham MR, as he then was, in *Roache v News Group Newspapers Ltd*,[24] where he said this: **18-06**

> "The judge must look closely at the facts of the particular case before him and ask: Who, as a matter of substance and reality, has won? Has the Plaintiff won anything of value which he could not have won without fighting the action through to a finish? Has the Defendant substantially denied the Plaintiff the prize which the Plaintiff fought the action to win?"[25]

Any such assessment of costs must not however be carried out as if it were an assessment under Pt 36. Calderbank offers may have been the blueprint for Pt 36 but, as the Court of Appeal affirmed in *Coward v Phaestos Ltd*[26], the consequences of failing to beat such an offer was not to be assessed by reference to CPR r.36.14(1A). As it made clear, CPR Pt 36 is a self-contained code,[27] and is distinct from the separate and general costs discretion contained within CPR Pt 44, which as David Richards J explained "contains no rules as to the way in which the court is to have regard to offers."[28] Consequently, when assessing the costs consequences: -

> "The task of the judge in any particular case is to exercise his or her discretion as to the just order for costs, having regard to all the circumstances of the case, including those specified in 44.2(4). Clearly a payment into court or an admissible offer to settle is unlikely in normal circumstances to be of much if any relevance, if the offeree has achieved significantly more at trial."[29]

Exercise of that discretion may, however, as the Court of Appeal affirmed in *Capita (Banstead 2011) Ltd, Capita Hartshead Benefit Consultants Ltd v Rfib Group Ltd*[30], quite properly result in the court reaching the same decision on an assessment of costs under CPR Pt 44 as it would have done under CPR Pt 36. Explaining the approach, Flaux LJ said that:

---

19 RSC Ord.22 r.14; CCR Ord.11 r.10.
20 See para.14-07.
21 See para.18-03.
22 26 April 1999.
23 *Butcher v Wolfe* [1999] C.P.L.R. 112; *Hobin v Douglas* [2000] P.I.Q.R. Q1.
24 *Roache v News Group Newspapers Ltd* [1998] E.M.L.R. 161.
25 This test was accepted as the correct test in the two cases noted in fn.23.
26 [2014] EWCA Civ 1256; [2015] C.P. Rep. 2, at [93]–[101].
27 See para.14-02.
28 [2014] EWCA Civ 1256; [2015] C.P. Rep. 2, at [98].
29 [2014] EWCA Civ 1256; [2015] C.P. Rep. 2, at [98].
30 [2017] EWCA Civ 1032; [2017] C.P. Rep. 38.

"It is well-established that, in an appropriate case, the court may treat a Calderbank offer as having the same effect as regards costs as a Part 36 offer. Whether or not the case is an appropriate one is quintessentially a matter for the discretion of the trial judge ..."[31]

18-07 The review of Calderbank offers in ordinary civil litigation shortly prior to the introduction of the CPR led to the rejection of the approach adopted previously, namely, that the recipient of such an offer was under no duty to seek clarification of the offer if it was unclear or ambiguous or to engage in any further negotiation.[32] This approach was rejected as being "altogether too narrow and inflexible".[33] Some meaningful engagement would thus be required. This approach to such an offer continues. In *Codent Ltd v Lyson Ltd*,[34] which involved an offer "in the nature of ... a Calderbank offer", May LJ said[35] that "[a] party who ... refused a Calderbank offer point-blank and failed to negotiate might be penalised in costs if such refusal was unreasonable". The obligation was to negotiate.

AN OPEN OFFER

18-08 This means exactly what its title conveys: it is not the subject of the privilege associated with the expression "without prejudice" and is available for all to see at all times. It is usually made or confirmed in a letter. It could be made in a witness statement prepared for the purposes of an interim application or indeed the substantive case. It is not unknown for it to be made or confirmed by an advocate during the course of proceedings.

18-09 The particular value of the open offer (other, of course, than its relevance to the issue of costs) is that it serves to demonstrate to the tribunal dealing with the substantive case (or any interim application) that a party who might otherwise be thought to be adopting a wholly unreasonable stance in the litigation is not doing so.[36] It also obviates the embarrassment caused by a witness who, forgetful of previous advice, refers to a "without prejudice" proposal. Its disadvantage is that the terms of the offer are known to the tribunal which might be influenced (or, more likely, be thought to be influenced) accordingly. The tendency, therefore, amongst practitioners is to reserve the making of such an offer to a case where it is felt that the offeree is being unduly optimistic about the outcome of the case and that there is virtually no prospect of the offer being bettered by the ultimate decision of the tribunal.

18-10 One potential matter arising from the existence of an open offer is the extent, if any, to which the tribunal is entitled to draw inferences from it about the merits of the case. Can the offeree point to it (or cross-examine upon it) for the purpose of suggesting it displays a weakness in the offeror's case? Since this is likely to arise very rarely there is no direct authoritative guidance on the point. Clearly, if the open offer contains an express admission of fact, that fact could without more be relied upon. The mere fact, however, that an open offer had been made would not, of itself, amount to an admission. In *Dorchester Group Ltd (t/a Dorchester Collection) v Kier*

---

31 [2017] EWCA Civ 1032; [2017] C.P. Rep. 38 at [45].

32 *C & H Engineering v F. Klucznik & Son Ltd* [1992] F.S.R. 667 (Aldous J).

33 In *Butcher v Wolfe* [1999] C.P.L.R. 112, per Simon Brown LJ.

34 *Codent Ltd v Lyson Ltd* [2005] EWCA Civ 1835; [2006] C.P. Rep. 33.

35 *Codent* [2005] EWCA Civ 1835; [2006] C.P. Rep. 33; [2006] C.P. Rep. 33 at [30].

36 In *Sampson v John Boddy Timber Ltd* (1995) 145 N.L.J. 851, noted at para.19-14, Evans LJ said that an open offer might be used by the party making it "to claim credit for being reasonable if no settlement is achieved and the dispute comes to trial".

Construction Ltd,[37] Coulson J held that the open offer made in that case did not constitute an admission for the purposes of CPR Pt 14. For judgment to be entered under r.14.1, "the admission has to be clear and unequivocal" and it was not so in that case.[38]

While an express concession of an issue is clearly available for consideration, can it go further than that? Does the opening of the offer enable investigation of the basis upon which the offer was made? It is thought that the answer to that question must generally be 'no' unless, and to the extent that, the wording of the offer is clearly and unequivocally an admission. In the absence of such an admission within the offer, it is likely that the open offer does no more than set out, as Coulson J stated was the situation in the *Dorchester Group* case, that the party making it was accepting certain propositions in their opponent's case for the purposes of making the offer.[39] This would in turn suggest that the ability of a tribunal to draw inferences from an open offer, or for a party to cross-examine on it, will be limited by the extent to which the offer contains formal admissions.

One reason for upholding the traditional meaning given to a "without prejudice" offer is to prevent the use by the party to whom it is made of the existence of the offer as some form of admission;[40] it thus avoids questions whether an admission in an offer was a formal admission. Arguably, discarding the "without prejudice" tag, which is, of course, the choice of the offeror, could legitimately lead to an investigation whether an admission in an open offer was a formal admission. Most questions asked further to such an investigation would be likely to trespass, however, on the privilege given to legal advice and other communications relating to litigation.[41] Each case would doubtless depend upon its own circumstances and, in particular, on the phraseology of the communication making the offer.[42] But it is thought that little, if any, investigation of the offer would appear to be profitable and few, if any, legitimate inferences drawn from its existence are likely to be possible. **18-11**

37 [2015] EWHC 3051 (TCC); [2016] C.I.L.L. 3753.

38 [2015] EWHC 3051 (TCC); [2016] C.I.L.L. 3753 at [15], and see e.g. *Technistudy v Kelland* [1976] 1 W.L.R. 1042.

39 [2015] EWHC 3051 (TCC); [2016] C.I.L.L. 3753 at [13].

40 See para.18-04.

41 *Phipson on Evidence*, 19th edn (2017), Ch.23.

42 See the views of Sir Thomas Bingham MR on the without prejudice letter in *Sampson v John Boddy Timber Ltd* (1995) 145 N.L.J. 851. An open letter from a defendant in a defamation action offering to make an apology on terms may be highly relevant to the issue of damages and can, therefore, be referred to and form the subject of questions to the plaintiff: *Dixons Stores Group Ltd v Thames Television Plc* [1993] 1 All E.R. 349 (Drake J). Presumably, such a letter could be the subject of questions to the defendant.

CHAPTER 19

The "Without Prejudice" Rule

INTRODUCTION

The "without prejudice" rule is one of long-standing. Its parameters have been revisited by the House of Lords twice and the UK Supreme Court once in recent years,[1] but the earliest cases to which reference continues to be made from time to time[2] are cases derived from the late 18th century.[3] Its longevity reflects its importance in the civil litigation landscape, an importance that continues to be emphasised when suggested exceptions to its operation are advanced.[4] **19-01**

The net effect of negotiations, including those conducted during mediations,[5] being "without prejudice" is that, subject to certain exceptions,[6] a privilege[7] attaches to the content of those negotiations rendering it inadmissible at the trial of the action to the settlement of which they were directed.[8] **19-02**

The foundation for the rule has traditionally been seen as lying partly in public policy and partly in the express or implied agreement of the parties to the relevant negotiations.[9] In *Muller v Linsley and Mortimer*,[10] Hoffmann LJ, as he then was, having referred to *Cutts v Head*,[11] said this: **19-03**

"*Cutts v Head* shows that the rule has two justifications. First, the public policy of

---

1 *Bradford & Bingley Plc v Rashid* [2006] 1 W.L.R. 2066, *Ofulue v Bossert* [2009] 1 A.C. 990 and *Oceanbulk Shipping & Trading SA v TMT Asia Ltd & Ors* [2010] UKSC 44; [2011] 1 A.C. 662. The occasion prior to those cases in which the operation of the rule had been considered by the House of Lords was in *Rush & Tomkins Ltd v Great London Council* [1989] 1 A.C. 1280.

2 See *Bradford & Bingley Plc* [2006] 1 W.L.R. 2066 at [12] and *Ofulue v Bossert* [2009] 1 A.C. 990 at [26], [39], [58] and [92]–[93].

3 *Waldridge v Kennison* (1794) 1 Esp. 142 and *Turner v Railton* (1796) 2 Esp. 474, both cases in which the views of Lord Kenyon CJ are recorded.

4 See, in particular, para.19-51.

5 *Aird v Prime Meridian Ltd* [2006] EWCA Civ 1866; [2007] C.P. Rep. 18 at [5].

6 See para. 19-23 onwards.

7 *Sampson v John Boddy Timber Ltd* (1995) 145 N.L.J. 851, noted at para.19-14, per Sir Thomas Bingham MR, the relevant quotation from whose judgment appears in para.19-07.

8 For a case concerning the admissibility or otherwise in a criminal case of evidence of things said in "without prejudice" discussions concerning a civil case, see *R v K (A)* [2009] EWCA Crim 1640; [2010] 1 Cr. App. R. 3. For a case that extended the application of the "without prejudice" rule by analogy to discussions in the context of regulatory proceedings, see *Property Alliance Group Ltd v The Royal Bank of Scotland Plc* [2015] EWHC 1557; [2016] W.L.R. 361.

9 *Cutts* [1984] Ch. 290 at 306; *Rush & Tomkins Ltd v Great London Council* [1989] 1 A.C. 1280 at 1300, *Unilever Plc v The Procter & Gamble Co* [2000] 1 W.L.R. 2436 at 2442, *Oceanbulk Shipping & Trading SA v TMT Asia Ltd & Ors* [2010] UKSC 44; [2011] 1 A.C. 662 at [19].

10 *Muller v Linsley & Mortimer* (1996) 1 P.N.L.R. 74 at 77.

11 *Cutts* [1984] Ch. 290 In *Sternberg Reed Solicitors v Andrew Paul Harrison* [2019] EWHC 2065 (Ch), HHJ David Hodge QC, sitting as a High Court Judge, confirmed that authority makes it "absolutely clear that communications expressly made on a 'without prejudice' basis are inadmissible, even for the purpose of costs arguments" and "that the court has no general discretion to disapply the 'without prejudice' rule." For such communications to be admissible on costs, it is neces-

encouraging parties to negotiate and settle their disputes out of court and, secondly, an implied agreement arising out of what is commonly understood to be the consequences of offering or agreeing to negotiate without prejudice. In some cases both of these justifications are present; in others, only one or the other."

In *Ofulue v Bossert*[12] Lord Neuberger of Abbotsbury put the matter thus[13]:

> "The normal rule is, of course, that statements made in negotiations entered into between parties to litigation with a view to settling that litigation are inadmissible and therefore cannot be given in evidence. In *Rush & Tompkins Ltd v Greater London Council* ... Lord Griffiths explained that the rule was "founded upon the public policy of encouraging litigants to settle their differences rather than litigate them to a finish". As stated by Robert Walker LJ in *Unilever plc v The Procter & Gamble Co*[14] ... the rule also rests on "the express or implied agreement of the parties themselves that communications in the course of their negotiations should not be admissible in evidence."

In *Oceanbulk Shipping & Trading SA v TMT Asia Ltd & Ors* Lord Clarke of Stone-cum-Ebony made the same point[15]:

> "Robert Walker LJ observed ... that, while ... the rule was recognised as being based at least in part on public policy, its other basis or foundation is in the express or implied agreement of the parties themselves that communications in the course of their negotiations should not be admissible in evidence if, despite their negotiations, a contested hearing ensues. Robert Walker LJ further noted that these two justifications for the rule are referred to in some detail by Hoffmann LJ in *Muller v Linsley & Mortimer*."

As Hoffmann LJ's comments in *Muller v Linsley and Mortimer* suggest, the extent to which the public policy foundation for the rule and/or a foundation based upon the express or implied agreement of the parties in a particular case may influence its operation will vary according to the nature of the case and the true nature of the discussions involved.[16]

19-04 The essence of the rule and the authorities is set out in the following summary in Andrews J's judgment in *Willers v Joyce*[17]:

> "1. The "without prejudice" rule is a rule governing the admissibility of evidence. It is separate from, and independent of the rules relating to legal professional privilege. Although "without prejudice" negotiations have sometimes been referred to in the authorities as "privileged", that is simply shorthand for the protection afforded them, which is similar to the protection afforded to privileged communications.
>
> 2. The rule is founded partly in public policy (the encouragement of parties to speak freely with a view to promoting settlement) and partly in the agreement of the parties: *Unilever plc v The Proctor & Gamble Co* [2000] 1 W.L.R. 2436 per Robert Walker LJ at 2442.

---

sary to provide expressly for that eventuality. However, he went on to conclude that "where communications take place to resolve a live dispute [which] are not expressly labelled 'without prejudice', then they will be treated as impliedly 'without prejudice' on the substantive dispute, and they may not be referred to until after the determination of that dispute, but they may thereafter be referred to on questions of costs".

12 *Ofulue v Bossert* [2009] 1 A.C. 990.

13 *Ofulue* [2009] 1 A.C. 990 at [85].

14 See paras 19-49–19-51.

15 [2010] UKSC 44; [2011] 1 A.C. 662 at [24]. *Briggs v Clay* [2019] EWHC 102 (Ch) at [42]–[74] sets out a detailed analysis of the leading authorities.

16 cf. *Bradford & Bingley Plc* [2006] 1 W.L.R. 2066 per Lord Brown of Eaton-under-Heywood at [62]–[67].

17 [2019] EWHC 937 (Ch) at [32].

3. It applies to render inadmissible evidence of what was said and/or done during the course of negotiations genuinely aimed at settlement: see *Rush & Tompkins Ltd v GLC* [1989] AC 1280 per Lord Griffiths at 1299-1300.
4. It is not limited to admissions made against a party's interest, although the protection of admissions against interest is its most important practical effect: *Unilever* per Robert Walker LJ at 2443-2444. Thus, "without prejudice" negotiations will normally be inadmissible in their entirety.
5. The rule is not limited to statements made in the course of settlement negotiations with the other party to those negotiations. It protects statements that were made to reach settlement with a different party within the same litigation, irrespective of whether settlement was achieved: *Rush & Tomkins Ltd* per Lord Griffiths at 1301.
6. The rule also extends to:
   a) statements made in settlement negotiations in earlier proceedings between the same parties concerning a matter that remains in issue between them: *Ofulue v Bossert* [2009] AC 990;
   b) proceedings between one of the parties to the negotiations and a third party concerning the same subject-matter as the proceedings in respect of which the settlement negotiation took place: Rush & Tompkins Ltd per Lord Griffiths at 1301.
7. The rule is an important one whose boundaries should not be lightly eroded. The protection afforded by the rule should be enforced unless it can be shown that there is a good reason for not doing so (or, as it is sometimes put, "justice clearly demands it"): see *Oceanbulk Shipping SA v TMT Ltd* [2011] 1 AC 662 per Lord Clarke, reviewing observations to that effect made in earlier authorities at [28]-[29].
8. Insofar as the rule depends on the agreement of the parties as well as on policy considerations, there is no reason why the parties cannot enter into an agreement varying its effect (by, for example, broadening or narrowing its scope): see the observations of Lord Rodger and Lord Walker in *Ofulue* at [37] and [55], and of Lewison LJ in *Avonwick Holdings Ltd v Webinvest Ltd and another* [2014] EWCA Civ 1436 at [17].
9. It is not open to one party to "without prejudice" negotiations to waive the protection afforded by the rule unilaterally: see *Avonwick Holdings Ltd* at [21]. The other party may expressly or implicitly consent to the deployment of the "without prejudice" material in evidence or, as Clarke LJ put it in *Somatra Ltd v Sinclair Roche & Temperley (No 1)* [2000] 1 W.L.R. 2436 at [38] they may accept a repudiatory breach of the implied contract that neither party will rely on what was said and done in the negotiations as bringing that contract to an end, freeing them to deploy the previously protected evidence themselves.
10. The rule is not an absolute one and there are several recognised exceptions to it."

THE ISSUES THAT ARISE FOR CONSIDERATION

A number of issues need to be addressed in the context of the "without prejudice" rule. They can be enumerated as follows: **19-05**

(i) When are negotiations without prejudice?
(ii) When will the without prejudice veil be lifted or disregarded?
(iii) When will the disclosure of documents be protected by operation of the rule?
(iv) When can without prejudice negotiations be referred to during interim applications?

(v) At what stage in proceedings may objection be taken to a proposal to adduce evidence of the content of without prejudice negotiations?

WHEN ARE NEGOTIATIONS WITHOUT PREJUDICE?[18]

19-06 Negotiations may be conducted in writing (whether in "hard" or electronic form) or orally (by telephone or other means of electronic or video communication, in a specially arranged meeting or outside court) or in a combination of both. Parties may, of course, have agreed to alternative dispute-resolution (ADR), including mediation.[19] Whatever form the negotiations may take, it is clear on the highest authority that genuine negotiations with a view to settlement are protected from disclosure whether or not the "without prejudice" stamp has been applied expressly to the negotiations. In *Rush & Tomkins Ltd v Great London Council* Lord Griffiths put the matter thus[20]:

> "The ... rule applies to exclude all negotiations genuinely aimed at settlement whether oral or in writing from being given in evidence. A competent solicitor will always head any negotiating correspondence 'without prejudice' to make clear beyond doubt that in the event of the negotiations being unsuccessful they are not to be referred to at the subsequent trial. However, the application of the rule is not dependent upon the use of the phrase 'without prejudice' and if it is clear from the surrounding circumstances that the parties were seeking to compromise the action, evidence of the content of those negotiations will, as a general rule, not be admissible at the trial and cannot be used to establish an admission or partial admission."

19-07 The impression of the "without prejudice" stamp upon the negotiations may, therefore, either be achieved expressly or by implication from the fact that the parties are genuinely seeking to compromise their dispute. This statement of principle lays to rest the possibility of an argument that the failure to use the well-known phrase "without prejudice" means that the party making the offer (or otherwise being engaged in negotiations) intends the offer (or the negotiations) to be open. It follows that any party who wishes an offer of settlement to be regarded as an open one[21] must say so expressly. In *Sampson v John Boddy Timber Ltd*,[22] Sir Thomas Bingham MR, as he then was, said that

---

[18] A thorough and authoritative analysis of without prejudice communications and the earlier UK and Commonwealth authorities was made by (Professor) David Vaver (1974) *University of Columbia Law Review* 85. Although some of the learning in this article has now been overtaken by later authorities, it remains a "learned" and "exhaustive" analysis of the earlier cases (per Robert Walker LJ in *Unilever Plc* [2000] 1 W.L.R. 2436 at 2445) and merits continued attention by all interested in this field: see per Lord Mance in *Bradford & Bingley Plc v Rashid* [2006] 1 W.L.R. 2066. See also McEwan, "Without Prejudice–Negotiating the Minefield" (1994) 13 C.J.Q. 133.

[19] See para. 13-03 onwards and see Ch.35.

[20] *Rush & Tomkins Ltd* [1989] 1 A.C. 1280 at 1299. Lord Griffiths' formulation was accepted by Lord Brown of Eaton-under-Heywood in *Bradford & Bingley Plc* [2006] 1 W.L.R. 2066 at [62]. See also *Sampson v John Boddy Timber Ltd* (1995) 145 N.L.J. 851, noted at para.19-14. The expression "genuinely aimed at settlement" means that the negotiations are aimed at the avoidance of litigation: *Forster v Friedland* (1992) CAT 1052, noted at para.19-47, per Hoffmann LJ. Cf. *Prudential Insurance Co of America v Prudential Assurance Co Ltd* [2003] EWCA Civ 1154.

[21] See para. 18-08 onwards.

[22] *Sampson* (1995) CAT 552. In *Cheddar Valley Engineering Ltd v Chaddlewood Homes Ltd* [1992] 1 W.L.R. 820, Jules Sher QC, sitting as a deputy judge of the High Court, held that where one party to without prejudice negotiations wishes to change the basis of the negotiations and to make an open offer, it is incumbent on that party to spell out that changed basis to the other party with clarity. It was, however, said that if this changed basis "is made in circumstances in which the change would

"the rule is clear that unless a party makes plain its intention that such an offer should be treated as an open offer it is covered ... by the cloak of privilege".

Express stipulation

19-08 The most common means by which negotiations are rendered without prejudice is by express stipulation to this effect. The communication will be headed "without prejudice" or the position made clear at some suitable point within it. A telephone conversation or other visual or oral electronic communication tin which negotiations are conducted will be prefaced with words such as "these discussions are 'without prejudice' and so would any offer made". Provided the material in the negotiations is such that the law permits the cloak of privilege to cover it,[23] an express stipulation of this nature will be upheld by the court.[24]

Implied stipulation

19-09 Where the first of a series of letters is marked "without prejudice" it is likely that the rest of the series will be regarded impliedly as of the same character[25] unless it appears that there is a clear break in the chain of the subsequent correspondence showing that the privilege is not claimed.[26] Where without prejudice negotiations take place and it is agreed that further information should be obtained from a third

---

be brought home to the mind of a reasonable man in the position of the recipient of that information that would be enough". It was further suggested that the mere use of the word "open" may not be enough. It should, perhaps, be observed that these views were expressed in the context of a case where the representative of the party wishing to make the "open" offer did indeed use that expression when the relevant telephone call was made, but it was accepted that the legal executive receiving the offer did not hear it or realise its significance. The facts were somewhat unusual and, it is submitted, the use of the word "open" would in most circumstances operate to displace the without prejudice basis of the negotiations simply because it is a word the significance of which would be understood by the vast majority of practitioners. In *Williams v Hull* [2009] EWHC 2844 (Ch), Arnold J noted that it was "common ground between counsel that the question whether a particular communication is a without prejudice communication is a question which must be assessed objectively as at the date of the communication having regard to the relevant factual circumstances". He referred to *Schering Corp v Cipla Ltd* [2005] EWHC 2597 (Ch), see fn.31, where Laddie J held that where: "[The] court has to determine whether or not a communication is bona fide intended to be part of or to promote negotiations ... [it] has to work out what, on a reasonable basis, the intention of the author was and how it would be understood by a reasonable recipient." In *Pearson Education Ltd v Prentice Hall India Private Ltd* [2005] EWHC 636 (QB), Crane J said, at [17]–[22], that these words did not connote any subjective element in the evaluation.

23 See para. 19-18 onwards.

24 *Rush & Tompkins Ltd* [1989] 1 A.C. 1280, *Walker v Wilsher* (1889) L.R. 23 QBD 335. In *Bradford & Bingley Plc v Rashid* [2006] 1 W.L.R. 2066 Lord Brown of Eaton-under-Heywood (at [63]) said that where communications in question are "expressly made 'without prejudice' ... generally speaking, such communications will attract the privilege even without the public policy justification of encouraging parties to negotiate and settle their disputes out of court". Lord Mance (at [87]) disagreed with that proposition saying that it "is not open to a party or parties to extend at will the reach of the 'without prejudice' rule or of the 'privilege' it affords as regards admissibility or disclosure". Lord Mance's view was followed in *Williams v Hull* [2009] EWHC 2844 (Ch) at [18], and *Avonwick Holdings Ltd v Webinvest Ltd* [2014] EWHC 3322 (Ch) per David Richards J at [26]: "I take the view that the correct approach is that stated by Lord Mance. Marking a document as 'without prejudice' is a strong indication that there is a genuine dispute and a genuine attempt to settle the dispute, but it is not conclusive."

25 *Paddock v Forrester* 3 Sc. N. R. 715 at 734, *Walker v Wilsher* (1889) L.R. 23 QBD 335, per Lindley LJ at 337: "Supposing that a letter is written without prejudice then, according both to authority and to good sense, the answer also must be treated as made without prejudice."

26 The case of *Dixons Stores Group Ltd v Thames Television Plc* [1993] 1 All E.R. 349 is an example of this. It will be important to ensure that an analysis of this nature does not involve the "dissecting out" of particular parts of the correspondence: see para.19-51.

party, the court may hold that the resulting documents are impliedly without prejudice and cannot be referred to.[27]

19-10 The statement of principle in *Rush & Tompkins Ltd v GLC*[28] applies to negotiations conducted by parties to a dispute, whether or not assisted by legal advisers. The character of the discussions, not the character of the participants, leads to the application of the "without prejudice" rule.[29] On one view, it could be said that the agreement giving rise to the application of the "without prejudice" rule is to be implied from the circumstances in which the parties find themselves, namely, that of seeking to negotiate a settlement. However, this may not represent the foundation for such an implication. In *Bradford & Bingley Plc v Rashid* Lord Brown of Eaton-under-Heywood said this[30]:

> "In the present case, of course ... the exchanges in question were *not* marked without prejudice, so there can be no question of any implied agreement here. Rather the critical question here is whether (in Lord Griffiths's words in *Rush & Tompkins Ltd v Greater London Council* ...) 'it is clear from the surrounding circumstances that the parties were seeking to compromise the action'—whether, as Sir Robert Megarry V-C put it in *Chocoladefabriken Lindt & Sprungli AG v Nestlé Co Ltd* [1978] RPC 287, 288, 'there is an attempt to compromise actual or impending litigation'."

The precise juridical basis for the application of the rule will not ordinarily matter when the parties are clearly and unequivocally involved in trying to settle disputed litigation, whether actual or potential. In that situation the rule *will* apply unless any of the grounds for exempting its application is established[31] or unless the negotiations have been expressly stated to be "open".

19-11 The question of when it can be said that the parties are truly negotiating or merely exchanging assertions of their respective positions may not always be easy to determine. This issue has arisen in the context of what have become known as the "opening shots" in litigation,[32] "parting shots" and responses to "without prejudice" communications and admissions and acknowledgements.

"Opening shots"

19-12 As is plain from the foregoing discussion, statements (including specific offers) made in negotiations genuinely aimed at settlement are generally protected from revelation at any subsequent trial of the action in the event that the negotiations do

---

27 *Rabin v Mendoza & Co* [1954] 1 W.L.R. 191 at 293, per Denning LJ, who referred to a "tacit agreement" that the documents should not be used to the prejudice of either party.

28 *Rush & Tompkins Ltd* [1989] 1 A.C. 1280.

29 This also lays to rest consideration of the question of whether negotiations between members of the Bar and/or the solicitors' profession are impliedly without prejudice merely because of the professional status of the participants in the negotiations. See, e.g. *Chocoladefabriken Lindt & Sprungli AG v Nestle Co* [1978] R.P.C. 287 at 289, where Megarry VC recalled his experience of practice at the Bar which was to the effect that discussions "outside the doors of the Court" were never expressed to be without prejudice because it was "so plain ... that the discussions were upon that footing".

30 *Bradford & Bingley Plc* [2006] 1 W.L.R. 2066 at [64].

31 See para. 19-23 onwards.

32 Litigation does not have to exist for the "without prejudice" privilege to arise "[T]he crucial consideration would be whether in the course of negotiations the parties contemplated or might reasonably have contemplated litigation if they could not agree. Confining the operation of the rule ... to negotiations of a dispute in the course of, or after threat of litigation on it, or by reference to some time limit set close before litigation, does not ... fully serve the public policy interest underlying it of discouraging recourse to litigation and encouraging genuine attempts to settle whenever made." per Auld LJ in *Barnetson v Framlington Group Ltd* [2007] 1 W.L.R. 2443 at [34].

not produce a resolution. The question has arisen from time to time as to whether an "opening shot" or an intimation of a willingness to negotiate is similarly privileged. It is, perhaps, axiomatic that discussions cannot be treated as being "aimed at settlement" if at the time they take place there is no dispute (or no extant dispute) to settle.[33] The dividing line between that situation and one when the first tentative steps towards negotiations are taken may not always be that easy to determine. Cases on each side of the line are to be found reported.

In *South Shropshire DC v Amos*,[34] C made a claim for compensation against the district council pursuant to s.120 of the Town and Country Act 1971 following a discontinuance order in respect of the business use of premises occupied by C. C's agents submitted a substantial document to the district council's district valuer containing full particulars of the claim with submissions in support of the claim. It was headed "without prejudice". The submission of this document had been preceded by a direct communication from C to the district council which stated that he wished the amount of compensation "to be negotiated with his agent". The Court of Appeal held that, given C's expressed intention to negotiate, the common practice for such claims to be the subject of negotiation before referral to the Lands Tribunal and a concession that there had been an ongoing dispute prior to the submission of the document, the document was protected by the without prejudice privilege even though it was an "opening shot". **19-13**

In *Sampson v John Boddy Timber Ltd*,[35] an issue arose in a wasted costs application as to the status of a letter written by D's insurers. C had been injured at work and, through solicitors, intimated a claim against D. D's insurers, in a standard form letter, sought details of the claim which C's solicitors provided promptly. After a delay of some weeks C's solicitors wrote to D's insurers asking if they "were prepared to deal with the matter", failing which an application for legal aid would be made. D's insurers wrote back in the following terms: **19-14**

> "We have now completed our investigations into the circumstances of your client's accident and confirm that we are prepared to negotiate a settlement on a compromise basis, arguing that your client ought not to have used the platform as a means of access. If you will provide us with a copy of any medical evidence you have in this case ... our representative will arrange to discuss [the case]."

C's solicitors responded saying that they looked forward to meeting the insurers "and engaging in further negotiations". Eventually, some negotiations took place, but no agreement was reached. At the trial, at which liability was contested by D, C's counsel sought to rely upon the initial letter as an admission of liability subject to an argument about contributory negligence. The Court of Appeal *held* that the letter was to be regarded as without prejudice even though not marked as such. Sir Thomas Bingham MR stated: "the letter was a bona fide offer by the insurers to explore the possibilities of settlement on a compromise basis". Evans LJ stated: "the letter was intended as an acknowledgement and as an offer to negotiate". Aldous LJ stated:

> "[T]he use of the words 'negotiate a settlement on a compromise basis' indicate that the writer was attempting to negotiate a settlement."

---

33 *Daintrey Ex p. Holt, Re* [1893] 2 Q.B. 116 at 119, *Standrin v Yenton Minster Homes Ltd* (1991) CAT 634; *Buckingham CC v Moran* [1990] 1 Ch. 623, noted at para.19-15. See also Ch.2.

34 *South Shropshire DC v Amos* [1986] 1 W.L.R. 1191. The Court of Appeal disapproved *Norwich Union Life Insurance Society v Tony Waller Ltd* (1984) 190 E.G. 42 (Harman J). In *Schering Corp v Cipla Ltd* [2004] EWHC 2587 (Ch), Laddie J ruled as inadmissible an "opening shot" in seeking to initiate negotiations about a possible infringement of patent. C had sought to rely upon a without prejudice letter to obtain an injunction preventing an alleged infringement of patent.

35 *Sampson* (1995) CAT 552.

19-15 In *Buckinghamshire CC v Moran*,[36] a plot of land acquired in 1955 by C for possible use for a proposed road diversion adjoined D's property. In 1967 D's predecessors in title began using the plot of land for their own purposes. In 1971 D acquired the property together with such rights as the vendors may have had over the plot of land. D continued to use the plot as his own. In late 1975 C questioned D's use of the plot of land and he replied in January 1976 saying that it had always been his

> "firm understanding that the [plot] should be kept by the owner of the [property] if and until the [proposed road diversion] was built".

The letter was marked "without prejudice". C challenged this view in subsequent correspondence, but took no action to evict D from the plot of land. In proceedings for possession commenced by C in October 1985 D argued that he had acquired title to the plot by adverse possession. The question of the admissibility of D's letter of January 1976 arose. The Court of Appeal held that the letter was not an "opening shot" in negotiations: it was an assertion of D's rights and contained no or no clear indication of a willingness to negotiate.

"Parting shots" and responses to "without prejudice" communications

19-16 Whilst examples from decided cases are thin on the ground, it would not be impossible to conceive of a situation where an issue as to the admissibility of a closing salvo in an exchange of correspondence might arise. The test must be similar to that relating to "opening shots",[37] namely whether the letter is part of a sequence of correspondence aimed at the avoidance of litigation or whether it merely represents an assertion of the rights of the sender of the letter. However, an obstacle in the path to admissibility is the fact that most letters of the nature described will be in response to without prejudice letters and thus will be privileged from exposure as a result.[38]

19-17 The question of the evidential significance or otherwise of letters written in response to without prejudice letters arises from time to time. The answer to the question is normally quite straightforward: any letter in response to a without prejudice letter will itself form part of the negotiations and thus will be privileged. The privilege, albeit to a degree imposed by the sender of the first letter, is in fact that of the writer of the response. Unless the writer of the response waives the privilege, the other party is not entitled to refer to it.[39] The same principles applies in respect of Calderbank offers.[40] The recipient of a Calderbank offer has no right to refer to that letter on any issue, including the issue of costs. The privilege remains that of the maker of the Calderbank offer.

Acknowledgments and admissions

19-18 An essential feature of the "without prejudice" rule is that something com-

---

36 *Buckinghamshire CC v Moran* [1990] 1 Ch. 623. In *Standrin v Yenton Minster Homes Ltd* (1991) CAT 634, Lloyd LJ, after referring to *Norwich Union Life Insurance Society v Tony Waller Ltd, South Shrophsire DC v Amos and Moran* [1990] 1 Ch. 623, said as follows: "The principle to be derived from those authorities, if it can be called a principle, is that the opening shot in negotiations may well be subject to privilege where, for example, a person puts forward a claim and in the same breath offers to take something less in settlement, or ... where a person offers to accept a sum in settlement of a yet unquantified claim. But where the opening shot is an assertion of the person's claim and nothing more than that, then prima facie it is not protected."

37 See para.19-12.

38 See para.19-17.

39 See, e.g. *C & H Engineering v F. Klucznik & Son Ltd* [1992] F.S.R. 667 at 669–670.

40 See para. 18-05 onwards.

municated on a truly "without prejudice" basis should not be capable of being treating subsequently as an admission or acknowledgment of fact if the negotiations fail.[41] The question of the effect on limitation issues (which arise through the intervention of statute) of things said or stated in what were arguably without prejudice communications arose in each of the cases considered by the House of Lords in recent years.[42]

In *Bradford & Bingley Plc v Rashid*[43] C had been mortgagee of a property formerly occupied by D. D had fallen behind with his mortgage payments, the last payment being made on 3 January 1991. A possession order was made and the property sold in October 1991 leaving an outstanding debt of £15,583. Section 20(1) of the Limitation Act 1980 allows a period of 12 years for an action brought to recover "any principal sum of money secured by a mortgage". The 12-year period began to run on 3 January 1991 when D made his last payment on account. On 14 June 1994 C (which had had difficulties in tracing D) notified D of the debt, indicating that it might be prepared to waive part of it were he to make a substantial immediate payment. Nothing material occurred until 2001 when C asked D to complete a draft income/expenditure form and to make an "offer of repayment". D completed and returned the form, but with no offer of repayment. Solicitors for C wrote to D on June 25, 2001 saying that that was not acceptable and invited his "proposals for repayment as a matter of urgency". On 26 September 2001 an advice centre wrote to C's solicitors on D's behalf in the following terms: **19-19**

"Please find attached [D's] financial statement, which clearly indicates that at present he is not in a position to repay the outstanding balance, owed to you. However, my client requests that once his financial situation is stable he will start to repay. This could be in year 2003/04. Please could you take the above into consideration and reassess this matter and of course his financial situation."

On 2 October 2001 C's solicitors replied as follows:

"Our client is not willing to hold this matter without payment. Our client requires [D's] proposals for repayment. Should your client be in a position to raise a lump sum payment in full and final settlement, our client is willing to consider writing off a substantial amount of this debt."

On 4 October 2001 the advice centre replied saying that D "is willing to pay approximately £500 towards the outstanding amount as a final settlement" and that "[he] is only able to afford this amount by borrowing from friends and family". None of these letters was headed "without prejudice". There was no further correspondence thereafter and on 17 June 2003 C issued proceedings claiming £15,583 plus statutory interest. D took the point that the proceedings were statute-barred and indeed but for any "acknowledgment" of the debt within the terms of s.29(5) of the 1980 Act time would have expired before the issue of the proceedings. C argued that the letters of 26 September 2001 and 4 October 2001 constituted acknowledgments for the purposes of the 1980 Act. D argued that they did not constitute acknowledgments and, in any event, were "without prejudice" communications and should not be admitted in evidence. The House of Lords *held* that the letters of 26 September and 4 October 2001 had constituted clear acknowledgments of C's claim and that neither was to be treated as "without prejudice".

Their Lordships were not entirely unanimous in the reasons given for holding that the letters were not to be treated as "without prejudice". However, the majority (Lords Walker of Gestingthorpe, Brown of Eaton-under-Heywood and Mance) held that: **19-20**

"[T]he without prejudice rule has no application to apparently open communications, such

[41] See para. 19-26 onwards.

[42] *Bradford & Bingley Plc* [2006] 1 W.L.R. 2066.

[43] *Bradford & Bingley Plc* [2006] 1 W.L.R. 2066.

> as those here, designed only to discuss the repayment of an admitted liability rather than to negotiate and compromise a disputed liability."
>
> "No 'statements or offers' were made here with a view to settling a dispute. Since the debt was admitted, there was no dispute.... [D] was simply asking for a concession; he was not giving one."[44]

19-21 A different view of the relevant communications was taken in *Ofulue v Bossert*.[45] The facts of the case were these:

> C1 and C2 were had been the registered proprietors of the freehold of a property since 1976. Thereafter they went to Nigeria and let the property to tenants. In 1981 D1 and his daughter, D2, were permitted to occupy the property by one of those tenants. After C1 and C2 became aware of the occupation of the property by D1 and D2 various meetings and discussions between the parties took place, but on 15 June 1989 C1 and C2 began possession proceedings against D1 and D2 in the High Court. C1 and C2 asserted that they were "the owners and entitled to possession of the property" and that D1 and D1 and D2 were trespassers. In their defence and counterclaim they admitted C1 and C2's title, but denied their right to possession on two alternative grounds: (i) they said that they had taken an assignment of the previous tenant's tenancy; and (ii) they claimed that they had carried out substantial work to the property on the understanding that they would be granted a 14-year lease. Accordingly, they contended either that they had a protected tenancy or that they were entitled to a 14-year lease of the property. They counterclaimed a declaration as to "extent and nature of" their interest in the property. C1 and C2 served a reply and defence to counterclaim in December 1990 and the proceedings were transferred to the Shoreditch County Court in February 1991. During 1991 further and better particulars of the case of each of the parties were provided and lists of documents were exchanged, but nothing then happened in relation to those proceedings for nearly 10 years. However, in a letter dated 12 August 1991 headed "without prejudice" D1 and D2, through their solicitors, wrote to C1 and C2's solicitors stating that they were prepared to buy the property for £20,000. This offer was rejected, but was followed by further correspondence. In a further letter headed "without prejudice" dated 14 January 1992 D1 and D2's solicitors asserted that C1 and C2 would "at the most ... be entitled to six years arrears of rent" and then set out their assessment of the value of the property and of the work carried out to it. The letter concluded as follows:
>
> > "In these circumstances, our client would be willing to make an offer of £35,000 to your client for the purchase of the property."
>
> This offer was promptly rejected by C1 and C2's solicitors. That is where matters rested. In August 1996 D1 died and on April 26, 2000 the proceedings were automatically stayed under the provisions of the CPR. An application to re-instate the proceedings failed and on September 30, 2003 C1 and C2 issued fresh proceedings in the Bow County Court for possession of the property against D2. D2 contended that she had obtained title to the freehold of the property by adverse possession on the basis that any claim that she and her father had had any legal or equitable interest in the property was abandoned and that she (together with her father until August 1996) had been in uninterrupted possession, as trespassers, for more than 12 years before the present proceedings for possession had been begun. Although other arguments were raised, the only relevant answer to this contention was that D2 had acknowledged C1 and C2's title within s.29(2)(a) of the Limitation Act 1980 during that 12-year period: (a) in the defence in the earlier proceedings; and/or (b) in the letter of 14 January 1992. The House of Lords held that both documents relied upon constituted acknowledgments of C1 and C2's title, but (a) was not a continuing acknowledgment so as to cause the accrual of a right of action from day to day for the purposes of s.29. However, (b) remained an acknowledgment but

---

44 *Bradford & Bingley* [2006] 1 W.L.R. 2066 per Lord Brown of Eaton-under-Heywood at [73].
45 *Ofulue* [2009] 1 A.C. 990.

(Lord Scott of Foscote dissenting) was inadmissible (and thus ineffective for this purpose) because it was made in a "without prejudice" offer to settle the earlier proceedings.

Lord Neuberger of Abbotsbury (with whom Lords Hope of Craighead, Rodger of Earlsferry and Walker of Gestingthorpe agreed on this issue) said this[46]: **19-22**

"[I]t is indisputable that the letter was written with a view to settling the earlier proceedings, and that [C1 and C2] can have been in no doubt but that the without prejudice rule was intended to apply to it. Nor is there any question of [D2's] reliance on the rule amounting to some sort of abuse. Further, the fact that the rule is being invoked in relation to negotiations involving earlier proceedings involves no new extension of the rule.... In my view, it is strongly arguable that the principles which govern the admissibility in subsequent proceedings, of a statement made in without prejudice negotiations to settle earlier proceedings, should be the same as those which would govern its admissibility in the earlier proceedings. Indeed, I find it hard to see how the contrary could even be argued in a case such as this, where the two sets of proceedings involve the same parties and very closely connected issues, namely, in each case, whether the [D1 and D2] had any interest in, or right to possession of, the property.

...

The fact that [C1 and C2's] freehold title to the property was not directly in dispute in the earlier proceedings is not ... a good ground for admitting the without prejudice offer to purchase into evidence ... for two reasons ... The first reason is that the only sentence in the letter on which [C1 and C2] seek to rely must ... be covered by the without prejudice rule on any view. That sentence, after all, is the one which contains the actual offer to settle the earlier proceedings. It appears to me that, even if an admission of title in the letter could be admissible because it went to a point which was not in issue in the earlier proceedings, a sentence which implies or contains such an admission could not be admissible if that sentence contains the offer to settle those proceedings. After all, there can be nothing in a without prejudice letter or conversation which is more clearly within the scope of the rule than the actual sentence containing the offer to settle the proceedings in question.

Quite apart from this, it appears to me that, save perhaps where it is wholly unconnected with the issues between the parties to the proceedings, a statement in without prejudice negotiations should not be admissible in evidence, other than in exceptional circumstances such as those mentioned in *Unilever* ... It is not only that the offer contained in the relevant sentence of the letter was connected with the issue between the parties in the earlier proceedings. It is also that the title to the property was in issue in the earlier proceedings in the sense that [C1 and C2] claimed the unencumbered freehold, whereas [D1 and D2] were contending that the freehold was subject to their legal or equitable interest ... it seems to me that it would set an unfortunate precedent [to hold] that an admission of [C1 and C2's] title in a without prejudice letter was sufficiently remote from the issues in a possession action relating to the same land as to be outside the rule."

WHEN WILL THE WITHOUT PREJUDICE VEIL BE LIFTED OR DISREGARDED?

The circumstances in which communications are properly to be regarded as without prejudice have already been considered. In the course of that review it has emerged that unless at the time of the relevant communications there was an extant dispute between the parties, the communications are not covered by the privilege.[47] **19-23**

46 *Ofulue* [2009] 1 A.C. 990 at [87], [90] and [91].

47 See paras 19-12 and 19-19 onwards.

In one sense this does not in reality form any kind of exception to the "without prejudice" rule: it represents a manifestation of circumstances in which the rule never truly comes into play. When attention is focused upon apparent departures[48] from the rule, a somewhat similar analysis is revealed.[49]

19-24 When seeking to identify the circumstances in which the revelation of the contents of what are apparently without prejudice communications may be permitted, it is necessary to have regard to the underlying rationale for the "without prejudice" rule.[50] In *Rush and Tomkins v GLC*[51] the House of Lords endorsed the following appraisal of the rule by Oliver LJ, as he then was, in *Cutts v Head*, an appraisal that continues to influence all analyses of situations where issues concerning "without prejudice" material arise[52]:

> "That the rule rests, at least in part, upon public policy is clear from many authorities, and the convenient starting point of the inquiry is the nature of the underlying policy. It is that parties should be encouraged so far as possible to settle their disputes without resort to litigation and should not be discouraged by the knowledge that anything that is said in the course of such negotiations (and that includes, of course, as much the failure to reply to an offer as an actual reply) may be used to their prejudice in the course of their proceedings. They should, as was expressed by Clauson J. in *Scott Paper Co. v Drayton Paper Works Ltd* [1919] 44 R.P.C. 151 at 156, be encouraged fully and frankly to put their cards on the table ... The public policy justification, in truth, essentially rests on the desirability of preventing statements or offers made in the course of negotiations for settlement being brought before the court of trial as admissions on the question of liability."

19-25 Lord Griffiths said that the

> "underlying purpose of the rule ... is to protect a litigant from being embarrassed by any admission made purely in an attempt to achieve a settlement".[53]

He also emphasised[54] that the rule applies to "a genuine attempt to reach a settlement" and to "genuine negotiations".

19-26 The foregoing statement of the rationale for the rule was analysed further by Hoffmann LJ in *Muller v Linsley and Mortimer*,[55] when considering the basis for exceptions to the rule. That analysis forms a backdrop to the discussion of certain of the exceptions to the general rule. Hoffmann LJ said this[56]:

> "If one analyses the relationship between the without prejudice rule and the other rules of evidence, it seems to me that the privilege operates as an exception to the general rule

---

48 See para. 19-28 onwards.

49 See para.19-26.

50 In *Muller v Linsley and Mortimer* (1996) 1 P.N.L.R. 74, noted at para.19-03, Hoffmann LJ said that: "[Some] of the decisions on the without prejudice rule show a fairly mechanistic approach, but the recent cases, most notably ... *Cutts v Head* ... and *Rush & Tomkins v G.L.C* ... are firmly based on the analysis of the rule's underlying rationale." For Hoffmann LJ's appraisal of the apparent exceptions to this rule and their relationship with its underlying rationale, see para.19-26. Though see para.19-27.

51 *Rush and Tomkins* [1989] 1 A.C. 1280.

52 *Rush and Tomkins* [1989] 1 A.C. 1280, quoting from [1984] Ch. 290 at 306.

53 *Rush and Tomkins* [1989] 1 A.C. 1280 at 1300. In *Muller* (1996) 1 P.N.L.R. 74, noted at para.19-61, Hoffmann LJ said that "the public policy rationale is ... directed solely to admissions".

54 *Rush and Tomkins* [1989] 1 A.C. 1280 at 1301 and 1305.

55 *Muller* (1996) 1 P.N.L.R. 74.

56 *Muller* (1996) 1 P.N.L.R. 74 at 79–80. Swinton Thomas and Leggatt LJJ agreed with the judgment. The analysis did not purport to deal with the exception based upon the revelation of "unambiguous impropriety" perpetrated during without prejudice negotiations to which Hoffmann LJ referred to in *Forster v Friedland* (1992) CAT 1052: see para.19-47.

on admissions (which can itself be regarded as an exception to the rule against hearsay) that the statement or conduct of a party is always admissible against him to prove any fact which is thereby expressly or impliedly asserted or admitted. The public policy aspect of the rule is not ... concerned with the admissibility of statements which are relevant otherwise than as admissions, i.e. independently of the truth of the facts alleged to have been admitted.

Many of the alleged exceptions to the rule will be found on analysis to be cases in which the relevance of the communication lies not in the truth of any fact which it asserts or admits, but simply in the fact that it was made. Thus, when the issue is whether without prejudice letters have resulted in an agreed settlement, the correspondence is admissible because the relevance of the letters has nothing to do with the truth of any facts which the writers may have expressly or impliedly admitted. They are relevant because they contain the offer and acceptance forming a contract which has replaced the cause of action previously in dispute. Likewise, a without prejudice letter containing a threat is admissible to prove that the threat was made. A without prejudice letter containing a statement which amounted to an act of bankruptcy is admissible to prove that the statement was made: *Re Daintrey*. Without prejudice correspondence is always admissible to explain delay in commencing or prosecuting litigation. Here again, the relevance lies in the fact that the communications took place and not the truth of their contents. Indeed, I think that the only case in which the rule has been held to preclude the use of without prejudice communications, otherwise than as admissions, is in the rule that an offer may not be used on the question of costs; a rule which, as I have said, has been held to rest purely upon convention and not upon public policy.

This is not the case in which to attempt a definitive statement of the scope of the purely convention-based rule, not least because ... it depends upon customary usage which is not immutable. But the public policy rationale is, in my judgment, directed solely to admissions."[57]

This analysis was pursued by Lord Hoffmann in *Bradford & Bingley Plc v Rashid* and whilst its validity has been accepted in some respects, it has not commanded unqualified support.[58] In *Ofulue v Bossert* Lord Neuberger of Abbotsbury said of the suggestion that the **19-27**

"public policy aspect of the rule is not ... concerned with the admissibility of statements which are relevant otherwise than as admissions, i.e. independently of the truth of the facts alleged to have been admitted"

that, attractive intellectually as the distinction was, he was "inclined to think that it is a distinction which is too subtle to apply in practice" and "that its application would often risk falling foul of" the need not to dissect out identifiable admissions from the rest of the material.[59]

The fact of agreement

One aspect of Hoffmann LJ's analysis that survives these reservations is the **19-28**

---

57 As Lord Hoffmann acknowledged in *Bradford & Bingley Plc* [2006] 1 W.L.R. 2066 (at [18]) in the *Unilever* [2000] 1 W.L.R. 2436 case (see para.19-49): Robert Walker LJ expressed some doubt as to whether the "large residue of communications which remain protected [as being outside the recognised exceptions to the without prejudice rule] can all be described as admissions." Lord Hoffmann said that he: "[W]ould certainly accept that the without prejudice rule is capable of excluding statements which are not being used as evidence of the truth of what they expressly or impliedly admit."

58 See, e.g. per Lord Walker of Gestingthorpe in *Ofulue* [2009] 1 A.C. 990 at [47]–[52].

59 See para.19-51. In *Oceanbulk Shipping & Trading SA v TMT Asia Ltd & Ors* [2010] UKSC 44; [2011] 1 A.C. 662, Lord Clarke of Stone-cum-Ebony at [32] (with whom Lord Rodger, Lord Walker, Lord Brown, Lord Mance and Lord Dyson JSC agreed) summarised the main exceptions to the "without prejudice" rule identified by Robert Walker LJ in *Unilever Plc* [2000] 1 W.L.R. 2436.

proposition that the evidence showing that an agreement had been concluded is simply relevant to a fact that needs to be proved and there is no countervailing public policy requirement that the evidence to support the fact should be excluded. On any analysis it has always been the position that the contents of without prejudice negotiations can be revealed and considered by the court if an issue arises as to whether an agreement has been concluded.[60] The whole purpose of the privilege would be negated if it were not possible to lift the veil on the negotiations to determine whether an agreement had crystallised. If the result of that determination is that no agreement was concluded, the veil can be drawn again over the contents of the negotiations.[61]

The interpretation of the agreement

19-29 Where the negotiations between the parties to a settlement agreement are or may be relevant to the interpretation of that agreement, the mere fact that the antecedent negotiations were conducted "without prejudice" does not preclude reference to them on the issue of interpretation where evidence of the negotiations is otherwise admissible.[62] While there was some doubt about this, the Supreme Court of the United Kingdom in *Oceanbulk Shipping & Trading SA v TMT Asia Ltd & Ors*[63] affirmed this to be correct. As Lord Phillips of Worth Matravers PSC said[64]:

> "The principle ... can be shortly stated. When construing a contract between two parties, evidence of facts within their common knowledge is admissible where those facts have a bearing on the meaning that should be given to the words of the contract. This is so even where the knowledge of those facts is conveyed by one party to the other in the course of negotiations that are conducted 'without prejudice'. This principle applies both in the case of a contract that results from the without prejudice negotiations and in the case of any other subsequent contract concluded between the same parties."

Lord Clarke of Stone-cum-Ebony JSC explained the position in greater detail,[65]

> "... I see no reason why the ordinary principles governing the interpretation of a settlement agreement should be any different regardless of whether the negotiations which led to it were without prejudice. The language should be construed in the same way and the question posed by Lord Hoffmann should be the same, namely what a reasonable person having all the background knowledge which would have been available to the parties would have understood them to be using the language in the contract to mean. That background knowledge may well include objective facts communicated by one party to the other in the course of the negotiations. As I see it, the process of interpretation should in principle be the same, whether the negotiations were without prejudice or not. In both cases the evidence is admitted in order to enable the court to make an objective assessment of the parties' intentions.
>
> The parties entering into such negotiations would surely expect the agreement to mean the same in both cases. I would not accept the submission that to hold that the process of interpretation should be the same in both cases would be to offend against the principle underlying the without prejudice rule. The underlying principle, whether based in public

---

60 *Rush & Tomkins Ltd* [1989] 1 A.C. 1280, *Tomlin* [1969] 1 W.L.R. 1378, *Oceanbulk Shipping & Trading SA* [2010] UKSC 44; [2011] 1 A.C. 662 at [32].

61 The misconception does still exist amongst some practitioners (and, perhaps, more widely amongst lay persons) that an agreement reached in without prejudice negotiations is not binding until confirmed by an "open" agreement. This is not so: see para.3-67.

62 See paras 5-10—5-16.

63 [2010] UKSC 44; [2011] 1 A.C. 662.

64 [2010] UKSC 44; [2011] 1 A.C. 662 at [48].

65 [2010] UKSC 44; [2011] 1 A.C. 662 at [40]–[42].

policy or contract, is to encourage parties to speak frankly and thus to promote settlement. As I see it, the application in both cases of the same principle, namely to admit evidence of objective facts, albeit based on what was said in the course of negotiations, is likely to engender settlement and not the reverse. I would accept the submission made on behalf of TMT that, if a party to negotiations knows that, in the event of a dispute about what a settlement contract means, objective facts which emerge during negotiations will be admitted in order to assist the court to interpret the agreement in accordance with the parties' true intentions, settlement is likely to be encouraged not discouraged. Moreover this approach is the only way in which the modern principles of construction of contracts can properly be respected.

Any other approach would be to introduce an unprincipled distinction between this class of case and two others which have already been accepted as exceptions to the without prejudice rule ..."

Delay and Adverse Inferences from Apparent Lack of Communication

Reference to the existence (though not normally the contents) of without prejudice communications may be made to rebut any suggestion of delay or laches[66] or, it seems, any adverse inference upon which a party seeks to rely derived from the apparent lack of correspondence or discussion of an issue.[67] The relevant fact is the delay and the negotiations explain it. 19-30

Where a Without Prejudice Document Would Prejudice the Recipient

It is often said that a without prejudice communication cannot be used to the disadvantage of the recipient. This proposition is derived from the case of *Daintrey Ex p. Holt, Re*.[68] It is not wholly clear whether the principle underlying the case should be regarded as being in a different category of exception to the general rule from that referred to below (threats, abuse of rule and lack of good faith), or whether it should be seen as one example of the court not permitting the "without prejudice" rule to be abused. 19-31

In *Daintrey Ex p. Holt, Re*,[69] C commenced proceedings against D for recovery of a sum of money. In a letter headed "without prejudice", sent a short while after, D offered to compound the debt due from him to C. He also stated that he was unable to pay his debts and would suspend payment unless the composition was accepted. C presented a bankruptcy petition relying upon the letter as an act of bankruptcy. It was held[70] that the letter was admissible to prove the act of bankruptcy. It was said[71] that it was not possible to give a notice of bankruptcy without prejudice because 19-32

> "the document in question was one which, from its character, might prejudicially affect the recipient whether or not he accepted the terms offered thereby".

---

66 *Walker v Wilsher* (1889) L.R. 23 Q.B.D. 335.

67 *McFadden v Snow* (1952) 69 W.N. N.S.W. 8, *Pitts v Adney* [1961] N.S.W.R. 535.

68 *Daintrey Ex p. Holt, Re* [1893] 2 Q.B. 116.

69 *Daintrey Ex p. Holt, Re* [1893] 2 Q.B. 116.

70 Vaughan Williams and Bruce JJ.

71 *Daintrey* [1893] 2 Q.B. 116 at 120. In *Cutts* [1984] Ch. 290, both Oliver LJ and Fox LJ treated *Daintrey Re* as establishing that a without prejudice letter cannot be used to the disadvantage of the recipient. Oliver LJ also said (at 304–305) that the Divisional Court in bankruptcy had, in holding that the letter was admissible, "relied upon the fact that there was no dispute and no offer of compromise". In fact, although stating that the existence of a dispute was necessary before a letter headed without prejudice could be regarded as such, the Divisional Court regarded the existence of the proceedings, commenced shortly prior to the letter, as constituting a "dispute" for this purpose: see [1893] 2 Q.B. 116 at 120.

19-33 Hoffmann LJ regarded this as an illustration of the principle that the evidence necessary to prove the fact of an act of bankruptcy was admissible. Whilst that may indeed be so, it is respectfully submitted that *Daintrey* may, on one view, simply be seen as an exception to the general rule which is not easily categorised. Another view is that "the real point of the decision is that the veil was never there in the first place".[72] In *Ofulue v Bossert* Lord Walker of Gestingthorpe said[73] that the

> "sending of the without prejudice letter was an act of bankruptcy, and its character could not be altered simply by affixing a without prejudice label to it."

Lord Neuberger of Abbotsbury said that "a person's act of bankruptcy has an impact on all the creditors and potential creditors of that person" and that, although not mentioned in the judgment of Vaughan Williams J:

> "[T]here is therefore a pretty strong case for saying that the public interest in ensuring that an act of bankruptcy can be referred to and acted on as such, should outweigh the public interest in the without prejudice rule being observed."

19-34 Whatever its precise juridical basis, the decision has stood unchallenged for over 100 years and, it is thought, will probably be followed on similar or analogous facts.

Matters independent of or collateral to the subject matter of the dispute?

19-35 An admission of a fact independent of, or collateral to, the subject-matter of the instant dispute between the parties has traditionally been treated as admissible in evidence subsequently to prove that fact. The foundation for this exception to the general rule is the ancient case of *Waldridge v Kennison*.[74] In that case an admission by one of the parties to a without prejudice discussion that his handwriting appeared on the bill of exchange upon which the action was based was held to be admissible evidence on that issue. Lord Kenyon CJ justified the exception to the general rule on the grounds that,

> "it was a matter no way connected with the merits of the cause, and which was capable of being easily proved by other means".

19-36 However, in *Rush & Tompkins Ltd v GLC*[75] Lord Griffiths made the following observation on *Waldridge v Kennison*:

> "I regard this as an exceptional case and it should not be allowed to whittle down the protection given to the parties to speak freely about all issues in the litigation both factual and legal when seeking compromise and, for the purpose of establishing a basis of compromise, admitting certain facts. If the compromise fails the admission of the facts made for the purpose of the compromise should not be held against the maker of the admission and should not therefore be received in evidence."

19-37 That cautious view of the breadth of this apparent exception has been repeated subsequently. In *Ofulue v Bossert* Lord Rodger of Earlsferry[76] said that:

> "[T]here must indeed be a significant danger that allowing in evidence of admissions of

---

72 *Unilever Plc* [2000] 1 W.L.R. 2436 at 2448, per Robert Walker LJ. But see fn.71.
73 *Ofulue* [2009] 1 A.C. 990 at [53].
74 *Waldridge v Kennison* (1794) 1 Esp. 142.
75 *Rush & Tompkins Ltd* [1989] 1 A.C. 1280 at 1300.
76 *Rush & Tompkins* [1989] 1 A.C. 1280 at [39].

'independent facts' would undermine the effectiveness of the rule as an encouragement to parties to speak freely when negotiating a compromise of their dispute."

Lord Neuberger of Abbotsbury expressly[77] left open

"the question of whether, and if so to what extent, a statement made in without prejudice negotiations would be admissible if it were 'in no way connected' with the issues in the case the subject of the negotiations."

Vaver[78] draws attention to a case which would seem to illustrate a clear example of an admission which, if this exception exists, was rightly received in evidence, although it is questionable whether it would now survive the observations of the House of Lords in *Ofulue v Bossert*: **19-38**

In *Barden v Barden*,[79] C and D were brothers who had been co-defendants in an action against them to recover judgment for goods supplied. During a without prejudice discussion between C and D, on the one hand, and the solicitor representing the plaintiff in the action, on the other, designed to discover whether D was also liable for the debt, D admitted that C was entitled to a half-share in a wheat-crop growing on certain land. This was irrelevant to the subject matter of the discussion. Subsequently, C sued D for a declaration that the two had been partners in connection with the crop of wheat and sought to rely upon the admission. It was held that he was entitled to rely on the admission because it had nothing to do with the issues in the then pending action, but was only incidental thereto.

"Unambiguous impropriety"

The expression "unambiguous impropriety" is a convenient generic description applied to a variety of things said or done during without prejudice negotiations which may, in certain circumstances, be admitted in evidence. It was first used by Hoffmann LJ in *Forster v Friedland*[80] and has since become part of the legal lexicon in this context. It may be helpful to put this exception to the general rule in its historical context. **19-39**

In a brief review of circumstances in which the "without prejudice" label may be disregarded by the court, Lord Griffiths in *Rush & Tompkins Ltd v GLC*[81] referred to the case of *Kitcat v Sharp*[82] as authority for the proposition that a threat will not be subject to the privilege. In fact that case involved letters written by a defendant to a clergyman plaintiff, marked "private and confidential", in which he threatened to publish the statement of claim with his abusive marginal comments appended to it to, amongst others, the plaintiff's bishop. The court treated this as a threatened contempt of court and granted the plaintiff an injunction. Whilst analogous to a threat made in a without prejudice letter, it is not, perhaps, the most direct example. **19-40**

---

[77] *Rush & Tompkins* [1989] 1 A.C. 1280 at [92].

[78] See fn.18.

[79] *Barden v Barden* (1921) 21 S.R.N.S.W. 588 SC, cf. *Field v Commissioner for Railways for New South Wales* (1957) 32 A.L.J.R. 110. See also *McDowall v Hirschfield Lipson & Rumney* [1992] 2 F.L.R. 126.

[80] See para.19-47. In *Unilever Plc* [2000] 1 W.L.R. 2436 at 2444, Robert Walker LJ identified an exception to the general rule as being one where "one party may be allowed to give evidence of what the other said or wrote in without prejudice negotiations if the exclusion of the evidence would act as a cloak for perjury, blackmail or other 'unambiguous impropriety'". And see *Oceanbulk Shipping & Trading SA* [2010] UKSC 44; [2011] 1 A.C. 662 at [32].

[81] See fn.9.

[82] *Kitcat v Sharp* (1882) 48 L.T. 64 (Fry J).

Vaver[83] draws attention to two Commonwealth cases where threats, lack of good faith and abuse of the rule led the court to disregard the without prejudice tag.

19-41 In *Underwood v Cox*,[84] a brother secured the agreement of his sister to, in effect, a rearrangement of the terms of their late father's will under a threat to expose the alleged illegitimacy of one of her children. The threat was made in a letter marked "without prejudice" which was sent in an envelope marked "Personal". When the brother sought to enforce the agreement the sister alleged misrepresentation, fraud, intimidation, undue influence and non est factum. When the brother denied the threats in cross-examination the trial judge disallowed reference to the letter because it had been written without prejudice. The Divisional Court held, without hesitation, that the letter should have been exposed since it contained no bona fide inducement to settle but a "dishonourable threat".

19-42 In *Greenwood v Fitts*,[85] D, during without prejudice negotiations, told C that if the matter went to trial he would perjure himself if necessary and bribe witnesses to perjure themselves to defeat the claim. He further threatened to leave the jurisdiction if C obtained judgment so as to defeat their entitlement. The trial judge disallowed C's attempt to rely on these matters to impeach D's credibility. The Court of Appeal held that the material should have been admitted since the without prejudice rule was never intended to protect threats of this nature. The evidence would tend to show that D did not believe that he had a good case or that on the issue in the case (i.e. whether D had made a fraudulent representation) he was not telling the truth.

19-43 In his commentary on these two cases, Vaver says this:

> "Compromises are regularly induced by such considerations as the desire to preserve good relations between the parties (especially if they are commercial men), the supposed weaknesses of a party's case, the supposed strength of the opponent's case, the costs and risks of litigation, etc. These are part and parcel of settlements in everyday life. On the other hand, misrepresentations, libels, threats of insolvency or bankrup[t]cy in the event of non-acceptance, blackmail, threats of perjury, suborning or flight from the jurisdiction must all amount to the sort of improper pressure which ought to be admitted in evidence if relevant to some matter in issue—this notwithstanding they occur during 'without prejudice' negotiations."[86]

19-44 The issue to which matters of this nature would go in most instances would be the belief or otherwise in the merits of his case by the party engaging in such conduct.[87] The approach in these two Commonwealth cases has been reflected in subsequent decisions in the English courts.

---

83 See fn.18.

84 *Underwood v Cox* (1912) 4 D.L.R. 66 (Ontario Div Ct).

85 *Greenwood v Fitts* (1961) 29 D.L.R. 260 (British Columbia Court of Appeal). See also *Kurtz and Co v Spence & Sons* (1877) L.J. Ch. 238 (a patent case). In the latter case, D contended that C's manufacture of sulphate of alumina infringed D's patent and, during without prejudice negotiations to resolve the dispute, threatened legal proceedings if the manufacture was not abandoned. The Patents, Designs and Trade Marks Act 1883 s.32 enabled a party who was not in fact infringing the legal rights of a person claiming to be a patentee of an invention, to bring an action against that person if that person had himself threatened proceedings for infringement of patent. Kekewich J held that C was entitled to rely upon D's threat for the purposes of injunction proceedings against D. This case was, it is submitted, one which turned very much on the application of the relevant statutory provisions and could not have been seen as having any wider application Indeed, in *Unilever Plc* [2000] 1 W.L.R. 2436 at 2450, it was held that the decision "should no longer be regarded as good law".

86 Vaver (1974) *University of British Columbia Law Review* 85, 152–153.

87 In *Moriarty v London, Chatham and Dover Railway Co* (1870) 5 Q.B.D. 314 at 319, Cockburn CJ said that the: "[C]onduct of a party to a cause may be of the highest importance in determining whether the cause of action ... or the ground of defence ... is honest and just ... [I]t is always evidence which ought to be submitted to the consideration of the tribunal which has to be judged

In *Finch v Wilson*,[88] C had sold D one of two adjacent plots of land and, by a separate contract, had undertaken to construct upon it a bungalow for the occupation of D. Various disputes arose and C brought an action for the unpaid balance of the price under the building contract. D contested C's right to this sum and counterclaimed for damages, including damages in respect of the cost of employing another builder to finish the works. C alleged that they were entitled to extensions under the building contract. A further element of D's counterclaim was for an injunction restraining C from carrying out threats made of assaults and trespass. One of the allegations made was that at a without prejudice meeting between C and D and their respective solicitors, C1 had threatened that he would "ruin the lives of [D] and their family if the issues between him and them were not resolved". An order for exchange of proofs was made pursuant to the then RSC Ord.38 r.2A. D's solicitor had made a proof dealing with the circumstances of the without prejudice meeting and, inter alia, referred to C1's threats of the ruination of D's lives by harassment derived from C's intention to occupy the adjoining plot of land. As a preliminary point, C objected to the admissibility of this aspect of the proof. H.H. Judge Stannard, official referee, held: (a) that the evidence was relevant both to the allegation of alleged threats of trespass and assault and to the question of C's belief or otherwise in the strength of their case; and (b) that "since the purpose of the [without prejudice] privilege is only to protect negotiations bona fide entered into for the settlement of disputes", threats of the nature involved in the instant case were not privileged and the passage in the proof was admissible in evidence.

In *Hawick Jersey International Ltd v Caplan*,[89] C claimed repayment of a loan to D of £10,000 made by means of a cheque. D denied that the transaction was a loan because he had supplied £10,000 cash. D secretly tape-recorded a without prejudice meeting at which: (a) C did not dispute (and indeed accepted) D's repeated assertions that the transaction was not a loan but one involving an exchange for £10,000 in cash; and (b) C expressly or impliedly said that the proceedings were brought to persuade D to reach a fairer settlement and to settle other differences. Anthony May QC, as he then was, sitting as a deputy High Court judge, held that C was threatening to persist with dishonest proceedings and, accordingly, the without prejudice privilege did not apply to the discussion. **19-45**

Each of the foregoing cases has illustrated how impropriety perpetrated under the cover of without prejudice discussions may properly be revealed at a subsequent trial[90]. There is, however, a clear trend in the authorities reflecting the desirability of restricting the occasions when this is permissible to clear cases of "unambiguous impropriety". **19-46**

In *Forster v Friedland*,[91] C (who were eight individuals) owned 4.5 million shares in S Plc. C alleged that on 31 July 1989 D1 agreed with C1 that he (D1) and others for whom he acted would purchase the shares at 73p each. £100,000 was paid at once and completion, it was alleged, was to take place by 31 October 1989. D1 and D2 denied the existence of any legally binding agreement, saying that it was merely an agreement in principle. No completion took place on 31 October 1989 and a letter before action was written a few **19-47**

---

of the facts."

88 *Finch v Wilson* unreported 8 May 1987.

89 *Hawick Jersey International Ltd v Caplan, The Times,* 11 March 1988. In *Forster v Friedland* (1992) CAT 1052, noted at para.19-36, Hoffmann LJ said that a party cannot use the without prejudice rule "as a cloak for blackmail" and, having referred to *Greenwood v Fitts* and *Hawick Jersey International Ltd v Caplan*, described them as "clear cases of improper threats".

90 For an example of where the Hong Kong court admitted evidence on the basis of this exception, see *Crane World Asia Pte Ltd v Hontrade Engineering Ltd* [2016] HKCA 737: in a "without prejudice" letter from D's solicitors to Y in respect of another set of proceedings in which D advanced claims against Y, D made as one of the terms of the offer the stipulation that Y should agree not to prepare any witness statements for C in the present action. That offer was not accepted by Y and C wished to rely upon the evidence at trial.

91 *Forster* (1992) CAT 1052.

days later threatening proceedings if completion did not take place shortly. Various meetings and telephone conversations between the parties took place thereafter, all of which were covertly tape-recorded by C. D1 made his position clear that, if the matter came to litigation, he would deny that there was any legally binding agreement. However, he sought to reassure C that he regarded himself as honour bound to go through with the deal but that he wanted time to so arrange matters as to avoid the need to offer 73p to all the other shareholders in accordance with the City Takeover Code. At first instance the judge held that the discussions were intended to be without prejudice but that they did not fall within the policy of the rule because there was no dispute which the parties sought to resolve and their purpose was merely for D1 to gain time. The Court of Appeal held that the discussions were protected by the "without prejudice" rule in that they were "genuinely aimed at settlement" in the sense of being aimed at the avoidance of litigation. There was an underlying dispute about whether the agreement was legally binding. Hoffmann LJ stated:

> "Provided that this criterion is met, the nature of the proposals put forward or the character of the arguments used to support them are irrelevant."

An argument that D1 was threatening to advance what he knew to be a sham defence, namely that there had been no agreement, whether legally binding or not, was rejected. Hoffmann LJ stated:

> "The value of the without prejudice rule would be seriously impaired if its protection could be removed from [sic] anything less than unambiguous impropriety."

19-48 In *Fazil-Alizadeh v Nikbin*,[92] C and D1 became involved in a dispute, and proceedings ensued, about the circumstances of the acquisition and subsequent refurbishment of a house. In a second action issues concerning a cheque for £150,000 drawn in C's favour by D1 on D2's account arose. In July 1990 a settlement agreement was reached and was reduced to writing. Very considerable disputes arose thereafter about what had been agreed in that agreement. D1 alleged that the agreement had been altered in certain highly material respects by C. C contended that the alterations were made on the very day that the agreement had been drawn up. D2 covertly tape-recorded various conversations between the parties aimed at resolving their differences in the sense of resolving the underlying disputes reflected in the two actions. During one of the conversations, C made observations which, on one interpretation, could be seen as an acceptance that the alterations to the agreement were made at a date later than the date upon which the original agreement had been concluded. D1 and D2 wished to rely upon the contents of that conversation and that issue had been dealt with as a preliminary issue at an interlocutory stage by the county court judge. The Court of Appeal held that the observations in the conversation were ambiguous and did not represent "an unambiguous impropriety". Simon Brown LJ stated:

> "There are powerful policy reasons for admitting in evidence as exceptions to the without prejudice rule only the very clearest of cases. Unless this highly beneficial rule is most scrupulously and jealously protected, it will all too readily become eroded."

19-49 This theme was taken up subsequently again by the Court of Appeal in *Unilever Plc v The Procter & Gamble Co*.[93]

C sought to bring proceedings against D under s.70 of the Patents Act 1977 for threatening C with proceedings for infringement of patent in relation to a particular product or process, the threat relied upon being asserted to have been made during a without prejudice meeting set up to discuss a number of issues between the parties. D applied to strike out C's claim on the grounds that it was an abuse of the process of the court for C to rely upon anything said during the without prejudice meeting. The Court of Appeal upheld the judge's decision to strike out the claim since what occurred at the meeting did

---

92 *Fazil-Alizadeh v Nikbin* (1993) CAT 205.

93 *Unilever Plc* [2000] 1 W.L.R. 2436.

not fall within the recognised exceptions to the normal "without prejudice" rule. There was nothing "oppressive, or dishonest, or dishonourable" in what was said on D's behalf.

Apart from its importance in the particular field of litigation to which it related, the *Unilever* case is also significant for the emphasis it places on the utility of the without prejudice privilege in encouraging full and frank exchanges between the parties. Robert Walker LJ, as he then was, drew attention to the way in which practitioners treated the "without prejudice" rule, particularly in the context of meetings set up to discuss settlement. He said this[94]: **19-50**

> "I have no doubt that busy practitioners are acting prudently in making the general working assumption that the rule, if not 'sacred' ... has a wide and compelling effect. That is particularly true where the 'without prejudice' communications in question consist not of letters or other written documents but of wide-ranging unscripted discussions during a meeting which may have lasted several hours.
>
> At a meeting of that sort the discussions between the parties' representatives may contain a mixture of admissions and half-admissions against a party's interest, more or less confident assertions of a party's case, offers, counter-offers, and statements (which might be characterised as threats or as thinking aloud) about future plans and possibilities."

Robert Walker LJ's general conclusions are also of importance in what might be termed the post-Woolf culture. Having reviewed the earlier authorities he said this[95]: **19-51**

> "They show that the protection of admissions against interest is the most important practical effect of the rule. But to dissect out identifiable admissions and withhold protection from the rest of without prejudice communications (except for a special reason) would not only create huge practical difficulties but would be contrary to the underlying objective of giving protection to the parties, in the words of Lord Griffiths in the *Rush & Tompkins* case ... 'to speak freely about all issues in the litigation both factual and legal when seeking compromise and, for the purpose of establishing a basis of compromise, admitting certain facts.' Parties cannot speak freely at a without prejudice meeting if they must constantly monitor every sentence, with lawyers ... sitting at their shoulders as minders."

He continued by saying that:

> "[The] expansion of exceptions should not be encouraged when an important ingredient of Lord Woolf's reforms of civil justice is to encourage those who are in dispute to engage in frank discussions before they resort to litigation."[96]

---

94 *Unilever Plc* [2000] 1 W.L.R. 2436 at 2443–2444.

95 *Unilever Plc* [2000] 1 W.L.R. 2436 at 2448–2449.

96 *Unilever* [2000] 1 W.L.R. 2436 at 2449–2450. This theme was reinforced in *W.H. Smith Ltd v Colman* unreported 20 March 2000 CA, *Dora v Simper* unreported 15 March 1999 CA, noted at para.19-59, *Berry Trade Ltd v Moussavi* [2003] EWCA Civ 715 and *Savings & Investment Bank v Fincken* [2003] EWCA Civ 1630. In the latter case the issue in effect arose of whether C could give evidence at the trial of an alleged admission by D at a without prejudice meeting held a few days after D had sworn an affidavit inconsistent with the alleged admission. The circumstances were complicated, but the Court of Appeal held that the evidence could not be given. The policy approach referred to in the text was re-emphasised. In *Belt v Basildon & Thurrock NHS Trust* [2004] EWHC 783 (QB), Cox J referred, inter alia, to paras 19-39 and 19-40, and concluded that she did not: "[A]ccept [the] broad submission that the CPR and the Pre-Action Protocol require that an admission or partial admission made in the course of genuine 'without prejudice' negotiations aimed at settling a personal injury claim should automatically lose the cloak of privilege. In any event the approach being suggested by the claimant in this case, it seems to me, would have the effect of deterring parties from genuine attempts to settle claims, which would run completely contrary to the aims of the CPR and the Protocol." The comments of Robert Walker LJ have been expressly approved and adopted by the

19-52 Some of the cases considered above[97] involve the covert recording of without prejudice discussions. This seems to be occurring with greater frequency. In *Fazil-Alizadeh v Nikbin*, Simon Brown LJ issued a timely warning about how readily the court should entertain the reception of evidence obtained in this way. Having expressed himself as noted above,[98] he said as follows:

> "Not least requiring of rigorous scrutiny will be claims for admissibility of evidence by those ... who have procured their evidence by clandestine methods and who are likely to have participated in discussions with half a mind at least to their litigious rather than their settlement advantages. That distorted approach to negotiation ... is itself to be discouraged, militating, as it inevitably must, against the prospects of successful settlement."

19-53 The criterion of "unambiguous impropriety" before the reception of evidence of what was said during without prejudice communications, and the need to protect admissions made during those communications, would seem to rule out from subsequent admissibility a number of things which, said in different circumstances, would either go to an issue in the case or to the credibility of a witness. For example, a changed version of the circumstances of an accident or a changed emphasis on material facts between the time of the without prejudice discussions and the trial would almost certainly not be admissible although plainly relevant.[99] A previous inconsistent statement of a witness could, from the purely evidential point of view, be relied upon as an admission that what was said previously was true and, of course, admissions made in without prejudice discussions are generally protected from subsequent disclosure.[100] Equally, the maintenance of a position during without prejudice negotiations designed to prevent subsequent litigation which is inconsistent with a position necessary to the success of that subsequent litigation if the negotiations fail, is not something that can be revealed in that litigation:

19-54 In *Independent Research Services v Catterall*[101] A brought proceedings for unfair dismissal before an industrial tribunal based upon the assertion that R, his employers, had acted in such a way as to cause a breakdown in the relationship of mutual trust and confidence that ought to subsist between employer and employee. R wished to put before the industrial tribunal at the substantive hearing evidence of a without prejudice letter written by A in which he put forward an offer of settlement which, inter alia, involved him remaining as a full-time employee of the company. This, it was suggested, was inconsistent with the basis of the claim he wished to advance before the industrial tribunal. The Employment Appeal tribunal held that the negotiations were privileged and that none of the exceptions to the "without prejudice" rule permitted the reception of this evidence.

19-55 The authorities referred to in the foregoing analysis have set the parameters within which the issue of the reception of without prejudice material falls to be determined. It would be surprising if every potential scenario in which the issue will arise for consideration has been foreseen. New factual situations will almost

---

House of Lords in *Ofulue* [2009] 1 A.C. 990: see per Lord Rodger of Earlsferry at [43] and Lord Neuberger of Abbotsbury at [89]. Lord Hope of Craighead agreed with both opinions (see [1]). In *Williams v Hull* [2009] EWHC 2844 (Ch), Arnold J rejected a submission that what had been said in a "without prejudice" letter constituted an "unambiguous impropriety".

97 For example, *Hawick Jersey International Ltd v Caplan*, *The Times*, 11 March 1988, *Forster* (1992) CAT 1052 above and *Fazil-Alizadeh v Nikbin* (1993) CAT 205.

98 i.e. the quotation at the conclusion of the note of the case set out in para.19-48.

99 cf. *Williams* [2009] EWHC 2844 (Ch). In *Bradford & Bingley Plc v Rashid* [2006] 1 W.L.R. 2066 Lord Hoffmann said (at [18]): "I do not think that a litigant could be cross-examined to credit on without prejudice correspondence to show that he has made previous inconsistent statements."

100 See para.19-19.

101 *Independent Research Services v Catterall* [1993] I.C.R. 1.

inevitably arise which will require close consideration and, perhaps, adaptation of the present parameters. The court will doubtless have to adopt a pragmatic approach, balancing the primary consideration of ensuring protection for parties involved in true settlement negotiations against the need to ensure that the privilege afforded by the rule is not abused.[102] In *Briggs v Clay*, Fancourt J summarised the manner in which the court should approach the question of accepting the existence of a new exception to the "without prejudice" rule,[103]:

> "As long as without prejudice privilege is not being abused ..., the exclusion of relevant evidence will be normally be the result. As explained in the *Unilever* and *Ofulue* cases, the rule is designedly broad in its effect and the exceptions are narrow. Though the list of exceptions is not closed, any exception must be of the same character or a principled and incremental extension of an existing exception: see *Single Buoy Moorings* at [54], per Teare J."[104]

No broad "interests of justice" exception to the "without prejudice" has yet been accepted.[105] Moreover, the court will not redact material or separate out "without prejudice" material to enable a party to deploy material concerning negotiations, while enabling material that might be taken as admissions concerning the underlying dispute remain inadmissible.[106]

---

[102] A proposition to like effect in the 3rd edition of this work was referred to without disapproval in *Independent Research Services v Catterall* [1993] I.C.R. 1 at 4 The Hong Kong Court of Appeal referred to this sentence in *Crane World Asia Pte Ltd v Hontrade Engineering Ltd* [2016] HKCA 737 at [17]. In *BNP Paribas v Mezzotero* [2004] I.R.L.R. 50 the EAT (Cox J) upheld the decision of the chairman of the Employment Tribunal who ruled as admissible in her claim for sex discrimination what she alleged was said to her by her employers following her return from maternity leave at what they described as a "without prejudice" meeting at which she was told that her job was no longer viable and that it would be best for both parties if her contract was terminated. Cox J held that there was no extant dispute at the time of the meeting and that the discussion was not genuinely aimed at settlement. She also held that it was "very much in the public interest that allegations of unlawful discrimination in the workplace are heard and properly determined by the Employment Tribunal to whom complaint is made, as the appropriate forum under the legislation". An application for permission to appeal was rejected: [2004] EWCA Civ 477. Pill LJ said at [21]: "At the meeting the complainant was plainly vulnerable and at a disadvantage. In the course of the meeting, the proposal is made to her, purportedly under without prejudice protection. Sensibly and reasonably she asked that it be put in writing. That request was refused. I simply do not understand how, if this was a genuine attempt at a without prejudice discussion with a view to settling the case, the applicants could refuse, as they did, to put the suggestion in writing. Indeed, their case would have been stronger had a properly worded letter been sent to her under a without prejudice heading." Cf. *Cowen v Rentokil Initial Facility Services (UK) Ltd T/A Initial Transport Services* unreported March 6, 2008 EAT, Elias J.

[103] [2019] EWHC 102 (Ch) at [118] citing *Unilever* [2000] 1 W.L.R. 2436; *Ofulue* [2009] UKHL 16; [2009] 1 A.C. 990, and *Single Buoy Moorings Inc v Aspen Insurance UK Ltd* [2018] EWHC 1763 (Comm); [[2018] B.L.R. 616 at [54], where Teare J stated, "his summary of the law shows that third parties, in this case the Defendant, can be affected by without prejudice privilege and that the privilege continues notwithstanding that the dispute in question has been settled, as the disputes between SBM and Talisman were in this case. There are however exceptions to the rule where the justice of the case demands it. Mr. Schaff accepted that he could not submit that the court should in any particular case decide whether it was just and equitable to relax the without prejudice privilege. In my judgment an exception can only be allowed where it is of the same character as one already established or where it is an incremental but principled extension of an existing exception, as was the exception in *Oceanbulk v TMT*."

[104] Although note that the requirement for an incremental approach was doubted by Andrews J in *Willers v Joyce* [2019] EWHC 937 (Ch) at [37].

[105] Such an exception was specifically rejected by Fancourt J in *Briggs* [2019] EWHC 102 (Ch) at [119]. cf. *Ofulue* [2009] UKHL 16; [2009] 1 A.C. 990 at [103].

[106] *Briggs* [2019] EWHC 102 (Ch) at [122].

Estoppel

19-56 Evidence may be given of a clear statement made by one party during without prejudice negotiations upon which the other is intended to act (and did act) so as to give rise to an estoppel.[107]

Waiver and mutuality

19-57 Where a party entitled to claim the privilege associated with the "without prejudice" rule waives the privilege by relying on parts of the material at trial, it is established law that the whole of the without prejudice material may be admitted,[108] As Fancourt J observed in *Briggs v Clay*, "waiver cannot be partial or limited".[109] Waiver would thus render all of the "without prejudice" communications admissible.[110] One consequence of this is that ordinarily any waiver must be made expressly. The court will thus not generally imply a waiver of the privilege.[111] Waiver must be consented to by both parties to the settlement negotiations.[112] One party may by, for instance, their conduct in seeking to place material subject to the privilege in evidence at trial, or by referring to it in their pleadings. The other party may then choose to accept such a breach of implied contract not to deploy such material. Equally, they may consent to its use, and thus to the waiver.[113] Where the question arises whether one party has impliedly agreed to the other party's attempt to waive the privilege the court must assess the question whether there was implied consent or agreement objectively. That objective assessment must take account of all the circumstances of the case.[114] In *Property Alliance Group Ltd v The Royal Bank of Scotland Plc*,[115] Birss J accepted the proposition that where a party had waived privilege by referring to material in their pleadings that would otherwise have been subject to the "without prejudice" privilege and hence the waiver had been accepted or impliedly consented to by the other party, that waiver could be set aside should the party make a successful application to amend their pleadings. Where such an amendment, which would result in the party no longer relying on the material at trial, is allowed "no waiver will have taken place merely by virtue of having been pleaded before."[116]

Where a party has relied on without prejudice material at an interim application (e.g. when seeking a freezing order) for the purposes of undermining the merits of the other party's case, the other party is entitled to deploy the contents of the without

---

107 *Hodgkinson & Corby Ltd v Wards Mobility Services Ltd* [1997] F.S.R. 178 at 191, per Neuberger J, referred to in *Unilever Plc v The Procter & Gamble Co* [2000] 1 W.L.R. 2436 at 2444 and noted as an established category of exception to the "without prejudice" rule in *Oceanbulk Shipping & Trading SA* [2010] UKSC 44; [2011] 1 A.C. 662 at [32].

108 *Great Atlantic Insurance Co v Home Insurance Co* [1981] 1 W.L.R. 529 as applied by concession in *Somatra Ltd v Sinclair Roche & Temperley* [2000] 1 W.L.R. 2453 at 2462–2463. Also see *Avonwick Holdings Ltd v Webinvest* [2014] EWCA Civ 1436.

109 [2019] EWHC 102 (Ch) at [77], citing *Somatra* [2000] 1 W.L.R. 2453.

110 Ibid.

111 *Sang Kook Suh v Mace (UK) Ltd* [2016] EWCA Civ 4; [2016] 2 P. & C.R. DG3, *Briggs* [2019] EWHC 102 (Ch) at [78].

112 *Avonwick Holdings Ltd v Webinvest Ltd* [2014] EWCA Civ 1436 at [21], *Cammack v Gresham Pension Trustees* [2016] EWCA Civ 655; [2016] 4 Costs L.O. 691 at [19].

113 *Somatra Ltd v Sinclair Roche & Temperley (No 1)* [2000] 1 W.L.R. 2453 at 2465–2467.

114 *Sang Kook Suh* [2016] EWCA Civ 4; [2016] 2 P. & C.R. DG3 at [37].

115 [2015] EWHC 3272 (Ch).

116 [2015] EWHC 3272 (Ch) at [68].

prejudice discussions or communications to advance its case at trial.[117] Following *Property Alliance Group Ltd*[118], where the party that relied on such material amends their pleadings, such that an order made at an interim application is set aside, assuming the interim application did not go to the merits of the underlying dispute, any waiver of the privilege would also be set aside.[119]

Rectification

In *Oceanbulk Shipping & Trading SA v TMT Asia Ltd & Ors* Lord Clarke of Stone-cum-Ebony JSC accepted that the parties were correct in acknowledging rectification as a further instance where without prejudice communications can be admitted. As he put it[120]: **19-58**

> "A party to without prejudice negotiations can rely upon anything said in the course of them in order to show that a settlement agreement should be rectified. It was so held at first instance in Canada in *Pearlman v National Life Assurance Co of Canada* (1917) 39 OLR 141 and in New Zealand in *Butler v Countrywide Finance Ltd* (1992) 5 PRNZ 447. Neither case contains much reasoning but both courts treated the point as self-evident. In my opinion the parties correctly recognised such an exception because it is scarcely distinguishable from the [fact of agreement exception]. No sensible line can be drawn between admitting without prejudice communications in order to resolve the issue of whether they have resulted in a concluded compromise agreement and admitting them in order to resolve the issue of what that agreement was. This can be seen most clearly where the alleged agreement is oral but, in my opinion, must equally apply where the agreement is partly oral and partly in writing and where the agreement is wholly in writing but the issue is whether it reflects the common understanding of the parties."

WHEN WILL THE DISCLOSURE OF DOCUMENTS BE PROTECTED BY OPERATION OF THE RULE?

In *Rush & Tompkins Ltd v GLC*[121] the issue was whether without prejudice communications between parties to litigation are protected from disclosure to other parties in the litigation. The House of Lords upheld the claim for privilege contended for by one of the parties to a compromise achieved after without prejudice negotiations. Although the distinction between discoverability of a document and its admissibility was recognised, it was felt that the "without prejudice" rule (which essentially goes to the latter) should protect such communications from disclosure **19-59**

---

117 See *Somatra* [2000] 1 W.L.R. 2453 at 2465 where Clarke LJ, said: "[W]here, in support of its case on the merits of an action, a party deploys material which would not be admissible because it forms part of without prejudice communications the other party is entitled to refer to the contents of those same communications in order to advance its own case on the merits. It does not seem to me to be just to allow the first party to obtain an advantage by relying on the without prejudice material in one part of the litigation, as here on an application for *Mareva* relief, where the merits are relevant, and to rely upon the without prejudice nature of the communications when the other party wished to rely upon, say, an admission made in the same without prejudice discussions at the trial, where the merits are of course also relevant." He had previously said: "It seems to me that no party which has taken part in without prejudice discussions should be entitled to use them to his advantage on the merits of the case in one context, but then assert a right to prevent its opponent from doing so on the merits at the trial." And see *Oceanbulk Shipping & Trading SA* [2010] UKSC 44; [2011] 1 A.C. 662 at [32].

118 See fn.131.

119 [2015] EWHC 3272 (Ch) at [71]–[73].

120 [2010] UKSC 44; [2011] 1 A.C. 662 at [32].

121 *Rush & Tompkins* [1989] 1 A.C. 1280.

to third parties.[122]

19-60 The facts were that D1 engaged C as main contractor in respect of a large housing development and C engaged D2 as subcontractors for the ground works. The completion of the contract was much delayed and D2 claimed for loss and expense against C who, in turn, sought to pass these claims on to D1. D1 would not agree D2's claim and, accordingly, C would not pay it. In August 1979 C commenced proceedings against D1 and D2 in which an inquiry as to the loss and expenses to which D2 were entitled under the subcontract was sought and a declaration that C was entitled to be reimbursed that sum by D1. Before the proceedings came to trial C and D1 reached an agreement whereby C accepted £1.2 million in settlement of all outstanding claims under the main contract. It was a term of the agreement that C would accept direct responsibility for all the sub contractor's claims. The terms of settlement were disclosed to D2, but the settlement did not disclose what valuation had been put on D2's claim in carrying out the global settlement. D2 sought specific discovery of the without prejudice correspondence leading to the settlement agreement. The House of Lords held that D2 could not have discovery of the documents. Lord Griffiths stated:

> "I would therefore hold as a general rule that the 'without prejudice' rule renders inadmissible in any subsequent litigation connected with the same subject-matter proof of any admissions made in a genuine attempt to reach a settlement. It of course goes without saying that admissions made to reach settlement with a different party within the same litigation are also inadmissible whether or not settlement was reached with that party.[123]"

19-61 Where, however, the reasonableness of a compromise arrived at as a result of without-prejudice negotiations is put in issue in subsequent proceedings, the without-prejudice correspondence is admissible in those subsequent proceedings.

In *Muller v Linsley and Mortimer*[124] C1 was a director and shareholder in a computer software company, S company. He consulted D, solicitors, about a dispute with other directors and shareholders. D gave him advice about a certain course of action he should take in connection with his fear that the majority of the Board might dismiss him from his employment and thereby activate a provision that he be obliged to sell all his shares to the other shareholders at a fair value. Notwithstanding having attempted to take the advised course of action, C1's fears were realised. C1 and C2 brought proceeding against S company which, in due course, were settled in return for a cash payment and shares which became worth over £2 million when the company was floated. C1 and C2 then brought proceedings against D in connection with the advice alleging that, as a result of that advice, they became dispossessed of their original shares which would have been worth more than £4 million. C1 and C2 asserted that the earlier proceedings, and the settlement of those proceedings, had represented reasonable steps to mitigate their loss. As part of their defence, D denied the reasonableness of the settlement. D sought discovery of the without prejudice correspondence leading to the settlement. The Court of Appeal held that the correspondence was not privileged in the second action. The purpose of the revelation of the correspondence was not to establish the truth or otherwise of any express or implied admissions it might contain, but to determine the reasonableness of C's actions in reaching a settlement. Furthermore, by putting the reasonableness of the settlement in issue, C had impliedly waived any privilege that might exist.

19-62 In *Murrell v Healy*,[125] C was involved in two separate accidents six months apart. His claim in respect of the first accident, which included a claim for loss of earnings, was set-

---

[122] *Rush & Tompkins* [1989] 1 A.C. 1280 at 1305.

[123] *Rush & Tompkins* [1989] 1 A.C. 1280 at 1301.

[124] *Muller* (1994) CAT 1461; *The Times,* 8 December 1994.

[125] *Murrell v Healy* [2001] EWCA Civ 486. See also *Gnitrow Ltd v Cape Plc* [2000] 1 W.L.R. 2319 CA, cf. *V.S.E.L. v Cape Contracts* [1998] P.I.Q.R. P207.

tled before the trial of the assessment of damages in relation to the second accident, his damages claim in that action also containing a claim for loss of earnings. The Court of Appeal held that the trial judge had been correct to admit documents showing how the compensation in respect of the first accident had been agreed. The settlement was relevant to the inquiry as to what injury C had suffered in the first accident.

A document created for the purpose of without prejudice discussions is privileged and an order for production in favour of one of the parties to the litigation will not be made.[126] **19-63**

WHEN CAN "WITHOUT PREJUDICE" MATERIAL BE REFERRED TO AT INTERIM APPLICATIONS?

Want of prosecution

Most substantive trials are preceded by various interim applications. The question arises as to the extent to which it is permissible for a without prejudice communication to be used as an aid to the determination of the outcome of a contested interim application. **19-64**

Consistent with the principle that the existence of without prejudice negotiations may be referred to in order to rebut any inference of delay or laches that may otherwise arise,[127] without prejudice communications have frequently been referred to for that purpose on applications to dismiss for want of prosecution.[128] The practice was approved expressly by the Court of Appeal in *Family Housing Association v Michael Hyde & Partners*[129] in which the public policy considerations underlying the "without prejudice" rule generally[130] were held to have "little or no application"[131] in the particular context of applications to strike out for want of prosecution. Indeed, the content of the negotiations, as opposed merely to their existence, was recognised as having potential relevance in some cases.[132] Without-prejudice communications may have a particular relevance in this context if a claimant seeks to argue[133] that a defendant is precluded from relying upon delay induced by the defendant's willingness for the case to proceed as manifested in those communications.[134] **19-65**

---

[126] *Rabin v Mendoza & Co* [1954] 1 W.L.R. 191 CA. In *Prudential Assurance Co Ltd v Fountain Page Ltd* [1991] 1 W.L.R. 756, Hobhouse J held that witness statements served on D4 by P, pursuant to a direction under the then RSC Ord.38 r.2A, in an action which was subsequently settled, were not to be used by D4 in other proceedings because they remained privileged documents. The same limitation did not arise in relation to an expert's report served by P on D4 pursuant to a direction under what was then RSC Ord.38 r.37.

[127] See para.19-30.

[128] For example, *Phipson on Evidence*, 14th edn (1990), pp.554–555, quoted in *Family Housing Association* [1993] 1 W.L.R. 354 at 361. See also per HH Judge John Newey QC, official referee, in *Simaan General Contracting Co v Pilkington Glass Ltd* [1987] 1 W.L.R. 516 at 519 and the current edition of *Phipson*, 19th edn (London: Sweet & Maxwell, 2017), para. 24–28.

[129] *Family Housing Association* [1993] 1 W.L.R. 354.

[130] See para.19–19.

[131] *Family Housing Association* [1993] 1 W.L.R. 354 at 363, per Hirst LJ.

[132] *Family Housing Association* [1993] 1 W.L.R 354.

[133] See *Roebuck v Mungovin* [1994] 2 A.C. 224.

[134] *Family Housing Association* [1993] 1 W.L.R. 354 at 363.

Security for costs[135]

19-66 It would seem that the normal "without prejudice" rule continues to apply in respect of things said and done by a defendant who applies for security for costs against the claimant. In *Kristjansson v R. Verney & Co Ltd*,[136] the Court of Appeal expressly said that it did

> "not wish to give any encouragement whatsoever to the notion that there is some general relaxation of the 'without prejudice' rule on an [interim] application for security for costs."

The following reasoning of HH Judge Newey QC, official referee, was approved[137]:

> "To allow one party to give evidence of 'without prejudice' communications without the consent of another would be in direct conflict with the general rule excluding such evidence and with the public policy which supports it. Defendants sued by plaintiffs resident abroad or by companies likely to get into financial difficulties would be deterred from exploring possibilities of settlement and making sensible offers for fear of prejudicing their prospects of being able to obtain security for costs. In particular a defendant who has obtained an order for security intended to relate to preparations for trial only would be most unwilling to take any action which might prevent him from obtaining a second order for security in respect of trial costs."

19-67 The court is, however, entitled to take into account an open offer.[138] It was formerly the case that a Pt 36 payment could be taken into account.[139] On that basis, given that no payment of money into court is now required and that a Pt 36 offer is in substance equivalent to a Calderbank offer albeit subject to the provisions of Pt 36,[140] it is arguable that account could be taken of a Pt 36 offer.[141] Nonetheless, the strictures endorsed by the Court of Appeal in *Kristjansson v R. Verney & Co Ltd*[142] would doubtless be regarded as material.

Interim payment applications

19-68 Where an application for an interim payment on account of damages is made in circumstances in which the defendant has not admitted liability or had judgment for damages to be assessed entered against him,[143] it will be necessary for the claimant to show that, if the action proceeded to trial, he,

---

135 For the duty of disclosure, including disclosure of "without prejudice" material, on the part of a claimant for a freezing order, see *Gulf Interstate Oil Co v Ant Trade & Transport Ltd of Malta (The "Giovanna")* [1999] 1 Lloyd's Rep. 867, Rix J.

136 *Kristjansson v R. Verney & Co Ltd* unreported 18 June 1998 CA.

137 *Simaan General Contracting Co* [1987] 1 W.L.R. 516 at 520. It would seem that the case of *Rogers and Parry Ltd (In Liquidation) v Thornham Construction Co Ltd* referred to in para.9–49 of the 4th edn of this work, must be treated as wrongly decided.

138 *Sir Lindsay Parkinson & Co Ltd v Triplan Ltd* [1973] Q.B. 609. See also *Keary Developments Ltd v Tarmac Construction* [1995] 3 All E.R. 534 at 540, per Peter Gibson LJ. The open offer in the *Sir Lindsay Parkinson* case had been made in terms that were designed to give it the same effect as a payment into court.

139 On the basis that the practice prior to the CPR enabled a payment into court to be considered: see *Sir Lindsay Parkinson & Co Ltd* [1973] Q.B. 609.

140 See Ch. 14 onwards.

141 In *Simaan General Contracting Co* [1987], Judge Newey QC said (at 520) that Lord Denning MR (in *Sir Lindsay Parkinson & Co Ltd* [1973] Q.B. 609) would "[no] doubt ... today add Calderbank letters, which are the equivalent of payments in".

142 See fn.129.

143 CPR r.25.7(1)(a) and (b).

"would obtain judgment for a substantial amount of money ... against the defendant from whom he is seeking an order for an interim payment".[144]

Whilst it might arguably be permissible to have regard to a without prejudice offer in order to see the extent to which a defendant has been prepared to entertain the claim,[145] some considerable caution would need to be applied to attaching too great a significance to it. To do so might be tantamount to treating the offer as some form of partial admission which, bearing in mind the express reference to an admission of liability as justifying the making of an order for an interim payment in the rules,[146] and to the rationale for the "without prejudice" rule generally,[147] would result in too liberal an approach. Issues of this nature are probably better determined on an overall analysis of the nature of the cases to be advanced on either side rather than on the consideration of without prejudice material. Where liability has been admitted, or a judgment has been obtained, it was held possible when the RSC governed the practice to have regard to a payment into court when determining the amount of an interim payment.[148] It would follow that a Pt 36 or Calderbank offer (both of which are "without prejudice except as to costs"[149]) could also be relevant in this context.

AT WHAT STAGE IN PROCEEDINGS MAY OBJECTION BE TAKEN TO A PROPOSAL TO ADDUCE EVIDENCE OF THE CONTENT OF WITHOUT-PREJUDICE NEGOTIATIONS?

In the normal course of events, questions concerning the admissibility of evidence at trial are taken before the trial judge at a convenient point during the proceedings, normally when the evidence is about to be tendered.[150] Not infrequently, it is necessary for the judge to hear (or hear about) the evidence *de bene esse* in order to decide the question. If ruled inadmissible, a judge will exclude it from his consideration of the case. This is a familiar judicial exercise[151] even though on occasions it may require what has been described as "mental gymnastics" in order to ensure exclusion of the material from the evaluation of the case.[152] Notwithstanding this generally adopted practice, there are cases where it has been regarded as desirable to determine issues of admissibility prior to the trial.[153] It can save a considerable amount of time and expense both in preparation for, and at, trial if inadmissible evidence is identified and excised early. It may also serve to preempt those rare cases where a party is, by having the issue determined by the trial judge, endeavouring to influence the judicial mind. **19-69**

---

144 CPR r.25.7(1)(c).

145 cf. para.19–65.

146 See para.19–68.

147 See para.19–06.

148 *Fryer v London Transport Executive* unreported 30 November 1982.

149 It should be noted that where parties intend material to be "without prejudice save as to costs" they must make that explicit at the outset of their communications; see *Cammack v Gresham Pension Trustees* [2016] EWCA Civ 655; [2016] 4 Costs L.O. 691 at [15]–[17].

150 *Mason v Walton-on-Thames Charity & Ors* [2010] EWHC 1688 (Ch).

151 Characterised as "controlled forgetfulness" by Knox J in *An action for negligence (1992) (C No.3063), Re*, *The Times*, 5 March 1993.

152 *Savings and Investment Bank Ltd v Gasco Investments (Netherlands) BV* [1984] 1 W.L.R. 191 at 198.

153 *Gasco* [1984] 1 W.L.R. 191; *Chocaladefabriken Lindt and Sprungli v Nestlé Co* [1978] R.P.C. 287, *Finch v Wilson* noted at para.19-44. See also *Crane World Asia Pte Ltd v Hontrade Engineering Ltd* [2016] HKCA 737.

19-70 There is, of course, much to be said for having an issue such as this determined before the trial. Once determined, it will enable the parties to concentrate on deployment of the admissible evidence at the trial. However, it has been said that a decision to exclude evidence at an interim stage on the basis that to admit it would offend the "without prejudice" rule should be made only if the evidence is "plainly and obviously inadmissible". If it is "reasonably arguable" that the evidence is admissible, it may be more just and convenient that the final decision is left to the trial judge who, in the normal way, is better placed to appreciate the significance of the issues in the action and the relevance of the proposed evidence to those issues.[154] If, on the other hand, the preparations for trial would be seriously affected by the question being left to be resolved finally in this way, or substantial unnecessary costs would be incurred by this course, the balance might be tipped back in favour of making a clear decision at an interim stage.[155] The issue tends to come before the court either on the basis of an application by a party to exclude evidence of "without prejudice" material referred to in a witness statement or witness statements put forward by an opposing party or on the basis of an application for permission to rely on such material by a party who seeks to do so.[156]

19-71 In *Dora v Simper*,[157] C sought relief from D1 and others arising from an alleged transfer of assets from a company of which they were directors, the transfer being alleged to have been at an undervalue. C also sought damages for conspiracy. The company had gone into liquidation. C obtained a freezing order against the defendants based upon an affidavit in which the contents of a without prejudice meeting were given during which, it was alleged, D1 had made an improper threat. The defendants sought to set aside the freezing order and, in a preliminary application, sought to exclude the evidence of the alleged improper threat. The Court of Appeal held that it should decide whether the evidence as it stood was capable of disclosing unambiguous impropriety. If it was, it would be for the judge hearing the application to discharge the freezing order to decide whether the threat was made and whether it was an improper threat. The court held that the alleged statement (namely that assets would be transferred so as to render any judgment nugatory) was capable of amounting to unambiguous impropriety.

19-72 In *Williams v Hull*[158] the issue appears to have been raised by a preliminary application to the trial court for permission to rely upon the letter in issue.[159]

---

[154] *Redifusion Simulation Ltd v Link Miles Ltd* [1992] F.S.R. 195, per Mummery J.

[155] *Redifusion* [1992] F.S.R. 195 at 200.

[156] In *Chaudhary v Secretary of State for Health* [2006] EWCA Civ 1648 the Court of Appeal entertained (and granted) an application by a third party (the Secretary of State) to exclude from inclusion in the court papers in an appeal to which the Secretary of State was not a party a "without prejudice" letter written on the Secretary of State's behalf. In *Stuart Midgeley v Oakland Glass Ltd* [2009] EWHC 1100 (QB) a preliminary application to remove certain letters from the trial bundle in a forthcoming trial was refused because there was "nothing in them which can be said to disclose a dispute between the parties".

[157] *Dora v Simper* (1999) CAT 458.

[158] See fn.22.

[159] See *Williams v Hull* [2009] EWHC 2844 (Ch) at [1] of the judgment of Arnold J.

PART 5: ROLE OF LEGAL ADVISERS IN COMPROMISE

This part is devoted to the role that a party's legal adviser, whether barrister, solicitor or other appropriate representative, plays in the process of compromise. Undoubtedly, many skills are required by those engaged in that process: not only the skills of negotiation which result in a compromise on satisfactory terms for the client, but also the skills of persuading a reluctant client to come to a compromise which is undoubtedly in his or her best interests. The role of a legal adviser can be looked at in terms of duties, obligations and responsibilities: to the client, to other members of the profession, to the court and, in some cases, to the public purse. It is from this standpoint that this part is constructed.

CHAPTER 20

Professional Ethics and Responsibilities

GENERAL

The tradition of the Bar and of the solicitors' profession is one of honesty and fair dealing.[1] This extends over many areas, not the least important of which is the course of negotiation with a view to compromise. Dishonest conduct will, of course, carry liability to disciplinary action, but a reputation for untrustworthiness, unreliability and sharp practice is easily gained and by no means readily displaced. It will result in an opponent aware of the reputation being far less disposed to engage in compromise negotiations than might otherwise be the case. Cases in which litigants' interests are not served by the arrival of their cases in court do as a result arrive there. **20-01**

Putting forward a false proposition on behalf of a client is often inevitable if it forms part of instructions received in good faith. Any deliberate attempt to deceive an opponent in negotiations must, however, never occur[2]. From the purely legal point of view, once discovered such a deception would afford grounds for setting aside the agreement.[3] **20-02**

"CONFIDENTIAL" MATTERS DISCLOSED BY CLIENT OR OPPONENT

There are occasions when the legal profession's traditions and standards, as well as the law of misrepresentation,[4] seem to conflict with the duty to keep confidential matters disclosed by a client. Equally, the service of a client's interests may sometimes conflict with the convention of confidence between members of the profession when a conversation is said to be "off the record". Often decisions about the appropriateness or otherwise of a course of action have to be taken instantane- **20-03**

---

1 Hilberry, *Duty and Art in Advocacy* (1959), pp.21–22; See *The Solicitors Regulation Authority (SRA) Handbook* (2018, version 21) and specifically The SRA Principles 2011, esp. Principles 2 and 6. See also *Bolton v The Law Society* [1994] 1 W.L.R. 512 at 518–519.

2 From a regulatory perspective such conduct would arguably conflict with Outcome 11.1, which requires solicitors not to have taken unfair advantage of third parties, see The SRA Code of Conduct 2011, O.11.1. Where counsel is concerned such conduct would arguably fall foul of core duty 3, conduct rule 9.1 of the Bar Code of Conduct: see Bar Standards Board, *Bar Handbook 2019*, 4th edn (April 2019). Such conduct may also, depending on the circumstances conflict with other regulatory requirements that apply, such as those set out in *CEDR's Code of Conduct for Third Party Neutrals* (2018), and particularly its clause 4.1.

3 See Ch.4. For an illuminating analysis of the issues that can arise in contemporary times and the duties of those involved in negotiations, see *Thames Trains Ltd v Adams* [2006] EWHC 3291 (QB).

4 *Thames Trains* [2006] EWHC 3291 (QB).

ously without the opportunity for consultation with more experienced colleagues.[5] Sometimes the opportunity of testing a judgment against that of others is available. Occasionally, recourse may be had to the organs of the professional regulators responsible for assisting on such matters.[6]

20-04 Two past rulings of these professional bodies which impinge on the process of compromise illustrate the issues that can arise:

(a) Although negotiations between counsel with a view to compromise are impliedly "without prejudice",[7] certain admissions of fact made during the course of such negotiations are not so privileged and may be used by an opponent if it be in his client's interests. For example, where a wife's counsel discloses to a husband's counsel that the wife is to remarry and this is of significance to the compromise of financial proceedings between them, it is legitimate for the husband's counsel to use this information in his client's interest.[8]

(b) Where a solicitor acts for a claimant in a personal injuries case and the defendants pay into court[9] a sum arrived at on the basis of the plaintiff's medical condition shown in reports disclosed to them, he is entitled to act on the claimant's instructions to accept the sum paid in even if a further report becomes available showing that the client has only a short while to live, provided the defendants had originally been offered the opportunity of examining the claimant and had declined to do so.[10]

CONFLICTS OF INTEREST[11]

20-05 A solicitor or barrister must not act for or advise a client when an actual or potential conflict of interest arises, whether the conflict of interest arises from some personal interest of the solicitor or barrister himself or by reason of having advised or represented some other party whose interests conflict with the client in question.[12] The most likely cause of such a problem in the context of compromise is where the legal adviser to a party is possessed of confidential information received from the other party to the dispute when previously acting for that other party.[13]

20-06 Clearly, it would be wrong for a legal adviser to act for a client in compromise

---

5 cf. the comments of Lord Diplock in *Saif Ali v Sidney Mitchell & Co* [1980] A.C. 198.

6 For example, the Bar Council's Ethics and Practice Hub (*https://www.barcouncilethics.co.uk*) and its Ethical Enquiries Service (*https://www.barcouncilethics.co.uk/ethical-enquiries-service/*) or The Law Society's Practice Advice Service (*https://www.lawsociety.org.uk/support-services/help-for-solicitors/practice-advice-service/*) [Accessed 28 April 2019].

7 cf. para.19-10 fn.29.

8 Boulton, *Conduct and Etiquette at the Bar*, 6th edn (1975) p.80.

9 No longer required as a matter of practice: see para.14-01.

10 The Law Society, *The Guide to the Professional Conduct of Solicitors* (1974), p.52. See also *Thames Trains Ltd* [2006] EWHC 3291 (QB).

11 See Hollander and Salzedo, *Conflicts of Interest*, 5th edn, and the SRA Code of Conduct 2011 Ch.3; *The Law Society Practice Note on Conflicts of Interest* (25 August 2015).

12 Presumably, it is open to all relevant parties expressly to consent to the solicitor or barrister acting, although it would be rare for such consent to be forthcoming and, in any event, most practitioners would prefer not to be placed in a potentially embarrassing position.

13 In *Bolkiah v KPMG* [1999] 2 A.C. 222 at 235–236 Lord Millett said this of a solicitor's duty of confidentiality to a former client: "Whether founded on contract or equity, the duty to preserve confidentiality is unqualified. It is a duty to keep the information confidential, not merely to take all reasonable steps to do so. Moreover, it is not merely a duty not to communicate the information to a third party. It is a duty not to misuse it, that is to say, without the consent of the former client to

negotiations when possessed of information about the other party's position in relation to the litigation, relevant to the negotiations, obtained when acting for that other party. Equally, a legal adviser is entitled to use, for the purpose of advancing his client's cause, only material which forms part of his instructions.[14] It would follow, it is thought, that it would be improper to seek to assist negotiations on behalf of a client by utilising information about the other party obtained other than by instructions received.[15]

UNFOUNDED CLAIMS

Reference was made at the beginning of this work[16] to the principle that a person who makes a claim knowing it to be unfounded shall not be entitled to retain any advantage derived from its compromise. A legal adviser instructed to pursue a claim acknowledged by a client to be baseless is entitled to refuse to act and indeed should not act. To do otherwise would conflict with his duty to the court where proceedings are involved and, whether or not proceedings are involved, would amount to complicity in his client's fraudulent attempt to obtain some wholly unjustified advantage.[17] It follows that a legal adviser should not act for a client who has intimated the hope that the assertion of a baseless claim will result in some offer of compromise by the other party.[18] Needless to say, there is nothing improper in acting for a party who has some arguable case, though not one thought to have much prospect of success, in the hope that some compromise will result.[19] **20-07**

Equally, it appears that there is nothing professionally improper in acting for a party who pursues a claim or a defence which is plainly doomed to fail,[20] although the distinction between acting in that fashion and continuing unreasonably with an action with "no or no substantial chance of success"[21] is not always easy to define. The dividing line between that which is proper and that which is improper in this context is determined by distinguishing between the pursuit of a hopeless case, on the one hand, and the pursuit of one which amounts to an abuse of the process of the court, on the other.[22] Where either situation confronts a practitioner representing a legally aided client, there is a clear obligation to inform the Legal Aid Agency, **20-08**

---

make any use of it or to cause any use to be made of it by others otherwise than for his benefit. The former client cannot be protected completely from accidental or inadvertent disclosure. But he is entitled to prevent his former solicitor from exposing him to any avoidable risk; and this includes the increased risk of the use of the information to his prejudice arising from the acceptance of instructions to act for another client with an adverse interest in a matter to which the information is or may be relevant." Also see the SRA Code of Conduct 2011 Ch.4; Barmark Requirements (2011), Section 2, para.XII (*https://www.barcouncil.org.uk/media/50412/barmark_req_apr_2011.pdf*) [Accessed 28 April 2019]; Bar Code of Conduct, core duty 6, conduct rule 15.5, 21.4 and guidance notes; Bar Standards Board Confidentiality Guidance (March 2019); and, Hollander and Salzedo, *Conflicts of Interest*, 5th edn (2016), paras 1-009 and 4-015 onwards.

14 cf. Hilberry, *Duty and Art in Advocacy*, (1959) p.11.

15 cf. *A Firm of Solicitors, Re* [1992] Q.B. 959 CA. Also see The SRA Code of Conduct 2011 Ch.4.

16 See para.2-19.

17 See para.2-19.

18 See also the discussion on the question of an intention to proceed with a claim at para.3-10 onwards.

19 cf. *Abraham v Jutsun* [1963] 1 W.L.R. 658. See para.2-19 fn.37 and fn.21.

20 *Ridehalgh v Horsefield* [1994] Ch. 205 at 253.

21 *Davy-Chiesman v Davy-Chiesman* [1984] Fam. 48 at 67, per Dillon LJ.

22 *Ridehalgh* [1994] Ch. 205 at 234 per Bingham MR, "Legal representatives will, of course, whether barristers or solicitors, advise clients of the perceived weakness of their case and of the risk of failure. But clients are free to reject advice and insist that cases be litigated. It is rarely if ever safe for a court to assume that a hopeless case is being litigated on the advice of the lawyers involved. They are there

through a relevant Area Director, so that the interests of the Legal Aid Fund may be protected.[23]

INFORMING CLIENT OF OFFER OF SETTLEMENT

20-09 A legal adviser must inform his client of an offer of compromise.[24] The obligation does not appear to go as far as reasoning the whole matter with the client and quoting authority,[25] although assistance in weighing balancing considerations would, and should, be undertaken.[26]

OVERALL DUTIES TO CLIENT IN COMPROMISE

20-10 How is the advisory role to be played in the context of compromise? The fact that the great proportion of disputes are resolved by agreement before being contested in court,[27] not to mention those which are resolved before proceedings are even instituted, testifies to the existence of pressures on litigants or potential litigants to compromise. Such pressures may come from the litigant himself, from his family and friends, from his legal advisers, or from a combination of each. Despite the existence of some who are prepared to see the whole process of litigation through to its ultimate conclusion, many would prefer simply not to be involved in it at all. They are prepared to concede to the other side simply to avoid the personal anxiety involved. Others are more concerned about the problems of the uncertainties of litigation, the incidence of costs and, in some cases, the publicity associated with the litigation process. Even the best prepared case on paper crumbles when the principal witness gives evidence. Tribunals are composed of human beings who are fallible. In many cases, particularly where a large element of discretion is conferred upon the tribunal, the uncertainties are even greater.[28] One advantage of a

---

to present the case; it is ... for the judge and not the lawyers to judge it. It is, however, one thing for a legal representative to present, on instructions, a case which he regards as bound to fail; it is quite another to lend his assistance to proceedings which are an abuse of the process of the court ... It is not entirely easy to distinguish by definition between the hopeless case and the case which amounts to an abuse of the process, but in practice it is not hard to say which is which and if there is doubt the legal representative is entitled to the benefit of it." These words were quoted with approval by the Privy Council in *Harley v McDonald* [2001] 2 A.C. 678 at [57]. The same approach would presumably apply in other contexts. An area in the context of compromise in which the question arises of whether proceedings represent an abuse of the process of the court is that of the statutory demand procedure and the subsequent issue of a winding-up petition: see Ch.23. The tension between what is proper and improper in this context is reflected upon in *Philex Plc v Golban* [1994] Ch. 205 at 250–253, one of the individual cases decided along with *Ridehalgh.*

23 Civil Legal Aid (General) Regulations 1989 (SI 1989/339) regs 67–69; *R. (Machi) v Legal Services Commission* [2001] EWCA Civ 2010; [2002] 1 W.L.R. 983.

24 *Sill v Thomas* (1839) 8 C. & P. 762 (solicitor).

25 *Blair v Assets Co* [1896] A.C. 409 at 431. For a detailed analysis of the role of a barrister in giving advice on a settlement at court, see *Moy v Pettmann Smith (A Firm)* [2005] 1 W.L.R. 581, especially [59]–[60], and see *Fraser v Bolt Burdon* [2009] EWHC 2906 (QB).

26 See paras 20-10—20-11. See also The Law Society, *Civil Litigation—A Guide to Good Practice*, para.5.1.

27 See para.13-01.

28 "I appreciate that ... it is difficult for practitioners to advise clients in these cases because the rules are not very firm. That is inevitable when the courts are working out the exercise of the wide powers given by a statute like the Matrimonial Causes Act 1973. It is the essence of such a discretionary situation that the court should preserve, so far as it can, the utmost elasticity to deal with each

compromise, provided it is put into effect correctly, is that each party knows his position. Neither party may be completely satisfied with the result but that is far better in many cases than one party facing a bill for legal costs far in excess of that which he ever really conceived as being his liability.

The vast majority of legal advisers will take an early opportunity of warning clients who have embarked, or are about to embark, on litigation of the uncertainties associated even with what may appear to be a good case and the costs which may be involved. In some cases, of course, such advice is unnecessary or goes unheeded. But a failure to give such warnings, particularly when clients of limited means are involved in a dispute the outcome of which, by its very nature, is even more uncertain than what might be termed the mainstream of litigation, would be a serious dereliction of professional duty.[29] **20-11**

KEEP COURT INFORMED

Finally, in the context of professional responsibilities, members of both branches of the profession are required to keep the appropriate court officials informed of possible and actual settlements in cases in which they are involved.[30] **20-12**

---

case on its own facts. Therefore, it is a matter of trial and error and imagination on the part of those advising clients": per Ormrod LJ in *Martin v Martin* [1978] Fam. Law 12 at 20.

29 Due to the operation of CPR PD-Pre-Action Conduct and Pre-Action Protocols (see para.13-06 onwards) the need for legal advisers to give advice about the merits of settlement at an early stage has assumed even greater prominence as a professional obligation. It remains important, of course, that sufficient information about the dispute is available to enable an informed view to be taken of any settlement proposal. A legal adviser who counsels settlement without such information runs the risk of an allegation of professional negligence: see Ch.21.

30 See para.10-25.

CHAPTER 21

Authority to Compromise and the Liabilities of Legal Advisers Arising from Compromise

AUTHORITY TO COMPROMISE—GENERAL

An extremely important topic for discussion in the context of compromise is the extent to which a legal adviser may bind a client to such an agreement.[1] It will be apparent from the discussion that follows that there may be circumstances in which a client is bound by a compromise entered into on his behalf which is not in accordance with his wishes or instructions. The question of the possible liability of the legal adviser to his client is dealt with later.[2] **21-01**

A review of the law in this area prior to the decision of the House of Lords in *Arthur J.S. Hall v Simons*[3] revealed in some instances subtle differences between the extent to which a solicitor might bind a client to a compromise and that to which a barrister might bind a client.[4] Although not clearly articulated in the cases, it was thought that these distinctions arose at least to a degree because of the immunity from suit of barristers in relation to certain work undertaken by them compared with the lack of such immunity in relation to solicitors. There may have been a greater inclination to release a client from a compromise entered into on his behalf by a barrister because of the lack of remedy against the barrister. **21-02**

If that is the true explanation for the subtle differences that existed, then the justification for those differences was removed by the repudiation by the House of Lords of the continued immunity from suit for barristers in relation to civil litigation.[5] Whether or not it was the true justification, the need for continued subtle distinctions in this area hardly seems appropriate with the developments in contemporary legal practice. Furthermore, many of the authorities in this area were decided in an era when the instantaneous and accessible means of communication that now represent everyone's everyday experience were not available. This should mean that, when it matters, no legal adviser (whether barrister or solicitor) should be without express instructions from the client when the question of either making or accepting an offer arises. Whilst that ought to be the norm in contemporary times, it is possible that circumstances will continue to arise when that is not the case. The older authorities and the principles established by them may, therefore, still need **21-03**

---

1 Persons other than legal advisers (e.g. partners and directors) may have authority to compromise. Generally speaking, the normal principles of agency apply, though see Ch.4. For the position of insurers in relation to compromise, see Ch.22.

2 See paras 21-22 onwards.

3 *Arthur J.S. Hall v Simons* [2002] 1 A.C. 615.

4 See 4th edn of this work, para.12-04 onwards.

5 *Arthur J.S. Hall* [2002] 1 A.C. 615.

to be addressed when seeking an answer to problems that arise when communications have broken down.

THE LAW

Actual authority and ostensible (or apparent) authority to compromise[6]

21-04 A barrister or solicitor may be given express authority by a client in connection with a compromise. Vested with such authority he will be able to bind the client to a compromise. Although what follows is a discussion of situations in which a legal adviser may act in connection with a compromise without express authority, as already indicated,[7] it is very unusual nowadays for a solicitor or barrister to take any step towards concluding an agreement of compromise without obtaining their client's express authority. Given the possibility of a claim in negligence this is plainly the only sensible course to adopt.[8]

In circumstances in which it may become relevant to inquire into the question whether a client has given express authority in connection with a compromise,[9] the obtaining of information and relevant documentation will be permitted for the purpose. Such an area of inquiry is not covered by legal professional privilege.[10]

21-05 Where express authority to compromise is given, no question can arise as to the binding nature of the agreement entered into on a client's behalf. The authority of the legal adviser as the client's agent is conferred directly by the client's express instructions. The law of agency does, however, in certain circumstances clothe an agent with actual authority even though the principal has not conferred it directly and expressly upon the agent. The authority is *implied* from the nature of the agent's position or profession.[11] In this sense barristers and solicitors, according to the law as it stands, do possess certain implied powers to compromise on a client's behalf even though not given express powers to do so.[12]

21-06 The difference between an implied authority to compromise and an ostensible (or apparent) authority to do so needs to be noted. It was brought into relief in *Waugh v HB Clifford and Sons Ltd.*[13] As Brightman LJ said[14]:

> "[I]t is … necessary to bear in mind the distinction between on the one hand the implied

---

6 For a general account of agency see, P. Watts and F. Reynolds, *Bowstead & Reynolds on Agency*, 21st edn, (London: Sweet & Maxwell, 2017).

7 See para.21-03.

8 *Waugh v HB Clifford & Sons Ltd* [1982] Ch. 374 at 387 and 389.

9 See para.21-23 onwards.

10 *Conlon v Conlons Ltd* [1952] 2 All E.R. 462 CA: C's solicitors settled his personal injuries claim with D before proceedings were issued. When C subsequently commenced proceedings for damages generally, D raised the settlement by way of defence. C's reply alleged that the solicitors had acted without authority. D sought to interrogate on the scope of C's instructions in connection with the settlement. Although pre-CPR authorities in relation to matters of practice are generally to be treated as of no great assistance, the general approach of this case would probably be followed in a similar situation. It would be impossible to arrive at a just result without the kind of information and documentation sought.

11 *Chitty*, Vol.2, para.31-043 onwards.

12 But see the considerations referred to in para.21-11 onwards. See *Bankfield Farm Ltd v Hart and MacFarlane as Trustees of the Harvest Trust* [2009] NZCA 297.

13 *Waugh* [1982] Ch. 374. See also *Debtors No.78 of 1980, Re, The Times,* May 11, 1985, cf. *Thompson v Howley* [1977] 1 N.Z.L.R. 16. And see *Harford v Birmingham City Council* (1993) 66 P. & C.R. 468; *Leymunlall Nandrame v Lomas Ramsaran (Mauritius)* [2015] UKPC 20; [2015] 4 WLUK 527 at [9].

authority of a solicitor to compromise an action without prior reference to his client for consent: and on the other hand the ostensible or apparent authority of a solicitor to compromise an action on behalf of his client without the opposing litigant being required for his own protection either (1) to scrutinise the authority of the solicitor of the other party, or (2) to demand that the other party (if an individual) himself signs the terms of compromise or (if a corporation) affixes its seal or signs by a director or other agent possessing the requisite power under the articles of association or other constitution of the corporation."

In *Waugh v HB Clifford and Sons Ltd*, by an error, a specific instruction from D to his solicitors not to agree to a matter which would conclude a compromise did not come to the attention of the person dealing with the matter until after he had sent a letter to C's solicitors confirming the agreement. The Court of Appeal held that D's solicitors had been able to agree the terms of the agreement within their ostensible authority, but not within their actual authority. The agreement was held to be binding on D. **21-07**

In the course of his judgment, Brightman LJ reviewed a number of the authorities on implied authority and said this[15]: **21-08**

"The law has become well established that the solicitor or counsel retained in an action has an implied authority as between himself and his client to compromise the suit without reference to the client, provided that the compromise does not involve matters 'collateral to the action'; and ostensible authority, as between himself and the opposing litigant to compromise the suit without actual proof of authority, subject to the same limitation."

Attention was drawn to the proposition that the implied authority may not be as extensive as the ostensible authority. It would be possible for a legal adviser to compromise a claim for a very substantial sum within his ostensible authority, whereas to do so may well be outside his implied authority. Agreeing a substantial figure without reference to the client might result in an allegation of negligence, but it would not affect the validity of the compromise as such. **21-09**

It was emphasised that the only question an opposing litigant needs to ask himself is whether the compromise contains matters "collateral to the suit". The magnitude of the compromise, or the burden which its terms impose on the other party, is irrelevant.[16] Too restrictive an interpretation of "collateral" is not to be given.[17] **21-10**

The judgments in *Waugh v HB Clifford & Sons Ltd* were given in December 1981. All the principles reflected in those judgments in relation to implied authority were derived from decisions towards the end of the nineteenth century or the early part of the twentieth century.[18] The principles thus established arose from events that took place long before the modern world of communications technology became inhabited by all lawyers and their lay clients.[19] As already indicated,[20] no legal adviser would now regard it as appropriate to reach a final settlement of a client's case relying upon an implied authority to do so: express instructions would **21-11**

---

14 *Waugh* [1982] Ch.374 at 387.
15 *Waugh* [1982] Ch. 374 at 387.
16 *Waugh* [1982] Ch. 374 at 387.
17 *Waugh* [1982] Ch. 374 at 388.
18 See para.21-13.
19 Sir David Foskett recalls that the first fax machine was installed in his Chambers in 1988. Fax machines have, of course, long since ceased to be at the cutting edge of modern technology.
20 See para.21-04.

be sought. Choosing a settlement figure within parameters previously agreed by a client[21] is, of course, somewhat different.

21-12 So far as issues of authority are concerned, the same or similar considerations would apply in relation to a significant agreement at the interim stages of a case. For example, an agreed resolution of a freezing-order application or an application for a substantial interim payment would almost certainly not now be concluded without express authority from the client. However, some of the more everyday decisions that need to be made in the context of litigation (for example, extensions of time) will undoubtedly continue to be made as part of the incidental authority[22] of the particular level or status of the legal adviser concerned. Should the matter ever fall to be tested in contemporary times, the implied authority to settle matters within contemplated[23] or actual litigation will probably be confined to relatively mundane procedural issues and not to the resolution of the substantive case.

21-13 If the foregoing analysis is correct, it is unlikely that the ambit of the residual implied authority will be held to be different as between solicitors and barristers. It has always been the case that no implied authority to settle a claim existed until proceedings are in existence[24] and, in relation to barristers, not until the barrister is present at court, either conducting or about to conduct the client's case.[25] The justification for that rule appears to have been that counsel is retained "to advise his client out of court, and to act for him in court".[26] Where counsel is indeed retained purely in that capacity, then an approach to the same effect is likely to apply in current practice, although express confirmation of the making or acceptance of a proposed agreement is invariably obtained either from the instructing solicitor if present or by some other form of communication if not. However, any approach to the extent of the implied authority would almost certainly be one molded by the realities of present-day practice where barristers play a more direct part (often unattended at court by an instructing solicitor) in the affairs of the client.

21-14 A barrister instructed in an interim application or in respect of a case management conference some days before it takes place may communicate with his opposite number in order to resolve matters. Whilst it would now be normal practice for the barrister to obtain authority from his instructing solicitor before agreeing anything, it is at least possible that in this kind of situation an implied authority equivalent to that of the solicitor would be accorded to the barrister.

OSTENSIBLE (OR APPARENT) AUTHORITY

21-15 As already indicated,[27] a legal adviser's ostensible (or apparent) authority may be more extensive than his actual authority, whether the actual authority is express or implied. It follows that ordinarily it is not necessary for the advisers for the other side in a dispute to question the extent of the actual authority when a settlement

---

21 cf. *Thames Trains Ltd* [2006] EWHC 3211 (QB).

22 *Chitty*, Vol.2, para.31-045.

23 Given the emphasis placed in the post-CPR culture upon pre-action steps (including pre-action exchanges of information and possible alternative dispute-resolution (ADR)), it would be difficult to draw a distinction between the content of the implied authority to settle at that stage and the content of the implied authority to settle at the stage when proceedings have commenced.

24 *Macaulay v Polley* [1897] 2 Q.B. 122 CA.

25 *Green v Crockett* (1865) 34 L.J. Ch.606, *Harvey v Croydon Union Rural Sanitary Authority* (1884) 26 Ch. D. 249 CA.

26 *Matthews v Munster* (1887) 20 Q.B.D. 141 at 143, per Lord Esher MR. See also *Richardson v Peto* (1840) 1 Man. & G. 896. Counsel may, of course, be given express authority to negotiate a compromise at an earlier stage.

27 See para.21-09.

proposal is discussed. If the legal representative agreeing to a settlement is doing so on behalf of a party who needs to execute certain formal procedures before even he can be bound by the settlement,[28] then the ostensible authority of the legal representative will not be sufficient to make good that deficiency if it exists. Equally, if the other party knows that the actual authority of the representative acting for the opposing party is limited notwithstanding the position apparently being taken, the ostensible authority will not be operative.[29]

The other limitation upon the operation of the principle of ostensible authority is that it does not extend to "collateral matters".[30] A matter obviously outside the ambit of the dispute being discussed would be regarded as "collateral" for this purpose, but presumably a legal representative may bind his client by the operation of the principle of ostensible authority to a general release of all claims, whether foreseen or unforeseen at the time of the settlement.[31] **21-16**

Misunderstandings between client and legal adviser

Except in the circumstances indicated above,[32] the relationship between an opposing party and his legal adviser in relation to settlement discussions should be of no consequence to the other party. The remedy for a client whose legal adviser has agreed something in excess of his authority would ordinarily be a claim against the legal adviser. As the law now stands,[33] such a remedy is available against both solicitor and barrister.[34] Where, therefore, does the jurisdiction established in the following cases now fit into the picture? **21-17**

In *Neale v Gordon Lennox*,[35] C authorised her counsel to compromise an action subject to a specified condition. He entered into a compromise which did not incorporate that condition. The order giving effect to the compromise was drawn up by C with a view to applying to set it aside. The House of Lords held that there was jurisdiction to set aside the order and, in the circumstances of the case, this should be done. **21-18**

In *Shepherd v Robinson*,[36] counsel for D, with the agreement of D's solicitor, who was present, consented to judgment being entered against his client for part of the total sum claimed, the balance being abandoned. Unbeknown to that counsel, D had decided not to compromise and sent a message to her solicitor at court to that effect. The message had not arrived by the time of the agreement. Prior to the judgment being perfected D, in effect, applied to set it aside. The Court of Appeal held that there was jurisdiction to do so and exercised it in the circumstances of the case. **21-19**

Both the foregoing cases concerned a situation where, on the facts, counsel misapprehended the extent of his authority. The jurisdiction is discretionary and exercised with caution.[37] As has been noted,[38] it has been extended to cover a situation where counsel has deliberately ignored instructions not to compromise. **21-20**

---

[28] See, e.g. para.4-09 onwards.

[29] *Welsh v Roe* (1918) 87 L.J.K.B 520 (McCardie J), following *Brady v Curran* (1868) I.R. 2 C.L. 314, and reviewing fully all the authorities, *Scheyer v Wontner* (1890) 90 L.T. Jo. 116, *Marsden v Marsden* [1972] Fam. Law 280.

[30] See para.21-10.

[31] See para.5-22 onwards. Though cf. *Gardiner v Moore (No.2)* [1969] 1 Q.B. 55.

[32] See paras 21-15 and 21-16.

[33] Following *Arthur J.S. Hall* [2002] 1 A.C. 615.

[34] *Arthur J.S. Hall* [2002] 1 A.C. 615.

[35] *Neale v Gordon Lennox* [1902] A.C. 465.

[36] *Shepherd v Robinson* [1919] 1 K.B. 474.

[37] *Marsden* [1972] Fam. 280.

[38] *Marsden* [1972] Fam. 280.

21-21 As suggested above, the logical position is to say that the remedy of the wronged client in this situation is against his legal adviser. That having been said, it is not difficult to envisage situations in which "wires become crossed" without obvious fault on the part either of the client or the legal adviser. It would be unfortunate if there was no way of resolving a genuine misunderstanding. This jurisdiction, which until overruled by either the Court of Appeal or the Supreme Court, is one which offers the potential for a pragmatic solution to such a situation. Whilst it continues to exist,[39] it will doubtless continue to be exercised with considerable caution and only where a clear injustice would arise if it were not exercised.[40]

LIABILITIES OF LEGAL ADVISERS ARISING FROM COMPROMISE

21-22 A legal adviser, whether barrister (following the abolition of any forensic immunity in relation to civil litigation) or solicitor, can be sued by their client for negligence in connection with advice given and work done in relation to the compromise of litigation.[41]

WHAT CONSTITUTES NEGLIGENCE IN THIS CONTEXT?

21-23 Without intending to be exhaustive, it is submitted that the following actions of a legal adviser would be capable of amounting to negligence:

(a) giving positive advice to a client on a compromise having overlooked some matter (for example a limitation point) which would completely or significantly undermine the case advanced by the other party;
(b) compromising in defiance of express instructions on the matter[42];
(c) (a solicitor) failing to communicate to counsel some express limitation of the client on compromise;
(d) giving positive advice to a client to settle, upon terms which no reasonably competent and well-informed member of the profession would have agreed or advised[43];
(e) failing to insist on a machinery of compromise under which the client's interests are adequately protected.[44]

21-24 These examples merely illustrate situations in which prima facie a breach of duty may arise. Proving one or another will not necessarily mean that a breach of duty is thereby established: that will depend on the circumstances of the case. In relation to points (b) and (c) there will be no breach of duty if the client acts in a way

---

39 The jurisdiction certainly continues to exist: *Balcarran Bundhoo v State of Mauritius* [2007] 4 WLUK 420, PC.

40 *Marsden* [1972] Fam. 280.

41 See fn.34.

42 *Newen, Re* [1903] 1 Ch. 812, per Farwell J.

43 See *Saif Ali* [1980] A.C. 198; *Chown v Parrott* (1863) 14 C.B.(n.s.) 74, *Prestwich v Poley* (1865) 18 C.B.(n.s.) 806; *Newen, Re* [1903] 1 Ch.812, *Waugh v Clifford* [1982] Ch. 374. See, in particular, in the context of advice on settlement, *Moy v Pettmann Smith (A Firm)* [2005] 1 W.L.R. 581 HL. For an example of a case where considerations of advice given at court about a settlement fell for consideration, see *Walker v Chruszcz* [2006] EWHC 64 (QB).

44 This might be regarded as an aspect of (d) above. See Ch.9.

which reasonably leads his legal adviser to believe that he has authorised the compromise.[45]

Furthermore, in any case it will be necessary for the dissatisfied client to establish that the breach of duty caused him some loss or damage. It may be necessary to show that, given proper advice, he would have acted differently.[46] In many cases the issue will be whether the client has, as a result of the negligence, lost the chance of a better result and, if so, what is the measure of that lost chance.[47] Where a breach of duty is established but no loss has been occasioned, nominal damages only will be awarded.[48] **21-25**

In *Butler v Knight*,[49] a solicitor, who thought that a judgment debtor had no funds, compromised the debt despite having instructions to enforce the judgment and not to accept any compromise. The solicitor was held liable for the difference between the whole amount of the judgment debt and the amount received under the compromise. **21-26**

In *McNamara v Martin Mears & Co*,[50] Peter Pain J awarded W £8,000 against her solicitors who negligently advised her to accept £12,000 as a once-for-all settlement with H when she should have been looking for £24,000. The award was discounted for the costs and risks of litigation and for accelerated receipt. **21-27**

In *Dickinson v Jones Alexander & Co*,[51] C was negligently advised in connection with the financial aspects of her divorce from her husband. He was an extremely wealthy man, but the result of the advice she received in connection with the financial affairs was that she, together with the two children, found herself living in a small house in an unsatisfactory area with a mortgage she was unable to service as she was on supplementary benefit. At one stage she started selling her few assets and personal possessions to make ends meet. Douglas Brown J held that the primary measure of damages was what a judge or registrar would have ordered C's husband to pay or transfer to her under the matrimonial legislation, taking into account subsequent variation orders. There was a negligible risk of C having obtained less than a proper award and the damages should be assessed on that basis. Since it was not clear that C's damages would not be taxable in her hands, she should receive the full sum, and not a sum which was assessed on the basis of tax having been deducted. Equally, since it was likely that supplementary benefits paid to her would be recoverable, it was not appropriate for credit to be given for those payments. In addition, she should be awarded damages for the distress and anxiety caused to her as a result of the inadequate settlement. In total she was awarded over £330,000.[52] **21-28**

Where a compromise is concluded as a result of negligent legal advice or representation, but where no identifiable pecuniary loss can be identified, the court will be faced with seeking to place a monetary value on the consequences that flowed from the negligence, provided those consequences were reasonably foreseeable.[53] **21-29**

---

45 *Little v Spreadbury* [1910] 2 K.B. 658.

46 cf. *West Wallasey Car Hire Ltd v Berkson & Berkson (A Firm)* [2010] P.N.L.R. 14.

47 *Allied Maples Group Ltd v Simmons & Simmons* [1995] 1 W.L.R. 1602 CA.

48 *Fray v Voules* (1859) 1 E. & E. 839.

49 *Butler v Knight* (1867) L.R. 2 Exch. 109.

50 *McNamara v Martin Mears & Co* (1983) 127 S.J. 69.

51 *Dickinson v Jones Alexander & Co* [1993] 2 F.L.R. 521. See also *Sharples v Coole & Haddock* [1995] C.L.Y. 1832 CA, and *Beswarick (formerly Bulpin) v Ripman* [2001] 4 WLUK 488 (QBD), HH Judge John Griffith Williams QC sitting as a High Court judge.

52 An appeal by the defendants was settled on the basis of a reduction in the amount of damages awarded.

53 See, e.g. *Heywood v Wellers* [1976] Q.B. 446 CA, *Al-Kandari v J.R. Brown & Co* [1988] 1 Q.B. 665 CA, *Dickinson v Jones Alexander & Co* [1993] 2 F.L.R. 521.

LEGAL ADVISERS IN THE INVESTIGATION OF NEGLIGENCE

21-30 Where a legal adviser is a party to proceedings brought by a former client concerning a compromise, he will be entitled to give evidence in the usual way.[54] Where a legal adviser is called upon by a client to state the circumstances of a compromise in which he was involved, a solicitor may give evidence. It was once the view that the correct course for counsel was to make a statement from his place at the Bar without being sworn, but this does not now seem to reflect the current practice. Written statements by counsel have been received in such circumstances[55] and oral evidence is given in the usual way.[56]

---

54 The duty of confidentiality would not operate in this context either by way of an express or implied waiver. A claim would be stayed if the former client refused to release the duty of confidence.

55 *Gardiner v Moore (No.2)* [1969] 1 Q.B. 55.

56 See, e.g. *Green v Collyer-Bristow and Pointer* [1999] Lloyd's Rep. P.N. 798.

PART 6: INSURANCE INTERESTS AND COMPROMISE

CHAPTER 22

Insurance Interests and Compromise

INTRODUCTION[1]

A great deal of litigation is carried on by insurers exercising their rights of subrogation. The rights to which an insurer is subrogated are those of the insured with the result that any claim made by the insurer in pursuance of those rights must be brought in the name of the insured.[2] Equally, any resistance by an insurer to a claim brought by another party against its insured will be in the name of the insured. Given the volume of disputation that is conducted by or on behalf of insurers, it is clearly of importance to examine the effects that an insurance interest may have upon the settlement of a dispute. **22-01**

In many cases, the existence of an insurer behind a party to a dispute will cause no complications in the context of the compromise of that dispute. However, problems may arise when both insured and uninsured losses constitute the subject matter of the dispute.[3] Furthermore, the settlement of a dispute by either the insurer, on the one hand, or the insured, on the other, may have an impact upon the claims which the one may have on the other.[4] These two situations fall to be examined briefly. **22-02**

SETTLEMENT WITH THIRD PARTY—THE EFFECTS FOR THE THIRD PARTY

THE GENERAL PRINCIPLE

So far as a third party is concerned, the insurer and the insured represent a single **22-03**

---

[1] The Consumer Insurance (Disclosure and Representations) Act 2012 came into force on 6 April 2013. It has not obviously altered the law applicable to settlements. In particular, s.10, which prohibits insurers from contracting out of the provisions of the Act, does not apply to contracts for the settlement of claims: s.10(3). The Insurance Act 2015 received Royal Assent on 12 February 2015, with the majority of its provisions coming into force 18 months later. It was not intended to alter the law applicable to settlement: See the *Law Commission Report* (Law Com No. 353), paras 23.23 and 29.57–29.59. Sections 15 and 16, which prohibit insurers from contracting out of certain provisions of the Act, do not apply to contracts for the settlement of claims: ss.15(3), 16(4).

[2] See, e.g., *Morris v Ford Motor Co* [1973] 1 Q.B. 792, 800, *Smith (M.H.) (Plant Hire) Ltd v Mainwaring (D.L.) (t/a Inshore)* [1986] 2 Lloyd's Rep. 244 CA; *Esso Petroleum Co Ltd v Hall Russell & Co Ltd* [1989] A.C. 643 at 663G, 677A; *Coles v Hetherton* [2013] EWCA Civ 1704; [2015] 1 W.L.R. 160, 173 at [35].

[3] See para.22-04 onwards.

[4] See para.22-11 onwards.

entity or a composite unit.[5] Consequently, any compromise by the insured which constitutes a complete settlement of all issues between him and the third party will be effective as such as between the third party and the composite unit, even though the insurer may not have authorised the settlement of the matters in respect of which it has interests.[6] Equally, it is likely that a similar form of settlement by the insurer will bind the insured.[7] However, the settlement may not be, or purport to be, a settlement of all issues including both insured and uninsured losses.[8]

INSURED AND UNINSURED LOSSES

22-04 Usually the insurer will pay the insured his insured losses under the policy and then seek to recover its outlay against the party (often, of course, his insurers) responsible for causing those losses. The insured may have other claims against that party for which he was not covered by his insurance policy—in other words, the uninsured losses. Parallel (though, not infrequently, disjointed and disconnected) negotiations may be pursued by each in respect of each set of losses. It does happen, from time to time, that a settlement is concluded by either the insurer or the insured which seems to suggest that it represents a complete settlement of both sets of losses. However, where it is plain from the course of the negotiations that only one set of losses was intended to be embraced by the settlement, there will be no bar to the other claims being pursued.[9]

22-05 In *Capon v Evans*,[10] the facts of which have been given previously,[11] the Court of Appeal held that the settlement concluded in correspondence embraced only the uninsured losses and that the insured losses remained capable of being pursued.

22-06 The position becomes a little more complicated if proceedings are commenced in respect of one or other set of losses and a Pt 36 offer is made and accepted, since

---

5 MacGillivray, *Insurance Law*, 14th edn (2018), para.24-052. See, in the context of limitation issues, *Kelly v Bastible & Ors (Executors of The Estate of Christopher Bastible, Deceased)* [1997] P.N.L.R. 227 CA.

6 MacGillivray, *Insurance Law*, 12th edn (2018), para.24-052; *West of England Fire Insurance Co v Isaacs* [1897] 1 Q.B. 226 CA. See also *Buckland v Palmer* [1984] 1 W.L.R. 1109 CA and *Hayler v Chapman* [1989] 1 Lloyd's Rep. 490 CA.

7 This will depend on whether the insurer had authority (actual or ostensible) to settle the whole of the claim, including those matters not strictly the concern of the insurer. In *Kitchen Design and Advice Ltd v Lea Valley Water Co.* [1989] 2 Lloyd's Rep. 221, the policy conferred on the insurer the right "to undertake in the name of, and on behalf of, the Insured the absolute conduct, control and settlement of any proceedings". This was sufficient to confer the necessary authority onto the insurer to settle claims even before any proceedings were commenced. The Insured argued that there was no basis for finding that the insurer had implied or ostensible authority to settle the claim. In light of the finding of actual authority, it was not necessary to decide that issue. However, Phillips J. commented that there was "some force" in that argument. Cf. the position of a legal representative at para.21-04 onwards. The facts of *Kitchen Design and Advice Ltd v Lea Valley Water Co.* [1989] 2 Lloyd's Rep. 221 have been given at para.2-09.

8 See para.22-04 onwards.

9 And note the comment (obiter and in a different context) of Longmore LJ in *B v B* [2005] EWCA Civ 237 at [12] that "Such cases are not common but can happen in a road traffic context where a claimant sues for his uninsured loss and a sum of money is paid into court in respect of that loss, which the claimant accepts without informing his insurers of the existence of proceedings. In such a case it would be axiomatic that one way or another the insurer should be able, in the name of the claimant, to proceed, by way of subrogation, to claim for the loss which is insured and for which he has indemnified the claimant." See also *Buckland v Palmer* [1984] 1 W.L.R. 1109 CA, and *Hayler v Chapman* [1989] 1 Lloyd's Rep. 490 CA, referred to at para.22-08 and fn.18.

10 *Capon v Evans* (1986) CAT 413. See also *Taylor v Wray & Co Ltd* [1971] 1 Lloyd's Rep. 497 CA.

11 See para.3-24.

the effect of acceptance of such an offer is to stay the further pursuit of the action.[12] The stay may be lifted in exceptional circumstances, for example where one party took unconscionable advantage of an error by the other party.

In *Lambert v Mainland Market Deliveries Ltd*,[13] C's stationary motor car was struck and severely damaged by a motor vehicle driven by D's employee. The accident occurred in January 1975. C's insurers paid C £982.97 in respect of the damage to his car and in March 1975 notified D's insurers of the amount they had paid to C and which they sought to recover from them (there being no "knock-for-knock" agreement between the two insurers). On July 2, 1975 C, acting personally, issued proceedings in the county court to recover his uninsured losses of £72.80, although the summons concerning this was not served on D until 22 July 1975. In the meantime, on 3 July, C's insurers had written to D's insurers threatening to instruct C's own solicitors (whom C had previously consulted) to "include our claim" in proceedings to be brought on C's behalf unless payment was made within 14 days. On 29 July, D's insurers, who were then unaware of the proceedings instituted by C, replied offering 50% of the outlay. On 7 August, by which time C's insurers had not responded to the letter of 29 July, D's insurers became aware of C's personal claim. Immediately, they: (a) paid £72.80 into court in respect of C's claim; and (b) wrote to C's insurers withdrawing the offer previously made. C accepted the payment into court. When C's insurers, acting in C's name, sought to have the automatic stay of the proceedings lifted to enable them to pursue their outlay, D's insurers, acting in D's name, argued that there was no jurisdiction to lift the stay, but that if there was, it should not be lifted. The Court of Appeal held that there was jurisdiction to set aside the stay, albeit a jurisdiction that would be exercised "with very great care". It was appropriate to set aside the stay in this case as D's insurers were fully aware that C's insurers were pursuing the (much larger) balance of the claim and that D's insurers were simply trying to take advantage of a procedural provision to bar the pursuit of the rest of the claim. The stay was set aside on the undertaking of C's insurers to repay D's insurers the amount paid into court.[14] **22-07**

In *Buckland v Palmer*,[15] C's car was damaged in an accident caused by D's negligent driving in February 1982. When notified by C, C's insurers told her that they had a "knock-for-knock" agreement with D's insurers and that they (C's insurers) would meet the costs of the damage to her car less a £50 excess. In April 1982, C issued county court proceedings against D seeking to recover that £50. Within a few days D paid into court the full amount of the claim without admission of liability. At some stage after this, C's insurers discovered that D was not insured by the insurers he had mentioned to C at the time of the accident. In September 1982, C's insurers, acting in C's name, began county court proceedings against D personally for the amount of their outlay (some £1,142) less the sum of £50. D sought to strike out the action as an abuse of the process of the court. The Court of Appeal held that the second action should be struck out as an abuse of the process of the court since it constituted the bringing of two actions in respect of the same cause of action, but that the striking out should be without prejudice to an application by C's insurers to remove the stay on the first action imposed when the payment into court was accepted. **22-08**

The position is less clear when one of the two types of claim proceeds to a consent judgment. In the normal course of events, a consent judgment would be **22-09**

---

[12] CPR r.36.14(1).

[13] *Lambert* [1977] 1 W.L.R. 825.

[14] In *Houghton v British Coal Corp* [1997] 1 WLUK 376, referring to *Lambert*, the Court of Appeal stated that this jurisdiction should "be exercised very sparingly and limited to instances of the kind that were there cited, such as a typing error or some misconduct amounting to bad faith or foul play".

[15] *Buckland v Palmer* [1984] 1 W.L.R. 1109.

seen as extinguishing the cause of action by merger.[16] This was recognised by Sir John Donaldson MR in *Buckland v Palmer*,[17] but who went on to say this[18]:

> "I should be surprised and disappointed if this left the courts powerless to do justice if, for example, advantage had been taken of an ill-informed plaintiff by an experienced defendant who offered to submit to judgment in a small sum, well knowing that the plaintiff was under some misapprehension as to the effect upon his right thereafter to proceed with his substantial claim ... I would expect the courts to re-appraise the circumstances in which a judgment could be set aside, if justice so required."

22-10 Although the position is, perhaps, not entirely free from doubt,[19] it would seem that jurisdiction does exist for setting aside a consent judgment for one or other of the two types of loss (the matter usually arising with the settlement of uninsured losses) if the justice of the case requires it.[20] It is thought likely, however, that the jurisdiction would be exercised sparingly[21] and with particular circumspection if third-party interests proper would be affected.[22]

SETTLEMENTS WITH THIRD PARTY—THE EFFECT AS BETWEEN INSURER AND INSURED

22-11 Under the general law of insurance, the insured is required not to do anything which would prejudice the insurer's rights. Indeed, most insurance policies contain express conditions concerning the insured's duties in this regard. Where, contrary to these duties, the insured compromises with a third party, he will be liable to the insurer for the full value of the rights he has compromised.[23]

22-12 Whilst there does not appear to be any direct authority on the point, it is thought that there would be an implied term in any contract of insurance to the effect that the insurer would not exercise its rights of subrogation so as to cause damage to the insured.[24] If an insurer mistakenly binds the insured to an overall compromise in a way that would leave the insured with no direct remedy against the third party, it is submitted that the insured should have a remedy against the insurer.

22-13 Where an insurer settles an insured's claim pursuant to the insured's policy and the insured then sues the person responsible for the loss and settles that claim, the insurer has, by virtue of the doctrine of subrogation, an equitable proprietary right

---

16 *Chitty*, Vol.1, para.25-007.

17 Noted at para.22-08.

18 *Buckland* [1984] 1 W.L.R. 1109 at 1115.

19 In *Hayler v Chapman* [1989] 1 Lloyd's Rep. 490, a case where C, unknown to his insurers, recovered his uninsured losses against D following a contested county court arbitration hearing, the Court of Appeal assumed, without deciding, that the jurisdiction to set aside the award existed, but considered it right not to have done so in the circumstances.

20 There is some support for this jurisdiction existing in respect of a default judgment. In *Holmes v Barnes* [2001] 2 WLUK 725, the claimant's insurers wrongly assumed that the parties' insurers were party to a knock-for-knock agreement. They claimed only uninsured losses and judgment was entered in default. When the defendant's insurers paid only the uninsured losses, the claimant applied to set aside the judgment on grounds of mistake. The Court allowed the application and permitted the claimant to revive the claim and plead the insured losses.

21 cf. *Lambert* [1997] 1 W.L.R. 825, per Megaw LJ at 833.

22 See para.6-84.

23 *West of England Fire Insurance Co v Isaacs* [1987] 1 Q.B. 226, *Horse, Carriage and General Insurance Co v Petch* (1916) 33 T.L.R. 131, *Boag v Standard Marine Insurance Co* [1937] 2 K.B. 113. See also *Faircharm Investments Ltd v Citibank International Plc* [1998] Lloyd's Rep. 127 CA, and *Ballast Plc, Re* [2006] EWHC 3189 (Ch).

24 MacGillivray, *Insurance Law*, 14th edn (2018), para.23-059.

in the form of a lien over the settlement monies.[25] The insurer does not, however, have any proprietary interest in the insured's cause of action itself.[26]

A policy may require that the insured (or re-insured) obtain the prior approval of the insurer (or re-insurer) before settling a claim. Where such a requirement exists, there may be implied a duty on the insurer (or re-insurer) not to withhold approval unreasonably, arbitrarily or capriciously.[27] In *Gan Insurance Co Ltd v Tai Ping Insurance Co Ltd (No.2)*,[28] considering such a provision in a re-insurance policy, the Court of Appeal held that "any withholding of approval by reinsurers should take place in good faith after consideration of and on the basis of the facts giving rise to the particular claim and not with reference to considerations wholly extraneous to the subject-matter of the particular reinsurance".[29] **22-14**

SETTLEMENT WITH THIRD PARTY—THE EFFECT ON A CO-INSURER

An insured may be covered for the same risk in the same interest in the same subject-matter by more than one policy of insurance. In the normal course of events, where one insurer reasonably settles the claim of a third party brought against the insured, that insurer is entitled in equity to a contribution from the co-insurer.[30] Where, however, the insurer that settles the claim of the third party in full has in its policy with its insured a rateable proportion clause, it was held in *Legal & General Assurance Society Ltd v Drake Insurance Co Ltd*[31] that the insurer was precluded from claiming a contribution from its co-insurer because the amount paid to the third party in excess of the appropriate rateable proportion was to be regarded as a voluntary payment and the right to claim a contribution in equity arises only where an insurer has been obliged under its policy to pay more than its rateable proportion. However, in *Eagle Star Insurance Co Ltd v Provincial Insurance Plc*[32] the Judicial Committee of the Privy Council held that where two insurers were under a statutory liability to indemnify a third party, the right of one insurer to a contribution from the other had to be determined in accordance "with the extent of their respective liabilities to the ... insured under the separate contracts of insurance".[33] The decision in *Legal & General v Drake* was further doubted by the **22-15**

[25] *Napier and Ettrick (Lord) v Hunter* [1993] A.C. 713.

[26] *Re Ballast Plc* [2007] Lloyd's Rep. I.R. 742 at [40]–[51]. This was followed in *Dornoch Ltd v Westminster International BV* [2009] 2 Lloyd's Rep. 191, albeit Tomlinson J noted at [52] that the issue of whether the insurer's interest in the cause of action might have been an equitable lien or charge was only "faintly pressed".

[27] This may be seen as an application of the wider principle subsequently endorsed by the Supreme Court in *Braganza v BP Shipping* [2015] UKSC 17, [2015] 1 W.L.R. 1661.

[28] *Gan Insurance Co Ltd v Tai Ping Insurance Co Ltd (No.2)* [2001] EWCA Civ 1047; [2001] Lloyd's Rep. I.R. 667.

[29] Per Mance LJ (as he then was) at [67].

[30] MacGillivray, *Insurance Law*, 14th edn (2018), para.25-032; *Chitty*, 33rd edn (2015), Vol.2, para.42-118.

[31] *Legal & General Assurance Society Ltd v Drake Insurance Co Ltd* [1992] Q.B. 887 CA, overruling *Monksfield v Vehicle & General Insurance Co Ltd* [1971] 1 Lloyd's Rep. 139.

[32] *Eagle Star Insurance Co Ltd v Provincial Insurance Plc* [1994] 1 A.C. 122.

[33] *Eagle Star* [1994] 1 A.C. 122 at 141. This approach was said to be more appropriate than that of determining the issue on the basis of their respective statutory liabilities because their respective contractual liabilities to the insured "will indicate the scale of the double insurance". The case of *Monksfield v Vehicle General Insurance Co Ltd* [1971] 1 Lloyd's Rep. 134, was said to have been correctly decided and *Legal & General Assurance Society Ltd v Drake Insurance Co Ltd* [1992] Q.B.

Court of Appeal in *Drake v Provident*[34] where Rix LJ made clear[35] that the mere existence of a rateable proportion clause will not exclude the operation of the equitable rule of contribution.

REINSURANCE AND "FOLLOW THE SETTLEMENTS" CLAUSES[36]

22-16 Reinsurance is the process by which an insurer of a risk takes out insurance of that risk with another insurer.[37] The original insurer is called the reinsured (or the reassured). A standard clause in the London reinsurance market between the reinsured and the reinsurer (called the "follow the settlements" clause) is in these terms:

> "All loss settlements by the reassured including compromise settlements and the establishment of funds for the settlement of losses shall be binding upon the reinsurers, providing such settlements are within the terms and conditions of the original policies and/or contracts and within the terms and conditions of this reinsurance."

22-17 The effect of the provisos in the above clause was considered by the House of Lords in *Hill v Mercantile and General Reinsurance Co Plc*.[38] A "compromise settlement" of the reassured will be excluded from the "follow the settlements" clause

---

887 CA, was not followed. In *Bolton MBC v Municipal Mutual Insurance Ltd* [2006] 1 W.L.R. 1492, the CA expressed preference for the reasoning in the *Eagle Star Insurance* case. "An insurer is entitled to say that he has only agreed to insure on certain terms and he ought to be able to rely on that position not only against his insured but also as against a co-insurer. Indeed it is hardly a case of double insurance at all if one insurer agrees to be liable without imposing any condition precedent to liability in relation to a notice requirement and another insurer says he will only be liable if due notice of accident or claim has been given." Per Longmore LJ, with whom Auld and Hallett LJJ agreed.

34 [2003] EWCA Civ 1834; [2004] Q.B. 601.

35 At [114].

36 See MacGillivray, *Insurance Law*, 14th edn (2018), para.35-080 onwards. "[The] effect of a clause binding reinsurers to follow settlements of the insurers, is that the insurers agree to indemnify insurers in the event that they settle a claim by their assured, i.e., when they dispose, or bind themselves to dispose, of a claim, whether by reason of admission or compromise provided [1] that the claim so recognised by them falls within the risks covered by the policy of reinsurance as a matter of law, and provided [2] also that in settling the claim the insurers have acted honestly and have taken all proper and business like steps in making the settlement": per Robert Goff LJ in *The Insurance Co of Africa v Scor (UK) Reinsurance Co Ltd* [1985] 1 Lloyd's Rep. 312 at 322. "The commercial purpose of a follow settlements clause is that from the insurers' point of view it saves time and costs and also makes co-insurance more marketable which is attractive to those seeking insurance. It simplifies claims settlement; see *Roar Marine v Bimeh Iran Insurance* [1998] 1 Lloyd's Reports 423": per Teare J in *San Evans Maritime Inc, Livanbros Maritime SA, Mrs Chariklia Livanou v Aigaion Insurance Co SA* [2014] EWHC 163 (Comm).

37 *Chitty*, Vol.2, para.42-127. See generally *Wasa International Insurance Co Ltd v Lexington Insurance Co* [2010] 1 A.C. 180 HL.

38 *Hill v Mercantile and General Reinsurance Co Plc* [1996] 1 W.L.R. 1239: "There are only two rules, and both obvious. First, that the reinsurer cannot be held liable unless the loss falls within the cover of the policy reinsured and within the cover created by the reinsurance. Second, that the parties are free to agree on ways of proving whether these requirements are satisfied": per Lord Mustill at 1251. See also *Assicurazioni Generali SPA v CGU International Insurance Plc* [2004] EWCA Civ 429, *Eagle Star Insurance Co Ltd v J.N. Cresswell* [2004] EWCA Civ 602, *CGU International Insurance Plc v Astrazeneca Insurance Co Ltd* [2005] EWHC 2755 (Comm), Cresswell J, and *English and American Insurance Co Ltd (in a scheme of arrangement) v Axa Re SA* [2006] EWHC 3323 (Comm), Gloster J. See also *Wasa International Insurance Co Ltd v Lexington Insurance Co* [2009] UKHL 40; [2010] 1 A.C. 180. While there is a presumption that the re-insurance is intended to be

only if the provisos apply. Lord Mustill said this of the provisos[39]:

> "The intent of these seems clear in broad outline, although it may be difficult to apply on the margins. The crucial words are 'within the terms and conditions' of the original policies and of the reinsurance. To my mind these draw a distinction between the facts which generate claims under the two contracts, and the legal extent of the respective covers: the purpose of the distinction being to ensure that the reinsurer's original assessment and rating of the risks assumed are not falsified by a settlement which, even if soundly based on the facts, transfers into the inward or outward policies, or both, risks which properly lie outside them. This restriction is perhaps more clearly visualised in relation to the second proviso. Here, the reinsurers are entitled to say that they rated the policy by reference to its chronological and geographical extent, to the types of casualty insured, to the boundaries of the insured layer, the mode of calculating the loss, and so forth. These variables, defined by the terms of the policy, founded the bargain between reinsurers and reinsured on the basis of which the premium and other terms were set. The purpose of the second proviso is ... to keep this foundation intact, and it would be undermined if an honest attempt by those further down the chain to ascertain the legal consequences of the facts could impose on the reinsurers responsibilities beyond those expressed in the policies. So also with the first proviso. The reinsurers undertake to protect the reinsured against risks which they have written, not risks which they have not written. To allow even an honest and conscientious appraisal of the legal implications of the facts embodied in an agreement between parties down the chain to impose on the reinsurers risks beyond those which they have undertaken and those which the reinsured have undertaken would effectively rewrite the outward contract: and it is this ... which the provisos are designed to forestall."

The burden of establishing that an exception to the reinsurer's obligation to follow the reinsured's settlements exists lies upon the reinsurer.[40] **22-18**

NATURE OF THE "SETTLEMENT" OF AN INSURED'S CLAIM

Where an insured makes a claim upon his insurer pursuant to the contract of insurance between them and the insurer makes a payment in respect of that claim, it is traditional to refer to that payment as being "in settlement of" the claim. As previously indicated,[41] it has been suggested that this situation constitutes an "implied settlement" having a contractual status similar to that of a true compromise even though no articulated dispute between insurer and insured has emerged. However, as Clarke[42] has succinctly and pertinently stated, "[there] is a difference between settling a claim and settling a dispute". For reasons previously given,[43] "settlements" of claims made under insurance policies should be seen as forming a category of their own, some of which will have all the characteristics of the compromise of a dispute either as to liability or as to quantum or both, and some **22-19**

---

co-extensive with the insurance, that will not always be the case. It was not the case in *Wasa*, where the relevant language of the contracts was virtually identical, but they were governed by different systems of law, which took different approaches to their construction.

39 *Hill* [1996] 1 W.L.R. 1239 at 1252–1253.

40 *Charman v Guardian Royal Exchange Assurance* [1992] 2 Lloyd's Rep. 607, per Webster J.

41 See paras 2-12 onwards.

42 Clarke, *The Law of Insurance Contracts* (London: Informa), para.30-06.

43 See fn.39.

of which simply reflect the performance by the insurer of the obligations under the insurance contract.[44]

22-20 Unless there is evidence of bad faith or collusion between an insured and his insurer aimed at prejudicing a third party who has a claim against the insured, the court will not intervene to prevent the insured from accepting a sum in settlement of his claim against his insurer arising from the third party's claim against him even if that sum is substantially less than the amount of the third party's claim.[45]

---

44 Clarke, *The Law of Insurance Contracts* (London: Informa), para.30-06.

45 *Normid Housing Association Ltd v Ralphs, Mansell* [1989] 1 Lloyd's Rep. 265 CA. This case involved a professional negligence claim by C against D (architects) who were insured in relation to claims of this nature.

PART 7: CHANCERY LITIGATION

This section is devoted to the settlement of disputes which are ordinarily dealt with within the Chancery jurisdiction of the court.

CHAPTER 23

The Settlement of Chancery Litigation

This chapter concerns the settlement of disputes which, when pursued to litigation, are likely to result in proceedings in the Chancery Division of the High Court, which since October 2017, has formed part of the Business and Property Courts.[1] Certain business is assigned directly by statute to that division of the High Court[2]; other business has been so assigned by virtue of rules and orders made pursuant to statutory authority.[3] A claimant may, of course, elect to commence proceedings in any division of the High Court, subject to the powers of the court to transfer those proceedings elsewhere[4] ; and certain types of litigation[5] are commonly to be found in both the Chancery Division and the Queen's Bench Division. Furthermore, some 23-01

---

1 The *Chancery Guide* gives practical guidance on the conduct of cases in the Chancery Division. Its provisions are reproduced in *White Book*, Vol.2 at para.1A-0 onwards. The current edition of the *Chancery Guide* was published in February 2016, with amendments made in January 2018, April 2018, September 2018, January 2019, April 2019 and August 2019. It is available on the gov.uk website at *https://www.gov.uk/courts-tribunals/chancery-division-of-the-high-court* [Accessed August 2019]. Also relevant are CPR Practice Direction 57AA—Business and Property Courts (*White Book*, Vol.1, para.57 AAPD.0) and the Business and Property Courts Advisory Note (*White Book*, Vol.1, para.57 AA.1). The *Chancery Guide* provides guidance as to (and specimen draft orders for) early neutral evaluation (at paras 18.7–18.15) and financial dispute resolution (at paras 18.16–18.19). These topics are considered more fully in Ch.35 at para.35-28 onwards.

2 By virtue of s.61(1) of, and Sch.1 to, the Senior Courts Act 1981 the following matters are assigned specifically to the Chancery Division:

(a) the sale, exchange or partition of land, or the raising of charges on land;
(b) the redemption or foreclosure of mortgages;
(c) the execution of trusts;
(d) the administration of the estates of deceased persons;
(e) bankruptcy;
(f) the dissolution of partnership or the taking of partnership or other accounts;
(g) the rectification, setting aside or cancellation of deeds or other instruments in writing;
(h) probate business, other than non-contentious or common form business;
(i) patents, trade marks, registered designs, copyright or design right;
(j) the appointment of a guardian of a minor's estate;

and all causes and matters involving the exercise of the High Court's jurisdiction under the enactments relating to companies.

3 For example, High Court claims for the possession of land subject to a mortgage: Practice Direction 55A—Possession Claims para.1.6 (*White Book*, Vol.1, para.55APD.1); landlord and tenant claims in the High Court: Practice Direction 56—Landlord and Tenant Claims and Miscellaneous Provisions About Land para.2.6 (*White Book*, Vol.1, para.56PD.1); arbitration claims relating to a landlord or tenant or partnership dispute: Practice Direction 62—Arbitration para.2.3(2) (*White Book*, Vol.2, para.2E-46); probate claims in the High Court: CPR r.57.2(2); claims and applications for the substitution or removal of a personal representative: CPR r.57.13(2); and all proceedings in the High Court relating to the administration of the estates of deceased persons, trusts and charity proceedings: CPR r.64.1(3).

4 Senior Courts Act 1981 ss.64 and 65.

5 For example, professional negligence actions against solicitors, accountants, valuers or other professionals and claims by an employer for breach of a contract of employment by a former employee. The cases of *Platform Home Loans Ltd v Oyston Shipways Ltd* [2000] 2 A.C. 190 HL, and *Fac-*

types of litigation, most notably in this context disputes under the Inheritance (Provision for Family and Dependants) Act 1975, are assigned to alternative divisions.[6] In addition to proceedings in the Chancery Division of the High Court (in London and in the District Registries in Birmingham, Bristol, Cardiff, Leeds, Liverpool, Manchester, Newcastle-upon-Tyne, Preston, Mold and Caernarfon[7]), a number of county courts have specific "chancery lists" where specialist judges deal with chancery disputes which fall within the County Court's jurisdiction. Such work should be marked "Business and Property work". The range of cases heard in the Chancery Division is wide and varied, the major part of the caseload today involving business or property disputes of one kind or another. Often these are complex and involve substantial sums of money and many cases have an international element to them.[8] The discussion that follows, however, relates to those forms of dispute that are truly to be regarded as the exclusive province of the Chancery Division.[9]

23-02 As stated elsewhere,[10] the underlying legal basis for any compromise is the law of contract. That applies as much to the matters with which this chapter is concerned as to any other. However, in some aspects of Chancery business the law demands attention to matters beyond the merely contractual; and, in some respects, the practice differs from that to be observed in relation to common law disputes. It is proposed to examine briefly certain aspects of Chancery business in which disputes may fall to be resolved by agreement and to deal with relevant matters of Chancery practice.

INSOLVENCY

23-03 Unlike other forms of inter-party litigation, the presentation of a winding-up or bankruptcy petition involves the invocation of a class remedy which is intended to be for the benefit of the general body of creditors of the company or debtor concerned. As a result, the court's approach to the compromise of insolvency litigation will have regard to the wider interests of the general body of creditors. This is reflected (by way of example) in the court's general practice (referenced below) of refusing to permit a winding-up petition to be withdrawn after it has been advertised or of refusing to grant long or repeated adjournments of winding-up petitions. Parties seeking to compromise insolvency proceedings should always bear in mind the potential for another creditor to apply to be substituted for the original petitioning creditor and (in that event) the potential implications for any settlement of a winding-up petition of Insolvency Act 1986 s.127 invalidating post-petition dispositions of the company's property and assets (including cash) without the specific approval of the court.

---

cenda Chicken Ltd v Fowler [1987] Ch. 117 CA, for example, were commenced and pursued in the Chancery Division.

6 CPR r.57.15(1). The settlement of these disputes is dealt with in Ch.25.

7 There are Business and Property Courts in the District Registries in Birmingham, Bristol, Cardiff, Leeds, Liverpool, Manchester and Newcastle-upon Tyne but not in Preston, Mold or Caernarfon.

8 *Chancery Guide*, para.1.8.

9 And, in analogous cases, the preserve of the equity jurisdiction of the county court: County Courts Act 1984 ss.23 and 24. With effect from 22 April 2014 the equity jurisdiction of the county court under s.23 was increased from £30,000 to £350,000. The county court's jurisdiction in respect of contentious probate matters is limited to cases where the value of the deceased's net estate at the date of death did not exceed £30,000 (although this is likely to be increased in the near future). See generally the County Court Jurisdiction Order 2014 (SI 2014/503) and the High Court and County Court Jurisdiction (Amendment) Order 2014 (SI 2014/821).

10 See Chs 1 and 3.

Companies

The presentation and service of a creditor's petition seeking the compulsory winding-up of a corporate debtor may provoke the company to discharge the debt. If the company has repaid the debt out of its own moneys, it will be in the interests of the petitioner as well as the company to seek to prevent the court from making any order to wind up the company,[11] because the winding-up will be deemed to have commenced at the time of the presentation of the petition for winding-up on which the order is based,[12] and the payment will thereupon be invalidated unless the court otherwise orders.[13] If the petition has not been advertised, no notices (whether in support or in opposition) have been received by the petitioner with reference to the petition, and the company consents, the petitioner may, at least five days before the date fixed for the hearing, apply for permission to withdraw the petition, on such terms as to costs as the parties may agree.[14] An order may also be made without the company's consent if it has not been served. The application may be made without notice by ordinary application, and, if made at least five days before the hearing, it will generally be dealt with in the High Court in London by a clerk authorised to deal with such applications or, in the High Court outside London or the County Court, by a district judge. Permission to withdraw a petition will almost never be given after the petition has been advertised or heard in court.[15] Alternatively, the petitioner may appear at the hearing of the petition and ask for it to be dismissed. The usual practice, where a winding-up petition is dismissed on late payment of a debt by the company, is to make an order for costs in the petitioner's favour as against the company, even if it does not appear. The petitioner is seen as having succeeded, and the normal rule applies that costs follow the event. This general principle also applies to the costs of applications connected with the petition (such as applications to stay advertisement), unless there is good reason to the contrary.[16] The onus is on the company to lay before the court material as to why an order for costs should not be made against it; but this material does not have to be formal evidence properly so described. The court adopts a pragmatic approach to the acceptability of whatever material is put before it where an order for costs, other than in the petitioner's favour, is sought upon payment of the debt in full.[17] In earlier times, the threat by a petitioner who had been paid the petition debt that, if his costs were not paid in full, he would nonetheless press on with his petition and ask for a compulsory order, was very effective to avoid the airing of disputes as to costs, to avoid assessment of costs, and to avoid the risk of failure to honour an order for costs. However, the modern practice of dismissing the petition with an order for costs against the company is now so entrenched that it has been said that the threat 23-04

---

11 Possibly after the substitution of another creditor for the petitioner under Insolvency Rules 2016 r.7.17.

12 Insolvency Act 1986 s.129.

13 Insolvency Act 1986 s.127.

14 Insolvency Rules 2016 r.7.13.

15 Insolvency Rules 2016 r.7.13 and *White Book*, Vol.2, para.3E-64.1. See Precedent No.4, at para.A1-04, for an appropriate form of order. The process for submitting consent orders, including Tomlin Orders, in Chancery proceedings is explained in "Practice Note - Chancery Division - production of orders for Masters and Judges", dated 2 January 2015, available at *https://www.judiciary.gov.uk/wp-content/uploads/2014/12/judges-and-masters-orders-final-02012015l.pdf* [Accessed July 2019]. See, in relation to Tomlin orders specifically, para.23-34 and *https://www.judiciary.uk/wp-content/uploads/2016/10/sealing-of-tomlin-orders-03-10-2016-amended-24-10-2016.pdf* [Accessed July 2019].

16 *Ryan Developments Ltd, Re* [2002] 2 B.C.L.C. 792 at [22], per Neuberger J.

17 *Nowmost Co Ltd, Re* [1996] 2 B.C.L.C. 492 following *Shusella Ltd, Re* [1983] B.C.L.C. 505; for a recent application of *Nowmost*, see *Reliance Wholesale Ltd v AM2PM Feltham Ltd* [2019] EWHC 1079 (Ch).

that the petitioner would press on with his petition and ask for a compulsory winding-up order after the payment of his debt unless his costs are also paid has ceased to be a truly effective threat, at all events for the time being.[18]

23-05 If at the hearing of the petition the company seeks an adjournment with a view to paying the petitioning creditor, the court may stand the petition over to a future date. Whatever may be the rights of the parties to agree to the deferment of the hearing of other forms of litigation, the special considerations which apply to creditors' winding-up petitions require, as a general rule, that they should be heard promptly. Thus, the court is reluctant to grant long or repeated adjournments, even with the consent of all concerned, unless there are cogent grounds for the application. In normal cases where the debt is not disputed, a period of a few weeks from the date of the first hearing will usually be regarded as sufficient to enable the petitioning creditor, if still unpaid, to decide whether to press for a winding-up order or to rely on other arrangements. Usually this period will also be regarded as sufficient to enable the company to decide whether or not to propose other arrangements (such as a company voluntary arrangement) or to apply for an administration order.[19] Shorter or longer periods may be granted by the court, depending on the circumstances of the case.

23-06 Where the debt on which the petition is based is disputed by the company and the petition is dismissed pursuant to an agreement between the petitioner and the company, the court will imply a term into that agreement that no further winding-up petition will be presented in respect of the same debt. If thereafter the petitioning creditor successfully sues the company to judgment, the debt will merge in the judgment and may be relied upon to found a fresh petition.[20] An order in Tomlin form[21] is not appropriate to embody the terms of any compromise of a winding-up petition: it is inappropriate that the proceedings should be stayed while the terms of compromise are carried into effect since, if an order for the compulsory winding-up of the company were subsequently to be made, it would relate back to the service of the petition, thereby invalidating any intervening dispositions of the company's property in accordance with s.127 of the Insolvency Act 1986.[22]

Individuals

23-07 In suitable cases the Bankruptcy Court may make a consent order without at-

---

18 *Nowmost Co Ltd, Re* [1996] 2 B.C.L.C. 492 per Lindsay J at 496b–d.

19 *Practice Note (Companies: Winding Up)* [1977] 1 W.L.R. 1066 suggested that four weeks would usually be the appropriate period. Although para.1.2, Practice Direction—Insolvency Proceedings (made on 26 April 1999) replaced all previous Practice Notes and Practice Directions relating to insolvency proceedings, it was suggested in the previous edition of this book that the former practice would still apply. The 1999 Practice Direction has itself been superseded and replaced by later Practice Directions, most recently Practice Direction—Insolvency Proceedings (*White Book*, Vol.2, para.3E-1 onwards) which came into force on 4 July 2018. The 2018 Practice Direction does not say anything specific about the length of adjournments of creditors' winding-up petitions, but it is suggested that the rationale for avoiding lengthy adjournments as explained by Brightman J in the 1977 Practice Note remains relevant. A summary of the most important updates in the Practice Direction—Insolvency Proceedings, July 2018, can be found at *White Book*, Vol.2, para.3E-21.1.

20 *A Company (No.00928 of 1991) Ex p. City Electrical Factors Ltd, Re* [1991] B.C.L.C. 514. For a suggested form of order dismissing a winding-up petition by consent, see Precedent No.5 at para.A1-05.

21 See para.9-23 onwards.

22 cf. *A Company (No.003324 of 1979), Re* [1981] 1 W.L.R. 1059 at 1060, per Vinelott J, considered at para.23-12.

tendance by the parties in personal insolvency matters.[23] The written consent of the parties will be required. Examples of such orders are as follows:

(1) On applications to set aside a statutory demand, orders:
  (a) dismissing the application, with or without an order for costs as may be agreed (permission will be given to present a petition on or after the seventh day after the date of the order, unless a different date is agreed); or
  (b) setting aside the demand, with or without an order for costs as may be agreed.
(2) On petitions: where there are no support or opposing creditors (see r.10.19 of the Insolvency Rules 2016) and there is a statement signed by or on behalf of the petitioning creditor that no notices have been received from supporting or opposing creditors, orders:
  (a) dismissing the petition, with or without an order for costs as may be agreed; or
  (b) if the petition has not been served, giving permission to withdraw the petition (with no order for costs).[24]
(3) On other applications, orders:
  (a) for sale of property, possession of property, disposal of proceeds of sale;
  (b) giving interim directions;
  (c) dismissing the application, with or without an order for costs as may be agreed; or
  (d) giving permission to withdraw the application, with or without an order for costs as may be agreed.

If (as may often be the case with orders under sub-paras 14.3(3)(a) or (b) of the 2018 Practice Direction above), an adjournment is required, whether generally with liberty to restore or to a fixed date, the order by consent may include an order for the adjournment. If adjournment to a date is requested, a time estimate should be given, and the court will fix the first available date and time on or after the date requested.[25]

The above lists should not be regarded as exhaustive, nor should it be assumed that an order will be made without attendance as requested.[26] Applications for consent orders without attendance should be lodged at least two clear working days (and preferably longer) before any hearing date.[27] Whenever a document is lodged or a letter sent, the correct case number should be quoted. A note should also be given of the date and time of the next hearing (if any).[28] **23-08**

As in the case of winding-up petitions,[29] where, following the service of a bankruptcy petition, the debt is paid, the petitioning creditor will ordinarily be entitled to his costs on the dismissal of the petition: he has in substance succeeded in his proceedings against the debtor. However, that inference can be displaced in **23-09**

---

23 Practice Direction—Insolvency Proceedings 2018, paras 14.3 and 14.4 (*White Book*, Vol.2, para.3E-14).

24 For an appropriate form of order, see Precedent No.6 at para.A1-06.

25 Practice Direction—Insolvency Proceedings para.14.4 (*White Book*, Vol.2, para.3E-14).

26 Practice Direction—Insolvency Proceedings para.14.5.

27 Practice Direction—Insolvency Proceedings para.14.6.

28 Practice Direction—Insolvency Proceedings para.14.7.

29 See para.23-03.

a particular case, as where avoidable defects in the creditor's proceedings have led to costs being incurred unnecessarily by the debtor.[30]

23-10 Where the petitioning creditor and the bankrupt compromise an application for the annulment (or review) of a bankruptcy order, they should expressly address the issue of who should be liable for the costs of the trustee in bankruptcy (or official receiver). This had not been done in *Butterworth v Soutter*[31]; and Neuberger J held that "the least unjust result" was to order that both the petitioning creditor and the bankrupt should be equally responsible for the trustee in bankruptcy's costs.

Appeals

23-11 The destination of appeals in insolvency proceedings is set out in Table 2 at para.3.5 of Practice Direction A to CPR Pt 52. Further detail as to applications for permission to appeal and to appeals themselves in the corporate and personal insolvency context is set out in *Part Four of the Practice Direction—Insolvency Proceedings* [2018] B.C.C 421 (which came into effect on 4 July 2018).

In summary:

1. an appeal from a decision of the county court (whether made by a district judge, a recorder or a circuit judge) in insolvency proceedings lies to a single High Court judge of the Chancery Division in accordance with s.375(2) of the Insolvency Act 1986 and r.12.59(2)(a) of the Insolvency Rules 2016; the one exception is that in corporate insolvency proceedings, the appeal from a decision of a district judge in the County Court on the South Eastern Circuit lies to a single Insolvency and Companies Court Judge[32] of the High Court (in accordance with r.12.59(2)(a) of and Schedule 10 to the Insolvency Rules 2016);
2. an appeal from a decision of a district judge sitting in a district registry of the High Court, a master or an Insolvency and Companies Court Judge at first instance in insolvency proceedings lies to a single High Court judge in accordance with r.12.59(2)(b) of the Insolvency Rules 2016;
3. an appeal from a decision of an Insolvency and Companies Court Judge whose decision was an appeal from a decision of a district judge lies to the Civil Division of the Court of Appeal in accordance with r.12.59(2)(c) of the Insolvency Rules 2016;
4. an appeal from the decision of a High Court Judge lies to the Civil Division of the Court of Appeal in accordance with r.12.59(2)(d) of the Insolvency Rules 2016.

The permission requirement in CPR r.52.3[33] and the procedure set out in CPR Part 52 and Practice Directions 52A, 52B and 52C apply to appeals in insolvency proceedings.[34] Such an appeal may be dismissed by consent; but the appeal court

---

[30] *A Debtor (No.510 of 1997), Re* [1999] B.C.C. 446. On the facts, the proper order was that there should be no order as to costs.

[31] *Butterworth v Soutter* [2000] B.P.I.R. 582. For guidance as to the principles to be applied in determining who should pay the costs arising on the annulment of a bankruptcy order, see *London Borough of Redbridge v Mustafa* [2010] EWHC 1105 (Ch); [2010] B.P.I.R. 893 (Sir Andrew Morritt C).

[32] Under The Alteration of Judicial Titles (Registrar in Bankruptcy of the High Court) Order 2018 (SI 2018/130), from 26 February 2018, the name of the office of "Registrar in Bankruptcy of the High Court" became "Insolvency and Companies Court Judge", commonly known as an ICC Judge.

[33] See Practice Direction—Insolvency Proceedings 2018 para.18 (*White Book*, Vol.2, para.3E-18) and *Chancery Guide*, paras 24.3 and 24.14.

[34] See Practice Direction—Insolvency Proceedings 2018 para.18 (*White Book*, Vol.2, para.3E-18) and

will not make an order allowing an appeal unless it is satisfied that the decision of the lower court was wrong.[35]

LIQUIDATORS AND TRUSTEES IN BANKRUPTCY

A liquidator's power to compromise claims against the company is exercisable only: **23-12**

(1) in the case of a members' voluntary winding-up, with the sanction of a special resolution of the company[36];
(2) in the case of a creditors' voluntary winding-up, with the sanction of the court or the liquidation committee (or, if there is no such committee, a meeting of the company's creditors)[37]; and
(3) when the company is being wound up by the court, with the sanction of the court or the liquidation committee.[38]

A trustee in bankruptcy's power to compromise claims against the bankrupt or his estate is only exercisable with the permission of the creditors' committee or the court.[39]

A liquidator or trustee in bankruptcy may apply to the court for it to sanction a compromise in the face of a refusal to do so by the liquidation or creditors' committee.[40]

A liquidator or trustee in bankruptcy does not require any sanction to compromise claims by the company or the bankrupt or arising out of or incidental to his estate.[41]

The proper approach to the exercise of the court's power to sanction a compromise by a company liquidator was considered by the Court of Appeal in *Greenhaven Motors Ltd, Re*.[42] The decision whether or not to sanction a proposed compromise was one for the court and not for the liquidator. It was therefore wrong in principle for the court to approach its task on the basis that the liquidator's wish to exercise the power should prevail unless it was satisfied that the liquidator was not acting bona fide, or that he was acting in a way in which no reasonable liquidator should act. The correct approach was for the court to consider whether or not the interests of those creditors or contributories who had a real interest in the assets of the company in liquidation were likely to be best served by permitting the company to enter into the proposed compromise. In reaching its decision the court was entitled to give weight to the wishes of those creditors and contributories who would be affected by the decision and to the views of the liquidator; but ultimately it was for the court to decide whether or not to sanction the proposed compromise. If the exercise of the power was sanctioned, it was for the liquidator, in the absence

---

Chancery Guide, para.24.3.

35 See PD 52A—Appeals: General Provisions, paras 6.1–6.4. See Ch.34.

36 Insolvency Act 1986 s.165(2)(a), Sch.4 para.2.

37 Insolvency Act 1986 s.165(2)(b), Sch.4 para.2.

38 Insolvency Act 1986 s.167(1)(a), Sch.4 para.2.

39 Insolvency Act 1986 s.314(1)(a), Sch.5 paras 7 and 8.

40 *Re North-Eastern Insurance Co Ltd* (1915) 113 LT 989 (Sargant J).

41 Insolvency Act 1986 ss.165(3), 167(1)(b), Sch.4, para.6A (liquidation); Insolvency Act 1986 s.314(1)(b), Sch.5 paras 9A, 9B (bankruptcy).

42 *Greenhaven Motors Ltd, Re* [1999] 1 B.C.L.C. 635. It is submitted that the same principles would apply to a trustee in bankruptcy.

of a direction from the court, to decide whether or not actually to exercise the power of compromise.[43]

UNFAIR PREJUDICE

23-13 Provided a petition under s.994 of the Companies Act 2006 (formerly s.459 of the Companies Act 1985) does not seek an order for the compulsory winding-up of the company,[44] agreed terms of compromise may be embodied in an order in Tomlin form[45] and the petition allowed to remain on the file whilst the terms of compromise are implemented, subject to an undertaking by the petitioner to apply to dismiss the petition when the terms of the compromise have been fully implemented.[46]

RESTORATION OF A COMPANY TO THE REGISTER

23-14 Claims for an order restoring the name of a company to the register are made under s.1029 of the Companies Act 2006. With effect from 6 April 2015, such proceedings will be issued and heard in the County Court sitting in Central London, a District Registry of the High Court with Chancery jurisdiction or certain county courts (where the registered office of the company is within its jurisdiction, the issued share capital of the company does not exceed £120,000 and the court has not been excluded from having winding-up jurisdiction).[47]

DISQUALIFICATION ORDERS[48]

23-15 The Company Directors Disqualification Act 1986 empowers the court to make a disqualification order, that is to say an order that for a period specified in the order

---

43 See especially *Greenhaven Motors Ltd, Re* [1999] B.C.L.C. 635, per Chadwick LJ at 642h–643h. For a case in which the court sanctioned a compromise despite the opposition of preference shareholders on the grounds that they had no real or tangible interest in the assets available for distribution in the winding-up in any foreseeable circumstances, see *Barings Plc (No.7), Re* [2002] 1 B.C.L.C. 401. For a case where the court sanctioned a compromise despite the opposition of the company's largest creditor, see *Coote v Rubin* [2011] EWCA Civ 106; [2011] BCC 596.

44 See Practice Direction 49B—Order Under s.127 Insolvency Act 1986 para.1 (*White Book*, Vol.2, para.2G-53.1) and para.22 of the Practice Direction—Insolvency Proceedings, July 2018, (*White Book*, Vol.2, para.3E-21) as to the undesirability of asking as a matter of course for a winding-up order as an alternative to an order under s.994 of the Companies Act 2006. The petition should not ask for a winding-up order unless that is the remedy which the petitioner prefers or it is thought that it may be the only remedy to which the petitioner is entitled. The same Practice Direction also draws attention to the need to state whether the petitioner consents or objects to an order under s.127 in the standard form whenever a winding up order is asked for in a contributory's petition; and it contains provisions governing applications for, and the making of, orders under s.127 in such cases in both the standard or a modified form.

45 See para.9-23 onwards and para.23-34.

46 *Re A Company (No.003324 of 1979), Re* [1981] 1 W.L.R. 1059; see also *Willcox v Willcox* [2010] EWHC 3764 (Ch). See Precedent No.7 at para.A1-07.

47 *White Book*, Vol.2, para.3E-22 (regarding proceedings issued in London); information relating to the procedure for such applications both in and outside London is given on the gov.uk website at *https://www.gov.uk/guidance/company-restoration-guide* (updated 30 May 2018) [Accessed August 2019].

48 For a more detailed discussion, see Walters and Davis-White, Directors' Disqualification and Insolvency Restrictions, 3rd edn (London: Sweet & Maxwell, 2010), Ch.9.

a person:

(a) shall not be a director of a company, act as a receiver of a company's property or in any way, whether directly or indirectly, be concerned or take part in the promotion, formation or management of a company unless (in each case) he has the leave of the court; and
(b) shall not act as an insolvency practitioner.[49]

In *Secretary of State for Trade and Industry v Rogers*[50] the Court of Appeal endorsed the summary form of procedure sanctioned by Ferris J in *Carecraft Construction Co Ltd, Re*[51] which enables disqualification proceedings to be dealt with summarily in cases where: **23-16**

(1) facts regarding the director's conduct in managing the company or companies in question are either agreed or, at least, are not disputed;
(2) the Secretary of State is willing for the case to be dealt with by the judge on the agreed (or not disputed) facts and does not consider it necessary to endeavour to prove the additional facts that have been alleged in the evidence filed in support of the application;
(3) the director is willing for the case to be dealt with by the judge on the agreed (or not disputed) facts and does not dispute that those facts require the court to make a disqualification order; and
(4) the Secretary of State and the director have reached agreement either as to the length of the disqualification period that would be appropriate or, at least, as to the bracket of years into which the disqualification period should fall.

As explained by the Court of Appeal,[52] the *Carecraft* procedure can effectively, and without the judge's consent, limit the facts on which the judge can base his judgment as to the order that should be made[53]; but the *Carecraft* procedure cannot oblige the judge to make a disqualification order, and cannot bind him as to the period of disqualification to be imposed. If the judge, on reading the papers in advance, has any doubts as to whether a disqualification order should be made, or as to whether the period should fall within the agreed bracket, those doubts should be voiced at the earliest possible moment so that the parties can consider whether they, or either of them, would prefer a full trial. The Court of Appeal anticipated that it would be a very rare case in which any such doubts would be entertained.

If the parties decide to invite the court to deal with the application under the *Carecraft* procedure they should inform the court immediately and obtain a date for the hearing of the application. Whenever this procedure is adopted, the claimant must submit a written statement of agreed or undisputed facts and an agreed period **23-17**

---

49 The wording of the 1986 Act is reproduced with the amendments introduced by s.5 of the Insolvency Act 2000 as from 2 April 2001.

50 *Secretary of State for Trade and Industry v Rogers* [1996] 1 W.L.R. 1569.

51 *Carecraft Construction Co Ltd, Re* [1994] 1 W.L.R. 172.

52 *Secretary of State for Trade & Industry v Rogers* [1996] 1 W.L.R. 1569 at 1574H–1575B, per Sir Richard Scott VC, as he then was.

53 In this regard, the Court of Appeal differed from the approach of Ferris J in *Carecraft Construction Co Ltd, Re* [1994] 1 W.L.R. 172 at 181B–C and 183G–H: see *Secretary of State for Trade & Industry v Rogers* [1996] 1 W.L.R. 1569 at 1574A–C. Sir Richard Scott VC said this: "There is no impropriety in directors disqualification cases or in any other civil proceedings in placing before the court an agreed statement of facts and inviting the court to deal with the case on the basis of that statement."

of disqualification or an agreed range of years (e.g. 2 to 5 years, 6 to 10 years, 11 to 15 years).[54]

Unless the court otherwise orders, a hearing under the *Carecraft* procedure will be held in private.[55] If the court is minded to make a disqualification order having heard the parties' representations, it will usually give judgment and make the disqualification order in public. Unless the court otherwise orders, the witness statement referred to above will be annexed to the disqualification order.[56] If the court refuses to make the disqualification order under the *Carecraft* procedure, it will give further directions for the hearing of the application.

23-18 In *Secretary of State for Trade and Industry v Banarse*[57] it was said that a *Carecraft* statement of facts should not "mince its words". Either the parties were in agreement as to the facts or they were not. If not, a trial would in the long run be the appropriate course. But if they were in agreement, the facts should be spelt out clearly and should leave no room or need for infilling or interpretation by way of inference of secondary fact. Where the court was faced with an admission that a respondent knew or ought to have known something, it could not proceed on the basis of actual knowledge. A defendant who wants to dispose of disqualification proceedings under the *Carecraft* procedure should consider insisting on the inclusion in the written statement of a provision limiting any admissions and concessions made by him to the purpose of facilitating a *Carecraft* disposal of the proceedings, and stating that they are wholly without prejudice to his position in relation to any other proceedings which may be brought against him, such as proceedings brought on behalf of the creditors of a company by its liquidator (or other office holder).[58]

The then Vice Chancellor (Sir Richard Scott) had recommended amending legislation enabling disqualification to be imposed by a formal undertaking entered into by the director without the necessity of a court order.[59] Section 6 of the Insolvency Act 2000 accordingly amended the Company Directors Disqualification Act 1986 (as from April 2, 2001) by inserting a new s.1A, relating to disqualification undertakings. Directors whom the Secretary of State considers unfit may consent to a period of disqualification without the need for court involvement by giving a disqualification undertaking. The Secretary of State has an unfettered discretion as to whether to accept an undertaking which has been offered, and he is entitled to refuse to accept an otherwise satisfactory disqualification undertaking on the grounds that it does not refer to, or incorporate, a statement setting out (usually in the form of a schedule) the grounds of the director's unfitness.[60] The director should always seek expressly to limit the use of any admitted or undisputed facts recorded in a schedule of unfit conduct solely to the purposes of the Company Directors Disqualification Act 1986, or any purposes consequential thereto, so as to prevent them from being used against him in other proceedings brought, for example, by an administrator, receiver or liquidator. The general rule is that the

---

[54] Practice Direction—Directors Disqualification Proceedings para.12.1 (*White Book*, Vol.2, para.3J-34; commentary updated 11 December 2018). This Practice Direction came into effect on 9 December 2014.

[55] Practice Direction—Directors Disqualification Proceedings para.12.2.

[56] Practice Direction—Directors Disqualification Proceedings para.12.3.

[57] *Secretary of State for Trade and Industry v Banarse* [1997] 1 B.C.L.C. 653, especially at 658, per Jules Sher QC, sitting as a deputy High Court judge.

[58] The propriety of such a provision was accepted in *Official Receiver v Cooper* [1999] B.C.C. 115 per Jonathan Parker J.

[59] See *Practice Note* [1996] 1 All E.R. 442 and *Secretary of State for Trade and Industry v Rogers* [1996] 1 W.L.R. 1569 at 1574G–H.

[60] *Blackspur Group Plc (No.3), Re* [2001] EWCA Civ 1595; [2002] 2 B.C.L.C. 263.

court will order the defendant to pay the costs of the Secretary of State (or official receiver) if a pending disqualification application is discontinued because the Secretary of State has accepted a disqualification undertaking; but the general rule will not apply where the court considers that the circumstances are such that it should make another order.[61] Apart from the issue of costs, the Practice Direction—Directors Disqualification Proceedings (9 December, 2014) does not address the subject of disqualification undertakings because they are a matter between the parties, and (unlike the *Carecraft* Procedure) they do not require the sanction of the court. Since the introduction of disqualification undertakings, the use of the *Carecraft* procedure has largely dropped away, principally because undertakings have advantages in terms of reduced expense. However, it remains open to the parties to use the *Carecraft* procedure. Indeed certain defendants prefer it because the opportunity to include matters of mitigation is not (as a matter of the Secretary of State's policy) available in respect of disqualification undertakings, but (at least as matters currently stand) it is available under the *Carecraft* procedure.

Section 8A of the 1986 Act enables a person who is subject to a disqualification undertaking to apply to the court to reduce the period for which it is to be in force, or to provide for it to cease to be in force.[62] In the case of *INS Realisations Ltd, Re*[63] Hart J held that an applicant for such relief should not be permitted to seek to controvert the facts which had been agreed at the time of the undertaking as the basis on which it had been given unless either: (i) some ground was shown which would be sufficient to discharge a private law contract; or (ii) some ground of public interest was shown which outweighed the importance of holding a party to his agreement. Although the court had an apparently unfettered discretion, the jurisdiction under s.8A should only be sparingly exercised where the application was based on arguments of a general kind, such as cases in which a director pleaded that he only gave the undertaking because he could not afford legal advice and assistance, or where an undertaking had been given for a period in excess of that subsequently found by the court to be appropriate in relation to other directors who had been involved in the same insolvency and the same misconduct. There must be some new event (uncontemplated at the date of the applicant's undertaking) which entitled him to ask the court to consider whether there remained any good reason why he should continue to be subject to the undertaking which he had voluntarily given. In that case, the court acceded to the application of a director who had taken no active part in the affairs of the company, and declared that her undertaking should cease to be in force, where, in the light of the evidence presented by the director who had actually caused the matters complained of, the Secretary of State no longer considered that it was in the public interest for that director to be subject to a disqualification order. **23-19**

61 Practice Direction—Directors Disqualification Proceedings paras 25.1 and 25.2 (*White Book*, Vol.2, para.3J-51). Thus the normal rule on discontinuance (in CPR 38.6) that the claimant should pay the costs is reversed where the claimant discontinues following the acceptance of a disqualification undertaking.

62 The procedure is governed by Part Eight of the Practice Direction—Directors Disqualification Proceedings (*White Book*, Vol.2, paras 3J-54–3J-61).

63 *INS Realisations Ltd, Re, Secretary of State for Trade & Industry v Jonkler* [2006] 1 W.L.R. 3433.

COURT-APPOINTED RECEIVERS

23-20 The procedure for the appointment of a receiver[64] is set out in CPR 69 and Practice Direction 69—Court's Power to Appoint a Receiver. The main function of a court-appointed receiver is to protect the assets received by him (or her) pending the court proceedings. A court-appointed receiver must obtain directions from the court when appointed or at any time afterwards, including in relation to whether the receiver can bring, defend or compromise legal proceedings or compromise a claim.[65]

A receiver appointed by the court has a right to be indemnified in respect of his costs and remuneration out of all of the assets subject to the receivership, and not merely those in his possession. That right is not extinguished even though the receivership is discharged by consent, and the receiver hands back control of the assets to their legal owners. Accordingly, the receiver can obtain an order charging all the assets over which he was appointed receiver with the amount of his costs and remuneration, whether or not he has ever reduced those assets into his possession.[66]

TRUSTEES AND PERSONAL REPRESENTATIVES

23-21 By s.15 of the Trustee Act 1925 a personal representative, or two or more trustees acting together, or (subject to the restrictions imposed in regard to receipts by a sole trustee, not being a trust corporation) a sole acting trustee where, by the instrument (if any) creating the trust, or by statute, a sole trustee is authorised to execute the trusts and powers reposed in him, may, if and as he (or they) think fit, compromise any debt, account, claim or thing whatever relating to the testator's or intestate's estate, or to the trust, without being responsible for any loss occasioned by any act or thing so done by him (or them) if he has (or they have) discharged the duty of care set out in s.1(1) of the Trustee Act 2000.[67] The powers conferred by this section extend to a judicial trustee,[68] and to the trustee of a deed of arrangement.[69] They also extend to the compromise by the trustees of an occupational pension scheme of a statutory debt from the employer arising under s.75 of the Pensions Act 1995.[70] These powers are to be given a wide construction.[71] Thus, trustees have power under s.15 to compromise a claim to property in the

---

64 Under Senior Courts Act 1981 s.37 and County Courts Act 1984 ss.38, 107.

65 Practice Direction 69 paras 6 and 8 and *Chancery Guide* paras 29.72–29.76.

66 *Mellor v Mellor* [1992] 1 W.L.R. 517, applied in *Glatt v Sinclair* [2013] EWCA Civ 241, [2013] 1 W.L.R. 3602. For the position where the original receivership order was wrongly made, see *Barnes v Eastenders Cash & Carry Plc* [2014] UKSC 26; [2015] A.C. 1. The sum involved may be substantial: the receiver in *Mellor v Mellor* was seeking (in 1992) to recover a sum of a little under £40,000 (inclusive of VAT) in respect of his time, costs and disbursements during a receivership lasting three-and-a-half weeks.

67 The reference to the statutory duty of care is substituted for the words "in good faith" which appeared in the original section by Trustee Act 2000 s.40(1), Sch.2, Pt II, para.20, as from 1 February 2001. For a discussion of the statutory duty of care, see *Lewin on Trusts*, 19th edn (London: Sweet & Maxwell, 2015), para.34–001 onwards.

68 *Ridsdel, Re* [1947] Ch. 597.

69 *Shenton, Re* [1935] Ch. 651.

70 *Bradstock Group Pension Scheme Trustees Ltd v Bradstock Group Plc* [2002] EWHC 651 (Ch); [2002] I.C.R. 1427. It has been held that Pensions Act 1995 s.91 (inalienability of occupational pension) does not prevent the parties from making, or the court from approving or enforcing, a bona fide compromise of disputed or doubtful entitlements or rights under an occupational pension

hands of a beneficiary by abandoning part of their claim in consideration of a beneficiary giving up a beneficial interest under the trust, provided the trustees consider, in good faith, that such a compromise would be beneficial to the trust estate, that is to say, to all of the beneficiaries in accordance with their several interests in the trust estate, holding the scale fairly between them.[72] However, neither the statutory power of compromise, nor the court's inherent jurisdiction to sanction a compromise by an infant in a suit to which he is a party,[73] can be extended to cover cases in which there is no real dispute as to rights, but in which it is sought, by way of bargain between the beneficiaries, to rearrange the beneficial interests under the trust instrument, and to bind infants and unborn persons.[74] Section 15 is concerned with what may be called external disputes, in the sense of cases in which there is some issue between the trustees, on behalf of the trust as a whole, and a claimant whose claim is adverse to the trusts. It is not concerned with internal disputes, where one beneficiary under the trusts is at issue with another beneficiary under the trusts.[75]

In exercising their powers under s.15 the trustees must listen to the beneficiaries and pay full attention to their views and wishes; but the decision whether or not to compromise rests with the trustees, and even if all of the beneficiaries oppose the proposed compromise the trustees have power to agree a proposed compromise.[76] However, the trustees must exercise some active discretion, and must not adopt the merely passive attitude of leaving matters alone, as by failing to collect debts due to the trust.[77] In the case of a private (but not a public or charitable)[78] trust, no majority of trustees can bind a minority[79] unless the trust instrument expressly provides to the contrary.[80] Thus, where there are two or more trustees of a private trust they must all act together under s.15 unless the trust instrument expressly empowers the majority to bind the minority. But it is competent for an executor in a proper case to compromise a claim by his co-executor against the estate.[81] **23-22**

The court has the jurisdiction to exercise the discretion given to the trustees by s.15 and to direct them whether or not they should proceed with the compromise; and in exercising the jurisdiction the court will act in just the same way as any trustee, on the balance of possibilities and apparent advantages.[82] As stated elsewhere,[83] provided rights are in dispute, the court also has the power to ap- **23-23**

---

scheme: *International Management Group (UK) Ltd v German* [2010] EWCA Civ 1349; [2011] I.C.R. 329; [2011] P.L.R. 11, CA.

71 *Earl of Strafford, Re* [1980] Ch. 28 CA.

72 *Earl of Strafford, Re* [1980] Ch. 28 CA.

73 See, e.g. Ch.27.

74 *Chapman v Chapman* [1954] A.C. 429 HL. The Variation of Trusts Act 1958 gives the court an extensive jurisdiction to approve variations of trusts (including beneficial interests thereunder) on behalf of minors, unborn persons and others: see, generally, *Snell's Equity*, 33rd edn (London: Sweet & Maxwell, 2015), para.29-047 onwards, and *Lewin on Trusts*, 19th edn (2015), para.45-038 onwards.

75 *Earl of Strafford, Re* [1980] Ch. 28 CA at 32–33 and 46.

76 *Ezekiel's Settlement Trusts, Re* [1942] Ch. 230 CA.

77 *Greenwood, Re* (1911) 105 L.J. 509.

78 *Whiteley, Re* [1910] 1 Ch. 600.

79 *Luke v South Kensington Hotel Co* (1879) 11 Ch. D. 121 CA at 125–126 per Sir George Jessel MR, *Roth, Re* (1896) 74 L.T. 50.

80 *Butlin's S.T., Re* (1974) 118 S.J. 757.

81 *Houghton, Re* [1904] 1 Ch. 622.

82 *Ezekiel's Settlement Trusts, Re* [1942] Ch. 230 CA.

83 See, e.g. Ch.27.

prove, on behalf of beneficiaries under a disability, compromises proposed by the beneficiaries who are sui juris.[84]

23-24 Clearly trustees cannot effect a compromise pursuant to the statutory power conferred by s.15 where they are affected by a conflict of interests or duties. In such a case, the trustees may apply to the court for its approval to the compromise by way of a Pt 8 claim form without naming any defendants, and without the court's prior permission; and the court may be requested to determine the claim without a hearing. The procedure is governed by para.1A of the Practice Direction 64A—Estates, Trust and Charities. The claim form must be accompanied by: (a) a witness statement setting out the material facts justifying determination without a hearing, and in particular identifying those affected by the remedy sought, and detailing any consultation of those so affected and its result; (b) the advice of a lawyer having a 10-year High Court qualification on the merits of the claim; (c) a draft order for the remedy sought; and (d) a statement of costs. If the court considers that the case does not require an oral hearing, it will proceed to consider the claim on the papers; otherwise, it will give appropriate directions. If the court considers it appropriate, it will make the order sought, and may direct that the claimant must: (a) serve notice of the order on the interested parties in accordance with CPR r.19.8A; and (b) file a certificate of service within seven days of doing so.

23-25 By CPR r.19.7(1) and (2), in a claim about the estate of a deceased person, property subject to a trust, or the meaning of a document (including a statute), the court may make an order appointing a person to represent any other person or persons in the claim where the person or persons to be represented:

- (a) are unborn;
- (b) cannot be found;
- (c) cannot easily be ascertained; or
- (d) are a class of persons who have the same interest in a claim and either:
  - (i) one or more members of that class are within subparas (a), (b) or (c); or
  - (ii) to appoint a representative would further the overriding objective of enabling the court to deal with cases justly and at proportionate cost.[85]

Where a party is acting as a representative under this rule, the court's approval of any settlement of the claim is required.[86] The court may approve such a settlement where it is satisfied that the settlement is for the benefit of all the represented persons.[87] The former rules[88] expressly provided that in approving a compromise, the court could further order that the compromise should be binding on absent persons; but that such an order could be set aside where it was subsequently shown that the compromise order had been obtained by fraud or non-disclosure of material facts (thus making it unnecessary for absent persons to commence an action to set aside that order). CPR r.19.7(7) now provides that, unless the court otherwise directs, any judgment or order given in a claim in which a party is acting as a representative under CPR r.19.7 is binding on all persons represented in the claim, but may only be enforced by or against a person who is not a party to the claim with the permission of the court. Where, under the former rules, proceedings between a single claimant and a single defendant, the latter of whom could not be found, raised issues of disputed fact, it was held that it was not appropriate to order that a third

---

84 *Chapman v Chapman* [1954] A.C. 429 at 457 HL.
85 See CPR Pt 1.
86 CPR r.19.7(5).
87 CPR r.19.7(6).
88 RSC Ord.15 r.13(4); and CCR Ord.5 r.6(3).

party, such as the Official Solicitor, should be appointed to represent the missing defendant with a view to the approval of a compromise binding on the latter.[89]

CPR r.19.8A gives the court power to make judgments binding on non-parties. Its terms should always be borne in mind when considering the compromise of any claim to which its provisions apply. In any claim relating to: (a) the estate of a deceased person; or (b) property subject to a trust; or (c) the sale of any property, the court may at any time direct that notice of any judgment or order given in the claim be served on any person who is not a party, but who is, or may be, affected by it.[90] Any person served with notice of a judgment or order under this rule: (a) shall be bound by the judgment or order as if he had been a party to the claim; but (b) may, provided he acknowledges service: (i) within 28 days after the notice is served on him, apply to the court to set aside or vary the judgment or order, and (ii) take part in any proceedings relating to the judgment or order.[91] **23-26**

CHARITIES

Charity trustees enjoy the wide powers conferred by s.15 of the Trustee Act 1925 to compromise claims relating to the assets of the charity.[92] Exceptionally, these powers may be exercised by a majority of the trustees.[93] In cases where the trustees disagree, or in complicated cases, they may consider it appropriate to apply to the Charity Commission for an order sanctioning the proposed compromise pursuant to s.105 of the Charities Act 2011. Anything done under the authority of such an order is deemed to be properly done in the exercise of the trustees' powers. The Charity Commission will normally require such an application to be supported by an opinion of properly instructed, and suitably qualified, counsel recommending the proposed compromise as expedient in the interests of the charity or (in a simpler case) by a letter from the charity's solicitors analysing the legal issues and commending the expediency of the proposed compromise. **23-27**

The powers of charity trustees to compromise claims should be contrasted with the making of ex gratia payments. In *Snowden, Re*[94] it was held that the court, and the Attorney General, had the power to authorise charity trustees to make ex gratia payments out of funds held on charitable trusts; but that it was a power which was not to be exercised lightly, or on slender grounds, and only in circumstances where it could fairly be said that, if the charity were an individual, it would be morally wrong of him to refuse to make the payment. Subject to the supervisory and directive powers of the Attorney General, the Charity Commission is now empowered[95] to authorise charity trustees to make any application of the charity's property, or to waive to any extent, on behalf of the charity, its entitlement to receive any property, in any case where the charity trustees (apart from s.106) have no such power but, in all the circumstances, regard themselves as being under a moral obligation to do so. *Snowden, Re* contains guidance as to the circumstances in which the power to make ex gratia payments may be exercised. In particular, Cross J distinguished between cases where it appeared that the testator had never intended the charity to receive so large a gift as it did receive, and cases where the testator intended the **23-28**

---

89 *Cotton v Official Solicitor* [1989] C.L.Y. 3045, cited in *White Book*, Vol.1, para.19.7.5.

90 CPR r.19.8A(1) and (2).

91 CPR r.19.8A(8).

92 See paras 23-20–23-22.

93 *Whiteley, Re* [1910] 1 Ch. 600.

94 *Snowden, Re* [1970] Ch. 700.

95 By the Charities Act 2011 s.106.

charity to receive what it had received but the testator's relatives considered that he was not morally justified in leaving his money to charity rather than to them; and he suggested that cases in which an ex gratia payment would be justified might be rarer in the second category than in the first.[96]

PROBATE CLAIMS

23-29 The procedure for contentious probate is now to be found in Section 1 of CPR Pt 57 and the Practice Direction supplementing Pt 57.[97] Because a probate claim is of the nature of a claim in rem a default judgment cannot be obtained in a probate claim[98]; and CPR Pt 38 (relating to discontinuance) does not apply to a probate claim.[99] A probate claim may be compromised in one of three possible ways.[100]

(1) By obtaining an order for the claim to be discontinued or dismissed under CPR r.57.11(2) (leading to a grant in common form)

23-30 At any stage of a probate claim the court, on the application of the claimant, or of any defendant who has acknowledged service, may order that the claim be discontinued, or dismissed, on such terms as to costs, or otherwise, as it thinks just; and may further order that a grant of probate of the will, or letters of administration of the estate, of the deceased person (as the case may be) which is the subject of the claim, be made to the person entitled thereto.[101] An application for such an order may be made by application notice in accordance with CPR Pt 23. An order for the discontinuance or dismissal of a probate claim under CPR r.57.11(2) will lead to a grant of probate, or of letters of administration, in common form. It should provide that on application for such a grant, any relevant caveat do, if still subsisting, cease to have effect. The advantage of this method of compromising a probate claim is that there is no need to ensure that all potential beneficiaries are either parties to the claim or have had notice thereof (pursuant to CPR r.19.8A)[102]; and the order will be made without the expense of a trial of the claim on written evidence. The disadvantage of this method of compromising a probate claim is that since it leads only to a grant in common form, it will only bind the parties to the compromise. It is therefore sensible to ensure that the compromise will be acceptable to any non-parties who may be affected by it. This method of compromise may only be used where it is the last will of the deceased person which is to be admitted to probate in common form. If it is an earlier will which is to be admitted to

---

96 *Snowden, Re* [1970] Ch. 700 at 710–711.

97 See also *Chancery Guide*, paras.29.47–29.58.

98 CPR r.57.10(1) and *Chancery Guide* para.29.51.

99 CPR r.57.11(1) and *Chancery Guide* para.29.54.

100 Practice Direction 57—Probate para.6.1. And see *Chancery Guide*, para.29.54. For a suggested form of order, which should be adapted as appropriate, see Practice Form No.38CH (*White Book*, Forms Volume), reproduced as Precedent No.8 at para.A1-08.

101 CPR r.57.11(2). The court retains a greater degree of control over probate claims than over ordinary litigation and permission to discontinue can be refused. In *Green v Briscoe* [2005] EWHC 3455 (Ch), David Richards J held that in the circumstances the master had been entitled to take the view that it was not appropriate to give permission to a named executrix to discontinue her counterclaim seeking an order of the court pronouncing in favour of a will. At the later trial of the counterclaim, Peter Leaver QC (sitting as a deputy judge of the Chancery Division) pronounced in favour of the will in solemn form: see *Briscoe v Green* [2006] EWHC 2116 (Ch).

102 See para.23-25.

probate, later wills will have to be pronounced against, and the earlier will pronounced for, all in solemn form.[103] If the parties wish to alter any of the dispositions effected by the will which is to be admitted to probate, it is suggested that this may be done (with the consent of all persons who are thereby affected) by incorporating the agreed variations in the form of a schedule to a Tomlin Order.[104] If it is intended that the variations should be retrospective to the date of the deceased's death for the purposes of either Inheritance Tax or Capital Gains Tax, care should be taken to ensure that the relevant statutory requirements are observed.[105]

(2) By means of an order under section 49 of the Administration of Justice Act 1985

This section permits a probate claim to be compromised without a trial if every "relevant beneficiary"[106] has consented to the proposed order. It is only available in the High Court. Applications under s.49 may be heard by a master or district judge, and must be supported by written evidence identifying the "relevant beneficiaries" and exhibiting the written consent of each of them. The written evidence of testamentary documents will still be necessary.[107] The advantage of this method of compromising a probate claim is that it leads to a grant in solemn form, yet it avoids the expense of a trial of the claim on written evidence. The disadvantage is that the consent of every "relevant beneficiary" must be obtained. **23-31**

(3) Following a trial of the claim on written evidence

Where the parties to the claim agree to a compromise, the court may order the trial of the probate claim on written evidence.[108] The written evidence of testamentary documents required by CPR r.57.5 will still be necessary. It will also normally be necessary for an attesting witness to sign a witness statement or swear an affidavit of due execution of any will or codicil sought to be admitted to probate.[109] Since a trial of the claim on written evidence will lead to an order for a grant in solemn form, the court will generally ensure that all persons with any potential interest in the proceedings are either joined as parties or served with notice under CPR r.19.8A.[110] If the claim comes within CPR r.19.7,[111] the court can make a representation order with a view to approving the settlement if satisfied that it is for the benefit of all the represented persons. When satisfied that the matter is ready for trial, the master will order the case to be tried in the General List. Where any **23-32**

---

103 See *White Book*, Vol.1, para.57.11.1. This is said to be one important reason why there are the different methods of settling a probate claim referred to in Practice Direction 57—Probate para.6.1.

104 See para.23-34.

105 As to which see Inheritance Act 1984 s.142; Taxation of Chargeable Gains Act 1992 s.62(6).

106 By Administration of Justice Act 1985 s.49(2) "relevant beneficiary" in relation to a pronouncement relating to a will, or wills, of a deceased person means: (a) a person who under any such will is beneficially interested in the deceased's estate; and (b) where the effect of the pronouncement would be to cause the estate to devolve as on an intestacy (or partial intestacy), or to prevent it from so devolving, a person who under the law relating to intestacy is beneficially interested in the estate.

107 Practice Direction 57—Probate, para.6.2.

108 Practice Direction 57—Probate, para.6.1.

109 *Chancery Guide*, para.29.55. At this stage, the will or codicil will be in the court's possession and cannot be handed out for use as an exhibit. The solution to the practical difficulties to which this gives rise is to be found at paras.29.55 and 29.56 of the *Chancery Guide*.

110 See para.23-25.

111 See para.23-24.

party to the proposed compromise is under a disability, or is represented under CPR r.19.7, it will be necessary for the court to approve the compromise on their behalf. The application to have the compromise approved will be heard by the judge in private; and the evidence to prove the will can be heard immediately thereafter in open court.

23-33 In *Di Placito v Slater*[112] a claim by executors to distribute the deceased's estate in accordance with a particular will was compromised on the basis of an undertaking by the claimant not to bring proceedings to challenge the validity of that will after a specified date. The claimant breached the undertaking by commencing proceedings shortly after that date, and he then applied to the court to vary the undertaking by retrospectively extending the specified time so as to validate the proceedings. In dismissing an appeal from an order refusing the extension of time, the Court of Appeal emphasised the need for the claimant to demonstrate "special circumstances", in the sense of circumstances so different from those which might properly be regarded as contemplated or intended to be governed by the order at the time that it was made, that it was appropriate to release the claimant from the burden of his undertaking.

PRACTICE AND PROCEDURE

Agreed orders

23-34 CPR r.40.6 and para.3 of Practice Direction 40B—Judgments and Orders[113] apply where all the parties agree the terms in which a judgment should be given or an order should be made. Unlike the former RSC Ord.42 r.5A, these provisions apply to claims proceeding in the Chancery Division. All consent orders filed in the Chancery Division, and in respect of which a fee has been paid, are referred to the Master for approval before the order is sealed. The procedure for filing consent orders for sealing has changed by reason of the creation of electronic files and electronic filing and Ch.22 of the *Chancery Guide* (August 2019) explains what is required in order for consent orders (including Tomlin orders) to be sealed in the Chancery Division. Paragraph 10.4 of Practice Direction 23A—Applications[114] which supplements CPR r.23.8 (providing for applications to be dealt with without a hearing), emphasises that the parties to an application for a consent order must ensure that the court is provided with any material it needs in order to be satisfied that it is appropriate to make the order. By para.10.5 of the same Practice Direction, the parties must inform the court immediately when a judgment or order has been agreed in respect of an application or claim where a hearing date has been fixed. Indeed, para.41 of the standard draft case management directions for Chancery cases in Form CH1[115] expressly provides that if the claim or part of the claim is settled, the parties must immediately inform the court, whether or not it is then possible to file a draft consent order to give effect to the settlement.

Tomlin orders

23-35 Where proceedings are to be stayed on agreed terms to be scheduled to the order,

---

112 *Di Placito v Slater* [2004] 1 W.L.R. 1605. See further para.23-42.

113 *White Book*, Vol.1, para.40BPD.3. See para.10–17 onwards.

114 *White Book*, Vol.1, para.23APD.10.

115 Referred to at para.1.13 of the *Chancery Guide* and available on the gov.uk website via a link set out therein.

the *Chancery Guide* provides that the draft order in the form of a Tomlin order[116] should be headed "Tomlin Order" (not simply "consent order") and drawn so as to read as follows[117]:

> "And the parties having agreed to the terms set out in [the attached schedule][a [confidential] schedule/agreement dated........, copies of which are held by the parties' solicitors/the solicitors for the (*party*)] [and to there being no order for costs
>
> [AND the solicitors having certified that the only relief sought in this claim/ counterclaim is the payment of money including any interest and costs, and that no ancillary relief has been sought at any stage]
>
> *IT IS BY CONSENT ORDERED that*
>
> (1) all further proceedings in this claim be stayed except for the purpose of carrying the terms of the agreement into effect
>
> AND for that purpose the parties have permission to apply [without the need to issue fresh proceedings].
>
> (2) [any provision in respect of costs] (*unless in preamble*)"

According to the *Chancery Guide*, if the order refers to a confidential schedule or agreement this should not be lodged with the court with the order, but the order must identify clearly the agreement which forms the schedule and where it is held.[118]

Consent orders (including Tomlin Orders) lodged with the court will only be accepted and referred to the Judge or Master for approval if: **23-36**

(a) the word "draft" or "minute" does not appear in the order and the title and preamble are in the correct format;
(b) the signed order, together with a "clean" copy of the order in Word format excluding the signature provisions, is submitted by email to ChanceryJudgesListing@justice.gov.uk for Judges' orders or; Chancery.mastersappointments@justice.gov.uk for Masters' orders;
(c) the email contains an undertaking that the court fee will be paid within two working days;
(d) the order specifies the party who will receive the order for service from the court;
(e) the order includes a service note (see paras 5–7 of the *Chancery Guide*) in the correct format.

The order will not be sealed until the court fee has been paid.[119]

It is not the normal practice of the judges of the Chancery Division to inspect schedules or agreements annexed to Tomlin Orders. The judge who makes the order undertakes no responsibility for the scheduled terms, and cannot be taken to have approved them.[120] If a Tomlin order is concerned only with claims for money (i.e. debt or damages, including interest and costs) and no other relief has been sought, they may be sealed by the court associate under CPR rule 40.6(3) without reference to the Master or Judge, but, in order to obtain sealing by the court associate, the solicitors for the parties must include in the preamble to the order the follow- **23-37**

---

116 See para.9-21 onwards.

117 *Chancery Guide*, para.22.12.

118 *Chancery Guide*, para.22.11(b).

119 *Chancery Guide*, para.22.9. Further information regarding the sealing of Tomlin orders can be found in a Note approved by the Chief Master on 3 October 2016 and amended on 24 October 2016, available as a PDF on the judiciary.uk website — *https://www.judiciary.uk/wp-content/uploads/2016/10/sealing-of-tomlin-orders-03-10-2016-amended-24-10-2016.pdf* [Accessed July 2019].

120 *Chancery Guide*, para.22.13.

ing wording (on which the court associate will rely)[121]:

> "AND the solicitors having certified that the only relief sought in this claim/counterclaim is the payment of money including interest and costs, and that no ancillary relief has been sought at any stage".

The embodiment of a settlement in a consent order does not constitute the court's approval of the settlement for the purposes of CPR r.21.10 (compromise, etc by or on behalf of a child or protected party), the purpose of which is to impose an external check on the propriety of the settlement.[122]

Appeals

23-38 The practice for compromising all appeals to the Chancery Division is set out in section 6 of Practice Direction 52A—Appeals: General Provisions[123] supplementing CPR Pt 52. Where an appellant does not wish to pursue an application or an appeal, he may request the appeal court to dismiss the application or the appeal.[124] If such a request is granted, it will usually be subject to an order that the appellant pays the costs of the application or appeal.[125] If the appellant wishes to have the application or appeal dismissed without costs, his request must be accompanied by a consent, signed by the respondent, stating that the respondent so consents.[126] Where the appeal is proceeding in the High Court, a document signed by all the parties, or their legal representatives, must be lodged with the Chancery Judges' Listing Office (ground floor, Rolls Building) requesting dismissal of the appeal. The appeal can be dismissed without any hearing by an order made in the name of the Chancellor. Any orders with directions as to costs will be drawn by the Chancery associates.[127] The appeal court will not normally make an order allowing an appeal unless satisfied that the decision of the lower court was wrong or unjust because of a serious procedural or other irregularity; but the appeal court may set aside or vary the order of the lower court by consent, and without determining the merits of the appeal, if it is satisfied that there are good and sufficient reasons for so doing. Where the appeal court is requested by all the parties to allow an application or an appeal, the court may consider the request on the papers. The request should set out the relevant history of the proceedings and the matters relied on as justifying the proposed order, and should be accompanied by a copy of the proposed order.[128] Where one of the parties is a child or protected party, any disposal of an application or the appeal requires the court's approval. A draft order signed by the

---

121 *Chancery Guide*, paras.22.14-22.15.

122 *Dunhill v Burgin (Nos 1 & 2)* [2014] UKSC 18; [2014] 1 W.L.R. 933.

123 *White Book*, Vol.1, paras 52APD12–14. See also para.24.19 of the *Chancery Guide*. Even appeals in insolvency proceedings are now governed by the procedure set out in CPR Part 52: see para.23-10.

124 This reflects the former practice under which the court was reluctant to allow an appeal to be withdrawn (as opposed to the appeal being dismissed by consent) because once an appeal was dismissed that was an end of the matter, whereas if the appeal was merely withdrawn, the appellant could (subject to obtaining any necessary extension of time) subsequently change his mind and launch the appeal again: *Buckbod Investments Ltd v Nana-Otchere* [1985] 1 W.L.R. 342.

125 Practice Direction 52A—Appeals: General Provisions para.6.1.

126 Practice Direction 52A—Appeals: General Provisions para.6.2.

127 *Chancery Guide*, para.24.19. But under the new procedure for Chancery orders (see Ch.22 of the *Chancery Guide*), the parties should provide the court with the order in a form which may be approved and sealed by the court without amendment. A nominated party will be required to serve the order once it has been sealed.

128 Practice Direction 52A—Appeals: General Provisions para.6.4.

parties' solicitors should be sent to the appeal court, together with an opinion from the advocate acting on behalf of the child or protected party and, in the case of a protected party, any relevant documents prepared for the Court of Protection.[129]

If a claim is compromised at a time when an appeal is pending or contemplated, and the terms of compromise expressly identify different specified results if the appeal is either dismissed or allowed, care should be taken to ensure that the terms of compromise clearly and adequately cater for all the possible outcomes of the hearing of the appeal. In *Bayoumi v Women's Total Abstinence Educational Union Ltd (No.2)*[130] the court held that, since neither of the two prescribed results of the appeal had in fact occurred, the judgment embodied in a consent order was not applicable in the events that had happened. 23-39

DECLARATIONS[131]

By CPR r.40.20 the court may make binding declarations, whether or not any other remedy is claimed. It is not the normal practice of the Chancery Division to make a declaration when giving judgment by consent.[132] But the rule is one of practice only, and not of law, and will give way to the paramount duty of the court to do the fullest justice to the claimant to which he is entitled, particularly where the declaration sought cannot affect the rights of anyone other than the parties and persons claiming through them.[133] Thus, where a contract has been brought to an end by reason of the defendant's repudiation of it, by consent the court may declare that the contract is at an end, and that the claimant is no longer bound by it.[134] Where the appellant had entered into an agreement compromising pending litigation as part of a bona fide commercial bargain to avoid the need for a trial on terms whereby in certain circumstances (which had occurred) he would not oppose the respondents applying for an order which would include the grant of declaratory relief, the Court of Appeal upheld the lower court's conclusion that this was one of those rare cases in which it was necessary to grant the relevant declarations in order to do justice between the parties.[135] The Court of Appeal confirmed that the rule that declarations should not be granted by consent was one of practice, and was not an immutable rule, so that declarations could be granted by consent where this was necessary to do justice in the case. Where the parties consent to (or agree not to oppose) the grant of declaratory relief, and that consent forms part of a bona fide commercial bargain entered into between them to avoid the need for a trial, the court is likely to consider it necessary to grant the declarations sought in order to do justice between the parties. Before it accedes to an application to make a declaration by consent, the court will need to be satisfied: 23-40

(1) that the claim which has been compromised was seriously arguable;
(2) that if that claim had succeeded at trial, the court would have been likely

---

129 Practice Direction 52A—Appeals: General Provisions para.6.5.

130 *Bayoumi v Women's Total Abstinence Educational Union Ltd (No.2)* [2005] EWHC 3417 (Ch), Simon Berry QC, sitting as a deputy High Court judge.

131 See also para.10-02.

132 *Wallersteiner v Moir* [1974] 1 W.L.R. 991, per Buckley LJ at 1029 and per Scarman LJ at 1030.

133 *Patten v Burke Publishing Ltd* [1991] 1 W.L.R. 541. In *Lever Faberge Ltd v Colgate-Palmolive Ltd* [2005] EWHC 2655 (Pat); [2006] F.S.R. 333 at [4], Lewison J indicated that the reluctance of the court to grant declarations without full investigation of the facts was less strong now that the CPR required allegations to be verified by a statement of truth than was formerly the case. See also para.10-02.

134 *Patten v Burke Publishing Ltd* [1991] 1 W.L.R. 541 per Millett J at 544C.

135 *Animatrix Ltd v O'Kelly* [2008] EWCA Civ 1415 at [53]–[54] per Arden LJ (delivering the judgment of the Court of Appeal).

to have considered that the declarations sought were necessary to afford justice to the claimant; and

(3) that the grant of the declarations sought is not likely to have any adverse repercussions for third parties.[136]

INTERIM APPLICATIONS

23-41 If all the parties to an interim application agree, it can be adjourned for not more than 14 days by counsel's clerks or solicitors attending the Chancery Judges' Listing in the Rolls Building at any time before 4.00 pm on the day before the hearing of the application and producing consents signed by solicitors or counsel for all parties agreeing to the adjournment. A litigant in person must attend before Judges' Listing as well as signing a consent.[137] This procedure may not be used for more than three successive adjournments, and no adjournment may be made by this procedure to the last two days of any term.[138]

23-42 This procedure should also be used where the parties agree that the application will take two hours or more and that, in consequence, the application should be adjourned to be heard as an Interim Application by Order. In that event, the consents set out above should also contain an agreed timetable for the filing of evidence, or confirmation that no further evidence is to be filed. Any application arising from the failure of a party to abide by the timetable, and any application to extend the timetable, must be made to the judge.[139]

Undertakings given to the court may be continued unchanged over any adjournment. If, however, on an adjournment, an undertaking is to be varied, or a new undertaking given, then that must be dealt with by the court.[140]

23-43 It is commonly the case that on an interim application the respondent does not appear, either in person or by solicitors or counsel, but the applicant seeks a consent order based upon a letter of consent from the respondent, or their solicitors, or a draft statement of agreed terms signed by the respondent's solicitors. This causes no difficulty where the agreed relief falls wholly within the relief claimed in the application notice. If, however, the agreed relief goes outside that which is claimed in the application notice, or even in the claim form, or when undertakings are offered, then difficulties can arise. A procedure has been established for this purpose, to be applied to all applications in the Chancery Division.[141] Subject always to the discretion of the court, no order will be made in such cases unless a consent signed by, or on behalf of, the respondent to the application is put before the court in accordance with the following provisions:

(1) Where there are solicitors on the record for the respondent, the court will normally accept as sufficient a written consent signed by those solicitors on their headed notepaper.

(2) Where there are solicitors for the respondent who are not on the record, the court will normally accept as sufficient a written consent signed by those solicitors on their headed notepaper only if in the consent (or some other

---

[136] *Hayim v Couch* [2009] EWHC 1040 (Ch) at [17]–[18], per Stephen Smith QC; followed and applied in *Singh v Singh* [2014] EWHC 2762 (Ch), per Simon Monty QC, also holding that the court should be cautious before it makes a declaration by consent (at [9]); and that HM Revenue & Customs should not be considered a third party for these purposes (at [23]).

[137] cf. para.10-03, fn.20.

[138] *Chancery Guide*, para.16.22.

[139] *Chancery Guide*, para.16.23.

[140] *Chancery Guide*, para.16.24.

[141] *Chancery Guide*, paras.16.36–16.39.

document) the solicitors certify that they have fully explained to the respondent the effect of the order and that the respondent appeared to have understood the explanation.

(3) Where there is a written consent signed by a respondent acting in person, the court will not normally accept it as sufficient unless the court is satisfied that the respondent understands the effect of the order, either by reason of the circumstances (for example, that the respondent is himself a solicitor or barrister) or by means of other material (for example, that the respondent's consent is given in reply to a letter explaining, in simple terms, the effect of the order).

(4) Where the respondent offers any undertaking to the court:
   (a) the document containing the undertaking must be signed by the respondent personally;
   (b) solicitors must certify on their headed notepaper that the signature is that of the respondent; and
   (c) if the case falls within (2) or (3) above, solicitors must certify that they have explained to the respondent the consequences of giving the undertaking, and that the respondent appeared to understand the explanation.

If the parties to an application are able to agree an order by consent without the parties attending, they should also agree a figure for costs to be inserted in the order, or agree that there should be no order as to costs. If the costs position cannot be agreed, then the parties will have to attend on the appointment; but unless good reason can be shown for the failure of the parties to deal with costs, no costs will be allowed for that attendance. The court usually finds it unsatisfactory if the parties agree the terms of a consent order but not the provision for costs. Depending on the facts and circumstances, the court may not be able to decide on the question of costs without hearing the application fully; but it is not likely to be consistent with the overriding objective to allow the necessary amount of court time to the dispute on costs in such a case. The court may then have to decide the costs issue on a broad brush approach, making an order against one party or the other only if it is clear, without spending too much time on it, that such an order would be appropriate, and otherwise making no order as to the costs.[142] **23-44**

Even in interlocutory matters it is not permissible to reopen an issue that that been disposed of unless there has been a significant change of circumstances of an unforeseen kind. Thus where, on an application for an interim injunction, the respondent chooses not to seek an adjournment of the application, but instead accepts that it should be dealt with and disposed of then and there by offering undertakings until trial or further order, there must be good grounds before the respondent is able to apply to discharge or modify the undertakings. Good grounds can consist of a significant change of circumstances, or becoming aware of new facts which could not reasonably have been known, or found out, before the undertakings were given; but not a subsequent decision of the Court of Appeal which has undermined the applicant's case.[143] Where, however, an application for an interim injunction is not stood over to the trial of the action, but is adjourned **23-45**

---

142 In previous editions of the *Chancery Guide*, these principles were specifically set out (see *Chancery Guide* 2013, para.11.11). The *Chancery Guide* 2018 does not set them out but it is suggested that the Court's approach to costs where the application is agreed will remain broadly the same. See also paras 9-03 – 9-07.

143 *Chanel Ltd v F.W. Woolworth & Co Ltd* [1981] 1 W.L.R. 485 CA; *Butt v Butt* [1987] 1 W.L.R. 1351 at 1353 CA, per Nourse LJ. For a case where the *Chanel* case was distinguished, see *Kensington*

generally, it has not been dealt with and disposed of as an interim matter; and the respondent does not have to show any such grounds before he can apply to the court to modify the terms of the undertaking, or to discharge it.[144] Often the party against whom an injunction is sought gives to the court an undertaking which avoids the need for the court to grant the injunction. In these cases, there is an implied undertaking in damages by the party applying for the injunction in favour of the other.[145] The position is less clear where the party applying for the injunction also gives an undertaking to the court. The parties should consider, and, if necessary, raise with the judge, whether the party in whose favour that undertaking is given must give a cross-undertaking in damages in those circumstances. Consideration should also be given to the question whether a cross-undertaking should be given in favour of a person who is not a respondent to the application.[146] If the action is later compromised, the parties should expressly provide for their release from any cross-undertakings as to damages.[147]

23-46 There was a practice of long-standing in the Chancery Division whereby an ordinary interlocutory motion might, by agreement, be treated as a motion for judgment, or as the trial of the action. Where an interim application was not contested, and an agreed order was sought, the application might be treated as an application for final judgment. The order would recite the agreement of the parties that the application was to be treated as an application for judgment.[148] Where the application was contested, the consent of the parties was required for it to be treated as the trial of the action; and the order would contain a recital to this effect. If the judge was satisfied with the written evidence, he would be free to give final judgment thereon. The appropriate fee had to be paid before the order would be passed and entered. This practice is now probably obsolete but practitioners may nevertheless find the precedent useful.

Masters and District Judges

23-47 The former procedural restrictions on the power of a High Court Chancery Master to approve compromises and settlements have now disappeared.[149] In district registries of the Chancery Division (in Birmingham, Bristol, Leeds, Liverpool, Manchester, Newcastle, and Cardiff), in proceedings in the Chancery Division, without the consent of the relevant Supervising Judge or their nominee, a District Judge may not deal with approving compromises (other than applications under the Inheritance (Provision for Family and Dependants Act) 1975[150]) (i) on behalf of a person under disability where that person's interest in a fund, or if there is no fund, the maximum amount of the claim exceeds £100,000 or any larger sum specified

---

International Ltd v Republic of Congo [2007] EWCA Civ 1128; [2008] 1 W.L.R. 1144. See also para.6-22.

144 *Butt v Butt* [1987] 1 W.L.R. 1351 CA.

145 *Chancery Guide*, para.16.29.

146 *Chancery Guide*, para.16.29. If, exceptionally, a freezing order is to be extended to assets held by the defendant as a trustee or nominee for a third party, it will usually be appropriate for the cross-undertaking in damages to be extended in terms to cover the purported beneficiary for any loss caused by the injunction which is subsequently varied or discharged in respect of any trust assets: *JSC BTA Bank v Solodchenko* [2010] EWCA Civ 1436; [2011] 1 W.L.R. 888.

147 And see paras 5-41 and 6-05.

148 See Precedent No.9 at para.A1-09.

149 See PD 2B (Allocation of Cases to Levels of Judiciary), para.7B.1.

150 See Ch.25.

by the Chancellor of the High Court and (ii) on behalf of absent, unborn and unascertained persons.[151]

When hearings before masters or Insolvency and Companies Court Judges are compromised or settled, the Court Office in the Rolls Building should be informed in writing immediately. 23-48

Release from undertaking

For the correct approach to considering an application to be released from an undertaking which has been incorporated in a consent order settling an action not to bring proceedings after a specified date, reference should be made to *Di Placito v Slater*.[152] 23-49

Costs

For possible approaches where the parties have compromised an interim application or the entire litigation but have been unable to reach a settlement on the issue of costs, reference should be made to the authorities cited in the *White Book*, Vol.1, paras 44.2.6 and 44.2.17.[153] These authorities were reviewed by Henry Carr J in *Conversant Wireless Licensing SARL v Huawei Technologies Co Ltd*[154] when determining the issue of costs following the compromise of an interim application. The court noted that two earlier cases had considered the approach the court should take when considering the incidence of costs following a compromise. In *Brawley v Marczynski (No 1)*,[155] it was said that the court should look to secure justice between the parties without incurring unnecessary court time and additional costs, thereby applying the overriding objective. If it was obvious which of the parties would have succeeded on the substantive issue, that party ought to be awarded their costs. If it was not obvious, then it would depend on the circumstances whether the court would look at the substantive issue to determine the question of costs but in the absence of good reason to do so, no order as to costs would be the approach taken. In *BCT Software Solutions Ltd v C Brewer & Sons Ltd*[156] it was stressed that in such a situation it remained open to the court to take the approach that if costs were not compromised, then the action was not compromised and must continue. Those authorities were said to be distinguishable from the present case. Previous authorities had concerned a compromise reached during the course of a trial, where witnesses might have been called and cross-examined. The present case concerned the compromise of an interim application, with no witnesses and no cross-examination. The application had been fully argued before it was compromised. As such, the judge was in a position to determine who would have succeeded on the application but for the compromise; and he was also in the position to form a view about the parties' conduct. Moreover, significant costs were at stake. In the event, the judge awarded costs to the claimant as it had, in substance, succeeded on the application. 23-50

---

[151] See PD 2B (Allocation of Cases to Levels of Judiciary), para.7B.2.
[152] *Di Placito v Slater* [2004] 1 W.L.R. 1605: see para.23-32.
[153] See also paras 9-03–9-07.
[154] [2018] EWHC 2549 (Ch).
[155] [2002] EWCA Civ 756; [2003] 1 W.L.R. 813.
[156] [2003] EWCA Civ 939. See also para.9-04.

PART 8: MATRIMONIAL, FAMILY AND INHERITANCE DISPUTES

CHAPTER 24

Compromise of Disputes between Husband and Wife and Civil Partners

Not every marriage or civil partnership breakdown ends in divorce/dissolution, although many of course do. It is necessary, therefore, to consider a number of areas in which disputes may fall to be resolved by agreement. They can be enumerated as follows: **24-01**

(1) Agreements when no divorce, dissolution or judicial separation proceedings are proposed or contemplated or, if proposed or contemplated, where they are likely to be delayed for a time.
(2) Agreements concerning the disposal of the divorce, dissolution or judicial separation suit itself.
(3) Agreements involving the interim stages of divorce, dissolution or judicial separation proceedings, particularly those involving interim financial provision.
(4) Agreements relating to the final disposal of financial and property applications.
(5) Agreements relating to children.

By far the most difficult of these areas is that relating to final financial and property applications. In relation to each area enumerated, it is proposed to examine briefly the law applicable and the manner in which such agreements are reached, effectuated, enforced and, where necessary, set aside.

AGREEMENTS NOT NECESSARILY INVOLVING DIVORCE OR JUDICIAL SEPARATION

There is a growing encouragement for parties in dispute to settle their differences by way of compromise. The changes in procedure and recent Supreme Court decisions underline the importance that is now attached to enabling and encouraging parties to think about compromising their difficulties without court intervention. **24-02**

Before any claim for financial relief or private law proceedings relating to children can be issued, the proposed applicant must demonstrate that he/she has attended a meeting (a "MIAM"[1]) which will provide information about mediation and at which the suitability of mediation would have been assessed.[2] Moreover, at every stage the court is required to consider whether non-court dispute resolution is appropriate and, if so, may adjourn for the parties to obtain advice about non-court **24-03**

---

1 (Family) Mediation Information and Assessment Meeting.
2 Family Procedure Rules 2010 rr.3.6, 3.7 and 3.8.

dispute resolution and, where the parties agree, to enable it to take place.[3] Non-court dispute resolution includes a number of different processes—collaborative, mediation, arbitration,[4] and private FDRs. In recent years, the private FDR system[5] has, in particular, gained in popularity and received judicial endorsement.[6]

24-04 It is perhaps not surprising, therefore, that the courts have increasingly acknowledged the importance of allowing parties to determine how they would like their financial affairs to be arranged in the event that they were to divorce. In this context, one is looking not only at agreements that are made in the knowledge that divorce is likely but also at agreements that are made in the contemplation and expectation that the marriage or civil partnership will survive but which provide, in the event that it does not, how the financial resources should be distributed between the parties.

24-05 Although the encouragement for the parties to resolve their financial differences without court intervention is clear, it remains the case that any agreement they might reach may be subject to interference from the court. Thus, the only way to achieve absolute financial certainty, on the breakdown of the marriage or civil partnership, is to seek an approved order from the court. Pension Sharing Orders and a "clean break" (i.e. the dismissal of potential financial claims under the Matrimonial Causes Act 1973 (or Civil Partnership Act 2004) and the Inheritance (Provision for Family and Dependants) Act 1975) require a court order in any event.

24-06 There has been significant development of the jurisprudence in recent years considering the weight that should be attached by a court dealing with financial provision following divorce to earlier agreements of the parties. Agreements reached in contemplation of divorce or as part of the process following divorce are dealt with later.[7] This section will deal with "nuptial agreements" and agreements reached within the context of the Married Women's Property Act 1882 or s.66 of the Civil Partnership Act 2004. Historically, "maintenance agreements" (governed by ss.34 and 35 of the Matrimonial Causes Act 1973) were agreements that fell for consideration in this context. However, the consensus would appear to be that they no longer have any meaningful role.[8]

---

3 Family Procedure Rules 2010 rr.3.3 and 3.4. Mostyn J considered these rules in *Mann v Mann* [2014] 2 F.L.R. 928 at [25]–[28]. He identified where r.3.4 (then r.3.3) differed from the Civil Procedure Rules 1998 r. 26.4(2A) and, in particular, noted that the power under the FPR to adjourn so as to enable non-court dispute resolution to take place, while capable of being exercised on the court's own initiative, can only be exercised if the parties agree whereas under the CPR counterpart the court can impose a stay in favour of ADR whether the parties agree or not. Mostyn J suggested that the Family Procedure Rules Committee give consideration to deleting the words "if the parties agree" from the FPR rule so that it is put on the same footing as its CPR counterpart. This amendment has not yet been made. The Court of Appeal has held (on appeal from a decision by Parker J reported at [2019] EWHC 1267) that in the civil context the consent of the parties is not necessary for a case to be referred to Early Neutral Evaluation (*Lomax v Lomax* [2019] EWCA Civ 1467).

4 Available in finance cases since 2012 and in private law children cases since 2016.

5 The parties select, and pay for, a private FDR tribunal. That tribunal may be a solicitor, barrister or retired judge. The private FDR will take place at a time and place of the parties' choosing. If (as is usually the case) the private FDR takes the place of an in-court FDR, a short directions hearing will normally be listed to take place after the private FDR. That directions hearing can either be vacated if agreement is reached at the private FDR (with the draft consent order filed for the court's approval) or otherwise directions can be sought for a Final Hearing. Unlike a court FDR, at the conclusion of a private FDR the "judge" cannot make an appropriate consent order or give directions for the future course of the proceedings.

6 Munby P. in "*President's Circular: Financial Remedies Court Pilot Phase 2*" (paras 7-11), 27 July 2018 and the Financial Remedies Courts Good Practice Protocol (paras 9 and 10), 7 November 2019.

7 See para.24-15 onwards.

8 Wilson LJ (as he then was) suggested in *Radmacher v Granatino* [2009] 2 F.L.R. 1181 at [134] that

NUPTIAL AGREEMENTS DEALING WITH FINANCIAL PROVISION UPON DIVORCE

The court should give effect to any agreement, either before the marriage (ante-nuptial) or after the marriage (post-nuptial), freely entered into by each party with a full appreciation of its implications unless in the circumstances prevailing it would not be fair to hold the parties to their agreement.[9] Thus the ability exists for parties to compromise any claims for financial relief, should divorce occur, even though divorce is not contemplated at the time of the agreement. The procedure for, and interplay between, an application for financial provision upon divorce in cases where a nuptial agreement exists, is explored fully in the section entitled "Securing an order reflecting a prior agreement".[10] For the purposes of this section it is sufficient to record that any concern that such agreements would offend public policy was swept away by *Radmacher*.[11] Indeed, the Supreme Court was keen to emphasise that respect should be given to the parties' autonomy and their ability to agree what is right for them.[12] **24-07**

One other matter falls to be considered in this context: the compromise of proceedings brought under s.17 of the Married Women's Property Act 1882 (as amended) or s.66 of the Civil Partnership Act 2004. **24-08**

COMPROMISE OF PROCEEDINGS UNDER MARRIED WOMEN'S PROPERTY ACT 1882 SECTION 17 AND CIVIL PARTNERSHIP ACT 2004 SECTION 66

Preliminary

Though much less important now than it was prior to the implementation of the Divorce Reform Act 1969 and its associated legislation, s.17 still has a role to play in the resolution of disputes between husband and wife (or engaged parties) concerning "the title to or possession of property". "Property" for this purpose is defined as including "real or personal property and any estate or interest therein, any money, negotiable instrument, debt or other chose in action and any other interest whether in possession or not".[13] Section 66 of the Civil Partnership Act 2004 confers the same rights on civil partners. Most commonly the matter in issue is the family home. What proportion does each party own?[14] Has the share of one party increased by virtue of improvements carried out by that party?[15] What money did each contribute and what was the intention of the parties as to ownership? Should **24-09**

---

maintenance agreements have "long since become virtually dead letters". Although the Supreme Court did not examine the proposition further, Wilson LJ's view was recorded without disagreement: [2010] 2 F.L.R. 1900 at [36]. A different view had been taken by Baroness Hale in the earlier Privy Council decision of *MacLeod v MacLeod* [2009] 1 F.L.R. 641. For an analysis of the law concerning maintenance (and separation) agreements, see paras 24-08–24-19 of the 7th edition of this work.

9 *Radmacher v Granatino* [2010] 2 F.L.R. 1900 at [75].

10 See para.24-47 onwards.

11 *Radmacher v Granatino* [2010] 2 F.L.R. 1900 at [52] and [66].

12 *Radmacher v Granatino* [2010] 2.F.L.R 1900 at [78].

13 The definition was added by the Matrimonial Causes (Property and Maintenance) Act 1958 s.7.

14 In *Hallman v Harkins (Land Registration—Beneficial Interests, Trusts and Restrictions)* [2019] UKUT 245 (LC) the Upper Tribunal (Lands Chamber) held that the First Tier Tribunal lacks the jurisdiction to determine the *size* of a beneficial interest in property. Its jurisdiction is limited to determining the *existence* of a share so as to fulfil the statutory function of entering a restriction to protect a beneficiary under a trust. Civil litigation (or arbitration) is therefore required to determine the size of such a share.

15 Matrimonial Property and Proceedings Act 1970 s.37.

the property be sold either immediately or at some stage in the future?[16] However, issues concerning the ownership of property or rights in a family company or partnership can also be dealt with, as can issues relating to chattels.[17] Section 17 may assume particular importance in circumstances where a claim for a financial remedy cannot be made—for example, when the claimant has remarried before issuing an application for a financial remedy. Equally, s.17 may be utilised where it is important to establish the beneficial and legal interests of the parties—say, when bankruptcy has occurred or is threatened or there are proceedings under Proceeds of Crime Act 2002.[18] Section 17 proceedings should not be started where there are proceedings that have already been brought under the Matrimonial Causes Act 1973, it having been established that it is unnecessary to bring claims under this section when the courts have all necessary powers under the MCA 1973 to determine the issues identified.

Jurisdiction of the court and the parties' agreement

24-10 The jurisdiction of the court under s.17 of the Married Women's Property Act 1882 concerns primarily the declaration of existing rights, although the court has the power to prevent one party from enforcing those rights if to do so would be unjust to the other.[19] Likewise, s.66 of the Civil Partnership Act 2004. Under both Acts, within the scope of the powers available to it, the court has the power to make any order that it thinks fit.[20] The court has power to order a sale of the property in question,[21] to assess the value of one party's share in that property and to order the other party to pay that assessed value.[22] It can also direct, in appropriate circumstances, that one party gives to the other credit in respect of the whole or part of mortgage instalments paid by the party who remains in occupation of a property subject to a mortgage and require the party in occupation to pay an occupation rent to the other.[23]

This statement of the powers of the court is important because any provisions of an agreement compromising s.17 or s.66 proceedings which come to be reflected in a consent order must be within the jurisdiction of the court.[24] Any terms outside the normal jurisdiction would have to be dealt with by means of undertakings or in some other way (e.g. making the agreement the subject of a Tomlin order).[25]

---

16 Matrimonial Causes (Property and Maintenance) Act 1958 s.7(7). See, e.g., *Jackson v Jackson* [1971] 1 W.L.R. 1539 and *Burke v Burke* [1974] 1 W.L.R. 1063.

17 Forever etched in Sir David Foskett's memory is an occasion when two parties to Married Women's Property Act 1882 s.17 proceedings were contesting bitterly the "custody" of a stuffed woodpecker! ("Correspondence", *The Times*, 19 January 1995).

18 For examples of the interplay between POCA 2002 (or its predecessor the Criminal Justice Act 1988) and family law see *Ahmad v Ahmad* [1999] 1 F.L.R. 317 and *Webber v Webber (CPS Intervening)* [2007] 2 F.L.R. 116.

19 *Pettitt v Pettitt* [1970] A.C. 777; *Gissing v Gissing* [1971] A.C. 886.

20 Civil Partnership Act 2004 s.66(2) and Married Women's Property Act 1882 s.17.

21 There remains a difference of opinion between Mostyn J and Moor J as to whether the court has the power to make an interim order for sale under FPR 2010 r.20.2(1)(c)(v). In *SR v HR (Property Adjustment Orders)* [2018] 2 F.L.R. 843 Mostyn J therefore suggested that until the question was resolved by a higher court such applications should be made under s.17.

22 *Bothe v Amos* [1976] Fam. 46.

23 For example, *Leake v Bruzzi* [1974] 1 W.L.R. 1528, and *Suttill v Graham* [1977] 1 W.L.R. 819. In relation to the payment of an occupation rent, see *Dennis v McDonald* [1982] Fam. 63 which is a claim brought under s.30 of the Law of Property Act 1925.

24 *Livesey v Jenkins* [1985] A.C. 424, *Hinde v Hinde* [1953] 1 W.L.R. 175. See also Ch.10.

25 See Ch.9.

Ousting the jurisdiction?

As will be observed in due course,[26] the parties to an agreement over financial matters in the context of actual or contemplated divorce, dissolution or judicial separation proceedings cannot oust the jurisdiction and ultimate discretion of the court. However, any concluded agreement[27] compromising s.17 or s.66 proceedings does not require the sanction of the court[28] and it binds the parties and the court.[29] It would seem to follow that any consent order made would not be susceptible to future variation on account of changed circumstances, the agreement underlying the order being the governing factor.[30] **24-11**

Setting aside—practice

If any grounds exist for setting aside the agreement underlying a consent order, the route of challenge is now governed by Family Procedure Rules 2010 r.9.9A.[31] Nonetheless there may still be scope to bring a fresh action to set aside the agreement which resulted in a compromise of "no order" being made.[32] If, of course, the view is taken (contrary to that suggested above) that even a consent order of this nature was susceptible to "a continuing power to vary its terms",[33] it would be regarded as an interlocutory order[34] and thus amenable to an appropriate application in the s.17 and s.66 proceedings,[35] and not only would there be jurisdiction to vary the order on account of changed circumstances,[36] but also to set it aside on appeal on any of the usual grounds[37] and the availability of fresh evidence. **24-12**

If any part of the order remains executory (i.e. has still to be carried out), the court may be persuaded to intervene if circumstances arise suggesting that the agree- **24-13**

---

26 See para.24-35.

27 See, e.g. *Shears v Shears* (1973) CAT 288, considered at para.3-23.

28 *Shears v Shears* (1973) CAT 288.

29 *Steadman v Steadman* [1976] A.C. 536. It should be observed, however, that the Married Women's Property Act 1882 s.17 and the Civil Partnership Act 2004 s.66(2) each provide that the judge "may make such order ... as he thinks fit" which suggests a discretion of sorts concerning a proposed agreed order notwithstanding what the parties may have agreed.

30 In *Gee v Gee* (1972) 116 S.J. 219, the Court of Appeal held that there was jurisdiction to vary an order made, apparently, after a contested hearing.

31 Proceedings under the Married Women's Property Act 1882 are family proceedings, as defined by Sch.1 to the Senior Courts Act 1981. Family Procedure Rules 2010 rr.8.12–8.17 provide the procedure for initiating claims under the Married Women's Property Act 1882 s.17 and the Civil Partnership Act 2004 s.66. PD 30A para.14.1 (headed "Appeals against consent orders") provides as follows "The rules in Part 30 and the provisions of this Practice Direction apply to appeals relating to orders made by consent and in addition orders which are not made by consent." As originally drafted the rule went on to state that: "An appeal is the only way in which a consent order can be challenged". However, in *CS v ACS (Consent Order: Non-Disclosure: Correct Procedure)* [2016] 1 F.L.R. 131 Munby P held that this final sentence was ultra vires and hence a nullity. This decision led to the deletion of this sentence and the introduction of a new FPR 2010 r.9.9A which came into force on 3 October 2016. This is considered later: see para.24-131 onwards.

32 *Page v Page* (1972) CAT 383: "no order" was made on W's Married Women's Property Act 1882 s.17 application upon certain agreed terms. H sought to appeal on the basis of W's non-disclosure of what he suggested was a material matter. The Court of Appeal held that even if H was right on the substantive matter there was no order from which to appeal—he should have brought an action to set aside the agreement.

33 *De Lasala* [1980] A.C. 546 at 561, per Lord Diplock.

34 *De Lasala* (1980) A.C. 546. See para.4-28.

35 See para.24-25.

36 Akin to the jurisdiction in Matrimonial Causes Act 1973 s.31.

37 See Ch.4.

ment should not be enforced (the so-called "*Thwaite* jurisdiction").[38] This jurisdiction has been considered in three recent cases (the first two of which are not easily reconciled).[39] Whilst there is no specific procedural guidance on the point, it would appear that a *Thwaite* application is procedurally akin to an application for set aside, which is made to the first instance court using the Pt.18 procedure pursuant to the new FPR 2010 r.9.9A.

Intervention of third parties

24-14 Unless any grounds existed for impeaching a compromise of s.17 (or s.66) proceedings, it would be binding on both parties to it. It is clear that a transfer of property made in financial remedy proceedings under a court order is to be regarded as having involved the giving of consideration in money or money's worth and would not be set aside under the Insolvency Act 1986 in the event of a subsequent bankruptcy unless shown to be the product of collusion between the spouses, designed to affect the creditors adversely, or some other vitiating factor exists.[40] By analogy a declaration made by consent by the court in proceedings under s.17 (or s.66) will not be set aside at the instance of a third party (such as a trustee in bankruptcy) unless it is the product of an agreement designed to injure third parties and is not justified by the realities of the dispute between the parties.

AGREEMENTS CONCERNING DISPOSAL OF APPLICATIONS FOR DIVORCE, DISSOLUTION, NULLITY, JUDICIAL SEPARATION OR SEPARATION ORDERS

24-15 Generally speaking, little dispute will arise between the parties on the "fact" required to be proved before a decree or order can be granted in matrimonial or civil partnership proceedings.[41] This enables the obtaining of a decree or order in an undefended case,[42] with the whole procedure, except for the making of the decree or order, being dealt with in private in most cases.[43] Even allegations that the respondent to a petition has behaved in such a way that the petitioner cannot reasonably be expected to live with the respondent are seldom disputed since "conduct" rarely has any great significance in relation to an application for financial remedies. The full rigours of the doctrine of res judicata probably do not apply to undefended allegations of this nature and thus no detriment is suffered by a respondent who does not defend such allegations.[44]

However, there may be cases where a respondent feels sufficiently strongly to

---

[38] *Thwaite v Thwaite* [1982] Fam. 1.

[39] *Bezeliansky v Bezelianskaya* [2016] EWCA Civ 76 (which, as a decision refusing permission to appeal, cannot strictly speaking be cited as authority (Practice Direction (Citation of Authorities [2001] 1 W.L.R. 1001 para. 6.2) although it is still likely to be persuasive), *SR v HR (Property Adjustment Orders)* [2018] 2 F.L.R. 843 per Mostyn J, and *US v SR (No.4) (Executory Mainframe Distribution Order: Change in Circumstances: Extent of the Court's Ability to Revisit Terms)* [2018] EWHC 3207 (Fam) per Roberts J.

[40] *Hill v Haines* [2008] 1 F.L.R. 1192.

[41] Matrimonial Causes Act 1973 s.1(2) and Civil Partnership Act 2004 s.44(5).

[42] Family Procedure Rules 2010 r.7.1(3): "undefended case".

[43] Family Procedure Rules 2010 r.7.20.

[44] See *Rowe v Rowe* [1980] Fam. 47 In practice the respondent's advisers either secure the petitioner's advisers agreement that the allegations will not be relied upon any financial remedy proceedings or state that, although the respondent denies the allegations, for the purposes of the divorce suit he does not intend to contest them but if they are raised in any ancillary financial remedy proceedings he

wish to defend: he or she may simply dispute the allegations or, in addition, make cross-allegations of his or her own. If a case is defended,[45] the court must list the matter for a case management hearing.[46] Sometimes the strong feeling about the allegations can be assuaged by a "toning down" or deletion of some of them but they must remain sufficient to justify a court granting the decree sought.[47] More often than not, the nature of the allegations against a respondent will be forgotten if the cross-allegations are not contested and each party obtains a decree on their own petition.

Occasionally, the application will not have been compromised prior to being listed for trial. Perhaps the case management hearing will have failed in its objective.[48] However, further judicial encouragement towards agreement can be anticipated, and even where the parties have not reached agreement the court may, in certain circumstances, impose its own will on the situation.[49] **24-16**

A court will be slow to declare an agreement seeking to avoid a contested suit as contrary to public policy:

> In *N v N (Divorce: Agreement Not to Defend)*,[50] W presented a petition for divorce based upon H's alleged unreasonable behaviour. Some three or four weeks later, H and W agreed that there should be a five-month moratorium in which the possibility of a reconciliation should be explored. W agreed not to pursue her divorce suit for the agreed period so that the possibility of a reconciliation could be examined. H agreed that if at the end of the agreed period W did not withdraw her petition and proceeded with the suit, he would not defend the petition. At the end of the five-month period W decided to proceed with her petition. Ewbank J held that she was entitled to proceed and H was bound by his agreement not to defend. There was nothing contrary to public policy in H agreeing not to defend the petition. The agreement was "entirely proper and indeed encouraged the possibility of a reconciliation".

Where agreement on the disposal of the application is reached before trial or "at the doors of the court" and the agreement involves amendment of the petition (for example on the basis of the fact of two years' separation and the consent of the other party), this may occur with the written consent of the parties or permission of the Court.[51] **24-17**

Where the parties acknowledge that the marriage or civil partnership has broken down irretrievably, circumstances would be rare indeed in which a contested application would be justified.[52] Sensible advice from legal advisers will always receive judicial backing. In some cases, of course, a third party or parties will have been introduced into the proceedings and thus a compromise will have to provide for those wider interests. However, that should not render agreement impossible provided satisfactory arrangements as to costs can be made.

---

reserves the right to defend them fully and make cross-allegations.

45 Family Procedure Rules 2010 r.7.1(3): "defended case".

46 Family Procedure Rules 2010 r.7.20(4), r.7.22(2).

47 *Owens v Owens* [2018] 2 F.L.R. 1067.

48 Family Procedure Rules 2010 r.7.22, r.1.4, r.4.1.

49 *Grenfell v Grenfell* [1978] Fam. 128 (where an undisputed allegation of adultery appeared in the proceedings).

50 [1992] 1 F.L.R. 266.

51 Family Procedure Rules 2010 r.7.13(4).

52 cf. *Welfare v Welfare* (1977) 121 S.J. 743; (1978) Fam. Law 55. There will be some rare cases where a grave hardship defence is being maintained in response to a five-year separation petition: see Matrimonial Causes Act 1973 s.5.

AGREEMENTS INVOLVING INTERIM STAGES OF DIVORCE OR JUDICIAL SEPARATION PROCEEDINGS, INCLUDING INTERIM FINANCIAL PROVISION

INTERIM APPLICATIONS PROPER

Preliminary

24-18 There are two principal areas in which interim[53] applications proper are made to the court during the pendency of divorce or judicial separation proceedings—one relating to the occupation of the matrimonial home and the non-molestation of one party by the other and the other relating to the preservation and discovery of the assets of one of the parties.

Occupation of matrimonial home and non-molestation

24-19 Applications relating to the occupation of the matrimonial home are made frequently.[54] When resolved by agreement they are usually so resolved by the giving of appropriate undertakings. For example, undertakings may be given unilaterally or by both parties as to the times when use will be made of certain rooms in the house or to the effect that certain rooms will not be entered. Equally, however, one party may be prepared to leave after a period of time and an undertaking to this effect may be given. Of course, it is open to a party to consent or submit to an appropriate order being made against him, usually on the basis of an express recital that the court heard no evidence and/or no findings were made, although the provision of undertakings is more common.[55] There are now prescribed forms of undertaking contained within the Family Procedure Rules 2010.[56]

The same applies to applications for non-molestation orders. Undertakings will frequently be offered. Often the party against whom such an application is made does not accept the allegations relied upon by the applicant. Strictly speaking, a party against whom allegations are made who gives an undertaking is not taken as admitting the allegations. There are restrictions on the court's ability to accept undertakings in the context of non-molestation orders.[57] When an undertaking is offered and accepted it is not necessary for the court to have read or heard the evidence in support. However, a party sometimes wishes to emphasise his or her non-acceptance of allegations by introducing the words "without admission" into the undertaking. This occurs frequently without objection and is a useful way of arriving at an interim compromise of what can be difficult and sensitive cases.

Preservation of assets and discovery of resources

24-20 The second area concerns the preservation of financial resources and assets. Section 37 of the Matrimonial Causes Act 1973 affords one jurisdiction for obtaining orders preserving family assets; s.37 of the Senior Courts Act 1981 provides

---

53 cf. interim financial provision at para.24-22 onwards.

54 Usually under the Family Law Act 1996.

55 An undertaking to the court is the equivalent of an order and does not, unlike an order, have to be served on the person who gave it before enforcement steps can be taken: *D v A & Co* [1900] 1 Ch. 484; *Launder, Re* (1908) 98 L.T. 554.

56 Family Procedure Rules 2010 PD 33A paras 2.2 and 2.3 and PD 37A paras 2.1 and 2.2.

57 Family Law Act 1996 s.46.

another. In addition (and, in some respects, more useful and flexible) is the court's inherent jurisdiction.[58] That jurisdiction also affords the basis for the grant in the Family Court (and Family Division) of a search order.[59] Again, any agreement concerning these matters will usually be dealt with by way of undertakings to the court.[60]

Effect of undertakings "until further order"

One matter should be observed in relation to undertakings (or consent orders) of this nature: they are (if orders) interim orders or (if undertakings) equivalent to interim orders. They do not represent compromises of the substantive applications: they merely dispose of matters which arise in the course of proceedings. To that extent the court is likely to intervene and regulate such an order even if made pursuant to an agreement. In any event, parties usually consent to or undertake certain things "until the hearing of the substantive applications (or trial) or further order". Those last three words show that the parties are agreeable to placing themselves at the mercy of the court in the sense of recognising that some discharge, release or other variation of their agreement might be ordered at some later stage but prior to the hearing of the substantive issues.[61] **24-21**

Interim financial provision

Preliminary and nature of agreement

Pending the resolution of the final financial issues between the parties, interim arrangements may be contemplated and made. Many of the issues which fall for consideration in relation to final orders arise in this context and it is not proposed to duplicate the discussion.[62] **24-22**

Broadly speaking, the orders with which the court is likely to be concerned on an interim basis are those for maintenance pending suit, orders for legal services payments orders (i.e. an order that the respondent contributes to the applicant's legal costs) and, to the extent permitted by the Child Support Act 1991,[63] interim periodical payments for any children of the family.[64] Where agreement concerning interim financial provision is reached, that agreement will usually be reflected or embodied in a consent order, suitable undertakings being given where appropriate in connection with, for example, the continued payment of mortgage instalments and other outgoings on the matrimonial home pending the final applications. The essential approach in contested matters of this nature has historically been to preserve the status quo so far as possible pending final disposal of the financial issues[65] and to ensure that the recipient has sufficient provision to meet immediate needs, including the **24-23**

---

58 *Roche v Roche* (1981) 11 Fam. Law 243. See also *Shipman v Shipman* [1991] 1 F.L.R. 250.

59 See *Anton Piller KG v Manufacturing Processes Ltd* [1976] Ch. 55.

60 In *UL v BK (Freezing Orders: Safeguards: Standard Examples)* [2013] EWHC 1735 Mostyn J provided models of a s.37 order, a freezing order and a search order.

61 cf. *Chanel Ltd v F.W. Woolworth & Co Ltd* [1981] 1 W.L.R. 485, *Thompson v Thompson* [1986] Fam. 38.

62 See para.24-31.

63 Child Support Act 1991 s.10.

64 Matrimonial Causes Act 1973 ss.22 and 23(2)(d). There is also jurisdiction, pre-decree, to make secured periodical payments and lump sum provision for a child. The jurisdiction is rarely invoked, whether by consent or otherwise.

65 See *Moore v Moore* [2010] 1 F.L.R. 1413 at [22] and *MET v HAT (Interim Maintenance) (No.2)* [2015] 1 F.L.R. 576 at [10]. See also *Poon v Poon* [1994] 2 F.L.R. 857.

payment of legal fees.[66] In recent years emphasis has been placed on "reasonableness" (the applicable statutory guidance) as being synonymous with fairness and that the parties' standard of living may be an important feature in this.[67] There has also been an increased focus on the fact that interim applications are expensive and should only be pursued when, on a broad assessment, "the court's intervention is manifestly required."[68] Agreements relating to these matters will, presumably, be directed towards these ends and since, even in these matters, the ultimate discretion as to whether to make the proposed interim consent order remains with the court notwithstanding the parties' agreement,[69] it is important that this should be so. Doubtless, however, the fact that the parties have arrived at an agreement will be regarded by the court as important and will not lightly be disturbed.[70]

The court's practice

24-24 Since the ultimate discretion is that of the court, it is important that the court has the "correct, complete and up-to-date" information concerning the relevant matters in order that it can "lawfully and properly" exercise that discretion.[71] Since 1984[72] it has been necessary to lodge a statement of information with the court when applying for a consent order for interim financial provision so that the relevant information is available to the court before making the order sought.

Setting aside and variation

24-25 An order of this nature is clearly interim[73] and parties agreeing to one must be taken as submitting themselves to the jurisdiction of the court to interfere with such an order and to vary, discharge or suspend it or any part of it having regard to

> "all the circumstances of the case ... [which] shall include any change in any of the matters to which the court was required to have regard when making the order to which the application relates".[74]

It appears that this statutory jurisdiction, and the inherent jurisdiction of the court to control interim orders (even those made by consent), enables the court, on an application in the suit,[75] to alter or discharge a consent order ab initio (or from some other date) where it is clear that the original order was inappropriate and it would

---

66 Matrimonial Causes Act 1973 ss. 22(ZA) and 22(ZB) and *Rubin v Rubin* [2014] 2 F.L.R. 1018.

67 *TL v ML (Ancillary Relief: Claim Against Assets of Extended Family)* [2006] 1 F.L.R. 1263.

68 *BD v FD (Maintenance Pending Suit)* [2014] EWHC 4443 (Fam); [2016] 1 F.L.R. 390 at [34].

69 *Livesey* [1985] A.C. 424.

70 See para.24-47 onwards. In *BN v MA* [2013] EWHC 4250 Mostyn J held at [33] that "when adjudicating a question of interim maintenance, [in a case] where there has been a prenuptial agreement, the court should seek to apply the prenuptial agreement as closely and practically as it can, unless the evidence of the wife in support of her application demonstrates, to a convincing standard, that she has a likely prospect of satisfying the court that [the] agreement should not be upheld. In the absence of any evidence of that nature from the wife, it is my judgment that it is appropriate for me to seek to apply the agreement to this case as closely as I can, provided that the wife is not left in any real predicament of need."

71 *Livesey* [1985] A.C. 424 per Lord Brandon of Oakbrook at 437.

72 When Matrimonial Causes Rules 1977 r.76A became operative. See now Family Procedure Rules 2010 r.9.26(1)(b).

73 The court has a "continuing power to vary its terms" which in *De Lasala v De Lasala* [1980] A.C. 546 at 56 was held to be the appropriate test for an "interlocutory" order.

74 Matrimonial Causes Act 1973 s.31(7).

75 Unlike certain final orders it may not be necessary or appropriate to appeal in these cases: if, e.g. the original consent order was a district judge's order, it would be appropriate to issue the application to vary or discharge before him.

be unjust to insist on its continuance.[76] Although it is clear that once a consent order of this nature has been made, the legal effect of the agreement which led to it is to be derived from the order, not the agreement,[77] it is likely that the grounds upon which such an agreement would have been set aside had it remained in the realm of contract[78] would be entertained as grounds for discharging or varying the order under the foregoing jurisdiction. Indeed, a mistake on one side only has afforded grounds for intervention[79] and, presumably, any non-disclosure of a material fact to the other side (and, in due course, indirectly to the court) would constitute a reason for intervention.[80] A party may, however, prefer simply to put the other side on notice of the alleged non-disclosure or mistake, not to incur the costs of an application to set aside or vary an interim order, but instead seek to remedy the wrong at the final hearing with appropriate backdating.[81] In any case where intervention of this nature is sought, it is clear that the party seeking the intervention must show that the matter raised (for example, mistake or non-disclosure) led to the making of an order substantially different from that which otherwise would have been made.[82]

Consent orders "without prejudice" to final orders

The approach of the court to the making of interim financial provision orders following contested applications has been referred to above.[83] As a result of this approach it is not infrequently the case that an interim periodical payments order is different in quantum from the final order (the former being normally lower because of a concentration at the interim stage on meeting immediate needs). Furthermore, in the case of a consent order, a full appreciation of the evidence and the issues is not undertaken by the court. To that extent it would be wrong to suppose that the level of payments agreed should be regarded as influencing in any way those to be agreed or ordered in the final disposal.[84] However, in these cases the parties may prefer that fact to be acknowledged on the face of the order lest it be thought that positions are being "given away". At some suitable place in the agreed order (usually in the preamble) words such as "without prejudice to the final orders herein" can appear in order to make the position clear. **24-26**

---

76 *Brister v Brister* [1970] 1 W.L.R. 664 (Ormrod J), *Beighton v Beighton* (1974) 4 Fam. Law 119, and *Stephenson v Stephenson* (1974) 4 Fam. Law 124.

77 *Livesey* [1985] A.C. 424, *De Lasala v De Lasala* [1980] A.C. 546.

78 See Ch.4.

79 *Brister* [1970] 1 W.L.R. 664.

80 *Livesey* [1985] A.C. 424.

81 See fn.84.

82 *Brister* [1970] 1 W.L.R. 664 and *Livesey v Jenkins* [1985] A.C. 424. See further the discussion in relation to setting final orders at para.24-89 onwards.

83 See para.24-22.

84 See also *F v F (Ancillary Relief: Substantial Assets)* [1995] 2 F.L.R. 45 where Thorpe J (as he then was), suggested that on an interim provision application the court should not indulge in an in-depth investigation and that any shortfall or over-provision could be compensated for at the final hearing. Further, in *BD v FD (Maintenance Pending Suit)* [2014] EWHC 4443 (Fam); [2016] 1 F.L.R. 390 Moylan J (as he then was) applied similar remarks made by him in *G v G (Child Maintenance: Interim Costs Provision)* [2010] 2 F.L.R. 1264 when determining an interim application under Sch.1 to the Children Act 1989 to applications for maintenance pending suit or interim maintenance.

AGREEMENTS RELATING TO FINAL DISPOSAL OF FINANCIAL AND PROPERTY APPLICATIONS

Preliminary

24-27 As previously observed,[85] this is by far the most difficult area concerning compromises in the matrimonial sphere. As long ago as December 1980, the Court of Appeal was reminded by leading counsel[86] of the "confusion prevailing in the profession about consent orders in the matrimonial jurisdiction."[87] Practically speaking, the resolution by agreement of the financial and property affairs of the parties to a marriage breakdown assumes far greater significance than the resolution by agreement of the divorce or judicial separation itself. The process itself is one which commands full judicial support: "The law now encourages spouses to avoid bitterness after family breakdown and to settle their money and property problems."[88]

24-28 However, the context in which agreements of this nature operate is one in which a number of particular problems can arise in addition to those associated with compromises in other spheres. At all stages both parties may be exposed to emotional and financial pressures which result in unwise decisions being made in respect not only of themselves, but also of such children as there may be.[89] Equally, the bitterness sometimes associated with these situations can result in one or other or both of the parties seeking to conceal from the other the existence of resources. There is also the temptation to conceal proposed plans for remarriage or new relationships which may have an influence on the future resources of one or other or both of the parties. Sometimes, of course, circumstances may change after parties conclude an agreement (and a consent order) which makes continued reliance upon it (or the order) seem inappropriate.

24-29 The foregoing shows the need for the court to retain a fair degree of control over agreements and consent orders in this context. On the other hand, consistent with the approach which encourages settlement,[90] it is important that the court's control should not be used as a vehicle by which parties break their bargains and seek to reopen matters which were fairly and properly concluded. It is inevitable that the legal principles applicable in this area endeavour to strike a balance between these competing considerations. The certainty, therefore, which legal advisers prefer to see in the statements of applicable principle is unlikely to be found to the extent seen in other contexts. That factor may have led to some of the confusion referred to above. Unfortunately, however, some of the earlier decisions in this area (all undoubtedly correct on their merits) often failed to reveal consistent statements of principle, whether relating to the law or practice applicable, leading to further confusion.[91]

24-30 Happily, a greater degree of clarity has emerged from a number of subsequent decisions, and certain propositions, particularly concerning the principles of law applicable, can now be advanced with a degree of confidence. There has also been the

---

85 See para.24-01.

86 Joseph Jackson QC, then principal editor of *Rayden on Divorce* and co-author of Jackson's *Matrimonial Finance and Taxation*.

87 *Thwaite v Thwaite* [1982] Fam. 1, per Ormrod LJ.

88 *Minton v Minton* [1979] A.C. 593 at 608, per Lord Scarman. See also *Harris (formerly Manahan) v Manahan* [1997] 1 F.L.R. 205, per Ward LJ.

89 See, e.g. *Backhouse v Backhouse* [1978] 1 W.L.R. 243 per Balcombe J, *Edgar v Edgar* [1980] 1 W.L.R. 1410 at 1418, per Ormrod LJ, *Camm v Camm* (1983) 4 F.L.R. 577.

90 See para.24-02.

91 See also the comments of Lord Diplock in *De Lasala* [1980] A.C. 546.

additional statutory intervention in the form of s.33A of the Matrimonial Causes Act 1973.[92]

NATURE AND RELEVANCE OF AN AGREEMENT IN THIS CONTEXT

Nature

It should be recalled at the outset that the topic under discussion is the compromise of *proposed* or *actual* applications for financial provision ancillary to a suit for divorce or judicial separation. In the past a "maintenance agreement" as defined in s.34(2) of the Matrimonial Causes Act may well have contained provisions seeking to compromise applications of this nature, but such an agreement did not necessarily do so. However, as noted above such agreements in practice no longer have a meaningful role. **24-31**

In *De Lasala v De Lasala*[93], at a time when the relevant jurisdiction of the court[94] provided for the making merely of periodical payment orders (secured and unsecured) and lump sum orders, W consented to the dismissal of those claims when H had (a) paid to her a substantial lump sum referred to in a deed of arrangement which was approved by the court; and (b) settled upon trustees certain other substantial sums for the benefit of W and one child of the family, the relevant trust deeds being annexed to the deed of arrangement. These terms represented part of a global settlement which dealt with the manner in which W should obtain a decree of divorce, matters relating to the care and control of, and access to, the child and the basis upon which the outgoings of any residence purchased for W pursuant to the trusts were to be met. It is clear, therefore, that the parties contemplated the intervention of a court in relation to these arrangements. The agreement did represent a compromise of proposed (and actual) applications to the court. It is not clear whether the Judicial Committee of the Privy Council decided that the agreement was a "maintenance agreement", but it is clear that, if it was, it was no longer "subsisting" to the extent that it was susceptible of variation in its own right. The reason given was this[95]: **24-32**

> "Financial arrangements that are agreed upon between the parties for the purpose of receiving the approval and being made the subject of a consent order by the court, once they have been made the subject of the court order no longer depend upon the agreement of the parties as the source from which their legal effect is derived. Their legal effect is derived from the court order."

In the context of a case[96] concerning the basis upon which such a consent order could be set aside subsequently, the Court of Appeal interpreted the above statement of principle as representing "a significant departure" from the general principle applicable to consent orders in non-matrimonial cases and said that it had the effect of "eliminating the contractual basis" of matrimonial consent orders.[97] Whether or not that interpretation, for the purposes for which it was advanced, survived the reaffirmation of the approach of the Privy Council by the House of Lords in *Livesey* **24-33**

---

92 Introduced by the Matrimonial and Family Proceedings Act 1984 s.7.

93 [1980] A.C 546.

94 The consent order was made in May 1970 when the relevant Hong Kong Ordinance reflected the terms of the English Matrimonial Causes Act 1965.

95 *De Lasala* [1980] A.C. 546 at 560.

96 *Thwaite* [1982] Fam. 1.

97 *Thwaite* [1982] Fam. 1 at 8. In *Tommey v Tommey* [1983] Fam. 15, Balcombe J said that the effect of *Thwaite v Thwaite* was that the "contractual basis of matrimonial consent orders is to be disregarded".

v Jenkins[98] is a matter to which it will be necessary to return in due course.[99] However, one thing is clear from the quotation from the judgment of the Privy Council, namely, that prior to the making of the consent order embodying the agreement of the parties the agreement of the parties must have *some* legal effect.

24-34 This, again, follows from the restatement of the principle in *Livesey v Jenkins*. A full analysis of the implications of that case appears below.[100] For present purposes, all that needs to be recorded is that it concerned the circumstances in which a consent order, reflecting a previously negotiated compromise of financial provision and property adjustment applications, could be set aside and the duty of disclosure of the parties.[101] In the speech with which all their Lordships agreed, Lord Brandon of Oakbrook, referring to *De Lasala v De Lasala*,[102] said this[103]:

> "[W]hen parties agree the provisions of a consent order, and the court subsequently gives effect to such agreement by approving the provisions concerned and embodying them in an order of the court, the legal effect of those provisions is derived from the court order itself, and does not depend *any longer* on the agreement between the parties." (Emphasis added.)

24-35 Since the court's ultimate discretion cannot be ousted by an agreement between the parties, but an agreement arrived at is a very significant factor in exercising that discretion,[104] what is the legal effect of the agreement prior to the making of the consent order? Is it binding on the parties? If so, how is it enforced? What happens if the party entitled to apply for the relevant financial or property provision fails to bring the agreement before the court to enable the agreed orders to be made?

The agreement

24-36 Logically, the first step must be to decide if agreement has been reached at all. The nature of an agreement in this context was considered by the Court of Appeal in *Xydhias v Xydhias*.[105]

> There were lengthy pre-trial negotiations for settlement of W's ancillary relief claim. A series of draft consent orders were settled by counsel as working documents as the parties moved towards settlement. They had agreed the principal terms but were still at odds as to the terms of security and the duration of certain continuing obligations. The court was told that the imminent final hearing would not be needed but that a short appointment should be preserved for approval of a consent order or to allow time for negotiation of outstanding points. At that short appointment H withdrew from all negotiations. W sought to enforce an agreement which she asserted had been reached "between 22–29 August 1996". The district judge found that,
>
> > "by some time probably on 29 August 1996 (it is difficult to isolate clearly a defining moment) the essential building blocks of an agreement were in place".

---

98 *Livesey* [1985] A.C. 424.

99 See para.24-88 onwards.

100 See para.24-89 onwards.

101 The position as to when set aside (as distinct from appeal) is now the appropriate application is as set out in Family Procedure Rules 2010 PD 30A para.14.1 and r.9.9A.

102 [1980] A.C. 546.

103 At p.560.

104 *Hyman v Hyman* [1929] A.C. 601; *Brockwell v Brockwell* (1975) 6 Fam. Law 46, and *Dean v Dean* [1978] Fam. 161. However also see *Soulsbury v Soulsbury* [2008] 1 F.L.R. 90 in which an agreement was upheld following the court determining that the agreement was not intended to oust the jurisdiction of the court, because W had not attempted to pursue an application through the courts. See also para.24-47 onwards.

105 [1999] 1 F.L.R. 683. H was granted permission to appeal to the House of Lords, but did not pursue the appeal.

He excised from the final draft order those matters which H had not agreed. H's appeal to the judge was dismissed, as was his appeal to the Court of Appeal.

In dismissing the appeal Thorpe LJ expressed himself thus[106]: **24-37**

"My cardinal conclusion is that ordinary contractual principles do not determine the issues in this appeal. This is because of the fundamental distinction that an agreement for the compromise of an ancillary relief application does not give rise to a contract enforceable in law. The parties seeking to uphold a concluded agreement for the compromise of such an application cannot sue for specific performance. The only way of rendering the bargain enforceable, whether to ensure that the applicant obtains the agreed transfers and payments or whether to protect the respondent from future claims, is to convert the concluded agreement into an order of the court. The decision of the Privy Council in *De Lasala v De Lasala* ... demonstrated that thereafter the rights and obligations of the parties are determined by the order and not by any agreement which preceded it. The order is absolute unless there is a statutory power to vary or unless vitiated by a fact that would vitiate an order in any other division. Additionally, as was demonstrated in *Robinson v Robinson* ... an order in ancillary relief proceedings may be set aside if the product of a material breach of the duty of full and frank disclosure. An even more singular feature of the transition from compromise to order in ancillary relief proceedings is that the court does not either automatically or invariably grant the application to give the bargain the force of an order. The court conducts an independent assessment to enable it to discharge its statutory function to make such orders as reflect the criteria listed in s.25 of the Matrimonial Causes Act 1973, as amended ...

In consequence, it is clear that the award to an applicant for ancillary relief is always fixed by the court. The payer's liability cannot be ultimately fixed by compromise as can be done in the settlement of claims in other divisions. Therefore the purpose of negotiation is not to finally determine the liability (that can only be done by the court) but to reduce the length and expense of the process by which the court carries out its function. If there is a dispute as to whether the negotiations led to an accord that the process should be abbreviated, the court has a discretion in determining whether an accord was reached. In exercising that discretion the court should be astute to discern the antics of a litigant who, having consistently pressed for abbreviation, is seeking to resile and to justify his shift by reliance on some point of detail that was open for determination by the court at its abbreviated hearing. If the court concludes that the parties agreed to settle on terms then it may have to consider whether the terms were vitiated by a factor such as material non-disclosure or tainted by a factor within the parameters set in *Edgar v Edgar*. Finally in every case the court must exercise its independent discretionary review applying the s.25 criteria to the circumstances of the case and to the terms of the accord. This approach particularly applies to accords intended to obviate delivery of briefs for trial. Different considerations may apply to agreements not negotiated in the shadow of an impending fixture ...

Litigants in ancillary relief proceedings are subjected to great emotional and psychological stresses, particularly as the date of trial approaches. In my opinion there are sound policy reasons supporting the conclusion that the judge is entitled to exercise a broad discretion to determine whether the parties have agreed to settle. The pilot scheme depends on judicial control of the process from start to finish. The court has a clear interest in curbing excessive adversariality and in excluding from trial lists unnecessary litigation. A more legalistic approach, as this case illustrates, only allows the inconsistent or manipulative litigant to repudiate an agreement on the ground that some point of drafting, detail, or implementation had not been clearly resolved. Ordinarily heads of agreement signed by the parties or a clear exchange of solicitors' letters will establish the consensus. Hopefully a case such as this requiring the exercise of the judge's discretion will be a rarity ...

In ancillary relief litigation a clear distinction has always been drawn between the

---

[106] At p.691 onwards.

determination of the liability and the determination of the security for the performance of the obligation. In the years when secured provision orders were commonplace counsel regularly settled cases on the footing that if the quantum of the annual payment could be agreed the mechanism that would be triggered to secure the recipient in the event of the payer's default would be separately and subsequently put into place either by further agreement or by determination of the court. I have no doubt that that long-established practice informs and explains the communications between counsel as well as their readiness to regard the detail of the properties to be included within the schedule as ancillary and not precedent to a concluded agreement. Of course if the issue had to be decided on the stricter basis of pure contractual principle then the saga of the developing drafts and the complementary exchanges between the solicitors would have to be examined in much greater detail. The ambiguities and the inconsistencies that such an analysis would reveal would all tell against a finding of concluded contract on *Pagnan*[107] principles. However on the evidence before me I am in no doubt that the district judge rightly held that the parties had concluded a compromise during the week before the hearing. Throughout that week it was the husband who was pressing for a settlement and plainly there came a point at which the wife agreed his terms. All that remained unresolved was either mechanics or trivial."

24-38 This statement of the approach to agreements of this nature is, of course, important. Indeed, the merits of the case were such as undoubtedly justified the outcome. However, it is respectfully submitted that there are troubling uncertainties arising from the case. In *Soulsbury v Soulsbury*[108] Ward LJ said that "[o]ne has to say that there are some who are critical of the 'cardinal conclusion that 'ordinary contractual principles' do not apply to determine whether or not the parties had reached a concluded agreement".[109] The concern (which he expressly associated himself with) was that rather than the court only having a discretion to exercise whether or not to sanction an agreement and make the order *once* the agreement was established, the court now also exercised its discretion in determining *whether or not* an accord was reached. That the *effect* of a compromise should receive different treatment in the Family Division from the other divisions was established in *Thwaite*,[110] but (said Ward LJ) *Xydhias*[111] had given the Family Division a different and unique test for establishing the very formation of the underlying agreement itself.[112] However the correctness of that part of the decision was not a matter which arose for determination in the case itself.

Although Ward LJ made it clear that it was not for the Court of Appeal to pronounce upon the correctness of the "cardinal conclusion", he did consider Thorpe LJ's reason for arriving at that conclusion. The reason given was, he said, "the fundamental distinction that an agreement for the compromise of an ancillary relief application does not give rise to a contract enforceable in law." He considered that in expressing this view Thorpe LJ had ignored the dictum of Butler-Sloss LJ,

---

107 *Pagnan SpA v Tradax Ocean Transport SA* [1987] 3 All E.R. 565.

108 [2007] EWCA Civ 969; [2008] 1 F.L.R. 90.

109 [2008] 1 F.L.R. 90 at [40].

110 *Thwaite v Thwaite* [1982] Fam. 1, per Ormrod LJ.

111 [1999] 1 F.L.R. 683.

112 In turn, Keehan J may be said to have taken a different view in *TW v PL (Agreement)* [2013] EWHC 3078 (Fam); [2014] 2 F.L.R. 106 where, in the context of a father seeking to resile from an agreement under Sch.1 of the Children Act 1989 shortly before the final hearing was due to begin, he said (after consideration of *Xydhias* and *Edgar*) at [8] that there was "no authority which entitles me to find that there is a concluded agreement, but then to impose on one or other of the parties different terms from those which have been incorporated within the agreement." It is submitted that it is not easy to reconcile these observations with the other authorities.

as she then was, in *Kelley v Corston*[113] and the opinion of Lord Diplock in *De Lasala*[114] which confirmed that an agreement *can* be enforced. He noted that Thorpe LJ was of the view that "[t]he parties seeking to uphold a concluded agreement for the compromise of such an application cannot sue for specific performance" but in *Merritt*[115] the Court of Appeal allowed specific performance. Further Ward LJ noted that in his judgment in *Xydhias*[116] Thorpe LJ had stated that the only way of rendering a bargain to make payment of money enforceable would be to convert the concluded agreement into an order of the court. In Ward LJ's view, "[s]tated in those terms, it cannot be correct".[117] He therefore concluded that "the cardinal conclusions expressed by Thorpe LJ are stated in terms which are too wide".[118] The reason for this was that although "if there are negotiations to compromise a claim for ancillary relief, then there is a duty to seek the court's approval as is stated in *Smallman*".[119] But as *Smallman v Smallman*[120] states "even an agreement subject to the approval of the court is binding on the parties to the extent that neither can resile from it." It is, perhaps, surprising that there has not been further judicial exploration of the differences of opinion between Thorpe LJ and Ward LJ in relation to this issue over the last 20 years.

An example of *Xydhias* being applied in practice is *G v S (Children Act 1989: Schedule 1)*.[121]. The parties attended a round table meeting which resulted in heads of agreement and the parties agreed that they should be bound by the *Xydhias* principles. However, issues remained including that the father sought to restrict the possibility of the mother moving from London, seeking the incorporation of a clause that prevented her from obtaining a replacement property outside England and Wales in any circumstances before the parties' daughter completed her primary education. The mother contended that the restriction was inappropriate in principle, that there was a variety of scenarios in which she might need to move to a different jurisdiction and further, the court ought not insert a term that removed all discretion from a court charged in future with making decisions about the child's welfare. Hayden J approved the draft order in terms that permitted the mother to relocate. He stated, inter alia, that if he had found that the heads of agreement, strictly construed in the way that the father sought, truly represented both its philosophy and objectives, then it would have been wrong in principle. He stated that where a court at the second stage of the process determined that an agreement between the parties was irreconcilable with the best interests of a subject child, it was likely that the *Xydhias* principles would be disapplied. **24-39**

In *Xydhias* the court felt unable to define the moment when agreement was reached. More importantly, it is clear that no complete agreement was reached. Whilst it might be straightforward in theory to distinguish between that which is substantive (i.e. upon which agreement is necessary for a party to be held to their bargain) and that which is procedural (i.e. upon which agreement is not necessary), in practice that which to one person may be very important may to another be trivial. For example, the nature of the security might be critical to the husband who had to give it, but purely a matter of mechanics to the wife. As a consequence,

---

113 [1998] 1 F.L.R. 986.
114 [1980] A.C. 546.
115 [1992] 2 F.L.R. 140.
116 [1999] 1 F.L.R. 683.
117 [2008] 1 F.L.R. 90 at [44].
118 [2008] 1 F.L.R. 90 at [45].
119 [2008] 1 F.L.R. 90 at [45].
120 [1972] Fam. 25.
121 [2017] 2 F.L.R. 1207.

defining where the line is to be drawn between quantification and principle on the one hand and mechanics and mode of performance on the other may be very difficult.

24-40 The spectre of one party seeking to claim the existence of a concluded agreement relying upon *Xydhias*, whilst the other denies having reached that stage, is not illusory. It may be avoided if the parties agree to the two-stage process advocated by Thorpe LJ whereby the agreement is concluded upon the heads of agreement being signed. However, negotiations are often not that formal and take place through a chain of correspondence and conversations, with new matters emerging as negotiations develop.[122] Whilst it is normally not too difficult to determine whether a complete agreement is reached at any point, it may be far more difficult to discern if the principles of agreement are agreed at some earlier stage.

24-41 From a practical point of view, it is suggested that it is now particularly important for negotiators to ensure that all material issues are raised at an early stage and that it is made clear that no agreement is to be regarded as concluded until final agreement is reached on all those issues. Negotiations should remain expressly "subject to final agreement" until agreement is reached on all the material terms.

24-42 What other conclusions can be drawn from *Xydhias* and other authorities in this area?

24-43 First, there must be a sufficient agreement reached on the principal terms for it to have any impact at all on the court's discretion. If the parties are still negotiating, or they conclude an agreement and then agree to ignore it, there is no agreement to put forward for the court's consideration.

24-44 Secondly, it is beyond doubt that any provision in an agreement thus identified which seeks to restrict the right of a party to apply to the court for financial provision is unenforceable.

24-45 Thirdly, if some legal effect is to be attributed to such a compromise it must, it is submitted, be along the following lines: a concluded compromise of proposed or actual applications for financial relief carries with it the express or, at the very least, implied agreement of the parties to invite the court in due course to exercise its discretion in accordance with the agreement unless some new circumstances, material in substance to the exercise of that discretion, arise between the conclusion of the agreement and the time when the court is invited to exercise it.[123] It follows, given the court's ultimate discretion, that the agreement is subject to the approval of the court. By analogy, therefore, with an agreement which is made expressly "subject to the approval of the court" the agreement:

(a) is not operative until approved by the court and made the subject of an order[124]; but
(b) is binding on the parties in the sense that it may be disavowed by neither pending the application to the court.[125]

FDR hearings

24-46 All financial remedy applications are required to be listed for a financial dispute resolution (FDR) hearing unless the court otherwise orders.[126] An FDR hearing is

---

[122] cf. *FSHC Group Holdings Ltd v Glas Trust Corporation Ltd* considered at para.24-97.
[123] cf. *Livesey* [1985] A.C. 424.
[124] Whence, thereafter, will be derived its legal effect: see para.24-32.
[125] *Smallman* [1972] Fam. 25 and *Soulsbury v Soulsbury* [2008] 1 F.L.R. 90 (see para 24-38). In *Amey v Amey* [1992] 2 F.L.R. 89 H had purchased an inn for £12,000 which he and W improved and ran

governed by FPR 2010 r.9.17. Where a FDR is ordered attendance by the parties is compulsory—r.9.17(10). In *Mann v Mann*[127] Mostyn J noted that he had never heard of a party refusing to attend—and so could not say from experience what would happen if someone did—but that "[i]t would be a serious contempt of court were a party recalcitrantly to refuse to do so".[128] It is a privileged appointment. It is to be treated as a meeting held for the purposes of discussion and negotiation,[129] and parties must use their best endeavours to reach agreement on matters in issue between them.[130] The judge will seek to advise the parties on the likely outcome if the matter were contested and examine the issues between them in light of the overriding objective.[131] The judge hearing the FDR appointment must have no further involvement with the application other than to conduct a further FDR, to make a consent order or to make further directions.[132]

Sometimes, FDR hearings result in consent orders which are drafted and approved on the day.[133] Often, agreement is reached but the full order is not drafted there and then, either because of the lateness of the hour, anticipated complexity of the drafting, or the need to obtain further advice, e.g. to minimise tax liabilities. In such circumstances, it is good practice to draw up heads of agreement, which should be signed by both the parties and their advisers. If parties have elected to have a private FDR, the same good practice applies.[134] An order reflecting the heads of agreement is then subsequently drafted and filed at court for approval. If one party subsequently seeks to resile from the agreement the practice and procedure set out at para.24-59 onwards is usually followed.

What is the status of an agreement (whether or not embodied in signed heads of agreement) that is expressly approved by the court? This was considered in *Rose v Rose*.[135] Having reconsidered the matter, the husband sought to withdraw his consent to what had been agreed. The Court of Appeal concluded that the product of such a hearing is an unperfected order of the court, not merely a contractual *Xydhias*-type agreement between the parties. Although Thorpe LJ noted that no authority had been cited in the field of financial remedies where one party sought

together in partnership. H and W were divorced in 1986 and an agreement as to their financial affairs was reached. In effect the agreement was to a 50:50 split of their assets. In pursuance of the agreement H paid £120,000 to W on 1 October 1986. On 9 October 1986, W's counsel drafted minutes of order with a view, as had been agreed, to an order being made by the court in due course. On 8 December 1986, W acquired the lease of another public house using, as H knew, part of the £120,000 for the purpose. On 9 December 1986, suddenly and unexpectedly, W died. The intended consent order had not by that time been made. H sought rescission of the agreement. Scott Baker J, as he then was, held (a) that there was a binding agreement notwithstanding the fact that the proposed consent order had not been made; (b) the agreement stood or fell by reference to common law; (c) there was no basis in mistake or frustration to justify setting aside the agreement and; in any event (d) it had already been performed. See also the comments of Hoffmann LJ, as he then was, in *Pounds v Pounds* [1994] 1 F.L.R. 775. As to the choices available to the "innocent party" in the event of the other seeking to resile from any such agreement, see para.24-78 onwards.

126 Family Procedure Rules 2010 r.9.15(4).

127 [2014] 2 F.L.R. 938.

128 [2014] 2 F.L.R. 938 at [21].

129 Family Procedure Rules 2010 r.9.17(1).

130 Family Procedure Rules 2010 r.9.17(6).

131 Family Procedure Rules 2010 r.1(1).

132 Family Procedure Rules 2010 r.9.17(2). The scope of this rule has been considered in *Myerson v Myerson* [2009] 1 F.L.R. 826 and *Shokrollah-Babaee v Shokrollah-Babaee* [2019] EWHC 2135 (Fam).

133 Family Procedure Rules 2010 r.9.17(8). At the conclusion of the FDR appointment, the court may make an appropriate consent order.

134 See para.24-03.

135 *Rose v Rose* [2002] 1 F.L.R. 978.

release between the making of the order in court and its perfection and noted leading counsels' disagreement as to whether such an application should be decided on *Edgar*[136] or *Barder*[137] principles, he expressed the view that it was "perhaps wiser"[138] to avoid stating a general principle but that, even if the lower threshold of "exceptional circumstances" or "strong reasons" was applied, the husband could not on the facts satisfy it. The whole purpose of an FDR is undermined if parties are free to re-evaluate their decisions and suggest that they have made the wrong choice.

Securing an order reflecting a prior agreement

Where both parties are still in agreement

Practice on seeking an order

24-47 An application to the court should be made by the party having the carriage of the applications for financial relief to which the other party gives consent. The consent may be personal or by a legal adviser. In reality the application is often regarded as a joint application.[139]

24-48 The manner in which the application is made depends upon when agreement is reached. Where, for example, agreement is reached during negotiations between solicitors before any substantive hearing takes place, an application for a consent order will be made under Family Procedure Rules 2010 r.9.26. Unless the court directs otherwise, the parties need not attend the hearing of an application for a consent order.[140] Agreement may, of course, be reached before any notice of application for financial relief is issued by or on behalf of either party. In this event, a notice of application in Form A[141] should be issued seeking an order in the terms agreed. The applicant must file two copies of the draft order in the terms sought, one of which must be endorsed with a statement signed by the respondent to the application signifying agreement.[142] Further, each party must file with the court and serve on the other party, a statement of information in the form referred to in Family Procedure Rules 2010 PD 5A.[143] The statement of information must set out the necessary personal information about the parties, their means and resources. Where each party's statement of information is contained in one form, it must be signed by each party to certify that they have read the contents of the other's statement.[144] Where each party's statement of information is in a separate form, the form of each party must be signed by the other party to certify that they have read the contents of the statement contained in that form.[145] There is currently an HMCTS pilot for the online filing of applications for consent orders which is supported by Family Procedure Rules 2010 PD36I. Where all or any of the parties attend the court hearing, the court may dispense with the filing of a statement of information, and give

136 *Edgar v Edgar* [1980] 1 W.L.R. 1410.
137 *Barder v Barder* [1988] A.C. 20.
138 [2002] EWCA Civ 208; [2002] 1 F.L.R. 978 at [40].
139 *Livesey* [1985] A.C. 424 at 437.
140 Family Procedure Rules 2010 r.9.26(4).
141 Family Procedure Rules 2010 PD 5A.
142 Family Procedure Rules 2010 r.9.26(1)(a), PD 9A, para.7(1).
143 Family Procedure Rules 2010 r.9.26(1)(b). Form D81.
144 Family Procedure Rules 2010 r.9.26(2).
145 Family Procedure Rules 2010 r.9.26(3).

directions for the information which would otherwise be required to be given in such a statement in such a manner as it thinks fit.[146]

Merely because these provisions have been complied with correctly does not mean that the judge is obliged to make the order sought or to deal with the application without attendance. The court retains its ultimate discretion in these matters[147] and has a discretion as to whether to deal with the application on the basis only of the information provided in the statement.[148] In *L v L*[149] Munby J (as he then was) endorsed the earlier comments of Ward LJ[150] that "whilst the court is no rubber stamp, nor is it some kind of forensic ferret". Where there is "reason to think that there are other circumstances into which it ought to inquire",[151] the court will undoubtedly decline to deal with the application in this way and will make further enquiries to be dealt with in writing or may require the personal attendance of the parties and/or their representatives. **24-49**

Where either or both of the parties do not have solicitors acting for them, it is unlikely that a court would make a consent order without the personal attendance of the parties or, at the very least, clear evidence of their genuine and informed consent (such as a signed statement to the effect that that they have been advised to take independent legal advice, that they have (or have not) done so, that they understand the meaning and consequences of the draft consent order and that they wish for an order to be made in its terms).[152] This would be particularly so if the dismissal (or a restriction of the right to apply for a variation) of the periodical payments claims of the financially weaker party is contemplated. In any event, the court would need to see compliance with r.9.26 as discussed at para.24-48 before acting on an application for a consent order in such a situation. **24-50**

An agreement may not be concluded until arrival by the parties "at the doors of the court". When agreement is concluded in the discussions which take place, it is normal for the parties' legal representatives to draw up an agreed draft order for presentation to the court. The parties may choose simply to draft heads of agreement to put before the court before filing a perfected order.[153] In such circumstances, the court may dispense with the filing of a statement of information, and give directions for the information which would otherwise be required to be given in such a statement in such a manner as it thinks fit.[154] **24-51**

Contents and phraseology of agreed order

It is essential that all the terms of the proposed consent order should come clearly within the court's powers conferred by ss.23 and 24 of the 1973 Act. Any terms which cannot be brought within that jurisdiction should be formulated as undertakings or reflected in the recitals to the order to the court.[155] The parties cannot, by **24-52**

---

146 Family Procedure Rules 2010 r.9.26(5).

147 See *Hyman v Hyman* [1929] A.C. 601, *Brockwell v Brockwell* (1975) 6 Fam. Law 46, and *Dean v Dean* [1978] Fam. 161.

148 The use of the word "may" in s.33A(1) yields the basis for this further discretion: see para.24-30.

149 [2008] 1 F.L.R. 26.

150 *Harris (formerly Manahan) v Manahan* [1997] 1 F.L.R. 205 at 213.

151 Matrimonial Causes Act 1973 s.33A(1).

152 cf. para.10-03.

153 See the discussion at para.24-46.

154 Family Procedure Rules 2010 r.9.26(5). cf. para.24-46.

155 *Jenkins v Livesey* [1985] A.C. 424 at 444. In *CH v WH (Power to Order Indemnity)* [2018] 1 F.L.R. 495 Mostyn J approved a consent order that had previously been rejected by two judges as it had included provisions in the body of the order—requiring one party to release the other party from a

consent, confer on the court a jurisdiction which it does not otherwise possess.[156] Strictly speaking, the court can (and should) decline to make an order outside its jurisdiction.[157] If an order containing such provision is made, the provision will almost certainly be unenforceable unless it can be enforced in contract.[158]

24-53 It is important also that the proposed consent order truly reflects the agreement of the parties so that its essential purpose—the final resolution of the parties' differences—is not frustrated by future (costly) disputes about what the order was intended to achieve. In *Dinch v Dinch*[159] Lord Oliver of Aylmerton said this[160]:

> "I feel impelled once again to stress in most emphatic terms that it is in all cases the imperative professional duty of those invested with the task of advising the parties to these unfortunate disputes to consider with due care the impact which any terms that they agree on behalf of their clients have and are intended to have upon any outstanding application for ancillary relief and to ensure that such appropriate provision is inserted in any consent order made as will leave no room for any future doubt or misunderstanding or saddle the parties with the wasteful burden of wholly unnecessary costs."

24-54 The problem has arisen not infrequently when the consent order does not make plain whether an outstanding claim for financial remedies has, or has not, been dismissed. It has often been said[161] that where it is intended to dismiss a claim for any particular relief that should be stated clearly in the order and that the expression "no order" should be avoided since it is ambiguous. A claim can, of course, be "kept alive" specifically by adjourning the application for it with liberty to restore.[162]

24-55 When a court is subsequently called upon to determine what was the true effect of an order for financial relief, the question is one of construction.[163] The court will look at all the surrounding circumstances to give effect to its spirit and purpose. The

---

mortgage or indemnify them against the liability—that were thought to be outside of the 1973 Act. Mostyn J held the terms were within the power of the court to order as the Family Court had all the powers of the High Court and the High Court had such powers. Further the provisions in question were (he said) inside the parameters of the 1973 Act in any event. *CH v PH (Power to Order Indemnity)* was relied upon by Moor J in *AP v ALP* [2018] EWHC 2758 (Fam); [2019] 1 F.C.R. 380 at [140] so as to order one party to indemnify the other in relation to a tax liability.

156 *Hinde v Hinde* [1953] 1 W.L.R. 175, and *Masefield v Alexander* [1995] 1 F.L.R. 100 at 102. See also Ch.10. There is jurisdiction to dismiss one party's claims whilst keeping alive those of the other: *Thompson v Thompson* [1988] 1 W.L.R. 562 (Ewbank J).

157 *Noel* [1971] 1 W.L.R. 355. It is important that an order for financial relief is not made until after the decree nisi: *Pounds v Pounds* [1994] 1 F.L.R. 775. See most recently *K v K (Financial Remedy: Final Order Prior to Decree Nisi)* [2017] 1 F.L.R. 541 where the district judge's order which was to take immediate effect—prior to decree nisi—was held by Cobb J to be a nullity.

158 *Hinde* [1953] 1 W.L.R. 175. If the underlying agreement ceases to have effect once reflected in an order (see para.24-32), the provision cannot be enforced as an agreement.

159 [1987] 1 W.L.R. 252.

160 At 255.

161 In *Gee v Gee* (1976) CAT 278, *Rushforth v Rushforth* (1976) CAT 91, *Carter v Carter* [1980] 1 W.L.R. 390 and *Dipper v Dipper* [1981] Fam. 31.

162 cf. *Davies v Davies* [1986] 1 F.L.R. 497.

163 See, for example, *Hamilton v Hamilton* [2014] 1 F.L.R. 55 where an issue arose as to whether the consent order as drafted accurately reflected the underlying agreement that was approved by the judge. The Court of Appeal (where Baron J gave the lead judgment) held (at [41]) that where there is a disagreement as to whether the terms of the order are, in reality, correct then the court retains jurisdiction and must assess what the parties agreed against the objective factual matrix of what occurred during the relevant period. It was said that ordinarily the language of the order will settle matters but, in the event of a dispute as to the nature of the agreement, the court is entitled to look at the surrounding facts and circumstances which bear upon the terms as drafted. This investigation was perfectly proper because it is evidence of the stages that preceded the perfection of the court order. The Court of Appeal emphasised, however, that the test is objective as the court is not look-

view has been expressed[164] that the court will not readily imply or infer a dismissal of a wife's claim for financial remedies (assuming for these purposes that she is the financially weaker party) when no express order was made in relation to that claim in the original order and that the burden of establishing the dismissal of that claim should be on the husband. However the House of Lords has emphasised that the matter is one of construction to determine what the parties intended[165]:

> "There cannot ... be any irrebuttable presumption that an order which is silent as to a claim which, on the record, appears to have been put in issue necessarily and always has to be construed as containing a dismissal of that claim. It must, in each case, be a question of construction of the particular order under consideration, and whilst I do not dissent from the proposition that a proper caution should be exercised before reaching a conclusion that will effectively preclude a wife from making a further claim for relief, I do not ... derive much help from consideration of where the burden lies. One has ... simply to look at the order and any admissible material available for its construction, and determine ... in the case of a consent order, what the parties intended ... to effect by the order. If the conclusion is that what was intended was a final and conclusive once-for-all settlement, either overall or in relation to a particular property, then it must follow that that precludes any further claim in relation to that property."

A related issue arose in *Wyatt v Vince*.[166] In 1992, in the Sunderland County Court, the wife had issued a petition for divorce which resulted in a decree absolute dated 26 October 1992. As the court file had subsequently been destroyed or mislaid it was not known whether the wife had included in her petition applications for the full range of financial orders for the benefit of herself. The Supreme Court made an "educated guess" that she did so as such was the usual practice. However, as she had not subsequently remarried, (which would have precluded her doing so: s.28(3) of the Matrimonial Causes Act 1973) it was open to her to initiate applications for them in 2011 (when she did) or at any time. However the question that then arose, assuming that in her petition the wife included applications for financial orders, as to what orders, if any, were then made upon them? The husband asserted a clear recollection that, following the transfer of the proceedings to the Gloucester and Cheltenham County Court, it ordered that "[he] did not have to pay [the wife] any money". This asserted recollection was consistent with each of three hypotheses (i) that the court made only a nominal order for the husband to make periodical payments to the wife; (ii) that its order on her applications was "no order" or (which amounts to the same thing) that it never addressed them; or (iii) that it dismissed all the wife's applications; in that event it would not be open to her to have brought her 2011 application. The Court of Appeal considered it "likely" that no order was sought or made, i.e. it favoured hypothesis (ii). The Supreme Court agreed. The Court of Appeal added that hypotheses (i) and (iii) were possible. The Supreme Court considered hypothesis (i) to be a significant possibility but hypothesis (iii) to be so remote a possibility as entirely to be discounted given the facts of the case **24-56**

---

ing to assess the subjective beliefs of the parties rather it is looking at the objective factual matrix to interpret what was agreed in the light of the words used and communications that passed.

[164] *Brown v Kirrage* (1981) 11 Fam. Law 141, a case involving the question of whether an application for a lump sum had in fact been dismissed or left open. See also *Atkinson v Atkinson* (1984) 14 Fam. Law 305, a case involving a consent order.

[165] *Dinch* [1987] 1 W.L.R. 252 at 263. See also *Banyard v Banyard* (1985) 15 Fam. Law 120, *Sandford v Sandford* [1986] 1 F.L.R. 412, *Potter v Potter* [1990] 2 F.L.R. 27 and *Richardson v Richardson* [1994] 1 F.L.R. 286.

[166] [2015] UKSC 14; [2015] 1 F.L.R. 972.

in the absence either of the wife's consent or of a capital payment by the husband, neither of which is suggested to have been forthcoming.

Undertakings

24-57 The status of undertakings in financial remedy orders has been the subject of debate. Much of this debate has now been resolved following the detailed guidance as to enforcement within FPR 2010 PD 33A. Undertakings are routinely given by parties to cover matters which the court has no power to order: for example, the taking out of an insurance policy. The enforcement of an undertaking to do or abstain from doing any act other than the payment of money is governed by Pt 37 and PD 37A. The undertaking must be endorsed with a penal notice[167] (unless it is contained within an order or judgment[168]). The court may decline to accept an undertaking, or deal with disobedience in respect of an undertaking by contempt proceedings, unless the party has given a signed statement as detailed in PD 37A para.2.2, or in words to substantially the same effect.

24-58 Any undertaking for the payment of money that has effect as if it was an order made under Pt 2 of the 1973 Act may be enforced as if it was an order.[169] It must be endorsed with a notice setting out the consequences of disobedience as prescribed.[170] The person giving the undertaking must make a signed statement to the effect that he understands the terms of the undertaking being given and the consequences of failure to comply with it.[171] The statement need not be given before the court in person. It may be endorsed on the court copy of the undertaking or may be filed in a separate document.[172] There is no requirement for the undertaking to be contained within a general form of undertaking, as emphasised in *Bakir v Downe*.[173] However, in order to minimise difficulties in enforcement it is suggested that the party giving the undertaking should give it to the court as well as agreeing to like effect with the other party.

Where one party is resiling from the agreement

24-59 The circumstances in which a court would feel entitled, either before or after a consent order is made, to disregard the prior agreement of the parties will be considered in due course.[174] The following discussion concerns the situation where parties agree on the orders (or the basis of the orders) which they would invite the court to make, but one of the parties has a change of heart. The change of heart may simply be of a wilful nature or may derive from a genuinely held belief that, on reflection, the agreement was not fair. How should the party who wishes to abide by the agreement react? What procedural steps can be taken?

24-60 In the first place it is clear that, even though the agreement may not have what might be termed "full contractual force",[175] such a party should go on acting, so far as possible, as if the agreement stood. Without seeking to introduce into this area

167 PD 37A, para.2.1.
168 Family Procedure Rules 2010 r.37.9(2).
169 PD 33A para.2.1.
170 PD 33A para.2.2.
171 PD 33A para.2.3.
172 PD 33A para.2.4.
173 [2014] EWHC 3318, per Mostyn J.
174 See para.24-67 onwards.
175 In the sense that no "cause of action" arises on the "breach" (or, more accurately, the "anticipatory breach") of the agreement: see para.24-31 onwards.

all the usual contractual concepts,[176] it is undeniably correct for the party not repudiating the agreement to show clearly that the other party's repudiation is not accepted; otherwise there would be a mutual abandonment of a previously agreed position to which it is not possible for either party to return with conviction.

Since the court's approach is to require the party trying to abandon the agreement to show good reason for the court to disregard it, the normal form of application made by the party seeking to uphold the agreement is one requiring the resiling party[177] "to show cause" why an order reflecting, or in the terms of, the previous agreement should not be made.[178] Once prima facie evidence of an agreement is adduced, the onus is placed squarely on the shoulders of the party resiling from it to adduce evidence of sufficient reasons to compel the court to ignore it. If, for example, an applicant for financial relief is satisfied with the provisions of the agreement, there is no reason why an order such as this should not be sought. Equally, however, the substantive application could be pursued, an appropriate witness statement making it clear that all that is pursued, if the court thinks it right, is an order reflecting the previous agreement. If it is the respondent to an application who wishes to uphold the agreement, an application for a "show cause" order could be made even if the applicant by then is not actively pursuing the substantive applications. If the substantive applications are being pursued, in effect in breach of the agreement, an order of this nature can be sought, coupled, perhaps, with an application for an order staying those applications save for the purpose of making orders reflecting, or in the terms of, the agreement.[179] **24-61**

The court must be careful not to consider the agreement as a preliminary issue in isolation without any consideration of the s.25 factors. This occurred in *Smith v Smith*[180] which led to an order being made that held the wife to an agreement which failed to meet her basic needs. Thorpe LJ said[181]: **24-62**

> "My greatest criticism of this judgment is one that is perhaps not directed against the judge himself. I believe that the omissions in the judgment are probably the product of the way the case was presented and argued. It seems as if it was almost presented to the judge as a preliminary issue for him to decide whether the existence of the contract in September 1996 disentitled the wife, as a matter of either law or discretion, from an investigation of her statutory claims. That was simply not the judicial function. ... when a wife brings to the court her statutory claims for determination the existence of an earlier contract is only one of the considerations to which the judge must give weight ..."

In *S v S (Ancillary Relief)*,[182] Eleanor King J (as she then was) said that she "[did] not take *Smith v Smith* to be saying that the court must always hear a case as a full blown ancilliary relief hearing where there is an alleged agreement, but rather as a "trenchant reminder that an agreement forms part of all the circumstances of a case and that, even if such an agreement be found to be of magnetic importance, the court should only ever consider such an agreement against the backdrop of all the s.25 factors".[183] The 'notice to show cause' mechanism, she said, "can appropriately be regarded as the proportionate and just route by which to determine the extent to which that factor should be determinative of the action". **24-63**

---

176 cf. *Edgar v Edgar* [1980] 1 W.L.R. 1410 at 1417, per Ormrod LJ.

177 See para.24-59.

178 This was done in *Dean v Dean* [1978] Fam. 161. See also *Crossley v Crossley* [2008] 1 F.L.R. 1467, *S v S (Ancillary Relief)* [2009] 1 F.L.R. 254, and *T v T* [2013] EWHC B3.

179 In *Harte v Harte* (1976) CAT 423 the argument that the appeal had been compromised was raised by way of preliminary motion to stay the appeal.

180 [2000] 3 F.C.R. 374.

181 [2000] 3 F.C.R. 374 at 381f.

182 [2009] 1 F.L.R. 254.

183 [2009] 1 F.L.R. 254 at [23 (ii)].

Pursuant to the overriding objective, the court should seek actively to case manage the "show cause" application. In *S v S (Ancillary Relief)* the court declined to order further disclosure or responses to questionnaires, on the basis the agreement was a matter of such magnetic importance, it must necessarily dominate the discretionary process.

24-64 On the assumption that the court considers that the agreement was, and remains, fair, what can it do? On one view an order "by consent" could not be made because the consent of one of the parties would not be forthcoming on the day the court was invited to make the order. On the other hand, the necessary consent could arguably be found in the agreement itself and an order "by consent" made.[184] This approach reflects the robust attitude which, it is submitted, a court can and should adopt when satisfied that an unmeritorious position is being adopted by the party seeking to resile from the agreement.

24-65 Nonetheless, whether or not the order made by the court is prefaced by the words "by consent", it will not allow itself to be frustrated by technical problems in connection with the order. Problems will arise only where terms going beyond the jurisdiction conferred by the Matrimonial Causes Act 1973[185] were included in the agreement. Matters such as these are usually dealt with by way of undertakings to the court.[186] It is extremely unlikely that a court would feel able, notwithstanding its desire to give effect to the agreement, to incorporate undertakings as such in the order made because:

(a) no undertaking is being volunteered to the court; and
(b) it would be inappropriate to bind a party to an obligation the breach of which could result in immediate steps for committal being taken.

24-66 A degree of ingenuity may have to be shown in utilising the jurisdiction of the court to secure the desired result. Although of no direct coercive effect, the preamble to the order can make it clear, for example, why a particular level of periodical payments or lump sum order is being made, reflecting, perhaps, some additional element (e.g. premiums payable in respect of a life policy or private medical insurance) which had been agreed but which cannot be made the subject of an order.[187]

Disregarding Agreements and Setting Aside Consent Orders

Disregarding agreements before an order is made

Preliminary

24-67 The nature and effect of a compromise of proposed or actual financial remedy applications has been stated.[188] So too has the influence which such an agreement will have on the court's ultimate discretion.[189] A number of factors have emerged which can be regarded as preliminary to a consideration of the circumstances in which the court is entitled to disregard a previously negotiated position:

---

184 *Cook* (1984) 14 Fam. Law 121. See also Ch. 5, para.5-58.
185 Or Married Women's Property Act 1882 if invoked, s.17. See para.24-52.
186 See paras 24-57 and 24-58.
187 *Milne v Milne* [1981] 2 F.L.R. 286.
188 See para.24-31 onwards.
189 See para.24-36.

(1) Clearly, if the negotiations never crystallised into a sufficient agreement there would be no agreement to put before the court.[190]
(2) If an agreement had been concluded, but both parties subsequently abandon reliance upon it, there will be no extant (and thus relevant) agreement to put before the court.[191]
(3) If there is no agreement to put before the court, it cannot be taken into account in exercising its discretion. The matter must be dealt with at large.

Grounds for disregarding

Even though full contractual force is not to be given to a compromise of this nature, the fact of an agreement is significant. As a matter of principle, the argument should be available to a party that, notwithstanding an agreement apparently concluded and not subsequently abandoned, such agreement should be regarded as of no significance because it was entered into on the basis of some ground which would invalidate an ordinary compromise such as an operative mistake, an effective misrepresentation (fraudulent or otherwise), duress or undue influence.[192] Whilst it may be right not to try to adhere too strictly to precise common law contractual principles, regard must be had to the circumstances leading to the agreement and the parties' subsequent conduct. The matter was put thus in *Edgar v Edgar*[193]: **24-68**

"To decide what weight should be given, in order to reach a just result, to a prior agreement ... regard must be had to the conduct of both parties, leading up to the prior agreement, and to their subsequent conduct, in consequence of it. It is not necessary in this connection to think in formal legal terms, such as misrepresentation or estoppel; *all*[194] the circumstances as they affect each of two human beings must be considered in the complex relationship of marriage. So, the circumstances surrounding the making of the agreement are relevant. Undue pressure by one side, exploitation of a dominant position to secure an unreasonable advantage, inadequate knowledge, possibly bad legal advice, an important change of circumstances, unforeseen or overlooked at the time of making the agreement, are all relevant to the question of justice between the parties."

THE AGREEMENTS TO WHICH EDGAR APPLIES

In *Radmacher (formerly Granatino) v Granatino*[195] the distinction between ante-nuptial agreements and post-nuptial agreements, including separation agreements, was considered by the Supreme Court. **24-69**

H was French and W was German. They were married in London in 1998 having entered into an ante-nuptial agreement three months prior to the marriage. The agreement was entered into at the instigation of W, to whom a further portion of her family's considerable wealth would be transferred if the agreement were signed. H, who was working as a

[190] See paras 24-36 – 24-45.
[191] It is not clear to what extent, if any, reference to the previously concluded agreement, which is thereafter abandoned by both parties, may be made at the hearing of a substantive application. It would not be inadmissible as such if relevant to any issues arising. It might, it is thought, be relevant to explain questions of delay or even, perhaps, the manner in which one party organised his or her finances or plans for a time.
[192] See Ch.4. Cf. *Pounds v Pounds* [1994] 1 F.L.R. 775.
[193] *Edgar* [1980] 1 W.L.R. 1410 at 1417, per Ormrod LJ (with whom Oliver LJ agreed). cf. *Allsop v Allsop* (1981) 11 Fam. Law 18, where the expression "misrepresentation" was used. See also *H v H* [1994] 2 F.L.R. 94.
[194] Ormrod LJ's emphasis.
[195] [2011] 1 A.C. 534.

banker at the time, declined the opportunity to take independent legal advice on the agreement. H knew that W had substantial wealth but had shown no interest in ascertaining its approximate value. There were no negotiations on the agreement. The parties separated in 2006 after having two children together. By the time the parties separated H had left banking and embarked upon research studies at Oxford.

24-70 In the leading judgment in the Supreme Court, Lord Phillips of Worth Matravers observed that historically it was contrary to public policy for a married couple or a couple about to get married to make an agreement for the contingency that they may separate.[196] He reviewed the cases in which, increasingly, significant weight had been attached by the courts to separation agreements.[197] He contrasted that with the approach taken to cases involving nuptial agreements, which merely anticipated the possibility of separation or divorce. The courts had not attached weight to those agreements as they were considered to be contrary to public policy.[198] Consideration was given to *MacLeod v MacLeod*,[199] in which the Privy Council took the view that it was not open to that court to reverse the longstanding rule that ante-nuptial agreements were contrary to public policy and thus not valid or binding. *Radmacher* swept away the distinction between ante-nuptial and post-nuptial agreements. The distinction was tested by comparing an agreement concluded the day before the wedding with one concluded the day after it.[200] The focus of the Supreme Court was upon the circumstances surrounding the agreement and whether the circumstances at the time of the final order made it fair or just to depart from it, rather than whether the agreement was ante-nuptial or post-nuptial.[201] In relation to the weight to be accorded to an agreement Lord Phillips stated:

> "If an ante-nuptial agreement, or indeed a post-nuptial agreement, is to carry full weight, both the husband and wife must enter into it of their own free will, without undue influence or pressure, and informed of its implications...
>
> Sound legal advice is obviously desirable, for this will ensure that a party understands the implications of the agreement, and full disclosure of any assets owned by the other party may be necessary to ensure this. But if it is clear that a party is fully aware of the implications of an ante-nuptial agreement and indifferent to detailed particulars of the other party's assets, there is no need to accord the agreement reduced weight because he or she is unaware of those particulars. What is important is that each party should have all the information that is material to his or her decision, and that each party should intend that the agreement should govern the final consequences of the marriage coming to an end."[202]

24-71 Lord Phillips continued as follows:

> "71. In relation to the circumstances attending the making of the nuptial agreement, this comment of Ormrod LJ in *Edgar v Edgar* at p.1417, although made about a separation agreement, is pertinent:
>
> > 'It is not necessary in this connection to think in formal legal terms, such as misrepresentation or estoppel; all the circumstances as they affect each of two human beings must be considered in the complex relationship of marriage.'
>
> The first question will be whether any of the standard vitiating factors: duress, fraud or misrepresentation, is present. Even if the agreement does not have

---

196 [2011] 1 A.C. 534 at [31].
197 [2011] 1 A.C. 534 at [37]–[41].
198 [2011] 1 A.C. 534 at [42]–[44].
199 [2010] A.C. 298.
200 [2011] 1 A.C. 534 at [57]–[61].
201 [2011] 1 A.C. 534 at [61].
202 [2011] 1 A.C. 534 at [68]–[69].

contractual force, those factors will negate any effect the agreement might otherwise have. But unconscionable conduct such as undue pressure (falling short of duress) will also be likely to eliminate the weight to be attached to the agreement, and other unworthy conduct, such as exploitation of a dominant position to secure an unfair advantage, would reduce or eliminate it.

72. The court may take into account a party's emotional state, and what pressures he or she was under to agree. But that again cannot be considered in isolation from what would have happened had he or she not been under those pressures. The circumstances of the parties at the time of the agreement will be relevant. Those will include such matters as their age and maturity, whether either or both had been married or been in long-term relationships before. For such couples their experience of previous relationships may explain the terms of the agreement, and may also show what they foresaw when they entered into the agreement. What may not be easily foreseeable for less mature couples may well be in contemplation of more mature couples. Another important factor may be whether the marriage would have gone ahead without an agreement, or without the terms which had been agreed. This may cut either way.

73. If the terms of the agreement are unfair from the start, this will reduce its weight, although this question will be subsumed in practice in the question of whether the agreement operates unfairly having regard to the circumstances prevailing at the time of the breakdown of the marriage."

In the case of ante-nuptial agreements the court will go beyond the merely contractual grounds for setting the agreement aside, such as fraud, non-disclosure or undue pressure and look at the matter in the round. The court will typically ask: **24-72**

(1) Were there circumstances attending to the making of the agreement that detract from the weight that should be accorded to it?
(2) Were there circumstances attending to the making of the agreement that enhance the weight that should be accorded to it?
(3) Do the circumstances now prevailing make it fair or just to depart from the agreement?[203]

In relation to the question of fairness, the fact of the agreement may alter what is fair. The starting point is that the court should give effect to an agreement that is freely entered into by each party with a full appreciation of its implications unless in the circumstances prevailing it would not be fair to hold the parties to their agreement.[204] There is nothing inherently unfair in an agreement as to the disposal of non-matrimonial property at the termination of the marriage and there may be good objective justification for it.[205] **24-73**

The Supreme Court upheld the ante-nuptial agreement between the parties. Since *Radmacher* it will be natural to infer that parties who enter into an ante-nuptial agreement to which English law is likely to be applied will intend that effect will be given to it.[206] Whilst it remains the case that nuptial agreements are not binding and cannot oust the jurisdiction of the court, the Supreme Court's decision appears to shift the presumption in favour of upholding ante-nuptial and post-nuptial agreements fairly entered into. **24-74**

In *Versteegh v Versteegh*[207] the Court of Appeal rejected the argument that once one party chose to make an offer in excess of that to which the other party would be entitled under the strict terms of an ante-nuptial agreement, then that agree- **24-75**

---

203 [2011] 1 A.C. 534 at [67].
204 [2011] 1 A.C. 534 at [75].
205 [2011] 1 A.C. 534 at [79].
206 [2011] 1 A.C. 534 at [70].
207 [2018] 2 F.L.R. 1417.

ment (and its agreed intention) must be ignored. It was said by King LJ at [78] that such an approach runs against the fundamental tenet of *Radmacher*. "Fairness" does not, she said, require a court to ignore the precept upon which the parties have governed their affairs for (on the facts of that case) over 20 years, anchored as they were to an ante-nuptial agreement, simply because the one party, for whatever reason, chose not to hold the other party to that agreement in its entirety.

24-76 Most recently the Court of Appeal held in *Brack v Brack*[208] that, whilst the courts at first instance post-*Radmacher* have consistently resolved cases where there is a valid ante-nuptial agreement by only interfering with the agreement so as to ensure the economically weaker party's needs are met, the court is not constrained only to making a needs-based award. Indeed, even in circumstances where there is a valid ante-nuptial agreement the court remains under an obligation to take into account all of the factors in MCA 1973 s.25(2), together with a proper consideration of all the circumstances. That approach may lead a court to make an order which, contrary to the terms of the ante-nuptial agreement, provides a party with an award in excess of their needs.[209]

24-77 In *Radmacher* the broad approach applied to the issue of whether or not an ante-nuptial agreement should be upheld was very similar to that applied in the case of a separation agreement in *Edgar v Edgar*. It is submitted that *Edgar* is authority for the proposition that, when considering one party's contention that an agreement has been made which should influence the court's discretion, it is open to the other party to raise, inter alia, suggestions akin to misrepresentation or undue influence.[210] In *De Lasala v De Lasala*[211] the Privy Council did not demur from the proposition that, as a matter of principle, an agreement to a consent order obtained by fraud or mistake was susceptible to being set aside. So far as fraud, mistake or misrepresentation are concerned in this context, they will often be embraced by the wider concept of the need for full and frank disclosure of all material facts between the parties when engaged in seeking to compromise proposed or actual applications for financial relief.[212]

24-78 Although it is submitted that it is clear that circumstances akin to the usual grounds for setting aside a compromise may be raised at some appropriate stage, it is equally clear, as a matter of practice, that the party relying on any of these grounds need not apply to the court to set aside an agreement of this nature.[213] He or she may simply make it clear to the other party that the agreement is, for the relevant reason, no longer regarded as having effect. This may be emphasised, if it is the applicant for relief who takes this course, by taking active steps to pursue the substantive applications. Should the other party take any of the procedural steps suggested previously as being appropriate,[214] the matter of the invalidating ground can be raised then as the reason advanced for the court disregarding the agreement.

24-79 However, it is plain that wider grounds than merely those referred to above may be available in order that an agreement may be disregarded. The lack of full and frank disclosure of all material facts may, if significant to the agreement, cause the court to disregard it at the invitation of the party to whom the full disclosure was

---

208 [2019] 2 F.L.R. 234.

209 *Brack v Brack* [2019] 2 F.L.R. 234 at [102]–[104].

210 cf. the position after the making of an order. See also para.4-66 onwards.

211 *De Lasala* [1980] A.C. 546.

212 *Livesey* [1985] A.C. 424.

213 The relevance of the grounds for setting aside a consent order based upon the prior agreement is considered at para.24-88 onwards.

214 See para.24-60 onwards.

not made.[215] A material and unforeseen or overlooked change in circumstances since the agreement is another ground, although that, of course, represents an ex post facto basis for saying that the agreement is to be ignored. A "material change of circumstances" for this purpose may be one of many things. The most obvious example would be a significant change in the financial position of one or other or both of the parties, particularly if this had an adverse impact upon any children of the family.[216] Equally, of course, anything which occurs that invalidates the basis, or fundamental assumption, upon which the agreement was concluded would constitute a material change in circumstances.[217]

Bad legal advice and "internal" undue pressure

A further ground referred to in *Edgar v Edgar* was where a party entered into a disadvantageous agreement of this nature on the basis of "bad legal advice".[218] One of the factors held against Mrs Edgar by the Court of Appeal was that she entered into an agreement which was arguably less than generous to her against strong advice from her solicitor. Clearly, she did not receive bad legal advice.[219] One of the factors which led the Court of Appeal in *Camm v Camm*[220] to disregard an agreement made some seven-and-a-half years previously was that Mrs Camm had not received sufficiently strong and carefully thought-out legal advice. In *B v B (Consent Order: Variation)*[221] Thorpe LJ extended the term for maintenance in the case of a wife where her solicitor had unilaterally offered a term order which was accepted by the other side in a case despite her being in need of periodical payments for life. **24-80**

The extent to which a court ought to investigate the quality of legal advice received is debatable.[222] Once embarked upon, the task is a difficult and sensitive one in an area of the law which is itself particularly difficult and sensitive.[223] Examination of the issue may be a prolonged affair.[224] Judges at first instance are, of course, bound to investigate these matters if raised[225] and the court is bound to apply the approach established authoritatively in *Edgar v Edgar* and *Camm v* **24-81**

---

215 cf. *Livesey* [1985] A.C. 424.

216 *N v N* [1994] 2 F.C.R. 275.

217 By analogy with such a change of circumstances after a consent order is made: *Barder v Barder* [1988] A.C. 20. See para.24-112 onwards.

218 See paras 24-104 – 24-105.

219 A client who, against advice, insists on a speedy settlement without a prolonged investigation into the other party's resources cannot sustain a negligence claim against his or her solicitor alleging that the settlement was unsatisfactory: *Dutfield v Stephens (Gilbert H.) and Sons* (1988) 18 Fam. Law 473. See generally Ch.21.

220 (1983) 4 F.L.R. 577.

221 [1995] 1 F.L.R. 9.

222 The nature of the bargain struck should be manifest from its terms and the circumstances of the parties as revealed in the negotiations leading to it. If unfairness is to be a ground for rejecting an agreement, it would be unfair whether it was entered into against good advice or on the basis of bad legal advice. However, in *B v B* [1995] 1 F.L.R. 9, the quality of the advice received by W was examined in some detail and taken into account upon her application to vary and extend a consent order for periodical payments made some years earlier. See also *H v H* [1994] 2 F.L.R. 94 and *Smith v McInerney* [1994] 2 F.L.R. 1077.

223 cf. the comments of Omrod LJ, recorded at in para.24-68.

224 This appears to have been so in *Pounds v Pounds* [1994] 1 F.L.R. 775. It may involve the kind of detailed examination that the Court of Appeal has expressly said should be avoided in the "wasted costs" jurisdiction: *Ridehalgh v Horsfield* [1994] Ch. 205.

225 See, e.g. *B v B* [1995] 1 F.L.R. 9.

Camm.[226] However, it is clear that there is not universal enthusiasm for the kind of investigation required, nor for the result which may emerge from that investigation. In *Pounds v Pounds*,[227] where the issue did not in the event fall for determination,[228] Hoffmann LJ, as he then was, when reflecting on the grounds upon which a court might refuse to give effect to a concluded agreement between the parties, said this[229]:

> "The result of the decision of this Court in *Edgar v Edgar* ... and the cases which have followed it is that we have, as it seems to me, the worst of both worlds. The agreement may be held to be binding, but whether it will be can be demonstrated only after litigation and may involve, as in this case, examining the quality of the advice which was given to the party who wishes to resile. It is then understandably a matter for surprise and resentment on the part of the other party that one should be able to repudiate an agreement on account of the inadequacy of one's own legal advisers, over whom the other party had no control and of whose advice he had no knowledge."

24-82 It cannot be pretended that the resolution of the problems thrown up by cases in this jurisdiction where poor legal advice has been given is easy. If bad legal advice is alleged, the file of the apparently offending solicitor is ordinarily made open to inspection and privilege is waived.[230] The provision of a satisfactory legal framework within which these problems can appropriately be addressed is also not easily achieved. A simplistic (though not, it is submitted, an unrealistic) solution in a case where a plainly unfair and disadvantageous agreement has been reached following bad advice is for the court which comes to that conclusion simply to say so.[231] The route by which it came to be unfair is, perhaps, of very much less relevance. The same comment might be made of the "undue pressure" which was also relied upon by the Court of Appeal in *Camm v Camm*, certainly in so far as reliance was placed upon the "undue pressure" which came from "within" Mrs Camm. Where H took advantage of a W's conscience to persuade her to sign over the house, the document was disregarded.[232] Where W was suffering from severe mood swings and was conducting an affair with another man, she was not held to an agreement signing away all her rights to maintenance and to the house.[233] Where a post-nuptial agreement was offered on a "take it or leave it" basis at the time of and in the throes of an "emotional melt down" and was stipulated to be the only way in which to save the marriage, the agreement was not upheld.[234]

24-83 The court has to take special care when assessing the manner in which each party's conduct affected the other: if a wife has been accustomed to placing reliance upon her husband's decisions she might be much more easily influenced than

---

226 (1983) 4 F.L.R. 577.

227 [1994] 2 F.L.R. 1055.

228 Because the Court of Appeal decided, contrary to the decision at first instance, that the order for financial relief was made with jurisdiction: *Pounds v Pounds* [1994] 1 F.L.R. 775.

229 [1994] 2 F.L.R. 1055 at 1073. In *Harris (formerly Manahan)* [1997] 1 F.L.R. 205, discussed at para.24-104, Ward LJ having reviewed *Edgar*, *Camm*, *Pounds* and *B v B*, said this: "The effect of these authorities seems to me to amount to this: because the Court is under a duty imposed by s.25 of the Matrimonial Causes Act 1973 to have regard to all the circumstances, and then under the duty itself to decide whether it will exercise any of its powers and if so how they are to be exercised, 'bad legal advice' must be taken into account whether as a good justification or as a weak excuse for a party not being held to his or her bargain. The quality of advice clearly has a part to play."

230 *Conlon v Conlons Ltd* [1952] 2 All E.R. 462. See para.21-04.

231 Indeed, the Court of Appeal did, in effect, say this in *Camm* (1983) 4 F.L.R. 577.

232 *Backhouse v Backhouse* [1978] 1 W.L.R. 243.

233 *Evans v Evans* (1981) 2 F.L.R. 33.

234 *NA v MA* [2007] 1 F.L.R. 1760.

an individual in a commercial transaction.[235] If an agreement is so plainly at variance with what would be fair having regard to the considerations set out in s.25, there is little need to conclude other than that a wholly unwise decision was made, for whatever reason, from which the court will relieve the party having made it. If it was unfair, it was unfair. Needless to say, the court will take a broad, rather than a particular, approach to whether the agreement was fair.[236]

The question of whether or not bad legal advice can justify a court disregarding an agreement is to be contrasted with the question of whether bad legal advice can ever be a justification or ground for setting aside a consent order.[237]

Other factors even if an "invalidating ground" exists

Merely because one of the "invalidating grounds" has been raised and indeed proved does not necessarily mean that the agreement will be disregarded wholly or partially. First, it will be necessary to conclude that the ground was sufficiently important materially to affect the agreement.[238] Secondly, consideration will presumably have to be given to how long it has taken the party raising the issue to do so after discovering its existence and the extent to which the agreement has already been acted upon by both parties.[239] This should not be looked at in the strict common law way of affirmation or laches, but more as part of the general appraisal of the conduct of the parties or the general circumstances of the case.[240] **24-84**

Setting aside consent orders—law and practice

1. Preliminary

The foregoing discussion has been directed at the circumstances in which a prior agreement could come to be disregarded by the court when invited to make an order by consent or where it is alleged that the parties have agreed terms concerning their financial affairs. It is now necessary to consider the position *after* a consent order has been made. Because the order is made by consent, it is made expressly at the joint invitation of the parties.[241] In what circumstances, if any, may the court, at the invitation of one of the parties, set aside the whole or part of that order and substitute another one? **24-85**

Before embarking on that discussion two things should be emphasised: first, the discussion relates to, for want of a better expression, "getting rid" of the original order. It is not concerned as such with the subsequent variation of an order which is recognised as having been validly obtained in the first instance. The jurisdiction to vary orders appears in s.31 of the Matrimonial Causes Act 1973. As observed previously,[242] that jurisdiction has been invoked to vary a prior consent order for periodical payments on the ground of a mistake as to the practical effect of the **24-86**

---

235 *NA v MA* [2007] 1 F.L.R. 1760.

236 *Dean v Dean* [1978] Fam. 161, cf. *Wachtel v Wachtel* [1973] Fam. 72.

237 See para.24-104.

238 cf. para.24-89.

239 cf. *Smallman* [1972] Fam. 25, *Camm* (1983) 4 F.L.R. 577, and *X v X (Y and Z intervening)* [2002] 1 F.L.R. 508.

240 See para.24-68.

241 Or, using the phraseology of Matrimonial Causes Act 1973 s.33A(1), "an order in the terms applied for to which the respondent agrees".

242 See para.24-25.

order.[243] The mistake was one of "all the circumstances" which the court was entitled to take into account. Presumably, the same considerations could apply in relation to the other orders which s.31 ordains as being variable for this purpose.[244]

24-87 Secondly, the discussion does not relate to the situation where consent is given to an order containing arrangements for the use of a property until its subsequent disposition in certain events, one of those events being the "further order of the court", liberty to apply for such order being provided for.[245] Sometimes this is seen, incorrectly it is submitted, as a basis upon which the original agreement reflected in the order can be altered. Parties agreeing to such an order are expressly (or, at the very least, impliedly) submitting themselves to the jurisdiction of the court to make provision for the earlier disposition of the property in circumstances other than those otherwise provided for specifically in the parties' agreement.[246] The provision of "liberty to apply" generally, whether in a consent order or otherwise, does not give the court power to set aside, alter or vary the original order. It merely relates to applications for the implementation and enforcement of the original order.[247]

2. Grounds for setting aside a consent order

General

24-88 Subject to one area of uncertainty,[248] the grounds upon which a consent order in this jurisdiction may be set aside are now reasonably clear. The series of cases comprising *De Lasala v De Lasala*,[249] *Livesey v Jenkins*,[250] *Barder v Barder*,[251] *Sharland v Sharland*,[252] and *Gohil v Gohil*[253] represents the source of much of the authoritative guidance on these matters. Two broad propositions may be advanced on the basis of these authorities from which certain subsidiary propositions can be derived:

(a) once the provisions of the parties' agreement have become embodied in an order of the court, the legal effect of those provisions is thenceforth derived from the order and not from the agreement[254]; and
(b) any factor which undermines to a significant degree, or otherwise invalidates, the basis upon which one or other or both of the parties agreed to the making of that order may constitute a ground for setting aside the order.[255]

It is the second of these propositions from which the subsequent subsidiary propositions are to be derived.

---

243 *Brister* [1970] 1 W.L.R. 664 cited in *De Lasala* [1980] A.C. 546, but not referred to in the judgment.
244 *De Lasala* [1980] A.C. 546.
245 *Alonso v Alonso* (1974) 4 Fam. Law 164, *Carson v Carson* [1983] 1 W.L.R. 285, and *Thompson v Thompson* [1986] Fam. 38.
246 cf. *Chanel v F.W. Woolworth & Co Ltd* [1981] 1 W.L.R. 485 CA, at para.6-22, fn.57.
247 *Cristel v Cristel* [1951] 2 K.B. 725 and *Potts v Potts* (1976) 6 Fam. Law 217.
248 See para.24-100.
249 [1980] A.C. 546.
250 [1985] A.C. 424.
251 [1988] A.C. 20.
252 [2015] UKSC 60.
253 [2015] UKSC 61; [2015] 2 F.L.R. 1289.
254 *De Lasala* [1980] A.C. 546 at 560, *Livesey* [1985] A.C. 424 at 435, *Barder* [1988] A.C. 20 at 40.
255 *Livesey* [1985] A.C. 424 at 443, *Barder* [1988] A.C. 20 at 40–43.

Failure to disclose all material facts before the order is made

The failure of either or both of the parties to make full and frank disclosure of all material facts before the consent order is finally made will yield the basis for an application to set aside the order, provided, of course, the order made was substantially different from that which would have been made had the proper disclosure occurred.[256] Many of the older cases arise from a failure to disclose an intention to remarry; many of the more modern cases from a failure to disclose assets. **24-89**

In *Livesey v Jenkins*,[257] W obtained a decree nisi of divorce in an undefended suit in March 1982, the decree being made absolute the following month. Negotiations concerning financial matters, which had commenced before then, continued until about 12 August when the form and terms of the consent order were agreed. The essential terms were to the effect that H would transfer to W all of his half share in the matrimonial home in return for the dismissal of all W's claims for herself. The purpose of the transfer of H's half share was to enable W to have a house of her own in which she could reside with the two children. On 18 August, she became engaged to a man whom she had met on 12 July. On 19 August, the parties' solicitors issued a joint application to the court for the agreed order. On 2 September, the registrar made the consent order as applied for and made no inquiries about its nature or basis. The order provided for the transfer to be made within 28 days and, on 22 September, H executed the appropriate conveyance. On 24 September, W remarried. Neither the fact of, nor the possibility of, W's remarriage had ever been mentioned in the negotiations. After H learned of W's remarriage (on 10 October), in due course, an application was made on his behalf for leave to appeal out of time against the original consent order, coupled with an application to set aside that order. The application was, in the first instance, dealt with by a circuit judge who gave leave, but dismissed his appeal. The Court of Appeal dismissed H's appeal. The House of Lords allowed H's appeal.

On the matters of principle directly of concern in the case, the decision of the House of Lords can be summarised thus: **24-90**

(a) Whenever the court is invited to exercise the jurisdiction conferred by ss.23 and 24 of the Matrimonial Causes Act 1973 it is bound by s.25 to take into account all the circumstances of the case including the particular matters therein specified.[258]
(b) Unless the parties inviting the court to exercise its jurisdiction under these provisions provide the court, directly or indirectly, with correct, complete and up-to-date information about all the circumstances of the case, including the particular matters specified,

> "the court is not equipped to exercise and cannot therefore lawfully and properly exercise, its discretion in the manner ordained by section 25(1)".[259]

(c) The parties owe to each other and the court a duty "to make full and frank disclosure of all material facts".[260]
(d) If there is a failure in any case to comply with the duty referred to in (c)

---

[256] *Livesey* [1985] A.C. 424 at 445–446 and 430. For cases in which it was held that the non-disclosure would not have made any substantial difference, see *Cook* (1988) 18 Fam. Law 163, *Chaudhuri v Chaudhuri* (1992) 22 Fam. Law 385, and *B v B (Financial Provision: Leave to Appeal* [1994] 1 F.L.R. 219. Cf. *Hope-Smith v Hope-Smith* [1989] 2 F.L.R. 56.
[257] [1985] A.C. 424.
[258] [1985] A.C. 424 at 436–437.
[259] [1985] A.C. 424.
[260] [1985] A.C. 424 at 437–438. See also *Imerman v Tchenguiz* [2010] EWCA Civ 908; [2011] 2 W.L.R.

above which has led the court into making, whether by consent or otherwise, an order substantially different from the order which it otherwise would have made, the order actually made is liable to be set aside.[261]

24-91 On the facts of the case it was held:

(a) that, although not guilty of a misrepresentation, W was in breach of the duty referred to above by not disclosing the fact of her engagement as soon as it took place[262];
(b) that her failure to do so undermined the whole basis on which the consent order was agreed since H would undoubtedly have withdrawn his consent to the making of the order had he known[263];
(c) that in consequence the consent order was "invalid" and H was "entitled, in order to prevent injustice, to have it set aside".[264]

24-92 The courts have also underscored the *ongoing* duty to provide full and frank disclosure during financial proceedings.[265] For example, where a husband failed to disclose negotiations in which he has engaged, prior to the making of the final consent order, which led to a significant improvement in his financial circumstances after the making of the order, he was in breach of the duty of disclosure at the time the order was made. Although it was uncertain at the time of the hearing which resulted in a consent order whether the husband would in fact be offered a new job or, if he was, whether the terms would be acceptable to him, the Court of Appeal held that he was under a duty to disclose the negotiations and that if he had done so the hearing would have been adjourned to await the outcome of the negotiations. The duty extends beyond what is certain at the date of the order to any fact relevant to the foreseeable future. The order was set aside because the wife would have "raised her sights" had she known of the negotiations taking place.[266] However, such non-disclosure will not be sufficient if the events were foreseeable or if the effects of the non-disclosure were avoidable by reasonable enquiry.[267] In *Burns v Burns*[268] Thorpe LJ considered that there was a "duty of candour", which extended beyond the making of the substantive order, to inform the other party of an event which occurred shortly after a consent order had been made, if that event had the effect (as in *Barder*) of fundamentally altering the basis upon which the original order had been made or which may form the basis of an appeal. Failing to provide full and frank disclosure may result in a consent order being set aside.[269] However, whether the non-disclosure will justify the consent order being set aside will be a question of degree as to how relevant the non-disclosure is to the outcome.[270] There is not

---

592 at [25]–[27].

261 [1985] A.C. 424 at 445–446.

262 [1985] A.C. 424 at 438.

263 [1985] A.C. 424 at 434 and 438.

264 [1985] A.C. 424 at 438.

265 *Livesey* [1985] A.C. 424 at 437E, *Vernon v Bosley (No.2)* [1999] Q.B. 18 at 32–36, *S v S (No.2) (Ancillary Relief: Application to Set Aside Order)* [2010] 1 F.L.R. 993 at [20].

266 *Bokor-Ingram v Bokor-Ingram* [2009] 2 F.L.R. 922 (allowing an appeal from *I v I (Ancillary Relief: Disclosure)* [2009] 1 F.L.R. 201).

267 *B v B (Ancillary Relief Consent Order: Appeal Out Of Time)* [2008] 1 F.L.R. 1279 at [38] and *Walkden v Walkden* [2010] 1 F.L.R. 174 at [93].

268 [2004] 3 F.C.R. 263 at [22].

269 *Vicary v Vicary* [1992] 2 F.L.R. 271 and *T v T (Consent Order: Procedure to Set Aside)* [1996] 2 F.L.R. 640.

270 *P v P (Consent Order: Appeal Out Of Time)* [2002] 1 F.L.R. 743.

necessarily however the equivalent positive duty to disclose any change of financial circumstances during any appellate process.[271]

A particularly striking example is *Sharland v Sharland*.[272] In the course of the final hearing the husband gave evidence confirming that there was no Initial Public Offering (IPO) in relation to his business "on the cards today". The parties then reached a settlement, the judge approved the agreement, and a draft consent order was drawn up. The wife subsequently became aware that the husband's company was in fact being actively prepared for an IPO. On the wife's application not to seal the consent order and resume the final hearing the judge, Sir Hugh Bennett, found that the wife had been deliberately misled into agreeing to compromise her claims and the court had been misled into approving the consent order. The court considered that had the husband disclosed the true position it would have adjourned the final hearing to establish whether the IPO was going ahead. However, by the time of the hearing of the wife's application, the IPO had not taken place and was not now in prospect. The judge therefore declined to set aside the consent order on the ground that he would not have made a substantially different order. The Court of Appeal, by a majority, upheld the judge's decision. In allowing the wife's appeal, the Supreme Court held that in a case of fraud or deliberate non-disclosure, there is a presumption of materiality. The burden of satisfying the court that the presumption does not apply lies with the perpetrator of the fraud. The exception to the principle that "fraud unravels all" is where the court is satisfied that, at the time when it made the consent order, the fraud would not have influenced a reasonable person to agree to it nor, had it known what it knows now, would the court have made a significantly different order (whether or not the parties had agreed to it).[273] On the facts it was clear that the judge would not have made the order he did, when he did, in the absence of the husband's fraud, and the consent order should have been set aside. The judge had misinterpreted *Livesey*, which had drawn a distinction between triviality and materiality at the date of the order and not at some later date.[274] He had also been wrong to deprive the wife of a full and fair hearing of her claims by re-making his decision at the hearing of the application on the basis of the evidence then before him.[275]

At the same time as it heard the appeal in *Sharland v Sharland*, the Supreme Court considered *Gohil v Gohil*[276] In *Gohil v Gohil*, the Court of Appeal found that a judge had erred by allowing an order to be set aside for non-disclosure without having *found as a fact* that there had been material non-disclosure. The court confirmed that there were two stages that would need to be passed if an order were to be set aside on this ground; (i) a factual determination of whether there had been material non-disclosure; and (ii) if so, a determination of whether the order should be set aside. In allowing the wife's appeal, the Supreme Court held that where a party's non-disclosure was inadvertent there is no presumption that it was material. The onus lies with the other party to show that proper disclosure would, on the balance of probabilities, have led to a different order.[277] **24-93**

[271] *N v N* [2015] 1 F.L.R. 241.
[272] [2015] 2 F.L.R. 1367.
[273] [2015] 2 F.L.R. 1367 at [32]–[33].
[274] [2015] 2 F.L.R. 1367 at [34].
[275] [2015] 2 F.L.R. 1367 at [35].
[276] [2015] UKSC 61; [2015] 2 F.L.R. 1289.
[277] [2015] UKSC 61; [2015] 2 F.L.R. 1289 at [44].

Moreover, in *Gohil v Gohil* the Court of Appeal considered that the judge had erroneously applied the test in *Ladd v Marshall*[278]—i.e. that there was new evidence which would probably have an important influence on the result of the case. The Court of Appeal confirmed that this test was applicable only to an appellate court and had no application to an application to set aside. The Supreme Court held that the test in *Ladd v Marshall* had no relevance to the determination of an application to set aside a financial order on the ground of fraudulent non-disclosure.

Fraud and misrepresentation

24-94 Fraud was recognised in *De Lasala v De Lasala*[279] as a ground for impeaching a financial consent order. Even though there is some authority[280] for saying that it is not necessary to talk in terms of "misrepresentation" as such in this context, the House of Lords did not expressly eschew the expression in *Livesey v Jenkins*.[281] Instances of a party failing to disclose relevant facts will involve differing levels of culpability depending on the scale of the undisclosed asset or the length to which the offender has gone. However, in practice distinctions important in other fields such as that between innocent and false misrepresentation will have less impact in financial remedies.[282] At all events, this semantic discussion is of little relevance: any misrepresentation (whether fraudulent, negligent or innocent) of a material factor is almost bound to result in the failure of the duty to disclose in full all material facts.

Mistake

24-95 A sufficiently significant mistake may operate to undermine an ordinary compromise[283] and it has been acknowledged to be an invalidating ground so far as orders of the sort under consideration are concerned.[284] In most cases the mistake will lead to a situation in which the parties, and thus the court, are misinformed as to a material fact which itself will affect the validity of the consent of the parties and the order made pursuant to it. *Fallon v Fallon* is an example of an order being set aside on the basis of a fundamental mistake as to the amount needed by the wife to enable her to rehouse.[285] The problem of mistake is most likely to arise where mistaken valuations of property are relied upon in negotiations.[286] A simple a change in fortunes post-trial through, for example, volatility in share values or money markets would not constitute a mistake, as the possibility of that happening is foreseeable.[287] In the same vein, where parties proceeded on the basis that the husband would have to meet a liability estimated at £14m, it being accepted the estimate was riddled with uncertainty, the wife was not permitted to reopen the mat-

---

278 (1954) FLR Rep 422.

279 [1980] A.C. 546.

280 *Edgar* [1980] 1 W.L.R. 1410, referred to at para.24-68.

281 [1985] A.C. 424.

282 *Shaw v Shaw* [2002] 2 F.L.R. 1204 at [44], *S v S (No.2) (Ancillary Relief: Application to Set Aside Order)* [2010] 1 F.L.R. 993; cf. *Judge v Judge* [2009] 1 F.L.R. 1287 at [4].

283 See Ch.4.

284 *De Lasala* [1980] A.C. 546, *Robinson v Robinson* (1983) 4 F.L.R. 102. In *Harris (formerly Manahan)* [1997] 1 F.L.R. 205, noted at para.24-104. Ward LJ said that he could "imagine circumstances where the bad advice gives rise to a mistaken belief which, if shared by the other side, may enable the underlying agreement to be attacked on the ground of mistake".

285 [2010] 1 F.L.R. 910.

286 See para.4-19. See also *Hope-Smith v Hope-Smith* [1989] 2 F.L.R. 56, *Thompson v Thompson* [1991] 2 F.L.R. 530 and *Rundle v Rundle* [1992] 2 F.L.R. 80. See also para.24-117 onwards.

287 *Walkden v Walkden* [2010] 1 F.L.R. 174 and *Myerson v Myerson (No. 2)* [2009] 2 F.L.R. 147.

ter on the basis of mistake when the husband was, in the result, only required to pay £600,000. The liability had been a "known unknown" and it could have been significantly more than the estimated figure: indeed the wife had sought an outcome which protected her against that eventuality.[288] In a case where both parties were proceeding on the assumption that the whole of a liability would be met by an insurance policy but, in the event, the consequence of the order left the husband exposed to an unforeseen liability, due to the insurer's avoidance of the policy; the court took the view that the possibility that the insurance company would avoid the policy was not contemplated. It was an "unknown unknown" and therefore a vitiating mistake. However, conversely there was a portion of the claim which, in any event, exceeded the limit of the insurance cover about which the husband was ignorant. This was not a mistake as the husband could have discovered it on enquiry.[289]

In *DB v DLJ (Challenge to Arbitral Award)*[290] Mostyn J stated that where a case of mistake, as opposed to supervening event, was being advanced the question of the ability of the claimant, by exercising due diligence, to have discovered the true facts is critically important. In this regard the burden will be on him to show that he could not have discovered the true state of affairs. He went on to state that the applicable principles in relation to mistake can be formulated as follows[291]: **24-96**

i) the court may set aside an order on the ground that the true facts on which it based its disposition were not known by either the parties or the court at the time the order was made;
ii) the claimant must show that the true facts would have led the court to have made a materially different order from the one it in fact made;
iii) the absence of the true facts must not have been the fault of the claimant;
iv) the claimant must show, on the balance of probabilities, that he could not with due diligence have established the true facts at the time the order was made;
v) the application to set aside should be made reasonably promptly in the circumstances of the case;
vi) the claimant must show that he cannot obtain alternative mainstream relief which has the effect of broadly remedying the injustice caused by the absence of the true facts;
vii) the application if granted should not prejudice third parties who have, in good faith and for valuable consideration, acquired interests in property which is the subject matter of the relevant order.

In *FSHC Group Holdings Ltd v Glas Trust Corporation Ltd*[292] the Court of Appeal to be applied in deciding whether the written terms of a contract may be rectified because of a common mistake. In particular, the key question was whether, in a situation where at the time the parties executed the document, they had a common intention in respect of a particular matter which, by mistake, the document did not accurately record, Lord Hoffmann was correct in obiter dicta in *Chartbrook Ltd v Persimmon Homes Ltd*[293] to have said that the relevant test of intention is purely "objective" i.e. what a reasonable observer (with knowledge of the background facts and prior communications between the parties) would have thought the parties common intention at the time of contracting to be. The Court of Appeal concluded that **24-97**

---

[288] *Judge v Judge* [2009] 1 F.L.R. 1287.
[289] *Richardson v Richardson* [2011] 2 F.L.R. 244.
[290] [2016] 2 F.L.R. 1308.
[291] [2016] 2 F.L.R. 1308 at [57].
[292] [2019] EWCA Civ 1361. See Ch.4, fn.81.
[293] [2009] UKHL 38.

these remarks did not correctly state the law. Leggatt LJ (with whom Flaux and Rose LJJ agreed) said that "[w]e consider that we are bound by authority, which also accords with sound legal principle and policy, to hold that, before a written contract may be rectified on the basis of a common mistake, it is necessary to show either (1) that the document fails to give effect to a prior concluded contract or (2) that, when they executed the document, the parties had a common intention in respect of a particular matter which, by mistake, the document did not accurately record. In the latter case it is necessary to show not only that each party to the contract had the same actual intention with regard to the relevant matter, but also that there was an "outward expression of accord"—meaning that, as a result of communication between them, the parties understood each other to share that intention."[294]

24-98 It is likely that this decision will mean that a claimant seeking rectification on the basis of common mistake will in practice face a more significant task than he or she would were *Chartbook* to have been followed. This is because in most cases it will be harder to prove the necessary subjective consensus (which will depend solely on the actual communications passing between the parties) than it would an objective consensus (i.e. what an objective person would reasonably consider to be the consensus). In the absence of any written or actual proof of those communications, this may be very difficult to demonstrate, especially where there are conflicting witness testimonies from both parties. As a result, successful cases of rectification will be rarer. The Court of Appeal recognised[295] these practical consequences, but made clear that as a matter of policy rectification should be difficult to prove. The presumption should be that formal written contracts are to be upheld. Any other approach would undermine the importance commercial parties put on the final written agreement.

24-99 In future it will, therefore, be of great importance to (i) ensure that the written terms of any agreement accurately reflect the parties' intentions and the agreement reached; and (ii) keep a detailed record of any negotiations prior to entering into an agreement (such as meeting minutes, notes, emails and non-binding heads of terms). It may become crucially important in future to show the court what was agreed, discussed and intended by the parties should a dispute arise. When negotiations are taking place at an FDR hearing best practice is therefore to put all material terms of an offer in writing and record the time that the offers were made and, assuming that agreement is reached, use these written documents as a checklist of the agreed terms when explaining the terms to the FDR judge.

Undue influence

24-100 On the basis of the second of the general propositions referred to previously,[296] anything that undermines significantly the consensual basis of the order must constitute a prima facie ground for setting aside the order. Where one party's agreement has been obtained as the result of the duress or undue influence of the other there would seem no reason in principle why any consent order made in pursuance of that agreement should not be vulnerable to attack by the party subjected to whatever pressure may have been applied. It has certainly been recognised as a

---

294 [2009] UKHL 38 at [176].
295 [173].
296 See para.24-88(b). See also para.4-66 onwards.

ground for ignoring an apparently concluded agreement prior to an order being sought.[297]

24-101 In *Tommey v Tommey*[298] Balcombe J (as he then was) concluded that undue influence could not, as a matter of law, afford a basis for setting aside a consent order in this jurisdiction. That decision, however, was made before *Livesey v Jenkins* and, though carefully declining to express any concluded view on the matter, the House of Lords did venture the comment that it was "not persuaded that [the] decision on the question was necessarily correct".[299] Balcombe J felt obliged, as he plainly was, to apply the decision of the Court of Appeal in *Thwaite v Thwaite*[300] to the problem in hand. As recorded previously,[301] the Court of Appeal interpreted the judgment of the Privy Council in *De Lasala v De Lasala*[302] as requiring the elimination of the "contractual basis" of consent orders in this jurisdiction and that "so far as possible" they should be dealt with, for the purpose of being set aside, in the same way as non-consensual orders.[303] That conclusion, it was said, followed from the proposition that the legal effect of agreed financial arrangements made the subject of a court order derived from the court order and not the prior agreement. However, the conclusion does not necessarily follow from the premise. The legal effect of something is one thing; the basis upon which that something is deprived of legal effect is another. Merely because a party submits himself consensually to the exercise of this jurisdiction of the court in a particular way does not, it is submitted, mean that thereby he deprives himself of the right to say subsequently that his consent to that course was improperly obtained. There would be little justice in that. That principle is recognised clearly in *Livesey v Jenkins*, *De Lasala v De Lasala*, and *Sharland v Sharland* in the sense that agreements to orders resulting from fraud, mistake or non-disclosure of material facts should be deprived of effect. It is but a small step to hold that an order obtained following an agreement induced by undue influence should similarly be deprived of effect. It may well be, as Balcombe J said in *Tommey v Tommey*,[304] that it "will be a rare case where undue influence can be shown to exist right up to the making of the order", but if it can be shown that the prior agreement was induced by undue influence it is, with respect, difficult to see why the law should deprive the person subjected to it of remedy. It may well be that the particular part of *Thwaite v Thwaite* which Balcombe J was bound to follow cannot stand in the light of the approach of, and the principles enunciated by, the House of Lords. It must be noted, however, that, though cited both in *Livesey v Jenkins* and *Barder v Barder*,[305] no expression of disapproval of any part of the judgment in *Thwaite v Thwaite* is to be found in either of the speeches of Lord Brandon of Oakbrook.

The bad deal

24-102 Will a consensual "bad deal" afford grounds for the subsequent intervention by the court at the request of the victim of the "bad deal"? Whilst the logic behind cases like *Livesey v Jenkins* might suggest so, it is hard to see circumstances where a "bad deal" alone (i.e. without the presence of any other invalidating ground) might be

---

297 *Edgar* [1982] 1 W.L.R. 1410, *Camm* (1983) 4 F.L.R. 577.
298 [1983] Fam. 15.
299 [1985] A.C. 424 at 440.
300 [1982] Fam. 1.
301 See para.24-33.
302 [1980] A.C. 546.
303 *Thwaite* [1982] Fam. 1 at 8.
304 [1983] Fam. 15 at 24–25.
305 [1988] A.C. 20.

grounds for setting aside a consent order. A "bad deal" is likely to arise from bad legal advice or from a refusal to accept reasonable legal advice, in which case the harm is self-inflicted. However there may be circumstances, particularly where children's interests have not been properly protected, where such a ground might be entertained.[306]

24-103 That a party may have done better by going to court will not, of itself, generally be a basis for permitting that party to be relieved of their bargain.[307] What is or is not a good bargain will not depend entirely on financial aspects; the court may take into account the social, personal, religious or cultural considerations.[308] The court should also take into account the fact that some parties are prepared to pay a price for finality and the undesirability of reopening matters between parties who have reached an agreement.[309]

Bad legal advice

24-104 Although bad legal advice is a factor to be taken into account by the court in determining whether to give effect to the parties' agreement before a consent order is made,[310] it is not something which per se affords a basis for setting aside a consent order.

In *Harris (formerly Manahan) v Manahan*,[311] H and W attended a pre-trial review with their legal advisers, the purpose of which was to explore settlement. A clean-break agreement was reached on the basis that the former matrimonial home should be sold and H should receive a fixed sum of £25,000 if the property was sold for more than £185,000, and approximately 13 per cent of the gross sale price if sold for less than £185,000. A consent order reflecting this agreement was made. For some time prior to the making of the agreement the property had been the subject of an offer of £195,000, but W's solicitors advised against sale until the ancillary relief proceedings had been concluded. If a sale at that price had proceeded, W would have received about £29,000 net and H between £10–15,000 net. H, who was in his 50s, was still earning. W had no income of any significance and no prospect of such an income. Shortly before the making of the consent order, and because of the delay caused by the advice to W not to sell until the financial proceedings were concluded, the purchasers of the property withdrew. By the time of the consent order the parties had been separated for just over one year during which time H, despite being in employment, failed to pay the instalments due under the mortgage of about £87,000. With no further purchaser having been found, and given the increasing mortgage arrears, the building society secured a possession order in August 1994. Execution of this order was postponed for a while but, in due course, possession was obtained. At the price at which the property was likely to be sold, and given the parties' indebtedness, neither would receive anything once the property was sold. W had been advised badly about agreeing to the consent order and, after a period of about 17 months, she sought to set aside the consent order on the grounds of the bad legal advice she had received. The court directed the determination as a preliminary point the question whether

306 In *L v L* [2008] 1 F.L.R. 26 H attempted to extricate himself from a consent order which was still executory on the basis that he had been under pressure and had thereby become so over-generous as to make the order unfair to him. Munby J (as he then was) held that pressure short of undue influence or duress could not suffice as grounds to set aside. The need for finality and certainty made any lower hurdle inappropriate. Over-generosity was not a ground for setting aside although it might justify a variation of the periodical payments element of the order (which by s.31 of MCA 1973 are capable of being varied).

307 *Edgar v Edgar* [1980] 3 All E.R. 887 at 897 and *Dean v Dean* [1978] Fam 161 at 172c.

308 *X v X (Y and Z intervening)* [2002] 1 F.L.R. 508.

309 *X v X (Y and Z intervening)* [2002] 1 F.L.R. 508.

310 See para.24-80 onwards.

311 [1997] 1 F.L.R. 205; *Tibbs v Dick* [1998] 2 F.L.R. 1118.

the ground relied upon by W for seeking to set aside a consent order was available to her. The Court of Appeal held that this ground was not available to her, principally on policy grounds that there must be finality in litigation. Ward LJ stated:

> "To allow a bargain struck to be set aside is inevitably to fuel recrimination. Bitterness and anger are inevitable concomitants of the conflict which arises from contested claims. Parties suffer. So do their children. It is inevitable that the focus of recrimination will swing from the incompetent solicitor and will be heaped upon the other party even though his conduct in the negotiations may not fairly be capable of being impeached. If the policy of the law is to encourage the clean break, then the law should also ensure that break with the past is final and that there is no turning back."

In *L v L*[312] Munby J (as he then was), following a complete review of the relevant authorities, came to the conclusion that bad legal advice can never be a justification or ground for setting aside a consent order. Such an allegation it was said "is barred."[313] **24-105**

This approach should be compared with the situation when a consent order is attacked by way of variation, as in *B v B*.[314] In that case a periodical payments order which was due to expire was extended. The order was entered into after bad legal advice. In *L v L*[315] Munby J similarly stated that a party could, in principle, rely upon bad legal advice in support of an application to vary, discharge or suspend such order(s) as are potentially so susceptible under s.31 of the Matrimonial Causes Act 1973. **24-106**

Whether or not a lump sum order payable by instalments entered into as a result of bad legal advice could be attacked likewise by way of variation is a moot point. As with an order for periodical payments, such an order is variable under s.31 of the Matrimonial Causes Act 1973, albeit the power to vary is only exceptionally utilised.[316] It is anticipated that a court would strain to avoid such a result, but the issue has yet to be tested.[317] **24-107**

A failure to observe s.33A and the "prescribed rules"

A consent order made following failure to lodge the statement of information with the application for it may result in the court being held subsequently not to have exercised its discretion on the basis of the required information and that the order is ipso facto invalid. The requirement for the statement of information appears to be mandatory.[318] However, if the information is available in any other manner—e.g. by counsel giving it orally—or if no injustice is done by the lack of information, the absence of it would be unlikely on its own to vitiate the order. **24-108**

The "moving target"

The duty of ongoing financial disclosure during the currency of proceedings is discussed above.[319] **24-109**

This problem becomes acute when there is (as is not uncommon) a delay of some **24-110**

312 [2008] 1 F.L.R. 26.
313 [2008] 1 F.L.R. 26 at [57].
314 [1995] 1 F.L.R. 9. See also *Richardson v Richardson* [1994] 1 F.L.R. 286 and *R v R (No. 2)* [1996] 2 F.L.R. 617.
315 [2008] 1 F.L.R. 26.
316 *Tilly v Tilly* (1979) Fam. Law 79 and *Westbury v Sampson* [2002] 1 F.L.R. 166.
317 See also para.24-81.
318 See para.24-24, but subject to Family Procedure Rules 2010 r.9.26(1)(b).
319 See para.24-92.

weeks between agreement being reached and the draft order which has been sent into the Court being approved by the judge. During that time events may occur of significance—for example, an offer to purchase a business or property significantly in excess of what had been disclosed as a likely value. In those circumstances, the continuing duty to disclose remains alive, notwithstanding that the agreement was reached without any breach of the disclosure requirements.

24-111 However, such non-disclosure will not be sufficient if the events were foreseeable or if the effects of the non-disclosure were avoidable by reasonable enquiry.[320]

Supervening events

24-112 The foregoing discussion has been directed generally to events which precede the making of the consent order and which, if established subsequently, may lead to the setting aside of that order. The question arises of whether supervening events which falsify the basis upon which the consent order was made can be relied upon to have the order set aside and a fresh order made. The issue was raised starkly in the tragic circumstances of *Barder v Barder*[321]:

> In that case a consent order was made by the county court registrar whereby H was to transfer his interest in the jointly owned former matrimonial home to W in full and final settlement of all her claims. H also agreed to an order for substantial periodical payments in favour of the two children of whom W had previously been granted the custody, care and control. There were certain other ancillary undertakings concerning life policies held by the mortgagees. After the time limit for appealing against the order had expired, but before the order had been executed, W killed the two children and then committed suicide. H applied to the county court judge subsequently for, and was granted, leave to appeal out of time against the registrar's order. The judge allowed the appeal and set aside the order on the ground that it was made on the basis that for an appreciable time after the order was made W and the children would continue to live and benefit from the order. The House of Lords held that the judge had the jurisdiction to act as he did and that he was correct in setting aside the original order.

24-113 Lord Brandon of Oakbrook, with whom all the members of the House agreed, referred[322] to the conflicting principles of the need for finality in litigation and the need, in justice, for cases to be decided upon their true facts,

> "and not on assumptions or estimates with regard to those facts which are conclusively shown by later events to have been erroneous".

Having reviewed various authorities, Lord Brandon identified four conditions that would need to be satisfied to enable a court properly to exercise its discretion to grant leave to appeal out of time against an order for financial provision or property adjustment.[323] These can be summarised as follows:

(a) the supervening events invalidate the basis, or fundamental assumption, upon which the order was made;
(b) the events should have occurred within a relatively short time from the making of the order, usually "no more than a few months";
(c) the application for permission to appeal out of time should be made reasonably promptly;

---

320 *B v B (Ancillary Relief Consent Order: Appeal Out Of Time)* [2008] 1 F.L.R. 1279 at [38] and *Walkden v Walkden* [2010] 1 F.L.R. 174 at [93].
321 [1988] A.C. 20.
322 *Barder* [1988] A.C. 20 at 41.
323 *Barder* [1988] A.C. 20 at 43.

(d) third-party rights in connection with property which is the subject-matter of the order should not be prejudiced.

Lord Brandon also emphasised[324] that the question of leave to appeal out of time should not be treated separately from the question of the merits of the appeal if leave is granted. This arose out of the first condition referred to above because, if established, it would mean that the appeal itself would be "certain, or very likely, to succeed".[325] **24-114**

These principles have formed the basis for the court's consideration of applications in a number of cases since then, mostly[326] in less tragic circumstances than in *Barder v Barder* itself. These applications have arisen largely where a property valuation adopted at the time of the original consent order has been shown to have been erroneous, a subsequent unexpected death has occurred or where there has been an unanticipated remarriage or cohabitation by one of the parties.[327] The introduction of the Child Support Act 1991[328] led to an argument that the statutory provision for extra-judicial maintenance assessments it brought into effect represented a supervening event which undermined previously concluded "clean break" settlements.[329] It must be borne in mind, of course, that the principles enunciated in *Barder v Barder* are as applicable to cases where the original order followed a contested hearing as those where it followed an agreement between the parties. Cases in which a "Barder event" can be argued successfully are rare and should be regarded as such by the specialist profession.[330] **24-115**

A "crucial distinction" between a mistake (considered above) and supervening events (*Barder*) was made in *DB v DLJ (Challenge to Arbitral Award)* by Mostyn J.[331] In his view, the distinction is that in the former the relevant facts will exist at the time of the order, but will be unknown; while in the latter, the relevant facts will arise after the order. **24-116**

Erroneous valuations

There is an initial need to distinguish for this purpose between those situations in which the original order was based upon a valuation which was erroneous at the time because of a mistaken valuation[332] and those where some supervening event (which may be no more than a radical change in the property market) has caused a change in the valuation relied upon.[333] Strictly speaking, those cases which fall to be determined by reference to the principles set out in *Livesey v Jenkins*.[334] However, there is clearly some scope for overlap between the two[335] and cases which, on analysis, appear to fall into the first category have been determined on *Barder v Barder* principles: **24-117**

---

324 *Barder* [1988] A.C. 20.
325 *Barder* [1988] A.C. 20.
326 Though see *Smith v Smith* [1992] Fam. 69, noted at para.24-123.
327 See *Salter* (1992) 22 Fam. Law 50. For a case in which two of these factors were alleged (unsuccessfully) by H to apply, see *B v B (Financial Provision: Leave to Appeal)* [1994] 1 F.L.R. 219.
328 See para.24-127.
329 See *Crozier v Crozier* [1994] Fam. 114, referred to at para.24-127.
330 *Richardson v Richardson* [2011] 2 F.L.R. 244.
331 [2016] 2 F.L.R. 1308 at [54].
332 See para.24-115.
333 The distinction was clearly articulated by the Court of Appeal in *Thompson* [1991] 2 F.L.R. 530, noted below.
334 See para.24-89 onwards.
335 cf. in *Cornick v Cornick* [1994] 2 F.L.R. 530 per Hale J (as she then was), noted at para.24-119.

24-118 In *Thompson v Thompson*,[336] H and W were divorced in 1990 after 17 years of marriage, the decree being made absolute in January 1990. There were two children who continued to live with W. The ancillary relief proceedings were heard by the district judge on 1 June 1990. The matrimonial home was valued at £75,000 (provided that £3,000 repairs were carried out) subject to a mortgage of £5,600. H had life policies worth £8,500 and the equity of another house amounting to £9,800. H also had a travel agency business which was taken by the district judge to be worth £20,000. H had an indebtedness to the bank of £27,600 secured by way of second charge on the home, together with further debts of £6,000. Each party had liabilities for costs, quantified at £6,500 on W's side. The district judge transferred the matrimonial home to W subject to the first mortgage and ordered her to pay a lump sum of £7,500 to H, the basis of the order being a clean break. The time for appealing against the order expired on 8 June 1990. One week later H sold his business for £45,000. W applied for leave to appeal out of time against the district judge's order when she discovered what had happened. The judge rejected W's application on the basis that, although on the merits he would have granted it, he had no jurisdiction to entertain it because the valuation of £20,000 had been agreed by W. She had commissioned a valuation of the business prior to the hearing before the district judge which revealed a figure of £45,000, but her expert (who was present but not called at the hearing) did not feel able to sustain it. The Court of Appeal held that the sale at £45,000 represented a "new event" that changed the situation radically and which required a reconsideration of the district judge's order. Where an altered valuation is relied on, it may be relevant to inquire into whether the applicant was in some way responsible for the erroneous valuation because, if that be the case, it may (though it is not conclusive) be a reason for not granting the applicant the indulgence underlying an application for leave to appeal out of time (as in *Edmonds v Edmonds*).[337] Furthermore, if the cause of the altered valuation was foreseen and taken into account at the time of the original order, the altered valuation cannot be "new". Neither of these factors operated against W in this case since it was said that "all concerned acted reasonably on the assumption that the business was worth £20,000 at most". It was also said in this context that "percentages should be used with caution" and that it was "much better for the reviewing court, when considering the questions of degree to look in broad terms at the balance of the financial relationship created by the order under review, and then ask itself how this balance has been affected by the new state of affairs.

24-119 A general review of those cases in which this kind of issue has arisen was conducted by Hale J, as she then was, in *Cornick v Cornick*.[338]

In that case the original order (not made by consent) in December 1992 was that the matrimonial home should be sold and H should pay W a lump sum of £240,000 and periodical payments for herself at the rate of £20,000 per annum. Periodical payments for the two children were ordered at the rate of £4,200 per annum, with further provision for the payment by H of their school fees. The value of each of H's shares in the company of which he was deputy chairman was taken by the court as £2.17. Excluding the value of certain share options of H falling due in 1996, the net assets of the parties in December 1992 totalled £649,000. The effect of the court order was to give W 51% of those net assets or 36% if the share options were taken into account. The value of H's shares increased substantially after the order was made. In the light of these increases the net effect of the order by November 1993 was to give W 26% of 15% of the assets, depending on whether the share options were taken into account. By May 1994 (when the application for leave to appeal was heard) the proportions were 20% and 11% respectively. W did not suggest that this dramatic rise in share value could reasonably have been foreseen at the time of the hearing in December 1992. Hale J held that W's application for leave to appeal out of time should be rejected because what occurred was nothing more than "a natural albeit

---

336 *Thompson* [1991] 2 F.L.R. 530.

337 *Edmonds v Edmonds* [1990] 2 F.L.R. 202.

338 [1994] 2 F.L.R. 530.

dramatic change in the value of [H's] shareholding" reflecting a "natural process of price fluctuation.

Following her review of the authorities,[339] Hale J drew the following conclusions: **24-120**

"(1) An asset which was taken into account and correctly valued at the date of the hearing changes value within a relatively short time owing to natural processes of price fluctuation. The court should not then manipulate the power to grant leave to appeal out of time to provide a disguised power of variation which Parliament has quite obviously and deliberately declined to enact.

(2) A wrong value was put upon that asset at the hearing, which had it been known about at the time would have led to a different order. Provided that it is not the fault of the person alleging the mistake, it is open to the Court to give leave for the matter to be reopened. Although falling within the *Barder* principle it is more akin to the misrepresentation or non-disclosure cases than to *Barder* itself.

(3) Something unforeseen and unforeseeable has happened since the date of the hearing which has altered the value of the assets so dramatically as to bring about a substantial change in the balance of assets brought about by the order. Then, provided that the other three conditions are fulfilled, the *Barder* principle may apply. However, the circumstances in which this can happen are very few and far between. The case law, taken as a whole, does not suggest that the natural processes of price fluctuation, whether in houses, shares or any other property, and however dramatic, fall within this principle."

Changing economic climate

In recent times, and faced with a potential flood of cases caused by the rise and then the collapse of the financial and property markets, the courts have taken a more analytical approach and have been less willing to reopen cases simply because an asset has fluctuated substantially in value.[340] **24-121**

---

[339] The following cases, inter alia, are referred to in the judgment: *Chaudhuri* [1992] 2 F.L.R. 73, *Cook* [1988] 1 F.L.R. 521, *Edmonds* [1990] 2 F.L.R. 202, *Hope-Smith* [1989] 2 F.L.R. 56, *Penrose v Penrose* [1994] 2 F.L.R. 621, *Rundle v Rundle* [1992] 2 F.L.R. 80, *Thompson* [1991] 2 F.L.R. 530 and *Worlock v Worlock* [1994] 2 F.L.R. 689. *Heard v Heard* [1996] 1 F.C.R. 33, decided on 20 June 1994, was not referred to. It appears, however, to be consistent with Hale J's analysis. The original order (not a consent order) was made with the intention that H should have enough money from the sale of the former matrimonial home to re-house himself. It became apparent that the value upon which this expectation had been based was wrong. Sir Thomas Bingham MR (with whom Kennedy and Millett LJJ agreed) said that "the discovery that the valuation was unsound, or alternatively the discovery that the house could not be sold at the price which had been assumed as its market price, did amount to new events sufficient to satisfy Lord Brandon's first condition".

[340] In *Walkden v Walkden* [2010] 1 F.L.R. 174 the Court of Appeal refused to allow a wife to reopen an award when a business was sold for more than anticipated and in consequence her award was worth 18% of the total assets rather than 42% of the declared assets pursuant to the consent order. The value of the shares had never been agreed and the court held that the agreement was based on the unknown value with each party expressing rival views and that a sale at some stage was in the anticipation of the parties. Likewise the sale of a property at a significantly enhanced value in *B v B* [2008] 1 F.L.R. 1279 was a product of the market which was not an event which justified reopening. It should be noted that in *Walkden*, as in *Judge v Judge* [2009] 1 F.L.R. 1287, the court emphasised that a mistake as to value is not a supervening event (as in *Barder*) but is more akin to mistake or misrepresentation. In *Myerson v Myerson (No 2)* [2009] 2 F.L.R 147. the Court of Appeal refused to permit a husband to reopen a consent order the effect of which was said to leave him with less than nothing, having already paid the wife over £7 million. The court commented that the husband had chosen to keep control of the speculative assets. A price fluctuation, however dramatic, was not a *Barder* event. The husband could apply if he wished to vary the unpaid lump sum instalments.

Delaying tactics

24-122 In certain circumstances the delaying tactics of one of the parties in connection with the implementation of a consent order (e.g. in the sale of a property) can operate to invalidate or falsify the basis upon which that order was made.[341] However, the other party will, in the normal course of events, be expected to take steps to enforce the order and a failure to do so will negative the suggestion that the delay constitutes a material supervening event.[342]

Unexpected death of a party

24-123 This kind of event was, of course, illustrated starkly by the case of *Barder v Barder* itself.[343]

In *Smith v Smith*,[344] H and W, who had been married in 1955, divorced in 1988, the decree having been made absolute on 6 October 1988. W's application for ancillary relief was heard by the registrar on 7 December 1988. At that time H was 62 and W was 52. The total family assets were approximately £107,000, comprising the equity in the house (which was in H's name and in which both parties were still living) of £63,000 and the balance of £46,000 representing accumulated savings and H's pension lump sum. H was earning £12,400 per annum and would receive a further pension of £5,300 per annum on his eventual retirement. H was not in good health. W was treated as having a potential income of £5,000 per annum. The registrar ordered H to pay W a lump sum of £54,000 in full and final settlement of her claims for ancillary relief and directed that upon payment W should vacate the matrimonial home. The order was complied with by both parties. On 17 May 1989 W committed suicide. The Court of Appeal held, applying *Barder v Barder*, that it was correct in the circumstances for the judge to have granted leave to appeal out of time against the registrar's order and to allow H's appeal, but wrong to restrict himself to what was the predominant consideration before the registrar, namely the needs of the parties. It was necessary to consider the position in the light of the changed circumstances prevailing at the time when the reassessment was carried out. Having regard to all the criteria set out in s.25, the proper lump sum award in W's favour would be £25,000.

24-124 Where the calculation of and obligation to pay the amount awarded is not referable to the wife's needs or to her future expectation of life (which would be the case, for example, if the award were made by reference to the "sharing" principle alone) the court will be unlikely to hold the unexpected death of the wife to be a *Barder* event.[345] The question is whether the unexpected death of the party undermines the basis on which the order was made.[346] In such circumstances it may be appropriate to start again.[347]

Remarriage

24-125 An undisclosed intention to remarry or cohabit at the time the original order was made will operate as a failure to make full disclosure.[348] If the possibility of an event of this nature was not or could not have been foreseen at the time of the original

---

341 *Hope-Smith* [1989] 2 F.L.R. 56.
342 *Rooker v Rooker* (1988) 18 Fam. Law 55.
343 See para.24-112.
344 *Smith v Smith* [1992] Fam. 69.
345 *Amey v Amey* [1992] 2 F.L.R. 89; *Richardson v Richardson* [2011] 2 F.L.R. 244.
346 *Reid v Reid* [2004] 1 F.L.R. 736.
347 *Barber v Barber* [1993] 1 F.L.R. 476.
348 See para.24-89.

order, it is, of course, important that, had it been known or foreseen, it would have made a material difference to the order made and would have thus invalidated it.[349] If, of course, the possibility of remarriage by one of the parties had been foreseen at the time of the order and had been taken into account, then the fact that it took place subsequently could not be a supervening event within the *Barder v Barder* principle:

In *Chaudhuri v Chaudhuri*,[350] H and W had separated in 1984 and the initial ancillary relief proceedings took place in February 1988. The principal issue was the matrimonial home. H wanted it sold so that both parties could rehouse themselves. W wished to remain there with the children. The registrar ordered that H should have one-third of the net equity, which was to be realised by an immediate lump sum payment of £27,000, out of which he was to discharge the mortgage on the house, and that he should have a charge on the house (which was then to be transferred to W) for one-sixth of the net proceeds of sale, the charge not to be realised without W's consent, or until the older child ceased full-time education, or until W's death or remarriage or permanent cohabitation with another man, whichever event should first occur. On H's appeal to the President in May 1988 the registrar's order was confirmed save that H's share in the proceeds of sale of the house was to be increased to one-quarter. W's case before the registrar and the President was that she needed to stay in the matrimonial home in order to provide a secure home for the children in a neighbourhood where she would have the support of friends. The house was transferred to her in July 1988. In June 1989 W's solicitors informed H that she intended to remarry and move to Chester. She did so in September 1989 and the elder son went to live with H. On H's application for leave to appeal against the order out of time the Court of Appeal held: **24-126**

(1) that the order contemplated the possibility of W remarrying and nothing was said as to what might happen in that event save that H's charge became realisable and, accordingly, it could not have been a fundamental assumption of the order that in the event of W remarrying she necessarily always had to stay in the same home with the children;
(2) that the time which had elapsed, although near the borderline, was too great for it proper to grant leave to appeal out of time;
(3) a suggestion that W had failed to disclose that she had opened a joint bank account with another man before the hearing before the President should be rejected as being something of no great significance.

Child Support Act 1991

In *Crozier v Crozier*[351] Booth J rejected the suggestion that the introduction of the administrative machinery, outside the jurisdiction of the courts, for the assessment of a father's liability to maintain his children constituted a new event **24-127**

---

349 *B v B (Financial Provision: Leave to Appeal)* [1994] 1 F.L.R. 219.

350 (1992) 22 Fam. Law 385. See also *Cook* [1988] 1 F.L.R. 521. See the comments of Hale J (as she then was) in *Cornick v Cornick* [1994] 2 F.L.R. 530 at 534 noted at para.24-119. In *Dixon v Marchant* [2008] 1 F.L.R. 655 the Court of Appeal held (by a majority) that a compromise by way of a negotiated clean break settlement must have envisaged that the wife might marry her boyfriend (about whom questions had been asked and truthfully answered) and that that remarriage on its own was not an event justifying reopening. A distinction was drawn between this case and others where a wife had been granted funds to house children which monies she would not otherwise have received and which the new event made unnecessary. In *Williams v Lindley* [2005] 2 F.L.R. 710 the court held that the wife's engagement within a few months of the order did constitute a supervening event where the basis for the lump sum order was the wife's need to re-house herself and the children.

351 [1994] Fam. 114.

undermining the basis of a consensual attempt at a clean-break order made before the introduction of this machinery. Booth J expressed herself in this way:

> "The fact that Parliament has chosen a new administrative method by which the State may intervene to compel a parent to contribute towards the maintenance of a child, by-passing the jurisdiction of the Courts, does not fundamentally alter the position as it was in law in February 1989. The parties were then unable to achieve a clean financial break in respect of their son. The legal liability to maintain him remained on them both as his parents. While the wife was prepared to assume that responsibility as between herself and the husband, she could not in fact fulfil that obligation without the assistance of State moneys. The State was never bound by the agreement or the order. At any time it could have intervened, through the Secretary of State, to seek an order through the Courts and the parties were not entitled to assume for the purposes of their agreement that it would not do so. I consider that it is immaterial for this purpose that the same parental liability will now be enforced through an agency outside the Courts. That is a difference only in the means by which the State may proceed to relieve itself of the obligation which it is the duty of the parents to discharge. The fact that the sum required of a parent may be greater under the new procedure than under the old is a consequence of the procedural change and not of any new and unforeseen power vested in the State. In my judgment, neither the existing order made in March 1993 under the statutory machinery which existed in February 1989 nor any anticipated liability which may be levied under the new machinery introduced by the Act of 1991, constitutes a new event, in fact or in law, sufficient to invalidate the basis of the consent order."

Change in the law

24-128 In *S v S (Ancillary Relief: Consent Order)*[352] a wife sought to argue that the effect of the House of Lords' decision in *White v White*[353] was so fundamental that she should be entitled to reopen an order into which she entered by consent shortly before the decision. It was held that the decision could be deemed so fundamental as to entitle a party to reopen matters but that (i) the decision was so widely speculated upon that it was foreseeable and thus failed to meet the *Barder v Barder* criteria; and (ii) a mistake of law as a vitiating factor ab initio had no place in consent orders for ancillary relief. Public policy was against adopting an argument that would lead to the floodgates being opened.[354]

Delay

24-129 It is incumbent upon an applicant to proceed expeditiously with an application to set aside, or appeal out of time, a consent order. An applicant who, having ascertained the material facts, delays, is likely to be unsuccessful.[355] The court is inclined to be far more rigorous in applying Lord Brandon's test in *Barder v Barder* of a probable deadline of one year to cases of supervening events than it will be in cases of non-disclosure, the existence of which may not emerge for many years. In *Benson v Benson*,[356] a case in which a husband delayed for 15 months after his wife's death before applying to vary an order, Bracewell J held the delay to be fatal to the application. Indeed, the husband had, through his former solicitors,

---

352 [2002] 1 F.L.R. 992.
353 [2001] 1 A.C. 596.
354 Cf. para.4-20.
355 *Burns v Burns* [2004] 3 F.C.R. 263.
356 [1996] 1 F.L.R. 692. See also *Rose* [2003] 2 F.L.R. 197, *Chaudhuri v Chaudhuri* [1992] 2 F.L.R. 73, *B v B (Financial Provision: Leave to Appeal)* [1994] 1 F.L.R. 219, and *Worlock v Worlock* [1994] 2 F.L.R. 689.

compromised a variation of the order subsequent to the wife's death, before receiving fresh legal advice to challenge the original order. A party taking any step that may be regarded as an affirmation of the order is likely to undermine their attempt to set aside.[357]

This approach can be contrasted with cases such as *T v T*[358] and *C v C*[359] where serious cases of fraudulent non-disclosure were discovered 9 and 14 years respectively after the consent orders. The court permitted the orders to be reopened. It remains clear, however, that once non-disclosure is discovered, the applicant must act with reasonable alacrity, although the court will not have much sympathy with a deliberate concealer of assets.[360] **24-130**

It is suggested that there is balance to be struck. An applicant to reopen cannot stand by indefinitely. Even if the respondent declines to give information, once the applicant is put on notice that a supervening event or a breach of disclosure has taken place which might justify setting aside, if an enquiry does not produce a helpful reply from the respondent reasonable promptitude must be exercised if the non-variable element of a settlement is to be attacked.[361]

3. Practice

The procedure for set aside applications has been much-simplified by the Family Procedure (Amendment No.2) Rules 2016 which came into force on 3 October 2016. It inserted a new rule, Family Procedure Rules 2010 r.9.9A, which sets out the procedure for applications to set aside financial remedy orders. The accompanying FPR 2010 PD 9A provides, inter alia, that the grounds on which a financial remedy order may be set aside include fraud, material non-disclosure, certain limited types of mistake or a subsequent event, unforeseen and unforeseeable at the time the order was made, which invalidates the basis on which the order was made (i.e. the circumstances described in *Barder*[362]). An application under r.9.9A is to be made in accordance with the Pt 18 procedure as modified by the rule. The Practice Direction includes guidance as to the appropriate court to which the application is to be made depending on whether the financial remedy order was made before or after 22 April 2014 (i.e. the date of the creation of the Family Court).[363] **24-131**

In *Sharland v Sharland*,[364] the Supreme Court confirmed that where an order is varied or set aside the court, in the renewed financial remedy proceedings, does not need to start from scratch. Instead, it may be possible to isolate the issues to which the non-disclosure or misrepresentation related and deal only with those. Ultimately, however, the court has enormous flexibility to enable the procedure to fit the case.[365] **24-132**

In *Roocroft v Ball*,[366]the Court of Appeal held the principle that the court is not **24-133**

---

[357] *Walkden v Walkden* [2010] 1 F.L.R. 174.

[358] [1996] 2 F.L.R. 640.

[359] [1994] 2 F.L.R. 272.

[360] In *Den Heyer v Newby* [2006] 1 F.L.R. 1114 the court declined to disentitle W from reopening her claim when H, who was not criticised for any breach of disclosure prior to the making of the order, brushed off her enquiries as to the terms of the subsequent sale of his company and declined to give information. The duty to disclose a substantial change was held to be magnified because of the ongoing and variable periodical payments order.

[361] See, for example, cases such as *Burns v Burns* [2004] 3 F.C.R. 263 and *Shaw v Shaw* [2002] 2 F.L.R. 1204.

[362] [1988] A.C. 20.

[363] See paras 13.3 and 13.4 of PD9A.

[364] [2015] 2 F.L.R. 1367.

[365] [2015] 2 F.L.R. 1367 at [43].

[366] [2017] 2 F.L.R. 810.

constrained from exercising its case management powers to direct there to be some form of abbreviated hearing following a provisional evaluation of the issues could be drawn from the Supreme Court's decision in *Wyatt v Vince*.[367] Care should, however, be taken to avoid the situation that led to the appeal in *Roocroft v Ball* whereby the Court of Appeal found that the judge at first instance erred in conducting not an abbreviated hearing (as he would have been entitled to do), but rather in conducting a hearing that had the hallmarks of summary judgment (for which there is no provision in the FPR 2010).

AGREEMENTS RELATING TO CHILDREN

24-134 It is difficult to conceive of an agreement between parents concerning their child as being a compromise in the usually accepted sense of that term. Hopefully, parents agree on a particular course of action because they both regard it as in the child's best interests without regard to their own selfish concerns. Unhappily, experience in practice suggests that this is not always the case. However, agreements concerning children are frequently made, whatever might be said of the motives of the parties. The Child Arrangements Programme[368] requires any person who is considering making a "relevant family application" to attend a Mediation Information and Assessment Meeting (known as a "MIAM")[369] with some limited exceptions.[370] Further, the court is now required to consider, at every stage of court proceedings, whether non-court dispute resolution is appropriate.[371]

24-135 It appears that the discretionary jurisdiction conferred by s.8 of the Children Act 1989 in respect of agreed Child Arrangement Orders,[372] could be exercised irrespective of the wishes or agreement of the parties.[373] Since, however, co-operation between parties over a child is clearly in the child's interests, it would be unusual for a court to decline to reflect an agreement in an order if an order was required. That said, under the Child Arrangements Programme, the court shall not make a Child Arrangements Order by consent, or give permission for an application to be withdrawn, unless the parties are present in court, all initial safeguarding checks have been obtained, and an officer of CAFCASS has spoken the parties separately, except where it is satisfied that there is not risk of harm to the child in so doing.[374] It must be noted that the enforcement of an order which did not reflect the wishes of the parties would be virtually impossible.[375] Nevertheless, it is not unknown for a judge to ask parents to think again over, say, arrangements for a very young child involving frequent changes of primary carer or an agreement whereby children are to be split, if the view is taken that the plans have not been adequately considered. It is likely that the order sought will be made if it has been fully considered even if the judge might not regard it as entirely sensible.

---

[367] [2015] 1 F.L.R. 972.

[368] Family Procedure Rules 2010, PD 12B.

[369] Children and Families Act 2014 s.10(1). Family Procedure Rules 2010, PD 12B, para.5.3.

[370] Family Procedure Rules 2010, r.3.8(1).

[371] Family Procedure Rules 2010, PD 12B, para.6.1.

[372] Children and Families Act 2014 Sch.2, Pt 1, para.3.

[373] By s.10(1) of the Children Act 1989 it is said that the court "may make a section 8 order" at the instance of the parties specified and s.1(1) and 1(5) appear to be applicable in relation to consideration of a proposed agreed order.

[374] Family Procedure Rules 2010, PD 12J, para.6.

[375] Though see s.11J–N of the 1989 Act for enforcement provisions.

A court faced with a dispute between parents over a child or children will, understandably perhaps, find itself even more frustrated than in other cases that the dispute cannot be resolved by agreement. A judge with great experience of this kind of jurisdiction has said this[376]: **24-136**

> "Whilst in other jurisdictions it is open and often desirable for the Court to exercise its influence to induce parties to compromise, it can only be in the rarest of cases an appropriate course to take where sensitive and delicate decisions must be taken to achieve the welfare of children."

Consent orders entered into in this sphere are not, or do not always remain, satisfactory to one or other of the parties. Any challenge to such a consent order must be in accordance with Family Procedure Rules 9.9A and PD9A. If the appropriate route is to appeal, then unless the consent order was made by a bench of lay justices, permission to appeal is also a requirement.[377] In most cases, certainly where interim orders are concerned, an application to vary the order would be the most appropriate course to follow.[378] The court will always be guided by what is in the best interests of the child irrespective of what may have been agreed at some earlier stage in his or her life. **24-137**

---

[376] *Re R* [1995] 1 F.L.R. 123 at 135, per Sir Francis Purchas.

[377] Family Procedure Rules 2010, Pt 30.3.

[378] cf. *TF v PJ* [2015] 1 F.L.R. 861 in which Mostyn J applied r.4.16 of the Family Procedure Rules 2010, and the Supreme Court judgment in *Re L-B* [2013] 2 F.L.R. 859, and set aside a return order where there had been a significant change of circumstances.

CHAPTER 25

Settlement of Inheritance Act Disputes

PRELIMINARY

The Inheritance (Provision for Family and Dependants) Act 1975 provides the court with jurisdiction, in appropriate circumstances,[1] to make orders that alter the provisions of a will or the effect of the laws of intestacy where no will was made. Claims under the Act can be heard either in the county court or the High Court. Such claims can be dealt with as Chancery or Family business. In the High Court claims under the Act are more often dealt with in the Property and Business Court, Property Trusts and Probate List. However, where the significant beneficiaries include minors claims can and maybe more appropriately dealt with in the Family Divisions. Orders under the Act may be made at the instance of a limited class of persons[2] and a time limit is applicable to claims advanced.[3] A range of orders may be made which is very similar to the range available under the financial remedy jurisdiction provided for by the Matrimonial Causes Act 1973.[4] A number of questions arise in connection with the law and practice applicable to the settlement of potential or actual disputes under this jurisdiction. The settlement of disputed claims arising under the Act should be seen against the background of the general proposition that such claims are claims against the individual rights of the beneficiaries of the estate and not against the estate as a whole. The consequence is that the personal representatives have no power to compromise claims under the Act pursuant to s.15 of the Trustee Act 1925 without reference to the beneficiaries. Accordingly, although necessarily parties to the proceedings, in the majority of cases the personal representatives take a neutral stance confining themselves to providing information about the estate and where they have it, of the deceased and his or her intentions. The appropriate course for the personal representatives to adopt in relation to settlement (if the beneficiaries wish them to assume that role) is to seek to negotiate a compromise with the authority of the beneficiaries (with suitable indemnities as to costs) and (if any children or protected persons are affected or if any real doubt exists as to the propriety of any negotiated compromise) for the personal representatives to apply to the court for its approval to any resulting **25-01**

---

1 Inheritance (Provision for Family and Dependants) Act 1975 s.2.

2 Inheritance (Provision for Family and Dependants) Act 1975 s.1(1), as amended by the Law Reform (Succession) Act 1995 and the Civil Partnership Act 2004. In this chapter, where the context so admits, references to a spouse or former spouse include a civil partner or former civil partner and references to a marriage include a civil partnership.

3 Inheritance (Provision for Family and Dependants) Act 1975 s.4.

4 Inheritance (Provision for Family and Dependants) Act 1975 s.2. cf. Matrimonial Causes Act 1973 ss.23 and 24.

compromise using the procedure available under para.1A of PD 64A—Estates, Trusts and Charities.[5]

CONTRACTING OUT

25-02 It is not clear whether a potential applicant other than a spouse or former spouse may, during the deceased's lifetime, "contract out" of the right to apply to the court for an order under the Act.[6] Under the general law, spouses or former spouses cannot do so.[7] Provision is, however, made under the Act to enable the making (by consent or otherwise) of an order disentitling recourse to this jurisdiction on or after a decree of divorce, judicial separation or nullity[8] or on the making of a financial provision or property adjustment order following an overseas decree to like effect.[9] Section 15(1) of the Act[10] provides that the court:

> "[I]f it considers it just to do so, may on the application of either party to the marriage, order that the other party to the marriage shall not on the death of the applicant be entitled to apply for an order under s.2 of this Act."

25-03 The "court" in question is the court dealing with the parties' financial remedy applications. Plainly, it has a discretion whether or not to make an order in the terms indicated notwithstanding that the parties agree. However, since the previous phraseology of s.15(1) permitted such an order only if the parties were in agreement and the court thought it right, it is unlikely, except in the most exceptional circumstances, that the court would stand in the way of making such an order. Where parties contemplate that their property and capital settlement is "once for all", it is a provision which will doubtless find its way into most consent orders. Where the disentitlement provision is incorporated by agreement, the usual order will provide for it to come into operation only upon the final dismissal of the periodical payments claim, whether immediately or at some future date.

25-04 It has been said[11] that it is not possible for the court to be satisfied that it is "just" to make such an order unless it is given,

> "some indication of what the estate is likely to consist of and some details of the persons whom the applicant considers to have a prior claim on his estate in the event of his decease".

This comment was made in the context of a somewhat unusual situation[12] and,

---

5 See para.23-23.

6 The position was not clear under the Inheritance (Family Provision) Act 1938: see *Zamet v Hyman* [1961] 1 W.L.R. 1442, where the Court of Appeal expressed no view on the matter in relation to a dependant.

7 *M, Re* [1968] P. 174. See also *S, Re* [1965] P. 165.

8 s.15. Section 15ZA makes similar provision where a domestic civil partnership is dissolved, etc.

9 s.15A. Section 15B makes similar provision where an overseas civil partnership is dissolved, etc.

10 As introduced by the Matrimonial and Family Proceedings Act 1984 s.9, with effect from 12 October 1984. Section 15A was introduced by s.25 of that Act. The order may be made "on making an order under section 17" of the 1984 Act. Subject to that, s.15A(1) is in identical terms to s.15(1).

11 *Whiting v Whiting* [1988] 1 W.L.R. 565 at 577, per Balcombe LJ at 577, with whom, on this issue, Stocker and Slade LJJ agreed.

12 H had applied to the court for an order discharging a consent order for nominal periodical payments in favour of W, made several years previously following their divorce, and at the same time applied for an order under s.15(1). All the evidence adduced by H before the judge was directed to his application to discharge the periodical payments order. The judge rejected his application in toto.

whilst strictly speaking applicable also to a consensual application for such an order, it is very unlikely that any very detailed (and specific) information on these matters would be required by the court. No specific provision was made in the statement of information required to be lodged in support of an application for a consent order in financial remedy proceedings[13] relating to these matters, but it is thought that the information required in such a statement would give the court sufficient material in all but the most exceptional cases upon which to approve the making of the order requested.

It should, perhaps, be said that even in cases where parties may not "contract out" of the Act, the fact that they made an agreement to that effect may be one of the "relevant" matters which the court may consider in exercising its jurisdiction.[14] **25-05**

EFFECT OF PREVIOUS COMPROMISE OR CONSENT ORDER

If two spouses have not "contracted out" of the Act pursuant to s.15(1) at the time of their divorce, will the fact that they have compromised everything else at that time be of any significance on an application under the Act by the surviving former spouse? The question at the heart of the Court's decision whether to exercise its discretion in any claim under the Act is whether the will or the intestacy regime (whichever applies) fails to make reasonable financial provision for the claim.[15] That question is asked and answered at the time the Court decides the claim.[16] Whilst the deceased may have acted reasonably when making a will, subsequent events involving either of the former spouses and/or the estate after the date of the will or even after the death may be highly relevant to a claim under the Act. **25-06**

It is therefore unsurprising that whilst every case would, in the final analysis, depend upon its own facts, the answer to the question posed in the context of a divorce settlement must clearly be "yes". In terms of the divorce settlement it will be very significant when a claim is considered and maybe a determinative factor, but not necessarily. The prior agreement is obviously one of the circumstances the court must take into account. In *Fullard, Re*[17] Ormrod LJ said this[18]: **25-07**

> "Where the application is made by an ex-wife (or ex-husband) of the deceased, the fact that the parties have been divorced and the result of that divorce in financial terms is plainly [a] matter which is relevant–and which is highly relevant."

In that case, in answering the question whether it was reasonable for the deceased to make no provision for his former wife upon his death, the court took into account the size of the estate (which was modest) and the consideration that the deceased had "made arrangements with his former wife which settled their financial affairs". It was held emphatically that the deceased had acted perfectly reasonably. **25-08**

On his appeal against this rejection, the Court of Appeal by a majority dismissed his appeal "on the simple ground that [H had] not made out a case to support his application under section 15". The appeal was dismissed "without prejudice to [H's] right to renew his application under section 15".

13 See para.24-48 onwards.

14 s.3(1)(g). Cf. *Fullard, Re* [1982] Fam. 42 CA. But see *Farrow, Re* [1987] 1 F.L.R. 205 (Hollings J).

15 s.1(2)(b).

16 *In Re Hancock (deceased)* [1998] 5 WLUK 15; [1998] 2 F.L.R. 346 as approved in*Ilott v Mitson* [2017] UKSC 17; [2018] A.C. 545; [2017] 2 W.L.R. 979.

17 *Fullard, Re* [1982] Fam. 42 CA.

18 *Fullard, Re* [1982] Fam. 42 at 46–47.

A similar conclusion was reached in *Brill v Proud*.[19] However, it should be noted, as discussed above, that strictly the question is not whether the deceased acted reasonably, but whether disposition (by will or intestacy) failed to make reasonable provision even if, when the deceased acted, he or she did so reasonably.

EFFECT AND VARIATION OF PREVIOUS "MAINTENANCE AGREEMENT"

25-09 Consistent with the approach referred to above,[20] the existence of a "maintenance agreement" and its terms would be taken into account by the court considering the exercise of its jurisdiction. There is specific provision, in relation to a maintenance agreement which subsisted at the deceased's death and which provided for the continuation of payments after his death, for the court to vary or revoke the agreement. In exercising its power in such matters the court must have regard,

> "to all the circumstances of the case, including any order which the court proposes to make under section 2 or section 5 of this Act and any change (whether resulting from death of the deceased or otherwise) in any of the circumstances in the light of which the agreement was made".[21]

Likewise the court has the jurisdiction, in the context of applications under the Act to vary a pre-existing order for secured periodical payments or a maintenance agreement, to exercise its powers under s.2.[22]

COMPROMISE PROPER OF CLAIMS UNDER THE ACT[23]

25-10 Any compromise by virtue of which the parties seek the making of a consent order under the Act must ensure that the order made is within the jurisdiction conferred on the court by the Act.[24]

25-11 The jurisdiction conferred by the Act, in the sense of the reliefs available, is very similar to that conferred by the Matrimonial Causes Act 1973. The differences for present purposes are immaterial, but there is one difference between the jurisdictions in the wider sense which is of some relevance: once the divorce court comes to adjudicate on applications for financial relief, the sine qua non of those applications (the decree) will have been pronounced. In virtually all such cases the parties will have co-operated in relation to the obtaining of the decree. By implication they will have exposed themselves to the jurisdiction of the court in relation to ancillary matters.

25-12 Under the 1975 Act what has been described as the equivalent "two-tier process"

---

19 *Brill v Proud* (1984) 14 Fam. Law 59 CA.

20 para.25-07.

21 s.17(2). Maintenance agreements are an increasing rarity: see para.24-06, fn.8.

22 s.18.

23 It is an area where early neutral evaluation ("ENE") may be requested by the parties: see, e.g., *Seals v Williams* [2015] EWHC 1829 (Ch); [2015] 5 WLUK 405, Norris J and indeed the Court of Appeal has held that there is "no reason to imply into rule [CPR 3.1(2)(m)] any limitation on the court's power to order an ENE hearing to the effect that the agreement or consent of the parties is required": *Lomax v Lomax* [2019] EWCA Civ 1467. This provision came into effect on 1 October 2015. See further at Ch.35.

24 cf. *Livesey* [1985] A.C. 424; *Hinde v Hinde* [1953] 1 W.L.R. 175. See para.24-52 onwards.

is almost always carried out at one and the same time. The right to make application and the making by order of provision, if appropriate, is dealt with by the same tribunal at the same time. Furthermore, the factors to be taken into account by the court in deciding whether an applicant is within the jurisdiction conferred by the Act are the same as those to be taken into account by the court in determining what, if any, provision should be made.[25]

For the court to exercise its jurisdiction to make orders there is a condition precedent[26] which states that the court must be satisfied that the financial provision made for the applicant (whether by testamentary disposition or the rules of intestacy) is not reasonable.[27] That is, almost by definition, an area ripe for argument. It may, therefore, be that the parties to an application of this nature, recognising the uncertainty of this matter (putting aside for the moment the uncertainties associated with the exercise of the discretionary jurisdiction conferred by the Act so far as orders are concerned), will wish to reach an overall settlement without putting to the test whether the applicant can surmount the first hurdle associated with an application.[28] This is unlikely to be discouraged by the court, particularly having regard to the question of costs, but equally, strictly speaking, the court could not make orders within its jurisdiction unless satisfied of this first matter. Whilst bona fide admissions of fact[29] would doubtless be accepted to bring an applicant within the Act, there are always those cases where such an admission will not be forthcoming and yet a compromise be desired. This, it is thought, is a situation where the compromise might be best effectuated by means of a Tomlin order[30] or by making the agreement a rule of court.[31] **25-13**

When the court is invited to exercise its powers by consent it will be under a dual duty: **25-14**

(a) to consider whether the financial provision actually made for the applicant is reasonable; and, if not;
(b) to consider how, if at all, its powers are to be exercised.

The duty is carried out by means of a yet further duty, namely, that of having regard to the specific matters enumerated in s.3(1), the last of which being "any other matters ... which in the circumstances of the case the court may consider relevant"[32].

Although no rules have been made[33] ordaining the information which the parties should put before the court when applying for a consent order, the court will need to have sufficient up-to-date and accurate information to enable it to exercise **25-15**

---

25 s.3.
26 *Fullard, Re* [1982] Fam. 42, per Ormrod LJ at 46.
27 s.2(1).
28 Indeed, some intending applicants may be concerned as to whether they can show that they were being "maintained" for the purposes of the Act: s.1(1)(e).
29 cf. *Carecraft Construction Co Ltd, Re* [1994] 1 W.L.R. 172 at 182, per Ferris J. See para.23-16 onwards.
30 See Ch.9, para.9-20 onwards.
31 Since the practice of "filing and making an agreement a rule of court" found its origin in the old Probate practice, this might be thought the appropriate course. There is, however, some doubt about how such an agreement is enforced (see paras 9-11 and 11-06 onwards) and the practice has largely fallen into disuse. See for historical purposes *Practice Direction (Probate: Compromised Action)* [1972] 1 W.L.R. 1215.
32 For an example of the considerations taken into account by the court when approval to a proposed settlement of a claim under the Act is sought, see *Simonetta v Lovell-Tomon* [2018] EWHC 3904 (Fam), Williams J.
33 cf. Family Procedure Rules 2010 r.9.26(1)(b).

its discretion.[34] The scheme of the Act is so similar to that of the Matrimonial Causes Act 1973 that it must be presumed that Parliament intended commensurate concern to be shown for the disposition of the assets of the dead as for those of the living. As a matter of practicality, claims under the Act are made as Pt 8 claims and as a result the initial evidence filed by the parties, as required under Pt 8, will generally be sufficient for the Court's consideration of any consent order.

SETTING ASIDE AND ENFORCEMENT

25-16 It is thought that grounds similar to those available for setting aside a compromise of matrimonial ancillary relief applications will be available to set aside the compromise of these proceedings.[35] It should, however, be noted that an order for provision under the Act is to be treated as a legacy or something which devolves on intestacy.[36] Any such provision is not, therefore, to be treated for the purposes of enforcement as an order. The correct way to enforce such a provision is to take proceedings for the administration of the estate.[37]

PRACTICE

25-17 Rules exist to facilitate the identification of all relevant parties and their incorporation as parties into the proceedings. Where all the parties who are or may be interested in the estate are not parties to the proceedings, it seems that the correct course to adopt is to ask the court for administration of the estate which will enable it to authorise the executors to enter a compromise on agreed terms.[38]

25-18 Where an applicant or a beneficiary is a child or a protected party, he or she will be represented by a litigation friend. As with all compromises affecting the rights of such persons, the court will have to approve any proposed settlement and will be guided by the views of the legal advisers.[39]

25-19 A copy of any consent order made under the Act, whether in the Family Division or the Property and Business Court (or, of course, the county court), must be sent to the Principal Registry of the Family Division for entry and filing, and a memorandum of the order is to be endorsed on, or permanently annexed to, the grant of probate or letters of administration under which the estate is being administered.[40] Applications under the Act may be made in either the Family or the Property and Business Court of the High Court, or in a county court. Where an application in the Property and Business Court Division is compromised, special requirements apply to the terms of any Tomlin order.[41]

TAX CONSIDERATIONS

25-20 Fiscal considerations frequently loom large in the compromise of proceedings under the Act and any settlement should be structured so as to take the maximum

---

34 cf. *Livesey* [1985] A.C. 424.

35 See Ch.24.

36 s.19(1).

37 *Jennery, Re* [1967] Ch. 280 CA.

38 *Knowles, Re* [1966] Ch. 386, *Lofts, Re* [1968] 1 W.L.R. 1949.

39 See generally CPR Pt 21. For example, *Simonetta v Lovell-Tomon* [2018] EWHC 3904 (Fam).

40 s.19(3); *Practice Direction (Family Provision: Endorsement of Order)* [1979] 1 W.L.R. 1.

41 *The Chancery Guide* (February 2016), paras 22.9-22.15. See para.23-34.

advantage of any available exemptions and reliefs. Without an order of the court, any variation of the deceased's estate will not be retrospective to the date of death for the purposes of either Inheritance Tax[42] or Capital Gains Tax[43] unless it is effected within two years of the deceased's death. Even then, all those persons whose interests are affected by the variation must be ascertained, in being and of full age and capacity. They must all agree to the variation. An out-of-court variation will not be retrospective for the purposes of income tax. A court order made under s.2 of the 1975 Act, and relating to any property forming part of the deceased's net estate, may have retrospective effect for Inheritance Tax purposes whenever it is made.[44] Indeed, such an order would appear to have retrospective effect for *all* tax purposes.[45]

---

42 Inheritance Tax Act 1984 s.142.

43 Taxation of Chargeable Gains Act 1992 s.62.

44 Inheritance Tax Act 1984 s.146.

45 Inheritance (Provision for Family and Dependants) Act 1975 s.19(1).

CHAPTER 26

Offers of Settlement in Matrimonial Finance and Children Cases

PRELIMINARY

The costs involved in contested financial proceedings have always been a matter of concern. In almost all cases the costs are met from the family's resources. Except where those resources are very substantial, their division, in whatever proportions, involves sufficient hardship in its own right without the need for aggravating the position by running up legal bills beyond that which is necessary. **26-01**

Irrespective of whether or not the parties' resources are substantial, legal costs can assume disproportionately high levels.[1] The direction of the lay client's mind towards the question of costs in this context has received repeated judicial encouragement.[2] **26-02**

> In *Evans v Evans*,[3] Booth J found herself unable to make the appropriate provision for the parties and the children because of the very substantial costs of each party. The parties had assets of £350,000 and had incurred costs of £60,000. With the concurrence of the then President of the Family Division, Sir Stephen Brown, the judge issued a series of guidelines for the preparation of substantial ancillary relief cases. Of those guidelines two related specifically to the duties of the parties' legal advisers in connection with the possibility of settlement. Booth J said this[4]:
>
> "(10) Solicitors and counsel should keep their clients informed of the costs at all stages of the proceedings and, where appropriate, should ensure that they understand the implications of the legal aid charge ...
>
> (11) The desirability of reaching a settlement should be borne in mind throughout the proceedings. While it is necessary for the legal advisers to have sufficient knowledge of the financial position of both parties before advising their clients on a proposed settlement, the necessity to make further inquiries must always be balanced by a consideration of what they were realistically likely to achieve and the increased costs which were likely to be incurred by making them.[5]"

---

1 *Re T (Divorce: Interim Maintenance: Discovery)* [1990] 1 F.L.R. 1, *Newton v Newton* [1990] 1 F.L.R. 33, *Piglowska v Piglowski* [1992] 2 F.L.R. 763 (where the parties had assets of c. £128,000 and incurred costs in the same amount), *A v A (No 2) (Ancillary Relief: Costs)* [2008] 1 F.L.R. 1428 (where 41.5% of matrimonial assets of £2,669,715 was spent on costs), *Whig v Whig* [2008] 1 F.L.R. 453 *Mekarska v Ruiz and Boyden* [2011] 2 F.L.R. 1351 (where the liabilities were said by Peter Jackson J (as he then was) at [2] to "virtually extinguish" the assets), and *Seagrove v Sullivan* [2015] 2 F.L.R. 602 (where c. £1.3 million was expended in a dispute over c. £500,000).

2 See, e.g. *Singer (formerly Sharegin) v Sharegin* [1984] F.L.R. 114.

3 *Evans v Evans (Practice Note)* [1990] 1 F.L.R. 319.

4 *Evans v Evans (Practice Note)* [1990] 1 F.L.R. 319.

5 See further at para 26–04 onwards.

26-03 The concerns and encouragements to economy have continued [6]:

> "Something must be done about the problems highlighted by this and by too many similar cases. We simply cannot go on as we are. The expenditure of costs on the scale exemplified by this and too many other such cases is a scandal which must somehow be brought under control."

26-04 The Family Procedure Rules 2010 introduced an 'Overriding Objective' modelled on that included in the Civil Procedure Rules 1998. The court is obliged to deal with the case "justly" which includes "saving expense".[7] The parties are required to help the court to further the overriding objective.[8]

The costs-focussed approach in *Evans v Evans* was one adopted by the ancillary relief (now financial remedies) procedures introduced in 2000. These required costs estimates to be produced at every hearing or appointment so that the court and the parties could be aware of the extent of the costs incurred.[9] Further, the first appointment must be conducted with the objective of defining the issues and saving costs.[10]

However, notwithstanding initiatives of this nature the level of costs has continued to be a major problem confronting judges dealing with all but those cases involving the wealthiest parties and anxiety has continued to be expressed over the level of costs incurred in relation to the value of the assets in issue.[11] In *J v J*[12], a case where the asset base was c. £2.9 million and the parties had spent £920,000 in costs, Mostyn J commented:

> "Although the mantra 'something must be done' is repeated time and again, nothing ever is. In the ancillary relief field the mantra has been incanted over and over ever since the iconic judgment of *Evans v Evans* [1990] 1 FLR 319. The procedural reforms of 1996 and 2000 tried to address the problem, but with only limited success, as this and many other egregious cases show only too clearly."

Mostyn J advocated two measures to arrest what he described as "the grotesque leaching of costs"[13] namely (i) fixed pricing for cases for each of the three phases of a financial remedies case (i.e. Form A to First Appointment, First Appointment to FDR, and FDR to final hearing; and (ii) for the court to be able to impose at the beginning of the case a costs cap on what may be charged by the lawyers to their client for each of the three phases. As yet, these measures have not been introduced.

---

6 *KSO v MJO and JMO (PSO Intervening)* [2009] 1 F.L.R. 1036, per Munby J, as he then was, at [81], a case where the parties spent £553,000 out of matrimonial assets of £771,000.

7 Family Procedure Rules 2010 r.1.2(d).

8 Family Procedure Rules 2010 r.1.3.

9 Now Family Procedure Rules 2010 r.9.27.

10 Family Procedure Rules 2010 r.9.15(1).

11 See, e.g. *S v B (Ancillary Relief: Costs)* [2005] 1 F.L.R. 474, *P v P (Financial Relief: Illiquid Assets)* [2005] 1 F.L.R. 548, and *KSO v MJO and JMO (PSO Intervening)* [2009] 1 F.L.R. 1036.

12 [2014] EWHC 3654 at [11].

13 [16]

GENERAL APPROACH TO COSTS

In family disputes, there is often no obvious successful or unsuccessful party.[14] This is particularly so in relation to disputes about children, but may also extend to financial matters. A party may lose on some issues and win on others. A degree of flexibility in costs is, therefore, exercised: **26-05**

> "The practice as to costs in the Family Division especially at first instance is, and rightly, much less rigid than it has become in ordinary litigation."[15]

Save in relation to financial remedy proceedings (for which see para.26-07), CPR Parts 44 (except rr.44.2(2) and (3) and 44.10(2) and (3)), 46 and 47 and r.45.8 apply to costs in family proceedings.[16] The exceptions are important, in particular the "general rule" that the unsuccessful party will be ordered to pay the costs of the successful party is displaced. Thus in family proceedings, apart from financial remedy proceedings, the court starts from a neutral starting point, often described as a "clean sheet".[17] **26-06**

With effect from 3 April 2006 the procedural rules were changed so as to introduce a "general rule" in financial remedy proceedings that "the court will not make an order requiring one party to pay the costs of another party"[18] and made Calderbank offers (i.e. offers made "without prejudice save as to costs") inadmissible in such proceedings except in the context of FDR hearings.[19] "Financial remedy proceedings" are defined by r.28.3(4)(b). They include all applications for a "financial order"[20]" but exclude interim applications including maintenance pending suit, an order for maintenance pending outcome of proceedings; an interim periodical payments order, and an order for payment in respect of legal services. Such interim orders are therefore governed by the "clean sheet" rule. **26-07**

In *J v J* Mostyn J described the fact that no order as to costs was the normal order following a final hearing in financial remedy proceedings as being "our Jackson reform, seven years ahead of its time."[21] **26-08**

Notwithstanding the general presumption in financial remedy proceedings that there should be no order as to costs, the court may make such a costs order at any stage of the proceedings because of the conduct of a party in relation to the proceedings (whether before or during them).[22] In deciding what, if any, order to make, the court must have regard to the matters set out at r.28.3(7).

---

14 *Gooday v Gooday* [1969] P. 1, *Povey v Povey* [1972] Fam. 40, and *Martin v Martin* [1976] Fam. 335.

15 *McDonnell v McDonnell* [1977] 1 W.L.R. 26, per Ormrod LJ at 37. And see *Grenfell v Grenfell* [1978] Fam. 128 per Ormrod LJ at 143.

16 Family Procedure Rules 2010 r.28.2(1).

17 See para.26-09

18 Family Procedure Rules 2010 r.28.3(5).

19 Family Procedure Rules 2010 r.28.3(8) and rr.9.17(3) and (4) See para.24-46.

20 A financial order is defined in Family Procedure Rules 2010 Part 2 as (a) an avoidance of disposition order; (b) an order for maintenance pending suit; (c) an order for maintenance pending outcome of proceedings; (d) an order for periodical payments or lump sum provision as mentioned in s.21(1) of the Matrimonial Causes Act 1973, except an order under s.27(6) of the Act; (e) an order for periodical payments or lump sum provision as mentioned in para.2(1) of Sch.5 to the Civil Partnership Act 2004, made under Pt 1 of Sch.5 to that Act; (f) a property adjustment order; (g) a variation order [as defined in r.9.3]; (h) a pension sharing order [as defined in r.9.3] ; (i) a pension compensation order [as defined in r.9.3]; or (j) an order for payment in respect of legal services.

21 [18].

22 Family Procedure Rules 2010 r.28.3(6).

In *J v J* Mostyn J went on to observe that the 2006 reforms had done nothing to curb the disfiguring impact of excessive costs.[23] Whether as a result of these comments or otherwise, Family Procedure Rules 2010 PD28A was amended with effect from 27 May 2019 to add at the end of paragraph 4.4 that "The court will take a broad view of conduct for the purposes of this rule and will generally conclude that to refuse openly to negotiate reasonably and responsibly will amount to conduct in respect of which the court will consider making an order for costs. This includes in a 'needs' case where the applicant litigates unreasonably resulting in the costs incurred by each party becoming disproportionate to the award made by the court. Where an order for costs is made at an interim stage the court will not usually allow any resulting liability to be reckoned as a debt in the computation of the assets." It is yet to be seen whether this leads to open (as opposed to without prejudice) offers being made earlier than the date when the parties are under a duty to serve their open proposals (14 days before the date of the final hearing for the applicant and 7 days after service of the applicant's proposals for the respondent).[24]

This amendment may reflect in part the decision in *WG v HG*[25] where Francis J rejected the "rather remarkable proposition" that in a needs case the applicant is entitled to a full indemnity in respect of all of his (or her) costs, the rationale for this being that these costs are a debt that needs to be paid and that, in a needs case, needs must be met.[26] He expressed the view that "people cannot litigate on the basis that they are bound to be reimbursed for their costs ... no one enters litigation simply expecting a blank cheque".[27] Francis J ordered the husband to pay an additional lump sum of £400,000 leaving the wife to find some £500,000 towards her costs. He answered whether this was fair in the following way: "It might be said that I have assessed her needs at a given figure. If I have done that, then how can I leave her with a lower sum which, by definition, does not meet her needs? This conundrum happens in so many cases. People who engage in litigation need to know that it has a cost. The wife ... will have to make the sort of decisions about budget managing that other people have to make day in day out, but I am satisfied that people who adopt unreasonable positions in litigation cannot simply do so confident that there will be an indemnity for the costs of the litigation behaviour, however unreasonable it may have been."[28]

As noted above, one of the consequences of the 2006 reforms was to make Calderbank offers inadmissible in financial remedy proceedings except in the context of FDR hearings. The Costs Working Group of the Family Procedure Rules Committee (FPRC) is (as at the time of writing) undertaking a review of the functioning of the current costs regime in financial remedies cases, with a view to making recommendations for further reform. The FPRC has expressed concern that insufficient emphasis is given to encouraging parties to engage reasonably in negotiations. As a result the FPRC is currently considering the question of if (and, if so, how) Calderbank offers might be taken into account as "conduct" when the court is considering making an order for one party to pay, or contribute towards, the costs of another.[29] It is presently proposed that any new provision would be

---

23 [18].
24 Family Procedure Rules 2010 r.9.28.
25 [2018] EWFC 70.
26 [15].
27 [91].
28 [93].
29 The consultation period ran from 16 July 2019 to 31 October 2019. At the time of writing the outcome of the consultation is unknown.

made on the basis that the general 'no order' rule should remain. The consultation states that "in this way, excessive weight ought not to be attached only to whether one party has 'won' or 'lost' but proper account could be taken of whether either party has acted reasonably or unreasonably in the course of their negotiations (including those undertaken "without prejudice save as to costs") having regard to all of the matters to which the court is required to have regard under FPR 2010 r.28.3(7) when deciding whether it is 'appropriate' to make an order requiring one party to pay the costs of another party having regard to 'conduct of the party in relation to the proceedings' under FPR 2010 r.28.3(6)".[30]

Although an application for a variation of a financial order is not excluded from the definition of financial remedy proceedings, and is therefore governed by the 'no order' presumption, Practice Direction 28A at para.4.4 reminds the parties that the court will, when considering the conduct of the parties for the purposes of r.28.3(6) and (7), have regard to the obligation on the parties to help the court to further the overriding objective. Moreover the court will take into account the nature, importance and complexity of the issues in the case. The paragraph highlights that this may be of particular significance in variation applications where "there is a risk of the costs becoming disproportionate to the amounts in dispute." In practice these words have had little (if any) effect in making courts more willing to make costs orders in variation applications.

In proceedings not within the definition of "financial remedy proceedings", the CPR 2008 apply with the modifications set out at para.26-06. So for example, in *Judge v Judge*[31] (an appeal against a refusal of an application to set aside a financial order) Wilson LJ (as he then was) took the view that although the application did not come within the definition of "ancillary relief proceedings" (now financial remedy proceedings), it did come within the definition of "family proceedings". In consequence no general rule applied and the court was able to start with a clean sheet. The Court of Appeal held that on the facts of the case the judge was entitled to award the successful respondent only half the costs of his defence. Moreover, courts have at times been drawn to making issue-based orders, penalising a party who has pursued and lost a particular issue[32] or where a party's conduct has otherwise led to substantial costs being incurred.[33] **26-09**

MAKING AN OFFER THAT MAY AFFECT THE COSTS ORDER

As indicated at para.26–07, under the Family Procedure Rules 2010, Calderbank correspondence is (at least currently) not admissible within financial remedy proceedings before a court except at an FDR. At that stage the court has no power to impose an order upon the parties and all "without prejudice" correspondence, whether Calderbank or otherwise, is admissible. That does not mean that the parties cannot still negotiate "without prejudice". It remains public policy that parties should try to settle their differences. However, (at least at present) only open of- **26-10**

---

30 *https://consult.justice.gov.uk/digital-communications/treatment-of-calderbank-offers-consultation/consultation/subpage.2019-06-26.5019030536/* [Accessed 30 October 2019].

31 *Judge v Judge* [2009] 1 F.L.R. 1287. See also *Baker v Rowe* [2010] 1 F.L.R. 761.

32 *M v M (Costs)* [2010] 1 F.L.R. 256.

33 *Imerman v Imerman (Costs)* [2010] 2 F.L.R. 802.

fers may be put before the court on occasions other than an FDR and relied upon when seeking an order for costs.

26-11 In proceedings that are not financial remedy proceedings but which are still consequent on the breakdown of the marriage (for example applications for interim provision, preliminary issue applications, applications for legal services payment orders, cases relating to interveners/those joined to the proceedings, set aside applications (such as *Judge v Judge* referred to at para.26-09) and enforcement applications) Calderbank offers can be made as these are "clean sheet" cases. This ensures that they can properly be considered when it comes to the question of costs. Calderbank offers are also admissible in financial applications under Sch. 1 of the Children Act 1989.[34]

Although not wholly free from doubt (as some commentators have interpreted the rules differently) it is commonly (and it is submitted rightly) understood that Calderbank offers are also admissible on appeals in financial remedy cases either because "financial remedy proceedings" is to be given a similarly narrow interpretation to that given in *Judge v Judge* and *Baker v Rowe* (i.e. appeals are proceedings *about* a financial order and not *for* a financial order)[35] and/or although r.28.3(8) states that only open offers to settle are admissible "at any stage of the proceedings" this refers solely to first instance proceedings.[36]

CHILDREN'S CASES

26-12 In children's cases concerning welfare issues the usual order is that there is no order as to costs. This is because the court does not wish a party to feel punished with the resulting ill-feeling between the parties, the likelihood of non-co-operation and consequential effect on the child's welfare. Exceptionally, an order may be made and the general approach may be displaced if one party has been behaving particularly unreasonably or there is a large disparity between the respective means of the parties.[37] The court will take into account the risk of an order in such a case exacerbating hostility between the parents, to the child's detriment.[38]

The more recent cases have tended to emphasise that the unreasonableness which leads to a costs order is in the context of the conduct of the litigation rather than the welfare of the child.[39] Different treatment will be given to legitimate litigation over reasonable disagreements on the one hand and irrational conduct which brings unnecessary litigation on the other.[40] In *Re G (Contact Proceedings: Costs)*[41] the Court of Appeal dismissed the father's appeal against a costs order made within contact proceedings on the basis that he had used the proceedings as a vehicle for "getting at" the mother and had presented a case totally lacking in merit. In *E-R (Child Arrangements)*[42] having reviewed the relevant authorities, Cobb J ordered

---

34 *KS v ND (Schedule 1: Appeal: Costs)* [2013] 2 F.L.R. 698.

35 *H v W (Cap on Wife's Share of Bonus Payments) (No 2)* [2015] 2 F.L.R. 161.

36 *WD v HD* [2017] 1 F.L.R. 160.

37 For example, *M v H* [2000] 1 F.L.R. 394.

38 See *London Borough of Sutton v Davis (Costs) (No.2)* [1994] 2 F.L.R. 569, *R v R (Costs: Child Case)* [1997] 2 F.L.R. 95, *Q v Q* [2002] 2 F.L.R. 668, *C v FC* [2004] 1 F.L.R. 362, and *Re T (Children: Care Proceedings: Serious Allegations Not Proved)* [2013] 1 F.L.R. 133.

39 *Re T (Order for Costs)* [2005] 2 F.L.R. 681.

40 *Re S (Leave to Remove: Costs)* [2010] 1 F.L.R. 834 and *EM v SW* [2009] EWCA Civ 311.

41 [2014] 1 F.L.R. 517.

42 [2017] 2 F.L.R. 501.

that the father should make a contribution towards the mother's costs given that he had behaved unreasonably in respect of some aspects of the litigation.

PART 9: SETTLEMENT OF SERIOUS PERSONAL INJURY CLAIMS INVOLVING CHILDREN OR PROTECTED PARTIES

CHAPTER 27

Settlement of Serious Personal Injury Claims Involving Children or Protected Parties

INTRODUCTION

Cases involving serious personal injury to the claimant present special problems for practitioners.[1] The settlement of any such claim will invariably involve consideration of how best to provide for the claimant's future needs out of the compensation received. The problems are accentuated where the claimant cannot conduct the litigation on his own behalf, either because he is a child (i.e. he is under 18)[2] or because he is a "protected party" under the Mental Capacity Act 2005 and CPR Pt 21. **27-01**

As has already been noted,[3] the foundation of the law of compromise is the law of contract. The general law makes special provision for those who may be incapable of entering into valid contracts or whose ability to make contracts may be restricted by age.[4] **27-02**

The Mental Capacity Act 2005 and a new version of Pt 21 have now been in force for over 12 years. There were no transitional provisions and the Act had immediate effect. Whilst the Act concerns capacity in general (and deals with, for example, capacity to execute documents and to marry) the focus of the following discussion is upon the implications of the Act and Pt 21 for the purposes of litigation. The most significant early authority on its interpretation was *Masterman-Lister v Jewell*[5] to which those required to consider capacity in the present context should refer.[6] **27-03**

Section 1 of the Act introduced five key principles governing the assessment of capacity, the most important for present purposes being that capacity will be assumed until the contrary is established.[7] In order to prove lack of capacity, medical evidence (normally from a psychiatrist, a neuropsychiatrist or neurologist, depending upon the circumstances) will be essential. The standard of proof is the **27-04**

---

1 See, generally, *Kemp & Kemp*, Vol.1. As this chapter does not set out to deal in detail with the underlying law, the reader is referred for more detailed discussion to *Kemp & Kemp*, which should be the vade mecum of all practitioners in this field.

2 CPR r.21.1(2)(a).

3 See, e.g. Ch.1.

4 For a general discussion of contractual capacity see *Chitty*, Vol.1, Ch.8, and para.4-02 onwards. The normal principle is that contracts made by minors are, with some exceptions, voidable at their instance.

5 [2002] EWCA Civ 1889.

6 The test in *Masterman-Lister* was applied in *Bailey v Warren* [2006] EWCA Civ 51; [2006] C.P. Rep. 26 and approved by the Supreme Court in *Dunhill v Burgin* [2014] UKSC 18; [2014] W.L.R. 933.

7 Mental Capacity Act 2005 s.1(2).

balance of probabilities.[8] A person is not to be treated as unable to make a decision merely because he makes an unwise decision.[9] The Act provides expressly that a "best interests" test applies to all things done or decisions made under it.[10] It provides also[11] that a person lacks capacity in relation to a matter if at the material time he is unable to make a decision for himself in relation to the matter because of "an impairment of, or a disturbance in the functioning of, the mind or brain." This may be permanent or temporary.[12] Inability to make decisions stems from an inability: (a) to understand the information relevant to the decision; (b) to retain that information; (c) to use or weigh that information as part of the process of making the decision; or (d) to communicate that decision.[13] Relevant information covers the consequences of both making and not making a decision.[14]

27-05 A defendant to a claim for personal injuries is entitled to dispute an alleged lack of capacity and may well wish to do so since the cost of administering any recovered compensation will itself be the subject of claim within the litigation. However, a defendant does not appear to have the right to challenge by medical evidence the appointment of a litigation friend.[15] Any challenge to a lack of capacity would be mounted within the substantive hearing and not at the case management stage. Where capacity is in issue, the court may be assisted by the intervention of the Official Solicitor.[16]

27-06 The new version of Pt 21 introduced two new terms of art, "protected party" and "protected beneficiary". A protected party is one who "lacks capacity to conduct the proceedings" whilst a protected beneficiary is one who "lacks capacity to manage and control any money recovered by him or on his behalf or for his benefit in the proceedings".[17]

27-07 The procedure governing actions brought by or against protected parties or children is set out in Pt 21 and its accompanying Practice Direction.[18] A protected party must proceed through a litigation friend.[19] A child will normally proceed through a litigation friend, although the court may dispense with this in appropriate circumstances.[20]

27-08 No settlement, compromise or payment and no acceptance of any money paid into court is valid, so far as it relates to a claim by, on behalf of, or against a child or protected party without the approval of the court.[21] This includes the making of

---

8 Mental Capacity Act 2005 s.2(4).

9 Mental Capacity Act 2005 s.1(4).

10 "An act done, or decision made, under this Act for or on behalf of a person who lacks capacity must be done, or made, in his best interests." Mental Capacity Act 2005 s.1(5). See also s.4.

11 Mental Capacity Act 2005 ss.2 and 3.

12 Mental Capacity Act 2005 s.2(2).

13 Mental Capacity Act 2005 s.3(1).

14 Mental Capacity Act 2005 s.3(4).

15 *Folks v Faizey* [2006] EWCA Civ 381.

16 *Lindsay v Wood* [2006] EWHC 2895, Stanley Burnton J. The Official Solicitor cannot be compelled to act if he is not put in funds to carry out his duties: see *Bradbury v Paterson* [2014] EWHC 3992 (QB).

17 CPR r.21.(2)(d) and (e).

18 There have been various changes over time to Pt 21 and the Practice Directions, the latest having come into force on 1 October 2014. It is important always to observe the requirements of the latest version when considering the procedure to be followed.

19 CPR r.21.2(1).

20 CPR r.21.1(2) and (3).

21 CPR r.21.10(1).

a voluntary interim payment. A step taken before a child or protected party has a litigation friend will be of no effect unless the court orders otherwise.[22]

The effect of this rule is that a defendant who "settles" a claim against a protected party or child which does not have the approval of the court does not secure a discharge from liability. **27-09**

A claimant who, through a litigation friend, reaches an agreement to settle a claim before proceedings are begun must nevertheless seek the approval of the court. An application for this purpose must be issued. The procedure is governed by Pt 8 of the CPR.[23] **27-10**

Where a settlement of a personal injury claim is reached during proceedings, approval of the proposed settlement may be sought from a district judge, master or judge, depending on the circumstances of the case.[24] The court will require information (amongst other things) as to: **27-11**

- (i) whether and to what extent the defendant admits liability;
- (ii) the age and occupation of the child or protected party;
- (iii) the litigation friend's approval of the terms of settlement;
- (iv) the circumstances of the incident or state of affairs giving rise to the claim;
- (v) relevant medical reports;
- (vi) a schedule of loss and damage;
- (vii) details of the evidence on liability, if it is not admitted, and an appreciation of the perceived litigation risks, with an assessment of the discount against a full liability award considered appropriate having regard to those risks;
- (viii) an opinion from counsel or the solicitor acting for the child or protected party endorsing the settlement figure[25] ;
- (ix) in a complex case, a draft order[26] ;
- (x) suggestions as to investment, where appropriate;
- (xi) (where the claim contains an element to reflect future pecuniary loss) information as to whether an order for periodical payments is sought and an explanation, if not, as to the reason no such claim is being made.[27]

Where a settlement includes provision for periodical payments, certain other details must be provided to the court when approval is sought.[28]

Circumstances may dictate that further information needs to be put before the court. For example, where the claim has been discounted to reflect the risk of defeat on a difficult and undecided point of law, it may be necessary to provide the court with authorities. It is not, however, necessary to obtain the approval of the Court of Protection to any proposed settlement. **27-12**

---

22 CPR r.21.3(4).

23 But see the discussion of *Drinkall v Whitwood* [2004] 1 W.L.R. 462 at para.27-15 onwards. for the procedure governing approval of a partial settlement arrived at before proceedings. See CPR r.21.10(2)(a) and (b) and PD 21 para.6.1.

24 See para.10-22 onwards.

25 CPR PD 21 para.6. This opinion should also deal, where appropriate, with the amount to be paid out to those who have provided gratuitous care.

26 See Precedent No.10 at A1–10 in Appendix 1.

27 The court is required in all such cases to consider whether such an order is appropriate: see the Damages Act 1996 s.2(1)(b).

28 Pt 21 PD para.5.5.

CONSEQUENCES OF FAILING TO OBTAIN APPROVAL/ FAILING TO APPOINT A LITIGATION FRIEND

27-13 Until such time as approval has been given it is open to either side to withdraw from the agreement.[29] Once the court has given its approval it seems that even if the order has not been drawn the agreement will still be binding.[30] Neither party would, on this analysis, be permitted to withdraw its consent. It is arguable, however, that even after this point, and even once the consent order has been drawn, the court may still allow the terms to be set aside and the action to proceed.

27-14 The court's approval must be sought to the making of interim payments to or on behalf of a protected party.[31]

27-15 It should be appreciated that the restriction on enforceability applies not only to an overall settlement but also to a compromise of individual issues within a case. The very great importance of securing the court's approval to a settlement of even a single issue to ensure that it is binding is shown by the case of *Drinkall v Whitwood*.[32]

> C was a minor who suffered serious injuries when the bicycle she was riding collided with a car. The issue of contributory negligence arose before proceedings were issued and the parties agreed an 80:20 settlement in C's favour. No agreement was reached on quantum and proceedings were issued. About 18 months later, and just before C reached her majority when she would have been capable of adopting the agreement and making it binding, D sought to resile from the agreement to allege a higher degree of contributory negligence, the ground being that C had not been wearing a cycle helmet. C opposed the right of D to withdraw from what she said was a binding agreement. The Court of Appeal, applying *Dietz v Lennig Chemicals*,[33] held that the acceptance of a partial settlement offer in these circumstances did not constitute a binding agreement until and unless the settlement was approved by the court. The court went on to say that advisers of claimants in such circumstances would be well advised to issue proceedings with the specific purpose of securing approval of a partial settlement. Where this occurred pre-proceedings it seems that this should be done by proceedings under CPR Pt 7 rather than Pt 8. It should also be noted that the court left open the possibility, not raised in this case, of an argument based on estoppel and change of position.

27-16 In a case where proceedings have been issued, a concession such as was made in *Drinkall*[34] could be secured by obtaining an approved consent judgment on liability in a specified proportion with damages to be assessed.

27-17 In *Dunhill (a Protected Party be her Litigation Friend Tasker) v Burgin Nos 1 and 2*[35] the Supreme Court had to consider the meaning of "capacity to conduct proceedings" and the effect on a negotiated settlement of a claim of a failure to have the court approve the settlement and the related failure to appoint a litigation friend where one was required.

> The claimant had been injured in 1999 in a road traffic accident. She suffered a significant brain injury. In 2002, shortly before the primary limitation period expired, she issued

---

29 *Dietz* [1969] A.C. 170 at 190, per Lord Pearson. This common law principle is not in conflict with the rights of the protected party under the ECHR art.14 as read with art.6: see *Revill v Damiani* [2017] EWHC 2630 (QB), per Dingemans J.

30 *Barrell Enterprises, Re* [1973] 1 W.L.R. 19 CA.

31 CPR PD 21 para.1.7.

32 *Drinkall* [2004] 1 W.L.R. 462.

33 *Dietz* [1969] A.C. 170.

34 *Drinkall* [2004] 1 W.L.R. 462.

35 [2014] 1 W.L.R. 933.

proceedings, limited in value to £50,000. She did not claim to be a protected party and no litigation friend had been appointed. The matter was listed for trial on liability only in January 2003. On the day of trial one of the claimant's witnesses did not attend, presumably—though this is not entirely clear from the judgments—weakening her case. Negotiations took place and the claim was settled for £12,500 plus costs. The negotiated settlement was enshrined in a consent order shown to and made by the court. Neither side asked for the court's approval of that settlement or the order based upon it and such approval was not, therefore, given. In 2006 the claimant sought new legal advice and an action was issued against her former lawyers. That claim was stayed pending the outcome of an application to set aside the original consent order and resurrect the original claim.[36] By the time of the appeal to the Supreme Court [February 2014] the claimant's new advisers were asserting that the claim, had it been properly understood, put and evidenced, would have had and did have a value of in the region of £2 million.

Two points arose for decision: first, what is the proper test of capacity in such a case? For the claimant it was argued that "capacity to conduct proceedings" meant capacity to understand and give instructions on the claim as a whole, including capacity to understand the way the claim was put, but extending also to the way in which the claim might have been put and the possibility of a gross undervalue. The defendant argued that in this context capacity meant the capacity to make the actual decision demanded of the claimant in January 2003, namely, how far the claim as actually put was harmed by the non-attendance of the witness and what, in the circumstances, was a reasonable settlement. **27-18**

Baroness Hale of Richmond, giving the sole judgment of the Supreme Court, ruled on this point as follows at [18]: **27-19**

"I would hold, therefore, that the test of capacity to conduct proceedings for the purpose of CPR Part 21 is the capacity to conduct the claim or cause of action which the claimant in fact has, rather than to conduct the claim as formulated by her lawyers. Judged by that test, it is common ground that [the claimant] did not have the capacity to conduct this claim."

The claimant accordingly lacked capacity to conduct the proceedings even if she had capacity in relation to the relatively narrow issue that faced her in January 2003.

Baroness Hale rejected the argument advanced by the defendant that CPR r.21.10(1) applied only where a litigation friend had in fact been appointed (with the result, it was argued, that only then would the defendant be put on notice that the settlement required the approval of the court) because to "disapply the rule where there was no litigation friend would ... require the words 'having a litigation friend' to be written into the rule" and also rejected as inconsistent with authority and otherwise incorrect as an argument that the rule was ultra vires the rule-making body. **27-20**

Dunhill is, therefore, a very significant statement of the law in this area. The purpose of CPR r.21.10 is to protect parties from improvident bargains and applies as much to those suggested by their lawyers as to any other. Whilst capacity is to be defined by reference to the task in question, when that test is applied to conducting proceedings a claimant—or for that matter (though this will be rarer) a defendant—who lacks capacity is unable to understand the litigation as a whole, both as in fact presented but also as it should have been presented. Where a party does lack such capacity any compromise of any issue requires the approval of the court before it is binding and absent such approval is liable to be set aside. **27-21**

---

[36] Subject to evidential difficulties caused by any delay this may well usually be the preferable course as within any secondary litigation against the retained legal advisers there will be a discount to reflect the chance that the primary litigation would have failed. Full compensation, the aim of the law of tort, will therefore rarely if ever be achieved.

27-22 In *Dunhill* the primary litigation, i.e. the original dispute between the claimant and the driver, was re-opened.That may be some relief to legal advisers and their insurers in those circumstances, but it remains important to appreciate that those legal advisers may be liable if they fail to detect and investigate a lack of capacity on the part of their client. A failure to recognise a potential lack of capacity and to investigate it properly may lead to unnecessary litigation and, at the very least, a wasted costs order.

27-23 From the above it can be seen that a defendant is at risk in settling a claim of its being re-opened later for lack of capacity even if a) the defendant has acted in good faith and b) neither the defendant nor the claimant's advisers had thought that lack of capacity arose. Some comfort may be taken by such defendants from the fact that the presumption of capacity means that the claimant must prove a lack of capacity at the time in order to succeed. For a case where this was tried and failed, including some judicial comments on the applicability of the rule in *Ladd v Marshall*, see *Wadhwani v Ingenious Media Holdings Ltd*.[37]

EFFECT OF APPROVAL AND SETTING ASIDE CONSENT ORDERS ON THE BASIS OF A CHANGE OF CIRCUMSTANCES

27-24 A consent order is, for all that it is made by agreement, nevertheless an order of court. Where a child or protected party is involved, the court, in making the order, is exercising a supervisory jurisdiction and is anxious to scrutinise the terms of the proposed settlement: it is not performing a mere rubber-stamping exercise. It requires information to be placed before it to enable it to fulfil its function. The order thus made reflects the view and decision of the court: an appeal against it may lie. The right to appeal against a consent order has existed since 1873[38] and is now contained in s.18(1)(f) of the Senior Courts Act 1981. With few exceptions[39] there is no distinction between appealing against a final and an interim consent order. Permission is required to appeal against a consent order.

27-25 Where there has been a contested trial, it has long been accepted that an appeal may lie if the factual basis for the decision is falsified by events, even if those events occurred after judgment and could not possibly have been predicted at the time of trial.[40] Granted that the vitiating events have, in all the reported cases, occurred during the currency of appeals on other grounds, this does not seem to be a reason in principle for restricting the operation of the doctrine to cases where there is coincidentally an extant appeal.

27-26 In the matrimonial jurisdiction, it is well established that a consent order providing for ancillary relief may be appealed, even out of time, on the grounds of a change of circumstances which falsifies the basis upon which the order was made.[41] As when it is dealing with protected parties and children, the court, in family matters, is exercising a supervisory jurisdiction. It was expressly recognised in *Barder*

---

37 [2018] EWHC 350 (QB).

38 Supreme Court of Judicature Act 1873 s.49.

39 For example, as to appealing an order extending time for a step to be taken within proceedings.

40 See *Murphy v Stone-Wallwork (Charlton) Ltd* [1969] 1 W.L.R. 1023 HL, *Mulholland v Mitchell* [1971] A.C. 666 HL, *Curwen v James* [1963] 1 W.L.R. 748, *McCann v Shepherd* [1973] 1 W.L.R. 540, *Hughes v Singh* (1989) CAT 276; *The Times*, 21 April 1989 CA.

41 See *Barder v Caluori (Barder)* [1988] A.C. 20 and *Burns v Burns* [2004] EWCA Civ 1258. See also the discussion at Ch.24.

v Caluori (Barder)[42] that the principles expounded in *Mulholland v Mitchell*[43] and *Murphy v Stone-Wallwork (Charlton) Ltd*[44] applied to cases involving financial relief on divorce.[45]

It is suggested that there is no good reason why the court should not, in appropriate circumstances, allow an appeal against a consent order or judgment where there has been a change of circumstances such that the basis upon which the order or judgment was made has been falsified. It is, however, likely that this jurisdiction will be used rarely and with caution and, in the personal injury context, it is probable that an event only as extreme as the death of the claimant shortly after the order is made will suffice.[46] The courts will, of course, strive to ensure that parties keep to bargains freely struck except where it would be grossly unfair (and, perhaps, contrary to the public interest) to hold them to the consequences of those bargains. Equally, the courts will recognise no doubt that settlement of any personal injury claim involves a great deal of speculation and unscientific prediction. **27-27**

It is submitted that an appeal will ordinarily be allowed only where: **27-28**

(i) a change of circumstances has occurred which renders the terms of the consent order manifestly and significantly unfair; provided that
(ii) the changed circumstances relate to matters which were the subject of an assumption common to both parties[47] ;
(iii) the changed circumstances were not foreseeable at the time the consent order was made and falsify the common assumption upon which both parties had acted[48] ;
(iv) the changed circumstances occur within a short time of the order[49] ;
(v) the party seeking to set aside the order acts promptly on discovering the changed circumstances[50] ;
(vi) third party rights will not be affected significantly by the setting-aside of the order.

In *Roult v North West Strategic Health Authority*[51] C brought a high value claim against D based on clinical negligence. At one point C's case was that he required adapted housing and he sought to recover the cost of this from D. Before the action was concluded, however, C's case changed as it was accepted that a group home, where accommodation was provided at no cost, was more suitable to his needs and would in fact be chosen for him. Certain heads of loss were compromised during the action whilst others went to trial. One of the heads of loss that was settled related to the private accommodation costs which, consistent with the then understanding, were agreed to be nil, although any additional costs associated with being housed in a group home were left to be claimed. The agreement to settle this head of loss and some others was approved by the court with the outstanding quantum issues to be tried. In fact C moved into group accommodation after approval of those heads that had been compromised, but before trial. His stay there was, it was said, not a success. Accordingly, C sought to resurrect his accommodation claim in a subsequent **27-29**

42 *Barder* [1988] A.C. 20.

43 *Mulholland* [1971] A.C. 666.

44 *Murphy* [1969] 1 W.L.R. 1023 HL.

45 *Barder* [1988] A.C. 20 at 41, per Lord Pearson.

46 Assuming, of course, that the settlement figure contained a large element for future loss, particularly for the claimant's care.

47 i.e. they were not part of the litigation risk posed by rival contentions.

48 For example, a change in the multiplier discount rate would normally be foreseeable and foreshadowed by debate, a first instance decision or consultation exercise.

49 It is probable that this will be measured in months rather than years.

50 For a matrimonial case in which it was held that the proposed appellant had waited too long, see *Burns* [2004] EWCA Civ 1258.

51 *Roult v North West SHA* [2010] 1 W.L.R. 487.

schedule of loss and damage. D argued that this was impermissible because of the court's earlier approval of the compromise of this specific item of claim. C sought to persuade the court to set aside its earlier order under CPR r.3.1(7).[52] The Court of Appeal held that this rule did not confer upon a court of first instance the power to set aside a consent order settling part (or all) of a claim for damages where that consent order had been approved by the court. The court held that that rule was most likely to be of use where procedural or case management orders were involved rather than orders disposing of substantive issues.

27-30 The Court of Appeal also, however, considered the issue of whether an appeal could lie in such circumstances. No concluded view was expressed, but Hughes LJ[53] said this:

> "19. The broader question of whether an order approving a settlement could ever be one in respect of which an appellate court would be justified in granting leave to appeal out of time if there had been either erroneous information given to the judge, or a supervening event had destroyed the basis on which he had made the order does not arise and accordingly we should not attempt to answer it in the abstract. Erroneous information is not suggested, but if it were to arise it might involve features such as fraud, mistake or misrepresentation which could be capable of vitiating the underlying contract of settlement and/or the approval, and the defendants did not contend otherwise. As to a Barder supervening event, I am in no doubt ... that even if the principles enunciated in that case could ever apply to an order approving settlement, whatever happened in this case is incapable of being such an event.
>
> 20. All serious personal injuries litigation involves an attempt to predict the future in order to quantify claims for future loss. The quantification of a care claim, as here, is perhaps the largest single example, but the same applies to the assessment of future career paths, lost future earnings and future expense of living, to name but three. What has happened in this case is not that there has been any event which destroys the basis of the order approving the settlement. The most that has happened is that in one (important) respect the prediction of the future has changed so far as the claimant's parents are concerned. Whether they are right or wrong is necessarily uncertain. The Judge was prepared to proceed upon the assumption (without deciding) that at a future trial the claimant would be able to establish that he should be awarded damages based upon the cost of future care in privately provided accommodation. But even if he could now prove that, that would not be capable of being a new event shattering the basis of the settlement, which, like all such settlements, proceeded upon the best prediction of the future which could be made at the time. It was always foreseeable that the prediction might turn out to be erroneous; this is simply unavoidable. The financing of care homes might be changed fundamentally by government or other action. The claimant might be refused admission to the kind of care which had been anticipated. These uncertainties are inevitable in the settlement of any claim for future loss which is going to endure over many years. For that matter, medical advances or sudden fatal illness may ... unexpectedly falsify the predictions of expectation of life on which a settlement is based. I would moreover add that before any application for leave to appeal could be mounted on the basis of fresh evidence of a dramatic Barder-type event, the case must, as Lord Brandon held, be so clear that it is plain that such appeal would be certain or very likely to succeed. The right test therefore is not to be based on an assumption about disputed facts or the outcome of a hypothetical appeal; it must be clear that it would almost certainly succeed."

27-31 The question thus remains unanswered, but it is suggested that nothing in *Roult*

---

[52] "(7) A power of the court under these Rules to make an order includes a power to vary or revoke the order."

[53] With whom Carnwarth and Smith LJJ agreed.

should preclude the appeal route in appropriate cases though it is to be expected that any court, even if persuaded that the jurisdiction existed, would require a truly significant falsification of a genuinely fundamental assumption and would further require that it occurred within a short time of the approval. The jurisdiction may be therefore of more apparent than real utility. It is a jurisdiction that will most normally assist a defendant rather than a claimant who will not be able to return to court if, for example, he or she significantly outlives their predicted life expectancy at the date of settlement. If the jurisdiction does exist, the appropriate procedure is to appeal the consent order (for which permission is, as noted above, required) rather than to ask the court to vary or revoke the order under CPR r.3.1(7).

It is perhaps also worth emphasising that to settle a head of loss based on a parental choice for an option that has not yet been put to the test, and whose suitability may be uncertain, may be unwise before a trial of the regime has taken place if, of course, time and circumstances allow such a trial. **27-32**

COURT OF PROTECTION[54]

Section 45(1) of the Mental Capacity Act 2005 established a new Court of Protection as a superior court of record. It has wide powers to protect the interests of those who lack capacity. Its work is supported by the Office of the Public Guardian and its procedures have since 1 December 2017 been governed by the Court of Protection Rules 2017.[55] **27-33**

Where the involvement of the Court of Protection is appropriate, it is common for a Deputy to be appointed to manage the affairs of a protected beneficiary.[56] Frequently, this is achieved by recruiting an experienced solicitor to perform the function of Deputy. That solicitor's charges may form part of the claim for damages. They will in each case be the subject of evidence as charges are known to vary. **27-34**

Equally, the Court of Protection will charge for the administration and management of funds entrusted to it. Those charges should always be claimed by the claimant in personal injury proceedings, although precise quantification of the anticipated costs will often not be possible until the overall damages sum is known. **27-35**

It is no longer necessary to seek the approval of the Court of Protection for any settlement of a relevant claim for damages for personal injury. **27-36**

VARIOUS PRINCIPLES IN SETTLEMENT IN PERSONAL INJURY CASES

Whilst it is not appropriate in this work to consider in detail the quantification of claims for personal injury of the utmost severity, there are some areas which are of particular importance to the question of compromise. These are now dealt with. **27-37**

---

54 See Heywood and Massey, *Court of Protection Practice*, Looseleaf edn (London: Sweet & Maxwell, latest update 30 May 2019).

55 Replacing the Court of Protection Rules 2007.

56 But note that s.18(3) of the 2005 Act provides that a "deputy can only be appointed for a person not yet 16 if the Court considers it likely that [that person] will still lack capacity to make decisions when he reaches 18". Deputies are therefore suitable for those whose need for protection arises from 2005 Act considerations rather than by virtue of their age alone.

A. Provisional damages

27-38 It is well known that in most personal injury cases where there is uncertainty about the future duration and extent of the claimant's losses the court will make the best estimate it can on the evidence and award damages for future loss on a once-for-all basis. As has been acknowledged by the House of Lords, the one inevitable feature of such a process is that it will be shown in time to have been wrong.[57] The courts compensate for lost chances when considering quantum, if not in relation to matters of causation.[58]

27-39 Where, however, the claimant at the time of trial has simply a possibility of a significant deterioration in health which, if it occurred, would markedly increase his losses beyond what could legitimately then be claimed, statute provides that he can protect himself by seeking an award of provisional damages.[59]

27-40 A detailed examination of the criteria for an award of provisional damages is beyond the scope of this work,[60] but the general principle is that the claimant must show

> "a chance[61] that at some definite or indefinite time in the future [he] will, as a result of the act or omission which gave rise to the cause of action, develop some serious disease or suffer some deterioration in his physical or mental condition."

Even if the claimant can demonstrate a risk of the development of a serious disease or deterioration the court still retains a discretion as to whether to make an award of provisional damages.[62]

27-41 A claim for provisional damages must be pleaded.[63] If a claim which includes a claim for provisional damages is settled before proceedings are commenced then, whether or not approval would otherwise be necessary, proceedings under CPR Pt 8 should be issued. Whenever, and at whatever stage, a claim is settled on terms which include an award of provisional damages it is vital to comply with the requirements of CPR Pt 41, in particular the requirement for an agreed statement of facts.[64] By definition in such a case there will not have been a reasoned judgment on quantum and, equally plainly, the case may not be reactivated until many years after the settlement is reached. The judge dealing with the case then will have to reconstruct the way in which the immediate damages figure was reached and determine the nature of the condition(s) agreed to be capable of triggering a claim for further damages. Although the court is obliged to keep the case file safe, it would

---

57 "There is only one certainty: the future will prove the award to be either too high or low": *Lim Poh Choo v Camden and Islington Health Authority* [1980] A.C. 174 at 184, per Lord Scarman. See also *Thompson v Smiths Shiprepairers (North Shields) Ltd* [1984] Q.B. 405 at 443E, per Mustill J: "The whole exercise of assessing damages is shot through with imprecision."

58 See *Davies v Taylor* [1974] A.C. 207 HL, *Doyle v Wallace* [1998] P.I.Q.R. Q147, *Langford v Hebran & Nynex Cablecom* [2001] EWCA Civ 361 CA.

59 Senior Courts Act 1981 s.32A, inserted by the Administration of Justice Act 1981 s.6, as from 1 July 1985 and County Courts Act 1984 s.52.

60 See *Kemp & Kemp*, Vol.1, Ch.25.

61 The chance must be "measurable rather than fanciful": *Willson v Ministry of Defence* [1991] 1 All E.R. 638. There is no conclusive definition of how large a chance must be before it gives grounds for such a claim. In *Mitchell v Royal Liverpool and Broadgreen University Hospitals NHS Trust* Queen's Bench Division District Registry (Manchester) unreported 17 July 2006, Beatson J held that a chance assessed at 0.15 per cent was "measurable" and thus qualified for this purpose notwithstanding the remoteness of the possibility.

62 *Willson v Ministry of Defence* [1991] 1 All E.R. 638.

63 CPR r.41.2(1)(a).

64 The application itself is made under CPR Pt 23: see PD 41 para.4.1.

be good practice for the solicitors acting for the parties to make special archiving arrangements for the whole file, at least for the period specified in the order as being the time within which the claimant could return to court.

Under Practice Direction: Provisional Damages,[65] the consent order submitted to the court being invited to approve an award of provisional damages must: **27-42**

- (i) specify the disease or type of deterioration, or diseases or types of deterioration, which for the purposes of the immediate award have been assumed will not occur and will entitle the claimant to further damages if they do occur;
- (ii) give an award of immediate damages;
- (iii) specify the period or periods within which an application may be made in respect of each disease or deterioration[66] ;
- (iv) contain a direction as to the documents to be preserved (which will normally be the consent judgment itself, the statements of case, an agreed statement of facts and the agreed medical reports).

Where the only issue is provisional damages, there is nothing to stop the parties agreeing a lump sum award as appropriate whether or not provisional damages are awarded and litigating solely the claim for provisional damages.[67] This may reduce costs and provide both parties with the ability to protect themselves on costs.[68] **27-43**

Like provisions apply where a periodical payments order has been made against the background that a future significant change in health status may render the amount excessive or inadequate. The Damages (Variation of Periodical Payments) Order 2005[69] permits the court in such circumstances to include a term permitting variation of the periodical payments order. Aside from the fact that a variable periodical payments order may—unlike a provisional damages order—entitle the defendant to vary the order if there is a significant improvement in the claimant's condition, there is no material difference in practice between the requirements for a provisional damages order and those for a variable periodical payments order.[70] **27-44**

For a case of an application to vary a consent order giving the claimant liberty to apply within 20 years for an award of provisional damages see *Ministry of Defence v Blythe*.[71] The application, made beyond the 20-year limit, succeeded both at first instance and on appeal. **27-45**

B. Orders for periodical payments

The uncertainty which accompanies once-for-all awards of damages can also affect the mechanics of settlement in some high-value cases. Where the severely injured claimant depends upon his compensation for amelioration of his condition (particularly in respect of his care regime), then as soon as that compensation runs out (which it is likely to do if he outlives the life-expectancy predictions of the medical experts or if his investments do not perform as expected) he will be left dependent upon publicly funded or charitable services. **27-46**

---

65 CPR PD 41 para.4.1. See also para.15-04.

66 Although it is far from clear that a fixed cut-off point could or should be inserted into all such orders: see *Middleton v Elliott Turbomachinery* (1990) CAT 910.

67 See *Chewings v Williams* [2009] EWHC 2490 (QB), Slade J.

68 See Ch.15.

69 SI 2005/841.

70 See for example *Kotula v EDF & Others* [2011] EWHC 1546 (QB) Irwin J and *Loughlin v Singh* [2013] EWHC 1641 (QB) Kenneth Parker J.

71 [2013] EWHC 1422 (QB) HH Judge Allan Gore QC.

27-47 This plainly undesirable prospect was initially addressed in appropriate cases by way of a structured settlement. Until April 2005 a structured settlement could not be imposed by the court on either party[72] nor, even if the defendant was in principle prepared to agree to such a settlement, could the defendant be forced to purchase an annuity rather than to fund the structure itself.[73] A decision by a defendant not to offer a structured settlement (or structured settlements generally) was not amenable to judicial review.[74]

27-48 The area in which structured settlements operated was changed fundamentally by the amendment to s.2 of the Damages Act 1996 effected by ss.100 and 101 of the Courts Act 2003. Since the implementation of these provisions the court is required in all cases involving claims for future pecuniary loss in respect of personal injury to consider making an order that the damages are paid wholly or partly by way of periodical payments. The court may also order periodical payments in respect of other damages (i.e. those not in respect of future pecuniary loss) with the consent of the parties.

27-49 It is now routine in high-value personal injury actions for damages for future care and case management[75] to be claimed by way of periodical payments. It should never be assumed, however, that this will inevitably be in the claimant's best interests. In particular, changing economic (and particularly investment) conditions may make such an order disadvantageous. Financial advice should be sought in all such cases.

27-50 CPR Pt 41 and the Practice Direction set out the matters to which the court should have regard when considering making such an order, e.g. the scale of annual payments, the form of award preferred by the claimant and defendant, the nature of financial advice received and continuity of payment.

27-51 The parties may, in their statements of case, set out whether they consider an order for periodical payments or lump sum to be more appropriate. Particulars may be ordered by the court of any such plea.[76] The court will give an indication "as soon as practicable" as to which way it is thinking.[77] This is likely to be at a case management conference and at an early stage.

27-52 Part 36 has been amended to reflect the changes effected by the system of periodical payments.[78] Costs consequences follow if the claimant fails to secure an award which is "more advantageous" than a Pt 36 offer including an offer in relation to periodical payments (or, as the case may be, does secure an award which is "more advantageous"), but the phrase "more advantageous" is not defined in the rule.[79]

27-53 CPR r.36.18(4) provides that an offer must state the amount of the lump sum element, what part of the offer (if any) relates to periodical payments, the amount and duration of any such periodical payments, the basis of variation (i.e. by reference to what indexation) and the security of the funding. A party may also state what part

---

72 See *Cowan v Kitson Insulation Ltd* [1992] P.I.Q.R. Q19, *Clegg v Burnley, Pendle and Rossendale HA* Unreported July 17, 2001, Penry-Davey J. The Law Commission rejected a suggestion that claimants be given the right to insist on a structure and the court the power to impose one: *Law Com. No.224.*

73 *Clegg v Burnley* unreported 17 July 2001.

74 See *R. (on the application of Hopley) v Liverpool HA* [2002] EWHC 1723 (Admin); [2002] Lloyd's Rep. Med. 494.

75 And increasingly, though not in most cases, other heads such a Deputyship costs and loss of earnings.

76 CPR r.41.5.

77 CPR r.42.6.

78 Civil Procedure (Amendment No.3) Rules 2004.

79 See para.17-05 onwards.

of the offer relates to future pecuniary loss in the form of a lump sum and what amount relates to other damages by way of lump sum.

Such offers may only be accepted as a whole and not in part[80] and the defendant must actually pay the lump sum element to have costs protection.[81] **27-54**

It is of the first importance that care is taken in relation to the terms of any consent order put before the court where there is a claim for periodical payments, whether these are absolute, stepped and/or variable. The courts have considered the appropriate form of order in cases where litigation is settled in part for a lump sum and in part for an order for periodical payments. Various draft precedents exist and at Appendix 1, section 3, is a draft order appropriate under the Clinical Negligence Scheme for Trusts using ASHE as the appropriate index.[82] Arguments may arise as to which is the appropriate indexation measure and as to the types of future losses that are to be made subject of a periodical payments order. **27-55**

Typically, claimants in receipt of a periodical payments order have to give a certificate that they are still alive in the relevant year to qualify for continuing payments. It is routine for such a certificate to be given by the claimant's GP. In *Wallace v Follett*[83] the Court of Appeal considered of a failure to provide such a certificate, the claimant arguing that it was appropriate to stop payments only with a prior court order permitting this step. Leveson LJ suggested that the following form of words would be suitable: **27-56**

> "Following a request by the Defence Insurer in writing on or before 1 November each year, the Claimant shall obtain and provide to the Defence Insurer by 1 December each year, commencing 01/12/2012, written confirmation from his GP or other medical adviser dated not before 1 November of the same year confirming that the GP or medical adviser has seen the Claimant on or after that date and that the Claimant is still alive, in default of which the obligation of the Defence Insurer to make instalment payments to the Claimant shall be suspended until 7 days after the written confirmation (dated not more than one month before the date of its submission) is provided to the Defence Insurer."[84]

In the same case, the court had to consider the perhaps rather more significant issue of whether an insurer could require a claimant in receipt of a periodical payments order to undergo a general medical examination with a view to updating the life expectancy estimate so that that insurer could maintain reserves that were as accurate as possible. The claimant argued that this was an unjustified invasion of his personal autonomy from which he would derive no benefit. Once again, Leveson LJ suggested a form of words that would be appropriate, effectively upholding the insurer's right as claimed to periodic health reviews. At paragraph 19 he gave the following suggested specimen clause: **27-57**

> "The Defence Insurer shall be entitled to require the Claimant to undergo medical examination at its request upon reasonable notice being given to the Claimant at any time during the Claimant's life time, such medical examinations to be limited to obtaining a medical opinion as to the Claimant's general health in order to obtain a quotation for the purchase cost of an annuity to fund the periodical payments and/or (not more frequently than once every seven years) for the express purposes of reviewing its reserve. The cost of any such examination, to include any reasonable costs and any loss of earnings incurred

---

80 CPR r.36.18(6).

81 CPR r.36.18(7).

82 This draft was approved in *RH (A Child by his Mother and Litigation Friend LW) v University Hospitals Bristol NHS Foundation Trust (Formerly United Bristol Heathcare NHS Trust* [2013] EWHC 299 (QB).

83 [2013] EWCA Civ 146.

84 [2013] EWCA Civ 146 at [25].

by the Claimant in attending the examination, shall be paid by the Defence insurer. The Claimant shall have permission to apply to the court in the event of reasonable concern as to the nature or extent of any such examination."

C. The recoupment of benefits[85]

27-58 The Social Security (Recovery of Benefits) Act 1997, and the very many different regulations made under it form a detailed code dealing with the recoupment by the State from a tortfeasor of benefits paid to an injured person by reason of injuries caused by the tort. Recovery of NHS charges incurred is in certain circumstances possible.

27-59 So far as settlement is concerned, the following points should be noted:

(1) No case should be settled without sight of a current certificate of recoverable benefits.[86]
(2) A Pt 36 offer must state either that the offer is made without regard to recoverable benefits or that it is intended to include deductible benefits.[87] It must also state the net amount of compensation. This is important because it is failure to beat this net sum that triggers the adverse costs consequences provided by Pt 36.[88]
(3) If a certificate is appealed after the settlement of an action, it seems that the benefit of such an appeal (subject to any agreement to the contrary) will inure to the claimant. Where, however, the agreement is for payment of a sum of money only and the benefits position is not addressed, it seems that the claimant is entitled only to the net sum after deduction of benefits.[89]

D. Costs

27-60 A litigation friend must give an undertaking to be responsible for any costs awarded against the child or protected party, subject to a right to recoupment from the assets of the claimant under a disability. The litigation friend does, however, enjoy the protection afforded by the existence of a Legal Services Commission funding agreement.

27-61 Just as the court will be careful to ensure that the claim of a protected party or child has not been undervalued, whether negligently or otherwise, by his legal advisers, so too will it look to see that he is not overcharged by those same advisers.

27-62 Wherever an order is made for money to be paid to or by a protected party or child the court will generally assess the costs payable by the protected party or child to his solicitor as well as those payable by any other party to the protected party or child. This latter step is not necessary where there has been a default costs certificate. Only that which the court assesses as payable may be paid to the solicitor by or on behalf of the protected party or child.[90]

27-63 A detailed assessment of the solicitor/client costs may be dispensed with: (a) where one is not necessary to protect the protected party or child; (b) where another

---

85 For further reading, see The Means Tested Benefits Legislation (Sweet & Maxwell). See also the DWP's own Guidance, *https://www.gov.uk/government/publications/recovery-of-benefits-and-or-lump-sum-payments-and-nhs-charges-technical-guidance* [Accessed 30 October 2019].

86 Where a Part 36 offer is intended to take account of recoverable benefits, before making the offer the offeror "must" apply for a certificate of recoverable benefits CPR r.36.22(5).

87 CPR r.36.22(3).

88 CPR r.36.22(6)(c) and 36.22(8).

89 *Rees v West Glamorgan County Council* [1994] P.I.Q.R. P37 noted at para.5-13.

90 CPR r.46.4.

party has agreed to pay those costs and the solicitor has waived any right to seek more from his client; (c) where there has been a summary assessment and a waiver by the solicitor of any right to claim more; and (d) where there is a legal expenses or other insurer liable to pay those costs and the court is satisfied that it has the means to do so.[91]

There is a continuing interest in, and encouragement for, alternative dispute resolution (ADR). In serious personal injury cases, for example major clinical negligence actions, it is routine for the Queen's Bench masters to make an order requiring the parties to address their minds to ADR well in advance of trial and, if they cannot agree upon it, to set out their reasons in a sealed document to be opened by the trial judge only when costs come to be considered.[92] Costs consequences can, though not always will, follow a refusal to enter into ADR.[93] It is now routine in serious personal injury and clinical negligence cases for Joint Settlement Meetings (JSM) to be ordered. These meetings are without prejudice and offers made at such meetings cannot be brought to the court's attention during any subsequent costs disputes, unless they were specifically said to be without prejudice save as to costs.[94] If offers intended to have costs consequences have been made orally at a JSM it is prudent to repeat or record them immediately in correspondence. **27-64**

E. Exaggeration

Whilst it is unlikely that a protected party would ever be guilty of conscious and culpable exaggeration in order to inflate a claim it is possible that a child could do so. To that extent the consequences of doing so against the background of a Pt 36 offer needs to be considered.[95] **27-65**

The starting point must be r.36.17(1) and (2) and r.44.3. As noted above,[96] a claimant secures a "more advantageous" result than an offer if he beats that offer by any sum, however small. Nevertheless, a party's conduct can be relevant when making an order for costs and the court retains a wide discretion on costs.[97] Provided that the court has regard to the relevant principles a variety of results is possible in the exercise of judicial discretion.[98] **27-66**

The introduction of the qualified one-way costs shifting regime and the enactment of s.57 of the Criminal Justice and Courts Act 2015 has generated a volume of authority on when a claim can be described as "fundamentally dishonest", a reason for disapplying the QOCS regime. This is outside the scope of this chapter but the interested reader is referred to *Howlett v Davies and Ageas Insurance*[99] for an appellate decision on the principles and *London Organising Committee of the* **27-67**

---

[91] CPR r.46.4.(2.1).

[92] See para.35-11 onwards.

[93] See generally Ch.35.

[94] *Jackson v Ministry of Defence* [2006] EWCA Civ 46.

[95] See Chs 14–18.

[96] See para.27-52.

[97] *Straker v Tudor Rose (A firm)* [2007] EWCA Civ 368.

[98] *Widlake v BAA Ltd* [2009] EWCA Civ 1256 (no order for costs of trial), *Hullock v East Riding of Yorkshire CC* [2009] EWCA Civ 1039 (where C was ordered to pay D's costs from date of earlier interim payment); *Morgan v UPS* [2008] EWCA Civ 1476 (where D was ordered to pay C's costs in circumstances where initial "gross exaggeration" had been abandoned following service of video evidence and C had beaten a CPR Pt 36 payment by a small amount). For an appellate case where exaggeration was not held to be a reason not to award full costs see *Fox v Foundation Piling* [2011] EWCA Civ 790. See generally, Ch.17.

[99] [2017] EWCA Civ 1696; [2018] 1 W.L.R. 948.

Olympic and Paralympic Games (in Liquidation) v Sinfield[100] for a first instance decision on the mechanics.

F. Anonymity

27-68 Protected parties may have particular vulnerability to exploitation. Concern is especially acute where the protected party will not, perhaps on reaching his majority, be a protected beneficiary. The risks in such a case are too obvious to need stating. It is not only the potential activities of the unscrupulous or criminal that are of concern, however, the publication of the identity and medical condition of someone who by definition is vulnerable and cannot give lawful consent to such a step raises clear questions about the invasion of such a person's privacy. It is to be noted, of course, that settlements reached by those with full capacity do not require any hearing at all and it is entirely normal in such cases for the public to know nothing about the existence or outcome of any litigation. For the protected party to be required to submit to the publication of his or her identity and medical state would be a curiosity.

27-69 There have been various methods employed to conceal the claimant's identity and any identifying details. The Court of Appeal has given definitive guidance on the matter in the case of *JX MX (By her mother and litigation friend AX MX) v Dartford & Gravesham NHS Trust*.[101] Having considered balance between open justice and an individual's right to privacy the Court of Appeal concluded that:

> "In our view the court should recognise that when dealing with an approval application of the kind now under consideration it is dealing with what is essentially private business, albeit in open court, and should normally make an anonymity order in favour of the claimant without the need for any formal application, unless for some reason it is satisfied that it is unnecessary or inappropriate to do so. Such an order should be drawn in terms that prohibit publication of the name and address of the claimant and his or her immediate family and also (if not already covered) the name of his or her litigation friend."[102]

27-70 The court went on to state eight principles:

(i) Anonymity orders should be the norm in cases requiring the court's approval;

(ii) Unless an anonymity order has already been made, the approval hearing should be listed under the name in which the proceedings were issued;

(iii) The public and press have a right to be present at approval hearing, which will continue to be held in public;

(iv) The press may freely report the proceedings subject to any order "restricting publication of the name and address of the claimant, his or her litigation friend (and, if different, the names and addressed or his or her parents) and restricting access by non-arties to documents in the court record other than those which have been anonymised";

(v) The court should invite submissions from the parties and press before making any such order; but

(vi) Unless the court is "satisfied after hearing argument that it is not necessary to do so" an anonymity order should be made;

(vii) If the court declines to make an anonymity order it should give its reasons; and

---

[100] [2018] EWHC 51 (QB), per Julian Knowles J.
[101] [2015] EWCA Civ 96.
[102] [2015] EWCA Civ 96 at [34].

(viii) If an order is made the court should go on to give a brief judgment on the application explaining the circumstances giving rise to the claim and should make a copy available to the press on request.

It would be an extremely rare case in which a defendant, particularly an institutional defendant, could ask for and get an anonymity order.

The right of the press—acting on behalf of the public—to make representations as to the making of an anonymity order are no mere cipher. The court will ensure that the procedure required to give them notification of any such application are followed. In *Zeromska-Smith v United Lincolnshire Hospital NHS Trust*[103] Martin Spencer J, whilst refusing to make an anonymity order in favour of a claimant who was neither a child nor a protected party, said that any application for anonymity should be made well in advance of trial and on proper notice. **27-71**

There may be occasions, rare it is anticipated, where the best interest of the protected party/beneficiary require that (s)he be not told of the amount of the compensation paid, even if (s)he is aware that some award has been made. For a case where the Court permitted the withholding of this information from the protected beneficiary see *EXB v FDZ*.[104] **27-72**

---

[103] [2019] EWHC 552 (QB).

[104] [2018] EWHC 3456 (QB), per Foskett J.

PART 10: EMPLOYMENT CONTRACTS AND COMPROMISE

CHAPTER 28

Employment Contracts and Compromise

INTRODUCTION

For many years the common law contractual relationship between employer and employee has been augmented by a number of statutory protections provided to employees and workers. This process of statutory protection has increased such that it now includes, by way of example only, protection in regard to dismissal (i.e. the right not to be unfairly dismissed); on the transfer of the business in which the employees have been employed under the Transfer of Undertakings (Protection of Employment) Regulations 2006[1]; against discrimination based on, again by way of example only, sex, race, disability or age and in connection with the conditions of employment (for example, under the Working Time Regulations 1998[2] and National Minimum Wage Age 1998) and in terms of the right to equal pay which is part of the law relating to sex discrimination but which is structured around implying "a sex equality clause" into contracts of employment. **28-01**

It follows that, when considering the settlement of disputes arising in the employment setting, it is frequently necessary to consider both contractual claims (for example, for wrongful dismissal or alleged breach of restrictive covenants) and statutory claims. This distinction is reflected in the different forums in which such disputes can be heard. Generally, contractual claims are heard in the ordinary civil courts (although employment tribunals have a limited jurisdiction to determine some claims of breach of contract).[3] Statutory claims are in the overwhelming generality of cases determined by employment tribunals. However, at least in theory the civil courts do have jurisdiction to hear claims for equal pay in addition to those claims being heard in employment tribunals. It is understood that in practice equal pay claims are still overwhelmingly heard in employment tribunals. **28-02**

In regard to the compromise of claims arising from disputes in the employment setting, important differences exist between the compromise of contractual and common law claims, on the one hand, and the settlement of statutory claims, on the other. In essence, contractual claims (including contractual claims which can be heard by employment tribunals) are subject to the same general principles that apply to compromise agreements in other civil disputes. This is in sharp contrast to the settlement of statutory claims. With regard to the latter, stringent limitations on the ability to settle such claims are in place which are designed to protect employees from entering into ill-advised settlement agreements. **28-03**

---

1 Transfer of Undertakings (Protection of Employment) Regulations 2006 (SI 2006/246).
2 Working Time Regulations (SI 1998/1833).
3 See the Industrial Tribunal Extension of Jurisdiction Orders 1994.

CONTRACTUAL CLAIMS

28-04 Relatively little needs to be said in this chapter about the compromise of these claims, because, as already stated, they are subject to the general principles that apply to the compromise of other civil law claims. Reference should, however, be made to four particular matters. Before moving to these, it should be made clear that these are matters dealt with in the context of settling contractual claims because the matters relate to general settlement agreements rather than the specific rules that define the conditions that must be met in order to achieve a valid and effective settlement of statutory claims that would be heard by employment tribunals. However, naturally, the general principles discussed below apply equally to the drafting of settlements under the statutory structures which apply to the effective settlement of statutory claims that would be heard in employment tribunals. The four matters dealt with immediately below are:

(1) the insertion of a general release clause in a settlement agreement;
(2) the need for care before including what used to be a standard provision in settling employment related claims which was to exclude from the scope of the settlement claims for personal injuries;
(3) considerations relating to a term in a settlement agreement which obliges the employer to provide a reference for the employee;
(4) the use of non-disclosure or confidentiality clauses in settlement agreements.

General release

28-05 The first of these matters arises from the decision of the House of Lords in *Bank of Credit and Commerce International SA v Ali*,[4] the facts of which have been given elsewhere.[5] As indicated previously,[6] the majority of the House of Lords (Lord Hoffmann dissenting) held that, on its true construction, the settlement agreement did not extend to claims for stigma damages. In particular, the majority held that, whilst a party was capable of agreeing to release claims of which he was not, and could not have been, aware, any such agreement had to use clear and unambiguous terms to that effect. That was not the case with the settlement agreement of 1990 involved in that case. Lord Hoffmann dissented. He was of the view that the compromise agreement of 1990 was sufficiently wide in its terms to include a claim for stigma damages. Lord Hoffmann did recognise that, in the context of a general release, a party should not be allowed to rely on that release when that party has failed to disclose the existence of a claim of which it had knowledge and of which it believes the other party is unaware. However that did not, in Lord Hoffmann's view, apply to the facts of the *Ali* case. The other members of the House of Lords did not express any view on this aspect of the case.

28-06 As is apparent from the above, a variety of views were expressed by the individual members of the House of Lords in the *Ali* case. At present there is no doubt that those who wish to compromise all possible claims (whether or not those claims are known by the parties and/or recognised by the law at the time of the compromise) must be careful to use extremely clear and comprehensive express terms to obtain this effect. Further, a party seeking to obtain a general release from another who is aware of the existence of some possible claim of which the other

---

4 *Ali* [2002] 1 A.C. 251.

5 See para.5-24.

6 See paras 5-23–5-28.

party is unaware, is at risk of being prevented from relying on that general release on the basis that any such reliance would be unconscionable, unless, of course, the first party informs the other of the potential claim in advance of entering into the settlement. It is appropriate to add in the above context some comments on the drafting of settlements which seek to apply to, and settle, "future claims"—in other words, claims that do not exist at the time of the settlement, but which might arise at a later date. It appears that, at least in principle, such future claims can be validly and effectively settled.[7] However, whilst such claims can in principle be settled, it was emphasised in that case that to obtain such an extreme result would require the clearest express terms to that effect.

Stress-related personal injury

The second of the four particular matters to be discussed in the context of contractual or common law claims between employers and employees (although these matters discussed in this section of this chapter can also arise in regard to settlements of statutory claims as already noted above) arises from the recognition of claims for stress-related injury caused by unreasonable working practices. **28-07**

It has long been a common practice to exempt from the scope of a "full and final settlement" between an employer and employee any claim that the employee has or may have in regard to personal injury. This practice may need to be considered with greater care in the light of the development of the line of authority that employees may be able to claim damages for personal injury from their employer for breach of duty of care in relation to failing to protect the employee from work-related stress.[8] However, it is envisaged that it will continue to be expected that some kind of exemption from the scope of a settlement in the area of employment law will apply in regard to personal injury claims. As a result, care should be taken in defining the scope of any such exemption, for example by excluding from the exemption the settlement claims of alleged work related stress or psychiatric conditions. **28-08**

References

Thirdly, in this context of dealing in this section of this chapter with issues that can arise in the settlement of common law and civil claims as well as statutory employment claims reference should be made to the following. A well-established development in the law of employment has been the blossoming of a duty of care in regard to the giving of references by an employer. The employer owes a duty of care both to the employee (or ex-employee) with regard to whom the reference is provided and to the recipient of the reference. The basis for this liability was set out by the House of Lords in *Spring v Guardian Assurance Plc*.[9] **28-09**

It is not uncommon for a settlement agreement in the employment setting to include a term that the employer will provide a reference in regard to the employee to any interested parties and will do so in agreed terms. An agreement of this nature can give rise to difficult issues. Thus, for example, it is often the case that those seeking references will require the referee to complete a questionnaire relating to the employee. Indeed, in some professional activities (such as the provision of financial services) the completion of a questionnaire about the employee is manda- **28-10**

---

7 *Royal National Orthopaedic Hospital v Howard* [2002] I.R.L.R. 849.

8 See *Hartman v South Essex Mental Health and Community Care NHS Trust* [2005] EWCA Civ 6.

9 *Spring v Guardian Assurance Plc* [1995] 2 A.C. 296.

tory—for example, as to their compliance or non-compliance with financial regulations. The issue may arise as to whether completion of any such questionnaire in addition to providing the agreed reference constitutes a breach of the settlement agreement.

28-11 Again, difficult questions can arise as to the relationship between the duty of an employer to provide an agreed reference and the duty of honesty owed to the recipient of that reference. The range of difficult questions that can arise in the context of an agreement to provide a particular reference was recognised by the Court of Appeal in *Cox v Sun Alliance Life Ltd*.[10] However, those issues did not need to be determined on the facts of that case.

28-12 Those involved in settling employment disputes in which the settlement includes an agreement to provide an agreed reference would be well advised to bear in mind the words of Mummery LJ in that case:

> "I would add a final word for the benefit of employers and employees who prefer to avoid time consuming, costly litigation about job references. In a case where the terms of an agreed resignation or of the compromise of an unfair dismissal claim make provision for the supply of a reference, the parties should ensure as far as possible that the exact wording of a fair and accurate reference is fully discussed, clearly agreed and carefully recorded in writing in COT3 at the same time as other severance terms."

Non-disclosure agreements

28-13 The fourth and final issue of potential importance relating to the settlement of both civil/common law claims and statutory claims relating to employment law concerns the inclusion of non-disclosure terms. In essence, these clauses seek to keep a range of issues confidential as part of the settlement agreement. Very often they include the attempt to prevent the disclosure of the allegations that provided the context for the employment dispute. A classic example of the above is an attempt to impose a duty of confidentiality in regard to allegations of discrimination and/or sexual harassment that the ex-employee has raised in the claims that are being settled. Another common example is where the confidentiality clause would seek to prevent disclosure of concerns that the ex-employee has raised, for example in regard to health and safety issues.

28-14 Unsurprisingly, the use of such clauses has given rise to concerns. At the same time it is recognised that the inclusion of confidentiality clauses is often a vital part of allowing the parties to reach a settlement. In terms of the degree of concern that exists about non-disclosure agreements, not only has the House of Commons Women and Equalities Committee published reports that raise concerns about attempts to silence employees but also on 21 July 2019 the Business, Energy and Industrial Strategy Department announced that the Government intended to introduce legislation to strengthen protections around non-disclosure agreements in the workplace. That strengthening would include a duty to make clear to employees that such clauses cannot prevent disclosures of perceived wrongdoing to appropriate bodies and a duty to ensure that those entering into such a confidentiality agreement are given the opportunity to receive legal advice.

28-15 Despite the above concerns the courts have also recognised that the existence of a well- drafted confidentiality clause in a settlement agreement can and should provide some protection from disclosure of the information subject to such clauses not being effective to prohibit disclosure of what would be protected disclosures within the law of "whistleblowing" to appropriate bodies. The above was

---

[10] *Cox v Sun Alliance Life Ltd* [2001] EWCA Civ 649; [2001] I.R.L.R. 448.

recognised and applied by the Court of Appeal in the case of *ABC v Telegraph Media Group Ltd*[11] which concerned the grant of an interim injunction preventing disclosure of allegations where that disclosure would have been in breach of a well-drafted confidentiality clause. The Court of Appeal was of the clear view that where there was such a clause and where the disclosure would appear to be a breach of that clause then there would need to be a strong case on behalf of those who wished to make the disclosure before the court would decline to grant an interim injunction preventing the disclosure. The case is a reminder of the benefits that can come from a well-drafted confidentiality clause.

A FINAL POINT IN THIS SECTION OF THIS CHAPTER

Before leaving the compromise of contractual, common law claims in the context of employment law, it should be noted that, as already mentioned, in respect of the limited jurisdiction enjoyed by employment tribunals to determine claims for breach of contract, the same rules apply in regard to settlement agreements of those claims as apply to the settlement of contractual and common law claims in the civil courts.[12] **28-16**

STATUTORY CLAIMS

As indicated above,[13] the rules that apply to the settlement of statutory claims by employees are very different from those applicable to the compromise of common law claims. The basic scheme adopted in connection with the settlement of statutory claims is for these to be rendered void and ineffective unless certain conditions are met as to the involvement of third parties in the making of those agreements, whose involvement is intended to ensure a degree of protection for the interests of the employee. Two broad categories of third parties are recognised for these purposes: conciliation officers of ACAS and "independent advisers". **28-17**

STATUTORY CLAIMS: SOME PRELIMINARY COMMENTS

Before setting out the central rules that apply in terms of achieving valid and effective settlements of statutory claims, mention should be made to the fact that 2013 and 2014 saw considerable legislative activity in connection with the provisions relating to the settlement of statutory claims. First, as a matter of nomenclature, the vocabulary of "settlement" has replaced the previous vocabulary of "compromise agreements" and "compromise contracts"[14] and that new vocabulary is adopted in this chapter. However, the reforms and changes introduced during that period included matters of far greater substantive significance than that change in vocabulary. Those other changes are dealt with (in so far as they are still relevant) in detail at paras 28-51 to 28-62. However, it can be stated at this stage that the apparent purpose of those changes and reforms has been to encourage the settlement **28-18**

---

[11] [2018] EWCA Civ 2329; [2019] 2 All E.R. 684.

[12] *Sutherland v Network Alliance Ltd* [2000] I.R.L.R. 12. In that case a compromise agreement that did not meet the statutory requirements to be an effective compromise of statutory claims was held to be effective in barring a claim for breach of contract brought in the employment tribunal.

[13] See para.28-03.

[14] The expression used in the SDA 1975 and RRA 1976.

of disputes and the reduction in claims and hearings before Employment Tribunals and indeed the Employment Appeal Tribunal. The two most important of these changes in recent years have been the introduction of a system of mandatory consideration of early (i.e. pre-action) conciliation and the introduction of fees for instituting and pursuing claims in the Employment Tribunals and Employment Appeal Tribunal. However, whilst the introduction of fees had a major impact on the number of claims presented to employment tribunals that issue is now of only historical relevance because the system of fees introduced was found to be unlawful by the Supreme Court in the case of *R. (Unison) v Lord Chancellor*[15] and no alternative system of fees has been introduced since then. As to the issue of introducing pre-action conciliation that issue is dealt with at paras 28-52–28-55.

STATUTORY CLAIMS – THE GENERAL STRUCTURE

28-19 Section 203(1) of the Employment Rights Act 1996 (ERA 1996) sets out the general prohibition against contracting out of rights contained within the Act. Section 203(1) declares "void" any contractual term that purports to exclude the operation of the ERA 1996 or which precludes a person from bringing proceedings thereunder before an employment tribunal. This provision, and its predecessors, have been given a liberal interpretation by the courts against the background of arguments designed to escape from its consequences.[16]

28-20 In *Igbo v Johnson Matthey Chemicals Ltd*,[17] A wished to visit her husband and children in Nigeria and R, her employers, agreed to an extended holiday entitlement (by some three days) to enable her to do this. She was required to agree to a term of this arrangement to the effect that if she did not return to work on the day following the termination of the extended holiday her contract of employment would "automatically terminate on that date". She was unwell on her return from the holiday and unable to return to work as required. She had a medical certificate confirming her illness, but R decided to treat her contract as terminated in accordance with the agreement. The Court of Appeal held, rejecting the suggestion that there had been a consensual termination of the contract, that she had been dismissed and that the effect of the agreement was to "limit the operation" of the provisions in the Act that gave A the right not to be unfairly dismissed. Hence the agreement was void.

28-21 In *Courage Take Home Ltd v Keys*,[18] A was dismissed and an industrial tribunal adjudged that the dismissal was unfair. The question of the remedy was adjourned. Before the restored hearing, and without the intervention of a conciliation officer, A accepted the sum of £9,500 from R in full and final settlement of his claim. Subsequently, A sought to pursue his claim for compensation. The Employment Appeal Tribunal held that the agreement concerning the £9,500 was void within s.140(1)(b) of the Employment Protection (Consolidation) Act 1978 (the predecessor to s.203 ERA 1996) in that it precluded or sought to preclude A from bringing proceedings for compensation under the Act. A was, nonetheless, held not entitled to seek further compensation as it would not be "just and equitable" under s.74 of that Act.

28-22 However, the broad terms of s.203(1) of the ERA 1996 are subject to s.203(2), which sets out a number of exceptions to this general prohibition against contract-

---

15 [2017] UKSC 51; [2017] 3 W.L.R. 409.

16 *Council of Engineering Institutions v Maddison* [1977] I.C.R. 30, *Naqvi v Stephens Jewellers Ltd* [1978] I.C.R. 631 EAT.

17 *Igbo v Johnson Matthey Chemicals Ltd* [1986] I.C.R. 505.

18 *Courage Take Home Ltd v Keys* [1986] I.C.R. 874.

ing out of rights accorded to employees within the Act. By far the two most important of these exceptions are set out at s.203(2)(e) and (2)(f). These provide:

> "(2) Subsection (1)—
>
> ...
>
> (e) does not apply to any agreement to refrain from instituting or continuing proceedings where a conciliation officer has taken action under section 18 of the Employment Tribunals Act 1996; and
>
> (f) does not apply to any agreement to refrain from instituting or continuing proceedings within section 18(1) of the Employment Tribunals Act 1996 if the conditions regulating settlement agreements under this Act are satisfied in relation to the agreement."

The reference to a "conciliation officer" is, of course, a reference to an ACAS conciliation officer. The reference to "the conditions regulating settlement agreements" includes reference to the involvement of "independent advisers" in the making of those agreements as well as a range of other requirements that must be met in order to give rise to a valid and effective settlement agreement within s.203(2)(f) of the ERA 1996. **28-23**

Hence, there can be a valid and effective settlement of various employment related statutory rights, which rights are or can be enforced before an Employment Tribunal, only if the settlement agreement has been made under the auspices of ACAS or with the involvement of an independent adviser acting on behalf of the employee. The particular rights enjoyed under the ERA 1996 that fall within these terms are: **28-24**

(1) the right to an itemised pay statement per s.8 of the ERA 1996;
(2) the right not to suffer unauthorised deductions from wages per s.13 of the Act;
(3) the right not to have to make payments to an employer per s.15 of the Act;
(4) the right not to be obliged to be subject to more than the maximum permitted deductions from wages in retail employment per ss.18 and 21 of the Act;
(5) the right to guarantee payments per s.28 of the Act;
(6) the right to parental leave per s.80 of the ERA;
(7) the right to a written statement of reasons for dismissal per s.92 of the Act;
(8) the right to a redundancy payment per s.135 of the Act;
(9) protection from suffering detriment in employment under Pt V of the Act;
(10) the right to time off from work under Pt VI of the Act;
(11) rights in connection with suspension from work under Pt VII of the Act;
(12) the right not to be unfairly dismissed under Pt X of the Act.

Provisions similar to those found in the ERA 1996 apply in regard to the settlement of rights enjoyed under other legislation. These are in particular: **28-25**

(1) the Equality Act 2010;
(2) the National Minimum Wage Act 1998 (s.49 of that Act);
(3) the Working Time Regulations 1998[19] (reg.35);
(4) the Transnational Information and Consultation of Employees Regulations 1999[20] (reg.41);

[19] Working Time Regulations 1998 (SI 1998/1833).
[20] Transnational Information and Consultation of Employees Regulations 1999 (SI 1999/3323).

(5) the Part-Time Workers (Prevention of Less Favourable Treatment) Regulations 2000[21] (reg.9);
(6) ss.10–13 of the Employment Relations Act 1999 which are concerned with rights associated with the right to be accompanied at a disciplinary or grievance hearing. These sections are to be treated as provisions within Pt 5 of the ERA 1996 for the purposes of s.203;
(7) the Fixed-Term Employees (Prevention of Less Favourable Treatment) Regulations 2002[22];
(8) the Employment Equality (Sexual Orientation) Regulations 2003[23];
(9) the Employment Equality (Religion or Belief) Regulations 2003[24];
(10) the Merchant Shipping (Working Time: Inland Waterways) Regulations 2003[25];
(11) the European Public Limited Liability Company Regulations 2004[26];
(12) complaints under the Fishing Vessels (Working Time: Sea-fishermen) Regulations 2004 (see reg.20);
(13) complaints under the Information and Consultation of Employees Regulations 2004 (see reg.40);
(14) complaints under the Transfer of Undertakings (Protection of Employment) Regulations 2006 (see reg.18) (as to which the only method of effective settlement is through the involvement of an ACAS officer; the "compromise agreement" method, involving an "independent adviser" does not apply);
(15) complaints under the Employment Equality (Age) Regulations 2006 (see Sch.5 para.2(b));
(16) complaints under the Occupational and Personal Pension Schemes (Consultation by Employers and Miscellaneous Amendment) Regulations 2006 (see Sch. para.12(3));
(17) complaints under the European Co-operative Society (Involvement of Employees) Regulations 2006 (see reg.41(3));
(18) complaints under the Companies (Cross-Border Mergers) Regulations 2007 (see reg.62);
(19) complaints under the Cross-Border Railway Services (Working Time) Regulations 2008 (see reg.18(2)(b));
(20) complaints under the European Public Limited-Liability Company (Employee Involvement) (Great Britain) Regulations 2009;
(21) complaints under the Agency Workers Regulations 2010 (reg.18);
(22) complaints under the Employee Study and Training (Procedural Requirements) Regulations 2010 (reg.17);
(23) complaints under the Employment Relations Act 1999 (Blacklists) Regulations 2010 (regs 5, 6 or 9);
(24) the Exclusivity Terms in Zero Hours Contracts (Redress) Regulations 2015;

---

21 Part-Time Workers (Prevention of Less Favourable Treatment) Regulations (SI 2000/1551).
22 Fixed-Term Employees (Prevention of Less Favourable Treatment) Regulations 2002 (SI 2002/2034).
23 Employment Equality (Sexual Orientation) Regulations 2003 (SI 2003/1661).
24 Employment Equality (Religion or Belief) Regulations 2003 (SI 2003/1660).
25 Merchant Shipping (Working Time: Inland Waterways) Regulations 2003 (SI 2003/3049).
26 European Public Limited Liability Company Regulations 2004 (SI 2004/2326).

(25) the Posted Workers (Enforcement of Employment Rights) Regulations 2016.

Likewise a number of rights accorded by the Trade Union and Labour Relations (Consolidation) Act 1992 (TULRCA 1992) are subject to the same scheme whereby settlement agreements are rendered void unless made through the officers of ACAS or with the involvement of an independent adviser on behalf of the employee.[27] Those rights under TULRCA 1992 are: **28-26**

(1) the right of trade union members not to be unjustifiably disciplined or suffer unauthorised or excessive deductions from subscriptions, per ss.64, 68 and 86;
(2) the rights in regard to union membership and activities set out at ss.137, 138, 146, 168–170 and 164, being rights not to suffer detriment in relation to union membership or expulsion or exclusion from a union and rights in connection with time off for trade union duties and activities;
(3) rights in connection with the recognition of unions within s.70(B) and para.156 of Sch.A1.

In addition, there can be an effective settlement of rights in connection with consultation with employers' representatives (see ss.188 and 190 of TULRCA 1992) through an ACAS-conciliated agreement, but not through a settlement agreement effected with the involvement of an independent adviser.[28] **28-27**

So far in this chapter only the general scheme that applies to the settlement of both potential and actual statutory claims has been described. The details relating to agreements achieved both with the assistance of ACAS conciliation officers and through the involvement of independent advisers will now be addressed. **28-28**

SETTLEMENT ACHIEVED THROUGH INTERVENTION OF CONCILIATION OFFICER

Under what was s.18(2) of the Employment Tribunals Act 1996 and is now s.18C of that Act[29] it is the duty of a conciliation officer, where he has been invited to act, or where he decides that he should act, "to endeavour to promote a settlement" and to do so with the aim of bringing the proceedings or potential proceedings to an end through that settlement without the complaint being determined by an Employment Tribunal.[30] When an agreement has been achieved through the intervention of a conciliation officer, the usual procedure is for the conciliation officer to record the terms on what is known as Form COT3, a document that each of the parties or his representative[31] is asked to sign before onward transmission to the Employment **28-29**

---

27 TULRCA 1992 s.288.

28 TULRCA 1992 s.288(2c). Similar restrictions in regard to the scope of a valid settlement agreement in connection with the provisions in TUPE relating to providing information and holding consultations in regard to a transfer are dealt with at para.28-38.

29 See also ETA 1996 s.18(1) in relation to the matters in respect of which employment tribunal proceedings can be brought which fall within s.18. Section 18C was introduced by the Enterprise and Regulatory Reform Act 2013.

30 The meaning of this expression and the scope of a Conciliation Officer's duties in this regard were considered by the House of Lords in *Moore v Duport Furniture Products Ltd* [1982] I.C.R. 84. See also *Hennessey v Craigmyle & Co Ltd* [1996] I.C.R. 461 CA.

31 The signature of a representative will bind the party upon whose behalf it is purportedly written provided the representative has ostensible authority to act: *Freeman v Sovereign Chicken Ltd* [1991]

Tribunal. Consistent with ordinary principles,[32] the reduction of the agreement to writing is not essential to its enforceability unless, of course, it is a condition of the agreement that a form of document such as form COT3 is executed.[33] As has been referred to above, the concept of "early conciliation", i.e. mandatory consideration of conciliation before any proceedings have been lodged, has been introduced into the law.The details of those provisions are dealt with below. However, those new provisions do not affect the continuing duties of ACAS and its Conciliation Officers in terms of seeking to promote settlements if proceedings are in fact lodged despite the provisions as to early conciliation. Reference should also be made to the fact that discussions involving ACAS in connection with proceedings or potential proceedings are confidential and may not be referred to in a court or tribunal.

28-30 A settlement achieved through the medium of a conciliation officer is extremely difficult to challenge subsequently. This is particularly so where the challenge is based on the supposed failure of the ACAS officer to comply with the duties and parameters of his or her functions set out in the statutory provisions relating to the involvement of ACAS officers in settlements.[34] It would probably require evidence that the conciliation officer acted in bad faith or adopted unfair methods in seeking to achieve a settlement before consideration would be given to setting aside the agreement.[35] However, as is dealt with at para.28-47, it appears that ACAS settlements (and settlement agreements involving independent advisers) can be challenged on the standard common law bases such as duress. It should be noted that, unlike the situation which had obtained prior to the passing of s.39 of the Trade Union Reform and Employment Rights Act 1993,[36] a conciliation officer will not simply "nod through" an agreement already concluded between the parties. His or her active involvement[37] in promoting the agreement is required for an agreement to be regarded as one made through his or her intervention and thus binding by virtue of s.203(2)(e) of the ERA 1996. An agreement entered into other than with the active intervention of the conciliation officer will need to fulfil the statutory requirements of a "settlement agreement" for it to be binding. Indeed, it was because of ACAS's refusal to "nod through" agreements reached between the parties that the alternative method of settling disputes through the involvement of an independent adviser was introduced.

28-31 As has already been noted, conciliation officers may be called upon to assist in connection with a wide range of disputes. Not infrequently a settlement of proceedings is achieved through the intervention of a conciliation officer and a payment is made by the employer said expressly to be,

> "in full and final settlement of all claims which [the employee] has or may have against [the employer] arising from [his/her] employment or out of its termination".

However, those drafting COT3 agreements should be wary about using this once

---

I.C.R. 853, where the signature of a representative of the Citizens Advice Bureau was held by the Employment Appeal Tribunal to bind the party on whose behalf it was written. However, in *Gloystarne & Co Ltd v Martin* [2001] I.R.L.R. 15, the trade union representative was found to lack ostensible authority to conclude a settlement agreement on behalf of the employee through ACAS.

32 See Ch.3.

33 *Gilbert v Kembridge Fibres Ltd* [1984] I.C.R. 188, *Gloystarne & Co Ltd v Martin* [2001] I.R.L.R. 15.

34 See, for example, *Moore v Du Pont Furniture Products Ltd* [1982] I.C.R. 84, *Slack v Greenham (Plant Hire) Ltd* [1983] IC 617 and *Clarke v Redcar and Cleveland BC* [2006] I.C.R. 897.

35 *Slack* [1983] I.C.R. 617.

36 This section of the Act became operative on 30 August 1993.

37 ERA 1996 s.203(2)(e) refers to an agreement concluded after the conciliation officer has "taken action" under s.18 of the Employment Tribunals Act 1996.

commonplace formulation. The Employment Appeal Tribunal has held[38] that the use of such a formula in an unfair dismissal case will not operate to prevent the pursuit of claims which otherwise might be settled through the intervention of a conciliation officer. The use of such words will be confined to "those matters which are within [the parties'] presumed intention at the time". On that basis it would seem, therefore, that express reference to the other possible claims for relief would need to be made in any such formulation to achieve also a final resolution of those matters in addition to the issue to which the actual or potential claim relates such as unfair dismissal.

The role of ACAS officers was extended by regs 22–24 of Sch.1 to the Employment Tribunals (Constitution and Rules of Procedure) Regulations 2004.[39] In essence these provisions imposed a compulsory period of conciliation through ACAS before there could be a substantive hearing of a relevant claim presented to an employment tribunal. A relevant claim was any claim in which ACAS would otherwise have authority to seek to effect conciliation other than a claim for discrimination (including a claim in connection with the protected disclosure provisions) or a claim for national security proceedings. Relevant claims either fell within the category of claims to which the "standard period" of imposed conciliation applied (i.e. 13 weeks) or within those to which the shortened period applied (i.e. seven weeks). Provisions existed which allowed for the extension or abbreviation of those periods and, indeed, for the removal of the compulsory period of conciliation. Those provisions were repealed with effect from 6 April 2009.[40] However, as dealt with at paras 28-52 to 28-55, new provisions came into effect on 6 April 2013 which, in general terms, require the involvement of ACAS in terms of seeking to achieve a settlement before any claim has been presented to the Employment Tribunal. However, before examining those recent changes, the traditional scheme relating to the settlement of statutory claims will be examined. **28-32**

SETTLEMENT AGREEMENTS

For an agreement between the parties settling statutory claims, achieved other than through the intervention of a conciliation officer, to be binding, it must satisfy the conditions that regulate the form and content of a "settlement agreement". Section 203(3) of the ERA 1996 provides that: **28-33**

"(a) the agreement must be in writing;
(b) the agreement must relate to the particular complaint;
(c) the employee must have received advice from a relevant independent adviser as to the terms and effect of the proposed agreement and in particular its effect on his ability to pursue his rights before an employment tribunal;
(d) there must be in force, when the adviser gives the advice, a policy of insurance covering the risk of a claim by the employee in respect of loss arising in consequence of the advice;
(e) the agreement must identify the adviser; and
(f) the agreement must state that the conditions regulating settlement agreements under the Act are satisfied."

As already made clear, similar provisions apply to settling claims through the **28-34**

---

[38] *Livingstone v Hepworth Refractories Ltd* [1992] I.C.R. 287. This case might have to be looked at afresh in the light of *Ali* [2002] 1 A.C. 251. See paras 28-05–28-06.

[39] Employment Tribunals (Constitution and Rules of Procedure) Regulations 2004 (SI 2004/2351).

[40] SI 2008/3240.

involvement of an independent adviser under a wide range of other legislation such as the Equality Act 2010. In regard to each type of claim settled through the involvement of an independent adviser, it is vital that the settlement agreement stipulates that the conditions relating to each relevant enactment have been satisfied. A number of further matters need to be discussed in regard to these statutory settlement agreements or contracts.

Independent advisers

28-35 Originally the requirement was that the employee be assisted by a legal adviser (a solicitor or barrister). However, the definition of relevant advisers has been extended (and can be further extended by order of the Secretary of State).

"Independent advisers" currently comprise:

(1) qualified lawyers (which includes certain legal executives);
(2) representatives of trade unions who have been certified to be competent to give advice;
(3) advisers who work for an advice centre so long as that advice is provided without charge and they have been certified as competent to give advice.

28-36 As to the expression "qualified lawyers", anyone acting for the employer or an associated employer involved in the matter in dispute does not constitute an "independent" adviser. Similarly, representatives of trade unions and advisers from advice centres are not "independent" if the trade union or advice centre is the employer or an associated employer of the employee.

The particular complaint or proceedings

28-37 The legislation confines the scope of effective "settlement agreements" to the settlement of the particular "complaint" or "proceedings". The intention behind this restriction is to ensure that settlement agreements cannot be used effectively to constitute a blanket "full and final settlement" of all claims that an employee "has or might have" against an employer. The involvement of an independent adviser can only render effective settlement agreements which seek to settle the specific dispute or disputes raised between employee and employer. However, if a number of disputes exist between an employee and an employer, each can be settled in the single settlement agreement provided the proper formulation is used in connection with each claim. There is no need for separate agreements in relation to each.[41] The confinement of a "settlement agreement" to the particular complaint or proceedings involved means that such an agreement is more limited in its scope than an agreement effected through an ACAS conciliation officer. It should be emphasised that the specific claims settled must be identified in the agreement. The points of contrast referred to in this Chapter between settlements achieved under the auspices of ACAS and settlement agreements involving independent advisers

---

[41] See *Lunt v Merseyside TEC Ltd* [1999] I.C.R. 17. The nature of the requirements for a valid compromise agreement was considered by an employment tribunal in Scotland in *McWilliam and Others v Glasgow City Council* S/135430/2007. The employment tribunal, chaired by the Vice-President of Scottish Employment Tribunals, held that the adviser need only explain what the terms of the agreement are and what they mean; there was no duty to advise on the merits of the agreement. The employment tribunal also held that the claims settled did not have to have been presented to the employment tribunal and that the solicitors used as independent advisers were sufficiently independent notwithstanding the fact that their fees had been paid by Glasgow City Council. The Employment Tribunal's decision was upheld by the EAT see UKEATS/0036/10.

reveal how much more flexible and broad is the scope of ACAS settlements. For this reason, in addition to the benefit parties can obtain through the involvement of ACAS Officers, there is much to commend the use of the ACAS method of settlement when parties wish to settle statutory claims.

STATUTORY SETTLEMENT AGREEMENTS, ACAS CONCILIATION AND CONTINUITY OF EMPLOYMENT

In a number of circumstances where an employee has been dismissed but has been reinstated or re-engaged by his or her employer, continuity of employment is preserved. These circumstances include those where an employee who has alleged unfair dismissal or sex or race discrimination is re-employed after the intervention of an ACAS conciliation officer or after the making of a settlement agreement through the involvement of an independent adviser. The full provisions are set out in the Employment Protection (Continuity of Employment) Regulations 1996.[42] **28-38**

TRANSFER OF UNDERTAKINGS (PROTECTION OF EMPLOYMENT) REGULATIONS 2006 (TUPE)

The 2006 Regulations replaced the TUPE Regulations of 1981. TUPE govern the rights and duties of employees where the undertaking in which they work is transferred as a going concern to another undertaking (the transferee) or responsibility for performing services which the employees had provided for a transferor are transferred to be performed by the potential transferee. Regulation 4 of TUPE has the effect of transferring automatically those employees who worked in the entity transferred on their existing terms and conditions to the transferee. TUPE also makes provision in respect of such matters as dismissals in connection with transfers and the provision of information to workers' representatives. TUPE provides that the parties are not able to contract out of its protections.[43] There is authority,[44] based both on the EC Directive on which TUPE are based and under TUPE, that the prohibition against contracting out demands that agreements with employees entered into as a result of, or in connection with, a transfer which alters those employees' rights are void and ineffective. This has important implications. Thus, a transferee employer, and staff automatically transferred to it as a result of TUPE, cannot enter into a binding and effective agreement to vary the transferred employees' terms and conditions if a reason for that agreement is the existence of the transfer, unless that is as a result of an "economic, technical or organisational reason entailing changes in the workforce". However, the EAT has held in *Solectron Scotland Ltd v Roper*[45]: **28-39**

> "[T]hat this principle does not apply to a compromise agreement entered into after the employment has ended which settles a financial claim of transferred ex-employees that arose at the end of the employment. This is because the compromise agreement cannot

---

[42] Employment Protection (Continuity of Employment) Regulations 1996 (SI 1996/3147).

[43] See TUPE reg.18.

[44] *Foreningen of Arbeijdslederei Danmark v Daddy's Dance Hall AS* [1988] E.C.R. 739; [1988] I.R.L.R. 315, *Credit Suisse First Boston (Europe) Ltd v Lister* [1998] I.R.L.R. 700.

[45] *Solectron Scotland Ltd v Roper* [2004] I.R.L.R. 4.

be said to have arisen out of the transfer and the agreement did not purport to alter terms and conditions of employment because the employment had terminated. As a result, the compromise is in principle capable of being valid even though it compromised a claim which related to a transferred right to enhanced redundancy payments."

28-40 TUPE is anomalous in that, apart from regs 11–16A (which concern the provision of information and consultation), neither TUPE nor legislation such as the ERA 1996 nor the Employment Tribunals Act 1996, nor indeed the enactments dealing with discrimination, contain any provision extending the provisions relating to ACAS agreements or settlement agreements to TUPE. This may well reflect the fact that, in general, the claims of employees who come within TUPE will be made either against the transferor or the transferee based upon the substantive rights provided by other legislation—for example, the right not to be unfairly dismissed or the right not to be discriminated against on grounds of sex, race or disability.

28-41 The exception to the above concerns regs 11–16A of TUPE, which create a distinct cause of action justiciable in an Employment Tribunal. Regulations 13 and 14 deal with the right of representatives of affected staff to be kept informed (and, in some circumstances, consulted) about the effect of a transfer of an undertaking and reg.11 concerns the provision of information by the transferor to the transferee. Regulations 12 and 16 permit disputes relating to claims under regs 11, 13 and 14 to be resolved by a conciliation officer from ACAS. No provision exists, however, which allows effective settlement agreements of these claims through the involvement of "independent advisers". In this respect TUPE mirrors the provisions that relate to ss.188 and 190 of TULRCA 1992, discussed at para.28-27.

28-42 In regard to the remainder of TUPE, as already noted, there are no express provisions dealing with the settlement of claims of employees who fall within TUPE. As already indicated, this may be because any statutory claims such employees make will be through other substantive legislation (such as the ERA 1996). Nevertheless, it is surprising that the (potentially complex) relationship between TUPE and settlement agreements (both at common law and under the statutory provisions) has given rise to such little litigation.[46] In the absence of case law, it is suggested that tribunals and courts may well adopt the following approach:

(1) Where employees who are embraced within the provisions of TUPE institute statutory claims (for example, for unfair dismissal) which fall within the existing structure of the resolution of such claims through ACAS or settlement agreements, then the statutory provisions which permit ACAS settlements or settlement agreements through independent advisers of those claims will apply.

(2) Where employees who are embraced within TUPE seek to compromise common law claims against their employers then, for so long as the reason for that compromise agreement is not connected with the transfer, the compromise will be an effective common law compromise.

(3) Where employees who are embraced within TUPE purport to compromise common law claims against their employers, and those claims and the

[46] An exception to this lack of case law is the case of *Thompson v Walon Car Delivery* [1997] I.R.L.R. 343. The case concerned an ACAS agreement entered into between the transferor and the employees, but not with the transferee. The agreement was not concluded until after the transfer. It was held that the benefit did not transfer to the transferee of the undertaking.

compromise agreement arise as a result of, or for a reason connected with, the transfer, the purported compromise will be void.

MECHANICS OF SETTLEMENT IN EMPLOYMENT TRIBUNALS

A settlement achieved through the intervention of a conciliation officer is, as previously indicated, usually embodied in Form COT3, although this is not a requirement of a valid ACAS agreement: indeed, the same can be oral. "Settlement agreements" in contrast must be reduced to writing. Any agreement of this nature would have its own contractual status and could, without more, be enforced as such. Where there are extant proceedings before an Employment Tribunal, or where the settlement is not achieved until the parties are "at the doors of the tribunal", some form of consent order may be considered appropriate, often involving the dismissal of the claims by the Employment Tribunal. **28-43**

The consent order may consist of a simple dismissal of the complaint, the applicant having agreed to withdraw upon terms agreed.[47] If that course is adopted, the terms of settlement will have a simple contractual status and will be susceptible to enforcement only by the bringing of a fresh action in the civil courts. Another possibility is the imposition of a "stay" on the proceedings.[48] This would also, without more, mean that the terms of settlement would fall to be enforced by a fresh action in the civil courts. **28-44**

Where an applicant is prepared to allow his claim to be adjourned to enable the respondent to comply with the terms of an agreement, an appropriate order to that effect can be made.[49] **28-45**

It is always open to the parties, of course, to agree a consent order to the effect that the former employer should pay an agreed sum by way of compensation. However, the disadvantage of this course from the claimant's point of view is that it will almost certainly activate the recoupment provisions concerning certain benefits received,[50] provisions which will not come into play if a settlement not involving an order for payment (a "monetary award") is concluded. **28-46**

SETTING ASIDE AN AGREED SETTLEMENT

As observed previously at para.28-30, it is difficult to set aside an agreement entered into pursuant to the intervention of a conciliation officer on the basis of his or her supposed failure to comply with his or her statutory duties or the ambit of his or her statutory functions. This proposition is largely derived from the obstacles that exist in the path of suggesting that such an officer exceeded his duties or car- **28-47**

---

47 A decision by an employment tribunal to dismiss an originating application on withdrawal gives rise to the application of the principles of cause of action estoppel: see *Barber v Staffordshire CC* [1996] I.C.R. 379.

48 Whilst there is no specific reference to a power to order a stay in the Employment Tribunals (Constitution and Rules of Procedure) Regulations 1993 (SI 1993/2687) r.13(1) provides employment tribunals with the ability to administer wide powers including, it is submitted, the imposition of a "stay".

49 cf. *The Milestone School of English Ltd v Leakey* [1982] I.R.L.R. 3 EAT.

50 Employment Protection (Recoupment of Jobseekers' Allowance and Income Support) Regulations 1996 (SI 1996/2349).

ried them out improperly. However, as already mentioned, there would seem to be no reason in principle why an agreement thus concluded (or, of course, a settlement agreement involving an independent adviser) could not be set aside if any of the usual invalidating grounds for a contract[51] could be established as between the parties to the agreement. Indeed this is recognised implicitly in the decision of the Court of Appeal in *Hennessey v Craigmyle & Co Ltd*[52] where an allegation that the agreement was concluded following "economic duress" was entertained, albeit rejected.[53] Naturally, the same principle would apply to compromise agreements relating to contractual and common law claims which fall outside the statutory provisions. Further, where a contracting party (in practice the employer or ex-employer) is a statutory body, any settlement must be made intra vires. An irrationally generous settlement agreement, or one which was based on the consideration of irrelevant or improper matters, could, in principle, be ultra vires and void[54] although the Court of Appeal, in allowing the appeal of the claimant (Ms Gibb), held that the settlement agreement in that case did not stand to be set aside on either of the above bases.

SETTING ASIDE A CONSENT ORDER

28-48 It has been said[55] that in order to justify the setting aside of a consent order, whether made by an employment tribunal or by the Employment Appeal Tribunal, it is necessary to set aside the underlying agreement and that, accordingly, since the Employment Appeal Tribunal has no jurisdiction to do that, it has no jurisdiction to set aside a consent order made pursuant to that agreement. However, there can be little doubt that it would be open to a party to seek to challenge a consent order made either by an employment tribunal or by an Employment Appeal Tribunal by instituting a fresh action for the purpose.[56] This is the normal course to adopt in relation to a consent order designed to dispose finally of a case, and there would seem to be no reason why such a course should not be available.

28-49 An employment tribunal and the Employment Appeal Tribunal each possesses

---

51 See Ch.4.

52 *Hennessey v Craigmyle & Co Ltd* [1986] I.C.R. 461. In the EAT judgment in *Hennessey*, it was specifically held that an agreement within s.140 of the Employment Protection (Consolidation) Act 1978 could be avoided on all the grounds available at common law: see [1995] I.C.R. 879.

53 Insofar as the decision of the Employment Appeal Tribunal in *Larkfield of Chepstow Ltd v Milne* [1988] I.C.R. 1 at 7 tentatively suggests the contrary, it is respectfully submitted that it is wrong. It does appear that the passage in the judgment was more directed to the question of whether the Employment Appeal Tribunal had the jurisdiction (in the narrow sense of the term) to entertain an appeal designed to secure the setting-aside of a concluded settlement rather than to the broader issue of whether, if established in the appropriate forum (see below), the usual invalidating grounds could afford a reason for setting aside such an agreement. Indeed the EAT has confirmed in the case of *Industrious Ltd v Vincent* [2009] UKEAT 1478109 that the approach in *Hennessy* [1986] I.C.R. 461 is correct and should be followed rather than the approach in *Larkfield of Chepstow Ltd v Milne*.

54 *Gibb v Maidstone & Tunbridge Wells NHS Trust* [2010] EWCA Civ 678 where it was recognised that a public body "... in entering into a contractual obligation to make payments to an employee or ex-employee ... is constrained by a general duty arising in public law not to enter into undertakings which may be described as 'irrationally generous'." Laws LJ at [4] said that the expression "irrationally generous" was "a term of art, since the reference to irrationality is to unreasonableness in the *Wednesbury* ... sense—a decision so unreasonable that no reasonable decision-maker could have arrived at it."

55 *Times Newspapers Ltd v Fitt* [1981] I.C.R. 637 at 642. The decision rested partly upon *Eden v Humphries & Glasgow Ltd* [1981] I.C.R. 183 which is discussed at paras 28-49 and 28-50.

56 This is effectively what the EAT invited the appellant in *Eden* [1981] I.C.R. 183, to do if he wished to pursue the matter further.

jurisdiction under the rules applicable to them to review and revoke any decision or order if "the interests of justice" require such a review.[57] In the absence of authority to the contrary, these words would seem to confer a wide discretionary jurisdiction to intervene and revoke or vary a consent order in appropriate circumstances. One such circumstance, it is submitted, would be where the consent to the making of the order is shown to have been invalidated. In *Larkfield of Chepstow Ltd v Milne*,[58] the Employment Appeal Tribunal appeared to confirm that an employment tribunal does have power under the relevant rule to review a consent order staying proceedings following a settlement, although in the particular case it held that the employment tribunal was wrong to have set aside the order.[59] In *Eden v Humphries & Glasgow Ltd*,[60] however, whilst apparently entertaining an application under the equivalent rule dealing with its own proceedings to review a consent order giving leave for an appeal to be withdrawn, the Employment Appeal Tribunal declined to say that the interests of justice required a review of the order since its jurisdiction did not extend to setting aside the agreement underlying that order.[61]

Neither of these two decisions is, with respect, very satisfactory, a situation possibly contributed to by the fact that there may not have been the fullest argument on what are, it is submitted, important issues. However, insofar as the jurisdiction of an employment tribunal to review a consent order is confirmed by *Larkfield*, it is submitted that the case is correct. Insofar as the Employment Appeal Tribunal in *Eden* said that it did not have jurisdiction to review one of its own consent orders, it is submitted that, with respect, it was fettering its own powers unnecessarily. Each of the rules relating to the powers to review would, it is submitted, afford a satisfactory alternative to the institution of a fresh action. **28-50**

THE REFORMS AND CHANGES OF 2013 AND 2014

It is now appropriate to provide an account of the substantive changes to the law which have been introduced in 2013 and 2014 which were alluded to at para.28-18, although there will be no further analysis herein in regard to the introduction of fees for bringing claims in the Employment Tribunal because that system of fees no longer applies. Some of these are directly related to the settlement of statutory **28-51**

---

57 Employment Tribunals (Constitution and Rules of Procedure) Regulations 1993 (SI 1993/2687) r.11, and Employment Appeal Tribunal Rules 1993 (SI 1993/2854) r.33, respectively.

58 *Larkfield* [1988] I.C.R. 1.

59 The circumstances of the case were very unusual. At the conclusion of the hearing on whether the dismissals had been unfair the employment tribunal reserved its decision, but encouraged the parties to consider the possibility of settlement. As a result they did agree, following the conciliation procedure, on effectively a 50:50 basis, and a consent order staying the proceedings was made. Some while later the employment tribunal contacted the parties and indicated that prior to reserving its decision it had already reached a unanimous decision in favour of the applicants. The applicants were, in effect, invited by the tribunal to apply for a review under what was then r.10(1)(e) of the 1985 Procedural Regulations. When they did so the tribunal removed the stay and directed that the issue of compensation be dealt with by a different tribunal. The Employment Appeal Tribunal drew a clear distinction between the agreement (which was reflected in Form COT3) and the order, but did acknowledge that if the agreement could be attacked (e.g. on the basis of a mistake or misrepresentation) then the consent order could also be attacked. The judgment, however, seemed to be based at least partly on the question of whether the Employment Appeal Tribunal itself could set aside the agreement. Plainly, it could not do that, but the essential question (which was not very clearly addressed) was whether the employment tribunal had the power to set aside the order if satisfied that the agreement was invalidated for some reason.

60 *Eden* [1981] I.C.R. 183.

61 *Eden* [1981] I.C.R. 183 at 186.

claims and others are less directly so but are likely to have a significant effect in terms of encouraging settlement of such claims. The new provisions fall within the following categories:

(1) the introduction of conciliation before the institution of any proceedings in the Employment Tribunals ("Early Conciliation" or "EC");
(2) the (limited) protection of confidentiality of discussions between employer and employee relating to attempts to agree terms as to the termination of an existing contract of employment;
(3) the introduction of the system of "employee-shareholders" where employees can waive their rights to bring certain claims in exchange for a shareholding in their employing company.

Each of the above will be considered in turn.

(1) Early Conciliation ("EC")

28-52 Sections 7–9 of the Enterprise and Regulatory Reform Act 2013 introduced a compulsory system of EC, i.e. consideration of conciliation before any claim within the scope of s.18(1) of the ETA 1996 can be lodged before an Employment Tribunal.[62] In particular, s.7 has inserted new ss.18A and 18B into the ETA 1996. Section 8 of the 2013 Act makes consequential amendments to the running of time limits for instituting claims in the Employment Tribunal (effectively "stopping the clock" during the early conciliation period). Section 9 extends the powers of the Secretary of State and Lord Chancellor to amend the list of claims to which s.18A of the ETA applies. The system of EC came into effect on April 6, 2014 but only became mandatory in regard to claims presented to Employment Tribunals from 6 May 2014.

28-53 The effect of the new s.18A inserted into the ETA 1996 is the following.

28-54 A potential claimant in the Employment Tribunal is obliged to contact ACAS giving his or her name and contact details, and the same information as to each of the potential respondent(s). Once these details have been received ACAS is to contact the offices of the Employment Tribunal to give notice of the above. ACAS will also appoint a Conciliation Officer who will liaise with the potential claimant in regard to the issue of engaging in conciliation. A potential claimant has the right to inform the Conciliation Officer that he or she refuses to participate in conciliation. In that event the Conciliation Officer will issue "an early conciliation certificate", the effects of which are set out below. However, if that is not the case, the Conciliation Officer will seek to promote a settlement between potential claimant and potential respondent of the potential claim. If those attempts are successful then, naturally, the claim will not proceed and a COT3 ACAS agreement will be entered into between the parties. Naturally, the rules that relate to the conditions that must be met for a settlement of statutory claims that would have been heard in the Employment Tribunal will apply to any such settlement even though that settlement is achieved before any proceedings have been presented.

28-55 If, however, the Conciliation Officer decides that no settlement can be reached, or if no settlement is reached within the statutory period (one month with a potentially agreed two-week extension), then the Conciliation Officer will again issue "an early conciliation certificate" to that effect. On receipt of that certificate by

---

[62] These provisions are subject to detailed rules set out in the Employment Tribunals (Early Conciliation: Exceptions and Rules of Procedure) Regulations 2014 (SI 2014/254) and the Early Conciliation Rules of Procedure are set out in Sch.1 of those Regulations.

the potential claimant, or on the earlier receipt of such a certificate where the potential claimant has informed ACAS that he or she does not wish to pursue conciliation at all, the potential claimant will be allowed to bring a claim. However, subject to very limited exceptions, a claimant can only bring a claim in the Employment Tribunal in regard to any cause of action which falls within s.18(1) of the ETA 1996 if he or she has received an early conciliation certificate.[63] As has been indicated above, if proceedings are instituted, ACAS will continue to seek to achieve a settlement of the claim.

(2) The Limited Protection of Confidentiality

Section 14 of the Enterprise and Regulatory Reform Act 2013 introduced, with effect from 29 July 2013, a scheme whereby communications between employers and employees concerning the potentially agreed termination of an existing contract of employment cannot be referred to in legal proceedings. It did so by the insertion of s.111A into the ERA 1996. Those potential communications are referred to as "confidential pre-termination negotiations". That protection of confidentiality applies even if there is no existing dispute and, therefore, even where there can be no protection of confidentiality as a result of the "without prejudice" privilege.[64] **28-56**

However, the limitations that apply to "confidential pre-termination negotiations" are very significant. The protections only apply in regard to claims for unfair dismissal within s.111 of the ERA 1999, i.e. those protections do not apply to claims that a dismissal was automatically unfair. Further, the protection does not apply to any other claims than unfair dismissal and, therefore, by way of example only, does not apply to any claim for discrimination, wrongful dismissal or the like. **28-57**

What is more, the protection is lost to the extent which an Employment Tribunal deems "reasonable" even in regard to claims for unfair dismissal under s.111 of the ERA 1996 as against a party who an Employment Tribunal concludes is guilty of "improper conduct" under the relevant regulations in regard to the negotiations relating to the possible termination of the contract of employment. ACAS has issued a Code under s.199 of TULRCA 1992 dealing with the scope of "improper conduct". It identifies such behaviour as including harassment, bullying, threats of, or actual, assaults, discrimination and threats to damage the employer's reputation as constituting "improper conduct". It is clear that "improper conduct" has a wider application than the scope of "unambiguous impropriety" which is a standard formulation of when a party can lose the protection of the "without prejudice" privilege as a result of improper conduct if that privilege would otherwise apply.[65] **28-58**

Emphasis has been set out above as to the limitations on the protections offered by the new s.111A of the ERA 1996 inserted by s.14 of the 2013 Act. Further, it is well known that potential claims often mutate in their nature (from, for example, a claim for "ordinary" unfair dismissal to a claim for discrimination or automatically unfair dismissal). The latter fall outside of the scope of the protection of **28-59**

---

[63] The limited exceptions to the requirement to have been issued with an early conciliation certificate as a condition of being able to lodge a claim in the Employment Tribunal are set out at reg.3 of the Employment Tribunal (Early Conciliation) Regulations referred to above and are the following: (1) claims against the intelligence services; (2) claims involving multiple claimants; (3) claims made in the same Claim Form as contains other types of claim to which dismissal; and (5) as a result of new s.18B inserted into the ETA 1996 by s.8 of the 2013 Act, when others, particularly the potential employer, have involved ACAS in early conciliation.

[64] See Ch.19.

[65] See para.19-39 onwards.

confidentiality. As a result, many may well be of the view that often the wisest course will be not to act on the basis of this supposed protection of confidentiality.

The Remaining Reform

28-60 The next matter, and final issue identified at para.28-51, falls outside of the rules directly relating to the conclusion of settlement agreements. However it would be remiss not to make reference to the following in this chapter. The issue relates to "employee-shareholders".

(3) Employee-Shareholders

28-61 On 1 September 2013 the concept of the "employee-shareholder" was introduced into employment law by s.31 of the Growth and Infrastructure Act 2013 through the insertion of s.205A into the ERA 1996. In essence those provisions allow employees to waive their rights to bring certain claims in exchange for shares to a value of between £2,000–£50,000 in their employing company. Such employees can waive their rights to claim for:

(1) unfair dismissal (other than claims for automatically unfair dismissal or claims of unfair dismissal involving a breach of the Equality Act 2010 or claims relating to dismissal where there has been a requirement for the employee's suspension on medical grounds within s.64 of the ERA 1996);
(2) redundancy payments;
(3) flexible working;
(4) time off for training.

In addition employee-shareholders are subject to a duty to provide extended notice of a return date for working when they have been on maternity or paternity or adoption leave. However, it should be emphasised that the waiver agreement in regard to the above rights in exchange for receipt of shares described above is only valid if the employer-shareholder has received advice from an independent adviser as defined in ss.203(3)(c) of the ERA 1996.

28-62 On 22 August 2019 the EAT handed down the first Appellate Court decision on s.205A of the ERA 1996 and employee-shareholder status. That case was *Barrasso v New Look Retailers Ltd*.[66] It concerned whether the entry of the affected individual into a service agreement terminated his previous status as an employee-shareholder. The Employment Tribunal and the EAT held that it did not do so because the service agreement was not inconsistent with the continuation of that employee-shareholder status.

STATUTORY ARBITRATION SCHEME

28-63 On 25 May 2001 a new scheme was introduced in England and Wales for arbitration in claims of unfair dismissal. The scheme was subsequently applied to Scotland. It was also extended with effect from 6 April 2003 to apply to claims relating to flexible working arrangements.[67] Further, the Secretary of State may extend the scheme to other kinds of claim.

---

[66] [2019] 8 WLUK 137.

[67] See TULRCA 1992 s.212A, introduced under the power set out in s.7 of the Employment Rights (Dispute Resolution) Act 1998, and the ACAS Arbitration Scheme (Great Britain) Order 2004 (SI

An agreement to engage in such an arbitration is, of course, an agreement to oust the jurisdiction of the employment tribunal. This is an effective ouster for so long as the arbitration agreement is in writing, and is made either through an ACAS-conciliated agreement or a settlement agreement involving an independent adviser. The parties must agree to a written waiver of rights, including the waiver of the right to return to the employment tribunal in regard to the dispute. ACAS appoints the arbitrator from its panel of arbitrators, although the arbitrator cannot be an ACAS employee. **28-64**

Provision was made in the ACAS Arbitration Scheme (England and Wales) Order 2004[68] to deal with the situation where the parties to a valid arbitration agreement are able to settle their dispute. Paragraphs 31–34 of the Schedule to the Order provide that: **28-65**

> "**31.—** Parties are free to reach an agreement settling their dispute at any stage.
>
> **32.—** If such an agreement is reached:
>
> (i) upon the joint written request of the parties to the arbitrator or the ACAS Arbitration Section, the arbitrator (if appointed) or the ACAS Arbitration Section (if no arbitrator has been appointed) shall terminate the arbitration proceedings;
>
> (ii) if so requested by the parties, the arbitrator (if appointed) may record the settlement in the form of an agreed award (on a covering pro forma).
>
> **33.—** An agreed award shall state that it is an award of the arbitrator by consent and shall have the same status and effect as any other award on the merits of the case.
>
> **34.—** In rendering an agreed award, the arbitrator:
>
> (i) may only record the parties' agreed wording;
>
> (ii) may not approve, vary, transcribe, interpret or ratify a settlement in any way;
>
> (iii) may not record any settlement beyond the scope of the Scheme, the Arbitration Agreement or the reference to the Scheme as initially accepted by ACAS."

The scheme can be seen as representing an attempt to return, in appropriate cases, to the philosophy that underpinned employment tribunals (or, as they were originally called, "industrial tribunals") when first established (i.e. that they were to represent a quick, cheap and informal method of dispensing justice in the context of employment disputes). **28-66**

CONCLUSION

It is clear from the review of the law and practice associated with the resolution by agreement of disputes in the employment setting that the rules surrounding the settlement of statutory rights enforced in employment tribunals are considerably more tightly defined than those that govern the compromise of contractual and other common law claims between employers and employees. That there should be this difference of emphasis is, of course, consistent with the philosophy of the protection of workers that underpins the ever-increasing (and increasingly EC-led) edifice of employees' rights. **28-67**

2004/753) which replaced the original order of 2001 (SI 2001/1185) and the ACAS (Flexible Working) Arbitration Scheme (Great Britain) Order 2004 (SI 2004/2333).

68 ACAS Arbitration Scheme (England and Wales) Order 2004 (SI 2004/753) which replaced the 2001 Order.

PART 11: LANDLORD AND TENANT AND DISPUTES OVER LAND

CHAPTER 29

Landlord and Tenant

Landlord and tenant relationships remain at the root of a wide range of litigation. The parties involved generally have significantly different interests in the property concerned and often have different perceptions of its future. The tenancies involved may be business tenancies or residential tenancies; the law involved may be common law, statute-based or both. The common law principles involved are those related to property, contract and/or equity. 29-01

Many landlord and tenant disputes are resolved by compromise. In some instances the complex statutory intervention complicates the settlement process. In other instances it is necessary to focus upon the exact nature of the landlord and tenant relationship which may result from the compromise and its impact on the rights and obligations of the parties or the rights of third parties. It is also necessary to appreciate that if a compromise involves a disposition of land it must comply with s.2(1) of the Law of Property (Miscellaneous Provisions) Act 1989.[1] 29-02

As indicated above, the two broad areas of landlord and tenant litigation that are subject to differing statutory control are, of course, those involving: 29-03

(a) business tenancies; and
(b) residential tenancies.

BUSINESS TENANCIES

INTRODUCTION

The Landlord and Tenant Act 1954 (the 1954 Act) Pt II, as amended by the Regulatory Reform (Business Tenancies) 2003 Order,[2] provides significant security of tenure for business tenants and, in some instances, compensation in the event that the tenant's security of tenure is lost. The 1954 Act enables a business tenant or landlord to apply to the court for a new tenancy, or the landlord to apply for termination of the existing tenancy following the service of notices by either the landlord or the tenant seeking such determination. It then restricts the circumstances in which a landlord can successfully refuse to grant a new tenancy. Given the commercial background to the premises and their use and the valuable nature of protection under the 1954 Act, it is an area ripe for both dispute and compromise. It follows those entering into such compromises need to understand the 1954 Act, the significance of a tenancy being subject to the provisions of the 1954 Act or not and the mechanisms involved in ensuring the protection of the 1954 Act is excluded if that is the aim. 29-04

---

1 See Ch.30.

2 Regulatory Reform (Business Tenancies) 2003 Order (SI 2003/3096).

Contracting out and surrendering of 1954 Tenancies Act

29-05 Agreements to contract out of the security of tenure provisions (ss.24–28) of the 1954 Act, or to surrender a tenancy that is subject to its provisions, are void save as provided for by the Act, as amended with effect from 1 June 2004. Section 38(A) of the 1954 Act contains the current provisions for effective contracting out and valid surrenders.[3] The relevant part of s.38(A) which relates to tenancies or agreements for tenancies granted on or after 1 June 2004, reads as follows:

"(1) The persons who will be the landlord and the tenant in relation to a tenancy to be granted for a term of years certain which will be a tenancy to which this Part of this Act applies may agree that the provisions of ss.24 to 28 of the Act shall be excluded in relation to that tenancy.
(2) The persons who are the landlord and the tenant in relation to a tenancy to which this Part of this Act applies may agree that the tenancy shall be surrendered on such date or in such circumstances as may be specified in the agreement and on such terms (if any) as may be so specified.
(3) An agreement under subs.(1) above shall be void unless:
 (a) the landlord has served on the tenant a notice in the form or substantially in the form, set out in Sch.1 to the Regulatory Reform (Business Tenancies) (England and Wales) Order 2003; and
 (b) the requirements specified in Sch.2 to that Order are met.
(4) An agreement under subs.(2) above shall be void unless:
 (a) the landlord has served on the tenant a notice in the form or substantially in the form, set out in Sch.3 to the Order 2003; and
 (b) the requirements specified in Sch.4 to that Order are met.
(5) The requirements specified in Sch.2 to that Order are met."

29-06 This provision, like its predecessor, is of considerable commercial importance and is widely invoked. Prior to 1 June 2004 an agreement to contract out was only valid if it was authorised by the court. An application to either the County Court or High Court could be made under s.38(4). An application to the County Court was made by a Pt 8 claim form in which both the landlord and tenant-to-be would be named as applicants. Where the application was made to the High Court it was to be issued in the Chancery Division. This application was also made under Pt 8 of the CPR. Where previously it was common for agreements for leases or their surrender to be entered into conditional upon the parties obtaining the requisite authority from the court under the now repealed s.38(4) but not otherwise,[4] the exclusion of the security of tenure under the Act now lies solely within the parties' control. Despite being of such importance and a purely paper exercise, no doubt the apparently straightforward requirements of the section will be subject to interpretation and errors will be made. This can give rise to a number of unwanted consequences including costly litigation. It is worth noting that the structure and content of the section and the procedure to be adopted will not fit well with a last-minute compromise of litigation that involves the grant of a new tenancy excluded from the protection of the 1954 Act.

29-07 Under the scheme in operation since 1 June 2004, a business tenancy can be granted outside the provisions of the Act provided that certain conditions are complied with. First:

(a) The intended landlord must serve on the intended tenant a notice in writ-

---

[3] The Landlord and Tenant Act 1954 (LTA 1954) s.38(1). Prior to 1 June 2004 the relevant exceptions were contained in s.38(4).

[4] *Essexcrest Ltd v Evenlex Ltd* [1988] 1 E.G.L.R. 69 at 71, per Dillon LJ. For the effect of an agreement "subject to the approval of the court", see para.3–61.

ing 14 days before the tenancy is to start, or before the tenant becomes contractually bound to enter into it, in prescribed form containing a "health warning" to the effect that the proposed tenancy does not enjoy the protection of the 1954 Act. There is a prescribed form of landlord's notice.[5] The notice contains a "health warning" informing the intended tenant clearly that the security of tenure given by the 1954 Act will not apply.

(b) The intended tenant must sign a declaration to the effect that the notice has been served on him, read by him and that he accepts the consequences of the notice. There is a prescribed form of the tenant's simple declaration.[6] This is referred to as a "simple" declaration because the intended tenant simply makes the declaration by signing it and need not formalise it by swearing to it.

(c) If the landlord's notice is served less than 14 days before the grant of the tenancy the tenant may still accept it by confirming receipt, reading and acceptance of the notice including the "health warning", but in this case the statement must be supported by statutory declaration. There is a prescribed form of the tenant's statutory declaration.[7] The tenant is thereby forced into the arms of a solicitor even if only for the purpose of having his declaration sworn. Nothing in the Order or the form of the declaration requires the tenant to seek, or the solicitor to give, advice.

(d) The notice, the declaration or statutory declaration, and the agreement to contract out (or at least a reference to it) have to be endorsed on the instrument creating the tenancy.

A similar structure of pre-conditions is imposed upon the making of an enforceable agreement to surrender a tenancy subject to the 1954 Act regime.

It follows that if a proposed settlement includes the grant of a new tenancy outside the Act, or the surrender of one within it, the settlement must accommodate the giving of the necessary notices and declarations. Where a tenant provides a statutory declaration, and the grant of the tenancy or the agreement for surrender is then delayed so that more than 14 days has passed, the statutory declaration will operate in place of a simple declaration by the tenant, enabling a valid exclusion of the 1954 Act without another declaration being obtained.[8] However, where a statutory declaration is required a simple (non-statutory) declaration will not suffice.[9]

Secondly, the court has jurisdiction to make an order excluding the effect of the 1954 Act only if s.38(A) applies. As with the previous regime, if the tenancy is one in respect of which the statute confers no jurisdiction (e.g. where the proposed tenancy is not for a term of years certain) the effect of the 1954 Act will not be excluded in relation to any tenancy granted on the basis of an agreement made in the mistaken belief that there was jurisdiction to make the order.[10] Even where the parties have proceeded in the belief that the effects of the 1954 Act have been **29-08**

---

5 See the Regulatory Reform (Business Tenancies) (England and Wales) Order 2003 (SI 2003/3096) Sch.1.

6 Regulatory Reform Order 2003 Sch.1.

7 Regulatory Reform Order 2003 Sch.1.

8 *The Chiltern Ry Co Ltd v Patel* [2008] EWCA Civ 178; [2008] Bus L.R. 1295; [2008] 2 P. & C.R. 225.

9 *The Chiltern Ry Co* [2008] 2 P. & C.R. 225.

10 *Nicholls v Kinsey* [1994] Q.B. 600; [1994] W.L.R. 622; [1994] 1 E.G.L.R. 131, *Co-operative Insurance Society v Hastings BC* (1993) 91 L.G.R. 608 and *Newham LBC v Thomas-Van Staden* [2008] EWCA Civ 1414; [2009] 1 E.G.L.R. 21. The same approach was adopted following a failure to serve a notice under s.17 of the Landlord and Tenant (Covenant) Act 1995 when a claim for arrears under

excluded, and so have entered the tenancy on that basis, any tenancy granted will nevertheless attract the protection of the 1954 Act.[11] An agreed tenancy for a fixed term continuing from period to period thereafter, or a tenancy where the term includes a fixed term and any period of holding over under the 1954 Act, is not a tenancy for a term of years certain, and accordingly, cannot be excluded from the protection of the 1954 Act. Parties wishing to agree an initial fixed term followed by a degree of flexibility may be able to achieve that result by agreeing a longer fixed term and a rolling break clause without creating a 1954 Act tenancy.

29-09 In addition, s.38(A)(1)[12] expressly relates to persons "who will be" the landlords and tenants. It follows that only those who are going to enter into to proposed tenancies can rely on that provision: it is not open to parties to tenancies already granted. Thus it should be noted that compliance with the notice regime can be effective to exclude a tenancy from the protection of the 1954 Act only if that compliance *predates* the grant of the tenancy (namely the execution of the lease) itself.[13] Conversely, agreements for the surrender of a tenancy to which the 1954 Act applies may only be made by those who are currently landlords and tenants.[14] They must be made by those who are, at the time of agreement, the landlord and tenant, not by those anticipated or contracted to become landlord and tenant.

29-10 Finally, it is essential that the notice and declaration or statutory declaration and the agreement to contract out or reference to the same be endorsed on the instrument creating the tenancy.[15] It has been said, in relation to the equivalent requirement under the old regime,[16] that this requirement exists "in order that third parties, prospective assignees, or prospective mortgagees of the tenant's interest under a lease" of this nature should know that the provisions of Pt II of the Act have been excluded. Whatever the rationale for the requirement, compliance with it would seem to be a condition precedent to the efficacy of the exclusion of the protection under the 1954 Act in relation to any lease granted pursuant to the parties' agreement and notice procedure. In the normal course of events, a provision will be included in the lease when executed to the effect that the parties have agreed that the provisions of ss.24–28 of the Act are excluded from the tenancy and that the necessary notice and declaration were given on specified dates pursuant to s.38(A).[17]

29-11 The case of *Tottenham Hotspur Football & Athletic Co Ltd v Princegrove Publishers Ltd*,[18] demonstrated the additional dangers under the old regime for those compromising on the basis the grant of a new tenancy.

> In that case C and D compromised proceedings for a new business tenancy brought by D on the basis that a new lease for one year should be granted upon certain agreed terms. One of those terms was that C and D should apply jointly for an order under s.38(4) authorising an agreement excluding the provisions of ss.24–28. The county court judge made a consent order granting D the new tenancy upon the agreed terms and authorising the agreement to be included in the new lease. No formal lease was executed in pursuance of the order but D, pursuant to the agreement and the order, remained in occupation

---

an AGA was held to be validly compromised: see *Lee v Sommer* [2015] EWHC 3889 (Ch).

11 *Newham LBC v Thomas-Van Staden* [2008] EWCA Civ 1414.

12 The provision that enables parties to exclude the operation of the security of tenure provisions in the 1954 Act (ss.24–28).

13 LTA 1954 s.38A and, by analogy, *Essexcrest Ltd v Evenlex Ltd* [1988] 1 E.G.L.R. 69.

14 Such agreements are permitted by LTA 1954 s.38(A)(2).

15 See para.29–05. Sch.2 of the Order requires the agreement, or a reference to the agreement, to be contained in and endorsed upon the instrument creating the tenancy: para.6.

16 *Tottenham Hotspur Football & Athletic Co Ltd v Princegrove Publishers Ltd* [1974] 1 W.L.R. 113; [1974] 1 All E.R. 17; (1974) 27 P. & C.R. 101 at 119, per Lawson J.

17 It will be necessary to draw this with care.

18 *Tottenham Hotspur* [1974] 1 W.L.R. 113.

of the premises and paid rent accordingly. In proceedings for possession brought by C after the expiration of the term provided for in the agreement and order, D sought to argue that the agreement authorised by the order was not valid since it was not contained in or endorsed on the instrument specified in the order, namely the new lease. Lawson J held that since D continued to occupy the premises following the agreement and consent order on the basis of the agreement embodied in that order, they were to be taken as occupying pursuant to an agreement for a lease in accordance with the principle of *Walsh v Lonsdale*.[19] Accordingly, the consent order itself was to be regarded as the "instrument creating the tenancy" and, since the order contained the agreement excluding ss.24–28, the requirements of s.38(4) had been met.

It follows that, since the event necessary for exclusion of the 1954 Act protection was a court order and the consent order both created the tenancy and amounted to compliance with the steps for exclusion, those steps were treated as meeting the requirement to pre-date the grant of the tenancy. Under the new regime the steps required are to be taken by the parties and not the court. If a consent order has the effect of creating a tenancy, and the necessary notice and declaration have not been given prior to the consent order, it appears that the tenancy created will not be excluded from the 1954 Act regardless of any express indication in the consent order that it was to be.

Parties agree upon the grant of a new tenancy or surrender of a current tenancy

Previously, where a tenant's claim for a new tenancy was properly before the court and the parties were agreed on the period and terms of a new tenancy and desired the new tenancy to be outside the provisions of the 1954 Act, then the court could authorise the agreement under s.38(4) and the tenancy would be outside of the Act.[20] Under the new regime for contracting out of the protection of the 1954 Act, the parties have to take the necessary steps themselves and cannot achieve the desired result simply by court order.[21] The parties will normally seek a consent order embodying the agreed terms, although there is no reason why an appropriately drafted Tomlin order[22] might not be utilised. Where the parties are agreed and the necessary notice and declaration have been dealt with, the master or district judge can make the appropriate order depending on whether the proceedings are in the High Court or County Court, and the grant of the tenancy will be complete subject to any requirement to register the lease.[23] In the alternative, the parties may elect to embody their agreement in a Tomlin order that does not amount to the grant of a tenancy but provides a timetabled process for the grant of the tenancy they have agreed will be granted. **29-12**

It follows even more than ever that parties who reach an agreement in principle for the grant of a new tenancy or surrender of an existing one in a business context need to appreciate whether they have in fact concluded a legally binding agreement and, if so, whether all formalities have been undertaken and, if they have not, how to protect their position pending the finalisation of all necessary formalities. **29-13**

---

19 *Walsh v Lonsdale* (1882) 21 Ch. D. 9. See also *Shelley v United Artists Corp Ltd* [1989] 7 WLUK 272; (1990) 60 P. & C.R. 241 and *Stockport MBC v Punj Lloyd Ltd* [2018] EWHC 3776 (Admin); [2019] 1 W.L.R. 2269.

20 LTA 1954 s.29.

21 See para.29–11.

22 See para.9–21 onwards.

23 Land Registration Act 2002 s.4(2)(b) —new leases for a term of more than seven years must be registered.

An appreciation of the nature of the contractual relationship they may or may not be entering is the key to these matters. In the past many landlords and tenants have taken a very relaxed attitude both to the proceedings for the grant of a new tenancy and to their negotiations, often allowing the status quo to drift on for years. That approach can cause problems if one or other changes his mind, third parties acquire rights in the property, one enters into contractual arrangements with third parties that depend on the validity of an agreement between the landlord and tenant, or the court steps in before anything is formalised.

29-14 However, in the absence of express agreement the courts have demonstrated in recent years an increasing reluctance to infer an agreement that creates a new tenancy from the parties' conduct.[24] When invited to draw such inferences the courts have emphasised the need to consider all the surrounding circumstances. Where those circumstances include the fact that any new tenancy inferred to have been agreed and would not be contracted out of the 1954 Act, that fact is relevant. In asking if it is correct to infer that the parties intended to create a new tenancy, the nature of that tenancy and the associated benefits and burdens will be taken into account. That situation occurs most commonly where a tenant holds over after the expiry of an expressly granted and contracted out tenancy.[25]

29-15 Where an agreement is void pursuant to s.38 of the 1954 Act, it is void as between the landlord and tenant or proposed landlord and tenant. However, contractual obligations owed to a third party which may be impossible to perform due to the void tenancy may remain as effective obligations giving rise to liability for their breach. The effect of s.38 is to render void the relevant landlord and tenant agreement, not other related agreements or severable parts of the same agreement. So in *Ultimate Leisure Ltd v Tindle*,[26] where a landlord and tenant together granted a third party an option to purchase the freehold of property free of the tenant's lease, which necessarily required the tenant to surrender, but the preconditions required by s.38A were not met, the agreement to surrender could not be enforced against the tenant. Nevertheless the landlord remained contractually bound to transfer the unencumbered freehold to the purchaser. As that was an obligation the landlord could not fulfil, an order for specific performance could not be obtained. The purchaser's remedies were therefore confined to claims for damages for breach of contract and/or restitution. The fact the landlord was willing, but unable, to fulfil the contract does not relieve the landlord of that liability.

29-16 Given the greater court management of litigation and the drive to bring proceedings to a conclusion within a reasonable period, there is a tension created by the traditional approach to 1954 Act claims for a new tenancy as being more akin to a conveyancing transaction which can have unwanted consequences. Prior to the making of an order for the grant of a new tenancy or the creation of an enforceable contract for the grant of a new lease, a tenant who relaxes simply because there is broad agreement between him and his landlord, and allows his time to commence proceedings to pass, or his proceedings to be struck out for failing to take such steps as the court requires, loses his legal right to a new tenancy altogether. Once agreement has been reached in principle the tenant and his legal advisers need to ensure that the position is secured either by court order or the creation of an enforceable contract as soon as possible. Pending either of those events, it is essential that the tenant takes care to ensure that his ability to commence or continue proceedings is protected.

---

24 *Barclays Wealth Trustees (Jersey) Ltd v Erimus Housing Ltd* [2014] EWCA Civ 303; [2014] 2 P. & C.R. 4 and *Gilpin v Legg* [2017] EWHC 3220 (Ch).

25 *Barclays Wealth Trustees (Jersey) Ltd v Erimus Housing Ltd* [2014] EWCA Civ 303; [2014] 2 P. & C.R. 4.

26 *Ultimate Leisure Ltd v Tindle* [2007] EWCA Civ 1241; [2008] 1 P. & C.R. D28.

In this context it may be important to distinguish between the two types of agreement that the parties may actually have made, namely: 29-17

(i) an agreement for the grant of a new lease; or
(ii) a contract of compromise which compromises proceedings under the Act or any dispute about the tenant's rights under the Act.

The distinction between the two types of agreement is brought into relief by two cases: 29-18

In *Stratton Ltd v Wallis Tomlin & Co*,[27] L1 served on T a notice to terminate the business tenancy between them in accordance with s.25, to which T responded by serving a counter-notice indicating an unwillingness to give up possession at the end of the tenancy. Thereafter solicitors and surveyors instructed by both parties sought to achieve an agreed position. In correspondence in January 1982 the surveyors for both parties agreed the terms "of the new lease which ... will commence on March 26, 1982". In February 1982 a receiver of L1 was appointed and shortly thereafter the premises were conveyed, subject to the residue of the existing lease, to L2. The land upon which the premises were sited was unregistered land and the agreement reached previously had not been registered before the transfer of the reversion to L2. The question arose of whether the agreement constituted an agreement for a new lease and, if so, whether its existence precluded T's application to the court for a new tenancy under the Act. The Court of Appeal held: 29-19

(1) that there was nothing in the correspondence to suggest that the agreement was "subject to the execution of a formal lease" and hence not binding until such a lease had been executed;
(2) that the agreement was a binding agreement for a new lease within s.28; and, accordingly,
(3) T was precluded from invoking the Act.

Furthermore, since the agreement had not been registered, it was not binding on L2. Accordingly the court concluded T's entitlement to a new lease had been concluded by a compromise that was not binding on L2 and T had no other entitlement under the Act.

In *Behar v Territorial Investments Ltd*,[28] T made an application for a new tenancy and proceedings were adjourned pending negotiations. The correspondence showed that the parties were agreed on all the terms, the expression "subject to contract" or "subject to lease" never being used. L sought to resile from the agreement and contended that, even though it was clear that the parties' solicitors intended to short-circuit the problems of going to court and obtaining an order for a new tenancy, he was not bound to execute the lease because it was contemplated during negotiations that the parties would not be bound until formal execution of it had taken place. The Court of Appeal held that L was bound by the agreement: it was a case of trying to compromise pending litigation and not one of a proposed lessor and lessee negotiating for a lease. 29-20

Where the parties' agreement in principle operates purely as an agreement to grant a new lease and does not extend to compromising the proceedings for the 29-21

---

[27] *Stratton Ltd v Wallis Tomlin & Co* [1986] 1 E.G.L.R. 104. In *Derby & Co Ltd v ITC Pension Trust Ltd* [1977] 2 All E.R. 890; [1978] 1 E.G.L.R. 38, T applied to the court for the grant of a new tenancy under the 1954 Act. Negotiations ensued during which terms were agreed, but those terms were expressly stated by T to be without prejudice to their rights under the Act and subject to contract. Oliver J, as he then was, held that L could not in those circumstances insist on the grant of a new tenancy on those terms. This was affirmed in *Newham LBC* [2008] EWCA Civ 1414.

[28] *Behar v Territorial Investments Ltd* (1973) CAT 229. See also *Boots the Chemists Ltd v Pinkland Ltd* (1992) 28 E.G. 118; [1992] 2 E.G.L.R. 98, for the position where T's counsel referred to an agreement between the parties about a particular period of tenure in the opening of proceedings for a new tenancy which the court concluded was either an agreement or a concession from which T could not resile.

tenant's claim for a new tenancy, it is necessary to consider whether the agreement is legally enforceable in the first instance against the other party and also against third parties. It is particularly important for a tenant, who does not commence proceedings on the basis that the matter has been resolved, to ensure that the agreement reached is enforceable against the landlord and any successor in title, thus enabling him to obtain his new lease even after his ability to apply to the court for one has been lost. The necessity to protect the tenant as against third parties acquiring the landlord's interest or an interest derived from the landlord's interest was highlighted by *Stratton v Wallis Tomlin & Co.*[29]

29-22 As with all other transactions relating to dispositions of land since 27 September 1989, an agreement for the grant or surrender of a lease of more than three years will only be enforceable as such if it is in writing, the document contains all the terms expressly agreed, both parties have signed a single copy or signed copies and the written agreement has been exchanged.[30]

29-23 Even a written agreement, copies of which have been signed by both parties, may not create a binding and enforceable contract for the grant of the lease if the agreement was "subject to contract" and has not been "exchanged" in the technical conveyancing sense.

29-24 In *Salomon v Akiens*,[31] L served a s.25 notice objecting to a new tenancy on the basis of persistent delay in the payment of rent, to which T served a counternotice. The parties then proceeded to negotiate the terms of a new tenancy. In correspondence marked "Subject to contract" and "Subject to lease" the parties agreed the form of the lease. L's solicitors sent a counterpart lease for signature which was, after some delay, signed and returned. L refused to proceed. No claim for a new tenancy had ever been issued on behalf of T. It was held that there was nothing in the circumstances to justify a departure from the well-established principle that the expressions "subject to contract" and "subject to lease" mean that either party may withdraw at any point prior to exchange of the lease and the counterpart. Further, since L made no promise to grant a lease there was no consideration for T not commencing proceedings and no estoppel was created. Such representation would be very unlikely to have been made in the face of the indication that the negotiations and agreement were "subject to contract" or "subject to lease.

29-25 Provided the compromise between the parties is enforceable as an agreement for a lease, it will be open to either party, in the event of any subsequent difficulty, to rely on that contract and seek specific performance as between themselves. The tenant who has protected his position by registering[32] the agreement for a lease, will also be able to enforce that agreement against any third party purchaser from the landlord. It is rare that such a step is taken.

29-26 Where the agreement reached is a compromise of the proceedings and one party seeks to resile from the agreement, it will be possible for the other to be able to rely on the compromise so as to prevent the resiling party seeking anything other than that which has been agreed in the proceedings. That would usually be achieved by raising the compromise as a preliminary issue and seeking an appropriate declaration or other relief so as to give effect to the compromise.[33]

29-27 Whether a party can use an agreement compromising 1954 Act proceedings to

---

29 See para.29–17.

30 Law of Property (Miscellaneous Provisions) Act 1989 s.2. See paras 3–72 and 3–73, and Ch.30.

31 *Akiens v alomon* [1993] 1 E.G.L.R. 101; (1992) 65 P. & C.R. 364.

32 Where the land is unregistered an agreement for a lease can be registered as a class C(vi) land charge and where the land is registered an agreement for a lease can be protected by an agreed notice, a unilateral notice or a restriction.

33 See para.11–03.

insist on the grant of a new lease when that agreement does not itself amount to an enforceable agreement for a lease remains to be tested in the courts. However, the safest course is clearly to ensure that the agreement settling the proceedings contains all the terms agreed, all the necessary terms of the new tenancy or mechanisms for determining them and that it is signed by all parties or their representatives authorised for that purpose. It is also wise to consider what is required where any such agreement requires registration so that the compromise can include all necessary provisions.[34] Clearly, practitioners acting for tenants involved in negotiations with a view to settling 1954 Act proceedings should think very carefully before allowing the tenant's statutory rights to cease, whether by bringing no claim or by allowing the claim to be struck out, until the new tenancy is actually granted.

Parties agree that a business tenant will vacate

The resolution of a dispute under or in connection with an existing business tenancy may involve the surrender of the tenancy. As discussed above, in the normal course of events any such surrender is void.[35] However, s.38(A) permits the parties to make an effective agreement with such effect if certain conditions are complied with.[36] Similar procedural provisions and requirements apply in this situation as exist in relation to an agreement to exclude the provisions of ss.24–28 of the 1954 Act in relation to a proposed business tenancy and are discussed above.[37] **29-28**

Some tenants quitting business premises on the termination of their tenancy are entitled to compensation. The right to compensation arises where the tenant's potential right to a new tenancy fails in the face of the landlord's reliance on only grounds (e), (f) and/or (g) under s.30 of the 1954 Act.[38] The entitlement to compensation arises only upon "quitting" the premises where a new tenancy could not be ordered on those grounds alone, or no application was made, or such an application was withdrawn in the face of an objection on those grounds alone.[39] It is not unusual in such cases for a landlord who does not actually require the premises immediately to be willing to allow the tenant a short-term lease provided it is excluded from the Act.[40] In such circumstances the tenant actually quits upon the termination of the new short lease outside the statutory regime and not on the termination of his business tenancy. There is a good argument that, as the quitting of the premises is not connected to the termination of the business tenancy, the loss of his statutory rights or the grounds raised by the landlord, the tenant's right to compensation never arose as the preconditions to compensation did not result in a quitting, and the prospect of the right arising was lost when the short intervening lease was taken so that no compensation ever becomes payable.[41] **29-29**

If it is the intention in these circumstances that the tenant should receive both the value of his compensation and a short lease, care should be taken to ensure that a binding agreement is reached which places the landlord under a contractual obliga- **29-30**

---

34 For instance the Land Registry guidance provides for surrenders of registered leases to be completed on a standard transfer form providing for the transfer of the lease from tenant to landlord.

35 LTA 1954 s.38(1).

36 LTA 1954 s.38(A).

37 See para.29–06 onwards.

38 LTA 1954 s.29.

39 *International Military Services v Capital and Counties* [1982] 1 W.L.R. 575; (1982) 44 P. & C.R. 83, *Cardshops v John Lewis Properties* [1983] Q.B. 161; [1982] 3 W.L.R. 803; (1983) 45 P. & C.R. 197.

40 See para.29–05 onwards.

41 See *Woodfall*, Vol.2, Ch.22, para.22.170.2.

tion to pay a sum of money such as would have been paid in connection with the right to compensation.

RESIDENTIAL TENANCIES

INTRODUCTION

29-31 For many years the relationship of landlord and tenant in the field of residential lettings has been almost exclusively governed by statute.[42] The statutory structure by virtue of which tenants have received qualified security of tenure has remained essentially the same since the early days, although the emphasis of the grounds upon which: (a) rents have been controlled; and (b) possession of premises may be regained has changed from time to time according to the economic and political climate. As things stand, the relationship of landlord and tenant in this area is likely to be regulated by one of a number of Acts depending on when the relationship commenced.

29-32 In the context of private residential landlord and tenant relationships most tenancies are governed by the Housing Act 1988, as amended from time to time. Tenancies entered into after 28 February 1997 will be assured shorthold tenancies, and those entered into after 15 January 1989, but before 28 February 1997, will be assured tenancies (unless the parties had complied with the necessary formalities to make the tenancy an assured shorthold tenancy). Any such relationship formed prior to 15 January 1989 would be dependent upon the Rent Act 1977 and/or the Rent (Agriculture) Act 1976. In the context of a residential landlord and tenant relationship where the landlord is a local authority or other registered social landlord the relationship is likely to be governed by the Housing Act 1985.[43]

NO CONTRACTING OUT

29-33 It has long been an established principle that parties cannot contract out of the protection afforded by the Rent Acts.[44] This principle does not prevent parties engaged in a genuine dispute of fact that impacts on the application of a statutory provision compromising that dispute.[45] So where there is a genuine dispute about whether or not the tenancy with which the parties are concerned is fully protected by the Acts they can compromise the underlying factual dispute which will then determine whether the tenant has or had that protection. When taking that approach it is preferable to record the resolution of the factual dispute reached between the parties.

---

[42] The first rent controls were introduced in 1915 and the first major statutory intervention was the Increase of Rent and Mortgage Interest (Restrictions) Act 1920.

[43] The 1985 Act consolidated a large number of enactments including, in this context, the Housing Act 1980.

[44] See, e.g. *AG Securities v Vaughan* [1990] 1 A.C. 417; [1988] 3 W.L.R. 1205; (1989) 21 H.L.R. 79; (1989) 57 P. & C.R. 17. See also *Appleton v Aspin* [1988] 1 W.L.R. 410 CA; (1988) 20 H.L.R. 182; (1988) 56 P. & C.R. 22.

[45] cf. *Binder v Alachouzos* [1972] 2 Q.B. 151; [1972] 2 W.L.R. 947, considered at para.2–17 and affirmed in *Attorney General v British Museum Trustees* [2005] EWHC 1089; [2005] Ch. 397; [2005] 3 W.L.R. 396; [2005] W.T.L.R. 781; (2005) 155 N.L.J. 865. See also *Syed Hussain bin Abdul Rahman bin Shaik Alkaff v AM Abdullah Sahib & Co* [1985] 1 W.L.R. 1392 PC.

In *Bruce v Worthing BC*,[46] T was a disabled man who, at all material times, owned a specially adapted property in Kent. In March 1983 he obtained the tenancy of a flat from L, a local authority in Sussex, for a period of 11 months. At the expiration of that term the tenancy was extended and T remained in occupation. In 1985 T sought to exercise a right to buy the freehold of the flat from L pursuant to the provisions of the Housing Act 1985 which conferred such a right upon someone having a "secure tenancy". For a person to have a "secure tenancy" it was for the premises to be occupied "as his only or principal home" (s.81 of the Housing Act 1985). L entertained T's application for a while until the view was taken that T had not occupied the flat as his sole or principal residence. L served a notice to quit on T, and sought possession of the premises and arrears of rent. T issued proceedings seeking, inter alia, a declaration that he was and had always been a "secure tenant". After T and three other witnesses had given evidence in the county court proceedings over a period of two days, an agreement was concluded which was reflected in the consent order which provided, inter alia, that "[T's] claim be dismissed with no order as to costs". Subsequently, T sought to contend that this order should not have been made since he had not made an express admission to the effect that he was not a secure tenant and that the judge should have made inquiries as to T's status before making the order. The Court of Appeal held that the judge was not required to make any further inquiry in the circumstances. The consent order amounted to an express admission that T did not enjoy the protection of the Housing Act 1985 or, if it did not, it amounted to an implied admission to the same effect, which was sufficient. **29-34**

It is also established by authority[47] that a landlord and tenant may agree that the tenant will vacate premises of which he is a statutorily protected tenant in return for the payment by the landlord to him of a sum of money. In the event of the tenant complying with the obligation to vacate, he will be able to enforce recovery of the promised sum of money even though in many instances the landlord would not have been able to enforce the agreement to vacate. The inability of the parties to contract out of the protection afforded by the Acts that confer protection is derived from the way in which those Acts have been structured. **29-35**

Statutory framework and the court's jurisdiction

Each of the Acts[48] capable of conferring a degree of protection on a residential tenant contains a mandatory obligation on the court not to make an order for possession except where the circumstances prescribed in the relevant Act are established and even then in some instances the court retains a discretion.[49] In this context, as in others,[50] the courts have held that the parties cannot, by agreement or default, confer upon the court a jurisdiction which it does not otherwise have.[51] It is, therefore, incumbent on the court to satisfy itself and be seen to satisfy itself that the statutory provisions are met irrespective of any agreement between the parties.[52] **29-36**

---

46 *Bruce v Worthing BC* (1994) 26 H.L.R. 223.

47 *Rajbenback v Mamon* [1955] 1 Q.B. 283 CA; [1955] 2 W.L.R. 21; [1955] 1 All E.R. 12; cf. comments of the Privy Council in *Syed Hussain v AM Abdullah Sahib & Co* [1985] 1 W.L.R. 1392 at 1397. See Stocker, "Compromise of possession claims", 83 L.S. Gaz. 1701.

48 See para.29–29.

49 Rent Act 1977 s.98(1); Rent (Agriculture) Act 1976 s.6(1); Housing Act 1985 s.84; Housing Act 1988 s.7; Housing and Regeneration Act 2008 s.299 and Sch.11.

50 See para.10–09 onwards.

51 *Barton v Fincham* [1921] 2 K.B. 291 CA, *R. v Bloomsbury and Marylebone County Court Ex p. Blackburne* [1985] 2 E.G.L.R. 157 CA, *R. v Newcastle upon Tyne County Court Ex p. Thompson* [1988] 2 E.G.L.R. 119; (1988) 20 H.L.R. 430, *Wandsworth v Fadayomi* [1987] 1 W.L.R. 1473 CA.

52 *Barton v Fincham* [1921] 2 K.B. 291, *Salter v Lask* [1924] 1 K.B. 754, *Smith v Poulter* [1947] K.B.

29-37 In *Plaschkes v Jones*,[53] the judge gave possession of a flat subject to a protected tenancy effectively "by consent", although this did not appear in the order, without having considered the validity of the notice to quit (which had been put in issue in a defence and a letter from the defendants' solicitor to the court) or whether it was reasonable to make an order. Contrary to expectations, the housing authority "looked behind" the order, considered that it should not have been made and declined to re-house the defendants. On the defendants' appeal, the Court of Appeal held that the judge should have considered these matters. A re-trial was ordered.

29-38 In *R. v Newcastle upon Tyne County Court Ex p. Thompson*,[54] L issued proceedings against T seeking possession of a flat. L accepted that the premises were premises to which the Rent Act 1977 applied and sought possession on the ground that the flat was reasonably required by them for occupation as a residence for themselves and their two sons. This assertion was put in issue in T's defence and the issue of greater hardship raised. At the hearing before the district registrar an order was made by consent (although not so expressed) to the effect that T should give up possession of the flat by a specified date approximately six months later. No order for costs was made. None of the matters that it would have been necessary for L to establish in order to obtain an order for possession were admitted or conceded on T's behalf, and no evidence was called. McNeill J held that in the absence of any admissions or concessions of the grounds entitling L to possession, the order was made without jurisdiction and should be quashed.

29-39 In *Baygreen Properties Ltd v Gil*[55] the Court of Appeal recognised the desirability of the ground for possession being recorded on the face of the order. That is particularly so where the order was based on one of the mandatory grounds. However in a discretionary case, whilst an order would be bad for want of jurisdiction if the judge had not considered whether it was reasonable to make the order when he did, if it was shown that the matter was in fact considered by the court when the order was made, the order would not be bad for want of jurisdiction because that was not expressly recorded on the face of the order. Where the order was made pursuant to the tenant's consent, the recording of admissions in the order may be necessary. The court would only have jurisdiction to order possession if there were express or implied admissions affording the basis for sufficient grounds. Accordingly, the court would only have jurisdiction if the material before it contained such admissions. It follows that where a consent order is simply presented to the court without any other material on which the court could exercise its discretion, the consent order itself would need to contain the admissions in order for it to be effective.

29-40 Essentially, the court must be satisfied that grounds for possession are made out including, where applicable, the requirement that the making of an order is reasonable. The tenant's agreement to an order for possession may indicate an admission that there are grounds and that the making of an order is reasonable, but it may simply constitute a submission to the giving-up of possession. Consequently, the court cannot simply rely on the fact that the order for possession is effectively by consent to satisfy itself that the order should be made.[56] The court must have material upon which to form a view as to its jurisdiction to grant the order. That material might be evidence in the form of statements, admissions made expressly,

---

339; [1947] 1 All E.R. cf. *Bruce v Worthing BC* (1993) 26 H.L.R. 223.

53 *Plaschkes v Jones* (1983) 9 H.L.R. 110.

54 *R. v Newcastle upon Tyne County Court Ex p. Thompson* [1988] 2 E.G.L.R. 119; (1988) 20 H.L.R. 430.

55 *Baygreen Properties Ltd v Gil* [2002] EWCA Civ 1340; [2003] H.L.R. 12.

56 *Hounslow LBC v McBride* (1999) 31 H.L.R. 143.

or which can be implied from the documentation or other matters put before the court. The ability to point to the material from which the court's jurisdiction derived is important. For the landlord who wishes to avoid any prospect of the tenant subsequently challenging the jurisdiction of the court to have made the order for possession recording admissions by the tenant that establish grounds for and the reasonableness of the order is the safest way of dealing with the matter.

Obtaining an "agreed" order in practice

The jurisdictional matters referred to above[57] can present difficulties in obtaining an effective order for possession. Not infrequently, a protected tenant will desire to have an order for possession against him with a view to assisting his position over re-housing by the local authority. Such a tenant will be concerned to ensure that the terms of the order, including any admissions, will not enable a local authority to conclude that he is intentionally homeless.[58] Whatever the merits or otherwise of the matter may be (and, from the strictly legal point of view, it is of no concern to the court), the jurisdictional problems to which reference has been made can arise. This has been recognised on the highest authority[59] as being overcome by admissions of fact by the tenant of the basis of the landlord's claim[60]: **29-41**

> "If the parties before the court admit that one of the events has happened which give the court jurisdiction and there is no reason to doubt the bona fides of the admission, the court is under no obligation to make further enquiry as to the question of fact; but apart from such an admission the court cannot give effect to an agreement, whether by way of compromise or otherwise, inconsistent with the provisions of the Act." **29-42**

The matter was put in similar terms subsequently[61]: **29-43**

> "If it is desired to reach terms of agreement to be embodied in an order whereby possession of premises covered by section 98 of the Rent Act 1977 is to be given up, for the court to have jurisdiction to make an order there must be plain admissions of the qualifying conditions which must be fulfilled before such an order can be made. That is to say, a concession that it is reasonable for the order to be made, that, whichever the case may be, suitable alternative accommodation is or will be available to the tenant, or that the relevant circumstances specified in the appropriate case exist, and, where relevant, that it is accepted by the tenant that greater hardship would not be caused by granting the order than by refusing to grant it."

Where such admissions of fact are made in good faith, it is open to the court to regard the tenant as submitting in the sense of conceding the absence of a defence (rather than consenting) to an order for possession and to drawing the order as such. Such difficulties as the tenant might face with the local authority by having "consented" to an order for possession are at least reduced.[62] The tenant's legal representatives will need to consider carefully with the tenant how such admissions will be viewed. **29-44**

---

57 See para.29–36.

58 Housing Act 1996 s.191.

59 *Barton* [1921] 2 K.B. 291, per Atkin LJ at 299.

60 See Precedent No.12 at para.A1–12.

61 *R. v Newcastle upon Tyne County Court Ex p. Thomson* [1988] 2 E.G.L.R. 119 at 122.

62 It is apparent from cases such as *Plaschkes v Jones* (1983) 9 H.L.R. 110, that even in cases where the words "by consent" are omitted from an order, some housing authorities will look closely at whether any admissions or concessions made were correctly and appropriately made.

Residential occupants without statutory protection or with "restricted contracts"

29-45 Where a residential occupant has never had any statutory protection[63] no jurisdictional obstacles exist in the path of securing an agreed order for possession. Similarly, where the longstanding occupant occupies under a "restricted contract",[64] i.e. where a degree of protection is afforded by virtue of the right to apply to a rent assessment committee (when sitting as a rent tribunal) for limited security of tenure, it is possible for the tenant to contract out of that right if he chooses to do so. It follows that where the parties agree that there never was any basis on which the tenant's status attracted statutory protection or they compromise a genuine dispute about that issue, the court has no duty to investigate the facts before it makes the order for possession which the parties seek.[65]

29-46 In *Alcove Properties v Fraser and Fraser*,[66] the defendants were tenants under a furnished tenancy to which the Furnished Houses (Rent Control) Act 1946 applied. At a time when they had a clear defence to the possession proceedings brought against them,[67] and a further application to the rent tribunal for time was pending, they consented to an order for possession, suspended until a specified date, a claim for damages being abandoned. Subsequently, they applied to set aside the consent order on the basis that it was made without jurisdiction and that they could not contract out of their rights under the Act. The Court of Appeal held that there was nothing in the Act to deprive the consent order of having "its full efficacy". Russell LJ emphasised that under the Act in question it was,

> "entirely for the individual to decide whether to put the Rent Tribunal procedure into operation and whether and when to withdraw from that procedure".

Such an individual is in no way debarred from bargaining away his right to invoke that procedure if he wishes to do so.[68]

Subsequent variation and enforcement of orders

29-47 It should be recalled that a possession order may be enforced against any person on the premises when it is executed.[69]

29-48 It should be borne in mind that where a tenant is a protected tenant, the court retains a statutory jurisdiction to vary an order for possession even if it is made by consent.[70] In addition, the fact that the court retains jurisdiction to vary an undertak-

---

63 For example, where there is a genuine licence or a genuine holiday letting.

64 Rent Act 1977 s.19. By virtue of the Housing Act 1988 s.36, s.140 and Sch.18 no new "restricted contracts" may be made after the commencement of the Act save where the contract is granted pursuant to a contract made before the commencement of the Act.

65 *Syed Hussain Bin Abdul Rahman Bin Shaikh Alkaff v AM Abdullah Sahib & Co* [1985] 1 W.L.R. 1392.

66 *Alcove Properties v Fraser and Fraser* (1966) CAT 124A.

67 The proceedings were premature.

68 In *R. v Bloomsbury and Marylebone County Court Ex p. Blackburne* [1985] 2 E.G.L.R. 157, Sir John Donaldson MR, at 158, explained the case on the basis that "the Rent Acts operated in relation to premises, whereas the rent tribunal scheme operated in personam and it was open to the tenant to agree to waive his personal contractual rights".

69 See para.6–33.

70 See Rent Act 1977 s.100; Housing Act 1988 s.9; Housing Act 1985 s.85. See also *Rossiter v Langley* [1925] 1 K.B. 741, *Mouat-Balthasar v Murphy* [1967] 1 Q.B. 344; [1966] 3 W.L.R. 695; [1966] 3 All E.R. 477.

ing or release a party from his undertaking even where the undertaking is given in conjunction with a consent order[71] should not be forgotten.

The compromise of a claim for possession may provide for the making of a possession order suspended on terms. If it be alleged that the order ought to be enforced because of some failure to observe those terms, leave to issue execution proceedings may be required and the requirements under the CPR[72] must be complied with. Where an application for permission must be made, whether actual notice must be given to every person in occupation is unclear on the authorities. As the law stands, it should be assumed that it is necessary to do so, so that every occupant who would be affected by the proposed eviction is given an opportunity to be heard.[73] **29-49**

An order for possession secured with the agreement of a party may be set aside on the same grounds, as may other orders obtained by consent.[74] Where a landlord obtains a possession order by misrepresentation a tenant may have a statutory right to compensation.[75] The fact that the tenant effectively consented to the order does not prevent the court making an order for compensation.[76] **29-50**

The status of the tenancy after a possession order

Where possession proceedings have run their course, whether in connection with a tenancy protected under the Rent Act 1977, the Housing Act 1985 or an unprotected tenancy, it is not unknown for the parties to make an arrangement whereby the tenant remains in occupation of the premises on the basis of a commitment to pay the current rent and a regular sum in reduction of the arrears or any damages payable. There was once uncertainty about status of such occupiers who came to be known as "tolerated trespassers". Their tenancies having been determined, it was possible for new tenancies to be created, although the courts were generally slow to impute the necessary intention to create a new tenancy. Parties entering into a consent order when contemplating some continued occupation could, therefore, assist themselves by an expression of their intentions. **29-51**

The law has been changed, however. The existence of residential occupiers who were not tenants and remained in occupation, being liable to pay for their occupation but without rights, was causing significant difficulties. The position of tolerated trespassers has for the most part been addressed by the Housing and Regeneration Act 2008 s.299 and Sch.11, which came into force on 20 May 2009. Any tenant under a secure, assured, introductory or demoted tenancy, who is made the subject of a possession order now remains a tenant under their original tenancy until the order for possession is executed. Those who were the subject of a possession order which was not executed prior to the implementation of s.299 of the Act, but whose tenancies were not ended, fall within the scope of the Act. In line with the principles discussed above, that extension of the original tenancy having been imposed by statute, it appears the parties can no longer prevent the occupying party remaining as a tenant. **29-52**

---

71 *Kensington Housing Trust v Oliver* (1998) 30 H.L.R. 608, *Mid Suffolk DC v Clarke* [2006] EWCA Civ 71; [2007] 1 W.L.R. 980.

72 CPR 83.

73 *Fleet Mortgage and Investment Co Ltd v Lower Maisonette 46 Eaton Place Ltd* [1972] 1 W.L.R. 765; [1972] 2 All E.R. 737, *Partridge v Gupta* [2017] EWHC 2110 (QB); [2018] 1 W.L.R. 1 and *Hall v Oraki* [2019] EWHC 1515 (Ch).

74 See Ch.4.

75 Rent Act 1977 s.2; Housing Act 1988 s.12.

76 *Thorne v Smith* [1947] K.B. 307; [1947] 1 All E.R. 39.

FORFEITURE AND RELIEF FROM FORFEITURE

29-53 Proceedings seeking forfeiture of a lease and proceedings seeking relief from forfeiture are frequently compromised. It is important for the parties compromising such claims to be clear in their understanding and intent so far as the impact of the compromise on the existence of the lease and of third parties' interests are concerned.

29-54 The issue of forfeiture proceedings by a landlord is an act of forfeiture like peaceable re-entry. However, as against the tenant the lease and its covenants are not immediately determined. Unless it is established that the claim to forfeiture is unsustainable in law[77] then pending judgment of the claim for forfeiture or relief from forfeiture there is a "twilight period"[78] or "period of limbo"[79] when the lease has a shadowy existence during which the landlord cannot rely upon the covenants, but the lease and covenants have not actually been brought to an end.[80] If the forfeiture proceedings are compromised then, as long as the compromise does not provide for a forfeiture, the landlord may then rely on obligations under the lease which arose during that twilight period.

29-55 In *Ivory Gate Ltd v Spetale*,[81] L served a s.146 notice and commenced forfeiture proceedings which were compromised on the basis that L discontinued the forfeiture proceedings without releasing any of its rights against the sureties, and the lease itself would be transferred to L. The lease was transferred to L. L commenced proceedings against the sureties claiming rent arrears up to the date of the transfer. It was held that the issue of forfeiture proceedings itself did not determine the lease. The lease was determined only by merger upon the transfer, and until that point the sureties' obligations subsisted.

29-56 In *Weaver v Mogford*,[82] L commenced forfeiture proceedings against the current tenant on the basis of rent arrears. L obtained a default judgment which was challenged subsequently. The proceedings were ultimately compromised on the basis that L obtained an order for possession which would not be executed for three months on conditions, it being acknowledged that the current tenant and its mortgagee had no further interest in the property. L had taken proceedings against the original lessee for damages for disrepair, who claimed that the effect of the order was a waiver of the forfeiture followed by a surrender, thereby relieving him of his obligations. It was held that the order for possession in the forfeiture proceeding confirmed that the lease was forfeit. The fact that in correspondence there had been discussion of reinstating the lease did not alter the effect of the order made. The original lessee remained liable until the date of the forfeiture.

29-57 Similarly, dismissal of a claim for forfeiture, even by consent, has the effect of restoring the lease fully, the legitimacy of the act of forfeiture not having been established with the effect that it is to be treated as a nullity.[83] It follows that both parties are then treated as having the same rights and obligations they would have had if the forfeiture proceedings had never taken place.

29-58 Where the effect of the compromise of such proceedings is a forfeiture and the granting of relief subject to conditions, the position is not so clear. It is clearly

---

77 *Lambeth LBC v Vincent* [2000] 2 E.G.L.R. 73, where forfeiture proceedings did not affect T's title because the s.146 notice was invalid and accordingly the forfeiture claim was unsustainable in law.

78 *Associated Deliveries v Harrison* (1985) 50 P. & C.R. 91; [1984] 2 E.G.L.R. 76.

79 *Liverpool Properties v Oldbridge Investments* [1985] 2 E.G.L.R. 111.

80 See *Woodfall*, Vol.1, Ch.17, para.17.091.1

81 *Ivory Gate Ltd v Spetale* (1999) 77 P. & C.R. 141; [1998] 2 E.G.L.R. 43.

82 *Weaver v Mogford* [1988] 2 E.G.L.R. 48.

83 *Hynes v Twinsectra* [1995] 2 E.G.L.R. 69; (1996) 28 H.L.R. 183; (1996) 71 P. & C.R. 145.

established that if the court itself decides to grant relief from forfeiture subject to conditions, the court retains jurisdiction to modify those conditions by extending time, if not varying the conditions, insofar as it considers that it would be just and equitable even if the order itself did not preserve a "liberty to apply".[84] The power of the court to intervene and extend time or otherwise modify the conditions of relief expressly agreed between the parties and incorporated in a consent order has been doubted judicially, but not conclusively ruled out.[85] Similarly, the ability of the tenant to seek to avoid his failure to comply with the conditions for relief in a consent order by making a second application for relief has been doubted. However, if it appears to the court that the tenant submitted to an order for relief upon terms, rather than genuinely consenting to such an order, it would seem that the court does retain the power to intervene.[86]

In this regard it appears that a distinction may need to be drawn between a final order by consent and an interim order by consent. Where the parties agree an adjournment of forfeiture proceedings upon compliance with conditions and provide in default of compliance that there will be an order for possession against the tenant, it is possible that the court's case management powers will enable it, if it concludes that it is necessary to satisfy the overriding objective, to intervene.[87] **29-59**

---

84 *Chandless-Chandless* [1942] 2 K.B. 321; [1942] 2 All E.R. 315.

85 *Chandless-Chandless* [1942] 2 K.B. 321, *Crawford v Clark* [2000] E.G. 33 (C.S).

86 *Chandless-Chandless* [1942] 2 K.B. 321.

87 *Ropac Ltd v Inntrepreneur Pub Co (CPC) Ltd* [2001] C.P. Rep. 31. But see para.6–23.

CHAPTER 30

Disputes over Land

GENERAL

As previously discussed,[1] where a compromise agreement involves a disposition of land, or of an interest in land, the formalities affecting transactions involving land or interests in land need to be taken into account. An understanding of the requirements and implications that impact on such transactions is essential. A compromise agreement involving the disposition of land or an interest in land must satisfy the formalities required by s.2 of the Law of Property (Miscellaneous Provisions) Act 1989[2]. A contract for the disposition of an interest in land entered into after 27 September 1989 will not be valid or enforceable unless the statutory formalities are complied with. An agreement that does not so comply is void and unenforceable unless it can be said that the underlying communications between, and conduct of, the parties in all the circumstances operate so as to create a constructive or resulting trust or they give rise to a lease for three years or less.[3] **30-01**

The actual instruments that dispose of legal interests in land are controlled by ss.51–55 of the Law of Property Act 1925. Generally such instruments are required to be in writing and by way of deed. Under the Land Registration Act 2002 transactions that create or dispose of registrable interests in land require registration to be completed. If such transactions are not completed by registration a third party benefiting under another transactions for valuable consideration once registered will take free of the earlier transaction. In addition the Law of Property Act 1925, particularly ss.61–63 and ss.77–83, operate to imply provisions into conveyances or provide for the construction of particular provisions that may appear in conveyances unless expressly excluded. It follows that, when drafting the terms of a compromise agreement that disposes of land or an interest in land, provision should be made for the necessary formalities to make the agreement enforceable, for the execution of the necessary transfer, assignment, grant or surrender and for the subsequent applications to HM Land Registry. **30-02**

It is the nature of land and interests in land that they are readily transferable and are frequently disposed of. Further, some interests over land may be acquired without a transaction or the active participation of some or all of those who may be adversely affected by that interest.[4] Some interests need to be shown on the register by means of a notice or restriction in order to ensure protection against third **30-03**

---

1 See paras 3-72–3-73.

2 See, e.g., *Abberley v Abberley* [2019] EWHC 1564 (Ch). See Ch.3, fn.124.

3 An agreement for a lease of less than three years is exempt from Law of Property (Miscellaneous Provisions) Act 1989 s.2: see para.3-73.

4 For example, easements acquired by prescription or title acquired by adverse possession.

parties, but some still do not need to be shown on the register.[5] Those acquiring interests in land as a result of a compromise need to make enquiries (just as those purchasing such interests do) to ensure they are able to secure and then protect the interest they expect to acquire.

30-04 Disputes over land in a commercial context will often involve issues surrounding ownership, enforcement of contracts for the disposition of land, mortgages, easements, options and restrictive covenants. The compromise of such matters will often involve a disposition or potential disposition of land or an interest in it. Land disputes between co-owners of land or neighbours are a practitioner's nightmare. Ownership, boundaries, fences, adverse possession, rights of way and so on, are a fertile source of acrimonious litigation into which, strive as he might, the practitioner finds it well-nigh impossible to inject a modicum of common sense and rationality. With the possible exception of co-ownership disputes, costs can escalate out of all proportion to the nature and significance of the dispute and to the value of the land or rights at stake.[6] That fact will occasionally lead parties to see sense and come to an amicable compromise, although all too often at the doors of the court.

30-05 Ensuring that a contract or consent order embodying the compromise of a dispute over land is properly enforceable demands an understanding of the technical and practical requirements to achieve a binding contract, completion and registration of any necessary transaction. An appreciation of any potential tax implications may also be important.

30-06 The issue of the need for a compromise involving the disposition of land or an interest in it to comply with s.2 of the 1989 Act has arisen from time to time. It has been considered most extensively in the context boundary disputes.

30-07 In *Joyce v Rigolli*,[7] the Court of Appeal concluded that boundary agreements fall into two categories: (i) those involving an exchange of land and (ii) those by which the parties identify or demark the extent of their respective parcels of land. The second category does not ordinarily involve any disposition of an interest in land with the consequence that s.2 does not apply. The Court of Appeal indicated that ordinarily a boundary agreement would be within the second category and, whilst it was not necessary to consider whether s.2 would apply to a compromise agreement, the court's reasoning clearly proceeded on that assumption. That approach is also supported by the approach of Park J in *Styles v Smith*[8] in which he concluded, albeit obiter, that the fact that an agreement formed part of a compromise of court proceedings would not exempt it from s.2 if the section would otherwise apply. He again concluded that the compromise of the boundary dispute in that case fell into the demarcation category rather than the disposition category with the result that it was outside of the ambit of s.2 of the 1989 Act.[9]

30-08 In *Yeates v Line*[10], Kevin Prosser QC, sitting as a Deputy High Court Judge, drew

---

5 See Schs 1 and 3 of the Land Registration Act 2002 for overriding interests.

6 cf. *Jones v Price* [1965] 2 Q.B. 618 CA; [1965] 3 W.L.R. 296; [1965] 2 All E.R. 625. It is an area where mediation at an early stage in a dispute would often be sensible.

7 *Joyce v Rigolli* [2004] EWCA Civ 79. In *Melhuish v Fishburn* [2008] EWCA Civ 1302, it was said that *Joyce v Rigolli* established "that, where an agreement is made merely to demarcate a boundary, it is not a contract for the sale or other disposition of an interest in land for the purposes of Section 2 of the 1989 Act, simply because a trivial transfer or transfers of land were consciously involved".

8 *Styles v Smith* [2005] EWHC 3224 (QB); [2005] PLSCS 232.

9 "[A]n agreement to resolve an unresolved issue about the true location of a boundary … [is] not one for the disposition of an interest in land": *Styles v Smith* [2005] EWHC 3224 (QB) at [14].

10 *Yeates v Line* [2013] Ch. 363; [2013] 2 W.L.R. 844; [2013] 1 P. & C.R. 22.

a distinction between the actual effect on the ground of an agreement and its purpose. He concluded that it was the purpose of an agreement, not what turned out to be its actual effect, that was important when ascertaining whether the agreement was "a contract for the ... disposition of an interest in land ..." and so subject to s.2. Accordingly, he concluded that even if a boundary agreement had a "disposing effect", provided its purpose was one of demarcation rather than dispositions s.2 would not apply.

By way of contrast, in *Orton v Collins*,[11] in the context of a Pt 36 offer being accepted where a contract had not arisen given the failure to comply with s.2, it was held that the resulting "sui generis obligation", which arose out of the parties' voluntary use of the Pt 36 regime, could be enforced by the court notwithstanding the absence of an enforceable contract. The court ordered the parties to sign a single document that incorporated the terms of the compromise so that an enforceable contract came into existence. There was no suggestion that an agreement to compromise proceedings which did not comply with s.2 and was outside the Pt 36 regime would nevertheless be enforceable by the court. However, it may be argued that when the parties submit voluntarily to a consent order they accept a similar obligation as was found to arise upon their voluntary engagement with the Pt 36 regime by the making and acceptance of a Pt 36 offer. **30-09**

The prudent course for all those advising upon and drafting a compromise which provides for, or will or may amount to, a disposition of land or an interest in land is to assume that it is necessary to comply with s.2. It is also necessary to be conscious of the potential implied terms[12] and the fact that the transaction may have taxation implications.[13] Any consent order should comply with s.2 or, at the very least, provide mechanisms for its subsequent compliance including immediate execution of the necessary deeds. Any settlement agreement or consent order should include provisions that ensure that registration requirements[14] can be satisfied promptly, and drafted, taking account of the usual due diligence associated with a conveyancing transaction that may not be taking place. Consideration should be given to the use of warranties to give protection where the due diligence is absent or limited. [15] **30-10**

In light of the change from the "voluntary" system of stamp duty to stamp duty land tax[16] which gives rise to a liability for tax for the "purchaser" upon the occurrence of a "land transaction", parties need to understand the potential for liability. Any acquisition of a chargeable interest in land, including a transfer of the legal and/or beneficial interest in land or the grant, release or surrender of a lease, will be an event that gives rise to potential liability.[17] **30-11**

---

11 *Orton v Collins* [2007] EWHC 803 (Ch); [2007] 1 W.L.R. 2953; [2007] 3 All E.R. 863. See Ch.15 fn.87.

12 i.e. ss.61–63 and ss.77–83 of the Law of Property Act.

13 See para.30-11.

14 Land Registration Act 2002.

15 See para.30-20.

16 See Finance Act 2003 Pt 4 ss.42–56. Stamp Duty Land Tax (SDLT) is generally payable on the purchase or transfer of property of land in the United Kingdom where the amount is above a certain threshold.

17 In general, a "chargeable interest" means (a) an estate, interest, right or power in or over land in the United Kingdom, or (b) the benefit of an obligation, restriction or condition affecting the value of any such estate, interest, right or power and an acquisition can take the form of the creation, surrender, release or variation of a chargeable interest.

THE REQUIREMENTS OF SECTION 2

30-12 Where s.2 applies, it is necessary that the contract is in writing, that all express terms are in (or incorporated into) one document, that all parties to the contract sign such a document and if the parties each sign a different document, those documents must also be exchanged. It should be noted that any material variation to a contract that falls within s.2 must itself comply with s.2,[18] and the grant of an option (as opposed to its exercise) must also comply.[19] Further, mutual wills which require the sale or disposition of an interest in land must also comply with s.2.[20] Where parties enter into a composite agreement, only part of which constitutes an agreement for the disposition of an interest in land, that part must comply with s.2, although it is not always necessary for the agreement relating to other subject matter to comply with s.2.[21] However, difficulties can arise in identifying the extent of the part of the agreement relating to land. Where parties have agreed terms which in reality all form part of a single agreement, but which are contained in two distinct agreements, the resulting contract, at least in so far as it relates to the disposition of land, will be void.[22] Even if the parties proceed to complete the disposition of land the remaining obligations related to that transaction will continue to be unenforceable and part performance will not cause a void agreement to mature into one which is enforceable.[23] If a compromise provides for a transfer of land and a number of actions or payments related to the land, the failure to incorporate all those terms in one compliant agreement may leave the subsequent obligations to act or pay unenforceable notwithstanding the fact the benefit of the property has passed. It follows that extreme caution is required in order to ensure that all the terms relating to that aspect are expressly recorded in the necessary document. The question whether a document signed document records all the terms of a disposition of land when there is a supplemental agreement is a question of fact which will generally require determination at trial.[24]

30-13 It should be noted that whilst both the High Court and county court have power to grant declarations concerning land, and whilst it has not been the general practice of the court to grant such declarations by consent, that practice is not an immutable rule and increasingly where a declaration is necessary to do justice in a case, even where it may affect the interests of third parties, the courts are willing to take that step.[25] The court will be concerned not to make a declaration where it is an academic or pointless exercise. However if the declaration serves to narrow the issues between the parties, it is likely to be made. An entitlement to a declara-

---

[18] *McCausland v Duncan Lawrie Ltd* [1997] 1 W.L.R. 38; [1996] 4 All E.R. 995; (1997) 74 P. & C.R. 343.

[19] *Spiro v Glencrown Properties Ltd* [1991] Ch. 537; [1991] 2 W.L.R. 931; [1991] 1 All E.R. 600.

[20] *Goodchild, Re* [1997] 1 W.L.R. 1216; [1997] 3 All E.R. 63; [1997] 2 F.L.R. 644.

[21] *Tootal Clothing Ltd v Guinea Properties Ltd* (1992) 64 P. & C.R. 452, *Godden v Merthyr Tydfil Housing Association* [1997] 1 N.P.C. 1.

[22] *North Eastern Properties Ltd v Coleman* [2010] 1 W.L.R. 2715; [2010] 3 All E.R. 528 as qualified and explained by *Keay v Morris Homes (West Midlands) Ltd* [2012] EWCA Civ 900; [2012] 1 W.L.R. 2855; [2012] 2 P. & C.R. 18.

[23] *Keay v Morris Homes (West Midlands) Ltd* [2012] EWCA Civ 900; [2012] 1 W.L.R. 2855; [2012] 2 P. & C.R. 18.

[24] *Keay v Morris Homes (West Midland) Ltd* [2012] EWCA Civ 900; [2012] 1 W.L.R. 2855; [2012] 2 P. & C.R. 18

[25] *Wallersteiner v Moir* [1974] 1 W.L.R. 991 at 1029 and 1030 CA, *Patten v Burke Publishing Ltd* [1991] 1 W.L.R. 541, *Crystal Decisions (UK) Ltd v Vedatech Corp* [2007] EWHC 1062 (Ch), *Animatrix Ltd v O'Kelly* [2008] EWHC 438 (Ch) and [2008] EWCA 1415 (CA) and *Hayim v Couch* [2009] EWHC 1040 (Ch). See also paras 10-02 and 23-40.

tion in the event that one party to the transaction fails to complete a disposition provided for will generally be enforceable. However, where the court refuses to grant a declaration by consent, the parties should ensure that the recital to the consent order (or a schedule to it) records all matters agreed between them.

Whilst it is often said that a "bare right to litigate" is ordinarily not assignable, that statement has been qualified in several ways.[26] It is clear that a right to litigate ancillary to a transfer of property can be assigned.[27] This probably means that rights arising from the compromise of a dispute over interests in land or boundaries are capable of assignment provided that some transfer of property is involved in it. **30-14**

It would seem consistent with the position under the general law[28] that, where a compromise involving a possible change of title is contemplated, all defects in the transferor's title must be disclosed to render the agreement fully effective. **30-15**

Given the significant implications that flow from the fact that a contract of compromise contains a contract for the disposal of any interest in land, it is important accurately to characterise compromises in property disputes. A compromise providing for the sale of a property to a third party, as opposed to a disposition between the parties to the compromise, does not amount to a contract for the disposition of land. A contract for the disposal of the interest in land is made between parties which include a "vendor", someone obliged to dispose of the interest (whether by creation, transfer or surrender) and a "purchaser", someone obliged to take it or take it back.[29] The essence of a contract for the disposition of land is the creation of an obligation to pass a proprietary interest between the two parties to the contract or for the surrender/release of a proprietary interest between those parties, one being the holder of the interest and the other being the party whose interest is immediately burdened by it. **30-16**

BOUNDARIES

If, as is normal, the compromise agreement in a boundary dispute involves a redefinition of the boundaries, the most prudent approach is to finalise the agreement by deed in case, in reality, some small part of the land changes ownership. However as discussed above,[30] the courts have demonstrated an increasing willingness to treat parties and their successors as bound by a boundary agreement which does not comply with s.2 provided their purpose can be characterised as demarcation. In any event, a properly prepared plan, having certain fixed points of reference, should be drawn up and incorporated in the agreement, and the agreement should comply with the relevant formalities.[31] For registered land the title plans do not purport to define with precision the position of the boundary between separate titles. Unless and until formal application for a determined boundary is granted, the title plan is subject to the general boundaries rule.[32] A boundary agreement compromising a boundary dispute will not result in a determined boundary for the purposes of registration. Nevertheless, within the parameters of the "general boundary rule" the title may be adjusted by HM Land Registry. In addition, or in **30-17**

---

26 *Chitty*, 33rd edn Vol.1, para.19-050 onwards.
27 *Chitty*, 33rd edn Vol.1, para.19-050 and 16-92.
28 *Chitty*, 33rd edn Vol.1, paras 7-175-7-175.
29 *Nweze v Nwoke* [2004] EWCA Civ 379.
30 See para.30-05.
31 Law of Property (Miscellaneous Provisions) Act 1989 s.2(1) and para.3-72.
32 Land Registration Act 2002 s.60.

the alternative, the existence of the boundary agreement may be noted on the title of both properties affected. In any event, the plan produced by the parties will not be substituted for the title plan. It follows that, in order to ensure that any detailed agreed plan can practically be enforced as between the parties and their successors, it is wise to keep the consent order or agreement and plan with the title deeds and to apply to note the existence of a consent order or deed and ideally to incorporate the plan on the registered title.

30-18 When the implementation of a consent order defining a boundary results in practical difficulties, the court is always available to assist in interpreting orders and will strive to ensure certainty. Whilst a consent order might be void for uncertainty, the mere fact that difficulty exists in interpreting the agreement and plan, and indeed applying it to the ground so as to implement the agreement, will not of itself result in the setting aside of the compromise entered into with due formality and embodied in an order. The court will however, declare such an agreement and order void if there was a failure to agree an essential term such that it is impossible to implement the consent order without further agreement being reached between the parties.[33]

30-19 If the agreement involves a clear reorganisation of the boundary which provides for land to change ownership, for instance as a result of a trade of different areas of land, the need to comply with s.2 becomes acute and consideration should be given (a) to the need for a formal transfer which can be registered to achieve completion and (b) to whether any liability for stamp duty land tax arises.[34]

DURING COURT PROCEEDINGS

30-20 Where court proceedings are extant and there is any question of land changing hands, the best and safest course is, usually, for an order in the Tomlin form[35] to be prepared, one of the agreed terms being that the parties will execute a deed giving effect to their agreement so far as the boundary is concerned. Drafting such an agreement without the benefit of the due diligence usually undertaken during the conveyancing process is not straightforward or easy. The general law gives parties and their drafting representatives a good degree of protection against an unknown and undisclosed defect in title.[36] Frequently the defect will mean the "vendor" is unable to comply with their obligation. Accordingly, it is wise to give serious consideration as to what will happen if completion of the proposed transferred or granted is not possible, or the interest transferred or created is defective. Consideration should be given to the use of warranties (as to title and authority) and to including default provisions which assist in any potential remedial action and/or provision for compensation. All terms necessary to implement the compromise including steps to achieve registration should be provided for. The incorporation of a relevant set of the Law Society standard terms with such omissions or variations as the situation calls is often a practical and effective way to proceed. It is sensible to expressly provide which party will have carriage of any documentation, make any applications to HM Land Registry and at whose expense it will be undertaken. In any event this is one situation in which, for several reasons, it would be sensible

---

33 *Dicker v Scammell* [2005] EWCA Civ 405; [2005] 3 All E.R. 838; [2006] 1 P. & C.R. 4.
34 See para.30-08.
35 See para.9-21.
36 See *Chitty*, 33rd edn, Vol.1, para.7-175.

for the parties themselves to be required by their legal advisers to sign the schedule to the order. This approach to the settlement will enable eventual recourse to s.9 of the Senior Courts Act 1981 in the event of one party failing or refusing to execute the deed. Equally, insofar as the provisions of the agreement concern positive steps to be taken by one party or the other, or the prevention of interference or trespass, they can be enforced within the action provided the necessary steps are taken.[37]

---

[37] See Ch.11.

PART 12: CONSTRUCTION LITIGATION

CHAPTER 31

Construction Disputes

INTRODUCTION

Construction disputes are usually dealt with in the Technology and Construction Court,[1] by arbitration,[2] by dispute boards[3] and by adjudication under the Housing Grants Construction and Regeneration Act 1996 s.108. **31-01**

Particular issues

The general law of compromise applies to construction disputes in the same way as it does to any other form of dispute. However, certain problems occur frequently by reason of the complexity of the subject matter and the interaction of dispute-resolution machinery which often highlight particular issues. These issues include problems associated with: **31-02**

(i) the long-term nature of construction contracts;
(ii) certificates and retentions;
(iii) the presence of multiple issues;
(iv) claims for contribution to settlements reached with other parties;
(v) other issues associated with the involvement of multiple parties;
(vi) adjudication.

LONG-TERM ISSUES

Problems often arise during the course of a construction project as to the contractor's progress and/or responsibility for defects. As a result, mechanisms for dispute resolution have evolved to deal with disputes on an interim basis, pending final agreement or determination. Pursuant to the Housing Grants Construction and Regeneration Act 1996 s.108, parties to a construction contract (as defined) are entitled to refer a dispute under the contract for adjudication. Increasingly, contracts also provide for the appointment of dispute boards.[4] These disputes may be settled **31-03**

---

1 See CPR Pt 60.

2 See Ch.32.

3 Dispute boards are a standing panel of independent adjudicators often appointed at the start of a project, before any dispute has arisen. They will generally undertake regular visits to site to familiarise themselves with the works with a view to helping the parties to avoid and, if necessary resolve quickly, any disputes. Dispute boards may issue decisions which are binding until final determination of the dispute. For an overview of the role of dispute boards, see *Keating on Construction Contracts*, 10th edn (London: Sweet & Maxwell, 2016), Ch.17, section 12.

4 See, for example, the DAB ("Dispute Adjudication Board") provisions in the FIDIC (the

by agreements intended either to be a temporary resolution pending final determination, or to be final and binding.

DISPUTES CONCERNING PROGRESS

31-04 Disputes concerning progress are often compromised by an "acceleration agreement" by which the contractor or subcontractor undertakes to adopt accelerative measures. The term "acceleration agreement" may be used to mean either an agreement to bring forward the contractual completion date or an agreement to catch up on existing delays.[5] In the former case, the contractor or subcontractor will normally be paid additional sums for the deployment of the additional resources required to accelerate progress. Often the payment is made conditional upon the achievement of the new completion date. Where the purpose is to catch up on existing delays, the terms of the agreement will inevitably depend on which party is responsible for the delays and, in particular, whether or not the contractor or subcontractor already has the benefit of an extension of time. If an extension of time has been granted or claimed, it may be agreed that the extension of time or the claim be withdrawn; if no extension of time has been granted, the original contract may be varied to provide a different completion date.

31-05 It will be important for the parties to make clear whether the acceleration agreement is intended to compromise any existing actual or potential claims for delay or extensions of time. In the absence of express words, the agreement may well be construed as compromising those disputes. Difficulties can arise, however, where there is a disputed claim for an extension of time and the contractor accelerates works, so as not to risk incurring liability for liquidated damages. It may be arguable that, if the contractor is later found to have been entitled to an extension, the employer should be required to pay for the acceleration. This may turn on whether, in the circumstances, the employer's conduct can be construed as giving implicit instructions for acceleration.[6]

31-06 In the negotiation of acceleration agreements it is essential that the parties consider what is to happen if progress is delayed further and to specify whether the original allocation of risk in the underlying contract is to remain or whether, having regard to the additional rewards available to the contractor or subcontractor, a reallocation of risk is required.

Disputes concerning defects

31-07 Disputes concerning defects often arise during the course of the works. The parties may recognise that liability will require extensive investigation and may agree that rectification of the defects is necessary in the meantime so as to ensure satisfac-

---

International Federation of Consulting Engineers) suite of contracts.

5 See the comments of HH Judge Hicks QC in *Ascon Contractors Ltd v Alfred McAlpine Construction Isle of Man Ltd* (2000) 16 Const. L.J. 316 at [50] and [51]. See also Andrew Tweeddale, "What are Acceleration Costs?" (2004) 20 C.L.J. 115.

6 In *Ascon Contractors Ltd v Alfred McAlpine Construction Isle of Man Ltd* (2000) 16 Const. L.J. 316 at [52]-[54], HHJ Wicks QC considered that, had it been pleaded and had the facts supported it, it might have been arguable that instructions to accelerate works could be "discerned" from the employer's conduct. In that case, however, the claim could not succeed on that basis. In *Motherwell Bridge Construction Ltd v Micafil Vacuumtechnik* 81 Con. L.R. 44, HHJ Toulmin QC found that a contractor was entitled to recover acceleration costs incurred as a result of keeping the works to schedule in light of the increased scope of work instructed by the employer.

tory and timely completion of the project. In such circumstances, they may wish to enter into an interim agreement by which the contractor will undertake the necessary remedial works, the employer will continue making payments to the contractor and the question of responsibility for the defects will be resolved subsequently.

It has been pointed out[7] that the following issues should be borne in mind when negotiating such an agreement: **31-08**

(i) whether the agreement is intended to be without prejudice to the parties' rights or without prejudice in the sense that it will be privileged from production[8];
(ii) whether existing rights of set-off should be excluded. An employer might take the benefit of the remedial works, but thereafter refuse to make payment on the ground that the remedial works were going to have to be undertaken by the contractor in any event. The employer could not, of course, refuse to make payment for the works in accordance with the contract in those circumstances, but might seek to raise by way of set-off losses consequent on the delay in remedying work not in conformity with the contract;
(iii) when and in what manner the dispute as to the quality of the works should be determined.

Additionally, the parties should be careful to ensure that the agreement is either expressed as a deed or supported by consideration.[9] Where, for example, the purpose of the acceleration agreement is simply to achieve the contractual completion date, it may be arguable that one of the parties is obliged to do no more than it had agreed to do under the construction contract and therefore that the agreement fails for lack of consideration.[10] **31-09**

CERTIFICATES AND RETENTIONS

Structure of construction contracts

The traditional construction contract is one where there is "an entire contract for the sale of goods and work and labour for a lump sum price payable by instalments as the goods are delivered and the work is done".[11] The contract is likely to provide for the timing or regularity of the contractor's performance. Where it does not, the Courts have generally been reluctant to imply any additional terms prior to the contract completion date.[12] The price and its instalments will often (although not invariably) be paid throughout the course of the contract upon the issue of certificates, either by a third party acting fairly and impartially as between the par- **31-10**

---

7 Fenwick Elliott, *Building contract disputes: practice and precedents*, Ch.14.

8 See Ch.19.

9 See Ch.3 and cf. Ch.30.

10 See, by way of example, *Westminster Building Co v Beckingham* [2004] B.L.R. 163 in which an adjudicator held that a variation agreement was unenforceable because it was not supported by consideration. It was held that the adjudicator had jurisdiction to decide as he did.

11 *Gilbert Ash (Northern) Ltd v Modern Engineering (Bristol) Ltd* [1974] A.C. 689 at 717, per Lord Diplock.

12 See the discussion in *Leander Construction Ltd v Mulalley and Co Ltd* [2011] EWHC 3449 (TCC); [2012] B.L.R. 152 at [26]–[39] and the cases cited there.

ties,[13] or by one of the parties itself acting under a duty to act honestly, fairly and reasonably, in accordance with the terms of the contract.[14] Often an agreed percentage is paid up front as an advance payment, to be earned out over the course of the contract in the certified amounts. Another percentage is generally held back from certified amounts by way of "retention" to be released in stages after satisfactory completion of the works.

31-11 In many forms of contract, certificates issued during the course of the works are not conclusive of whether the work certified complies with the contract. The certificates have "provisional validity".[15] The fact that a certificate has been issued does not prevent a subsequent claim that the works or the materials are substandard, for example, or that the certificate has under or over valued the work. However, there may be a provision requiring the issue of a final certificate which gives rise to evidential or procedural bars to claims by any party. Whether or not the certificate has that effect will be a matter of construction of the relevant provisions of the contract.[16]

31-12 Some standard forms attempt to accommodate settlement agreements reached between the parties. An example is cl.30.2.2 of the *JCT Standard Form of Building Contract* (1998 edn):

> "If any adjudication, arbitration or other proceedings have been commenced by either Party before the Final Certificate has been issued the Final Certificate shall have effect as conclusive evidence as provided in clause 30.9.1 after either:
>
> 2.1 such proceedings have been concluded, whereupon the Final Certificate shall be subject to the terms of any decision, award or judgment in or settlement of such proceedings; or
>
> 2.2 a period of 12 months after the issue of the Final Certificate during which neither Party has taken any further step in such proceedings, whereupon the Final Certificate shall be subject to any terms agreed in partial settlement, whichever shall be the earlier."

31-13 Although the expression "agreed in partial settlement" is somewhat obscure, it is suggested that if proceedings have been commenced before the issue of a final certificate, but have lain dormant for 12 months, the final certificate will be conclusive,[17] subject to any issue that may have been compromised during the course of those proceedings. The terms of any settlement may of course override the conclusive effect of the certificate.

---

13 See *Sutcliffe v Thackrah* [1974] A.C. 727, 737 (in relation to an architect issuing interim certificates). See also the analysis of Lord Hoffmann in *Beaufort Developments (NI) Ltd v Gilbert-Ash (NI) Ltd* [1999] 1 A.C. 266 at 275-282. For a discussion of the role of the engineer or architect in a construction contract more generally, see *Keating on Construction Contracts*, 10th edn (London: Sweet & Maxwell, 2016), Ch.14, section 4.

14 *Balfour Beatty Civil Engineering Ltd v Docklands Light Railway Ltd* (1996) 78 B.L.R. 42 at 57, per Sir Thomas Bingham M.R. The employer conceded that it was subject to such a duty when exercising its powers. In the light of that, the Court did not feel it necessary to imply a term imposing a more wide-ranging duty of good faith on the employer. In *Scheldebouw BV v St. James Homes (Grosvenor Dock) Ltd* [2006] B.L.R. 113 at [46], Jackson J noted that "It is such an unusual state of affairs for the employer himself to be the certifier and decision-maker that this can only be achieved by an express term."

15 Per Lord Hoffmann in *Beaufort Developments (NI) Ltd v Gilbert-Ash (NI) Ltd* [1999] 1 A.C. 266 at 275.

16 *Crown Estate Commissioners v John Mowlem & Co Ltd* (1994) 70 B.L.R. 1, *Matthew Hall Ortech v Tarmac Roadstone* (1997) 87 B.L.R. 96, *Barking & Dagenham LBC v Terrapin Construction Ltd* [2000] B.L.R. 479. See also *Keating on Construction Contracts*, 10th edn (2016), Ch.5, Pt B, section 4.

17 As was the case in *Blackpool BC v F Parkinson Ltd* (1991) 58 B.L.R. 85 (see p.108).

In *Henry Boot Construction Ltd v Alstom Combined Cycles Ltd*[18] the Court of Appeal considered the effect of the certification provisions in the ICE standard conditions (6th edn). The case emphasises the importance of identifying in any particular case the effect of the certificates already issued (or though not issued, that ought to have been issued), the parties' accrued rights under those certificates or for the failure to issue those certificates and the extent to which those accrued rights are intended to be affected by any settlement agreement. **31-14**

The contractor was employed by the defendant to undertake civil engineering works in the construction of a gas turbine power station. The contract was made in 1994 under the ICE standard conditions (6th edn). Under cl.60(2) of the contract, relating to interim certificates, the engineer was required within 28 days of the delivery of the monthly statement to certify and the employer to pay the amount which in the opinion of the engineer "on the basis of the monthly statement" was due on account. Under cl.60(4), relating to the final certificate, the contractor was required to submit a statement of final account,

> "showing in detail the value in accordance with the contract of the works executed together with all further sums which the contractor considers to be due to him up to the date of the defects correction certificate".

Within three months after receipt of the final account, the engineer was required to issue his final certificate stating the amount which in his opinion was finally due under the contract. By May 1996 the works had been substantially completed and in October 2002 the engineer issued a final certificate in the sum of £44.43 million. The employer served a notice of dispute for the consideration of the engineer pursuant to cl.66(2) of the contract, challenging the valuation in the final certificate and raising the issue that the contractor's claim was statute-barred under s.5 of the Limitation Act 1980. The contractor then served two notices of dispute, the first of which related to the employer's refusal to pay the sum certified as due under the final certificate. The engineer decided in relation to the employer's notice that the value of the final account was £44.38 million but made no decision on the limitation issue. In relation to the contractor's first notice, he decided that a sum of at least £2.9 million had become overdue for payment to the contractor on 8 December 2002. Arbitration proceedings were commenced on 27 May 2003, and the limitation defence tried as a preliminary issue. The judge-arbitrator decided that all or almost all the claims were statute-barred because the relevant causes of action had arisen when the work had been done or when the events on which the claims were based had occurred, which was more than six years before the arbitration proceedings were started. The Court of Appeal allowed the contractor's appeal in part: (1) on the true construction of the contract, certificates were not merely evidence of the engineer's opinion but were a condition precedent to the contractor's entitlement to an interim payment under cl.60(2) and final payment under cl.60(4); the right to payment arose not when the work was done but when a certificate was issued or ought to have been issued, but that it did not follow from the fact that a certificate was a condition precedent that the absence of a certificate was a bar to the right to payment; and, accordingly, the judge-arbitrator had erred in concluding that the contractors' entitlement arose when the work was done; (2) the cause of action in respect of the engineer's failure to include a sum in an interim certificate was separate and different from the cause of action in respect of the failure to include the sum in the final certificate, even if the sums were for the same amount; interim certificates were no more than provisional estimates to which the contractor was entitled by way of instalment payments; and the nature of the exercise required to be performed by the contractor and the engineer under the contract at the interim certificate stage was so different from that required at the final certificate stage that it could not be said that a failure by the engineer to perform his obligations at the interim stage could start time running in relation to a cause of action based on the failure by the engineer to perform his obligations in relation to the final certificate; the position would be otherwise in a contract for the pay-

[18] *Henry Boot Construction Ltd. v Alstom Combined Cycles Ltd.* [2005] 1 W.L.R 3850.

ment of fixed monthly instalments which were due and certain and not provisional sums; but (3) once a sum was overdue for payment in a particular month the cause of action was complete in respect of that overdue payment, whether the overdue payment resulted from a failure to pay the contractor the sum due or from the engineer's failure to certify the sum; that the right to claim interest on a sum which should have been certified became statute-barred six years after that right accrued; and that, accordingly, any claim for interest was statute-barred insofar as it was based on amounts that should have, but had not, been certified before 27 May 1997.

31-15 In non-standard form contracts it can be a matter of argument whether certificates are intended to be conclusive on particular matters, or whether the issue of such a certificate is intended to be a condition precedent to a right to payment. In *London & Regional (St George's Court) Ltd v Ministry of Defence*[19] the Court of Appeal considered the criteria for determining these questions. It may sometimes be a conclusive certification regime, although that is much less common and requires the clearest possible terms.[20]

Settlement where certificates are to be issued

31-16 If the parties have agreed to settle a dispute arising under a contract containing certification provisions, they must consider whether their agreement is intended to operate within the context of those provisions or whether it is intended to replace them. Generally, construction contracts provide, either through the evolution of standard forms or through individual negotiation, a complex interaction of the allocation of risk. Parties should be cautious of interfering with the structure of a contract, particularly during the course of the works to which it relates.

Agreements as to the content of certificates

31-17 An agreement operating within the context of the provisions of the contract will allow specific issues to be compromised while preserving the contractual machinery for dealing with outstanding matters in the manner agreed between the parties. This may be achieved by an agreement that operates only to settle the content or quantum of a certificate to be issued by the certifier.

31-18 Parties must exercise care when dealing with certificates from which deductions have been made. They otherwise run the risk of compromising the disputes inherent in such a certificate or of otherwise prejudicing their ability subsequently to claim the sums deducted.

"Clean break" agreements

31-19 Parties are often attracted by "clean break" agreements (often by agreement of the final account after allowance for cross-claims), particularly after the works are

---

19 *London & Regional (St George's Court) Ltd. v Ministry of Defence* [2008] EWCA Civ 1212; [2009] B.L.R. 20.

20 See *Henry Boot Construction Ltd v Alstom Combined Cycles Ltd* [2005] 1 W.L.R. 3850 at [36]-[37] where Dyson LJ, as he then was, made clear that to assert that a certificate (a) is a condition precedent to a right of action but (b) is not conclusive since it can be reviewed by an arbitrator or court is not to advance inconsistent propositions. But any certification regime will ordinarily be attended by provisions designed to ensure fairness, such as what exactly the certifier is to decide, what information he is to have, and what opportunity the potential payer is to have to make representations or provide information.

physically, although not contractually, complete. Such an agreement may discharge the contract and also the jurisdiction of the certifier. Parties should ensure that the agreement addresses all contractual provisions which would normally apply after the final account, such as retentions, liability for latent defects and whether the provisions of the original contract giving a discharge by way of final certificate are to apply[21] or whether liability is to be preserved.[22]

Retentions

As indicated above, retentions should not be overlooked in a "clean break" settlement. If the payment of a single further sum is agreed, it is advisable to state whether it is inclusive or exclusive of retentions. While the employer might be negotiating on the basis of the actual payments made to date, the contractor might regard the retentions as a fund of money that has already been earned, but has not yet been paid. Under certain forms of contract, the employer is entitled to have recourse to the retention fund and to deduct, for example, liquidated damages for delay.[23] **31-20**

MULTIPLE ISSUES

Historically, construction disputes have involved multiple issues. This has given rise to the development of techniques such as the Scott Schedule and the use of preliminary issues and sub-trials. The compromise of discrete issues in construction cases raises two particular issues: **31-21**

(i) multiple causes of action causative of the same or similar damage; and
(ii) latent defects.

Multiple causes of action causative of the same or similar damage

It is not uncommon for a party to a construction dispute to frame its claim not only in terms of breach of the substantive contract, but also in tort (for misrepresentation, negligence or breach of statutory duty), in quasi-contract (for restitutionary remedies) or for breach of a collateral contract. These causes of action may be advanced in the alternative. However, the claim may be put on the basis that damage suffered by the claimant was caused, for example, both by the defendant's breach of contract and by his negligence. The rationale for such a strategy is to take advantage of the limitation periods applicable in tort[24] or equity. Parties have also previously sought to take advantage of the differing measures of damage applicable in tort and contract. However, in *Wellesley Partners LLP v Withers LLP*[25], the Court of Appeal confirmed that, where it would make a difference, parties claiming in contract and tort concurrently should be limited to the stricter contractual test **31-22**

---

21 For an example of the difficulties that can arise where this is not done see *Tameside MBC v Barlow Securities Group Services Ltd* [2001] B.L.R. 113.

22 See for example *Jim Ennis Construction Ltd v Combined Stabilisation Ltd* [2009] EWHC B37 (TCC), where the subcontractor was not entitled to open up or revise the final account value stated in a final account agreement or to receive any further payment under the subcontract.

23 See *Henry Boot Building Ltd v The Croydon Hotel & Leisure Co Ltd* (1985) 36 B.L.R. 41.

24 *Henderson v Merrett Syndicates Limited* [1995] 2 A.C. 145, 191C-D.

25 *Wellesley Partners LLP v Withers LLP* [2015] EWCA Civ 1146; [2016] Ch. 529.

of the parties' reasonable contemplation, rather than the tortious test of reasonable foreseeability.[26] If particular issues are to be compromised, the parties should ensure that they are clearly identified in any agreement or order embodying the compromise. The problems associated with failing to do so have been addressed elsewhere.[27]

LATENT DEFECTS

31-23 Problems can arise in connection with the compromise of claims for defects where there is the potential for further claims in respect of existing defects or for further defects to manifest themselves at some point in the future.

31-24 In *Brunsden v Humphrey*[28] it was said that it is a "well settled rule of law that damages resulting from one and the same cause of action must be assessed and recovered once for all".[29] The settlement of a claim is therefore likely to preclude a further claim based on the same cause of action.

31-25 The principle in *Brunsden* was applied in a construction context in *Conquer v Boot*.[30]

> In that case D contracted to build a bungalow for C in a good and workmanlike manner. C brought an action in the county court "for breach of contract to complete in a good and workmanlike manner", setting forth particulars of what he alleged required to be done to fulfil the contract, and he obtained damages. He afterwards brought another action, claiming in identical terms for breach of the same contract except as to amount claimed, and the addition that the contract was to build "with proper materials". This was followed by particulars different from, but of the same character as, those in the first action. D pleaded res judicata.
>
> Sankey LJ said[31]:
>
> "The cause of action here is: (1) the contract to complete in a good and workmanlike manner a bungalow, and (2) the breach of it. I do not think that every breach of it—every particular brick or particular room that is faulty—gives rise to a separate cause of action. I am of opinion that the cause of action here was the contract and the breach of it, both

---

26 And note the comments, obiter, of HHJ McKenna in *Obsession Hair and Day Spa Limited v Hi-Lite Electrical Limited* [2010] EWHC 2193 at [66]–[67]. See also *McGregor on Damages* 20th edn (London: Sweet & Maxwell, 2014), para.24-009. See also the lecture given by Jackson LJ to the Technology & Construction Bar Association and the Society of Construction Law on 30 October 2014 and entitled "Concurrent Liability: Where have things gone wrong?"—*http://www.judiciary.gov.uk/wp-content/uploads/2014/10/tecbarpaper.pdf* [Accessed 31 October 2019]. The position may be different where the concurrent tort concerned is conversion: *McGregor on Damages*, 20th edn (London: Sweet & Maxwell, 2014), para.24-014.

27 See para.6-07 onwards.

28 *Brunsden v Humphrey* (1884) 14 Q.B.D. 141 at 147, per Bowen LJ. *Brunsden* concerned a claim arising out of a road traffic accident. By a majority, the Court of Appeal found that the plaintiff's claim for damage to his cab relied on a different cause of action to his claim for personal injuries. The cogency of this aspect of the decision has subsequently been doubted and has not been followed in the United States, Canada or Scotland—see *Buckland v Palmer* [1984] 1 W.L.R. 1109, 1115-1116, noted at para.22-08; *Smith v Sabre Insurance* [2013] CSIH 28 at [30]–[39].

29 In *Grieves v FT Everard & Sons Ltd* [2007] 3 W.L.R. 876, Lord Hoffmann, referring to *Brunsden*, put the principle in these terms (at [14]): "A defendant should not have to answer more than once for the consequences of the same act. A corollary of the rule is that if a claimant does have a cause of action, he may recover damages for the risk that he may suffer further injury in consequence of the same act of negligence, even though (under the principle in *Gregg v Scott*), such risk would not be independently actionable."

30 *Conquer v Boot* [1928] 2 K.B. 336.

31 *Conquer v Boot* [1928] 2 K.B. 336 at 342.

of which had been assigned in the original action. I do not think it is possible to say that every one of these breaches is a separate cause of action."

Talbot J said[32]:

"Here, there is but one promise, to complete the bungalow; and the question whether or not it has been performed is to be decided by the state in which the bungalow was when it was handed over by the defendant to the plaintiff as complete ... The plaintiff could not alter the fact that he was recovering damages for the breach of this single promise by failing to specify in his action all the particulars of breach and all the damages for which he was entitled. The test whether a previous action is a bar is not whether the damages to be recovered are different, but whether the cause of action is the same."[33]

In *Steamship Mutual Underwriting Association Ltd v Trollope & Colls (City) Ltd*,[34] however, Lloyd LJ held that in each case it will depend on the facts as to whether or not damage gives rise to a separate cause of action. He said that cases such as *Brunsden* and *Conquer* were simply examples of well-settled principles being applied to particular facts. In his view **31-26**

"if the appellants had succeeded against the contractors and the architects in respect of defects to the central heating system in the original action, and then subsequently the brickwork defects had shown themselves—or indeed let us say foundation defects had shown themselves—and the appellants had brought a second action against those same contractors and architects in respect of those further defects, it is inconceivable that they could have been met with a successful plea of res judicata."

In *Secretary of State for Transport v Pell Frischmann*,[35] after reviewing the authorities, Jackson J set out a number of principles which might be applied to determine whether a claim raised a new cause of action: **31-27**

"(i) If the claimant asserts a duty which was not previously pleaded and alleges a breach of such duty, this usually amounts to a new claim.
(ii) If the claimant alleges a different breach of some previously pleaded duty, it will be a question of fact and degree whether that constitutes a new claim.
(iii) In the case of a construction project, if the claimant alleges breach of a previously pleaded duty causing damage to a different element of the building, that will generally amount to a new claim."

The Court of Appeal approved this statement in *Co-Operative Group Ltd v Birse Developments Ltd*.[36] Longmore LJ noted (at [22]) that the courts have often had great difficulty in deciding whether a new cause of action is pleaded and this is particularly true of construction cases. Longmore LJ also noted the tension between the decision in *Steamship Mutual Underwriting* and previously decided cases. He went on to endorse the statement of Lloyd LJ in *Steamship Mutual Underwriting* that "in most cases it will be easy to say on which side of the line the case falls". Despite this, these cases illustrate the difficulties there can be in deciding whether **31-28**

---

32 *Conquer v Boot* [1928] 2 K.B. 336, 344.
33 This passage was cited with approval by Lord Goff in the House of Lords in *Republic of India v India Steamship Co Ltd ("The Indian Endurance")* [1993] A.C. 410.
34 *Steamship Mutual Underwriting Association Ltd v Trollope & Colls (City) Ltd* (1986) 33 B.L.R. 81 at 101.
35 *Secretary of State for Transport v Pell Frischmann* [2007] B.L.R. 46 at [38].
36 *Co-Operative Group Ltd v Birse Developments Ltd* [2013] B.L.R. 383.

or not a new claim for defects is founded on a cause of action which has already been decided or settled.[37]

31-29 An employer is not bound to set up a defects claim by way of defence to a claim for the contract price.[38] It is therefore open to the employer to admit the claim for the price without being precluded from advancing a defects claim.[39]

31-30 Whether or not a settlement releases other claims will however depend on its terms. Absent an express exclusion, a general release is likely to include claims for latent damage:

> In *Mostcash Plc (formerly UK Paper Plc) v Fluor Ltd (No.1)*,[40] the parties had compromised earlier proceedings,
>
> > "in full and final settlement of all claims and in satisfaction of all causes of action ... arising out of or in connection with [the project] ... excluding only any cause of action that may in future accrue to [Mostcash] (a) for any latent defect arising from [Fluor's] design".
>
> Mostcash commenced subsequent proceedings claiming damages for breach of contract or negligence in respect of Fluor's design. The Court of Appeal found that the claim was barred by the settlement.

31-31 In reaching this conclusion the Court of Appeal emphasised a number of points in construing releases in this context[41]:

(1) First, the case of *Bank of Credit and Commerce International SA v Ali*[42]

---

37 In *Co-Operative Group Ltd v Birse Developments Ltd* [2013] B.L.R. 383 at [22], after his review of the authorities, Tomlinson LJ added his own "gloss", observing that there is not likely to be a new cause of action unless the "new breach does not arise out of the same or substantially the same facts as those already in issue". In *PJSC Tatneft v Bogolyubov* [2016] EWHC 2816 (Comm), Picken J clarified that this was not a reference to the test in CPR 17.4(2), which provides for amendments to statements of case where a limitation period has expired. Picken J added (at [91]) that it was "important, therefore, not to overfocus on Tomlinson LJ's "gloss" and instead to have proper regard to the helpful review which precedes it".

38 *Davis v Hedges* (1871) L.R. 6 Q.B. 687 where, in an action for damages for the non-performance and improper performance of certain work, the defence raised was that the defendant had sued the claimant for the price of the work and the claimant had settled by paying the whole amount then sued for. The defendant claimed that the claimant could have raised the defects as a defence to that action and therefore the claimant was precluded from bringing a cross action for them. It was held that, though the claimant might have used the defects claim in reduction of the claim in the former action, he was not bound to do so, but could maintain a separate action for them. See also: *Bow, McLachlan & Co Ltd v The Camosun* [1909] A.C. 597, 610, 611 and *Henriksens Rederi A/S v T.H.Z. Rolimpex (The Brede)* [1974] Q.B. 233, 248. For a recent application of the latter case, see *Schenker Ltd v Negocios Europa Ltd* [2018] 1 W.L.R. 718.

39 *Keating on Building Contracts*, 10th edn (2015), para.19-161. But note the dicta of Clarke MR in *Stuart v Goldberg Linde* [2008] EWCA Civ 2 at [96]: "For my part, I do not think that parties should keep future claims secret merely because a second claim might involve other issues. The proper course is for parties to put their cards on the table so that no one is taken by surprise and the appropriate course in case management terms can be considered by the judge. In particular parties should not keep quiet in the hope of improving their position in respect of a claim arising out of similar facts or evidence in the future. Nor should they do so simply because a second claim may involve other complex issues. On the contrary they should come clean so that the court can decide whether one or more trials is required and when. The time for such a decision to be taken is before there is a trial of any of the issues. In this way the underlying approach of the CPR, namely that of co-operation between the parties, robust case management and disposing of cases, including particular issues, justly can be forwarded and not frustrated."

40 *Mostcash Plc (formerly UK Paper Plc) v Fluor Ltd (No.1)* [2002] B.L.R. 411.

41 And see the summary of these principles by the Court of Appeal in *Priory Caring Services Limited v Capita Property Services Limited* (2010) 129 Con L.R, 81 at [62].

42 *B.C.C.I. v Ali* [2002] 1 A.C. 251. See para.5-22 onwards.

turned on its own "very particular" facts[43]. The court was not required, as a result of that case, to approach the compromise on the basis that the parties intended to exclude future causes of action of which they would not have had knowledge at the date of the compromise. The claim in *Ali* was excluded from the compromise because it could not have been within the contemplation of the parties at the time of the release—the claim was unknown to the law at that time.[44]

(2) By contrast, claims arising out of latent defects are just the sort of claims that may be expected to be within the contemplation of parties to a construction contract.[45] Claims for latent defects would have fallen squarely within the general release, but for proviso (a) in the settlement agreement.[46]

(3) Properly construed, proviso (a) did not exclude the claims for latent damage as it referred only to "any cause of action that may *in future* accrue". The date on which a cause of action accrued was not postponed as a result of the claimant being unaware of the damage.[47]

A similar approach was taken by the Court of Appeal in *Priory Caring Services Ltd v Capita Property Services Ltd*.[48] **31-32**

In that case, the claimant claimed for damages said to have been caused by the alleged negligence of the defendant surveyor in the design, specification and supervision of refurbishment works to a hotel following a fire. Some time after the work was carried out, it was discovered that the hotel had been seriously affected by damp penetration. The defendant relied on the terms of a prior agreement between the parties, which stated that, save in relation to certain fees:

> "it is agreed that Capita will not issue proceedings against Priory Caring Services Limited"

The Court of Appeal reviewed the authorities, including *Mostcash* and found that the agreement, properly construed, extended to the present claim. The parties knew that there was a question mark over the competence and honesty of the relevant individual. The fact that damp penetration did not emerge until two years after the agreement did not take the resulting claim outside the contemplation of the parties or the scope of the agreement. The claim was therefore struck out.

CLAIMS FOR CONTRIBUTION TO SETTLEMENTS REACHED WITH OTHER PARTIES

Construction disputes frequently involve multiple parties including employers, occupiers, contractors, subcontractors, materials suppliers, professional advisors, guarantors and insurers. The presence of numerous parties with different relationships, liabilities and interests complicates the settlement process.[49] Arbitration clauses are prevalent in construction contracts and it is generally impossible to join further parties to an arbitration without their agreement.[50] As a result, it is not uncommon for parties to settle an arbitration and then pursue other parties for a **31-33**

---

43 *Mostcash* at [52].
44 *Mostcash* at [59].
45 *Mostcash* at [53].
46 *Mostcash* at [47].
47 *Mostcash* at [55], [61].
48 *Priory Caring Services Ltd v Capita Property Services Ltd* (2010) 129 Con L.R. 81.
49 See para.6-26 onwards.
50 Arbitration Act s.35. Where the parties identify institutional rules for the arbitration, consent may

contribution or indemnity.[51] This has led to a considerable jurisprudence on the topic arising from construction disputes.

A REASONABLE SETTLEMENT

31-34 Where one party claims a contribution to a settlement from a third party, the question arises of the relevance of the settlement in quantifying the claimant's loss.

31-35 Ramsey J reviewed the authorities in *Siemens Building Technologies FE Ltd v Supershield Ltd*[52] and stated the following principles:

(1) For C to be liable to A in respect of A's liability to B which was the subject of a settlement it is not necessary for A to prove on the balance of probabilities that A was or would have been liable to B or that A was or would have been liable for the amount of the settlement.
(2) For C to be liable to A in respect of the settlement, A must show that the specified eventuality (in the case of an indemnity given by C to A) or the breach of contract (in the case of a breach of contract between C and A) has caused the loss incurred in satisfying the settlement in the manner set out in the indemnity or as required for causation of damages and that the loss was within the loss covered by the indemnity or the damages were not too remote.
(3) Unless the claim is of sufficient strength reasonably to justify a settlement and the amount paid in settlement is reasonable having regard to the strength of the claim, it cannot be shown that the loss has been caused by the relevant eventuality or breach of contract. In assessing the strength of the claim, unless the claim is so weak that no reasonable party would take it sufficiently seriously to negotiate any settlement involving payment, it cannot be said that the loss attributable to a reasonable settlement was not caused by the eventuality or the breach.
(4) In general if, when a party is in breach of contract, a claim by a third party is in the reasonable contemplation of the parties as a probable result of the breach, then it will generally also be in the reasonable contemplation of the parties that there might be a reasonable settlement of any such claim by the other party.
(5) The test of whether the amount paid in settlement was reasonable is whether the settlement was, in all the circumstances, within the range of settlements which reasonable people in the position of the settling party might have made. Such circumstances will generally include:
    (a) The strength of the claim;
    (b) Whether the settlement was the result of legal advice;
    (c) The uncertainties and expenses of litigation;
    (d) The benefits of settling the case rather than disputing it.
(6) The question of whether a settlement was reasonable is to be assessed at the date of the settlement when necessarily the issues between A and B remained unresolved.

This statement of the law was not challenged in the Court of Appeal[53], where

---

be found in those rules. See, for example, the LCIA Rules 2014, art.22(x); ICC Arbitration Rules 2017, art.10.

[51] See para.6-49 onwards.

[52] *Siemens Building Technologies FE Ltd v Supershield Ltd* (2009) 124 Con. L.R. 158.

[53] *Siemens* [2010] EWCA Civ 7; [2010] 1 Lloyd's Rep. 349 at 353.

Toulson LJ said[54]:

> "Megarry J once described the law reports as charts of the wrecks of unsinkable cases. Because of its uncertainty and expense, prudent parties usually try to avoid litigation where possible. It has to be borne in mind that the "settlement value" of a claim is not an objective fact (or something which can be assessed by reference to an available market) but a matter of subjective opinion, taking account of all relevant variables. Often parties may have widely different perceptions of what would be a fair settlement figure without either being unreasonable. The object of mediation or negotiation is then to close the gap to a point which each finds acceptable. When a judge is considering the reasonableness of a settlement he will have in mind these factors and another: that he is likely to have a less complete understanding of the relative strengths of the settling parties than they had themselves (unless he is to embark on a disproportionately detailed investigation), and especially so in complex litigation. The issue which the judge has to decide is not what assessment he would have made of the likely outcome of the settled litigation, but whether the settlement was within the range of what was reasonable. If he decides that it was, an appellate court will not interfere with his decision unless persuaded that he erred in principle or (which is intrinsically unlikely) that his decision was incapable of justification on any reasonable view."

Ramsey J's summary of the law was adopted in *125 OBS (Nominees1) v Lend Lease Construction (Europe) Ltd*.[55] After reciting the summary, Stuart-Smith J added the following points[56]: **31-36**

(i) The Court encourages reasonable settlements, particularly where strict proof would be very expensive.
(ii) The test of reasonableness is generous, reflecting the fact that the paying party has put the other in a difficult situation by its breach.
(iii) Reasonableness is evaluated as at the time of the settlement and in the chances of litigation at that time.
(iv) A claim will generally have to be so weak as to be obviously hopeless before it can be said that settling it is unreasonable.
(v) The evidential burden of proving unreasonableness of any settlement falls upon the defendant: see *Mander v Commercial Union Assurance* [1998] Lloyds Rep IR 93, 148 col 2 per Rix J, *BP Plc v AON* [2006] EWHC 424 (Comm) at [281]–[282].

In many cases, it will be sufficient to cite the principles stated by Ramsey J in *Siemens Building Technologies FE Ltd v Supershield Ltd* and by Stuart-Smith J in *OBS (Nominees1) v Lend Lease Construction (Europe) Ltd*. However, it is important to have an understanding of how these principles have developed. **31-37**

The principle in Biggin v Permanite

The leading case on the relevance of a settlement to quantum is *Biggin v Permanite*.[57] **31-38**

> In that case, the claimant had settled an arbitration arising out of its supply of defective roofing materials to the Dutch Government. The claimant then brought proceedings against its suppliers to recover that sum as damages for breach of warranty. The defend-

---

[54] *Siemens* [2010] EWCA Civ 7; [2010] 1 Lloyd's Rep. 349 at [28].
[55] *OBS (Nominees1) v Lend Lease Construction (Europe) Ltd* [2017] EWHC 25 (TCC) at [186].
[56] *OBS (Nominees1) v Lend Lease Construction (Europe) Ltd* [2017] EWHC 25 (TCC) at [187].
[57] *Biggin v Permanite* [1951] 2 K.B. 314.

ant admitted liability but disputed quantum. At first instance,[58] Devlin J found that the settlement sum was irrelevant to quantum and dismissed the claim for the settlement sum. The claimant was obliged to prove its actual loss, which was its actual liability to the Dutch Government. The Court of Appeal reversed this decision and held that the settlement sum, if reasonable, should be taken as the measure of damages. Whether or not the settlement was reasonable was a question to be determined by evidence. In the circumstances, the evidence in the case established that it was reasonable.

31-39 Somervell LJ said this[59]:

> "I think that the judge here was wrong in regarding the settlement as wholly irrelevant. I think, though it is not conclusive, that the fact that it is admittedly an upper limit would lead to the conclusion that, if reasonable, it should be taken as the measure. The result of the judge's conclusion is that [the claimants] must prove their damages strictly to an extent to show that they equal or exceed £43,000; and that if that involves, as it would here, a very complicated and expensive inquiry, still that has to be done. The law, in my opinion, encourages reasonable settlements, particularly where, as here, strict proof would be a very expensive matter."

31-40 This principle has been applied to contribution claims advanced both on the basis of the third party's breach of duty,[60] pursuant to a contractual indemnity[61] and pursuant to the Civil Liability (Contribution) Act 1978.[62]

31-41 The principle was also applied in relation to costs in *Construction and Property Consultants LLP (Arcadis Homola Project Management AG, Part 20 defendant)*,[63] where a defendant claimed its costs of third party proceedings from the claimant after the main claim was struck out.

31-42 It is necessary, but not of itself sufficient, for a party to demonstrate that the settlement was reasonable. The claimant must first show that the third party is liable on the usual principles. In *Fletcher & Steward v Jay & Partners*,[64] the Court of Appeal confirmed that the principle in *Biggin* was concerned only with the relevance of a settlement sum to the quantum of the claimant's damages. A defendant cannot impose liability on a third party by settling the claimant's claim against him. Geoffrey Lane LJ pointed out that *Biggin* has nothing to do with proving the liability of a third party to a defendant.[65]

WHAT MUST BE PROVED TO DEMONSTRATE A REASONABLE SETTLEMENT?

31-43 The question of what must be proved to demonstrate a reasonable settlement has been addressed in a series of cases decided since *Biggin v Permanite*.

---

58 *Biggin & Co Ltd v Permanite Ltd* [1951] 1 K.B. 422.

59 *Biggin* [1951] 2 K.B. 314 at 321.

60 As was the case in *Biggin v Permanite* itself.

61 See, for example, *Siemens Building Technologies FE Ltd v Supershield Ltd* (2009) 124 Con. L.R. 158, where liability arose both for breach of contract and pursuant to a contractual indemnity. The decision was upheld on appeal: [2010] EWCA Civ 7; [2010] 1 Lloyd's Rep. 349.

62 See, for example, *Demco v Interamerican Life Assurance (International) Ltd* [2012] EWHC 2053 (Comm) at [55] and *Gilman v UPS Ltd* [2013] EWHC 2341 (TCC) at [163]–[165], where HHJ Stephen Davies (sitting as a High Court Judge) expressly rejected the submission that the principle should not have been extended to contribution claims under the 1978 Act.

63 *German Property 50 Sarl v Summers-Inman Construction and Property Consultants LLP v Arcadis Homola Project Management AG* [2009] EWHC 2968 (TCC).

64 *Fletcher & Steward v Jay & Partners* (1976) 17 B.L.R. 38.

65 *Fletcher & Steward* (1976) 17 B.L.R. 38 at 44 and 46.

In *Biggin v Permanite*, Somervell LJ said[66]: **31-44**

"The question, in my opinion, is: what evidence is necessary to establish reasonableness? I think it relevant to prove that the settlement was made under advice legally taken. The client himself could do that, but I do not think that the advisers would normally be relevant or admissible witnesses. I say 'normally'. It may be that in special cases they might be. [The claimant] must, I think, lead evidence, which can be cross-examined to, as to facts which the witnesses themselves prove and as to what would probably be proved if, as here, the arbitration had proceeded, so that the court can come to a conclusion whether or not the sum paid was reasonable. The defendant may, by cross-examination, as was done here, seek to show—and perhaps successfully show—that it was not reasonable. He may do so, or call evidence which leads to the same conclusion. He might in some cases show that some vital matter had been overlooked."

Singleton LJ said[67]: **31-45**

"The claimants must establish a prima facie case that the settlement was a reasonable one. If the defendants fail to shake that case, the amount of the settlement can properly be awarded as damages. The position is much the same, though perhaps not quite so strong, as in a case in which damages have been assessed in a suit between other parties involving the same facts. The judgment is not binding, but the court will not lightly disregard it in the absence of fresh evidence or new factors ...

The question is not whether the claimants acted reasonably in settling the claim, but whether the settlement was a reasonable one; and, in considering it, the court is entitled to bear in mind the fact that costs would grow every day the litigation was continued. That is one reason for saying that it is sufficient for the purpose of the claimants if they satisfy the judge that somewhere around the figure of settlement would have been awarded as damages."

Comyn Ching & Co (London) Ltd v Oriental Tube Co Ltd[68] concerned a claim for a contribution pursuant to a contractual indemnity. Goff LJ said[69]: **31-46**

"It is clear that in *Fisher v Val de Travers*, Lord Coleridge, CJ, put two questions to the jury: (1) Was it reasonable to compromise, and (2) Was the sum paid reasonable (see page 480). In *Biggin v Permanite* Somervell LJ said (at p.320) the two questions are really only one, and so of course, for his purpose they were because in his case the defendant admitted that he was liable to indemnify the plaintiff and the only issue was that of quantum. In practice I think they will generally be found to merge into one another, although for example, if the point was one which could be speedily and cheaply determined, it might not be reasonable as against the indemnifier to settle, though if there were going to be a settlement, the amount might be perfectly reasonable.

I will consider the problem in the present case on the basis that there are two separate questions which are the most favourable to the defendants. So far as the first question is concerned, it has in my judgment only to be asked to be seen to require an affirmative answer. Ching were advised to settle by competent and experienced legal advisers. That is not conclusive, but clearly important. Ching were facing long and complex litigation which was bound to be costly, and the outcome of which they could not foresee with any certainty."

In *Holland Hannen v WHTSO*,[70] the Court of Appeal emphasised that the court has to consider the reasonableness of the compromise itself, not the reasonableness of the conduct of the parties. **31-47**

---

66 *Biggin* [1951] 2 K.B. 314 at 321.

67 *Biggin* [1951] 2 K.B. 314 at 325–326.

68 *Comyn Ching & Co (London) Ltd v Oriental Tube Co Ltd* [1979] 17 B.L.R. 56.

69 At p.89.

70 *Holland Hannen v Welsh Health Technical Services Organisation* (1985) 35 B.L.R. 1 at 15.

31-48 *Seven Seas Properties Ltd v Al-Essa (No.2)*[71] is an example of a case where the settlement was held not to be reasonable. Gavin Lightman QC (as he was), sitting as a deputy High Court judge, held that it is not sufficient for the claimant merely to plead the compromise without any explanation as to how the settlement figure was made up or arrived at, or any evidence as to how or why or on what advice it was entered into. He rejected the claim because he considered that it over-valued certain matters.

31-49 In *P&O Developments v Guy's and St Thomas' National Health Service Trust*[72] HH Judge Bowsher QC held that an agreement made with a person not a party to the action is relevant and admissible on two bases: (a) as a rule of evidence—the settlement may be some evidence of the true value of the claim settled, it sets a maximum to the claim and may reduce the degree and detail of evidence required to prove the claim; and (b) the reasonable settlement of claims may be a matter which parties may be held to have in their reasonable contemplation under the second rule in *Hadley v Baxendale*.[73] By "reasonable settlement" the judge meant that it was based on an assessment of what was legally due to the third party.

31-50 In *Royal Brompton National Health Service Trust v Hammond (No 1)*[74] HH Judge Hicks QC held, after a detailed analysis of what was in dispute in *Biggin*[75], that the principle extends not only to cases where liability is not in dispute, but also where the settlement involves a compromise of issues of liability on a claim and counterclaim as well as issues of quantum.[76]

31-51 In *General Feeds v Slobodna Plovidba Yugoslavia*,[77] Colman J said:

> "assuming that loss attributable to a payment in settlement is not too remote, the plaintiff must prove that the fact and amount of the settlement were reasonable in all the circumstances. Unless he proves that, he fails to establish that the loss was caused by the relevant breach of contract by the defendant, for if and to the extent that an unreasonable settlement has been entered into, the loss has been caused not by the breach but by the plaintiff's voluntary assumption of liability under the settlement …
>
> … when properly analysed, the overall exercise which the Court must do is to consider whether the specified eventuality (in the case of an indemnity) or the breach of contract (in a case such as the present) has caused the loss incurred in satisfying the settlement. Unless the claim is of sufficient strength reasonably to justify a settlement and the amount paid in settlement is reasonable having regard to the strength of the claim, it cannot be shown that the loss has been caused by the relevant eventuality or breach of contract. That is not to say that unless it can be shown that the claim is likely to succeed it will be impossible to establish that it was reasonable to settle it. There may be many claims which appear to be intrinsically weak but which common prudence suggests should be settled in order to avoid the uncertainties and expenses of litigation. Even the successful defence

---

71 *Seven Seas Properties Ltd v Al-Essa (No.2)* [1993] 1 W.L.R. 1083 at 1089.

72 *P&O Developments v Guy's and St Thomas' NHS Trust* [1999] B.L.R. 3 at 13.

73 *Hadley v Baxendale* (1854) 9 Ex. 341.

74 *Royal Brompton NHS Trust v Hammond (No 1)* [1999] B.L.R. 162 at 170.

75 As noted by Edwards-Stuart J in *Fluor v Shanghai Zhenhua Heavy Industry Co Ltd* [2018] EWHC 1 (TCC) at [467], it had been wrongly assumed in some other cases that liability was not in issue when Biggin settled its claim.

76 In *Hammond*, HHJ Hicks QC considered that the effect of *Biggin* was to preclude any argument that a party had failed to mitigate its loss in settling a claim: see [19]–[20]. Warren J expressed "serious doubts" about that view in *Codemasters Software Co Ltd v Automobile Club de L'Ouest* [2009] EWHC 3194 (Ch) at [27]–[28]. *Biggin* was concerned with the measure of loss and mitigation was not considered. There was nothing in *Biggin* to prevent a party from saying that, even though the settlement was reasonable, the claimant had failed to mitigate the loss by failing to take steps which would have reduced it.

77 *General Feeds Inc Panama v Slobodna Plovidba Yugoslavia (The Krapan J)* [1999] 1 Lloyd's Rep. 688, 691.

> of a claim in complex litigation is likely to involve substantial irrevocable costs ... Unless it appears on the evidence that the claim is so weak that no reasonable owner or club would take it sufficiently seriously to negotiate any settlement involving payment, it cannot be said that the loss attributable to a reasonable settlement was not caused by the breach by reason of which the goods are in a damaged condition."

In *CFW Architects v Cowlin Construction*[78] the contractor sought damages from the architect under a design and build contract representing sums paid to the employer in settlement of the contractor's liability for liquidated damages for delay. The employer had agreed a generous extension of time in return for the contractor abandoning its claim that the liquidated damages provisions represented a penalty. HH Judge Anthony Thornton QC held that the settlement represented a sum reasonably incurred as a direct result of the delays caused by the architect since it was a sum resulting from a reasonable settlement of a dispute between the contractor and the employer for the delay caused by the architect. Notwithstanding that the judge found that the arguments that the liquidated damages constituted a penalty would not have succeeded, those arguments were available during the settlement negotiations and therefore contributed to the reasonableness of the settlement. **31-52**

In *John F Hunt Demolition Ltd v ASME Engineering Ltd*[79] HH Judge Peter Coulson QC (as he then was) expressed the view that it must be reasonably foreseeable, at the time that the contracts were made between A and C, that A might settle a claim brought by B arising out of the same subject matter, even if, on a detailed analysis, A's legal liability to B might actually be hard or even impossible to establish. It was not necessary to prove that the settled claim would probably have succeeded. **31-53**

RELEVANCE AND ADMISSIBILITY OF ADVICE RECEIVED

In *Biggin*, the Court of Appeal commented that it was relevant, but not conclusive, that the claimant had entered into the settlement agreement on advice from its lawyers. However, evidence from the advisers themselves explaining the advice would not normally be relevant or admissible.[80] **31-54**

In *Oxford University Press v John Stedman Design Group*[81] HH Judge Esyr Lewis QC held that it was neither necessary nor indeed permissible to call evidence from any legal adviser to explain why the settlement was made and its basis. The court has to decide whether the settlement was reasonable in the light of the circumstances that are shown to have obtained when the settlement was made. The opinion of the lawyers who advised the party who settled is irrelevant. **31-55**

In *DSL Group v Unisys International*[82], HH Judge Hicks QC went one stage further, finding that the content of the advice was also irrelevant and inadmissible. He noted that the defendant to the original claim must prove that the settlement was reasonable, not that he acted reasonably and found that the advice he received will go to the latter not the former. Accordingly, the nature of the advice is legally irrelevant and, therefore, privilege in respect of it is not waived automatically by any reference to it. This analysis was said to be "lucid and helpful" by HH Judge **31-56**

---

78 *CFW Architects v Cowlin Construction* (2006) 105 Con. L.R. 116 at 168.

79 *John F Hunt Demolition Ltd v ASME Engineering Ltd* [2007] EWHC 1507 (TCC); [2008] 1 All E.R. 180.

80 See para.31-44.

81 *Oxford University Press v John Stedman Design Group* (1990) 34 Con. L.R. 1 at 101.

82 *DSL Group v Unisys International* (1994) 67 B.L.R. 117 at 137.

Humphrey Lloyd QC in *J Sainsbury Plc v Broadway Malyan*.[83] He went further still, holding that the test is an objective one and so the fact that settlement was reached following legal advice is also irrelevant.[84]

31-57 In the *P&O*[85] case, HH Judge Bowsher QC expressly disagreed with that conclusion. He held that advice received by a party might go either to the question whether the claimants acted reasonably or to the question whether the settlement was reasonable, or both. Moreover, whether the claimants acted reasonably may have an evidential bearing on whether the settlement was reasonable. HH Judge Anthony Thornton QC reviewed the authorities in *Bovis Lend Lease Ltd (formerly Bovis Construction Ltd) v RD Fire Protection Ltd*,[86] and concluded that evidence that may be adduced to establish reasonableness may include, if the claimant so elects, evidence of advice given by relevant professionals to the claimant which was relied on in deciding to settle. Warren J took the same view in *Codemasters Software Co Ltd v Automobile Club de L'Ouest*.[87] He also disagreed with the views of HHJ Hicks QC. He agreed that the correct question was whether the settlement was reasonable, not whether the claimant had acted reasonably in settling. He further agreed that the fact that advice had been received by the claimant might go only to the excluded issue of whether the claimant had acted reasonably. However, the advice itself could be relevant to whether the settlement was reasonable.[88]

31-58 Despite the judgment of HH Judge Hicks QC in *DSL Group*, it appears to be right that the fact and content of legal advice may be relevant in determining whether a settlement was reasonable. However, this will not be sufficient to establish that the settlement was reasonable.[89] In practice, it may be of limited probative value.

31-59 Where a party contends or accepts that the existence, nature and terms of any advice received are facts material to the issue of the reasonableness of the settlement, privilege in respect of that advice is waived.[90] The extent of such waiver will depend on the manner in which the advice is deployed.[91]

Global settlements

31-60 The *Biggin* principle continues to apply where a settlement incorporates multiple heads of claim for only some of which the third party is liable.[92] In those circumstances, however, the court will need to make an assessment of which parts of the settlement are attributable to the third party's breach of duty or other liability.

---

83 *J Sainsbury Plc v Broadway Malyan* (1998) 61 Con. L.R. 29 at 64.

84 This statement appears to go somewhat further than HH Judge Hicks QC went in the *DSL* case and is difficult to reconcile with Somervell LJ's statement in Biggin that "I think it relevant to prove that the settlement was made under advice legally taken" and Singleton LJ's that "It is a matter for consideration that the settlement was arrived at under advice".

85 *P&O* (1999) B.L.R. 3 at 14.

86 *Bovis Land Lease Ltd (formerly Bovis Construction Ltd) v RD Fire Protection Ltd* (2003) 89 Con. L.R. 169.

87 *Codemasters Software Co Ltd v Automobile Club de L'Ouest* [2009] EWHC 3194 (Ch)

88 *Codemasters Software Co Ltd v Automobile Club de L'Ouest* [2009] EWHC 3194 (Ch) at [24]–[26].

89 See for example, *Mirant Asia-Pacific Construction (Hong Kong) Limited v Ove Arup and Partners International Ltd* [2007] EWHC 918 (TCC) at [44].

90 *The Society of Lloyds v Kitson's Environmental Services* (1994) 67 B.L.R. 102 at 116.

91 *Bovis Lend Lease Ltd (formerly Bovis Construction Ltd) v RD Fire Protection Ltd* (2003) 89 Con. L.R. 169 at [80], point 5.

92 *P&O* (1999) B.L.R. 3 at 11 onwards, *Royal Brompton* (1999) B.L.R. 162 at 168-169. See also Lewis Cohen, "Reasonableness of Settlements Revisited" (2005) 21 Const. L.J. 216.

In *Bovis Lend Lease Ltd (formerly Bovis Construction Ltd) v RD Fire Protection Ltd*,[93] C had settled claims and counterclaims brought by C against the employer. Certain preliminary issues fell to be determined between C and its subcontractors, D1 and D2. C contended that defaults by both D1 and D2 had caused it to be in breach of the main contract, which had led the employer to bring substantial claims against C. It fell to be determined whether the global settlement between C and the employer precluded C from claiming for the alleged defaults against D1 and D2 where the settlement did not provide a means of determining the fault attributable to each of them and, further, whether C could rely on hypothetical remedial schemes instead of on the settlement to support its loss claims. **31-61**

HH Judge Anthony Thornton QC considered the law concerning reliance on settlement agreements. He derived eight conclusions from the *Biggin* line of authorities. His eighth principle addressed multi-party cases[94]: **31-62**

> "8. The *Biggin* principles are not confined to cases where there is only one party causing the loss being settled or where the claims being settled are confined to those based on the defendant's breaches of contract. It is necessary, however, for the court to determine what part of an overall settlement of a multi-party or multi-issue dispute is attributable to the relevant breaches of contract of the defendant, or to each separate defendant where a *Biggin* claim is being made against more than one defendant. Any allocation of part of a reasonable overall settlement must itself be reasonable."

He then went on to answer six disputed issues as to the application of the *Biggin* principles that arose on the facts of the case, but will arise in many other cases: **31-63**

(1) Where a settlement has been entered into, it is for the claimant to establish the sum or loss caused by relevant claims or causes of action.
(2) Where the wording of a settlement does not identify what sum is included for the settlement of relevant claims or causes of action and there is no allocation of the overall sum to the relevant claims or causes of action, it ought to be possible for a court to undertake the two necessary tasks of placing an appropriate value on the settlement and of apportioning from that an appropriate and reasonable overall value for the works in respect of which contribution is being sought. The court should not accept the assertion that these tasks are impossible unless there is clear and satisfactory factual and expert evidence to support it.
(3) Even if a claimant elects to prove its claim in some other way than by relying on a settlement, it is prevented from recovering more than the sum included in the settlement, even if a greater sum is proved by that alternative means. The settlement amount attributable to the claim against the third party is a cap on the third party's liability.
(4) If a claimant cannot establish what part of the settlement related to or could be allocated to the defendant's breaches of contract, then either the claimant fails to establish that any sum is included in the settlement, or the evidence might establish that something was included in the settlement and the court should assess a reasonable sum. However, it might not be possible or reasonable to make such an assessment; if the unreasonableness had been the result of inequitable or self-induced conduct of the claimant, the claim would fail because the claimant could not establish what sum it lost.

---

[93] *Bovis Lend Lease Ltd (formerly Bovis Construction Ltd) v RD Fire Protection Ltd* (2009) 89 Con L.R. 169.

[94] *Bovis Lend Lease Ltd (formerly Bovis Construction Ltd) v RD Fire Protection Ltd* (2009) 89 Con L.R. 169 at [80].

On the other hand, if the unreasonableness arose from factors outwith the claimant's control, it might be concluded that there was no significant reduction in the loss incurred by the claimant as a result of the settlement and the claimant may proceed to seek damages unconstrained by the settlement.

(5) Following *Comyn Ching & Co (London) Ltd v Oriental Tube Co Ltd*,[95] the inclusion of unpleaded claims does not automatically render a settlement unreasonable but must depend on the possibility that the claimant's ultimate liability might include those claims. The fact that the third party is liable for only a small element of the dispute which was settled is a matter of evidence which goes to the question of what part of the settlement (if any) should be attributed to the third party's breach.

(6) If the settlement is unreasonable, it can provide no evidential foundation to establish the claimant's loss, but it would still provide a ceiling on recovery if the claim were sought to be established by conventional means. On the other hand, if it could be shown that the settlement constituted a break in the chain of causation or was a wholly unreasonable failure to mitigate the claimant's loss, nothing would be recoverable.

31-64 Where a settlement agreement does allocate sums to particular claims or causes of action, that will not necessarily be conclusive. The court will look behind the form or words used in a global settlement to ascertain the underlying position and to ensure that third parties rights are not unjustly affected.

31-65 The preceding paragraph was considered by Edwards-Stuart J in *Fluor v Shanghai Zhenhua Heavy Industry Co Ltd*[96] and the approach was endorsed in his reasoning.[97]

In *Fluor v Shanghai Zhenhua Heavy Industry Co Ltd*, a contractor had been engaged to construct the foundations and infrastructure for offshore wind turbines. Cracking in the welds of steel elements had been caused by the sub-contractor's breach of contract. As a result, the employer had demanded testing which the contractor and sub-contractor considered went beyond what was required by the contract. The contractor and subcontractor had settled certain aspects of the dispute between them. The contractor then entered into a settlement agreement with the employer. According to the terms of that agreement (a) the employer agreed to pay the contractor £42.65m in respect of unpaid milestone payments and variation orders (b) the contractor agreed to pay the employer £32.325m in respect of "Counterclaim Damages"; (c) the contractor agreed to provide an extended warranty in relation to certain unrepaired steel elements, capped at £28m; and (d) the parties otherwise agreed to "walk away" and mutual release[98]. The contractor claimed that it had given up approximately £20m in claims against the employer, with the result that the cost of the settlement was approximately £53.325m. It therefore claimed approximately £50m from the sub-contractor as losses arising from its breach. The sub-contractor did not deny the bona fides of the settlement, but contended that the expression "Counterclaim Damages" did not reflect the true nature of the sums agreed to be paid under that head and could not be relied on. Edwards-Stuart J considered that the Court's task was to establish what proportion of the sum paid or foregone (a) was attributable to the breaches of contract by the sub-contractor and (b) was in respect of costs or delays which had not been waived in the settlement between the contractor and sub-contractor. The Court then needed to assess whether that proportion of the settlement was reasonable, taking into account the extended warranty. The exercise was not the same as construing the settlement contract between the contractor and employer, with the result that the

---

95 *Comyn Ching & Co (London) Ltd v Oriental Tube Co Ltd* (1979) 17 B.L.R. 47.
96 *Fluor v Shanghai Zhenhua Heavy Industry Co Ltd* [2018] EWHC 1 (TCC).
97 *Fluor v Shanghai Zhenhua Heavy Industry Co Ltd* [2018] EWHC 1 (TCC) at [477]–[480].
98 *Fluor v Shanghai Zhenhua Heavy Industry Co Ltd* [2018] EWHC 1 (TCC) at [458].

Court was entitled to look at evidence of the negotiations leading to the settlement which would otherwise have been excluded in construing the agreement.[99] The Judge found that he was not bound by the label applied to the "Counterclaim Damages". Of the sum claimed, £13.825m was attributable to claims arising from the defective welding which had not been waived by agreement between the contractor and sub-contractor.[100] That was a reasonable settlement and so the sub-contractor was liable to the contractor in that amount.

The point arose in a different context in *Durabella Ltd v Jarvis & Sons Ltd*.[101] **31-66**

In that case, C was a subcontractor to D on "pay when paid" terms. D had been involved in previous proceedings with the employer which had been compromised on terms which, at the behest of D, included the following,

> "no value is included within the settlement figure for works undertaken in connection with the Development by [C] the subject of [the action by C] and [the employer] has taken account of its counterclaim ... in calculating the sum to be paid to [D]".

HH Judge Humphrey Lloyd QC held that the settlement had no evidential value whatsoever as showing whether or not D received payment for C's work. The relevant clause inserted by D had the deliberate intention of misleading readers as to the employer's supposed position.

Liability under the Civil Liability (Contribution) Act 1978[102]

Where a party (D) settles a claim or proposed claim against it by C, it may seek to claim a contribution from a third party under the Civil Liability (Contribution) Act 1978, s.1, on the ground that the third party is liable to the claimant for the same damage.[103] The meaning of the phrase "the same damage" has been addressed by the Courts on a number of occasions.[104] Two of the most important cases concerned construction contracts. **31-67**

In *Birse Construction Ltd v Haiste Ltd*,[105] C was engaged to design and construct a reservoir. The employer appointed its own employee, N as the engineer responsible for issuing certificates. The reservoir was defective and C settled on terms including its agreement to build a replacement reservoir. C sued its sub-contractor, D, who in turn brought a third party claim against N. It was held that D's claim failed. D and N could not be liable for the same damage. Any liability N might have had would have been to the employer. D's liability was to C. The term "the same damage" referred to damage suffered by the same person. **31-68**

In *Royal Brompton Hospital NHS Trust v Hammond (No.3)*,[106] a contractor was employed to construct a hospital. The employer and the contractor settled, inter alia, claims by the employer for late delivery of the building. The employer then brought proceedings against the architect for negligence in issuing an instruction and granting extensions of time which imposed a liability on the employer to the contractor. The architect brought third party proceedings against the contractor. The claims by the employer against the contractor and the architect were not claims in respect of the same damage. **31-69**

---

99 *Fluor v Shanghai Zhenhua Heavy Industry Co Ltd* [2018] EWHC 1 (TCC) at [480]–[483].

100 *Fluor v Shanghai Zhenhua Heavy Industry Co Ltd* [2018] EWHC 1 (TCC) at [529]–[540].

101 *Durabella Ltd v Jarvis & Sons Ltd* (2001) 83 Con. L.R. 145.

102 See para.6-49 onwards.

103 It is not necessary to establish that D was in fact liable to C. D must show that it would have been liable to C if the factual basis of the claim against it could be established: Civil Liability (Contribution) Act 1978, s.1(4).

104 See para.6-52.

105 *Birse Construction Ltd v Haiste Ltd* [1996] 1 W.L.R. 675.

106 *Royal Brompton Hospital NHS Trust v Hammond (No.3)* [2002] UKHL 14; [2002] 1 W.L.R. 1397.

31-70 Lord Bingham referred to "the obvious justice of requiring that a common liability should be shared between those liable". He went on to say:

> "5. It is plain beyond argument that one important object of the 1978 Act was to widen the classes of person between whom claims for contribution would lie and to enlarge the hitherto restricted category of causes of action capable of giving rise to such a claim. It is, however, as I understand, a constant theme of the law of contribution from the beginning that B's claim to share with others his liability to A rests upon the fact that they (whether equally with B or not) are subject to a common liability to A...
>
> 6. When any claim for contribution falls to be decided the following questions in my opinion arise:
> (1) What damage has A suffered?
> (2) Is B liable to A in respect of that damage?
> (3) Is C also liable to A in respect of that damage or some of it?
>
> ... I do not think it matters greatly whether, in phrasing these questions, one speaks (as the 1978 Act does) of "damage" or of "loss" or "harm", provided it is borne in mind that "damage" does not mean "damages" (as pointed out by Roch LJ in *Birse Construction Ltd v Haiste Ltd* [1996] 1 W.L.R. 675, at p 682) and that B's right to contribution by C depends on the damage, loss or harm for which B is liable to A corresponding (even if in part only) with the damage, loss or harm for which C is liable to A. This seems to me to accord with the underlying equity of the situation: it is obviously fair that C contributes to B a fair share of what both B and C owe in law to A, but obviously unfair that C should contribute to B any share of what B may owe in law to A but C does not."

31-71 Lord Steyn referred to the earlier judgment of Sir Richard Scott VC in *Howkins & Harrison v Tyler (a firm)*,[107] at p.4, para.17:

> "Suppose that A and B are the two parties who are said each to be liable to C in respect of 'the same damage' that has been suffered by C. So C must have a right of action of some sort against A and a right of action of some sort against B. There are two questions that should then be asked. If A pays C a sum of money in satisfaction, or on account, of A's liability to C, will that sum operate to reduce or extinguish, depending upon the amount, B's liability to C? Secondly, if B pays C a sum of money in satisfaction or on account of B's liability to C, would that operate to reduce or extinguish A's liability to C? It seems to me that unless both of those questions can be given an affirmative answer, the case is not one to which the 1978 Act can be applied. If the payment by A or B to C does not pro tanto relieve the other of his obligations to C, there cannot, it seems to me, possibly be a case for contending that the nonpaying party, whose liability to C remains unreduced, will also have an obligation under section 1(1) to contribute to the payment made by the paying party."

Payment in kind

31-72 Where a contractor has agreed with an employer to carry out remedial works, that will nevertheless amount to "payment" within the meaning of s.1(4) of the Civil Liability (Contribution) Act 1978, at least where the payment in kind was capable of valuation in monetary terms. Accordingly, the contractor would not be precluded from seeking contribution under the 1978 Act from another party alleged to be liable in respect of the same damage.[108]

---

107 [2001] Lloyd's Rep. PN 1.

108 *Baker & Davies Plc v Leslie Wilks Associates (A Firm)* [2005] EWHC 1179 (TCC); [2005] 3 All E.R. 603.

Indemnities

The existence of indemnities in the contract between the claimant and those from whom contribution is sought will affect the circumstances and extent of recovery. An indemnity may be expressed to be against claims made, as opposed to liabilities[109] or be limited to specific liabilities. It remains to be decided whether the existence of a limited contractual right of indemnity will also limit the right of recovery under the *Biggin* principle. Some indication of the answer may be given by analogy to contracts of insurance. **31-73**

In *Lumbermans Mutual Casualty Co v Bovis Lend Lease Ltd*[110] D was insured by C under a construction engineering and design professional liability policy and a commercial excess liability policy. D commenced proceedings against its employer relating to the design and construction of a leisure and retail complex. The employer served a defence and counterclaim alleging, amongst other things, mismanagement of the project. The litigation was settled, but the settlement agreement did not identify how the sum paid to D was calculated or what elements of the counterclaim were recognised as valid. D then made claim under the policies. C sought a negative declaration. In the course of the argument C relied on the *Biggin* and *P&O* cases. The Commercial Court held that the function of ascertainment of loss in the context of liability insurance is not identical to the process of proving the amount of loss caused by breach of contract where the consequence of such breach is liability of the claimant to a third party with whom a settlement has been entered into. In the context of liability insurance the process of ascertainment is not merely the process of evidencing loss, but represents that stage in the assured's relationship with the third party by which he sustains those compensatory liabilities to the third party specifically identified by the judgment, award or settlement agreement which, by the terms of the policy, is an essential element in the cause of action against insurers. There is no similar mechanism which operates as a precondition to the cause of action for an ordinary breach of contract. The claimant has his cause of action regardless of whether there was a judgment, award or settlement of a third party's claim against him. His only concern is to establish the measure of damages, and for this purpose the judgment, award or settlement is likely to provide the necessary evidence, although, as appears from the *P&O* case, this may not be of great weight in the case of the settlement agreement, especially if it is a global settlement. **31-74**

OTHER ISSUES ASSOCIATED WITH MULTIPLE PARTIES

As a result of the involvement of numerous parties, certain problems arise regularly in the settlement of construction proceedings. **31-75**

Release of third parties

Parties should be alive to the possibility that settling a claim against one party (D) may preclude a claim against a third party (T). This may arise because D and T are joint tortfeasors[111] or joint contractors[112] or because the sum received from B **31-76**

---

[109] See *Comyn Ching & Co Ltd v Oriental Tube Co Ltd* (1979) 17 B.L.R. 47, 92, per Brandon LJ. In other words, it is not necessary to establish primary liability on the part of the person against whom secondary liability under the indemnity is sought.

[110] *Lumbermans Mutual Casualty Co v Bovis Lend Lease Ltd* [2004] EWHC 2197 (Comm); [2005] B.L.R. 47.

[111] See para.6-41 onwards.

[112] See para.6-45 onwards.

compensates the claimant for the full extent of his loss.[113] The case of *London & Regional (St George's Court) Ltd v Ministry of Defence*[114] is an example of a construction case where, on the wording of the settlement agreement between the claimant and a third party, the claims against the defendant were preserved.

31-77 A different issue arose in *Safeway Stores Ltd v Interserve Project Services Ltd.*[115]

In that case the contractor and developer reached a settlement concerning payment under the building contract but did not settle the developer's claims for defects in the works. The developer went into liquidation before making the payments due under the settlement. The tenant expended sums remedying defects in the works and sought to recover those sums from the contractor under the collateral warranty. It was held that since the contractor was owed a greater sum by the developer than the cost of the remedial works, the contractor was entitled to assert equitable rights of set off in order to extinguish its liability to the developer and therefore the contractor had no liability to the tenant under the warranty.

31-78 It will be a matter of commercial negotiation and agreed risk allocation whether the contractor's liability for defects to the tenant is intended to be independent of its liability to the developer. If that is what is intended, the *Safeway* case demonstrates that consideration must be given to rights of set off as between the contractor and the developer, especially in the event of the developer's insolvency.

Impugning settlements for duress

31-79 The existence of multiple contracts may place particular pressure on a party to settle, so as not to miss contractual deadlines and attract liability to third parties. In such circumstances, where a settlement is concluded as a result of threats to withhold performance, the settlement may be voidable for duress.

31-80 In *Carillion Construction Ltd v Felix (UK) Ltd*[116] C was the main contractor and engaged D as a subcontractor. D breached its delivery obligations and told C that future deliveries were dependent on agreement by C of its final account in the sum of £3.3 million. C did not agree to that amount. C considered its position but was advised that adjudication would take too long and that an application for injunctive relief was unlikely to succeed. Accordingly, C reached an agreement with D to settle the final account in the sum of £3.2 million. C made a written complaint to D, mentioning duress. The settlement agreement was put into effect and D completed its deliveries. C sought an order rescinding the agreement on the grounds of duress. Dyson J held, allowing the application, that duress required illegitimate pressure to be applied which compelled the victim's agreement to enter into a contract, following *DSND Subsea Ltd (formerly DSND Oceantech Ltd) v Petroleum Geo Services ASA*.[117] D's threat to withhold deliveries until settlement of its final account was a threat to breach the contract when it was already guilty of culpable delay. The pressure exerted by D in threatening to withhold deliveries was illegitimate and gave C no real choice but to enter into the settlement agreement.

---

113 *Heaton v AXA Equity and Law Life Insurance Security Plc* [2002] 2 A.C. 329. See para.6-39 onwards.

114 *London & Regional (St George's Court) Ltd* [2008] EWCA Civ 1212; [2009] B.L.R. 20.

115 *Safeway Stores Ltd v Interserve Project Services Ltd* (2005) 105 Con. L.R. 60.

116 *Carillion Construction Ltd v Felix (UK) Ltd* [2001] B.L.R. 1.

117 *DSND Subsea Ltd (formerly DSND Oceantech Ltd) v Petroleum Geo Services ASA* [2000] B.L.R. 530.

ADJUDICATION

Interim nature of adjudication

The law of compromise generally applies equally to disputes which are the subject of adjudication as it does to any other form of dispute resolution. However, the decision of the adjudicator is binding until the dispute is finally determined by legal proceedings, by arbitration (if the contract provides for arbitration or the parties otherwise agree to arbitration) or by agreement.[118] If a dispute referred to adjudication is to be compromised, it must therefore be decided whether the compromise is intended to be final or whether the dispute can be reopened in subsequent litigation or arbitration proceedings. **31-81**

The effect of compromise on the adjudicator's jurisdiction

It is no defence to a claim for enforcement of an adjudicator's decision that it is wrong.[119] However, it will not be enforced if the adjudicator lacked jurisdiction. The adjudicator can investigate the challenge and decide whether he has jurisdiction. However, that decision will not be binding on the parties when the court comes to consider enforcement unless the defendant has agreed[120] not only that the adjudicator should rule on the issue of jurisdiction but also that he would then be bound by that ruling.[121] There is some tension between the authorities on whether a dispute about a compromise would be likely to fall within the adjudicator's jurisdiction and so whether an arguable case that a dispute has been compromised would be sufficient to resist summary judgment on an adjudicator's decision. **31-82**

In *McConnell Dowell Constructors (Aust) Pty Ltd v National Grid Gas Plc*,[122] Jackson J found that, where the settlement agreement operates as a variation of the original construction contract, disputes as to the settlement will still fall to be determined by adjudication, pursuant to any adjudication provision in the construction contract or pursuant to the statutory scheme.[123] By contrast, where the settlement operates as a stand-alone agreement, which does not incorporate and is not subject to adjudication provisions, the adjudicator will not have jurisdiction.[124] **31-83**

---

118 Housing Grants, Construction and Regeneration Act 1996 s.108(3).

119 *Carrillion Construction Ltd v Devonport Royal Dockyard Ltd* [2006] B.L.R. 15.

120 Participation without reservation will amount to such agreement. It is desirable for a reservation to state the specific basis of objection. However, a general reservation on jurisdiction might be sufficient. It may not be sufficient if the objecting party fails to articulate specific grounds of which it knows or should know or if the reservation is worded simply to try to keep all options open: *Bresco Electrical Services Ltd (In Liquidation) v Michael J Lonsdale (Electrical) Ltd* [2019] EWCA Civ 27 at [92]. And see *GPS Marine Contractors Ltd v Ringway Infrastructure Services Ltd* [2010] B.L.R. 377 at [31]-[41].

121 See *Pegram Shopfitters Ltd v Tally Wiejl (UK) Ltd* [2004] 1 W.L.R. 2082 at [10]-[12]. This is consistent with the position of an arbitrator: see *Dallah Real Estate & Tourism Holding Co v Ministry of Religious Affairs* [2011] 1 A.C. 763 at [24]. In the arbitration context, it has been said that conduct consistent merely with the parties dealing with a dispute on jurisdiction will not by itself create jurisdiction to issue a binding award on that issue: *LG Caltex Gas Co Ltd v China National Petroleum Corp* [2001] EWCA Civ 788 at [52]–[68].

122 *McConnell Dowell Constructors (Aust) Pty Ltd v National Grid Gas Plc* [2006] EWHC 2551 (TCC); [2007] B.L.R. 92.

123 See also *GPS Marine Contractors Ltd v Ringway Infrastructure Services Ltd* [2010] EWHC 283; [2010] B.L.R. 377, *Lee v Chartered Properties* [2010] EWHC 1540 (TCC); [2010] B.L.R. 500 at [22].

124 Per Jackson J in *McConnell* at [42]. Note that, where a stand-alone settlement agreement includes

31-84 In this way, Jackson J resolved apparent tensions between three earlier decisions: *Shepherd Construction v Mecright Ltd*,[125] *Quarmby Construction Co Ltd v Larraby Land Ltd*[126] and *Westminster Building Co v Beckingham*.[127] In *Shepherd* and *Quarmby*, the settlement had operated as a stand-alone agreement which did not incorporate adjudication provisions. The adjudicator's jurisdiction therefore depended on whether the dispute survived the settlement. If it did not, the adjudicator had no jurisdiction to determine the dispute. By contrast, in *Beckingham*, the settlement operated as a variation of the construction contract. The adjudicator therefore had jurisdiction to determine disputes arising under either agreement, including the question of whether the existing dispute had been compromised.

31-85 In *McConnell*,[128] Jackson J found that the settlement agreement was an amendment to the contract, not a stand-alone contract. As such, the question was one which the adjudicator had jurisdiction to resolve. In reaching that conclusion, Jackson J said the following:

> "The officious by-stander test, which Mr Baatz has invited me to apply, supports this conclusion. The contract and the Supplemental Agreement are mutually intertwined. It would not make commercial sense to have one procedure for resolving disputes under the contract and a different procedure for resolving disputes under the Supplemental Agreement."

He relied on the reasoning of Ramsey J in *L. Brown & Sons Limited v Crosby* at [51]:

> "I bear in mind that it is quite common in the construction industry for parties to enter into side or supplemental agreements which add to or vary the terms when matters arise during the course of the contract. Those agreements frequently do not have their own provisions for dispute resolution, including adjudication. If the officious bystander had asked such parties what dispute resolution methods applied, I consider that they would invariably assume that those in the underlying contract would apply. The idea that different or no provisions applied to such additional changed obligations would, in my judgment, be an impossible situation and make adjudication unworkable for such projects."

31-86 In *J Murphy & Sons Ltd v W Maher & Sons Ltd*[129], Akenhead J reviewed the authorities in light of the decision in *Fiona Trust & Holding Corp v Privalov*.[130] In that case, the House of Lords had found that arbitration agreements should be construed broadly, without undue regard to fine distinctions of language. Given the arbitration agreement was a separate contract to the substantive agreement between the parties, factors vitiating the contract would not necessarily also vitiate the arbitration agreement. As such, an allegation that the contract had been procured by bribery fell within the terms of a valid arbitration agreement, which was unaffected by that allegation. In *J Murphy & Sons*, Akenhead J emphasised that, in *Mc-*

---

obligations to carry out works, it may qualify as a construction contract and so give rise to a right to refer disputes to adjudication under the Housing Grants, Construction and Regeneration Act 1996 s.108.

125 *Shepherd Construction v Mecright Ltd* [2000] B.L.R. 489.

126 *Quarmby Construction Co Ltd v Larraby Land Ltd* unreported 14 April 2003 Leeds Technology and Construction Court.

127 *Westminster Building Co v Beckingham* [2004] EWHC 138 (TCC); [2004] B.L.R. 163.

128 *McConnell Dowell Constructors (Aust) Pty Ltd v National Grid Gas Plc* [2006] EWHC 2551 (TCC); [2007] B.L.R. 92 at [44].

129 *J Murphy & Sons Ltd v W Maher & Sons Ltd* [2016] EWHC 1148; [2017] Bus. L.R. 916 at [16]–[34].

130 *Fiona Trust & Holding Corp v Privalov* [2007] UKHL 40; [2007] 4 All E.R. 951.

Connell, Jackson J had not said that the only way in which a later settlement agreement could be adjudicated upon was if it was classifiable other than as some sort of stand-alone agreement. In any event, Jackson J had not had the benefit of the *Fiona Trust* decision. The Judge extended the reasoning in *Fiona Trust* to adjudication, finding that a broad construction of the statute and the adjudication agreement was required. A dispute as to whether all or some of the alleged entitlements which one contractual party has against the other has been settled in a binding way generally arises "under" the original contract. Had it been necessary to decide the issue, he would have found that the agreement concerned was a variation of the original agreement.

The reasoning in *Fiona Trust* was similarly extended to the construction of an adjudication agreement in *Air Design (Kent) Ltd v Deerglen (Jersey) Ltd*.[131] By contrast, in *Hillcrest Homes Ltd v Beresford and Curbishley Ltd*,[132] HHJ Raynor QC saw "considerable force" in the submission that the reasoning in *Fiona Trust* had no application to the construction of the statutory scheme. He found that claims for misrepresentation and negligent misstatement were not claims "under" the contract within the meaning of the Act and so were not within the jurisdiction of the adjudicator. **31-87**

It is suggested that the approach of Akenhead J in *J Murphy & Sons* is to be preferred. As the Judge pointed out,[133] many of the factors relied upon to justify a broad construction of arbitration agreements also apply to the construction both of adjudication agreements and of the statutory scheme.[134] The full effects of the *Fiona Trust* decision may not, however, apply to statutory adjudication. In part, the reasoning in *Fiona Trust* was based on the fact that arbitration agreements are separate contracts from the substantive agreement between the parties. Factors vitiating the main contract (in that case bribery) will not necessarily also vitiate the arbitration agreement. In some cases, however, they will, for example where the dispute is about whether the parties ever reached agreement at all. Under the statutory scheme, an adjudicator has jurisdiction to decide disputes arising under a construction contract. If it is arguable that the effect of a settlement agreement is to extinguish and replace the original contract in its entirety, it may then be arguable that there is no longer any construction contract under which the dispute can arise.[135] **31-88**

It may be appropriate to have the issue of whether or not a compromise has had the result that there is no dispute that can be referred to adjudication determined by the court before the adjudication is commenced so as to forestall the inevitable issues that will arise on any attempted enforcement of the adjudicator's decision.[136] **31-89**

Jurisdiction and duress

Where the contract containing the adjudication provision is void or voidable, does that deprive the adjudicator of jurisdiction? HH Judge Wilcox found that it did in *Capital Structures Plc v Time & Tide Construction Ltd*.[137] He held that there was an arguable case that a settlement was procured by economic duress. There was **31-90**

---

131 *Air Design (Kent) Ltd v Deerglen (Jersey) Ltd* [2008] EWHC 3047 (TCC) at [24].

132 *Hillcrest Homes Ltd v Beresford and Curbishley Ltd* [2014] EWHC 280 (TCC) at [50]–[52].

133 *J Murphy & Sons Ltd v W Maher & Sons Ltd* [2016] EWHC 1148; [2017] Bus. L.R. 916 at [31].

134 Housing Grants, Construction and Regeneration Act 1996 s.108.

135 And see paras 31-91–31-92 as to the effect of an argument that the contract is void or voidable.

136 *Quality Street Properties (Trading) Ltd v Elmwood (Glasgow) Ltd* (2002) S.C.L.R. 1118.

137 *Capital Structures Plc v Time & Tide Construction Ltd* [2006] EWHC 591 (TCC); [2006] B.L.R. 226.

therefore a triable issue as to whether the settlement was voidable. He held that if the settlement were avoided, the adjudication provisions within the agreement would also become void. Consequently he refused to grant summary judgment of an adjudicator's decision given in respect of sums due under the settlement on the grounds that the adjudicator arguably lacked jurisdiction. He decided the question by analogy to the status of arbitration clauses in voidable contracts. It is submitted that the case would have been decided differently in the light of the decision of the House of Lords in *Fiona Trust & Holding Corp v Privalov*.[138].

31-91 Where, by contrast, the right to refer a dispute to adjudication arises from statute, rather than by express agreement, the answer may be different. The statutory right arises only where there is a dispute arising under a construction contract. Unlike an agreement to arbitrate or adjudicate, the statutory right to adjudication stands or falls with the underlying contract. If the contract is void or has been avoided, the right may not arise. As a result, an arguable case to that effect may be sufficient to avoid summary enforcement of an adjudicator's decision.

Forbearance from adjudication

31-92 Forbearance to sue has long been recognised as furnishing consideration for a compromise.[139]

> In *Joseph Finney Plc v Vickers (t/a Mill Hotel)*,[140] HH Judge David Wilcox gave summary judgment in a claim based on a compromise whereby the defendant agreed to pay an interim certificate in consideration of the claimant's promise not to proceed with an adjudication to enforce the claimant's rights under the contract.

---

[138] *Fiona Trust & Holding Corp v Privalov* [2007] UKHL 40; [2007] 4 All E.R. 951. Referred to at para.31-87

[139] See para.3-03 onwards.

[140] *Joseph Finney Plc v Vickers (t/a Mill Hotel)* unreported 7 March 2001.

PART 13: ARBITRATIONS

CHAPTER 32

Settlement of Arbitrations

GENERAL

Throughout the world a great many disputes which otherwise would fall to be resolved by litigation within the courts of a particular domestic jurisdiction are dealt with by arbitration, the confidentiality of the process being one feature that makes arbitration attractive to many parties. Equally, some disputes are thought more appropriate to an arbitral process. Within the domestic jurisdiction of England and Wales arbitration is the dispute resolution mechanism of choice for many parties in a number of areas, principally in the context of commercial disputes and those giving rise to technical issues. Many construction disputes[1], for example, are resolved within an arbitral process. Such an arbitration usually arises by agreement pursuant to an arbitration clause within the contract between the parties that governs their relationship in respect of a transaction or series of transactions between them. Sometimes parties to a dispute may not be subject to a binding arbitration clause in the contract between them, but will agree to submit their dispute to arbitration after it has arisen. In certain cases, statute provides for compulsory or optional arbitration[2]. Where there is an arbitration agreement, it is almost invariably written with the result that the Arbitration Act 1996 ("the 1996 Act") applies to it[3]. **32-01**

A great many international commercial contracts[4] contain arbitration clauses that commit the parties to arbitration in the event of disputes arising. The agreement will usually specify the law that is to govern the resolution of any such dispute and the location (the "seat") of the arbitration. A full discussion of the implications of these matters is beyond the scope of this work[5]. However, the relevance of these matters to the practice and enforceability of a settlement of an international commercial dispute is discussed in Ch. 36. **32-02**

Many international commercial contracts specify the law of England and Wales **32-03**

---

1 See Ch.31.

2 For an overview of statutory arbitrations in England and Wales, see *Russell on Arbitration*, 24th edn (London, Sweet & Maxwell, 2015), Appendix 3.

3 See section 5. Furthermore, s.5(5) provides as follows: "An exchange of written submissions in arbitral or legal proceedings in which the existence of an agreement otherwise than in writing is alleged by one party against another party and not denied by the other party in his response constitutes as between those parties an agreement in writing to the effect alleged."

4 For this purpose, such a contract may be defined as one between parties each of whose place of business is in a different country from that of the other. A party may, of course, be the state itself. Any dispute between them is termed a "cross-border dispute".

5 See, e.g., *Handbook on International Commercial Arbitration*, 2nd edn (Jurisenet LLC, 2014); *The Principles and Practice of International Commercial Arbitration*, 3rd edn (Cambridge University Press, 2017). See also '*The Proper Law of the Arbitration Agreement*', Peter Ashford, in Arbitration, August 2019.

as the law to be applied to the resolution of the dispute and London as the seat of the arbitration. Where that is the case any settlement of the dispute is likely to be governed by the law and practice of England and Wales. The focus of this Chapter is upon the settlement of "pure" domestic arbitrations and those where the law and practice of England and Wales applies to the settlement of an international dispute that is the subject of a pending arbitration within that jurisdiction. There is a degree of overlap between those two situations and situations where the issue of the enforcement in England and Wales of a settlement of an international commercial dispute arises, but, as indicated above, that latter situation will be addressed in Ch.36.

32-04 Since the process of arbitration is similar in many respects to the litigation process, the essential principles and practice of the compromise of an arbitration are similar, albeit with subtle differences broadly based upon the principle that the overall arbitration process is consensual and thus depends to a large extent upon what the parties have agreed should form the subject-matter of the arbitration[6]. The structure of an institutional arbitration[7] may be governed by the rules of the institution such that any settlement would need to take account of those rules.

32-05 Three areas merit particular discussion:

(1) Agreed awards and their enforcement;
(2) The effect of a settlement on the arbitral tribunal's jurisdiction; and
(3) Offers of settlement.

AGREED AWARDS AND THEIR ENFORCEMENT

32-06 Where parties settle arbitration proceedings, they may agree that their settlement be given effect in an arbitral award. The 1996 Act s.51 provides that:

> "(1) If during arbitral proceedings the parties settle the dispute, the following provisions apply unless otherwise agreed by the parties.
> (2) The tribunal shall terminate the substantive proceedings and, if so requested by the parties and not objected to by the tribunal, shall record the settlement in the form of an agreed award.
> (3) An agreed award shall state that it is an award of the tribunal and shall have the same status and effect as any other award on the merits of the case."

These provisions are based on Article 30 of the UNCITRAL Model Law on International Commercial Arbitration[8]. Parties can agree that s.51 shall not apply.[9]

32-07 It has been suggested that s.51 might not apply where the parties do not settle the whole of the dispute.[10] Notwithstanding that suggestion, an arbitral tribunal may

---

6 *Premium Nafta Products Limited and others v Fili Shipping Company Limited and others* [2007] UKHL 40 (the '*Fiona Trust* case').

7 In other words, an arbitration administered by an institution such as The London Court of International Arbitration, The International Chamber of Commerce or the Chartered Institute of Arbitrators.

8 *Departmental Advisory Committee on Arbitration report on the Arbitration Bill* (the DAC Report), §240. A copy of the Model Law (as amended) is in Appendix 7. See further in Ch. 36 at para.36-10.

9 1996 Act s.51(1). These statutory provisions are mirrored in the rules of many of the well-known arbitral institutions: Article 26.9 of the LCIA Arbitration Rules (2014), Article 33 of the ICC Arbitration Rules and Article 36 of the CIArb Arbitration Rules (2015).

10 *Russell on Arbitration*, para.6-023 and footnote 98, p.300.

embody a settlement of part only of a reference in an award relating to that part under s.47 of the 1996 Act.[11]

Section 51(2) of the Act requires the tribunal to record the settlement in the form of an agreed award "if not objected to by the tribunal". There is no statutory guidance as to when the tribunal may object to recording a settlement. In its report on the Arbitration Bill (the 'DAC Report'), the Departmental Advisory Committee on Arbitration suggested that arbitrators might object if the award "contains an objectionable feature, e.g. is structured to mislead third parties."[12] It will be recalled that ordinarily a judge has no right to interfere with a proposed settlement of litigation unless what is proposed is illegal or a consent order or judgment is proposed that is outside the normal jurisdiction of the court[13]. One area of potential concern in relation to *illegality* would be where the arbitral tribunal considers that a proposed agreed award was a cloak for a money-laundering purpose. The DAC Report preceded the Proceeds of Crime Act 2002. That Act (particularly s. 328) raised concerns within the legal profession about its disclosure responsibilities which were considered by the Court of Appeal in *Bowman v Fels*[14], a case which led other professionals (including arbitrators) to consider their position if presented with suspicions about arrangements made. The Chartered Institute of Arbitrators gave guidance to its arbitrators in this way[15]: 32-08

> "Following *Bowman v Fels*, it appears that the only situation in which an arbitrator may be at risk of becoming concerned in an arrangement prohibited by Section 328 is if, at the request of the parties, he issues an agreed award following a settlement: see Section 51 of the Arbitration Act 1996. It is not unknown for parties to an illegal operation to use an agreed arbitration award as a way of "laundering" the proceeds of crime. If an arbitrator knows or suspects that a request for an agreed award is, or may be, a prelude to an arrangement by which criminal property is to be acquired, retained, used or controlled he should of course refuse to issue such an award ...."

That represents a clear example of a situation in which an arbitral tribunal would be justified in declining to make an agreed award if asked to do so (and indeed plainly should so decline). Where there is doubt in any such situation, it is thought that an arbitral tribunal should be guided by the practice of the courts where legality issues form the basis of binding or, at the very least, persuasive legal authority[16]. 32-09

Is there any situation in which an arbitral tribunal could properly decline to make an agreed award on *jurisdictional* grounds? Generally speaking, it is the parties' agreement that confers jurisdiction on the tribunal. In those circumstances, it would seem surprising for a tribunal to refuse to make an agreed award when both parties desire it to do so. Section 51 is concerned with a settlement "during arbitration proceedings" and not with the position where arbitration proceedings had not been commenced at the time of the settlement. Where that occurs, the strict legal position is that when the settlement has been concluded there is no longer any dispute between the parties[17] and thus no dispute to refer to arbitration[18]. This could, in some circumstances, give rise to the question of whether an arbitral tribunal, ap- 32-10

---

11 A previous version of this paragraph was cited with approval in *Dawes v Treasure and Son Ltd* [2010] 2 CLC 907; [2010] EWHC 3218 (TCC) at [28].

12 DAC Report, §242.

13 See Ch.10 at para.10-02.

14 *Bowman v Fels (Bar Council and Others intervening)* [2005] 1 W.L.R. 3083.

15 CIArb '*Guideline 12: The Proceeds of Crime Act 2002: Guidance for arbitrators and mediators.*'

16 See Ch. 4, para. 4-71–4-83.

17 See para.36-10.

18 Unless the agreement resolving the dispute is construed, expressly or impliedly, as not being final unless and until a consent award is made: cf. para. 5-48–5-55.

pointed by the parties solely for the purpose of making an agreed award to embody their settlement, has the power to do so[19]. However, no such issue arises if the arbitration is commenced prior to the settlement. Nevertheless, if the settlement includes (as many commercial settlements do) a general release[20], where no specific dispute between the parties has been identified, would an arbitral tribunal be justified in declining to make an agreed award embodying such a release on the basis that without a dispute there can be no award? It is difficult to give an all-embracing answer to the question, because it would depend largely on the way the arbitration clause in the particular case was drawn and/or on the way the rules of an institutional arbitration were drafted. At the end of the day, the term would be contractually binding and enforceable by the court, but not necessarily pursuant to enforcement of the provision in the consent arbitral award if made by the tribunal.

32-11 Where the arbitrator refuses to issue an agreed award where there is no basis for refusing to do so, the parties may apply to the court to remove him under s.24 of the Act. An arbitrator who seeks to impose impermissible provisions in a proposed settlement between the parties is likely to be removed:

> In *Wicketts v Brine Builders & Siederer*[21], the arbitrator issued directions as to the terms on which the parties were required to conclude any settlement. The arbitrator directed that the settlement was not to be implemented and no money was to be paid under it until his own fees had been settled. In granting the claimants' application to remove the arbitrator under s.24 of the 1996 Act, HHJ Seymour QC described the directions as "quite the most outrageous that I have ever seen given in any arbitration proceedings."[22]

32-12 The agreed award shall state that it is an award of the tribunal and shall have the same status and effect as any other award on the merits of the case.[23] There is no requirement that the award should state on its face that it is an agreed award.[24] The tribunal is not required to state its reasons for making an agreed award.[25] The provisions of the Act relating to awards generally[26] apply to agreed awards and, unless the parties have also settled the matter of the costs of the arbitration, the provisions of the Act relating to costs[27] will also apply.

32-13 Where the arbitrator issues an agreed award disposing of the entire dispute, he becomes functus officio, subject to any power to correct clerical errors or slips.[28]

SETTING ASIDE AN AGREED AWARD

32-14 It is unclear whether all of the grounds which would justify the setting-aside of a contract would be sufficient to justify the setting-aside of an arbitral award made

---

19 See paras 36-10 and 36-67 onwards. "Furthermore, the whole of Clause 51 is based upon the assumption that there is a dispute between the parties which has been referred to arbitration and then settled": DAC Report, para. 242.

20 See para. 2-08–2-14 and 5-22–5-33.

21 [2002] CILL 1805.

22 *Wicketts v Brine Builders*, at [52].

23 1996 Act s.51(3).

24 See the DAC Report, §§241–244.

25 1996 Act s.52(4).

26 ss.52–58.

27 ss.59–65.

28 *Sutherland & Co v Hannevig Bros Ltd* [1921] K.B. 336, *CNH Global NV v PGN Logistics & Ors* [2009] 1 CLC 807. For the power to correct awards, see 1996 Act s.57.

by consent.[29] The 1996 Act does not expressly provide for an agreed award to be set aside in such circumstances. It is likely that a party seeking to set aside an agreed award would need to bring itself within the provisions of the Act which deal with challenging awards generally.[30]

Section 68(1) of the Act provides that a party may apply to the court to challenge an award in the proceedings on the ground of serious irregularity affecting the award. A serious irregularity will exist where the award was obtained by fraud or where the award or the way in which it was procured is contrary to public policy.[31] However, difficult procedural questions may arise as to whether the underlying issue giving rise to the challenge should be determined first in the Court or in accordance with the dispute resolution agreement in the settlement if the settlement contains such a provision. **32-15**

In *Minister of Finance (Inc) v International Petroleum Investment Company*,[32] an arbitration was settled by the parties agreeing two deeds ("the Settlement Deeds"). In accordance with their terms, the arbitrators issued an agreed award. The Settlement Deeds contained an arbitration agreement. The Claimants alleged that the Settlement Agreements and the arbitration agreements contained within them had been entered into in furtherance of a conspiracy to misappropriate in excess of US$3.5 billion. In relation to the arbitration agreements, each of which specified London as the "seat", it was said that they were agreed to conceal the fraud and so were themselves impeachable as part of the conspiracy. The Claimants applied to the Court to set aside the agreed award pursuant to the Arbitration Act 1996, ss.67 and 68 on the grounds (i) that the tribunal lacked jurisdiction to make the agreed award, (ii) that the award had been obtained by fraud and (iii) that the way in which it was procured was contrary to public policy. The Defendants commenced fresh arbitration proceedings pursuant to the arbitration agreement in the Settlement Deeds. They sought, amongst other relief, declarations that the Settlement Deeds were valid and binding and they applied to stay the Claimants' applications under s.9 of the Arbitration Act 1996 or, alternatively, as a matter of case management. Robin Knowles J. rejected the application for a stay under s.9. Although the issue of whether the Settlement Agreements were binding or void was common to the application to the Court and the claim before the second tribunal, the Claimants' challenge in Court was to the award, not to the Settlement Deeds. In any event, by agreeing to the first arbitration, the parties had agreed that any award arising from that arbitration could be challenged in Court. As a result, both the Court and the second tribunal had jurisdiction over claims in which the validity of the Settlement Deeds were in issue. However, he granted a stay on case management grounds to allow the second tribunal to investigate its own jurisdiction and the validity of the Settlement Deeds first.

There is no requirement that an arbitral tribunal should give reasons for an agreed award.[33] As a consequence, it will not generally be possible to appeal against an agreed award on a point of law under s.69 of the Act.[34] Where, however, it can be shown that the underlying settlement agreement is void, has been rescinded or is otherwise not binding, it may be arguable that the award was not an agreed award within the meaning of the Act. **32-16**

---

29 See Ch.4.

30 This is the approach which has been taken in the German Courts. A summary of the relevant judgment is at *http://www.dis-arb.de/en/47/datenbanken/rspr/bgh-case-no-iii-zb-55-99-date-2000-11-02-id2*. [Accessed 2 November 2019].

31 s.68(2)(g).

32 [2019] EWHC 1151.

33 s.52(4).

34 s.69(1).

32-17 By s.70(3) any application or appeal must be brought within 28 days of the date of the award, although that period may be extended by the court under CPR r.62.9.[35]

ENFORCEMENT OF AN AGREED AWARD

32-18 As indicated above[36], the focus of this Chapter is upon the settlement of "pure" domestic arbitrations and those where the law and practice of England and Wales applies to the settlement of an international dispute that is the subject of a pending arbitration within that jurisdiction. Where enforcement is sought within that jurisdiction, English law and practice will apply to the enforcement of any agreed award. Within that jurisdiction there are clear advantages to recording a settlement in an agreed award. Any settlement of a dispute referred to arbitration will be contractual in nature and, subject to its terms, enforceable by action on the contract[37]. An agreed award can, however, be enforced directly. Enforcement is therefore likely to be faster and easier where there is an agreed award. In addition, if it is intended to enforce overseas, it may be possible to seek recognition and enforcement of an agreed award under the New York Convention.[38]

32-19 The normal procedure to enforce an agreed award made in England and Wales is by the summary procedure under s.66 of the 1996 Act. Section 66 provides that an award made by a tribunal pursuant to an arbitration agreement may, by leave of the court, be enforced in the same manner as a judgment or order of the court to the same effect. Where leave is given, judgment may be entered in terms of the award.[39] The procedure extends to an agreed award.[40]

32-20 As recorded above, every arbitration award is enforceable by a fresh action brought for the purpose,[41] but in practice this would be very unusual as the procedure under s.66 is faster and cheaper. However, the s.66 procedure may not be available, for example, where the arbitration agreement was oral and not written.[42]

---

35 The circumstances in which the Court would grant such an extension were addressed in *Kalmneft v Glencore International AG* [2002] 1 Lloyd's Rep. 128 and *Terna Bahrain Holding Company WLL v Bin Kamil Al Shamsi & Ors.* [2012] EWHC 3283 (Comm); [2013] 2 C.L.C. 1 at [27] – [31].

36 para. 32-03.

37 See fn. 41.

38 The Convention on the Recognition and Enforcement of Foreign Arbitral Awards 1958. See Ch.36.

39 1996 Act s.66(2). For a consideration of the circumstances in which leave to enforce may be given, but judgment refused, see *Honeywell International v Meydan* [2014] B.L.R. 599.

40 CPR r.62.18(5) provides that where an application is made to enforce an agreed award both the arbitration claim form and the order itself must state that that the award which it is sought to enforce is an agreed award.

41 *Bremer Deltransport GmbH v Drewry* [1933] 1 K.B. 753 CA. As to the nature of the claim to enforce an award at common law, see *SC Rolinay Sea Star SRL v Compagnia de Navigatie Maritimie Petromin SA ("The Bumbesti")* [2000] Q.B. 559 at [10]: the preferred analysis was that a claim on an award is a claim for breach of an implied term in the submission to arbitration that any award made would be fulfilled. Many institutional rules contain express terms to that effect.

42 Or where the arbitration agreement otherwise does not fall within the broad statutory definition in ss.5 and 6 of the 1996 Act.

THE EFFECT OF A SETTLEMENT ON THE TRIBUNAL'S JURISDICTION

As has been mentioned above,[43] the issue of an agreed award disposing of the entire dispute brings an end to the arbitrator's jurisdiction. In the absence of an agreed award however, the settlement of a dispute which is the subject of arbitration proceedings does not necessarily bring an end to the arbitrator's jurisdiction. **32-21**

After settlement, the arbitrator retains jurisdiction to terminate the proceedings and determine issues of costs.[44] **32-22**

The tribunal may also retain jurisdiction over new claims referred to it after settlement has been achieved. **32-23**

> In *Dawes v Treasure and Son Ltd*,[45] the parties agreed a settlement of their substantive dispute, which was not recorded in an agreed award. Both parties then applied to the arbitrator for their costs. The arbitrator proceeded to make a series of costs awards. Shortly after the second of these, the respondent served a fresh notice of arbitration. This prompted a further notice of arbitration from the claimant seeking a finding that the claims advanced by the respondent had been settled. Akenhead J found that the arbitrator retained "unqualified" jurisdiction after the settlement and therefore had jurisdiction to decide whether the settlement encompassed the claims which the respondent sought to advance.[46] Under the applicable CIMAR rules[47] the claimant had the right to refer another dispute to the same arbitrator and had done so in its second notice of arbitration. Had "all facets of the dispute including costs and interest" been resolved by the arbitrator, however, the arbitrator would have ceased to have jurisdiction.

Where there is a dispute about whether arbitration proceedings have been settled, that dispute will generally fall within the reference to the tribunal.[48] The existence of the settlement does not generally deprive the tribunal of jurisdiction, but is a defence to the substantive claim which, like any other defence, the tribunal is required to determine. In *Sun United Maritime Ltd v Kasteli Marine Inc*,[49] the claimant challenged a costs award on the basis that the costs claim had been settled. Hamblen J, as he then was, dismissed the challenge. Even if made out, the settlement would not deprive the tribunal of jurisdiction. The award could not therefore be challenged on the basis that the tribunal lacked jurisdiction (the 1996 Act s.67). The claimant's remedies were confined to challenging the award under s.68 (serious irregularity) or s.69 (appeal on point of law)[50] of the 1996 Act. Where there is a question of whether a claim has been settled in the course of arbitration proceed- **32-24**

---

[43] See para.32-13.

[44] s.51

[45] [2010] EWHC 3218 (TCC).

[46] And see *Sun United Maritime Ltd v Kasteli Marine Inc* [2014] EWHC 1476 (Comm); [2015] 1 W.L.R. 1527 at [18].

[47] The Construction Industry Model Arbitration Rules.

[48] *Dawes v Treasure and Son Ltd* [2010] 2 CLC 907; [2010] EWHC 3218 (TCC) at [32](a), *Sun United Maritime Ltd v Kasteli Marine Inc* [2014] EWHC 1476 (Comm); [2015] 1 W.L.R. 1527 at [18], *Doshion Ltd v Sembawang Engineers and Constructors Pte Ltd* [2011] SGHC 46. For a similar decision in respect of adjudication, see *J. Murphy & Sons Ltd v W Maher & Sons Ltd* [2016] BLR 435. Per Akenhead J. at [32]: "a dispute as to whether all or some of the alleged entitlements which one contractual party has against the other has been settled in a binding way arises "under" the original contract." It therefore fell within the statutory scheme for adjudication.

[49] [2014] EWHC 1476 (Comm); [2015] 1 W.L.R. 1527.

[50] *Sun United Maritime Ltd v Kasteli Marine Inc* [2014] EWHC 1476 (Comm); [2015] 1 W.L.R. 1527 [18]–[20].

ings, it may also be possible to refer that question to the court under s.45 of the 1996 Act, where the parties agree or the tribunal gives permission.[51]

32-25 Where the parties go further than settling the substantive dispute and agree to terminate the arbitration proceedings, the result may be different. The effect of such an agreement may well be to withdraw the dispute from the tribunal's jurisdiction. In *Chimimport Plc v G D'Alesio SAS ("The Paola D'Alesio")*,[52] Rix J, as he then was, found that the effect of an alleged settlement agreement would, if effective, be to deprive the tribunal of jurisdiction. It was common ground that the tribunal could not determine its own jurisdiction. It therefore followed that the tribunal was not entitled to determine the respondent's case that the alleged settlement was voidable for duress. The case was decided before the 1996 Act. An arbitral tribunal does now have jurisdiction to determine its own jurisdiction.[53] However, the position now would be that the tribunal in *Chimimport* would be entitled to decide on the validity of the settlement, but that any such decision would be open to review afresh by the courts, as with any other jurisdictional challenge.[54]

32-26 The cases of *Dawes* and *Sun United Maritime* were concerned with settlement agreements reached after the commencement of arbitration proceedings. Where a disputed settlement is said to have been concluded before proceedings were started, the terms of the settlement agreement will determine whether the tribunal has jurisdiction to decide the issue. Where the settlement operates as a variation of the underlying contract or otherwise incorporates the arbitration agreement in the underlying contract, there can be little doubt that the arbitrator would have jurisdiction. Similarly, where the settlement agreement contains no dispute resolution agreement, a subsequent dispute about the settlement is likely to fall within the original arbitration agreement.[55] Where, by contrast, the settlement agreement contains its own dispute resolution provisions, those provisions are likely to be construed as superceding the earlier arbitration agreement and applying to all disputes arising under both the settlement agreement and the underlying contract.[56]

OFFERS AND COSTS

General

32-27 Unless an arbitration agreement provides to the contrary, the costs of the reference to arbitration and of the award are at the tribunal's discretion, subject to the general position that costs should follow the event.[57] An arbitral tribunal pos-

---

51 For an example of this, see *Goodwood Investments Holdings Inc. v Thyssenkrupp Industrial Solutions AG (M/Y "Palladium")* [2018] EWHC 1056 (Comm).

52 [1994] 2 Lloyd's Rep. 366.

53 s.30.

54 And see *Dallah Real Estate & Tourism Holding Co v Ministry of Religious Affairs* [2011] 1 A.C. 763.

55 See, for example, *Sonact Group Ltd v Premuda Spa "Four Island"* [2018] EWHC 3820 (Comm) at [14] – [20]. Per Males J. at [20]: "there is, in my judgment, no bright line rule that once the parties enter into a new legal relationship, here a settlement agreement, an arbitration clause in the underlying contract necessarily can no longer apply."

56 See *Monde Petroleum SA v Westernzagros Ltd* [2015] EWHC 67 (Comm), per Popplewell J at [38]-[39]. And see, by analogy, paras 31-81 — 31-89, where adjudication is addressed.

57 Arbitration Act 1996 s.61. This was intended to mirror the approach in the English courts: see DAC Report on Arbitration Bill, paras 268–269.

sessed of this discretion has the same discretion as a High Court judge.[58] The discretion must be exercised judicially and "without prejudice" offers may not be taken into account.[59] Furthermore, in considering the question whether the claimant has achieved more by rejecting the offer and continuing the arbitration than accepting it,[60] an arbitral tribunal should not have regard to the incidence of costs in the reference, but only to the claim for principal and interest.[61] Since the Civil Procedure Rules do not apply to arbitrations, the process of a Pt 36 offer[62] is not available as a protection on costs. How, then, can an offer be made which, if not bettered on the award, will influence the award as to costs?

The form and substance of an effective offer

As Donaldson J (as he then was) made clear in *Tramountana Armadora SA v Atlantic Shipping Co SA*,[63] there are two methods of making an offer potentially effective on costs in arbitration proceedings: **32-28**

(1) an "open offer"; and
(2) a "sealed offer".

The former will have a status identical to that in ordinary litigation.[64] The latter has been described as[65]:

> "... the arbitral equivalent of making a payment into court on settlement of the litigation or of particular causes of action in that litigation."

The procedures are not, of course, identical—and, of course, a payment into court in respect of a money claim is no longer required in ordinary civil litigation.[66] A "sealed offer" does not involve an actual payment of a sum of money as part of the offer of settlement. An offeree disposed to accept the sum of money proffered might be well advised to accept the offer on condition that the sum of money (or a banker's draft in the appropriate sum) is paid (or the banker's draft received) within a specified period. Any failure to observe this condition would leave the original claim open or, arguably, if he elected to waive the condition in his favour, enable recourse to a cause of action on the compromise. **32-29**

As with a Pt 36 or Calderbank offer, the fact that a sealed offer has been made is usually concealed from the tribunal. This is usually achieved by an invitation to the tribunal at the conclusion of the arbitration to make an interim award on the substance of the dispute and to receive further representations on the question of costs subsequently.[67] Another (rather archaic) means by which this is achieved is **32-30**

---

58 *Stotesbury v Turner* [1943] K.B. 370.

59 *Stotesbury*. See, generally, *L. Figueiredo Navegacas SA v Reederei Richard Schroeder KG* [1974] 1 Lloyd's Rep. 192. The rule preventing consideration of without prejudice offers is not confined to offers of settlement, but extends to efforts to resolve disputes by other means: *Reed Executive Plc v Reed Business Information Ltd* [2004] 1 W.L.R. 3026.

60 See paras 32-31 onwards.

61 *Everglade Maritime Inc v Schiffahrtgesellschaft* [1993] Q.B. 780 CA.

62 See Ch. 14 onwards.

63 *Tramountana Armadora SA v Atlantic Shipping Co SA* [1978] 1 Lloyd's Rep. 391, 396.

64 See paras 18-08 onwards.

65 *Tramountana* [1978] 1 Lloyd's Rep. 391, per Donaldson J.

66 See para.14-01 onwards.

67 *King v Thomas McKenna Ltd* [1991] 2 Q.B. 480, 492.

if the tribunal invites the parties to give it a sealed envelope, the contents of which would reveal whether an offer had been made and where so, in what terms.[68]

32-31 When the arbitral tribunal comes to consider the relevance of a "sealed offer" the approach for the arbitrator has been described thus[69] :

> "... he should ask himself the question: 'Has the claimant achieved more by rejecting the offer and going on with the arbitration than he would have achieved if he had accepted the offer?' This is a simple question to answer, whether the offer does or does not include interest. The arbitrator knows what the claimant would have achieved if he had accepted the offer. He would have received that sum and could not have asked the arbitrator to award any interest.[70] The arbitrator knows what he has in fact awarded to the claimant both by way of principal and interest. In order that like should be compared with like, the interest element must be recalculated as if the award had been made on the same date as the offer. Alternatively, interest for the period between offer and award must notionally be added to the amount of the sealed offer. But, subject to that, the question is easily answered.
>
> If the claimant in the end has achieved no more than he would have achieved by accepting the offer, the continuance of the arbitration after that date has been a waste of time and money. Prima facie, the claimant should recover his costs up to the date of the offer and should be ordered to pay the respondent's costs after that date. If he has achieved more by going on, the respondent should pay the costs throughout."

32-32 An important feature of a Pt 36 offer is that the offer constituted thereby includes an offer to pay the claimant's costs to the date when the "relevant period" expires.[71] For a "sealed offer" to have the equivalent effect in terms of protection on costs, the terms offered must make this plain.

32-33 In the *Tramountana* case,[72] the offer had been for a lump sum effectively to include interest and costs. The question of whether the offer was sufficient in relation to the capital sum and interest was a relatively easy exercise. But the costs to the date of the offer were an unknown factor and it was not possible for the arbitrator to make the comparison between the offer and the eventual award.[73]

The difficulty which arose in the *Tramountana* case led Donaldson J to say[74]:

> "If a party wishes to make a 'sealed offer' and to have it considered in the context of an order for costs, he must offer to settle the action for £x plus costs."

32-34 In *Archital Luxfer Ltd v Henry Boot Construction Ltd*[75] Peter Gibson J, as he then was, concluded that Donaldson J was merely "dealing with the essential substance and purpose of sealed offers and was not intending to lay down any universal requirements as to form". He continued thus[76]:

> "In order for the essential task of the arbitrator to be performed, namely, of deciding the question whether the party to whom the offer is made has achieved more by rejecting the

---

[68] *King* at 492–493.

[69] *Tramountana Armadora SA* [1978] 1 Lloyd's Rep. 391, 397.

[70] Since this comment in the *Tramountana* case, arbitrators have been given the power to award any interest: Arbitration Act 1996 s.49.

[71] See paras 14-03 onwards. In *Mitchell v James* [2004] 1 W.L.R. 158 it was held that as CPR r.36.1(2) states, nothing in Pt 36 prevents a party making an offer to settle in whatever way he chooses. However, nothing in r.36.1(1) (2) permits a party to include a term as to costs as part of a Pt 36 offer for the purpose of obtaining an order for costs on an indemnity basis.

[72] *Tramountana Armadora SA v Atlantic Shipping Co SA* [1978] 1 Lloyd's Rep. 391.

[73] See the quotation from the judgment of Donaldson J, at para.32-28.

[74] *Tramountana* [1978] 1 Lloyd's Rep. 391, 398.

[75] *Archital Luxfer Ltd v Henry Boot Construction Ltd* [1981] 1 Lloyd's Rep. 642.

[76] *Archital Luxfer* at 654.

offer and going on with the arbitration, than he would have achieved if he had accepted the offer, the offer must be in such terms as will enable the question to be answered. When the structure of the litigation is such that settlement on the terms offered will entitle the party to whom the offer is made, to payment of his costs to that date, then unless the offer includes an offer to pay the costs the arbitrator cannot in most circumstances know whether the claimant has or has not achieved more.

If an offer should be made in terms which specifically included a named sum to cover costs, and the arbitrator is satisfied that the amount so offered must without question have covered any costs therein incurred, there is no reason why the arbitrator should not give effect to the offer if the sum offered to settle the claim was insufficient. It will always be prudent to offer to pay taxed costs, because of the risk of error, but the sufficiency of an offer is concerned with its demonstrable substance and not with its form.

A party to whom an offer is made cannot be expected or required to enter upon any detailed investigations as to his position on costs in order to decide whether or not an offer made fairly reflects his prospect of success; nor, in my judgment, should an arbitrator enter upon any such investigation in order to discover whether an offer made was such that a claimant has or has not achieved more by rejecting it. Such offers are required to be plain and self-evident in their terms."

In *Archital Luxfer Ltd v Henry Boot Construction Ltd*, there was a claim and a counterclaim. The respondents made a sealed offer that they would allow the claimants £12,000 on their claim and accept £17,000 on their counterclaim. They proposed that the £5,000 thus owing to them be paid out of a sum of £12,000 held in a joint deposit account in the names of the parties pending the outcome of the proceedings with the accumulated interest in that account being duly apportioned on that sum. They proposed that there should be no order as to costs. At the end of the arbitration the claimants were awarded substantially less on their claim than the £12,000 offered and the respondents recovered a little more than the £17,000 they said they would accept. It was conceded that as at the date of the offer there was no reason to suppose that the costs of either side were significantly different. Peter Gibson J held that the offer was a valid and effective sealed offer and should have been acted upon by the arbitrator when considering his order as to costs. **32-35**

In that case the position on costs as at the time of the offer was clear. In other cases where the respondent is the net creditor of the claimant, it may not be and Peter Gibson J suggested[77] a means by which this problem could be resolved: **32-36**

"There is no reason ... why the substance of such an offer should not conclude with the proposal that there should be no order as to costs but that, if the party to whom the offer is made does not accept that part of the offer, the question of costs be referred to and decided by the arbitrator upon the basis that the other terms of settlement of the action are accepted. The offer could further provide that if the arbitrator then directed that the costs be paid in terms no more favourable to the offeree than as first proposed, the arbitrator would be asked to direct the offeree to pay the costs thus wasted. If the offer were in those terms and was rejected; and the claimant received no more than the sum offered in settlement the arbitrator could determine what costs ought to be allowed to the claimant on the basis that he had accepted the offer when made."

An offer that excludes the payment of costs may be given relatively little weight, although it may not be disregarded if its value can be ascertained relatively easily. In *Lindner Ceilings Floors Partitions Plc v How Engineering Services Ltd*[78] the respondent made an offer of a defined sum in respect of the claimant's claim exclusive of interest and costs, both of which were to be assessed by the arbitrator. The arbitrator took account of the offer notwithstanding that it was not in the form **32-37**

---

77 *Archital Luxfer* [1981] 1 Lloyd's Rep. 642, 655–656.

78 *Lindner Ceilings Floors Partitions Plc v How Engineering Services Ltd* [2001] B.L.R. 90.

"£X plus costs". On appeal the judge held[79] that the form of the offer allowed the tribunal to answer the question posed in the *Tramountana case*[80] and it was not difficult to see that the claimant should have accepted the offer.

32-38 Conversely, in determining whether the sum awarded exceeds the offer, the costs awarded are to be disregarded. In *Everglade Maritime Inc v Schiffahrtgesellschaft*[81] the arbitrators awarded US$16,215.99, plus interest. The respondent had made a sealed offer of US$15,000, plus interest and the claimant's costs to the date of the offer. The arbitrators found that, in the absence of an offer, they would have directed that each party bear its own costs and pay half of the costs of the reference. They concluded that the claimant would have received more by accepting the offer and therefore the claimant should pay the respondent's costs from the date of the offer. The Court of Appeal held that they were wrong, that they should have disregarded costs and simply considered whether the claimant had recovered more in the award than it would have recovered had it accepted the offer.

32-39 So far as interest is concerned, in the *Tramountana* case, Donaldson J suggested[82] that in order to compare the offer and the award on a "like for like" basis either the interest may be recalculated as if the award had been made on the same date as the offer, or the interest between the offer and the award may be added to the offer. An added complication is that by s.49(3) of the 1996 Act arbitrators now have the power to award compound interest. A prudent offeror may wish to take account of the possibility of an award of compound interest in the offer. In the *Lindner* case, HH Judge Seymour QC suggested the simpler approach of leaving interest out of account altogether.[83]

32-40 The question of whether the tribunal should take into account the impact of developments over time on other aspects of the relief awarded may be a question of fact which cannot be challenged in court.

In *Centreland Management Ltd v HSBC Pension Trust (UK) Limited*,[84] a landlord and tenant had participated in an arbitration to determine a rent under s.64 of the Landlord and Tenant Act 1954. The tenant made a Calderbank offer of £68,000 per annum. Nine months later, the arbitrator determined the rent at £69,000 per annum. In the interim, rents had risen and the arbitrator had concluded that, at the time the offer was made, it exceeded the market rate. However, it was nevertheless less than the rent subsequently awarded. The offer had therefore "failed". He ordered that each party bear its own costs and 50% of the arbitrator's costs. The tenant argued that the arbitrator was obliged to assess the merits of the offer at the date that it was made. If the offer exceeded market rate at the time it was made, it should be regarded as a "winning offer", regardless of any subsequent changes in the market. The tenant appealed to the court under s.69 of the 1996 Act. Vos J. (as he then was) rejected the appeal. The correct question was whether the offeree did better by refusing the offer and carrying on. The answer to that will be fact dependent. Even the correct approach to that question will be fact dependent. The court should not attempt to tie the hands of an arbitrator in deciding it.

32-41 *Angel Airlines SA v Dean & Dean Solicitors*[85] is an example of a case in which

---

79 *Lindner* at 96.
80 See para.32-28.
81 *Everglade Maritime Inc v Schiffahrtgesellschaft* [1993] Q.B. 780 CA.
82 See para.32-28.
83 *Lindner* [2001] B.L.R. 90 at [6].
84 [2013] EWHC 3238 (Ch).
85 [2009] 2 Costs L.R. 159.

the offer was found to be in a defective form as it failed to deal with the costs consequences of acceptance.[86]

The foregoing discussion, though reflecting on the form of a "sealed offer", has centred largely on its substance. The form is likely to vary from case to case. In the *Archital Luxfer* case the concluding paragraph of the respondent's offer was in these terms[87] : **32-42**

> "This offer is made on terms that its existence and contents are not to be disclosed to the Arbitrator until he has determined all issues of liability and debt or damages, and it will be brought to his attention on the issue of costs. The offer made in this letter is intended to have the effect of a payment into court pursuant to RSC, Ord.22. This offer will remain open for acceptance at any time, with the proviso that if it is not accepted within one month from the date upon which it is received, [our clients] will propose that [your clients] should pay any further costs incurred by [our clients] after the expiry of that period."

It is thought that this would provide a useful model upon which offers of this nature could be based save, of course, that RSC, Ord.22, has long since disappeared from the civil litigation arena. Presumably, a 21-day period for acceptance of the offer would be regarded as sufficient for this purpose: it is the period for acceptance of a Pt 36 offer. Arbitral tribunals may however, have an even wider discretion than the courts under CPR r.36.[88] **32-43**

The foregoing discussion has focused upon offers of settlement involving payment of money. If the terms of the arbitration agreement and the content of the dispute provide for other or additional remedies, considerations concerning the sufficiency of the offer would arise much as they arise in the context of Calderbank offers in the ordinary sphere of civil litigation.[89] **32-44**

---

86 *Angel Airlines* at [28].

87 *Archital Luxfer* [1981] 1 Lloyd's Rep. 642, 646.

88 *Argolis Shipping Co SA v Midwest Steel & Alloy Corp, The "Angeliki"* [1982] 2 Lloyd's Rep. 594 at 597, per Lloyd J.

89 See paras 18-05 onwards.

PART 14: ADMINISTRATIVE COURT PROCEEDINGS

CHAPTER 33

The Resolution by Agreement of Administrative Court Proceedings

INTRODUCTION

A wide variety of proceedings in which the decisions or actions of public bodies are challenged are allocated to the Administrative Court, formerly known as the Crown Office List.[1] Most significant of these is the application for judicial review.[2] It is beyond the scope of this work to consider the practice applicable to Administrative Court cases generally, or to consider in detail the circumstances in which relief may be granted by the court.[3] **33-01**

A very significant number of Administrative Court matters "settle". The Crown Office List Review chaired by Sir Jeffery Bowman, which reported in March 2000, obtained statistics for the year ending 30 June 1999.[4] Appendix E to the review team's report showed that in that year 1,622 cases had proceeded to the substantive hearing stage, of which 785 had been disposed of by consent or withdrawn. The rate of such disposals varied considerably between different categories of case. In 2009 the Public Law Project carried out a study of the resolution and determination of judicial review cases before reaching final hearing, so as to assess the impact of the procedural reforms implemented following the Bowman review.[5] In a sample of cases studied, 34 per cent of claims were withdrawn prior to the permission stage, and 56 per cent of claims for which permission was granted were subsequently withdrawn. The assessment of the authors is that "settlement activity as a whole has increased" and that a high proportion of cases that settled did so in favour of claimants. Like Bowman, the Public Law Project study found considerable variations between categories of case.[6] **33-02**

It is relatively unusual for the resolution of Administrative Court proceedings to **33-03**

---

1 *Practice Direction (QBD) (Trials in London)* [1981] 1 W.L.R. 1296; *Practice Direction (Administrative Court: Establishment)* [2000] 1 W.L.R. 1654.

2 Judicial review procedure is the procedure under Pt 8 of the Civil Procedure Rules as modified by CPR Pt 54: see CPR r.54.1(2)(e). Other Administrative Court business includes case stated appeals, certain statutory appeals and statutory applications to quash, habeas corpus proceedings and a miscellany of other matters.

3 See, e.g. De Smith, Woolf and Jowell, *Judicial Review of Administrative Action*, 8th edn (London: Sweet & Maxwell, 2018); Lewis, *Judicial Remedies in Public Law*, 5th edn (London: Sweet & Maxwell, 2014).

4 Although Ch.2 of the report expressed doubts as to the accuracy of the statistics. See also Eynon, "Uncontested Proceedings in the Crown Office" [1999] J.R. 153.

5 Bondy and Sunkin, *The Dynamics of Judicial Review Litigation; the resolution of public law challenges before final hearing*, Public Law Project [2009]. See also Bondy and Sunkin, Settlement in Judicial Review Proceedings [2009] PL 237.

6 The Ministry of Justice publishes civil justice statistics on a quarterly basis showing the volume of judicial review cases dealt with by the courts over time and the overall timeliness of those cases.

represent an instance of compromise in its true sense.[7] Generally speaking, one party or the other ceases to contest the claim, rather than there being a settlement involving an element of "give and take". This may be because the claimant or defendant comes to accept that its position is untenable, but often it is because it does not make sense in practical terms to take the matter further, irrespective of the merits. A particular reason for this is that many applications for judicial review and statutory appeals allocated to the Administrative Court seek to do no more than to compel a reconsideration of the original decision—inevitably so, because the court cannot normally substitute its own view of the proper outcome even if the decision-maker has erred in law. Where the claimant has a plausible case but the outcome of the litigation is uncertain, it will often be more sensible for the defendant to agree to take a fresh decision than to incur cost and delay by contesting the proceedings.

33-04 Nonetheless, there may be cases where the outcome accords more closely with a conventional compromise. For example, a claimant might be prepared to withdraw an application for judicial review of a housing authority's decision to take possession proceedings against him, in return for a commitment by the authority to permit him to remain in his present accommodation for longer than would have been the case if the decision under challenge had been upheld by the court. Another example is a case in which the parties agree upon an order granting some but not all of the relief originally claimed (e.g. a quashing order but no mandatory order). Another form of compromise, in a case where a decision has been challenged on a number of grounds (say, lack of jurisdiction and a failure to take account of relevant considerations), might involve the defendant consenting to a quashing order and to reconsideration of its decision in return for the claimant agreeing not to challenge the new decision for want of jurisdiction.

ALTERNATIVE DISPUTE RESOLUTION

33-05 It is a long-established principle that judicial review is a remedy of last resort, in the sense that permission to apply for judicial review will not normally be granted where there is some adequate alternative remedy open to the claimant.[8] Such alternative remedies may include not only other statutory rights of appeal or review, but also the ability to pursue the defendant's internal complaints procedures or to complain to some external regulator. A claimant should state in the claim form for judicial review whether an alternative remedy to judicial review exists, whether or not the claimant is pursuing such a remedy and, if not, why judicial review is appropriate despite the alternative remedy.[9] The detail of these matters is outside the

---

See *https://www.gov.uk/government/collections/civil-justice-statistics-quarterly* [Accessed 31 October 2019]. This includes data about summary statistics on the overall caseload in the Administrative Court from 2004-2019 and case progression data about individual cases. The data suggest that a significant number of cases continue to be disposed of by consent or withdrawn prior to any final determination.

7 See para.1-03.

8 *Kay v Lambeth LBC* [2006] UKHL 10; [2006] 2 A.C. 465 at [30] per Lord Bingham; *R. (Cart) v Upper Tribunal* [2011] UKSC 28; [2012] 1 A.C. 663 at [33] per Lord Phillips and *R. (Archer) v HM Revenue and Customs* [2019] EWCA Civ 1021 at [87]-[95]. See also *The Administrative Court: Judicial Review Guide 2019*, para.5.3.3.3 which states that if the court finds that a claimant has an adequate alternative remedy, it will generally refuse permission to apply for judicial review.

9 See *R. v Humberside County Council Ex p. Bogdal (No.2)* [1992] C.O.D. 467, *R. v Secretary of State for the Home Department Ex p. Swati* [1986] 1 W.L.R. 477 and *R. (Zahid) v The University of Manchester* [2017] EWHC 188 (Admin) at [53].

scope of this work. However, in *R. (Cowl) v Plymouth CC*[10] the Court of Appeal built upon the discretionary nature of the power to grant or withhold permission for judicial review proceedings, in order to encourage the use of alternative dispute resolution. The court held that even where no alternative remedy in the technical sense was available, there was no absolute right to proceed with an application for judicial review. It was held that except for good reason, the application should be stayed and not permitted to proceed "if a significant part of the issues between the parties could be resolved outside the litigation process". In *Cowl* itself the defendant had offered to establish a modified form of complaints procedure to deal with the matter. The rationale is obviously also capable of being applied to a proposal to mediate. The court has power to make costs orders which reflect the failure of a party to exhaust an alternative remedy before resorting to judicial review.[11] The court's power to make adverse costs orders against a party who unreasonably refuses to mediate is also capable of being applied in judicial review proceedings as elsewhere.[12]

Despite the considerable attention received by *Cowl* when first decided, it is not thought that a large number of cases have been stayed or refused permission on the basis there set out, nor that great use has been made of mediation in judicial review proceedings, by comparison with other forms of civil litigation.[13] The potential for mediation in public law disputes is probably greater than is often recognised, not least because it allows for a more substantive outcome than the mere reconsideration of a decision. Moreover, *The Administrative Court: Judicial Review Guide 2019* specifically refers to a continuing duty on the parties throughout the proceedings to settle the claim without requiring the intervention of the court. It identifies that the parties should consider using alternative dispute resolution, such as mediation, to explore settlement of the case, or at least to narrow the issues in the case.[14] Nonetheless, there are valid reasons why mediation may sometimes be inappropriate in judicial review. If the defendant believes that a particular course of action would be improper in public law, through lack of vires or otherwise, it will prob- **33-06**

---

10 *R. (Cowl) v Plymouth CC* [2001] EWCA Civ 1935; [2002] 1 W.L.R. 803. See also *Anufrijeva v Southwark LBC* [2004] Q.B. 1124 at [81], holding that damages claims under the Human Rights Act 1998 should normally be referred to ADR or pursued through internal procedures or referred to an ombudsman as complaints of maladministration. But see *R. (on the application of Paul Crawford) v The University of Newcastle Upon Tyne* [2014] EWHC 1197 (Admin) and *R. (RD (A Child)) v Worcestershire County Council* [2019] EWHC 449 (Admin).

11 See *R. (Archer) v HM Revenue and Customs* [2019] EWCA Civ 1021 at [88]-[96] where the Court of Appeal concluded that a statutory right afforded to a taxpayer to make representations to HMRC provided an alternative remedy which should have been exercised and failure to do so justified making no order as to costs in favour of the taxpayer on the successful claim.

12 See Ch.35. For an example of a successful defendant being refused its costs on this basis (in part), see *R. (Nurse Prescribers Ltd) v Secretary of State for Health* [2004] EWHC 403 (Admin). For examples the other way, see *R. (A, B, X and Y) v East Sussex CC* (2005) 8 C.C.L.R. 228 at [42]–[45] and *R. (Wildbur) v Ministry of Defence* [2016] EWHC 1636 (Admin). In *Halsey v Milton Keynes General NHS Trust* [2004] 1 W.L.R. 3002 at [34]–[35] the court rejected any suggestion that it should be more willing to impose costs sanctions against public bodies than against other litigants on this ground. Indeed, at [18(b)] of *Halsey* itself and in some subsequent decisions it has been recognised that large public bodies may need to contest what they reasonably regard as unfounded claims so as to deter the routine making of such claims: see, e.g. *Daniels v Metropolitan Police Commissioner* [2005] EWCA Civ 1312 at [30]–[32]. There seems to be no reason why this thinking should not apply equally to public law claims.

13 In *R. (Zahid) v The University of Manchester* [2017] EWHC 188 (Admin) at [65], Hickinbottom J noted that academic texts continue to exhort the message in *Cowl* but observed that it appeared to have become a largely forgotten authority in the Administrative Court itself. However, Hickinbottom J conclude that the observations of Woolf J in *Cowl* continued to be apt today.

14 See *The Administrative Court: Judicial Review Guide 2019*, para.12.2.1.

ably regard itself as barred from taking that step without a ruling of the court. Where a judicial or quasi-judicial decision is under challenge, then again the decision-maker may feel that this cannot appropriately be made the subject of negotiation or compromise. Finally, given the relatively short nature of most judicial review hearings, the incentive to spend money on mediation in the hope of avoiding hearing costs may be comparatively limited.[15] These issues are discussed in detail in another Public Law Project research study.[16]

THE POWER TO COMPROMISE

33-07 In most Administrative Court cases, the defendant will be a public body, and often a statutory corporation whose powers are therefore limited to those expressly or impliedly conferred upon it by statute.[17] It follows that such a body, before entering into a compromise, must be satisfied not only that the proposed compromise would represent a proper exercise of its powers having regard to the merits of the claim, the likely cost of the litigation and so forth,[18] but also that any positive step which the agreement requires it to take would be intra vires.[19] For example, if a local authority is forbidden by statute from allocating its housing stock to certain persons, it could not validly agree to make such an allocation as part of a compromise of litigation.

33-08 However, in the absence of some such express prohibition, it is thought that it will not generally be too difficult to identify a power to conclude a compromise. In the case of a local authority, such power may be found either in reading together s.222 of the Local Government Act 1972 (power to prosecute, defend or appear in legal proceedings) and s.111 of that Act (power to take steps incidental to discharge of functions), or in the very general "well-being" power now conferred by s.2 of the Local Government Act 2000. Also significant in local authority cases is the power under s.92 of the Local Government Act 2000 to make payments to, or provide other benefits for, persons whom an authority considers may have been adversely affected by action that may amount to maladministration.

33-09 In *R. (Hooper) v Secretary of State for Work and Pensions*[20] the court had to consider an argument that, having settled the claims of some individuals, the defendant was under a public law obligation to treat others in a like position in the

---

15 This commentary as to why mediation may sometimes be inappropriate in judicial review was specifically invoked in explaining why it was understandable, to an extent, that ADR is not prevalent in the sphere of public law disputes. See *R. (Zahid) v The University of Manchester* [2017] EWHC 188 (Admin) at [57] per Hickinbottom J.

16 Bondy and Mulcahy, *Mediation and Judicial Review—an empirical research study* (2009).

17 Ministers of the Crown, by contrast, are corporations sole having all the capacity of a natural person. For the implications of this status, and the extent to which any power to make payments might be cut down by the existence of statutory powers of more limited scope, see the discussion in *R. (Hooper) v Secretary of State for Work and Pensions* [2003] 1 W.L.R. 2623 at [120] to [137] (CA) and [2005] 1 W.L.R. 1681 at [6], [45]–[47] and [123] (HL); and cf. *Shrewsbury & Atcham BC v Secretary of State for Communities and Local Government* [2008] 3 All E.R. 548.

18 It is worth noting that a compromise agreement concluded with an authority which is subject to the Freedom of Information Act 2000 may be subject to public disclosure. Even if such an agreement were to contain a confidentiality provision, it might not attract the absolute exemption conferred by s.41 of the Act, since the agreement itself may not rank as "information obtained" by the authority, and it is also possible that there could be a sufficient public interest in the disclosure of the agreement that it would not involve any actionable breach of confidentiality.

19 See *Hazell v Hammersmith and Fulham LBC* [1992] 2 A.C. 1 at 38. See also para.4-10.

20 *R. (Hooper) v Secretary of State for Work and Pensions* [2003] 1 W.L.R. 2623 at [103] to [108]. This issue was not debated in the House of Lords.

same way. In relation to persons refused a certain type of benefit on allegedly discriminatory grounds, the state's policy had been to settle any such claim once it was brought to the European Court of Human Rights and declared admissible, but not otherwise. The court upheld this approach, saying that a settlement without admission of liability, whether at Strasbourg or in any other proceedings, did not require equivalent payments to be made to others in a like position:

> "A well recognised motive for settling a case is to avoid the risk of an adverse decision and a settlement cannot be considered as carrying the same consequences as such a decision."[21]

The Supreme Court has more recently considered the content of the public law principles of fairness and equal treatment and their practical consequences for a decision-maker in handling other parties in *R. (Gallaher Group Ltd) v Competition and Markets Authority*.[22] The appellants argued that the Office of Fair Trading had acted unlawfully in not offering them the same assurances that had been offered to another party. The Supreme Court concluded that the common law did not recognise equal treatment as a distinct principle of administrative law, but that administrative law requirements of consistency of treatment generally arose as an aspect of rationality. This could mean a general duty to offer equal treatment to those subject to a single set of legal and policy criteria in the same circumstances arose only as matter of rationality or legitimate expectation. Likewise, the Supreme Court concluded that whilst the principle of procedural unfairness is well-established and well-understood, there is no distinct legal criterion of "substantive unfairness" or "conspicuous unfairness" and this does not add anything to the ordinary principles of judicial review including irrationality and legitimate expectation. In the circumstances it found that it had not been irrational, nor a breach of any legitimate expectation, to have treated the appellants differently as the assurance offered to the other party had been a mistake.

In some cases where the claimant seeks the quashing of an existing decision **33-10** and/or the taking of a fresh decision, or the variation of some prior decision, the defendant may have no power to embark upon that course unless the existing decision is quashed by an order of the court.[23] In other words the decision-maker, having once reached a decision, is functus officio for so long as that decision continues to subsist[24]. This is most obviously true of judicial and quasi-judicial determinations involving the resolution of competing claims, but the doctrine may apply in other situations as well. This is notwithstanding the general rule that, unless the contrary intention appears, a statutory power may be exercised and a statutory duty

---

21 See also *R. (Ali) v Secretary of State for Justice* [2014] EWCA Civ 194; [2014] W.L.R. 3202 in which the Court of Appeal concluded that even where a subsequent decision establishes that previous decisions made by a public decision-maker may have been subject to a misunderstanding as to the law, a decision-maker may adopt a policy as to what previous decisions will be reconsidered (applying *R. v Hertfordshire County Council Ex p. Cheung* (1986) *The Times*, 26 March 1986). By logical extension of that principle, where a public authority decides to compromise proceedings on the basis that the underlying decision is legally flawed, this will not necessarily prevent the public authority adopting a policy not to re-open other decisions which might have been subject to the same legal error, but which were not subject to a judicial review claim.

22 [2018] UKSC 25, [2019] A.C. 96.

23 See, e.g. *R. v Parliamentary Commissioner for Administration Ex p. Balchin* [1998] 1 P.L.R. 1, where Sedley J, having found the ombudsman's decision on an investigation to be unlawful, indicated that he would quash it formally if this was necessary in order for the matter to be reconsidered.

24 See, e.g. *R. (Sambotin) v Brent LBC* [2018] EWCA Civ 1826; [2019] H.L.R. 5.

must be performed "from time to time as occasion requires".[25] In the context of a proposed compromise, the issue may be of practical importance if a change of heart by the decision-maker will affect a third party who may seek to persuade the court not to make a quashing order.[26]

NATURE, ENFORCEMENT AND EFFECT OF COMPROMISE

33-11 The nature of the compromise may be of importance where a term of the compromise is that the defendant should take certain positive steps, particularly where those steps entail something more complex than the mere retaking of a decision.

33-12 If the court is invited to, and does, make a mandatory order requiring certain steps to be taken, then the position is straightforward. The order of the court must be obeyed, and failure to comply with a mandatory order is a contempt of court. That is one reason why it is undesirable to agree terms of compromise which involve the court making an order against the defendant the effect of which is unclear.[27] Where the material terms of the agreement between the parties do not form part of an order of the court,[28] they may well amount to a contract of compromise, enforceable in the same way as any other contract to compromise civil proceedings. In other cases, the true construction of the "agreement" may be that it amounts to no more than a giving of an assurance by the defendant as to how it proposes to exercise its powers in future. Such an assurance would undoubtedly give rise to a legitimate expectation that it would be fulfilled, of a substantive and not merely a procedural kind,[29] so that a failure to do what had been promised without some compelling reason would constitute grounds for a fresh application for judicial review.[30]

33-13 It should be noted that, in *R. v Commissioner for Local Administration Ex p.*

---

25 Interpretation Act 1978 s.12.

26 See para.33-18, and the *Towry Law* case cited at para.33-23. In *R. v Aylesbury Vale DC Ex p. Chaplin*, *The Times*, 23 July 1996, Keene J and the Court of Appeal ([1997] 3 P.L.R. 55) rejected a submission that it was improper for a local planning authority to grant a fresh application for planning permission where its original refusal was under appeal, and the objector to permission would have been able to make representations in opposition to the appeal at the inquiry. However, Keene J did acknowledge that the grant of permission would have been unlawful if it had been motivated by the authority's desire to avoid the costs of the appeal rather than by its assessment of the likely outcome. In *R. (Council for the Regulation of Healthcare Professionals) v Health Professions Council* [2006] EWHC 890 (Admin) at [9], Jackson J raised a question as to whether it would be proper for a regulatory body to concede an appeal against a disciplinary decision where it considered that there were or might be good grounds for resisting the appeal.

27 See, e.g. *R. (Lloyd) v Barking and Dagenham LBC* (2001) 4 C.C.L.R. 196, where the defendant gave undertakings to the court as part of an agreement pursuant to which judicial review proceedings were adjourned, but disputes later arose as to whether there had been compliance with those undertakings. At 206A–C, the Court of Appeal criticised the undertakings on various grounds: in part they stated merely that the Council would comply with its duties under statute, which it was obliged to do in any event (see also *R. v ILEA Ex p. Ali* (1990) 2 Ad. L.R. 822 at 837B); they imposed positive obligations which it was outside the defendant's power to achieve; and they required the implication of terms as to reasonableness. The possibility of sanctions for contempt "merely complicates an already difficult situation".

28 The Tomlin form of order (see para.9-21 onwards) does not appear to be common in Administrative Court proceedings, but there is no reason in principle why it should not be used.

29 See the discussion in *R. v North & East Devon Health Authority Ex p. Coughlan* [2001] Q.B. 213.

30 Cf. the doubts expressed in *R. (Whapples) v Birmingham East and North PCT* [2008] EWCA Civ 465 as to whether a compromise agreement could give rise to any rights in public law rather than contract.

PH,[31] it was held by Turner J that the Local Government Ombudsman was not entitled to investigate a complaint of maladministration, with a view to the award of compensation, where the complainant had already ventilated the matters in question by way of judicial review.[32] That was a case in which the judicial review proceedings had led to a judgment, but the result would presumably have been the same if they had ended in settlement. Accordingly, a judicial review claimant who wishes to preserve the possibility of complaint to the Ombudsman or some similar avenue of redress should ensure that this is reflected in the terms of any compromise of the judicial review proceedings (even then it would be a matter for the Ombudsman's discretion whether to accept the complaint).

WITHDRAWAL OF PROCEEDINGS

Under the Civil Procedure Rules, an application for judicial review is a claim within the meaning of CPR Pt 38,[33] and so may be discontinued by the claimant filing and serving a notice of discontinuance at any point in the proceedings,[34] save in the specific cases where the consent of the court is needed pursuant to CPR r.38.2(2).[35] The discontinuance will take effect from the date on which the notice of discontinuance is served on the other parties.[36] By filing a notice of discontinuance the claimant accepts liability for the defendant's costs up until that date, unless the parties have agreed a different costs order, and a costs order will be deemed to have been made on the standard basis.[37] A claimant may apply to reverse that general rule or to seek costs, but any application will have to demonstrate good reason for departing from the general rule such as the defendant having behaved unreasonably.[38] Eynon[39] indicates that it is the practice of the Administrative Court 33-14

31 See *R. v Commissioner for Local Administration Ex p. PH, The Times*, 8 January 1999 (permission to appeal refused by Simon Brown L.J., 8 March 1999) and *R. (Scholarstica Umo) v Commissioner for Local Administration* [2003] EWHC 3202 (Admin); [2004] E.L.R. 265. See also *Gifford v Governor of Bure Prison* [2014] EWHC 911 (Admin) at [38] and *R. (B) v Office of the Independent Adjudicator* [2018] EWHC 1971 (Admin); [2019] P.T.S.R. 769 for the application of the same principle that the settlement of relevant proceedings may preclude the subsequent jurisdiction of a decision-maker and c.f. *R. (Parish) v Pensions Ombudsman* [2009] EWHC 32 (Admin); [2009] Pens L.R. 91.

32 Conversely, in *R. v Secretary of State for the Environment, Transport and the Regions Ex p. Garland* (Turner J, 10 November 2000) the claimant was held to be barred from applying for judicial review of a determination of the Secretary of State concerning his pension entitlement, where that would undermine the effect of a settlement entered into between the claimant and the district auditor in a way which would be inequitable.

33 The phrase "claim for judicial review" is specifically used in CPR Pt 54. This interpretation, if correct, means that the position is now significantly different from what it was held to be by Laws L.J. in *Estate of Kingsley (deceased) v Secretary of State for Transport* [1994] C.O.D. 358. The then RSC Ord.21, r.2(4) permitted the withdrawal of an action without the leave of the court if all the parties consented, but it was held that in the context an "action" did not include proceedings in the Crown Office List, because the role of the court in public law proceedings was to guard the public interest as it might be affected by the decision under challenge, and that on that account it was important for the withdrawal of proceedings to be subject to the court's approval.

34 For guidance, see *The Administrative Court: Judicial Review Guide 2019*, para.22.3 Discontinuance.

35 cf. para.9-38. A claimant who discontinues will be liable for the defendant's costs unless the court orders otherwise.

36 See CPR 38.5(1).

37 See CPR 38.6(1).

38 See guidance in *The Administrative Court: Judicial Review Guide 2019*, para.22.3.6.

39 See fn.4, at para.10-14 of the article. See now the 2008 Practice Statement referred to at para.33-17, para.3(b) of which provides for a claimant, where leave of the court is not necessary for proceed-

Office to permit applications to be withdrawn without consent,[40] but to seek written confirmation from other parties who have been given notice of the proceedings that they do not object to the withdrawal, and in particular that they do not seek any costs order, before closing the court file. If necessary, the case may be listed on the issue of costs alone.

33-15 In the case of statutory appeals assigned to the Administrative Court, CPR Pt 52 PD 52A para.6.1 will apply. The appellant may seek an order that the appeal be dismissed,[41] which will if it is granted usually be on the basis that the appellant pays the costs of the appeal. Again, this is reflected in para.3(d) of the 2008 Practice Statement. The request must contain a statement that the appellant is not a child or a protected party. If it is desired to have the appeal dismissed without costs, the request must be accompanied by a consent signed by the respondent or his legal representative, stating that the respondent is not a child or protected party and that he consents to the dismissal of the appeal without costs.

OBTAINING AGREED ORDER

33-16 In judicial review proceedings, the practice to be adopted when a consent order (as opposed to mere withdrawal of the proceedings) is required, and the parties are agreed on the terms of the order they seek, is set out in CPR Pt 54 PD 54A para.17, the terms of which are as follows:

> "17.1 If the parties agree about the final order to be made in a claim for judicial review, the claimant must file at the court a document (with 2 copies) signed by all the parties setting out the terms of the proposed agreed order together with a short statement of the matters relied on as justifying the proposed agreed order and copies of any authorities or statutory provisions relied on.
>
> 17.2 The court will consider the documents referred to in paragraph 17.1 and will make the order if satisfied that the order should be made.
>
> 17.3 If the court is not satisfied that the order should be made, a hearing date will be set.

---

ings to be withdrawn and no order as to costs is sought, simply to inform the Administrative Court Office in writing, confirming that all other parties to the proceedings have been notified. The court file will then be closed.

40 para.14 of Eynon's article (fn.4) indicates that the leave of the court is required to withdraw proceedings involving the liberty of the subject, i.e. applications for writs of habeas corpus or for committal for contempt. It is respectfully suggested that under the CPR there is no very clear basis for such a requirement in habeas corpus cases, and that the true reason for it in contempt cases may be the court's own interest in securing that its orders are upheld. No suggestion of a need for leave in proceedings of this nature appears in *The Administrative Court: Judicial Review Guide 2019* (July 2019). Paragraph 3(a) of the 2008 Practice Statement sets out the procedure to be followed where the parties are agreed that proceedings should be withdrawn but require the leave of the court to do so, but does not seek to define the cases in which such a requirement exists (the procedure also applies in cases of withdrawal by agreement where an agreed costs order is sought). *R. v Secretary of State for the Home Department Ex p. Gashi* [2000] EWHC Admin 356 is an example of a case in which the court appears to have accepted a defendant's argument that the withdrawal of certain claims should not be permitted, because they raised points on which a judgment was required in order to dispose of a large number of other outstanding applications for judicial review; see also *R. (B) v Asylum Support Adjudicator* [2005] EWHC 2017 (Admin).

41 Again, therefore, the position has changed under the CPR. Previously, in the absence of any express provision requiring it, the appellant was entitled to withdraw an appeal by way of case stated (and presumably a statutory appeal) without the permission of the court: see *Collet v Bromsgrove DC* [1997] Crim. L.R. 206.

17.4 Where the agreement relates to an order for costs only, the parties need only file a document signed by all the parties setting out the terms of the proposed order."

A Practice Statement[42] also exists, para.1 of which is in very similar terms. It adds the information that the agreed document will be submitted to the Master or Deputy Master of the Crown Office, and that if the court is satisfied, the order will be made without the need for attendance by the parties or their representatives, and will be publicised on the HMCTS website. Paragraph 2 makes similar provision in relation to agreed interim orders. Guidance in respect of consent orders and uncontested proceedings is also provided in *The Administrative Court: Judicial Review Guide 2019*, para.22.4. Any draft order must note that the order is made "By Consent".[43] Where the claim has been finally determined, the consent order must detail the manner of determination including whether the claim is withdrawn, as the effect of this will be to leave the challenged decision in place unless the defendant has withdrawn the decision. The consent order should make provision for determining costs, otherwise a deemed costs order will apply.[44] In practice, it is highly unusual for the court not to make the order sought, and the statement of matters relied upon can in most cases properly be made extremely concise.[45] Cases in which the court may require rather more by way of justification are likely to be those in which some unusual form of order is sought, or in which it is apparent that the order that the court is asked to make may have an impact upon third parties. That would include cases where the proposed form of relief includes a declaration which is not strictly limited to the relationship between the claimant and the defendant. **33-17**

Real difficulties are only likely to arise in cases where the defendant is amenable to the grant of certain relief sought by the claimant, but a third party is opposed to that relief being granted. There are numerous instances in which a third party will be more closely interested in the outcome of an application for judicial review than the nominal defendant. A challenge to a planning authority's grant of planning permission to a developer is an obvious example, as are most instances in which judicial review is sought of a decision made by magistrates. In *R. v Independent Appeals Tribunal of Hillingdon BC Ex p. Governing Body of Mellow Lane School*,[46] the statutory appeal panel decided to allow a pupil's appeal against his permanent exclusion from school. When faced with an application for judicial review by the school governing body for which permission was granted, the panel decided not to contest the matter, and signed a consent order providing for the original decision to be quashed. The consent order was made by the court notwithstanding the opposition of the pupil, and without an examination of the merits. It is respectfully submitted that to take this course was contrary both to principle and to authority.[47] **33-18**

---

42 Administrative Court: uncontested proceedings [2008] 1 W.L.R. 1377, which replaces the former practice note of 12 May 1997 ([1997] 1 W.L.R. 825).

43 CPR 40.6(7)(b).

44 See *The Administrative Court: Judicial Review Guide 2019*, para.22.4.3, para.23.5.4, para.23.8 and annex 5 to that Guide setting out the ACO Costs Guidance dated April 2016 as to what the consent order should state.

45 Note however the comments of Laws LJ in *R. (Anwar-Lindley) v Lancashire Justices* [2005] EWHC 1214 (Admin), emphasising "the importance that the court attaches to there being a proper explanation of the basis upon which it is asked to quash a decision of another public authority."

46 *R. v Independent Appeals Tribunal of Hillingdon BC Ex p. Governing Body of Mellow Lane School* [2001] E.L.R. 200.

47 Newman J appears to have taken the view that the pupil suffered no deprivation of rights, because he would be entitled to a fresh appeal panel hearing, and that the panel could have agreed to reconsider its decision regardless of any application for judicial review. It is respectfully suggested that neither of these propositions is sustainable.

In *Kingsley's* case,[48] Laws LJ said that where the defendant conceded that relief should be granted, there was "no question" but that the court had to approve any order carrying that into effect. In *R. (Wirral Health Authority) v Finnegan*[49] the Mental Health Review Tribunal was willing to agree to the quashing of its decision to discharge a patient, but the patient was not. The court held[50] that, in the circumstances, it was plainly not appropriate to make a consent order and the matter had to be "properly considered" by the court to see whether judicial review was appropriate.[51] Additionally, it is submitted that "the parties" within the meaning of para.17 of the Practice Direction include not only the claimant and the defendant, but also any interested party[52] who has been served pursuant to CPR r.54.7(b) and has filed an acknowledgment of service. In *R. (Reading BC) v Admissions Appeal Panel for Reading BC*,[53] the court adopted a procedure, when the defendant was willing to agree to a consent order quashing its decision, whereby interested parties were allowed a specified period in which to object to the order. The court's direction made provision for such objections to be considered on the papers, but the interested parties were regarded as enjoying a right to insist upon an oral hearing if they chose (which is what then occurred). Likewise, in *R. (Clare) v Independent Police Complaints Commission*[54] a consent order made in ignorance of an interested party's objection was set aside, and the matter fully argued between the interested party and the claimant. In *R. (Midcounties Co-Operative Ltd) v Forest of Dean District Council*[55] the court was confronted with a case where a defendant did not concede the claim, but decided not to take part in the proceedings for financial reasons and left it to the interested party to defend the decision. The court noted that this was unusual. Whilst noting that it was readily understandable where public authorities were facing increasing financial pressures, the court considered that the stance could lead to tension with certain fundamental aspects of the way in which judicial review proceedings are conducted. This is because judicial review litigation is not to be conducted in the same way as ordinary civil litigation and the relationship between a public authority defendant and the court is not the same as that between an ordinary litigant and the court. The court referred to the duty of candour and co-operation owed by a public authority defendant to assist the court in understanding the decision and in dealing with the issues fairly.[56] It stated that if a defendant finds itself in that position, it should at least consider whether: it had complied with its duty of candour and co-operation by disclosing all relevant documents; it should file any witness evidence to assist the court; it should file an acknowledgement of service with summary grounds of resistance even if only in outline form to justify its decision; a representative should be present in court at any

---

48 See fn.23.

49 Scott Baker J, 6 March 2001 (CO/202/01).

50 Judgment para.28. This was approved as a correct approach by the Court of Appeal in the same case (*R. (Wirral Health Authority) v Mental Health Review Tribunal* [2001] EWCA Civ 1901 at [7]).

51 Compare *R. v Bassetlaw DC Ex p. Oxby, The Times,* 18 December 1997, where the court was prepared to entertain an application for judicial review made by the leader of the defendant authority as a means of enabling that authority to attack one of its own earlier decisions, but held that the fact that the defendant was in substance seeking judicial review of its own decision was to be taken into account in deciding how the court should exercise its discretion. See also *R. (Meredith) v Merthyr Tydfil CBC* [2002] EWHC 634 (Admin).

52 Defined as any person (other than the claimant and defendant) who is directly affected by the claim: see *R. v Liverpool CC Ex p. Muldoon* [1996] 1 W.L.R. 1103.

53 *R. (Reading BC) v Admissions Appeal Panel for Reading BC* [2006] E.L.R. 186.

54 *R. (Clare) v Independent Police Complaints Commission* [2005] EWHC 1108 (Admin).

55 [2015] EWHC 1251 (Admin).

56 *R. v Lancashire County Council, Ex p. Huddleston* [1986] 2 All E.R. 941.

hearing to know what is going on and so as to be able to deal with any points that might arise unexpectedly or to answer judicial questions if required.

Where the proceedings are by way of a statutory appeal, CPR Pt 52 PD 52A para.6.3 permits the parties to make a joint request to the court for the appeal to be dismissed by consent. However, para.6.4 of the Practice Direction provides that the appeal court will not normally make an order allowing an appeal unless satisfied that the decision of the lower court was "wrong or unjust because of a serious procedural or other irregularity". It now also provides, although it did not do so originally, that the order of the lower court may be set aside or varied by consent without a determination of the merits of the appeal, if the appeal court is satisfied that there are good and sufficient reasons for doing so.[57] Where the appeal court is requested by all parties to allow an appeal, that request may be considered on the papers. The request should state that none of the parties is a child or patient and set out the relevant history of the proceedings and the matters relied on as justifying the proposed order and be accompanied by a copy of the proposed order. **33-19**

The parties have an obligation to inform the Administrative Court if they believe that a case is likely to settle as soon as they become aware of the possibility of settlement.[58] *The Administrative Court: Judicial Review Guide 2019* identifies that failure to do may result in the court making an adverse costs order against the parties.[59]

COSTS UPON WITHDRAWAL OR SETTLEMENT OF JUDICIAL REVIEW PROCEEDINGS

As noted above, some judicial review proceedings are inherently likely to be overtaken by events. Sometimes they will cease to be of practical utility to the claimant: for example, an application for judicial review is made in respect of the refusal to admit a pupil to a school, but before it can be heard the pupil obtains a place in another school and no longer wishes to go to the original school. Perhaps more frequently, the defendant will agree to take a fresh decision. In such circumstances, which party should bear the costs? There is an onus on the parties to reach agreement on costs wherever possible and in advance of asking the court to resolve the issue. *The Administrative Court: Judicial Review Guide 2019* states that the parties should not, therefore, make submissions to the court on costs following a compromise of proceedings without first seeking to agree them through reasoned negotiation, mindful of the overriding objective to the CPR, the amounts of costs actually at stake, and the relevant case law.[60] There is a significant body of authority as to the approach which the court will take if an application for costs comes before it. If the parties allow this case-law to inform their negotiations, it will usually be possible to agree what costs order should be made. **33-20**

The leading authority on the current approach of the court to this issue is now **33-21**

---

[57] For an example in a judicial review context of the court deciding to approve a consent order varying an inquisition without determining its unlawfulness, where satisfied that it was arguably unlawful, and that a full hearing would take several days, see *Ministry of Defence v HM Coroner for Wiltshire and Swindon* [2006] EWHC 309 (Admin). See Ch.34.

[58] See *Yell Ltd v Garton* [2004] EWCA Civ 87; [2004] C.P. Rep 29 and *The Administrative Court: Judicial Review Guide 2019*, paras 12.2.7 and 22.6.1.

[59] See *The Administrative Court: Judicial Review Guide 2019*, para.22.6.1

[60] See *The Administrative Court: Judicial Review Guide 2019*, para.23.5.1.

R. (M) v Croydon London Borough Council.[61] All previous guidance, including that given in *R. v Waltham Forest LBC Ex p. Boxall*,[62] must be read in the light of the observations of the Court of Appeal in this case. The court emphasised that the general rule in civil litigation (reflected in the then CPR r.44.3(2), now CPR r.44.2(2)) is that a successful party who obtained all the relief sought, whether by consent or after a contested hearing, is entitled to the payment of costs by the unsuccessful party unless there was good reason to the contrary and that it applied in the Administrative Court just as much as to other parts of the civil justice system and it made no difference that a defendant was a public body. Lord Neuberger of Abbotsbury MR reflected on these issues as follows:

> "60. Thus, in Administrative Court cases, just as in other civil litigation, particularly where a claim has been settled, there is, in my view, a sharp difference between (i) a case where a claimant has been wholly successful whether following a contested hearing or pursuant to a settlement, and (ii) a case where he has only succeeded in part following a contested hearing, or pursuant to a settlement, and (iii) a case where there has been some compromise which does not actually reflect the claimant's claims. While in every case, the allocation of costs will depend on the specific facts, there are some points which can be made about these different types of case.
>
> 61. In case (i), it is hard to see why the claimant should not recover all his costs, unless there is some good reason to the contrary. Whether pursuant to judgment following a contested hearing, or by virtue of a settlement, the claimant can, at least absent special circumstances, say that he has been vindicated, and, as the successful party, that he should recover his costs. In the latter case, the defendants can no doubt say that they were realistic in settling, and should not be penalised in costs, but the answer to that point is that the defendants should, on that basis, have settled before the proceedings were issued: that is one of the main points of the pre-action protocols. Ultimately, it seems to me that *Bahta*[63] was decided on this basis.
>
> 62. In case (ii), when deciding how to allocate liability for costs after a trial, the court will normally determine questions such as how reasonable the claimant was in pursuing the unsuccessful claim, how important it was compared with the successful claim, and how much the costs were increased as a result of the claimant pursuing the unsuccessful claim. Given that there will have been a hearing, the court will be in a reasonably good position to make findings on such questions. However, where there has been a settlement, the court will, at least normally, be in a significantly worse position to make findings on such issues than where the case has been fought out. In many such cases, the court will be able to form a view as

---

61 [2012] EWCA Civ 595; [2012] 1 W.L.R. 2607.

62 *R. v Waltham Forest LBC Ex p. Boxall* (2001) 4 C.C.L.R. 258. Scott Baker J, as he then was, indicated that, in cases which settled before permission was granted, it was only in plain and obvious cases that a costs order should be made against the defendant. In other cases, the extent to which the court would be prepared to look into the previously unresolved substantive issues would depend upon the circumstances of the particular case, including the amount of costs at stake and the conduct of the parties. The adverse impact of a failure to obtain a costs order upon the rate of remuneration payable to the lawyers of a publicly funded party is not in itself a sufficient reason to investigate the merits, although it does serve to emphasise that the court should be prepared to make a reasonable and proportionate attempt to analyse the situation. In *Boxall* itself, Scott Baker J considered the allegations and response "broadly", concluded that there was little doubt that the defendant would have been found to have acted unlawfully in at least some respects, and awarded the claimants their costs up to a particular point. The final (December 2009) report of Lord Justice Jackson's review of civil litigation costs recommended modification of the *Boxall* approach in the light of the fact that there is now a pre-action protocol for judicial review, so that if the defendant concedes any material part of the relief sought by the claimant after the issue of proceedings, the normal order should be that the defendant pays the claimant's costs. Particular circumstances might warrant a different order. That approach has generally been endorsed in *M*. *Boxall* had received more general approval, outside the public law field, in *Brawley v Marczynski* [2003] 1 W.L.R. 813.

63 *R (Bahta) v Secretary of State for the Home Department* [2011] 5 Costs L.R. 857.

to the appropriate costs order based on such issues; in other cases, it will be much more difficult. I would accept the argument that, where the parties have settled the claimant's substantive claims on the basis that he succeeds in part, but only in part, there is often much to be said for concluding that there is no order for costs. That I think was the approach adopted in *Scott*.[64] However, where there is not a clear winner, so much would depend on the particular facts. In some such cases, it may help to consider who would have won if the matter had proceeded to trial, as, if it is tolerably clear, it may, for instance support or undermine the contention that one of the two claims was stronger than the other. *Boxall* appears to have been such case.

63. In case (iii), the court is often unable to gauge whether there is a successful party in any respect, and, if so, who it is. In such cases, therefore, there is an even more powerful argument that the default position should be no order for costs. However, in some such cases, it may well be sensible to look at the underlying claims and inquire whether it was tolerably clear who would have won if the matter had not settled. If it is, then that may well strongly support the contention that the party who would have won did better out of the settlement, and therefore did win."

Lord Neuberger MR went on to agree with the following observation of Stanley Burnton LJ: **33-22**

"77. Where the parties are unable to agree costs, and they are left to be determined by the Court, it is important that both the work and costs involved in preparing the parties' submissions on costs, and the material the judge is asked to consider, are proportionate to the amount at stake. No order for costs will be the default order when the judge cannot without disproportionate expenditure of judicial time, if at all, fairly and sensibly make an order in favour of either party. This is not to say that there are not cases where the merits can be determined and no order for costs can be seen to be the appropriate order; but in such cases that order is not a default order, but an order made on the merits."

In *R. (TH) v East Sussex County Council*,[65] the Court of Appeal emphasised that the first principle stated by Lord Neuberger in *M* is not absolute and should not apply where there is good reason to the contrary. It was also noted that there is a high duty on both parties to public law litigation to take advantage of any reasonable and sensible opportunity for settlement which presents itself. In *R. (Tesfay) v Secretary of State for the Home Department*,[66] the Court of Appeal reaffirmed the principles in *M* and identified that in public law litigation, securing reconsideration of a decision which is challenged is usually considered a success for costs purposes. The fact that following reconsideration a decision may be taken which is against the interests of the claimant, which the claimant may also wish to challenge, will not generally be a reason for refusing the claimant's costs of the judicial review.

Guidance has been given by the Administrative Court Office on the content of the consent order in relation to costs and the manner in which an application to the court for costs should be prepared and presented following the decision in *M* and *Tesfay*.[67]. The submissions must, amongst other things, confirm that the parties have used reasonable endeavours to negotiate a costs settlement and identify what issues or reasons prevented the parties agreeing costs liability. The submissions are intended to be concise and not normally to exceed two A4 pages in length absent good reason.

There are some types of case, most typically a challenge by case stated or judicial **33-23**

---

64 *R (Scott) v Hackney London Borough Council* [2009] EWCA Civ 217.

65 [2013] EWCA Civ 1027.

66 [2016] EWCA Civ 415; [2016] 1 W.L.R. 4853.

67 See ACO Costs Guidance, dated April 2016, reproduced as annex 5 to *The Administrative Court: Judicial Review Guide 2019*. See Appendix 7

review to a decision of the magistrates' court, a coroner or a tribunal, in which the nominal respondent or defendant (the justices) is not normally expected to appear to defend its decision, and will not generally be liable for costs if it does not appear, even if the decision is overturned. The Administrative Court will generally not make costs orders against such a defendant where it has not acted obstructively or improperly and only makes representations neutrally on the procedure or law.[68]. However, such a party is under a duty to consider whether it is appropriate to sign a consent order quashing the decision, and if its refusal to do so is unreasonable in all the circumstances, it may be liable for the costs unnecessarily incurred.[69] It will often be appropriate in those circumstances for the court to make a costs order against the interested party which took the underlying administrative decision that generated the proceedings before the court or tribunal in question (such as the Secretary of State for the Home Department in judicial review proceedings against the Upper Tribunal in an immigration case). Conversely, it was held in *R. (Towry Law Financial Services Plc) v The Financial Ombudsman Service Ltd*[70] that the defendant ombudsman, although recognising a flaw in its determination, was not entitled to re-open the matter without the consent of both parties to the underlying complaint (see para.33-10). Since the ombudsman could not have done more to avoid or resolve the proceedings, no costs award against it would have been appropriate in any event.

CONTINUATION OF PROCEEDINGS AFTER FRESH DECISION

33-24 How far should the court permit a defendant to bring the proceedings to an enforced end by means of its own willingness to take a fresh decision? Apart from the issue of costs, the claimant may be reluctant to withdraw the claim because it suspects that it may wish to challenge the fresh decision, and would prefer to do so by way of amendment to the existing proceedings rather than by having to commence entirely fresh proceedings. Alternatively, the claimant may have an interest in obtaining the court's adjudication upon some question of principle.

33-25 The general approach of the court has been summarised in *R. (Bhatti) v Bury MBC*.[71] In short, where a defendant has agreed to reconsider the original decision challenged, so effectively agreeing to that decision being quashed without the intervention of the court, it may not be appropriate to stay the claim or seek to amend it. Instead, it may be more appropriate to end the claim by withdrawal or dismissal, with any appropriate costs order; if the claimant subsequently seeks to

---

[68] See also *The Administrative Court: Judicial Review Guide 2019*, para.23.12.

[69] *R. v Newcastle-under-Lyme Justices Ex p. Massey* [1994] 1 W.L.R. 1684. Relevant considerations include the attitude of the body which instituted the original proceedings before the magistrates, and the nature and obviousness of the flaw in the justices' decision. A similar approach was applied to the Special Educational Needs Tribunal whose decision was the subject of a statutory appeal in *S v Metropolitan Borough of Dudley* [2000] Ed. C.R. 410. The subject of the award of costs against inferior courts, tribunals and coroners in judicial review and statutory appeal proceedings was comprehensively reviewed in *R. (Davies) v HM Deputy Coroner for Birmingham (No.2)* [2004] 1 W.L.R. 2739. The present acknowledgment of service form in judicial review proceedings caters specifically for such defendants.

[70] *R. (Towry Law Financial Services Plc) v The Financial Ombudsman Service Ltd* [2002] EWHC 1603 (Admin).

[71] [2013] EWHC 3093 (Admin). See also *R. (Rathakrishnan) v Secretary of State for the Home Department* [2011] EWHC 1406 (Admin) and *R. (Yousuf) v Secretary of State for the Home Department* [2016] EWHC 663 (Admin).

challenge the new decision, it will normally be appropriate to commence a new claim. The exceptions to this approach are considered to be narrow. The court is only likely to be prepared to consider a challenge to the initial superseded decision where the case raises a point of general public importance and the point which was at issue in relation to the initial decision challenged remains an important issue in relation to the subsequent decision.[72]

Where a defendant has made a new decision in response to a claim in light of the evidence filed by the claimant which is again adverse to the claimant, then it may be more convenient for the parties to substitute the second decision for the first decision as the decision challenged in those proceedings, provided the claimant has a properly arguable challenge to the new decision.[73] In those circumstances, however, the court can impose a condition requiring the re-formulation of the claim and re-preparation of the relevant materials so as to eliminate any irrelevant surplus material; any application for such amendment should typically include a provision allowing for a new, amended claim bundle to be filed or, ideally, be accompanied by a copy of the proposed amended claim bundle. The court retains a discretion on whether to permit such amendments. It may make its own assessment that overall the proper conduct of proceedings will best be promoted by refusing permission to amend the claim and requiring a fresh claim to be brought. The court will consider whether a claimant may be seeking to avoid complying with any relevant time limits by seeking to amend the existing claim rather than commencing a fresh claim and that proper notice has been given to all relevant persons, including interested parties.[74]

Sometimes the defendant may purport to reconsider its decision or to perform its statutory duty at a very late stage before the substantive hearing of the judicial review, or otherwise in circumstances such that it is unclear whether the defendant's duty has now been properly performed. In *Parr v Wyre Forest BC*[75] Donaldson LJ indicated that the court should not refuse relief "merely because at the eleventh hour the authority had done something which might be, but was not necessarily, a compliance with their duty".

The leading case on the question of whether a case in which the claimant no longer requires substantive relief should go forward as a "test case" is the decision **33-26**
of the House of Lords in *R. v Home Secretary Ex p. Salem*[76]: there is a discretion to hear disputes in public law cases even when they are academic as between the parties, but it should be exercised with caution and only where there is a good reason in the public interest for doing so. Whether a case should proceed as a test case is a matter to be determined by the court, if the parties cannot agree, and not unilaterally by the claimant or its advisers.[77] In the case of a statutory application or appeal against a decision which can only be brought by a "person aggrieved", as for planning cases under the Town and Country Planning Act 1990, there are likely to be difficulties for the court in entertaining proceedings brought by the suc-

---

72 *R. v Secretary of State for the Home Department Ex p. Alabi* [1997] I.N.L.R. 124, applied in *R. v Entry Clearance Officer Ex p. Makkari*, Moses J, 18 February 1999.

73 See *R. v Secretary of State for the Home Department ex p. Turgut* [2001] 1 All E.R. 719 and *R. (Hussain) v Secretary of State for the Home Department* [2016] EWCA Civ 1111.

74 See *R. (Hussain) v Secretary of State for the Home Department* [2016] EWCA Civ 1111 at [22] and *The Administrative Court: Judicial Review Guide 2019*, para.6.10.4 and para.9.2.5.

75 *Parr v Wyre Forest BC* (1982) 2 H.L.R. 71 at 83. See also *R. v Lambeth LBC Ex p. A1 and A2* (1997) 30 H.L.R. 933 at 947.

76 *R. v Home Secretary Ex p. Salem* [1999] 1 A.C. 450. For further discussion of these principles, see *R. (Zoolife International Ltd) v Secretary of State for the Environment, Food and Rural Affairs* [2007] EWHC 2995 (Admin) and *R. (Raw) v Lambeth LBC* [2010] EWHC 507 (Admin).

77 *R. (Tshikangu) v Newham LBC, The Times*, 27 April 2001.

cessful party who nonetheless wishes to challenge the approach in principle of the decision maker in reaching that decision.[78]

AGREEMENT AT THE PERMISSION STAGE

33-27 There is no provision in the CPR for permission to apply for judicial review to be granted by consent, and CPR r.54.5(2) specifically provides that the time limit for filing the claim form may not be extended by agreement between the parties.[79] This no doubt reflects the wider interest in the speedy resolution of disputes concerning the validity of determinations by public bodies. But in cases where third-party rights are not materially affected, it is highly likely in practice that permission to apply for judicial review will be granted, along with any necessary extension of time, where the defendant raises no objection.[80]

33-28 There will often be scope for agreement between the parties at the permission stage concerning the directions which the court will be invited to give, particularly in relation to expedition and the abridgement of time for the defendant's evidence. Typically, in a case in which the claimant would otherwise seek interim relief, the defendant may be willing to give undertakings over to the substantive hearing if the court is prepared to expedite that hearing. When granting permission a judge will often give directions as to how the case will progress to the substantive hearing and such directions will supersede the standard directions that apply in default of specific directions.[81]

33-29 Finally, it should be noted that CPR r.54.18 enables the court to decide a claim for judicial review without a hearing (i.e. on the papers) where all the parties agree. To date, it is not thought that much use has been made of this facility.

SETTLEMENT AFTER DRAFT JUDGMENT SENT TO PARTIES

33-30 As in the general run of civil litigation, it is not unknown for parties to come to terms after receipt from the court of a draft judgment for suggested correction. On occasions the parties may seek to agree that the judgment is not handed down. The court is not obliged to give effect to any such agreement and has a discretion on the matter.[82]

---

78 See *Tewskbury Borough Council v Secretary of State for Communities, Housing and Local Government* [2019] EWHC 1775 (Admin), considering *GLC v Secretary of State for the Environment* [1985] J.P.L. 868.

79 The position on statutory appeals is the same: CPR r.52.6(2).

80 This is implicitly recognised in the judgment of Collins J in *R. (International Masters Publishers Ltd) v Revenue and Customs Commissioners* [2006] EWHC 127 (Admin) at [13].

81 See *The Administrative Court: Judicial Review Guide 2019*, para.9.1.

82 For a case where this occurred in the context of the Administrative Court, see *S, R (On the application of) v The General Teaching Council for England & Anor* [2013] EWHC 2779 (Admin).

PART 15: THE SETTLEMENT OF APPEALS, THE ROLE OF ADR AND THE SETTLEMENT OF CROSS-BORDER DISPUTES

CHAPTER 34

Settlement of Appeals

Parties may decide, even after trial, judgment and the filing of an appeal, to cut short the appellate process and compromise their differences. Such an agreement is as binding as if made at any other stage of the proceedings.[1] No additional court approval, other than that required by the nature of the particular proceedings, is required to validate such an agreement. The procedure may vary according to the appeal process and the stage in the process when the settlement is achieved.[2] **34-01**

COURT OF APPEAL

Parties may decide to settle a pending appeal by modifying the effects of the order or judgment obtained below. In some cases this can be achieved without the need for any formal variation of such an order or judgment. For example, an appeal by the defendant against the quantum of an award of damages may be compromised by agreement if the claimant is willing to accept a lower figure than the amount awarded by the award below. While the judgment might stand as the judgment between the parties, a contractual commitment to accept a lower sum is sufficient to dispose of the matter. In this situation the appeal may safely be dismissed by consent, the defendant relying upon that contractual commitment. **34-02**

Indeed, the procedure whereby an appeal is dismissed by consent is the preferred procedural course as it does not require an order from the appellate court allowing the appeal by consent.[3] This procedure can, of course, be employed in cases where the terms of settlement are more complex than foreshadowed in the example given in the preceding paragraph. The only drawback, unless a Tomlin order is agreed, is that a fresh action will be necessary for the purposes of enforcement.[4] **34-03**

Where parties are agreed that an appeal should be dismissed by consent, a joint request to the court to that effect should be made.[5] The procedure does not apply where any party to the proceedings is a child or a protected party or the proceedings are by way of an application or appeal to the Court of Appeal from a decision of the Court of Protection.[6] Unless there appear to be any difficulties, a Lord or Lady Justice or a Master or Deputy Master of Civil Appeals will initial the request, the effect being that the appeal will thereby be dismissed. An order to this effect will be drawn up and sent to the parties. Once this has been done the Court of Appeal **34-04**

---

1 *National Benzole Co Ltd v Gooch* [1961] 1 W.L.R. 1489, *Rothwell v Rothwell* [2008] EWCA Civ 1600 at [7].

2 See generally CPR Pt 52.

3 CPR Pt 52 PD 52A paras 6.1–6.5, and see further at para.34–06.

4 See para.9–19 onwards and also para.34–05.

5 CPR Pt 52 PD 52A para.6.3.

6 CPR Pt 52 PD 52A para.6.5. For provisions concerning cases involving a child or a protected party, see para.34–08.

will have no jurisdiction to reinstate the appeal or to permit the appellant to begin a fresh appeal.[7]

34-05 Where a Tomlin order is required by the parties it is likely that the practice prior to the introduction of the Civil Procedure Rules will be followed. The Court of Appeal is ordinarily prepared to make such an order if satisfied that the dismissal by consent procedure is not appropriate or sufficient. The parties would submit a draft order to the Master or a Deputy Master of Civil Appeals. If the office entertained any concerns about the matter that could not be dealt with relatively informally through the Civil Appeals Office or the clerk to the Lord or Lady Justice assigned to consider the proposed order, the application for the order could be listed for mention. Where a Tomlin order is made, it is usual for the permission to apply for the purpose of enforcing the agreed terms[8] to be directed to the court below.

34-06 Where the parties are agreed that the order of the court below was wrong and are agreed on the order that ought to be substituted they can invite the Court of Appeal to allow the appeal. This must be dealt with by means of a joint request to the court, setting out the relevant history of the proceedings and the matters relied on as justifying the proposed order, a copy of which must accompany the application.[9] If the Court of Appeal is satisfied that it is appropriate to make the order it will do so on the papers. It will list the appeal for mention only if it considers that there are problems about the proposed order which cannot be resolved in any other way.[10]

34-07 Solicitors and counsel, consistently with their duty under CPR Pt 1.3, will need to ensure that they inform the Court of Appeal Office if they enter into settlement negotiations and/or reach settlement at the earliest opportunity. Should an appeal settle outside the court's opening hours, the court would expect attempts to be made to communicate the fact of settlement to the court via the relevant court out-of-hours service.[11]

34-08 Where an appeal which relates to a child or a protected party is settled, the approval of the Court of Appeal to the settlement is required. In either case the parties' solicitors should send a copy of the proposed order to the Court of Appeal together with an opinion from the advocate representing the child or protected party and, in the case of a protected party, any relevant reports prepared for the Court of Protection and a document evidencing the formal approval of that court where required.[12]

COURT OF APPEAL MEDIATION SCHEME (CAMS)

34-09 The Court of Appeal promotes consensual settlement of appeals through the Court of Appeal Mediation Scheme (CAMS).[13] The scheme applies to non-family appeals. Personal injury, clinical and professional negligence claims, the value of

---

7 *Ogwr BC v Knight* [1994] T.L.R. 22 CA. "The general rule … is that once an order dismissing an appeal has been perfected the court has no jurisdiction to revive the appeal or to allow a fresh appeal to be brought." Per Peter Gibson LJ, referring to *Samuel, Re* [1945] Ch. 364.

8 See para.9–23.

9 CPR Pt 52 PD 52A para.6.4.

10 cf. *Hadfield v Knowles (Practice Note)* [1996] 1 W.L.R. 1003. For a case where an appeal was allowed by consent, see *W v Oldham MBC* [2005] EWCA Civ 1247; [2006] 1 F.L.R. 543 and, in particular, the observations of Wall LJ at [7].

11 *Tasyurdu v Secretary of State for the Home Department* [2003] EWCA Civ 447 at [13]–[14], *Yell Limited v Garton* [2004] EWCA Civ 87 at [1]–[2].

12 CPR Pt 52 PD 52A para.6.4.

13 HMCTS Form 56A and Form 56B (*http://hmctsformfinder.justice.gov.uk/HMCTS/GetForm.do?court_forms_id=996* and

which is up to £250,000, are referred to the scheme. Parties may, however, opt-out. Use of the scheme by parties to appeals in other cases may be recommended by the Court of Appeal. Such encouragement is to be given when permission to appeal is being considered, in which case the permission to appeal application may be adjourned pending the outcome of mediation if it is taken up by the parties, or following the grant of permission to appeal. Parties remain free to consider entry into the mediation scheme, even where the Court of Appeal makes no recommendation Costs penalties may be imposed on parties who refuse to act on such a recommendation.[14]

JUDGE

In addition to providing for appeals to the Court of Appeal, Pt 52 of the CPR applies to appeals within the County Court, from a district judge or equivalent to a circuit judge or equivalent,[15] from the County Court to the High Court and within the High Court from a Master or equivalent to a High Court judge.[16] **34-10**

Any such appeal will, if pursued, be limited to a **34-11**

> "review of the decision of the lower court unless—(a) a practice direction makes different provision for a particular category of appeal; or (b) the court considers that in the circumstances of an individual appeal it would be in the interests of justice to hold a rehearing."[17]

Parties may, of course, compromise any such appeal, subject only to the court's case management powers which may be exercised independently of the parties' agreement.[18] Since many appeals of this nature will be in relation to interim matters, those case management functions may result in the court looking carefully at what has been agreed when invited to make a consent order disposing of an appeal. **34-12**

Where an appeal is compromised, the same procedure as that described in relation to appeals to the Court of Appeal applies.[19] The Pt 52 PDs apply to "all appeals to which Pt 52 applies"[20] and, given that paras 6.1, 6.4 and 6.5 of PD 52A, which govern the dismissal and allow by consent procedures, refer to the "the appeal court",[21] it would appear that the procedure set out in those paragraphs should be followed when an appeal to a judge is resolved. **34-13**

---

http://hmctsformfinder.justice.gov.uk/HMCTS/GetForm.do?court_forms_id=997 [Accessed 2 May 2019]). cf. for further detail on how the scheme works, *https://www.cedr.com/docslib/56D_CA_Mediation_Scheme_rules_for_1_April_13_final.pdf* [Accessed 2 May 2019].

14 *Faidi v Elliott Corporation* [2012] EWCA Civ 287; [2012] H.L.R. 27 at [34]–[39]; *Ali Ghaith v Indesit Company UK Ltd* [2012] EWCA Civ 642 at [26] and [29]. See Ch.35.

15 For equivalence between judicial office holders see, CPR Pt 2 PD 2B para.1.3.

16 CPR Pt 52 PD 52B para.1.1. Also see Pt 52 PD 52C and 52D for further categories of appeals that lie to the Court of Appeal.

17 CPR Pt 52.21. A "review" connotes a narrower approach to an appeal than a "rehearing": *E.I. De Nemours & Co v S.T. Dupont* [2003] EWCA Civ 1368.

18 CPR Pt 3.

19 See para.34–04 onwards.

20 CPR Pt 52 PD 52A para.2.1.

21 The "appeal court" is defined as "the court to which an appeal is made": CPR r.52.1(3)(b).

CHAPTER 35

Settlement Through ADR

INTRODUCTION

The increased use of alternative dispute resolution (ADR) to achieve settlement has already been noted.[1] The true definition of ADR is much debated.[2] For the purposes of this work ADR is taken to be any process that ordinarily, although not invariably, involves the active intervention of a third party in helping to facilitate a settlement of a dispute between others.[3] The principal and best known process of this nature is mediation,[4] although conciliation needs also to be identified as a process within the working definition adopted. Early Neutral Evaluation (ENE) is, however, increasingly becoming well-known as a process by which settlement can be facilitated.[5] 35-01

Much has been written about the technique of mediation as a process.[6] This is outwith the scope of this work. The areas of legal and practical relevance that need to be considered can be summarised thus: 35-02

(i) the court's role in directing and encouraging mediation and the costs consequences to the parties of failing to embrace it;

---

1 See para.13–03.

2 See, e.g. Boulle and Nesic, *Mediation, Principles Process Practice* (2001), Ch.1. See also Sir Anthony Evan's presentation at the Annual Conference of the Association of Independent Construction Adjudicators on 17 April 2008.

3 This means that arbitration, adjudication, expert determination and other decision-making options are excluded. In *Halsey v Milton Keynes General NHS Trust* [2004] 1 W.L.R. 3002 at [5] it was said that the "term 'alternative dispute resolution' is defined in the Glossary to the CPR as a 'collective description of methods of resolving disputes otherwise than through the normal trial process'. In practice, however, references to ADR are usually understood as being references to some form of mediation by a third party".

4 In *Aird v Prime Meridian Ltd* [2006] EWCA Civ 1866; [2007] B.L.R. 105, May LJ said that "[it] is well-known and uncontentious in this case that mediation takes the form of assisted 'without prejudice' negotiation". Mediators tend to look for a broader definition: Cornes, 'Mediation Privilege and the EU Directive: An Opportunity' (2008) 74 *Arbitration* 4, 395. The Centre for Effective Dispute Resolution (CEDR) defines mediation in this way: "Mediation is a flexible process conducted confidentially in which a neutral person actively assists parties in working towards a negotiated agreement of a dispute or difference, with the parties in ultimate control of the decision to settle and the terms of resolution." cf. EU Directive on Mediation in Civil and Commercial Cases (Directive 2008/52 EC), arts. 3(a) and 3(b). See also the definition in the Singapore Convention: para.36-33.

5 W. Brazil, *Early Neutral Evaluation*, (American Bar Association, 2012), CPR r.3.1(2)(m).

6 See, Menkel-Meadow et al, *Dispute Resolution: Beyond the Adversarial Model* (Aspen Publishers, 2011); Brown and Marriott, *ADR Principles and Practice*, 3rd edn (London: Sweet & Maxwell, 2011); Spencer and Brogan, *Mediation: Law and Practice* (Cambridge University Press, 2007).

(ii) the legal parameters of a mediation and a mediated settlement.

COURT'S ROLE IN DIRECTING AND ENCOURAGING MEDIATION AND THE COSTS CONSEQUENCES TO PARTIES OF FAILING TO EMBRACE IT

35-03 Under the CPR there is an obligation on the court to "further the overriding objective by actively managing cases".[7] It further imposes a continuing duty on parties to assist the court in carrying out active case management to further the overriding objective.[8] "Active case management" includes:

> "(e) [E]ncouraging the parties to use an alternative dispute resolution procedure if the court considers that appropriate and facilitating the use of such procedure;
> (f) helping the parties to settle the whole or part of the case."[9]

35-04 These words do not confer upon the court an explicit power to order ADR against the wishes of the parties.[10] A number of cases decided shortly after the CPR came into force assumed that such a power existed.[11] In *Shirayama Shokusen Co Ltd v Danovo Ltd*,[12] Blackburne J went further, considered whether it did and held

> "that the court does have jurisdiction to direct ADR even though one party may not be willing to have the dispute submitted to ADR".

The power to do so was said to be derived from the overriding objective.[13] Notwithstanding this decision, the generally accepted position based upon judicial authority is that the court has no power to require parties to enter into an ADR process; it can do no more than to encourage them strongly to do so in appropriate circumstances. In giving the judgment of the court in *Halsey v Milton Keynes NHS Trust*[14] Dyson LJ said:

> "[It] seems to us that to oblige truly unwilling parties to refer their disputes to mediation would be to impose an unacceptable obstruction on their right of access to the court."

In other words, art.6 of the ECHR would be infringed if ADR was compulsory. It was also said that

> "if (contrary to our view) the court does have jurisdiction to order unwilling parties to refer their disputes to mediation, we find it difficult to conceive of circumstances in which it would be appropriate to exercise it".

---

7 CPR r.1.4(1).

8 CPR r.1(3). *Garritt-Critchley v Ronnan* [2014] EWHC 1774 (Ch); [2015] 3 Costs L.R. 453 at [25].

9 CPR r.1.4(2).

10 Neither does CPR r.26.4(1), which provides that the court may stay the proceedings at the "directions questionnaire" stage if both parties request the opportunity to "try to settle the case by alternative dispute resolution or other means" initially "for one month" and thereafter "for such specified period as it considers appropriate." ; *Mann v Mann* [2014] EWHC 537 (Fam); [2014] 1 W.L.R. 2807 at [13], the power to order a stay under this rule can be exercised at any time and not just at the directions questionnaire stage of proceedings. cf CPR r.26.4A, which also provides for referral of claims that would otherwise be allocated to the small claims track to the small claims mediation scheme. Such referral is only by consent of the parties.

11 See *Guinle v Kirreh* [2000] C.P. Rep. 62, per Arden J and *Muman v Nagasena* [2000]. In *Cable and Wireless Plc v IBM United Kingdom Ltd* [2002] EWHC 2059 (Comm); [2002] 2 All E.R. (Comm) 1041 Colman J noted that Commercial Court compulsory ADR orders were commonplace.

12 *Shirayama Shokusen Co Ltd v Danovo Ltd* [2004] 1 W.L.R. 2985.

13 [2004] 1 W.L.R. 2988 at [22] ff.

14 *Halsey v Milton Keynes NHS Trust* [2004] 1 W.L.R. 3002.

It was said that it

> "is one thing to encourage the parties to agree to mediation, even to encourage them in the strongest terms. It is another to order them to do so. It seems to us that to oblige truly unwilling parties to refer their disputes to mediation would be to impose an unacceptable obstruction on their right of access to the court".[15]

The decision in *Halsey* has not gone uncriticised. Writing extra-judicially, both Lord Phillips CJ[16] and Sir Anthony Clarke MR, as he then was, have argued that it was wrongly decided on the art.6 point, the latter suggesting that the court could, using a combination of powers within the CPR, oblige parties to enter into an ADR process[17]: **35-05**

> "To my mind the power [to order that the parties meet in the presence of a mediator] exists under a combination of the court's case management powers under CPR 1.4(2)(e) ... and CPR 3.1(2)(m), which enables the court to take any step in managing a case to further the overriding objective. It seems to me that furthering the overriding objective in this sense calls for the case management power to be applied consistently with the duty under CPR 1.1(2)(e) which requires the court to take account of the needs of all litigants and the court in furthering the overriding objective; to further access to justice for all. Equally, it is surely part of the parties' duty to assist the court in the furtherance of the overriding objective that they should take active steps to take part in mediation (CPR 1.3)."

Ward LJ, who was a member of the Court of Appeal in *Halsey*, has also suggested that the decision ought to be revisited.[18] Writing extra-judicially, Lord Dyson MR, has also queried whether the decision needs tempering, not least given the decision of the European Court of Justice in *Rosalba Alassini*, which held that a requirement to mediate before commencing proceedings did not in principle infringe art.6 of the ECHR.[19] **35-06**

Notwithstanding the fact that compulsory ADR, in the form of compulsory mediation, is permitted under the EU Mediation Directive,[20] In *PGF II SA v OMFS* **35-07**

---

15 *Halsey* [2004] 1 W.L.R. 3002 at [9].

16 Lord Phillips CJ, "*Alternative Dispute Resolution: An English Viewpoint*" (March 29, 2008, speech given in India); and cf. Lightman J, also writing extra-judicially, to the same effect, in "*Mediation: An Approximation of Justice*" (June 28, 2007, speech given at S.J. Berwin).

17 Sir Anthony Clarke MR "The Future of Civil Mediation" (2008) 74 *Arbitration* 419.

18 *Wright v Wright* [2013] EWCA Civ 234; [2013] C.P. Rep. 3 at [3].

19 *Alassini v Telecom Italia Spa* (Joined Cases C-317/08, C-301/08, C-319/08 and C-320/08) 3 C.M.L.R. 17 ECJ. The ECJ held that "... the principles of equivalence and effectiveness or the principle of effective judicial protection [do not] preclude national legislation which imposes, in respect of such disputes, prior implementation of an out-of-court settlement procedure, provided that that procedure does not result in a decision which is binding on the parties, that it does not cause a substantial delay for the purposes of bringing legal proceedings, that it suspends the period for the time-barring of claims and that it does not give rise to costs—or gives rise to very low costs—for the parties, and only if electronic means is not the only means by which the settlement procedure may be accessed and interim measures are possible in exceptional cases where the urgency of the situation so requires." The implications of this were discussed in Lord Dyson's speech entitled "*Halsey 10 years on— The Decision Revisited*" (Belfast, 9 May 2014) and see *Arbitration* (2011) 77(3) 375. cf. *Menini & Rampanelli v Banco Popolare Società Cooperativa* (Case C-75/16), in which the ECJ reiterated its reasoning on the approach needed to be taken to ensure that mandatory mediation did not infringe the right of access to justice, again described as the principle of effective judicial protection.

20 EU Directive on Mediation in Civil and Commercial Cases (Directive 2008/52 EC), art.5(2): "This Directive is without prejudice to national legislation making the use of mediation compulsory or subject to incentives or sanctions, whether before or after judicial proceedings have started, provided that such legislation does not prevent the parties from exercising their rights of access to the judicial system." The Directive appears to be consistent with the view expressed by Sir Anthony Clarke MR

Company 1 Ltd[21], where the issue was whether silence in the face of an invitation to participate in alternative dispute resolution was, as a general rule, of itself unreasonable, no argument challenging the approach to compulsory mediation in *Halsey* was advanced. The Court of Appeal specifically endorsed *Halsey*, including its conclusion concerning compulsory mediation.[22]

35-08 The traditional view, endorsed by the Jackson Review, is that mediation is or should be a voluntary process[23]: the prospects of settlement are, it is said, diminished if the parties are reluctant to engage in the process. However, there is evidence that even parties who engage in a mediation reluctantly do take advantage of the opportunity to settle thus afforded.[24] In any event, the distinction between ordering a reluctant party to engage in ADR and encouraging it "in the strongest terms" may be a fine one in some circumstances although the distinction continues to be maintained.[25]

35-09 Before *Halsey* a number of cases had given strong encouragement for the use of mediation.[26] *Halsey* provided the Court of Appeal the opportunity to review the general considerations applicable to the issue and to give guidance on the correct approach. Although the case itself was a clinical negligence case (and the other appeal heard at the same time was a personal injury case) the Court of Appeal said that whilst "mediation and other ADR processes do not offer a panacea, and can have disadvantages as well as advantages", nonetheless "most cases are not by their very nature unsuitable for ADR". It was said that,

> "[all] members of the legal profession who conduct litigation should now routinely consider with their clients whether their disputes are suitable for ADR".

(fn.17) at 422.

21 [2013] EWCA Civ 1288; [2014] 1 W.L.R. 1386.

22 See [22] ff.

23 R. Jackson, *Review of Civil Litigation Costs—Final Report* (December 2009), Ch.36, at 361.

24 Lord Phillips CJ, (fn.15), said this: "What are the pros and cons of compulsory mediation? Strong views are expressed about this on both sides. Those opposed argue that compulsion is the very antithesis of mediation. The whole point of mediation is that it is voluntary. How can you *compel* parties to indulge in a voluntary activity? 'You can take a horse to water, but you cannot make it drink'. To which those in favour of compulsory mediation reply, 'yes, but if you take a horse to water it usually does drink'. Statistics show that settlement rates in relation to parties who have been compelled to mediate are just about as high as they are in the case of those who resort to mediation of their own volition." While Lord Judge CJ chose not to enter into the debate concerning compulsion in his address to the Civil Mediation Council Conference on 14 May 2009, he did note: "… an underlying concern not so much directed at the mediation issue, which is about too many people telling too many other people what they must do and thus compel an additional step in the process of litigation." He also warned against the mediation process becoming "[E]ventually, and quite unintentionally, and by unforeseen accretion … increasingly formalised and procedural [otherwise it may] become just one more part of the expensive process that all of us are trying to avoid."

25 See, Ahmed "Implied Compulsory Mediation" (2012) 32 C.J.Q. 151.

26 See, in particular, *Dyson v Leeds City Council* [2000] C.P. Rep. 42, *R. (Cowl) v Plymouth City Council* [2002] 1 W.L.R. 803, *Dunnett v Railtrack Plc* [2002] 1 W.L.R. 2354, *Hurst v Leeming* [2003] 1 Lloyd. 2354, *Dunnett v Railtrack* was decided in February 2002: D, which had successfully defended a county court claim concerning C's horses brought in person by C, refused to consider mediation in the context of her appeal against the loss of her claim despite being encouraged to do so by the Court of Appeal prior to the appeal. D successfully resisted the appeal, but was not awarded its costs of the appeal, as would normally have been the case, because of its attitude to mediation. In *Royal Bank of Scotland v Secretary of State for Defence* [2003] EWHC 1841 (Ch), Lewison J took into account the "failure [by D] to abide by the formal pledge given on [the] part of the government … to settle cases by ADR techniques whenever the other side agrees to it" in making no order as to costs in a case where D was the substantial victor. See also *Leicester Circuits Ltd v Coates Brothers Plc* [2003] EWCA Civ 333.

In *PGF II SA v OMFS Company 1 Ltd*[27] the Court of Appeal reaffirmed this when concluding that the court's decision in the case, penalising the defendant for refusing to respond to an invitation to engage in ADR,

> "[sent] out an important message to civil litigants, requiring them to engage with a serious invitation to participate in ADR, even if they have reasons which might justify a refusal, or the undertaking of some other form of ADR, or ADR at some other time in the litigation."

In *OMV Petrom SA v Glencore International AG*[28] Sir Geoffrey Vos C reiterated this point, when he referred generally to the obligation imposed on parties to **35-10**

> "conduct litigation collaboratively and to engage constructively in the settlement process."

As he went on to state[29]:

> "A blank refusal to engage in any negotiating or mediation process, and the use of a vast asset base to seek to frustrate a claimant's attempts to reach a compromise solution should be marked by the use of the court's powers to discourage such conduct."

Active consideration must, therefore, be given in almost[30] every case at some stage[31] to the issue of whether it might be suitable for some form of ADR, particularly mediation. The use of ADR furthers the "policy of proportionality".[32]

In order to encourage such consideration the court will frequently give a direction to that effect at an appropriate case management stage. In the Admiralty and Commercial Courts the parties are directed "exchange lists of 3 neutral individuals who are available to conduct ADR procedures", to endeavour in good faith to agree a neutral individual or panel and to take[33] **35-11**

> "such serious steps as they may be advised to resolve their disputes by ADR procedures before the neutral individual or panel so chosen".

The order also provides that if the case is not settled

---

27 [2013] EWCA Civ 1288; [2014] 1 W.L.R. 1386 at [56].

28 [2017] EWCA Civ 195; [2017] W.L.R. 3465 at [39].

29 [2017] EWCA Civ 195; [2017] W.L.R. 3465 at [41].

30 As set out in para.35-09, in *Halsey* [2004] 1 W.L.R. 3002 it was said that "most cases are not by their very nature unsuitable for ADR". However, it was recognised that some disputes "do not lend themselves to ADR procedures". Examples given were where the parties want the court to determine issues of law or construction which may be essential to the future trading relations of the parties, or where the issues are generally important for those participating in a particular trade or market. Some issues involving allegations of fraud or other commercially disreputable conduct might not be mediated successfully. Other examples are cases where a party wants the court to resolve a point of law which arises from time to time, or cases where injunctive or other relief essential to protect the position of a party is sought. See, generally, *Halsey* [2004] 1 W.L.R. 3002 at [17] and *PGF* [2013] EWCA Civ 1288; [2014] 1 W.L.R. 1386.

31 Generally, it is submitted, there should have been a good degree of disclosure and exchange of information: see Ch.13, para.13–05.

32 *PGF II SA v OMFS Company 1 Ltd* [2013] EWCA Civ 1288; [2014] 1 W.L.R. 1386 at [39], and see [56].

33 The *Commercial Court Guide (incorporating the Admiralty Court Guide)* (2017), Appendix 3 (Draft ADR Order) ; and see Appendix 2 at [19]–[21]. The term "ADR procedures" is used to signify that the draft order applies to mediation, ENE, non-binding arbitration and other such ADR mechanisms.

> "the parties shall inform the Court by letter prior to [disclosure of documents/exchange of witness statements/exchange of experts' reports] what steps towards ADR have been taken and (without prejudice to matters of privilege) why such steps have failed".[34]

A direction devised by Master Ungley (an "Ungley Order") in the field of clinical negligence litigation, ordinarily made at a second or subsequent case management conference or pre-trial review,[35] which the Court of Appeal in *Halsey* said was a "less strong form of encouragement" but which should "also routinely be made at least in general personal injury litigation, and perhaps in other litigation too", is in these terms:

> "The parties shall by [specified date] consider whether the case is capable of resolution by ADR. If any party considers that the case is unsuitable for resolution by ADR, that party shall be prepared to justify that decision at the conclusion of the trial, should the judge consider that such means of resolution were appropriate, when he is considering the appropriate costs order to make.
>
> The party considering the case unsuitable for ADR shall, not less than 28 days before the commencement of the trial, file with the court a witness statement without prejudice save as to costs, giving reasons upon which they rely for saying that the case was unsuitable."[36]

35-12 It was said that where such a direction is given it will

> "bring home to [the parties] that, if they refuse even to consider [the question of whether the case is suitable for ADR], they may be at risk on costs[37] even if they are ultimately held by the court to be the successful party".[38]

More recently, there has been a shift in the Queen's Bench Division to the stronger approach taken by the Commercial and Admiralty Courts. A direction devised by Senior Master Fontaine (a "Fontaine Order"), commonly made at a first case management conference, stresses in mandatory terms the continuing requirement that parties consider the use of mediation, amongst other ADR mechanisms. It does so in the following terms:

> "At all stages the parties must consider settling this litigation by any means of ADR (including [round table conferences, early neutral evaluation] mediation [and arbitration]) and in any event no later than [date]: any party not engaging in any such means

---

34 ibid., and see *Halsey* [2004] 1 W.L.R. 3002 at [30].

35 Civil Justice Council, *ADR Interim Report*, (2017) at p.32.

36 CPR PD 29, 4.10(9) and see *Halsey* [2004] 1 W.L.R. 3002 at [32]. A variant on this theme is to require the reasons given for the unsuitability of ADR to be recorded in a sealed envelope to be filed with the court, which is not to be opened until the conclusion of the trial. The form commonly used at present is in the following terms: "At all stages the parties must consider settling this litigation by any means of Alternative Dispute Resolution (including Mediation); any party not engaging in any such means proposed by another must serve a witness statement giving reasons within 21 days of that proposal; such witness statement must not be shown to the trial judge until questions of costs arise."

37 Including an application for indemnity costs: see *Corby Group Litigation v Corby DC* [2009] EWHC 2109 (TCC) where Akenhead J rejected a claim on behalf of C for indemnity costs against D where D had declined to mediate. Having identified "the real question" as whether D acted "unreasonably in refusing ADR", Akenhead J concluded that D "did not act unreasonably" and that it "was not unreasonable [for D] to form the view that mediation would not have produced a settlement". For further discussion of indemnity costs, see Ch.13 paras 13–09-13–10. A failure to act positively in response to court encouragement of ADR may result in a reduction in costs: *Gaston, Boughton v Courtney* [2004] EWHC 600 (Ch).

38 *Halsey* [2004] 1 W.L.R. 3002 at [33]. cf. *Rolf v De Guerin* [2011] EWCA Civ 78; [2011] C.P. Rep. 24; and *Burchell v Bullard* [2005] EWCA Civ 358; [2005] C.P. Rep. 36.

> proposed by another must serve a witness statement giving reasons within 21 days of that proposal; such witness statement must not be shown to the judge until questions of costs arise."[39]

As the Court of Appeal's approach in *Halsey* indicates, the sanction available to the court if a party, despite encouragement from the court in the form of a direction such as an Ungley Order, or now a Fontaine Order, fails to agree to mediation, is to make some adverse order for costs at the end of the trial.[40] The order may deprive that party of its costs or require that party to pay the other party's costs despite the eventual result of the trial in favour of the party having refused mediation.[41] It should be noted that the court may consider delay in agreeing to mediate as a refusal. In *Nigel Witham Ltd v Smith & Isaacs*[42], for instance, a submission was accepted that late agreement to mediate could be treated as an unreasonable refusal to mediate and could lead to an adverse costs order.[43] It was noted, however, that such a finding would only arise in exceptional cases.[44] **35-13**

The Court of Appeal in *Halsey* emphasised, however, that deciding to deprive a successful party of their costs due to a failure to mediate required appropriate justification: **35-14**

> "In deciding whether to deprive a successful party of some or all of his costs on the grounds that he has refused to agree to ADR, it must be borne in mind that such an order is an exception to the general rule that costs should follow the event. In our view, the burden is on the unsuccessful party to show why there should be a departure from the general rule. The fundamental principle is that such departure is not justified unless it is shown (the burden being on the unsuccessful party) that the successful party acted unreasonably in refusing to agree to ADR. We shall endeavour in this judgment to provide some guidance as to the factors that should be considered by the court in deciding whether a refusal to agree to ADR is unreasonable."

The Court of Appeal identified the following, non-exhaustive, list of factors as being potentially relevant to the question of whether a party has unreasonably refused ADR: **35-15**

> "(a) the nature of the dispute; (b) the merits of the case; (c) the extent to which other set-

---

39 Cited in Civil Justice Council, *ADR Interim Report*, (2017) at p.26.

40 A further option, developed in South Africa, is to cap solicitor-client costs where a party's legal representatives fail to take appropriate steps to promote the use of ADR, see *Brownlee v Brownlee* 2008/25274 at [60] (South Gauteng High Court, South Africa).

41 CPR r.44.2(2) provides that "if the court decides to make an order about costs (a) the general rule is that the unsuccessful party will be ordered to pay the cost of the successful party; but (b) the court may make a different order". Rule 44.2(4) provides that "in deciding what order (if any) to make about costs, the court must have regard to all the circumstances, including—(a) the conduct of the parties". Rule 44.2(5) provides that the conduct of the parties includes, "(a) conduct before, as well as during, the proceedings and in particular the extent to which the parties followed any relevant pre-action protocol".

42 [2008] EWHC 12 (TCC); [2008] T.C.L.R. 3.

43 Cf. *S & Others v Chapman* [2008] EWCA Civ 800; [2008] E.L.R. 603. Discussed in Sorabji, "Costs—Further Developments from Halsey: Nigel Witham Ltd v Smith & Isaacs & S & Others v Chapman & Another" (2008) CJQ 27(4) 427.

44 At [36] per HH Judge Coulson QC: "It seems to me that the principles in *Halsey* might, in an exceptional case, be applicable to the situation where there was a mediation, but very late, when its chances of success were very poor, and that, if it could be shown that the successful party unreasonably delayed in consenting to the mediation, that might lead to an adverse costs order. But such considerations do not arise here on the facts, because there is nothing to demonstrate that the Defendants unreasonably delayed in consenting to the judicial settlement conference. Furthermore, I conclude that, even if there had been an earlier mediation, the Claimant's uncompromising attitude meant that it would not have had a reasonable prospect of success."

tlement methods have been attempted; (d) whether the costs of the ADR would be disproportionately high; (e) whether any delay in setting up and attending the ADR would have been prejudicial; and (f) whether the ADR had a reasonable prospect of success".[45]

Of these, (b), (c) and (f) are likely to be the most contentious, although (d) could certainly arise if the costs involved in a proposed mediation were disproportionately high compared with the sums at stake in the dispute.[46]

MERITS OF THE CASE

35-16 "The fact that a party reasonably believes that he has a strong case is relevant to the question whether he has acted reasonably in refusing ADR."

So stated the Court of Appeal when indicating that courts needed to be aware of the danger of a "claimant [using] the threat of costs sanctions to extract a settlement from the defendant even where the claim is without merit".[47] It was said that "the fact that a party reasonably believes that he has a watertight case may well be sufficient justification for a refusal to mediate". This approach was followed in *Swain Mason v Mills & Reeve*,[48] where the Court of Appeal held that the defendant, which throughout had contested the core issue of breach of duty advanced by the claimant, was not to be penalised for declining mediation.[49]

In *Halsey* the Court of Appeal agreed with the view of the trial judge, who had rejected the claimant's claim, that the defendant NHS Trust had been entitled to reject the repeated suggestions for mediation on the claimant's side because of the speculative nature of the claim to which it reasonably believed it had a strong defence. It was said that the claimant had "come nowhere near showing that the

---

45 *Halsey* [2004] 1 W.L.R. 3002 at [16]. cf. *Reed Executive Plc v Reed Business Information Ltd* [2004] EWCA Civ 887; [2004] 1 W.L.R. 3026.

46 *Halsey* [2004] 1 W.L.R. 3002 at [21].

47 *Halsey* [2004] 1 W.L.R. 3002 at [26]. cf *Daniels v Commissioner of Police for the Metropolis* [2005] EWCA Civ 1312; [2006] C.P. Rep. 9; at [32]–[33]: "... It seems ... to be entirely reasonable for a defendant, especially a public body ... to take the view that it will contest what it reasonably considers to be an unfounded claim in order to deter other, similarly unfounded, claims ... If defendants, who routinely face what they consider to be unfounded claims, wish to take a stand and contest them rather than make payments (even nuisance value payments) to buy them off, then the court should be slow to characterise such conduct as unreasonable so as to deprive defendants of their costs, if they are ultimately successful ... this may mean (and in the present case did mean) that litigation is sometimes contested whose costs are wholly disproportionate to the sums claimed. The court will always seek to ensure that all litigation is conducted in a reasonable and proportionate manner. But that does not mean that, in a case where costs are necessarily disproportionate to the amount claimed, a defendant is acting unreasonably and should be penalised in costs if he reasonably considers that the claim is without foundation and insists on a trial, any more than it means that a claimant is acting unreasonably and should in some way be penalised for issuing proceedings in respect of a claim, the cost of which is unavoidably out of all proportion to its size." And cf. *Hickman v Blake Lapthorn* [2006] EWHC 12 (QB) at [21]–[22].

48 [2012] EWCA Civ 498.

49 [2012] EWCA Civ 498 at [76], "In *Halsey*, ... [it] was ... emphasised that where a party reasonably believes that he has a watertight case that may well be a sufficient justification for a refusal to mediate. That has obvious resonance ... given the judge's finding that on the core issue of breach of duty the defendant's assessment of the strength of its case and weakness of the claimants' case had been vindicated. That, to my mind, remains very much in point: even if on some (non-core) issues the defence case proved to have weaknesses. After all, it is indeed a relatively rare case where a party succeeds on every issue raised."

trust acted unreasonably in refusing to agree to a mediation", nor had it been established that "mediation had a reasonable prospect of success".[50]

OTHER ATTEMPTS AT SETTLEMENT

> "The fact that settlement offers have already been made, but rejected, is a relevant factor. It may show that one party is making efforts to settle, and that the other party has unrealistic views of the merits of the case." **35-17**

This is the way that the Court of Appeal put the matter in *Halsey*.[51] However, only negotiations conducted under the rubric or principle of "without prejudice except as to costs" could be referred to on this issue.[52] In *Halsey* it was recognised that the issue of previous attempts at settlement was "in truth no more than an aspect of" the issue of whether "ADR had a reasonable prospect of success".

WHETHER MEDIATION HAD REASONABLE PROSPECTS OF SUCCESS

In *Halsey* the Court of Appeal identified "the fundamental question" as being "whether the successful party acted unreasonably in refusing to agree to mediation".[53] As already indicated,[54] the burden of showing a reason for departing from the normal rule as to costs lies on the unsuccessful party in the litigation. It follows from that that the burden should be on the "unsuccessful party to show that there was a reasonable prospect that mediation would have been successful".[55] This was said to be "not an unduly onerous burden to discharge" because "he does not have to prove that a mediation would in fact have succeeded". **35-18**

It is, of course, important to identify where the true responsibility for declining mediation rests. As was said in *Halsey*, a "successful party cannot rely on his own unreasonableness in such circumstances".[56] If, however, the successful party reasonably took the view that a mediation would have had no reasonable prospect of success because the party that ultimately lost the case was "most unlikely to accept a reasonable compromise" then that would constitute a basis for concluding that the refusal to mediate was reasonable.[57] The question whether a party has acted unreasonably in refusing to agree to mediate is not to be determined "purely objectively" as the Court of Appeal affirmed in *PGF II SA v OMFS Company 1 Ltd*.[58] As Briggs LJ[59] put it, the test established in *Halsey* required a consideration of the party's own perceptions: **35-19**

---

[50] *Halsey* [2004] 1 W.L.R. 3002 at [36]–[54].

[51] *Halsey* [2004] 1 W.L.R. 3002 at [20].

[52] In *Reed Executive Plc v Reed Business Information Ltd* [2004] EWCA Civ 887; [2004] 1 W.L.R. 3026 at [21]-[34], the Court of Appeal reaffirmed the principle established in *Walker v Wilsher* (1889) L.R. 23 Q.B.D. 335, that without prejudice negotiations cannot be referred to on questions going to the issue of costs. To that extent, the without prejudice correspondence was inadmissible on the issue of the reasonableness or otherwise of a party's stance to mediation.

[53] *Halsey* [2004] 1 W.L.R. 3002 at [25].

[54] See para.35–10.

[55] *Halsey* [2004] 1 W.L.R. 3002 at [28].

[56] *Halsey* [2004] 1 W.L.R. 3002 at [26].

[57] *Halsey* [2004] 1 W.L.R. 3002. A case that preceded *Halsey* in the Court of Appeal and which indicates the approach of the court where parties have "postured" and "jockeyed for position" in respect of the issue of mediation is *Macmillan Williams v Grange* [2004] EWCA Civ 294.

[58] [2013] EWCA Civ 1288; [2014] 1 W.L.R. 1386 at [36].

"The thrust of [the] submission for the defendant was that the *Halsey* tests for the unreasonableness of a refusal were to be assessed purely objectively, by reference to the material facts about the litigation at the time, so that it made no difference whether the refusing party provided or withheld its reasons at the time of the invitation. I disagree. When the question concerns the reasonableness or otherwise of a party's conduct, the party's own perceptions may play an important part in the analysis, as is apparent from the treatment of a party's reasonable belief in the strength of its case, in the *Halsey* case at para 26, rejecting as too narrow the purely objective approach applied by Lightman J in *Hurst v Leeming* [2003] 1 Lloyd's Rep 379."

The Court of Appeal in *PGF II SA v OMFS Company 1 Ltd* went on to affirm that a party could not rely on its own silence in the face of an offer to enter into ADR. It was, as a general rule, unreasonable conduct not to reply to such an offer. The general rule could, however, be set aside where, for instance, the party had not received the offer or where the failure to reply was a consequence of a mistake on the part of the party's lawyers. It also suggested that, "there may be rare cases", where silence in the face of an offer might not be unreasonable. Those cases would arise "where ADR [was] so obviously inappropriate that to characterise silence as unreasonable would be pure formalism".[60]

35-20 Silence in the face of an offer is only one way in which a party can act unreasonably. A non-response can also arise where a party deliberately procrastinates in getting on with a mediation process. In *Thakkar v Patel*,[61] Jackson LJ emphasised in a case where the prospects of success in a mediation were good, that an unreasonable failure to engage with an offer to mediate could arise not only where a party was silent in the face of an offer, but equally where they "dragged their feet" in providing an answer to the offer— i.e., there was a tacit refusal to engage through their conduct. As he put it[62]:

"The defendants did not refuse to mediate, but they dragged their feet and delayed until eventually the claimants lost confidence in the whole ADR process. The judge held that most but not all of the blame for the abortive mediation lay with the defendants."

35-21 In *Gore v Naheed*,[63] however, the Court of Appeal took an arguably more relaxed view to the question of whether silence in the face of an offer to mediate should be treated in the way it had previously set out in *PGF II*. The case raised complex issues of law and the first instance decision that it was not unreasonable of a party to fail to respond to an offer to mediate where his view was that "mediation had no realistic prospect of succeeding and would only add to the costs" was not itself unreasonable. Patten LJ[64] said this[65] of the approach adopted by Briggs LJ in *PGF II*:

"... Briggs LJ emphasised the need, as he saw it, for the courts to encourage parties to embark on ADR in appropriate cases and said that silence in the face of an invitation to participate in ADR should, as a general rule, be treated as unreasonable regardless of whether a refusal to mediate might in the circumstances have been justified. Speaking for myself, I have some difficulty in accepting that the desire of a party to have his rights

---

59 With whom Maurice Kay and Macfarlane LJJ agreed.

60 [2013] EWCA Civ 1288; [2014] 1 W.L.R. 1386 at [34]–[35]. Cf, *Burchell v Bullard* [2005] EWCA Civ 358; [2005] C.P. Rep. 36 at [43], parties cannot ignore offers to mediate made prior to proceedings being issued.

61 [2017] EWCA Civ 117; [2017] 2 Costs L.R. 233.

62 [2017] EWCA Civ 117; [2017] 2 Costs L.R. 233 at [29].

63 [2017] EWCA Civ 369; [2017] 3 Costs L.R. 509.

64 With whom Lewison and Underhill LJJ agreed.

65 [2017] EWCA Civ 369; [2017] 3 Costs L.R. 509 at [49].

determined by a court of law in preference to mediation can be said to be unreasonable conduct particularly when, as here, those rights are ultimately vindicated. But, as Briggs LJ makes clear in his judgment, a failure to engage, even if unreasonable, does not automatically result in a costs penalty. It is simply a factor to be taken into account by the judge when exercising his costs discretion."

It is respectfully thought that this observation should be treated with a degree of caution because it might, at first blush, be seen as undermining the strong support for the need for active consideration to be given by parties to ADR as set out in earlier judgments of the court. The better approach to *Gore v Naheed*, it is submitted, is to regard it as one decided on its own facts and which does not establish any binding principle. The case merely illustrates the proposition that a refusal to mediate may (not necessarily will) be reasonable where the dispute raises complex issues of law.[66] However, many cases do raise complex issues of law and that, it is submitted, does not automatically exclude them from the scope of mediation.

FAILURE TO ACT REASONABLY IN THE COURSE OF A MEDIATION

Generally speaking, that which takes place at a mediation is covered by the "without prejudice" privilege (and by the confidentiality terms agreed).[67] To that extent it is ordinarily impossible for the court to take account of the conduct of the parties during the mediation when deciding costs. Where, however, the parties agree to waive privilege in respect of all "without prejudice" matters, as occurred in *Carleton v Strutt & Parker*,[68] the opportunity for the court to consider these issues may arise. In that case Jack J considered that C's position at the mediation was "plainly unrealistic and unreasonable" and took it into account in the order made. In expressing the general position he said this[69]: **35-22**

> "As far as I am aware the courts have not had to consider the situation where a party has agreed to mediate but has then taken an unreasonable position in the mediation. It is not dissimilar in effect to an unreasonable refusal to engage in mediation. For a party who agrees to mediation but then causes the mediation to fail by his reason of unreasonable position in the mediation is in reality in the same position as a party who unreasonably refuses to mediate. In my view it is something which the court can and should take account of in the costs order in accordance with the principles considered in *Halsey*."

---

66 cf. *R (Crawford) v Newcastle upon Tyne University* [2014] EWHC 1197 (Admin) applying *PGF II*, but not applying a costs sanction in response to silence in the face of an offer to mediate. In that case the parties were already within the scope of an adjudication scheme, and hence another form of ADR.

67 See para.35–23 onwards.

68 *Carleton v Strutt & Parker* [2008] EWHC 424 (QB); 118 Con. L.R. 68. In *Hall v Pertemps* [2005] EWHC 3110 (Ch); *The Times*, 23 December 2005, Lewison J decided, in a different context, that there had been a "mutual waiver by both parties of the without prejudice protection so far as concerns [a particular] discrete matter which took place in the course of a discrete meeting" which gave rise to an issue between the parties, though the same did not apply to the "circumstances in which the Part 36 offer came to be withdrawn". Discussed in Sorabji "Costs: unreasonable conduct within a mediation—Carleton (Earl of Malmesbury) v Strutt & Parker (A Partnership)" (2008) CJQ 27(3) 288.

69 [2008] EWHC 424 (QB); 118 Con. L.R. 68 at [72].

LEGAL PARAMETERS OF A MEDIATION AND MEDIATED SETTLEMENT

35-23 In *Halsey* the Court of Appeal recognised the importance of respecting the integrity and confidentiality of the mediation process itself. It was put in this way[70]:

> "We make it clear at the outset that it was common ground before us (and we accept) that parties are entitled in an ADR to adopt whatever position they wish, and if as a result the dispute is not settled, that is not a matter for the court … if the integrity and confidentiality of the process is to be respected, the court should not know, and therefore should not investigate, why the process did not result in agreement."

35-24 This is an important policy statement. Leaving aside all other actual or potential advantages of embarking on a mediation in a particular case, the twin advantages of the confidential and the "without prejudice" nature of the process, allied to its informality, are fundamental. If the courts are to encourage parties to engage in mediation to maximum effect, the principles underlying the process will need to be respected fully.[71]

35-25 Since any mediation taking place against the background of actual or threatened litigation will almost invariably be designed to achieve a settlement, either in whole or in part, of the underlying disputes, the discussions forming part of the mediation will be impliedly without prejudice.[72] However, most mediators, whether acting on behalf of one of the main service providers[73] or as an individual, will ask the parties to sign a mediation agreement incorporating an express provision confirming the without prejudice nature of the process. The confidentiality of the process is secured in a similar fashion.[74]

---

70 *Halsey* [2004] 1 W.L.R. 3002 at [14].

71 In *Venture Investment Placement Ltd v Hall* [2005] EWHC 1227 (Ch), HH Judge Reid QC, sitting as a High Court judge, said this: "Mediation proceedings do have to be guarded with great care. The whole point of mediation proceedings is that the parties can be frank and open with each other, and that what is revealed in the course of the mediation proceedings is not to be used for or against either party in the litigation, if mediation proceedings fail." In *Cumbria Waste Management Ltd v Baines Wilson* [2008] EWHC 786 (QB), HH Judge Frances Kirkham, sitting as a High Court judge, said that: "[W]hether on the basis of the without prejudice rule or as an exception to the general rule that confidentiality is not a bar to disclosure, the court should support the mediation process by refusing, in normal circumstances, to order disclosure of documents and communications within a mediation."

72 See paras 19–06 onwards. Documents generated for and within the process are similarly privileged: see *Cumbria Waste Management Ltd v Baines Wilson* [2008] EWHC 786 (QB). However, a joint experts' statement ordered in the litigation between the parties and used in an unsuccessful mediation between them is not a privileged document such that it cannot be used in the resumed litigation: see *Aird v Prime Meridian Ltd* [2006] EWCA Civ 1886. The privilege is not the privilege of the mediator, but that of the parties: *Farm Assist Ltd in liquidation) v The Secretary of State for the Environment, Food and Rural Affairs (No.2)* [2009] EWHC 1102 (TCC).

73 For example, CEDR, ADR Group or the Chartered Institute of Arbitrators.

74 An obligation of confidentiality will be implied as a matter of law into an arbitration agreement: *Ali Shipping Corp v Shipyard Trogir* [1999] 1 W.L.R. 314 CA. Perhaps a fortiori in relation to a mediation agreement. The standard CEDR confidentiality clause in use at the time was considered in *Instance v Denny Bros Printing* [2000] F.S.R. 869, Lloyd J, as he then was. It was in these terms: "Every person involved in the mediation will keep confidential and not use for any collateral or ulterior purpose all information, (whether given orally, in writing or otherwise), produced for, or arising in relation to, the mediation including the settlement agreement (if any) arising out of it, except insofar as it is necessary to implement and enforce any such settlement agreement." It was held that "communications preceding the mediation agreement that … led to it [were] within the scope of the confidentiality clause". Lloyd J said that: "[G]iven that embarking on mediation is a consensual

As set out elsewhere in this work,[75] there are exceptions to the "without prejudice" rule. If called upon to permit an exception to apply in respect of some aspect of a mediation, the courts will have to tread a fine line between seeing that justice is done in the individual case and ensuring that precedents are not set which undermine the whole foundation, and thus the consequent strength, of the mediation process. Too ready a willingness to permit an exception to apply, particularly the "unambiguous impropriety" exception,[76] could have that effect. It is likely that the general approach of the Court of Appeal in *Unilever Plc v The Procter & Gamble Co*,[77] followed in subsequent cases,[78] will be the approach adopted when this kind of issue arises. Robert Walker LJ's description of a without prejudice meeting as consisting of "wide-ranging unscripted discussions ... which may have lasted several hours"[79] is a description which could be applied readily to many mediations. **35-26**

One exception to the "without prejudice" rule is that which permits evidence of without prejudice discussions to be given in order to prove that an agreement has been reached.[80] Technically, this exception could be called into play in the context of a mediation, but it is the almost invariable practice for a mediation to be conducted on the basis that an agreement will only be treated as having been concluded when it is reduced to writing and signed by or on behalf of the parties.[81] **35-27**

It is not, of course, an exception to the "without prejudice" rule to permit the reception in evidence of something said during without prejudice negotiations which is alleged to have constituted a material misrepresentation inducing the settlement achieved. This is a natural consequence of the law that entitles a party to seek to set aside a compromise on the basis of a misrepresentation or indeed any other ground capable of vitiating an otherwise apparently concluded agreement.[82] **35-28**

---

process which may well, as it did in this case, involve quite lengthy discussion before an agreement is reached for mediation, let alone any ultimate settlement agreement, it seems to me that it would be natural to read the phrase 'arising in relation to the mediation' as not being limited to things done after the signature of the mediation agreement. Mediation is defined as the attempt to settle the dispute by mediation. The process of getting to entry into the mediation agreement is itself, albeit at a preliminary stage, an attempt to settle the dispute by mediation. No doubt in practice all or most discussions at such a stage will be on a without prejudice basis." See also de Berti, 'The Model Mediation Agreement of the Chartered Institute of Arbitrators' (2010) 76 *Arbitration* 1, 136–144. The present standard CEDR clause is as follows: "Every person involved in the Mediation ... will keep confidential all information arising out of or in connection with the Mediation, including the terms of any settlement, unless otherwise agreed by the Parties in writing but not including the fact that the Mediation is to take place or has taken place or where disclosure is required by law, or to implement or to enforce terms of settlement or to notify their insurers, insurance brokers and/or accountants; and ... acknowledges that all such information passing between the Parties, the Mediator and/or CEDR, however communicated, is agreed to be without prejudice to any Party's legal position and may not be produced as evidence or disclosed to any judge, arbitrator or other decision-maker in any legal or other formal process, except where otherwise disclosable in law."

75 See Ch.19.

76 See para.19–39 onwards.

77 *Unilever Plc v The Procter & Gamble Co* [2000] 1 W.L.R. 2436.

78 See paras 19–50-19–51.

79 See para.19–50. See Sir David Foskett's Keynote address to the Professional Negligence Lawyers Association Annual Conference in December 2014: *http://www.judiciary.gov.uk/announcements/speech-by-mr-justice-foskett-pnla-annual-conference-keynote-address/* [Accessed 31 October 2019].

80 See para.19–28.

81 In *Brown v Rice & Patel* [2007] EWHC 625 (Ch); (2008) 24 Const. L.J. 238, the issue arose as to whether an express provision to this effect had been impliedly waived when an offer made in a mediation had been held over until midday on the following day. In the circumstances it was held that it did not operate as a waiver.

82 See Ch.4. In *Ruttle Plant Hire v The Secretary of State for the Environment and Rural Affairs* [2007] EWHC 2870 (TCC); [2008] 2 All E.R. (Comm) 264, C has pleaded a case against D seeking the set-

The extent to which a mediator may be drawn into this process, directly or indirectly, is considered below.[83]

35-29 So far as confidentiality is concerned, whether it springs from an express or implied contractual provision,[84] the remedy for breaching such a provision will usually be, in the first instance, a claim for an injunction and then damages or restitutionary relief.

35-30 As things stand in the United Kingdom, no particular privilege or immunity attaches to the position of a mediator under the general law.[85] On that basis a mediator could be called as a witness to speak about what occurred at a mediation subject, of course, to matters of objection available to the parties themselves. Many mediators would undoubtedly see the prospect of being called as a witness for or against a party to a mediation as inconsistent with his or her role as the trusted intermediary between the parties. To that extent most mediation agreements provide expressly that the parties will not call the mediator as a witness in any proceedings concerning the matters in dispute or what occurred at the mediation. Indeed the policy statement enunciated in *Halsey*[86] would suggest that the courts would ordinarily be reluctant to see a mediator being required to testify about such matters.[87] However, as already observed,[88] where something said or done at a mediation is sought to be relied upon to set aside an agreement reached during the mediation the court will need to receive evidence about it in order to determine whether the invalidating ground is made out. In that situation, it is difficult to see how the mediator could not be said to be potentially a material witness. Is there any basis upon which the mediator could resist attempts by one or other (or indeed all) of the parties to secure his or her attendance at a trial of such an issue?

---

ting aside of a mediated settlement between the parties based upon an allegation of economic duress; *Farm Assist Ltd (In Liquidation) v The Secretary of State for the Environment, Food and Rural Affairs (No.2)* [2009] EWHC 1102 (TCC); [2009] B.L.R. 399.

83 See para.35–25.

84 cf. *CEDR Model Mediation Agreement* (*https://www.cedr.com/about_us/modeldocs/*) [Accessed 31 October 2019].

85 The position varies worldwide and views differ about the desirability and/or need for such a privilege within the domestic jurisdiction. In *Rice & Patel* [2007] EWHC 625 (Ch); (2008) 24 Const. L.J. 238, Stuart Isaacs QC, sitting as a deputy High Court judge, held that the case could be decided under the existing without prejudice rule and without deciding if "a distinct mediation privilege" does or should exist. He said that: "[T]he existence of [such a] privilege [may] require to be considered by either the legislature or the courts but that is not something which arises for decision now." The argument in support of the existence of such a privilege in that case was based upon the approach of the courts in cases such as *McTaggart v McTaggart* [1948] 2 All E.R. 754 and *D v National Society for the Prevention of Cruelty to Children* [1978] A.C. 171. There are those who argue that, either by way of legislation (perhaps building on the EU Mediation Directive, which relates only to mediations of cross-border disputes involving parties from EU countries) or the development of the common law, that a discrete form of mediation privilege should be fashioned: see, e.g., Cornes, 'Mediation Privilege and the EU Directive: An Opportunity', (2008) 74 *Arbitration* 4, 395; Koo, 'Confidentiality of Mediation Communications' (2011) 30 CJQ 192. See also Briggs, 'Mediation Privilege?' Parts 1 and 2, (2009) 159 NLJ 506 and 550. See Sir David Foskett's Keynote address to the Professional Negligence Lawyers Association Annual Conference in December 2014: *http://www.judiciary.gov.uk/announcements/speech-by-mr-justice-foskett-pnla-annual-conference-keynote-address/* [Accessed 31 October 2019]. Notwithstanding such suggestions the courts have not as yet recognised the existence of a discrete "mediation privilege".

86 See para.35–19.

87 In *Cumbria Waste Management Ltd v Baines Wilson* [2008] EWHC 786 (QB); [2008] B.L.R. 330, HH Judge Kirkham noted "that the disclosure sought by the defendant is of such wide scope that it would include documents held by the mediator" which she said "the court should be very slow to order" because "[mediators] should be able to conduct mediations confident that, in normal circumstances, their papers could not be seen by the parties or others".

88 See para.35–24.

The question raised in the previous paragraph fell to be answered in *Farm Assist Ltd (In Liquidation) v The Secretary of State for the Environment, Food and Rural Affairs (No.2)*[89] in the context of the particular mediation agreement entered into in that case. The relevant clause was in these terms: 35-31

> "None of the parties to the Mediation Agreement will call the Mediator as a witness, consultant, arbitrator or expert in any litigation or arbitration in relation to the Dispute and the Mediator will not voluntarily act in any such capacity without the written agreement of all the Parties."

Ramsey J held that agreement not to call the Mediator as a witness "in relation to the Dispute" is limited to "litigation or arbitration in relation to the underlying dispute", and since the issue to which the mediator's evidence would be directed was whether the agreement reached at the mediation had been arrived at under duress, there were no grounds upon which the mediator could avoid giving evidence. He also said that even had the clause covered the mediation itself, it would simply "be a factor for the court to take into account in deciding whether, in the interests of justice, a mediator should be called as a witness."

COURT'S ROLE IN DIRECTING AND ENCOURAGING EARLY NEUTRAL EVALUATION (ENE)

Since the 1990s the courts, and particularly the Commercial Court, have promoted the use of ENE as a technique capable of securing settlement.[90] It is not a form of mediation, nor is it a mediation technique. Its aim is to provide parties to a dispute with an independent, neutral, evaluation of the merits of their dispute by an expert in the subject matter of, or issues in, the dispute. The neutral tests the evidence and the legal arguments, and provides an evaluation of the respective cases of the parties in the light of that. ENE does not seek, as mediation does, to promote communication between the parties, to help facilitate the identification of interests underpinning the dispute or to help formulate options to settle the dispute. 35-32

ENE's utility is not confined to commercial cases.[91] Experience from other jurisdictions have demonstrated its utility in personal injury disputes, clinical negligence disputes, contractual and business disputes, employment and property disputes.[92]

The obligation imposed by CPR r.1.4(1) on the court, to "further the overriding objective by actively managing cases" includes promoting the use of ENE. That obligation was acknowledged by amendment to CPR r.1.4(2)(m) in 2015, so that it now provides that the court may 35-33

> "(m) take any other step or make any other order for the purpose of managing the case and furthering the overriding objective, including hearing an Early Neutral Evaluation with the aim of helping the parties settle the case."

---

89 *Farm Assist* [2009] EWHC 1102 (TCC); [2009] B.L.R. 399. See also *Chu Chung Ming v Lam Wai Dan* [2012] HKCFI 1250.

90 cf. *Practice Statement (Commercial Cases: Alternative Dispute Resolution) (No.2)* [1996] 1 W.L.R. 1024.

91 Financial Dispute Resolution in family proceedings and Chancery proceedings as they focus on a judge facilitating negotiation are not forms of ENE (cf. *The Chancery Guide 2016* (April 2019 edn) at para.18.16).

92 W. Brazil, *Early Neutral Evaluation*, (American Bar Association, 2012) at p.42.

In some jurisdictions, such as California where ENE originally developed,[93] the court has the power to direct parties to engage in ENE as part of the court process. The Court of Appeal in *Lomax v Lomax* confirmed that that is also the case under the CPR and will exercise the power in do so in suitable cases.[94] Suitable cases would include those where the parties have entrenched positions or apparently unrealistic assessments of the merits of their respective cases, where an objective third party assessment of those merits, or where the costs of litigation are disproportionate to the value of the claim. The court may thus order parties to take part in judge-led ENE process notwithstanding best practice guidance in the various court guides that emphasise that ENE will only be ordered with party consent.[95] Following *Lomax v Lomax* it remains an open question whether the court does have the power to direct unwilling parties to engage in ENE outside the court process—i.e., to engage an independent third party to carry out the ENE. It is likely that as such an order would take place outside the court process and would require the parties to engage and pay for the services of the independent third party to carry out the ENE, the court is likely to view it as more closely akin to mediation carried out by a third party outside the court process. Hence, there is no power to mandate such a form of ENE for the same reason *Halsey v Milton Keynes NHS Trust*[96] concluded that the court could not order unwilling parties to engage in mediation. This would be an unfortunate consequence because it may be thought that full-time judicial resources are better deployed trying disputed issues than effectively engaging in an ADR process. However, that appears to be the position as matters stand. Nonetheless, it is submitted that there is no reason, in principle, why the court should not take a similar position in relation to costs where a party refuses to agree to ENE by a suitably experienced independent party.[97]

THE ENE PROCESS

35-34 ENE is an informal, flexible, process. It has no set procedure. As with mediation, the exact nature of the process can be designed and agreed by the parties and the evaluator, whether that is a judge or other independent, neutral, third party.

The starting point of the process will be for the parties to determine that they wish to take part in an ENE process and select whether they want the evaluator to be a judge or some other evaluator, such as an independent lawyer or ENE practitioner, who has expertise in the subject matter of the dispute. If a judge is to carry out the ENE the parties, or if one of the parties seeks an ENE, it ought then to apply to the court seeking an order to that effect. Otherwise the parties will need to identify and appoint an independent third party to carry out the ENE. Where an ENE takes place outside the court process, the parties may need to stay the proceedings pending the outcome of the ENE process. Once the evaluator has been decided upon, the parties with the evaluator will determine the exact nature and scope of the ENE process. If a judge is to evaluate, the nature of the process should be set out in a

---

93 W. Brazil, *Early Neutral Evaluation*, (American Bar Association, 2012) at p.157.

94 [2019] EWCA Civ 1467, overruling Parker J's decision to the contrary in *Lomax v Lomax (Referral to Early Neutral Evaluation)* [2019] EWHC 1267 (Fam).

95 See, for instance, Chancery Guide (fn.75) at paras 18.7 to 18.9.

96 [2004] 1 W.L.R. 3002.

97 For example, a QC who practises in the sphere, particularly one who sits as a Deputy High Court Judge or a Recorder, or a retired judge who has experience of the particular area of dispute.

court order. If some other form of evaluator is appointed, the parties and the evaluator should enter into an agreement setting out the terms of the process.[98]

A standard form case management order directing that an ENE take place, based on that used in Chancery proceedings and adapted for general use is set out at Appendix 6.[99] Model ENE agreements, where the ENE is to be carried out by someone other than a judge are also available.[100]

Generally, the process will require the parties to provide the evaluator with written case summaries and their submissions on the evidence and any legal issues. A limited amount of evidence may also be submitted. It is unusual for expert evidence to be submitted, however if it is necessary for determining an issue in dispute it may be submitted.[101] The evaluation may be based on the papers alone, or it may take place after a short hearing. Evaluation after a hearing is preferable, as it enables the parties to develop specific points orally and the evaluator to clarify issues with the parties. Witness evidence is generally not given or tested at the hearing. It also has the advantage of enabling the parties, who ought to be present at the hearing, to appreciate their and the other party's points and evidence directly. This puts them in a better position to appreciate the evaluator's opinion, and particularly their assessment of the issues and the merits of the parties' respective cases. At the conclusion of the hearing the evaluator may give their opinion orally or may provide a written opinion at a later date. **35-35**

Where a judge conducts an ENE, unless the parties expressly and on an informed basis agree otherwise,[102] the judge cannot take any further part in the claim.

ENE—Privacy and without prejudice

The ENE process is, unless the parties agree otherwise, ordinarily private. Any ENE hearing ought therefore to be held in private, particularly where a judge is the evaluator. The ENE process should also be without prejudice. Both these aspects of the process should be reflected in any order directing an ENE process to take place before a judge or any ENE agreement appointing a third party to act as the evaluator. **35-36**

Binding ENE process

ENE is ordinarily a non-binding process. There is, however, no reason in principle why parties to a dispute cannot agree that the opinion provided in an ENE process will bind them in respect of the entire dispute or to an issue or issues in it.[103] **35-37**

Party agreement to engage in ADR

It is increasingly the case that contracts will contain provision for disputes to be **35-38**

98 Ibid.

99 See Chancery Guide (fn.75) at para.18.15 for the original specimen order.

100 cf. *CEDR Model Early Neutral Evaluation Agreement* (*https://www.cedr.com/about_us/modeldocs/?id=9* [Accessed 31 October 2019].

101 If the dispute turns on an issue on which expert evidence, expert determination may be the more appropriate form of ADR process.

102 Having an opinion on the merits of the dispute or an issue or issues in it would lead to a judge being subject to, at the least, apparent bias, any waiver of the bias would need to be informed, see *Smith v Kvaerner Cementation Foundations Ltd* [2006] EWCA Civ 242; [2007] 1 W.L.R. 370.

103 Chancery Guide (fn.75) at paras 18.12 and 18.8 acknowledges the possibility that the parties may agree the opinion will bind them.

referred to ADR, whether a sole ADR method or a multi-tiered dispute resolution process, prior to litigation. In *Ohpen Operations UK Ltd v Invesco Fund Managers Ltd* [2019] EWHC 2246 (TCC) at [28]-[32] O'Farrell J summarised the case law on the approach to be taken to determine whether a contractual clause that purports to require a party to engage in ADR as a condition precedent to commencing proceedings is in fact binding on the parties. She summarised the test as follows,

"(i) The agreement must create an enforceable obligation requiring the parties to engage in alternative dispute resolution.

(ii) The obligation must be expressed clearly as a condition precedent to court proceedings or arbitration.

(iii) The dispute resolution process to be followed does not have to be formal but must be sufficiently clear and certain by reference to objective criteria, including machinery to appoint a mediator or determine any other necessary step in the procedure without the requirement for any further agreement by the parties.

(iv) The court has a discretion to stay proceedings commenced in breach of an enforceable dispute resolution agreement. In exercising its discretion, the Court will have regard to the public policy interest in upholding the parties' commercial agreement and furthering the overriding objective in assisting the parties to resolve their disputes."

CHAPTER 36

The Settlement of International Commercial Disputes

INTRODUCTION

The principal focus of this work has been the law and practice relating to the settlement of disputes arising within the jurisdiction of England and Wales. This law and practice has influence in other jurisdictions, particularly those with a common law tradition. Chapter 32 dealt specifically with the law and practice associated with the settlement of international commercial disputes that have proceeded to arbitration when the seat of the arbitration is London and English law is the law applicable to determining the outcome of the arbitration. That situation largely engages the law and practice of England and Wales. **36-01**

The vast number of international transactions that take place, whether purely of trade or in other respects, inevitably means that from time to time disputes will arise between the parties. Most contracts between parties whose places of business are in different countries provide that any dispute arising from the contract (or indeed more widely between the parties) shall be referred to arbitration in a jurisdiction other than the domestic jurisdiction of either of the parties. This is to overcome the perception (and, in some situations, the reality) that "playing at home" will give one party an unfair advantage. Not infrequently the parties will identify an arbitral institution such as the International Chamber of Commerce ("the ICC") or The London Court of International Arbitration ("the LCIA")[1] as the organisation that will set up and oversee any arbitration that may be required in accordance with the institution's rules. Those rules provide for the procedures to be adopted and are designed to ensure the integrity and fairness of the process. Where the arbitration clause does not identify such an institution, any resulting arbitration is often termed an ad hoc arbitration[2] and the parties will have to agree upon the arbitrator(s). Ordinarily, in that situation, the parties will specify the seat of the arbitration and the law to be applied to the resolution of any dispute. It does not, of course, follow that London will be the seat of the arbitration or where the arbitration physically takes place. Other choices include New York, Paris, Singapore or Hong Kong and other major cities throughout the world. It does not necessarily follow that the law to be applied to the resolution of the dispute will be the law of the country where the arbitration is destined to take place although frequently it is. **36-02**

That general backdrop sets the scene for consideration of the resolution by agreement of the disputes that would otherwise lead to a contested arbitration hearing **36-03**

---

[1] There are many others: see, e.g., M. Moses, *The Principles and Practice of International Commercial Arbitration*, 3rd edn (Cambridge University Press, 2017), pp.11–15.

[2] This is one of the two senses in which the term is used: see *Russell on Arbitration*, 24th edn (London: Sweet & Maxwell, 2015), para.2-006.

between parties to a commercial dispute. A flavour of this background can be seen in *Sulamérica Cia Nacional de Seguros SA v Enesa Engelharia SA*[3] where Lord Neuberger of Abbotsbury MR said this[4]:

> "It is not uncommon for a commercial contract to contain (i) a choice of law clause stating that it 'will be governed exclusively by the laws of' one country ..., (ii) a jurisdiction clause providing that the courts of the same country will have exclusive jurisdiction in relation to disputes arising out of the contract ..., and (iii) an arbitration clause providing that all, or certain, disputes arising out of the contract are to be referred to arbitration the seat of which is in a quite different country ...."

36-04 As with many disputes that would otherwise proceed to contested litigation in a domestic court, there is an impetus in most international commercial disputes for a settlement of the dispute before a contested arbitration hearing takes place. Indeed there will be cases where a settlement is achieved before arbitration proceedings are commenced, either through direct negotiations between the parties or with the assistance of a mediator. The same can occur, of course, during the pendency of arbitration proceedings. This Chapter focuses on the law and practice applicable to the settlement process in all those situations. It needs to be noted at the outset that the intervention of a *mediator*[5] may make a difference to the way in which a settlement agreement can be enforced (or utilised in some other way) if the need for enforcement (or utilisation) arises. This will depend upon whether the Singapore Convention[6] is observed in the country where appropriate relief is sought. The potential role of the Convention is dealt with separately in paras 36-32 to 36-61. Paragraphs 36-05–36-31 should be read on the basis that the Convention has no application.

SETTLEMENT BEFORE THE COMMENCEMENT OF ARBITRATION PROCEEDINGS

36-05 A concluded settlement of a dispute will have a contractual status in whichever jurisdiction it is concluded. It follows that a settlement achieved before (or indeed after[7]) the commencement of arbitration proceedings *and which does not thereafter become embodied in an agreed arbitral award*[8] is simply a contract that falls to be enforced as a contract.[9] The settlement agreement itself is very likely to contain an arbitration or other dispute resolution clause which will identify the applicable laws[10] or which will identify the legal system under which any dispute arising under the settlement agreement is to be determined[11]. Where it does not do so, some difficult issues may arise[12].

---

3 [2012] EWCA] Civ 638; [2013] 1 W.L.R. 102.

4 [2012] EWCA] Civ 638; [2013] 1 W.L.R. 102 at [50].

5 An independent facilitator. See para.36-32.

6 See paras 36-32–36-61.

7 See paras 36-20–36-31.

8 For the practice where a settlement of arbitration proceedings does become embodied in an agreed or consent award, see paras 36-09–36-14 for the circumstances in which such an award might be made in this situation.

9 If the agreement has resulted from a successful mediation, then, if applicable, the Singapore Convention (see Appendix 11 and paras 36-32–36-61) may afford a basis for obtaining enforcement of its provisions or seeking some other form of relief arising from them.

10 See paras 36-09–36-15.

11 In *Monde Petroleum SA v Westernzagros Ltd* [2015] EWHC 67 (Comm), for example, the settle-

It will, of course, be important for a party to such a settlement who considers that recourse to enforcement processes may be required at some stage to ensure, in the first instance, that the proposed agreement itself complies with all the requirements of the law governing the validity and enforceability of the agreement. This would be a prerequisite in whichever jurisdiction the agreement was in due course sought to be enforced. A settlement agreement that contains a provision that the agreement "shall be governed by and construed in accordance with the laws of England and Wales"[13] must meet all the relevant requirements of English law.[14] The same would apply if, for example, the law chosen by the parties as governing the settlement agreement was French law or German law. From a purely practical perspective, the party who contemplates the possibility of the need for enforcement action to enforce payment of monies due will want to ensure that the agreement is enforceable in a jurisdiction where the other party has traceable assets. **36-06**

On the assumption that the settlement is, in principle, valid and enforceable by reference to the law governing the settlement agreement, what steps are open to the party seeking to enforce the terms of the settlement? If the settlement agreement specifies that the judicial system of the country whose laws are to apply to the settlement agreement is also to have exclusive jurisdiction over the agreement, it is unlikely that the courts of that country would decline jurisdiction to enforce the agreement.[15] The quickest and most effective way in which an enforceable judgment can be obtained in that jurisdiction would doubtless be taken by the enforcing party. In England and Wales, that is likely to be by way of a summary judgment application.[16] This can, of course, be resisted on the basis that there is a real prospect of successfully defending the claim or there is some other compelling reason why the issue should be disposed of at a trial.[17] However, generally the court will take a robust view of insubstantial arguments concerning non-fulfilment of freely undertaken obligations. **36-07**

If the settlement agreement contains an arbitration clause that specifies that the law to be applied to the agreement is the same law as will govern the procedure of the arbitration itself (the "curial law"), there is ordinarily no doubt that these choices would be respected by the arbitrators. On the assumption that they did so, they could decide whether the agreement should be enforced and could issue an award accordingly. If the decision was in favour of enforcement this could be achieved pursuant to the New York Convention.[18] That would, however, involve the courts of a particular domestic jurisdiction effectively converting the award into an enforceable court order or judgment. Where there is, in reality, no credible defence to the enforceability of the prior settlement, this overall process is expensive and time-consuming and may simply have the effect of delaying the fulfilment of the **36-08**

---

ment agreement "contained a clause conferring exclusive jurisdiction on the courts of England and Wales" [5] and also provided that the agreement "shall be governed by and construed in accordance with the laws of England and Wales" [15]. Under the original agreement there was an arbitration clause that provided that any "arbitration was to be held in London under the ICC Rules": [10].

[12] See paras 36-15–36-19.

[13] See fn.11.

[14] See Chs 2–4.

[15] This will of course depend on the rules for establishing jurisdiction in the forum concerned. While most will accept jurisdiction on the basis of an exclusive jurisdiction agreement, that will not necessarily be true in every case. For example, a jurisdiction agreement in favour of the Dubai International Financial Centre Courts was originally not sufficient to establish that Court's jurisdiction. The relevant legislation was amended in October 2011 to provide for "opt in" jurisdiction.

[16] CPR Pt 24.

[17] CPR Pt 24.2.

[18] See paras 36-29–36-31 and Ch.32.

particular obligation(s) sought to be enforced. This is a strong reason for any party concerned about enforcement, if the relevant law and/or the relevant institutional arbitral rules permit,[19] insisting that any settlement is incorporated in an agreed arbitral award.

36-09 Where an agreed settlement of potential arbitration proceedings has been achieved *before* those proceedings have commenced, can the agreed settlement be made the subject of an agreed (or consent) arbitral award? If so, and the New York Convention recognises it, is enforcement pursuant to the Convention possible?

36-10 It is not easy to give an all-embracing answer to the questions thus posed, but the general position appears to be that an agreed or consent award may be made *only whilst arbitral proceedings are pending*. In other words, the institution of arbitration proceedings *after* a settlement has been concluded simply in order to embody the settlement in an agreed award will not be effective. In essence, this is because, once a settlement has been concluded, there is no extant dispute between the parties[20] and without a dispute there can be no grounds for instituting an arbitration. By way of example, art.30(1) of the UNCITRAL Model Law on International Arbitration (1985), on which many countries base their approach, says this:

> "If, *during arbitral proceedings*, the parties settle the dispute, the arbitral tribunal shall terminate the proceedings and, if requested by the parties[21] and not objected to by the arbitral tribunal, record the settlement in the form of an arbitral award on agreed terms." (Emphasis added.)

In the UNCITRAL 2012 Digest of Case Law on the Model Law on International Commercial Arbitration, the following observations were made:

> "Article 30 only applies if arbitral proceedings have commenced and the final award has yet to be made. Where a full and final settlement of any claim has been reached before arbitral proceedings have commenced, a dispute no longer subsists to be referred to arbitration .... It follows that such an agreed settlement may not be made in the form of an award under article 30. However, some States have, in their legislation enacting the Model Law, extended that article to include a settlement agreement reached in the course of conciliation/ mediation proceedings to be made in the form of an arbitral award .... In contrast, where the parties have commenced the arbitral proceedings and subsequently enter into a settlement agreement (prior to oral hearing), the dispute over the existence of a settlement agreement still falls under the jurisdiction of the arbitral tribunal ...."

36-11 Whilst this might be seen as a somewhat technical issue that arguably impedes a settlement process that ought to be encouraged and supported, the juridical basis

---

19 See para.36-23.

20 cf. paras 6-01–6-02. See, e.g., *Castro v Tri Marine Co*, US Court of Appeals for the 9th Circuit, 27 February 2019, the Opinion in which, delivered by Judge Margaret McKeown, contains the memorable passage: "... this appeal involves [the] fundamental question—whether we are presented with a foreign arbitral award at all. In the mine run of cases, the answer is uncontroversial: when it looks, swims, and quacks like an arbitral award, it typically is. Yet, in this unusual appeal, we have an arbitral award in name only." The court held that, by the time the arbitrator was approached to make the agreed award (during "an impromptu meeting in a building lobby"), "the parties had fully settled their claims" and "[there] was no dispute to arbitrate". It was held that the New York Convention could not be relied upon to enforce the "award". The judgment goes on to say that "our decision does not encroach on the common practice of reducing settlements reached during arbitration into arbitral awards, frequently termed 'consent awards'."

21 The Report of the 18th session of UNCITRAL (1985) records the following: "Another proposal was that the request to record the settlement as an award needed to be made by only one of the parties. The Commission, after deliberation, was agreed that there must be the dual will of the two parties that the settlement be recorded as an award, but that the formal request needed to be made by only one of them."

for the approach, given the premise that arbitration is a means of resolving a *dispute*, is sound. On the other hand, since arbitration is a consensual process,[22] it is difficult to see why, in principle, parties are not entitled to confer power on a subsequently-appointed arbitrator to make an agreed award. There are, it is thought, a number of ways of avoiding the prospect of not being able to obtain a consent award in the event of settlement negotiations being concluded satisfactorily when no substantive steps have been taken in an arbitration. It depends upon when arbitrations proceedings are deemed to have commenced. Once commenced, the proceedings are *pending* and there would seem no obstacle to making a consent award within cl.30 or any national variation to similar effect.

Article 21 of the Model Law[23] provides as follows: **36-12**

> "Unless otherwise agreed by the parties, the arbitral proceedings in respect of a particular dispute commence on the date on which a request for that dispute to be referred to arbitration is received by the respondent."

Given that the parties may agree upon the date when arbitration proceedings begin, all that needs to be done before negotiations either commence or are concluded satisfactorily is that the parties agree that arbitration proceedings between them are to be regarded as having commenced. As long as this is evidenced appropriately, there does not appear to be any principled objection to appointing a sole arbitrator (or the sole arbitrator accepting appointment) subsequently to make, if he/she has no principled objection,[24] a consent award embodying the settlement. If there is concern that evidencing the agreement as to commencement of the arbitration will be insufficient (which it should not be), the parties could agree on the formal appointment of a sole arbitrator[25] before negotiations commence with an invitation to that arbitrator to hold him or herself available to make a consent award if the negotiations succeed.[26] In the event of one party not agreeing to such an approach, the other party might be entitled to see this as an indication of potential non-cooperation after a substantive settlement has apparently been achieved and would, in those circumstances, be justified (and well advised) to serve a request for a referral of the dispute to arbitration upon that party before negotiations commence.

Under the law of England and Wales arbitration proceedings "commence" when **36-13**
the appropriate provision in s.14 of the Arbitration Act 1996 is met. Subsection (1) provides that the "parties are free to agree when arbitral proceedings are to be regarded as commenced for the purposes of" the Act. There are other specific provisions that deem the proceedings "commenced" when certain notices in writing have either been "served" or "given" by one of the parties[27] if agreement under subsection (1) cannot be reached. Nothing aggressive should be seen in the conduct of one party serving or giving such notice before any negotiations take place or are concluded since it would simply be to preserve the opportunity of obtaining a consent award in due course if the negotiations succeed.

---

22 See para.32-04.

23 See Appendix 7.

24 See paras 36-23–36-27 and 32-05–32-10.

25 It may be thought sensible to appoint a legally qualified sole arbitrator for this purpose since such an arbitrator will understand the process being adopted (and its rationale) and will be best placed to decide whether to agree to the making of the consent award in due course if the negotiations succeed: see paras 36-23–36-27.

26 This is a similar approach to the approach adopted in the Singapore "Arb-Med-Arb" procedure described in paras 36-67–36-71.

27 Subsections (3)–(5). These subsections are to be interpreted "broadly and flexibly": per Thomas J, as he then was, in *Seabridge Shipping AB v AC Orssleff's Eftf's A/S* [1999] 2 Lloyd's Rep. 685. This approach has been followed: see, e.g., *Easybiz Investments v Sinograin & Chinatex ("The Biz")* [2010] EWHC 2565 (Comm); [2011] 1 Lloyd's Rep 688–692, Hamblen J, as he then was.

36-14 Another (though, it is submitted, probably less satisfactory) approach would be for the parties to agree at the outset of their negotiations that their arbitration would be deemed to commence before they reached any concluded settlement. Since the parties control the process, it is difficult to see any objection in principle to such a course if the law under which they are conducting their negotiations permits it.

36-15 The foregoing discussion has been directed to situations where the parties' settlement agreement contains an arbitration or other dispute resolution clause which identifies the applicable laws or the legal system under which any dispute arising under the settlement agreement is to be determined.[28] If it does not do so, a number of factors will need to be considered by the courts of the jurisdiction where enforcement of the agreement is sought.

36-16 There are three discrete relationships to consider: (1) the law governing the settlement agreement itself; (2) the law governing the dispute resolution agreement, whether a jurisdiction or arbitration agreement; and (3) the law governing the dispute resolution process by which any disputes about the settlement agreement will be determined. While these will often be the same, this is not always the case. The approach to resolving which system of law applies will depend on the conflict of laws rules in the forum in which the question is being addressed.

36-17 In England, where there is an express choice of the law governing the substantive contract, there will generally be found to be an implied choice of the same system of law for any arbitration agreement contained within the same contract, unless there is some indication to the contrary[29]. Where there is no such choice, the court will consider which system of law has the closest and most real connection with the dispute resolution agreement.[30] That is likely to be the law of the seat of the arbitration, being the place where the arbitration agreement is to be performed.[31]

36-18 Where there is no choice of law in the main contract or the arbitration agreement, the selection of a seat for the arbitration may be treated as an implied choice of the law of the contract.[32] If there is no choice of law or seat, the governing law of the contract will be determined in accordance with the provisions of the Rome I Regulation.[33] The law so chosen will also be likely to govern the arbitration agreement.[34]

36-19 The law governing the dispute resolution procedure will almost always be the law of the forum in which the dispute is to be resolved. In the case of a jurisdiction agreement, that would appear to follow inevitably. It is almost inconceivable that a foreign court would apply the procedural law of another jurisdiction in determining a dispute before it. In the case of an arbitration agreement, it is possible, but highly unlikely, for parties to agree to apply a curial law other than the law at the seat. Such a choice would create "complexities and inconveniences" because the

---

28 See para.36-05.

29 *Sulamérica Cia Nacional de Seguros SA v Enesa Engelharia SA* [2012] EWCA Civ 638; [2013] 1 W.L.R. 102 at [29]–[31].

30 The Rome I Regulation (Regulation (EC) 593/2008) on the law applicable to contractual obligations does not apply to arbitration agreements: Article 1(2)(e).

31 *Sulamérica* at [32].

32 See Dicey, Morris and Collins, *The Conflict of Laws*, 15th edn (London, Sweet & Maxwell, 2018), para. 16-019 and fn.41.

33 Regulation (EC) No 593/2008 of the European Parliament and of the Council of 17 June 2008 on the law applicable to contractual obligations. See generally, Dicey, Morris and Collins, *The Conflict of Laws*, 15th edn, Ch.32.

34 Dicey, Morris and Collins, *The Conflict of Laws*, 15th edn, para.16-019 and fn.42.

curial law deals primarily with the relationship between the courts and the arbitral process.[35] A very clear express agreement would therefore be required.

SETTLEMENT AFTER THE COMMENCEMENT OF ARBITRATION PROCEEDINGS

Article 30(1) of the UNCITRAL Model Law on International Arbitration[36] contemplates that an agreed award may be made if a settlement is achieved "during arbitral proceedings". Article 30(2) spells out the status to be accorded to such an award: 36-20

> "An award on agreed terms shall be made in accordance with the provisions of article 31[37] and shall state that it is an award. Such an award has the same status and effect as any other award on the merits of the case."

Notwithstanding the terms of the Model Law, the New York Convention itself does not refer expressly to an agreed (or consent) award. It is sometimes said that since the *travaux préparatoires* of the New York Convention do not clarify the extent to which it applies to agreed or consent awards[38] (indeed neither term is mentioned): 36-21

> "[this] silence raises the question of whether consent awards qualify as arbitral awards under the Convention. The answer to this question may turn on whether a consent award is, in fact, an arbitral award, or if it is something [definitely] distinct to be given the same status and effect as an arbitral award."[39]

The extension of the argument has been described thus[40]:

> "It has been argued that some consent awards should not be enforceable under the New York Convention because they are not arbitral awards per se; they are only to be treated like arbitral awards. The word choice providing for the "same status and effect" as arbitral awards suggests that these consent awards are not technically arbitral awards. Under this line of reasoning, the reference to "same status and effect" applies to domestic enforcement. However, since these consent awards are not arbitral awards, they cannot fall within the New York Convention."

If that argument prevailed, an agreed or consent arbitral award could not be enforced under the Convention and there would be little, if anything, to gain from making a settlement the subject of such an order. Many would not see an argument such as that outlined above as possessing much intrinsic merit. Just as a judg- 36-22

---

35 See *Naviera Amazonica Peruana SA v. Compania Internacionale de Seguros* [1988] 1 Lloyd's Rep 116 at pp.120–121. See also the discussion of Hamblen J (as he was) in *Shagang South-Asia (Hong Kong) Trading Co. Ltd. v Daewoo Logistics* [2015] 1 Lloyd's Rep 504 at [25]–[28].

36 See para.36-10. In the law of England and Wales, s.51(3) of the Arbitration Act 1996 provides as follows: "An agreed award shall state that it is an award of the tribunal and shall have the same status and effect as any other award on the merits of the case." cf. fn.41.

37 Article 31 provides that the award "shall be made in writing and shall be signed by the [arbitrator(s)]", "shall state its date and the place of arbitration" and that copies signed by the arbitrator(s) "shall be delivered to the parties".

38 See, e.g., Yaraslau Kryvoi and Dmitry Davydenko, "Consent Awards in International Arbitration: From Settlement to Enforcement", (2015) 40 Brook. J. Int'l L., 850–851.

39 Brette L. Steele, "Enforcing International Commercial Mediation Agreements as Arbitral Awards under the New York Convention", (2007) 54 UCLA L. REV. 1385–1399, 1397.

40 Steele, op cit, 1397–1398.

ment in England and Wales is a judgment, whether made by consent or otherwise,[41] an arbitral award should, it is submitted, be regarded as an award, whether made pursuant to the agreement of the parties or otherwise. The United States District Court for the Southern District of Texas has adopted this approach and rejected the foregoing argument in *Transocean Offshore Gulf of Guinea VII Ltd v Erin Energy Corp*.[42] In resisting the making of an order enforcing an agreed arbitral award under the Convention, the respondent sought to argue that the Convention did not apply to such an award, drawing attention, inter alia, to what was said in the *UNCITRAL Secretariat Guide on the Convention on the Recognition and Enforcement of Foreign Arbitral Awards* (2016 edition) which referred to the diplomatic Conference held in May and June 1958. The Guide said this[43]:

> "The Convention is silent on the question of its applicability to decisions that record the terms of a settlement between parties. During the Conference, the issue of the application of the Convention to such decisions was raised, but not decided upon. Reported case law does not address this issue."

It was argued that "the Convention's silence meant that it was not intended to apply to consent awards" and that "a consent award is fundamentally different from other arbitral awards because an arbitral award represents the tribunal's conclusions, not the parties' agreement." The court[44] followed the "persuasive" analysis of the District Court for the Southern District of New York[45] in *ALBtelecom SH.A v Unifi Commc'ns, Inc.*,[46] where it was held that there was no reason to take a consent award outside the Convention. The District Judge in that case said this:

> "There is no reason for such an exception. On the contrary, the opposite rule would discourage resolution of disputes in mid-arbitration. Parties who initiate arbitration under the [arbitral court] might be less willing to settle, were the implication of a settlement that the resulting Award would lose its enforceability under the New York Convention. There is indeed limited law on this point, presumably because Awards achieved following the parties' consent are less likely to result in later disputes. But the limited available precedents reflect recognition and enforcement of Awards entered into based on stipulations by the parties."

In *Transocean* the District Judge said this:

> "No binding or persuasive statutory language or case law requires a court to hold that a tribunal must reach its own conclusions, separate from the parties' agreement, to make a valid, binding award subject to the Convention. As the *Albtelecom* court noted, this rule would dissuade parties from seeking arbitration in the first place or benefitting from the efficiencies it is meant to provide."

Whilst these authorities are not binding in other parts of the international com-

---

41 *Re South American and Mexican Co* [1895] 1 Ch 37, CA. "The truth is, a judgment by consent is intended to put a stop to litigation between the parties just as much as is a judgment which results from the decision of the Court after the matter has been fought out to the end": per Lord Herschell LC, with whom Lindley and A.L. Smith LJJ agreed. See also *Naraji v Shelbourne* [2011] EWHC 3298 (QB) at [126].

42 12 March 2018.

43 At [36].

44 Judge Lee H. Rosenthal, Chief United States District Judge.

45 Judge Paul A. Engelmayer, District Judge.

46 16 Civ. 9001 (PAE) (S.D.N.Y. 30 May 2017).

munity, it is submitted that they provide powerful, persuasive support for the contention that the Convention does apply to agreed or consent arbitral awards.[47]

As indicated above, the well-recognised utility of the New York Convention would be significantly diminished if it was inapplicable to agreed awards. Most arbitral institutions provide within their rules for the making of agreed awards. The LCIA Rules provide as follows[48]: **36-23**

> "In the event of any final settlement of the parties' dispute, the Arbitral Tribunal may decide to make an award recording the settlement if the parties jointly so request in writing (a "Consent Award"), provided always that such Consent Award shall contain an express statement on its face that it is an award made at the parties' joint request and with their consent. A Consent Award need not contain reasons ...."

The ICC Rules provide thus[49]:

> "If the parties reach a settlement after the file has been transmitted to the arbitral tribunal ..., the settlement shall be recorded in the form of an award made by consent of the parties, if so requested by the parties and if the arbitral tribunal agrees to do so."

As with the position in respect of domestic (or indeed international) arbitrations conducted in England and Wales[50], there is a residual discretion on the part of the arbitrator(s) not to make a proposed agreed award to be found in the words "and not objected to by the arbitral tribunal".[51] During the 18th session of UNCITRAL in 1985,[52] a suggestion was made that these words should be deleted, the rationale for the suggestion being that "if the parties wanted their settlement to be in the form of an award, rendering it enforceable as an award under the 1958 New York Convention or other applicable procedures, the arbitral tribunal should not be able to disagree."[53] The view of the Commission was encapsulated in the following paragraph: **36-24**

> "It was stated in reply that a distinction should be drawn between the right of the parties to have the arbitral proceedings terminate as a result of their settlement and their right to have their settlement recorded as an award. It was pointed out that arbitrators should not be forced to attach their signatures to whatever settlement the parties have reached since the terms of such settlement might, in exceptional cases, be in conflict with binding laws or public policy, including fundamental notions of fairness and justice. Furthermore, even if the words were deleted, arbitrators who felt sufficiently strongly that they should not record the settlement in the form of an award might resign. After discussion, the proposal was not adopted."[54]

According to the view expressed in the "[analytical] commentary on draft text of a model law on international commercial arbitration (1985)"[55], this provision in the Model Law is "based on the view that the arbitral tribunal, although it would normally accede to such a request, should not be compelled to do so in all **36-25**

---

47 When interpreting legislation based on treaty, the courts of England and Wales will take into account the decisions of foreign courts on the interpretation of that treaty: see, in an arbitration context, *Rainstorm Pictures Inc v Lombard-Knight* [2014] EWCA Civ 356; [2014] 2 Lloyd's Rep 74 at [3].
48 Article 26.9.
49 Article 33.
50 See paras 32-06–32-10.
51 See para.36-10.
52 See fn.21.
53 See para.248 of the report.
54 See para.249 of the report.
55 See Yearbook, Volume XVI: 1985.

circumstances (e.g. in case of suspected fraud, illicit or utterly unfair settlement terms)."[56]

36-26 These observations indicate the general nature of the kind of issue that might persuade an arbitrator not to agree to the embodiment of a settlement in an agreed award bearing his or her name. Experience suggests that it is rare for this to occur[57] and the circumstances in which an arbitral tribunal would be entitled to characterise a settlement as "utterly unfair" as between the parties[58] would, it is thought, be extremely rare: as with a court in England and Wales when invited to make a Tomlin order,[59] the circumstances in which the merits of a proposed settlement can be the subject of legitimate concern are extremely limited. Some authoritative guidance from a distinguished international arbitral tribunal (the Iran-US Claims Tribunal) can be found in the reasoning in *Iran v United States*,[60] a case that inevitably involved some extremely difficult and politically sensitive issues. The Tribunal's Rules of Procedure were modelled on the UNCITRAL rules. Article 34(1) of the Tribunal's Rules of Procedure provided as follows:

> "If, before the award is made, the parties agree on a settlement of the dispute, the arbitral tribunal shall either issue an order for the termination of the arbitral proceedings or, if requested by both parties and accepted by the tribunal, record the settlement in the form of an arbitral award on agreed terms. The arbitral tribunal is not obliged to give reasons for such an award."

There was an issue between the parties about the approach the Tribunal should adopt to a proposed settlement. Iran contended inter alia that the Tribunal should make an award on agreed terms, if the claim was, prima facie, within the jurisdiction of the Tribunal. The United States contended that the Tribunal should make an award "only after it has reviewed the settlement and found that [it] represents a reasonable determination of the claim". The unanimous view of the Tribunal[61] was expressed as follows:

> "The legal history of the UNCITRAL Rules demonstrates that Article 34 confers upon a tribunal the power to refuse to record a settlement as an award on agreed terms .... This power is not limited or defined. In drafting the Rules, UNCITRAL repeatedly declined to accept proposals to limit the grounds for refusal to a situation in which the arbitrators found that the settlement violated law or public policy .... However, it is at the same time clear that the power to refuse to record a settlement cannot be exercised in an arbitrary manner.
>
> Although the Tribunal, when deciding on a request under Article 34, *should not attempt to review the reasonableness of the settlement in the place of the arbitrating parties*, the Tribunal can refuse to record a settlement in the form of an award, provided that it does not act arbitrarily ...." (Emphasis added.)

---

56 See para.2 of the commentary on art.30.

57 See, e.g., G. Born, *International Commercial Arbitration*, 2nd edn (Kluwer Law International, 2014), p.3025.

58 Where it is plain that the proposed agreement is unfair on a third party (someone or some entity not a party to the agreement), the position is unclear. If the agreement amounts to an obvious fraud on that party, then it is certain that the arbitrator(s) would not make the award. If, however, the effect on a third party seems harsh and thus, on one view, unfair because the party has not had the opportunity to take part in the arbitration and influence the terms of the settlement agreement, the position is more nuanced. There may be such cases where the arbitrator(s) could legitimately take the view that the remedy would lie in the hands of the third party by way of appropriate applications to a court.

59 See paras 9-23–9-35.

60 Decision (DEC 8-A1-FT).

61 Presided over by President Gunnar Lagergren.

The assessment by the arbitral tribunal of a proposed settlement will, it is thought, be governed primarily (though not exclusively[62]) by the law and practice of the seat of the arbitration because it is that law and practice which will govern the conduct of the arbitration and thus the way in which a settlement is viewed. Public policy issues would probably also be viewed through that prism, the focus in any event being upon "international" public policy issues. As noted below,[63] it would require a very serious issue to arise before an arbitral tribunal would decline to make an award on this ground. Given the generality of the discretion conferred by rules such as this, it is impossible to postulate every situation in which an arbitral tribunal might justifiably decline to embody a proposed settlement in an agreed award. However, any settlement that the tribunal considers may involve criminal illegality (particularly money laundering, support for terrorist activities or fraud) or civil illegality (for example, breach of restraint of trade and/or anti-competition provisions) would almost certainly not be made the subject of an agreed award.[64] Corruption is generally seen as an important, if difficult, issue in the context of international commercial arbitration and an arbitral tribunal will inevitably be alive to the need not to sanction or appear to sanction any arrangement based upon corrupt practices in a consent award.[65] There is a degree of practical overlap between the considerations applicable to whether a consent award should be made and whether such an award should be enforced in another State pursuant to the Convention[66] although the two processes are, strictly speaking, distinct. **36-27**

In terms of the practice to be adopted by parties who want their settlement embodied in a consent award, alerting the arbitrator(s) to the fact that a settlement has been achieved would be the first step to take. It is thought that the preparation of a draft award for submission to the arbitrator(s) would be the next step with, where appropriate, an explanation for any apparently unusual provisions and a demonstration of the jurisdiction to make the award (or any parts of it that are, at first sight, unusual). **36-28**

On the assumption that a consent award is prima facie recognised within the jurisdiction where it is sought to be enforced as an award that falls within the New York Convention,[67] the party seeking enforcement will need to make the appropriate application to the courts within that jurisdiction for the recognition and enforcement of the award. That will usually be for some kind of summary judgment or order[68] following the obtaining of which an appropriate execution process will ensue. The Convention provides in Article V[69] for certain circumstances in which "the competent authority" in the enforcing State may (not "must") decline to enforce the award. It is beyond the scope of this work to consider those provisions **36-29**

---

62 The law applicable to the substance of the dispute, if different from the law of the seat of the arbitration, would need to be considered.

63 See fn.72.

64 See para.32-08.

65 In April 2019, the Basel Institute on Governance published "Corruption and Money Laundering in International Arbitration—A Toolkit for Arbitrators" which is designed "to help arbitrators who suspect, or are confronted with, alleged corruption or money laundering in relation to the underlying dispute, to address these issues in a systematic and comprehensive manner, and to find a solution in accordance with the applicable laws." Whilst focused on the "underlying dispute", the need for such a publication demonstrates the concerns felt at all levels of the practice of arbitration about the involvement of corruption.

66 See paras 36-55–36-56.

67 See paras 36-20–36-23.

68 See para.32-19.

69 See Article 36(1)(b)(ii) of the UNCITRAL Model Law on International Commercial Arbitration set out in Appendix 7.

in detail,[70] but attention needs to be drawn to one provision in particular.[71] Before doing so, it is to be noted that the exceptions to enforcement are ordinarily construed very narrowly by the courts of the State where enforcement is sought,[72] demonstrating a "strong pro-enforcement bias" and "a pragmatic, flexible and non-formalistic approach".[73] It is well-recognised that it is not open to the court called upon to enforce the award to review the merits of the arbitral tribunal's decision.[74]

36-30 Under Article V(1)(c) an award that "deals with a difference not contemplated by or not falling within the terms of the submission to arbitration, or ... contains decisions on matters beyond the scope of the submission to arbitration" may not be enforceable as such. A question raised elsewhere[75] is whether a general release in a consent award would be enforceable as part of the award. A release which deals with issues that were not in the contemplation of the parties at the outset of the arbitration proceedings may thus only be enforceable contractually. If such a provision is not enforceable as part of the award, provided that it is capable of being separated from other enforceable parts of the agreed award, those other parts "may be recognized and enforced" in the enforcing State[76].

36-31 For completeness for present purposes, it should be noted that there are exemptions from the obligation of enforcement where the "subject matter of the difference is not capable of settlement by arbitration under the law of" the enforcing State or the "recognition or enforcement of the award would be contrary to the public policy of that country".[77] The general position in relation to the "public policy" exemption has already been noted,[78] but this and the other exemptions will be considered more fully when considering similar exemptions under the Singapore Convention.[79]

---

70 See, e.g., N. Blackaby et al, *Redfern & Hunter on International Commercial Arbitration*, 6th edn. (Oxford University Press, 2015), paras 11.66–11.123; D. St John Sutton, J. Gill, M. Gearing, *Russell on Arbitration*, 24th edn (London: Sweet & Maxwell, 2015), paras 8-037–8-050.

71 Article V(1)(c).

72 The International Council for Commercial Arbitration ("ICCA") produced in 2011 the *Guide to the Interpretation of the 1958 New York Convention: A Handbook for Judges* in which the following was said about Article V: "The general rule to be followed by the courts is that the grounds for refusal defined in Article V are to be construed narrowly, which means that their existence is accepted in serious cases only. This is especially true with respect to claims of violation of public policy, which are often raised by disappointed parties but very seldom accepted by the courts. For example, although London is one of the great financial centres of the world where parties often seek enforcement, there is no recorded case of an English court ever rejecting a foreign award on the grounds of public policy ..."

73 See the above Handbook.

74 See *UNCITRAL Secretariat Guide on the Convention on the Recognition and Enforcement of Foreign Arbitral Awards* 2016 at p.126: "The grounds for refusal under article V do not include an erroneous decision in law or in fact by the arbitral tribunal. A court seized with an application for recognition and enforcement under the Convention may not review the merits of the arbitral tribunal's decision. This principle is unanimously confirmed in the case law and commentary on the New York Convention."

75 See para.32-10.

76 See para.32-10.

77 Article V(2)(a).

78 See fn.72.

79 See paras 36-55–36-56.

MEDIATED SETTLEMENT AGREEMENTS

As indicated above,[80] an international commercial dispute may be resolved by direct negotiation between the parties and/or their lawyers before or during the pendency of arbitration proceedings without the intervention of a mediator. This has been the case for many years and indeed remains so. However, the intervention of a mediator has become more prevalent in recent years and it is perceived to have advantages as well as some disadvantages, the latter including potential difficulties over the enforcement of any agreement reached.[81] **36-32**

Various attempts have been made to define "mediation" and the role of a mediator,[82] but for present purposes the definition in the Singapore Convention should be noted: **36-33**

> ""Mediation" means a process, irrespective of the expression used or the basis upon which the process is carried out, whereby parties attempt to reach an amicable settlement of their dispute with the assistance of a third person or persons ("the mediator") lacking the authority to impose a solution upon the parties to the dispute."[83]

The end result of a successful mediation of an international commercial dispute is, in law in most jurisdictions, the same as if no mediator had been involved in the negotiations, namely, the conclusion of a binding contract of settlement of the dispute. Prima facie, and subject to any international Conventions, it will fall to be enforced (or otherwise relied upon) as a contract in whatever jurisdiction may be relevant for the purpose.[84] As previously indicated[85], this can give rise to complex questions about the law and practice to be applied to the process of enforcement and can prove to be an expensive and time-consuming process. If, however, the agreement is embodied in an agreed arbitral award then, subject to the various exemptions set out in the Convention, it may be enforced internationally pursuant to the New York Convention.[86] **36-34**

UNCITRAL had, for a number of years, recognised the utility of what was then called "conciliation" in resolving international commercial disputes and in 1980 had produced the Conciliation Rules and then in 2002 the Model Law on International Commercial Conciliation. With the increasing interest in mediation[87] in this context, proposals for considering "the enforceability of settlement agreements resulting from international commercial conciliation" were initially advanced in 2014 and the consequent work of UNCITRAL eventually came to fruition with the signing by 46 countries of the Singapore Convention on 7 August 2019[88]. The Convention will come into force six months after three countries have ratified, accepted, approved **36-35**

---

80 See para.36-04.

81 For a useful appraisal of where matters stood in 2013, see Thomas Gaultier. "Cross-Border Mediation: A New Solution for International Commercial Dispute Settlement" (2013) 26 *International Law Practicum* 1, Spring 2013, Vol. 26, No.1.

82 See para.35-01.

83 Article 2 para.3.

84 See Chs 2 and 3.

85 See paras 36-16–36-19.

86 See paras 36-29–36-31 and Ch.32. If, unusually, the dispute is being litigated in the courts of a particular jurisdiction, then a mediated settlement agreement may provide for the terms of the agreement to be embodied in an agreed order or judgment of the domestic court which could then be enforced appropriately.

87 Which UNCITRAL equated with conciliation: see UNCITRAL, 47th session, New York, 7–18 July 2014, A/CN.9/822.

88 The 46 countries that signed the Convention on that day were Afghanistan, Belarus, Benin, Brunei Darussalam, Chile, China, Colombia, Congo, Democratic Republic of Congo, Eswatini, Fiji,

or acceded to the Convention.[89] At the time of writing, the extent to which other countries will adopt the Convention remains uncertain, but the text of what follows is written on the basis that increasing numbers of countries will in due course adopt it.[90] Equally, the position of the UK in relation to the EU and the role of the EU Mediation Directive[91] in the future post-Brexit situation is unclear. Some guidance on its present relevance will be given below.[92]

36-36 On the day the Singapore Convention was signed, UNCITRAL stated its objective as follows[93]:

> "... By providing for the first time a cross-border enforcement mechanism for settlement agreements that result from mediation, the Convention brings certainty and stability to the international framework on mediation, thereby promoting more prosperous, stable and sustainable international trade relationships among States and regions. The Convention will undoubtedly enhance the use of mediation and will therefore foster access to justice.
>
> The Singapore Convention on Mediation is complemented by the UNCITRAL Model Law on International Commercial Mediation and International Settlement Agreements resulting from Mediation (2018), which was developed by UNCITRAL in parallel to the Singapore Convention. This provides States with the flexibility in implementing the cross-border enforcement mechanism and achieving a comprehensive legal framework on mediation."

36-37 How are these objectives to be achieved for international commercial disputes?[94] The commitment of each country to adopt the Convention is to "enforce a settlement agreement in accordance with its rules of procedure and under the conditions laid down in this Convention".[95] Each country acts through a "competent authority" which, for this purpose, will be the relevant judicial authority. It is the "competent authority" that will decide whether to grant an application for relief[96] under the Convention. It follows that, as with the New York Convention, for the Convention to achieve its intended purpose the courts called upon to grant the

---

Georgia, Grenada, Haiti, Honduras, India, Iran, Israel, Jamaica, Jordan, Kazakhstan, Laos, Malaysia, Maldives, Mauritius, Montenegro, Nigeria, North Macedonia, Palau, Paraguay, the Philippines, Qatar, Republic of Korea, Samoa, Saudi Arabia, Serbia, Sierra Leone, Singapore, Sri Lanka, Timor-Leste, Turkey, Uganda, Ukraine, United States of America, Uruguay and Venezuela. The UK was not a signatory and neither was any EU country. The up-to-date position can be found at *https://treaties.un.org/pages/ViewDetails.aspx?src=TREATY&mtdsg_no=XXII-4&chapter=22&clang=_en* [Accessed 3 November 2019].

89 Article 14(1).

90 160 countries have adopted the New York Convention to date albeit, in some cases, with reservations. It has taken a good number of years for the total number to rise to the present number.

91 Mediation Directive 2008/52/EC.

92 See paras 36-62–36-66.

93 Press Release issued on 7 August 2019.

94 Unlike the New York Convention, the Singapore Convention contains a definition of what constitutes an "international" dispute (Article 1(1) and Article 2(1)), but does not contain a definition of "commercial". It exempts from its provisions disputes arising from "transactions engaged in by one of the parties (a consumer) for personal, family or household purposes" and "family, inheritance or employment law" issues (art.1(2)).

95 Article 3(1). For a helpful analysis of the meaning of "commercial" in the context of the New York Convention, see A. Redfern and M. Hunter, *The Law and Practice of International Commercial Arbitration*, 6th edn (Oxford: Oxford Univeristy Press, 2015) paras 1.35–1.38.

96 The expression "granting relief" in the Convention is "intended to encompass both the right of a party to seek enforcement and to invoke a settlement agreement" under Article 3 Report of Working Group II (Dispute Settlement) on the work of its 65th session (New York, 6-10 February 2017), A/CN.9/901, para.57. It was said that that "it would be appropriate for the [Convention] to address situations where a party might not be necessarily seeking enforcement of a settlement agreement but instead would be seeking to rely on the settlement agreement as a defence or for other procedural purposes": para.18.

relevant relief will need to be astute to ensure that insubstantial arguments against granting relief do not succeed.[97] When considering an application for relief, "the competent authority shall act expeditiously".[98] The Convention makes clear that it applies only when the settlement agreement has been concluded with the assistance of a mediator[99] and it does not apply to an agreement that has been embodied in an agreed court order or arbitral award or has otherwise been "concluded in the course of proceedings before a court".[100]

The first threshold requirement for a party seeking relief under the Convention is to establish that the settlement agreement[101] "resulted from mediation" by supplying to the competent authority evidence to that effect.[102] This evidence includes[103] the following: **36-38**

"(i) The mediator's signature on the settlement agreement;
(ii) A document signed by the mediator indicating that the mediation was carried out;
(iii) An attestation by the institution that administered the mediation; or
(iv) In the absence of (i), (ii) or (iii), any other evidence acceptable to the competent authority."

These requirements seem relatively straightforward, but go largely to the form in which the evidence is or may be supplied to the competent authority. There will rarely be any dispute about whether a settlement "resulted" from a mediation, but there are occasions when settlement is not achieved at a mediation, but in the weeks or possibly months thereafter. It may prove to be a question of fact and degree as to whether such a settlement "resulted" from the mediation. Provided that the word "resulted" is not interpreted too narrowly and is construed in "a pragmatic, flexible and non-formalistic" way,[104] an issue such as this ought not to trouble a competent authority that adopts a broadly pro-relief approach. **36-39**

Some concern may be felt by mediators about being asked to provide evidential support for the fact that a settlement agreement did result from a mediation, the principal concern being that it might be said to represent an incursion into their obligation of confidentiality. Equally, it is not the practice of all mediators to sign settlement agreements, the rationale largely being that the actual terms of the agreement are a matter for the parties. It is likely that concerns such as these will be overcome by incorporating into the mediation agreement provisions that absolve the mediator from any responsibility beyond meeting the bare requirements of the Convention if a mediation is successful. **36-40**

Plainly, it is (or should be) the desire of all parties to a mediated settlement agreement prima facie covered by the Convention to ensure so far as possible that the agreement will be valid and acceptable for relief purposes in any country where pursuit of relief might be sought in due course. An eye must be kept on possible **36-41**

---

97 cf. para.36-29.
98 Article 4(5).
99 Article 2(3).
100 Article 1(3). That is so even if the agreement was concluded with the assistance of a mediator.
101 Signed by both parties: Article 4(1)(a).
102 Article 4(1)(b). The "signatures" may be in electronic form if a means of authenticating the signature(s) has been agreed: Article 4(2).
103 This is to be deduced from the words "such as" at the commencement of this list, but it would seem that ultimately it is for the "competent authority" to decide what evidence is sufficient if one of (i)-(iii) is not fulfilled. It was apparently intended that the list should be regarded as "open" rather than "closed": A/CN.9/929, para. 58.
104 cf. para.36-29.

avenues for contending that relief should not be given. Those avenues are set out in Article 5.[105] Each will be examined below.

CAPACITY

36-42 It is unlikely that any party to the settlement agreement "was under some incapacity"[106] at the time the agreement was concluded. Any incapacity issues are likely to have been identified before the mediation takes place or before the settlement agreement is concluded. On the assumption that what constitutes incapacity is characterised broadly in the same way as "capacity" is interpreted within the New York Convention, one possible area of concern is in relation to the authority of those representing a corporate or other non-personal legal entity to enter into the settlement agreement and/or where a corporate entity acts beyond the scope of its corporate constitution. Most mediation agreements require the parties attending a mediation to warrant that those present have full authority to enter any agreement concluded and it is likely that the parties (if not the mediator) will raise any concerns about capacity issues at the time. That is why it is thought that this response to an application for relief will arise in a meritorious way extremely rarely.

36-43 However, if any such issue is raised at the stage when relief is sought, the question arises as to the law by which the issue as to capacity is judged. The equivalent provision in the New York Convention[107] provides an exception to enforcement where "[the] parties to the [arbitration agreement] were, under the law applicable to them, under some incapacity".[108] Although the word "parties" is in the plural, this provision has generally been interpreted as being referable to the incapacity of one party. The Singapore Convention is explicit in this respect. In relation to the issue of capacity under the New York Convention, the ICCA Guide[109] says this:

> "The Convention does not indicate how to determine the law applicable to the capacity of a party ("the law applicable to them"). This law must therefore be determined by applying the conflict-of-laws rules of the court where recognition and enforcement are sought, usually the law of the domicile of a physical person and the law of the place of incorporation of a company."

It appears that UNCITRAL intended the same in relation to the question of capacity within the Singapore Convention. The Working Group[110] considered how the law applicable in relation to "defences" in the enforcement procedure should be addressed in the Convention, but concluded that it "raised complex issues, particularly as different laws might be applicable depending on the defences." It was noted that the competent authority "might need to consider the law applicable to the parties

---

105 See Appendix 8.

106 Article V(1)(a).

107 Article V(1)(a).

108 The words "under the law applicable to them" were not incorporated in the Model Law because "they appeared to contain a conflict of laws rule which in fact was either incomplete or misleading in that the rule might be understood as referring to the law of the nationality, domicile or residence of the parties": see *UNCITRAL Yearbook*, Vol. XVI (1985), para.280. The adopted recommendation was to provide for a defence to enforcement where "a party to the arbitration agreement ... was under some incapacity", an issue ordinarily determined by reference to the law of the country where an individual is domiciled or a company is incorporated.

109 See fn.72.

110 *Report of Working Group II (Arbitration and Conciliation) on the work of its 63rd session* (Vienna, 7-11 September 2015), A/CN.9/861, paras 100-102.

(in relation to capacity) ..."[111] and the general approach adopted (in relation to all "defences") was that the Convention "should not address the laws applicable with respect to defences in the enforcement procedure, with the assumption that the enforcing authority or the court seized with the matter would usually apply the conflict-of-law rules at the place of enforcement and where relevant, consideration of the parties' choice of law in the settlement agreement."[112]

Ordinarily, it is submitted that this issue, if it falls to be considered, should be addressed by reference to the law of the country where the relevant party is situated.

The onus of establishing this (or indeed any) "defence" is on the party seeking to rely upon it.[113]

SETTLEMENT AGREEMENT VOID, INOPERATIVE OR INCAPABLE OF PERFORMANCE

Relief may be denied if the party resisting relief demonstrates that the settlement agreement is "null and void, inoperative or incapable of being performed under the law to which the parties have validly subjected it or, failing any indication thereon, under the law deemed applicable by the competent authority ... where relief is sought".[114] This is based upon art.V(1)(a) of the New York Convention which refers to an arbitration agreement being "invalid" by reference to the same considerations as those set out in the Singapore Convention. According to the Working Group on the Singapore Convention, the word "invalid" had been amplified in art.8(1) of the Model Law on Arbitration, which referred to arbitration agreements being deprived of effect when found to be "null and void, inoperative or incapable of being performed". The Working Group suggested that those terms "had been interpreted by courts in a number of jurisdictions in a harmonized fashion and therefore could be used in the [Convention]."[115] To the extent that assistance is required from previous authorities to the interpretation of this provision, it will be found in the reported cases under the equivalent provision of the New York Convention.[116] **36-44**

---

111 *Report of Working Group II (Arbitration and Conciliation) on the work of its 63rd session* (Vienna, 7-11 September 2015), A/CN.9/861, para.100.

112 *Report of Working Group II (Arbitration and Conciliation) on the work of its 63rd session* (Vienna, 7-11 September 2015), A/CN.9/861, para.102.

113 Article 5(1) provides that the "competent authority of the Party to the Convention where relief is sought ... may refuse to grant relief at the request of the party against whom the relief is sought *only if that party furnishes to the competent authority proof*" of the relevant defence. (Emphasis added.)

114 Article 5(1)(b)(i).

115 *Report of Working Group II (Arbitration and Conciliation) on the work of its 63rd session* (Vienna, 7–11 September 2015), para.92.

116 See, e.g., *Redfern and Hunter on International Arbitration*, 6th edn (Oxford: OUP, 2015) paras 11.66–11.70 and *Recognition and Enforcement of Foreign Arbitral Awards—The Interpretation and Application of the New York Convention by National Courts*, G. Bermann (ed.), (Springer 2017), para.3.1. And see *Dallah Real Estate & Tourism Holding Co v Pakistan* [2010] UKSC 46; [2011] 1 A.C. 763.

AGREEMENT NOT FINAL OR BINDING

36-45 If the party resisting relief can establish that the settlement agreement is not final or binding "according to its terms", relief may be denied to the other party.[117] The word "binding" finds expression in the New York Convention where enforcement of an award may be resisted if it "has not yet become binding on the parties".[118] The ICCA Guide[119] says this about that provision:

> "The use of the word "binding" was intended to make it clear that a party was entitled to apply for recognition and enforcement of an award once it was issued by the arbitral tribunal. This meant that this party did not need to obtain *exequatur* or leave to do so from the court of the State in which, or under the law of which, the award was made (known as a double exequatur), as was required under the 1927 Geneva Convention."

It is difficult satisfactorily to equate the use of the word "binding" in the Singapore Convention with its use in the New York Convention. Where there has been a mediated settlement agreement, the inevitable inference is that the parties thereto will regard themselves as "bound" by what they have agreed. It is, of course, always possible that, for example, they agree specifically that the agreement will only become binding upon them on the happening of some further event or upon the action of a third party.[120] If such an agreement was made, it is at least arguable that relief might be declined if that further event or action has not taken place. It appears that this was, at least in part, the reason for the inclusion of the word in the Convention[121] and the expression "according to its terms" might be thought to support this. The difficulty is that the words "binding" and "final" may have differing meanings within different national jurisdictions. Under the law of England and Wales, a settlement agreement may be binding on the parties even if a condition remains to be fulfilled[122] whereas that may not be so under the laws of other jurisdictions.

36-46 The disjunctive word "or" between "binding" and "not final" in the Singapore Convention might be taken as suggesting that the two concepts are distinct although reference to the *travaux preparatoires* can also suggest that in some jurisdictions they are regarded as interchangeable.[123] Whatever implications there may be arising from that, or indeed the phraseology of the Convention, one matter of potential concern in the context of a mediated settlement arises from the fact that not

---

[117] Article 5(1)(b)(ii).

[118] Article V(i)(e). See N. Blackaby et al, *Redfern & Hunter on International Commercial Arbitration*, 6th edn. (Oxford: Oxford University Press, 2015), paras 11.87–11-100.

[119] See para.36-43. See also D. St John Sutton, J. Gill, M. Gearing, *Russell on Arbitration*, 24th edn (London: Sweet & Maxwell, 2015), para. 8-046. "Exequatur" is a private international law concept that means the decision by a court of a particular country authorising the enforcement in that country of a judgement, arbitral award or court settlement given abroad. cf. The definition given by the European Judicial Network in civil and commercial matters. https://ec.europa.eu/civiljustice/glossary/glossary_en.htm#Exequatur [Accessed 3 November 2019].

[120] cf. paras 3-59–3-60.

[121] *Report of Working Group II (Arbitration and Conciliation) on the work of its 64th session* (New York, 1-5 February 2016, A/CN.9/867), para.162: the provision should be retained to "encompass other situations, such as when the settlement agreement contained conditional … obligations". The Working Group returned to this issue (and associated issues) in October 2017 and the report (A/CN.9/929) shows that there was considerable debate about these matters: see para.77-93 of the report. Although not eventually incorporated into the Convention, one suggestion at that time was that "final" should be defined as meaning "that the implementation of the agreement shall not be dependent on a condition that has not yet been achieved, or a specific date that has not yet been reached".

[122] See paras 3-61–3-64.

[123] cf. fn.110.

infrequently parties will agree about a large number of issues, but will leave certain issues outstanding to be resolved, if necessary, at a later stage. Will that be regarded as an agreement that is "not final"? The Convention speaks of "an agreement resulting from mediation ... to resolve a commercial dispute"[124] and there are no added words such as "or relevant part thereof".[125] There are features of the *travaux preparatoires* that suggest that the Working Group was approaching matters on the basis that any settlement agreement should be "a final resolution of the dispute".[126] However, it does not appear that the Working Group regarded the presence in a settlement agreement of a dispute resolution clause as of itself resulting in the agreement not being final and constituting grounds for a defence since "there were existing mechanisms to address those issues".[127]

It is to be hoped that competent authorities will adopt a liberal and purposive attitude to a mediated settlement agreement that expressly "parks" certain issues otherwise the utility of the Convention may be diminished. If a mechanism for resolving those issues is contained in the settlement agreement, there is no reason why the agreement should not be regarded as "final" (and indeed "binding") such that "relief" in relation to the issues actually resolved could be granted even if the mechanism for resolving the other matters has not been invoked at the time the relief is sought. **36-47**

AGREEMENT SUBSEQUENTLY MODIFIED

The purpose of this provision is to ensure that an agreement that has subsequently been modified should not be the subject of relief.[128] In other words, seeking relief in relation to the original form of the agreement which can be shown to have been modified by the parties subsequently is not permitted. In the *travaux préparatoires* it is recorded that "the purpose of the clause was to ensure that only the latest version of the settlement agreement "concluded by the parties" should be enforced".[129] **36-48**

OBLIGATIONS IN THE SETTLEMENT AGREEMENT HAVE BEEN PERFORMED

There can be little controversy about this provision.[130] If the party against whom relief is sought can show that the relevant provision in the settlement agreement has been performed, there is no basis for granting relief. **36-49**

---

124 Article 1(1).

125 Words that were in the initial draft: *Report of Working Group II (Dispute Settlement) on the work of its 65th session* (Vienna, 12–23 September 2016), para.89.

126 *Report of Working Group II (Dispute Settlement) on the work of its 65th session* (Vienna, 12–23 September 2016), para.88, A/CN.9/929, para.84 and A/CN.9/861, para.91.

127 See A/CN.9/896, para.95.

128 Article 5(1)(b)(iii).

129 A/CN.9/929, para.86.

130 Article 5(1)(c)(i).

OBLIGATIONS IN THE SETTLEMENT AGREEMENT ARE NOT CLEAR OR COMPREHENSIBLE

36-50 It is a well-established proposition, certainly in the law and practice applied in England and Wales,[131] that a court needs to determine what it is that a party has agreed to do before deciding whether there has been a breach of that obligation and granting a remedy in respect of the alleged breach. It is, therefore, unsurprising that an agreement that is not clear or comprehensible is not to be regarded as susceptible of relief within the Convention.[132] There was broad support for that proposition within the Working Group, but there were unresolved concerns about how this provision (or other drafts of the provision) would be interpreted in particular jurisdictions.[133]

36-51 Whilst the competent authority in the State where relief is sought will doubtless pay attention to the law of the settlement agreement, it will doubtless also be influenced by the approach of its own law to such issues. It will generally be necessary to balance the need to ensure that a party is not expected to do more than what was clearly undertaken as an obligation in the settlement agreement with the need also to ensure that specious arguments about the interpretation of the agreement do not prevail.

GRANTING RELIEF WOULD BE CONTRARY TO THE TERMS OF THE SETTLEMENT AGREEMENT

36-52 Where it is established that granting relief would be contrary to the terms of the settlement agreement,[134] it would plainly be inappropriate for relief to be granted. An example would be where the obligation sought to be enforced was one that did not arise until some other event took place or some other obligation on the part of the other party had been performed and that neither had occurred.

SUBJECT MATTER OF THE DISPUTE NOT CAPABLE OF SETTLEMENT BY MEDIATION UNDER THE LAW OF THE COUNTRY WHERE RELIEF IS SOUGHT

36-53 This is taken out of the order in which the "defences" appear in Article 5 so that issues concerning the way in which the mediated settlement was arrived at can be addressed at the conclusion.[135] This "defence" is set out in Article 5(2)(b) which provides that the competent authority of the relevant State "may also[136] refuse to grant relief if it finds that[137] ... [the] subject matter of the dispute is not capable of

---

131 See, e.g., *Chitty*, Ch.21.

132 Article 5(1)(c)(ii).

133 See, e.g., A/CN.9/934, para.47-53.

134 Article 5(1)(d). The view of the Working Group was that the phraseology of this provision "was broad enough to encompass situations in which the obligations in a settlement agreement would be conditional or reciprocal, and their non-performance could be justified for a variety of reasons": A/CN.9/934, para.57.

135 See paras 36-57–36-61.

136 And thus in addition to any of the grounds set out previously in art.5.

137 The words "if it finds that" indicate that, according to the Working Group, "this defence could be

settlement by mediation under the law of that" State. This mirrors art.V(2)(a) of the New York Convention and affords a discretionary ground for declining relief in respect of the settlement of a commercial dispute that could not have been settled by mediation in that State.

It is difficult to postulate examples of situations where this might occur in the general commercial field. Any application of this defence will depend on a close analysis of the domestic law of the State concerned. It is thought that States that are in favour of mediated settlements will not be astute to find this "defence" established. **36-54**

PUBLIC POLICY OF THE STATE WHERE RELIEF IS SOUGHT

There is a similar "public policy" defence to that provided in the New York Convention[138] if granting the relief sought would be "contrary to the public policy" of the State where relief is sought. The defence on this basis to enforcement of an arbitral award rarely succeeds[139] and it is thought that a similar response can be anticipated in respect of a mediated settlement agreement. **36-55**

A relatively straightforward example of a situation where this issue might legitimately arise would be an attempt to obtain relief concerning the payment of interest in a State where the payment of interest is prohibited as a result of the application of Shariah law. It is possible that issues of national interest and security might arise.[140] A State might have a particular policy concerning money-laundering which differs from that governing the settlement agreement, but it is thought that this would be an exceptionally rare occurrence. **36-56**

MEDIATOR ISSUES

Where the party resisting relief demonstrates one or other of the following circumstances, the competent authority may refuse relief. Those circumstances are: **36-57**

(i) a serious breach by the mediator of standards applicable to the mediator or the mediation without which breach that party would not have entered into the settlement agreement[141]; or

(ii) a failure by the mediator to disclose to the parties circumstances that raise justifiable doubts as to the mediator's impartiality or independence and such failure to disclose had a material impact or undue influence on a party without which failure that party would not have entered into the settlement agreement.[142]

The first matter to note is that it must be shown in either case that without the **36-58**

considered by the enforcing authority ex officio" (A/CN.9/WG.II/WP.198, para.41), thus reflecting the strict position under the New York Convention. In practice, however, the onus may well be placed on the party resisting relief.

138 See paras 36-24, 36-27 and 36-55–36-56. And see Redfern and Hunter, op cit, paras 11.106–11.122, *Recognition and Enforcement of Foreign Arbitral Awards—The Interpretation and Application of the New York Convention by National Courts*, see fn.116, para.4.27 and *Practitioner's Handbook on International Commercial Arbitration*, 3rd ed., F. Weigand and A. Baumann (eds.), paras 21.489–21.497.

139 See fn.72.

140 A/CN.9/929, para.100.

141 Article 5(1)(e).

142 Article 5(1)(f). Both these matters were the subject of considerable debate within the Working Group:

relevant default on the part of the mediator the party seeking relief would not have entered into the settlement agreement. Any default of the type described plainly would need to have had a material impact upon the entry into the settlement agreement by the party seeking relief. This may prove a significant hurdle. Parties to the kind of dispute with which the Convention is concerned will almost invariably have their lawyers present at the mediation, or otherwise available for consultation, and it will be extremely difficult in those circumstances to suggest that a party would not have entered into a settlement agreement because of some conduct or non-disclosure on the part of the mediator unless some egregious conduct can be demonstrated that had a decisive influence on that party.

36-59 These provisions were initially drafted as providing a defence to an application for relief if "[the] conciliator failed to maintain fair treatment of the parties, or did not disclose circumstances likely to give rise to justifiable doubts as to its impartiality or independence".[143] The route by which the discussions of the Working Group arrived at the final formulation was quite extended[144] and the formulation itself was described in the *travaux préparatoires* as a "compromise proposal".[145] The expression "standards applicable to the mediator or the mediation" is unexplained anywhere else in the Convention and the expectation of the Working Group was as follows:

> "... that [(i) above] would allow the competent authority to determine the standards applicable, which could take different forms such as the law governing conciliation and codes of conduct, including those developed by professional associations."[146]

It is respectfully suggested that this represents a very vague analysis of the situation. That may well have been the view of the Working Group because the next sentence in the same document reads as follows:

> "It was further confirmed that the text accompanying the [Convention] would provide an illustrative list of examples of such standards."

No such list has been provided. Equally, no examples of "circumstances that raise justifiable doubts as to the mediator's impartiality or independence" have been provided.

36-60 As to what constitute "circumstances that raise justifiable doubts as to the mediator's impartiality or independence", that issue is not of itself to be judged by any standards set by a professional organisation or representative institution[147] because the test is set by the words of the provision itself. Doubtless a competent authority would take account of professional standards set by reputable institutions. For example, the European Code of Conduct for Mediators says this:

> **2.1. "Independence**
>
> If there are any circumstances that may, or may be seen to, affect a mediator's independence or give rise to a conflict of interests, the mediator must disclose those circumstances

---

see, e.g., A/CN.9/896, paras 103-109 and 191-194.

143 A/CN.9/WG.II/WP.198, para.35. This was based partly on art.6(3) of the Model Law on Conciliation (2002) which said that "[in] any case, in conducting the proceedings, the conciliator shall seek to maintain fair treatment of the parties and, in so doing, shall take into account the circumstances of the case." That model law said nothing more about the conduct to be expected of a conciliator (now known as a mediator) and reference to "proceedings" would now be regarded as inappropriate.

144 See A/CN.9/901, paras 44-50 and 72-88 and A/CN.9/929, para.96-98.

145 A/CN.9/901, para.52.

146 A/CN.9/929, para.96.

147 For example, the American Bar Association, the Australian Mediation Association, the Centre for Effective Dispute Resolution (in the UK), the Civil Mediation Council (in the UK) or the European Code of Conduct for Mediators.

to the parties before acting or continuing to act.

Such circumstances include:–

- any personal or business relationship with one or more of the parties;
- any financial or other interest, direct or indirect, in the outcome of the mediation;
- the mediator, or a member of his firm, having acted in any capacity other than mediator for one or more of the parties.

In such cases the mediator may only agree to act or continue to act if he is certain of being able to carry out the mediation in full independence in order to ensure complete impartiality and the parties explicitly consent.

The duty to disclose is a continuing obligation throughout the process of mediation.

2.2. Impartiality

Mediators must at all times act, and endeavour to be seen to act, with impartiality towards the parties and be committed to serve all parties equally with respect to the process of mediation."

Whilst there is plainly an obligation on the mediator to ensure that all appropriate disclosure is made of anything that might be construed as a conflict of interest, it will be incumbent on the parties also to reveal anything to each other that might be thought to compromise the mediator's independence. Whilst the provision is, of course, part of the Convention, it is difficult to envisage a situation in which parties to a mediation of an international commercial dispute and the mediator will all have overlooked disclosure of some apparent conflict. A mediator does not, of course, make any decision that binds the parties, unlike an arbitrator, and that will represent one factor that a party who seeks to raise such an issue at the relief stage will have to address when trying to establish the causal link between the alleged failure to disclose and the conclusion of the settlement agreement.

There are few published standards of conduct by a mediator at a mediation other **36-61**
than the obligation of confidentiality and the need to act impartially. There is one area of standard mediator practice that could, if not understood by a competent authority (namely, a court), lead to some unjustified refusals to grant relief. Part of the standard mediation process in a commercial mediation is for the mediator to invite each party to engage in "reality checking". This involves asking pertinent questions about the strengths and weaknesses of each party's stance on the issues at stake. That is almost invariably undertaken in a caucus session (in other words, in the absence of the other party and its representatives). Each mediator will have his or her own style. Most will explain that he/she will not be doing a proper job as a mediator if this process is not pursued, but it can sometimes be uncomfortable for a party to be confronted with some difficult questions. It is not impossible to envisage such a party trying to make something out of such a session to suggest that the mediator was showing bias or was acting in a way that failed to meet "standards applicable to the mediator or the mediation", an expression which, as indicated above, is extremely vague. It is to be hoped that courts are alive to the realities of mediation practice otherwise this could represent a serious problem so far as obtaining relief in respect of a mediated settlement agreement is concerned and would undermine the whole process that the Convention is designed to encourage and support. As emphasised above, it will also have to be borne in mind that mediation is a fundamentally different process from arbitration: unlike an arbitrator a mediator does not make the final decision at the end of the mediation process. It is for the parties to decide whether they wish to resolve their differences and, if so, how they will do so.

THE EUROPEAN MEDIATION DIRECTIVE

36-62 The European Mediation Directive[148] was adopted on 21 May 2008. The ultimate aim of the Directive is to promote the use of mediation and so facilitate better access to justice. The Directive applies to cross-border[149] civil and commercial disputes, with limited exceptions.[150] The Directive imposes a number of requirements intended to achieve its aim. Of these, the requirements imposed by three Articles were considered already satisfied by English law and so required no further implementing legislation.[151] They were art.4 (ensuring the quality of mediation); art.5 (the encouragement of recourse to mediation); and art.9 (the provision of information to the public about how to contact mediators and mediation organisations).

36-63 By art.6, the Directive required that it be possible for the parties (or one of them with the explicit consent of the others) to request that a mediated settlement be made enforceable. This was implemented by the addition of Section III to Pt 78 of the Civil Procedure Rules. In qualifying cases, parties may apply to the Court for an order making the settlement agreement enforceable. The application is made by application notice if the settlement is made in existing proceedings, or by Pt 8 Claim Form if it is not.[152]

36-64 Article 7 provides that mediators and those involved in the administration of mediations may not be compelled to provide evidence about the mediation proceedings unless it is necessary (a) for reasons of public policy, such as to protect a child or (b) in order to implement or enforce the settlement.[153]

36-65 Article 8 provides that parties who attempt to settle a qualifying dispute by mediation should not subsequently be prevented from starting court proceedings as a result of the expiry of a limitation period during the mediation. This has been implemented in English Law by extending the applicable limitation period to a specified time after the mediation ends.[154] In the majority of cases, the extension will be until 8 weeks after the end of the mediation.[155]

36-66 The Directive has attracted a somewhat mixed reception,[156] but little controversy

---

148 Directive 2008/52/EC of the European Parliament and of the Council of 21 May 2008 on certain aspects of mediation in civil and commercial matters.

149 Defined to include cases in which at least one of the parties is domiciled or habitually resident in a Member State other than that of any other party on the date of which mediation is agreed, ordered or required by national law: "art2(1)".

150 Ibid, art1(2).

151 *Explanatory Memorandum to the Cross-Border Mediation (EU Directive) Regulations 2011/1133*, para.4.3.

152 CPR Rule 78.24.

153 These provisions were implemented by the Cross Border Mediation (EU Directive) Regulations 2011/1133, regs 9 and 10. The Regulations will be revoked by the Cross-Border Mediation (EU Directive) (EU Exit) Regulations 2019 (SI 2019/469) when the United Kingdom exits the European Union, if no other arrangements are put in place. The procedure for any application to obtain such evidence is set out in CPR Rules 78.26 to 78.28.

154 Cross Border Mediation (EU Directive) Regulations 2011/1133, Pts 3 and 4. These Regulations are currently due to be revoked by the Cross-Border Mediation (EU Directive) (EU Exit) Regulations 2019 (SI 2019/469) when the United Kingdom exits the European Union, if no other arrangements are put in place.

155 See, for example, Limitation Act 1980 s.33A(3). The circumstances in which a mediation is deemed to "end" are defined at s.33A(7).

156 The confidentiality provisions have been received positively by some. See, for example, Agapiou and Clark, "The Practical Significance of Confidentiality in Mediation" (2018) 37(1) *Civil Justice Quarterly* 74, where the authors suggest that the provisions in art.7 should be extended in English law to purely domestic mediation. Others have been more critical. See, e.g. Derek Roebuck, "Keep-

in England and Wales. The European Parliament appears to consider the Directive a qualified success,[157] albeit accepts that difficulties in obtaining data on mediation make progress difficult to assess and achieve.[158]

"ARB-MED-ARB"

The Singapore Convention was seen as necessary by UNCITRAL because there was no internationally-recognised mechanism for enforcing (or for obtaining relief in relation to) pure mediated settlement agreements—in other words, a settlement agreement arising from a mediation, but which did not then become embodied in an agreed arbitral award. **36-67**

One way to obviate the need to use the Singapore Convention would be for the parties to engage in what is known as the "Arb-Med-Arb" procedure available principally (somewhat ironically) in Singapore. In Singapore there is the Singapore International Mediation Centre (SIMC) and the Singapore International Arbitration Centre (SIAC). These two bodies have collaborated to offer parties to a cross-border dispute an arrangement known as the Arbitration-Mediation-Arbitration service (or, as indicated, more colloquially, the "Arb-Med-Arb" service). It enables the parties to attempt mediation after the commencement of formal arbitration proceedings before a single arbitrator. That arbitrator does nothing more than give a few preliminary directions and refers the matter to the SIMC for mediation. If the mediation succeeds, the mediated settlement is referred back to the single arbitrator who then makes a consent award embodying the agreement. **36-68**

The consent award is valid and enforceable because it does not offend the principle that applies to the New York Convention, namely, that there is no power to make a consent arbitral award when there is no extant dispute or difference between the parties at the time the arbitration begins.[159] In the Arb-Med-Arb scenario there was a genuine dispute at the time when the arbitration began.[160] **36-69**

If the mediation fails, the continuing dispute is referred back to the single arbitrator and the arbitration continues, usually with two more arbitrators appointed, as if nothing had happened. It does not give rise to the complications that can sometimes arise when an arbitrator is asked to perform (or assumes) the role of **36-70**

---

ing an eye on fundamentals" (2012) 78(4) *Arbitration* 375, where it is suggested that the Directive "risks inhibiting natural development" and is "ill thought out". A more limited criticism may be detected in the remarks of Sir Vivian Ramsey in his presentation "Mediation 2020: a presentation to the Chartered Institute of Arbitrators' 4th Annual Mediation Symposium, October 19, 2011" (2012) 78(2) *Arbitration* 159–162, where he points out that 6 pages of Directive generated 23 pages of implementing regulations in the UK. In his view, increased regulation of mediation represented a threat to its flexibility and confidentiality.

157 European Parliament resolution of 12 September 2017 on the implementation of Directive 2008/52/EC of the European Parliament and of the Council of 21 May 2008 on certain aspects of mediation in civil and commercial matters (the "Mediation Directive") (2016/2066(INI)).

158 Ibid., para 6.

159 See para.36-10.

160 SIMC describes the process in this way: "A process where a dispute is referred to arbitration before mediation is attempted. If the parties settle their dispute through mediation, their mediated settlement may be recorded as a consent award. If mediation fails, they may continue with the arbitration proceedings." "A settlement agreement obtained through the Arb-Med-Arb process may be made a consent award. The consent award is accepted as an arbitral award, and, subject to any local legislation and/or requirements, is generally enforceable in 150 countries under the New York Convention. Parties can achieve finality whether through the mediation process or arbitration process."

mediator and vice versa[161] because, unless the parties otherwise agree, the arbitrator(s) and the mediator(s) will generally be different persons.

36-71 Whilst this arrangement is available in Singapore, there is no reason, in principle, why it should not be made elsewhere provided the relevant facilities and personnel (in the form of willing arbitrators and mediators) were available.[162]

---

161 Variously called "Arb-Med" or "Med-Arb" depending on the proposed sequence of events. For cases demonstrating the problems that can arise, see, e.g., *Ku-ring-gai Council v Ichor Constructions Pty Ltd* [2018] NSWSC 610 and *Gao Haiyan v Keeneye Holdings Ltd* [2011] HKCA 459.

162 For example, the Cairo Regional Centre for International Commercial Arbitration offers the arrangement and the rules of the Hong Kong International Arbitration Centre permit it if the parties agree.

TABLE OF CONTENTS

APPENDICES

APPENDIX 1

Precedents

SECTION 1 DRAFT CONSENT ORDERS AND JUDGMENTS—GENERAL

Contents

1 General form of draft consent order

[Title of action]

[BEFORE, etc.] **A1-01**

UPON the parties having agreed terms of settlement

BY CONSENT

IT IS ORDERED/DIRECTED

[SET OUT PRECISE TERMS OF ORDER]

AND IT IS FURTHER ORDERED that the costs of this matter/application are [agreed in the sum of £X] [to be the subject of a detailed assessment if not agreed] and to be paid by the claimant/defendant [or such other agreed order as to costs even if it is that "there shall be no order as to costs"].

[AND IT IS FURTHER ORDERED that the claimant's/defendant's costs shall be the subject of [a]/[an immediate] detailed assessment on the standard basis in accordance with Regulation 107 of the Civil Legal Aid (General) Regulations 1989, as amended, Article 5 of the Access to Justice Act 1999 (Commencement No.3) Order 2000, Article 4 of the Community Legal Services (Funding) Order 2000 and the Civil Legal Aid (General) (Amendment) Regulations 2000].[1]

[AND IT IS FURTHER ORDERED that either party shall have permission to apply][2]

Dated, etc.

Counsel/Solicitor for Claimant	Counsel/Solicitor for Defendant

---

[1] If one or other of the parties is in receipt of assistance from the Legal Services Commission.

[2] If this is appropriate.

2 General form of draft consent judgment for a sum of money

[Title of action]

A1-02 [BEFORE, etc.]

UPON the parties having agreed terms of settlement

BY CONSENT

IT IS ORDERED/DIRECTED/ADJUDGED that the defendant do pay the claimant the sum of £X, inclusive of interest[3] [to be paid within Y days] [to be paid by equal weekly/monthly instalments of £Z, commencing on …, the whole sum to be immediately payable if the defendant should fail to make any one payment].

[continue as in Precedent 1]

3 Tomlin order—general

[Title of case]

A1-03 UPON [hearing Counsel for the parties] [hearing the solicitors for the parties] [reading the letter from the claimant's solicitor and the defendant's solicitor/defendant in person]

AND UPON the parties having agreed terms of settlement

BY CONSENT

IT IS ORDERED that all further proceedings in this [matter/case] be stayed upon the terms set out in the [Schedule to this order] [document entitled "Settlement of Claim No. between [C] and [D]" dated and signed by (counsel for each party) (the solicitors for each party) (the solicitor for C and the defendant in person), the original of which has been retained by (C's solicitors) and a copy of which has been retained by (D's solicitors)(D)][4] except for the purpose of enforcing those terms.

AND IT IS FURTHER ORDERED that either party may be permitted to apply to the court to enforce the terms upon which this [matter/case] has been stayed without the need to bring a new claim.

AND IT IS RECORDED that the parties have agreed that any claim for breach of contract arising from an alleged breach of the terms set out in the [Schedule to this order] [the above-mentioned document] may, unless the Court orders otherwise, be dealt with by way of an application to the Court without the need to start a new claim.[5]

AND IT IS FURTHER ORDERED [set out agreed order as to costs and include any Legal Aid assessment]

Schedule

[set out terms of agreement here unless they are to be recorded on a separate document]

---

3 If the terms of the judgment continue no further than this point, the judgment will be enforceable after 14 days: CPR r.40.11.

4 If the parties wish to keep the terms of their agreement confidential by recording it elsewhere than in a Schedule to the order, which is part of a record that can be made public, then a formula such as that suggested will need to be adopted.

5 This agreement may be necessary if the parties wish to avoid the consequences of the case of *Hollingsworth* (1987) CAT 1244. See paras 9-28 onwards.

SECTION 2 CHANCERY PRECEDENTS

Contents

4 Order for permission to withdraw winding-up petition

[Title of petition]

Winding-up petition presented on ... **A1-04**

UPON the Without Notice Application of ...

AND UPON reading the evidence recorded in the Schedule

AND UPON HEARING ...

AND the Court being satisfied that the petition has not been advertised, that no notices in support of or in opposition to the petition have been received by the Petitioner and that the Company consents to this Order

IT IS ORDERED that the Petitioner have permission to withdraw the said petition and that [insert any further terms of the order]

Schedule

[list the evidence before the court]

5 General form of order dismissing a winding-up petition by consent

[Title of petition]

UPON THE PETITION OF ... a creditor of the above-named Company presented on **A1-05**

AND UPON HEARING Counsel for the Petitioner and for the Company

AND UPON reading the written evidence filed

IT IS BY CONSENT ORDERED

1. That the said Petition do stand dismissed out of this Court.
2. That the Petitioner be restrained, whether by himself or by his servants or agents or otherwise howsoever, from presenting any further petition for the winding-up of the above-named Company based on the sum of £X claimed in the said Petition.
3. That the costs of and occasioned by the said Petition be treated as costs in the cause in any subsequent court proceedings for the recovery of the said sum.

6 General form of order dismissing or giving permission to withdraw a bankruptcy petition

[Title of petition]

A1-06 IN THE MATTER of a bankruptcy petition presented on …
UPON THE APPLICATION of …
AND UPON HEARING …
AND UPON reading the written evidence filed
BY CONSENT
IT IS ORDERED that [this petition be dismissed] [the petitioner has permission to withdraw this petition]
and that [insert any further terms of the order, e.g. as to costs]
AND IT IS ORDERED that the registration of the petition as a pending action at the Land Charges Department of the Land Registry on … under Reference No … be vacated upon the application of the debtor under the Land Charges Rules.
DATED …
NOTICE TO DEBTOR
It is your responsibility, and it is in your interest, to ensure that the registration of the petition as an entry, both in the Land Charges Register and your registered titles, is cancelled.

7 General form of Tomlin order compromising a petition under s.994 of the Companies Act 2006

[Title of petition]

A1-07 UPON THE PETITION OF … presented on …
AND UPON HEARING Counsel for the Petitioner and for the Respondents
AND UPON reading the written evidence filed
AND the Parties having agreed to the terms set out in the attached Schedule.
AND the Petitioner by his Counsel undertaking to apply to dismiss the Petition when the said terms have been fully implemented.
IT IS BY CONSENT ORDERED that all further proceedings herein be stayed upon the terms set out in the said Schedule except for the purpose of carrying such terms into effect and for that purpose the parties have permission to apply.

Schedule

[set out the agreed terms]

8 Order in probate claim involving compromise

[Title of claim]

A1-08 AN APPLICATION by notice dated … was made on … by [Counsel/Solicitor] for … and was attended by …
THE COURT HEARD … for …
THE COURT read the written evidence filed
[Probate of the alleged last will and testament dated … /Letters of administration of the estate] of deceased [was/were] granted on … to …
THE COURT is satisfied that:

(1) consents by or on behalf of every relevant beneficiary (as defined by s.49 of the Administration of Justice Act 1985) have been given to the making of this order; and

(2) this order is for the benefit of the relevant beneficiaries who are children.

THE COURT pronounces for/against the force and validity of the last will and testament of the deceased a completed copy of which is the testamentary document dated ... and marked exhibit ... referred to in the [witness statement/affidavit] of testamentary documents of ... [made/sworn] on ... and against the force and validity of the last will and testament of the deceased a completed copy of which is the testamentary document dated ... and marked exhibit ... referred to in the [witness statement/affidavit] of testamentary documents ... [made/sworn] on ...

IT IS ORDERED that

(1) this claim [and counterclaim] be discontinued.
(2) the probate/letters of administration be revoked.
(3) the terms set out in the Schedule be carried into effect.
(4) [probate of the will] [and codicil(s)] [letters of administration of the estate] of deceased late of [address] be granted to [the claimant/the defendant] named as executor if entitled thereto.
(5) on application for such a grant the caveat numbered and entered on [date], do if still subsisting cease to have effect.
(6) there be assessed if not agreed
    (a) the costs of this claim [and counterclaim] of the claimant/defendant the executor named in the will;
    (b) the costs of this claim [and counterclaim] of the claimant/defendant; and
    (c) the costs of the claimant/defendant for public funding purposes.
(7) the costs specified in 6(a) and (b) above be raised and retained or paid out of the estate of the deceased in the due course of administration.

Schedule

[set out the agreed terms]

9 Agreed order in passing-off action where hearing of interim application treated as application for judgment

[Title of claim]

UPON APPLICATION for an injunction made by Counsel for the Claimant on ... **A1-09**

AND UPON HEARING Counsel for the Defendant

AND UPON reading the written evidence filed

AND the Parties by their respective Counsel

(a) agreeing to the application being treated as an application for judgment and
(b) consenting to this Order

IT IS BY CONSENT ORDERED

1. That the Defendant be restrained (whether by itself, its directors, officers, servants or agents or otherwise howsoever) from using or carrying on business under the name or style of ... or under any name or style which includes the word or so nearly resembles the same as to be calculated to deceive members of the public into or to induce the belief that the business carried on by the Defendant is the same as the business presently carried on by the Claimant or is in any way connected therewith.
2. That the operation of this injunction be suspended until after so as to enable the Defendant to take all necessary steps to change the name of the Defendant company to one not containing the word... .

3. That the Defendant do pay to the Claimant its costs of this action in the agreed sum of £ ..., such costs to be paid on or before... .

SECTION 3 DOCUMENT 1: CNST: PPO CARE AND CASE MANAGEMENT ONLY: FIX ASHE 6115

IN THE HIGH COURT OF JUSTICE

Claim No:

QUEEN'S BENCH DIVISION
BEFORE THE HONOURABLE MR/MRS JUSTICE
BETWEEN

A
(A child/protected party proceeding by his/her Mother/Father and Litigation Friend B)

Claimant

And
C NHS FOUNDATION TRUST

Defendant

ORDER

Before The Honourable Mr/Mrs Justice [..........] sitting in [..........] on [..........] **A1-10**

UPON HEARING [..........] one of Her Majesty's Counsel, on behalf of the Claimant and [..........] one of Her Majesty's Counsel, on behalf of the Defendant

WHEREAS the Claimant has made a claim (the "Claim") against the Defendant for personal injuries suffered by him/her arising out of the Defendant's negligence on or about the [..........] and in respect of which proceedings were commenced by the Claimant against the Defendant in the High Court of Justice Queen's Bench Division on [..........]

AND WHEREAS the Claimant is a Child/Protected Party and brings the Claim by his/her Mother/Father and Litigation Friend, B

AND WHEREAS the National Health Service Litigation Authority ("NHSLA") shall be responsible for and make the payments set out in the Schedule to this Order and for the benefit of the Claimant (referred to below as "periodical payments")

AND WHEREAS the NHSLA has entered into an agreement with the Defendant which permits the NHSLA to be responsible for and make the periodical payments under this Order

AND WHEREAS the NHSLA is a Special Health Authority within the meaning of section 70 of the National Health Service Act 2006

AND WHEREAS the Defendant and the NHSLA agree with the Claimant that in the event of any failure to make the periodical payments or any alteration in the method or change in the identity of the source of payment the same shall give rise to a direct right of the Claimant to enforce the Order and all rights arising under it against the NHSLA in consideration of the Claimant agreeing to the terms of this Order

AND UPON READING the Advice from Counsel for the Claimant dated [..........] and the report of [..........] dated [..........]

AND UPON the Court being satisfied that:

(a) The continuity of payment under the Order is reasonably secure pursuant to section 2(3) of the Damages Act 1996 and/or pursuant to section 2(4)(c) of the Damages Act 1996 and under the terms of the Order as herein set out
(b) The periodical payments are to be paid free of taxation under section 731-734 of the Income Tax (Trading and Other Income) Act 2005
(c) The Order set out below is agreed by the Claimant and the Defendant as being the preferred Order that should apply
(d) The form of the Order is that which best meets the Claimant's needs and CPR 21 and 41 have been complied with

AND UPON the Claimant having given the following undertakings to the Court

1. A Deputy has been appointed for the Claimant [*Alternatively: A Deputy will be appointed within 28 days*]
2. The Claimant whether acting by his/her Litigation Friend or his/her Deputy will take all necessary steps to seek to stay the Claim and any proceedings which have begun or have been threatened against the Defendant in connection with the Claim
3. The Claimant, his/her Litigation Friend and/or his/her Deputy will not institute any proceedings against the Defendant or any other party or person whomsoever in connection with the Claim save by way of enforcement of this Order

[Here insert any further series of undertakings relating to indemnities or otherwise or any reference to additional schedules to be annexed to the order with appropriate numbering]

AND UPON the parties having agreed in full and final settlement of the claim that the Defendant shall pay to the Claimant the sum of [£..........] (..........] inclusive of interim payments of [£..........] (..........) and CRU of [£..........] (..........) and interest to 28 days after the date of the Order approving the agreement together with the periodical payments contained in the Schedule annexed to this Order

AND UPON the Court having approved the terms of this Order and the Schedule annexed to this Order

BY CONSENT

(1) *IT IS ORDERED* that the Defendant shall make payments to or for the benefit of the Claimant as follows in full and final settlement of the claim

(a) By the [..........] of [..........] the Defendant shall pay (having taken into account any interim payments and/or CRU and/or interest to that date) the sum of £ [..........] (..........)

Either in the event of no Deputy being appointed: into Court subject to a first charge pursuant to Section 16(6) of the Legal Aid Act 1988 or Section 10(7) of the Access to Justice Act 1999, which sum shall upon the appointment of a Deputy be transferred immediately to the Court of Protection there to be dealt with as a fund of a protected beneficiary and as that Court in its discretion shall think fit. Pending the transfer the sum paid into court shall be placed in the special investment account standing to the credit of the Claimant

Or in the event of a Deputy being appointed: into the Account of the Deputy (complete details) subject to a first charge pursuant toSection 16(6) of the Legal Aid Act 1988 or Section 10(7) of the Access to Justice Act 1999, which sum shall be there to be dealt with as a fund of a protected beneficiary and as the Deputy in his/her discretion shall think fit

Or alternatively in the event of a Deputy being appointed: into the Court of Protection in the Protection Division into account numbered [details to be inserted] subject to a first charge pursuant to Section 16(6) of the Legal Aid Act 1988 or Section 10(7) of the Access to Justice Act 1999, there to be dealt with as a fund of a protected beneficiary and as that Court in its discretion shall think fit

(b) The Defendant shall pay to the Department of Work and Pensions the CRU benefits amounting to £ [..........] ([..........] pounds and [..........] pence)

(c) By the [..........] of [..........] the Defendant shall pay to the Claimant's solicitors free of any statutory charge the sum of £ [..........] which sum shall include interest thereon to 28 days after the date of this order in respect of damages to be held on trust for the Claimant's parents in respect of gratuitous past care

(d) Further, the sums as specified in the attached Schedule be paid by the Defendant as stipulated in the Schedule and be funded in accordance with section 2(4)(c) of the Damages Act 1996 with the sums payable to comprise damages for future care and case management, such that the NHSLA shall be responsible to the Claimant for and make such payments to the Claimant

(2) *AND IT IS FURTHER ORDERED* that the Defendant do pay the Claimant's costs on the standard basis such costs to be the subject of a detailed assessment, if not agreed

(3) *AND IT IS FURTHER ORDERED* that there be permission to have a detailed assessment of the Claimant's costs in accordance with Regulation 107 of the Civil Legal Aid (General) Regulations 1989 as amended, Article 5 of the Access to Justice Act 1999 (Commencement No.3) Order 2000, Article 4 of the Community Legal Service (Funding) Order 2000 and the Civil Legal Aid (General) (Amendment) Regulations 2000 as amended, save that in the event that the Claimant's solicitors waive any claim to any further costs beyond those referred to above, they have permission to dispense with any Legal Aid Assessment

(4) *AND IT IS FURTHER ORDERED* that all further proceedings in this action be stayed except for the purpose of implementing the terms of this Order and the terms set out in the attached Schedule, for which purpose there be permission to apply to the Claimant, the Defendant and to the NHSLA, and if necessary to add the NHSLA as a party to enforce the terms of this Order

(5) *AND IT IS FURTHER ORDERED* that there be permission to restore

Dated [..........]

Schedule to the Order

Part 1 of the Schedule to the order

Each sum payable under part 2 of this schedule is a "periodical payment" subject to the conditions set out in paragraphs 1–8 of this part

1. Unless specifically stated, all the periodical payments under part 2 of this schedule will continue during the lifetime of the Claimant

2. No minimum number of periodical payments under part 2 of this schedule shall be made

3. Payment of the periodical payments under part 2 of this schedule will cease on the death of the Claimant

4. The final periodical payment under part 2 of this schedule will be pro-rated for so much of the final year that the Claimant had survived and any balance owing to the NHSLA or its successor will be repayable to it out of the Claimant's estate, subject only to deduction by the Claimant's estate of such sums as the Claimant's estate may be liable for in respect of the termination of the employment of any persons employed to care for the Claimant

5. The NHSLA shall be entitled to require the Claimant to produce evidence in a form reasonably satisfactory to the NHSLA that the Claimant remains alive before making any periodical payment

6. The periodical payments under part 2 of this schedule are to be made by BACS to the Court of Protection (or its successor) for the benefit of the Claimant under reference [..........] (where applicable)

7. Under part 2 of this schedule the NHSLA shall provide to the Claimant and/or the Deputy in writing:
7.1 At the time of each periodical payment an explanation of how it has been calculated;
7.2 If reclassification or a change of methodology occurs within the meaning of part 2 of this schedule then when a periodical payment is made or in the event of a deferred periodical payment as soon as practicable following such a reclassification or a change of methodology, the relevant calculation(s) under paragraph 6 and the numerical value of '*AR*' as defined in paragraph 7.1.4 of that part applicable to any current and/or future periodical payment to be made under that part

8. The NHSLA shall pay the relevant annual sums set out in part 2 of this schedule on 15th December of each year, save that:
8.1 If the Office for National Statistics ['*ONS*'] does not publish by 17th November in the relevant year all the relevant data and as a result the NHSLA is unable to perform the relevant calculations under part 2 to recalculate the periodical payment due to the Claimant before 15th December of the relevant year, the NHSLA shall on 15th December of the relevant year make the periodical payment: (a) in the same sum as that paid in the previous year; or (b) in the increased/decreased sum recalculated in accordance with the relevant data for the previous year where in the relevant year the annual sum was due to be increased or decreased or commenced under the relevant sub-paragraph of paragraph 1 of part 2
8.2 Any balancing payment due to the Claimant or the NHSLA shall be made within 28 days after the publication of all the relevant data by the ONS
8.3 The NHSLA shall pay interest at the then applicable Judgment Act rate on any outstanding periodical payment or part of a periodical payment not paid on 15th December in any year from 16th December in that year until full payment is made, except that in the circumstances contemplated in paragraphs 8.1-2 interest due on any balancing payment shall only be payable by the NHSLA from 28 days after publication of all the relevant data until full payment is made

9. For the period from [the date when the future loss period accrues assuming periodical payments relate only to future loss] to [14th December of the relevant year when the periodical payments will commence] to represent the periodical payment under part 2 of this schedule for that period the Defendant do pay the sum of [£..........] (..........) due as the balance of the periodical payment for the above period and that sum shall be paid by 4.00 pm on the [..........]

Part 2: The ASHE 6115-Linked Periodical Payments

1. The following present value annual sums as recalculated in accordance with paragraphs 3-10 shall be paid in advance
1.1 The annual sum of [£..........] (..........) payable on 15th December in each year from [..........] until 15th December [..........] inclusive, with the first such payment to be made on 15th December [..........]
1.2 The annual sum of [£..........] (..........) payable on 15th December in each year

from [..........] until 15th December [..........] inclusive
1.3 The annual sum of [£..........] (..........) payable on 15th December in each year from [..........]

The expiry of one period and the commencement of another period under the above sub-paragraphs constitutes a "step change" under this Schedule

2. The relevant earnings data are the gross hourly pay for "*all*" employees given by the present Standard Occupational Category ['*SOC*'] for (Care assistants and home carers) ['*6115*'] at the relevant percentile shown below (currently in table 26.5a at the tab for "*all*" employees) of the Annual Survey of Hours and Earnings in the United Kingdom ['*ASHE*'] published by the ONS. The original relevant percentiles are:
2.1 [..........] percentile shall be applied to paragraphs [..........] above
2.2 [..........] percentile shall be applied to paragraphs [..........] above

First payment of periodical payments under each step

3. Unless paragraphs 5-10 below apply, the annual periodical payments referred to in paragraph 1 *[1.1 to 1.3]* above shall be recalculated in November prior to payment on 15th December of the same year from November [..........] in accordance with the following formula

$$PP = C \times \frac{NP}{A}$$

3.1 Where
3.1.1 '*PP*' = the amount payable by way of periodical payment in each year being calculated in November and paid on 15th December the first '*PP*' being the payment on 15th December [..........]
3.1.2 '*C*' = the relevant annual sum set out in paragraph 1 *[1.1 to 1.3]* above respectively
3.1.3 '*NP*' = the "*first release*" hourly gross wage rate published by the ONS for the relevant percentile of ASHE SOC 6115 for "*all*" employees for the year in which the calculation is being carried out, the first *NP* being the figure applicable to the year [..........] published in or around October [..........]
3.1.4 '*A*' = the "*revised*" hourly gross wage rate for the relevant percentile of ASHE SOC 6115 for all employees applicable to [..........] and published by the ONS in or around October [..........]. In the event of a correction by the ONS it will be the replacement "*revised*" figure issued by the ONS

Subsequent payment of periodical payments under each step

4. Unless paragraphs 5-10 below apply, the annual periodical payments referred to in paragraph 1 *[1.1 to 1.3]* above shall be recalculated annually in subsequent years in November in each year prior to payment on 15th December of the same year from November [..........] in accordance with the following formula

$$PP = C \times \frac{NP + (NF - OP)}{A}$$

4.1 Where in addition to the definitions previously set out
4.1.1 '*NF*' = the "*revised*" hourly gross wage rate published by the ONS for the relevant percentile of ASHE SOC 6115 for "*all*" employees for the year prior to the year in which the calculation is being carried out, the first *NF* being that applicable to the year [..........] and published in or around October [..........]

4.1.2 'OP' = the "*first release*" hourly gross wage rate published by the ONS for the relevant percentile of ASHE SOC 6115 for "*all*" employees for the year prior to the year in which the calculation is being carried out, the first OP being the figure applicable to the year [..........] published in or around October [..........]

Payments upon reclassification of the SOC or a change of methodology by the ONS

5. Reclassification for the purposes of paragraphs 6-9 below occurs when the ONS publishes for the same year "*revised*" hourly gross wage rates for both:

5.1 the previously applied SOC (for which the "*revised*" wage rate is defined as 'AF' in paragraph 6.1.1 below) and

5.2 for a new SOC (for which the "*revised*" wage rate is defined as 'AR' in paragraph 7.1.4 below) that includes those currently defined as "*home carers*" in ASHE SOC 6115

In that event the new SOC shall be applied

6. The relevant annual sum referable to the sums at paragraph 1 *[1.1 to 1.3]* above following reclassification shall be known as 'CR' and shall be calculated only in the year of reclassification, in accordance with the following formula

$$CR = C \times \frac{AF}{A}$$

6.1 Where in addition to the definitions previously set out

6.1.1 'AF' = the final published "*revised*" hourly gross wage rate for the relevant percentile of the previously applied SOC for "*all*" employees

7. When reclassification occurs the first payment only shall be

$$PPR = \left[CR \times \frac{NPR}{AR} \right] + \left[C \times \frac{AF - OPF}{A} \right]$$

The second bracket of the above formula shall not apply where at the time of reclassification, either (a) there has been no periodical payment made in the previous year or (b) where at that time a step change in the annual sum is due under paragraph 1 above and in those circumstances the first payment shall be calculated in accordance with the following formula

$$PPR = \left[CR \times \frac{NPR}{AR} \right]$$

7.1 Where in addition to the definitions previously set out

7.1.1 'PPR' = the amount payable by way of periodical payment in each year following reclassification

7.1.2 'NPR' = the "*first release*" hourly gross wage rate published for the relevant percentile of the new SOC following reclassification for the year in which the calculation is being carried out

7.1.3 'OPF' = the final "*first release*" hourly gross wage rate published for the relevant percentile of the previously applied SOC for "*all*" employees

7.1.4 'AR' = the "*revised*" hourly gross wage rate for the relevant percentile of the new SOC, when first published, which is closest to AF, and the new percentile of the new SOC shall be the percentile to which AR corresponds

8. Until further reclassification the formula for calculating subsequent values of PPR shall be

$$PPR = CR \times \frac{NPR + (NFR - OPR)}{AR}$$

8.1 Where in addition to the definitions previously set out

8.1.1 *'NFR'* = the "*revised*" hourly gross wage rate published for the relevant percentile of the new SOC following reclassification for the year prior to the year in which the calculation is being carried out

8.1.2 *'OPR'* = the "*first release*" hourly gross wage rate published for the relevant percentile in the new SOC following reclassification for the year prior to the year in which the calculation is being carried out

9. Further reclassifications shall be dealt with in the same way by the application of paragraphs 5-8 above

10. For the purposes of this part a change of methodology occurs when the ONS publishes two sets of data for the applied SOC. In that event, the same process as set out in paragraphs 6-9 above shall be undertaken. However, in these circumstances references to

10.1 '*reclassification*' shall be treated as being a reference to '*a change of methodology*',

10.2 '*the new SOC*' shall be treated as being a reference to '*the existing SOC using the new methodology*', and

10.3 '*the previously applied SOC*' shall be treated as being a reference to '*the existing SOC using the old methodology*'

Miscellaneous

11. In the event of a dispute between the parties arising out of the application of this part, there be liberty to apply

SECTION 4 LANDLORD AND TENANT CASES AND BOUNDARY DISPUTES

Contents

11 Agreed order for possession relating to premises outside any statutory protection

[Title of action]

A1-11 *Use Form N 26 and insert*

UPON hearing counsel/solicitors for the parties

AND UPON the parties having agreed

insert agreed facts that establish the tenancy is not subject to statutory protection eg

(1) the defendant's tenancy was granted on ....;

(2) that the defendant does not have the protection of [the Rent Act 1977, etc]; and

(3) terms of settlement.

[*OR use a schedule to record the admitted facts and agreement]*

AND UPON counsel [or the solicitor] for the defendant expressly admitting the several matters set out in the schedule to this order

BY CONSENT IT IS ORDERED that

1. The defendant give the claimant possession of the land and premises known as and situated at [*set out details*] and mentioned in the Particulars of Claim attached to the claim form in this action.
2. The defendant pay the claim £.......... for the period .... to .... and £.......... per day from .... until possession is given to the claimant.

12 Agreed order for possession relating to residential premises with Housing Act or other statutory protection[6]

[Title of action]

A1-12 *Use Form N 26 and insert*

UPON hearing counsel/solicitors for the parties

AND UPON the parties having agreed and the defendant having expressly admitted by counsel that

insert agreed facts that establish the grounds for possession notwithstanding the statutory protection eg

(1) the defendant's tenancy was granted on ....;

(2) the defendant does not have the protection of [the Rent Act 1977, etc]; and

---

6 See para.29-40 above.

(3) [terms of settlement].

[*OR use a schedule to record the admitted facts and agreement]*

AND UPON counsel [or the solicitor] for the defendant expressly admitting the several matters set out in the schedule to this order

BY CONSENT IT IS ORDERED that

1. The defendant give the claimant possession of the land and premises known as and situated at [*set out details*] and mentioned in the Particulars of Claim attached to the claim form in this action.
2. The defendant pay the claim £.......... for the period .... to .... and £.......... per day from .... until possession is given to the claimant.
3. ....

[Schedule

1. That suitable alternative accommodation will be available to him when the order for possession takes effect, namely [here set out the relevant details of the accommodation available] or [set out in this paragraph the ground or grounds relied upon by the claimant which is or are admitted by the defendant]

2. That it is reasonable for the court to make an order for possession.[7]]

13 Agreed order for new tenancy under Landlord and Tenant Act 1954

[Title of application]

BEFORE District Judge ... **A1-13**

UPON hearing counsel/solicitors for the parties

BY CONSENT

IT IS ORDERED that a new tenancy of the premises described in the schedule to this order be granted to the applicant for the period, at the rent and on the terms set forth in the said schedule.

AND IT IS FURTHER ORDERED that [*insert agreed provision as to costs*]

DATED, etc.

14 Agreed order for possession by reason of forfeiture[8]

[Title of action]

Use Form N 27 and insert **A1-14**

UPON hearing counsel/solicitors for the parties

AND UPON the parties having agreed and the defendants expressly admitting by counsel that

insert agreed facts that establish the grounds for possession notwithstanding the statutory protection eg

(1) the defendant's tenancy was granted on ....;

(2) that the defendant does not have the protection of [the Rent Act 1977, etc]; and

(3) terms of settlement.

[*OR use a schedule to record the admitted facts and agreement]*

AND UPON counsel [or the solicitor] for the defendant having expressly admitted by counsel the several matters set out in the schedule to this order

---

7 This admission is necessary when any of the grounds in Pt II of Sch.2 to the Act are relied upon and admitted: s.7(4).

8 See para.29-53 above.

BY CONSENT IT IS ORDERED that
1. … in accordance with N 27] …
2. …

15 An offer in a boundary dispute

A1-15 Our Client: [name]
Our Client's Property: [address and title number]
Your Client: [name]
Your Client's Property: [address and title number]

Our client proposes a settlement of the current boundary dispute with your client relating to the boundary between their respective properties identified about on the following terms.

1. Our client will abandon his counterclaim for damages if your client will abandon his claim for damages.
2. The true boundary between our respective clients' properties identified above is agreed to be in the location shown on the scale plan enclosed by the red line between points X and Y.
3. Our client will remove or have removed the existing [type] fence erected along with the line shown by a blue line on the plan enclosed within 14 days of the making of the order we suggest below.
4. Our client will have erected at his own expense within 28 days of the making of the order suggested below a sound [type] fence along the line of the true boundary between points X and Y shown as defined above and will maintain the same in good condition so long as he remains the owner of his property adjoining the boundary. We should, of course, emphasise that he cannot impose an obligation on his successors in title to maintain the fence in good condition or at all.
5. The agreement as to the location of the boundary will be submitted to the Land Registry with a request that it be noted on our client's respective registered titles.
6. Notwithstanding in mind the expense to which our client will be exposed in relation to 4 above, we would propose that each party should bear his own costs.
7. If agreement is reached it will be in full and final settlement of all claims between the parties relating to the boundary between their properties including any use made.

If the terms set out above are accepted, we would suggest a consent order in Tomlin form, terms 1 to 4 being incorporated as specific terms of the schedule, a further term of the schedule being that both parties will execute a deed giving effect to the agreement in paragraph 2.

The provision as to there being no order as to costs would appear on the face of the court order. We would suggest that our respective clients personally sign the schedule to the order. If the terms set out above are acceptable, but our suggested consent order is not, please advise us of any alternative proposal so that we can consider the matter.

SECTION 5 ADMINISTRATIVE COURT PROCEEDINGS

Contents

16 Document in support of agreed order

IN THE HIGH COURT OF JUSTICE

NO.

QUEEN'S BENCH DIVISION
ADMINISTRATIVE COURT
IN THE MATTER OF AN APPLICATION FOR JUDICIAL REVIEW
BETWEEN

R
on the application of
AB

Claimant

v
CD

Defendant

1. Subject to the approval of the court, the Claimant and the Defendant jointly seek an order that [set out terms of order sought]. **A1-16**

Either

2. For the reasons set out in paragraph 3 below, each party accepts that the decision of CD cannot stand/the order made by CD cannot stand [or as appropriate] and that the relief sought under paragraph 1 above is the appropriate relief in the circumstances.

3. The reasons why the decision/order of CD cannot stand are agreed by AB and CD to be as follows: [*set out reasons, referring to any authorities or statutes as may be necessary*].

or

AB and CD differ on why the decision/order of CD cannot stand, but do not consider that the time of the Court could properly be utilised in determining which of the competing views is correct. In summary the competing views are as follows: [*set out the situation*].

or

2. AB contends that the decision of CD is unlawful. CD disputes that, but accepts that in the interests of avoiding delay and costs, it is appropriate to reconsider its decision. No third party interests will be materially affected by such reconsideration.

Solicitors for AB | Solicitors for CD

DATED, etc.

APPENDIX 2

Civil Procedure Rules Part 36[1]

Scope of this Part

36.1(1) This Part contains a self-contained procedural code about offers to settle made pursuant to the procedure set out in this Part ("Part 36 offers"). **A2-01**

(2) Section I of this Part contains general rules about Part 36 offers.

(3) Section II of this Part contains rules about offers to settle where the parties have followed the Pre-Action Protocol for Low Value Personal Injury Claims in Road Traffic Accidents ("the RTA Protocol") or the Pre-Action Protocol for Low Value Personal Injury (Employers' Liability and Public Liability) Claims ("the EL/PL Protocol") and have started proceedings under Part 8 in accordance with Practice Direction 8B.

SECTION I

PART 36 OFFERS TO SETTLE

General

Scope of this Section

36.2(1) This Section does not apply to an offer to settle to which Section II of this Part applies. **A2-02**

(2) Nothing in this Section prevents a party making an offer to settle in whatever way that party chooses, but if the offer is not made in accordance with rule 36.5, it will not have the consequences specified in this Section.

(Rule 44.2 requires the court to consider an offer to settle that does not have the costs consequences set out in this Section in deciding what order to make about costs.)

(3) A Part 36 offer may be made in respect of the whole, or part of, or any issue that arises in—

(a) a claim, counterclaim or other additional claim; or

(b) an appeal or cross-appeal from a decision made at a trial.

(Rules 20.2 and 20.3 provide that counterclaims and other additional claims are treated as claims and that references to a claimant or a defendant include a party bringing or defending an additional claim.)

Definitions

36.3 In this Section— **A2-03**

(a) the party who makes an offer is the "offeror";

---

1 NB: The provisions in CPR Pt 36 and PD36A came into force, subject to transitional provisions, on April 6, 2015: see Civil Procedure (Amendment No. 8) Rules 2014 (SI 2014/3299) and the 78th Update, Practice Direction Making Document.

(b) the party to whom an offer is made is the "offeree";
(c) a trial means any trial in a case whether it is a trial of all issues or a trial of liability, quantum or some other issue in the case;
(d) a trial is "in progress" from the time when it starts until the time when judgment is given or handed down;
(e) a case is "decided" when all issues in the case have been determined, whether at one or more trials;
(f) trial judge includes the judge (if any) allocated in advance to conduct a trial; and
(g) the relevant period means—
 (i) in the case of an offer made not less than 21 days before a trial, the period specified under rule 36.5(1)(c) or such longer period as the parties agree;
 (ii) otherwise, the period up to the end of such trial.

Application of Part 36 to appeals

A2-04 **36.4**(1) Except where a Part 36 offer is made in appeal proceedings, it shall have the consequences set out in this Section only in relation to the costs of the proceedings in respect of which it is made, and not in relation to the costs of any appeal from a decision in those proceedings.

(2) Where a Part 36 offer is made in appeal proceedings, references in this Section to a term in the first column below shall be treated, unless the context requires otherwise, as references to the corresponding term in the second column—

Term	Corresponding term
Claim	Appeal
Counterclaim	Cross-appeal
Case	Appeal proceedings
Claimant	Appellant
Defendant	Respondent
Trial	Appeal hearing
Trial judge	Appeal judge

Making Offers

Form and content of a Part 36 offer

A2-05 **36.5**(1) A Part 36 offer must—
(a) be in writing;
(b) make clear that it is made pursuant to Part 36;
(c) specify a period of not less than 21 days within which the defendant will be liable for the claimant's costs in accordance with rule 36.13 or 36.20 if the offer is accepted;
(d) state whether it relates to the whole of the claim or to part of it or to an issue that arises in it and if so to which part or issue; and
(e) state whether it takes into account any counterclaim.

(Rule 36.7 makes provision for when a Part 36 offer is made.)

(2) Paragraph (1)(c) does not apply if the offer is made less than 21 days before the start of a trial.

(3) In appropriate cases, a Part 36 offer must contain such further information

as is required by rule 36.18 (personal injury claims for future pecuniary loss), rule 36.19 (offer to settle a claim for provisional damages), and rule 36.22 (deduction of benefits).

(4) A Part 36 offer which offers to pay or offers to accept a sum of money will be treated as inclusive of all interest until—

(a) the date on which the period specified under rule 36.5(1)(c) expires; or

(b) if rule 36.5(2) applies, a date 21 days after the date the offer was made.

Part 36 offers - defendant's offer

36.6(1) Subject to rules 36.18(3) and 36.19(1), a Part 36 offer by a defendant to pay a sum of money in settlement of a claim must be an offer to pay a single sum of money. **A2-06**

(2) A defendant's offer that includes an offer to pay all or part of the sum at a date later than 14 days following the date of acceptance will not be treated as a Part 36 offer unless the offeree accepts the offer.

Time when a Part 36 offer is made

36.7(1) A Part 36 offer may be made at any time, including before the commencement of proceedings. **A2-07**

(2) A Part 36 offer is made when it is served on the offeree.

(Part 6 provides detailed rules about service of documents.)

Clarifying, Withdrawing and Changing the Terms of Offers

Clarification of a Part 36 offer

36.8(1) The offeree may, within 7 days of a Part 36 offer being made, request the offeror to clarify the offer. **A2-08**

(2) If the offeror does not give the clarification requested under paragraph (1) within 7 days of receiving the request, the offeree may, unless the trial has started, apply for an order that the offeror do so.

(Part 23 contains provisions about making an application to the court.)

(3) If the court makes an order under paragraph (2), it must specify the date when the Part 36 offer is to be treated as having been made.

Withdrawing or changing the terms of a Part 36 offer generally

36.9(1) A Part 36 offer can only be withdrawn, or its terms changed, if the offeree has not previously served notice of acceptance. **A2-09**

(2) The offeror withdraws the offer or changes its terms by serving written notice of the withdrawal or change of terms on the offeree.

(Rule 36.17(7) deals with the costs consequences following judgment of an offer which is withdrawn.)

(3) Subject to rule 36.10, such notice of withdrawal or change of terms takes effect when it is served on the offeree.

(Rule 36.10 makes provision about when permission is required to withdraw or change the terms of an offer before the expiry of the relevant period.)

(4) Subject to paragraph (1), after expiry of the relevant period—

(a) the offeror may withdraw the offer or change its terms without the permission of the court; or

(b) the offer may be automatically withdrawn in accordance with its terms.

(5) Where the offeror changes the terms of a Part 36 offer to make it more advantageous to the offeree—

(a) such improved offer shall be treated, not as the withdrawal of the original offer; but as the making of a new Part 36 offer on the improved terms; and

(b) subject to rule 36.5(2), the period specified under rule 36.5(1)(c) shall be 21 days or such longer period (if any) identified in the written notice referred to in paragraph (2).

Withdrawing or changing the terms of a Part 36 offer before the expiry of the relevant period

A2-10 **36.10**(1) Subject to rule 36.9(1), this rule applies where the offeror serves notice before expiry of the relevant period of withdrawal of the offer or change of its terms to be less advantageous to the offeree.

(2) Where this rule applies—

(a) if the offeree has not served notice of acceptance of the original offer by the expiry of the relevant period, the offeror's notice has effect on the expiry of that period; and

(b) if the offeree serves notice of acceptance of the original offer before the expiry of the relevant period, that acceptance has effect unless the offeror applies to the court for permission to withdraw the offer or to change its terms—

(i) within 7 days of the offeree's notice of acceptance; or

(ii) if earlier, before the first day of trial.

(3) On an application under paragraph (2)(b), the court may give permission for the original offer to be withdrawn or its terms changed if satisfied that there has been a change of circumstances since the making of the original offer and that it is in the interests of justice to give permission.

Accepting Offers

Acceptance of a Part 36 offer

A2-11 **36.11**(1) A Part 36 offer is accepted by serving written notice of acceptance on the offeror.

(2) Subject to paragraphs (3) and (4) and to rule 36.12, a Part 36 offer may be accepted at any time (whether or not the offeree has subsequently made a different offer), unless it has already been withdrawn.

(Rule 21.10 deals with compromise, etc. by or on behalf of a child or protected party.)

(Rules 36.9 and 36.10 deal with withdrawal of Part 36 offers.)

(3) The court's permission is required to accept a Part 36 offer where—

(a) rule 36.15(4) applies;

(b) rule 36.22(3)(b) applies, the relevant period has expired and further deductible amounts have been paid to the claimant since the date of the offer;

(c) an apportionment is required under rule 41.3A; or

(d) a trial is in progress.

(Rule 36.15 deals with offers by some but not all of multiple defendants.)

(Rule 36.22 defines "deductible amounts".)

(Rule 41.3A requires an apportionment in proceedings under the Fatal Accidents Act 1976 and Law Reform (Miscellaneous Provisions) Act 1934.)

(4) Where the court gives permission under paragraph (3), unless all the parties have agreed costs, the court must make an order dealing with costs, and may order that the costs consequences set out in rule 36.13 apply.

Acceptance of a Part 36 offer in a split-trial case

36.12(1) This rule applies in any case where there has been a trial but the case has not been decided within the meaning of rule 36.3. **A2-12**

(2) Any Part 36 offer which relates only to parts of the claim or issues that have already been decided can no longer be accepted.

(3) Subject to paragraph (2) and unless the parties agree, any other Part 36 offer cannot be accepted earlier than 7 clear days after judgment is given or handed down in such trial.

Costs consequences of acceptance of a Part 36 offer

36.13(1) Subject to paragraphs (2) and (4) and to rule 36.20, where a Part 36 offer is accepted within the relevant period the claimant will be entitled to the costs of the proceedings (including their recoverable pre-action costs) up to the date on which notice of acceptance was served on the offeror. **A2-13**

(Rule 36.20 makes provision for the costs consequences of accepting a Part 36 offer in certain personal injury claims where the claim no longer proceeds under the RTA or EL/PL Protocol.)

(2) Where—

(a) a defendant's Part 36 offer relates to part only of the claim; and

(b) at the time of serving notice of acceptance within the relevant period the claimant abandons the balance of the claim,

the claimant will only be entitled to the costs of such part of the claim unless the court orders otherwise.

(3) Except where the recoverable costs are fixed by these Rules, costs under paragraphs (1) and (2) are to be assessed on the standard basis if the amount of costs is not agreed.

(Rule 44.3(2) explains the standard basis for the assessment of costs.)

(Rule 44.9 contains provisions about when a costs order is deemed to have been made and applying for an order under section 194(3) of the Legal Services Act 2007.)

(Part 45 provides for fixed costs in certain classes of case.)

(4) Where—

(a) a Part 36 offer which was made less than 21 days before the start of a trial is accepted; or

(b) a Part 36 offer which relates to the whole of the claim is accepted after expiry of the relevant period; or

(c) subject to paragraph (2), a Part 36 offer which does not relate to the whole of the claim is accepted at any time, the liability for costs must be determined by the court unless the parties have agreed the costs.

(5) Where paragraph (4)(b) applies but the parties cannot agree the liability for costs, the court must, unless it considers it unjust to do so, order that—

(a) the claimant be awarded costs up to the date on which the relevant period expired; and

(b) the offeree do pay the offeror's costs for the period from the date of expiry of the relevant period to the date of acceptance.

(6) In considering whether it would be unjust to make the orders specified in paragraph (5), the court must take into account all the circumstances of the case including the matters listed in rule 36.17(5).

(7) The claimant's costs include any costs incurred in dealing with the defendant's counterclaim if the Part 36 offer states that it takes it into account.

Other effects of acceptance of a Part 36 offer

A2-14 **36.14**(1) If a Part 36 offer is accepted, the claim will be stayed.

(2) In the case of acceptance of a Part 36 offer which relates to the whole claim, the stay will be upon the terms of the offer.

(3) If a Part 36 offer which relates to part only of the claim is accepted, the claim will be stayed as to that part upon the terms of the offer.

(4) If the approval of the court is required before a settlement can be binding, any stay which would otherwise arise on the acceptance of a Part 36 offer will take effect only when that approval has been given.

(5) Any stay arising under this rule will not affect the power of the court—

(a) to enforce the terms of a Part 36 offer; or

(b) to deal with any question of costs (including interest on costs) relating to the proceedings.

(6) Unless the parties agree otherwise in writing, where a Part 36 offer that is or includes an offer to pay or accept a single sum of money is accepted, that sum must be paid to the claimant within 14 days of the date of—

(a) acceptance; or

(b) the order when the court makes an order under rule 41.2 (order for an award of provisional damages) or rule 41.8 (order for an award of periodical payments), unless the court orders otherwise.

(7) If such sum is not paid within 14 days of acceptance of the offer, or such other period as has been agreed, the claimant may enter judgment for the unpaid sum.

(8) Where—

(a) a Part 36 offer (or part of a Part 36 offer) which is not an offer to which paragraph (6) applies is accepted; and

(b) a party alleges that the other party has not honoured the terms of the offer,

that party may apply to enforce the terms of the offer without the need for a new claim.

Acceptance of a Part 36 offer made by one or more, but not all, defendants

A2-15 **36.15**(1) This rule applies where the claimant wishes to accept a Part 36 offer made by one or more, but not all, of a number of defendants.

(2) If the defendants are sued jointly or in the alternative, the claimant may accept the offer if—

(a) the claimant discontinues the claim against those defendants who have not made the offer; and

(b) those defendants give written consent to the acceptance of the offer.

(3) If the claimant alleges that the defendants have a several liability to the claimant, the claimant may—

(a) accept the offer; and

(b) continue with the claims against the other defendants if entitled to do so.

(4) In all other cases the claimant must apply to the court for permission to accept the Part 36 offer.

Unaccepted Offers

Restriction on disclosure of a Part 36 offer

36.16(1) A Part 36 offer will be treated as "without prejudice except as to costs". A2-16

(2) The fact that a Part 36 offer has been made and the terms of such offer must not be communicated to the trial judge until the case has been decided.

(3) Paragraph (2) does not apply—

(a) where the defence of tender before claim has been raised;

(b) where the proceedings have been stayed under rule 36.14 following acceptance of a Part 36 offer;

(c) where the offeror and the offeree agree in writing that it should not apply; or

(d) where, although the case has not been decided—

(i) any part of, or issue in, the case has been decided; and

(ii) the Part 36 offer relates only to parts or issues that have been decided.

(4) In a case to which paragraph (3)(d)(i) applies, the trial judge—

(a) may be told whether or not there are Part 36 offers other than those referred to in paragraph (3)(d)(ii); but

(b) must not be told the terms of any such other offers unless any of paragraphs (3)(a) to (c) applies.

Costs consequences following judgment

36.17(1) Subject to rule 36.21, this rule applies where upon judgment being entered— A2-17

(a) a claimant fails to obtain a judgment more advantageous than a defendant's Part 36 offer; or

(b) judgment against the defendant is at least as advantageous to the claimant as the proposals contained in a claimant's Part 36 offer.

(Rule 36.21 makes provision for the costs consequences following judgment in certain personal injury claims where the claim no longer proceeds under the RTA or EL/PL Protocol.)

(2) For the purposes of paragraph (1), in relation to any money claim or money element of a claim, more advantageous means better in money terms by any amount, however small, and at least as advantageous shall be construed accordingly.

(3) Subject to paragraphs (7) and (8), where paragraph (1)(a) applies, the court must, unless it considers it unjust to do so, order that the defendant is entitled to—

(a) costs (including any recoverable pre-action costs) from the date on which the relevant period expired; and

(b) interest on those costs.

(4) Subject to paragraph (7), where paragraph (1)(b) applies, the court must, unless it considers it unjust to do so, order that the claimant is entitled to—

(a) interest on the whole or part of any sum of money (excluding interest) awarded, at a rate not exceeding 10% above base rate for some or all of the period starting with the date on which the relevant period expired;

(b) costs (including any recoverable pre-action costs) on the indemnity basis from the date on which the relevant period expired;

(c) interest on those costs at a rate not exceeding 10% above base rate; and

(d) provided that the case has been decided and there has not been a previous order under this sub-paragraph, an additional amount, which shall not exceed £75,000, calculated by applying the prescribed percentage set out below to an amount which is—

(i) the sum awarded to the claimant by the court; or

(ii) where there is no monetary award, the sum awarded to the claimant by the court in respect of costs—

Amount awarded by the court	Prescribed percentage
Up to £500,000	10% of the amount awarded
Above £500,000	10% of the first £500,000 and (subject to the limit of £75,000) 5% of any amount above that figure.

(5) In considering whether it would be unjust to make the orders referred to in paragraphs (3) and (4), the court must take into account all the circumstances of the case including—

(a) the terms of any Part 36 offer;

(b) the stage in the proceedings when any Part 36 offer was made, including in particular how long before the trial started the offer was made;

(c) the information available to the parties at the time when the Part 36 offer was made;

(d) the conduct of the parties with regard to the giving of or refusal to give information for the purposes of enabling the offer to be made or evaluated; and

(e) whether the offer was a genuine attempt to settle the proceedings.

(6) Where the court awards interest under this rule and also awards interest on the same sum and for the same period under any other power, the total rate of interest must not exceed 10% above base rate.

(7) Paragraphs (3) and (4) do not apply to a Part 36 offer—

(a) which has been withdrawn;

(b) which has been changed so that its terms are less advantageous to the offeree where the offeree has beaten the less advantageous offer;

(c) made less than 21 days before trial, unless the court has abridged the relevant period.

(8) Paragraph (3) does not apply to a soft tissue injury claim to which rule 36.21 applies.

(Rule 44.2 requires the court to consider an offer to settle that does not have the costs consequences set out in this Section in deciding what order to make about costs.)

Personal Injury Claims

Personal injury claims for future pecuniary loss

A2-18 **36.18**(1) This rule applies to a claim for damages for personal injury which is or includes a claim for future pecuniary loss.

(2) An offer to settle such a claim will not have the consequences set out in this Section unless it is made by way of a Part 36 offer under this rule.

(3) A Part 36 offer to which this rule applies may contain an offer to pay, or an offer to accept—

(a) the whole or part of the damages for future pecuniary loss in the form of—

(i) a lump sum;
(ii) periodical payments; or
(iii) both a lump sum and periodical payments;
(b) the whole or part of any other damages in the form of a lump sum.
(4) A Part 36 offer to which this rule applies—
(a) must state the amount of any offer to pay or to accept the whole or part of any damages in the form of a lump sum;
(b) may state—
(i) what part of the lump sum, if any, relates to damages for future pecuniary loss; and
(ii) what part relates to other damages to be paid or accepted in the form of a lump sum;
(c) must state what part of the offer relates to damages for future pecuniary loss to be paid or accepted in the form of periodical payments and must specify—
(i) the amount and duration of the periodical payments;
(ii) the amount of any payments for substantial capital purchases and when they are to be made; and
(iii) that each amount is to vary by reference to the retail prices index (or to some other named index, or that it is not to vary by reference to any index); and
(d) must state either that any damages which take the form of periodical payments will be funded in a way which ensures that the continuity of payments is reasonably secure in accordance with section 2(4) of the Damages Act 1996 or how such damages are to be paid and how the continuity of their payment is to be secured.

(5) Rule 36.6 applies to the extent that a Part 36 offer by a defendant under this rule includes an offer to pay all or part of any damages in the form of a lump sum.

(6) Where the offeror makes a Part 36 offer to which this rule applies and which offers to pay or to accept damages in the form of both a lump sum and periodical payments, the offeree may only give notice of acceptance of the offer as a whole.

(7) If the offeree accepts a Part 36 offer which includes payment of any part of the damages in the form of periodical payments, the claimant must, within 7 days of the date of acceptance, apply to the court for an order for an award of damages in the form of periodical payments under rule 41.8.

(Practice Direction 41B contains information about periodical payments under the Damages Act 1996.)

Offer to settle a claim for provisional damages

36.19(1) An offeror may make a Part 36 offer in respect of a claim which includes a claim for provisional damages. **A2-19**

(2) Where the offeror does so, the Part 36 offer must specify whether or not the offeror is proposing that the settlement shall include an award of provisional damages.

(3) Where the offeror is offering to agree to the making of an award of provisional damages, the Part 36 offer must also state—
(a) that the sum offered is in satisfaction of the claim for damages on the assumption that the injured person will not develop the disease or suffer the type of deterioration specified in the offer;
(b) that the offer is subject to the condition that the claimant must make any claim for further damages within a limited period; and
(c) what that period is.

(4) Rule 36.6 applies to the extent that a Part 36 offer by a defendant includes an offer to agree to the making of an award of provisional damages.

(5) If the offeree accepts the Part 36 offer, the claimant must, within 7 days of the date of acceptance, apply to the court for an award of provisional damages under rule 41.2.

Costs consequences of acceptance of a Part 36 offer where Section IIIA of Part 45 applies

A2-20 **36.20**(1) This rule applies where a claim no longer continues under the RTA or EL/PL Protocol pursuant to rule 45.29A(1).

(2) Where a Part 36 offer is accepted within the relevant period, the claimant is entitled to the fixed costs in Table 6B, Table 6C or Table 6D in Section IIIA of Part 45 for the stage applicable at the date on which notice of acceptance was served on the offeror.

(3) Where—
- (a) a defendant's Part 36 offer relates to part only of the claim; and
- (b) at the time of serving notice of acceptance within the relevant period the claimant abandons the balance of the claim, the claimant will be entitled to the fixed costs in paragraph (2).

(4) Subject to paragraphs (5), (6) and (7), where a defendant's Part 36 offer is accepted after the relevant period—
- (a) the claimant will be entitled to the fixed costs in Table 6B, Table 6C or Table 6D in Section IIIA of Part 45 for the stage applicable at the date on which the relevant period expired; and
- (b) the claimant will be liable for the defendant's costs for the period from the date of expiry of the relevant period to the date of acceptance.

(5) Subject to paragraphs (6) and (7), where the claimant accepts the defendant's Protocol offer after the date on which the claim leaves the Protocol—
- (a) the claimant will be entitled to the applicable Stage 1 and Stage 2 fixed costs in Table 6 or Table 6A in Section III of Part 45; and
- (b) the claimant will be liable for the defendant's costs from the date on which the Protocol offer is deemed to have been made to the date of acceptance.

(6) In a soft tissue injury claim, if the defendant makes a Part 36 offer before the defendant receives a fixed cost medical report, paragraphs (4) and (5) will only have effect if the claimant accepts the offer more than 21 days after the defendant received the report.

(7) In this rule, fixed cost medical report and soft tissue injury claim have the same meaning as in paragraph 1.1(10A) and (16A) respectively of the RTA Protocol.

(8) For the purposes of this rule a defendant's Protocol offer is either—
- (a) defined in accordance with rules 36.25 and 36.26; or
- (b) if the claim leaves the Protocol before the Court Proceedings Pack Form is sent to the defendant—
  - (i) the last offer made by the defendant before the claim leaves the Protocol; and
  - (ii) deemed to be made on the first business day after the claim leaves the Protocol.

(9) A reference to—
- (a) the "Court Proceedings Pack Form" is a reference to the form used in the Protocol; and

(b) "business day" is a reference to a business day as defined in rule 6.2.

(10) Fixed costs shall be calculated by reference to the amount of the offer which is accepted.

(11) Where the parties do not agree the liability for costs, the court must make an order as to costs.

(12) Where the court makes an order for costs in favour of the defendant—

(a) the court must have regard to; and

(b) the amount of costs ordered must not exceed, the fixed costs in Table 6B, Table 6C or Table 6D in Section IIIA of Part 45 applicable at the date of acceptance, less the fixed costs to which the claimant is entitled under paragraph (4) or (5).

(13) The parties are entitled to disbursements allowed in accordance with rule 45.29I incurred in any period for which costs are payable to them.

Costs consequences following judgment where section IIIA of Part 45 applies

36.21(1) Where a claim no longer continues under the RTA or EL/PL Protocol pursuant to rule 45.29A(1), rule 36.17 applies with the following modifications. **A2-21**

(2) Subject to paragraphs (3), (4) and (5), where an order for costs is made pursuant to rule 36.17(3)—

(a) the claimant will be entitled to the fixed costs in Table 6B, 6C or 6D in Section IIIA of Part 45 for the stage applicable at the date on which the relevant period expired; and

(b) the claimant will be liable for the defendant's costs from the date on which the relevant period expired to the date of judgment.

(3) Subject to paragraphs (4) and (5), where the claimant fails to obtain a judgment more advantageous than the defendant's Protocol offer—

(a) the claimant will be entitled to the applicable Stage 1 and Stage 2 fixed costs in Table 6 or 6A in Section III of Part 45; and

(b) the claimant will be liable for the defendant's costs from the date on which the Protocol offer is deemed to be made to the date of judgment; and

(c) in this rule, the amount of the judgment is less than the Protocol offer where the judgment is less than the offer once deductible amounts identified in the judgment are deducted.

("Deductible amount" is defined in rule 36.22(1)(d).)

(4) In a soft tissue injury claim, if the defendant makes a Part 36 offer or Protocol offer before the defendant receives a fixed cost medical report, paragraphs (2) and (3) will only have effect in respect of costs incurred by either party more than 21 days after the defendant received the report.

(5) In this rule fixed cost medical report and soft tissue injury claim have the same meaning as in paragraph 1.1(10A) and (16A) respectively of the RTA Protocol.

(6) For the purposes of this rule a defendant's Protocol offer is either—

(a) defined in accordance with rules 36.25 and 36.26; or

(b) if the claim leaves the Protocol before the Court Proceedings Pack Form is sent to the defendant—

(i) the last offer made by the defendant before the claim leaves the Protocol; and

(ii) deemed to be made on the first business day after the claim leaves the Protocol.

(7) A reference to—

(a) the "Court Proceedings Pack Form" is a reference to the form used in the Protocol; and

(b) "business day" is a reference to a business day as defined in rule 6.2.

(8) Fixed costs must be calculated by reference to the amount which is awarded.

(9) Where the court makes an order for costs in favour of the defendant—

(a) the court must have regard to; and

(b) the amount of costs ordered shall not exceed, the fixed costs in Table 6B, 6C or 6D in Section IIIA of Part 45 applicable at the date of judgment, less the fixed costs to which the claimant is entitled under paragraph (2) or (3).

(10) The parties are entitled to disbursements allowed in accordance with rule 45.29I incurred in any period for which costs are payable to them.

Deduction of benefits and lump sum payments

A2-22 **36.22**(1) In this rule and rule 36.11—

(a) the 1997 Act means the Social Security (Recovery of Benefits) Act 1997;

(b) the 2008 Regulations means the Social Security (Recovery of Benefits)(Lump Sum Payments) Regulations 2008;

(c) recoverable amount means—

(i) "recoverable benefits" as defined in section 1(4)(c) of the 1997 Act; and

(ii) "recoverable lump sum payments" as defined in regulation 1 of the 2008 Regulations;

(d) deductible amount means—

(i) any benefits by the amount of which damages are to be reduced in accordance with section 8 of, and Schedule 2 to the 1997 Act ("deductible benefits"); and

(ii) any lump sum payment by the amount of which damages are to be reduced in accordance with regulation 12 of the 2008 Regulations ("deductible lump sum payments"); and

(e) certificate—

(i) in relation to recoverable benefits, is construed in accordance with the provisions of the 1997 Act; and

(ii) in relation to recoverable lump sum payments, has the meaning given in section 29 of the 1997 Act, as applied by regulation 2 of, and modified by Schedule 1 to, the 2008 Regulations.

(2) This rule applies where a payment to a claimant following acceptance of a Part 36 offer would be a compensation payment as defined in section 1(4)(b) or 1A(5)(b) of the 1997 Act.

(3) A defendant who makes a Part 36 offer must, where relevant, state either—

(a) that the offer is made without regard to any liability for recoverable amounts; or

(b) that it is intended to include any deductible amounts.

(4) Where paragraph (3)(b) applies, paragraphs (5) to (9) will apply to the Part 3 offer.

(5) Before making the Part 36 offer, the offeror must apply for a certificate.

(6) Subject to paragraph (7), the Part 36 offer must state—

(a) the gross amount of compensation;

(b) the name and amount of any deductible amounts by which the gross amount is reduced; and

(c) the net amount of compensation.

(7) If at the time the offeror makes the Part 36 offer, the offeror has applied for, but has not received, a certificate, the offeror must clarify the offer by stating the matters referred to in paragraph (6)(b) and (c) not more than 7 days after receipt of the certificate.

(8) For the purposes of rule 36.17(1)(a), a claimant fails to recover more than any sum offered (including a lump sum offered under rule 36.6) if the claimant fails upon judgment being entered to recover a sum, once deductible amounts identified in the judgment have been deducted, greater than the net amount stated under paragraph (6)(c).

(Section 15(2) of the 1997 Act provides that the court must specify the compensation payment attributable to each head of damage. Schedule 1 to the 2008 Regulations modifies section 15 of the 1997 Act in relation to lump sum payments and provides that the court must specify the compensation payment attributable to each or any dependant who has received a lump sum payment.)

(9) Where—

(a) further deductible amounts have accrued since the Part 36 offer was made; and

(b) the court gives permission to accept the Part 36 offer,

the court may direct that the amount of the offer payable to the offeree shall be reduced by a sum equivalent to the deductible amounts paid to the claimant since the date of the offer.

(Rule 36.11(3)(b) states that permission is required to accept an offer where the relevant period has expired and further deductible amounts have been paid to the claimant.)

Miscellaneous

Cases in which the offeror's costs have been limited to court fees

36.23(1) This rule applies in any case where the offeror is treated as having filed a costs budget limited to applicable court fees, or is otherwise limited in their recovery of costs to such fees. **A2-23**

(Rule 3.14 provides that a litigant may be treated as having filed a budget limited to court fees for failure to file a budget.)

(2) "Costs" in rules 36.13(5)(b), 36.17(3)(a) and 36.17(4)(b) shall mean—

(a) in respect of those costs subject to any such limitation, 50% of the costs assessed without reference to the limitation; together with

(b) any other recoverable costs.

SECTION II

RTA Protocol and EL/PL Protocol Offers to Settle

Scope of this Section

36.24(1) Where this Section applies, Section I does not apply. **A2-24**

(2) This Section applies to an offer to settle where the parties have followed the RTA Protocol or the EL/PL Protocol and started proceedings under Part 8 in accordance with Practice Direction 8B ("the Stage 3 Procedure").

(3) A reference to the Court Proceedings Pack Form is a reference to the form used in the relevant Protocol.

(4) Nothing in this Section prevents a party making an offer to settle in

whatever way that party chooses, but if the offer is not made in accordance with this Section, it will not have any costs consequences.

Form and content of a Protocol offer

A2-25 **36.25**(1) An offer to settle which is made in accordance with this rule is called a Protocol offer.

(2) A Protocol offer must—

(a) be set out in the Court Proceedings Pack (Part B) Form; and

(b) contain the final total amount of the offers from both parties.

Time when a Protocol offer is made

A2-26 **36.26**(1) The Protocol offer is deemed to be made on the first business day after the Court Proceedings Pack (Part A and Part B) Form is sent to the defendant.

(2) In this Section business day has the same meaning as in rule 6.2.

General provisions

A2-27 **36.27** A Protocol offer—

(a) is treated as exclusive of all interest; and

(b) has the consequences set out in this Section only in relation to the fixed costs of the Stage 3 Procedure as provided for in rule 45.18, and not in relation to the costs of any appeal from the final decision of those proceedings.

Restrictions on the disclosure of a Protocol offer

A2-28 **36.28**(1) The amount of the Protocol offer must not be communicated to the court until the claim is determined.

(2) Any other offer to settle must not be communicated to the court at all.

Costs consequences following judgment

A2-29 **36.29**(1) This rule applies where, on any determination by the court, the claimant obtains judgment against the defendant for an amount of damages that is—

(a) less than or equal to the amount of the defendant's Protocol offer;

(b) more than the defendant's Protocol offer but less than the claimant's Protocol offer; or

(c) equal to or more than the claimant's Protocol offer.

(2) Where paragraph (1)(a) applies, the court must order the claimant to pay—

(a) the fixed costs in rule 45.26; and

(b) interest on those fixed costs from the first business day after the deemed date of the Protocol offer under rule 36.26.

(3) Where paragraph (1)(b) applies, the court must order the defendant to pay the fixed costs in rule 45.20.

(4) Where paragraph (1)(c) applies, the court must order the defendant to pay—

(a) interest on the whole of the damages awarded at a rate not exceeding 10% above base rate for some or all of the period starting with the date specified in rule 36.26;

(b) the fixed costs in rule 45.20;

(c) interest on those fixed costs at a rate not exceeding 10% above base rate; and

(d) an additional amount calculated in accordance with rule 36.17(4)(d).

Deduction of benefits

36.30 For the purposes of rule 36.29(1)(a) the amount of the judgment is less than the Protocol offer where the judgment is less than that offer once deductible amounts identified in the judgment are deducted. **A2-30**

("Deductible amount" is defined in rule 36.22(1)(d).)

PRACTICE DIRECTION 36A—OFFERS TO SETTLE

THIS PRACTICE DIRECTION SUPPLEMENTS CPR PART 36

1. Formalities of Part 36 offers and other notices under this Part

A2-31 **1.1** A Part 36 offer may be made and accepted using Form N242A.

1.2 Where a Part 36 offer, notice of acceptance or notice of withdrawal or change of terms is to be served on a party who is legally represented, the document to be served must be served on the legal representative.

2. Application for permission to withdraw or change the terms of a Part 36 Offer

A2-32 **2.1** Rule 36.10 makes provision as to the circumstances in which the offeror must seek the permission of the court in order to withdraw a Part 36 offer or change its terms to be less advantageous to the offeree before expiry of the relevant period.

2.2 The permission of the court must, unless the parties agree otherwise, be sought—

(1) by making an application under Part 23, which must be dealt with by a judge other than the trial judge;

(2) at a trial or other hearing, provided that it is not to the trial judge.

(Rule 36.3 defines "the trial judge".)

3. Acceptance of a Part 36 offer

A2-33 **3.1** Where a Part 36 offer is accepted in accordance with rule 36.11(1), the notice of acceptance must be served on the offeror and filed with the court where the case is proceeding.

3.2 Where the court's permission is required to accept a Part 36 offer, the permission of the court must, unless the parties agree otherwise, be sought—

(1) by making an application under Part 23, which must be dealt with by a judge other than the trial judge;

(2) at a trial or other hearing, provided that it is not to the trial judge.

(Rule 36.3 defines "the trial judge".)

3.3 Where rule 36.11(3)(b) applies, the application for permission to accept the offer must—

(1) state—

  (a) the net amount offered in the Part 36 offer;

  (b) the deductible amounts that had accrued at the date the offer was made; and

  (c) the deductible amounts that have subsequently accrued; and

(2) be accompanied by a copy of the current certificate.

APPENDIX 3

CPR Part 21—Extract

Compromise etc. by or on behalf of a child or protected party

21.10(1) Where a claim is made— A3-01

(a) by or on behalf of a child or protected party; or

(b) against a child or protected party,

no settlement, compromise or payment (including any voluntary interim payment) and no acceptance of money paid into court shall be valid, so far as it relates to the claim by, on behalf of or against the child or protected party, without the approval of the court.

(2) Where—

(a) before proceedings in which a claim is made by or on behalf of, or against, a child or protected party (whether alone or with any other person) are begun, an agreement is reached for the settlement of the claim; and

(b) the sole purpose of proceedings is to obtain the approval of the court to a settlement or compromise of the claim, the claim must—

(i) be made using the procedure set out in Part 8 (alternative procedure for claims); and

(ii) include a request to the court for approval of the settlement or compromise.

(3) In proceedings to which Section II or Section III of Part 45 applies, the court will not make an order for detailed assessment of the costs payable to the child or protected party but will assess the costs in the manner set out in that Section.

(Rule 46.4 contains provisions about costs where money is payable to a child or protected party.)

CPR PRACTICE DIRECTION 21—EXTRACT

Settlement or compromise by or on behalf of a child or protected party before the issue of proceedings

A3-02 **5.1** Where a claim by or on behalf of a child or protected party has been dealt with by agreement before the issue of proceedings and only the approval of the court to the agreement is sought, the claim must, in addition to containing the details of the claim and satisfying the requirements of rule 21.10(2), include the following—

(1) subject to paragraph 5.3, the terms of the settlement or compromise or have attached to it a draft consent order in Practice Form N292;
(2) details of whether and to what extent the defendant admits liability;
(3) the age and occupation (if any) of the child or protected party;
(4) the litigation friend's approval of the proposed settlement or compromise,
(5) a copy of any financial advice relating to the proposed settlement; and
(6) in a personal injury case arising from an accident—
  (a) details of the circumstances of the accident,
  (b) medical and quantum reports and joint statements material to the opinion required by paragraph 5.2,
  (c) where appropriate, a schedule of any past and future expenses and losses claimed and any other relevant information relating to the personal injury as set out in Practice Direction 16 (statements of case), and
  (d) where considerations of liability are raised—
    (i) any evidence or reports in any criminal proceedings or in an inquest, and
    (ii) details of any prosecution brought.

5.2(1) An opinion on the merits of the settlement or compromise given by counsel or solicitor acting for the child or protected party must, except in very clear cases, be obtained.
(2) A copy of the opinion and, unless the instructions on which it was given are sufficiently set out in it, a copy of the instructions, must be supplied to the court.

5.3 Where in any personal injury case a claim for damages for future pecuniary loss is settled, the provisions in paragraphs 5.4 and 5.5 must in addition be complied with.

5.4 The court must be satisfied that the parties have considered whether the damages should wholly or partly take the form of periodical payments.

5.5 Where the settlement includes provision for periodical payments, the claim must—

(1) set out the terms of the settlement or compromise; or
(2) have attached to it a draft consent order,

which must satisfy the requirements of rules 41.8 and 41.9 as appropriate.

5.6 Applications for the approval of a settlement or compromise will normally be heard by—

(1) a Master or a district judge in proceedings involving a child; and
(2) a Master, designated civil judge or his nominee in proceedings involving a protected party.

(For information about provisional damages claims see Part 41 and Practice Direction 41A.)

Settlement or compromise by or on behalf of a child or protected party after proceedings have been issued

6.1 Where in any personal injury case a claim for damages for future pecuniary loss, by or on behalf of a child or protected party, is dealt with by agreement after proceedings have been issued, an application must be made for the court's approval of the agreement. **A3-03**

6.2 The court must be satisfied that the parties have considered whether the damages should wholly or partly take the form of periodical payments.

6.3 Where the settlement includes provision for periodical payments, an application under paragraph 6.1 must—

(1) set out the terms of the settlement or compromise; or
(2) have attached to it a draft consent order,

which must satisfy the requirements of rules 41.8 and 41.9 as appropriate.

6.4 The court must be supplied with—

(1) an opinion on the merits of the settlement or compromise given by counsel or solicitor acting for the child or protected party, except in very clear cases; and
(2) a copy of any financial advice; and
(3) documentary evidence material to the opinion referred to at paragraph 6.4(1).

6.5 Applications for the approval of a settlement or compromise, except at the trial, will normally be heard by—

(1) a Master or a district judge in proceedings involving a child; and
(2) a Master, designated civil judge or his nominee in proceedings involving a protected party.

Apportionment under the Fatal Accidents Act 1976

7.1 A judgment on or settlement in respect of a claim under the Fatal Accidents Act 1976 must be apportioned between the persons by or on whose behalf the claim has been brought. **A3-04**

7.2 Where a claim is brought on behalf of a dependent child or children, any settlement (including an agreement on a sum to be apportioned to a dependent child under the Fatal Accidents Act 1976) must be approved by the court.

7.3 The money apportioned to any dependent child must be invested on the child's behalf in accordance with rules 21.10 and 21.11 and paragraphs 8 and 9 below.

7.4 In order to approve an apportionment of money to a dependent child, the court will require the following information:

(1) the matters set out in paragraphs 5.1(2) and (3), and
(2) in respect of the deceased—
    (a) where death was caused by an accident, the matters set out in paragraphs 5.1(6)(a), (b) and (c), and

(b) his future loss of earnings, and

(3) the extent and nature of the dependency.

APPENDIX 4

CPR Part 40—Extract

Consent judgments and orders

40.6(1) This rule applies where all the parties agree the terms in which a judgment should be given or an order should be made. **A4-01**

(2) A court officer may enter and seal (...) an agreed judgment or order if—

(a) the judgment or order is listed in paragraph (3);

(b) none of the parties is a litigant in person; and

(c) the approval of the court is not required by these Rules, a practice direction or any enactment before an agreed order can be made.

(3) The judgments and orders referred to in paragraph (2) are—

(a) a judgment or order for—

(i) the payment of an amount of money (including a judgment or order for damages or the value of goods to be decided by the court); or

(ii) the delivery up of goods with or without the option of paying the value of the goods or the agreed value.

(b) an order for—

(i) the dismissal of any proceedings, wholly or in part;

(ii) the stay(...) of proceedings on agreed terms, disposing of the proceedings, whether those terms are recorded in a schedule to the order or elsewhere;

(iii) the stay of enforcement of a judgment, either unconditionally or on condition that the money due under the judgment is paid by instalments specified in the order;

(iv) the setting aside under Part 13 of a default judgment which has not been satisfied;

(v) the payment out of money which has been paid into court;

(vi) the discharge from liability of any party;

(vii) the payment, assessment or waiver of costs, or such other provision for costs as may be agreed.

(4) Rule 40.3 (drawing up and filing of judgments and orders) applies to judgments and orders entered and sealed by a court officer under paragraph (2) as it applies to other judgments and orders.

(5) Where paragraph (2) does not apply, any party may apply for a judgment or order in the terms agreed.

(6) The court may deal with an application under paragraph (5) without a hearing.

(7) Where this rule applies—

(a) the order which is agreed by the parties must be drawn up in the terms agreed;

(b) it must be expressed as being 'By Consent';

(c) it must be signed by the legal representative acting for each of the parties to whom the order relates or, where paragraph (5) applies, by the party if he is a litigant in person.

CPR PRACTICE DIRECTION 23A—EXTRACT

Consent orders

10.1 Rule 40.6 sets out the circumstances where an agreed judgment or order may be entered and sealed. **A4-02**

10.2 Where all parties affected by an order have written to the court consenting to the making of the order a draft of which has been filed with the court, the court will treat the draft as having been signed in accordance with rule 40.6(7).

10.3 Where a consent order is made by a judge, the order must be drawn so that the judge's name and judicial title can be inserted.

10.4 The parties to an application for a consent order must ensure that they provide the court with any material it needs to be satisfied that it is appropriate to make the order. Subject to any rule or practice direction a letter will generally be acceptable for this purpose.

10.5 Where a judgment or order has been agreed in respect of an application or claim where a hearing date has been fixed, the parties must inform the court immediately.

(Note that parties are reminded that under rules 28.4 and 29.5 the case management timetable cannot be varied by written agreement of the parties.)

APPENDIX 5

Guidance as to how the Parties should Assist the Court when Applications for Costs are Made Following Settlement of Claims for Judicial Review—April 2016

When this guidance applies

1. This guidance is applicable where the parties to judicial review have agreed to settle the claim but are unable to agree liability for costs and have submitted that issue for determination by the Court. **A5-01**

2. It applies to all consent orders submitted for approval by the court after 18 April 2016.

3. Previous guidance is withdrawn.

The problem

4. The Court faces a significant number of cases, poorly considered and prepared by the parties, which can consume judicial time far beyond what is proportionate to deciding a costs issue after the parties have settled the case. The judicial and other Court resources applied to these cases must be proportionate to what is at stake. That requires efficiency and co-operation from the parties. At the same time, parties want to have the costs orders resolved fairly and quickly. **A5-02**

How the parties should assist the court before sending in submissions on costs

5. The onus lies on the parties to reach agreement on costs wherever possible, and in advance of asking the Court to resolve the issues, in order to support the overriding objective and ensure that efficient use is made of judicial time. See *M v Croydon* [2012] EWCA Civ 595, paragraphs 75-77. **A5-03**

6. The parties should not make submissions to the Court on costs following a compromise of the proceedings without first seeking to agree the allocation of costs through reasoned negotiation, mindful of the overriding objective to the CPR, the amount of costs actually at stake and the principles set out in *M v Croydon*, paragraphs 59-63. This should give them a clear understanding of the basis upon which they have failed to reach agreement, so as to focus their submissions to the court on the points in dispute.

7. Liability for costs between the parties will depend on the specific facts in each case but the principles are set out in *M v Croydon*, paragraphs 59-63 (annexed at the end of this guidance) and *Tesfay* (2016) EWCA Civ 415.

8. The fair and efficient operation of this Guidance and the Timetable detailed below assume that in the 28 day period between the date of the Court's order and the Defendant's submissions, the parties will have ascertained by communication between themselves who is seeking what costs order and why as well as the basis of any disagreement between them, so that all submissions are then as focused and succinct as possible to assist the Court in speedier decision-making.

9. The procedure timetabled below starts with the Defendant because it is so often said that the Claimant does not know why a costs order in its favour is resisted. However it is to be hoped that only one set of submissions per side will be necessary. The cost correspondence between the parties can be annexed to the submissions. Submissions are expected not to exceed 2 sides of A4 at reasonable font size, in the absence of very good reason.

The terms of consent orders

A5-04 **10.** Following a settlement the terms of consent orders require the approval of the court. Unless there are specific contrary reasons given with the proposed consent order, the court is very unlikely to approve the draft without varying its terms so as to expressly incorporate the provisions of this Guidance.

Timetable

A5-05 **11.** Within 28 days of the service of the order upon the parties, the Defendant may file with the Court, and serve on all other parties, submissions as to what the appropriate order for costs should be.

12. Where the Defendant does not file submissions in accordance with 11 above the Defendant will be ordered to pay the Claimant's costs of the claim on the standard basis and for these to be the subject of detailed assessment if not agreed. However, if the Court considers that such an order would be wrong or unfair in all the circumstances, it shall make such other costs order as it sees fit, or it may require submissions from any party in the case within a specified time, or extend time for the service of the Defendant's submissions.

13. Where submissions are filed and served by the Defendant, the Claimant or any other party may file and serve submissions in reply within 14 days of the service of those submissions.

14. Where no submissions are filed by the Claimant or by any other party in accordance with the above, the Court will make the Order sought by the Defendant. However, if the Court considers that such an order would be wrong or unfair in all the circumstances, it shall make such other costs orders as it sees fit, or it may require submissions from any party in the case within a specified time, or extend time for the service of the Claimant's or other party's submissions.

15. Where submissions are filed by the Claimant or by any other party, the Defendant shall have 7 days in which to file and serve a reply. If the Court thinks it necessary in the interests of justice, it may seek any further submissions from any party. A party may also apply for permission within 14 days of the service of previous submissions to lodge further submissions provided it explains what new point has arisen in those previous submissions to which it needs to reply. A short timetable can be expected for any such submissions.

Content of submissions

16. Submissions should: A5-06
- confirm that the parties have used reasonable endeavours to negotiate a costs settlement;
- identify what issues or reasons prevented the parties agreeing costs liability;
- state the approximate amount of costs likely to be involved in the case;
- clearly identify the extent to which the parties complied with the pre-action
- protocol;
- state the relief the claimant (i) sought in the claim form and (ii) obtained;
- address specifically how the claim and the basis of its settlement fit the principles in *M v Croydon*, and *Tesfay* including the relationship of any step taken by the defendant to the claim.

Documents

17. Submissions should be of a normal print size and should not normally exceed two A4 pages in length unless there is compelling reason to exceed this which is properly explained in the submissions. A5-07

18. Submissions should be accompanied by the pre-action protocol correspondence (where this has not previously been included as part of the documents supporting the claim), the correspondence in which the costs claim is made and defended, along with any other correspondence necessary to demonstrate why the claim was brought in the light of the pre-action protocol correspondence or why the step which led to settlement was not taken until after the claim was issued.

19. Unless advised otherwise, the parties should assume that the Court has the claim form and grounds, the acknowledgment of service and evidence lodged by the parties. Further copies of these should not be provided unless requested by the Court.

APPENDIX 6

Standard form case management order for Early Neutral Evaluation

Upon [reading (state the documents read by the Judge) and on the court's own initiative] [the claimant/defendant's application] [the parties requesting at a Case Management Conference] [the parties joint application] that [insert title and name of Judge] provide an opinion about the likely outcome of the claim [or the issue defined in the appendix]

IT IS ORDERED THAT:

1. The Claimant and Defendant shall exchange position papers by 4pm on [date].
2. The parties shall agree a core bundle of documents for the Judge which shall be filed with the court by 4pm on [date]
3. The parties shall attend before the Judge in private at [time] on [date].
4. The parties estimate the judicial pre-reading to be [x] hours.
5. The Judge shall consider the submissions made by the parties and provide an informal non-binding opinion about the likely outcome of [the claim] [the issue].
6. The opinion shall remain confidential to the parties.
7. The opinion shall be without prejudice to the claim.
8. The court shall not retain any papers filed for the ENE hearing or any record of the opinion provided by the Judge. No non-party shall be entitled to obtain a transcript of the hearing.
9. The Judge shall have no further involvement with this claim or any associated claim.
10. The costs incurred by the ENE shall be costs in the case.

APPENDIX 7

UNCITRAL Model Law on International Commercial Arbitration[1]

1985

With amendments as adopted in 2006

Contents

[1] Reprinted with permission of the UNCITRAL Secretariat.

RESOLUTIONS ADOPTED BY THE GENERAL ASSEMBLY

40/72. Model Law on International Commercial Arbitration of the United Nations Commission on International Trade Law

The General Assembly,

Recognizing the value of arbitration as a method of settling disputes arising in international commercial relations,

Convinced that the establishment of a model law on arbitration that is acceptable to States with different legal, social and economic systems contributes to the development of harmonious international economic relations,

Noting that the Model Law on International Commercial Arbitration[2] was adopted by the United Nations Commission on International Trade Law at its eighteenth session, after due deliberation and extensive consultation with arbitral institutions and individual experts on international commercial arbitration,

Convinced that the Model Law, together with the Convention on the Recognition and Enforcement of Foreign Arbitral Awards[3] and the Arbitration Rules of the United Nations Commission on International Trade Law[4] recommended by the General Assembly in its resolution 31/98 of 15 December 1976, significantly contributes to the establishment of a unified legal framework for the fair and efficient settlement of disputes arising in international commercial relations,

1. *Requests* the Secretary-General to transmit the text of the Model Law on International Commercial Arbitration of the United Nations Commission on International Trade Law, together with the *travaux préparatoires* from the eighteenth session of the Commission, to Governments and to arbitral institutions and other interested bodies, such as chambers of commerce;

2. *Recommends* that all States give due consideration to the Model Law on International Commercial Arbitration, in view of the desirability of uniformity of the law of arbitral procedures and the specific needs of international commercial arbitration practice.

112th plenary meeting
11 December 1985

[ON THE REPORT OF THE SIXTH COMMITTEE (A/61/453)]

61/33. Revised articles of the Model Law on International Commercial Arbitration of the United Nations Commission on International Trade Law, and the recommendation regarding the interpretation of article II, paragraph 2, and article VII, paragraph 1, of the Convention on the Recognition and Enforcement of Foreign Arbitral Awards, done at New York, 10 June 1958

The General Assembly,

Recognizing the value of arbitration as a method of settling disputes arising in the context of international commercial relations,

---

2 *Official Records of the General Assembly, Fortieth Session, Supplement No. 17* (A/40/17), annex I.

3 United Nations, *Treaty Series*, vol. 330, No. 4739, p. 38.

4 United Nations publication, Sales No. E.77.V.6.

Recalling its resolution 40/72 of 11 December 1985 regarding the Model Law on International Commercial Arbitration,[5]

Recognizing the need for provisions in the Model Law to conform to current practices in international trade and modern means of contracting with regard to the form of the arbitration agreement and the granting of interim measures,

Believing that revised articles of the Model Law on the form of the arbitration agreement and interim measures reflecting those current practices will significantly enhance the operation of the Model Law,

Noting that the preparation of the revised articles of the Model Law on the form of the arbitration agreement and interim measures was the subject of due deliberation and extensive consultations with Governments and interested circles and would contribute significantly to the establishment of a harmonized legal framework for a fair and efficient settlement of international commercial disputes,

Believing that, in connection with the modernization of articles of the Model Law, the promotion of a uniform interpretation and application of the Convention on the Recognition and Enforcement of Foreign Arbitral Awards, done at New York, 10 June 1958,[6] is particularly timely,

1. *Expresses its appreciation* to the United Nations Commission on International Trade Law for formulating and adopting the revised articles of its Model Law on International Commercial Arbitration on the form of the arbitration agreement and interim measures, the text of which is contained in annex I to the report of the United Nations Commission on International Trade Law on the work of its thirty-ninth session,[7] and recommends that all States give favourable consideration to the enactment of the revised articles of the Model Law, or the revised Model Law on International Commercial Arbitration of the United Nations Commission on International Trade Law, when they enact or revise their laws, in view of the desirability of uniformity of the law of arbitral procedures and the specific needs of international commercial arbitration practice;

2. *Also expresses its appreciation* to the United Nations Commission on International Trade Law for formulating and adopting the recommendation regarding the interpretation of article II, paragraph 2, and article VII, paragraph 1, of the Convention on the Recognition and Enforcement of Foreign Arbitral Awards, done at New York, 10 June 1958,[2] the text of which is contained in annex II to the report of the United Nations Commission on International Trade Law on the work of its thirty-ninth session;[3]

3. *Requests* the Secretary-General to make all efforts to ensure that the revised articles of the Model Law and the recommendation become generally known and available.

64th plenary meeting
4 December 2006

PART ONE

(United Nations documents A/40/17, annex I and A/61/17, annex I)

(As adopted by the United Nations Commission on International Trade Law on 21 June 1985, and as amended by the United Nations Commission on International Trade Law on 7 July 2006)

---

5 *Official Records of the General Assembly, Fortieth Session, Supplement No. 17* (A/40/17), annex I.

6 United Nations, *Treaty Series*, vol. 330, No. 4739.

7 *Official Records of the General Assembly, Sixty-first Session, Supplement No. 17* (A/61/17).

CHAPTER I.

GENERAL PROVISIONS

Article 1.

Scope of application[8]

(1) This Law applies to international commercial[9] arbitration, subject to any agreement in force between this State and any other State or States.
(2) The provisions of this Law, except articles 8, 9, 17 H, 17 I, 17 J, 35 and 36, apply only if the place of arbitration is in the territory of this State.
(Article 1(2) has been amended by the Commission at its thirty-ninth session, in 2006)
(3) An arbitration is international if:
(a) the parties to an arbitration agreement have, at the time of the conclusion of that agreement, their places of business in different States; or
(b) one of the following places is situated outside the State in which the parties have their places of business:
(i) the place of arbitration if determined in, or pursuant to, the arbitration agreement;
(ii) any place where a substantial part of the obligations of the commercial relationship is to be performed or the place with which the subject-matter of the dispute is most closely connected; or
(c) the parties have expressly agreed that the subject matter of the arbitration agreement relates to more than one country.
(4) For the purposes of paragraph (3) of this article:
(a) if a party has more than one place of business, the place of business is that which has the closest relationship to the arbitration agreement;
(b) if a party does not have a place of business, reference is to be made to his habitual residence.
(5) This Law shall not affect any other law of this State by virtue of which certain disputes may not be submitted to arbitration or may be submitted to arbitration only according to provisions other than those of this Law.

Article 2.

Definitions and rules of interpretation

For the purposes of this Law:
(a) "arbitration" means any arbitration whether or not administered by a permanent arbitral institution;
(b) "arbitral tribunal" means a sole arbitrator or a panel of arbitrators;
(c) "court" means a body or organ of the judicial system of a State;
(d) where a provision of this Law, except article 28, leaves the parties free to

---

8 Article headings are for reference purposes only and are not to be used for purposes of interpretation.
9 The term "commercial" should be given a wide interpretation so as to cover matters arising from all relationships of a commercial nature, whether contractual or not. Relationships of a commercial nature include, but are not limited to, the following transactions: any trade transaction for the supply or exchange of goods or services; distribution agreement; commercial representation or agency; factoring; leasing; construction of works; consulting; engineering; licensing; investment; financing; banking; insurance; exploitation agreement or concession; joint venture and other forms of industrial or business cooperation; carriage of goods or passengers by air, sea, rail or road.

determine a certain issue, such freedom includes the right of the parties to authorize a third party, including an institution, to make that determination;

(e) where a provision of this Law refers to the fact that the parties have agreed or that they may agree or in any other way refers to an agreement of the parties, such agreement includes any arbitration rules referred to in that agreement;

(f) where a provision of this Law, other than in articles 25(a) and 32(2) (a), refers to a claim, it also applies to a counter-claim, and where it refers to a defence, it also applies to a defence to such counter-claim.

Article 2 A.

International origin and general principles

(As adopted by the Commission at its thirty-ninth session, in 2006)

(1) In the interpretation of this Law, regard is to be had to its international origin and to the need to promote uniformity in its application and the observance of good faith.

(2) Questions concerning matters governed by this Law which are not expressly settled in it are to be settled in conformity with the general principles on which this Law is based.

Article 3.

Receipt of written communications

(1) Unless otherwise agreed by the parties:

(a) any written communication is deemed to have been received if it is delivered to the addressee personally or if it is delivered at his place of business, habitual residence or mailing address; if none of these can be found after making a reasonable inquiry, a written communication is deemed to have been received if it is sent to the addressee's last-known place of business, habitual residence or mailing address by registered letter or any other means which provides a record of the attempt to deliver it;

(b) the communication is deemed to have been received on the day it is so delivered.

(2) The provisions of this article do not apply to communications in court proceedings.

Article 4.

Waiver of right to object

A party who knows that any provision of this Law from which the parties may derogate or any requirement under the arbitration agreement has not been complied with and yet proceeds with the arbitration without stating his objection to such non-compliance without undue delay or, if a time-limit is provided therefor, within such period of time, shall be deemed to have waived his right to object.

Article 5.

Extent of court intervention

In matters governed by this Law, no court shall intervene except where so provided in this Law.

Article 6.

Court or other authority for certain functions of arbitration assistance and supervision

The functions referred to in articles 11(3), 11(4), 13(3), 14, 16(3) and 34(2) shall be performed by ... [Each State enacting this model law specifies the court, courts or, where referred to therein, other authority competent to perform these functions.]

CHAPTER II.

ARBITRATION AGREEMENT

Option I

Article 7.

Definition and form of arbitration agreement

(As adopted by the Commission at its thirty-ninth session, in 2006)

(1) "Arbitration agreement" is an agreement by the parties to submit to arbitration all or certain disputes which have arisen or which may arise between them in respect of a defined legal relationship, whether contractual or not. An arbitration agreement may be in the form of an arbitration clause in a contract or in the form of a separate agreement.

(2) The arbitration agreement shall be in writing.

(3) An arbitration agreement is in writing if its content is recorded in any form, whether or not the arbitration agreement or contract has been concluded orally, by conduct, or by other means.

(4) The requirement that an arbitration agreement be in writing is met by an electronic communication if the information contained therein is accessible so as to be useable for subsequent reference; "electronic communication" means any communication that the parties make by means of data messages; "data message" means information generated, sent, received or stored by electronic, magnetic, optical or similar means, including, but not limited to, electronic data interchange (EDI), electronic mail, telegram, telex or telecopy.

(5) Furthermore, an arbitration agreement is in writing if it is contained in an exchange of statements of claim and defence in which the existence of an agreement is alleged by one party and not denied by the other.

(6) The reference in a contract to any document containing an arbitration clause constitutes an arbitration agreement in writing, provided that the reference is such as to make that clause part of the contract.

Option II

Article 7.

Definition of arbitration agreement

(As adopted by the Commission at its thirty-ninth session, in 2006)

"Arbitration agreement" is an agreement by the parties to submit to arbitration all or certain disputes which have arisen or which may arise between them in respect of a defined legal relationship, whether contractual or not.

Article 8.

Arbitration agreement and substantive claim before court

(1) A court before which an action is brought in a matter which is the subject of an arbitration agreement shall, if a party so requests not later than when submitting his first statement on the substance of the dispute, refer the parties to arbitration unless it finds that the agreement is null and void, inoperative or incapable of being performed.

(2) Where an action referred to in paragraph (1) of this article has been brought, arbitral proceedings may nevertheless be commenced or continued, and an award may be made, while the issue is pending before the court.

Article 9.

Arbitration agreement and interim measures by court

It is not incompatible with an arbitration agreement for a party to request, before or during arbitral proceedings, from a court an interim measure of protection and for a court to grant such measure.

CHAPTER III.

COMPOSITION OF ARBITRAL TRIBUNAL

Article 10.

Number of arbitrators

(1) The parties are free to determine the number of arbitrators.

(2) Failing such determination, the number of arbitrators shall be three.

Article 11.

Appointment of arbitrators

(1) No person shall be precluded by reason of his nationality from acting as an arbitrator, unless otherwise agreed by the parties.

(2) The parties are free to agree on a procedure of appointing the arbitrator or arbitrators, subject to the provisions of paragraphs (4) and (5) of this article.

(3) Failing such agreement,

(a) in an arbitration with three arbitrators, each party shall appoint one arbitrator, and the two arbitrators thus appointed shall appoint the third arbitrator; if a party fails to appoint the arbitrator within thirty days of receipt of a request to do so from the other party, or if the two arbitrators fail to agree on the third arbitrator within thirty days of their appointment, the appointment shall be made, upon request of a party, by the court or other authority specified in article 6;

(b) in an arbitration with a sole arbitrator, if the parties are unable to agree on the arbitrator, he shall be appointed, upon request of a party, by the court or other authority specified in article 6.

(4) Where, under an appointment procedure agreed upon by the parties,

(a) a party fails to act as required under such procedure, or

(b) the parties, or two arbitrators, are unable to reach an agreement expected of them under such procedure, or

(c) a third party, including an institution, fails to perform any function entrusted to it under such procedure,

any party may request the court or other authority specified in article 6 to take the necessary measure, unless the agreement on the appointment procedure provides other means for securing the appointment.

(5) A decision on a matter entrusted by paragraph (3) or (4) of this article to the court or other authority specified in article 6 shall be subject to no appeal. The court or other authority, in appointing an arbitrator, shall have due regard to any qualifications required of the arbitrator by the agreement of the parties and to such considerations as are likely to secure the appointment of an independent and impartial arbitrator and, in the case of a sole or third arbitrator, shall take into account as well the advisability of appointing an arbitrator of a nationality other than those of the parties.

Article 12.

Grounds for challenge

(1) When a person is approached in connection with his possible appointment as an arbitrator, he shall disclose any circumstances likely to give rise to justifiable doubts as to his impartiality or independence. An arbitrator, from the time of his appointment and throughout the arbitral proceedings, shall without delay disclose any such circumstances to the parties unless they have already been informed of them by him.

(2) An arbitrator may be challenged only if circumstances exist that give rise to justifiable doubts as to his impartiality or independence, or if he does not possess qualifications agreed to by the parties. A party may challenge an arbitrator appointed by him, or in whose appointment he has participated, only for reasons of which he becomes aware after the appointment has been made.

Article 13.

Challenge procedure

(1) The parties are free to agree on a procedure for challenging an arbitrator, subject to the provisions of paragraph (3) of this article.

(2) Failing such agreement, a party who intends to challenge an arbitrator shall, within fifteen days after becoming aware of the constitution of the arbitral tribunal or after becoming aware of any circumstance referred to in article 12(2), send a written statement of the reasons for the challenge to the arbitral tribunal. Unless the challenged arbitrator withdraws from his office or the other party agrees to the challenge, the arbitral tribunal shall decide on the challenge.

(3) If a challenge under any procedure agreed upon by the parties or under the procedure of paragraph (2) of this article is not successful, the challenging party may request, within thirty days after having received notice of the decision rejecting the challenge, the court or other authority specified in article 6 to decide on the challenge, which decision shall be subject to no appeal; while such a request is pending, the arbitral tribunal, including the challenged arbitrator, may continue the arbitral proceedings and make an award.

Article 14.

Failure or impossibility to act

(1) If an arbitrator becomes *de jure* or *de facto* unable to perform his functions or for other reasons fails to act without undue delay, his mandate terminates if he withdraws from his office or if the parties agree on the termination. Otherwise, if a controversy remains concerning any of these grounds, any party may request the court or other authority specified in article 6 to decide on the termination of the mandate, which decision shall be subject to no appeal.
(2) If, under this article or article 13(2), an arbitrator withdraws from his office or a party agrees to the termination of the mandate of an arbitrator, this does not imply acceptance of the validity of any ground referred to in this article or article 12(2).

Article 15.

Appointment of substitute arbitrator

Where the mandate of an arbitrator terminates under article 13 or 14 or because of his withdrawal from office for any other reason or because of the revocation of his mandate by agreement of the parties or in any other case of termination of his mandate, a substitute arbitrator shall be appointed according to the rules that were applicable to the appointment of the arbitrator being replaced.

CHAPTER IV.

JURISDICTION OF ARBITRAL TRIBUNAL

Article 16.

Competence of arbitral tribunal to rule on its jurisdiction

(1) The arbitral tribunal may rule on its own jurisdiction, including any objections with respect to the existence or validity of the arbitration agreement. For that purpose, an arbitration clause which forms part of a contract shall be treated as an agreement independent of the other terms of the contract. A decision by the arbitral tribunal that the contract is null and void shall not entail *ipso jure* the invalidity of the arbitration clause.
(2) A plea that the arbitral tribunal does not have jurisdiction shall be raised not later than the submission of the statement of defence. A party is not precluded from raising such a plea by the fact that he has appointed, or participated in the appointment of, an arbitrator. A plea that the arbitral tribunal is exceeding the scope of its authority shall be raised as soon as the matter alleged to be beyond the scope of its authority is raised during the arbitral proceedings. The arbitral tribunal may, in either case, admit a later plea if it considers the delay justified.
(3) The arbitral tribunal may rule on a plea referred to in paragraph (2) of this article either as a preliminary question or in an award on the merits. If the arbitral

tribunal rules as a preliminary question that it has jurisdiction, any party may request, within thirty days after having received notice of that ruling, the court specified in article 6 to decide the matter, which decision shall be subject to no appeal; while such a request is pending, the arbitral tribunal may continue the arbitral proceedings and make an award.

CHAPTER IV A.

INTERIM MEASURES AND PRELIMINARY ORDERS

(As adopted by the Commission at its thirty-ninth session, in 2006)

SECTION 1.

Interim measures

Article 17.

Power of arbitral tribunal to order interim measures

(1) Unless otherwise agreed by the parties, the arbitral tribunal may, at the request of a party, grant interim measures.
(2) An interim measure is any temporary measure, whether in the form of an award or in another form, by which, at any time prior to the issuance of the award by which the dispute is finally decided, the arbitral tribunal orders a party to:

- (a) Maintain or restore the status quo pending determination of the dispute;
- (b) Take action that would prevent, or refrain from taking action that is likely to cause, current or imminent harm or prejudice to the arbitral process itself;
- (c) Provide a means of preserving assets out of which a subsequent award may be satisfied; or
- (d) Preserve evidence that may be relevant and material to the resolution of the dispute.

Article 17 A.

Conditions for granting interim measures

(1) The party requesting an interim measure under article 17(2)(a), (b) and (c) shall satisfy the arbitral tribunal that:

- (a) Harm not adequately reparable by an award of damages is likely to result if the measure is not ordered, and such harm substantially outweighs the harm that is likely to result to the party against whom the measure is directed if the measure is granted; and
- (b) There is a reasonable possibility that the requesting party will succeed on the merits of the claim. The determination on this possibility shall not affect the discretion of the arbitral tribunal in making any subsequent determination.

(2) With regard to a request for an interim measure under article 17(2)(d), the requirements in paragraphs (1)(a) and (b) of this article shall apply only to the extent the arbitral tribunal considers appropriate.

SECTION 2.

Preliminary orders

Article 17 B.

Applications for preliminary orders and conditions for granting preliminary orders

(1) Unless otherwise agreed by the parties, a party may, without notice to any other party, make a request for an interim measure together with an application for a preliminary order directing a party not to frustrate the purpose of the interim measure requested.
(2) The arbitral tribunal may grant a preliminary order provided it considers that prior disclosure of the request for the interim measure to the party against whom it is directed risks frustrating the purpose of the measure.
(3) The conditions defined under article 17A apply to any preliminary order, provided that the harm to be assessed under article 17A(1)(a), is the harm likely to result from the order being granted or not.

Article 17 C.

Specific regime for preliminary orders

(1) Immediately after the arbitral tribunal has made a determination in respect of an application for a preliminary order, the arbitral tribunal shall give notice to all parties of the request for the interim measure, the application for the preliminary order, the preliminary order, if any, and all other communications, including by indicating the content of any oral communication, between any party and the arbitral tribunal in relation thereto.
(2) At the same time, the arbitral tribunal shall give an opportunity to any party against whom a preliminary order is directed to present its case at the earliest practicable time.
(3) The arbitral tribunal shall decide promptly on any objection to the preliminary order.
(4) A preliminary order shall expire after twenty days from the date on which it was issued by the arbitral tribunal. However, the arbitral tribunal may issue an interim measure adopting or modifying the preliminary order, after the party against whom the preliminary order is directed has been given notice and an opportunity to present its case.

(5) A preliminary order shall be binding on the parties but shall not be subject to enforcement by a court. Such a preliminary order does not constitute an award.

SECTION 3.

Provisions applicable to interim measures and preliminary orders

Article 17 D.

Modification, suspension, termination

The arbitral tribunal may modify, suspend or terminate an interim measure or a preliminary order it has granted, upon application of any party or, in exceptional circumstances and upon prior notice to the parties, on the arbitral tribunal's own initiative.

Article 17 E.

Provision of security

(1) The arbitral tribunal may require the party requesting an interim measure to provide appropriate security in connection with the measure.
(2) The arbitral tribunal shall require the party applying for a preliminary order to provide security in connection with the order unless the arbitral tribunal considers it inappropriate or unnecessary to do so.

Article 17 F.

Disclosure

(1) The arbitral tribunal may require any party promptly to disclose any material change in the circumstances on the basis of which the measure was requested or granted.
(2) The party applying for a preliminary order shall disclose to the arbitral tribunal all circumstances that are likely to be relevant to the arbitral tribunal's determination whether to grant or maintain the order, and such obligation shall continue until the party against whom the order has been requested has had an opportunity to present its case. Thereafter, paragraph (1) of this article shall apply.

Article 17 G.

Costs and damages

The party requesting an interim measure or applying for a preliminary order shall be liable for any costs and damages caused by the measure or the order to any party if the arbitral tribunal later determines that, in the circumstances, the measure or the order should not have been granted. The arbitral tribunal may award such costs and damages at any point during the proceedings.

SECTION 4.

Recognition and enforcement of interim measures

Article 17 H.

Recognition and enforcement

(1) An interim measure issued by an arbitral tribunal shall be recognized as binding and, unless otherwise provided by the arbitral tribunal, enforced upon application to the competent court, irrespective of the country in which it was issued, subject to the provisions of article 17 I.
(2) The party who is seeking or has obtained recognition or enforcement of an interim measure shall promptly inform the court of any termination, suspension or modification of that interim measure.
(3) The court of the State where recognition or enforcement is sought may, if it considers it proper, order the requesting party to provide appropriate security if the arbitral tribunal has not already made a determination with respect to security or where such a decision is necessary to protect the rights of third parties.

Article 17 I.

Grounds for refusing recognition or enforcement[10]

(1) Recognition or enforcement of an interim measure may be refused only:
- (a) At the request of the party against whom it is invoked if the court is satisfied that:
  - (i) Such refusal is warranted on the grounds set forth in article 36(1)(a)(i), (ii), (iii) or (iv); or
  - (ii) The arbitral tribunal's decision with respect to the provision of security in connection with the interim measure issued by the arbitral tribunal has not been complied with; or
  - (iii) The interim measure has been terminated or suspended by the arbitral tribunal or, where so empowered, by the court of the State in which the arbitration takes place or under the law of which that interim measure was granted; or
- (b) If the court finds that:
  - (i) The interim measure is incompatible with the powers conferred upon the court unless the court decides to reformulate the interim measure to the extent necessary to adapt it to its own powers and procedures for the purposes of enforcing that interim measure and without modifying its substance; or
  - (ii) Any of the grounds set forth in article 36(1)(b)(i) or (ii), apply to the recognition and enforcement of the interim measure.

(2) Any determination made by the court on any ground in paragraph (1) of this article shall be effective only for the purposes of the application to recognize and

---

10 The conditions set forth in article 17 I are intended to limit the number of circumstances in which the court may refuse to enforce an interim measure. It would not be contrary to the level of harmonization sought to be achieved by these model provisions if a State were to adopt fewer circumstances in which enforcement may be refused.

enforce the interim measure. The court where recognition or enforcement is sought shall not, in making that determination, undertake a review of the substance of the interim measure.

SECTION 5.

Court-ordered interim measures

Article 17 J.

Court-ordered interim measures

A court shall have the same power of issuing an interim measure in relation to arbitration proceedings, irrespective of whether their place is in the territory of this State, as it has in relation to proceedings in courts. The court shall exercise such power in accordance with its own procedures in consideration of the specific features of international arbitration.

CHAPTER V.

CONDUCT OF ARBITRAL PROCEEDINGS

Article 18.

Equal treatment of parties

The parties shall be treated with equality and each party shall be given a full opportunity of presenting his case.

Article 19.

Determination of rules of procedure

(1) Subject to the provisions of this Law, the parties are free to agree on the procedure to be followed by the arbitral tribunal in conducting the proceedings.
(2) Failing such agreement, the arbitral tribunal may, subject to the provisions of this Law, conduct the arbitration in such manner as it considers appropriate. The power conferred upon the arbitral tribunal includes the power to determine the admissibility, relevance, materiality and weight of any evidence.

Article 20.

Place of arbitration

(1) The parties are free to agree on the place of arbitration. Failing such agreement, the place of arbitration shall be determined by the arbitral tribunal having regard to the circumstances of the case, including the convenience of the parties.
(2) Notwithstanding the provisions of paragraph (1) of this article, the arbitral tribunal may, unless otherwise agreed by the parties, meet at any place it considers appropriate for consultation among its members, for hearing witnesses, experts or the parties, or for inspection of goods, other property or documents.

Article 21.

Commencement of arbitral proceedings

Unless otherwise agreed by the parties, the arbitral proceedings in respect of a particular dispute commence on the date on which a request for that dispute to be referred to arbitration is received by the respondent.

Article 22.

Language

(1) The parties are free to agree on the language or languages to be used in the arbitral proceedings. Failing such agreement, the arbitral tribunal shall determine the language or languages to be used in the proceedings. This agreement or determination, unless otherwise specified therein, shall apply to any written statement by a party, any hearing and any award, decision or other communication by the arbitral tribunal.
(2) The arbitral tribunal may order that any documentary evidence shall be accompanied by a translation into the language or languages agreed upon by the parties or determined by the arbitral tribunal.

Article 23.

Statements of claim and defence

(1) Within the period of time agreed by the parties or determined by the arbitral tribunal, the claimant shall state the facts supporting his claim, the points at issue and the relief or remedy sought, and the respondent shall state his defence in respect of these particulars, unless the parties have otherwise agreed as to the required elements of such statements. The parties may submit with their statements all documents they consider to be relevant or may add a reference to the documents or other evidence they will submit.
(2) Unless otherwise agreed by the parties, either party may amend or supplement his claim or defence during the course of the arbitral proceedings, unless the arbitral tribunal considers it inappropriate to allow such amendment having regard to the delay in making it.

Article 24.

Hearings and written proceedings

(1) Subject to any contrary agreement by the parties, the arbitral tribunal shall decide whether to hold oral hearings for the presentation of evidence or for oral argument, or whether the proceedings shall be conducted on the basis of documents and other materials. However, unless the parties have agreed that no hearings shall be held, the arbitral tribunal shall hold such hearings at an appropriate stage of the proceedings, if so requested by a party.
(2) The parties shall be given sufficient advance notice of any hearing and of any meeting of the arbitral tribunal for the purposes of inspection of goods, other property or documents.
(3) All statements, documents or other information supplied to the arbitral tribunal by one party shall be communicated to the other party. Also any expert report or

evidentiary document on which the arbitral tribunal may rely in making its decision shall be communicated to the parties.

Article 25.

Default of a party

Unless otherwise agreed by the parties, if, without showing sufficient cause,
(a) the claimant fails to communicate his statement of claim in accordance with article 23(1), the arbitral tribunal shall terminate the proceedings;
(b) the respondent fails to communicate his statement of defence in accordance with article 23(1), the arbitral tribunal shall continue the proceedings without treating such failure in itself as an admission of the claimant's allegations;
(c) any party fails to appear at a hearing or to produce documentary evidence, the arbitral tribunal may continue the proceedings and make the award on the evidence before it.

Article 26.

Expert appointed by arbitral tribunal

(1) Unless otherwise agreed by the parties, the arbitral tribunal
(a) may appoint one or more experts to report to it on specific issues to be determined by the arbitral tribunal;
(b) may require a party to give the expert any relevant information or to produce, or to provide access to, any relevant documents, goods or other property for his inspection.

(2) Unless otherwise agreed by the parties, if a party so requests or if the arbitral tribunal considers it necessary, the expert shall, after delivery of his written or oral report, participate in a hearing where the parties have the opportunity to put questions to him and to present expert witnesses in order to testify on the points at issue.

Article 27.

Court assistance in taking evidence

The arbitral tribunal or a party with the approval of the arbitral tribunal may request from a competent court of this State assistance in taking evidence. The court may execute the request within its competence and according to its rules on taking evidence.

CHAPTER VI.

MAKING OF AWARD AND TERMINATION OF PROCEEDINGS

Article 28.

Rules applicable to substance of dispute

(1) The arbitral tribunal shall decide the dispute in accordance with such rules of law as are chosen by the parties as applicable to the substance of the dispute. Any designation of the law or legal system of a given State shall be construed, unless otherwise expressed, as directly referring to the substantive law of that State and not to its conflict of laws rules.

(2) Failing any designation by the parties, the arbitral tribunal shall apply the law determined by the conflict of laws rules which it considers applicable.
(3) The arbitral tribunal shall decide *ex aequo et bono* or as *amiable compositeur* only if the parties have expressly authorized it to do so.
(4) In all cases, the arbitral tribunal shall decide in accordance with the terms of the contract and shall take into account the usages of the trade applicable to the transaction.

Article 29.

Decision-making by panel of arbitrators

In arbitral proceedings with more than one arbitrator, any decision of the arbitral tribunal shall be made, unless otherwise agreed by the parties, by a majority of all its members. However, questions of procedure may be decided by a presiding arbitrator, if so authorized by the parties or all members of the arbitral tribunal.

Article 30.

Settlement

(1) If, during arbitral proceedings, the parties settle the dispute, the arbitral tribunal shall terminate the proceedings and, if requested by the parties and not objected to by the arbitral tribunal, record the settlement in the form of an arbitral award on agreed terms.
(2) An award on agreed terms shall be made in accordance with the provisions of article 31 and shall state that it is an award. Such an award has the same status and effect as any other award on the merits of the case.

Article 31.

Form and contents of award

(1) The award shall be made in writing and shall be signed by the arbitrator or arbitrators. In arbitral proceedings with more than one arbitrator, the signatures of the majority of all members of the arbitral tribunal shall suffice, provided that the reason for any omitted signature is stated.
(2) The award shall state the reasons upon which it is based, unless the parties have agreed that no reasons are to be given or the award is an award on agreed terms under article 30.
(3) The award shall state its date and the place of arbitration as determined in accordance with article 20(1). The award shall be deemed to have been made at that place.
(4) After the award is made, a copy signed by the arbitrators in accordance with paragraph (1) of this article shall be delivered to each party.

Article 32.

Termination of proceedings

(1) The arbitral proceedings are terminated by the final award or by an order of the arbitral tribunal in accordance with paragraph (2) of this article.
(2) The arbitral tribunal shall issue an order for the termination of the arbitral proceedings when:

(a) the claimant withdraws his claim, unless the respondent objects thereto and the arbitral tribunal recognizes a legitimate interest on his part in obtaining a final settlement of the dispute;
(b) the parties agree on the termination of the proceedings;
(c) the arbitral tribunal finds that the continuation of the proceedings has for any other reason become unnecessary or impossible.

(3) The mandate of the arbitral tribunal terminates with the termination of the arbitral proceedings, subject to the provisions of articles 33 and 34(4).

Article 33.

Correction and interpretation of award; additional award

(1) Within thirty days of receipt of the award, unless another period of time has been agreed upon by the parties:
(a) a party, with notice to the other party, may request the arbitral tribunal to correct in the award any errors in computation, any clerical or typographical errors or any errors of similar nature;
(b) if so agreed by the parties, a party, with notice to the other party, may request the arbitral tribunal to give an interpretation of a specific point or part of the award.

If the arbitral tribunal considers the request to be justified, it shall make the correction or give the interpretation within thirty days of receipt of the request. The interpretation shall form part of the award.

(2) The arbitral tribunal may correct any error of the type referred to in paragraph (1)(a) of this article on its own initiative within thirty days of the date of the award.

(3) Unless otherwise agreed by the parties, a party, with notice to the other party, may request, within thirty days of receipt of the award, the arbitral tribunal to make an additional award as to claims presented in the arbitral proceedings but omitted from the award. If the arbitral tribunal considers the request to be justified, it shall make the additional award within sixty days.

(4) The arbitral tribunal may extend, if necessary, the period of time within which it shall make a correction, interpretation or an additional award under paragraph (1) or (3) of this article.

(5) The provisions of article 31 shall apply to a correction or interpretation of the award or to an additional award.

CHAPTER VII.

RECOURSE AGAINST AWARD

Article 34.

Application for setting aside as exclusive recourse against arbitral award

(1) Recourse to a court against an arbitral award may be made only by an application for setting aside in accordance with paragraphs (2) and (3) of this article.

(2) An arbitral award may be set aside by the court specified in article 6 only if:
(a) the party making the application furnishes proof that:
(i) a party to the arbitration agreement referred to in article 7 was under some incapacity; or the said agreement is not valid under the law to which the parties have subjected it or, failing any indication thereon, under the law of this State; or

(ii) the party making the application was not given proper notice of the appointment of an arbitrator or of the arbitral proceedings or was otherwise unable to present his case; or

(iii) the award deals with a dispute not contemplated by or not falling within the terms of the submission to arbitration, or contains decisions on matters beyond the scope of the submission to arbitration, provided that, if the decisions on matters submitted to arbitration can be separated from those not so submitted, only that part of the award which contains decisions on matters not submitted to arbitration may be set aside; or

(iv) the composition of the arbitral tribunal or the arbitral procedure was not in accordance with the agreement of the parties, unless such agreement was in conflict with a provision of this Law from which the parties cannot derogate, or, failing such agreement, was not in accordance with this Law; or

(b) the court finds that:

(i) the subject-matter of the dispute is not capable of settlement by arbitration under the law of this State; or

(ii) the award is in conflict with the public policy of this State.

(3) An application for setting aside may not be made after three months have elapsed from the date on which the party making that application had received the award or, if a request had been made under article 33, from the date on which that request had been disposed of by the arbitral tribunal.

(4) The court, when asked to set aside an award, may, where appropriate and so requested by a party, suspend the setting aside proceedings for a period of time determined by it in order to give the arbitral tribunal an opportunity to resume the arbitral proceedings or to take such other action as in the arbitral tribunal's opinion will eliminate the grounds for setting aside.

CHAPTER VIII.

RECOGNITION AND ENFORCEMENT OF AWARDS

Article 35.

Recognition and enforcement

(1) An arbitral award, irrespective of the country in which it was made, shall be recognized as binding and, upon application in writing to the competent court, shall be enforced subject to the provisions of this article and of article 36.

(2) The party relying on an award or applying for its enforcement shall supply the original award or a copy thereof. If the award is not made in an official language of this State, the court may request the party to supply a translation thereof into such language.[11]

(Article 35(2) has been amended by the Commission at its thirty-ninth session, in 2006)

---

[11] The conditions set forth in this paragraph are intended to set maximum standards. It would, thus, not be contrary to the harmonization to be achieved by the model law if a State retained even less onerous conditions.

Article 36.

Grounds for refusing recognition or enforcement

(1) Recognition or enforcement of an arbitral award, irrespective of the country in which it was made, may be refused only:

(a) at the request of the party against whom it is invoked, if that party furnishes to the competent court where recognition or enforcement is sought proof that:

(i) a party to the arbitration agreement referred to in article 7 was under some incapacity; or the said agreement is not valid under the law to which the parties have subjected it or, failing any indication thereon, under the law of the country where the award was made; or

(ii) the party against whom the award is invoked was not given proper notice of the appointment of an arbitrator or of the arbitral proceedings or was otherwise unable to present his case; or

(iii) the award deals with a dispute not contemplated by or not falling within the terms of the submission to arbitration, or it contains decisions on matters beyond the scope of the submission to arbitration, provided that, if the decisions on matters submitted to arbitration can be separated from those not so submitted, that part of the award which contains decisions on matters submitted to arbitration may be recognized and enforced; or

(iv) the composition of the arbitral tribunal or the arbitral procedure was not in accordance with the agreement of the parties or, failing such agreement, was not in accordance with the law of the country where the arbitration took place; or

(v) the award has not yet become binding on the parties or has been set aside or suspended by a court of the country in which, or under the law of which, that award was made; or

(b) if the court finds that:

(i) the subject-matter of the dispute is not capable of settlement by arbitration under the law of this State; or

(ii) the recognition or enforcement of the award would be contrary to the public policy of this State.

(2) If an application for setting aside or suspension of an award has been made to a court referred to in paragraph (1)(a)(v) of this article, the court where recognition or enforcement is sought may, if it considers it proper, adjourn its decision and may also, on the application of the party claiming recognition or enforcement of the award, order the other party to provide appropriate security.

PART TWO

EXPLANATORY NOTE BY THE UNCITRAL SECRETARIAT ON THE 1985 MODEL LAW ON INTERNATIONAL COMMERCIAL ARBITRATION AS AMENDED IN 2006[12]

1. The UNCITRAL Model Law on International Commercial Arbitration ("the Model Law") was adopted by the United Nations Commission on International Trade Law (UNCITRAL) on 21 June 1985, at the end of the eighteenth session of the Commission. The General Assembly, in its resolution 40/72 of 11 December 1985, recommended "that all States give due consideration to the Model Law on International Commercial Arbitration, in view of the desirability of uniformity of the law of arbitral procedures and the specific needs of international commercial arbitration practice". The Model Law was amended by UNCITRAL on 7 July 2006, at the thirty-ninth session of the Commission (see below, paragraphs 4, 19, 20, 27, 29 and 53). The General Assembly, in its resolution 61/33 of 4 December 2006, recommended "that all States give favourable consideration to the enactment of the revised articles of the UNCITRAL Model Law on International Commercial Arbitration, or the revised UNCITRAL Model Law on International Commercial Arbitration, when they enact or revise their laws (...)".

2. The Model Law constitutes a sound basis for the desired harmonization and improvement of national laws. It covers all stages of the arbitral process from the arbitration agreement to the recognition and enforcement of the arbitral award and reflects a worldwide consensus on the principles and important issues of international arbitration practice. It is acceptable to States of all regions and the different legal or economic systems of the world. Since its adoption by UNCITRAL, the Model Law has come to represent the accepted international legislative standard for a modern arbitration law and a significant number of jurisdictions have enacted arbitration legislation based on the Model Law.

3. The form of a model law was chosen as the vehicle for harmonization and modernization in view of the flexibility it gives to States in preparing new arbitration laws. Notwithstanding that flexibility, and in order to increase the likelihood of achieving a satisfactory degree of harmonization, States are encouraged to make as few changes as possible when incorporating the Model Law into their legal systems. Efforts to minimize variation from the text adopted by UNCITRAL are also expected to increase the visibility of harmonization, thus enhancing the confidence of foreign parties, as the primary users of international arbitration, in the reliability of arbitration law in the enacting State.

4. The revision of the Model Law adopted in 2006 includes article 2 A, which is designed to facilitate interpretation by reference to internationally accepted principles and is aimed at promoting a uniform understanding of the Model Law.

---

[12] This note was prepared by the secretariat of the United Nations Commission on International Trade Law (UNCITRAL) for informational purposes only; it is not an official commentary on the Model Law. A commentary prepared by the Secretariat on an early draft of the Model Law appears in document A/CN.9/264 (reproduced in *UNCITRAL Yearbook*, vol. XVI — 1985, United Nations publication, Sales No. E.87.V.4).

Other substantive amendments to the Model Law relate to the form of the arbitration agreement and to interim measures. The original 1985 version of the provision on the form of the arbitration agreement (article 7) was modelled on the language used in article II (2) of the Convention on the Recognition and Enforcement of Foreign Arbitral Awards (New York, 1958) ("the New York Convention"). The revision of article 7 is intended to address evolving practice in international trade and technological developments. The extensive revision of article 17 on interim measures was considered necessary in light of the fact that such measures are increasingly relied upon in the practice of international commercial arbitration. The revision also includes an enforcement regime for such measures in recognition of the fact that the effectiveness of arbitration frequently depends upon the possibility of enforcing interim measures. The new provisions are contained in a new chapter of the Model Law on interim measures and preliminary orders (chapter IV A).

A. Background to the Model Law

5. The Model Law was developed to address considerable disparities in national laws on arbitration. The need for improvement and harmonization was based on findings that national laws were often particularly inappropriate for international cases.

1. Inadequacy of domestic laws

6. Recurrent inadequacies to be found in outdated national laws include provisions that equate the arbitral process with court litigation and fragmentary provisions that fail to address all relevant substantive law issues. Even most of those laws that appear to be up-to-date and comprehensive were drafted with domestic arbitration primarily, if not exclusively, in mind. While this approach is understandable in view of the fact that even today the bulk of cases governed by arbitration law would be of a purely domestic nature, the unfortunate consequence is that traditional local concepts are imposed on international cases and the needs of modern practice are often not met.

7. The expectations of the parties as expressed in a chosen set of arbitration rules or a "one-off" arbitration agreement may be frustrated, especially by mandatory provisions of applicable law. Unexpected and undesired restrictions found in national laws may prevent the parties, for example, from submitting future disputes to arbitration, from selecting the arbitrator freely, or from having the arbitral proceedings conducted according to agreed rules of procedure and with no more court involvement than appropriate. Frustration may also ensue from non-mandatory provisions that may impose undesired requirements on unwary parties who may not think about the need to provide otherwise when drafting the arbitration agreement. Even the absence of any legislative provision may cause difficulties simply by leaving unanswered some of the many procedural issues relevant in arbitration and not always settled in the arbitration agreement. The Model Law is intended to reduce the risk of such possible frustration, difficulties or surprise.

2. Disparity between national laws

8. Problems stemming from inadequate arbitration laws or from the absence of specific legislation governing arbitration are aggravated by the fact that national laws differ widely. Such differences are a frequent source of concern in international arbitration, where at least one of the parties is, and often both parties are, confronted with foreign and unfamiliar provisions and procedures. Obtaining a full and precise account of the law applicable to the arbitration is, in such circumstances often expensive, impractical or impossible.

9. Uncertainty about the local law with the inherent risk of frustration may adversely affect the functioning of the arbitral process and also impact on the selection of the place of arbitration. Due to such uncertainty, a party may hesitate or refuse to agree to a place, which for practical reasons would otherwise be appropriate. The range of places of arbitration acceptable to parties is thus widened and the smooth functioning of the arbitral proceedings is enhanced where States adopt the Model Law, which is easily recognizable, meets the specific needs of international commercial arbitration and provides an international standard based on solutions acceptable to parties from different legal systems.

B. Salient features of the Model Law

1. Special procedural regime for international commercial arbitration

10. The principles and solutions adopted in the Model Law aim at reducing or eliminating the above-mentioned concerns and difficulties. As a response to the inadequacies and disparities of national laws, the Model Law presents a special legal regime tailored to international commercial arbitration, without affecting any relevant treaty in force in the State adopting the Model Law. While the Model Law was designed with international commercial arbitration in mind, it offers a set of basic rules that are not, in and of themselves, unsuitable to any other type of arbitration. States may thus consider extending their enactment of the Model Law to cover also domestic disputes, as a number of enacting States already have.

(a) Substantive and territorial scope of application

11. Article 1 defines the scope of application of the Model Law by reference to the notion of "international commercial arbitration". The Model Law defines an arbitration as international if "the parties to an arbitration agreement have, at the time of the conclusion of that agreement, their places of business in different States" (article 1 (3)). The vast majority of situations commonly regarded as international will meet this criterion. In addition, article 1 (3) broadens the notion of internationality so that the Model Law also covers cases where the place of arbitration, the place of contract performance, or the place of the subject-matter of the dispute is situated outside the State where the parties have their place of business, or cases where the parties have expressly agreed that the subject-matter of the arbitration agreement relates to more than one country. Article 1 thus recognizes extensively the freedom of the parties to submit a dispute to the legal regime established pursuant to the Model Law.

12. In respect of the term "commercial", the Model Law provides no strict definition. The footnote to article 1 (1) calls for "a wide interpretation" and offers an illustrative and open-ended list of relationships that might be described as commercial in nature, "whether contractual or not". The purpose of the footnote is to circumvent any technical difficulty that may arise, for example, in determining which transactions should be governed by a specific body of "commercial law" that may exist in some legal systems.

13. Another aspect of applicability is the territorial scope of application. The principle embodied in article 1 (2) is that the Model Law as enacted in a given State applies only if the place of arbitration is in the territory of that State. However, article 1 (2) also contains important exceptions to that principle, to the effect that certain articles apply, irrespective of whether the place of arbitration is in the enacting State or elsewhere (or, as the case may be, even before the place of arbitration is determined). These articles are the following: articles 8 (1) and 9, which deal with the recognition of arbitration agreements, including their compatibility with interim measures ordered by a court, article 17 J on court-ordered interim measures, articles 17 H and 17 I on the recognition and enforcement of interim measures ordered by an arbitral tribunal, and articles 35 and 36 on the recognition and enforcement of arbitral awards.

14. The territorial criterion governing most of the provisions of the Model Law was adopted for the sake of certainty and in view of the following facts. In most legal systems, the place of arbitration is the exclusive criterion for determining the applicability of national law and, where the national law allows parties to choose the procedural law of a State other than that where the arbitration takes place, experience shows that parties rarely make use of that possibility. Incidentally, enactment of the Model Law reduces any need for the parties to choose a "foreign" law, since the Model Law grants the parties wide freedom in shaping the rules of the arbitral proceedings. In addition to designating the law governing the arbitral procedure, the territorial criterion is of considerable practical importance in respect of articles 11, 13, 14, 16, 27 and 34, which entrust State courts at the place of arbitration with functions of supervision and assistance to arbitration. It should be noted that the territorial criterion legally triggered by the parties' choice regarding the place of arbitration does not limit the arbitral tribunal's ability to meet at any place it considers appropriate for the conduct of the proceedings, as provided by article 20 (2).

(b) Delimitation of court assistance and supervision

15. Recent amendments to arbitration laws reveal a trend in favour of limiting and clearly defining court involvement in international commercial arbitration. This is justified in view of the fact that the parties to an arbitration agreement make a conscious decision to exclude court jurisdiction and prefer the finality and expediency of the arbitral process.

16. In this spirit, the Model Law envisages court involvement in the following instances. A first group comprises issues of appointment, challenge and termination of the mandate of an arbitrator (articles 11, 13 and 14), jurisdiction of the arbitral tribunal (article 16) and setting aside of the arbitral award (article 34). These instances are listed in article 6 as functions that should be entrusted, for the sake of centralization, specialization and efficiency, to a specially designated court or, with respect to articles 11, 13 and 14, possibly to another authority (for example, an arbitral institution or a chamber of commerce). A second group comprises issues of court assistance in taking evidence (article 27), recognition of the arbitration agreement, including its compatibility with court-ordered interim measures (articles 8 and 9), court-ordered interim measures (article 17 J), and recognition and enforcement of interim measures (articles 17 H and 17 I) and of arbitral awards (articles 35 and 36).

17. Beyond the instances in these two groups, "no court shall intervene, in matters governed by this Law". Article 5 thus guarantees that all instances of possible court intervention are found in the piece of legislation enacting the Model Law, except for matters not regulated by it (for example, consolidation of arbitral proceedings, contractual relationship between arbitrators and parties or arbitral institutions, or fixing of costs and fees, including deposits). Protecting the arbitral process from unpredictable or disruptive court interference is essential to parties who choose arbitration (in particular foreign parties).

2. *Arbitration agreement*

18. Chapter II of the Model Law deals with the arbitration agreement, including its recognition by courts.

(a) Definition and form of arbitration agreement

19. The original 1985 version of the provision on the definition and form of arbitration agreement (article 7) closely followed article II (2) of the New York Convention, which requires that an arbitration agreement be in writing. If the parties have agreed to arbitrate, but they entered into the arbitration agreement in a manner that does not meet the form requirement, any party may have grounds to object to the jurisdiction of the arbitral tribunal. It was pointed out by practitioners that, in a number of situations, the drafting of a written document was impossible or impractical. In such cases, where the willingness of the parties to arbitrate was not in question, the validity of the arbitration agreement should be recognized. For that reason, article 7 was amended in 2006 to better conform to international contract practices. In amending article 7, the Commission adopted two options, which reflect two different approaches on the question of definition and form of arbitration agreement. The first approach follows the detailed structure of the original 1985 text. It confirms the validity and effect of a commitment by the parties to submit to arbitration an existing dispute ("*compromis*") or a future dispute ("*clause compromissoire*"). It follows the New York Convention in requiring the written form of the arbitration agreement but recognizes a record of the "contents" of the agreement "in any form" as equivalent to traditional "writing". The agreement to arbitrate may be entered into in any form (e.g. including orally) as long as the content of the agreement is recorded. This new rule is significant in that it no longer requires signatures of the parties or an exchange of messages between the parties. It modernizes the language referring to the use of electronic commerce by adopting wording inspired from the 1996 UNCITRAL Model Law on Electronic Commerce and the 2005 United Nations Convention on the Use of Electronic Communications in International Contracts. It covers the situation of "an exchange of statements of claim and defence in which the existence of an agreement is alleged by one party and not denied by another". It also states that "the reference in a contract to any document" (for example, general conditions) "containing an arbitration clause constitutes an arbitration agreement in writing provided that the reference is such as to make that clause part of the contract". It thus clarifies that applicable contract law remains available to determine the level of consent necessary for a party to become bound by an arbitration agreement allegedly made "by reference". The second approach defines the arbitration agreement in a manner that omits any form requirement. No preference was expressed by the Commission in favour of either option I or II, both of which are offered for enacting States to consider, depending on their particular needs, and by reference to the legal context in which the Model Law is enacted, including the general contract law of the enacting State. Both options are intended to preserve the enforceability of arbitration agreements under the New York Convention.

20. In that respect, the Commission also adopted, at its thirty-ninth session in 2006, a "Recommendation regarding the interpretation of article II, paragraph 2, and article VII, paragraph 1, of the Convention on the Recognition and Enforcement of Foreign Arbitral Awards, done in New York, 10 June 1958" (A/61/17, Annex 2).[13] The General Assembly, in its resolution 61/33 of 4 December 2006 noted that "in connection with the modernization of articles of the Model Law, the promotion of a uniform interpretation and application of the Convention on the Recognition and Enforcement of Foreign Arbitral Awards, done in New York, 10 June 1958, is particularly timely". The Recommendation was drafted in recognition of the widening use of electronic commerce and enactments of domestic legislation as well as case law, which are more favourable than the New York Convention in respect of the form requirement governing arbitration agreements, arbitration proceedings, and the enforcement of arbitral awards. The Recommendation encourages States to apply article II (2) of the New York Convention "recognizing that the circumstances described therein are not exhaustive". In addition, the Recommendation encourages States to adopt the revised article 7 of the Model Law. Both options of the revised article 7 establish a more favourable regime for the recognition and enforcement of arbitral awards than that provided under the New York Convention. By virtue of the "more favourable law provision" contained in article VII (1) of the New York Convention, the Recommendation clarifies that "any interested party" should be allowed "to avail itself of rights it may have, under the law or treaties of the country where an arbitration agreement is sought to be relied upon, to seek recognition of the validity of such an arbitration agreement".

(b) Arbitration agreement and the courts

21. Articles 8 and 9 deal with two important aspects of the complex relationship between the arbitration agreement and the resort to courts. Modelled on article II (3) of the New York Convention, article 8 (1) of the Model Law places any court under an obligation to refer the parties to arbitration if the court is seized with a claim on the same subject-matter unless it finds that the arbitration agreement is null and void, inoperative or incapable of being performed. The referral is dependent on a request, which a party may make not later than when submitting its first statement on the substance of the dispute. This provision, where adopted by a State enacting the Model Law, is by its nature binding only on the courts of that State. However, since article 8 is not limited in scope to agreements providing for arbitration to take place in the enacting State, it promotes the universal recognition and effect of international commercial arbitration agreements.

22. Article 9 expresses the principle that any interim measures of protection that may be obtained from courts under their procedural law (for example, pre-award attachments) are compatible with an arbitration agreement. That provision is

[13] Reproduced in Part Three hereafter.

ultimately addressed to the courts of any State, insofar as it establishes the compatibility between interim measures possibly issued by any court and an arbitration agreement, irrespective of the place of arbitration. Wherever a request for interim measures may be made to a court, it may not be relied upon, under the Model Law, as a waiver or an objection against the existence or effect of the arbitration agreement.

3. Composition of arbitral tribunal

23. Chapter III contains a number of detailed provisions on appointment, challenge, termination of mandate and replacement of an arbitrator. The chapter illustrates the general approach taken by the Model Law in eliminating difficulties that arise from inappropriate or fragmentary laws or rules. First, the approach recognizes the freedom of the parties to determine, by reference to an existing set of arbitration rules or by an ad hoc agreement, the procedure to be followed, subject to the fundamental requirements of fairness and justice. Secondly, where the parties have not exercised their freedom to lay down the rules of procedure or they have failed to cover a particular issue, the Model Law ensures, by providing a set of suppletive rules, that the arbitration may commence and proceed effectively until the dispute is resolved.

24. Where under any procedure, agreed upon by the parties or based upon the suppletive rules of the Model Law, difficulties arise in the process of appointment, challenge or termination of the mandate of an arbitrator, articles 11, 13 and 14 provide for assistance by courts or other competent authorities designated by the enacting State. In view of the urgency of matters relating to the composition of the arbitral tribunal or its ability to function, and in order to reduce the risk and effect of any dilatory tactics, short time-periods are set and decisions rendered by courts or other authorities on such matters are not appealable.

4. Jurisdiction of arbitral tribunal

(a) Competence to rule on own jurisdiction

25. Article 16 (1) adopts the two important (not yet generally recognized) principles of "*Kompetenz-Kompetenz*" and of separability or autonomy of the arbitration clause. "Kompetenz-Kompetenz" means that the arbitral tribunal may independently rule on the question of whether it has jurisdiction, including any objections with respect to the existence or validity of the arbitration agreement, without having to resort to a court. Separability means that an arbitration clause shall be treated as an agreement independent of the other terms of the contract. As a consequence, a decision by the arbitral tribunal that the contract is null and void shall not entail *ipso jure* the invalidity of the arbitration clause. Detailed provisions in paragraph (2) require that any objections relating to the arbitrators' jurisdiction be made at the earliest possible time.

26. The competence of the arbitral tribunal to rule on its own jurisdiction (i.e. on the foundation, content and extent of its mandate and power) is, of course, subject to court control. Where the arbitral tribunal rules as a preliminary question that it has jurisdiction, article 16 (3) allows for immediate court control in order to avoid waste of time and money. However, three procedural safeguards are added to reduce the risk and effect of dilatory tactics: short time-period for resort to court (30 days), court decision not appealable, and discretion of the arbitral tribunal to continue the proceedings and make an award while the matter is pending before the court. In those cases where the arbitral tribunal decides to combine its decision on jurisdiction with an award on the merits, judicial review on the question of jurisdiction is available in setting aside proceedings under article 34 or in enforcement proceedings under article 36.

(b) Power to order interim measures and preliminary orders

27. Chapter IV A on interim measures and preliminary orders was adopted by the Commission in 2006. It replaces article 17 of the original 1985 version of the Model Law. Section 1 provides a generic definition of interim measures and sets out the conditions for granting such measures. An important innovation of the revision lies in the establishment (in section 4) of a regime for the recognition and enforcement of interim measures, which was modelled, as appropriate, on the regime for the recognition and enforcement of arbitral awards under articles 35 and 36 of the Model Law.

28. Section 2 of chapter IV A deals with the application for, and conditions for the granting of, preliminary orders. Preliminary orders provide a means for preserving the status quo until the arbitral tribunal issues an interim measure adopting or modifying the preliminary order. Article 17 B (1) provides that "a party may, without notice to any other party, make a request for an interim measure together with an application for a preliminary order directing a party not to frustrate the purpose of the interim measure requested". Article 17 B (2) permits an arbitral tribunal to grant a preliminary order if "it considers that prior disclosure of the request for the interim measure to the party against whom it is directed risks frustrating the purpose of the measure". Article 17 C contains carefully drafted safeguards for the party against whom the preliminary order is directed, such as prompt notification of the application for the preliminary order and of the preliminary order itself (if any), and an opportunity for that party to present its case "at the earliest practicable time". In any event, a preliminary order has a maximum duration of twenty days and, while binding on the parties, is not subject to court enforcement and does not constitute an award. The term "preliminary order" is used to emphasize its limited nature.

29. Section 3 sets out rules applicable to both preliminary orders and interim measures.

30. Section 5 includes article 17 J on interim measures ordered by courts in support of arbitration, and provides that "a court shall have the same power of issuing an interim measure in relation to arbitration proceedings irrespective of whether their place is in the territory of the enacting State, as it has in relation to proceedings in courts". That article has been added in 2006 to put it beyond any doubt that the existence of an arbitration agreement does not infringe on the powers of the competent court to issue interim measures and that the party to such an arbitration agreement is free to approach the court with a request to order interim measures.

5. Conduct of arbitral proceedings

31. Chapter V provides the legal framework for a fair and effective conduct of the arbitral proceedings. Article 18, which sets out fundamental requirements of procedural justice, and article 19 on the rights and powers to determine the rules of procedure, express principles that are central to the Model Law.

(a) Fundamental procedural rights of a party

32. Article 18 embodies the principles that the parties shall be treated with equality and given a full opportunity of presenting their case. A number of provisions illustrate those principles. For example, article 24 (1) provides that, unless the parties have agreed that no oral hearings be held for the presentation of evidence or for oral argument, the arbitral tribunal shall hold such hearings at an appropriate stage of the proceedings, if so requested by a party. It should be noted that article 24 (1) deals only with the general entitlement of a party to oral hearings (as an alternative to proceedings conducted on the basis of documents and other materials) and not with the procedural aspects, such as the length, number or timing of hearings.

33. Another illustration of those principles relates to evidence by an expert appointed by the arbitral tribunal. Article 26 (2) requires the expert, after delivering his or her written or oral report, to participate in a hearing where the parties may put questions to the expert and present expert witnesses to testify on the points at issue, if such a hearing is requested by a party or deemed necessary by the arbitral tribunal. As another provision aimed at ensuring fairness, objectivity and impartiality, article 24 (3) provides that all statements, documents and other information supplied to the arbitral tribunal by one party shall be communicated to the other party, and that any expert report or evidentiary document on which the arbitral tribunal may rely in making its decision shall be communicated to the parties. In order to enable the parties to be present at any hearing and at any meeting of the arbitral tribunal for inspection purposes, they shall be given sufficient notice in advance (article 24 (2)).

(b) Determination of rules of procedure

34. Article 19 guarantees the parties' freedom to agree on the procedure to be followed by the arbitral tribunal in conducting the proceedings, subject to a few mandatory provisions on procedure, and empowers the arbitral tribunal, failing agreement by the parties, to conduct the arbitration in such a manner as it considers appropriate. The power conferred upon the arbitral tribunal includes the power to determine the admissibility, relevance, materiality and weight of any evidence.

35. Autonomy of the parties in determining the rules of procedure is of special importance in international cases since it allows the parties to select or tailor the rules according to their specific wishes and needs, unimpeded by traditional and possibly conflicting domestic concepts, thus obviating the earlier mentioned risk of frustration or surprise (see above, paras. 7 and 9). The supplementary discretion of the arbitral tribunal is equally important in that it allows the tribunal to tailor the conduct of the proceedings to the specific features of the case without being hindered by any restraint that may stem from traditional local law, including any domestic rule on evidence. Moreover, it provides grounds for displaying initiative in solving any procedural question not regulated in the arbitration agreement or the Model Law.

36. In addition to the general provisions of article 19, other provisions in the Model Law recognize party autonomy and, failing agreement, empower the arbitral tribunal to decide on certain matters. Examples of particular practical importance in international cases are article 20 on the place of arbitration and article 22 on the language to be used in the proceedings.

(c) Default of a party

37. The arbitral proceedings may be continued in the absence of a party, provided that due notice has been given. This applies, in particular, to the failure of the respondent to communicate its statement of defence (article 25 (b)). The arbitral tribunal may also continue the proceedings where a party fails to appear at a hearing or to produce documentary evidence without showing sufficient cause for the failure (article 25 (c)). However, if the claimant fails to submit its statement of claim, the arbitral tribunal is obliged to terminate the proceedings (article 25 (a)).

38. Provisions that empower the arbitral tribunal to carry out its task even if one of the parties does not participate are of considerable practical importance. As experience shows, it is not uncommon for one of the parties to have little interest in cooperating or expediting matters. Such provisions therefore provide international commercial arbitration its necessary effectiveness, within the limits of fundamental requirements of procedural justice.

6. Making of award and termination of proceedings

(a) Rules applicable to substance of dispute

39. Article 28 deals with the determination of the rules of law governing the substance of the dispute. Under paragraph (1), the arbitral tribunal decides the dispute in accordance with the rules of law chosen by the parties. This provision is significant in two respects. It grants the parties the freedom to choose the applicable substantive law, which is important where the national law does not clearly or fully recognize that right. In addition, by referring to the choice of "rules of law" instead of "law", the Model Law broadens the range of options available to the parties as regards the designation of the law applicable to the substance of the dispute. For example, parties may agree on rules of law that have been elaborated by an international forum but have not yet been incorporated into any national legal system. Parties could also choose directly an instrument such as the United Nations Convention on Contracts for the International Sale of Goods as the body of substantive law governing the arbitration, without having to refer to the national law of any State party to that Convention. The power of the arbitral tribunal, on the other hand, follows more traditional lines. When the parties have not chosen the applicable law, the arbitral tribunal shall apply the law (i.e., the national law) determined by the conflict-of-laws rules that it considers applicable.

40. Article 28 (3) recognizes that the parties may authorize the arbitral tribunal to decide the dispute *ex aequo et bono* or as *amiables compositeur*. This type of arbitration (where the arbitral tribunal may decide the dispute on the basis of principles it believes to be just, without having to refer to any particular body of law) is currently not known or used in all legal systems. The Model Law does not intend to regulate this area. It simply calls the attention of the parties on the need to provide clarification in the arbitration agreement and specifically to empower the arbitral tribunal. However, paragraph (4) makes it clear that in all cases where the dispute relates to a contract (including arbitration *ex aequo et bono*) the arbitral tribunal must decide in accordance with the terms of the contract and shall take into account the usages of the trade applicable to the transaction.

(b) Making of award and other decisions

41. In its rules on the making of the award (articles 29-31), the Model Law focuses on the situation where the arbitral tribunal consists of more than one arbitrator. In such a situation, any award and other decision shall be made by a majority of the arbitrators, except on questions of procedure, which may be left to a presiding arbitrator. The majority principle applies also to the signing of the award, provided that the reason for any omitted signature is stated.

42. Article 31 (3) provides that the award shall state the place of arbitration and shall be deemed to have been made at that place. The effect of the deeming provision is to emphasize that the final making of the award constitutes a legal act, which in practice does not necessarily coincide with one factual event. For the same reason that the arbitral proceedings need not be carried out at the place designated as the legal "place of arbitration", the making of the award may be completed through deliberations held at various places, by telephone or correspondence. In addition, the award does not have to be signed by the arbitrators physically gathering at the same place.

43. The arbitral award must be in writing and state its date. It must also state the reasons on which it is based, unless the parties have agreed otherwise or the award is "on agreed terms" (i.e., an award that records the terms of an amicable settlement by the parties). It may be added that the Model Law neither requires nor prohibits "dissenting opinions".

7. Recourse against award

44. The disparity found in national laws as regards the types of recourse against an arbitral award available to the parties presents a major difficulty in harmonizing international arbitration legislation. Some outdated laws on arbitration, by establishing parallel regimes for recourse against arbitral awards or against court decisions, provide various types of recourse, various (and often long) time periods for exercising the recourse, and extensive lists of grounds on which recourse may be based. That situation (of considerable concern to those involved in international commercial arbitration) is greatly improved by the Model Law, which provides uniform grounds upon which (and clear time periods within which) recourse against an arbitral award may be made.

(a) Application for setting aside as exclusive recourse

45. The first measure of improvement is to allow only one type of recourse, to the exclusion of any other recourse regulated in any procedural law of the State in question. Article 34 (1) provides that the sole recourse against an arbitral award is by application for setting aside, which must be made within three months of receipt of the award (article 34 (3)). In regulating "recourse" (i.e., the means through which a party may actively "attack" the award), article 34 does not preclude a party from seeking court control by way of defence in enforcement proceedings (articles 35 and 36). Article 34 is limited to action before a court (i.e., an organ of the judicial system of a State). However, a party is not precluded from appealing to an arbitral tribunal of second instance if the parties have agreed on such a possibility (as is common in certain commodity trades).

(b) Grounds for setting aside

46. As a further measure of improvement, the Model Law lists exhaustively the grounds on which an award may be set aside. This list essentially mirrors that contained in article 36 (1), which is taken from article V of the New York Convention. The grounds provided in article 34 (2) are set out in two categories. Grounds which are to be proven by one party are as follows: lack of capacity of the parties to conclude an arbitration agreement; lack of a valid arbitration agreement; lack of notice of appointment of an arbitrator or of the arbitral proceedings or inability of a party to present its case; the award deals with matters not covered by the submission to arbitration; the composition of the arbitral tribunal or the conduct of arbitral proceedings are contrary to the effective agreement of the parties or, failing such agreement, to the Model Law. Grounds that a court may consider of its own initiative are as follows: non-arbitrability of the subject-matter of the dispute or violation of public policy (which is to be understood as serious departures from fundamental notions of procedural justice).

47. The approach under which the grounds for setting aside an award under the Model Law parallel the grounds for refusing recognition and enforcement of the award under article V of the New York Convention is reminiscent of the approach taken in the European Convention on International Commercial Arbitration (Geneva, 1961). Under article IX of the latter Convention, the decision of a foreign court to set aside an award for a reason other than the ones listed in article V of the New York Convention does not constitute a ground for refusing enforcement. The Model Law takes this philosophy one step further by directly limiting the reasons for setting aside.

48. Although the grounds for setting aside as set out in article 34 (2) are almost identical to those for refusing recognition or enforcement as set out in article 36 (1), a practical difference should be noted. An application for setting aside under article 34 (2) may only be made to a court in the State where the award was rendered whereas an application for enforcement might be made in a court in any State. For that reason, the grounds relating to public policy and non-arbitrability may vary in substance with the law applied by the court (in the State of setting aside or in the State of enforcement).

8. Recognition and enforcement of awards

49. The eighth and last chapter of the Model Law deals with the recognition and enforcement of awards. Its provisions reflect the significant policy decision that the same rules should apply to arbitral awards whether made in the country of enforcement or abroad, and that those rules should follow closely the New York Convention.

(a) Towards uniform treatment of all awards irrespective of country of origin

50. By treating awards rendered in international commercial arbitration in a uniform manner irrespective of where they were made, the Model Law distinguishes between "international" and "non-international" awards instead of relying on the traditional distinction between "foreign" and "domestic" awards. This new line is based on substantive grounds rather than territorial borders, which are inappropriate in view of the limited importance of the place of arbitration in international cases. The place of arbitration is often chosen for reasons of convenience of the parties and the dispute may have little or no connection with the State where the arbitration legally takes place. Consequently, the recognition and enforcement of "international" awards, whether "foreign" or "domestic", should be governed by the same provisions.

51. By modelling the recognition and enforcement rules on the relevant provisions of the New York Convention, the Model Law supplements, without conflicting with, the regime of recognition and enforcement created by that successful Convention.

(b) Procedural conditions of recognition and enforcement

52. Under article 35 (1) any arbitral award, irrespective of the country in which it was made, shall be recognized as binding and enforceable, subject to the provisions of article 35 (2) and of article 36 (the latter of which sets forth the grounds on which recognition or enforcement may be refused). Based on the above consideration of the limited importance of the place of arbitration in international cases and the desire of overcoming territorial restrictions, reciprocity is not included as a condition for recognition and enforcement.

53. The Model Law does not lay down procedural details of recognition and enforcement, which are left to national procedural laws and practices. The Model Law merely sets certain conditions for obtaining enforcement under article 35 (2). It was amended in 2006 to liberalize formal requirements and reflect the amendment made to article 7 on the form of the arbitration agreement. Presentation of a copy of the arbitration agreement is no longer required under article 35 (2).

(c) Grounds for refusing recognition or enforcement

54. Although the grounds on which recognition or enforcement may be refused under the Model Law are identical to those listed in article V of the New York Convention, the grounds listed in the Model Law are relevant not only to foreign awards but to all awards rendered in the sphere of application of the piece of legislation enacting the Model Law. Generally, it was deemed desirable to adopt, for the sake of harmony, the same approach and wording as this important Convention. However, the first ground on the list as contained in the New York Convention (which provides that recognition and enforcement may be refused if "the parties to the arbitration agreement were, under the law applicable to them, under some incapacity") was modified since it was viewed as containing an incomplete and potentially misleading conflict-of-laws rule.

Further information on the Model Law may be obtained from:

UNCITRAL secretariat

Vienna International Centre
P.O. Box 500
1400 Vienna
Austria
Telephone: (+43-1) 26060-4060
Telefax: (+43-1) 26060-5813
Internet: www.uncitral.org
E-mail: uncitral@uncitral.org

PART THREE

Recommendation regarding the interpretation of article II, paragraph 2, and article VII, paragraph 1, of the Convention on the Recognition and Enforcement of Foreign Arbitral Awards, done in New York, 10 June 1958, adopted by the United Nations Commission on International Trade Law on 7 July 2006 at its thirty-ninth session

The United Nations Commission on International Trade Law,

Recalling General Assembly resolution 2205 (XXI) of 17 December 1966, which established the United Nations Commission on International Trade Law with the object of promoting the progressive harmonization and unification of the law of international trade by, inter alia, promoting ways and means of ensuring a uniform interpretation and application of international conventions and uniform laws in the field of the law of international trade,

Conscious of the fact that the different legal, social and economic systems of the world, together with different levels of development, are represented in the Commission,

Recalling successive resolutions of the General Assembly reaffirming the mandate of the Commission as the core legal body within the United Nations system in the field of international trade law to coordinate legal activities in this field,

Convinced that the wide adoption of the Convention on the Recognition and Enforcement of Foreign Arbitral Awards, done in New York on 10 June 1958,[14] has been a significant achievement in the promotion of the rule of law, particularly in the field of international trade,

Recalling that the Conference of Plenipotentiaries which prepared and opened the Convention for signature adopted a resolution, which states, inter alia, that the Conference "considers that greater uniformity of national laws on arbitration would further the effectiveness of arbitration in the settlement of private law disputes",

Bearing in mind differing interpretations of the form requirements under the Convention that result in part from differences of expression as between the five equally authentic texts of the Convention,

Taking into account article VII, paragraph 1, of the Convention, a purpose of which is to enable the enforcement of foreign arbitral awards to the greatest extent, in particular by recognizing the right of any interested party to avail itself of law

---

[14] United Nations, *Treaty Series*, vol. 330, No. 4739.

or treaties of the country where the award is sought to be relied upon, including where such law or treaties offer a regime more favourable than the Convention,

Considering the wide use of electronic commerce,

Taking into account international legal instruments, such as the 1985 UNCITRAL Model Law on International Commercial Arbitration,[15] as subsequently revised, particularly with respect to article 7,[16] the UNCITRAL Model Law on Electronic Commerce,[17] the UNCITRAL Model Law on Electronic Signatures[18] and the United Nations Convention on the Use of Electronic Communications in International Contracts,[19]

Taking into account also enactments of domestic legislation, as well as case law, more favourable than the Convention in respect of form requirement governing arbitration agreements, arbitration proceedings and the enforcement of arbitral awards,

Considering that, in interpreting the Convention, regard is to be had to the need to promote recognition and enforcement of arbitral awards,

1. *Recommends* that article II, paragraph 2, of the Convention on the Recognition and Enforcement of Foreign Arbitral Awards, done in New York, 10 June 1958, be applied recognizing that the circumstances described therein are not exhaustive;

2. *Recommends also* that article VII, paragraph 1, of the Convention on the Recognition and Enforcement of Foreign Arbitral Awards, done in New York, 10 June 1958, should be applied to allow any interested party to avail itself of rights it may have, under the law or treaties of the country where an arbitration agreement is sought to be relied upon, to seek recognition of the validity of such an arbitration agreement.

---

15 *Official Records of the General Assembly, Fortieth Session, Supplement No. 17* (A/40/17), annex I, and United Nations publication, Sales No. E.95.V.18.

16 Ibid., *Sixty-first Session, Supplement No. 17* (A/61/17), annex I.

17 Ibid., *Fifty-first Session, Supplement No. 17* (A/51/17), annex I, and United Nations publication, Sales No. E.99.V.4, which contains also an additional article 5 bis, adopted in 1998, and the accompanying Guide to Enactment.

18 Ibid., *Fifty-sixth Session, Supplement No. 17* and corrigendum (A/56/17 and Corr.3), annex II, and United Nations publication, Sales No. E.02.V.8, which contains also the accompanying Guide to Enactment.

19 General Assembly resolution 60/21, annex.

APPENDIX 8

United Nations Convention on International Settlement Agreements Resulting from Mediation[1]

Contents

RESOLUTION ADOPTED BY THE GENERAL ASSEMBLY ON 20 DECEMBER 2018 [ON THE REPORT OF THE SIXTH COMMITTEE (A/73/496)]

73/198. United Nations Convention on International Settlement Agreements Resulting from Mediation

The General Assembly,

---

[1] Reprinted with permission of the UNCITRAL Secretariat.

Recalling its resolution 2205 (XXI) of 17 December 1966, by which it established the United Nations Commission on International Trade Law with a mandate to further the progressive harmonization and unification of the law of international trade and in that respect to bear in mind the interests of all peoples, in particular those of developing countries, in the extensive development of international trade,

Recalling also its resolution 57/18 of 19 November 2002, in which it noted the adoption by the Commission of the Model Law on International Commercial Conciliation[2] and expressed the conviction that the Model Law, together with the Conciliation Rules of the Commission[3] recommended in its resolution 35/52 of 4 December 1980, contributes significantly to the establishment of a harmonized legal framework for the fair and efficient settlement of disputes arising in international commercial relations,

Recognizing the value of mediation as a method of amicably settling disputes arising in the context of international commercial relations,

Convinced that the adoption of a convention on international settlement agreements resulting from mediation that is acceptable to States with different legal, social and economic systems would complement the existing legal framework on international mediation and contribute to the development of harmonious international economic relations,

Noting that the decision of the Commission to concurrently prepare a convention on international settlement agreements resulting from mediation and an amendment to the Model Law on International Commercial Conciliation was intended to accommodate the different levels of experience with mediation in different jurisdictions and to provide States with consistent standards on the cross-border enforcement of international settlement agreements resulting from mediation, without creating any expectation that interested States may adopt either instrument,[4]

Noting with satisfaction that the preparation of the draft convention was the subject of due deliberation and that the draft convention benefited from consultations with Governments as well as intergovernmental and non-governmental organizations,

Taking note of the decision of the Commission at its fifty-first session to submit the draft convention to the General Assembly for its consideration,[5]

Taking note with satisfaction of the draft convention approved by the Commission,[6]

Expressing its appreciation to the Government of Singapore for its offer to host a signing ceremony for the Convention in Singapore,

1. *Commends* the United Nations Commission on International Trade Law for preparing the draft convention on international settlement agreements resulting from mediation;

2. *Adopts* the United Nations Convention on International Settlement Agreements Resulting from Mediation, contained in the annex to the present resolution;

---

2 Resolution 57/18, annex.

3 *Official Records of the General Assembly, Thirty-fifth Session, Supplement No. 17* (A/35/17), para. 106; see also *Yearbook of the United Nations Commission on International Trade Law*, vol. XI: 1980, part three, annex II.

4 *Official Records of the General Assembly, Seventy-second Session, Supplement No. 17* (A/72/17), paras. 238–239; see also A/CN.9/901, para. 52.

5 *Official Records of the General Assembly, Seventy-third Session, Supplement No. 17* (A/73/17), para. 49.

6 Ibid., annex I.

3. *Authorizes* a ceremony for the opening for signature of the Convention to be held in Singapore on 7 August 2019, and recommends that the Convention be known as the "Singapore Convention on Mediation";

4. *Calls upon* those Governments and regional economic integration organizations that wish to strengthen the legal framework on international dispute settlement to consider becoming a party to the Convention.

62nd plenary meeting
20 December 2018

United Nations Convention on International Settlement Agreements Resulting from Mediation

Preamble

The Parties to this Convention,

Recognizing the value for international trade of mediation as a method for settling commercial disputes in which the parties in dispute request a third person or persons to assist them in their attempt to settle the dispute amicably,

Noting that mediation is increasingly used in international and domestic commercial practice as an alternative to litigation,

Considering that the use of mediation results in significant benefits, such as reducing the instances where a dispute leads to the termination of a commercial relationship, facilitating the administration of international transactions by commercial parties and producing savings in the administration of justice by States,

Convinced that the establishment of a framework for international settlement agreements resulting from mediation that is acceptable to States with different legal, social and economic systems would contribute to the development of harmonious international economic relations,

Have agreed as follows:

Article 1.

Scope of application

1. This Convention applies to an agreement resulting from mediation and concluded in writing by parties to resolve a commercial dispute ("settlement agreement") which, at the time of its conclusion, is international in that:

(a) At least two parties to the settlement agreement have their places of business in different States; or

(b) The State in which the parties to the settlement agreement have their places of business is different from either:

(i) The State in which a substantial part of the obligations under the settlement agreement is performed; or

(ii) The State with which the subject matter of the settlement agreement is most closely connected.

2. This Convention does not apply to settlement agreements:

(a) Concluded to resolve a dispute arising from transactions engaged in by one of the parties (a consumer) for personal, family or household purposes;

(b) Relating to family, inheritance or employment law.

3. This Convention does not apply to:

(a) Settlement agreements:

(i) That have been approved by a court or concluded in the course of proceedings before a court; and

(ii) That are enforceable as a judgment in the State of that court;

(b) Settlement agreements that have been recorded and are enforceable as an arbitral award.

Article 2.

Definitions

1. For the purposes of article 1, paragraph 1:

(a) If a party has more than one place of business, the relevant place of business is that which has the closest relationship to the dispute resolved by the settlement agreement, having regard to the circumstances known to, or contemplated by, the parties at the time of the conclusion of the settlement agreement;

(b) If a party does not have a place of business, reference is to be made to the party's habitual residence.

2. A settlement agreement is "in writing" if its content is recorded in any form. The requirement that a settlement agreement be in writing is met by an electronic communication if the information contained therein is accessible so as to be useable for subsequent reference.

3. "Mediation" means a process, irrespective of the expression used or the basis upon which the process is carried out, whereby parties attempt to reach an amicable settlement of their dispute with the assistance of a third person or persons ("the mediator") lacking the authority to impose a solution upon the parties to the dispute.

Article 3.

General principles

1. Each Party to the Convention shall enforce a settlement agreement in accordance with its rules of procedure and under the conditions laid down in this Convention.

2. If a dispute arises concerning a matter that a party claims was already resolved by a settlement agreement, a Party to the Convention shall allow the party to invoke the settlement agreement in accordance with its rules of procedure and under the conditions laid down in this Convention, in order to prove that the matter has already been resolved.

Article 4.

Requirements for reliance on settlement agreements

1. A party relying on a settlement agreement under this Convention shall supply to the competent authority of the Party to the Convention where relief is sought:

(a) The settlement agreement signed by the parties;

(b) Evidence that the settlement agreement resulted from mediation, such as:

(i) The mediator's signature on the settlement agreement;

(ii) A document signed by the mediator indicating that the mediation was carried out;

(iii) An attestation by the institution that administered the mediation; or

(iv) In the absence of (i), (ii) or (iii), any other evidence acceptable to the competent authority.

2. The requirement that a settlement agreement shall be signed by the parties or, where applicable, the mediator is met in relation to an electronic communication if:

(a) A method is used to identify the parties or the mediator and to indicate the parties' or mediator's intention in respect of the information contained in the electronic communication; and

(b) The method used is either:

(i) As reliable as appropriate for the purpose for which the electronic communication was generated or communicated, in the light of all the circumstances, including any relevant agreement; or

(ii) Proven in fact to have fulfilled the functions described in subparagraph *(a)* above, by itself or together with further evidence.

3. If the settlement agreement is not in an official language of the Party to the Convention where relief is sought, the competent authority may request a translation thereof into such language.

4. The competent authority may require any necessary document in order to verify that the requirements of the Convention have been complied with.

5. When considering the request for relief, the competent authority shall act expeditiously.

Article 5.

Grounds for refusing to grant relief

1. The competent authority of the Party to the Convention where relief is sought under article 4 may refuse to grant relief at the request of the party against whom the relief is sought only if that party furnishes to the competent authority proof that:

(a) A party to the settlement agreement was under some incapacity;

(b) The settlement agreement sought to be relied upon:

(i) Is null and void, inoperative or incapable of being performed under the law to which the parties have validly subjected it or, failing any indication thereon, under the law deemed applicable by the competent authority of the Party to the Convention where relief is sought under article 4;

(ii) Is not binding, or is not final, according to its terms; or

(iii) Has been subsequently modified;

(c) The obligations in the settlement agreement:

(i) Have been performed; or

(ii) Are not clear or comprehensible;

(d) Granting relief would be contrary to the terms of the settlement agreement;

(e) There was a serious breach by the mediator of standards applicable to the mediator or the mediation without which breach that party would not have entered into the settlement agreement; or

(f) There was a failure by the mediator to disclose to the parties circumstances that raise justifiable doubts as to the mediator's impartiality or independence and such failure to disclose had a material impact or undue influence on a party without which failure that party would not have entered into the settlement agreement.

2. The competent authority of the Party to the Convention where relief is sought under article 4 may also refuse to grant relief if it finds that:

(a) Granting relief would be contrary to the public policy of that Party; or

(b) The subject matter of the dispute is not capable of settlement by mediation under the law of that Party.

Article 6.

Parallel applications or claims

If an application or a claim relating to a settlement agreement has been made to a court, an arbitral tribunal or any other competent authority which may affect the relief being sought under article 4, the competent authority of the Party to the Convention where such relief is sought may, if it considers it proper, adjourn the decision and may also, on the request of a party, order the other party to give suitable security.

Article 7.

Other laws or treaties

This Convention shall not deprive any interested party of any right it may have to avail itself of a settlement agreement in the manner and to the extent allowed by the law or the treaties of the Party to the Convention where such settlement agreement is sought to be relied upon.

Article 8.

Reservations

1. A Party to the Convention may declare that:
- (a) It shall not apply this Convention to settlement agreements to which it is a party, or to which any governmental agencies or any person acting on behalf of a governmental agency is a party, to the extent specified in the declaration;
- (b) It shall apply this Convention only to the extent that the parties to the settlement agreement have agreed to the application of the Convention.

2. No reservations are permitted except those expressly authorized in this article.

3. Reservations may be made by a Party to the Convention at any time. Reservations made at the time of signature shall be subject to confirmation upon ratification, acceptance or approval. Such reservations shall take effect simultaneously with the entry into force of this Convention in respect of the Party to the Convention concerned. Reservations made at the time of ratification, acceptance or approval of this Convention or accession thereto, or at the time of making a declaration under article 13 shall take effect simultaneously with the entry into force of this Convention in respect of the Party to the Convention concerned. Reservations deposited after the entry into force of the Convention for that Party to the Convention shall take effect six months after the date of the deposit.

4. Reservations and their confirmations shall be deposited with the depositary.

5. Any Party to the Convention that makes a reservation under this Convention may withdraw it at any time. Such withdrawals are to be deposited with the depositary, and shall take effect six months after deposit.

Article 9.

Effect on settlement agreements

The Convention and any reservation or withdrawal thereof shall apply only to settlement agreements concluded after the date when the Convention, reservation or withdrawal thereof enters into force for the Party to the Convention concerned.

Article 10.

Depositary

The Secretary-General of the United Nations is hereby designated as the depositary of this Convention.

Article 11.

Signature, ratification, acceptance, approval, accession

1. This Convention is open for signature by all States in Singapore, on 7 August 2019, and thereafter at United Nations Headquarters in New York.
2. This Convention is subject to ratification, acceptance or approval by the signatories.
3. This Convention is open for accession by all States that are not signatories as from the date it is open for signature.
4. Instruments of ratification, acceptance, approval or accession are to be deposited with the depositary.

Article 12.

Participation by regional economic integration organizations

1. A regional economic integration organization that is constituted by sovereign States and has competence over certain matters governed by this Convention may similarly sign, ratify, accept, approve or accede to this Convention. The regional economic integration organization shall in that case have the rights and obligations of a Party to the Convention, to the extent that that organization has competence over matters governed by this Convention. Where the number of Parties to the Convention is relevant in this Convention, the regional economic integration organization shall not count as a Party to the Convention in addition to its member States that are Parties to the Convention.
2. The regional economic integration organization shall, at the time of signature, ratification, acceptance, approval or accession, make a declaration to the depositary specifying the matters governed by this Convention in respect of which competence has been transferred to that organization by its member States. The regional economic integration organization shall promptly notify the depositary of any changes to the distribution of competence, including new transfers of competence, specified in the declaration under this paragraph.
3. Any reference to a "Party to the Convention", "Parties to the Convention", a "State" or "States" in this Convention applies equally to a regional economic integration organization where the context so requires.
4. This Convention shall not prevail over conflicting rules of a regional economic integration organization, whether such rules were adopted or entered into force before or after this Convention: *(a)* if, under article 4, relief is sought in a State that

is member of such an organization and all the States relevant under article 1, paragraph 1, are members of such an organization; or *(b)* as concerns the recognition or enforcement of judgments between member States of such an organization.

Article 13.

Non-unified legal systems

1. If a Party to the Convention has two or more territorial units in which different systems of law are applicable in relation to the matters dealt with in this Convention, it may, at the time of signature, ratification, acceptance, approval or accession, declare that this Convention is to extend to all its territorial units or only to one or more of them, and may amend its declaration by submitting another declaration at any time.
2. These declarations are to be notified to the depositary and are to state expressly the territorial units to which the Convention extends.
3. If a Party to the Convention has two or more territorial units in which different systems of law are applicable in relation to the matters dealt with in this Convention:
- (a) Any reference to the law or rule of procedure of a State shall be construed as referring, where appropriate, to the law or rule of procedure in force in the relevant territorial unit;
- (b) Any reference to the place of business in a State shall be construed as referring, where appropriate, to the place of business in the relevant territorial unit;
- (c) Any reference to the competent authority of the State shall be construed as referring, where appropriate, to the competent authority in the relevant territorial unit.

4. If a Party to the Convention makes no declaration under paragraph 1 of this article, the Convention is to extend to all territorial units of that State.

Article 14.

Entry into force

1. This Convention shall enter into force six months after deposit of the third instrument of ratification, acceptance, approval or accession.
2. When a State ratifies, accepts, approves or accedes to this Convention after the deposit of the third instrument of ratification, acceptance, approval or accession, this Convention shall enter into force in respect of that State six months after the date of the deposit of its instrument of ratification, acceptance, approval or accession. The Convention shall enter into force for a territorial unit to which this Convention has been extended in accordance with article 13 six months after the notification of the declaration referred to in that article.

Article 15.

Amendment

1. Any Party to the Convention may propose an amendment to the present Convention by submitting it to the Secretary-General of the United Nations. The Secretary-General shall thereupon communicate the proposed amendment to the Parties to the Convention with a request that they indicate whether they favour a conference of Parties to the Convention for the purpose of considering and voting upon the proposal. In the event that within four months from the date of such communication at least one third of the Parties to the Convention favour such a conference, the Secretary-General shall convene the conference under the auspices of the United Nations.

2. The conference of Parties to the Convention shall make every effort to achieve consensus on each amendment. If all efforts at consensus are exhausted and no consensus is reached, the amendment shall, as a last resort, require for its adoption a two-thirds majority vote of the Parties to the Convention present and voting at the conference.

3. An adopted amendment shall be submitted by the depositary to all the Parties to the Convention for ratification, acceptance or approval.

4. An adopted amendment shall enter into force six months after the date of deposit of the third instrument of ratification, acceptance or approval. When an amendment enters into force, it shall be binding on those Parties to the Convention that have expressed consent to be bound by it.

5. When a Party to the Convention ratifies, accepts or approves an amendment following the deposit of the third instrument of ratification, acceptance or approval, the amendment shall enter into force in respect of that Party to the Convention six months after the date of the deposit of its instrument of ratification, acceptance or approval.

Article 16.

Denunciations

1. A Party to the Convention may denounce this Convention by a formal notification in writing addressed to the depositary. The denunciation may be limited to certain territorial units of a non-unified legal system to which this Convention applies.

2. The denunciation shall take effect 12 months after the notification is received by the depositary. Where a longer period for the denunciation to take effect is specified in the notification, the denunciation shall take effect upon the expiration of such longer period after the notification is received by the depositary. The Convention shall continue to apply to settlement agreements concluded before the denunciation takes effect.

DONE in a single original, of which the Arabic, Chinese, English, French, Russian and Spanish texts are equally authentic.

APPENDIX 9

UNCITRAL Model Law on International Commercial Mediation and International Settlement Agreements [1]

UNCITRAL Model Law on International Commercial Mediation and International Settlement Agreements Resulting from Mediation, 2018 (amending the UNCITRAL Model Law on International Commercial Conciliation, 2002)

SECTION 1 — GENERAL PROVISIONS

Article 1. Scope of application of the Law and definitions

1. This Law applies to international commercial[2] mediation[3] and to international settlement agreements.
2. For the purposes of this Law, "mediator" means a sole mediator or two or more mediators, as the case may be.
3. For the purposes of this Law, "mediation" means a process, whether referred to by the expression mediation, conciliation or an expression of similar import, whereby parties request a third person or persons ("the mediator") to assist them in their attempt to reach an amicable settlement of their dispute arising out of or relating to a contractual or other legal relationship. The mediator does not have the authority to impose upon the parties a solution to the dispute.

Article 2. Interpretation

1. In the interpretation of this Law, regard is to be had to its international origin and to the need to promote uniformity in its application and the observance of good faith.

---

1 Reprinted with permission of the UNCITRAL Secretariat.

2 The term "commercial" should be given a wide interpretation so as to cover matters arising from all relationships of a commercial nature, whether contractual or not. Relationships of a commercial nature include, but are not limited to, the following transactions: any trade transaction for the supply or exchange of goods or services; distribution agreement; commercial representation or agency; factoring; leasing; construction of works; consulting; engineering; licensing; investment; financing; banking; insurance; exploitation agreement or concession; joint venture and other forms of industrial or business cooperation; and carriage of goods or passengers by air, sea, rail or road.

3 In its previously adopted texts and relevant documents, UNCITRAL used the term "conciliation" with the understanding that the terms "conciliation" and "mediation" were interchangeable. In preparing this Model Law, the Commission decided to use the term "mediation" instead in an effort to adapt to the actual and practical use of the terms and with the expectation that this change will facilitate the promotion and heighten the visibility of the Model Law. This change in terminology does not have any substantive or conceptual implications.

2. Questions concerning matters governed by this Law which are not expressly settled in it are to be settled in conformity with the general principles on which this Law is based.

SECTION 2 — INTERNATIONAL COMMERCIAL MEDIATION

Article 3. Scope of application of the section and definitions

1. This section applies to international[4] commercial mediation.
2. A mediation is "international" if:
   (a) The parties to an agreement to mediate have, at the time of the conclusion of that agreement, their places of business in different States; or
   (b) The State in which the parties have their places of business is different from either:
      (i) The State in which a substantial part of the obligations of the commercial relationship is to be performed; or
      (ii) The State with which the subject matter of the dispute is most closely connected.
3. For the purposes of paragraph 2:
   (a) If a party has more than one place of business, the place of business is that which has the closest relationship to the agreement to mediate;
   (b) If a party does not have a place of business, reference is to be made to the party's habitual residence.
4. This section also applies to commercial mediation when the parties agree that the mediation is international or agree to the applicability of this section.
5. The parties are free to agree to exclude the applicability of this section.
6. Subject to the provisions of paragraph 7 of this article, this section applies irrespective of the basis upon which the mediation is carried out, including agreement between the parties whether reached before or after a dispute has arisen, an obligation established by law, or a direction or suggestion of a court, arbitral tribunal or competent governmental entity.
7. This section does not apply to:
   (a) Cases where a judge or an arbitrator, in the course of judicial or arbitral proceedings, attempts to facilitate a settlement; and
   (b) [...].

Article 4. Variation by agreement

Except for the provisions of article 7, paragraph 3, the parties may agree to exclude or vary any of the provisions of this section.

Article 5. Commencement of mediation proceedings[5]

1. Mediation proceedings in respect of a dispute that has arisen commence on the day on which the parties to that dispute agree to engage in mediation proceedings.

---

4 States wishing to enact this section to apply to domestic as well as international mediation may wish to consider the following changes to the text:
- Delete the word "international" in paragraph 1 of articles 1 and 3; and
- Delete paragraphs 2, 3 and 4 of article 3, and modify references to paragraphs accordingly.

5 The following text is suggested for States that might wish to adopt a provision on the suspension of the limitation period:

2. If a party that invited another party to mediate does not receive an acceptance of the invitation within 30 days from the day on which the invitation was sent, or within such other period of time as specified in the invitation, the party may elect to treat this as a rejection of the invitation to mediate.

Article 6. Number and appointment of mediators

1. There shall be one mediator, unless the parties agree that there shall be two or more mediators.
2. The parties shall endeavour to reach agreement on a mediator or mediators, unless a different procedure for their appointment has been agreed upon.
3. Parties may seek the assistance of an institution or person in connection with the appointment of mediators. In particular:
  (a) A party may request such an institution or person to recommend suitable persons to act as mediator; or
  (b) The parties may agree that the appointment of one or more mediators be made directly by such an institution or person.
4. In recommending or appointing individuals to act as mediator, the institution or person shall have regard to such considerations as are likely to secure the appointment of an independent and impartial mediator and, where appropriate, shall take into account the advisability of appointing a mediator of a nationality other than the nationalities of the parties.
5. When a person is approached in connection with his or her possible appointment as mediator, he or she shall disclose any circumstances likely to give rise to justifiable doubts as to his or her impartiality or independence. A mediator, from the time of his or her appointment and throughout the mediation proceedings, shall without delay disclose any such circumstances to the parties unless they have already been informed of them by him or her.

Article 7. Conduct of mediation

1. The parties are free to agree, by reference to a set of rules or otherwise, on the manner in which the mediation is to be conducted.
2. Failing agreement on the manner in which the mediation is to be conducted, the mediator may conduct the mediation proceedings in such a manner as the mediator considers appropriate, taking into account the circumstances of the case, any wishes that the parties may express and the need for a speedy settlement of the dispute.
3. In any case, in conducting the proceedings, the mediator shall seek to maintain fair treatment of the parties and, in so doing, shall take into account the circumstances of the case.
4. The mediator may, at any stage of the mediation proceedings, make proposals for a settlement of the dispute.

Article X. Suspension of limitation period
1. When the mediation proceedings commence, the running of the limitation period regarding the claim that is the subject matter of the mediation is suspended.
2. Where the mediation proceedings have terminated without a settlement agreement, the limitation period resumes running from the time the mediation ended without a settlement agreement.

Article 8. Communication between mediator and parties

The mediator may meet or communicate with the parties together or with each of them separately.

Article 9. Disclosure of information

When the mediator receives information concerning the dispute from a party, the mediator may disclose the substance of that information to any other party to the mediation. However, when a party gives any information to the mediator, subject to a specific condition that it be kept confidential, that information shall not be disclosed to any other party to the mediation.

Article 10. Confidentiality

Unless otherwise agreed by the parties, all information relating to the mediation proceedings shall be kept confidential, except where disclosure is required under the law or for the purposes of implementation or enforcement of a settlement agreement.

Article 11. Admissibility of evidence in other proceedings

1. A party to the mediation proceedings, the mediator and any third person, including those involved in the administration of the mediation proceedings, shall not in arbitral, judicial or similar proceedings rely on, introduce as evidence or give testimony or evidence regarding any of the following:

(a) An invitation by a party to engage in mediation proceedings or the fact that a party was willing to participate in mediation proceedings;

(b) Views expressed or suggestions made by a party in the mediation in respect of a possible settlement of the dispute;

(c) Statements or admissions made by a party in the course of the mediation proceedings;

(d) Proposals made by the mediator;

(e) The fact that a party had indicated its willingness to accept a proposal for settlement made by the mediator;

(f) A document prepared solely for purposes of the mediation proceedings.

2. Paragraph 1 of this article applies irrespective of the form of the information or evidence referred to therein.

3. The disclosure of the information referred to in paragraph 1 of this article shall not be ordered by an arbitral tribunal, court or other competent governmental authority and, if such information is offered as evidence in contravention of paragraph 1 of this article, that evidence shall be treated as inadmissible. Nevertheless, such information may be disclosed or admitted in evidence to the extent required under the law or for the purposes of implementation or enforcement of a settlement agreement.

4. The provisions of paragraphs 1, 2 and 3 of this article apply whether or not the arbitral, judicial or similar proceedings relate to the dispute that is or was the subject matter of the mediation proceedings.

5. Subject to the limitations of paragraph 1 of this article, evidence that is otherwise admissible in arbitral or judicial or similar proceedings does not become inadmissible as a consequence of having been used in a mediation.

Article 12. Termination of mediation proceedings

The mediation proceedings are terminated:

(a) By the conclusion of a settlement agreement by the parties, on the date of the agreement;

(b) By a declaration of the mediator, after consultation with the parties, to the effect that further efforts at mediation are no longer justified, on the date of the declaration;

(c) By a declaration of the parties addressed to the mediator to the effect that the mediation proceedings are terminated, on the date of the declaration; or

(d) By a declaration of a party to the other party or parties and the mediator, if appointed, to the effect that the mediation proceedings are terminated, on the date of the declaration.

Article 13. Mediator acting as arbitrator

Unless otherwise agreed by the parties, the mediator shall not act as an arbitrator in respect of a dispute that was or is the subject of the mediation proceedings or in respect of another dispute that has arisen from the same contract or legal relationship or any related contract or legal relationship.

Article 14. Resort to arbitral or judicial proceedings

Where the parties have agreed to mediate and have expressly undertaken not to initiate during a specified period of time or until a specified event has occurred arbitral or judicial proceedings with respect to an existing or future dispute, such an undertaking shall be given effect by the arbitral tribunal or the court until the terms of the undertaking have been complied with, except to the extent necessary for a party, in its opinion, to preserve its rights. Initiation of such proceedings is not of itself to be regarded as a waiver of the agreement to mediate or as a termination of the mediation proceedings.

Article 15. Binding and enforceable nature of settlement agreements

If the parties conclude an agreement settling a dispute, that settlement agreement is binding and enforceable.

SECTION 3 — INTERNATIONAL SETTLEMENT AGREEMENTS[6]

Article 16. Scope of application of the section and definitions

1. This section applies to international agreements resulting from mediation and concluded in writing by parties to resolve a commercial dispute ("settlement agreements").[7]

2. This section does not apply to settlement agreements:

(a) Concluded to resolve a dispute arising from transactions engaged in by one of the parties (a consumer) for personal, family or household purposes;

(b) Relating to family, inheritance or employment law.

---

6 A State may consider enacting this section to apply to agreements settling a dispute, irrespective of whether they resulted from mediation. Adjustments would then have to be made to relevant articles.

7 A State may consider enacting this section to apply only where the parties to the settlement agreement agreed to its application.

3. This section does not apply to:
   (a) Settlement agreements:
      (i) That have been approved by a court or concluded in the course of proceedings before a court; and
      (ii) That are enforceable as a judgment in the State of that court;
   (b) Settlement agreements that have been recorded and are enforceable as an arbitral award.

4. A settlement agreement is "international" if, at the time of the conclusion of the settlement agreement:[8]
   (a) At least two parties to the settlement agreement have their places of business in different States; or
   (b) The State in which the parties to the settlement agreement have their places of business is different from either:
      (i) The State in which a substantial part of the obligations under the settlement agreement is to be performed; or
      (ii) The State with which the subject matter of the settlement agreement is most closely connected.

5. For the purposes of paragraph 4:
   (a) If a party has more than one place of business, the relevant place of business is that which has the closest relationship to the dispute resolved by the settlement agreement, having regard to the circumstances known to, or contemplated by, the parties at the time of the conclusion of the settlement agreement;
   (b) If a party does not have a place of business, reference is to be made to the party's habitual residence.

6. A settlement agreement is "in writing" if its content is recorded in any form. The requirement that a settlement agreement be in writing is met by an electronic communication if the information contained therein is accessible so as to be useable for subsequent reference.

Article 17. General principles

1. A settlement agreement shall be enforced in accordance with the rules of procedure of this State, and under the conditions laid down in this section.
2. If a dispute arises concerning a matter that a party claims was already resolved by a settlement agreement, the party may invoke the settlement agreement in accordance with the rules of procedure of this State, and under the conditions laid down in this section, in order to prove that the matter has already been resolved.

Article 18. Requirements for reliance on settlement agreements

1. A party relying on a settlement agreement under this section shall supply to the competent authority of this State:
   (a) The settlement agreement signed by the parties;
   (b) Evidence that the settlement agreement resulted from mediation, such as:
      (i) The mediator's signature on the settlement agreement;
      (ii) A document signed by the mediator indicating that the mediation was carried out;

---

[8] A State may consider broadening the definition of "international" settlement agreement by adding the following subparagraph to paragraph 4: "A settlement agreement is also 'international' if it results from international mediation as defined in article 3, paragraphs 2, 3 and 4."

(iii) An attestation by the institution that administered the mediation; or
(iv) In the absence of (i), (ii) or (iii), any other evidence acceptable to the competent authority.

2. The requirement that a settlement agreement shall be signed by the parties or, where applicable, the mediator, is met in relation to an electronic communication if:

(a) A method is used to identify the parties or the mediator and to indicate the parties' or mediator's intention in respect of the information contained in the electronic communication; and
(b) The method used is either:
  (i) As reliable as appropriate for the purpose for which the electronic communication was generated or communicated, in the light of all the circumstances, including any relevant agreement; or
  (ii) Proven in fact to have fulfilled the functions described in subparagraph (a) above, by itself or together with further evidence.

3. If the settlement agreement is not in an official language of this State, the competent authority may request a translation thereof into such language.

4. The competent authority may require any necessary document in order to verify that the requirements of this section have been complied with.

5. When considering the request for relief, the competent authority shall act expeditiously.

Article 19. Grounds for refusing to grant relief

1. The competent authority of this State may refuse to grant relief at the request of the party against whom the relief is sought only if that party furnishes to the competent authority proof that:

(a) A party to the settlement agreement was under some incapacity;
(b) The settlement agreement sought to be relied upon:
  (i) Is null and void, inoperative or incapable of being performed under the law to which the parties have validly subjected it or, failing any indication thereon, under the law deemed applicable by the competent authority;
  (ii) Is not binding, or is not final, according to its terms; or
  (iii) Has been subsequently modified;
(c) The obligations in the settlement agreement:
  (i) Have been performed; or
  (ii) Are not clear or comprehensible;
(d) Granting relief would be contrary to the terms of the settlement agreement;
(e) There was a serious breach by the mediator of standards applicable to the mediator or the mediation without which breach that party would not have entered into the settlement agreement; or
(f) There was a failure by the mediator to disclose to the parties circumstances that raise justifiable doubts as to the mediator's impartiality or independence and such failure to disclose had a material impact or undue influence on a party without which failure that party would not have entered into the settlement agreement.

2. The competent authority of this State may also refuse to grant relief if it finds that:

(a) Granting relief would be contrary to the public policy of this State; or

(b) The subject matter of the dispute is not capable of settlement by mediation under the law of this State.

Article 20. Parallel applications or claims

If an application or a claim relating to a settlement agreement has been made to a court, an arbitral tribunal or any other competent authority which may affect the relief being sought under article 18, the competent authority of this State where such relief is sought may, if it considers it proper, adjourn the decision and may also, on the request of a party, order the other party to give suitable security.

INDEX

LEGAL TAXONOMY

FROM SWEET & MAXWELL

This index has been prepared using Sweet & Maxwell's Legal Taxonomy. Main index entries conform to keywords provided by the Legal Taxonomy except where references to specific documents or non-standard terms (denoted by quotation marks) have been included. These keywords provide a means of identifying similar concepts in other Sweet & Maxwell publications and online services to which keywords from the Legal Taxonomy have been applied. Readers may find some minor differences between terms used in the text and those which appear in the index. Suggestions to *sweetandmaxwell.taxonomy@tr.com.*